Praise for

No Higher Honor

"Important...her stories [of the aftermath of 9/11] add texture to the well-known history of those days and weeks, sometimes movingly so."

—Wall Street Journal

"Condoleezza Rice has a lot in common with Henry A. Kissinger....Now, like Kissinger, Rice has written a memoir drenched in details of the daily work of diplomacy....hers is a great story."

—Bloomberg.com

"It is Rice's careful retelling of responses to an almost unending series of crises that will make most readers grateful never to have worked as national security advisor or secretary of state....*No Higher Honor* is a thoughtful, self-reflective, and informative account of foreign policy making and crisis management in the Bush administration. Rice is to be commended for a degree of honesty that makes the book a must-read."

—Washington Independent Review of Books

"*No Higher Honor* chronicles the immensely substantive work Rice did in Washington and abroad....she is ever-gracious and industrious....the hallmarks of *No Higher Honor* are the integrity of hard work and the ultimate joy in duty."

—PopMatters

No Higher Honor

A Memoir of My Years in Washington

Condoleezza Rice

BROADWAY PAPERBACKS

NEW YORK

BROADWAY

Copyright © 2011 by Condoleezza Rice

All rights reserved.
Published in the United States by Broadway Paperbacks,
an imprint of the Crown Publishing Group,
a division of Random House, Inc., New York.
www.crownpublishing.com

BROADWAY PAPERBACKS and its logo, a letter B bisected
on the diagonal, are trademarks of Random House, Inc.

Originally published in hardcover in the United States
by Crown Publishers, an imprint of the Crown Publishing Group,
a division of Random House, Inc., New York, in 2011.

Library of Congress Cataloging-in-Publication Data is
available upon request.

ISBN 978-0-307-98678-8
eISBN 978-0-307-95247-9

PRINTED IN THE UNITED STATES OF AMERICA

Book design by Elizabeth Rendfleisch
Map by David Lindroth
Cover photograph: Michael Collopy

10 9 8 7 6 5 4 3 2 1

First Paperback Edition

To my parents

⁓

To the men and women in uniform
who volunteer to defend us on the front lines of liberty

and

To the diplomats and other civilians
who serve in hard places to promote a balance of power
that favors freedom

Contents

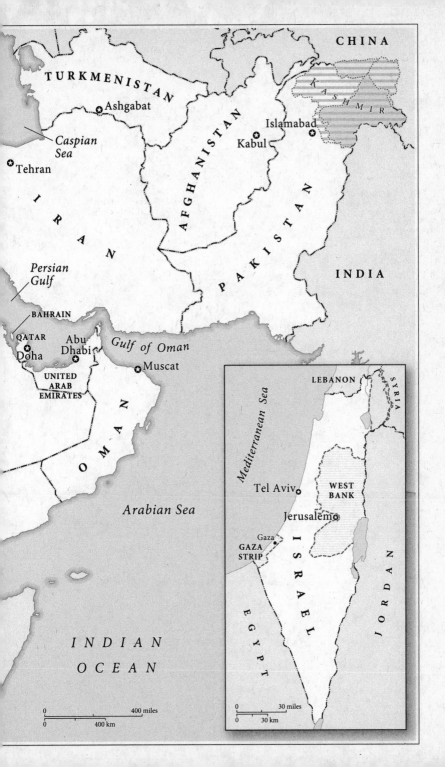

PROLOGUE

THE RIDE TO FOGGY BOTTOM from my Watergate apartment was short. I had the good fortune to live four minutes from the office, and I'd been grateful many times after late nights and tense days that I didn't have to commute.

On this, my last morning, I would have enjoyed a little more time to reflect. But I was quickly in the garage and then up the secretary's private elevator to the seventh floor, entering the ornate paneled hallway lined with portraits of my predecessors.

I met my staff for one final time to thank them. They had a gift for me: they'd purchased my White House Cabinet Room chair. Each member of the President's Cabinet sits in a large brown leather chair with a plaque on the back. I remember seeing "Secretary of State" for the first time and blushing at the thought that there had been a few others who had chairs like this before me. *Did Thomas Jefferson have his own chair?*

The ceremonial part of the meeting was short, though, because we had work to do. Tzipi Livni, Israel's foreign minister, was coming to negotiate a memorandum of understanding on terms for the withdrawal of Israeli troops from Gaza. Turmoil in the Middle East had been there when I arrived, and it was going to be there when I left. But it was a fundamentally different place than when we had entered office in 2001. So much had happened to shape the contours of a new Middle East.

Toward the end of my day, I stopped to look at the four portraits of former secretaries that I'd kept near me. There was Thomas Jefferson— everyone kept Thomas Jefferson—and George Marshall, arguably the greatest secretary of state and, well, everybody kept George Marshall too.

But I'd asked to have Dean Acheson and William Seward moved up the queue. Acheson graced my outer office. When he left as secretary in 1953, he was hounded by the question "Who lost China?" with many blaming him for America's inability to prevent Mao Zedong's victory. Now he was remembered as one of the founding fathers of NATO.

And I kept William Seward. Why would anyone keep Seward's portrait in a place of honor? Well, he bought Alaska. When the purchase was submitted for ratification in the Senate in 1867, Seward was excoriated: "Why would you pay the tsar of Russia seven million dollars for that icebox?" The decision quickly became known as "Seward's folly." One day I was talking with the then defense minister of Russia, Sergei Ivanov. He'd recently visited Alaska. "It's so beautiful," he said. "It reminds me of Russia." "Sergei, it used to *be* Russia," I quipped. We're all glad that Seward bought Alaska.

The portraits were not just decoration; they were a reminder of something that I often told the press and others: Today's headlines and history's judgment are rarely the same. If you are too attentive to the former, you will most certainly not do the hard work of securing the latter.

In that vein, Dean Acheson and I shared more than having had the honor of serving in turbulent times; we shared a favorite quote from the English historian C. V. Wedgwood: "History is lived forwards but it is written in retrospect. We know the end before we consider the beginning and we can never wholly recapture what it was to know the beginning only."

My, you've lived a lot of history, I thought. Then I headed down the hall to meet the Israeli foreign minister one last time.

INTRODUCTION

I<small>T HAD BEEN</small> a long two days. On Thursday morning, September 13, 2001, I stood looking at myself in the bathroom mirror. *How could this have happened? Did we miss something? Keep your focus. Just get to the end of today, then tomorrow, then the next day. There will be a time to go back. Not now. You have work to do.*

The time of reckoning—of facing the nation and myself about what had happened that day—would come in April 2004, when I testified before the 9/11 Commission. From the day the commission was announced, I knew that the administration would be asked the questions I'd asked myself. "How could you let it happen on your watch?" "Why didn't you see that the system was blinking red?"

I was familiar with past commissions of this type and had even taught about the investigations into the Roosevelt administration's failure to spot telltale signs of an impending attack on Pearl Harbor. But it's one thing to read about it and quite another to be a central, maybe the central, character in the drama.

"Isn't it a fact, Dr. Rice, that the August 6 PDB warned against possible attacks in this country?" Some forty-five minutes into my testimony, Richard Ben-Veniste, a seasoned prosecutor, abruptly pounced. He was referring to an intelligence report prepared for the President's Daily Briefing (PDB) on August 6, 2001. The report had been developed only after the President himself had asked whether there was any information on a possible al Qaeda attack on the U.S. homeland. The very fact that he'd had to ask suggested that the intelligence community thought it an unlikely event.

The report summarized historical information that had been contained in old intelligence documents and quoted a media interview that had already been public. It also said that the intelligence community could not corroborate a 1998 report about Osama bin Laden's desire to hijack a U.S. aircraft. None of us even remembered the PDB until May 2002, when *CBS Evening News* referred to its contents. I had talked to Bob Woodward and his colleague Dan Eggen of the *Washington Post* about it and had given a long White House press room briefing. The story had largely gone away.

The report, though, carried the eye-popping headline "Bin Ladin Determined To Strike in US." Since it had been issued only a month shy of 9/11, it commanded the spotlight during the hearings. In my opening statement before the commission, I said that the briefing item had not been prompted by any specific threat information. It noted some suspicious activity that we went to great lengths to investigate. But the report was not a warning, which I made clear at other points during the hearing. That did not prevent the commissioners from asking probing—and at times hostile—questions about its contents. I had to be careful with what I said because the report itself was still classified at the time. In fact, there are no more closely held documents than PDBs, which are seen only by the President, the Vice President, and a handful of other officials. Because PDBs usually deal with the most sensitive and current intelligence reporting, they are rarely declassified. But that fact did not prevent Commissioner Ben-Veniste from asking me to reveal the title of the August 6 memorandum. I knew I had to answer the question.

"I believe the title was 'Bin Laden Determined to Attack Inside the United States,' " I said. There were audible gasps in the chamber, particularly from victims' families who were in attendance. The report's title was suddenly the news of the hearings.

As the President's national security advisor, I had the responsibility of managing the various agencies involved in national security affairs at the time of the attacks. It helped to remember that I'd done everything that I thought necessary at the time. From the very beginning, I pressed for a strategy to disable al Qaeda and directed Richard Clarke, the White House's counterterrorism expert, to develop one. When threat levels began to spike in the summer of 2001, we moved the U.S. government at all levels to a high state of alert. Secretary of State Colin Powell and Secretary of Defense Donald Rumsfeld had secured our embassies and military bases abroad. After all, the intelligence assessment was that an attack would most likely come in Jordan, Saudi Arabia, Israel, or in Europe. The three of us talked almost every morning and assessed the situation and the need for further action. I asked Director of Central Intelligence George Tenet if there was more we could do, and we tried to find the key al Qaeda facilitator, Abu Zubaydah, with Vice President Dick Cheney asking the Saudis and Jordanians for help in doing so. With White House Chief of Staff Andrew Card present, I insisted that Dick Clarke inform domestic agencies of the heightened threat just in case an attack might come against the United States, despite the lack of intelligence pointing to the homeland. I did everything I could.

I was convinced of that intellectually. But, given the severity of what occurred, I clearly hadn't done enough. The hardest moment that morning was walking into the room and seeing the families of the 9/11 victims. Some were accusatory and others were supportive, but they were all hurting. And I hurt for them because the United States of America had failed to protect nearly three thousand of its innocent citizens.

The room was filled to capacity, and there were cameras and television lights everywhere. I felt surprisingly calm and said a little prayer before we started. I made my opening statement, acknowledging that the country had been poorly prepared—but because of *systemic* failures, not the negligence of any one administration or any one person. There was no silver bullet that could have prevented the 9/11 attacks. I concluded my prepared testimony by making the point that terrorists have to be successful just once, while the defender must be vigilant 100 percent of the time.

I had to make the policy case for what we'd done in response, place the blame squarely on al Qaeda, recommend changes to prevent another attack, and restore the American people's confidence in the Bush administration. A part of me wanted to apologize, but the collective view of my advisors was that to do so would overwhelm anything else that I said. So instead I expressed regret.

"I've asked myself a thousand times what more we could have done," I told the commission. "I know that had we thought there was an attack coming in Washington or New York, we would have moved heaven and earth to try and stop it."

. . .

YEARS LATER, in 2008, toward the end of our time in office, a terrorist attack took place in Mumbai, India. I traveled to New Delhi to lend support to the Indian government and to defuse tensions between India and Pakistan. I walked into Prime Minister Manmohan Singh's living room and came face to face with the Indian national security advisor. He was a slight man who wore huge dark-rimmed glasses that made him look like an owl. I had heard that he had offered to resign shortly after the attack and that the prime minister had refused to accept his resignation. He, M. K. Narayanan, had the same shell-shocked look that I remembered seeing in the mirror after the attacks on the Twin Towers and the Pentagon.

I took his hands. "It's not your fault," I said. "I know how you feel. It's like being in a dark room with doors all around and knowing anything might pop out and attack again. But now you have to concentrate on preventing the next attack."

I don't actually remember what he said in response because, in reality, I was very much inside myself. I was replaying those awful days in the wake of 9/11, days that had from that time forward been September 12 over and over again. Nothing was ever the same. It was as if there had been a crack in time.

Protest as you might to yourself, to the nation, and to the world, you never get over the feeling that you could have done better. And you resolve never to let it happen again.

BEFORE THE CRACK IN TIME

IN AUGUST 1998, President George H. W. Bush called and invited me to spend time with him and Mrs. Barbara Bush in Maine. I had become close to President Bush in the years after I'd served as his Soviet specialist in the National Security Council, and they had hosted me a few times before at their wonderful family home in Kennebunkport. The weathered, shingle-style house, decorated in calming pastel chintz, has an elegant yet understated decor and a spectacular view of the ocean. I'm not all that fond of being in the water. But I love to look at it, and there isn't a prettier place to view the Atlantic than Walker's Point. I promptly accepted the invitation.

Driving along the rocky New England coast to the entrance of the property, I was struck by two flags flying over the compound: the Texas state flag for the governor and the Stars and Stripes for the former President. (The Florida state flag would later join them when Jeb Bush was elected governor.) It was a subtle reminder that this was no ordinary family and it would be no ordinary weekend.

The elder Bush didn't hide his desire to get me together with his son George just so we could get to know each other better and talk a little about foreign policy. Before a casual lobster dinner that night, I joined Governor Bush on the back porch, where he told me that he was confident of reelection in November and that if he won impressively (which he fully expected), he'd likely run for the presidency.

A run for the White House by the Texas governor struck me as having long odds for success. President Clinton's years had been morally tarnished but peaceful and relatively prosperous. The governor was untested and would likely face a real pro in Vice President Al Gore. I was too polite to say those things that night, but I sure thought them.

Throughout the weekend, while fishing (he fished, I sat in the boat and watched) or exercising side by side in the small family gym on the compound, we talked about Russia, China, and Latin America. He wanted to start thinking about what to do in foreign policy if he got elected. I soon realized that he knew our southern neighbors, particularly Mexico, far better than I did. I made a mental note to read a few articles about Mexico when I got back to my home in California.

But we also talked about other things. He was interested in my upbringing in segregated Birmingham. I was attracted to his passion for improving education for disadvantaged youth. We compared notes on the problems of college admission and affirmative action. I was more traditional in my support of race-based admission; he'd tried to increase diversity at the University of Texas by other means. He proudly said that he would likely receive half of the Hispanic vote and more than a quarter of the African American vote.

I liked him. He was funny and irreverent but serious about policy. We e-mailed back and forth several times during the fall, mostly friendly chitchat about whatever was in the news—the growing conflict in the Balkans or the Clinton administration's efforts to expand NATO. Then, a couple of days after the November election and the landslide victory Governor Bush had hoped for, I received a note from him. He wanted to follow international events more closely.

Early in March 1999, Karl Rove, the governor's political advisor, called to ask if I'd come down to Austin and speak with the governor about the upcoming campaign. "Will you book a hotel room for me?" I asked.

"You won't need a hotel," he replied. "The governor wants you to stay at the residence." It was a signal that he expected me to support his campaign, which was quickly becoming a serious endeavor. A few weeks later, when my picture appeared on the front page of the *New York Times* as a member of the "exploratory committee" dedicated to electing George W. Bush President of the United States, I was momentarily stunned by the sudden exposure but committed to the cause.

My father was the first person I called after the governor asked me to join his campaign. John Wesley Rice, Jr., loved politics. He watched news shows, particularly C-SPAN, for hours at a time, and had been a loyal Republican ever since a clerk affiliated with the Grand Old Party had helped him register to vote in segregated Alabama. My father could barely contain his excitement.

The campaign itself proved professionally fulfilling, but early on I realized that it would require my full-time focus. For six years I had been the provost—the chief operating officer—of Stanford University. I was ready to step down independent of the chance to join the Bush campaign. Foreign policy would be the governor's Achilles' heel against more seasoned candidates in the primaries and eventually in the general election. I knew that George W. Bush would look to me to help answer the inevitable questions about his readiness to assume the mantle of commander in chief.

Throughout 1999 I worked to assemble a small group of foreign policy specialists to develop policy for the governor. My first call was to Paul Wolfowitz, who had been ambassador to Indonesia under President Ronald Reagan and under secretary for policy in the Pentagon during George H. W. Bush's administration. Paul was a cerebral, almost otherworldly intellectual. He'd done his undergraduate work at Cornell and gone on to complete a PhD in the intense academic environment of the University of Chicago. Though Paul had already had a distinguished public policy career, he was really most comfortable debating ideas. We'd been friends since the 1980s, and when I asked him to join me as cochair of the foreign policy group, he readily did so.

Richard Armitage and Stephen Hadley had also been in the first Bush administration. Rich was a muscular, stout former naval officer who had served in Vietnam and specialized in Asian affairs. Many people believed that the Rambo character had been based on Rich. Yet, there was another side to him: he and his wife had adopted numerous special-needs kids. He was Colin Powell's best friend, a fact that would later lead to considerable conflict within the administration.

Steve was a quiet, Yale-trained lawyer from Cleveland, Ohio, who at the time wore horn-rimmed glasses. He was smart and methodical, and when there was real work to be produced for the campaign (rather than just things to be said and debated), we all looked to Steve to write the first draft of the paper. He did so selflessly and effectively.

Robert Zoellick, Robert Blackwill, and I had worked closely together during the extraordinary days of 1989–1991 at the end of the Cold War.

They were among the best policy engineers I had ever known, capable of conceiving of a solution and then actually implementing it. Zoellick had been Secretary of State James Baker's closest aide at the State Department and the architect of many important initiatives concerning Central America and Europe. He had led the three-member U.S. delegation to the talks on German unification on which I had been the White House representative.

Bob Blackwill had been my boss for a while at the NSC the first time around as special assistant for European and Soviet affairs. He'd held numerous high-level positions. He was from Kansas, with very traditional values and a wicked sense of humor. But he could be abrasive and impatient, and he made enemies. Some thought that Bob would be high maintenance, but he would be valuable to the governor, and we were good enough friends to speak honestly about any problems that might arise.

I asked Richard Perle to join the group to represent the right wing of the Republican foreign policy establishment. Perle had been the bane of the party's foreign policy traditionalists such as Brent Scowcroft and Henry Kissinger. He had a well-deserved reputation for ruthlessness too. But Governor Bush needed all elements of the party united behind him, and the group that I assembled was broadly representative enough to demonstrate his commitment to a foreign policy big tent. Dov Zakheim, who did most of the work supporting our Pentagon reform plans, rounded out the group. And we were able, too, to draw on the regional expertise of others such as Jendayi Frazer, who developed our Africa policy.

In general, we got along well. My job was to organize the group and to deal with the personalities and egos—to keep everyone on board so that we could concentrate on the governor's campaign, not ourselves. If there was any resentment of my role (I had been the most junior of those who had served together in George H. W. Bush's administration), I couldn't tell. In any case, they all knew that I was the one who was closest to the governor. I was the point of access. We worked smoothly and with little drama, just getting the job done in standing Sunday-night phone calls to coordinate requests, policy positions, and responses for Governor Bush.

Just for fun we decided to adopt a nickname and called ourselves the Vulcans, after the Roman God and symbol of my home city of Birmingham, Alabama. The name meant nothing more than that, but many a conspiracy theorist tried to divine some deeper significance.

The work in the campaign was proceeding well. I made frequent visits to Austin to brief the candidate, developed policy papers on a half-dozen major initiatives, and helped write a couple of major speeches. I also began doing press appearances on behalf of candidate Bush. The question was always the same: "What makes you think that the one-term governor of Texas is ready to be President of the United States?"

My first televised interview was on Chris Matthews's *Hardball* in June. Chris was a relentlessly challenging interviewer who rarely gave a guest time to really answer a question. Asked at one point whether George W. Bush's being in the Oval Office would be "on-the-job training," I pointed out that my candidate was already dealing with considerable complexity as governor of Texas. Texas is a big, complicated state, and the person running it has to be able to ask the right questions, digest information, stick to principles, and make decisions. The Texas governor has to be tough.

Chris, sensing that I was contrasting George W. Bush's readiness with that of Bill Clinton when he had first run for President, said, "Right. You sound like the wife of the governor in *Primary Colors* where she said, 'And he's governor of a real state, not Arkansas.'" I don't know where it came from, but I shot back, "I come from Alabama, so I'm not going to talk about what *real* states are." Chris broke up laughing, and I thought that I'd passed my first media test on the campaign trail.

Anyone who is interested in politics should work on the ground floor of a campaign at least once. Early on we got stuck in traffic jams and carried our own bags. The crowds were enthusiastic but, in some places, quite small. The music track that introduced the governor at campaign rallies included Stevie Wonder's "Signed, Sealed, Delivered (I'm Yours)." I never understood why that song was chosen, but to this day I can't listen to it without vivid memories of stadiums, auditoriums, and cowboy bars full of early believers in George W. Bush.

I loved the pace and the sense of being a part of an adventure. Life had settled into a nice post-provost pattern, and I was quite content. When I arranged to have George W. Bush meet my father during a trip to Palo Alto in July of 1999, Daddy was hooked. He peppered me every night with questions about campaign strategy that I couldn't answer: "How in the world did we screw up in New Hampshire? George Bush isn't getting through to people that he is going to be a different kind of Republican. That's what people need to know!" He admired Governor Bush and was very proud of my association with the campaign.

In February 2000 I was back home, helping to rally the troops for the California primary in the wake of the disasters in New Hampshire and Michigan. I was getting ready to do an interview with a reporter named Ann Dowd for a profile of me. Ann had gone to interview my father that morning and was in the house when suddenly my father suffered cardiac arrest. She called 911 and then my longtime assistant, Marilyn Stanley. I was in a meeting, but Marilyn burst in and said that something had happened to my father and he was not breathing. I asked my assistant Ruth Elliott to come with me, rushed out, and sped to the house. It looked like a scene from *ER*. Daddy was on the floor, and they were shocking his heart. I heard the medic say, "I have a weak pulse." We all rushed to the hospital and waited. It hadn't been a heart attack, but his heart had stopped long enough to cause what his physician called an "anoxic brain event." Essentially, he'd been deprived of oxygen to his brain and was now in a coma. No one could say what the prognosis was.

Daddy continued in a coma for about a week and then began to stir. But he'd sustained significant brain damage. He never fully recovered, but he fought to live. Several times he was near death and refused to go. As I watched this giant of a man who'd loved me more than anyone in the world approach the end, it was hard to find much good in life. It seemed so unfair that I could no longer share stories of the campaign with my father. Here I was at the height of my professional career, and my father couldn't enjoy it with me. Not surprisingly, my absences from home became a source of guilt, and the campaign, which had been such a wonderful magical mystery tour, became something of a slog.

I kept going and told myself that Daddy undoubtedly approved of my decision to keep my commitment to the campaign. Slowly the governor was climbing in the polls, and he clearly had a real chance to be

President. But we had not erased the questions about his foreign policy competence. In fact, early in the campaign, one particular misstep created a deep hole, and it took a while to climb out of it.

I arrived at the Austin airport one November evening in 1999, and my cell phone was going crazy. It was Joel Shin, an incredibly dedicated young man who actually slept in the campaign office. (Joshua Bolten, the policy director for the campaign and later deputy chief of staff, director of the Office of Management and Budget (OMB), and chief of staff, finally made him get an apartment.) Joel asked if I'd seen the governor's interview with Andy Hiller. I said that I'd been on the plane and hadn't. He read the transcript. My heart sank. "Can you name the president of Taiwan?" Answer: "Lee." "Can you name the general who is in charge of Pakistan?" Answer: "General." "And the prime minister of India?" No answer.

"Well, that reads pretty badly," I commented.

"It's worse," Joel said. "It's on videotape and being played over and over."

I went to the hotel but decided not to call the governor, thinking it might be better to wait until I saw him the next morning to address what we might do. That evening, he called me. "Who is the prime minister of Italy?" he asked. I laughed and thought to myself that he'd be just fine. In truth, the failure to know the names of leaders said little about the governor's competence to lead the country. Indeed, even President Clinton said that if Governor Bush were to make it into the White House, he would "soon enough learn their names." It was not as debilitating an issue as the press was making it out to be. Still, when we had breakfast the next morning on the patio of the Governor's Mansion, I said exactly what I was thinking: "We've got to step it up."

"I know," he replied.

And step it up he did. We needed to fight to a draw in foreign policy so that the American people could concentrate on the governor's qualities and domestic achievements, not on what names of leaders he knew. We picked a few key issues on which to focus—missile defense, reduction of offensive nuclear arms, and relations with emerging democracies such as India—as well as trading on his extensive knowledge of Mexico and Latin America.

Some of the senior statesmen of the Republican Party backed the governor early, particularly Dick Cheney, Don Rumsfeld, and George Shultz, who held policy seminars in his home on the Stanford campus. After the primaries, other heavyweights joined forces with us, among them Colin Powell and Henry Kissinger. The work paid its greatest dividend in the second debate against Al Gore.

In the first debate, George Bush had been a bit shaky on foreign policy, but fortunately, Al Gore's sighing and orange makeup had obscured this fact. Moreover, there had been fewer foreign policy questions than expected. We all knew that international affairs would therefore dominate the next encounter. The afternoon of the second debate, Karen Hughes, the governor's close confidante and communications director for the campaign, and I sat in his suite in North Carolina, going over major foreign policy questions. After a while, the tired George Bush said, "That's enough."

By then, though, we'd armed him with a particularly good answer on issues of global development and poverty. When the question came up, he replied that the United States is a generous country and ought to participate in significant debt relief for the poorest countries. A few days later a *New York Times* article noted the backing of debt relief by an assortment of leaders, including Governor Bush and the Pope. With his crisp answers on other questions—and Al Gore's inexplicable near-catatonic state (lampooned on *Saturday Night Live*)—George Bush delivered the foreign policy performance he desperately needed. Foreign policy was no longer a liability.

He knew the significance of that too. After the debate I found him outside his room at the hotel. He hugged me and said, "Oh, baby!" I translated that as "Job well done."

Florida

THE TIME after the debates passed in an instant. I flew down to Austin the afternoon of the election. By the time I arrived at the Four Seasons Hotel, the news stations were chalking up state after state in the Gore column. When I made it downstairs to watch with a few Bush friends and family, everything was going against us: Michigan, Illinois, Pennsylvania, and Florida were all gone. I sat there with Doro Bush Koch, the governor's sister, and watched in dismay. "Let's change places," I said to Doro, employing a superstition from my days as an athlete and a sports fan: if your team is not winning while you're sitting on the right side of the sofa, move to the left. Yes, I know it doesn't matter, but it can't hurt.

We did change places. Almost magically, NBC News reported that we'd won Georgia. Then Jean Becker, the elder George Bush's assistant, got a call. Jean had been a reporter, and a friend from *USA Today* called to tell her that they were about to reverse the call on Florida. Within what seemed like minutes but was much longer, the TV screen suddenly began showing "George W. Bush, 43rd President of the United States." It was quite a moment, and my immediate impulse was to call my father. I decided not to, fearing that he would be too disoriented to share the moment with me.

I jumped into a minivan with other Bush supporters for the trip to the capitol for the victory speech. It was freezing cold in Austin, and we stood on the square, rocking to "Y'all Ready for This" from the Jock Jams album and hugging each other. But something was wrong. Al Gore hadn't conceded. I could also see the big screen displaying CNN's election coverage. The margin of victory in Florida was shrinking very fast.

Then Karen Hughes called her husband, Jerry, and reported that although Gore had called the governor to concede, he had subsequently withdrawn his concession. After another hour or so, we all shuffled back to the minivan and went back to the hotel. There was confusion but not really despair. I went to bed and awoke to the news that Florida would be contested.

When I spotted Fox News reporter Carl Cameron in the lobby, I asked him, "What's going on?"

"I thought *you* might know," he said and then went on to tell me that there would likely be a recount.

I also ran into Bob Blackwill. "You know what this is like?" he asked. "It's like eating a really spicy meal before bed and having a really bad dream. You think to yourself, 'Must have been what I ate last night. Boy, I'm glad to wake up from that one!' "

But of course it wasn't a dream. I stayed in Austin a few days. I hung out near Karl Rove, trying to understand what was really happening via his sophisticated county-by-county analysis of our chances in Florida.

Governor Bush called the morning after the election to say that he wanted me to be national security advisor but we'd obviously have to wait a bit on any announcement. It was surreal, but we went through the motions of planning a foreign policy transition that might never happen. One particularly bad idea was to have a photo op of the governor and me sitting in front of the fireplace discussing foreign policy. It looked like a faux Oval Office shot and was properly ridiculed. I decided to go home to California.

The return to California gave me a chance to spend quality time with my father. Meanwhile, I watched the ups and downs in Florida, my mood swinging with every court decision. I asked Steve Hadley to be the deputy national security advisor if I needed one. The two of us met with the Vulcans in Washington and talked about how to organize Bush's foreign policy, if we were given the opportunity. After the session, Steve and I were sitting in the conference room of his law office when we got word that the Florida Supreme Court had ordered a manual recount. The Bush lawyers had fought to prevent that, and though no one could know the outcome it seemed to portend a probable defeat.

We walked outside toward the restaurant for dinner. "Steve," I said, "I would have loved to serve with you. You would have been a great deputy national security advisor." I flew home to California the next day, believing that it was over. When I got off the plane and into the car, my driver, Mary Reynolds, gave me an update. The Supreme Court had, by a 5–4 decision, issued a stay, halting the manual recounts and setting a hearing for the matter on Monday, December 11. That meant that the judges in the majority were likely to rule in favor of Bush, certifying him as the winner of Florida's electoral votes. George W. Bush would indeed become the forty-third President of the United States.

That night I went to a birthday party for George Shultz at the Bohemian Club in San Francisco. The mood was very festive, and everyone congratulated me on my appointment. It hadn't been announced, but it had been assumed for a long time that I would accompany the governor to Washington as national security advisor. I accepted the thanks, but the next morning I called the governor and told him that I didn't think I could go to Washington. I explained that I could not leave my father in his current state. In fact, I'd already told a couple of close friends. I remember a conversation with Janne Nolan, with whom I'd been a research fellow at Stanford in 1981. "People would understand if I said I can't do it because of the children," I said. "They won't understand my obligations to my father."

"Rent a baby," Janne advised. We laughed, but she was one of the few who seemed to understand.

The governor called back and said that he understood but it was important I go. "I'm not asking you to leave your dad alone. He's always been there for you, and you want to be there for him. We'll make it work." We agreed that I would go to Washington but travel back to California every two weeks. In my heart I knew that it wasn't a practical solution, but I wasn't prepared to leave my father alone.

Three days before Christmas I went to have dinner at the home of my good friend and sports buddy Lori White. I stopped by to see Daddy on the way, and he seemed in pretty good spirits. I called a few hours later as I was leaving Lori's house, and Daddy got on the phone.

"I'm going home," he said.

"Daddy, you are at home," I answered.

"No, it's time for me to go home."

I knew in my heart what he meant, and it terrified me. My father, a Presbyterian minister and a man of great faith, believed that at the end of our earthly existence God calls us home to eternal life.

I rushed to his house. He seemed fine, and I left. I drove the ten minutes to my house. As I walked in the door, my stepmother, Clara, was calling. Daddy had stopped breathing. We rushed to the hospital. This time the physical and mental damage was irreparable. On Christmas Eve, after slipping into a coma, my father died.

I'd told Daddy just after the election that George W. Bush wanted me to go to Washington and become national security advisor. Daddy was able to communicate his understanding, but he also cried, and I couldn't tell whether they were tears of joy for my achievement or tears of despair because he knew that we would be separated. With his death he resolved my dilemma. Was it coincidence? I've always prayed that it was because I can't bear to think that John Wesley Rice, Jr., deliberately did that one last thing to make sure I fulfilled my dreams. Honestly, it would have been just like him.

Inauguration Day

I SAT ON the dais a few rows back of the President-elect, my feet freezing and covered in a plastic poncho to protect me from the sleet of that January day. I reflected on my journey to that point and ached to have my parents sitting on the Mall to see George W. Bush take the oath of office, ushering me into the White House with him. Still, it was a joyous day as I took in the sights and sounds of this most remarkable demonstration of the United States' democratic stability, despite the controversy surrounding the election. At the lunch in the National Statuary Hall, the new President entered for the first time to the strains of "Hail to the Chief." I felt chills of pride and excitement. And then the celebration was over. We returned directly to the White House and got down to work.

From that day on, my "routine" reminded me that nothing would, in fact, be routine. Entering through the guarded gate each morning, passing stiffly standing marine guards, walking through the corridors that Lincoln and Roosevelt, Truman and Kennedy and Reagan had frequented, gave me an extraordinary sense of a place—a small place—in history. But those who became too focused on the atmosphere didn't last very long. There was work to do, under enormous pressure, and missteps could have dire consequences. The White House was a hothouse, and everyone who worked in those highly coveted jobs knew the stakes.

2

HONEST BROKER

I'D GIVEN A LOT of thought to the type of organization that I wanted to form. The National Security Council was established by the National Security Act of 1947 when, after World War II, it became clear that the United States would be permanently and dominantly involved in world politics. There are four original statutory members of the National Security Council: the President, the Vice President, the secretary of state, and the secretary of defense. The only other statutory position created through the act is the executive secretary of the NSC, a largely administrative but very vital function. That person manages the paper flow, oversees the Situation Room, handles interagency communication, and often staffs the President during travel. The role requires a very good administrator who can "keep the trains running on time" internally and work seamlessly with the other agencies. But it also helps to have a seasoned foreign policy hand who can understand the context and meaning of the paper he's seeing. Our executive secretaries, Bob Bradtke, Steve Biegun, and then Greg Schulte, possessed both sets of qualifications.

Because of a very capable career administrative staff that works for the executive secretary, there is a kind of bureaucratic continuity. This allows for smoother functioning on the national security side of the White House than on the domestic side, which has essentially no standing career apparatus. When I returned to Washington, I was struck by the degree to which the paperwork looked exactly as it had when I had left as special assistant for Soviet affairs on the NSC staff of George H. W. Bush in 1991.

Given the prominence today of the national security advisor, it is surprising that the role, officially known as the assistant to the President for national security affairs, is not even mentioned in the 1947 legislation. McGeorge Bundy, who served President John F. Kennedy, is widely regarded as the first person to hold the position. Since then, there have been many variations in how the role is played. Some, such as Henry Kissinger, have sought—successfully—to become independent power centers. Others, such as Brent Scowcroft, have been honest brokers in representing the views of the secretaries to the President but giving him advice privately, never publicly.

The national security advisor is staff—rarified staff, to be sure, but staff nonetheless. There's no doubt that sitting a few feet from the Oval Office confers influence, but it is the reflected influence of the President and must be used sparingly. The national security advisor must find a way to get the secretaries to do what the President wants them to do. I once told the President that this was a bit like trying to execute policy with a remote control. You don't own troops, diplomats, or a budget. You have only your relationship with the President. I felt confident in mine and was sure that I knew what kind of NSC I would run.

We are all captives of our earlier experiences, and mine had been a very good and successful one when I had worked for Brent Scowcroft. I patterned my role after Brent, as an honest broker, not a separate power center. There would be a small staff, dedicated to doing the work that the Cabinet departments could not but avoiding the tendency of the NSC staff to duplicate their efforts. And never would the NSC become involved in operational matters. The execution of policy was to be left to the Cabinet secretaries, who carried the authority that Senate confirmation conferred. The NSC staff, on the other hand, cannot be held accountable by Congress because it is part of the President's personal staff. It is too small and too close to the President to actually act on behalf of the United States.

The imperative that secretaries (and their departments) handle operational matters was a conviction shared by everyone who'd studied the disasters that had befallen presidents when the NSC tried to be something more than a coordinating body. The most recent example had been the Iran-Contra affair, when the NSC staff had taken it upon itself to devise and then carry out a policy widely viewed as risky at best and likely illegal. As the facts emerged, it was clear that the plan to divert funds from covert Iranian arms sales to the Nicaraguan resistance (the Contras) had been cooked up secretly within the NSC staff—apparently without the knowledge of the secretary of state, let alone Congress. The fallout was disastrous; the affair almost brought down the Reagan presidency.

The counsel to the Tower Commission, which was chaired by former Texas Senator John Tower and investigated the affair on behalf of President Reagan, was none other than Steve Hadley, now the deputy national security advisor. He and I vowed that the NSC staff would play a limited but effective role, carrying out the agenda of the President through, not around, the Cabinet secretaries whom he'd appointed. As for my role in particular, I intended to keep a low public profile.

But if the NSC is to be an honest broker, it helps enormously to have Cabinet secretaries who work well together. The NSC should intervene when there is a policy disagreement among the departments or when they cannot coordinate among themselves. But the NSC cannot do so on every single issue every day, or the system would grind to a halt, wallowing in inefficiency. Most of the time the Department of Defense and the State Department need to find a way to work together—at all levels.

To be sure, tensions between Defense and State are almost endemic, and there have been some cases—Caspar Weinberger and George Shultz come to mind—where the two principals barely spoke to each other. That is not, as some might think, because State is from Venus and Defense from Mars. In fact, there are many times when the secretary of state is more willing to use force than the Pentagon, given the admirable conservatism of professional officers about the use of military power.

Nonetheless, secretaries of state find the Pentagon all too willing to exert influence in foreign policy. With a budget nearly forty times that of the State Department, the Defense Department possesses an awe-inspiring logistical capacity, and State sometimes finds itself dependent on and resentful of the military's reach. No U.S. response to a humanitarian crisis, such as the 2004 earthquake in Indonesia, is possible without the extraordinary capabilities of the Pentagon. The military undertakes humanitarian work around the world through, for example, the USNS *Mercy* hospital ship. In the best of circumstances, those capabilities merge seamlessly with the diplomatic expertise of the ambassador and his embassy, producing a unified U.S. response to a crisis or opportunity.

But that's not always the case. Combatant commanders exist for each region of the world, and they sometimes act quite independently, developing their own relationships with foreign leaders and bringing their influence to bear on issues that at best cross and at worst shatter the lines between diplomacy and security policy. Those commanders have enormous assets. For example, the commander in the Pacific (USPACOM) lives in Hawaii and travels on dedicated military aircraft across the Pacific and in Asia. By contrast, the assistant secretary of state for East Asian and Pacific affairs will often find himself in a web of connecting commercial flights that can take more than twenty-four hours to deliver him to the region.

There is also, of course, the tendency of civilians in the Office of the Secretary of Defense to have many different opinions about how diplomacy ought to be carried out. State Department officials must politely remind them that getting other countries to do what you want is no easy task. It is State that must deliver, but everyone has views about how to get it done, and often those individuals are vocally critical of how State is doing its work. It isn't surprising that the relationship between the two departments is sometimes a bit tense.

In the case of Colin Powell and Don Rumsfeld, it went beyond such almost inescapable tensions. The two men had known each other for years, and there was a good deal of personal respect. There was an equal measure of distrust, however. The two did not confront each other face-to-face, let alone in front of the President. Rather, Don would send memos (snowflakes, we called them) that implicitly—and sometimes explicitly—criticized what State or the NSC was doing. Often those memos reflected discussions that had already taken place, but they left the impression that it was Don imparting new wisdom or making an important recommendation. In meetings, he would ask Socratic questions rather than take a position. This led to tensions with and frustrations for Colin.

In addition, Colin had to battle the perception that State was not always on the same page with the White House. There is a tendency of

Foreign Service officers to regard the President and his political advisors as a passing phenomenon without the deep expertise that they, the professionals, bring to diplomacy. That sometimes led State to tell the world "What the President meant to say," usually in some leak to the *Washington Post* or the *New York Times*. The inclination of some in State to display what they regard as their superior expertise was especially strong in the first turbulent years of the Bush administration, but former Secretary of State Dean Acheson had talked about the appearance of the phenomenon decades before. As Acheson put it in his memoir *Present at the Creation,* "The attitude that presidents and secretaries may come and go but the Department goes on forever has led many presidents to distrust and dislike the Department of State."

The national security advisor is left to sort out those tensions. In general, I got along well with my colleagues. The Vice President had direct access to the President, and he used it. After those conversations, though, the President would fill me in on the Vice President's thinking, so that I was rarely blindsided. Often the Vice President and I talked directly about what was on his mind. Later, when I became secretary of state, he and I often disagreed and argued vociferously in front of the President. But it was never personal.

That was not always true of the Vice President's staff. At the start, there had even been one attempt to alter a long-standing tradition by having the Vice President chair the powerful Principals Committee, made up of the Cabinet secretaries, in place of the national security advisor. I went to the President and said, "Mr. President, this is what the NSA does: convene the national security principles to make recommendations to you." He agreed, and that was the end of that. Later, Steve Hadley told me that he'd spoken to the Vice President who'd acknowledged that it was a stupid idea.

The problem was that the Vice President's staff, which seemed very much of one ultra-hawkish mind, was determined to act as a power center of its own. Many things were done "in the name of the Vice President," whether he had directed them to be done or not. To be sure, he shared his staff members' views; they were not substantively out of line with his thinking. But some of the bureaucratic games that the

Office of the Vice President played were not characteristic of my dealings with their boss.

My relationship with Don Rumsfeld was considerably more complicated, though not in the ways that accorded with common wisdom in Washington. Don and I had been friends for a number of years. I first met him when we participated in a three-day "continuity of government" exercise to prepare for nuclear war. (The Cold War was not yet over.) He played the President, and I was his chief of staff. Over the years we remained in contact, and Don and his wife, Joyce, gave dinners for me or joined me for a meal when Stanford business took me to Chicago. Don tried to recruit me to a couple of corporate boards on which he served, and it was I who helped recruit Don to George W. Bush's cause in 1999. What's more, when initial secretary of defense candidates fell by the wayside during the transition, I recommended to the President-elect that he choose Don, pointing out that he was known to be a tough bureaucratic infighter but that he "knew where the bodies were buried in the Pentagon" and would be able to carry out the much-needed post–Cold War transformation of our military forces.

Throughout the ups and downs of the term, our relationship remained cordial. Don would come to my Christmas party and heartily sing "We Three Kings." For a long time I saved a letter that Don sent me in 2006 offering me his weekend home on Maryland's eastern shore should I want to get away from Washington. I knew that without proof no one would believe it. In other words, the tension that did build between us was not a problem of personal animosity but rather of professional conflict.

I am convinced that Don simply resented the role I had to play as national security advisor. He would become frustrated when my staff would reach out to military officers in the Pentagon to coordinate the particulars of a policy among the agencies. This was a routine responsibility for the NSC, but for some reason Don interpreted such actions as a violation of his authority.

In December 2002 he sent me a "snowflake" saying that I "was not in the chain of command"—a fact I well understood—and that if my staff and I did not stop "giving tasks and guidance" to the combatant commanders and the joint staff, he would take his objections to the President. I found the tirade amusing if slightly condescending and wished he had taken it to the President. I am confident that the President too would have found it bizarre.

This animosity toward my role resulted in complaints about the NSC process. Don wasn't party to my conversations with the President about matters before the NSC and assumed that I was substituting my own preferences for the views of the principals. He complained that I kept seeking consensus when the President should have been given a decision memo—so that he could just decide. Sometimes the President directed me to try one more time to find common ground. Sometimes he listened to the debate in the NSC and then told me what he wanted to do. George W. Bush had no trouble making decisions when the search for consensus failed. Often, though, it is preferable for the national security advisor to deliver the news that a Cabinet secretary has been overruled than to have the President do it. And sometimes a decision memo where the President checks a box fails to reflect the complexity of the reasoning that led to that decision—and, should it be leaked to the press, is sure to be misrepresented as a victory for one Cabinet secretary and a loss for another in the policy debate.

It is also not true as the press once reported that Don ever refused to return my phone calls. I would not have put up with that, and neither would the President. Don, Colin, and I spoke almost every morning, our travel schedules permitting. Don did dislike NSC Principals meetings, letting it be known that they were an unwelcome distraction from his day job of running the Pentagon, but our lines of communication were never closed.

Ironically, I came to have some sympathy with this view when I became secretary of state. The national security advisor's work is to coordinate various departments and to staff the President. The NSC staff numbers about a hundred people. The job is demanding but very different from the line responsibilities of the Cabinet secretaries, who must manage huge organizations (State has fifty-seven thousand employees worldwide, the Pentagon seven hundred thousand civilians alone) that are constantly in need of oversight, attention, and decision making. There is always some surprise landing on the secretary's desk, and frequently it is already public and largely beyond resolution. Big organizations are just difficult to manage, and as Secretary of Defense Bob Gates and I used to say to each other, only half jokingly, "You never know what your building is doing until it's too late."

Cabinet secretaries, as constitutional officers, also have responsibilities to Congress. Members of Congress expect a secretary to direct his or her attention to a host of issues ranging from the plight of individual constituents to major policy choices. There are constant reporting requirements, briefings, and sometimes hearings. Add to that press demands, ceremonial functions, and a demanding travel schedule, and there is never enough time. A two-hour NSC Principals meeting is core to the national security advisor's mission but a drain on the time of a secretary, who can end up making the trip to the White House two or three times a day.

The truth is that we would have had fewer Principals meetings had the distrust between Don and Colin not made the levels below the secretaries largely incapable of taking decisions. The two had dissimilar styles: Colin was a cautious consensus builder in international politics, and Don was confrontational. Don rarely saw shades of gray on an issue, while Colin almost always saw nuances. This, of course, reflected their different roles, but it was more than that; it was a matter of personality and worldview as well. Don's more black-and-white view of the world sometimes accorded more closely with that of the President in the early days, particularly after 9/11.

The other major challenge with Don was his secretiveness in running the Pentagon. He claimed to delegate decision making to lower levels, but then didn't always ratify what his lieutenants had done. The people who worked for him were fearful of his wrath. The atmosphere in the Pentagon was one where nothing was really settled until the secretary had opined. That handicapped the Deputies Committee (the number twos in the departments) that Steve chaired and made necessary the very Principals meetings that Don detested.

For the most part we managed the tensions between us. But we did clash with increasing frequency as time went on. It's always uncomfortable, particularly for the President, for a member of the President's staff to challenge a Cabinet secretary. Still, on a few occasions, Don and I did tangle in front of others. After one such episode, the two of us were walking side by side through the Rose Garden portico. I turned to Don and asked, "What's wrong between us?"

"I don't know," he said. "We always got along. You're obviously bright and committed, but it just doesn't work."

Bright? That, I thought to myself, is part of the problem. Don had been more comfortable in the old days, when he was the senior statesman championing my career. A relationship between equals was much harder for him.

Colin, on the other hand, always seemed very comfortable with my role and our personal relationship. I'd first met him in 1987, when he was deputy national security advisor and I was on a one-year fellowship with the Joint Chiefs of Staff. He invited me to a pleasant lunch, and we conversed about my future. He and his wife, Alma, became my friends. Alma and I shared familial ties in Birmingham, Alabama. My father had worked for Alma's uncle, who was the principal of the second largest black high school. Alma's father, Mr. R. C. Johnson, was the principal of the largest, Parker High, and was a legend in our middle-class, segregated community.

Colin knew how hard the NSA job was, and he tried to be supportive. But he also, I believe, thought that I was not strong enough in my support of him and the State Department agenda. He asked me many times why I didn't go to the President to "discipline" Defense for any number of sins of omission or commission, some imagined, some not. He probably didn't realize how often I took State's case to the President sympathetically.

But truthfully, I wondered why he did not take greater advantage of his extraordinary stature. Sometimes I would go to the President and suggest that it was time for him to sit down with Colin over dinner; the relationship between the two men was always better after they did. I often told the President before one of those sessions that Colin was very unhappy and would tell him so. He didn't, and the President sometimes had difficulty gauging the extent of Colin's dissatisfaction. I hate pop psychoanalysis, but I did sometimes wonder what held Colin back; perhaps the "soldier" felt constrained, and, of course, he had to be aware that he probably would have been President had he chosen to run. The relationship between George W. Bush and Colin Powell was thus respectful—genuinely so—but complicated.

In short, the President knew that Don and Colin did not get along, and decision making was difficult. My task was to work around the personal distrust between the two men, a task that became harder as the problems became more difficult. In the final analysis, Colin was probably right when he asked me one day, "Why doesn't the President just square the circle? One of us needs to go." I should have gone to the President and asked him exactly that. The President might have made a change, but where? Colin was essential to dealing with foreign governments, and the Pentagon was in the middle of a war under Don's leadership. I thought it was better to try to make it work. Despite the challenges, I learned important lessons from those bureaucratic struggles that I would take with me to State a few years later.

In the end we kept going, with Don complaining to the Vice President that I was slanting decision making toward State and Colin complaining to me that Defense was in league with the Vice President's office to undermine State's positions. And, mirroring what was going on at the top, the relationship between those at lower ranks grew increasingly unworkable. Sometimes the lower levels at Foggy Bottom (where the State Department is located) would, inexplicably, leak to the press that State was being outmaneuvered by Defense. Leaks are debilitating, sowing distrust among the officials who have to work together and coloring the President's options. People do it to show that they are in the know or to advance a position. But for the life of me, I could never understand why it was career-enhancing for State to tell the press that Colin was losing every bureaucratic battle. In fact, State was winning its share.

I've asked myself many times how I might have broken this cycle of distrust and dysfunction. Steve Hadley and I managed to make the creaky system work most of the time. We were able to do so in fighting the war in Afghanistan, helping to liberate Liberia, pushing a transformational agenda through NATO, sustaining peace in the Balkans, managing crises between India and Pakistan, launching the President's compassion agenda, and restructuring our approach to the Palestinian-Israeli conflict. But in the taxing issue of Iraq, the stress on the NSC system brought it—and our personal relationships—nearly to the breaking point.

3

POLICY BEGINS

E VERY PRESIDENT COMES to office determined to set a new course in foreign policy. This tends to be the case even when there is no change in party. When George H. W. Bush entered the White House in 1989, Brent Scowcroft instructed the NSC staff to initiate a series of policy reviews. The purpose was to give time to get new people into place and, in the case of European and Soviet policy, to slow down what was widely seen as Ronald Reagan's too-close embrace of Mikhail Gorbachev in 1988. The reviews, two of which I personally managed, seethed with distrust of the changes taking place in Eastern Europe and the Soviet Union. Yet the rapid collapse of communism got our attention in time to overcome our inherent caution. Fortunately, no one remembers that we wrote policy guidance questioning Gorbachev's motives and setting up careful "tests" of Moscow's intentions months before the collapse of Soviet power in Eastern Europe and the unification of Germany.

When there is a change of party on the heels of a hardfought campaign, the desire to seize the agenda is, of course, more pronounced. The Bush approach had been laid out in a series of speeches during the campaign, and we immediately set about executing the initiatives.

The most comprehensive of those speeches had been the governor's appearance at the Ronald Reagan Presidential Library and Museum in November 1999. The venue was as important as the speech, since the event represented a kind of laying on of hands by the Reagan establishment, in particular Nancy Reagan. She couldn't have been more gracious and remained so throughout the administration.

At the time, though, one subtext in the campaign was whether the presidency of George W. Bush would be, in effect, a second term for George H. W. Bush. This had important ramifications not only in domestic policy concerning taxes (Bush 41's nonfulfillment of his "no new taxes" pledge still rankled many Republicans, who were hoping for better from Bush 43) but also in foreign policy, where George H. W. Bush was viewed with suspicion in conservative circles. Until the end, the policies of the two men would be compared and contrasted: realism versus idealism; diplomacy versus confrontation; compromise versus absolutism; prudence versus plunging. In fact, I regarded—and still regard—the hyperbolic comparisons, drawn in stark shades of black and white, as unfair. Yes, there were differences in style and temperament, with George W. Bush quicker to anger and less given to shades of gray. But to the degree that the differences were sharp (and they sometimes were), it was in large part because 1989 and 2001 were worlds apart. George H. W. Bush is and always should be remembered for his tactful personal diplomacy that ended the Cold War. The successful—though inconclusive—Persian Gulf War is also part of his impressive legacy.

Yet the defining moments that laid the foundation for victory in the Cold War had come in the dark days of Josef Stalin and Nikita Khrushchev. Ronald Reagan had issued the final challenge to the Soviet Union at the dawn of the 1980s, calling it an evil empire and pushing through huge defense budgets that spent it into the Ice Age.

By the time George H. W. Bush came to power, the Soviet Union was a spent force. It was not easy to shepherd a dying but still dangerous superpower to collapse. Unifying Germany on Western terms and sustaining the forward momentum of freedom in Eastern Europe was difficult. But the Soviet Union was in its twilight, and enlightened leaders such as Mikhail Gorbachev and his foreign minister, Eduard Shevardnadze, knew it. In 2001 it fell to George W. Bush to confront a new and rising threat in al Qaeda and its extremist kin, full of bravado and revolutionary zeal, and to lead at the beginning of a new and dangerous historical epoch.

In 1999 the scope of that challenge was not yet evident. The Reagan Library speech laid out a broad, if somewhat conventional, foreign policy agenda, including a plan for dealing with great powers such as Russia and China. It also anticipated the arrival of India, the world's largest democracy, as a power of global significance, and vowed to strengthen U.S. ties by increasing trade and investment. I later elaborated on those themes in a *Foreign Affairs* article that winter. But a centerpiece of the foreign policy agenda drew on the governor's knowledge of and interest in Latin America and as such represented a departure. In a speech in Miami, Florida, in August 2000, the governor spoke about the central-ity of the "neighborhood." He vowed to make Latin America a funda-mental concern of his foreign policy, emphasizing strong ties to Mexico, renewed promotion of hemispheric free trade, and sustained support for freedom and democracy across the Americas.

Our first opportunity to put this promise into practice came in February 2001 with the President's first foreign trip. The President's foreign itinerary is made up both of trips that he must take—for ex-ample, to NATO summits and G8 meetings—and trips that he makes to push an initiative. The decision to make the first trip a visit to President Vicente Fox at his ranch in San Cristóbal, Mexico, was meant to send a strong signal that Latin America would be first among equals in Bush foreign policy.

The trip was intended to showcase not just the pivotal importance of Latin America in general but that of Mexico in particular. Fox and Bush had met in Dallas shortly after they had been elected. They'd sketched out a broad agenda: strengthening trade, modernizing the border, re-forming immigration, and pushing a free-market approach for the en-tire region. Years before as governors, they'd known each other and had great mutual respect.

Mexico was in the midst of a democratic transformation, marked by Fox's election win, the first time the opposition party had triumphed in seventy-one years. Fox's predecessor, Ernesto Zedillo, had ushered in a new brand of clean personal politics, telling people that he intended to leave office no richer than when he'd arrived. Fox stood for the next important step: Mexico's institutional maturation as a democracy and the peaceful transfer of power from one party to another.

George W. Bush understood the significance of Vicente Fox, and he wanted to be his friend and supporter as he took on the entrenched interests and corruption that prevented Mexico from moving forward economically and socially. Mexico and the United States have a long, mostly unhappy history with each other. We fully intended to highlight Mexico's importance and U.S. humility.

On the morning of February 16, 2001, we boarded Air Force One at 8:00 A.M. We landed in Guanajuato, Mexico, and were met by Fox and his soon-to-be wife, Marta Sahagún, who'd been his press secretary. Fox is a giant of a man, dark and handsome, and it struck me that he could easily have been cast in a movie as a Mexican hacienda owner of the late nineteenth century. In fact, he's a former international businessman who was the chief executive for Coca-Cola de México and speaks perfect English. Nonetheless, he looks as though he'd be right at home on a great stallion, and in fact, riding is an activity that he loves. He was reportedly disappointed when the White House let it be known that there would be no horseback riding, something President Bush did not enjoy.

Before going to the ranch, we stopped to say hello to President Fox's eighty-one-year-old mother. We all waited in the car while the two presidents went into a house that spoke volumes about Fox's modest beginnings. The short ride to the ranch was pleasant, with Mexican citizens out in significant numbers to greet the President. They were waving U.S. flags. Well, in every country the people along the motorcade route wave U.S. flags, unless they are protesting something that the United States has done. This time the spectators were all friendly.

We arrived at the ranch, which didn't look like a ranch at all—at least not my conception of one. It was a magnificent series of houses arrayed across a picturesque Mexican landscape. The discussions were held on the partially enclosed multicolored-tile-and-white-stucco patio of the largest house, overlooking the serene countryside. Sitting around the large wooden table, I thought, *All is going exactly as it should.* U.S.-Mexican relations were off to a terrific start.

About an hour into the discussion, I caught sight of Ari Fleischer, our peripatetic press secretary. Ari had sharp elbows and battled with the press on a daily basis, but our relationship was cordial and sound. We had talked early on about the need for the national security advisor and the press secretary to develop a relationship of trust. Ari would stop in every morning to get the latest updates and develop a line of attack—or defense—on the issues of the day. I told him that there would be times when I couldn't talk about issues but that I would never deceive him.

I couldn't imagine what Ari wanted, but he was clearly motioning, with increasing urgency, for me to leave the table and talk to him. I was reluctant since I was seated next to the President. But Ari was by now in some measure of distress. When I excused myself and reached him, he asked, "Why are we bombing Baghdad?"

"What?" I said.

"The press is telling me that we are bombing Baghdad," Ari said. "Their cell phones are going crazy."

I went back toward the table and motioned to Colin Powell, then Karen Hughes. Pretty soon it looked like one of those television shows where one participant after another leaves until there is only one. I can't imagine what the Mexicans thought. Here we were, writing a new chapter in U.S.-Mexican relations amid some very obvious distractions. The President finally stopped in midsentence and asked rather agitatedly, "What's going on?" I whispered to the President that something was happening in Iraq and I would get back to him. Needless to say, the moment was pretty much ruined.

I made a series of panicked phone calls to Washington and got Steve Hadley on the phone. He called the Pentagon and learned that during a "routine" overflight of Iraqi airspace we'd gotten, as he put it in his understated way, "a little close to the air defenses of Baghdad." We had, it seemed, set off every air-raid siren within shouting distance of the city. There wasn't much time for a full accounting of exactly how that had happened. We hurriedly wrote press guidance that explained that the United States, as a part of its obligations under the armistice terms that had ended the Persian Gulf War in 1991, was flying patrols to keep Saddam Hussein from using his aircraft against his own people or his neighbors. They were called "no-fly zones."

The press conference was a disaster. The President gamely made his points about the importance of U.S.-Mexican relations, our respect for Mexican democracy, and his desire for partnership with Vicente Fox. No one was listening. "Why are you bombing Baghdad?" "Are you going to war?" "Did you tell President Fox that you were going to war?"

I remember feeling sick from the afternoon heat, which was suddenly very pronounced. And I was so embarrassed by what was happening. The two presidents finished the press conference, and we said our good-byes.

The relationship between Fox and Bush never really reached its full potential. There were many reasons for that, including outsized Mexican expectations about immigration reform and our inability to deliver any change on this critical issue, despite the President's deep desire to do so.

There were also disappointments on both sides after September 11, 2001, shifted our focus and required from Fox support of U.S. priorities that he could not give. Indeed, 9/11 occurred just days after the Mexican state visit later in the year, which had included an historic joint meeting between the two countries' cabinets. The relationship with Mexico seemed destined to be overshadowed. Yet I have to think that that first encounter left its mark and contributed to the sense of lost opportunities that would follow.

That night we went to President Bush's ranch in Crawford, Texas. We were all a little shell-shocked. The television stations were playing the "attack" over and over, and Saddam Hussein, who was a master of public relations, Middle East style, had trotted out as many bloody bodies and scenes from hospitals as he could muster. The strikes against the air defenses had taken place near Baghdad, but it was unlikely that they had resulted in the civilian casualties now chronicled on the news. The President said, "I'm going to call Dick," perhaps seeking reassurance from an old foreign policy hand. The Vice President said that from his point of view it had been a good message, showing that we'd be tough on Saddam Hussein. I thought that it showed, once again, the United States' arrogance toward our Mexican hosts.

The next morning I was astonished to see that the *New York Times* had taken the line that the Vice President had predicted. The air strikes had "sent a timely signal," the paper said, that the new administration would "not shy away from using force to contain any new Iraqi military threat." The *Washington Post* called the strikes "a welcome reinvigoration of an existing policy that had been allowed to slide." I walked into breakfast with the President. "Mr. President," I said, "I want you to know that I know the difference between lucky and good."

We returned to Washington and conducted a postmortem on what had happened. A few days before departing for Mexico, the air force briefed Steve Hadley and me about an upcoming no-fly-zone mission. The general who briefed us did so in a very matter-of-fact way. Because it was our first experience with no-fly zones, we failed to ask a few key questions, such as "How routine is a mission of this type?" and "How close will it come to Baghdad?" The answers would have been "Not very routine" and "*Very* close." Even so, I doubt that the general would have said that we were likely to get into a "hot" fire exchange with weapons being fired. I blamed myself for not asking those questions. *I should have known,* I thought. How many times in my previous White House role had I seen the impact of unforeseen events involving military force? How many times had I taught about unintended consequences? That episode was an invaluable lesson.

The incident in Mexico was a reminder of the festering problem of Saddam Hussein's Iraq and its threat to our interests. Almost from the very beginning Iraq was a preoccupation of the national security team. Our focus was not, as common wisdom now has it, on the overthrow of Saddam Hussein. Rather, the early efforts were aimed at trying to strengthen the containment regime that had been put into place after the Gulf War. That war had ended inconclusively with Iraqi forces expelled from Kuwait but the regime still in power. The assessment of the George H. W. Bush administration in 1991 that Saddam was so weakened that he would either fall from power or stay in his box turned out to be wrong.

The no-fly zones were just one part of a complex web of constraints that the international system relied upon to keep Saddam from attacking his neighbors and his people and prevent him from rebuilding his weapons of mass destruction (WMD). And those constraints were being undermined on multiple fronts. For example, the Chinese were building a fiber-optic system in and around the capital, making it harder to track Iraq's military communications. Saddam was finding new ways to shield his forces.

At the end of the Gulf War in 1991, the international community had learned that Saddam's WMD capabilities were far more advanced than expected. When inspectors had arrived after Saddam's defeat, they had found that he was a little more than a year away from possessing a crude nuclear device. He had, of course, twice used chemical weapons, first against Iran and then against the Kurds, in both instances killing thousands of innocent civilians. The 1990s had been dominated by efforts to prevent him from restoring his capabilities. Resolution after resolution—sixteen in all—had demanded better access for weapons inspectors. But over the years, the inspection regime had been softened in myriad ways. Saddam wanted inspectors from the United States and Great Britain to be replaced by a mélange of nationals, some of whom had little experience in the WMD field. By the end of the 1990s, the Security Council would give in to his demands. The inspections themselves had at times lost the element of surprise when Saddam had insisted upon and gotten prior notification at designated sites. (Even when they could get in, inspectors often found themselves harassed by Saddam's forces.) The international community was slowly slipping into a posture of "respect for Iraqi sovereignty."

Over time, the Iraqis also became less and less compliant with even the scaled-back inspections, leading to multiplying questions about what was going on in Iraq. That ultimately led President Bill Clinton to order a military strike on suspected sites in December 1998. Just before the attack, inspectors left the country, not to return until 2002, and the Iraqi regime remained uncooperative.

Iraq had been, since 1991, under a comprehensive set of sanctions on prohibited items that could be used to rebuild military capabilities, including a prohibition against selling oil. That meant that there was no revenue to provide for basic goods such as food and medicine for the people. The effects on the population were growing increasingly harsh, with malnutrition rates exceeding 20 percent in the late 1990s. The Oil for Food program, which was created in 1996, permitted Iraq to sell a prescribed amount of oil. The money was then put into escrow, and food and medicines were purchased with that account. Compliance was the exception, however, not the rule. Saddam proved to be a master at developing front companies and shadow financing schemes to make illicit purchases. His bribery and cunning made the sanctions almost totally ineffective as he diverted funds to the priorities of the regime.

In an interview in early January, President Bush had talked about this situation and said that the sanctions against Saddam had become "Swiss cheese." Thus our first NSC meeting reviewed the state of the sanctions regime and also examined the problem of how to make the no-fly zones more effective. I prepared a memorandum for the Principals Committee summarizing the situation in Iraq as unsustainable and proposing a plan of action. The approach was adopted that day.

The State Department was tasked with the first issue, developing a program of "smart sanctions" that would target fewer items but really deny those that might benefit the regime and its efforts to rebuild its military capabilities.

Unfortunately, that would lead to a totally unsatisfying result. The effort was launched by the United States and Great Britain but quickly deadlocked over disagreements, for example, about whether to allow Iraq to have hechts (trailers for trucks), which, we argued, could be retrofitted for tanks. In fact, the Russians and to a lesser extent the French opposed any significant tightening of the sanctions.

Indeed, French and Russian companies were benefiting from the status quo. The United Nations' independent investigation into the corruption and mismanagement exposed this fact. The Oil for Food investigation found Iraq had subverted the program's controls and reaped nearly $13 billion in illicit income from kickbacks, surcharges, and oil smuggling. The investigation described the regime's "explicit policy" to sell oil to countries "friendly" to Iraq, particularly "if they were permanent members of the Security Council in a position potentially to ease the restrictions of sanctions." According to the report, Russian and French companies were, respectively, the largest and second largest purchasers of oil from Iraq under Oil for Food.

Beyond the challenge of forging international consensus, strengthening the sanctions to prevent Saddam from rearming was made more difficult because chemical or biological weapons can be made from items that may also have legitimate industrial uses. Chlorine is used both to purify swimming water and to produce lethal nerve agents.

Not surprisingly, the effort to make the sanctions smarter was maddeningly slow, and determining a single U.S. government position, let alone an international one, took the Deputies—and sometimes the NSC Principals—hours and hours.

This issue was so divisive that we once had a Sunday-afternoon NSC meeting with the President in the chair to decide whether or not to support a Security Council resolution that State had negotiated with the French, British, Russians, and Chinese. (Together with the United States, those countries are the permanent five Security Council members, who hold a veto on any action.) The resolution set the terms for "smart sanctions." Don and the Vice President believed that the resolution was too weak. I wasn't able to find consensus, so we met with the President.

Colin was instructed to do better, but the Russians had already made clear that they would veto the introduction of more robust sanctions. He could not overcome their resistance, and two days later we accepted essentially the same resolution that we'd rejected that Sunday.

While State labored at "smart sanctions," the Defense Department was asked to examine ways to improve the no-fly zones. U.S. and British pilots, flying from Kuwait and Turkey (though Ankara had begun to severely limit the number of missions) patrolled several times a week to keep the Iraqi air force grounded. Even though Saddam's air defenses were no match for high-performance aircraft, the Iraqis routinely fired on our planes, and there was a growing fear that they might bring a pilot down with a "lucky shot." Don Rumsfeld was told to develop options should this occur, including what the response might be if a pilot were taken hostage.

We also decided to intensify U.S. efforts, principally through intelligence channels, to build the capabilities of the opposition figures in exile and to help them unite. Frustrated with Saddam's constant flouting of his obligations under the armistice, Congress had passed and President Clinton had signed into law the Iraqi Liberation Act in 1998 that had put most of the machinery and funding into place. But the exiles were a mixed bag, ranging from the well-organized Kurds, who were already living and governing in the north of Iraq, to the Shia and Sunnis, who were scattered from Syria to Iran and from London to New York, with minimal indigenous support.

In truth, the patchwork of measures to enforce the armistice terms of 1991 had frayed badly. Although it is easy to forget now with the controversy surrounding the subsequent Iraq war, concerns had been growing for a decade, shared by the international community and both sides of the aisle in the United States that Saddam Hussein's Iraq was again emerging as a major threat to the Middle East. The air strike that President Clinton launched in December 1998 garnered a House vote of 417–5, resolving that the United States should "support efforts to remove the regime headed by Saddam Hussein from power in Iraq and to promote the emergence of a democratic government." Democratic senators such as Robert Byrd, Joseph Biden, and Dianne Feinstein all voiced their support for the Clinton administration's military action. Saddam held celebrations of his 1991 "victory" on the tenth anniversary of the Gulf War in 2001 and alarmingly continued to speak of Kuwait as a province of Iraq. That led Colin Powell to publicly reassure Kuwait that the United States and its friends would defend its freedom. Nonetheless, the use of U.S. military force to overthrow the regime was not, as I remember, even mentioned in our first NSC meeting or in subsequent ones in 2001.

The issue of North Korea, another rogue regime seeking weapons of mass destruction, came onto the agenda early as well. Days after the inauguration, South Korea requested a meeting for its president, Kim Dae-jung, with President Bush, forcing us to review where we stood on the North Korean issue.

During the campaign, we'd been critical of the Clinton administration's Agreed Framework between the United States and the Democratic People's Republic of Korea, the North's official name. After North Korea turned away weapons inspectors from the International Atomic Energy Agency, the United Nations' nuclear watchdog group, and threatened to withdraw from the Nuclear Non-Proliferation Treaty in 1993, the Clinton administration began on-and-off diplomatic negotiations with North Korea that would eventually last a year and a half and result in the 1994 Agreed Framework. Signed on October 21, 1994, the Agreed Framework aimed to eliminate North Korea's ability to make nuclear arms. It called on North Korea to suspend the construction and operation of nuclear reactors suspected of being part of a covert nuclear weapons program in exchange for U.S. fuel aid and assistance in building two reactors that would not further North Korea's ability to produce weapons. The two sides would then move toward full normalization of political and economic relations.

We'd been aware that the Clinton administration had been working in the last months to get a breakthrough deal with North Korea. Secretary of State Madeleine Albright's somewhat infamous visit to Pyongyang (complete with the stadium presentation of more than one hundred thousand North Koreans in a "cultural" performance) was intended to achieve enough to allow President Clinton to visit the "Hermit Kingdom."

Shortly after the election was decided, Colin received a call from Madeleine asking if he and I would take a briefing on their effort. In early January I accompanied the President-elect to Washington from Texas to begin the transition. After landing at Dulles, I broke off from the entourage and went directly to Colin's house. There, in Colin's dining room, Wendy Sherman, the counselor to the secretary, and Jack Pritchard, the senior director for Asian affairs at the National Security Council, told us of their plans. We didn't comment because President-elect Bush was adamant that there would be one President at a time. We did not communicate our skepticism either privately or publicly. In the end, the effort to get a common agenda for the meeting—including the North Koreans' promises to cease missile tests and development in return for U.S. compensation—failed, and President Clinton did not go to Pyongyang.

That was by far the most detailed policy encounter between the foreign policy advisors during the transition. When later there were claims of extensive briefings concerning al Qaeda during the transition, I recalled that North Korea, not terrorism, had been the Clinton administration's most pressing business with the incoming team.

The meeting with President Kim was set for March 7, 2001. Kim Dae-jung was a revered figure in many ways. He'd been a prisoner during the military regime of South Korean President Chun Doo-hwan in the 1980s. His life had quite literally been spared by U.S. entreaties to the authorities. A mild-mannered, aging statesman, Kim was also an idealist who believed that engagement with North Korea, through what he called the "Sunshine Policy," might eventually change the nature of the regime. The policy was built on large-scale assistance to the North with little demanded in return. South Korean policy and U.S. efforts to impose stricter requirements under the Agreed Framework were often at odds. One sensed that Kim Dae-jung simply wanted to avoid conflict with Kim Jong-il at almost any cost.

The day before Kim's arrival, we held a Principals meeting to go over the administration's approach. We all agreed that we would not publicly criticize the "Sunshine Policy" but that we would make it clear to Kim that the United States was looking for a different approach to North Korea. No one wanted to embarrass the South Korean, but he had to understand that we would not pursue the Agreed Framework. I walked down to the Oval that afternoon and reported our deliberations to the President. He concurred.

The next morning at five the phone rang in my temporary apartment on 7th Street in downtown Washington. It was before I resumed the practice of daily morning exercise that I'd established in California, and I was sound asleep. The apartment was tiny, but I had to get out of bed and go into the living room to answer the phone. The President had called directly, as he often did throughout the years. I was flattered to be on his speed dial, but I was robbed of that moment with the operator—"The President is calling"—to get my thoughts together. "Have you seen the *Washington Post*?" he demanded.

"No, Mr. President, I haven't," I said.

"Go outside and get it." He was speaking in short, declarative sentences—a sure sign that he was really upset.

I put on a robe and went to get the paper, thankful that for once it had been delivered a little early. "Go to page A20." There in bold headlines was an interview in which Colin had said that we'd tell the South Koreans that we'd take up the Clinton administration's approach to North Korea. "Do you want me to take care of this, or do you want to?"

"I'll take care of it, Mr. President." That, in a nutshell, is what the national security advisor does: takes care of it.

I called Colin and went through the same drill. "Get your newspaper." He did. He immediately saw the problem. Colin had intended to communicate that we were reviewing the policy but would not necessarily throw out all aspects of the Clinton approach. Truthfully, the *Post* had "overwritten" the story. The tendency of journalists to take a kernel and turn it into a full-blown scoop is one that I came to know well—and suffer from—throughout my eight years in Washington.

Colin was calm and thoroughly professional and said that he would take care of it. I went to the Oval immediately upon arriving at the White House and told the President that Colin would retract his statement by the time he arrived for the meeting. He did, calling the press to say that he "had gotten out a little forward on his skis." The damage had been done, though, and the public perception of Colin Powell being reined in by the White House lingered and festered.

The meeting with Kim Dae-jung was polite, but it was very clear that we were worlds apart on how to deal with the North. I do not doubt that Kim was a compassionate man and undoubtedly concerned about the human rights abuses and the misery of the North Korean people, whose malnutrition resulted in as much as a five-inch height differential with their South Korean brethren. Yet he gave every indication that he would never challenge the North in any way. We were convinced that the Agreed Framework was doing little to deal with Pyongyang's arsenal and that South Korea's largesse was helping to prop up the regime. George W. Bush was offended by the tyranny of Kim Jong-il and could not understand why South Korea's government seemed unmoved.

One of the hardest things about diplomacy is to put yourself into someone else's shoes without compromising your own principles. The United States, sitting on a protected continent away from the monstrous North Korean regime, could be more aggressive in confronting it. For South Korea, a relatively new and prosperous democracy, accommodating the regime was a price worth paying to maintain stability and peace. North Korea has thousands of missiles and artillery pieces that could reach Seoul, only thirty miles from the border. And too much focus on the plight of the North Korean people had another downside: what would happen at the time of unification of the North and South? Many years later a senior South Korean diplomat would tell me that his biggest worry about the North was that Seoul would be saddled with millions of "brain-damaged midgets." He was not being cruel; he was articulating the special vulnerability that South Korea felt.

The United States had different interests. North Korea's nuclear program was a global, not just a regional, issue. Its treatment of its own people offended not just the President personally but also our country's commitment to human rights. Those dueling perspectives would divide us until the ascent in 2008 of Lee Myung-bak, who placed greater public emphasis on North Korean abuses. But for the moment, there was little common ground on which to move forward.

That was painfully obvious in the press availability after the meeting. President Bush always did his best to cover over differences with his guests. As was the usual practice, the two sides got together before the press conference and agreed how to handle difficult questions so that there was not an obvious break. But the press, armed with Colin's comments of the day before, did not buy it. The visit ended sourly with a split between the United States and one of its closest Asian allies.

And the issue of how to deal with North Korea would soon cause some of the most divisive moments within the administration.

The Special Relationship Begins

RELATIONS WITH OUR European allies started somewhat more smoothly. The President's first meeting with a European leader, Prime Minister Tony Blair of Great Britain, scheduled for February 23, was greatly anticipated. The "special relationship," as the friendship between Great Britain and the United States is known, is as solid as any in international politics. There is a kinship and a deep sense of shared values forged through years of shared sacrifice, particularly during World War II. The relationship is so comfortable that I once had to remind a presidential speechwriter that Great Britain was *not* America's oldest ally; that would be France. It's not that no differences exist, but there *is* a deep feeling that if you cannot count on the Brits, you are really alone.

The political relationship transcends changes in administrations in London and Washington. Nevertheless, the personal relationships between British prime ministers and U.S. presidents have differed in terms of warmth and depth. Ronald Reagan and Margaret Thatcher were close because they were cut from the same ideological cloth and saw the world similarly. The relationship between Thatcher and George H. W. Bush was cooler and sometimes difficult, particularly during the period of German unification, about which Mrs. Thatcher harbored deep reservations.

Because Bill Clinton and Tony Blair shared, as Reagan and Thatcher had, an ideological kinship, their relationship came to symbolize the triumph of center-left politics, dubbed the "Third Way," and its revitalization of Labour Party politics in Britain and the Democratic Party in America. They were personally close, as were their wives, Hillary Clinton and Cherie Blair, both lawyers with the instincts of social activists of the late 1960s. In fact, I chuckled to myself when a few months later, during our first visit to Chequers, the British prime minister's equivalent of Camp David, I encountered a prominently displayed picture of the Blairs and the Clintons. I wondered if someone had forgotten to move it.

As Blair's visit approached, Washington (and for that matter London) chatter was about whether George W. Bush, a conservative Texan and foreign policy neophyte, would have anything at all in common with the sophisticated, smooth, and somewhat left-leaning Tony Blair. Tony Blair was a leader who exuded vast confidence and competence, a "rock star" in international politics. The press was intentionally setting up a test for the new U.S. President. Could he hold his own with Blair?

Since Franklin Delano Roosevelt's time in office, Camp David, nestled in Maryland's Catoctin Mountains, has been the presidents' weekend retreat from the pressures of Washington and the gilded cage of the White House. It is rustic in an elegant way, with individual cabins complete with fireplaces and large outdoor decks in a wooded setting. Over the years it has also become a place to take foreign leaders who merit the signal of importance and camaraderie that everyone reads into such an invite.

The Blairs arrived on Friday afternoon, February 23, 2001, becoming the Bushes' first foreign visitors to Camp David. There was a low-key welcoming ceremony at the helipad in keeping with the bucolic setting of Camp David: no national anthems, just the marine and navy honor guard displaying the national flags. As would become standard practice, the guests were given a little time to freshen up before the first meeting in Laurel Lodge, the main meeting cabin at Camp David.

Meetings between heads of government, particularly first meetings, are somewhat scripted. Any event of the kind sends the White House into hyperdrive. Briefing books have to be prepared by the NSC staff, covering every imaginable issue that might arise. Someone has to worry about the social arrangements: Who goes to dinner with the principals, and who entertains the rest of the staff? What press interviews need to be held to set the stage and by whom? The two-day visit takes many weeks of preparation. And if you are a smart national security advisor, you read every word and go over every detail, no matter how small.

Then there is the work to be done with the staff of the visiting leader. David Manning, Prime Minister Blair's exceptionally capable and trustworthy foreign policy advisor, and I had worked to put together a program. That was routine practice before the "bosses" met. But I knew that my relationship with David was not going to be routine. David was a career diplomat, elegant and urbane—and funny. He'd served as the counselor and head of the Political Section at the British embassy in Moscow, and we shared a fascination and frustration with Russia and Russians. We became very close, and I'm grateful to have found pals like David and Catherine Manning, a friendship that has outlasted our government service.

In the light of all that these men would do together after September 11, 2001, the agenda we put together for that first meeting at Camp David seems, in retrospect, very mundane. The two talked about the development of a European Security and Defense Policy (ESDP), which many American experts saw as a competitor of NATO. Blair wanted a nod from the President that the United States would support enhanced independent European forces. The President wanted to make sure that the Europeans, who were unwilling to spend more for defense, would not simply hollow out NATO by trying to make their already meager forces do double duty. And we wanted a reference to the importance of missile defense—or at least an acknowledgment of the importance of both offense and defense. They both got what they needed. There was a kind of review of the international landscape, including an agreement to work together to strengthen the sanctions on Saddam. They talked about Russian President Vladimir Putin and missile defense, the President telling Blair that he was determined to withdraw from the Anti–Ballistic Missile Treaty. Blair was calm, urging only that we try to work out a deal with the Russians rather than withdrawing unilaterally.

So the first encounter was pretty unremarkable, but I thought that the President was nervous, talking rapidly and in a staccato cadence that was a little hard to follow. When the discussion turned to a nettlesome trade dispute between the European Union and the United States concerning bananas, Blair did something that, either inadvertently or by design, broke the ice. It wasn't hard to tell that the President's knowledge of the issue was not, frankly, very deep. Blair made his two or three points in response and said, "And I have now just said everything that I know about this issue." With an agreement to kick the issue over to the "experts," everyone relaxed.

The two men continued their discussions over a walk around the grounds and then met the press. One of the final questions was "What do you two have in common?" The implication was, of course, that they had nothing in common. The President said, "We both use Colgate toothpaste." Okay. There has long been speculation about how, exactly, he knew that, but it was an amiable end to a very good day.

That night after dinner, all of us went to the small movie theater and watched *Meet the Parents*. Well, I watched part of it. As the President tells it, I was laughing robustly through the first half of the movie and then fell silent. I awoke to the prime minister of the United Kingdom and the President of the United States standing over me, saying, "Wake up, Dr. Rice." In my job, you slept when you could.

I believe that during those private talks, George W. Bush and Tony Blair began to see that they shared something more important than ideological kinship in the modern political sense. They shared values, and in time they would see that they shared a willingness to do difficult and controversial things. That was what they had in common, and it would soon make them undertake, together, actions to radically change the status quo in world politics.

A Crystalline Structure Called the Kyoto Protocol

IT WAS A good thing that the President had established a relationship with the British prime minister, because he would soon need friends in Europe. From the start George W. Bush was viewed with suspicion by the European powers, uncertain of how this brash Texan would exercise U.S. power. Ironically, it was not a matter of war and peace that led to the first confrontation with our European allies; it was climate change.

During the campaign the governor had been clearly opposed to the Kyoto Protocol, an agreement that would commit industrialized nations to reduce greenhouse gas emissions by 5.2 percent below their 1990s levels over the following decade. He opposed Kyoto because it exempted roughly 80 percent of the world, including major population centers such as China and India, from compliance. He also argued that it would have had an adverse effect on the U.S. economy. He was not alone. The U.S. Senate had, in a nonbinding resolution, rejected the accord 95 to 0, causing President Clinton to shelve the treaty.

Nonetheless, though skeptical of some of the more alarmist predictions about climate change, the governor had shown sensitivity to the issue of carbon emissions and had promised in the campaign to regulate power plants' emissions of four pollutants, including the greenhouse gas carbon dioxide.

I was in my office on March 13, 2001, when I got a phone call asking me to "clear" (sign off on) a letter from the President to four Republican senators who had asked the administration to clarify its position on limiting pollutants to address the greenhouse gas effect.

I immediately saw a problem with the letter, and since I knew that there was some urgency, I went directly to the President to tell him that we needed to change one sentence. That sentence criticized the Kyoto Protocol in the harshest possible terms and suggested we would have nothing to do with it. I wanted to add mitigating language saying that even though we could not support the treaty because it was fatally flawed, we would work with our allies to address the problem of climate change. I thought that it was the kind of standard line diplomats used all the time and that the President would have no problem with it.

When I walked into the Oval and described the approach, the President looked surprised and said, "But the letter is already gone. The Vice President is taking it up to the Hill because he has a meeting up there. I thought you cleared the letter." I was flabbergasted. I hurriedly called Colin and then Christine Todd Whitman, the EPA administrator, to tell them what had happened and to suggest that they call in immediately to protest. The President said, "It's too late."

Later, when it was clear that nothing could be done, I returned to the Oval to talk to the President. I said, "Mr. President, this is going to color your foreign policy from the outset, and that's a problem." I also said that I was appalled that the Vice President had been allowed to take a letter to Capitol Hill on a matter of international importance without my clearance or, more important, that of the secretary of state.

In fairness to the President, I think he had thought of the letter as addressing a *domestic* issue for our Congress. After all, we had been clear that we would not support Kyoto. What was the big fuss? But I knew better. As I predicted, we suffered through this issue over the years: drawing that early line in the sand helped to establish our reputation for "unilateralism." We handled it badly.

My immediate reaction was not to admit the mistake. It was my bad luck to have a meeting with the European Union ambassadors at the Swedish envoy's residence the very next day. I should have just said that the letter didn't fully reflect our view and that we'd work with them. Instead, because they were so aggressive in their questioning, I became combative too. "Kyoto is dead on arrival," I intoned. The meeting was "off the record" but obviously would be reported back to their capitals. In fact, it took a nanosecond for those words to ricochet around the European continent.

Unfortunately, the situation continued to get worse. The President was scheduled to visit Sweden for his first U.S.-EU summit. The European Union was at that time composed of fifteen countries and had several principal bodies, including the European Parliament, the European Commission, and the European Council, headed by a country presidency that rotated among the members every six months. At that point, Sweden held the presidency. The meeting with the commission president and the Swedes was deadly dull, with everyone reading their talking points and staff-produced "interventions" made on every conceivable issue. At one point we were discussing NATO's expansion into Eastern Europe, and I told the President that I wanted to say something. Much to my astonishment, he announced to the group, "Condi, you got something to say real quick." I was furious because his offhand tone seemed to belittle my participation.

In the early days, the President also had a tendency to finish my sentences for me. Finally one day, standing in the Oval, I said, "Mr. President, I know we're close and that you think you know what I'm going to say. I know you don't mean any harm, but I'm sure others see it as a sign of disrespect for my opinion." He was crestfallen. I felt bad bringing it up, but I was walking a fine line. I was staff, not a Cabinet secretary. At home and abroad, leaders and colleagues had to know that the President listened to me. As time went on I became very aware that no one doubted our relationship. The President would tell people that we were like brother and sister. Yet it wasn't always easy to get the balance right.

That evening in Sweden, the President went to dinner with the heads of government of the European Union. Colin was at a foreign ministers dinner. Karen Hughes and I were the "plus two," meaning the two staff allowed in the room with the President. Seated around a long table in a rather unattractive and quite cold room, the President was treated to lecture after lecture about climate change. The script didn't change; it was just delivered in different languages: "Climate change is a great international crisis, and the United States is turning its back on its responsibilities and its allies." "Don't you know that the whole planet is at stake and only Kyoto can save us?" It was as if no other subject existed. Though I'd predicted that this would happen, I too was appalled.

At one point the President took his translation earpiece out of his ear. *Uh oh*, I thought, *he's going to show them that he doesn't care what they think*. I was relieved when, moments later, he just shifted it to his other ear.

Fortunately, José María Aznar, the prime minister of Spain, who would become a close ally of the President, helped calm the atmosphere by lighting a cigar. A few others also helped. Prime Minister Blair made his points without the accusatory tone that dominated the evening. The Finnish participant made fun of the Danish intervention, which seemed to suggest that *windmills* were the answer to the world's climate problem.

But the President was really angry, and he never fully forgot what he saw as the disrespectful tone taken at that dinner. In time we produced policies that gave us a real voice in the climate change debate. The President's approach gained traction, with everyone realizing that the goal was to find sources of clean energy to protect the environment while still allowing for economic growth. Discussions of alternative fuel sources, from battery technology to cellulosic biomass, would animate the President as he poured over reports, listened to entrepreneurs, and engaged like-minded leaders such as Luiz Inácio Lula da Silva in Brazil. By the time we left office, the United States had spent more than $40 billion on programs related to climate change.

To be fair, the administration struggled to find a voice between the climate change alarmists who proposed draconian measures to confront the problem and those—even in the administration—who thought that any "concession" on the question was a slippery slope. I don't think there were any "deniers" among the key members of the President's team. But there was a wide divergence of opinion about how much the President should do.

In time, our willingness to engage the international community would lead to several breakthroughs: the Asia-Pacific Partnership on Clean Development and Climate, which brought China and India into the conversation in 2005; convening the largest emitters of greenhouse gases to chart a common way forward; and, perhaps most important, a public statement from the President that finally acknowledged the human element in climate change in July 2005. Still, we were never going to be seen as true believers, and it was hard to get attention for the pathbreaking work, especially in the second term, that the Council on Environmental Quality at the White House did, particularly under James Connaughton's leadership in partnership with State's under secretary for global affairs, Paula Dobriansky.

Years later the President and I talked about why the reaction in 2001 had been so sharp. "Mr. President," I said, "the Europeans had built this crystalline structure called Kyoto."

"I see; we came along and knocked it over," he said.

"No, it was worse than that," I told him. "We knocked it over and said, 'Did I hit something?' And we just kept on walking." That was a self-inflicted wound that could have been avoided.

The First Dangerous Crisis Unfolds

ISSUES LIKE climate change were ever present, particularly at the time of an international conference or meeting with a head of state. They formed the backdrop of steady daily work, carried mostly by the agencies and experts in the field. But the national security advisor's life is very different; there are spikes, brought on by crises that make you drop everything else until the danger passes. And they almost always begin with a phone call that seems like it came out of nowhere.

"Dr. Rice, the Situation Room is on the phone for you. You can take it in the commander's office." I always dreaded those words from the Camp David steward, particularly at 10 P.M. as we watched a Saturday-night movie in the Holly Cabin theater. Something had to be wrong.

I got up, went to the commander's office, and called the Situation Room. The senior duty officer said that the Pentagon was reporting an incident off the coast of China. The details were sketchy, but a U.S. maritime patrol aircraft on a routine surveillance mission had collided with one of two Chinese fighter jets. Both aircraft had been damaged in the collision, and the U.S. plane had made an emergency landing at an airfield on China's Hainan Island. Twenty-four crew members had been detained. I was told that the plane had been over international waters when the incident happened.

The crew was safe but in captivity, and they'd performed emergency security measures before going down. Those are steps to prevent the plane's technology from being stolen if it falls into foreign hands. The crippled U.S. plane had issued an emergency "Mayday" alert as it descended toward the airfield. A phone call among all relevant agencies of the government (called a "noiwon," for National Operations and Intelligence Watch Officer Network) had been convened and was in continuous session.

I started to go through my mental checklist as I sprinted back to

Holly Cabin just as the President was coming out. I said that I would call Colin and Don and get back to him. I reached the two. Don had only the information that I'd been given but was following up urgently. Colin began trying to reach the Chinese foreign minister.

The eleven days from April 1 until the release of the crew on April 11 were completely dominated by the Hainan Island crisis. Needless to say, that was not the way we'd hoped to start off our relationship with Beijing. In the campaign, we had referred to China as a strategic competitor, making clear that our first priority in Asia was to strengthen relationships with our longtime democratic friends Japan, South Korea, and Australia. It was not meant to be a signal of hostility to the PRC but some commentators in Beijing—and in Washington—took it as such.

The President was preparing to authorize a large arms sales package for Taiwan and there was press coverage already. The package would be significant enough to obviate the need to deal with the issue annually. Beijing would be angry but at least we wouldn't have to go through the upheaval every year. But the Hainan crisis came on the heels of the tensions over the arms sales and before we had established a productive basis for U.S.-China relations.

Still, neither China nor we wanted the crisis to escalate, but it was a very difficult one to defuse. First, the U.S. plane had been over international waters and it was important to defend freedom of navigation. The problem was exacerbated by the skewed information that the People's Liberation Army (PLA) fed the Chinese leadership. The PLA had every reason to paint itself as the victim and the United States as the aggressor. The Chinese civilian leadership appears to have been totally dependent on the military for information, especially at the start. That led to misplaced feelings of righteousness.

Second, and more important, the Chinese pilot who'd rammed our plane had been killed in the incident, making him an instant hero in the Chinese press. The Chinese wanted us to apologize for his death, something that we were unwilling to do—particularly once we learned that his hot-dogging had been a prime cause of the accident. But it became a matter of national pride in China. Time and again we would see this. China would stir up nationalist sentiment in the population through the state-controlled media, diminishing its own room for maneuver as it reacted to the very passions it had created. This tendency of authoritarian regimes to use manufactured "public opinion" is one of the most dangerous aspects of such regimes. In a democracy you don't have to create a public voice; citizens do that without prodding.

Finally, we were simply unable to establish proper communications with the Chinese leadership for several days. That first night, Colin couldn't get the foreign minister to return his phone call. We tried multiple channels for the better part of two days. Yet we were still having trouble maintaining consistent contact with the Chinese. On the second Sunday afternoon, I enlisted the Argentine and Chilean governments (the Chinese leadership was traveling in South America) to put us in touch with the Chinese by cell phone. In one bizarre incident, the Argentine put my counterpart on a cell phone, having tracked him down at a barbecue!

The reasons for this behavior continue to be a matter of speculation among those of us who managed this crisis. One theory is that the Chinese leadership was not on top of the facts and was trying to buy time until it could gather itself. That would correspond with what Clinton administration officials encountered in 1999 when the United States accidently bombed the Chinese Embassy in Serbia. That time, too, days passed before proper lines of communication could be established. Whatever the explanation, this behavior made the first few days very tense.

Once we returned to Washington from Camp David, we established a pattern for crisis management. I would talk to Colin at about 5:00 A.M. each day. As Colin noted, the Chinese seemed to make decisions at 4:30 P.M. their time because they always called him at 4:30 A.M. our time. I would then go to the White House at 6:00 A.M. or so, and at 7:00 A.M. the President and I would meet with Karen Hughes and Andy Card. Colin would often join us. We needed to keep our message under tight control while Colin sought an acceptable solution.

One problem in managing a crisis in today's media environment is that you are forced to say something each day. If you are not careful, your rhetoric escalates little by little and you create demands that must then be met by the other side. Since the other side is doing the same thing, it's easy to have the crisis spin out of control pretty quickly. For example, Dennis Blair, the head of the United States Pacific Command, reprimanded the Chinese air force for failing to intercept aircraft in a professional manner and playing "bumper cars in the air." We had to disavow that statement.

We were also concerned about the well-being of our people. We sent warnings privately to the Chinese not to do anything provocative, such as parading them in public to embarrass us. Our very able ambassador, the former Admiral Joseph Prueher, worked to get consular access to them so that we could reassure their families, and the nation, that they were safe.

The crux of the matter was to find a face-saving way out for the Chinese. We could not apologize for what was not our fault. But after several days, the Chinese sent a signal: if Colin would send a letter that said that we were sorry for the loss of their pilot's life, we could end the crisis. Don quipped that perhaps if Colin would say "pretty please," that would do it. The next days were consumed with efforts to find acceptable language. In the end we acknowledged the loss of life and the need to prevent further incidents without a hint of any wrongdoing on our part.

Word came that our people had been released early on the morning of April 11. I was with the President in Concord, North Carolina, later that day when he announced that he would shortly be visiting the family of one of the servicemen on board the plane. The nation's attention had been riveted on the fate of the crew, and when the President made the announcement, the crowd broke out into a chant: "USA, USA!"

My eyes welled up with tears, and I was pretty emotional when we met the crew several weeks later in the Oval Office. It was a relief to have them home. Eventually, a U.S. Air Force crew deployed to China and dismantled the aircraft so its pieces could be flown back to the United States. That was after a lot of back-and-forth about whether Beijing would return the plane at all. Chinese military personnel "monitored operations closely," according to the air force report, continuously photographing and videotaping the operation and reviewing photos and videos made by the Americans.

· · ·

THE REMAINDER of the spring was, for the most part, relatively straight-forward. Though the Balkans flared up, with violence in Macedonia that threatened stability in the region, it was not the kind of crisis that dominated the agenda of the White House every day. The State Department worked with the allies to defuse the crisis by the summer of that year.

And the Summit of the Americas in late April provided a much-needed second opportunity to highlight our agenda for Latin America. The meeting of the thirty-four countries of the Western Hemisphere (Cuba was excluded because it did not have a democratically elected president) took place in Quebec against a backdrop of anti-globalization demonstrations. As a result, security was tight as we drove along downtown streets that were eerily deserted, merchants largely having closed their doors for the day to avoid trouble.

However, inside the convention hall where we gathered, the meeting was surprisingly smooth. The summit declaration enshrined the support of the gathered for free enterprise and free trade, reaffirming the need to create a Free Trade Area of the Americas. The major governments of Latin America were center-right and like-minded. Hugo Chávez was a troubling but not yet central figure in the region. When we met him at a session for the Andean nations on the margins of the summit, he was all smiles and desperate to be seen in a photograph with the President. When George W. Bush entered the room, Chávez almost leapt across the table and offered a few words about their common interest in baseball. The President remarked afterward that Chávez was a "street thug," insecure in the clothing of a national leader. I thought he might be worse than that because he was animated by a certain crude charisma. Ultimately, the "street thug" would become a ruthless and surprisingly effective dictator, and his "insecurity" would give way to a relentless campaign against democratic principles, free markets, and, most important, U.S. influence in the region.

4

THE MIDDLE EAST

THE MIDDLE EAST WAS the exception to the sense of normalcy that spring. The low-intensity war between Palestinians and Israelis dominated our security agenda. The explosion in the region predated us. In 2000 the Clinton administration had convened the two sides at Camp David in a dramatic effort to solve the decades-old conflict. Ehud Barak, a former general who had become the leader of the Labor Party and was now Israel's prime minister, wanted a deal badly. The record is sketchy to this day, but he was apparently ready to withdraw from almost all of the West Bank and all of Gaza, permit a certain number of Palestinian refugees to return to Israel, and find a solution for Jerusalem that would cede, in some fashion, Israeli sovereignty over parts of the Holy City. It is easy to forget how far out on a limb Barak was at Camp David. After all, in 2000 there was no consensus in Israel that there should even *be* a Palestinian state.

In the summer before the failure of Camp David, I witnessed firsthand the ferment in Israel. I'd been invited to lecture at Tel Aviv University by my good friend Shai Feldman and took my first trip to the Holy Land in July of that year. For me it was literally a religious experience, visiting the Sea of Galilee and the Mount of the Beatitudes and walking where Christ had walked. But since it was well known by that time that I was advising George W. Bush, the visit took on a distinctly political character. I met with Barak and several of his ministers and discussed their efforts to make peace.

The air in Israel was thick with expectation that Camp David might succeed in ending the conflict with the Palestinians. I can well remember sitting with friends from the university in the courtyard of the King David Hotel in Jerusalem on a warm summer evening as they discussed how the Jewish state of Israel would develop in conditions of peace with the Palestinians. So much of Israel's young history had been defined by wars with the Arabs. "What would life be like without that conflict?" they asked.

On another occasion I sat with members of Israel's burgeoning high-tech community, drawing on my own experiences in Silicon Valley to engage them about Israel's economic future in the absence of permanent conflict. It was a time of uncertainty and questioning but, without a doubt, a time of optimistic anticipation.

Then I went to see Ariel Sharon, the leader of the conservative Likud Party, and his advisors, who were preparing to challenge Barak in upcoming elections. The encounter made it crystal clear that not all Israelis were willing to end the conflict on the basis of a deal like Camp David.

I met Sharon in the tiny offices of Likud, located on the top floor of a miserably hot building in Tel Aviv. I was immediately struck by the fact that he was as wide as he was tall. He had a slightly lazy eye and thick features, and he spoke in heavily accented English. Over the years I came to understand that Sharon was one of the few people who spoke English better than he understood it. This often led to misunderstandings and Sharon's tendency to repeat phrases over and over, whether they were connected to the conversation or not. But at the time I was impressed with what I took to be his fluency in English.

I also knew Sharon's reputation as an uncompromising defender of Israel and the terrible history of his role in the attack on Palestinian refugee camps at Sabra and Shatila, where many innocent Palestinians died during the war with Lebanon in 1982. He was the Israeli leader whom Arabs (and many liberal Israelis and Americans) hated most. Nothing in that first meeting suggested that his uncompromising hardliner reputation was undeserved, but I was a bit drawn to him nonetheless. He seemed to embody the Israeli experience because, in truth, without toughness, perseverance, and even ruthlessness, Israel would have ceased to exist in a neighborhood bent on its destruction.

When the conversation turned to Governor Bush, Sharon spoke warmly of him. George W. Bush had visited Israel two years before with several other American governors. Sharon had been his personal guide by helicopter of the West Bank and Gaza. Sharon's emphasis on the fragility of Israel's security situation had made a major and lasting impression on George W. Bush. The governor's sympathy for Israel's plight had an equally important impact on Sharon.

The meeting I had with him was taken up with Sharon's presentation of "maps" that essentially laid claim to all of the territory of the West Bank, Gaza, and Jerusalem. It was very clear that he would not support dividing the land and creating a Palestinian state, and I remember thinking that Barak would have a tough adversary to overcome if he succeeded in getting a deal with the Palestinians.

Sharon was especially anxious for me to meet his close advisor, a woman near my age, Tzipi Livni. She too exuded toughness and an uncompromising view of Israel's right to exist on the totality of its biblical lands. Sharon proudly noted that she was a child of the Irgun, the armed Israeli militia that had helped drive the British out of the Middle East after World War II. Her mother had been a "freedom fighter" who had spent time in a British jail. Her father had been an operational commander of Irgun at the time of the famous bombing of the British headquarters in the King David Hotel in 1946. Needless to say, the entire meeting was in stark contrast to my encounters with the intellectuals of the Israeli Left with whom I spent most of my time during that trip.

Throughout the summer and fall, the Clinton administration feverishly pursued an agreement, but Camp David failed. Palestinian leader Yasir Arafat maintained until his death that the deal was not a good one and that he had told the Clinton administration that he would have been "a dead man" for accepting it. Barak returned home to vicious criticism and certain defeat in the elections.

On September 28, 2000, Ariel Sharon decided to visit the Temple Mount, thereby asserting Israeli sovereignty over the holiest of Jewish places. Since the Six-Day War, the Israeli government had essentially barred practicing Jews from visiting the area. Both the Dome of the Rock (also known as Qubbat al-Sakhra) and Al-Aqsa Mosque are on the Temple Mount. The Dome of the Rock, from which the Prophet Mohammed is said to have ascended to heaven on a winged horse, is one of the holiest places of Islam. Some Jews, in turn, believe that it was built in the seventh century to defile the site of the ruins of the first and second temples of ancient Israel.

I had seen those places up close the summer before. As I walked through Jerusalem, I reflected that the world's great religions don't come together in the Holy City; they clash there, with Israeli soldiers securing the Dome of the Rock on top of the Temple Mount near the wailing wall—the Dome of the Rock having been built in a way to demonstrate dominion over the whole of the Old City—and various Christian sects squabbling about space in the Church of the Holy Sepulcher. I found Jerusalem enchanting but disturbing, a place where man's desire to use God for dominance over other human beings was very much on display.

In any case, Yasir Arafat, perhaps to cover his failings at Camp David, used Sharon's visit to the Temple Mount as a pretext and essentially condoned a return to the violence that the Palestinians had renounced in the Oslo Accords of 1993. The "second intifada" began with a rapid succession of attacks on Israelis: an Islamic Jihad suicide bomb attack on October 26; a car bombing on November 2; a school bus bombing on November 20; a car bombing on November 22; a suicide bombing on December 22; a car bombing on January 1; and the kidnapping and shooting of two Israelis in Tulkarm in the West Bank on January 23. Not surprisingly, Ariel Sharon defeated Ehud Barak for the position of prime minister on February 6, 2001. Sharon called for complete Israeli control of a unified Jerusalem and no negotiation until the Palestinians ceased their violence. A few days later, on February 14, Israel imposed a complete blockade on the Palestinian territories in response to the killing of eight soldiers and a civilian by a Palestinian bus driver.

It became fashionable during the Bush team's eight years in office to say that we did not come to power committed to the peace process and that we should have pursued the understandings at Camp David. It simply flies in the face of reality to believe that there was any room for negotiations between Palestinians and Israelis in 2001 or for some time afterward. Yasir Arafat had demonstrated that he would not or could not make peace. Ariel Sharon came to power to defeat the Palestinian resistance, not to negotiate.

That was the situation we inherited. I do not blame the Clinton administration for trying, but later, when we tried to reinvigorate the peace process, Arabs, Palestinians, and Israelis alike communicated the same message: don't let Camp David happen again!

WHEN WE took office, our goal was simply to calm the region. Still, a subtle split began to emerge within the administration. The President was determined that we would support Israel's right to defend itself. He believed that the constant attacks on Israeli civilians were intolerable for any democratic leader. He and I were both sympathetic to Sharon's view that peace with the Palestinians could not be achieved as long as their leadership wished to keep one foot in terrorism and the other in corruption.

The President and I began to discuss a different approach to the conflict, one that relied much more on fundamental change among Palestinians as the key to peace. Israel could not be expected to accept a deal while under attack or to agree to the establishment of a terrorist-led state next door. Though we remained committed to a peace process, we wanted to focus much more on what the nature of the Palestinian state would be. The President was disgusted with Yasir Arafat, whom he saw, accurately, as a terrorist and a crook.

The State Department had a much more traditional view that the United States would need to be even-handed in order to bring peace. Israel was occupying Palestinian lands and building settlements, and even in the face of violence, the peace process needed to be pursued. Yasir Arafat was, with all his failings, the leader of the Palestinian people and the key to any future peace.

Throughout the summer, it fell to Colin Powell to quell the fires burning in the Middle East. Each day he faced the press and the Arabs who wanted the United States to rein in Israel. Every day Ari Fleischer would come by my office and discuss press guidance. After a while he would say, "I know. Terrorism must stop. Israel has a right to defend itself, and we urge restraint so that innocent people don't die."

"Right," I would answer.

In the midst of the maelstrom, Colin decided to accept an invitation to address the American Israel Public Affairs Committee (AIPAC), the most pro-Israeli of the many interest groups, on March 19. The press billed the address as the first statement of U.S. policy on the Middle East. Though the speech essentially said nothing controversial or new, it was welcomed internationally since at least it affirmed our commitment to the peace process. We had decided to associate ourselves with the Mitchell Plan, named for former Senator George Mitchell, who'd been appointed in the last days of the Clinton administration to address the exploding violence. The Mitchell Plan called for a step-by-step set of commitments that each side would take, culminating in the restarting of peace negotiations.

But neither side was ready for even those modest interventions. When, on March 28, a Hamas suicide bomber killed two teenagers at a school bus stop, Sharon acted. Israeli helicopter gunships attacked Gaza and Ramallah (the governmental center of the Palestinian Authority). The gunship attack led to a wave of reprisals and counterattacks. To add fuel to the fire, the Israeli Housing Ministry announced plans to build more than seven hundred new homes for Jewish settlers near Qalqilya and Jerusalem. Such announcements were a constant problem throughout our years in office. Sometimes they were made despite the fact that construction was not to begin for years. Often they were a reiteration of old commitments in order to satisfy some coalition constituency at a particular point in time. But they were always disruptive and provocative, reminding the world of Israel's controversial settlement activity. And in the context of the violence of 2001, the announcement was even more toxic. Palestinians and Israelis were at war.

Those early events would shape our Middle East policy fundamentally, but in the spring and summer of 2001, I just wanted to avoid all-out conflagration in the region. The differences in the administration between the decidedly pro-Israel bent of the White House and the State Department's more traditional pro-Arab view percolated beneath the surface.

I know that Colin believed that we should resolve the differences in the administration and get the President to chart a course for our Middle East policy. I was sympathetic to him because he was on the front line every day. State and the White House were not on the same page, and everyone in the region—and in Washington—knew it. But I did not think that it was the time to try and resolve underlying tensions in the administration about the issue. I talked to the President every day, and I knew where he stood. The constant violence against Israeli civilians and Arafat's prevarication and unwillingness to break with terrorism led the President to tilt toward Tel Aviv. I think I convinced Colin that any attempt to chart a new course in 2001 was likely to result in an outcome that would be so pro-Israeli as to inflame an already bad situation.

So throughout the summer we struggled with the Palestinian-Israeli conflict, as we would for the next eight years. But for the most part, the spring was relatively calm. My life in Washington settled into a busy but predictable pattern. My Aunt Gee and my friend Louis Olave helped me move into my permanent home in the Watergate complex and I found occasions to enjoy Washington. On Sundays I would get into my car and drive to visit my friend Mary Bush or go to the shopping center, usually the Galleria in Chevy Chase, Maryland. In the days before 9/11 I was driven to work, so I always looked forward to getting into my car and heading out on my own on the weekends.

Most of all, I enjoyed living next door to the John F. Kennedy Center for the Performing Arts. I often took in concerts with friends, such as fellow White House staffer Harriet Miers and my adopted family, Steve and Ann Hadley and their daughters, Kate and Caroline.

On Good Friday of that first year, I joined the Hadleys for a performance of the Brahms *German Requiem*. Afterward, I walked home alone. The weather was warm, almost balmy. There was no security detail. Just me. I remember thinking how lucky I was to live next door to the Kennedy Center and that I would be able to enjoy many calm nights like this. After September 11, 2001, there would never be another one.

5

VLADIMIR PUTIN

I N 2001 IT WAS still the case that nothing in international politics was as newsworthy as the first meeting between the new president of the United States and the president of Russia. To a certain extent this was a holdover from the days of U.S.-Soviet summits, when the President and the general secretary of the Communist Party would meet. Kennedy-Khrushchev, Nixon-Brezhnev, Carter-Brezhnev, Reagan-Gorbachev, and the last one, Bush-Gorbachev: the very recounting of the names brings back vividly the drama associated with those encounters. At that time the meetings were valued, in part, for the signal that the conflict between the superpowers was under control. Since Moscow and Washington were talking, they could not possibly be contemplating nuclear war. Yet even without the tensions of the Cold War, the meetings retained their salience. And the President's first encounter with Vladimir Putin was highly anticipated.

The meeting was to be held in Slovenia prior to the G8 summit in Genoa, Italy. It was intended to allow the two men to get acquainted and to address, face-to-face for the first time, the issue of missile defense. One of Governor Bush's key campaign initiatives, laid out in a speech at the Citadel in Charleston, South Carolina, in September 1999, was to transform U.S. military forces, both conventional and nuclear. The conventional side of military transformation was largely driven by the belief that the United States should exploit its technological sophistication to build more agile, lethal, and readily deployable forces. The Cold War was over, but the U.S. military still looked as if it were waiting to engage Soviet forces across the north German plain. The then governor called for its modernization by leveraging innovations in stealth, precision weaponry, and information gathering and analysis. He said that as president he would direct the secretary of defense to improve the integration of the military and intelligence communities to enhance the military's special operations forces and long-strike capabilities. He also pledged to commit $20 billion to the research and development of new military technologies to replace outdated weapons programs.

A problem arose when we were asked what military systems we would actually cancel, a discussion bound to anger constituents in some states. We settled on the hapless Crusader, a much-maligned artillery system, and moved on to more fertile ground, such as advocating for greater readiness and for improvements in military housing. Don Rumsfeld would eventually embark on a campaign to fundamentally restructure U.S. conventional forces.

The nuclear side of the equation represented an even more dramatic break. The arcane nuclear strategy of the Cold War rested on the premise that the Soviet Union and the United States had to be vulnerable to each other to prevent nuclear war. "Mutually assured destruction" would deny the advantage in a conflict to both sides; it would not be possible to launch a first strike with offensive forces and then protect against a counterattack with missile defenses given the sheer size of the arsenals. Each side had tens of thousands of nuclear warheads adding up to tens of thousands of times the force of the bombs that had destroyed Nagasaki and Hiroshima, making it difficult to see how either country could have survived in any event. Nonetheless, the two sides entered into a web of arms control agreements aimed at maintaining this equilibrium, including the Anti–Ballistic Missile (ABM) Treaty of 1972, which limited defenses to negligible levels.

In 1983 Ronald Reagan challenged the premise of this strategy. He couldn't understand why defenses were bad and proposed the Strategic Defense Initiative (SDI), aimed at making nuclear weapons "impotent and obsolete." But among the high priests of arms control, SDI was a threat to strategic stability.

Even those who weren't wedded to the mutually assured destruction theology found the prospects for the success of Reagan's approach fairly dim. The U.S. defenses would have to literally knock down thousands of nuclear warheads. The science, they said, did not work, and even if it did, if even a few missiles leaked through, the destruction would be devastating. Reagan nevertheless pursued the initiative, which resulted in important breakthroughs in command and control that ironically improved U.S. conventional war-fighting capabilities. But the dream of a national shield to protect the United States from Soviet nuclear weapons died with the end of the Cold War. Reagan and Gorbachev went on to sign important arms control agreements, and the Anti–Ballistic Missile Treaty remained intact. The same approach—new agreements and maintenance of the treaty—remained true for George H. W. Bush and Bill Clinton.

For George W. Bush, however, the landscape had changed dramatically and brought a new set of urgent challenges and a reason to remake nuclear strategy. It had always been difficult to imagine a nuclear exchange between Moscow and Washington. The "bolt out of the blue," where one side launched an unprovoked attack, would have been suicidal. The slightly more plausible scenario was a nuclear exchange rising out of a conventional conflict in the center of Europe. After all, throughout the Cold War the most highly trained forces of the two alliances, NATO and the Warsaw Pact, had faced off across the line that divided Germany. The Soviet and U.S. militaries were thus prepared for the eventuality of a nuclear clash, and every president (and general secretary) had to be ready to think the unthinkable. I spent a good deal of my early career doing precisely that and served in 1986–1987 as a staff officer in the Nuclear and Chemical Division (NUCHEM, pronounced "nuke 'em") of the Joint Staff.

By 2001 this nightmare scenario was no longer imaginable. The Soviet Union had collapsed and the Red Army was out of Europe, withdrawn deep into Russian territory. Germany was unified, and the front-line states—Poland, the Czech Republic, and Hungary—were members of NATO. There was no Warsaw Pact. What possible scenario existed for nuclear conflict between the United States and Russia, which were no longer even enemies?

That question led President Bush to propose radical reductions in nuclear arsenals without the extensive and laborious negotiations of the Cold War period. The President was prepared to unilaterally reduce U.S.-deployed warheads to a reasonable level and let the Russians simply follow suit. That was to be accompanied by a revision to the ABM

Treaty or, better still, mutual abrogation, allowing the development of small-scale defenses to be used against the growing and very real missile threat from rogue nations such as North Korea and Iran.

That was too much for the national security establishment. Prior to the meeting with Putin, the hottest topic in Washington seemed to be whether to preserve the thirty-year-old ABM Treaty from an era long past. The arms control debates of years gone by were suddenly reborn in Moscow, Washington, and Europe. The discussion centered on "strategic stability," but I've come to believe that that was not the real issue for the Russians.

I do not mean to suggest that Moscow, particularly the Russian general staff, was unconcerned about the military balance. But in a larger sense, an end to arms control as we had come to know it also meant an end to the equality between the Kremlin and the White House that it had come to symbolize. The Russians liked the big, years-long negotiations, which then produced treaty signings and grand summits. The arms control regimes, dating back to the Nixon administration, had been accompanied by the Basic Principles of Relations Between the United States of America and the Union of Soviet Socialist Republics, a document that had essentially written the rules of the road for the two superpowers to "manage" international affairs.

Russia, the Soviet successor state, was a great power but not a superpower in the Cold War sense of the term. Only in terms of nuclear weapons was Russia by any stretch of the imagination equal to the United States. The Russian national security elite said all of the right things about cooperation in the post–Cold War era and even acted that way much of the time. But deep inside there was a nostalgia for the time when Moscow had stood astride the international system, challenging Washington and its allies with an alternative view of how human history would evolve. Arms control and the ABM Treaty were integral to that reality and thus talismans against decline.

It was against this backdrop that we arrived at the sixteenth-century castle of Brdo outside Ljubljana, Slovenia, quite a bit earlier than the Russian delegation did. George W. Bush had a well-deserved reputation for being on time, even early, for meetings. In fact, I once told the

President that he would be able to end his term six months sooner because he was so early for every engagement.

When the protocol chief announced that the Russians had arrived, the President walked out of the room and into the courtyard in order to meet them halfway. As Putin started toward him, I was struck by his physical bearing. He was not very tall, maybe five feet, eight inches, but had broad shoulders and an athlete's gait. He seemed a bit shy, even nervous. When I shook his hand and gave the customary Russian greeting, *"Ochen priyatno"* (Good to meet you), it suddenly occurred to me that we had met before.

In 1992 I had gone to St. Petersburg to meet with the reformist mayor, the late Anatoly Sobchak, who was seeking the advice of several Stanford professors about the creation of a new European University to be located in the grand former capital of the Russian Empire. That evening, Sobchak hosted a reception for our delegation. Sobchak and his wife were royalists who loved the aura of the nineteenth century and were doing all they could to channel the glorious past of St. Petersburg into modern Russia. The room was filled with people dressed in all black (as continental intelligentsia often did at the turn of the twentieth century). Many of them seemed to be named Tolstoy or Pushkin, having either real or appropriated familial connections to the great literary and artistic figures of the past. There was also one man who looked quite out of place, dressed in a suit befitting a high-ranking Soviet bureaucrat; he was introduced to me as the deputy mayor of St. Petersburg, Vladimir Putin.

I didn't say anything about that first encounter, focusing instead on the business at hand. The two presidents went into a room for a one-on-one session. Rarely are such sessions truly "under four eyes," and in that case I accompanied President Bush while Vladimir Rushailo attended with Putin. The Russian national security advisor was a former interior minister and general, who, like me, had only recently been appointed to the national security post. He looked like a wrestler, but his most noticeable characteristic was his eyebrows—or rather what seemed to be a single eyebrow that stretched across his forehead.

The two leaders started with pleasantries, but it did not take long for them to get down to business. President Bush said to Putin, "I have to know whom you trust. Who is the person we should turn to if there are sensitive matters between us?"

"Sergei Ivanov, the minister of defense," Putin answered.

The President nodded and said, "For me it will be Condi." I wondered if anyone else had noticed the asymmetry. I was the President's "go-to person"; Rushailo was apparently just along for the ride.

That was how my relationship with Sergei Ivanov began. Ivanov was, like Putin, a former KGB officer with extraordinary linguistic capability. He looked a little like Putin, blond and blue-eyed, but with more delicate features than his boss. He spoke English perfectly and with only the slightest accent, having, he said, listened to rock music to hone his skills. Sergei was tough and somewhat suspicious of the United States, but he was dependable. He never told me that he would do something that he did not do. He was an unfailing conduit to Putin on the most sensitive matters through changes in positions and titles. (He would later become first deputy prime minister and an unsuccessful candidate for Putin's endorsement for the Russian presidency, and I, of course, became secretary of state.) Our channel remained the most important and discreet one between the White House and the Kremlin.

During the meeting, Putin and the President talked about a variety of issues. The President said that he intended to get out of the ABM Treaty and would prefer to do so mutually. Calmly, Putin said that he could never agree to that but did not threaten any retaliation. They agreed to see if they could find a nonconfrontational way forward.

After touching on some other issues, Putin suddenly raised the problem of Pakistan. He excoriated the Pervez Musharraf regime for its support of extremists and for the connections of the Pakistani army and intelligence services to the Taliban and al Qaeda. Those extremists were all being funded by Saudi Arabia, he said, and it was only a matter of time until it resulted in a major catastrophe. We, of course, knew of the connections between Pakistan and the Taliban and had been hammering Islamabad, as the Clinton administration had, to break its ties with extremists. But I was taken aback by Putin's alarm and vehemence and chalked it up to Russian bitterness toward Pakistan for supporting the

Afghan mujahideen, who had defeated the Soviet Union in the 1980s. Putin, though, was right: the Taliban and al Qaeda were time bombs that would explode on September 11, 2001. Pakistan's relationship with the extremists would become one of our gravest problems. Putin never let us forget it, recalling that conversation time and time again.

During the meeting, Putin shared a rather syrupy story about a cross that his mother had given him; to be fair, the President was looking for a way to establish a more personal connection and asked about the cross that the Russian was wearing, so Putin did not initiate the story. It seems that a fire had consumed his dacha but workmen had retrieved the cross and returned it to Putin. I never really knew what to make of the story, because to this day it's hard for me to imagine Putin, this former servant of atheistic communism, as a religious man.

At the press conference afterward, President Bush was asked if he trusted Putin. The thought flashed through my mind that we hadn't covered that question in our preparation. It was a question fraught with pitfalls. The President answered, "Yes." That might have been okay, because "no" would have put the relationship on a pretty bad footing from the start. But then the President added, "I looked the man in the eye . . . I was able to get a sense of his soul." I visibly stiffened. It was an awkward way to get out of the predicament. We were never able to escape the perception that the President had naively trusted Putin and then been betrayed. There was little room to convince critics that the circumstances of 2001 and the relationship with Vladimir Putin then were very different from what would later come to pass.

False Alarm

IN FACT, Putin's warnings came as terrorism and al Qaeda were beginning to make their presence felt more acutely during the months of June and July.

When we first arrived in Washington after the election, we began a series of meetings with the outgoing Clinton national security team. I met Sandy Berger at the White House, and we talked about a variety of issues. He was very focused on the Middle East and the last throes of the Camp David process and on a possible presidential visit to North Korea.

Sandy and I talked about the functioning of the NSC and of the various departments. During one of our conversations, he said something that was often repeated after 9/11: he noted that I would spend far more time dealing with terrorism than I expected, recalling the 1993 World Trade Center bombing and the 1998 attacks on our embassies in Kenya and Tanzania. Not much more was said.

Sandy also offered to have Dick Clarke, the NSC's counterterrorism advisor, brief me separately. Sandy dropped by at the beginning of that meeting and then departed. I suspect that Clarke had wanted to have Sandy's imprimatur so that I would listen attentively to his concerns. He needn't have worried. I knew that there was a serious threat. I'd made that clear in a radio station interview in Detroit during the campaign, stating, "There needs to be better cooperation [among U.S. intelligence agencies] because we don't want to wake up one day and find that Osama bin Laden has been successful on our territory."

Nonetheless, I thought that Clarke's presentation was impressive, though short on operational content. There was a lot that described al Qaeda but not very much about what to do. He made the point that al Qaeda was a network dedicated to the destruction of the United States. There were numerous slides with the faces of al Qaeda operatives and a discussion of their safe haven in Afghanistan. There was very little discussion of Pakistan or Saudi Arabia. At the end I asked Clarke and his team whether we were doing all we could to counter al Qaeda. He made mention of some covert activities and said that he would later brief me on some other efforts.

That encounter solidified my view, shared by Steve Hadley, that we ought to keep the Clinton administration's counterterrorism team in place despite Dick Clarke's awful reputation with many who'd worked with him. In my first staff meeting, I asked the senior directors (the heads of the regional and functional directorates within the NSC) to give me their most urgent priorities. Dick Clarke sent such a memorandum to me on January 25, laying out the case for stepped-up efforts against al Qaeda. Ironically, only one paragraph, in an attachment to the memorandum, addressed al Qaeda and the homeland threat. It included a line that suggested that the FBI was following sleeper cells inside the United States. Most of the memo was devoted to two options: arming the Northern Alliance, the organized resistance to the Taliban, and increasing counterterrorism cooperation with Uzbekistan, the strategically located country from which many military and intelligence activities had to be carried out. Dick also favored the development of an "armed Predator," an intelligence drone that could locate a target and fire on it.

I called Clarke to my office on January 31 and essentially told him that he had a green light to develop a strategy. There was no need for a Principals Committee meeting because Don, Colin, and the Vice President had all been briefed on al Qaeda. I said that George Tenet had briefed the President during the transition. What was needed now was a strategy not to "roll back" al Qaeda but to eliminate the threat.

The President had made clear that he didn't want his administration to be put into the position of the Clinton administration after the bombing of the U.S. embassies in Dar es Salaam and Nairobi in 1998 and the bombing of the USS *Cole* in 2000. The only real option then had been a "standoff"—one in which cruise missiles or maybe bombers could be used from international waters or U.S. military bases, but nothing more because there was no regional support. In fact, our administration did not respond militarily to the *Cole* incident because we didn't want to launch a feckless cruise missile attack and leave al Qaeda intact, allowing Osama bin Laden to crow that he had survived the United States' military response. We needed a more comprehensive approach.

Steve and I discussed the need for a companion to the strategy Dick was developing that would address the problem of regional support for counterterrorism and the special role of Pakistan. Without a way to get Pakistan to shift from supporting the Taliban, any strategy would fail. We brought in Zalmay Khalilzad, who'd been born and educated in Afghanistan and who was a true South Asia expert, to lead that effort.

We were also concerned that we had too little contact with the south of the country. The warlords who composed the Northern Alliance were largely Uzbek and Tajik and occupied less than 10 percent of the territory of Afghanistan. The cultural, political, and geographic weight of the country was in the southern Pashtun belt in the strategic areas of Helmand and Kandahar. Though the CIA had well-developed relationships in the north, there was far less contact with opposition leaders in the Taliban's southern stronghold. Khalilzad and the CIA were told to develop a strategy for the south.

The work proceeded throughout the spring of 2001. There was an increased effort to pressure the Taliban to turn over Osama bin Laden to a country where he could face appropriate justice. The CIA also began developing a presidential finding to implement large-scale programs of covert aid to the Taliban's adversaries. Findings are authorized by the President and briefed to key members of Congress and members of the intelligence committees. It was important to get the work started, but we knew that nothing in the strategy was likely to have a short-term impact on al Qaeda. I told the President that the idea was to seriously damage al Qaeda in a period of three to five years. Any terrorist threat in the short term would have to be dealt with in the context of the existing strategy and operational structures.

Thus, when George Tenet told the President toward the end of May that he was worried about "chatter" among the terrorists concerning a coming attack, the existing counterterrorism machinery was mobilized.

The threat was assumed to be an overseas one. We were concerned about potential attacks in Jordan, Saudi Arabia, Israel, and Genoa, Italy, the site of the 2001 G8 summit. The period between late May and mid-July was intense as we tried to counter a maddeningly nebulous threat. Don and Colin and I discussed the situation almost daily during our morning phone call, and the two secretaries acted to secure U.S. assets and interests abroad. The State Department, for example, initiated a program in Saudi Arabia to issue express visas as a security measure to keep long lines of foreigners from forming at the embassy. By June 21, the U.S. Embassy in Yemen was closed and the U.S. Central Command had raised the force protection condition level for U.S. troops in six countries to the highest level in anticipation of an imminent attack. Special arrangements were made concerning Genoa, including shutting down the airspace over and around the city, since some of the potential plots involved airplanes.

George Tenet was in the Oval Office every morning and briefed the President about the threat situation. He and I met several times a week and reviewed what was being done. George contends in his book, *At the Center of the Storm,* that he called me on July 10 to sound the alarm about an impending attack, specifically claiming that increased numbers of Islamic extremists were traveling to Afghanistan. I do remember receiving a call from George in which he said, "I'm worried about the chatter." I asked what he wanted to do, and he suggested that he come over immediately. I readily agreed.

My recollection of the meeting is not very crisp because we were discussing the threat every day. There was a presentation that compiled the threat information that we had been reviewing daily along with some new intelligence. I remember asking George if there was more that the CIA could do to capture Abu Zubaydah, whom we believed to be al Qaeda's chief facilitator and who might therefore know the plot details. The Vice President made calls to Jordan and Saudi Arabia to solicit their help in finding him and to emphasize our concern for their security. Together with the raised levels of alert for State and Defense, I thought we were doing what needed to be done.

At the same time, Dick Clarke convened the Counter-terrorism Security Group (CSG) daily, sometimes twice in one day. The group was made up of senior counterterrorism experts from the counterterrorist departments of the CIA, the FBI, the Joint Chiefs of Staff, and the Departments of Defense, Justice, and State. It was their responsibility to sort through the intelligence and to make certain that all relevant agencies were taking steps to counter the threat.

Later, one of the accusations leveled at us was that we did not pay "high-level" attention to the terrorism threat in June and July. In 1999, as the millennium approached, there had been a spike in threat reporting, and indeed a plot had been disrupted before it could materialize. At that time, Sandy Berger had held daily Principals meetings. The theory post-9/11 was that had the Principals met every day and "shaken the trees," something might have fallen out to give us a clue that a homeland attack was coming.

The problem, however, was not the absence of effort to counter the threat; the weakness in our effort was systemic. One of its primary causes was the seam that existed between "domestic" and "foreign" intelligence. For example, electronic surveillance was artificially divided between the National Security Agency, which was responsible for monitoring the communications of terrorists outside the United States, and the FBI, which was supposed to conduct surveillance of suspected terrorists on U.S. soil. This split meant that no agency was responsible for collecting information transmitted between U.S.-based operatives and foreign terrorist cells.

The same foreign/domestic split kept the CIA and FBI from working well together. The FBI treated the internal terrorism problem as a law enforcement matter, not an intelligence mission. And the deliberations about internal threats were not well informed by information that the CIA was getting from foreign sources. Prevention was secondary to punishing terrorists after they were caught committing a crime. Agents had to be careful not to gather evidence in ways that might get a case thrown out of U.S. courts: think *Law and Order*. This law enforcement orientation led to a wall between criminal and intelligence investigations within the Bureau itself. And the FBI was very decentralized, with less-than-optimal communication between the powerful field offices and national-level officials. It is not surprising, therefore, that FBI headquarters did not act on recommendations from an agent in Phoenix who warned about Osama bin Laden sending students to the United States for flight lessons and failed to connect this alert with an investigation into Zacarias Moussaoui, who was himself taking flight lessons in Minnesota.

I found it particularly offensive during the 9/11 hearings that the former deputy attorney general in the Clinton administration, Jamie Gorelick, whom I otherwise admired, questioned the Bush administration's attention to terrorism. She had been the author of a famous memorandum that had had the effect of reinforcing the wall between criminal and intelligence investigations in 1995. The wall might have been put into place for good reasons (principally civil liberties), but it kept the FBI from moving quickly to follow the leads from Moussaoui before 9/11 and it undermined our ability to deal with transnational terrorist threats more generally.

The homeland threat was simply not sufficiently on anyone's radar screen at the national level before 9/11. The threat reporting pointed squarely to an attack on U.S. interests abroad. Nevertheless, it occurred to me that perhaps we should inform the domestic agencies about these reports just in case an attack might be launched against the American homeland. I asked to have the attorney general briefed after my meeting with George Tenet, since he oversaw the FBI. Moreover, I called Dick Clarke in on July 5, asking Andy Card to join us. I told Dick to convene the domestic agencies. The chief of staff was there to tell Dick that he would intervene with domestic agencies if necessary. Dick called a meeting and reported that the FBI, FAA, and other agencies were aware of the threat information and acting on it.

Several days after 9/11, Dick Clarke would send me an e-mail, unsolicited, reassuring me that the White House had supplied information to domestic law-enforcement and other authorities, including the FAA, and that we did ask that special measures be taken. That, of course, is not the impression he conveyed to *60 Minutes* when he suggested that we were somehow not focused enough on terrorism. Moreover, I learned on September 16 that there had been an after-action report on the homeland threat in the spring of 2000 in the wake of the breakup of the millennium plot. Ironically, given all the paper that he passed to the Bush administration, Clarke did not think this report on securing the homeland to be worthy of our attention.

The threat reporting spiked at the end of July and then receded. The President finally got an answer to his question about bin Laden and the homeland threat in the famous August 6 memo. Yes, everyone knew that bin Laden was determined to attack the United States. We were not told how he might carry out such an attack, only that he had been impressed by the partially successful attack on the World Trade Center in 1993.

That memo was the only PDB item that addressed the homeland threat in the 192 PDBs that the President had seen since assuming office. On August 6 the President was in Crawford and George Tenet was, as he put it to me in 2003, "on a beach in New Jersey." A homeland threat was simply not the focus of the myriad intelligence briefings the President received.

The fact is that the United States was poorly prepared for September 11, 2001, for systemic and psychological reasons. Our homeland had been spared a major foreign attack since the British burned the White House in the War of 1812. Yes, there had been the devastating attack on a military base in Pearl Harbor and there had been fears of a homeland threat during World War II. But the homeland had not been hit. No one was prepared for what happened on that awful day.

Ironically, the al Qaeda strategy was finally ready for the Principals' review on September 4. The meeting was fruitful. We were able to agree on a strategy of implementing an ambitious covert-action program in Afghanistan and launching the Predator drone for reconnaissance missions. Because its armed capabilities were not ready, the Predator, the Principals agreed, could provide us with actionable intelligence to target the locations of key al Qaeda leaders. I forwarded the strategy to the President for his approval on September 10.

6

"The United States Is Under Attack"

SEPTEMBER 11, 2001, began like every other day. The night before I'd dined with David Manning, Tony Blair's foreign policy advisor, after attending the President's meeting that day with John Howard, the prime minister of Australia.

I arrived at my office around 6:30 A.M. and read through the various news clippings, cables, and intelligence reports. There was nothing remarkable. I was to give a speech later in the day at the Johns Hopkins School of Advanced International Studies.

I planned to make a case for missile defense, noting that we had to deal with both the low-tech terrorism threat and the high-tech missile capabilities of rogue states such as North Korea and Iran. To be fair, I did not dwell on the terrorist threat, which was being worked through the NSC system. Steve and I had talked about that and decided that he or I, or maybe the President, would give a speech when we revealed our new strategy for combating al Qaeda. Rather, I concentrated my remarks on missile defense, countering the critics who thought the President to be too focused on the missile threat.

The President was traveling that morning to Florida for an education event. Usually Steve or I traveled with him, but this was to be a short day trip and we sent the director of the Situation Room, U.S. Navy Captain Deborah Loewer, to accompany the President.

Shortly before 9:00 A.M., I was standing at my desk when my executive assistant, then U.S. Army Major Tony Crawford, came in and said that a plane had hit the World Trade Center. "That's odd," I said, thinking that it was probably a small plane that had gone off course. Not too long before, the golfer Payne Stewart had died in a crash when the cabin had depressurized and knocked the pilot unconscious. That was the kind of scenario that immediately came to mind.

A few minutes later, Tony came in and said that it was a commercial airliner that had hit the Trade Center. I got the President on the phone and told him what had happened. "That's a strange accident," he said. We agreed that I would be back in touch.

I went down to the Situation Room for my staff meeting. I was going around the table to hear from the senior directors when Tony burst in with a note. A second plane had hit the World Trade Center. People have told me that I said, rather calmly, "I have to go." Maybe. But at that moment I knew that there had been a terrorist attack, and I was shaken to my core.

The Situation Room at that time (it has since been remodeled) was just a paneled conference room abutted by a kind of operations center staffed by civilians and military officers who monitored intelligence traffic and managed the phone calls for the President and the National Security Council staff. They kept in constant communication with the operations centers at the CIA and at State and with the National Military Command Center at the Pentagon.

I headed into the operations center, where phones were ringing and people were talking loudly while watching multiple television screens playing the footage from New York. I tried to reach the NSC principals. George Tenet had already gone to a safe location at Langley. Colin Powell was in Latin America, and I had a momentary scare because I thought he was in Colombia, then a hotbed of terrorism. Fortunately, he was in Peru attending a meeting of the Organization of American States. I tried to reach Don Rumsfeld but couldn't. His phones were just ringing, I was told. I turned around and saw on the television screen that a plane had gone into the Pentagon.

Before I could do anything else, the Secret Service came and said, "Dr. Rice, you must go to the bunker. Now! Planes are hitting buildings all over Washington. The White House has got to be next." I turned to head toward the bunker, and there was suddenly a report (a false one) that there had been a car bomb at the State Department.

The next moments passed quickly. I did stop to call my Uncle Alto and Aunt Connie in Birmingham. "There will be awful pictures from Washington," I said. "Tell everyone I'm okay."

Then I called the President. "I'm coming back," he said.

"Mr. President," I said, "stay where you are. You cannot come back here."

Frank Miller, my trusted senior director for defense policy and arms control, was standing next to me. "Tell him he can't come back."

"I know," I said. I then did something that I never did again. I raised my voice with the President and in a tone as firm as I could possibly muster, I said, "Mr. President, you cannot come back here. Washington, I mean the United States, is under attack." He didn't answer, and the Secret Service lifted me physically and pushed me toward the bunker.

I know the routes to the Presidential Emergency Operations Center (PEOC) very well. But I don't remember how we got there that day. The first person I saw and acknowledged was the Vice President who was on the telephone with the President. I spotted Norman Mineta, the secretary of transportation and as decent a public servant as one would ever know. He had been the Democratic congressman from a district not far from my home in northern California. He is Japanese American with one of those amazing personal histories of a family that remained loyal to the United States despite despicable treatment by the U.S. government during World War II.

Norm was seated at the corner of the long table with a legal pad; he was tracking the tail numbers of aircraft! We had no idea how many planes had been designated to crash into buildings, so the first task was to get every plane out of the air and onto the ground as fast as possible. There was enormous confusion as several planes were reported to be "squawking" inappropriately, meaning that they were not giving the standard response when air traffic control contacted them. Other aircraft would appear in the communications and then disappear. At one point a plane was said to have taken off unauthorized from Madrid, headed for the United States. A few minutes later it was said to have landed in Portugal, then supposedly it was still in the air headed for New York, then inexplicably back in Madrid. Commercial airliners had become weapons, and we needed to know the location—and intention—of all 4,500 planes in U.S. airspace that day.

The Vice President had contacted the President and asked what he wanted to do if a plane did not identify itself. Should we shoot it down? The President gave the order, which the Vice President transmitted to the Pentagon: if a plane did not "squawk" properly, treat it as a foe and shoot it down. That was a chilling prospect. The President had just made the unthinkable decision to have the U.S. Air Force shoot down a commercial airliner, killing its innocent passengers. That, though, was the kind of Hobson's choice that we suddenly faced. Really, no choice at all.

Sometime after the order was given, Norm was told that a plane had disappeared from the air traffic control radar. It was United Airlines Flight 93. For a few awful minutes we all thought that we had shot it down. The Vice President was on the line with the Pentagon. Steve Hadley established a second contact with the National Military Command Center. "You must know if you engaged a civilian aircraft," the Vice President kept saying. "How could you not know if you engaged a civilian aircraft?" It took what seemed like an eternity to get an answer: no, the air force had not shot down a civilian aircraft. We learned later, of course, that the passengers and crew of Flight 93 had driven it into the ground so that the terrorists could not destroy another building—most likely the Capitol or perhaps the White House. Those brave souls had saved hundreds of their fellow citizens.

A year later I went to a memorial service in Pennsylvania for the victims of Flight 93. One of the families was African American, a group of sisters who reminded me of my own relatives. Their brother LeRoy Homer, Jr., clearly the apple of their eye, had been the copilot on that flight. I told them that I wanted them to know that their brother had quite possibly saved my life, along with many others.

On 9/11, though, I do not remember feeling any sense of personal danger. I've been asked many times whether I was frightened, but frankly I didn't have time to entertain such thoughts. Rather, I fell into a mode consistent with all that I'd been taught and that I had taught myself about crisis management.

Not long after I got to the bunker, it occurred to me that we should contact the Russians. Russian military forces operate worldwide and sometimes in close proximity to our own. There was always a concern during the Cold War that raising the alert level of U.S. forces would spark the Soviet Union to do the same, causing a dangerous spiral of alerts.

As it turned out, Putin had been trying to reach the President, who by now was somewhere between Florida and a secure location in

Louisiana. I asked to speak to Sergei Ivanov, but Putin got on the phone. "Mr. President," I said, "the President is not able to take your call right now because he is being moved to another location. I wanted to let you know that American forces are going up on alert."

"We already know, and we have canceled our exercises and brought our alert levels down," he said. "Is there anything else we can do?"

I thanked him, and for one brief moment the thought flashed through my head: *the Cold War really is over.*

Another priority was to make sure that the world knew that the United States was still functioning. I could imagine the pictures being viewed in other countries around the world and the uncertainty provoked by the silence of the U.S. government. With buildings going down in New York and an attack on the Pentagon in Washington, we needed to send a message to friend *and* foe that the United States of America had not been decapitated: our leadership was intact, and we were functioning properly. Steve Hadley asked the State Department to send a cable to all posts to convey those important facts.

In retrospect it is amazing that we functioned as well as we did. There were certainly difficulties: we learned that the screens in the bunker could display the Situation Room or television channels but not both simultaneously. There was a moment when there were so many people in the room that the oxygen level dropped precipitously and we had to expel a number of "nonessential" personnel.

In the first few hours, we also failed to communicate convincingly with the outside world and, more important, the country. That was in large part due to the President's being out of Washington. Looking back, I can see that the first statement by the President, which Karen Hughes cobbled together with Ari Fleischer, was neither informative nor reassuring. But at the time no one wanted to say too much or too little about what might happen next.

In the final analysis, we just kept going. We were all veterans of the Cold War. I was grateful that I never had to use my training in nuclear war survival for the purpose for which it was intended. But it sure helped to have those instincts kick in reflexively when I was suddenly forced to deal with a different kind of "unthinkable" event.

The remainder of that day was a blur. The President arrived at

Barksdale Air Force Base in Louisiana and then decided that we had insufficient secure communications there. He was transferred to Offutt Air Force Base in Nebraska, where we held a video-conference meeting of the National Security Council at about 3:00 P.M. Colin Powell was still in the air, returning from Peru, so Rich Armitage represented State. Don and George managed to get to the White House. The meeting was brief, with the President saying only that this was an act of war and that combating terror was the new priority of his administration. At the moment, though, the most important task was to protect the country from further attack and deal with the injured. The victims in New York and at the Pentagon were to get any and all help they needed, but we were surprised at how few injured there were. The attack had been so devastating that most of the victims had never had a chance.

A few hours after the meeting, the President called me. "I'm coming back," he said. "And I don't want to hear any argument about it!" I knew it was fruitless to say anything more.

The President landed on the South Lawn of the White House by helicopter at about 7:00 P.M. I walked out toward him and he asked, "Where's Laura?" She was in the emergency operations center. He headed to the Oval and then immediately down to see the First Lady. When he returned, he joined Karen Hughes, Ari Fleischer, and me in his small private dining room located off the hallway from the Oval. We'd told the networks that the President would speak to the nation at 9:00 P.M., and a CBS crew was already in the process of transforming the Oval for the broadcast.

Mike Gerson had done a draft of the speech, which said what one might expect: the President was at once mourning the dead and reassuring the nation that the United States would be just fine. But the question arose regarding what to say about the terrorists. Though we could have a more considered policy discussion later, the first message would be read everywhere, particularly in the circles of al Qaeda and those who would do us more harm.

The statement said categorically that we would find the terrorists and bring them to justice. But the important issue was what to say about the state sponsors that supported them. One of the problems with terrorists is that they have little at stake in a conventional sense. Unlike states, they have no territory to threaten and no sovereignty to lose. We could, however, send a message to the states that supported them.

Thus we decided to put state sponsors on notice: "We will make no distinction between the terrorists who committed these acts and those who harbor them." The President paused over that line and looked at me. I asked him if he felt that he needed to say that now. He said that he did but asked if I had a different view. I told him that I thought he had to say it in the first message because later on it would lose its impact. I consulted with the Vice President and called Colin and Don and read the line to them. Everyone agreed, and that line became known as one of the most important elements of the "Bush Doctrine."

After the President delivered his address, we held another meeting of the National Security Council, which ended at about 10:00 P.M. Colin had returned from Peru and attended in person along with the other principals. Each principal gave a brief situation report, and George Tenet said that he was sure that al Qaeda had been the culprit but would wait until the next morning to make a definitive call.

I was struck that the President didn't even look tired. He was determined to keep everyone focused on what we needed to do in the immediate aftermath. He kept saying that we would punish those who attacked us. That, however, was a matter for another day. I remember thinking that he was absolutely in control and showing no strain whatsoever.

I'd been told earlier in the evening that the Secret Service didn't want me to go home to my Watergate apartment. I did not have a security detail, and their agents would assign me one the next day. Until then it was better that I stay at the White House. I didn't question them on this point and had planned to just sleep in my office. But the President nicely invited me to stay in the residence, so I asked a member of my staff, Sarah Lenti, to go to my apartment and pick up a change of clothes for the next day. From that time on, I kept a packed suitcase in my office, just in case I needed it again.

After the NSC meeting, Steve Hadley and Andy Card joined me in my office. I was finally tired. Bone tired. We were about to outline the tasks for the next day when a Secret Service agent burst into the office. "Go to the bunker! Another plane is headed for the White House!" We jumped up and walked quickly back toward the emergency operations center. The first "evacuees" I saw were Barney the dog and then Spot, the other dog. I then noticed the President's brother Neil, who happened to be staying at the White House, Maria Galvan, the Bushes' housekeeper, and then Laura and the President. Laura was in her bathrobe and, she later told me, *without* her contacts—so she couldn't see. The President was dressed for bed in a T-shirt and shorts. It was a motley crew.

It turned out to be a false alarm, but in solemn tones the Secret Service agent said, "Mr. President you should sleep here tonight." They had planned for him to sleep on a creaking, moth-eaten pullout sofa bed that looked as though it hadn't been opened since the 1960s. The President took one look at it and said, "I'm going to bed," whereupon he turned and started upstairs, Laura and the family and pets trailing after him. Steve, Andy, and I followed. It was for me a moment of comic relief. "No one would believe this," I whispered to Steve.

I went upstairs to one of the bedrooms on the residential floor. I turned on the television, which was playing the attack over and over, but I didn't really watch. Though I was really tired, I slept only a little, maybe a couple of hours. At about 4:30 A.M., I gave up, got dressed, and went downstairs to my office.

When I arrived, I had a message from Nicholas Burns, our ambassador to NATO. I returned his call, and Nick said that the NATO allies wanted to vote an Article V resolution: "An armed attack against one or more of them in Europe or North America shall be considered an attack against them all." I choked back tears at that one and told him that we would welcome the action. As a longtime student of NATO, I knew immediately that it would be the first time that NATO had ever invoked the collective-defense clause that was the essence of the Alliance. When the North Atlantic Treaty, which established NATO, was signed in 1949, Article V was the source of much debate because it committed the United States to defend Europe at a time of great tension and what was believed to be almost certain conflict with the Soviet Union. Now, ten years after the collapse of the Soviet Union, the Alliance was expressing the highest form of solidarity with us. I was deeply moved. *It's really good to have friends*, I thought.

As time went on, the allies felt frustrated that they hadn't been fully included in our response to 9/11. I have wondered many times if we somehow missed an opportunity to make the declaration of Article V have meaning for the Alliance. It is true that we were capable largely on our own to initiate war against the Taliban. It is also true that, after years of neglecting their military capabilities and concurrent failure to modernize for the war we'd eventually fight, most members of the Alliance were unable to move their military forces quickly. And we were single-minded, bruised, and determined to avenge 9/11 and destroy al Qaeda and its dangerous sanctuary as quickly as possible. Nonetheless, I've always felt that we left the Alliance dressed up with nowhere to go. I wish we'd done better.

"Every Day Since Has Been September 12"

THAT'S THE PHRASE that has always come to mind when, over the years, I've tried to explain the impact of the attack on the Bush administration's thinking and on me personally. No security issue ever looked quite the same again, and every day our overwhelming preoccupation was to avoid another attack. The United States was the most powerful country in the world—militarily and economically. And yet, we had not been able to prevent a devastating attack by a stateless network of extremists, operating from the territory of one of the world's poorest countries. Our entire concept of what constituted security had been shaken. The governmental institutions simply didn't exist to deal with a threat of this kind. And so in the first days and months ad hoc arrangements had to fill the void.

For the first time, the FBI director and the attorney general attended the President's intelligence briefing along with the CIA director. The divide between domestic and foreign intelligence was for a while bridged, literally, in the Oval Office. The threat report was hair-raising because overnight every conceivable threat, no matter how unlikely, seemed to come to the President. Having missed the attacks, the intelligence agencies were determined not to be wrong again.

That morning of September 12, George Tenet briefed us on the evidence of al Qaeda's complicity in the attacks. The President listened to the recitation of the case against al Qaeda and let the War Council know that we'd crossed a Rubicon and we would destroy them. The most important task, however, was to make sure that it could not carry out another attack.

I remember being struck by the President's clarity concerning priorities. First, secure the country. Second, reassure the American people and get the country back to normal as soon as possible. If America's way of life ground to a halt, the terrorists would have won. Third, plan to destroy the terrorist networks and give their sponsors a choice to be with us or against us. Fourth, prepare to go to war against al Qaeda in a meaningful way—that meant destroying its safe haven in Afghanistan. There would be no spasm attack, lashing out with cruise missiles into empty tents. He wanted an option for boots on the ground. We would go after al Qaeda at a time of our choosing.

THE PRESIDENT'S clarity stood in stark contrast to the chaotic decision-making structures supporting him. After calls to several world leaders and the intelligence briefing, the President called the NSC together in the Cabinet room. The attendance had been expanded dramatically because of the multifaceted nature of the problem we faced. In addition to the NSC core—State, Defense, Joint Chiefs of Staff, and CIA—there were several other agencies present: the FBI and the Justice Department to deal with domestic intelligence and security; Treasury and the National Economic Council (NEC) to deal with the shock to the economy; Transportation to deal with the airports and highways.

There seemed to be people everywhere, and the more clarity the President sought, the more chaotic the meeting became. The Australian prime minister, John Howard, was stuck in the United States and needed to get back home. We needed to get Alan Greenspan, the chairman of the Federal Reserve, back from Europe. The President wanted to know how soon he could safely open the airports. How long would it be before Wall Street and the banking system were up and functioning? Did we have any plans for protection of power plants, which had been named as a target in the threat reporting? Who was dealing with the forty-seven governors whose states had not been hit but who were desperate to hear from the White House concerning what they should do? I looked around and thought, *I'm the national security advisor. I'm supposed to make sense of this for the President!*

A second meeting that afternoon was only marginally better. New problems had arisen. We'd essentially closed our borders, and it was already evident that economic activity was grinding to a halt. The integrated nature of our industrial supply chain with Canada was evident as calls began to come in from Detroit that GM and other automakers, shut off from their Canadian suppliers, would soon cease to produce. The President was pushing very hard to reopen the airports and to find a way to assure the American people that it was safe to fly.

Josh Bolten, the deputy chief of staff, Steve Hadley, and I decided to develop "pods," groups of officials who would take responsibility for different elements of the response. Josh took over domestic issues and relations with the states. We turned to Larry Thompson, the deputy attorney general, to develop a plan for the protection of critical infrastructure. Larry Lindsey of the NEC took charge of trying to coordinate the many aspects of economic survival and then revival. Steve and I turned to managing the suddenly overwhelming work of the War Council. Years later, Larry Thompson and I were having lunch. "Why did you assign me critical infrastructure?" he asked. "I didn't know anything about it." I told him that no one knew how to protect critical infrastructure. He was capable, and everyone trusted him. In the immediate days after 9/11, that was enough.

On the afternoon of September 12, I accompanied the President to the Pentagon. As we drove toward it, we could see where the plane had slammed into the side of the building. Where there had once been a wall, now there was just a gaping hole of twisted metal and concrete. There were rescue workers still there, and the President wanted to thank them. I walked alongside him for a while and then broke off and began to talk to the doctors, nurses, and other first responders who'd pulled victims from the rubble—both those who could be saved and those who'd already perished. I was shaking when I got back into the motorcade. I returned to the White House and worked until after ten that night. When I got out of the car at the Watergate, I thought, *What is that smell?* It was my clothes, deeply penetrated by the soot and smoke of the Pentagon.

I just kept going the next day, not devoid of emotion but holding my feelings in check. There was work to be done. But slowly my emotions were emerging. I tried to ground myself by going back to some of my daily routines, such as exercising. I finally set aside time to get a long overdue haircut. As I sat there, John Lennon's "Imagine" came on the radio. I choked back tears, went back to the White House, and focused again on my work. I left that night at 11:49 P.M.; seventeen-hour days were now routine.

When I woke up the next morning, I turned on the TV. The scene was from London, and the Coldstream Guards were playing in the square outside Buckingham Palace. It took me a moment to focus, but then I realized that they were playing our national anthem. I broke down and cried.

I HAVE always felt as if I operated in a kind of fog, a virtual state of shock, for two days after 9/11. That was my state of mind on September 14 as we prepared for the National Day of Prayer and Remembrance service at National Cathedral. The presidential motorcade felt like a funeral procession. I was in the "control" or communications car with Andy Card; the national security advisor and chief of staff always rode together, along with the President's military aide. As we made our way up Massachusetts Avenue, I spotted a man holding a sign that said, "God Bless America. We will not be terrorized." We passed the Russian Orthodox church, where the priests were ringing the huge bells. Slowly we pulled into the circle in front of the cathedral. Entering the church, I saw an exceptional gathering: former presidents and Cabinet secretaries, Supreme Court justices, members of Congress, the military, all there together in a national day of mourning. It was an interfaith service with the three great monotheistic religions represented, including Islam. The nation's preacher, Billy Graham, was very frail, but he rallied to deliver a sermon at the service.

Just before the President spoke, the magnificent mezzo-soprano Denyce Graves sang the Lord's Prayer. I didn't see how the President would get through his remarks without breaking down. At the Cabinet meeting preceding the service, he had been emotional. Colin Powell, seated next to him as the secretary of state always is, passed him a note that said, in essence, "Dear Mr. President, don't break down at the service." The President, relating this to the Cabinet, said that he would be okay. He was right. He delivered his remarks sensitively but was completely in control. I thought to myself that I could never have done that.

The service was cathartic. I am the daughter of a Presbyterian minister, and my mother was a church organist. Music has been at the center of my life since I was born. I cannot to this day sing "O God Our Help in Ages Past," without flashing back to National Cathedral. I focused on the music and the extraordinary words of our great national songs. What had begun as a day of sadness ended, for me, with a sense of rising defiance. The last hymn was "The Battle Hymn of the Republic." The original words of the Civil War hymn had been "As he died to make men holy, let us die to make men free." Over the years congregations (hoping not to sound offensive, I guess) had changed the words to "As he died to make men holy, let us *live* to make men free." Much to my surprise, we sang the original version. As the military choir sang the climatic "Amen, Amen," I could feel my own spirit renewed. We'd mourned the dead. Now it was time to defend the country.

THE PRESIDENT left for New York after the service. I had asked if I should accompany him, but he said that he wanted me to go directly to Camp David to meet the Vice President, Colin, and Don. I flew up to Camp David with Don on a military helicopter. That evening the four of us had a dinner of buffalo steak (a favorite of the Vice President's) and discussed how we'd organize the next morning's session with the President. We all knew that the outcome would be a declaration of war against the Taliban and an invasion of Afghanistan. But the discussion was useful in teasing out questions the President would need to address.

For the first time, though, I felt a bit out of place. These men, who collectively had accumulated decades of experience in government, had known one another for years. They'd been through numerous crises separately and together. The enormity of what had happened on 9/11 and the sheer weight of the challenge that we now faced hit me very hard. These were not normal times and not exactly what I'd envisioned doing that March day in Austin, Texas.

The next morning the President called at about 6:30, as he often did when we were at Camp David. He asked how the evening had gone and said that he would listen to the presentations from the various Principals and then decide what to do. We came up with the idea of a morning session for presentations, an afternoon break, and then a wrap-up session for recommendations. He was worried about how people were doing under the circumstances. I assured him that the night before had been relaxed despite everything. I asked how he was doing. He said that he was just fine.

The President's phone call also steadied me. He was relying on me, and I was determined to be there for him. I had to set aside any personal doubts and fears and get on with doing my job.

After the President's daily intelligence briefing in the Laurel Lodge conference room, the NSC members and their deputies gathered. We put a map down in the middle of the huge oak conference table. There it was: Afghanistan, the place where great powers go to die. Not only was Afghanistan surrounded by troubled and hostile neighbors (in some cases, such as Iran, hostile to us), its rugged terrain was immediately obvious. On the other hand, I thought, a successful campaign in Afghanistan could help redraw the map of the region.

South-Central Asia, starting at the southern tip of India and continuing through Pakistan and Afghanistan and into the "stans" (Uzbekistan, Turkmenistan, Kyrgyzstan, Tajikistan, and, most important, Kazakhstan), formed the spine of the region. It in turn opened out to the Middle East and Iran on one side and western China on the other. An American military presence in Afghanistan and surrounding states—necessitated by the events of 9/11—could ultimately contribute to stability in South-Central Asia. And the emergence of a friendly government in Afghanistan and stronger relations with the "stans" would anchor American geostrategic influence in what had once been called by Zbigniew Brzezinski "the arc of crisis." I told Steve Hadley that we should start to think of the area as an arc of opportunity instead.

But getting to that point would take a lot of work over many years. Afghanistan had been ravaged by decades of warfare. When the Soviet Union invaded the country in 1979, Arab fighters joined local resistance forces who had set aside tribal and ethnic differences to form a loose alliance that became broadly known as the mujahideen. With the assistance of U.S. and Saudi funding and weapons funneled through Pakistan, the mujahideen succeeded in defeating the Soviet forces in the late 1980s.

In the absence of a common enemy, however, the rivalries among feuding warlords resurfaced, and their militias plunged the country into civil war. In the midst of this fighting, the Taliban, a group of Islamist militants led by Mullah Muhammad Omar, swept through the Pashtun South and in 1996 seized control of Kabul.

As the Taliban consolidated its control over the capital city, Osama bin Laden arrived in eastern Afghanistan. Having left Sudan and with his Saudi Arabian citizenship revoked, bin Laden returned to the country where he had once fought in the anti-Soviet resistance to build a base of operations for his terrorist network. Sharing some degree of ideological kinship with the terrorist leader, the Taliban condoned and at times supported bin Laden's efforts to establish al Qaeda training camps and recruit extremists to his cause.

For its part, Pakistan had trained extremist militants who fought in the resistance against the Red Army in Afghanistan, and it maintained ties to many of them after the Soviet withdrawal. As the Taliban rose to power, officials within Pakistan's military and security forces, particularly its elite Directorate for Inter-Services Intelligence (ISI), reached out to the group and developed bonds that grew over time. The links were generally ethnic in origin, uniting Pashtuns across the borders that the British had drawn with little regard for cultural or tribal identity. Pakistan largely paid lip service to U.S. demands, dating back to George H. W. Bush, to relinquish ties to the extremists.

The immediate problem we faced after 9/11 was to find a strategy to defeat the Taliban. We were all conscious of the Soviet experience there, and the Pentagon's presentation of military plans noted the importance of a "light footprint" for U.S. troops. That would turn out to be a crucial decision. The United States would not fight a big ground war in Afghanistan, even though we needed "boots on the ground." We would rely largely on Afghan fighters and U.S. Special Forces, intelligence and airpower. The U.S. commitment would contribute to a historical narrative in which we helped the Afghan people gain their freedom from the Taliban, not another foreign invasion of Afghanistan. The discussion was orderly, noting the need to turn Pakistan into an ally in the war on terror and to secure basing rights in Central Asia.

After a series of presentations and some discussion of how to proceed, Don Rumsfeld suddenly turned the floor over to his deputy, Paul Wolfowitz, who started talking about Iraq. His argument was not without merit, focusing on the relative strategic importance of Iraq over Afghanistan. Saddam was clearly an enemy of the United States and had supported terrorism. The war in Afghanistan would be so much more complicated than a "straightforward" engagement against a real army such as Saddam's.

The problem was that everyone had come into the room knowing that our war would be in Afghanistan, which had been the staging ground for the attack on the United States. I remember thinking that Paul's comment was a huge distraction when there was so much to be done. The President listened but did not comment.

As planned, after several hours the President called for a break. He told everyone to go to lunch (spouses had been invited) and then to take a couple of hours off. "Go for a walk, exercise, clear your minds," he said. We would reconvene at 4:00 P.M., and he would ask for recommendations.

After lunch, I asked the President what he wanted from me. Did he want my recommendation in the meeting or privately? "Privately," he said. I also overheard the President tell Andy Card to call Paul aside and tell him not to interject in that way again; he expected to hear from his principal advisors, not their deputies. I don't know what Andy said, but in the afternoon session, Paul said nothing.

After the break, the President asked each member of the War Council for a recommendation. Colin said that we would, of course, have to go to war. He suggested that the Taliban be given an ultimatum because no decent country goes to war without warning the other side. Indeed, there was a lot of discussion of the Japanese attack on Pearl Harbor and a desire to avoid a "sneak attack." We needed to deliver an ultimatum to the Taliban and then issue a declaration of war. Colin took on the task of giving the Pakistanis a choice: would they be with us or against us? There was no middle ground. Colin was fundamentally opposed to action in Iraq. He warned that the time was not right and that it would fracture the very strong coalition against the Taliban.

Don never really made a recommendation. He just asked rhetorical questions that made it clear that he believed in the war option. The chairman of the Joint Chiefs of Staff, Hugh Shelton, reassured the President that the military could develop a plan for boots on the ground but emphasized the importance of regional cooperation. George Tenet, appropriately for the CIA director, did not express an opinion. Andy Card said that the American people would expect us to go to war against Afghanistan, not Iraq.

The President turned to the Vice President, who also affirmed the war option and the need for an ultimatum. Then, gently rebuking Paul, he joined Colin and Andy in dismissing the idea of war against Iraq as a part of the response to 9/11. Despite all that has been written about the Vice President and his claims concerning Iraq and 9/11, he was resolute at Camp David in his belief that Iraq would be a distraction in the aftermath of the attacks.

The President said that he would let everyone know on Monday morning what he'd decided. He needed some time to mull over what he'd heard. The United States had been grievously injured, but he would not just lash out. The response had to be considered, and this time al Qaeda had to be defeated.

That night before dinner, Attorney General John Ashcroft played spirituals on the piano and we all sang. Contrary to type, John plays wonderful gospel piano, while I play Brahms and Mozart. So John provided the accompaniment and I sang "His Eye Is on the Sparrow." The comforting song proclaims that God's eye is on the sparrow and "I know He watches me." It was a deep, mournful moment. At dinner, the President asked me to say the prayer. "We have seen the face of evil but we are not afraid," I prayed. "For you, O Lord, are faithful to us."

The church service at Camp David was, of course, devoted to 9/11.

There were prayers for the victims and for the country. The Camp David chapel is very special, completed during George H. W. Bush's presidency as a place of worship for the President during stays at Camp David. The congregation is made up of the military people and their families stationed there. Thus the President and his family and aides worship side by side with the officers and enlisted personnel and their families. It is a beautiful expression of American democracy and its egalitarian character. That day, the commander in chief worshipped with those whom he would soon order to defend our wounded country in a most distant land.

After church we returned to the White House. The President asked me to accompany him to his office in the residence. He returned a call to Vicente Fox and said he needed to get some exercise. He asked me to come back at about 6:00 P.M. so that we could talk about what to do. At the agreed hour, I arrived and went back up to the office.

The President asked what I thought. I told him that we obviously had to go to war in Afghanistan but expressed my concern about the difficulty of getting Central Asian leaders to give us the basing rights we needed. When I had finished, the President talked for about thirty minutes without a break. The country had been deeply wounded, he repeated from the Saturday session, but we could not engage in a spasm attack. He needed boots on the ground, but he was worried about fighting in Afghanistan. We couldn't fail. This was different from any other war in our history. Using a sports analogy (he was fond of doing so), he said that he just didn't know how many more punches al Qaeda could throw.

As he talked, I felt that he was carrying a weight heavier than any other President, at least since Abraham Lincoln. There had been war presidents since then, but they had not experienced a devastating attack in Washington and New York. It is easy to forget that in those dark days we assumed that another attack was imminent. We had been talking in the Treaty Room, which had for a time been the U.S. Presidents' office before the Oval Office was built in the West Wing. It is dark, with heavy furniture and gloomy paintings, including Lincoln with his generals during the Civil War. I had never seen George W. Bush so somber.

The President asked me to record formally his decisions that night. He said that he'd distribute the paper at the meeting the next morning. I left him sitting alone and went back to my office about 9:00 P.M. to prepare the document. And then I went home feeling very much the weight of what we were about to do.

7

War Planning Begins

O UR DAILY ROUTINE, post 9/11, started the next day. We began each morning with the President's Daily Briefing. The session was now more operational, with both the CIA and the FBI reporting on threats and efforts to disrupt them. This in fact complicated decision making, because the President had a tendency to ask policy questions that were prompted by intelligence information. With neither the secretary of state nor the secretary of defense present, it fell to me to keep the conversation focused on what intelligence professionals are supposed to deliver: a policy-neutral assessment of various situations. I found myself constantly reminding the President that it would be up to his national security team to give him answers to the policy dilemmas raised by what he was hearing.

After the intelligence briefing, the President took several phone calls from other heads of state, largely expressions of solidarity that had been stacking up over the hectic days in the aftermath of 9/11. Among the calls, though, was another call with Putin. The two men had a remarkable conversation in which the Russian pledged assistance, particularly in securing the cooperation of the Central Asian states. The advantages were immediately clear: we needed the kind of help that we expected Russian intelligence to be able to deliver from its vast networks throughout South and Central Asia.

After the call, the National Security Council gathered for the first in-depth consideration of how to prepare for war in Afghanistan. The President distributed the document that I'd prepared the night before, making it clear that our primary consideration was to protect the country from further attack. That meant dealing with the al Qaeda sanctuary in Afghanistan.

Moreover, we quickly established a few principles for our outreach to the people of Afghanistan. We felt an obligation to leave them better off than when we had come. Thus freeing Afghan women emerged early as a policy goal. The women of Afghanistan had been brutally oppressed under the Taliban. They were prohibited from getting an education, working outside the home, and appearing in public without a male escort. In a stadium renovated by the United Nations, the Taliban would gather crowds to witness the execution of women who were accused of committing crimes against the regime's extreme interpretations of Islamic law. The regime's bizarre nature was evident in the sarcastic request of one Taliban leader for the United Nations to build a separate facility for their executions so that their stadium could be used for soccer. First Lady Laura Bush delivered the President's radio address on November 17, placing the fate of women at the center of the Afghanistan agenda.

We then turned to the diplomatic strategy, which, though obvious, was difficult to execute. Pakistan had to be convinced to end its long-standing support for the Taliban. Rich Armitage was dispatched with a message for President Musharraf. The United States would not tolerate shades of gray any longer: Pakistan must be with us or against us. President Musharraf responded forcefully that he would join us.

At that first meeting, the President said that he wanted to show the Afghan people a different face than the Soviet Union had at the beginning of its war. He asked early on whether the first "bombs" could be food drops to deal with the impending famine in much of the country. Andrew Natsios, who headed the U.S. Agency for International Development (USAID), was able to coordinate a huge international relief effort to complement military action.

Meanwhile, we prepared an ultimatum to the Taliban and reviewed the initial plans for the war. The President repeated the view that Colin had expressed at Camp David: decent countries don't launch surprise attacks, as Japan had done at Pearl Harbor.

As we considered our options, it was clear that the CIA was well prepared for operations in Afghanistan. But as we'd become aware well before 9/11, the Agency's contacts were better with the Northern Alliance than with the Pashtuns in the South.

The President rejected any strategy based on a large U.S. ground presence, deciding instead to have the Afghans take the lead in the ground campaign, with U.S. intelligence and special operations forces and U.S. airpower supporting them. This required an unprecedented level of integration of intelligence capability and military power, leading to some uncertainty about who was in charge.

As the planning progressed, there was an uncomfortable moment several days later when the President, frustrated by the lack of clarity in the chain of command, asked pointedly, "Who has the lead?" John McLaughlin, George Tenet's deputy at the CIA, was sitting in for George that day. John pointed at Don, and Don pointed at John. The President turned to me and said, "Fix this!" He ended the meeting somewhat abruptly, and I asked the Principals to stay behind. I didn't have to say much. Don and the CIA got the message. They worked out a flexible arrangement that largely shifted responsibility to the Pentagon after the invasion began.

That was one of several indications that the national security structures, dating as they did from the Cold War, were not a very good fit for the new kind of war that we were facing. To their credit, after that embarrassing moment, George and Don worked through the issues, and though military and intelligence coordination was not always seamless, it grew increasingly more effective. The enhanced cooperation would culminate in the successful operation to track and kill Osama bin Laden in 2011, but it found its origins in this early work among the agencies as we approached the war in Afghanistan.

Early on, collaboration was accomplished largely through personal relationships and daily attention from the highest levels of both organizations and the White House. That is often the way that institutions adapt in the early stages of a new challenge. In fact, the widely admired structures authorized by the National Security Act of 1947, including the NSC and the CIA, were at first ad hoc arrangements, whose predecessors were referred to as the War Council and the Office of Strategic Services. They had been created by Franklin D. Roosevelt to improve wartime planning during World War II.

Despite the new challenges, on balance the machinery of the NSC functioned smoothly. Colin and Don worked well together, with State both willing and capable of carrying out the diplomacy to support the military mission. The most important task was to obtain basing rights in and around Afghanistan from the hardnosed leaders in Central Asia, most especially Islam Karimov of Uzbekistan. After many sessions that apparently resembled a bazaar, the bargaining was done and we had the access we needed—and Karimov had a big financial package to show for his support.

THE RUSSIANS maintain to this day that they gave the "green light" to Karimov and to Tajikistan and Kyrgyzstan to work with us. Undoubtedly, Russia's support for a "temporary" U.S. presence in the region removed any anxiety that the leaders of Central Asia might have had about Moscow's reaction.

Ironically, the same cooperation created the conditions that would later lead to some of our most contentious issues with the Kremlin. As the U.S. presence in the region matured over the years, resulting in larger and more permanent military bases in Uzbekistan and Kyrgyzstan, Moscow became wary. When, in 2003, the "color revolutions" began to sweep through former Soviet satellite states, prompting the removal of corrupt officials and the ascension of pro-Western, democratically elected leaders in Georgia, Ukraine, and Kyrgyzstan, Putin clearly regretted his early posture. He began speaking not of cooperation but of the "encirclement" of Russia by the aggressive United States.

I am convinced that after 9/11 Putin saw the struggle against terrorism as the new epicenter of Russia's relationship with the United States, one in which there would be shared principles, strategy, and tactics. He moved quickly to associate the attacks on the United States with the terrorism of Chechen fighters. Though we did not fully support that view or Russia's brutal tactics in Chechnya, it was true that the Chechens were increasingly in league with al Qaeda. Throughout the years of the Bush administration, counterterrorism cooperation with Russia was indeed good. When a school in Beslan, Russia, was attacked in 2004, President Bush was one of the first leaders to unequivocally call it terrorism and equate it with what we had experienced. The Russians appreciated that clarity.

But Putin's larger vision of a shared mission would run headlong into the United States' emphasis on democracy and the Freedom

Agenda as the ultimate answer to terrorism. Further complicating that shared mission was Russia's turn toward authoritarianism at home. But that clash would come later. The Russians were focused and effective in providing assistance as we prepared for war in Afghanistan. They had long-standing ties with the Northern Alliance and agreed to provide it with equipment.

George Tenet mentioned one day that the fighters of Muhammad Fahim Khan and Abdul Rashid Dostum, the Northern Alliance commanders who would lead the Afghan forces, hadn't received the provisions they needed. "Call Sergei Ivanov," the President told me. I did. Ivanov said that he was doing all that he could to fulfill their requests. "But it's not easy to find donkeys," he said.

"Donkeys?" I repeated.

"Yes. Donkeys. That's how they move on those narrow paths in the mountains," he told me. Later we would all chuckle at the photographs of twenty-first-century U.S. fighter planes providing air cover for our "cavalry"—men on donkeys.

"When Am I Going to Have a Battle Plan?"

THE MILITARY PLANNING was proceeding smoothly but slowly, and the President was getting frustrated. It seemed that every NSC meeting ended inconclusively, with the military not quite ready to present a final plan to the President. The President had told me that he felt no need to rush to war. We needed to be fully prepared. Yet he knew that there would come a time—soon—when the American people and the world would expect a response. Moreover, he did not want to wait too long, allowing al Qaeda to perhaps launch another attack from its sanctuary in Afghanistan.

Finally the President's patience ran out. I'd gone to the CIA for a briefing on the afternoon of September 27. I was called out of the meeting to take a call from the President. He was clearly agitated. "I want a plan tomorrow," he said. "Call Don, and make sure I have one."

"Yes, sir," I answered and decided to depart from the CIA immediately and return to the White House. My car was barely rounding onto

George Washington Parkway from the Langley gate when the phone in the car rang. The President was on the secure line, which never seemed to work, especially in an emergency. I could never figure it out. The United States is one of the most technologically sophisticated countries in the world, but government communications—even national security ones—were often bedeviled by malfunctions. I can't tell you how many times my morning conference call with Don at the Pentagon and Colin at the State Department suddenly dropped; that was still the case for Steve Hadley, Defense Secretary Bob Gates, and me years later. There were multiple efforts to fix the problem, and I suspect a good deal of money was thrown at it—but somehow the government just couldn't get it done.

The problem was never as annoying as on that day, however. The President was saying something about wanting a plan, but the phone kept breaking up. "I'm on my way to the White House, sir," I said. "I'll meet you in the residence."

When I got to my office, he was on the phone again. "You don't need to come over here," he said. "Just call Don."

I called Don immediately and told him about my discussions with the President. "Don, he's had it," I said. "There really needs to be a final plan tomorrow."

"Got it," Don answered.

That evening I met with Frank Miller, who served as senior director for defense policy at the NSC and was a twenty-year Pentagon veteran. "Use your contacts to make sure the military is getting the message," I told him. Then I went home, praying that we'd have a plan at the NSC meeting the next morning.

Don delivered the next morning with a very good presentation of a final plan for the President's approval. I was relieved, though already the tendency of the Pentagon to give military briefings that were lacking in detail was evident. After the meeting I followed the President into the Oval and said that he needed to insist on a review of the plans by the full Principals Committee. "They will ask more detailed and candid questions than you can," I told him. "People don't like to admit that they don't understand something—or to critique their colleagues—with you in the room." The Vice President resisted, saying that the military briefings of the President were enough. He was a former secretary of defense, personally close to Don Rumsfeld and very protective of the Pentagon's prerogatives.

"Mr. President," I said, "you need *political*-military plans, not just military plans, and that requires all of the expertise of the NSC." The President nodded in agreement and did insist on full vetting for issues such as collateral damage. But Don was resistant to a review of the actual battle plan with the NSC Principals, relying instead on briefings with the President that were sometimes short on operational detail. The President had read many histories of Vietnam, and he did not want to be Lyndon Johnson, picking targets from the basement of the White House. He tended to accept the military's representations—not unquestioningly, but with fewer probes than he would make later in his presidency.

Finally, with the planning done, the President went before the American people on October 7, 2001, to announce what had long been expected: the United States of America was declaring war on the Taliban because it had refused to meet our demands to surrender al Qaeda's leaders and close terrorist training camps. But the first phase of Operation Enduring Freedom, as the campaign was called, brought new frustrations. U.S. fighter planes bombed the few installations that could be hit from the air. Yet because Afghanistan was so rural and underdeveloped, the military quickly ran out of targets. It was time to begin the ground assault, but our "cavalry" wasn't moving. For days after October 7, every NSC meeting went as follows: "When is Fahim Khan going to move?" "They say they need more equipment and better intelligence," Tenet would answer. "Why don't they have the intelligence they need?" someone would ask. "The intelligence will come as they begin to move forward and engage the Taliban forces," Tenet would reply. Impatient, the President would complain, "They just need to *move!*" The absence of action on the ground led to days of news coverage trumpeting the "quagmire" into which U.S. forces had fallen.

Finally, in late October, General Dostum got tired of waiting for Fahim Khan and started an assault on Mazar-i-Sharif. The President had departed for Shanghai and the Asia-Pacific Economic Cooperation (APEC) meeting, which had been postponed after the September 11 attacks. Within days Taliban forces were being routed throughout Afghanistan. We were meeting with Vladimir Putin on the day that Kabul was about to fall. Together with the Russians, we discussed whether the alliance forces should take Kabul or invest (surround) the city and demand that the Taliban surrender. Because we worried that the Taliban might resist by laying waste to Kabul, there was a mild preference for the former. The Pakistanis had also registered their concern that the sudden appearance of the Tajik- and Uzbek-led Northern Alliance in the capital might upset the ethnic balance of the city.

Before that decision could be communicated, however, the Northern Alliance broke through the Taliban lines and took the capital. As the President told Putin, once the assault began, the Taliban unraveled "like a cheap suit." I wasn't quite sure of the Russian translation, but Putin clearly understood and roared his approval.

8

The War on Terror and the Home Front

W E DID NOT HAVE the luxury of concentrating exclusively on Afghanistan. In his address to the nation on the night of September 11, President Bush had made clear that the United States would be engaged in a "war against terrorism." The scope of the struggle, however, had yet to be determined. Was it a broad war against any terrorist group, no matter what its origin or justification, or was the enemy limited to al Qaeda and its affiliates? What were the implications of a narrow view? What about one that was broader?

In the end we held to a more expansive view, focusing on terrorists with global reach who threatened our way of life and that of our friends and allies. The President decided after much deliberation that only a broader global definition would enlist the international community in establishing the worldwide dragnet that we needed to stabilize the international system and secure the United States and its allies. How could we tell others to help us but not help them fend off terrorist attacks? The decision reflected the need both to establish an international norm against terrorism in order to delegitimize it as a tactic and to paint vividly an enemy against which the world could mobilize. That is, I believe, why some have failed to understand why we used the term "war on terror" rather than "war on al Qaeda." The war had to be fought against both the tactic and the people who practiced it.

In some cases, that led us to become involved in distant struggles that were in fact linked only loosely to al Qaeda. This was the case with Jemaah Islamiyah in Indonesia and the Abu Sayyaf group in the Philippines. Though organizationally distinct from Osama bin Laden's terrorist network, they sometimes collaborated with al Qaeda to launch attacks, such as the 2002 bombing of a Bali nightclub that killed more than two hundred people.

That also meant confronting Chechen terrorists, even though we were uncomfortable with Moscow's heavy-handed treatment of the conflict in the Caucasus. Occasionally we accepted a responsibility to respond to groups with no observable tie to al Qaeda and no global reach, such as the Basque separatist group ETA in Aznar's Spain, our close ally.

While defining the target broadly, we judged the tactics that we employed on a case-by-case basis. We would not rely exclusively or even primarily on military might but leverage all instruments of U.S. power—diplomatic, economic, intelligence—to defeat the terrorists. For instance, certain lethal options were reserved for groups and individuals directly and inextricably linked to al Qaeda. But when it came to rhetorical support and, in some cases, tools such as freezing terrorists' assets, we were liberal in the definition of who was in and who was out. We believed that we had to discredit terrorism as a weapon, with no exceptions. There would be no carve-out for "freedom fighters." No cause could justify the use of terror.

NEW TERRORIST PLOTLINES were surfacing almost daily as the intelligence agencies struggled to determine what was real and what was not. On October 15, an anthrax-laced letter was opened at the office of Senator Tom Daschle in the Hart Senate Office Building, shortly after a similar package was received at NBC News. The discoveries bolstered suspicions that a Florida man, who had died days earlier after mysteriously contracting anthrax, had been a victim of terrorism. The United States was again under attack. In all, five letters laced with anthrax entered the postal system that fall, each containing a cryptic handwritten note that made reference to 9/11. Five people would die in those attacks, making them the worst incidents of bioterrorism in U.S. history. The FBI would later determine that the anthrax attacks had been the work of a domestic, not foreign, actor. But one month after September 11, that seemed like a remote possibility. We were all convinced that it was al Qaeda's second wave.

We later learned of another plotline suggesting that the United States was facing the threat of a smallpox attack. Ironically, because the disease had been eradicated, the country was vulnerable, since there was no longer a program of general vaccination. I called together the NSC Principals and the newly created Homeland Security Council, led by former Pennsylvania Governor Tom Ridge, to review the situation.

The President was told that the inoculation of the whole country would be a herculean task and there was some nonnegligible risk of death to those who might be allergic to the vaccine. The thought of a significant number of fatalities due to an inoculation program—which might ultimately prove unnecessary, given the tenuous nature of the threat—haunted the President. Someone mentioned the potential for class-action lawsuits if the program went badly. The President let it be known that that was the least of his concerns.

The questions on the table were ones that we would face many times throughout the Bush presidency: How could we tell the American people of a possible threat without engendering panic? Was the information even solid enough to constitute a legitimate threat? What were the risks of acting? What were the consequences of inaction? I thought to myself that he was being confronted with unprecedented dilemmas.

Eventually we decided on an intermediate course. First responders and the military would be vaccinated, starting with those who were in the field. A division of the Centers for Disease Control and Prevention (CDC), under the exceptional leadership of Julie Gerberding, was tasked with developing a plan for widespread inoculation of the population should the intelligence warnings intensify. The Vice President was charged with overseeing the effort.

The question then arose of whether to vaccinate the President and his closest advisors. The decision was made to do so, and a list was developed of those who would be inoculated. We were each informed individually of whether we'd be vaccinated but not told who else was on the list.

When Dr. Richard Tubb, the White House doctor, asked whether I had ever been vaccinated and my reaction to it, I remembered vaguely having rolled up my sleeve in elementary school but didn't recall if it had been for smallpox in particular. My parents were deceased, so there was no one to ask. I took the vaccination with some trepidation but assumed that it would have no adverse effect. In that case, my sense of personal vulnerability was only fleeting. But occasionally we confronted it more directly.

IN OCTOBER 2001, I was with the President in Shanghai for the APEC summit. Each day we'd have a secure videoconference, with the Vice President and Steve Hadley in Washington and the President, Colin, Andy, and me in China. On that particular morning, the screen opened to the Vice President, dressed fully in white-tie attire for his coming speech that night at the Alfred E. Smith Memorial Foundation dinner in New York (it was twelve hours earlier on the East Coast). His face was tense and ashen.

"Good morning, Dick," the President said. Then, noticing the Vice President's demeanor, he asked if everything was all right.

"Mr. President," the Vice President intoned, "the White House biological detectors have registered the presence of botulinum toxin, and there is no reliable antidote. Those of us who have been exposed to it could die."

"What was that, Dick?" the President asked, sinking back into his chair.

Colin intervened. "What is the exposure time?" he asked, clearly calculating from his last time in the White House. After learning that he too had been exposed, Colin also sank back into his chair.

We hastily finished an abbreviated review of the situation in Afghanistan and a few other matters and closed the conference. "Go call Hadley and find out what the hell is going on," the President said to me.

I called Steve. Indeed, the White House detectors had registered the presence of the deadly nerve agent. The substance was being tested on laboratory mice, but it would take about twenty-four hours to get an answer. "Let's put it this way," Steve said. "If the mice are feet down tomorrow, we are fine. If they're feet up, we're toast." He would monitor the situation along with Attorney General John Ashcroft and Health and Human Services Secretary Tommy Thompson and call us as soon as they knew anything.

We went about our business in Shanghai as if nothing had happened.

I told myself that it was probably a false alarm, though darker thoughts would flash through my mind as I sat through the endless meetings and events. At one point I remember wondering whether we'd get home before the toxin acted. I didn't particularly want to die in China.

Finally, the next day at lunch, an aide handed me a note saying that Hadley was on the phone. I passed the President's table. "It's Steve," I said. "This is it." The President said nothing in reply.

"Hi," I said to Steve.

"The mice are feet down," he said. It had been a false alarm.

I went back to the table. "Feet down, not up," I said. The President smiled. I'm sure the Chinese thought it was some kind of coded message.

I've been asked many times if I worried about my personal safety in the aftermath of 9/11. Occasionally, a scare like that one would remind me of my own vulnerability. But for the most part, such thoughts were buried deep behind the need to just get the work done.

The more vexing problem was the moral dilemma posed by often knowing information that was both frightening and incomplete. The question of what to say to the American people so that they could protect themselves was a constant concern.

That dilemma came into full relief later that month, when reports pointed toward another potential attack on Washington, D.C. Some of the information even suggested that it might be a radiological or nuclear attack. We knew that al Qaeda had been trying to acquire a nuclear capability, even experimenting with homemade devices. The threat was very real.

At the beginning of the week, we convened the National Security and Homeland Security Council principals and took several steps to address the scare, including the moving of radiological detection equipment and teams from the West Coast to the East. After the meeting, I walked down to the Oval Office to brief the President and to tell him that he would get a more complete report at the NSC meeting the next day.

He was in a pensive mood. "I've invited some of my friends here to Washington for the weekend," he said. "Should I tell them not to come?" he asked, mostly rhetorically. I suddenly remembered that I'd invited my friend in California, Susan Ford, and her son Tommy to Washington as well.

I'd worked day after day without a break and under unspeakable pressure. Only a well-timed invitation three weeks after September 11 from Karen and Jerry Hughes and their son, Robert, had broken the string of seventeen-hour days. "You look like you need a home-cooked meal," Karen had said. Now, a few weeks later, I was looking forward to the release that having a friend in town would bring. I suspected that the President felt the same way.

The President continued, "How can I warn my friends not to come and not tell the American people of the danger?" I suggested that his situation was different since the White House was likely a target of attack. The President was having none of it. He felt an obligation to say something. But what should we tell the population? Would they assume we were recommending an evacuation of the nation's capital? Were we ready for such a thing?

I suggested that he should tell his friends not to come, not for their safety but because he should go to an undisclosed location. He reacted strongly. "Those bastards will find me right here in the Oval," he said.

I was taken aback but reflexively said, "Me too."

I always knew when to leave the President alone. I walked back to my office and called in Steve Hadley to tell him what had transpired. "Are you afraid?" I asked.

"Not for myself," he said. "But I can't bear the thought that something might happen to my daughters."

I decided that whatever the moral dilemma, I had to ask Susan not to come. And in any case it would be a tense and very busy weekend. "It's just not a good time," I said to her. Susan later told me that she hadn't known what was going on, but the tone of my voice had told her that it was indeed serious. We could get together some other time.

THAT WAS how we lived and worked in the months immediately after September 11. It has become fashionable years after the attacks to say that the Bush administration overreacted to 9/11 and took controversial and radical steps in the war on terrorism that were unwarranted. Early in his administration, President Barack Obama would say that in the days after the attacks on New York and Washington, the Bush administration "made decisions based on fear."

Well, yes, we did, but not from irrational fear or paranoia. Rather, the days after September 11 were marked by the uncertainty and unease that come from operating in dangerous and unchartered territory. We knew far too little about al Qaeda and how it operated. We knew even less about what it was planning next. We were without a map but not without a compass. Our guiding principle would be to do everything within our power—and within our laws—to prevent another attack.

A Framework for the War on Terror

THREE PRESSING ISSUES arose in the post-9/11 period that challenged traditional notions of security: the classification and treatment of detainees; how to try terrorism suspects; and how to gain access to information that they might hold through interrogation and electronic surveillance. We were at war against the people who'd launched the deadliest foreign attack on the U.S. homeland in the nation's history. I do not remember a single person questioning whether al Qaeda had committed an act of war; it simply never occurred to us that it had been anything else. From the beginning, therefore, there was no dissent from the view that we were operating on a war footing and acting under the President's authority as commander in chief. But that is where the consensus ended. What did it mean?

That was the question that was put to the lawyers who were charged with legal interpretations of historic significance. John Bellinger, who was the NSC lawyer, is as capable a person as one can find. John had worked for the CIA and the Justice Department and was loyal and thorough. But in terms of bureaucratic warfare, he was no match for David Addington, the Vice President's legal counsel. Addington, with the full support of the Vice President, had a view—an expansive view—of presidential prerogatives during wartime and, drawing on opinions by lawyers such as Jay Bybee and John Yoo in the Justice

Department's Office of Legal Counsel, was determined to push the boundaries of executive authority. The NSC staff (and sometimes the White House counsel) was at times cut out of the process. That meant that the State Department, the military, and even the attorney general were outflanked on occasion. I didn't fully realize this until, as we will see, the President signed a military order that I had not even seen. From then on, I was more attuned to the bureaucratic process for evaluating these issues. We were not dealing with purely legal matters; there were important policy implications for such decisions, both at home and abroad.

The first question we confronted was what to do with those whom the military had detained on the battlefield. We knew we couldn't release them because they could still pose a threat to our forces and our citizens. We decided that they should be detained under the laws of war. For those who had committed crimes, we felt that in many cases we could not try them in ordinary civil courts since traditional evidentiary standards might reveal our intelligence-gathering methods to our enemies. We wanted a system of justice that would protect our sources and methods, punish those who posed a threat to the United States, and responsibly release those who, after careful investigation, we concluded did not.

As the President's chief legal advisor on policy questions, White House Counsel Alberto Gonzales convened an interagency group to investigate the matter. Led by Pierre-Richard Prosper, the ambassador-at-large for war crimes issues at the State Department, lawyers from the NSC, Defense, Justice, and State began exploring options for trying the detainees.

Some in the administration, however, felt the group was not working fast enough. It's always a challenge to respond immediately to a crisis and simultaneously lay the foundations for new institutions and frameworks that adapt to that new reality. Hundreds of suspects were being captured on the battlefield in Afghanistan, and we urgently needed a legal framework in place to try them. But that need for urgency does not, in my mind, excuse what happened next.

On the evening of November 13, 2001, I learned that the President had signed a military order earlier that day that I had not even been given. The order directed the Defense Department to establish military commissions to try detainees and issue guidance on procedures that would govern them. I did not object to the substantive arguments behind military commissions; they had World War II–era precedents, and they seemed to resolve some of my own concerns about the protection of our intelligence-gathering methods.

What I couldn't accept was the circumvention of the President's top national security officials. The interagency process exists to ensure that all perspectives are represented so that the President gets a comprehensive look at the potential impact of his decisions. Colin apparently first heard about the order through CNN. The attorney general, the nation's chief law enforcement officer, was reportedly concerned that the Justice Department would be given no formal role in the process of setting up the tribunals and had the chance to raise his objections to the draft only days before the President signed it. Perhaps a more thorough review would have brought to the surface some of the procedural challenges that led the Supreme Court to halt the commissions in 2006. We will never know for sure, but that is why vetting of controversial ideas is important.

When I learned what had happened, I went to see the President. "If this happens again," I said, "either Al Gonzales or I will have to resign." The President apologized, but it was not his fault. Al Gonzales and I were friends, and I respected him. But in that case I told the President that the White House counsel and the Vice President's office had not served him well.

Then there was the question of where to hold the overwhelming number of people who were being captured on the battlefield. There was no secure location in which to detain them, and no one wanted to risk their escape in the still-volatile environment of Afghanistan—or in the U.S. homeland. The Vice President was, as I remember it, the one who suggested that we find an "offshore" facility. That would become the detention center in Guantánamo Bay, Cuba, which had the advantage of being administered by the United States but not on U.S. territory. The overwhelming consideration was to make sure that those dangerous people were not in the U.S. homeland only months after 9/11. There was no disagreement at the Principals level with the decision to establish Guantánamo, although there was some sparring about who would pay. The Defense Department eventually got the bill.

The military commissions debate raised a larger question of how the detainees were to be treated and what protections they were entitled to under international law. At the center of the debate was the applicability of the 1949 Geneva Conventions, a series of four treaties that address the treatment of armed forces and civilians in combat. The Third Geneva Convention sets basic standards for the treatment of prisoners of war, and Common Article 3, a provision common to all four treaties, states that individuals not otherwise covered by the conventions should at minimum be treated humanely and protected against "outrages upon personal dignity."

In a process coordinated by the White House Counsel's Office, the Justice Department was asked to evaluate whether the Geneva provisions would apply to our conflict with al Qaeda and the Taliban. In January 2002 the Justice Department's Office of Legal Counsel presented its conclusions. It argued that al Qaeda detainees were not entitled to prisoner-of-war status under Geneva because, as a nonstate, violent political movement, al Qaeda could not be party to a treaty between nations. There seemed to be general consensus among the NSC Principals on that point: al Qaeda operatives were not lawful combatants in the traditional sense of the term. They did not represent a state that was party to the convention; they did not wear uniforms; and they attacked civilians with impunity.

Disagreements became more marked on whether any Geneva provisions would apply to other detainees, particularly the Taliban. The Justice Department had concluded that Taliban prisoners were not entitled to prisoner-of-war status; that the President had the authority to suspend Geneva in its conflict with Afghanistan; and that Common Article 3 of the conventions would not apply to the detainees. The President had accepted the Justice Department's conclusions and was preparing to issue an order to that effect when Colin Powell, who had been traveling in Asia, raised some concerns. He was particularly worried about the policy consequences of determining that the Geneva Conventions would not apply to a conflict with a signatory such as Afghanistan. I made sure that the President knew that there was an objection, and Colin presented his case at a National Security Council meeting with the President in the chair.

The resulting presidential memorandum on the treatment of detainees attempted to bridge the differences between his principals. The President decided that the Geneva Conventions provisions would apply to the conflict in Afghanistan but accepted the Justice Department's legal conclusions that neither al Qaeda nor Taliban detainees could qualify for prisoner-of-war status or the protections under Common Article 3. He nevertheless stated that "As a matter of policy, the United States Armed Forces shall continue to treat detainees humanely and, to the extent appropriate and consistent with military necessity, in a manner consistent with the principles of Geneva." The Supreme Court subsequently reversed the administration's legal judgment on Common Article 3 in 2006.

BY THE END of the year, I felt that we were getting our bearings. The war in Afghanistan was going well, and we were working with the international community to create a functioning Afghan government. Under the auspices of the United Nations, members of Afghanistan's ethnic and political groups met in Bonn, Germany, to develop a plan for national reconciliation and the establishment of a fully representative national government. Over the course of the eight-day negotiations, delegates to the conference agreed to form an interim administration that would oversee the governance of Afghanistan until a *loya jirga,* a representative assembly of Afghan tribal leaders and ordinary citizens, could be convened to form a transitional government and draft an Afghan constitution.

To lead the interim administration, the delegates at Bonn selected Hamid Karzai, a Pashtun leader from Kandahar. He had led an internal resistance force against the Taliban in its southern stronghold during Operation Enduring Freedom, so we believed that the Afghans had selected a credible partner with whom the United States could work. My initial impression was largely affirmed by our first meeting in January 2002, when he attended the State of the Union address. Six months later, Karzai would be elected president of the country by a *loya jirga* that established Afghanistan's transitional government.

The Agreement on Provisional Arrangements in Afghanistan Pending the Re-Establishment of Permanent Government Institutions, also known as the Bonn Agreement, created an International Security Assistance Force (ISAF) to secure the environment in and around Kabul and to assist Afghans in establishing and training the country's national armed forces. The UN Security Council endorsed the Bonn Agreement and authorized the formation of ISAF on December 20, 2001. Two days later power was officially transferred to Afghanistan's interim administration, setting the country onto a path—not without its difficulties—toward representative governance.

With the political transition unfolding, we also devoted a great deal of attention to stabilization and reconstruction efforts in Afghanistan, working to enlist the support of the international community and making sure we got it right on the ground. At a donor conference in Tokyo in January 2002, more than sixty countries came together to pledge $1.8 billion to that year's reconstruction effort. Of the total, the United States contributed almost $300 million. Those funds went to a variety of vital short- and long-term needs in Afghanistan, including emergency humanitarian relief, road construction, women's programs, health, and education. Reconstruction efforts were important to achieving our ultimate goal, which was to empower Afghans and assist them in acquiring the capability to help themselves. But the truth is, it was more often *construction* than reconstruction in Afghanistan. And we were building on the weak foundations of an economy dominated by corruption and the narcotics trade.

After 9/11 it was very clear that weak and failing states were a grave security threat to the United States. They could not control their borders and risked becoming safe havens for terrorists. But rebuilding them was a monumental task, one for which the U.S. had inadequate institutions to integrate the military and civilian capabilities as such missions required. Finally, by late 2002, we developed a new model to help bring together the different pieces of the puzzle. Provincial Reconstruction Teams (PRTs) were designed to couple the military's protective forces with civil affairs officers and civilian personnel who were experts in development and reconstruction. Together with our coalition partners, we set up a number of PRTs in the following months and deployed them to the far reaches of the country. Although the PRTs varied in their composition and activities, they all shared the same goal: to extend the authority of the central Afghan government and help provide security and development to the Afghan people. It was a step in the right direction, but we had a long road ahead.

THUS THE national security structures were slowly evolving to reflect the new demands of the daily war on terror. As an academic, my work centered on institutions, particularly military institutions: their birth and how they adapted (or failed to adapt) to changing circumstances. I'd written in line with a school of thought in political science called "the new institutionalism," which held that institutions are created with jurisdiction over a set of issues and acquire expertise and competence to exercise that jurisdiction. But they also have traditions and norms—long-standing expectations of the way something ought to be done—that constrain their ability to adapt rapidly to change. When a new challenge arises, the immediate response is to try to handle it within existing structures; but sometimes what is needed is an entirely different set of arrangements.

My own work had focused on how militaries reacted to the mechanization of warfare after World War I and to the emergence of strategic (deep-strike) airpower and nuclear weapons during and after World War II. In some cases, new institutions, such as the air force and the Strategic Air Command (for nuclear weapons)—or, in the Soviet Union, the Strategic Rocket Forces Command—were born, but not without a fight from existing institutions and continuing overlap in functions. In some cases, for instance after World War I, institutional interests had forced bad decisions such as the integration of tanks into the cavalry in most countries. Germany (the defeated country) was the first to completely leverage the power of mechanization by creating separate, fully mechanized brigades.

I found myself, even in the midst of the daily turmoil after 9/11, reflecting on this problem as I watched the existing structures strain to cope with new challenges. The most serious institutional gap stemmed from the perceived absence of a homeland threat for almost two hundred years, suggesting that national security meant external security. The United States had military commands with responsibility for every part of the world but *not* for the United States. (Northern Command was created in October 2002 to fill that void.) Our Interior Department dealt with environmental preserves, parks, and Indian affairs. In most countries, though, it dealt with internal security, with a writ broader than the FBI's law enforcement role. I'd actually considered creating a deputy for homeland affairs at the NSC when we first came into office. John Hamre, the president of the respected Center for Strategic and International Studies (CSIS), had briefed me on a commission report that made the suggestion. We decided instead to place homeland issues in the Directorate for Proliferation Strategy, Counterproliferation and Homeland Defense and kept the counterterrorism function separate under Dick Clarke. In retrospect, that was a mistake, though I doubt that it would have made a difference in the eight months before 9/11.

It was in that context that I welcomed the creation of dedicated homeland security institutions. The Vice President, Andy Card, and I conferred with the President the day before his address to the nation on September 20, 2001. He had decided to create a position for homeland affairs analogous to that of the national security advisor and asked Tom Ridge, the governor of Pennsylvania, to take the job.

The President sought to reassure me that it would mean no diminution in my role as the principal advisor on security affairs. He needn't have worried; I had only to think back to that chaotic meeting on September 12, when agencies from transportation to energy to border protection to the U.S. Coast Guard had suddenly been necessary to secure the country. And what of the governors and leaders of municipalities who wanted to know what 9/11 meant for them and how responsibility would be apportioned between Washington and the states? The need for a new set of structures was crystal clear. I pointed out that we had to avoid the emergence of new seams between homeland and foreign policy. I was fortunate that the President chose Tom Ridge, who was a wonderful and dedicated partner. For the most part the Homeland Security Council and the National Security Council met in joint session on matters of terrorism.

The Office of Homeland Security was thus established on October 8, and the next day we appointed a new counterterrorism advisor, who would report jointly to Tom and to me. General Wayne Downing assumed that role, and Dick Clarke was moved to a position as special advisor to the President for cyberspace security. We established a Critical Infrastructure Protection Board as well, and Dick guided this important new effort to bridge the gaps between government and the private sector on this issue. It was a very good change.

NOT ALL of the institutional adjustments required new structures. When I became national security advisor, I was cognizant of the important role of international finance in foreign policy, one that was becoming increasingly important in the globalized economy. On February 13, 2001, President Bush issued his first National Security Presidential Directive (NSPD) and secured a regular seat for the treasury secretary at the meetings of the National Security Council. I was certainly glad that economic issues were represented at the NSC when the global financial crisis hit in September 2008, but I was even more grateful that we'd made the institutional adjustment before 9/11, because financial sanctions would become one of our most important tools.

In fact, the first strike in the war on terror was not military-led. On September 23, 2001, President Bush signed Executive Order 13224 to freeze terrorist assets and disrupt the flow of funds to terrorist organizations. Empowered by the executive order, John Taylor, the under secretary of the treasury for international affairs and a distinguished Stanford economist and friend, coordinated a unified counterterrorism policy among the G7, setting a standard for other countries to follow. The results were remarkable, and the level of international cooperation was unprecedented: 120 countries passed new laws on terrorist financing, and approximately 1,400 terrorist accounts with assets close to $137 million were frozen. The combined effort of the Treasury and our intelligence agencies to freeze and trace terrorist financing proved a powerful weapon in the war on terror.

Though it was important to cut off the terrorists' money, the process of following the finance trail through shady *hawala* (remittance systems) and "charity" front networks often yielded information that was invaluable for capturing the perpetrators. The PATRIOT Act added additional instruments to our economic arsenal. Among its provisions was Section 311, which enhanced the Treasury Department's ability to prevent, detect, and prosecute international money laundering and the financing of terrorism. Entities designated as being "of primary money laundering concern" under this provision faced economic sanctions and isolation from the U.S. financial system.

Those financial tools were useful but by no means sufficient. The fact that every day began with a review of a terrorist threat report that was pages long reinforced for us the precariousness of our situation. We all had the overwhelming sense that we were still one step behind the terrorists and in danger of another successful attack. There had indeed been close calls. On December 22 an airplane passenger, Richard Reid, had hidden explosives in his shoes that had fortunately failed to detonate aboard a commercial flight from Paris to Miami.

The PATRIOT Act had expanded the tools that the FBI and other agencies could use to fight terrorism. It helped eliminate the wall between law enforcement and intelligence officials by easing restrictions on information sharing that had prevented effective counterterrorism cooperation prior to 9/11. But the President sought to do more, and he asked his top security officials to give him more aggressive options.

The appeal sometimes resulted in good ideas with significant downsides. Attorney General John Ashcroft brought forward the possibility of greater involvement of local law enforcement officers in reporting suspicious activities and people. In general, this was fine, but when taken to the extreme it could result in overzealousness by local officials, who lacked proper training in the identification of actual terrorists—including what one might look like. As John described some of the ideas one day in the Situation Room, I felt the need to slow the momentum toward acceptance. "Mr. President," I said, "you and I come from parts of the country where you might want to be careful in empowering local sheriffs in this way." Enough said. The President noted that he didn't need every sheriff trying to win the Medal of Freedom in the hunt for terrorists. I felt badly because I thought that I might have embarrassed John. I called him that afternoon, and he jokingly said that he should have thought about how it sounded. "There are some places where I come from where you'd want to be careful too," he noted.

More consequentially, Michael Hayden, who was then the director of the National Security Agency (NSA), approached the President with a far-reaching but important proposal. The President had often wondered aloud whether intercepting terrorists' communications before 9/11 would have prevented the attacks. Although the NSA had traditionally conducted surveillance on foreign entities, Hayden sought the President's authorization to intercept the international communications of people affiliated with or supporting al Qaeda. The proposed Terrorist Surveillance Program, as it came to be known, would allow the NSA to conduct electronic surveillance of al Qaeda suspects even if one party to the conversation were in the United States. Despite the popular—and mistaken—perception, it was not designed to monitor communications between two parties who resided in the United States. A several-layer review process within the NSA was used to determine a suspect's affiliation with al Qaeda and suitability as a target for the program.

The NSA hoped to conduct such activities outside of the traditional court requirements for electronic surveillance. The 1978 Foreign Intelligence Surveillance Act (FISA) required the NSA to obtain a warrant from a special court that had been established to review such requests for surveillance of individuals within the United States. The relative speed of cell phones, e-mail, and other new communications technologies, however, had made it more difficult for the NSA to collect timely intelligence under this framework. As Attorney General Al Gonzales would later explain in discussing the program, "FISA is very important in the war on terror, but it doesn't provide the speed and agility that we need in all circumstances to deal with this new kind of threat."

I listened to the President discuss what he had in mind, meeting with Hayden that day. He wanted to ensure that the NSA had enough authority to collect actionable intelligence in a timely manner. He told Mike that he would authorize the program after a review of its legality by the Department of Justice and the Office of Legal Counsel. I made a mental note to follow closely the advice he was getting. This was going to be very controversial.

The Justice Department concluded that it fell within his authority as commander in chief to authorize the surveillance program, as other presidents had done in past times of war. President Bush also wanted to ensure that adequate safeguards were in place to protect the civil liberties of innocent Americans. If, despite its best efforts, the NSA inadvertently intercepted any purely domestic communication, the incident would be reported to the Justice Department for resolution. The President was also committed to making use of the program only as long as it proved necessary. He required that it be subject to his reauthorization approximately every forty-five days and that such reauthorizations would require a comprehensive review of current threat assessments by the intelligence agencies as well as a summary of intelligence gathered through the Terrorist Surveillance Program and other programs during the previous authorization period.

As national security advisor, I had been one of the few officials read into, or briefed on, this highly classified program. Given its sensitive nature, even some of the administration's top security officials had been left out of the loop. So I was a bit taken aback when Frances Townsend, then the President's chief counterterrorism advisor, approached me in March 2004 about a code word to a program that she didn't recognize. Fran had run into James Comey, the deputy attorney general, in the West Wing, and he had asked to speak with her privately. Guiding her into the hallway between the Roosevelt Room and the Cabinet Room, Comey turned to Townsend.

"I'm going to start talking to you about something," Comey said. "If you don't recognize anything I am saying, tell me to stop." Without going into specific details, he stated the code name for the Terrorist Surveillance Program.

"Stop," Fran said. She told him that I might know what he was referring to and that she would speak to me about their encounter. I had known Comey as an attorney who had earned a distinguished record as a New York prosecutor. If he was reaching out to someone who might not have been read into the program, it was clear to me that something must be wrong.

I spoke with the President on the morning of March 12 and recommended that he meet with Comey, though I didn't know the details of what concerned him. "He's a respectable guy," I said. "You need to hear him out."

After a counterterrorism briefing that morning, the President asked Comey to stay behind so that they could talk one-on-one. I would later learn that the President had signed a routine reauthorization of the Terrorist Surveillance Program despite an objection raised by the Justice Department to one aspect of the program. White House lawyers had apparently known about the objection for weeks, but the President had not been informed about it until the morning that the Terrorist Surveillance Program was set to expire. He had thus been placed in a difficult position: kill a program that had been important to our national security or override the objection of his Justice Department to keep the program alive.

The President opted for the latter course, but he didn't fully realize until the day he met with Comey just how serious the situation was: Comey and a number of other Justice Department officials, including FBI Director Robert Mueller, were planning to resign. It would have been a repeat of the "Saturday Night Massacre," when senior Justice Department officials, including the attorney general, resigned after President Richard Nixon fired special Watergate prosecutor Archibald Cox in October 1973.

The President would modify the program to address the Justice Department's objections, and Jim and the other officials withdrew their resignation threats. I'm awfully glad I helped arrange that meeting.

STILL, ALL OF these structural changes and new programs were no substitute for the information that could be gleaned from key al Qaeda figures themselves. Soon we got the break that we'd long hoped for. Abu Zubaydah, an al Qaeda affiliate who had reportedly helped facilitate the foiled millennium plot, was found in Faisalabad, Pakistan, on March 28, 2002. U.S. and Pakistani authorities had launched a predawn raid on his fortified safe house, a compound operated by the Pakistani terror group Lashkar-e-Taiba. A firefight broke out, and Zubaydah was shot three times in the ensuing chaos. He survived, thanks largely to the treatment he received from a top American doctor flown in by the CIA. Zubaydah's death would have cost the United States an invaluable source of information on al Qaeda's operations. One of bin Laden's most trusted lieutenants, Zubaydah had been the group's chief recruitment officer, responsible for managing the flow of militants into training camps in Afghanistan and giving them orders on their way out. In this capacity he had acquired unrivaled knowledge about al Qaeda's ranks, both inside Afghanistan and abroad. Zubaydah had literally written the al Qaeda manual on resisting interrogation techniques, and he proved a challenge to interrogators.

The intelligence agencies and those who were interrogating him were certain that he knew far more than he let on, perhaps even crucial information about impending plots. It was under those circumstances that the Central Intelligence Agency sought authorization to use particular procedures they referred to as "enhanced interrogation techniques." The President asked two questions: Would the proposed interrogation program be legal? Is it necessary?

The Vice President, the attorney general, Steve Hadley, and I were told to meet with Director of Central Intelligence George Tenet that afternoon. George said that he would argue to the President that the program was necessary, explaining why the CIA thought Zubaydah was the key to understanding impending plots. He described in general terms what techniques he'd recommend, including waterboarding, and the safeguards that would be employed, including the presence of medical personnel, to ensure that the interrogations were conducted safely. The DCI emphasized that the techniques were safe and effective and had been used in the military training of thousands of U.S. soldiers. The attorney general said that he'd ask the Justice Department to determine whether the program would be legal under applicable domestic and international law. I asked that Colin and Don be briefed. The President had asked a direct question, and the answers from the CIA (regarding necessity) and the Justice Department (regarding legality) would be forthcoming.

The CIA was soon pressing for an answer. The Agency was absolutely convinced that Zubaydah knew something crucial and that time was running out. I went to see the President, who asked if we'd heard from Justice. I said that the attorney general was still considering the case. In fact, I had asked the attorney general to review the case personally. The President needed that confirmation from the nation's top legal officer, not just the lawyers in the Office of Legal Counsel.

The President decided to tell George to make preparations for the interrogations but to hold off on them until the Justice Department had made its determination regarding their legality. I informed George of the President's decision. The CIA was to begin the program only after the Justice Department concluded that the proposed program was legal, which it did by early August.

Abu Zubaydah turned out to be an important source in his own right. But it was the fact that he provided information that helped lead to the capture of Khalid Sheikh Mohammed that turned out to be of great consequence. KSM, as he came to be called, was captured in an apartment building in Pakistan a year later, on March 1, 2003. We'd been closing in on him since early 2003, aided by intelligence gathered by electronic means and the interrogation of other high-ranking operatives. But the case broke open at the end of February, when the CIA cultivated an informant who clued us in to KSM's whereabouts. Hours later, acting on the tip from the CIA, Pakistani forces raided KSM's apartment in Rawalpindi, rousing him from sleep in the predawn hours and taking him into custody.

I was at Camp David that weekend in March with the President. The phone rang in the middle of the night. It was George Tenet. "We got Khalid Sheikh Mohammed," he said. George described the circumstances under which he'd been captured and promised an update the next morning.

I decided not to wake the President since there was nothing for him to do. But after I hung up I thanked God that we had Khalid Sheikh Mohammed. We suspected that KSM had been the mastermind of 9/11, the al Qaeda operational commander for North America, and the man we thought most likely to know what was coming next and who was plotting it. He had also boasted that he had been Daniel Pearl's executioner.

Pearl, a graduate of Stanford, was the South Asia bureau chief for the *Wall Street Journal*. While pursuing a story in Pakistan in January 2002, Pearl was abducted by a group of militants, who had lured him with the false promise of an interview with a prominent cleric. When Pearl arrived for the interview, however, they kidnapped him and held him hostage in a safe house on the outskirts of Karachi, where he remained until his murder. The world—and Pearl's pregnant wife, Mariane—watched the drama unfold over the next several days, as the kidnappers released a series of messages denouncing Pearl as a spy and showing pictures of him with a gun to his head. When the militants found out that Pearl was Jewish, they announced that they would execute him within twenty-four hours. Ahmed Omar Sheikh, the ringleader of the abduction, transferred Pearl to the custody of a group of al Qaeda militants, led by KSM, who made good on the threat. The killers released a stomach-turning videotape of Pearl's gruesome murder that was later used to corroborate KSM's confession.

One of the hardest phone calls I had to make in my time in government was to Mariane Pearl. I called to tell her that Khalid Sheikh Mohammed had confessed to her husband's murder but that, for the time being, we would make no public announcement. She was calm and gracious and, thankfully, did not ask much about the details, which I knew to be incredibly gruesome. It seemed that KSM had been happy to regale his captors with a graphic blow-by-blow of his murder of the journalist.

EVEN AFTER the capture of Abu Zubaydah, KSM, and others, we continued to hope we'd find Osama bin Laden. Some people contend that we had a chance to capture or kill him at Tora Bora in the waning stages of the initial Afghan campaign in 2001. In fact, there were conflicting reports about his whereabouts at the time, and as a result the military did not request additional forces to conduct a strike. To my knowledge, the President was never asked to make a decision about a possible operation. But one thing is certain: if we had known where bin Laden was, we would have done absolutely everything in our power to take him down.

Over the subsequent years there were multiple "sightings" of bin

Laden, but none of them panned out. That was a deep disappointment, since we dreamed of the day that the American people would have the closure that his capture would bring. I was encouraged in 2007 when Mike Hayden, who was now serving as CIA director, told the President that we had a new lead—a courier who could lead us to the al Qaeda chief. But once again the trail went cold. In May 2011 the United States finally got bin Laden. I felt a great sense of relief and pride as well as gratitude to President Obama for the bold decision to launch the raid that had led to his killing. And I felt vindication for putting into place many of the tools that had led to that day.

I always believed that we would get bin Laden. But two years after 9/11, it was the fact that KSM and Ramzi bin al-Shibh, a logistics planner of the 9/11 attacks, were in custody and feeding us important information, that made me rest a little easier. It was a bit like having Field Marshall Erwin Rommel, the brilliant and notorious Nazi general, under lock and key during World War II.

I knew at the time that the steps we took, particularly the CIA's interrogation program, would be controversial and second-guessed as the memories of 9/11 faded. Steve Hadley and I talked about it many times. Over the next years the CIA program would be modified, suspended, modified, and eventually resumed. Three different CIA directors would continue to recommend it as necessary, and three different attorneys general would assess and affirm its legality. Congressional leaders in the Senate and House intelligence committees were briefed on the program. I welcomed the debate—which was legitimate from my point of view—inside and outside the administration as circumstances changed. Great democracies have institutions that are constantly assessing and, if necessary, adjusting the course of the country in the pursuit of consistency with our values and our law, even under the most stressing conditions. In time I would, myself, play a role in the debates as secretary of state.

Yet looking back at those days of sheer horror in the aftermath of the attack on the Twin Towers and the Pentagon, I do not regret the decisions we made. I would never have engaged in—or encouraged the President to undertake—activities that I thought to be illegal. That was why the Justice Department was front and center in the assessment of the policies. I was not enthusiastic about all that was being done, but I accepted the DCI's recommendation that it was necessary. I also found compiling lists of people who were individually targeted for "kill or capture" disturbing, particularly because there sometimes seemed to be civilian casualties in such engagements.

But that was the hand we were dealt after 9/11. I do not believe that we should have rejected options that were legal and necessary. I could not have forgiven myself had there been another attack. And had that happened, there would have rightly been a different kind of second-guessing as Americans asked, "Why did you not do everything in your power to keep it from happening again?"

9

TROUBLE IN NUCLEAR SOUTH ASIA

HISTORY TENDS TO IMPOSE a kind of sequential order on events, but a participant does not have the luxury of paying attention to them sequentially. In the fall of 2001, even as every day started with the terrorist threat report, events were unfolding around the globe, particularly in South Asia and the Middle East, each with its own dynamic. Yet in this new security environment there were unmistakable connections among those events, the rise of extremism, and the war on terror.

The meeting in the Situation Room that mid-December morning in 2001 was extremely tense, perhaps more so than at any time since the attacks on the Twin Towers. Trouble between India and Pakistan was escalating in the wake of a December 13 attack on the Indian Parliament House in New Delhi, which had killed nine people. Pakistani President Pervez Musharraf had sent a letter of condolence to Indian Prime Minister Atal Bihari Vajpayee and under enormous pressure internationally—particularly from the United States and Britain—condemned the attack in a televised address two days later. But Musharraf had also warned India not to take any actions that might escalate tensions. "This would lead to very serious repercussions," he said. "It must not be done." The warning did not sit well with the Indians, who suspected that Lashkar-e-Taiba, an extremist organization based in Pakistan and known to be supported by the country's security service, the ISI, was the culprit. Vajpayee was facing significant domestic pressure to respond militarily to the devastating attack on the Parliament.

As the NSC gathered that morning, military preparations were under way in the region, a mobilization that in a matter of weeks would result in nearly a million troops facing off across the border. Ever since the independent state of Pakistan had been carved out of the Indian subcontinent in 1947, tensions between Islamabad and New Delhi, particularly over disputed territory in Kashmir, remained high. The two neighbors had fought four wars against each other, and as hostilities escalated in the winter of 2001, we were eager to avoid yet another conflict. But because the nuclear-armed rivals have their forces in a near-constant state of alert, they had managed to mobilize and reach a heightened state of alert in a matter of days.

Yet the challenge for a policy maker is to interpret the evidence, and that was proving to be difficult. Looking at the same events unfolding on the ground, the Pentagon and the CIA gave very different assessments of the likelihood of war. The Defense Department, relying largely on reporting and analysis from the Defense Intelligence Agency, viewed the preparations as steps similar to those that any military (including our own) would take given the circumstances. In the Pentagon's view, such a buildup was not necessarily evidence of a formal decision to launch an attack.

The CIA believed that armed conflict was unavoidable because India had already decided to "punish" Pakistan. That is likely the view that Islamabad held and wanted us to hold too. The fact is that after years of isolation from India, a country that had viewed the United States with suspicion for decades, the CIA was heavily reliant on Pakistani sources in 2001. After repeated crises on the subcontinent over the next seven years, it was an institutional limitation that I would come to understand far better than I did at the time.

The President and the NSC Principals were frustrated with the ups and downs of the assessment over the next three days. The Defense Department and the CIA remained very far apart. One morning we were presented with a report that there had been firing across the border in Kashmir, which our military attaché judged to be false. Thankfully, he was right. The Principals Committee met every day, trying to make sense of what was transpiring. But one thing was clear: whatever the intentions of the two sides, they could easily stumble into war whether they intended to or not. Those nuclear-armed adversaries could, within a matter of hours, plunge the region into chaos—possibly nuclear chaos.

The State Department led an urgent diplomatic effort to calm the situation. While trying to defuse tensions, we felt it necessary to affirm

India's right to self-defense. Ari Fleischer did so in a carefully worded press statement on December 18, which also urged New Delhi to take no action that would complicate the situation. It was a direct consequence of how we had come to view the terrorism issue after September 11. In this case we had to acknowledge the right of others to do what we had done in responding to the attack on the Twin Towers but also convince them not to actually do it.

The terrorists who'd committed the attack against India had clear links to al Qaeda through the web of relationships with extremist groups that Pakistan maintained in the region. The trend had been exacerbated by the war against the Soviets in Afghanistan, which had led the ISI, Pakistan's intelligence service, to develop an intertwined network of violent extremists in Kashmir and Afghanistan, who, together with the mujahideen, resisted the Soviet invasion. The ISI was, to say the least, not very careful in separating materiel and training for those extremist groups. When the Soviet Union was defeated in 1989, some of the equipment and support that the United States had provided to the mujahideen stayed behind and added significantly to the further militarization of the region.

In 2001 the most urgent task was to break the extremists' hold on Pakistan. President Musharraf was a flawed partner. He'd come to power in a military coup in 1999 and had limited domestic legitimacy. But he'd demonstrated an understanding of the post-9/11 realities in the immediate aftermath of the attack. Now, with India and Pakistan on the brink of war, he had to do more.

Not surprisingly, India rejected Pakistan's proposal for a joint investigation into the attacks on the Indian Parliament. On December 21 tensions escalated further as India recalled its ambassador in Islamabad. Through all of the ups and downs and even military confrontations between the two states, this was the first time in thirty years that India was without diplomatic representation in Pakistan. That was a sign of how grave the situation had become.

Together with the British, we decided to approach the problem on three fronts. First, we would pressure Musharraf to make a public break with extremism. But he could not just utter statements; Pakistani security forces had to go after the extremists and arrest them. Second, we would demonstrate that we were acting too. That resulted in the United States' freezing assets of some Pakistani terrorist groups, including Lashkar-e-Taiba as well as the "charity" front known as Ummah Tameer-e-Nau (UTN). The latter was suspected of helping al Qaeda develop a nuclear weapon. Buckling under U.S. pressure, Pakistan announced that it would freeze UTN's assets as well.

Finally, we knew that Musharraf faced deep internal resistance within his security services and even within the armed forces, which would perceive his actions as a capitulation to India. He had to move quickly but carefully enough not to bring about his own demise. Colin and Jack Straw, the British foreign minister, organized a brilliant diplomatic campaign that could be summed up as dispatching as many foreign visitors to Pakistan and India as possible. We reasoned that the two wouldn't go to war with high-ranking foreigners in the region. Every time they accepted a visit, we breathed a sigh of relief. We needed to buy time.

But the situation continued to deteriorate. I left for my Aunt Gee's house in Norfolk, Virginia, on December 23, figuring that the location was close enough to get back to Washington quickly if I needed to do so. On the night of December 25, with my family waiting downstairs for Christmas dinner, Colin, Jack, David Manning, and I conferred in a long telephone conversation. There were new reports of troop movements as well as a disturbing one that India was preparing to move short-range ballistic missiles capable of carrying nuclear warheads to the Indian-Pakistani border. We reviewed the list of dignitaries who had been deployed to the region, searching for possible intermediaries through whom we could send messages to the adversaries, and agreed to reconvene the next day. I went downstairs to dinner, but my appetite was gone. Excusing myself from the celebration, I checked in again with Colin, received a situation update from the White House, called the President, and went to bed. Needless to say, I went back to Washington the next day.

By December 27 the reports were confirmed: India had indeed moved nuclear-capable missiles to the border. Colin called Jaswant Singh, the Indian minister of external affairs, and asked that the two countries sit down and talk. The suggestion was flatly rejected. I called my counterpart, Brajesh Mishra, a senior and experienced Indian diplomat. Brajesh was right out of central casting, British-educated and urbane, unfailingly calm and reasonable. But this time he was on edge and agitated. Musharraf and the Pakistanis had done nothing, he said. War fever was rising in India. Finally, on December 31, Pakistan arrested the founder and leader of Lashkar-e-Taiba. A little over a week later, on January 12, President Musharraf delivered a televised address condemning terrorism in all forms, rejecting terrorist activity in the name of Kashmir, and pledging to ban terror groups. The speech was well received in the international community: we had arranged statements of support from numerous heads of state. India, though, reacted skeptically and kept its troops on the border.

The next day I suggested that President Bush telephone Musharraf and Vajpayee and thank them for preventing tensions from getting out of hand. "Are they in hand?" the President asked.

"No," I said, "but let's act as if we're confident that they are." The President dispatched Colin to South Asia, and he reported that the situation had indeed calmed considerably. The first of several India-Pakistan crises that we would experience in the eight years of the administration had calmed but not ended. A prospective conflict on the subcontinent between nuclear powers always posed grave dangers. With our forces fighting in Afghanistan and stability in Pakistan key to confronting al Qaeda, the outbreak of war in the region would have threatened our interests more directly than ever before.

A second flare-up would come in May, when three gunmen invaded the family quarters of a military camp in Kaluchak, Kashmir, killing more than thirty people, including ten children. Again, Lashkar-e-Taiba was the suspected culprit. The fact that Pakistan had released its founder just weeks before, claiming that he would be closely monitored, incensed the Indians. With a million troops still massed on the border, the situation became grave.

We again found ourselves managing a crisis that could lead to nuclear war. In fact, President Bush warned U.S. nationals to leave India due to the potential danger. Given that there were sixty thousand of them in India, this was no small matter.

President Bush was in Europe for bilateral meetings and a Russia-

NATO summit as the crisis heated up. I received an urgent call from Brajesh Mishra and was pulled from the President's meeting. "I cannot contain the war lobby here without some help," he said. Making it clear that he was acting on his own, he asked that the President make a statement, which he would use internally to try to hold the line. I went back and talked with Colin and the President, who readily agreed to make the statement, calling on Musharraf to live up to the promises he'd made in his earlier speech.

In fact, Musharraf had angered the President by conducting a series of tests of short- and medium-range missiles capable of carrying nuclear warheads. The President publicly expressed "deep concern" with Pakistan and used strong language to urge Musharraf to rein in the militants. Despite that, Musharraf continued to make the situation worse. After saying that Pakistan would "respond with full might" if provoked by India, he announced that he would bolster the troops in Kashmir by moving some from the Afghanistan border. The President then called Musharraf and told him in private what he had said in public: Pakistan had made a choice after September 11 and needed to act or risk losing U.S. support. Don Rumsfeld visited the region to help prevent further escalation. After weeks of dialogue and visits, the tensions between India and Pakistan appeared to cool. I'm quite certain that it was, in large part, due to the good work of Brajesh Mishra.

IN THE AFTERMATH of the two crises, we accelerated the changes in our policies toward India and Pakistan. Early in the presidential campaign, we'd talked about the importance of India as a rising, multiethnic democracy on the world stage. The President had foreshadowed his interest in strengthening relations with India in his campaign speech at the Reagan Library, and I'd written about the same in my 2000 *Foreign Affairs* article. In several sessions, the Vulcans had discussed the importance of discarding the Indo-Pak framework that saw relations with the two countries as a reflection of the conflict between them.

The wisdom of doing so could not have been clearer after the events of December 2001 and May to June 2002. Pakistan was a troubled state, riddled with extremism in its mosques, its madrassas, and, unfortunately, in its security services. The 1947 British "partition" plan carved a Muslim entity called Pakistan out of India. Whatever the motivation at the time, it created a state that defined itself in contradistinction to India. Some Pakistanis would thus see an existential interest in conflict with their neighbor and, since the presidency of Zia ul-Haq in the 1980s, a reliance on militancy as a source of legitimacy.

Our relationship with Pakistan would focus heavily on hunting down and capturing terrorists. We tried to broaden the agenda by supporting Musharraf's efforts to deal with extremism at its roots and build his country. For instance, we launched a broad $1.2 billion foreign assistance program for Pakistan, with more than $100 million dedicated to education in support of his program to reform the madrassas. We supported Pakistan in the World Bank, the International Monetary Fund (IMF), and the Asian Development Bank as it tried to make economic reforms. But it was an uphill climb. Musharraf seemed to understand that Pakistan had to change, but his lack of legitimacy and, at times, his hatred of India made it difficult for him to fully commit.

Pakistan was the source of the A. Q. Khan nuclear proliferation network, the place where we captured most of al Qaeda's leadership and eventually a safe haven for terrorists in the Afghan War. I once described it as taking care of a critically ill patient: you got up every day and dealt with the symptom of the moment, hoping over time to cure the underlying disease of extremism. Later, as secretary of state, I went to many dangerous places: Baghdad and Kabul in the middle of the war; Lebanon in 2006; the West Bank and Jerusalem many times; even Darfur in Sudan. But no place felt as volatile as Pakistan. Those places were riddled by conflict during my visits, so extreme tensions were to be expected; Pakistan was theoretically at peace. Yet the streets of Islamabad were lined with unemployed young men with few prospects and a seething anger. Extremism seemed deeply imbedded in the fabric of the country.

India felt and was different. It is a mature democracy that seeks to integrate its various ethnic and religious populations. It is not that Sikhs, Muslims, and Hindus (among others) have no problems among themselves, and certainly there is still considerable prejudice and discrimination against minority groups. But you couldn't help but notice that any Indian delegation, whether government or private, was pretty diverse. Whatever its problems, one had to be impressed with a country of a billion people that regularly held peaceful and consequential free and fair elections.

Moreover, despite large regions where there was crushing poverty and significant problems with corruption, India was beginning to emerge as a global economic force, based largely on the creativity of its people. Both President Bush, as the governor of Texas, and I, as Stanford's provost in Silicon Valley, had noted with admiration the contributions of the Indian diaspora to the information revolution. Those migrating, opportunity-seeking families maintained their ties to their homeland and were beginning to help India transform. India was not just Kashmir and Calcutta; it was also Bangalore and Mumbai and Bollywood.

The President thus sought a broad, deep relationship with India, which he saw as a natural fit for U.S. strategic interests. Throughout the spring of 2001 we began to put the infrastructure into place for a transformation in U.S.-India relations. The two countries launched the first political-military dialogue in April 2002. Moreover, the Indian navy began a six-month joint escort mission with the U.S. fleet in the Malacca Strait, one of the busiest maritime trade routes in the world. And the establishment of the Joint Working Group on Counterterrorism and Law Enforcement formalized the emerging common agenda in the war on terrorism.

There was one issue standing in the way of a true breakthrough in U.S.-Indian relations: cooperation in the realm of high technology. The web of sanctions and constraints, many dating back to New Delhi's first nuclear weapons test in 1974, made it impossible to engage the Indians in that sphere. The President and I talked about doing something about those barriers. Steve Hadley was fully on board too. But we knew that we'd have to move carefully. Though most in our administration agreed that it was time to move forward with India, the high priests and protectors of the Non-Proliferation Treaty in Congress (and in some corners of the State Department) would resist anything that looked like a change of U.S. policy in that area.

We all agreed that we could not launch any such initiative with so much on our plate in 2001–2002. But we did begin discussions with the Indians on those issues. The two sides launched the U.S.-India High Technology Cooperation Group in November 2002, pledging to enhance high-technology trade between the two countries. What came to be called the Next Steps in Strategic Partnership (NSSP) initiative was a turning point and the camel's nose under the tent in regularizing India's nuclear status and launching a new U.S.-India relationship as full strategic partners.

10

THE TWO-STATE SOLUTION

MICHAEL GERSON, the President's talented chief speechwriter, had a gift for translating the President's compassionate conservatism into compelling prose, perhaps because he believed in it strongly himself. I loved working with him, not just because he was a wordsmith but also because he was an intellectual sounding board. In late October 2001 we met to discuss what the President would say at the upcoming opening session of the UN General Assembly, which had been postponed for two months due to the September 11 attacks. In his first address to the world since that day, the President would obviously talk about terrorism. But he also wanted to reaffirm his support for peace between Israelis and Palestinians as a pillar of a new and more stable Middle East.

The initial draft of the speech avoided the word "state," saying instead that the Palestinians should govern themselves in line with what was at the time U.S. policy. When we showed the speech to President Bush, he asked with characteristic directness, "Does that mean they will have a state?" I answered that it did but that the United States had always treated the question of *how* the Palestinians would govern themselves as a final-status issue and thus a matter for negotiation.

The President had always found the indirect language of the Middle East peace process frustrating. A few days after he became President, he'd challenged me when I'd given him a carefully worded statement to deliver to the press on the South Lawn prior to boarding Marine One. "Why do I have to say it this way?"

We didn't have time for a long historical discussion, so I just said, "Mr. President, if you change one comma, you will have changed U.S. policy in the Middle East." He relented and read the statement as written.

But now, almost a year into his term and with significant experience in the matter, the President wanted to say what he meant and say it directly. We agreed that he would call for the establishment of a Palestinian state.

The President then asked if the state would be called "Palestine." That was even trickier because the Israelis had always imbued the name "Palestine" with deep historical meaning. They considered its use a prejudgment of the question of what parts of "Judea and Samaria," biblical names for territories in the West Bank, could be ceded by Israel, if any. I answered that it would likely be called Palestine but did my best to explain the somewhat circular Israeli logic on the matter. The President would have none of it. He wanted to talk about the establishment of the State of Palestine and how it would live in peace and freedom alongside the State of Israel.

Since the President had made a decision on the matter, there was no need for an interagency meeting. I called Colin, who quickly and happily agreed to this significant step forward in U.S. policy on the Middle East. The Vice President's staff grumbled to Steve Hadley, but there wasn't really much pushback.

The afternoon before leaving for New York, the President practiced his speech in the Family Theater, located in the East Wing of the White House. President Franklin D. Roosevelt had apparently come up with the idea of a family theater since the leader of the free world can hardly go to the cineplex to view the latest releases. But the theater also doubles as a rehearsal space for the President to practice with the teleprompter in the company of the chief of staff and several other key staff. Karen Hughes was in charge of the sessions, and they provided a last chance to make changes. The President hated such disruptions, especially what he called "cram-ins," last-minute ideas that someone had failed to think of earlier in the process.

The session went smoothly in this case. Yet after hearing the speech from start to finish, some of us found that the language concerning the "State of Palestine" sounded more radical than it had seemed on the written page. Steve Hadley whispered to me that I needed to give the Israelis a heads-up. The President overheard it and said that he wasn't going to make any changes. "No, sir," I said. "We just don't want them to be surprised."

I called Danny Ayalon, Israeli Prime Minister Sharon's foreign policy advisor. It was already late in the evening in Jerusalem, but it seemed as if the Israelis never slept. They worked late into the night, making it convenient to reach them. Danny had been educated in the United States, was married to an American-born woman, and spoke perfect, nuanced English. He was a fierce defender of Israeli interests and the prerogatives of the prime minister, but he was an excellent and reasonable partner for me, and he had direct access to Sharon.

"Danny, the President is going to give a speech tomorrow," I said. I could almost hear Danny tense up. "He is going to call for the establishment of a Palestinian state." Now I could hear Danny breathe a sigh of relief. A U.S. President had never called forthrightly for the establishment of a Palestinian state as a matter of U.S. policy, so this was a significant departure. Yet the statement was not as radical as Danny feared; at least the President wasn't calling for a peace conference or something like that. Then I added, "And he's going to call it Palestine."

"He can't do that," Danny protested. "Palestine is Judea and Samaria, the biblical home of the Jewish people."

I listened calmly for a while to the history lesson and repeated, "Danny, he is going to call it Palestine." Danny said that he needed to talk to the prime minister. I said that the President had made a decision.

When he called back, Danny asked if we could call it "New Palestine." I replied that "New Palestine" sounded dumb and that the President wouldn't accept any change in the language. "And Danny, don't lobby the Hill," I said. "It's not going to work." The reaction in the Israeli press after the speech was relatively muted. The President had established the creation of a Palestinian state as a goal of U.S. foreign policy. Colin would deliver a speech nine days later at the University of Louisville that reaffirmed the President's vision and appointed General Anthony Zinni as special envoy to the Middle East. The President's policy vision was memorialized in UN Security Council Resolution 1397 in March of the next year.

I relate this exchange in some detail because it was my first experience in the management of U.S.-Israeli relations. George W. Bush was already trusted in Israel thanks to his full-throated support of Israel's right to defend itself against terror early in his presidency. Sharon had visited the White House twice, and the President had backed the Israeli position that final-status negotiations were premature in the face of Palestinian violence.

I too had established myself as a friend of Israel, linking our efforts in the war on terror to Israel's struggle. "You can't condemn al Qaeda and hug Hamas," I'd said to the press, much to the Israelis' delight.

Yet even with this basis of trust, every hint of a change in the status quo was met with suspicion and an attempt to haggle over every word. And disagreements with Israel were often immediately broadcast to Capitol Hill and to lobbyists such as the American Israel Public Affairs Committee (AIPAC). Moreover, those groups had a direct line into the White House, particularly through the Vice President's office. This was frequently a problem for the State Department, which was viewed as a bastion of pro-Arab sentiment. Israeli efforts to find exploitable daylight between the President and the secretary of state had complicated matters for more than one U.S. administration.

Fortunately, I developed my own close ties to the Jewish community in Washington and to the Israelis as well. Such people as Abraham Foxman, the national director of the Anti-Defamation League; Malcolm Hoenlein, the executive vice chairman of the Conference of Presidents of Major American Jewish Organizations; Harold Tanner, the president of the American Jewish Committee; and Howard Kohr, the executive director of AIPAC, came to trust me and I them. Abe in particular would call occasionally and suggest that it was time to meet with the leaders of key organizations when too much distance was growing between the President and the Jewish community. It was not that the groups had a veto—far from it. But they often provided a good check on what we were doing, and in any case they needed to be kept informed and sometimes reassured. The sessions helped us get ahead of potential problems.

And whatever the problems, I reminded myself constantly that even if Israel's leaders were sometimes a nightmare to deal with, this important ally of ours was the only democracy in the Middle East. Our relationship really was based on more than strategic interests; we were friends, and that mattered.

The President's speech was not exactly front-page news in the Arab press. Egypt, Jordan, and Saudi Arabia were so focused on the "peace process" that they seemingly failed to notice that the President of the United States had called for the establishment of a State of Palestine. Years later, the Arabs would acknowledge the importance of what the President had done. But in this initial failure to credit the President's stance was an important lesson too: whatever you do for peace in the Middle East, it is never enough for the Arab parties.

Violence Flares Up Again

DESPITE THE HOPEFUL rhetorical support for a Palestinian state, the low-intensity war between Israelis and Palestinians continued. While our envoy Anthony Zinni tried to mediate, Hamas perpetrated a series of suicide bombings at the beginning of December 2001, killing twenty-six Israelis in twenty-four hours in Jerusalem and Haifa. In response, Israeli helicopters attacked Yasir Arafat's headquarters in Ramallah, and Sharon soon declared Arafat to be "out of play." Hearing that, I thought it necessary to reaffirm with the Israelis the prime minister's commitment to President Bush not to kill Arafat. We were back in crisis management mode, just trying to stem the violence and calm the region.

Then an incident in the Red Sea cemented our already dim view of Arafat's "leadership." I never met him, and neither did the President, but it was absolutely clear that he was not going to lead his people to peace. The President placed the blame for the failure of the Camp David negotiations on Arafat. He believed that Arafat was corrupt and unwilling to make difficult choices for peace. In January 2002 we added "committed terrorist" to the list of offenses. Arafat had ostensibly renounced terrorism in 1988 and again as part of the 1993 Oslo Accords, which had recognized the Palestine Liberation Organization (PLO) as the governing authority for the Palestinian people. But when on January 3 the Israeli navy, with tracking support from the United States, captured the

Palestinian Authority's *Karine A*, a freighter loaded with arms destined for Gaza, Arafat's duplicity was exposed.

The NSC gathered a few days later to review the evidence from the incident and to discuss the ramifications for U.S. policy in the Middle East. The fact that the arms had likely come from Iran was particularly troubling; the Palestinian leadership had sponsors that we could not tolerate. We began to discuss alternatives to Arafat. But we wanted to be careful, particularly with the Israelis, to make clear that we meant peaceful change—not Arafat's assassination.

The violence continued unabated with the Israeli assassination of a leading Palestinian militant in the West Bank city of Tulkharam. Two weeks later the first female Fatah suicide attacker struck in Jerusalem, killing one person and wounding more than a hundred others, including an American man who'd been in the World Trade Center on 9/11.

It was against that backdrop that Crown Prince Abdullah of Saudi Arabia released his "peace initiative" after a dinner with *New York Times* columnist Thomas Friedman. Friedman reported the existence of the plan in a column on February 17, 2002. The proposal was that a unified Arab world would end its conflict with Israel in exchange for the establishment of a Palestinian state based on the 1967 borders (roughly the territory occupied by Israel after the 1967 war against the combined Arab armies). It was a bold proposal and could have been an important point of departure for negotiations. The Saudis would later express their disappointment that we hadn't responded favorably to the crown prince's efforts. But the timing could not have been worse. Sharon had been elected to defeat the intifada—not to make peace. There was no trust in Arafat as a partner, an assessment we shared.

The cycle of violence in the region was deepening when the Saudi initiative came to light. In early March Sharon responded to a series of suicide bombings by ordering military incursions into a number of Palestinian towns in Gaza and the West Bank, determined to defeat the terrorists and secure the State of Israel. Frankly, no one, most especially the President, blamed him for doing so.

Yet as the violence escalated, the pressure from our Arab allies and European friends to do something grew. The Vice President visited the Middle East on March 12 to 19, 2002, holding out the possibility of meeting with Arafat if the Palestinians agreed to fully implement the security cooperation plan drafted by George Tenet, the CIA director.

During the Clinton administration, the CIA had taken the U.S. lead on security matters in the West Bank and Gaza. The Palestinian security forces operated in a shadowy manner. They were essentially intelligence forces that looked quite a bit like mafia bosses or perhaps street gangs. Arafat had a web of at least a dozen of these security organizations, each led by a "chief" and all loyal to him, while jockeying with and checking one another. Violence between the organizations competing for the spoils of Arafat's corruption or control of territory was fairly common. Needless to say, it was a world in which the CIA was more capable than the State Department or the Pentagon, and the Agency sometimes succeeded in quelling the violence. But that version of security cooperation didn't do much to democratize Palestinian institutions or root out corruption within them.

Because the Palestinians failed to fully implement the Tenet security plan, the Vice President did not meet with Arafat. When he returned to the White House and reported on his trip, our discussions turned again to how the Palestinians might find leadership that would make a two-state solution possible. We were frankly ready to tell the world that it would never happen with Arafat in power.

Then events took a radical turn. On Passover, Hamas carried out a suicide attack at the Park Hotel in Netanya, killing dozens of Israelis and wounding more than a hundred people. Even with that provocation the Israelis sent word that they would accept the Zinni security plan, based largely on Tenet's earlier work. The Palestinians refused to do so.

Thus, when the Israelis launched Operation Defensive Shield and reoccupied all of the West Bank, we were neither surprised nor critical. The President and Colin said yet again that Israel had a right to defend itself. Ari Fleischer reiterated the statement practically every day. But the Israelis always seem to go too far. They decided to lay siege to the Palestinian headquarters in Ramallah with Arafat in it. For days CNN showed pictures of the Palestinian leader at the mercy of the Israeli forces.

When the Israelis entered Bethlehem, dozens of fleeing militants broke into the Church of the Nativity, seeking refuge. The church, which marks the place of Jesus's birth, was damaged by errant Israeli gunfire during the ensuing siege. That prompted an angry phone call to me from the Vatican's secretary of state. He didn't mince words. Saying that the Holy Father himself had directed him to make the phone call, the cardinal called the incident an attack on one of the holiest shrines for Christians. I tried to protest that it had been an accident, but somehow the point seemed moot. The Arabs were threatening all manner of retaliation if the Israelis didn't stop. We were in the midst of a full-blown Middle East crisis and a deepening split with Israel.

THE NATIONAL SECURITY ADVISOR is almost always the focal point in the management of a crisis with Israel. This is in part structural. The Israeli foreign minister is often selected as a part of domestic co-alition building and sometimes lacks full authority on matters of war and peace. Moreover, because Israel believes that it exists in a state of siege (not without some justification), the prime minister and his office carry the foreign policy brief as if the country is in a perpetual state of war. And in relations with the United States, it is the prime minister, from David Ben-Gurion to Yitzhak Rabin to Benjamin Netanyahu, who "owns" the relationship with Washington. This is reinforced by the aforementioned suspicion of the State Department as "pro-Arab."

As the violence escalated, I convened the Principals and then the NSC to consider what the President should say and when. Five days had passed since the Israeli initiation of Operation Defensive Shield, and the Arab world was roiling. We were under enormous pressure to rein in the Israelis. There were three problems with this. First, there is an assumption, particularly among the Arabs and even the Europeans, that if the United States threatens Israel with diplomatic isolation or perhaps limitations on financial or military assistance, Israel will comply immediately and completely. That, of course, isn't true, particularly in the midst of a military operation deemed necessary for Israel's security by its democratically elected government. What is more, what U.S. President wants to threaten the United States' ally in this way when Israel is responding to an attack? Second, the President has to be careful because if he calls for the Israelis to stop and they do not, his credibility and that of the United States will be severely damaged. Finally, there was some sentiment within the administration, particularly on the part of the Vice President and Don Rumsfeld, that the Israelis had a right to crush the terrorists who were attacking them. The President shared this view but acknowledged Colin's point that the inevitable carnage among innocent Palestinians was also a serious problem and that the credibility of the United States was deteriorating. We laid out the options, which ranged from doing nothing to calling for an end to the Israeli operation.

The President decided, despite significant reservations by all involved, to give a speech on April 4, 2002, urging Israel to stop settlement activity and stop Operation Defensive Shield. Even Colin worried that the Israelis might ignore the calls, further undermining U.S. credibility. The President also did what presidents do under the circumstances: he sent the secretary of state to the region even though Colin had nothing that he could deliver. The President told Colin directly that he needed him to go and spend some of his personal credibility on behalf of the administration. Colin went despite having deep reservations.

The next three weeks were exceedingly difficult and filled with tension. Powell dutifully traveled to the Middle East, meeting with Arafat in the Muqata compound (the Palestinian headquarters in Ramallah) with Israeli tanks outside. He told Arafat that he might be the last U.S. official with whom he'd meet if he didn't rein in the terrorists. He learned too that the Israeli government had decided to build a security buffer between Israel and the West Bank from Mount Gilboa in the north to the Judean desert in the south. Though the ostensible purpose was to make it impossible for terrorists to enter Israel, we knew that the construction of a "wall" (or "fence," as the Israelis called it) would be read as an Israeli attempt to cement the territorial status quo and thereby prejudge the boundaries of a Palestinian state. The imagery was terrible too: an ugly barrier erected between peoples who were supposed to try to find a way to live in peace.

Colin returned from the region without any agreements. He'd tried to negotiate a document that might lay out a path to end the violence and that would result in a peace conference of some kind. But the President shared the Israelis' allergy to any nod toward negotiations with Arafat. I tried to make the case to the President that simply pointing toward negotiations would carry little cost. He was adamant, though, and I called Colin, who was still in the region, to tell him that the draft statement he'd sent to Washington was dead on arrival. Our diplomatic efforts were failing miserably. And when, on April 18, the President answered a question by calling the Israeli prime minister "a man of peace," I thought we'd done long-term damage to our relations in the Arab world.

Colin had been sitting next to the President when he made the comment. After the press left, he came over to me. "Do you have any idea how this plays on Arab TV?" he asked. "The Israelis are just thumbing their noses at the President. Why is he giving Sharon a pass?" The State Department went into overdrive trying to explain what the President had "meant to say."

I fully agreed at the time that the President had made a mistake. But later I would see that the vote of confidence in Sharon had had an effect on the tough, aging Israeli. Sharon would ultimately take important and unexpected steps toward the Palestinians, whom he distrusted and whose ambitions for statehood he'd always crushed. It was not the only time that George W. Bush took a rhetorical leap forward that was both unscripted and strategically wise.

But on that day the problem was that the Israelis were continuing to lay waste to the West Bank and Gaza. The images of dead innocent Palestinians, Palestinian men being rounded up by the Israel Defense Forces (IDF), and the siege of Ramallah played over and over on television. That the Israelis were not responding to the President's call to stop was increasingly frustrating and embarrassing. When asked on CNN on April 7, 2002, what the President had meant by "without delay" in calling for an end to the Israeli operation, I'd said, "It means now." An Israeli governmental official responded by saying that Israel would withdraw "without delay" when they'd finished their operation. That wasn't exactly the response we were looking for. The offensive continued.

On April 25, the President hosted Crown Prince Abdullah of Saudi Arabia at his ranch in Texas. During the meeting the Saudi leader asked to be left alone in the living room with his delegation. We were a bit surprised but moved to the screened porch adjacent to where they were meeting. After a few minutes, Gamal Helal, the able U.S. interpreter, rushed into the room where we were sitting. The Arabs trusted Gamal after more than ten years of his being an interpreter and advisor to secretaries of state. He'd somehow been allowed to remain with the Saudis for their confab. He told the President that the Saudis were threatening to go home immediately if the President didn't stop the Israelis and make them withdraw that day. The President asked rhetorically, "Does it matter if they leave?"

"It would be a disaster," I said. Colin nodded his agreement and was immediately told by the President to "go and fix it." He couldn't. The President, temporizing a bit, asked the Saudi leader to go for a tour of the ranch and talk about religion. As President Bush has written in his memoir, the atmosphere improved while they were riding together in his pickup truck. He and the Saudi encountered a wild turkey that Abdullah took as a sign from God and a bond of friendship between the two men. When the President related the incident that evening at dinner, I thought, *Whatever works.*

The momentary easing of tensions with the Saudis did not end their insistence that the United States deal with Israel. And we had been turning up the pressure, pushing the Israelis to pull back. I was calling Danny Ayalon every day, sometimes several times a day. He was clearly troubled, but the IDF had a green light to finish what it had started. I appealed to Danny to at least end the siege of the Muqata compound. "Arafat is on CNN speaking by candlelight. You're making him look like Mother Teresa. Turn on their electricity."

"They have electricity," Danny retorted. "He's just doing that to evoke sympathy."

"That's the point," I said. In another call, on April 27, I told him that the President had instructed me to say that there had better be some movement within twenty-four hours or he would publicly criticize Israel and the prime minister in the harshest terms. I reminded Danny that the President had taken a risk in calling Sharon a "man of peace." Now it was time for him to prove it.

Finally we got some movement forward. Working with the British, we were able to come to a solution with the Israelis on one part of the problem. Some terrorists had holed up along with Arafat in his compound in Ramallah. Among them were militants who had been convicted of assassinating the Israeli tourism minister a few months earlier. The Israelis wanted the militants, and the Palestinians wanted to keep them jailed but in Palestinian custody. We worked out a deal to have them transferred to British custody in the West Bank. Then the Israelis agreed to start pulling back from Palestinian cities one at a time (in fact, they had already withdrawn from a few) and to announce that they'd continue to do so as long as there were no more attacks. At last, on May 2, five weeks after it had laid siege to the Muqata compound, the IDF withdrew, permitting the smiling Arafat to emerge to a hero's welcome. The Israelis never seemed to manage public perceptions very well.

On June 10, Sharon visited the White House for the sixth time. The President told him that the United States would insist that the Palestinian Authority would have to reform before peace negotiations. There would have to be a new PA with new leadership. That was music to Sharon's ears and brought Israel and the United States into close alignment. I leaned over to the President and asked him to reiterate one point, however. "That doesn't mean that you can kill Arafat," the President said to Sharon, who nodded in agreement.

WITH THE immediate crisis receding, we returned again to the question of what to do in the Middle East. Colin and the State Department again proposed a peace conference; the President again said no, not with Arafat. The Palestinian Authority had launched a hundred-day reform plan for governance, but we had little confidence that it would actually implement it. Yet there was clearly a void. If we weren't ready to support negotiations, what were we prepared to do?

The question bothered the President, who was turning it over in his head almost daily. I would go to the Oval Office for our morning meeting, only to have him ask questions about the Palestinians. The one that was most on his mind was why the PA could not find decent leadership. He knew many Palestinians, mostly living in the United States, and they were entrepreneurial people. He just couldn't understand why, even under occupation, the Palestinians had not "found their Nelson Mandela," as he put it. The President wanted to give a speech to rally Palestinians and the world behind the cause of decent governance. Already at a press conference during an EU-U.S. summit, the President had called for elections in the Palestinian territories. The idea had gone nowhere and had barely been noticed amid the calls for a peace conference.

The President had become deeply convinced that the question wasn't whether to establish a Palestinian state; it was "What *kind* of Palestinian state?" He wanted to put on the agenda the right of the Palestinians to live in freedom both from Israel and from their own corrupt leaders. Ironically, one cornerstone of the administration's Freedom Agenda would come from the search for an enduring and sustainable end to the conflict between Israelis and Palestinians.

I called Mike Gerson, and we sat down to sketch out ideas for a presidential speech. In the address the President would call for the establishment of a provisional Palestinian state founded on democracy, institutional reform, and the renunciation of terrorism. He'd also call on Israel to cease building settlements in the occupied territories and to eventually withdraw its forces to positions held prior to September 28, 2000. Further, he'd say that the Israelis needed to take steps to restore freedom of movement in the territories to help improve the Palestinian economy. And he'd state directly that the Palestinians needed new leadership.

The speech clearance process proved to be an interagency nightmare. We dropped the idea of a provisional state, accepting State's view that the Palestinians would reject the proposal. They wanted permanent borders, not temporary ones. The debate continued over what the President should say. But the struggle over the wording was actually masking differences concerning policy. After almost two weeks, I told the President that we had a text but recommended that he hold an NSC meeting just to make sure.

We met for a final review of the speech on June 21. The Vice President was adamant that the speech should not be given because in the middle of the intifada it would give too much credibility to the Palestinian claims. Colin was concerned that in a speech denouncing Arafat, the United States would be seen as trying to choose Palestinian leaders. The President kept saying that he wanted to speak up for the Palestinians' rights to decent lives and decent governance. "Wouldn't it be amazing if democracy in the Middle East sprung first from the rocky soil of the West Bank?" he asked. The discussion continued, with Colin and the Vice President coming to the same conclusion for diametrically opposed reasons.

Finally I decided to speak up and voice my own opinion, something I rarely did in an NSC meeting. Usually I spoke only to clarify points for the President or to get agreement from him on a way forward. But he was struggling to find support for what he clearly and rightly wanted to do. "Mr. President," I started, but, noticing that my voice was quivering, I stopped and started again. "Mr. President, this is what the President of the United States *does*. He changes the terms of the debate, and heaven knows someone has got to do that in the Middle East." I could tell that the President was a bit startled since I generally shared my views in private. But I was glad I'd said it.

After a little more debate he sat back in his chair. "I'm going to give the speech," he said.

When the President makes a speech in the Rose Garden, it signals that the message is important. So, with the press gathered on the lawn facing the French doors of the Oval Office, the President delivered his speech. "I call on the Palestinian people to elect new leaders, leaders not compromised by terror," he said. "I call upon them to build a practicing democracy, based on tolerance and liberty. If the Palestinian people actively pursue these goals, America and the world will actively support their efforts."

After he finished, we walked back into the Oval Office. He was gratified by what he'd done, and so was I. It had been a good and consequential speech but different from the expected calls for negotiations between the sides that were characteristic of the stale ideas governing policy toward the Middle East.

I decided to check in with William Burns, the assistant secretary for Near Eastern affairs at the State Department. "How's the reaction?" I asked. Bill is a consummate professional and not given to hyperbole, so when he said that the reaction in the Arab world was "pretty rough," I knew what he really meant: "All hell has broken loose."

Indeed it had. I called Colin. He was doing everything he could to calm the waters in the Arab world and to get the President's true message out. But it was "tough," he said and rushed away to engage in "damage control."

We had a particular problem with President Hosni Mubarak of Egypt. President Bush had hosted Mubarak at Camp David on June 8 for what had been a pretty straightforward conversation about the Middle East. The aging Egyptian president considered himself an authority on the subject and, given his country's historic peace treaty with Israel in 1979, the key to a deal between the Israelis and Palestinians. Mubarak had a tendency to lecture his interlocutors about the region, and it often felt like a one-way conversation.

Nothing had been said to Mubarak about the President's upcoming speech, let alone its content, which had yet to be determined within the administration. Still, Mubarak felt double-crossed after the speech, given the proximity of his visit to its delivery. He worried that some people might even suspect that he'd endorsed the President's controversial call for Arafat's dismissal. We managed to work with Mubarak from then on, but he never forgot what had happened.

The Arabists in the State Department were appalled too. One diplomat who was serving in the Middle East told a reporter at a cocktail party that he could no longer do his job thanks to "that speech." Unfortunately the remark got back to the White House, shaking our confidence in him and adding to the perception that the professionals in the Foreign Service didn't really back the President.

On the other hand, a previously arranged phone call with the leadership of the Jewish community that evening was just a love fest. "Thank you. Thank the President. Tell him there has never been a more important speech about the Middle East." *Well*, I thought, *we certainly have everyone's attention.*

The next day the President left for Kananaskis in Alberta, Canada, for a G8 summit, and as I opened my front door at five that morning, I was greeted by a screaming newspaper headline: "Bush Demands Arafat's Ouster." Seated in the President's office aboard Air Force One, we reviewed the press line with Ari, who then left to face the traveling press corps. "Don't you back off what I said," the President had told him, aware of our diplomats' tendency to explain yet again "what the President meant to say."

I stayed behind, and we talked about the firestorm that was brewing. You could count on George W. Bush to stand firm even in the face of withering criticism. But our relationship of trust allowed me to probe a little deeper with him and to see how he was really feeling. For instance, in connection with bin Laden, when the President had delivered the famous retort about wanting him "dead or alive," he'd asked me when we were alone if it had been a mistake. "The language was a little white hot for the President of the United States," I'd said. He'd nodded his head in agreement and admitted that the First Lady agreed with me. He wouldn't acknowledge the error publicly for some years.

But on this day he was absolutely confident that he'd done the right thing. Arafat *did* have to go if there were ever to be peace in the Middle East. I agreed, but we both knew that the G8 meeting was going to be rocky. The Europeans thought Arafat was the key to peace. They would take the President's statement as a sign that he was pro-Israel to a fault. They weren't the only ones. Apparently, the President's mother had called him to ask how it felt to be the first Jewish President!

The first meeting when we arrived in Canada was with Prime Minister Junichiro Koizumi of Japan, who didn't even mention the Arafat matter. Jean Chrétien of Canada, however, was appalled by what the President had done, saying he had no "specific point of view" on whether Arafat should go. He kept his criticism within bounds but couldn't help but lecture the President on the history of Middle East peace negotiations and the critical role that Canada had always played. The President listened politely but didn't budge. Fortunately the evening was "downtime," and Andy Card, Karen Hughes, and I had a relaxed dinner with him where the issue of what to do about the reaction in the Middle East was put on hold.

The next morning I went down to the gym to exercise and found myself in the company of Tony Blair, with whom the President was to meet that morning. "Well, George has stirred it up a bit," he said with characteristic British understatement. The President came in a few minutes later and talked about the speech, explaining why he'd made it and that he had intended it as a clear indication of his dedication to Middle East peace.

Blair said that he thought he could help at the press availability after their meeting. He too thought Arafat to be a spent force. It was just that the Arabs and Europeans, who fully understood that fact, weren't willing to challenge the orthodoxy that he was the legitimate leader of the Palestinian people. When the press asked Blair about the President's speech, he masterfully found a way to support his friend. "I have tried as hard as anyone" to get Arafat to reform, he said, explaining that he had met with Arafat more than thirty times in recent years. "But we've got a situation where we have not been able to make progress, and there has been an attitude towards terrorism that is inconsistent with the notion of Israel's security."

The Arabs would soon settle down, and Colin successfully worked to build support for President Bush's vision of a democratic Palestine, work for which he has never gotten enough credit. In early July the foreign ministers of Jordan, Saudi Arabia, and Egypt visited President Bush to discuss how to achieve the goals set out in the President's address. The Jordanian foreign minister made a proposal, reiterated by the king of Jordan during a visit the next month, to translate the President's speech into a written plan with performance-based benchmarks. The proposal would eventually result in the "Road Map for Peace." The fact is that Blair was right: the Arabs knew that Arafat would never make peace, though they would never publicly acknowledge it. Given that they themselves were authoritarians, they were also somewhat uncomfortable with the emphasis on Palestinian democracy.

But the President had broken a taboo that needed to be broken. The Israelis had loved the speech, but they would soon find that the President expected Israel to support and engage a changing Palestinian leadership. The old Israeli claim that "there was no Palestinian partner for peace" would soon lose salience too. And the United States would be able to approach the question of Middle East peace on a fundamentally different basis: that of a two-state solution in which a democratic Palestine and a democratic Israel would live side by side.

11

THE WORLD'S MOST DANGEROUS WEAPONS

NOT EVERY DAY in the White House was taken up with a crisis, although it sometimes seemed that way. By the beginning of 2002 we needed to start to make sense, in a systematic way, of what the events of September 11, 2001, meant to U.S. security. The attacks on the World Trade Center and the Pentagon were no less consequential in our thinking than the attack on Pearl Harbor had been for U.S. policy makers in December 1941. Arguably the effect of the more recent assault on the American psyche was more disorienting because it had been not a powerful state but a well-organized network of stateless actors who'd successfully launched the most devastating attack on the U.S. mainland in modern history: and they'd done it at a cost of only several hundred thousand dollars, using commercial airplanes as a weapon and the territory of the failed state of Afghanistan as a base of operations.

We needed to call attention to the fundamental restructuring of U.S. security priorities necessitated by 9/11: how to defend ourselves in a world in which attacks came with little if any warning and with the possibility that such an attack might involve weapons of mass destruction. But defense in this new era required not just pursuing and defeating terrorists themselves but addressing the failed states that were breeding grounds for terrorism, human trafficking, and the illicit trading of arms and narcotics. In order to help failed states heal, we would come to see the importance of building stable democratic institutions that could provide for their people and prevent the use of their territory for dangerous transnational networks. Finally, those fledgling democratic states would need foreign assistance to achieve stability. The new security concept thus linked defense, democracy, and development— each integral to the success of the strategy.

The first opportunity for the President to set a new direction for our national security policy was the 2002 State of the Union address, the first since the events of September 11. Clearly the President would address the war on terrorism, but what else would he say?

At the time of the address to the nation on September 20, 2001, the NSC had considered the question of linking terrorism and weapons of mass destruction—that is, it had debated whether to raise the specter of a successor attack to 9/11, this one carried out with WMD. Sitting in the Situation Room reviewing the speech on September 19, though, the time simply didn't seem right to go there. The nation had just been through a devastating event, and the American people did not need to be further unsettled by the specter of a nuclear attack on our soil.

But now the President had to talk about that nexus. The proliferation of weapons of mass destruction had taken on new urgency after September 11. The world had to prevent the most dangerous weapons from ending up in the hands of the most dangerous people, be they terrorists or rogue regimes.

We were veterans of the Cold War and completely conversant with the efforts of responsible powers to prevent biological, chemical, and nuclear war. But North Korea and Iran, opaque and tyrannical regimes with a deep animus toward the United States, appeared to be closing in on the development of weapons of mass destruction, including nuclear weapons. Saddam Hussein sat astride the Middle East, increasingly unconstrained in his ability to buy or produce weapons of mass destruction, which he had previously used against his own people and against his neighbors. His link to WMD was not a theoretical one. And once in office, we learned with great alarm that A. Q. Khan, the father of the Pakistani nuclear program, had a business on the side: selling the technology and the know-how to produce nuclear weapons to whoever could afford to buy it.

The world had looked frightening enough on September 10, 2001, but after the attacks on the Twin Towers and the Pentagon, the threat took on greater urgency. We faced the reality that terrorists had many potential sources from which to buy or develop what we knew they wanted most: a nuclear weapon capable of making the next 9/11 catastrophic on an unthinkable scale. In October 2001 we'd seen credible reporting that terrorists would again attack the United States, perhaps with a radiological or nuclear weapon.

The President sought in the 2002 State of the Union to place all of this into context and to make clear that the United States could defend itself only by taking on the proliferation challenge. In that regard, he uttered one of the most often cited and, frankly, overdramatized phrases of his time in office. After describing the North Korean, Iranian, and Iraqi regimes and their links to terrorism and weapons of mass destruction, the President said, "States like these, and their terrorist allies, constitute an axis of evil, arming to threaten the peace of the world. By seeking weapons of mass destruction, these regimes pose a grave and growing danger. . . . We will work closely with our coalition to deny terrorists and their state sponsors the materials, technology and expertise to make and deliver weapons of mass destruction. . . . America will do what is necessary to ensure our national security."

The substance of the sentence was unremarkable, but the phrase "axis of evil," which was, in fact, inserted by a speechwriter, was only meant to vivify the point that certain kinds of regimes with WMD might transfer those weapons to terrorists. I don't remember a great deal of focus on the phrase during the speechwriting process. Steve and I had talked about whether "evil" sounded too dire but didn't think at all about "axis" and the fact that it might be over-interpreted to mean an alliance of rogue states. The speech was reviewed in the Pentagon and at the State Department, and no one raised even a yellow flag.

When I briefed the press before the President's speech, I focused on what we thought was the news in his message: "America will take the side of brave men and women who advocate these [democratic] values around the world, including the Islamic world." The President was calling for freedom from tyranny in a region in which many of our friends were authoritarians. I even made sure to call Saudi Ambassador Prince Bandar so that our friends in Riyadh would not be surprised.

So the next morning, when the media focused almost exclusively on the phrase "axis of evil," I was stunned and so was the President. Since many people believed that we'd already decided to go to war against

Iraq, sinister interpretations suggested that we were preparing to use military force against all three states. We had for all intents and purposes, some believed, declared war on North Korea, Iran, and Iraq.

As luck would have it, I was scheduled to give a speech on proliferation the next day. Working with Steve Hadley and Robert Joseph, the senior director at the NSC who dealt with proliferation policy, I hastily revised the speech to clarify what the President had meant, and I continued to offer clarification in subsequent press interviews. The President was not saying that the three nations were in formal alliance. Rather, they were illustrative of a class of states that share certain characteristics, including the pursuit of WMD, and the axis was between them and their potential terrorist allies. No, we did not believe that military action was the appropriate course in all cases. The President wouldn't take any options off the table, but he'd said we would work with our friends to deal with the problem; diplomacy was the first line of defense. But, admittedly, the harsh language suggested that negotiation was impossible. How could you negotiate with members of an "axis of evil"? The phrase helped brand the Bush administration as radical and bellicose, given to hot rhetoric and a preference for military force.

That perception was reinforced when the President delivered the 2002 commencement address at West Point. We'd used the usual speechwriting process, which always started with a conversation with the President about what he wanted to say. The President had said that he needed to address the question of how to avoid a surprise attack the next time. That had led to a discussion of whether we, as a nation, had waited too long to act in Afghanistan. Nothing in international history or law suggested that a country had to wait until it was attacked and then respond. Why not argue for the legitimacy of preemption as a strategy, which says that one can act in self-defense in anticipation of an attack, rather than simply trying to deter or contain terrorists and rogues? After a rather academic discussion of preemption, prevention, and deterrence, the President sent us on our way to work on the speech.

The follow-up session took place in my office with Steve Hadley, Mike Gerson, Andy Card, Karen Hughes, and Karl Rove. The group worked well together because we valued one another's opinions. But when it came to the substance of the speech, people stayed in their lanes. Karl, for instance, struck just the right balance in discussing how a speech would play politically yet never tried to act as the foreign policy expert, though he is extremely well read. I loved working with Karl, who is brilliant and funny and was completely committed to the President's success. When I said that something wouldn't work in foreign policy terms, he took it on board. When he said that something wouldn't work politically, I tried to accommodate his views. I know that Karl had developed a reputation as a "take-no-prisoners" political operative, a "zero-sum game" player. He did not, however, try to insert himself into the substance of foreign policy—a testament to both him and the President. Karl and I had an easy working relationship.

The speech that emerged stated, "Our security will require all Americans to be forward-looking and resolute, to be ready for preemptive action when necessary to defend our liberty and to defend our lives." But why should that have been controversial? The President was not saying that the United States would always act preemptively. He was simply stating what we thought to be obvious: it might not be possible to deter shadowy networks, and that containment might not be possible when unbalanced dictators can deliver weapons or secretly provide them to terrorists. The language was surrounded by talk of homeland defense, missile defense, and the need for good intelligence. Even reading the speech many years later, it does not seem to me to have a "hair-trigger" feel. Yet that is how it was taken, and again it was linked to Iraq: the United States was declaring the right to attack at a time of its choosing, even if it had not yet been attacked itself.

There would be one more opportunity to lay out a rationale for this policy as well as to broaden the discussion to other key elements of our strategy going forward. The administration was mandated by the National Security Act of 1947, as amended by the Goldwater-Nichols Department of Defense Reorganization Act of 1986, to deliver to Congress a national security strategy each year. The document had previously been a largely bottom-up bureaucratic exercise that had produced an unwieldy tome of several hundred pages. I myself had participated in the process when I was on Brent Scowcroft's NSC. People both inside and outside the administration failed to take it seriously; it was just a task to be finished with as little effort as possible so that one could get on to more important things.

But this time we decided that the national security strategy would be different and consequential. We took as the model the historic NSC-68, Paul Nitze's seminal statement of U.S. objectives and strategy at the outset of the Cold War.

We allowed the bureaucracy at State and Defense to beaver away in the traditional way while quietly drafting a short, clear document within the NSC staff. All of the key staff members were stretched thin, so I asked Philip Zelikow, with whom I'd worked previously and with whom I'd written a well-regarded book on German unification, to take the pen for the first draft. Over lunch with Mike Gerson, Steve Hadley, speechwriter Michael Anton, and several others, I asked Phil to hold nothing back in addressing the United States' changed circumstances. Controversy was a good thing. I wanted people to debate this document and believe that it mattered. I specifically said that he should address the nexus between terrorism and nuclear weapons and the question of how we would avoid being surprised again as we had been on September 11, 2001. But we wanted to address not just the negative side but also the United States' view of how the world ought to be. The document should express the country's confidence in its ability to win this struggle based on its values, just as it had won the Cold War.

Philip's draft was just like its author, brilliant but baroque. I decided to take the draft and try my hand at a simpler, more direct version. The draft was short and clear—or at least I thought so. When I sent it to President Bush for an early look, he asked me to come down to the Oval. "I thought this document was supposed to be *my* strategy," he said. I nodded. "The boys in Midland will never believe it. It doesn't sound like me."

I took up my pen again and, after several iterations, produced the document that largely survived an abbreviated interagency process piloted by Steve Biegun, the executive secretary of the NSC, who was also expert in matters of defense and foreign policy. The national security strategy began with a strong commitment on the part of the United States to "create a balance of power that favors human freedom." It cast our struggle against terrorism in stark ideological terms: much like the great struggles of the twentieth century between liberty and totalitarianism, the United States now confronted a world in which "[f]reedom and fear are at war." In this new age, the document stated, we must never forget "that we are ultimately fighting for our democratic values and way of life."

The strategy made clear that we would not shy away from using our "unparalleled military strength and great economic and political influence" to achieve those ends. The emphasis we placed on preserving our military dominance sparked some comment, especially when paired with our commitment to defend our interests "by identifying and destroying the threat before it reaches our borders." Our allies were particularly concerned with the statement that followed: "While the United States will constantly strive to enlist the support of the international community, we will not hesitate to act alone, if necessary, to exercise our right of self-defense by acting preemptively against such terrorists, to prevent them from doing harm against our people and our country."

As we noted later in the strategy, the United States has long maintained the option of preemptive action to counter threats to our national security, and international law has for centuries recognized that nations need not suffer an attack before they can take actions against an imminent threat. Contrary to popular view, the only novel aspect of our articulation of the preemption strategy was the way in which we had to adapt the concept of "imminent threat" to contemporary realities. As the strategy states, "The United States will not use force in all cases to preempt emerging threats, nor should nations use preemption as a pretext for aggression. Yet in an age where the enemies of civilization openly and actively seek the world's most destructive technologies, the United States cannot remain idle while dangers gather."

We needed to drive home the point that the "enemies of civilization" were of a different character than before. In the past, when the threats had come largely from states, there was some reasonable expectation that military preparations for attack would be visible. But terrorists operated in the shadows and could attack without warning—as they had on September 11. In light of this threat, limiting preemption to the occasions when we are sure an enemy is about to attack makes little sense.

Finally, the strategy committed the United States to "make use of every tool in our arsenal"—not exclusively military force—in countering the threat that terrorists and rogue regimes pose to our nation and our ideals. The strategy emphasized working with our allies to share intelligence and disrupt terrorist finances. It spoke of the importance of opening societies to free commerce and access to markets. Perhaps most innovatively, it recognized the importance of linking development assistance with good-governance reforms and shifts toward democratic governance. For too long, foreign aid had failed to spur economic development in the world's poorest countries. Success was measured in dollars spent rather than growth rates and the poverty reduction achieved by recipients.

Our strategy recognized that economic development would require greater transparency and respect for the rule of law and basic human rights, and it created various metrics by which we could assess success. All of the measures used came from third parties to make it clear that the United States was going to be objective and transparent itself in conducting the program. Through funding from a new Millennium Challenge Account, we would "reward countries that have demonstrated real policy change and challenge those that have not, to implement reforms." Ultimately, we would work to protect basic human rights and political and economic freedom so that these countries could "unleash the potential of their people and assure their future prosperity."

The reaction was just as the President, Steve Hadley, and I had hoped. The *Financial Times,* the *Washington Post,* and the *New York Times* all printed full-page articles debating the strategy. John Lewis Gaddis, the eminent Yale historian, called it the most important foreign policy document since NSC-68 of Harry Truman's administration. I have to admit that the academic in me was absolutely thrilled to have produced within the confines of government something viewed as so consequential. The principles in the national security strategy would be reinforced in the 2003 National Strategy for Combating Terrorism, drafted in part by William McRaven, a U.S. Navy officer who worked for me at the NSC and would later lead the Pentagon's Joint Special Operations Command. The world had been waiting to hear how the United States would react to the devastating events of 9/11. The President's speeches and the national security strategy left no doubt: we would be aggressive in confronting threats and assertive in pursuing the United States' national goals and values. This stance was meant to unsettle our foes. Apparently, it succeeded in unsettling many of our friends as well.

Taking on the Proliferation Challenge

THOUGH THE national security strategy addressed a broad range of issues, it was the issue of the proliferation of weapons of mass destruction that attracted most of the attention of the international press and ours as well. We approached the problem on three fronts. First, we needed a way to stop and, where possible, roll back the weapons programs of rogue states. Second, we needed to secure existing weapons as well as nuclear materials in places as diverse as Pakistan and Russia so they would not fall into the hands of terrorists or rogue states. Finally, we needed to defend the United States and our allies should the unthinkable happen.

The effort to secure existing stockpiles was largely without controversy. President Bush was committed to funding the Nunn-Lugar Cooperative Threat Reduction (CTR) Program, which had worked for the last two decades to safeguard and dismantle the large stockpiles of nuclear, chemical, and biological weapons in former Soviet states. After the collapse of the Soviet Union, Belarus, Kazakhstan, Ukraine, and Russia inherited a vast number of weapons stored in facilities that were insecure at best, with some sites protected with little more than a chain-link fence.

Recognizing the threat that those weapons could fall into the hands of terrorists or other hostile actors, Senators Sam Nunn and Richard Lugar led the effort in Congress to establish a program in 1991 that would help successor Soviet states dismantle their stockpiles, develop secure processes for the storage and transfer of the materials, and reduce the threat of proliferation not only of the weapons themselves but also of the scientific knowledge necessary to develop them. President Bush invested heavily in the non-proliferation aspects of Nunn-Lugar, requesting more than $3.2 billion in funding for the CTR Program and other initiatives such as enhanced export and border control programs, recovery of radiological materials, and construction of secure chemical weapons destruction facilities. The administration also oversaw the first expansion of the CTR Program beyond the former Soviet Union by providing assistance to Albania to eliminate its chemical weapons. The United States assisted Pakistan to secure its nuclear arsenal by providing assistance in the early days after 9/11 and by helping share best practices in securing nuclear material.

In addition, President Bush joined with the leaders of the G8 nations in Kananaskis, Canada, in June 2002 to establish the G8 Global Partnership Against the Spread of Weapons and Materials of Mass Destruction. Under what became known as the "10+10 over 10" program, the United States committed to providing $10 billion over ten years to support ongoing threat-reduction efforts in Russia and other former Soviet states and requested the other G8 nations to match the United States' pledge with up to $10 billion collectively to the program. Many other allies would join the partnership at subsequent summits as both recipient and donor nations.

Our emphasis on missile defense was not without controversy, but abrogating the ABM Treaty so that we could develop missile defenses without limitation made the road considerably easier. On June 13, 2002, despite a last-minute congressional attempt to save the agreement, the United States' withdrawal from the ABM Treaty officially went into effect. The Russians reacted calmly, issuing a statement of mild protest.

In January Donald Rumsfeld had restructured the Pentagon bureaucracy to streamline the development and procurement process for missile defense technologies by establishing the Missile Defense Agency. By December the President announced that the United States would begin fielding initial missile defense capabilities that included ground-based and sea-based interceptors as well as detection sensors located on land and sea, in the air, and in space.

By far the most controversial and difficult issues concerned how to check and control the suspected ambitions of North Korea, Iran, and

Iraq to pursue WMD programs. The three states were different both in their levels of development and in the regional implications of their programs.

As noted before, the President had rejected any return to the Agreed Framework with North Korea because he—and all of us—believed it to be flawed. The North Koreans had taken the benefits, including $4.5 billion to build two light-water reactors, but by late 2002 they were once again threatening to expel all nuclear inspectors and restart plutonium-reprocessing facilities at Yongbyon. That was a familiar pattern with the North Koreans. As President Bush put it, "He [Kim Jong-il] throws his food on the floor, and all the adults run to gather it up and put it back on the table. He waits a little while and throws his food on the floor again." It was an apt description, but, given the consequences of conflict on the Korean peninsula, there didn't seem to be many alternatives.

It was in this context that we set about the contentious process of developing a follow-on strategy to the Agreed Framework. The divisions were deep, with State on one side and Defense and the Office of the Vice President on the other. In fact, State suffered from disunity within its own ranks. John Bolton, the newly appointed under secretary for arms control and international security, oversaw the department's bureau that developed proliferation policy. John had been Colin's "neocon hire," in deference to the President's desire to have his administration reflect the full range of opinions in the Republican Party. But John was loyal to his ideological soul mates, not to the secretary of state, and was a constant source of trouble for Colin.

The schism would persist throughout the eight years of the administration. In part this was a structural problem. The secretary of state is the chief diplomat and not surprisingly tries to solve problems diplomatically. Sometimes this involves talking—and taking steps forward—with unsavory regimes, or even enemies, in order to see if there is an overlap of interests. One can hardly negotiate successfully with a regime if one is publicly committed to its destruction. The Vice President and, to a lesser extent, Don Rumsfeld believed that those regimes would never make a deal and that any deal that could be made was not worth having. They made a reasonable case for toughening sanctions and isolation to lay the groundwork for regime change.

Frankly, the President was squarely on the hawks' side of the fence. I too was drawn to the side of unrelenting pressure on those regimes, but I could also see two problems with the approach. First, back in 1994 some people in the Clinton administration had reasoned that the North Korean regime might collapse before the United States actually had to deliver the benefits of the Agreed Framework. It didn't and was as diabolically resilient as ever. If Kim Jong-il had to freeze his people to death in the face of a cutoff of fuel assistance, his view was "So be it." North Korea had plenty of ways to buy, steal, and smuggle what it needed to ensure the relative comfort of the regime and its military. The malnourished, oppressed, and isolated population was unlikely to rise up against the "Dear Leader."

Second, a U.S. policy of complete isolation of North Korea in the service of regime change was not, in the long term, one that others in the region, particularly China and South Korea, would likely abide. In that policy they would see only U.S. intransigence, and pursuing the strategy would create constant tension with those states. Though they might have feared that the United States would use military force, they needn't have worried: the Pentagon wanted no part of armed conflict on the Korean peninsula. We were without a workable policy.

By the beginning of 2002, it was already clear that we needed a new approach. In March, after much debate, we notified Congress that North Korea was not in compliance with the terms of the Agreed Framework because it had failed to make a complete and accurate declaration of its nuclear activities and refused to allow inspections of related facilities. The notification meant an end to the $95 million in foreign assistance to keep the program afloat. At the eleventh hour, the President made a decision to stand by the determination but to grant a waiver so that the $95 million in foreign assistance to the North was not affected. That gave us time to develop a new approach without setting off a firestorm of protest among our allies.

I convened the NSC Principals that April to see where we stood. The North had been blustering ever since the "axis of evil" speech. But unexpectedly, Donald Gregg, a former U.S. ambassador to Seoul under George H. W. Bush, returned from Pyongyang with a message: the North would welcome a U.S. envoy. After raucous debate, Colin won agreement to send Assistant Secretary of State for East Asian and Pacific Affairs James Kelly to Pyongyang. I personally intervened with the President to get his grudging acquiescence. But what would Kelly do once he got there?

Colin advocated a bold approach, as he called it, prescribing engagement through a series of step-by-step moves by each side. His hope was that they'd lead to a different (if somewhat vague) new relationship between the United States and North Korea. Then, as the preparations were under way, a bombshell dropped from the intelligence community. Incomplete but troubling reports linking North Korea to the A. Q. Khan network had emerged. Moreover, Pyongyang had been suspected of seeking the components for uranium enrichment around the globe. Very close to the first anniversary of September 11, John McLaughlin, the deputy director of the CIA, reported the Agency's assessment that North Korea had built a "production-scale" facility for uranium enrichment. Whatever the status of the Agreed Framework in slowing the plutonium program, the North appeared to be pursuing a second means of obtaining a nuclear weapon.

There was an unbridgeable disagreement within the administration about how acute the threat was. Everyone agreed that the North had been cheating, *seriously* cheating, but Colin didn't want to spark a new crisis on the peninsula by confronting the North. He agreed, though, that Kelly's trip could not go forward.

Yet our allies were moving forward with the North. As we were deliberating, Prime Minister Koizumi of Japan visited Pyongyang in an effort to normalize relations between the two adversaries and resolve the crisis over Japan's abducted citizens. In one of the more bizarre revelations in modern international history, the North admitted that it had in fact kidnapped Japanese citizens in the 1970s and '80s to steal their identities and use them to train North Korean spies how to speak Japanese. The issue was deeply emotional for the families of the abducted and for the Japanese people as a whole. Kim's promise to allow the citizens to leave (to this day only partially fulfilled) encouraged Koizumi, though of the thirteen who had been abducted only five were still alive. The Japanese foreign minister, Yoriko Kawaguchi, pressed both Colin and me to send a U.S. delegation to North Korea. Koizumi made the same request of the President a couple of days later in a phone call.

However, with the exception of State, there was little enthusiasm among the NSC Principals for a trip. I felt that we needed to be responsive to the Japanese and South Koreans and that a policy of isolation would go nowhere if it remained unilateral. After Koizumi's call, I stayed behind and talked to the President. "Why don't you just authorize Kelly to go?" I asked. I added that he could take a tough message but that it would help our friends. The President said he would think about it and the next morning told me that we could go ahead. But he wanted the North to understand that we had toughened our stance, not softened it. I did not mention my conversation with him to anyone except Steve Hadley. Before putting the issue of Kelly's trip back onto the table in the NSC, I'd wanted to have a "steer" from the President. I often did this with controversial matters put before the NSC because the likelihood of a good outcome was increased if I knew in advance the limits of the President's tolerance. In this case it was clear that he wouldn't tolerate very much.

After considerable debate, Kelly's trip was rescheduled for October. When a U.S. diplomat is about to engage in sensitive negotiations, the NSC provides a set of talking points to ensure that the discussions are carried on in accordance with the agreed policy. The instructions that State drafted for Kelly were immediately seen as "soft." The Bolton part of State reacted angrily, as did the Vice President's office and the Pentagon. Moreover, the points were considerably more accommodating toward the North than I believed the President would allow.

Steve Hadley took the pen and, together with Michael Green, the director for Asian affairs on the NSC, drafted a much tougher approach. Usually there is enough trust in an experienced negotiator that the guidance is used more as points of reference than as a script. But in this case, given the fissures, the points were to be read verbatim. There were literally stage directions for Kelly. He was not to engage the North Koreans in *any* side conversation in *any* way. That left him actually moving to the corner of the table to avoid Pyongyang's representatives.

Colin was angry about this infringement on his turf and what it said about how the State Department was viewed. We decided, too, that there should be no socializing, and I asked Colin to cancel a scheduled dinner with the North Korean delegation. He did so, unhappily. I'd at least helped get Kelly to Pyongyang, but he and the State Department were on a short leash. I made a mental note that this was no way to treat the secretary of state.

Jim Kelly's trip turned out to be extremely consequential but not for the reasons that we'd expected. Jim had laid out his case, including the indictment on uranium enrichment. Until that program was undone, he stressed, it wasn't possible to move forward. The North Koreans were not prepared for the news that we'd discovered their program and at first denied its existence. But the next day, the first vice foreign minister, Kang Sok-ju, gave a presentation effectively acknowledging our claims.

Jim contacted Colin, saying that everyone in the delegation had heard the same thing. They'd made sure that the native Korean speakers agreed that, in fact, the North Koreans had admitted to having a covert uranium enrichment program. Because his instructions were so constraining, Jim couldn't fully explore what might have been an opening to put the program on the table. He sent a cable to Washington describing the events. It soon leaked. It's clear to me that the hard-liners had leaked the cable to snuff out any hope of further negotiations. They succeeded because the North backpedaled furiously.

In the absence of any movement, the United States had to respond forcefully. We briefed our allies on what we knew and made clear that we would halt further U.S. funding for the fuel shipments promised under the Agreed Framework. Good work by the State Department secured the agreement of our principal partners, South Korea, Japan, and the European Union. On November 18 the last load of fuel to be delivered as part of the Agreed Framework docked at the port of Nampo in North Korea. Three days later, the North Koreans issued a statement blaming the United States for the collapse of the Agreed Framework. The last shred of the framework for dealing with the North Korean problem had been dismantled.

As the end of the year approached, we again returned to the question of a strategy for North Korea. This time Steve Hadley commissioned papers from within the White House staff. Mike Green wrote a paper suggesting that we had to internationalize the conflict and pursue policies principally aimed at bringing allies on board in a common approach. Samantha Ravich, from the Office of the Vice President, proposed that we explicitly announce that regime change was our goal and lay out a set of steps to get there. That was an interesting idea, but it would have had no support internationally and would have scared our already nervous allies even more. Finally, Bob Joseph proposed "tailored containment," aimed at changing the regime's behavior through pressure. At an NSC meeting on November 13, the President, at my urging, supported the third approach.

Before we went down to the Situation Room, however, he told me that he had come to the conclusion that nothing would work without getting China on board. That was clearly right, but at the time, we didn't have a way to enlist the Chinese, and the point just hung in the air. By the end of 2002 the North had blown up any chance for negotiation by announcing in a letter to the IAEA that it was restarting its reactor. The North further declared that its nuclear facilities were not subject to any agreement with the IAEA and were instead a matter between North Korea and the United States. Kim Jong-il had just thrown a big wad of food on the floor. For the time being, we made no effort to pick it up.

The Iranian Challenge

IRAN PRESENTED a different kind of challenge than North Korea. Pyongyang was certainly a threat to our regional interests and more directly to South Korea, but the United States also enjoyed a preponderance of force on the Korean peninsula with which to deter the North. There were certainly dangerous flashes of aggression from Pyongyang. Still, I always believed that Kim Jong-il was crazy but not suicidal. The more likely problem would be the transfer of North Korean nuclear materials and know-how to other rogue states or even terrorists, not an invasion across the 38th parallel. After all, North Korea would sell anything.

On the other hand, Tehran was the poster child for state sponsorship of terrorism in the Middle East and made persistent attempts to shift the balance of power in the region. The regime maintained a network of terrorist groups, including the ever-dangerous Hezbollah, which had the capability to commit terrorist acts anywhere in the world. Based in Lebanon, Hezbollah had made its reach felt as far away as Latin America with attacks in Buenos Aires, Argentina, in the 1990s. George Tenet had referred to the organization as terrorism's "A Team," contrasting it to al Qaeda, which was deadly but not as sophisticated as Hezbollah, literally translated as the "Party of God."

Because the Iranian regime was also Shia, many of our Sunni allies in the Middle East feared Iran's penetration into the region. The Iranians had been known to stir up trouble among the Shia populations in Saudi Arabia, Kuwait, and Bahrain, to name just a few countries. Iran, they believed, wanted to establish a "Shia crescent," uniting those populations across national borders and destroying the integrity of the Sunni-governed states. The "Persian" challenge, as our Sunni friends called it, had to be counterbalanced since it could not be destroyed. Iraq historically served as this buffer, which explains why the United States had backed Saddam in the Iran-Iraq War in a conflict that Baghdad's dictator had actually started.

Furthermore, the United States was for the Iranians the "great Satan," a view reciprocated by Washington since the searing events of the 444-day hostage crisis of 1979–1981. But most of the world, including Europe and Japan, did not share this political antipathy toward Iran. Unlike the isolated North Koreans, every major power maintained embassies in Tehran, and trade between Iran and the rest of the world was robust. Iran's two largest trading partners in 2002, Germany and Japan, were U.S. allies.

Internationally, then, there were fewer alarmist interpretations regarding Iran's nuclear program, and consequently a considerable distance existed between the United States and other countries on what to do about it. The policy line was set quickly and clearly in the Bush administration: *any* nuclear program in Iran was unacceptable. We spent considerable time and energy trying to convince Moscow to abandon the construction of the Bushehr nuclear power plant. The

Russians countered that the Iranians, as signatories to the Nuclear Non-Proliferation Treaty, had a "right" to civil nuclear power. In response to our concerns, they made the plant "proliferation-resistant" by insisting that all of the nuclear fuel would be made in Moscow and shipped to Tehran to run the plant. The spent fuel would then be returned to Russia.

In continuing to insist that there be no nuclear program in Iran, the United States pointed out the obvious: Iran was sitting on huge oil and gas reserves. Why not focus on enhancing its refining capabilities to make use of those holdings? Why instead seek nuclear power? Furthermore, the August 2002 discovery of undisclosed nuclear plants at Natanz and Arak only seemed to strengthen the U.S. case. If they were ostensibly pursuing nuclear technologies for peaceful purposes, why would they have anything to hide?

As troubling as the Iranian program was in 2002, it seemed to be at a relatively early stage of development. It was not that Iran was completely trusted by the international community, but there was so much normal economic and political interaction between Tehran and the rest of the world that, for most of our friends, there was little urgency to intervene. We were pretty lonely in calling out the growing dangers of the Iranian nuclear threat, which did not yet occupy center stage.

12

SADDAM AGAIN

T HAT WAS NOT the case with Saddam Hussein, who had plunged the region into war a second time in 1990 with his invasion of Kuwait. It was well understood that Iraq was systematically violating the ceasefire agreement that it had signed in 1991 and evading the sanctions that had been levied against it. Periodic crises had flared in the intervening years, leading arms inspectors to exit Iraq in 1998 and leaving Saddam's WMD programs unmonitored. Unlike the situation in Iran, the international community had already employed virtually every tool to deal with Saddam—diplomatic isolation, weapons inspections, economic sanctions, travel bans, oil and arms embargoes, military containment through no-fly zones, and even the use of military force (to reverse his aggression against Kuwait in 1991 and to destroy suspected WMD sites in 1998).

Upon taking office in 2001, that was the situation we inherited and tried to address by strengthening the containment of the regime. Those efforts were frustrating and largely unsuccessful. September 11 had diverted our attention from the problem of Saddam, with the President making clear that the immediate problem was the al Qaeda sanctuary in Afghanistan. Now, in the spring of 2002, examining the WMD threat and its nexus with terrorism, the question of what to do about Saddam—who had a record of using chemical weapons against Iranian targets and ethnic minorities within his own population—was on the table again.

The President was becoming deeply concerned about our inability to deal effectively with Iraq. The intelligence picture concerning Saddam's military programs and his intentions was darkening. There were indeed uncertainties about the precise state of Saddam's weapons of mass destruction. But it is rare that policy makers are fortunate enough to have incontrovertible evidence about adversaries' weapons programs. Rogue regimes seeking WMD will try feverishly to evade detection: they will build front companies to trade in illicit goods, ship equipment and materials under false flags, and make inspections—when they consent to them—difficult with cat-and-mouse games that almost always lead to deeply qualified assessments of the state of their programs. Unlike the Soviet Union, which was a declared nuclear weapons state and actually paraded much of its military hardware through Red Square, virtually nothing about rogue regimes' weapons proliferation activities is conducted out in the open. That means intelligence analysis of such covert activities is the art (not the science) of piecing together information and drawing a picture of what is transpiring.

For instance, it takes certain materials and equipment to produce chemical, biological, or nuclear weapons. But many of the materials can also be used for more conventional purposes. The international community was well aware of the problem, which is why restrictions were placed on Iraq's ability to import those so-called dual use items in the 1990s. Saddam violated the prohibitions. So an intelligence report might say that Saddam had established front companies that were purchasing chlorine used in producing nerve agents or high-quality aluminum tubes that could be used in either conventional weapons, such as artillery, or centrifuges for uranium enrichment. There was always the chance that Saddam had large numbers of swimming pools to clean, but that hardly seemed like the most probable explanation for large chlorine purchases.

The next step is to assess whether a country has the capability and know-how to build weapons from these materials. In the case of Saddam, the answer was yes—the scientists who'd produced Iraq's weapons of mass destruction before the first Gulf War were still alive and serving the regime.

Then there is the question of infrastructure, laboratories, warehouses, and production facilities. Because there had been no inspectors in the country since 1998, the United States and others were dependent on maps and satellite imagery to monitor Iraq's construction of complexes in which weapons could be produced. There was no doubt that many new buildings were springing up in places associated with military activities. But of course no one could actually go in and inspect them.

Finally, there is the issue of intent: does a country have an *incentive* to make weapons of mass destruction? The same facts about, say, Japan's capabilities would not lead to the same conclusions. Saddam had produced weapons of mass destruction in the past and used them. His desire for WMD was not a theoretical proposition.

That led the intelligence communities of the United States, Europe, and even Russia to assess that Saddam was skirting the sanctions and likely going down a path to rebuild his weapons of mass destruction. The question was how fast his WMD programs were proceeding and, most important, how soon he would have a nuclear weapons capability. That calculation was influenced by the fact that intelligence failures usually come from *underestimating* the maturity of such programs. In 1949 the Soviet Union exploded a nuclear weapon nearly five years ahead of intelligence estimates. Although the intelligence community had suspected that India was pursuing a nuclear weapons program, decision makers were caught off guard when New Delhi conducted its first nuclear test in 1974. And in 1991, after the first Gulf War, inspectors found an Iraqi nuclear program far more advanced than analysts had believed: Saddam was a little more than a year away from having a crude nuclear device.

The final step in the process of providing an intelligence estimate is for the various agencies (the United States had twelve at that time, seventeen today) to produce a joint assessment called a National Intelligence Estimate (NIE). There are almost always differences among the agencies. Some will be reconciled in the process. Others will be reported as unresolved in the text of the assessment. And some will be noted as dissenting footnotes. The process usually requires months and takes place wholly within the intelligence community; the National Security Council is not involved. The NIE is then delivered to the Congress and the executive branch.

From the time he took office, the President had been receiving, almost daily, increasingly alarming reports about Saddam's progress in reconstituting his weapons of mass destruction program. The director of the CIA, George Tenet, was at the time responsible for providing to the President the collective assessment of the intelligence agencies. George was a tough-talking, cigar-chewing easterner who stated his case compellingly. Even in retrospect I don't think he overstated the evidence; he drew conclusions that pointed clearly toward Saddam's progress in reconstituting his WMD.

The NIE, in October 2002, would sum it up this way: "Iraq has continued its weapons of mass destruction (WMD) programs in defiance of UN resolutions and restrictions. Baghdad has chemical and biological weapons as well as missiles with ranges in excess of UN restrictions; if left unchecked, it probably will have a nuclear weapon during this decade."

The NIE also included an alternative view from the State Department's assistant secretary for intelligence and research (INR) concerning *nuclear weapons*, though State joined the consensus on chemical and biological capabilities. While the INR view recognized Saddam's desire for a nuclear capability, it stated, "The activities we have detected do not, however, add up to a compelling case that Iraq is currently pursuing . . . an integrated and comprehensive approach to acquire nuclear weapons. Iraq may be doing so, but INR considers the available evidence inadequate to support such a judgment. Lacking persuasive evidence that Baghdad has launched a coherent effort to reconstitute its nuclear weapons program, INR is unwilling to speculate that such an effort began soon after the departure of UN inspectors or to project a timeline for the completion of activities it does not now see happening. As a result, INR is unable to predict when Iraq could acquire a nuclear device or weapon."

A policy maker confronted with one assessment that says that Baghdad "could make a nuclear weapon within several months to a year" should it "acquire sufficient fissile material from abroad" and the INR alternative view that could not speak to timing is not likely to take the risks of accepting the latter, particularly after 9/11 and the specter of WMD terrorism.

Saddam was known to support terrorists. He paid the families of Palestinian suicide bombers $25,000 apiece after attacks. He had harbored Abu Abbas, who'd hijacked the *Achille Lauro* and killed a paraplegic American. In the shadow of 9/11, the possibility that Saddam might arm terrorists with chemical or biological weapons or even a nuclear device and set them loose against the United States was very real to us. We'd failed to connect the dots on September 10 and had never imagined the use of civilian airliners as missiles against the World Trade Center and the Pentagon; that an unconstrained Saddam might aid a terrorist in an attack on the United States did not seem far-fetched.

Some observers said that Saddam would never transfer WMD to terrorists out of fear of retaliation should the weapons be traced back to their source. He had, however, established a pattern of recklessness, particularly in failing to anticipate the international community's strong response to his 1990 invasion of Kuwait and his 1993 attempt to assassinate former President George H. W. Bush. When coupling his proclivity toward miscalculation with his past support for terrorist activity, it was not unreasonable to suspect that he might supply extremists with a weapon that could be detonated in an American city. And in any case, it was a chance we were not willing to take.

Certainly, the debate was influenced briefly by the question of whether Saddam had a hand in the September 11 attacks. It was reasonable to ask whether this implacable enemy of the United States had aided and abetted the attack on the Twin Towers. Some suggested that Saddam and al Qaeda were unlikely allies, given the dictator's brutal secularism and his likely fear of bin Laden's ambition to change the status quo in the Middle East. I was never convinced by that argument. There had been too many times in history when the explanation was simply "the enemy of my enemy is my friend." But as the CIA reviewed the evidence, there was simply no convincing case to be made for a link between 9/11 and Saddam.

The Vice President and his staff, however, were absolutely convinced that Saddam was somehow culpable. Given to personally sifting through raw intelligence data (not assessments that have been analyzed, checked for credibility, and integrated with other intelligence, but undigested information coming straight from the field), the Vice President latched on to every report of a meeting between Iraqi agents and al Qaeda affiliates. Many of the reports were of highly questionable origin and reliability—so much so that the CIA felt strongly that there had been no complicity between Saddam and al Qaeda in the 9/11 attacks and said so. But the Vice President's office remained convinced that there had been. At one point the Vice President asked Lewis "Scooter" Libby to present the evidence to the President. That was highly unusual. We sat in the Oval and listened to Scooter, whose eloquence actually made the case sound plausible. But after he was done, much to my relief, the President just said, "You keep on digging."

I stayed behind to make sure that he knew that the presentation had not been vetted with the intelligence agencies. He assured me that he did. The President didn't use any of the reports in a speech, briefing, or private conversation. He believed that the problem was not a connection between Saddam and September 11 but rather a potential link between Iraq's WMD and terrorism going forward.

We began to reconsider our strategy toward Saddam on two separate tracks. The NSC Principals met repeatedly after January 2002 to consider our options: continuing the policy of containment, including establishing smart sanctions and no-fly zones; promoting regime change through expatriates and covert action; enhancing international pressure to get arms inspectors back into Iraq; persuading or pressuring Saddam to give up power; using military force to overthrow him. There was brief consideration of setting up a Kurdish protectorate in the North to pressure the regime from within, but that idea gained little credence. In any case, the prospect of an independent Kurdish political unit within Iraq would have been unacceptable to the Turks, who have tried for decades to calm the restive Kurdish population along their border and dismantle the Kurdistan Workers' Party (PKK) terrorist organization.

The discussion the first few times was inconclusive. Yet no one believed that Saddam would give up power peacefully, and overthrowing him using the mixed bag that was the Iraqi National Congress seemed highly unlikely. We were really down to two options if we wanted to change course: increasing international pressure to make him give up his WMD or overthrowing him by force.

On a separate track, the President had asked Don Rumsfeld to examine U.S. military options. Having witnessed the United States' decision not to push toward Baghdad at the end of the first Gulf War in 1991,

President Bush wanted to understand the feasibility of overthrowing Saddam. The President had also been highly frustrated with the military's lack of readiness prior to the invasion of Afghanistan and sought an early outline of the Iraqi battle plan if it ultimately proved necessary.

Don formally began that work with a secret order to General Tommy Franks on December 1, 2001. Franks farmed out pieces to various parts of the Joint Staff's planning apparatus, trying to prevent all but the highest levels of the Pentagon from knowing what question they were really asking. Tommy Franks gave a preliminary briefing to the NSC via videoconference on December 28. The prospect of a six-month buildup to 400,000 troops sounded daunting, and Tommy noted that he was examining options with a lighter footprint—a way to give U.S. forces a "generated start."

The President was at Camp David in February 2002 after addressing a Republican Congressional Retreat in West Virginia. On the Sunday morning after church, Andy Card and I were standing with him in his office. Iraq was on his mind, and he was wondering how to use the threat of force to compel Saddam to comply with his obligations and destroy his suspected WMD. "All he cares about is staying in power," the President said. "Maybe if he thinks we'll overthrow him, he'll change." I told the President that in political science we called that "coercive diplomacy." He loved the term, and in time the two remaining options—international pressure and military force—would merge into one.

Bringing the Europeans on Board

THE REASSESSMENT of the Iraq strategy proceeded at a steady pace. In April the President and Tony Blair had an extended discussion about Iraq and the need to do something about Saddam. The President was clear that Saddam had to fear the international community if he was ever going to comply. He and Blair found common ground in that assessment, but what about the other allies?

The big event of the late spring was the President's trip to Germany, Russia, and France, and then to Italy for a NATO summit. (NATO summits are convened in a member country or at NATO's headquarters in Brussels as needed.) The trip was memorable for an audience with the Holy Father, Pope John Paul II, and my first trip to the Vatican. I will always remember my Protestant faux pas. When the Holy Father took my hand, I said, "God bless you," and then immediately realized that it should have been the other way around: you don't bless the Holy Father—he blesses you. He simply said, "Thank you."

The trip also included the first time we were treated to the hospitality of Silvio Berlusconi. The dinner took place at the spectacular Villa Madama. The sixteenth-century house overlooks Roman ruins on one side and the Vatican on the other. Standing on the balcony as the sun set on Rome, Andy Card quipped, "I guess the view from the Truman Balcony [at the White House] isn't so great after all."

As we turned to go into a dinner consisting of tricolored pasta and beef and triflavored gelato matching the Italian flag, Berlusconi said, "Be sure to look at the ceiling frescos. They were painted by Raphael."

I turned to Andy and said, "I guess the ceiling in the White House isn't so special either."

But the trip to Russia was the highlight of the journey. As a student of Russia, I found it personally satisfying to ride through the Spassky Gate of the Kremlin in the limousine of the President of the United States. I couldn't help but flash back to my first time on Red Square as a somewhat insecure graduate student in 1979. I would never have dreamed then that I'd end up as the President's national security advisor. I was a little sad that my mom and dad couldn't see that moment.

For the national security advisor, presidential trips are always busy and anxiety-filled. There is just so much to do to bring all of the agencies on board for various initiatives while attending to every detail of the President's visit. But the trip to Moscow was relatively relaxed. We had the "deliverable" (that is, the breakthrough every President is expected to deliver during a major trip abroad), the Treaty Between the United States of America and the Russian Federation on Strategic Offensive Reductions, also known as the Moscow Treaty, which dramatically reduced the offensive arsenals of the two sides. It was quite an accomplishment, coming less than a year after the United States had abrogated the ABM Treaty. Our relations with Russia were calm, even warm. Putin had visited the President at his ranch a few months earlier, and this was a return engagement for two men who enjoyed a certain degree of personal chemistry.

Crawford, Texas, was the President's home, and an invitation to visit it signaled a personal commitment to a relationship with a head of state. That visit had been very successful, even though it had rained buckets upon Putin's arrival. The President was annoyed that the visit to his special place had begun in foul weather. He was even unhappier when Putin, who was staying in the guesthouse, showed up for dinner an hour early. As Putin politely returned to his room, the President turned to Karen Hughes and me and barked, "Somebody forgot to tell Vladimir about the time change." I knew that he meant me and I should have been chagrined. But for some reason I laughed. The thought that a former senior KGB officer somehow couldn't get the time of day right—having failed to set his watch to the time change—struck me as funny. No harm was done, and the dinner was a great success. The next day, when the two men held a press conference before students of Crawford High School, the relationship seemed to be in very good shape indeed.

Putin reciprocated with an agenda of unusually personal activities when we visited him in his hometown of St. Petersburg. There is significant rivalry between Russia's great cities, Moscow and St. Petersburg, inhabitants of the latter considering themselves far more refined than Muscovites. The President was treated to the magnificent cultural sights of the beautiful city that Peter the Great had built along the Neva River. While in the Hermitage, the President's staff was split off from his personal tour. I've been to the Hermitage numerous times, but Russia possesses so much fine art that the rotating exhibits always make the encounter fresh.

This time, though, we were shown one exhibit that I had not seen and will never forget: a life-sized doll of Tsar Peter the Great. The guide explained that the doll was wearing the tsar's real hair. We Westerners who were listening recoiled. "They scalped him?" Apparently so. It might have been the refined side of Russia, but it was still Russia. Several years later I returned to the Hermitage and saw the same exhibit. This time the guide said that the doll was wearing a wig. Perhaps too many guests had found the original explanation unnerving.

That evening Putin and his wife, Lyudmila, the President and Mrs.

Bush, and Sergei Ivanov and I sailed along the Neva to experience "white nights," the stunning phenomenon of bright daylight at midnight due to St. Petersburg's far-north location. During the caviar and champagne dinner, the President asked Putin about an old redbrick building on the other side of the river with the most extraordinary view of the Winter Palace. "That's the prison," Putin answered and went on to explain that he wanted to do something about the horrible conditions there. The President was incredulous. "The prison! You should give that land to a developer and put the prison somewhere outside the city." It was one of the times when you could see that the capitalist impulse was not quite developed in the Russian leadership.

The President then mentioned that he'd seen a ballet barre in Putin's gym in his Moscow dacha. "Yes," Putin replied. "Lyudmila is learning ballet. She is dancing *Swan Lake*. Of course, if I tried to pick her up, I would be a dead swan." It was impolite to laugh at this rather crude reference to his wife's girth. But everyone did laugh, even the embarrassed Lyudmila.

The President used the remainder of the visit abroad to take the temperature of the Europeans concerning Saddam. There was general support for raising the profile of the Iraq problem, and we returned to Washington confident that it was time to do so.

THE YEAR flew by, what with the President's landmark speech on the Middle East in June, preparations for the establishment of a transitional government in Afghanistan, and the continuing assessment of our Iraq strategy. The pace was hectic, and I constantly reminded myself to keep exercising and find occasions to take a little time off. After 9/11, the thirty-plus days in a row of late nights and no break had taken a toll on me. When you're single, you have to be careful not to be drawn into working every waking moment; there are no spouse and children demanding your time and attention. But there are many things that I love to do, and years ago I told myself that I wouldn't become a workaholic. Even if I had very little time, it was important to get away. I particularly enjoyed an occasional Sunday afternoon at the piano.

The spring of 2002 gave me one of the best imaginable reasons to practice. One day in March, my assistant Liz Lineberry had come in to say that Yo-Yo Ma was on the phone and wanted to speak to me. "You mean the cellist?" I asked. "I think so," she answered.

It was indeed the greatest living cellist of our time, and he had a proposition for me. He was receiving the National Medal of the Arts on April 22 and wondered if perhaps we could play something together at the ceremony. We'd met at Stanford several years earlier, when he'd given a concert there. At the time his "Let's play together sometime" comment had seemed to be just a polite throwaway line. But now here he was, asking me, the failed piano major, to play with him. I readily accepted, and after some back-and-forth we decided to perform the second movement of the Brahms *D Minor Violin Sonata,* a piece that cellists often poach for their repertoire.

On the morning of the concert, we met at Constitution Hall to run through the piece. He was wonderful with such an easy manner that I felt very relaxed almost immediately. There were a few rough places in the rehearsal, but after about an hour we felt ready for the 5:30 P.M. performance. I returned to work and went downstairs to chair a 2:00 P.M. meeting. Steve met me at the door. "Do you realize that you're playing with Yo-Yo Ma before the President of the United States and two thousand people in a few hours?" he asked. "Yes, but first I have to chair this meeting," I said. "Then I'll go to another place in my head and get ready."

The performance went very well. The President was beaming as he congratulated us after we finished. It was one of the most memorable days of my life. I'd come full circle and back to music. But I wasn't confused about what my real destiny was. I would never have played with Yo-Yo Ma had I stayed in music. He played with me because I was the national security advisor who could also play the piano. I had made a good decision when I changed my college major.

The experience was so enjoyable that I resolved to get more deeply into music again. Within a few months, I formed my own piano quintet. Robert Battey, Soye Kim, Lawrence Wallace, and Joshua Klein would become good friends and my "sanity" crew through the difficult times ahead. Bob, the cellist, and Soye, the first violinist, were practicing lawyers who had been professional musicians. Soye was a graduate of Juilliard, and Bob had been a professor of music at the University of Missouri at Kansas City. Bob still occasionally played with the Washington National Opera Orchestra and was our "player-coach." Larry, our violist, was a retired deputy solicitor general of the United States; he had tried more cases before the Supreme Court than anyone else in the twentieth century and still played the viola and violin professionally. Josh, the second violinist, was a Stanford Law grad who was Sandra Day O'Connor's clerk and, like me, a good amateur who had never played professionally.

I had met the members of the group when a friend, the former Stanford Law School Dean Paul Brest, visited me in Washington. Paul and I had been a part of a string quintet in Palo Alto, and he wanted me to keep playing. His introduction worked. The group stayed together after that first session with Paul. They were high-quality musicians, and with them I rediscovered the joys of making music. We even managed to play concerts, including one at the British Embassy with none other than my friend the acclaimed pianist Van Cliburn in the audience, and the *New York Times* music critic Anthony Tommasini did a profile of us in 2006. Playing was not an escape—it came with its own stresses—but it was transporting, a total immersion in the part of me that occasionally demanded attention and nourishment.

A Dangerous Cocktail

THROUGHOUT THE SPRING of 2002, we searched for a viable option concerning Saddam Hussein. The Principals were briefed again on the evolving military plan on May 10, and in the State Department, Colin launched the Future of Iraq Project, which researched and assessed various postwar reconstruction issues that the United States would confront after Saddam's reign ended. The project joined dozens of Iraqi exiles with public administration experts, and together they formed working groups on topics such as health, finance, water, and agriculture. There was a sense of urgency to do something about Iraq, but we wanted to get it right.

In the middle of these preparations we learned that Abu Musab al-Zarqawi, a terrorist affiliated with al Qaeda, was operating a lab in the

Zagros Mountains in northern Iraq. Zarqawi and his affiliates joined ranks with Ansar al-Islam, a Kurdish terrorist organization seeking to produce WMD. The briefing read, "Al-Zarqawi has been directing efforts to smuggle an unspecified chemical material originating in northern Iraq into the United States." There was some concern that Zarqawi and Ansar al-Islam were conducting unconventional weapons work, testing cyanide gas and toxic poisons on animals and even their own associates.

The President's advisors were split on what to do. The Vice President and Don favored military action, perhaps air strikes followed by "exploitation," meaning gathering up evidence at the site after the strike. Colin believed that military action would destroy any chance of building an international coalition to confront Saddam. After one key meeting in mid-June, I followed the President into the Oval Office and told him that I agreed with Colin. I also asked him if he was comfortable with the military option that had been presented to him. Were we really going to put "boots on the ground" after a strike to "exploit" territory inside Iraq—even Kurdish-controlled territory? What would the Turks think? I was relieved to learn that the President had the same reservations. He decided to wait and let the larger Iraq strategy play out over the following months. But the incident was a reminder to all of us that terrorism, WMD, and Iraq were a dangerous cocktail.

As the military planning progressed, Don and Tommy had to broaden the circle of those "in the know" about the effort to update military options for Iraq. With the "axis of evil" rhetoric in people's minds and our already established reputation for aggressive policies, those activities leaked into the press as the "march toward war."

All manner of people were opining about the risks of war—economic, political, regional, and domestic. But when Brent Scowcroft entered the fray with an opinion column arguing against war in the *Wall Street Journal* on August 15, the debate took on a different coloration. Brent was thought by many to be speaking as a surrogate for the President's father, who had, of course, in the first Gulf War, decided not to try to overthrow Saddam. I was known to be close to Brent, and some wondered whether he was speaking for me too. I found this particularly bizarre since I could, of course, speak for myself and enjoyed the President's confidence.

The morning that Brent's op-ed appeared, the President called me immediately upon opening his newspaper. It seemed early since I was on personal leave. "What is he doing?" he exclaimed.

I said that Brent was just extremely cautious on these matters but that I would call him.

"When are you going back to Washington?" he asked.

"Today," I answered.

"And when are you coming to Crawford?"

"Tomorrow," I answered. "But I'll call Brent right now."

When I later met with Brent, I explained to him that we were working through the issue of Iraq systematically and carefully. I told him that the day before his op-ed was published the Principals Committee had approved a National Security Presidential Directive on our goals and objectives for U.S. strategy. There was no rush to war, but the President felt that he could not leave the Iraq issues unaddressed. I also explained that the President had felt blindsided by the *WSJ* column. I asked him why he hadn't called me to express his views or even asked to see the President. Brent was flummoxed by the whole uproar and said that he'd never meant to criticize the President or put him into a box. He was just expressing his perspective and thought it might be helpful to calm down some of the war talk.

I fully believe to this day that Brent was being completely honest about his motives. But several more times the same thing happened, and each time the level of trust between the President and Brent plummeted until there was nothing left. It was a rift that extended to my own relationship with Brent, one of my most important and revered mentors. We've worked over the years to repair the damage and we remain very close friends.

BEFORE LEAVING for Crawford, I took advantage of an interview with the BBC to say that there was a moral case and a national security argument for overthrowing Saddam. "We certainly do not have the luxury of doing nothing," I said. That was taken as more evidence that the President was building his case for war.

Against that backdrop, the NSC met on August 16, and Colin

argued that we should go to the United Nations in September. There was unanimous agreement that our new strategy should be launched at the United Nations, but we did not decide the question of what the President would say.

Then, on September 7, the President met with the NSC Principals again and solicited their views. The Vice President and Don argued that there had already been many chances for Saddam to come clean and that there should be an ultimatum of thirty to sixty days and then the United States should remove him by force if he did not comply. The Vice President argued that with the gathering evidence that Saddam was reconstituting his WMD, there wasn't time for another resolution and more inspections. Colin pushed for a resolution, saying that it was the only way to get the allies to join and to gather support to execute the military plan if our "coercive diplomacy" failed.

It was the culmination of a debate that had been playing out over the summer, and the President knew going into the meeting where the Principals stood. In fact, in August the Vice President had publicly stated his case in a speech to the VFW. That had led the President to feel that he was being boxed in. "Call Dick and tell him I haven't made a decision," he told me. I went back to the Governor's House, a separate dwelling on the property where I stayed at the ranch. Once I had the Vice President on the phone, I said, "The President is concerned that your speech is being read as a decision to skip the UN and challenge Saddam unilaterally." The Vice President immediately responded that it hadn't been his intention to limit the President's options. He asked that I call Scooter Libby and give him the exact language to use in a second speech scheduled for a few days later. The Vice President read the text verbatim.

After listening to everyone at the September NSC meeting, the President said that he'd decided to seek a resolution. That would clear up any ambiguity about where the international community stood. He wanted to make the case in an upcoming speech to the UN General Assembly.

The President had decided on a policy of coercive diplomacy. He would give Saddam a chance to respond to the united pressure of the international community, and the buildup of U.S. forces would make that pressure credible. The next several months would be devoted to that effort. The reputation of the United States would be at stake. One way or another, the threat of Saddam Hussein's Iraq would finally be removed.

Some people have claimed that the President never asked his advisors whether he should go to war against Saddam. At that September meeting, with the Vice President, the secretary of state, the secretary of defense, the chairman of the Joint Chiefs of Staff, the director of Central Intelligence, and the national security advisor in attendance, the National Security Council, after a full and frank discussion, decided on a course of action. Everyone in that room heard the President say, "Either he will come clean about his weapons, or there will be war." There was no disagreement. The way ahead could not have been clearer.

A Different Kind of Crisis

AS THE IRAQ STRATEGY was unfolding, I found myself dealing daily with economic chaos in Latin America. Though what confronted us there was not war and peace, at times it felt like it, especially in Argentina, where the presidency had changed hands four times in less than two weeks before January 1, 2002. In the midst of violent riots throughout Buenos Aires, President Fernando de la Rúa resigned and fled the Casa Rosada by helicopter, triggering a turbulent succession process. Days later, the Republic of Argentina officially defaulted on its sovereign debt.

When I had arrived in Washington the year before, Argentina had been mired in a perilous public debt cycle that had grown worse in the 1990s and was ballooning out of control. IMF loans were absorbed without stimulating even short-term benefits, creative debt-restructuring programs continually postponed repayment, and the Argentine peso, pegged to the U.S. dollar, was depreciating. Washington is full of academics turned policymakers, which was nice for me, since I often got to work with old friends from Stanford. When I asked my Stanford friend Anne Krueger, a highly regarded economist who was then first deputy managing director of the IMF, what on earth was going on in Argentina, she aptly compared the country's embattled finance minister to Sisyphus: "Every time he pushes the stone up, it goes down a bit further in the wrong direction!"

The crisis posed serious risks to other fragile economies in the region. One might ask why this was an issue for the national security advisor since the President obviously had senior economic counselors. Well, the National Economic Council simply lacked the clout of the long-established NSC; my economic counterparts, Larry Lindsey and later Stephen Friedman, agreed that we should jointly convene the interagency process for resolution of these issues.

There were so many overlapping concerns that it was hard to separate foreign policy and economic considerations in any case. Was the United States willing to take the lead, through the IMF, in what amounted to a bailout of another country? Though the State Department was inclined to support a lending plan in order to mitigate the diplomatic fallout and back the President's efforts to establish a free-trade zone in the Western Hemisphere, Treasury and the IMF were reluctant to do anything more. After all, Argentina had already eaten up $22 billion of aid with little to show in the way of reform. Profligate spending and corruption plagued the Argentine government. And what about all the other countries in dire need, such as Brazil and Turkey?

I found myself in endless phone calls and meetings, trying to broker a reasonable solution. The process was still going back and forth, but Spanish Prime Minister Aznar's personal appeal to the President turned the tide at the close. "The President really wants to support Argentina," I told Anne when we met for dinner. "The U.S. can't be party to a default. We need you to find an arrangement with the Argentine government." The decision was unpopular among some in the administration as well as in the IMF. Still, Argentina got its deal. Though the Néstor Kirchner government showed no gratitude for what we had done, the Argentine economy improved with five consecutive years of positive GDP growth after the crisis.

13

CONFRONTING THE INTERNATIONAL
COMMUNITY WITH A CHOICE

As WE PREPARED the President's speech to the United Nations, we were mindful of two requirements. The first was that the President wanted to remind his audience of the dangers of Saddam's regime and of its long history of defying international opinion. The language of the speech was thus appropriately uncompromising and tough but broke no new ground.

The second purpose of the speech was to put the world on notice that the United States would act—alone if necessary—to deal with the threat. "We will work with the UN Security Council for the necessary resolutions," the President said before the General Assembly. "But the purposes of the United States should not be doubted. The Security Council resolutions will be enforced—the just demands of peace and security will be met—or action will be unavoidable. And a regime that has lost its legitimacy will also lose its power."

We had to be aware of the need to address various audiences. This is an enduring problem for policy makers; a message meant to rally and reassure allies that you will be firm but prudent has to simultaneously strike fear into your adversary. The same words need to be heard differently by different listeners. It isn't an easy balance to find.

Sitting in the UN chamber, Colin and I realized about halfway through the President's speech that there had been an editing error. The President was supposed to call for a *new* resolution; that had been the whole debate inside the administration. Somehow it had been left out. How could we get word to him on the podium? Fortunately, we didn't have to. The President had been deeply involved in the debate about the resolution. He immediately noticed the omission and ad-libbed a line that put the fate of Saddam into the hands of the UN Security Council.

A week before the UN speech, the President sought authorization from Congress for military action against Saddam. There had been a spirited debate inside the White House as to whether it was wise to go to the United Nations first or to Congress. The President decided that our hand would be strengthened with the international community and with Saddam if Congress had already approved the use of military force. That was very much in line with his belief that Saddam would finally comply with his obligations only if he believed that this time he had no choice.

Coercive diplomacy requires the simultaneous conduct of military preparations and diplomatic engagement, and the success of the latter is dependent on the intensity of the former. But the required choreography is complex and rife with contradictions. The mobilization of the military has a certain rhythm and inexorable movement forward, and it cannot be sustained indefinitely. On the other hand, the pace of diplomacy is uncertain and erratic, and it is rarely clear whether or not the desired breakthrough is going to be achieved.

Colin launched the negotiations for a new United Nations Security Council Resolution (UNSCR) almost immediately after the address to the General Assembly. Within days Resolution 1441 was predictably bogged down in haggling over its exact wording. There were arguments over who would carry out the inspections, what the inspectors would be allowed to challenge, how often there would be reports to the Security Council, and so on. Not surprisingly, the biggest bone of contention was what was meant when Saddam was threatened with "serious consequences," a phrase that is often understood to mean the use of force if necessary if he failed to comply. The United States and Great Britain wanted to make the resolution the only necessary step before action could be taken. The French and the Russians insisted on language that left open the need for a second resolution.

It took more than six weeks to resolve those issues, but when the resolution finally passed it did so unanimously. That was a triumph for U.S. diplomacy, for John Negroponte, our ambassador to the United Nations, and for Colin Powell. I felt good about it too because I'd run interference for State in the process, taking up practically every controversy directly with the President rather than allowing continued haggling among the various agencies. I know that caused some unhappiness in Defense and within the Office of the Vice President, but the process was taking long enough at the United Nations; we didn't need to slow it down with divisions within our own ranks.

Once the resolution was passed, events moved rather quickly—at least by UN standards. Iraq was given one month, until December 7, 2002, to make a full and accurate declaration of the state of its weapons programs and to receive international weapons inspectors to begin the process of verifying the declaration's claims.

The truth is, though, the clock was ticking. We were trying to do three things simultaneously: assess the progress of the weapons inspectors; refine military plans and begin the mobilization of our forces to pressure Saddam; and plan for a postwar, post-Saddam Iraq should diplomacy fail.

The job of monitoring the progress of the inspections fell largely to me. I established a relationship with both Hans Blix, the Swedish diplomat who oversaw the effort, and Mohamed ElBaradei, the director general of the International Atomic Energy Agency (IAEA), who had responsibility for the nuclear component of the inspections regime. The Pentagon and the White House regarded both men with deep suspicion. I therefore took responsibility for reassuring the President that Saddam was not being allowed to cut corners.

I was pleasantly surprised to find Blix to be honest and pretty tough. He would later, like many others, become a critic of the war and claim that we hadn't given him enough time to complete his inspections. But in our two key conversations, at the United Nations in January and in Washington in February, he was extremely skeptical of Saddam's veracity. His report to the UNSC on January 27 was telling: "Iraq appears not to have come to a genuine acceptance, not even today, of the disarmament which was demanded of it and which it needs to carry out to win the confidence of the world and to live in peace." The second report, on February 14, was more ambiguous. I know that he'd received significant criticism from the Europeans, who believed that his first presentation had given the United States a pretext for war.

ElBaradei and I established a reasonably good relationship as well. He told me that he did not believe that Saddam had reconstituted his nuclear program. I reported this to the President, but the fact that the IAEA had been wrong in 1991 made it difficult to accept the assessment at face value.

By the beginning of 2003 I was convinced that we would have to use military force. Saddam seemed to be playing games with the inspectors, refusing interviews with his scientists or sending "minders" along with them for their meetings with the inspectors. That was what passed for cooperation, and it seemed to be producing minimal information. Nonetheless, UN inspectors did, despite the limitations, gather evidence that Iraqi officials were moving various items and hiding them at suspect sites prior to inspection visits. The Iraqi dictator seemed to be up to his old tricks.

I frankly couldn't understand it. Maybe he just didn't believe us. In 1990 he had underestimated the world's reaction and invaded Kuwait. I was in the White House when Operation Desert Storm was launched in 1991 and helped manage the run-up to the invasion. It had been remarkable to watch Saddam, with U.S. and coalition forces sitting on his doorstep, refuse to withdraw from Kuwait despite the warnings from his friends, including the Russians, who told him that his days were numbered. In 1991 he had been either stubborn or delusional, and it seemed to me that he had not changed.

Still, the question of how to get Saddam out short of war was constantly on my mind and the President's. We reached out to Arab leaders, asking them to tell him that we would indeed overthrow him if he didn't comply. The Egyptians claimed at one point that Saddam's son had sent a message: Saddam would leave in exchange for one billion dollars. The President sent word that we would gladly pay. Nothing came of it. Frankly, I'm not sure it would have been a good idea to pay the dictator to leave. What kind of precedent would that have set? But sometimes you face unpalatable choices. That was not the first time the international community had faced the tension between bringing a murderous tyrant to justice and offering him exile to avoid violence and war. In this case, the President was prepared to opt for the latter.

A few weeks before the President's UN speech, I was visited by Charles Boyd, a retired air force general who had previously been in the employment of the Council on Foreign Relations. He had a novel idea:

perhaps the United Nations could authorize armed inspections of Iraq, giving them more credibility with Saddam's henchmen. The very sight of the humiliation of the Iraqi dictator might also lead someone, maybe even the army, to overthrow him. The President was attracted to the idea, and so was I. But we could never figure out how to make it work. What would armed inspectors do, shoot their way into restricted sites? What if Saddam's guards fired back? Moreover, it is hard to imagine the Russians and French agreeing to what they would have undoubtedly seen as a violation of Iraqi sovereignty. The idea didn't get to first base with the NSC Principals either. When I raised it at a Camp David meeting a few weeks before the war, Colin, Don, and the Vice President were united in their disdain for the concept.

The fact is, we invaded Iraq because we believed we had run out of other options. The sanctions were not working, the inspections were unsatisfactory, and we could not get Saddam to leave by other means. The President did not want to go to war. We had come to the conclusion that it was time to deal with Saddam and believed that the world would be better off with the dictator out of power. We thought that there was a small chance that Saddam without his WMD, disarmed before the world, might not last long. He ruled through fear and cunning. Stripped of that he couldn't survive, and if UN action could achieve that result, all the better. His ouster would give us time, having dealt with the WMD threat, to advocate for further steps such as a transition to elections.

Moreover, we did not go to Iraq to bring democracy any more than Roosevelt went to war against Hitler to democratize Germany, though that became American policy once the Nazis were defeated. We went to war because we saw a threat to our national security and that of our allies. But if we *did* have to overthrow Saddam, the United States had to have a view of what would come next. When the NSC had that discussion, some members, including Don, argued that we had no such obligation. If a strongman emerged, so be it. But the President believed that the use of U.S. military power had to be followed by an affirmation of the United States' principles. If war occurred, we would try to build a democratic Iraq. And democracy in the Arab heartland would in turn help democratize the Middle East and address the freedom gap that was the source of hopelessness and terrorism.

Preparing for War

AS THE INSPECTIONS dragged on, the military component of the strategy was gaining momentum. To carry out Tommy Franks's plan, Don was putting the lead elements of an invasion into place—moving equipment and supplies to forward bases, for example. Military forces also had to be mobilized and troops called up. That is usually done in neat packages, with the troops and their equipment moving together. But Don, sensitive to the President's concern that the military preparations not outstrip the pace of diplomacy, deliberately delinked those elements and tried to slow everything down. That was frustrating to the uniformed military but was one of the requirements of coercive diplomacy.

The NSC Principals reviewed the military plan at least once a week during the run-up to the war. Several questions arose in the discussions. We were worried about Saddam's potential use of WMD against our troops or, again, against his own people. That led the coalition to take extraordinary measures, including the deployment of specialized chemical warfare teams from the Czech Republic, Poland, Slovakia, and Ukraine. The Warsaw Pact had been better prepared against battlefield WMD than had NATO, a fact about which I had written as a young East Europeanist. There were always debates about the reason for that, some suggesting that it was because the Soviet military intended to initiate the use of their vastly larger store of the nasty weapons. Whatever the explanation, we had inherited the superior capabilities to protect against WMD when the former Warsaw Pact states had joined NATO. Now those assets would be very useful.

We were also concerned that Saddam and his forces might just withdraw to Baghdad (we called this the "Fortress Baghdad scenario"), leaving us to launch a bloody assault on a heavily civilian area. Don raised and we discussed the possibility of retribution killings and ethnic violence as the Shia turned on the Sunnis, who despite their minority status had held the power and most of the wealth of the country. That was one reason we hoped to bring along a multiethnic interim authority as quickly as possible.

But I was most concerned about what seemed to be the Pentagon's insufficient attention to two issues: first, plans for the North and the volatile Turkish/Kurdish mix, and second, the requirements of what we called "rear-area security." Who would be responsible for maintaining order as coalition forces pushed through against Saddam's military forces?

I was able to get the first of these issues addressed by going to the President with my concerns. We were having all kinds of problems with the Turks, who had initially agreed to let our forces transit through their territory but eventually refused to do so. That meant we had no northern entry into the country. After one of the briefings in the Situation Room, I followed the President into the Oval. I sat on the sofa to the right of the wing chair in which the President sat. The Vice President was on the other side. George Tenet was present too. "Mr. President," I said, "you don't have a northern strategy, and the Pentagon owes you one." The Vice President immediately objected, letting it be known that the President should trust Don and the generals to do the military planning. I held my ground, though, and the President raised the issue with Don in his next meeting.

The plan wasn't perfect by any means. Franks concluded that he could send the 4th Infantry Division through Kuwait if necessary but would, at the outset of the war, leave them on their transit ships in the north. That would give us a contingency force if there was trouble on the Turkish-Kurdish border or if Saddam's forces tried to turn north. Because the Turkish government ultimately denied us permission to pass the 4th Infantry Division through its territory, around one thousand paratroopers from the 173rd Airborne Brigade dropped into the North.

On the issue of rear-area security, though, I failed to get a workable plan for the President. That turned out to be a big problem in the days immediately following Saddam's overthrow. As our forces pushed through, chaos ensued behind them. Neither we nor the British had enough troops to keep order.

My several attempts to get the Pentagon to address the rear-area security issue seriously always led to uninformative slides and a rather dismissive handling of the question. When I finally arranged a briefing on the issue before the President in early February, he started the meeting in a way that completely destroyed any chance of getting an answer.

"This is something Condi has wanted to talk about," he said. I could immediately see that the generals no longer thought it to be a serious question. That is the weakness of the national security advisor's position: Authority comes from the President. If he wasn't interested in this issue, why should they care?

Steve Hadley followed me to my office after the disastrous meeting. "I would have resigned after that comment by the President," he said.

"No," I replied. "I'll talk to the President, but we'll just have to keep hammering away at the issue." We did, knowing that the President would eventually share our concern and want the matter dealt with. He started to ask the question about rear-area security himself. The Pentagon briefed him several more times, but it always resulted in the same answer: "We've got this covered." Maybe Defense thought it did. But this was an early indication that the military's Phase IV (post-invasion) plans were lacking. As the importance of the issue was revealed in the days after the war, I wondered if Steve had been right.

After Saddam

ON THE OTHER HAND, I felt confident about our postwar planning on the civilian side. There were several contingencies that we just didn't anticipate. But the idea that we did not take the postwar situation seriously is patently false. We examined war termination procedures, humanitarian issues, and reconstruction and political arrangements, producing hundreds of documents and almost as many meetings to review them.

Elliott Abrams of the NSC staff was charged with developing a plan for humanitarian relief with a careful ministry-by-ministry assessment of Iraq's capabilities to deliver goods to the population. The group was concerned that there could be up to two million displaced Iraqis, and plans were made to engage UN agencies to handle the load.

In August I asked Frank Miller, the senior director for defense programs, to coordinate postwar planning efforts across the government. Frank was an experienced and respected civilian who had served in the Pentagon for twenty-two years. I had first gotten to know him in 1986, when he was working in the Office of the Secretary of Defense and I was serving on the Joint Staff. Careful and earnest, he was a stickler for details and had a network of contacts and sources within the Pentagon.

That was crucial because responsibility for the execution of Phase IV would come to rest within the Defense Department. The decision to give unambiguous authority to the Defense Department would turn out to be one of the most consequential that the President and his advisors took—and it was not particularly controversial within the administration at the time.

The President wanted the United States to take the lead in the aftermath of the war. We considered two other options. The first was to let the United Nations and its various agencies lead the effort. But the President had been to Kosovo in 2001 and been appalled by the lethargic UN presence more than two years after the war had ended. The head of the mission, who frankly couldn't have looked more disinterested in the discussion, had told us that the economy was starting to perform but unemployment was still rampant at more than 55 percent. On the flight back the President had opined that Kosovo seemed to be where European governments sent their washed-up diplomats rather than their best and brightest. I couldn't disagree.

The second alternative for coordinating the war's aftermath would be to follow the model of the postwar effort in Afghanistan. There we had used an "adopt a ministry" plan, with allied governments taking responsibility for various functions: the Germans had the police, the Italians had the Justice Ministry, we had the army, and so on. That was already breeding conflict and incoherence, and no one wanted to repeat that approach.

Moreover, with large numbers of U.S. troops on the ground, the President wanted one authority with full responsibility; that would be the Defense Department. No one challenged this assumption, most especially not the State Department. Colin had said that there was a reason that Douglas MacArthur hadn't been a Foreign Service officer. The department was too small and was ill suited to oversee a complex operation in the middle of a war zone. Colin, for his part, wanted to make sure that State had an appropriate but supporting role. The President signaled in mid-October that the Defense Department would be the lead agency responsible for postwar planning in the immediate aftermath of the invasion, should one be necessary. This would be formalized in a National Security Presidential Directive (NSPD) that officially established an office in the Pentagon to coordinate these efforts.

On December 18, having watched the inspectors play cat and mouse with the Iraqi government, the President told Don to jump-start the civil administration office that would help manage postwar Iraq. When I mentioned to the President the need to ensure coordination from Washington, he agreed but said I needed to use a "light touch." He believed that once the Pentagon was given the authority on the ground, it had to be free to act.

But he didn't mean that it should do so in the high-handed, dismissive way that emerged. Almost immediately the under secretary of defense for policy, Douglas Feith, made clear that the Pentagon neither needed nor welcomed the opinions of others. He treated Franks's Executive Steering Group as a nuisance and the NSC Deputies Committee with only slightly more respect. At one point, Steve Hadley asked Doug if he realized that the President had given Don the Iraq ball and with it the future of his presidency. "Not only does he know it," Doug intoned, "he welcomes it."

Defense produced a lot of preparatory work, going so far as to issue a document called "Parade of Horribles," which presented twenty-nine catastrophes that the war in Iraq might unleash. We asked the intelligence agencies to examine the likelihood of potential disasters. Most of the points on the list were self-evident, such as possible sectarian violence and Iranian support for our enemies in Iraq, though I suspected that the Defense Department's motive was really to issue a documented warning just in case the whole endeavor failed. In any case, there were no implementation plans to address the conclusions.

On January 20, the President signed NSPD-24 that formally created the postwar planning machinery for postwar Iraq, including the Office of Reconstruction and Humanitarian Assistance (ORHA). The NSPD outlined nine tasks for ORHA to address, including humanitarian relief assistance, the reestablishment of key civilian services, the restructuring of the Iraqi military, and a variety of other political and economic issues. Retired General Jay Garner was put in charge of ORHA. He seemed the perfect choice, since he had overseen the successful implementation of Operation Provide Comfort in support of humanitarian relief for the Kurds after Saddam's attack on them in 1991. Jay Garner briefed the NSC after a "rock drill" (an exercise to simulate various contingencies) his office conducted with representatives of the military and civilian agencies that were to be involved in the administration of Iraq. The drill uncovered a number of problems, which were then sent back to the agencies for review and resolution.

All those plans were reviewed at the Principals Committee meetings on March 1 and March 7. At a full National Security Council meeting on March 10, Doug Feith briefed the President on a political plan to transfer governance to an Iraqi Interim Authority (IIA) composed of Iraqi exiles and Kurdish leaders. The interim authority, which would be charged with developing a constitution for the country and organizing the country's permanent elections, was designed to be representative of Iraq's Shia and Sunni sects. There were differing views about how long the transfer of authority and governance to the Iraqis would take. Defense, which was more willing to rely on exiles, believed that the United States would not have to bear responsibility for managing the country very long. State was less optimistic about the ability of the Iraqis to govern the country and concerned about too heavy a reliance on people who had not lived in Iraq for decades.

President Bush resolved the differences among his advisors by making clear that he wanted some government ministries placed under Iraqi control as soon as possible. But he also worried that placing Iraqi expatriates at the highest levels of government might stir resentment among locals who had suffered under Saddam's rule. The power dynamics of the country had likely shifted since those exiles had fled, he reasoned, preventing them from having any natural domestic constituencies that would align behind them and potentially denying the interim administration the legitimacy it needed. The President nevertheless agreed to the Iraqi Interim Authority framework on the condition that internals were "fully represented." The IIA was meant to cooperate with the U.S.-led military coalition in carrying out political and military tasks. Iraqis would take as much responsibility as they could demonstrate the ability to take.

Another challenge confronting us was how to restructure the institutions of a multiethnic Iraq to enfranchise and protect populations that had been suppressed under Saddam's regime without alienating those who had previously benefited from his rule. Frank Miller briefed the President on our plan for de-Baathification, a process designed to purge the government of Saddam's loyalists without crippling basic services necessary to keep the state running. Although Saddam's Baath Party had approximately 1.5 million associated members and supporters, Miller estimated that only 1 to 2 percent—or about 25,000—were "active and full" members who constituted the party elite. He argued that those full members should be removed from government posts and all positions of power and influence. The country had 2 million government employees, including military and police, and the de-Baathification process, as we conceived it, would eliminate only approximately 1 percent of them; as Frank put it, it "will not leave the public institutions without leadership."

Rounding out the meeting, Treasury Secretary John Snow outlined a plan for a new currency in Iraq to replace the two official ones that were now in place, a Swiss dinar in the north and a Saddam dinar in the south. John advocated the temporary use of the U.S. dollar as a stable replacement in the interim, and President Bush approved the plan. (By mid-October 2003, new Iraqi dinar banknotes were available and the U.S. dollar was phased out.)

Two days later, on March 12, Feith briefed the President on ORHA's postwar plans for the Iraqi military and intelligence services. It was clear that, like the existing government institutions, the country's security apparatus needed to be purged of its politicized elements and Saddam loyalists who had committed atrocities on behalf of his regime. The Defense Department planned to completely dismantle Iraq's paramilitary forces, including the Baath Party Militia, the Jaysh al-Tahrir al-Quds ("Jerusalem Liberation Army"), and Fedayeen Saddam ("Saddam's Martyrs"). He said that Iraq's entire intelligence service needed to be demobilized and consolidated and that Iraq's Republican Guard would be completely disarmed, detained, and dismantled, with some of its members prosecuted for war crimes, given its heinous record of abuse.

Regarding the regular standing Iraqi army, the plan presented to the President on March 12 did not call for its full dismantling but actually the retention and reintegration of some of its elements into Iraqi society. To be sure, Iraqi society needed to be demilitarized, with the armed forces subordinated to civilian control. The army was plagued by sectarian prejudices between Sunni senior officers and Shi'a conscripts. But the advantages of preserving some elements of the Iraqi military were its assets: a formal chain of command, trained personnel, and sophisticated infrastructure. Furthermore, it was clear that we would not be able to immediately demobilize 250,000 to 300,000 military personnel. No one wanted desperate, once armed, now-unemployed young men out in the streets.

The plan put before the President therefore called for the preservation of three to five army divisions that would form the "nucleus" of a new Iraqi army. Elements of the Iraqi army would be permitted to retain their current status in assembly areas and permanent garrisons. Those troops would be used as a national reconstruction force that would have the dual benefit of training and identifying new military leadership and rebuilding the country that they would work to protect.

Finally, together with Tom Ridge, the NSC developed a plan for security here at home just in case terrorist groups believed that there was a window of vulnerability during the war. That would likely never have been a consideration before 9/11, but the world had changed.

In short, we needed to get ready because the President was increasingly convinced that Saddam had blown his last chance. Now it was a matter of explaining to the American people and the rest of the world that "serious consequences" had to have meaning.

The Case for Action

THE PRESENTATION of the case against Saddam had three elements. First, we would review his transgressions against the international community and against his own people. Saddam had signed a ceasefire agreement in 1991 and was systematically violating every aspect of it. Second, we would inform the world of what we knew about his continuing pursuit of weapons of mass destruction, his support for terrorism, and his oppression of his own people. Finally, we would paint a picture of the dangers inherent in failing to address the decade-old threat of Saddam Hussein.

The President had begun this effort at the UN, but there was much more to say. The entire NSC team spoke to the issue in television appearances and print interviews. The "Sunday shows"—*Meet the Press, Fox News Sunday, Face the Nation, ABC This Week,* and *CNN Late Edition*—were particularly important venues. The audiences of those shows are not huge (*Meet the Press* is the largest, with only a few million viewers), but they're influential among policy elites and often drive the Monday headlines.

When I became national security advisor, I had planned to follow Brent Scowcroft's example and keep a low profile, deferring to the cabinet secretaries for public appearances. After September 11, though, I was pressed into action in large part because I could be a reliable surrogate for the President. In the run-up to the Iraq war, that became even more the case. Between September and March, I appeared on twelve Sunday shows.

I didn't mind doing the press interviews, though the appearances tended to ruin any remaining semblance of a weekend. Because of their importance, I devoted late Saturday afternoons to preparing for them after working in the morning and early afternoon. If more than one official was appearing, we participated in a long conference call to coordinate our responses. And then Sunday morning had to begin unusually early, with a full review of the news and updates from the press staff about overnight events. The President and I talked every Sunday morning anyway, and he sometimes passed along his thoughts about what I should try to achieve.

Most of the time, the goal of these interviews was to state current U.S. policy and take the slings and arrows of the very capable and experienced journalists who anchored the shows. But we adopted a practice that in retrospect I believe to have been a mistake. In support of the public case, the intelligence community began declassifying pieces of information in order to describe the emerging threat fully. That was the source of some of the claims that turned out to be controversial and in many cases wrong: the high-quality aluminum tubes that were thought to be components for uranium enrichment; mobile laboratories for biological weapons development; the acquisition of mapping software for the territory of the United States that could be used in conjunction with pilotless drones. In one now infamous case, we used the CIA's assessment that the aluminum tubes were for centrifuges—a key element in a nuclear weapons program. I misspoke during one of the interviews, saying that the tubes could *only* be for nuclear use. In fact, I had meant to say that they were *most likely* for nuclear use and corrected the language in subsequent statements. But the misstatement was taken as evidence that we were inflating the evidence. It was a lesson in the dangers of using individual intelligence points. As a result of this practice, these intelligence "nuggets" became too much the focus of the arguments about the dangers of Saddam. The entire case came to rest on those isolated intelligence statements about his programs.

The argument was really more straightforward: Saddam Hussein was a cancer in the Middle East who had attacked his neighbors, throwing the region into chaos. He had drawn the United States into conflict twice, once to expel him from Kuwait and a second time to deliver air strikes against suspected WMD sites because he would not allow arms inspectors to do their jobs. Saddam was routinely shooting at our aircraft patrolling under UN authority. The sanctions put into place to contain him had crumbled under the weight of international corruption and his considerable guile. He had tried to assassinate a former President of the United States and supported terrorists, harboring some of the most notorious of them in his country. There had been no arms inspections in Iraq for more than four years. And it was the unanimous view of the U.S. intelligence community that he had reconstituted his chemical and biological weapons programs. All but one agency believed that he was reconstituting his nuclear weapons capability as well and could have a crude nuclear device in one year if he got foreign help, by the end of the decade if he had to go it alone. Similar views were shared by many foreign intelligence organizations, including the British. The world had given Saddam one last chance to come clean about his weapons programs or face serious consequences. This time the word of the international community had to mean something.

In 2001 we had failed to connect the dots. We could not do so again. When I said, "We don't want the smoking gun to be a mushroom cloud," that is what I meant. Intelligence information is rarely certain. Waiting until a threat explodes was not an option after the experience of 9/11.

It is hard for many people now, knowing what subsequently occurred, to appreciate how compelling the overall intelligence case against Saddam appeared to be. I was a veteran of the Cold War, Gulf War I, and 9/11. I had served on the Joint Staff in the Pentagon and spent years trying to determine the direction of Soviet military programs. I had never seen a stronger case, and we knew Saddam had used weapons of mass destruction before. We reviewed the intelligence on numerous occasions. The NSC Principals, all experienced people, read the NIE cover to cover, and George Tenet repeatedly assured us of his own judgment that the intelligence was sound.

But what really should have anchored the argument was the problem of WMD in the hands of Saddam, not just the problem of WMD per se. In fact, Senator Robert Bennett of Utah reminded me that I had told a group of legislators exactly that. Russia had many times the number of WMD that Saddam was thought to possess, but there wasn't much worry about Moscow using it or passing it on to a terrorist. Saddam was a unique threat on both counts. Intelligence was an input but not a substitute for our strategic judgment about what he was doing and, more important, what he might do. One cannot reliably judge the intentions of an adversary, but Saddam had shown a willingness to act recklessly before. We didn't believe that we had the luxury of inaction.

Our public reliance on isolated intelligence nuggets was especially foolish when it turned the President of the United States into a "fact witness." No one is to blame for this but me. We worked closely with the White House communicators, and they, not surprisingly, pushed the President to be specific in describing the threat. They loved the sporadic declassified nuggets, which had the added attraction of giving the American people a sense of being "let behind the spy's curtain," as one person put it. But knowing the uncertainties that always attend intelligence and how it is especially true in intelligence that the whole is worth more than the sum of the parts, I should have resisted.

The practice came to a head in the State of the Union address on

January 28, 2003. The President knew that we were likely headed to war and wanted to give as detailed an assessment to the American people as possible. The speech included a long litany of what we knew about Saddam's WMD. One of the nuggets referenced a British report that Saddam was trying to purchase uranium from the African country of Niger.

Three months earlier, George Tenet had suggested in a memo clearing another presidential speech that this reference be removed. At the time of the elaborate process for vetting the State of the Union, however, the Agency did not make the same request for the reference. In fact, the reference appeared in the 2002 NIE. Steve Hadley and I had a firm policy: if the intelligence agencies couldn't support something the President was about to say, he wouldn't say it. This time the red flag was not raised, and the line would embolden our critics in the months to come.

Late in February, Steve Hadley and I realized belatedly that the President had not made the broader argument. Somehow all that Saddam had done and what he meant to stability in the Middle East was getting lost in the discussion. The President agreed to deliver one last speech on Iraq and did so at the American Enterprise Institute. But the die had been cast. This was a war that had been justified by an intelligence judgment, not a strategic one. The rationale would rise or fall accordingly.

A Coalition of the Willing

AS THE INSPECTIONS dragged on and military preparations accelerated, splits began to emerge within the international community. The President conducted almost daily phone calls with his counterparts and could hear firsthand the divergence among them. Colin reported the same. We had always known that France and Russia harbored deep reservations about action against Saddam. Their policies, quite frankly, had contributed to the weakening of the containment regime against Saddam, and they had been unwilling to strengthen those constraints earlier in 2001. Russia was at least honest in citing its economic interest as a principal rationale for avoiding war. But we were not sure whether Moscow and Paris would actually oppose military action if the United States and Great Britain decided on that course.

We decided to call for an extraordinary session of the UN Security Council on February 5 at which Colin would present the case against Saddam. At first Steve and I proposed two separate sessions: one on WMD and the other on the remainder of Saddam's behavior in violating terrorism and human rights resolutions. The State Department felt that the world would rally only on the charges concerning his weapons of mass destruction but agreed that there should be a second resolution charging him with the other violations. That resolution never happened, as attention shifted to refining and passing Resolution 1441.

So, with the subject matter chosen, it fell to the CIA to prepare a brief. Colin reviewed it and found it lacking. George Tenet and John McLaughlin presented the case to the President in an Oval Office meeting just before Christmas. He was equally underwhelmed and asked about the strength of the evidence. That was the context for Tenet's "slam dunk" comment, which was meant to convey, I think, that the intelligence was indeed strong. I didn't take it as anything more than that, but the President asked me to review the intelligence one more time. I did so with an analyst in a long session in the Situation Room on December 23. Scooter Libby and the Vice President, reacting to the CIA presentation, wrote a "litigator's case," which not only focused on WMD but reintroduced a good deal of the questionable evidence on al Qaeda and Saddam.

Colin decided that he had to take the pen and vet the intelligence personally. He devoted several days to sessions at Langley, where he examined every claim, asking about the underlying sources and methods and throwing out a significant portion of what had been written for him. Colin had been the chairman of the Joint Chiefs of Staff, and he knew the pitfalls of intelligence. I joined him for two nights and couldn't have felt more confident about the case he would make.

I watched the first part of Colin's presentation on TV in my office, eventually joining the President in the dining room adjacent to the Oval to view the end of it. I thought at the time that it was a tour de force. The evidence didn't allow for an "Adlai Stevenson moment," a reference to the U.S. ambassador to the United Nations and his surprise revelation of satellite photos showing Soviet nuclear missiles in Cuba in 1962. But it was impressive nonetheless, particularly in light of Saddam's record with the international community.

The response broke along expected lines, with Spain's fiery foreign minister, Ana Palacio, and Britain's Jack Straw calling for action and France and Russia arguing for giving the weapons inspectors more time. When Hans Blix gave a report on February 14 that was more ambiguous than the one of January 27, it was clear that we had our work cut out for us with the world community.

Our sense of urgency was driven by two factors. First, our military forces were approaching levels of mobilization that could not be sustained for very long. We were not on a hair trigger, but a decision was going to have to be made to keep moving forward with the mobilization or start to pull back. It wasn't possible just to stand still, since doing so would leave our forces vulnerable in-theater without sufficient logistical support. I found it ironic that some diplomats, including Hans Blix, liked the backdrop of U.S. military power as a means to force Saddam's hand. They seemed to have no idea that we couldn't stand ready forever while Saddam played cat and mouse as he always did. Second, the President believed that the only way to avoid war was to put maximum and unified pressure on Saddam. That argued for continued mobilization, not pulling back. Maybe he would get the message and decide to save his own skin.

Unfortunately, the international community was starting to send mixed messages. The moment was approaching when we would have to reconcile conflicting views over the admittedly ambiguous language in Resolution 1441 concerning the need for a second resolution to authorize war. Tony Blair came to the White House for a meeting on January 31. He made it clear that he would need a second resolution explicitly authorizing the use of force. It was not a matter of legality but politics: he would have to face the House of Commons in a vote on the use of force that could bring down his government. The President already had congressional authorization, but if the British needed a second resolution, we would seek a second resolution.

Colin believed that we had a strong chance of getting nine or ten votes in the UN Security Council and might be able to persuade the Latin Americans—Mexico and Chile—to go along. Yet if Russia, France, or China voted against the resolution, it would fail due to their veto as permanent Security Council members. Russia had made clear that it was concerned mostly about its economic interests in Iraq. France was more principled if patronizing, viewing the Iraqi dictator as a necessary evil in an area of the world that needed strongmen to ensure stability. China was difficult to read.

Therefore the emergence of a French, Russian, and German triumvirate publicly opposed to action in Iraq was the devastating last straw. The President was particularly shocked at the participation of Germany since, months before, Chancellor Gerhard Schroeder had led us to believe that he might support the United States against Saddam "as long as it was quick." Needless to say, it was also galling to see the United States' NATO allies hug Russia in opposition to the United States on a matter of national security. Colin still hoped that we might get a plain-vanilla resolution that would perhaps simply reaffirm the language of "serious consequences" in Resolution 1441.

The President decided to call Tony Blair. They agreed to forge ahead on the second resolution, even though the prospects were dwindling. French President Jacques Chirac had let it be known that "nothing justifies war." But there was still some hope that the French and Russians might abstain if enough members of the Council could be lined up. The resolution was introduced on February 24 and was almost dead on arrival.

The Latin Americans were proving to be more difficult than we had thought. The Chileans said they could not support a war resolution. When President Bush called Mexico's president, Vicente Fox, Fox asked, "What resolution?" When his promised return phone call to the President had not occurred some hours later, I checked in with my Mexican counterpart to learn that President Fox had gone in for back surgery and would not be available. The chance of passing a second resolution now seemed very remote.

In early March the President called Blair again. I assumed it was just to review the status of the resolution, but he had something else in mind. He was concerned that the war might bring down Blair's government and made clear that he would think no less of the prime minister if Britain did not participate in the invasion; perhaps there was some other way for the United Kingdom to be involved later in the conflict. Blair would have none of it, saying that he had promised to be by our side and had not changed his mind.

As I listened to that conversation, I remembered sitting with Margaret Thatcher in the Roosevelt Room in August 1990 as a young aide to President George H. W. Bush. The prime minister had come to the White House to discuss a response to Saddam's invasion of Kuwait. The President was tied up with a congressional delegation, and Richard Haass, then the special assistant for Near East and South Asian affairs, and I sat with Mrs. Thatcher until he was ready. She would tell the President not to go "wobbly" on Saddam. What irony! I left the President's office with the deepest respect and admiration for Tony Blair and the United Kingdom. It seems that when the chips are down, the British never go wobbly.

The President and Blair agreed to hold a meeting in the Azores for the key Security Council members who supported military action. President Bush, Prime Minister Blair, and Prime Minister Aznar were joined by Prime Minister José Barroso of Portugal, their host, who had offered the Azores as a quiet meeting place.

Aznar and his foreign minister, Ana Palacio, had become stalwart allies against terrorism and tough critics of Saddam Hussein. The Spanish had their own terrorism experiences with the Basque separatist group ETA, and the President's early support for their cause against the separatists had created a bond between the countries. Aznar's party would be defeated in 2004, however, after a terrorist attack that many read as retaliation for Spain's support of the war on terrorism and participation in the Iraq war. His successor, José Luis Rodríguez Zapatero, reversed course, precipitously withdrawing Spanish forces from Iraq and causing tensions in our relationship that were never overcome.

That Sunday evening in the Azores, we sat rather glumly, realizing that a united international community would not materialize. We would take on Saddam either with a coalition of the willing or not at all. The British had to leave early to prepare for Tony Blair's moment of truth in the House of Commons. As they bade us good-bye, I turned to Andy Card and said, "I hope it's not the last time we see them."

. . .

TONY BLAIR survived the vote of no confidence in the House of Commons. I watched that Tuesday morning as Blair delivered his case for enforcing Resolution 1441. British parliamentary debates are theatrical. I found myself nodding even when listening to those with whom I disagreed. There is something about the accent and the beautiful way the British use what is purported to be our common language. They just sound so impressive.

In the end Blair prevailed by a larger margin than expected and committed British forces to the initial campaign to overthrow Saddam and liberate Iraq. Prime Minister John Howard of Australia and President Aleksander Kwaśniewski of Poland did the same. While France, Germany, and Canada stood aside, eighteen NATO members (including seven states who gained formal ascension into NATO in 2004) and several other states joined the coalition. Some of "old Europe," as Don undiplomatically called them, refused to participate. But it was heartening to see the Baltic states, several of the East and Central Europeans, and even Georgia do what they could and with the best possible motive: they were finally free after years of tyranny and wanted to help others to achieve liberty. Japan and South Korea would anchor the effort in the north and south with forces carrying out humanitarian missions and helping to train Iraqi security forces. It was the first "overseas" mission for Japan in the post–World War II period. It was deeply offensive to those countries to see their contributions ridiculed by others as insignificant, and it was annoying to us that the military action against Saddam was dubbed unilateral. In fact, thirty-three countries from the coalition provided troops to support military operations in Iraq in 2003.

Neither was it the first time that the United States had acted without an explicit UNSC resolution. From the 1948 Berlin airlift under Truman to the 1999 NATO bombing of Yugoslavia, the coalitions involved were acting without that specific authority. But in this case, we believed that both Resolution 1441 and the sixteen before it were more than adequate to express the international community's view that Saddam Hussein was a threat to international peace and security. And in our view, "serious consequences" had to mean something.

14

48 Hours

JUST BEFORE OUR DEPARTURE for the Azores, the National Security Council met at Camp David on March 15 to review the situation. We decided that any military action had to be preceded by an ultimatum to Saddam. As had been the case with the Taliban, it was the unified view that decent nations do not go to war without warning. The President addressed the nation on March 17 from the Cross Hall in the White House. Flanked by a row of columns on one side and the flags of the presidency and the United States of America in the distance, the President issued a forty-eight-hour ultimatum to Saddam to leave the country or face attack. And on March 19 the National Security Council met one last time with the military commanders joining by videoconference from the field. The President asked each commander by name if he had everything that was needed. Each in turn answered affirmatively.

The President closed the meeting by saying, "God Bless America." I could tell that he was emotional, so I did not, as I usually did, follow him back to the Oval. Neither did Andy Card. When you work with the President of the United States, you come to see that being President is a very lonely job. Sometimes there is nothing that even the closest advisors can do or say to change that fact. At no time is that truer than when the commander in chief orders American men and women into battle. I never would have dreamed of encroaching on the moment when the President acknowledges that he, and he alone, is responsible for that decision.

"Maybe We Won't Have to Go to War"

I RETURNED to my office to review my to-do list. I had a number of calls to make to my counterparts around the world and several meetings scheduled about the war and its aftermath. The covert part of the operation was to commence that night with a lead element composed of British, Polish, Australian, and U.S. special forces.

At about 3:00 P.M. the President called and told me to come down to the Oval immediately. I always went immediately, and the fact that he said it that way was a bit strange. When I arrived, I saw George Tenet hovering over the desk, showing the President a map of a site near Baghdad. The Agency had gotten a tip that Saddam was moving to Dora Farms outside Baghdad. The source had revealed the approximate coordinates of the house in which he would be staying as well as an estimated time of arrival. We had even been told that he'd be traveling in a white vehicle. The question was whether to attack the site and try to kill Saddam before launching the military invasion.

Don Rumsfeld and Chairman of the Joint Chiefs of Staff Richard Myers were already there, but I looked around and didn't see Colin. "Get him here," the President said.

I excused myself, went into the President's little office adjacent to the Oval, and called him. "Get over here now!" I barked. I didn't have time to explain why.

The President was perplexed. The military operation had been set into motion a few hours before. How would this fit in with the plan? Were we being lured into a trap? Perhaps Saddam had filled the compound with women and children who would be killed in an air strike, filling the screens of Arab satellite TV with innocent victims of U.S. aggression. The decision was made more difficult by changing reports from the source, leaving George to try to draw the new coordinates on a piece of paper while leaning on the white Oval Office sofa. The President was skeptical, and frankly, so was I—but all of us agreed that it was worth a shot. The President asked Don to make sure Tommy Franks agreed. We all saw the upside: if we could kill Saddam, war could be avoided altogether.

An attack plan had to be developed immediately to give the bombers time to reach the target. Dick Myers ran between the Oval and Steve's office down the hall, communicating with the Joint Staff as it hastily developed a plan and readied the weapons package. The mission would be unorthodox, with minimal opportunity to suppress Iraqi air defenses before the bombers entered. The pilots would try to slip in and out undetected.

Around eight, I went to my office and woke up David Manning to tell him there had been a change in plans. I explained as best I could what we were trying to do. David in turn woke up the prime minister. The Brits were on board.

We all held our breath until the pilots completed the mission and left Iraqi airspace several hours later. The next day we received initial reports that a white vehicle had been hit and that "somebody important" had been taken out on a stretcher. Unfortunately, whoever it was, it was not Saddam. The planned military operation to liberate Iraq was launched that same day.

The next morning I was surprised to see our executive assistant Major Jen Easterly in her army uniform. The executive assistants at the NSC, which had included Kevin Moran, Michael Ma, Matt Waxman, and my former Stanford student Dave Travers, worked long hours and remained unflappable under great pressure. Steve and I were close to them.

"Jen, why are you in uniform?" I asked.

"We are at war and I am a soldier," she said humbly.

THE MILITARY CAMPAIGN went swiftly, with the Iraqi forces retreating and ultimately disintegrating. The President received briefings several times a day. We continued Principals and NSC meetings about the aftermath. But there was little for us or for the President to do. The operation was now in the hands of the commanders. In fact, looking back on those days, I am struck by what the President *did* do. The president of Cameroon made a visit, complete with an Oval Office meeting and lunch on March 20. In retrospect, I can't help wondering why. Perhaps my not remembering that the meeting even took place (until reviewing my calendar for this memoir) says something about the level of distraction that we really felt, even if on the surface things seemed normal.

Unlike during the early operations in Afghanistan, there was no sense of being bogged down. Coalition forces were making steady, even rapid, progress and were approaching Baghdad. We wondered whether Saddam would indeed make a stand there. He didn't, and on April 9

U.S. forces entered the capital city. There was pandemonium in the streets. I watched on TV as Saddam's statue toppled to the ground. Iraq had been liberated. But when a soldier climbed upon the rubble to plant a U.S. flag, he was quickly admonished to take it down. We did not want our presence there to be—or to seem to be—an occupation.

Seeing the images, I rushed down to the Oval Office. The Vice President and Kanan Makiya, one of the Iraqi exiles with whom we had worked, were there. Everyone was hugging. But the President was just sitting at his desk. "You did this," I said to him. He didn't really respond. Again I walked away because he was very much inside his own thoughts.

I later learned that a few nights later the Vice President had invited Scooter Libby, Paul Wolfowitz, and several other people to his house to celebrate the liberation of Iraq. I am not sure whether Don was invited, but Colin and I weren't included. For a brief time there was a kind of hubris among those who had been the most persistent and longstanding advocates for the overthrow of Saddam. It was summed up by the Vice President who, when challenged on the need for interagency coordination in the postwar period, said, "The Pentagon just liberated Iraq. What has the State Department done?" I knew that I had my work cut out for me. We all did.

"Where Are the Oil Workers?"

THE JOY of the liberation was short-lived. There was widespread looting, perhaps to be expected immediately after the overthrow of a hated dictator. But it went beyond that to systematic attacks on important buildings, including the museum containing Iraq's significant antiquities. Unidentified people were raiding weapons depots. At least there was no attempt as in 1991 to set the oil fields on fire, but the pictures from Iraq were very ugly.

I've always believed that those Baath party members loyal to Saadam, not ordinary Iraqis, created much of the chaos to embarrass us and sow the seeds of a comeback. Within a few days we began to get reports of armed thugs calling themselves "Fedayeen Saddam." "Who is Fedayeen Saddam?" I asked George, temporarily forgetting the somewhat cursory mention of the group in the prewar briefings.

In the midst of the increasing turmoil, we began carrying out the plans we'd made for the postinvasion period. It was immediately obvious that some of our assumptions had been faulty. No one could locate most of the civil servants who had been expected to keep the country running. I remember well standing at my desk a week after U.S. forces entered Baghdad and yelling, "Where are the oil workers?" Along with members of the army and police, they seemed to have vanished into thin air.

The problem was exacerbated by the fact that we could not get Jay Garner and his team into Iraq due to the security situation. That was hard to explain, given that we had just deployed almost 200,000 troops to Iraq, but the Pentagon insisted that it was too dangerous to send Garner in. Finally, almost three weeks after the invasion, he arrived and was almost immediately overwhelmed.

I called Margaret Tutwiler, our ambassador in Morocco. Margaret had been Jim Baker's closest confidante during his State Department years. She was a lot like Karen Hughes, a great communicator but also a savvy political advisor. "Go help Jay Garner," I implored her. "He can't seem to get a handle on what to do or what to say." She made clear that she didn't want the mission. But she is a patriot, and she agreed to go.

The Garner operation was to have worked hand in hand with an Iraqi Interim Authority (IIA) composed of exiled Sunni and Shia leaders and the Kurds. The President had been briefed on the concept before the war broke out. Doug Feith presented a more elaborate version on March 31, complete with principles for the authority and pledges by its members to uphold them. The Defense Department was given full authority to implement the plan, again with a caution from the President to make certain that indigenous, not just exiled, leaders were included.

In addition to planning for the new administration to have an Iraqi "face," Doug Feith's office had hired outside civilian experts to help run the government. Defense contracts had been awarded for various functions. Some of them made sense, and others did not. I learned later, for instance, that Science Applications International Corporation had been engaged to set up and run the Iraqi state television station. SAIC was a fine technical company, but it was hardly versed in media content, let alone Arab media content.

The State Department was prepared to deploy employees, many of whom were Arabists. Some were sent without incident, but Feith vetoed several State recommendations on what could only be called ideological grounds. When I learned of this, I went to the President and told him that it was an affront to Colin to act that way and we needed the expertise. But it was the Defense Department's show, and the President was reluctant to intervene. Steve dutifully worked to get as many State employees in as possible.

Unfortunately, the Pentagon had minimal ability to implement the elaborate IIA plans given the chaos on the ground. They managed to get some of the exiles into Iraq with the assistance of American military personnel. But the Garner mission collapsed almost on arrival and could barely manage itself, let alone the country and the Iraqi Interim Authority. The nightmare that we had tried to get Defense to avoid through planning for "rear-area security" was unfolding. There was a serious manpower shortage in Baghdad, and, though pressed by the President about the number of troops on the ground, Don continued to insist that there were enough.

Colin Powell had once said that military force has to be overwhelming in its application. That was known as the Powell Doctrine and certainly described the strategy in Gulf War I, when 500,000 forces had been used. He would later tell me that he had personally expressed concern to Tommy Franks about the troop levels. But the Pentagon had decided upon a different approach, using a so-called light footprint. It worked well for the defeat of Saddam's army and his overthrow, but we had too few troops to stabilize the postwar environment. As I watched the chaos unfold, I kept harkening back to all those briefings when the President had been told that the plan was "adequately resourced," meaning there were enough troops. If there were any objections in the ranks of the senior generals to the assessment, they were not made known to the President.

I caught up with Don outside the Situation Room after an NSC meeting as all of this was unfolding and asked him if he realized that the Garner mission was not working. "We can't even get Garner into the country," I told him. He said that he did see the problem and was considering a different model. On April 11, Don recommended that the President appoint a new presidential envoy, who would replace ORHA (Garner had finally arrived in the country the same day). Don and his staff put together a diverse and wide-ranging list of more than a hundred candidates, including Paul Wolfowitz, former Secretary of State George Shultz, former California Governor Pete Wilson, former Federal Reserve Chairman Paul Volcker, and L. Paul "Jerry" Bremer.

Bremer was well known to most of us and was working for Henry Kissinger's consulting firm. He seemed a reasonable choice and immediately impressed the President with his presence and can-do attitude. We did not, frankly, go through a long vetting process because the situation on the ground demanded an immediate response. On May 6 Jerry was appointed to lead the Coalition Provisional Authority (CPA). After a session with each of the NSC Principals and then alone with the President, Jerry Bremer was dispatched to Iraq. Don's instructions to Bremer empowered him with all executive, legislative, and judicial functions in Iraq. Jerry immediately did what Garner had not: he took control and brought a semblance of order.

That is how the Coalition Provisional Authority came into being. Some people in the Defense Department continued to argue that we needed to hand over more power to the Iraqi Interim Authority, but that contradicted the instructions Don had given Jerry. Did Don want Jerry to have all executive, legislative, and judicial functions or not? The issue wasn't between State and Defense. If there was a coordination problem, it was that Defense wouldn't or couldn't reconcile Doug Feith's Iraqi Interim Authority and Jerry's CPA within its own building.

In order to give maximum flexibility to the CPA, Steve Hadley "shut down" the Deputies process and Frank Miller's interagency Executive Steering Group. The coordination would be done in Baghdad under the direction and guidance of the Pentagon in Washington.

Upon his arrival Jerry made clear that the United States, at least for a while, needed to show a strong hand. It wasn't a matter of a binary choice: turn the country over to the IIA or not. It was a matter of how quickly the Iraqis could assume authority, particularly given the security situation on the ground and the fact that most of them hadn't been in the country for years, giving them no indigenous base. The President had confidence in Jerry and believed that he had to give his "man on the ground" flexibility to organize in the way he saw fit.

The Bremer mission could have been helped, nonetheless, by continuing to use Zalmay Khalilzad as a political envoy. Zal had been the very successful ambassador to Afghanistan and had long experience with exiles from all parts of Iraq. He was already working effectively with tribal and provincial leaders who had survived in Saddam's Iraq, calling them together for a conference in Salah ad-Din province. Together with the exiles, those leaders might have given the Baghdad-based interim authority greater legitimacy.

I'm not given to cultural arguments, but there was something about Zal's effectiveness that seemed attributable to his comfort level with the ways of the region and the region's comfort level with him. I asked the President to keep Zal on to help Jerry with the very difficult Iraqi personalities. The President said that it would be Jerry's call. Jerry demurred, saying that he would have to do the work himself. That was a mistake.

Yet Jerry would eventually become effective in dealing with the Iraqis. The criticism that the CPA became overblown and grandiose has some merit; at its height there were more than 1,200 people working for it. The CPA would make mistakes, including the decision to disband the army. But through the ups and downs of the next year, Jerry did heroic work under the most difficult of circumstances, including deteriorating security. The President appreciated that, and so did I.

"Punish France, Forgive Russia, and Ignore Germany"

IN THE immediate aftermath of the war, we began to consider how to restore at least a semblance of normalcy to our relations with the French, Germans, and Russians. The President was particularly concerned about the Russians, whom he saw as at least having been straightforward about their opposition to the war. I felt the same way but uttered what I thought was a clever quip in what I thought was a private moment with the President and a couple of aides standing in the Oval Office: "Punish France, forgive Russia, and ignore Germany," I said. We all laughed, but I was horrified to see that someone had passed the tidbit on to the press. I was reminded of a Benjamin Franklin saying that three people can keep a secret if two of them are dead. He must have been talking about Washington.

The President called Vladimir Putin and told him that he wanted to send me to Moscow. Putin appreciated the gesture and said that he would gladly receive me.

I arrived in Moscow on April 6 and went to my room in Spaso House, the U.S. ambassador's residence. The house is a beautiful neoclassical estate, which has been inhabited by the U.S. envoy since the establishment of relations between the Soviet Union and the United States in 1933. I turned on the television to a Russian news station. My Russian was once very good, but it is a difficult language to retain because of the peculiarities of its grammatical structure. I always found it helpful to get my Russian "ear" as soon as possible.

As I unpacked, I couldn't believe what I was hearing: a convoy of Russian diplomats and journalists had been wounded when their motorcade became trapped in a firefight while leaving Baghdad. *This is going to be a great trip,* I thought. I called the President, who said that we didn't have the facts but of course I should give Putin his deepest regrets.

Despite some back-and-forth about the responsibility for the accident, my meetings in Moscow went smoothly. I met with the secretary of the Russian Security Council and others and then made my way across the cobblestoned square to Putin's ornate Kremlin office. I had last been there on my own during a mission to smooth the diplomatic path before our withdrawal from the ABM Treaty in the summer of 2001.

Putin knew that I had been a student of Russia, a fact that he seemed to find reassuring—at least in the early days. Our personal chemistry was good, and though I always spoke to him in English (I wanted to be precise in delivering messages), I always listened to him in Russian. Putin spoke in a rough, unvarnished manner, and I wanted to hear him in his own language, not through translation. In any case, I told him that the President wanted to get relations back on track. He said that he wanted to do the same and then made clear that President Bush needed to be aware of Russian economic interests in the rebuilding of Iraq. Those included both the large debt that Saddam Hussein owed to Moscow and pending oil contracts. At least he was straight with me.

The first encounters with the French and Germans since the invasion would be on the margins of the G8 meeting in Evian, France, that June. The President began his trip in Poland and then went on to St. Petersburg for the three hundredth anniversary of the founding of the city. Millions of dollars had been spent to restore Peterhof, the spectacular palace of Peter the Great. Everywhere you looked there was gold: gold-leaf–covered cathedral domes, gold fountains, and gold people. Yes, gold people. What appeared at first to be statues were indeed human beings spray-painted gold. The grand performance following dinner featured those beings whirling around as classical ballet dancers performed *Swan Lake*. Not surprisingly, the finale was Tchaikovsky's *1812 Overture,* complete with cannons blasting across the river. The whole thing was a bit like the Bolshoi meets Caesar's Palace, but the Russians and Putin were bursting with pride. As we left, I noticed that the back of one of the cathedrals had not been painted. The phrase "Potemkin Village" came to mind: in days gone by, local officials would paint the fronts of houses whenever the tsar was passing through a village. They didn't bother with the part he couldn't see. Some things don't change.

During the event, President Bush approached German Chancellor Gerhard Schroeder and shook his hand. It was about as warm a moment as the two could ever manage, but they maintained cordial relations for the rest of Schroeder's term.

Prior to Evian, I had given an interview that was, in retrospect, a little brusque. Saying that our disappointment in our allies would not go away easily, I added that there were times it appeared that U.S. power was seen to be more dangerous than, perhaps, Saddam Hussein. I went to the President and said that I had been a little rough on the allies. He wasn't concerned, saying that it left him room to be the nice guy.

In fact, the G8 went very smoothly, everyone trying to demonstrate, as Colin said, that we were "starting to talk about the future and not just grind our teeth over the disappointments of the past." And people were starting to move on. The UN Security Council had been reunited with a resolution giving the United States and Great Britain a mandate to use Iraq's oil revenues to rebuild Iraq.

There had been a silly debate inside the administration about how much authority to give the United Nations. The Defense Department and the Vice President's office had scoured every word of the resolution to make sure that the United States had free rein to rebuild Iraq without the nettlesome advice of the international community. When I called Colin with yet one more "suggestion" from the White House, he said, "One day we're going to be trying to give this tar baby to the UN." He was, of course, right; our problem wouldn't be too much UN involvement but too little. I closed down the vetting process by the agencies and gave Colin the go-ahead to finalize the resolution.

The hubris didn't end there, however. As we were looking to the first proposals for the rebuilding of Iraq, we made what turned out to be a terrible and ultimately unenforceable decision. The Pentagon wanted the contracts to go to the countries that had supported the war. In theory that, of course, made some sense. But in practice it made the United States look petty. Eventually we would want help from everyone—a *lot* of help—to rebuild Iraq.

Again a Chance for Middle East Peace

THERE HAD LONG BEEN a belief that action in Iraq could be made more palatable for the region if accompanied by efforts to resolve the Palestinian-Israeli conflict. Though the connection is not obvious, the fact is that the perception had become the reality. After the Gulf War in 1991, then Secretary of State James Baker convened the Madrid Conference, which garnered international support for the peace process. What followed was the Oslo Accords between Arafat and the Israelis, which established the Palestinian Authority and a modicum of self-governance for the Palestinian people. Arafat would famously renounce violence and recognize Israel's right to exist. The accords were not directly related to the conference (in fact, they were conducted in secret and without U.S. participation). Nonetheless, the two events did establish a new foundation for the "peace process."

The overthrow of Saddam Hussein seemed to offer a similar opportunity. Since the end of the Israeli operations in the West Bank in the summer of 2002, there had been enormous pressure on Arafat to reform the Palestinian Authority. The adoption of a new Basic Law and the appointment of the moderate leader Mahmoud Abbas as prime minister were hailed worldwide as a real step forward.

The President decided to build on those developments, hoping that the "new" Palestinian leadership for which he had called in his Rose Garden speech was emerging. He would leave the G8 in Evian and go to the Middle East. To be sure, there was a kind of perverse pleasure in leaving Chirac's soirée a little early to go make Middle East peace.

We sought and gained agreement from the regional parties to hold two meetings: one would be held in Sharm el-Sheikh, where the key Arab leaders, Crown Prince Abdullah of Saudi Arabia, King Abdullah of Jordan, King Hamad of Bahrain, and President Mubarak of Egypt, would meet with Palestinian Prime Minister Abbas to signal support for him and for a new effort with the Israelis. Abbas would then go on to meet with Israeli Prime Minister Sharon in Aqaba, Jordan.

We wanted the effort to be bold, but there was unanimous agreement that the parties were not yet ready to launch final-status negotiations. Abbas was on something of a short leash from Arafat, and Sharon was still declaring that he had "no partner for peace." Our aims were modest but significant. We wanted the Palestinians to be clear that they sought a negotiated solution to the conflict and that there would be no more intifadas. We wanted the Israelis to acknowledge the rights of the Palestinians for statehood. We wanted the Arabs, particularly the Saudis, to show their brethren throughout the Arab world that the "Custodian of the Two Holy Mosques," as the king of Saudi Arabia is called, was fully behind this effort. We even hoped that the Saudis might make a gesture toward the Israelis, perhaps opening a trade office.

The negotiations for the meeting were a real slog, as is every attempt to find common language when dealing with those parties. I handled the negotiations on behalf of the President from Washington, prodding each of the Arabs, the Palestinians, and the Israelis to accept language that would move the process forward. It isn't unusual for the national security advisor to negotiate a document for a presidential visit. The State Department often steps back and supports such efforts rather than leading them. In this case, Colin and I worked closely together, sometimes tag-teaming our interlocutors to get the work done.

The Saudi ambassador to the United States, Prince Bandar, negotiated the Arab statement. Anything that the crown prince could accept would clearly work for the Egyptians and the Jordanians, who already had diplomatic relations with the Israelis. I'd known Bandar from my time in the George H. W. Bush administration. He was already twenty years into his tenure as Saudi ambassador, and despite his flamboyant lifestyle—he had a spectacular house in Virginia, another in Aspen, and a private plane—the talented diplomat enjoyed the confidence of both the crown prince and the White House. It was hard to get the Arabs to be bold enough, and I was pushing really hard. At one point, Bandar almost walked out on our deliberations, declaring that he'd done more than any other Saudi had ever even contemplated. I backed off, realizing that he was caught between Abdullah's reticence and Washington's expectations. We managed to get a good statement.

Negotiating with the Palestinians and the Israelis was no easier. Every encounter seemed to produce either a history lesson or a lecture about some UN resolution. One of my aides, seeing my frustration, noted that Israelis are among the most legalistic people on Earth; after all, the Torah is mostly about keeping the law, he said. I asked how one explained the Palestinians' behavior. "They are cousins," he answered.

We finally managed to produce the documents that would be issued at the summits. Only a fool goes to an important meeting in which the President will be involved without an agreed text. I would have to violate that rule once in a while, but it made for sleepless nights and the potential for embarrassment for the United States. This time we had the language locked down.

We arrived in Sharm el-Sheikh from Paris late in the evening. I had one last meeting with Prince Bandar and went to bed. The next morning we arrived at the meeting hall and were greeted by Mubarak. King Abdullah of Jordan and Mahmoud Abbas arrived shortly after. But the crown prince was not there. We waited and waited. I called Bandar, who wasn't answering his phone. Something had gone wrong. The press was antsy, knowing that the scheduled time of the meeting had come and gone.

Soon we learned from the Egyptians that the crown prince was at his hotel and threatening to go home. *Here we go again,* I thought. Fortunately, some last-minute changes to the document mollified him, and the meeting was completed successfully.

The follow-on meeting in Aqaba went more or less according to script in comparison with Sharm. The Palestinian delegation included Salam Fayyad, who was at the time finance minister. He impressed us all with his determination to do things right, including posting the budget of the Palestinian Authority on the Internet as a step toward greater transparency. The University of Texas–trained Fayyad was exactly the kind of leader the President had talked about in his June 24 speech: smart, honest, and capable. He would become our most important ally in helping to put Palestinian governance on a more democratic footing.

The President decided to take Sharon and Abbas on a little private stroll around the gardens to impress upon them the importance of moving forward for peace. The rest of us stayed behind with the delegations, which were busily engaging each other without our involvement. At one point, the Israeli intelligence chief turned to Mohammed Dahlan, one of Arafat's security heads, and complimented him on his Hebrew. "I learned it in one of your jails," Dahlan retorted. These folks knew each other very well indeed.

The Aqaba meetings ended with statements by Sharon and Abbas. Sharon pledged to improve the humanitarian situation in the Palestinian territories and to remove the unauthorized outposts that Israeli settlers had constructed in defiance even of Israeli law. He recognized the importance of territorial contiguity for a Palestinian state and said that it was not in Israel's interest to govern Palestinians. These were extraordinary statements for the "father of the settlement movement," as Sharon was called. At the time of Camp David in 2000, Ehud Barak had made pledges on behalf of Israel, but he was a Labor prime minister. The conservative Likud party had never countenanced a Palestinian state. A few months later, Sharon would deliver a pathbreaking address at the Herzliya Conference in which he talked about the need for compromise. "We are willing to proceed towards its [the Road Map's] implementation," he said. "Two states, Israel and a Palestinian state, living side by side in tranquillity, security, and peace." Sharon had arrived at the conclusion that it was time for Israel to make, as he had put it a few weeks earlier, "painful concessions." Now a broad swath of the Israeli body politic accepted the need for a two-state solution.

Abbas, for his part, made clear that a Palestinian state could not be born of terrorism and called it a deadly obstacle to Palestinian aspirations. He pledged to make Palestinian institutions, including the security services, more democratic and accountable.

The President appointed an experienced diplomat, John Wolf, to monitor the progress on the obligations the two sides had taken. I took direct responsibility for overseeing U.S. efforts, traveling to Jerusalem and the West Bank to carry the President's message to the region. I was concerned that I might be taking on too much of an operational role for a national security advisor. But it seemed to be one of those times when it was important to use my close relationship with the President to push the process forward. I felt bad that this produced press stories of a split between Colin and me. There was not. I kept him informed, and State supported my work. But some saw it as an affront to the nation's chief diplomat.

In any case, the effort soon bogged down. I would learn valuable lessons about how frustrating it can be to get the Israelis to actually carry through on promises relating to the Palestinians. The illegal outposts were always *going* to be moved but were never quite moved. Gratuitous "security" roadblocks that kept the Palestinians from moving around in the West Bank were always *going* to be taken down but were never quite taken down.

The Palestinians were frustrating too. Abbas meant well, but Yasser Arafat would soon grow jealous of the prime minister's new international stature. When the cautious Abbas tried to carry out reforms, he'd find resistance from Arafat's security chiefs and from the old guard of the ruling party, Fatah; he almost always backed off or simply postponed actions. Then, on September 6, 2003, Abbas abruptly resigned.

Meanwhile, Salam Fayyad's efforts to put PA finances on a more transparent footing continued, but he needed our help. The Israelis had long collected tax revenue on behalf of the Palestinians and then transferred it to the PA at their discretion. After the intifada began, the Israelis stopped the payments to the Palestinians, leaving them without their most important source of revenue. Fayyad had begged me to prevail on the Israelis. He was trying to build a decent economy, but the PA was out of legitimate funds and he did not want to be dependent on the somewhat suspect sources that Chairman Arafat had used to run the authority.

I called Dov Weisglass, Sharon's closest advisor. The prime minister always traveled with this lawyer, who, though not an elected official, was extraordinarily savvy in the snake pit of Israeli politics. Dubi, as he was called, was Sharon's fixer. When I described the problem with the Palestinians, he explained that the Israelis never knew where the money was going and couldn't take the chance that it was funding terrorists. I told him that Fayyad was different and asked him to meet with the finance minister.

After their meeting, Dubi called back to say that he was impressed with Fayyad's good intentions, particularly his decision to hire an American financial services company to improve the management and transparency of the PA's accounts. As Fayyad continued to implement sound financial reforms, the Israelis began to deliver the tax revenues. It was the first step in helping the new Palestinian leadership build a decent and honest government.

Thus, despite the setbacks, the period just after the Iraq war was important for the peace process. Long-standing conflicts are rarely resolved in one huge leap forward. Rather, progress is like a stepwise function, each step forward being followed by a plateau—but a new plateau.

The events of June put the Israeli-Palestinian conflict onto a new foundation, and after the terrible events of the intifada and its subsequent defeat, the two parties started, haltingly, to move forward. The international community would endorse the Road Map, a step-by-step plan in three phases that outlined the obligations of the two sides on the path to peace, in November 2003. Both the Israelis and the Palestinians would accept it, though the Israelis did so with stated reservations.

More important, we'd established that the character of the Palestinian state mattered as much as its boundaries. And most Israelis, as represented by Ariel Sharon, had accepted that the State of Palestine and the State of Israel should live side by side in peace and security. The Bush vision for a two-state solution was now the policy of the international community as a whole.

In Search of WMD

THE PRESIDENT DECLARED an end to major combat operations in Iraq on May 1, 2003 (under the unfortunate "Mission Accomplished" banner on the USS *Abraham Lincoln*), and, with the CPA established in Baghdad, our attention turned to finding Saddam's alleged WMD so that they could be destroyed. George Tenet selected David Kay to lead the Iraq Survey Group (ISG), which was to undertake a fact-finding mission concerning Saddam's weapons; no weapons caches or stockpiles had been uncovered by our forces as they pushed through the country. Occasionally someone would make a remark about the absence of weapons. David Manning called one morning to report that the inspectors had dug up some devices in the garden of one of Saddam's scientists. The devices turned out to be old, rusted pieces of weapons that were of no consequence. But despite finding nothing in the early days, we assumed that Saddam had simply been very good at hiding and dispersing weapons as war approached.

Yet around that time questions began to arise within the intelligence community about some of the prewar assessments on Iraq's WMD programs. For instance, on May 25, the DIA's civilian experts inspected two of the mobile labs that had been suspected of manufacturing biological weapons and concluded that they had not been used for that purpose, a fact that was not immediately reported to the President or the NSC.

Questions were arising about other reports as well. On May 6, *New York Times* columnist Nicholas Kristof published a column suggesting that in the lead-up to the war the administration had used intelligence that it had known to be false. Citing anonymous sources, Kristof wrote that the Vice President's office had asked for an investigation into a claim that Iraq had tried to buy uranium from Niger. As early as February 2002 the envoy had told the CIA and State Department that the information was "unequivocally wrong" and that the documents associated with the claim had been forged. International Atomic Energy Agency Director General Mohamed ElBaradei had expressed doubts regarding the documents' authenticity in his presentation before the UN Security Council on March 7.

George Stephanopoulos subsequently asked me on his Sunday-morning show on June 8 about Kristof's claim and how information that some in the administration knew to be false had ended up in the President's State of the Union address. I told him that it was possible that there had been some knowledge that the reports were not credible but that it might not have risen to our attention. I also reminded him that our entire case against Saddam did not hinge on a single statement in the President's speech.

A few weeks later, as the President was preparing to leave for a trip to Africa, the story erupted. Former ambassador Joseph Wilson wrote an op-ed in the *New York Times* revealing himself to be the "unnamed former envoy" who'd investigated the Niger claims, purportedly at the request of the Vice President's office. (The Vice President's office had not been involved in establishing the Wilson mission. In fact, Wilson's mission had been authorized by officials from the CIA's Counterproliferation Division.) He stated that he'd traveled to Niger and concluded that it was unlikely that the sale had occurred, given the layers of government oversight over uranium mines and the physical difficulty of transferring the uranium to Iraq. He further alleged that he'd briefed the CIA and the State Department about his findings after his return.

The first time I'd ever heard of Wilson was when George Tenet had mentioned that Wilson's wife, Valerie Plame, worked for the CIA. George didn't know her personally, but we both thought it an interesting coincidence, nothing more. Even George had not been aware of the mission.

The day before the President's departure, George and I met with the President and the Vice President. George was uncomfortable with the chatter about the Niger report, noting that his agency couldn't really vouch for the claim's veracity.

We decided on the spot that the White House should just take the issue off the table and say that the claim should not have been included in the President's speech. That seemed to me a pretty straightforward admission of a mistake. It was not that anyone had intended to mislead, but my view was that if the CIA couldn't stand behind the claim, the President should never have said it.

The Vice President was dead set against taking any responsibility, arguing that the information had been in the NIE and was therefore legitimate. Some on my staff agreed, including my press advisor Anna Perez, who believed that the President's critics would pounce on this one admission and draw a picture of a White House seeking to deceive. "They will smell blood in the water," she said. I somehow believed that the press would understand a mistake as just that—a mistake. The Vice President and Anna were absolutely right.

The next morning, as we departed for Africa, the headlines were screaming that the President had used false language in the State of the Union. Given that no WMD had yet been found, there was now a growing presumption that the intelligence had been wrong or, worse, that we'd somehow manipulated it in a rush to war.

Before leaving, I called George Tenet, who was in Idaho. "George," I said, "your people cleared that speech. You can't leave the President hanging." George said he would issue a statement that made clear that the Niger claim had come from intelligence sources. In other words, that the President hadn't been lying.

By the time we got on the plane, the situation was spinning out of control. Ari suggested that I go on the record to explain the origin of the statement. I agreed to do so. But what I intended as a defense of the President and a matter-of-fact statement that the CIA had cleared the language was seen as an effort to blame the Agency. After almost twenty-four hours of negotiations, George issued a statement that more or less took responsibility for the "sixteen words," but the story would not end there.

Throughout the Africa trip the traveling press hammered the President about the issue. Reporters can be that way, very much pack animals chasing one story relentlessly and then saying that the President can't escape scrutiny on the story. I always thought, *Well, that's a self-fulfilling prophecy, because you keep bringing it up.* I remember visiting an impressive AIDS clinic in Uganda later that day and hearing orphans singing "America the Beautiful" while the reporters stood to the side, peppering Ari and Karen with questions about Niger and uranium.

15

BUSH THE AFRICAN

D ESPITE THE CONTROVERSY, we were enjoying the chance to highlight the President's already exceptional record in Africa. We began the trip in Senegal, where we visited Goree Island, the port from which slaves had been shipped to the Americas. It was a deeply emotional experience for me as I walked through the archway that had led the slaves to the transit ship. I couldn't help but think of Dante's *Inferno*: "Abandon all hope, ye who enter here." And I couldn't help but wonder if any of my ancestors had crossed over from here into the tragic life ahead of them. I listened as the President acknowledged Africa's contribution to the birth of the United States of America. "The stolen sons and daughters of Africa helped to awaken the conscience of America," he said.

We had all looked forward to the trip, most especially the President, who'd been taken with the continent from the very beginning of the administration. I'd introduced the President to Jendayi Frazer, who'd become special assistant for African affairs for the NSC. Jendayi made a convincing case that Africa could be more than a charity case, and we set out to create a well-rounded policy that would deal with conflict resolution, economic development, and democratization. The events of September 11, 2001, added counterterrorism cooperation to that list. The President liked the African leaders and met with them frequently, seeing twenty-five African heads of state from 2001 to 2003 alone.

The President believed too that the United States had a special responsibility to show compassion toward those who were less fortunate. Some have said that he was convinced of this by his ties to the evangelical Christian community, and to a certain extent this is true. Yet he also believed that Africans bore at least some responsibility both for their dire conditions and for finding a way out of them. We set out to build the relationship with Africa as one of partnership, not patronage. That often set the President at odds with his European colleagues, particularly French President Jacques Chirac, who held a more paternalistic view. Chirac once told the President that we couldn't condemn corruption in Africa because "we," meaning the West, were responsible for it. The President reminded Chirac that the United States didn't have a colonial past in Africa and in any case the fight against corruption was on behalf of Africans, not the West.

The exchange had taken place in 2002 at the same contentious G8 meeting where the fate of Yasir Arafat had been discussed. The President had, three months before, announced a huge increase in U.S. foreign assistance to poor nations. But there was a condition: the money would go to countries that were governing wisely, investing in their people, and promoting economic freedom. The Millennium Challenge Account (MCA), which was to be administered by a new government entity, the Millennium Challenge Corporation, was an approach that addressed the well-founded concern that so much money had gone "down a rat hole" over decades of foreign assistance. The President's address at the Monterrey development summit in Mexico in March 2002 gave us an opportunity to redefine the bargain: we would provide new and substantial resources, but the recipients would be those who could spend the money well. We thought of the MCA not as rewarding good behavior, though it did. The point was that countries would never develop without good governance and a fight against corruption. Foreign assistance on any other basis was worse than wasted; it was creating permanent wards of the international system who could never deliver for their people. By giving large grants to well-governed states, the leaders of those states could address key constraints on development such as infrastructure or a system for titling land to encourage private farming. Those economies would then be able to take advantage of trade and foreign direct investment from the private sector. That would also mean that democratic governments could begin to deliver for their people, reinforcing freedom and liberty. The MCA would become a core piece of the 2002 National Security Strategy.

Gary Edson, the deputy national security adviser for economic affairs, oversaw the design of the program. Gary was one of the best "policy engineers" I'd ever known, one of those rare individuals who can take an idea from inception to implementation. He worked with Stephen Krasner, a professor of international relations whom I'd recruited to the NSC from Stanford. Steve and I had known each other for twenty years, and I knew that he was creative and could bring new ideas to stale bureaucratic thinking. Those two innovators produced a wonderful design, and after some wrangling with OMB we requested funding at a level of $1.3 billion. Together with other increases in aid, the funding authorization more than doubled the Bush administration's foreign assistance worldwide and quadrupled it for Africa.

The President announced the MCA initiative on March 14, 2002, in a speech at the Inter-American Development Bank in Washington shortly before departing for the development summit in Mexico. We wanted the MCA to receive due attention, and Josh Bolten, then deputy chief of staff, had an idea. We'd both met the Irish rocker Bono of U2, who'd been agitating for U.S. help in addressing the AIDS pandemic. Bono was also a major advocate of increased foreign assistance and debt relief for the poorest countries. The President's pledge to do something about the latter during the second debate with Al Gore had caught his attention, and he'd come to the White House several times to see if we really meant it.

I asked Bono to see me in my office a few days before the President's speech. He was a little reticent about endorsing the MCA. He agreed with its principles, but I suspect that standing with George W. Bush was not exactly what he or his constituencies had in mind. Bono was also concerned that the MCA would divert attention from AIDS relief. I assured him that we were working on that problem too and that he would not be sorry if he stood with us. He agreed to do so and became one of our staunchest supporters in the work. I told him that it was his job to be the "thorn in our side." He performed that role admirably. We all came to see that Bono was not just one of those luminaries who use a social issue to seize the spotlight and gain publicity. He really cared about the issues, and he was as well informed as anyone I knew. Bono is a religious man who shared with the President a sense of moral obligation to help those in need. He became and remains a really good friend.

And he was right about the need to address AIDS. At one of my first meetings with then Governor Bush in 1999, we agreed that our agenda in Africa would go nowhere if we did not address the scourge of AIDS. The disease was crippling a whole continent: from 2000 to 2003 alone, approximately nine and a half million people had died from it, and there were estimates of up to 100 million deaths over the next twenty years if something was not done to arrest the plague. One of the President's first decisions was to support the creation of a Global Fund to Fight HIV/AIDS, Malaria and Tuberculosis, which he announced with UN Secretary-General Kofi Annan in the Rose Garden on May 11, 2001. The United States committed $200 million. But the President quickly became frustrated both with the meager contributions of other countries and the slow pace of implementation. The United States would increase its commitment to the fund to $500 million, but the White House had begun working on even bigger initiatives.

In June 2002 the President unveiled a program to stem mother-to-child transmission of the disease. But the President was still not satisfied. He asked a small group, led by Josh Bolten, to develop a plan that could take advantage of new breakthroughs in the use of antiretroviral medicines to treat the disease. Gary Edson represented me on the task force. After several months of work, we all gathered in the Oval Office for the President to make a decision. Josh's group had recommended a $15 billion program over five years. It would be the largest international health initiative by any one country.

The President began by saying that the United States had been blessed with plenty. He went on to quote the Gospel of Luke, saying, "Everyone to whom much was given, of him much will be required." Anthony Fauci, the director of the National Institutes of Health, attested to the promising data on antiretroviral intervention. The budget folks did what they were supposed to do: they questioned such a big expenditure in light of other priorities and whether the American people would find it compelling to ship all of that money abroad. There was a brief discussion of whether the African countries could be counted on to spend the money efficiently and without corruption. Josh noted that most of the money would flow through U.S. nonprofits, including many that were faith based.

Finally the President turned to each of us and asked whether he should proceed. There had been one further question hanging in the air: antiretroviral drugs could prolong the life of an AIDS patient, but a cure was still far into the future. Was that enough?

When the President turned to me, I decided to address that question. "Mr. President," I said, "one of the saddest days of my life was when my mother died. But I have always been grateful that she survived her initial bout with cancer. She died when I was thirty, not fifteen. That meant that she saw me grow up, graduate from college, and become a professor at Stanford. You may not be able to cure those mothers in Africa, but maybe they'll live long enough to see their kids grow up. That will matter." Mike Gerson closed the meeting by saying, "If we can do this and we don't, it will be a source of shame."

As we left the Oval that day, the President warned us to tell no one of his decision, including the cabinet secretaries. He didn't want the departments to start fighting over the money. The President would announce the President's Emergency Plan for AIDS Relief (PEPFAR) in his State of the Union the next month.

Both sides of the aisle rose to applaud the announcement that evening, and PEPFAR has enjoyed bipartisan support for almost a decade. Before leaving office the President would seek congressional reauthorization to double the contribution to AIDS relief. The program met the goals that the President set: antiretroviral drugs for 2 million people, care for another 10 million, and testing and counseling for some 57 million. The President would go on to make a major push to eliminate 50 percent of malaria cases and to tackle the problem of other tropical diseases. But it is PEPFAR that will be remembered as one of the greatest acts of compassion by any country in history.

Charles Taylor Must Go

THE TRIP TO AFRICA coincided with what was becoming a devastating humanitarian and political crisis in Liberia. President Charles Taylor's roots as a brutal dictator traced back to the United States. Imprisoned in Massachusetts in the late 1980s, Taylor escaped from jail and dodged extradition when he faced charges of embezzlement.

Instead of returning to Liberia, Taylor went to Libya and received guerrilla warfare training under the guidance of Libyan dictator Muammar Qaddafi. With renewed financial support and military arms, Taylor led his armed militia back into Liberia in 1989 and waged a bloody civil war for nearly ten years.

Fearful that violence would otherwise continue, the Liberian people elected Taylor president in 1997. Under Taylor's regime, ruthless human rights violations and the support of regional militia groups continued unabated. Taylor kidnapped children, converted them into soldiers through the forced use of drugs, and terrorized the civilian population. His rapacious greed for diamonds also led him to support Sierra Leone's Revolutionary United Front, a militia that oversaw the murder and rape of tens of thousands in that country. Called "the Milošević of Africa," Charles Taylor became intolerable, and the international community demanded the formation of a transitional government in Liberia in 2003.

By mid-June, despite his promises to step aside, it was clear that Taylor had no intention of leaving. Violence peaked in the capital of Monrovia. I remember vividly a front-page photo in the *New York Times* on June 28 of a young boy wearing a teddy bear backpack on one arm and gripping an assault rifle in the other. He couldn't have been more than twelve years old.

Before leaving for Africa, we held an NSC meeting on Liberia. Colin was trying to assist Kofi Annan in bringing an end to the crisis but to no avail. The members of the Economic Community of West African States (ECOWAS) wanted Charles Taylor out to calm the situation and allow the entry of peacekeeping forces. Yet the African leaders were reluctant to say so publicly, maintaining an often counterproductive code of conduct of refusing to criticize one another no matter how egregious the behavior.

The President wanted to know what his options were in dealing with the Liberian crisis. He'd been involved in several efforts to defuse longstanding conflicts in Africa and during those previous engagements had preferred to work directly with African leaders and through African institutions. That had been done successfully at the UN General Assembly in New York in 2002, when he had teamed with President Thabo Mbeki of South Africa to bridge differences between President Laurent-Désiré Kabila of the Democratic Republic of the Congo and President Paul Kagame of Rwanda. That had given a push to moderating the Great Lakes Conflict and the raging violence affecting Rwanda, Burundi, and Congo that had claimed millions of lives since 1994.

Now, with Liberia, the President faced the question of how involved the United States should be. Before the meeting, Colin and I met with the President in the Oval. "Why should I do something in Liberia?" he asked.

"Because Liberia is ours, Mr. President," I replied. We talked about the history of the country that had been founded by freed American slaves.

"Even the Liberian flag imitates the Stars and Stripes," Colin added. I told the President that my Aunt Theresa had taught at the University of Liberia all the way back in 1961. The ties of the African American community to the country ran deep.

Jendayi had done a paper for me that suggested it would take only a few hundred Americans on the ground (and maybe a warship or two at sea) to intimidate the Liberian insurgents and stop them from fighting. "They respect America," she said. "It will be enough."

Sitting in the Situation Room, it was easy to read the body language of the Vice President and Don, who saw no earthly reason for U.S. involvement in the affair. They were particularly concerned when the President asked what military options he had, including perhaps joining the peacekeeping force. The NSC meeting ended with the Pentagon promising to get back to the President with options. In the meantime, the President would use his trip to Africa to rally the leaders in support of a political strategy: Charles Taylor would leave, peacekeeping forces would enter, and a transitional government would prepare for elections.

When the President returned home, he was even more determined to do something about Liberia. On July 14 Kofi Annan visited Washington, and the President took the opportunity to speak about the issue in a joint press conference. "Our government's position is a strong position. We want to enable ECOWAS to get in and help create the conditions necessary for the ceasefire to hold." The President reiterated that Taylor had to leave and said that the United States would "participate with troops." Ad-libbing the last part of the statement, the President had committed the United States to a military role.

Several days later I convened the Principals to see where the Pentagon stood on the President's request. It had been three weeks since he'd asked for military options. When the Defense Department doesn't want to do something, the options that the President receives make it seem as if he is about to launch World War III. Colin and I pushed back, saying that it shouldn't take thousands of U.S. soldiers to secure the airport and seaport so that humanitarian supplies could be distributed and peacekeepers could enter.

The second Principals Committee meeting a day later wasn't much better. Finally, on July 23, the Pentagon presented a realistic option. On July 25 the President ordered a naval amphibious force composed of 2,300 marines to sail from the Mediterranean into position off the coast of Liberia. Colin told reporters, "We do have some obligations as the most important, powerful nation on the face of the earth not to look away when a problem like this comes before us." The Pentagon's pique was obvious, as military "sources" told the New York Times that it had been caught off guard by the announcement.

In the face of international pressure and U.S. resolve, Charles Taylor resigned the presidency of Liberia on August 11 as three U.S. warships drifted into view and two U.S. helicopters hovered overhead. I watched on television as Ghanaian President John Kufuor, the chairman of ECOWAS, escorted Taylor out of the country. There had been a delay of several hours from his expected time of departure. I had called Colin to see what had gone wrong. He wasn't sure but suspected that the Africans were just taking a little time to "talk the brother into leaving for good." Sure enough, they soon emerged and the plane lifted off for Nigeria, where Taylor would live in exile until he was arrested and taken to The Hague in 2006 to stand trial for war crimes before the Special Court for Sierra Leone.

Two hundred marines went ashore several days after Taylor's resignation, and within a few weeks, African peacekeepers, under the command of an able Nigerian general, were deployed throughout the country. Liberia would become a true success story with the election two years later of Ellen Johnson Sirleaf, the first female head of state on the African continent. Though war-ravaged and poor, Liberia now ranks high on the Millennium Challenge criteria of political freedom and control of corruption. The United States had not looked away, and it paid off handsomely for the people of Liberia and for democracy's forward march in Africa.

16

NEW CHALLENGES IN IRAQ

B Y THE TIME we returned from Africa, the controversy over the "six-teen words" in the State of the Union was in full froth. I appeared on the Sunday shows the next day to face a torrent of accusations about the Niger statement. I tried fruitlessly to explain that the British stood by their report but there had been CIA concerns about its veracity— concerns of which I hadn't been made aware. People were saying that the President had taken the nation to war because of the Niger claim, which was ludicrous; at issue was one sentence in a long indictment against Saddam Hussein.

Bob Schieffer on *Face the Nation* was the most aggressive questioner: "How did the line get into the speech?" "Did your staff insist [over the objection of the CIA] on putting it in?" "Did the Vice President's office review it?" The entire three-thousand-word interview transcript went like that. So too did the encounters with Wolf Blitzer on CNN and Tony Snow on *Fox News Sunday*.

After the Schieffer interview I got into the car with Anna Perez, who was unflappable in the face of almost anything. She was worried. I'd come across as evasive, she thought, and perhaps as not taking respon-sibility for what had happened. By the time I got home to the Watergate, there were reports that Senator Jay Rockefeller was condemning my re-fusal to take personal responsibility. I was caught in a tsunami of criti-cism and, more troubling, questions about my personal integrity.

The situation didn't get better when the CIA suddenly produced the memorandum that had been sent to the White House at the time of the President's speech in Cincinnati, questioning the soundness of the British report. I didn't remember having seen it, but when Mike Gerson found the same document in his files, it was clear that it had indeed come across my desk. Perhaps I should have remembered one line in a long memo clearing a speech, but I didn't.

Steve Hadley then stepped forward and selflessly took responsibility for the whole mess. Though it was true that Steve oversaw the speech clearance process, what had happened was simply not his fault. If the Agency had had problems with the sixteen words in the State of the Union, it had only to say so at the time and we would have removed the words immediately. Full stop. But Tenet admitted that he hadn't read the speech.

I was attending a dedication of a library in Kansas for former Senator Robert Dole when Steve called the press together and methodically walked them through what happened. It was a searing experience for him—he the most honest of public servants.

Steve's "admission" did not, of course, stem the tide. The press wanted an admission from me. Anna had been right that I had created a perception of dodging responsibility. I called the late Tim Russert of NBC News, whose counsel I valued. "What do I need to do?" I asked him off the record. "The American people can always forgive," he said, "but they want to know that you feel remorse for what happened."

On July 30 I appeared on *The NewsHour with Jim Lehrer* with Gwen Ifill. I knew that Gwen would be tough but fair and, most important, credible. I stated clearly that I felt personally responsible for the whole flap. Earlier that day in a press conference the President had been asked whether he wanted me to resign. He gave me his strongest possible endorsement, but it really cut to hear the President have to give one of those "I have full confidence in . . ." statements that only demonstrate the depths of an official's troubles. I remember that evening receiving a phone call from a member of Congress who purported to be my friend. We were supposed to have dinner in a few days. "It wouldn't be good for us to be seen together," this person said. "I have to maintain my objectivity." Washington is a lonely place when the wolves turn on you.

Eventually my personal trials would abate, but the problems for the administration were just beginning. The weapons hunt continued, but no stockpiles were found. David Kay, the chief inspector, came to the White House and met with the President on July 27. Kay told the

President that it was likely that Saddam had a latent capability that he could have mobilized when the pressure from the international community lessened. There was still an infrastructure: scientists, laboratories, and front companies. Too, the air assault on Iraq's WMD in 1998 had been more successful than we had known, and serious damage had been done to Saddam's capabilities at the time.

After closed-door briefings to select Senate committees four days later, Kay publicly cautioned that the hunt for WMD was "going to take time" but that his team was making "solid progress" and that every day he was "surprised by new advances." To the critics on Capitol Hill who were anxious to find weapons, he said, "The Iraqis had over two decades to develop these weapons. And hiding them was an essential part of their program. So it's not an easy task, and we're not close to a final conclusion yet." But by the beginning of the next year, Kay told the Senate Armed Services Committee, "We were almost all wrong." In saying so he would become one of the administration's harshest critics.

I've replayed all of this over and over through the years. What could we have done differently? Where did I fail? Clearly, we had allowed the argument concerning WMD to get disconnected from the broader strategic case against Saddam. I should never have sanctioned the use of bits of intelligence, particularly by the President. The intelligence agencies were indeed wrong about the *extent* of the WMD threat from Saddam but not in saying that there was evidence of a threat. There were competing views in the intelligence community, but the Agency thought that he'd reconstituted his biological and chemical weapons capability and all but the State Department thought that he was doing so on the nuclear side. That assessment was shared by several foreign intelligence agencies too. I bristled as I listened to congressional critics accuse us of inflating the threat while forgetting their own prior statements of the impending doom posed by Saddam's WMD.

Ultimately the fallout took a toll on all of us. Colin has described the presentation at the United Nations on February 5 as a stain on his career. I am sorry that he feels that way, and it pains me to know that that is the moment that is often called up in reviewing the long and stellar record of service of this American hero and my friend. But Colin didn't seek to deceive anyone. None of us did. In retrospect, I wish I'd said over and over again that intelligence always carries uncertainties; that is the nature of the beast.

After 9/11, Saddam in possession of WMD in the world's most volatile region was a terrifying prospect; the Middle East would be a less frightening place without him. I still believe that the latter is true. I have many regrets about the run-up to the war, but I'm not sorry that we overthrew Saddam. And I'm grateful that today's concern is not an impending nuclear arms race between Iran's Mahmoud Ahmadinejad and Iraq's Saddam Hussein.

"The UN Headquarters Has Been Bombed!"

THE INTELLIGENCE FAILURE was unfolding simultaneously with the worsening security situation on the ground. Throughout the spring and early summer, the insurgency seemed to be gaining steam, and harrowing incidents were becoming commonplace. Tommy Franks stepped down in May 2003. I thought the world of Franks, but Don told several of us that the general was tired and wanted to retire. General John Abizaid was nominated to replace Franks on June 18 and assumed command July 7. I cannot be sure that the turnover in leadership mattered in the final analysis, but I remember thinking at the time that it was bizarre to change command in the middle of a war. Ricardo Sanchez, then a two-star general, was quickly promoted to lieutenant general to serve as the top commander in Iraq. Nonetheless, his staff lacked sufficient and experienced personnel to carry out the increasingly complex mission in Iraq during the early months of his command. John Abizaid would prove to be an exceptionally able commander of United States Central Command (CENTCOM), but the continuous shifting of military leadership in the field still strikes me as having been the wrong approach.

The CPA was also experiencing difficulty. Insurgents had begun to attack its incipient reconstruction projects, and Jerry Bremer was clearly struggling to reconcile the existing power structures and institutions with the political demands of the new Iraq. One of the first steps he'd taken was to issue CPA orders that removed full members of the Baath

Party from government posts and, more consequentially, dissolved the Iraq army, air force, navy, and other regular military services.

There has been a good deal of retrospective examination of whether the order to disband the Iraqi army was adequately reviewed by and co-ordinated with Washington. A postmortem conducted by the late Peter Rodman, the assistant secretary of defense for international security affairs, shows that the Pentagon was aware of Jerry's intentions to issue an order dissolving Iraqi security organizations, including the army, as a part of the de-Baathification effort. Don received a memorandum to this effect on May 19, but he did not bring it to my attention or that of the President. Jerry has said that he raised the issue at the NSC on May 22. Several participants remember that it was brought up only in general terms during a discussion of de-Baathification. It was certainly not a request for permission to issue the order.

By that point the army had largely melted away, and there was little left of a formal structure. But surely the decision to dissolve it explicitly ran counter to the earlier plans to retain as many as three to five divisions to form the nucleus of a new Iraqi army. We all knew that it was one of the pillars of Iraqi society and a source of pride. There were concerns, which I shared, that it was rife with Baathists and needed to be reformed. But I was surprised when I read in the newspaper on May 24 that the Iraqi military had been dissolved by order of the U.S. envoy.

I resolved at that moment to get a better handle on what was going on in Baghdad. The President had made clear that he wanted Jerry to have flexibility in dealing with conditions on the ground. But something was wrong when a decision of that magnitude could be made without Washington's full and considered deliberation.

Moreover, by June there were almost daily protests outside the CPA headquarters calling for elections to form a national government. The strong U.S. hand was already wearing on the population's nationalistic pride, and in response Jerry approved the formation of a twenty-five-member Iraqi Governing Council (IGC). Making clear that the Council was advisory, we hoped that it would begin to give the Iraqis more of a say in the development of their country. But it was a delicate balancing act because the IGC was a raucously divided group reflecting the political fissures of the country. The leaders decided to rotate the presidency of the IGC every month, adding to the chaos. More than a few times, Jerry had trouble even getting the Council to meet since some of its members greatly enjoyed traveling the world's capitals on behalf of the new Iraq.

Then, on August 20, the situation on the ground took a stunning turn for the worse. We'd long overcome our aversion to a UN role in Iraq. The President had come to the conclusion that Colin was right: we needed a substantial UN presence to help legitimize the steps we were taking toward the establishment of postwar order in Iraq.

I cannot say enough about the help that we received from UN Secretary-General Kofi Annan in this regard. Though he was clearly opposed to the war, he moved more quickly than I could have imagined to forge a good relationship between the United Nations and the United States concerning Iraq. He sought and received the UN Security Council's authorization for the appointment of a special representative of the secretary-general to carry out the difficult mission in Iraq. He chose a remarkable man, Sérgio Vieira de Mello, a Brazilian with long experience in conflict resolution. When Vieira de Mello at first refused the assignment, Kofi asked me to meet with him. We met in my office on March 5, and then I walked with him down the hall to the Oval Office to see the President. He returned to New York and agreed to take the job. That afternoon, Colin and I talked about the big leap forward that we had just achieved. Vieira de Mello would be a steady hand and bring international legitimacy as we pushed forward the transition to a new Iraqi government.

I'D DECIDED to take a short vacation in August at the Greenbrier in West Virginia. The lovely resort had become my quiet getaway every summer because it was a short drive home if I was needed in Washington. Colin and I once joked that a vacation spot is where you go to pay a lot of money, look out at the beautiful scenery, and take phone calls from the White House. But despite that, I still felt refreshed whenever I returned home from White Sulphur Springs.

On my last vacation day, I was playing tennis with a pro, Terry Deremer, and Missy Weiss, a woman who also vacationed at the Greenbrier every year. Missy had played number one for Ohio State and had been on tour. I was no match for her on the court but loved to rally with her. Once in a while I even won a point or two.

Literally midserve, one of my security agents sprinted onto the court. The Situation Room was on the phone. I yelled apologies while running toward the waiting cell phone and soon learned that the UN headquarters in Baghdad had been bombed. Initial reports indicated that there were many casualties, and the fate of Vieira de Mello was unknown. I rushed back to my room and packed, telling my aunt, cousin, and friends who were accompanying me that we were heading back to Washington immediately. A few minutes later I got a reassuring update concerning Vieira de Mello, who'd reportedly spoken with Kofi on the phone after the bombing. But by the time we drove away and onto Interstate 81, I got word that Vieira de Mello had perished along with twenty-one other people, including UN workers. I was devastated and felt personally responsible for having talked him into taking the job.

My friends and family were talking in the back of the van. "I can't hear," I said somewhat rudely as I listened to an update from the Situation Room. The chatter ceased. We drove home in silence, interrupted only by reports from the White House and a call from the President, whom I assured that I was headed home.

THE SITUATION would spiral downward after that terrible August attack. Coalition forces couldn't get a handle on the insurgency, which was gaining strength almost daily. The political situation wasn't stabilizing either, as Iraqis were becoming more insistent about retaking control of their country. We started to hear the word "occupiers" with greater frequency. I did not expect, as the Vice President and others naively suggested, that the Iraqis would joyfully greet us as liberators. I reckoned that the only place where soldiers had flowers thrown at their feet was in old movies about World War II. The Iraqi people are gritty and tough and have a reputation for being fiercely independent. "I know you want to bring democracy to the Middle East," Egyptian President Hosni Mubarak had told Steve Hadley. "But why did you start with the Iraqis? They are the worst."

But I didn't expect the United States to be thought of as an occupier, either. We'd gone to great lengths to avoid having a heavy military footprint in the country. A larger force would have given us much-needed manpower to deal with multiple contingencies—but there was also a downside to a big foreign presence.

At the time Tommy Franks sent a draft of his initial address to the Iraqi people to us for review, I remember turning to Anna Perez. "This sounds like a Roman emperor," I told her. We modified the address to make it sound friendlier. The British had no such qualms. They knew that for all intents and purposes we were occupying the country and constantly said so. It turned out that the Iraqis, even those who supported us, thought so too.

Obviously, we had to help the Iraqis find a path to sovereignty. Jerry understood this very well and proposed a road map that he published in the *Washington Post* on September 8, 2003. The problem was that he did so without fully consulting Washington. The seven-point plan he presented in the paper's op-ed pages touched off a firestorm in Iraq and consternation in the White House and State Department. Jerry had suggested that a new constitution be written through a process organized by the Iraqi Governing Council, with elections to follow. That drew a rebuke from perhaps the most powerful man in Iraq, the Ayatollah Ali al-Sistani, who objected to the sequence Jerry had outlined. Sistani believed that Iraq's new constitution had to be written by representatives elected by the Iraqi people, not through a process devised by an organization that emanated from the CPA.

The seventy-something Sistani was among the most revered clerics in the Shia faith. He'd been kept under house arrest during Saddam's reign but was now free to speak to his following. Sistani turned out to be a remarkable man. Insisting on "quietism" for clerics, he believed that religious men should eschew formal roles in politics. That, of course, stood in stark contrast to the ruling ayatollahs in Iran. When Sistani, sitting in Najaf, the holiest of Shia cities, was prohibited from speaking publicly, the Iranian mullahs in Qom had become the voice of the Shia people. But among the Arabs of Iraq, the Persian Iranians had long been viewed with suspicion, even hatred. And Najaf, not Qom, was the religious heart of the Shia sect, a kind of Vatican for that part of the Islamic faith.

So when Sistani spoke, it mattered. Ironically, he would not meet with nonmembers of the faith, particularly foreigners, so we had no direct contact with him. His son acted as a conduit for his views, which we came to regard as crucial to progress in Iraq. Yet this mysterious man always seemed to be on the right side of the issues; he was a voice for democracy and for the separation of religion from matters of the state. In private we called him Iraq's Benjamin Franklin—a wise man who never held or wished to hold elected office.

Within days it was clear that the road map that Jerry had outlined was untenable. The NSC met to consider the next steps, and there was a lot of talk around the table about whether Sistani was right about the sequence. The President cut through the debate. "How did I get on the wrong side of a demand for elections?" he asked. That shut everyone up, and we resolved to find a new path that would give the Iraqis a chance to elect the leaders who would draft their constitution.

INCIDENTS LIKE THOSE convinced me that we had to have better connectivity between Jerry and Washington. Colin and I had talked to Don about the problem of pronouncements popping out of Baghdad without due consideration in the NSC. I learned through Frank Miller that Jerry felt disconnected too, having only intermittent contact with Don. Jerry recruited Reuben Jeffery, a highly capable man who'd been a managing partner of Goldman Sachs, to run a Washington office for him and facilitate better contact with the Pentagon. But we just kept getting surprised by decisions—some small but some very large indeed.

I went to the President in late September and told him that I wanted to form a new steering group to bridge the divide between the CPA and Washington. He agreed. I drafted a memo, which I shared with Colin and Don, establishing the Iraq Stabilization Group (ISG). Robert Blackwill, with whom I had previously served in government, would lead the effort. Bob had just returned from a stint as ambassador to India, but it was his black belt in bureaucratic politics that made him the right person for the job. He was like a bull in a china shop, and I knew that there would be tensions with others. I could tolerate the turbulence, though, because Bob would make sure that the NSC had a voice.

A few days after the memo to Don and Colin, Anna called to say that David Sanger of the *New York Times* had caught wind of the formation of the group. She thought that we should give him the story so that it would be accurate. I know, too, that Anna thought it would make me look good—in control of what was a deteriorating situation in Iraq.

The story that emerged caused a sensation. My effort to explain that the Pentagon retained direct supervision and responsibility for the CPA was swept away by the perception that I'd shoved Don aside and taken operational control of the civilian effort in Iraq. The problem was exacerbated by the Defense Department, which conveyed the impression that Don had been caught off guard by the group's creation. This happened despite the fact that Larry Di Rita, Don's spokesman, had agreed to talk to Sanger so that it would be clear that we were all on the same page. I had talked to Larry personally about this issue.

The state visit of President Mwai Kibaki of Kenya took place the morning that Sanger's article appeared. As usual, I'd seen the President first thing that day, and he didn't seem too concerned by the press coverage. But an hour or so later, Andy Card found me as we waited to start the arrival ceremony and said that the President had heard screams of indignation from the Pentagon. "You need to talk to him," he said.

That afternoon I went to see the President. "You need to make it right with Don," he said. "The Pentagon is really spun up." I said that I hadn't intended to cause a problem and understood that the coverage was pretty sensational. "See if the Vice President can help," he said.

I went to see the Vice President right away, who said he would indeed talk to Don. The next morning at the NSC the President reaffirmed Don's role in overseeing the CPA and Jerry. It was the right thing to do under the circumstances, but I felt undermined and knew that it would be even more difficult to manage the situation in Iraq. Outside the Situation Room after the meeting, Don said, "What you did really hurt the President." I held my tongue, resisting the temptation to say, "You don't think that mess in Iraq is hurting the President?"

Much to my surprise, though, rather than doubling down on his authority over the CPA, Don took the opportunity to wash his hands of the political situation. In an earlier conversation, Don had told Colin and me that Jerry Bremer did not report to him but to the White House.

"That isn't right, Don," I insisted. But he didn't back down. "Look at the President's directive," I said. He let the issue drop. Then, after the ISG flap, he told everyone that Bremer now reported to me. This was a ludicrous statement. We needed better communication, but I couldn't be a substitute for the secretary of defense in overseeing the execution of policy.

I hadn't realized how much Don bristled at what he thought to be White House interference in the chain of command. He was unhappy that the President had met with Jerry alone at the time of his appointment. And he was furious that I called Jerry periodically to check in on developments in Iraq. I had no choice, because the difficult relationship between the two men became one of benign neglect by Don. Jerry and I started to talk every day as we began to map out a strategy to return sovereignty to the Iraqi people. Bob Blackwill deployed to Iraq, and the United Nations would soon appoint Lakhdar Brahimi, a seasoned diplomat, to help with that work.

Frankly, the situation was uncomfortable. I felt stuck with the Iraqi political transition and far deeper into operational matters than I believed wise for a national security advisor. Yet when Bob Blackwill called me in early November to say that Jerry was about to deliver another, revised schedule for the transition, I was very glad I'd intervened.

ON SUNDAY, November 9, 2003, I decided to attend a Redskins football game with my good friend Gene Washington. The team I liked to root for, the Cleveland Browns, was, as usual, already out of the playoff hunt, and I couldn't have cared less about the Redskins or the Seahawks. But I did look forward to a relaxing afternoon enjoying my favorite pastime—football.

A few minutes before halftime, my Secret Service agent said that Bob Blackwill was on the secure phone (we always carried one) from Baghdad. I thought to myself that it was pretty late on a Sunday evening in Iraq, so I was immediately concerned that something was really wrong. "Jerry is about to issue a new set of political guidelines tomorrow," Bob said.

"What?" I asked. After the "seven points" debacle, I couldn't believe my ears. "You have to tell him that the President has to see what he's going to say," I said.

"*You'd* better tell him," Bob replied.

I immediately put in a call to Jerry and said that I thought the President might have a view about the next steps in Iraq. Jerry agreed and said that he'd call him in the morning. "Jerry," I said, "maybe you'd better get on a plane and come to Washington." Again he agreed and said that he could arrive by Wednesday.

The next morning I went to the Oval and told the President about the conversation. "Why did you do that?" the President barked, perhaps still smarting from the ISG flap. "Does Don agree?"

"Mr. President," I said, "I wanted to tell you first, and I will call Don. And if you want me to tell Jerry not to come I'll do that too. But don't be surprised when the United States has a new plan for Iraq's political transition that you haven't seen." I immediately thought that this might have sounded insubordinate. But the President and I could speak frankly when we were alone.

He kind of smiled. "Okay, when is he coming?" he asked.

"Wednesday," I replied.

Jerry did come on Wednesday, and the NSC met with him. We agreed to develop a new plan that would satisfy Sistani's criteria. Eventually it would lead to the negotiation of the Transitional Administrative Law (TAL), which would provide direction for the country in preparation for elections. We would move toward the establishment of an interim government to oversee the transition. Elections would be held in 2005.

Through the ups and downs of that work, Jerry gently guided the Iraqis to write a political document that became the basis of the Iraqi Constitution. I was at a seder at the home of the Israeli ambassador on the night the TAL was completed. Jerry called me, I called the President, and we all celebrated that important step on the road to Iraqi self-rule. A grand ceremony was planned to launch the TAL on Friday, March 5, 2004. Jerry called that morning, saying that the Iraqis had turned out in droves for the event. Most of the leaders were there with their wives and children, he told me. "Some with several of their wives," he quipped. But by the time the children's choir had run out of songs to sing, the Shia leaders still had not arrived. It turned out there had been a last-minute disagreement about the document's language. Fortunately, the glitch was resolved over the weekend, and the TAL went into force on March 8, 2004.

This political progress came against a backdrop of increasing violence and a worsening security situation. The insurgents were able to disrupt the reconstruction effort seriously, exploiting vulnerabilities in the electrical grid that we were trying to rebuild. Bob Blackwill had sent a memo to me in September 2003 suggesting that the President deploy 40,000 more troops. I hadn't discussed it with the President at the time, but I went to him in November to suggest that he raise the possibility with the Pentagon again. He did and received the same answer: we had enough troops on the ground.

In part everyone was counting on the rebuilt Iraqi security forces to take on some of the burden. But the effort to establish a new Iraqi army was proceeding slowly. Reconstruction of the police forces was even more challenging. The problem was hardly unique to Iraq; the hardest job in a post-conflict environment is to build a reliable police force, free of corruption and competent to handle the full range of security threats from insurgencies to everyday crimes. We had seen the problem in places as different as the Balkans, Afghanistan, and Liberia.

Under Frank Miller's leadership, the defense policy arm of the ISG did its best to focus the Pentagon on the security problem but always received the same answer: the security situation will improve when the politics improve. But it's hard to win the hearts and minds of people when you can't protect them.

Still, a lot had been accomplished, and the President wanted to visit the troops in Baghdad to offer our men and women in uniform his gratitude and support. Joe Hagin, the deputy chief of staff, was put in charge of finding a way to get the President safely into and out of Baghdad. The feat Joe managed to pull off was extraordinary.

On the Wednesday before Thanksgiving, the President went to the ranch for what all but a few aides thought would be a well-deserved holiday weekend. That evening, the President and I climbed into an unmarked wine-colored van and left the ranch. We wore baseball caps, prompting the President to say later that we looked like a couple on the way to shop at Wal-mart. Only First Lady Laura Bush and the head of the President's Secret Service detail knew where we were headed.

Because the Secret Service couldn't use the usual motorcade procedures, our driver was forced to cope with heavy traffic on Interstate 35. "What is this?" the President asked.

"A traffic jam," I answered, thinking that he probably hadn't seen one in a while. Nonetheless, we made our way to the airstrip in Waco and flew to Andrews Air Force Base, where we'd board Air Force One.

The flight to Baghdad was surreal. Andy Card, Joe Hagin, and I sat with Dan Bartlett, the President's communications director, in the staff cabin. There were only four press representatives on board. As we approached Baghdad, Colonel Tillman, Air Force One's pilot, began to take evasive maneuvers that we could all feel. Then he lowered the lights so that the cabin was dark with the exception of the blue digital time display. It came to me that we should go up to the President's cabin and offer to pray with him. He is a religious man, and at times like that, religious people pray. There in the darkness on the presidential aircraft, we each offered a short prayer. When we returned to the cabin about ten minutes before landing, I closed my eyes to pray again. In my head I heard a voice say, "and keep them safe from hurt, harm or danger." They were words that I hadn't heard since my father died—the words of a prayer that he'd always uttered when someone was leaving on a trip. "Thank you, Daddy," I said softly to myself.

We landed at the airport and walked up the stairs to a makeshift dining hall. As we waited outside, I marveled at standing in Saddam Hussein's airport. Those thoughts were short-lived, though, as the President burst into a room filled with six hundred U.S. soldiers. The place went wild. George W. Bush had a way with the troops. Though the soldiers hadn't known he was coming, cameras started flying out of pockets all over the place. It was pandemonium.

I sat with several enlisted personnel and a couple of officers. We talked about their hometowns, how they had come to join the military, and a little about football. When I thanked them for their service, they returned the sentiment. It was a wonderful, reaffirming time for me—for all of us.

After two hours or so, we boarded Air Force One again and took off. About that time, news stations started reporting that the President of the United States had made a surprise visit to Baghdad.

Non-proliferation Breakthrough

DESPITE THE TRIALS and tribulations in Iraq, we registered some gains. For instance, the overthrow of Saddam Hussein was beginning to have a salutary effect on other parts of the non-proliferation agenda.

We'd been trying for some time to get the Chinese to play a more active role in reining in the North Korean nuclear program. The President had been right that only Beijing had enough leverage to convince Kim Jong-il to abandon his aggressive stance toward the international community. Much of the problem with the Agreed Framework was that it had left the United States negotiating bilaterally with the North Koreans, allowing Pyongyang to play the South Koreans, the Europeans, and the Chinese off of us by seeking concessions from each party individually.

Now we had a different idea. Rather than the bilateral negotiations with the North that were being urged on us by our allies, we proposed a six-party framework with China in the chair. Beijing had initially resisted the idea when Colin proposed it in March 2003. President Bush had been so frustrated with the Chinese that he'd raised the ante in a phone call with Chinese President Ziang Jemin. Before getting on the call, he had asked what more he could say to move Beijing. I suggested that he raise the specter, ever so gently, of a military option against North Korea. He liked the idea, and when Ziang began to recite the timeworn mantra about the need for the United States to show more flexibility with the North, the President stopped him. A bit more directly than I'd expected, he told Ziang that he was under a lot of pressure from hard-liners to use military force and added, on his own, that one also couldn't rule out a nuclear Japan if the North remained unconstrained.

We'll probably never know what role that conversation—or the action in Iraq—played in the obvious redirection of Chinese strategy toward the North Korean nuclear problem. By the summer Beijing had agreed to the establishment of the Six-Party Talks. That allowed us to unify our policy approach with our allies Japan and South Korea and put pressure on China to take an active role in solving the problem. We invited Russia to join as well, given its proximity to North Korea and its long-standing ties with Pyongyang. The forum met for the first time in Beijing in late August 2003.

Even more startling developments were emerging in Libya. In the spring of 2003 we heard through the British that Muammar Qaddafi wanted to open negotiations with the United States and the United Kingdom, with the carrot being an end to Libya's WMD programs. At first we didn't put much faith in the overture but we ultimately decided to send a joint CIA/MI5 team to assess the situation. It returned with a positive report: Qaddafi was serious.

The negotiations had to be conducted in absolute secrecy; any breach might lead the Libyan dictator to abandon the effort. So without the knowledge of most of the government, Bob Joseph from the NSC and William Ehrman and David Landsman from the United Kingdom, together with representatives from the intelligence agencies, led the negotiations with the Libyans. Bob is as tough and skeptical a conservative as one can imagine. So when he told me that we could get the deal done, I realized that we were going to achieve an incredible breakthrough. Nigel Sheinwald, who'd replaced David Manning in Tony Blair's office, and I oversaw the effort on behalf of our bosses.

As we were getting close to agreement, though, the Libyans started to balk at certain demands for transparency in the destruction of their WMD. It looked as if the whole effort was unraveling as Tripoli started to deny the existence of programs to which it had already admitted. Then we got a break: a ship from Malaysia carrying a suspicious cargo bound for Libya was stopped by German and Italian authorities and diverted for inspection. On board were five large shipping containers labeled "used machine parts" later determined to have been carrying thousands of centrifuge components—including some emanating from the A. Q. Kahn network. Exposed in the midst of negotiations, the Libyans retreated from their hard-line stance and an agreement was back within reach.

The successful interdiction had been the result of the President's Proliferation Security Initiative (PSI). Announced the previous May in

Poland, the PSI created a network of countries that shared intelligence information concerning suspicious air, sea, and land shipments. If the intelligence was strong enough, a country might agree to inspect the cargo in question or even deny overflight rights to a suspected trafficker. The PSI had no secretariat, no building, and no bureaucracy. It was a virtual institution and had been an unsung example of cooperation in the assault on proliferation worldwide. It was also an example of a coalition of the willing. The UN might have debated the details of such an arrangement for years. But the informality and flexibility of the PSI made it possible for countries as disparate as Russia and Japan, Australia and Saudi Arabia, to be members.

The Libyan affair also helped us understand better how the shadowy networks of proliferation were interacting with rogue regimes. The A. Q. Khan ring, about which we'd learned in 2001, was a big part of the story. The CIA, with the cooperation of several countries, would soon arrest key members of the network, and in 2004 A. Q. Khan himself would be put under house arrest in Pakistan. Though there would be many ups and downs with Musharraf about the nuclear scientist's fate, we were pretty certain that he was no longer plying his wares to rogue regimes. (In fact, he would be released in 2009.)

On December 19 we were set finally to tell the world about Libya's disarmament. That would show that dictators could be persuaded or perhaps coerced to give up their weapons of mass destruction. The announcement would be made by the Libyan foreign minister and Colonel Qaddafi, and then welcomed by President Bush and Prime Minister Blair.

As the day dragged on, Nigel and I had to manage the anxiety of our respective bosses, who were waiting to tell the world what had transpired. It was getting quite late in Britain, so we decided to have the prime minister go first. The President would still have time to catch the evening news feed in the United States. Nigel had an open line to U.K. sources in Libya, but there was nothing to report. As it turned out, there was an important soccer match underway in Libya that night and the "Brother Leader" was taking his time. Finally, the U.K. source read the Libyan statements to Nigel, who was on the phone with me.

"Well?" I asked.

"Good enough," he replied. Though Qaddafi's statement rambled on about a green revolution (Islamic, not environmental), the Libyan foreign minister's statement satisfied the explicit demands of the agreement and we had what we needed. Muammar Qaddafi would give up his WMD and seek to end Libya's isolation from the international community. These dangerous weapons would travel over 5,000 miles from Tripoli to Tennessee, where they would be dismantled at Oak Ridge National Laboratory.

The Saturday before the Libyan announcement, I'd called in Dan Bartlett to tell him about the coming good news. I was surprised when he looked disappointed. "I thought you were going to tell me that we had found Saddam," he said. "That will be next week," I said in jest. The truth is, I was more than a little annoyed that Dan did not seem to understand the importance of what we'd achieved.

ONE WEEK after that comment, I was preparing for the thirty or so friends who were coming to my house for a Christmas party and carol singing on Sunday, December 12. Just before the revelers were to arrive, I got a call from the President. "Don just called," he said. "The military thinks they've got Saddam."

Don and Steve were among the guests, and we huddled for a moment in the kitchen out of earshot of the others. Don said that he didn't want to say anything until they could get some more positive identification of the man, who'd been found hiding in a spider hole at a farmhouse outside Tikrit. We carried on singing, but I certainly had a hard time concentrating on the Christmas cheer. I'm sure the others did too.

The next morning at about 3:00 my phone rang. "We got him," Jerry Bremer said, waking me from a not-too-sound sleep. I called the President and woke him up. He called Don. It was true. The men of Task Force 121, assisted by troops from the First Brigade Combat Team of the army's 4th Infantry Division, had captured the dictator of Iraq. The man who'd launched wars against his neighbors and brutalized his people for more than twenty years was in our hands. "My name is Saddam Hussein," he'd said as he was captured. "I am the president of Iraq. And I want to negotiate."

I got up and dressed quickly to make my way to the office. There was a lot to do to prepare for Jerry's announcement, which would come in a matter of hours. I called the startled Dan Bartlett. This time he was excited by the news. Jerry went to the podium surrounded by members of the Iraqi Governing Council to tell the assembled press of Saddam's capture. "We got him," he said, repeating what he'd said to me hours earlier. The Iraqi press erupted in jubilation. It was a very satisfying moment, but I remember thinking that we'd made a mistake. *An Iraqi should have made that announcement,* I thought. But it was too late to make the capture of Saddam an Iraqi moment, not an American one.

AS CHRISTMAS APPROACHED, I was tired and ready for a break. So much had transpired, and most of it was of enormous historic significance, with all of the tension and stress that brought. But I was also enjoying experiences that had an almost fairy-tale quality. The most extraordinary of them had been the royal state visit to England in November 2003 and the chance to stay in Buckingham Palace. When we arrived, I was escorted to my room, where my own personal maid waited to unpack my belongings. I instinctively started to help her. Seeing that, Colin Powell, who, with his wife, Alma, was staying in the next room, said, "You're in her way. They've been doing this for three hundred years."

That night Colin, Alma, and I had a drink in the sitting room. *What would our parents think?* I thought. Then Alma and I drank a toast to her father and mine. Two little black girls from Birmingham had come a long way. Then, as Prince Charles escorted me into the elaborate dinner as the orchestra played "God Save the Queen," I once again wished that I could tell my parents about this incredible experience. And so I did in a little prayer just before going to sleep.

I left a few days before Christmas for my aunt's house in Norfolk, but work followed me, relentlessly triggered by a daily barrage of news—some good, some bad—from Iraq, Afghanistan, and the war on terror. Yet with the capture of Saddam, our year ended on a high note. Certainly, we believed, the news from Tikrit would soon bring an end to the insurgency. Earlier in the year, on the very day when Steve

Hadley had met the press concerning the Niger controversy, Saddam's sons, Uday and Qusay, had been killed in a violent shoot-out in Mosul. Surely the now-headless horsemen of the Baath Party would soon give up the fight.

We were also prepared for elections in Afghanistan and believed that we were about to put that country on a sound political footing. The Bonn process, which had set the country on a path toward representative government, was not yet showing the wear and incoherence that would soon become evident. In fact, the NATO allies were stepping forward to join us in the effort. New members from East-Central Europe were enthusiastically fighting in both Iraq and Afghanistan; the wisdom of extending NATO membership to the former Communist states had become increasingly clear.

The war on terror was progressing too, as we captured more and more important al Qaeda field generals. In Southeast Asia we were seeing results from counterinsurgency cooperation in the region. In 2002 new fronts in the war on terror had emerged as evidence linked al Qaeda to the Abu Sayyaf insurgency in the southern Philippines. Additionally, suspected al Qaeda affiliates threatened the stability of a struggling new democratic government in Indonesia by bombing a Bali nightclub. But by 2004 those threats would recede with the capture of terrorist mastermind Hambali and the election of Susilo Bambang Yudhoyono as president of Indonesia, which ushered in a new era of democratic stability in the country with the world's largest Muslim population.

The redesign of our national security structures was continuing too, with all of the growing pains that accompany major institutional change. In that regard, I'd made what would prove to be one of my most important and effective personnel changes. Wayne Downing, the first counterterrorism chief, had stepped down to be replaced by General John Gordon, with whom I'd worked in the administration of George H. W. Bush. They'd done good work in establishing the post-9/11 role. But when I met Fran Townsend, a tough-talking former prosecutor from New York, who also happened to be female, I knew I'd found the right person to take hold of all that was required in that position. Fran had won a conviction against the notorious Gambino crime family; she could handle al Qaeda and Washington, I reasoned. But Fran had also served in the Clinton Justice Department, leading some in the conservative punditry to question her loyalty to the President. Karl Rove gave me cover on this one, tamping down a brewing conflict with some of our friends on the Hill and in the press.

The country was not yet safe, but it was most certainly safer than it had been on September 11, 2001. We entered the election fray of 2004 ready to keep up the fight abroad and gearing up to defend the President's record at home.

M Y LAST YEAR as national security advisor began as my first year had: with a visit to Mexico. Yet, sitting in Monterrey at a special Summit of the Americas, it was obvious that the agenda that we'd so hoped to pursue in the hemisphere had slipped considerably.

Our relations with Mexico weren't bad, but they weren't good either. The high point had been the state visit of President Vicente Fox in September 2001 shortly before 9/11. The arrival ceremony and dinner had signaled a new day in U.S.-Mexican relations. But the literal downpour that had threatened the fireworks display may have been a small sign that not all would be as we had hoped. It wasn't long before the agenda with Mexico came to be dominated by important but seemingly intractable issues such as Mexican water deliveries to Texas and border modernization and safety. We formed a Cabinet-level commission to oversee the work, but frankly I came to refer to the interactions as "home owner's association meetings." We shared the same continent, and that was the basis of our cooperation. Somehow the once much-anticipated plans for hemispheric cooperation on the big issues of immigration, trade, and democratization faded.

The agenda of the Summit of the Americas, which had showed great promise in 2001, when the mostly center-right governments had united to support a Free Trade Area of the Americas, was stalling as well. At that time Hugo Chávez had seemed a quite isolated figure, but now three years later, Latin American leaders who castigated him in private lined up to hug him in public.

The Venezuelan had survived a coup attempt in April 2002, and at the time there had been lots of speculation about the role of the United States. We hadn't backed the coup plotters, as some alleged. In fact, we'd warned that the United States would not support extra-constitutional efforts against Chavez. The crisis had been managed largely by the State Department and the embassy in Caracas. They had done so effectively.

The jobs of the national security advisor and the secretary of state are very different in that regard. With a small staff and the daily demands of the President's schedule, I couldn't focus on every issue—even every important issue. The Venezuelan crisis was one of many that never quite got to the level that would produce intense White House involvement—phone calls with heads of state, for instance. I was certainly kept informed and in turn briefed the President. Colin talked with him about it as well. But as I would learn later, as secretary of state, there were many, many crises that Colin had spared us and handled ably himself. Yet when the coup failed, the Venezuelan dictator was left stronger at home and more active in the region.

Though our hemisphere-wide agenda was stalling, we successfully negotiated a free-trade agreement with five Central American countries and the Dominican Republic, as well as another one with Chile. We also made progress on the bilateral agendas with Brazil and Colombia. The President was able to develop close personal ties to the leaders of these two countries that served us well.

In the case of Colombian President Álvaro Uribe, the bond was forged around a common agenda against terrorism. When Uribe was elected, Colombia was very nearly a failed state. The Colombians told us that the army and police were unable to safely enter approximately 30 percent of the country. A decades-long struggle against the Communist-inspired FARC had left the country plagued by militants, and the paramilitaries that had emerged had left the Colombian state vulnerable and weak. FARC was holding numerous hostages, including three Americans. Uribe's predecessor, Andrés Pastrana, was an honorable man, but his effort to make a peace deal with the FARC had backfired when FARC had used the pause in military action to strengthen its grip on large parts of the country. Over the years, the FARC insurgency had produced a counterreaction and the development of paramilitary groups, the most powerful of which was the AUC. At times, the paramilitaries had been closely aligned with the security forces and even some members of the government. By the time of Uribe's election, they too had become a huge part of the problem.

The United States had trained and equipped Colombian security forces through Plan Colombia. The Clinton administration had begun a massive and comprehensive program to augment security aspects of the "war on drugs" with development assistance for Colombia and its neighbors. The idea was to help *all* of the Andean states so that the defeat of the druglords in one country wouldn't simply drive them to establish operations on the territory of a vulnerable neighbor.

Uribe wanted not only to continue this effort but to change its character. He came to power speaking of "democratic security," by which FARC would be defeated and power returned to the security forces of the state. He made clear that he'd go after the paramilitaries too, even though some of them had been associated with his political party. When he met with President Bush for the first time, he described the challenge and his commitment to confronting it. The President was immediately attracted to him and his toughness. "Do you really mean it?" the President asked. "Because if you do, you have to be prepared for really tough action. Kill their leadership, and they will start to fold." Uribe assured the President that he intended to do exactly that. Over the next years, Uribe would become one of our closest allies, and, more important, he'd deliver on his promise. Colombia is now widely recognized as a success, a state that was brought back from the brink of failure and chaos.

The President developed a somewhat different but also close relationship with President Luiz Inácio Lula da Silva of Brazil. Uribe was a man of center-right politics, and there was a natural fit with George W. Bush. Lula was a leftist, a former labor organizer who'd won a landslide victory to lead Brazil. Though the early signs were that he'd keep in place the market-oriented reforms of his predecessors, Lula was viewed with suspicion in global business communities—and in the White House.

When Lula first walked into the Oval Office as president-elect of Brazil on December 10, 2002, the President was, as always, warm and welcoming. But he couldn't take his eyes off the pin that Lula was wearing—the symbol of his party and one that displayed a decidedly socialist motif. The President would later say that Lula should have been wearing a Brazilian flag. Nonetheless, the chemistry between the two was immediately good. Lula has an easy manner and a twinkle in his eye that is endearing. I noticed too that he was missing a finger on his hand—he'd lost it in a lathe accident as a factory worker. There was an authentic feel to him, and unlike Chávez, a military officer turned ruling thug, Lula seemed to be someone we could work with.

With the outreach we'd done to Brazil, Colombia, Chile, and the countries of Central America, we had a good basis for a successful policy in Latin America. But sitting there in Monterrey at the Summit of the Americas, I recognized that, owing to the diversions of 9/11, Afghanistan, and Iraq, we'd done too little to help our friends. As a result of our inattention, our adversaries were gaining steam. The time would come later to do something about it—should the President get a second term.

"Strategery"

BEGINNING IN 2003, Karl Rove had begun convening the senior White House staff biweekly to review the totality of the President's agenda. Over cookies, cheese, fruit, and chips and dip, these early-evening meetings—dubbed "strategery," for a well-known malapropism uttered by then Governor Bush—were held to keep everyone on the same page. I found them extremely enlightening, learning, for instance, what Margaret Spellings, the domestic policy advisor, was doing to promote the No Child Left Behind program or how we were progressing on the economic agenda or in the Office of Faith-Based and Community Initiatives. The meetings added to the genuine comity that Andy Card successfully maintained in the White House. It was not unheard of in the annals of Washington, but it was unusual to be able to say that some of your best friends were other White House staffers. I simply never worried about what someone was doing behind my back. Margaret, Larry Lindsey, and later Steve Friedman at the NEC, Mitchell Daniels and his deputy Clay Johnson at OMB, Harriet Miers, Karen Hughes and Dan Bartlett, Karl, Josh, Ari, and most especially Andy were honest folk, and we supported one another in good times and bad. Al Gonzales and I repaired our relationship after he had allowed the presidential directive on military commissions to be signed without my knowledge. He too became and still is a good friend.

As the campaign approached, the "strategery" sessions became naturally intertwined with the politics of reelection. Karl and the domestic side of the White House wanted to reserve as sufficient a portion of the President's time as possible for the necessary work of seeking a second term. But the Bush presidency was a wartime one, and everyone understood that national security would continue to dominate his agenda.

The President's approval numbers had dropped but had not been disastrously affected by the course of the Iraq war despite the increasing difficulty there. But the controversy over the sixteen words and the suggestion by some in the media that the administration had been dishonest about prewar intelligence was clearly taking a toll. I found appalling, for instance, a *Time* magazine cover titled "Untruth & Consequences: How Flawed Was the Case for Going to War Against Saddam?" As amnesia set in on Capitol Hill among the many legislators who'd given fiery speeches about the threat of Saddam's WMD, we were suddenly very much alone in defending the premise for war. Clearly we had a credibility problem, but we also had a responsibility to examine what had gone wrong.

In February the President appointed a commission, led by Judge Laurence Silberman and former Democratic Senator Charles Robb, to examine the intelligence regarding weapons of mass destruction as well as the capabilities of the intelligence community. Although it concluded that many of the judgments of the intelligence community were flawed, the bipartisan Silberman-Robb Commission was sympathetic to those who supported the Washington consensus around Saddam's WMD. "Iraq's decision to abandon its unconventional weapons programs while simultaneously hiding this decision was, at the very least, a counterintuitive one," the report concluded. "And given the nature of the regime, the Intelligence Community can hardly be blamed for not penetrating Saddam's decision-making process. In this light, it is worth noting that Saddam's fellow Arabs (including, evidently his senior military leadership as well as many of the rest of the world's intelligence agencies and most inspectors) also thought he had retained his weapons programs." The intelligence failure was to some degree understandable, but there were still reforms we could implement.

THE SCRUTINY WE FACED on Iraq was intensified by the 9/11 Commission's inquiry into the September 11 terrorist attacks. In November 2002 President Bush and Congress had authorized the creation of a National Commission on Terrorist Attacks upon the United States, which would explore how the September 11 attacks had happened and issue recommendations on how to avoid future tragedies. Under the direction of former New Jersey Governor Thomas H. Kean and former Congressman Lee H. Hamilton, the commission reviewed more than 2.5 million pages of documents and interviewed more than 1,200 individuals as part of its investigation.

As the commission did its work in the spring of 2004, those who had been in positions of responsibility on September 11 did what people do: they sought to put their own actions in the best light. So too did Clinton administration officials, since the eight-month tenure of the Bush administration was arguably too short to merit full blame for what had happened.

Yet the attacks had happened on our watch, and a narrative of negligence began to develop. In those accounts, the Bush administration had come to office focused on Iraq and missile defense but not on terrorism. We had thus been slow to respond to "unmistakable" signals that an attack was coming. In hindsight, every e-mail, memo, or phone call that even mentioned, no matter how vaguely, the al Qaeda threat became evidence of negligence.

At the commission hearings, Clinton administration officials took some heat, particularly concerning their inaction against al Qaeda's sanctuary in Afghanistan. But Sandy Berger, President Clinton's national security advisor, had been able to give a thorough, well-rounded, and generally persuasive account of their fight against al Qaeda. On the other hand, Colin Powell, Don Rumsfeld, George Tenet, and Deputy Secretary of State Rich Armitage clearly had only pieces of the story from the perspective of individual departments, not the Bush administration as a whole. Only the national security advisor had that perspective.

I'd already given "testimony" to the commission in private, answering the commissioners' questions over a period of four hours. But there was no public record, and the interview was not under oath. The commission hearings were now a television event. My behind-closed-doors answers in the White House Situation Room were no match for critics seeking to show that the administration—now increasingly unpopular due to the Iraq war—had been asleep at the switch on September 11.

Despite a growing chorus of demands that I testify to answer the multiplying charges against the administration, the White House counsel, the Vice President, and indeed the President continued to cling to executive privilege, saying that the President's closest advisors (who had not been confirmed by the Senate) should not have to testify. There were elaborate arguments about the separation of powers and the President's right to confidential communication with his staff.

The press and Congress—frankly, the whole country—were having none of it. I'd been national security advisor on the day of the worst attack on U.S. soil in our history, and people wanted to know what I had known and when I had known it. The White House advisors came up with the idea of having me make my case directly to the American people on television and radio and in newspapers. I gave interviews to everybody—the *New York Times*, the *Washington Post*, AP, and Reuters, among others—on the record. I was almost always on background when speaking to the press, meaning that I was identified as a senior administration official, not by name, so being on the record attracted some attention in its own right. Coming out of a Situation Room meeting, Sean McCormack, the NSC spokesman, pulled me aside. "*Time* is doing a cover and maybe *Newsweek* too." The *Time* cover story was "Is Condi the Problem?" Clearly the strategy was backfiring horribly. The final nail in the coffin was an interview that I gave to *60 Minutes* on Sunday, March 28, 2004.

The late Ed Bradley did the interview, and I was pretty comfortable. We even did a bit of the taping on the balcony outside Mrs. Cheney's office overlooking the West Wing of the White House. Afterward, I told Sean McCormack that it had gone well. But the penchant of *60 Minutes* to edit liberally is well known. And when I saw the interview, it bore little resemblance to what I remembered in its immediate aftermath.

The next day, Jim Wilkinson, who was later my senior advisor at State, Sean McCormack, and Steve Hadley came to me and said that I had to convince the President to let me testify publicly before the 9/11 Commission. I was in complete agreement.

I called Ashley Hickey, the President's secretary, and asked when I might see him. He was available right then, minutes before his lunch with the Vice President. I went into the Oval. The President was standing behind his desk. He walked out toward me. "What's wrong?" he asked. He could always read me, and he knew this wasn't a visit to talk about the latest policy crisis. I told him that I felt I had to testify and that I would have no credibility going forward if I did not. The American people wanted to know the story. I'd asked to testify before and been denied. We had tried the strategy of "going directly to the people." It hadn't worked, and now even my own family and friends wondered what was going on. I didn't threaten to resign. My relationship with the President wasn't like that. But I would have had we not worked out a way for me to testify.

The President said that he was beginning to think that I should testify but that legal counsel and the Vice President were opposed. He nicely said that it was in his interest for me to testify because I was the best person to make the administration's case. He was worried about the precedent of a national security advisor testifying under oath.

I simply said, "Mr. President, we have to find a way." I left the Oval. Within twenty-four hours the decision had been made. I gave a heads-up to NBC News's Tim Russert, for whom I had enormous respect and whom I trusted. The story broke that same afternoon.

It was against that backdrop that my testimony took on a political importance that surprised me. "Bush's Credibility Now Rests on Her Shoulders" read a *New York Times* headline a few days before my testimony. " 'Warrior Princess' Goes to Full-Coverage Battle," said the *Washington Times*.

I studied hard, preparing as if I were going into an all-or-nothing exam. What had we done in response to the noise and chatter in the system about a coming attack? What signals had there been? What had we missed?

I put together a team to prepare me for the testimony: NSC lawyers

John Bellinger and Bryan Cunningham; policy advisers Steve Hadley and Bob Zoellick, who was serving as the U.S. Trade Representative; and communications specialists Dan Bartlett, Jim Wilkinson, and Sean McCormack. I made a mental catalog of the events. I read the biographies and personality sketches of the commission members to get a feel for their styles of questioning.

And then I put it all aside the day before. "I am an academic," I told my team. "I can't heal anyone or create jobs or invent products. But I do know how to talk. Now you'll just have to trust me."

I was pretty calm the morning of the testimony. I'd slept rather well and got up early. I went through my usual routine. I exercised; then my great hairdresser, Bruce Johnson, showed up really early and trimmed my hair while I read the blasting headlines in advance of . my testimony. I told myself to be conscious of how I entered the room (*with confidence,* I reminded the face in the mirror). Given the impact that a single picture—even a misleading one—can have, I even had to think about what the photograph would look like when I took the oath. (*You sometimes have a tendency to look wide-eyed,* I told myself. *Narrow your eyes.*)

In my testimony to the commission, I said that the failure to prevent the attacks had not been the fault of any one individual administration but was structural. The most critical issue was the stove-piping of information among government agencies and the seam between what we knew about foreign and domestic threats.

Better integrating intelligence would be critical to preventing the next attack. One example that I did not use in my testimony illustrated this point. There were phone calls made by two of the hijackers from San Diego to an al Qaeda safe house in the Middle East before September 11. Because of the legal and policy restrictions in place at the time, these calls were only intercepted overseas and neither the process of intercepting them nor their content revealed their U.S. origin. If other forms of collection had been permitted, as they were in the Terrorist Surveillance Program, it is possible we could have known the location of these two terrorists before September 11. The 9/11 Commission and the congressional Joint Inquiry into the Terrorist Acts of September 11, 2001, found the seam between foreign and domestic intelligence to be a crucial weakness. We did, too. Overcoming it would later become the rationale for the hotly debated Terrorist Surveillance Program, which permitted the government to monitor the international calls of a small number of terrorists, regardless of where the calls originated.

Though my confrontation with Commissioner Richard Ben-Veniste stood out, there were other memorable moments in the five-hour hearing. In a lighter one, former Senator Bob Kerrey inexplicably referred to me, not once but three times, as "Dr. Clarke," confusing me with the pale, graying white man who'd worked for me as the National Security Council staff's counterterrorism chief. In the run-up to the commission hearings, Dick had also taken on the role of chief accuser in insisting that the administration had been negligent in the days prior to the attacks of September 11. Finally I said, "I don't think I look like Dick Clarke." It provided some levity, at least for a moment.

In general, I felt good about the outcome. I had fought to at least a draw, maybe a little better. The President called when I returned to the White House to say that I had been "awesome." That evening, I joined my close friend Mary Bush for dinner and Maundy Thursday service at National Presbyterian Church. At the restaurant, a number of people came up and thanked me for my testimony. A small group applauded. My friend Barbara Harrison, the anchor of the local NBC affiliate morning news, called the next day. She related that they'd been told to stand by in the newsroom in case something broke. The networks had shown the testimony live. I had preempted the soaps.

THE FINDINGS of those two commissions were consistent with our own thinking about ways to restructure the nation's intelligence apparatus. I asked Brent Scowcroft, who was serving as the chairman of the President's Foreign Intelligence Advisory Board, to make recommendations on changes to the intelligence agencies, and we launched an effort internally to look at major institutional reforms. Those efforts resulted in the President's decision to create the position of director of national intelligence (DNI) to oversee the work of the nation's fifteen intelligence agencies. Since 1947 the CIA director had been simultaneously head of the CIA (as DCIA) and head of the whole intelligence community as director of central intelligence (DCI). This odd arrangement had drawn the attention of many a reform commission over the years. Finally, due to the twin intelligence failures of 9/11 and Iraq WMD, the DCIA was stripped of the larger intelligence community function and the distinct position of DNI was born.

I was given the task of presenting this new institutional arrangement to the press hours before the President first announced that he would ask Congress to create the DNI. The details were, to put it mildly, not fully fleshed out, but in general, the DNI was to make sure that an equal and full hearing was given to the views of all agencies. For instance, the CIA had been the agency most convinced that the high-strength aluminum tubes that Saddam surreptitiously ordered were for nuclear centrifuges. The Energy Department had disagreed. In retrospect, one could see that, though the dissent had been registered, the DCI, wearing also the hat of DCIA, gave considerably more weight to his own agency's findings. The DNI would level the playing field among the agencies.

The DNI was also to overcome the "silo" problem by ensuring cross-fertilization in the career paths of intelligence specialists. Everyone agreed that the "craft" of intelligence analysis needed to be reviewed and new training programs put into place. The country was short of linguists in such critical tongues as Arabic, Farsi, and Chinese. And someone needed to review the intelligence budget to eliminate redundancies and make certain that technical intelligence collection was balanced properly with human intelligence collection, which sometimes got short shrift. The most expensive intelligence operations—the National Security Agency, which oversees electronic intelligence, and the National Reconnaissance Office, which oversees satellite intelligence—both report to the secretary of defense. Their budgets are also highly compartmented (for secrecy) and pay for programs that frequently have long development times. That gave Defense the upper hand over other agencies in budgetary matters. The DNI would have a lot to do.

Yet most important, in my estimation, was a role for the DNI as the President's principal intelligence advisor, performing the same sort of function that the chairman of the Joint Chiefs of Staff was carrying out on the military side. On any given day, the President needed someone to sort through the various inputs and present him with a neutral, coherent analysis of the intelligence picture.

Congress would pass the law creating the DNI on December 8, 2004, and Fran Townsend, the deputy national security advisor for combating terrorism, would capably lead the many steps needed to implement it. To this day the DNI position remains a work in progress, and already there are calls to kill the position, calling it an unnecessary bureaucratic layer. This resistance is not surprising. Institutions take time to evolve and find their footing; given time, the right people, and presidential support, the DNI will, I believe, fulfill its promise. President Bush was very fortunate in this regard to have John Negroponte and later Mike McConnell serve as the nation's first and second directors of national intelligence. Their effective stewardship of the office in its early years would set the evolution of this venerable institution on a positive trajectory. The same is true of Tom Fingar, who had been my colleague at Stanford and served in various intelligence positions at the State Department before becoming deputy DNI for analysis and chairman of the National Intelligence Council. Their early leadership has left an indelible positive imprint on the DNI position.

18

"Iraqis Need to Govern Themselves"

T HE TRANSITIONAL administrative law that Jerry successfully shepherded through the Iraqi Governing Council gave Iraq an institutional framework for governance. But it's one thing to have a piece of paper that outlines principles and quite another to put those principles into practice. That needed to be done not by the United States but by Iraqis, who were increasingly anxious to assert their independence. I met with several members of the Iraqi Governing Council on January 20, 2004, and listened to their many complaints. It was clear that the representatives agreed on very little and were pressing largely sectarian agendas.

Ahmed Chalabi was one of my visitors. He was then and remains a controversial figure. There was no doubting his intelligence, and I found him an interesting—if somewhat manipulative—interlocutor. On this day, though, he crystallized something that I had been thinking and that drew approving nods from the others. "We need you to respect our need for sovereignty," he said simply. I walked down to the Oval and talked to the President, saying that I felt we were running out of time because the Iraqis were running out of patience. I don't know what I expected him to say, but it was clear that the Iraqis had an ally in the President of the United States. "They're right," he said. "The Iraqis need to govern themselves."

There was a lot to do to achieve that goal. The training and equipping of the Iraqi security forces were proceeding in fits and starts. Practical problems such as the fact that very few Iraqis had bank accounts meant that recruits would leave their units when they were paid to take money home to their families. Sometimes they didn't come back. When we received the weekly briefings about progress in building the forces, there seemed to be a contradiction: on one hand, a rising numbers of trained security forces and, on the other, a worsening security situation. I came to the conclusion that the Pentagon simply didn't have reliable metrics. That led me to employ a substantial "discount" factor whenever I listened to the briefings.

Rebuilding the economy was an equally difficult task. Oil production resumed shortly after the war, giving the Iraqis something that most new democracies lacked: resources. But attacks by insurgents against key pipelines were taking their toll, particularly in the south of the country, and it was hard to keep production steady. After falling from a prewar average of 2.5 million barrels per day, oil production climbed through the summer of 2003 but plateaued in October at about 2 million barrels per day. It remained at that level through June 2004, due largely to insurgent attacks.

Congress had approved a grant of $18.4 billion to help reconstruct Iraq. It had not been easy to argue for a grant to the oil-rich nation. Josh Bolten, by now the director of the Office of Management and Budget, and I carried the case to Congress in scores of individual meetings and group briefings. The United States, we said, needed to show generosity toward Iraq, which could use the grants to get back onto its feet and then use its own resources to sustain economic development and growth. Some very good work flowed from that commitment of money, particularly rehabilitation of agricultural lands and the construction of schools, hospitals, safe water sources, bridges, and the like. We made progress on pipeline renovation and rebuilding the electrical grid. But the larger projects were difficult to complete as insurgent attacks increased. The electrical grid was especially vulnerable. The creaky system was already overburdened by the decision after the invasion to distribute power more evenly throughout the country. We quickly learned that Saddam had been quite willing to starve most of Iraq of energy in favor of Baghdad. Countrywide demand increased too as Iraqis used their new freedom to buy goods such as satellite dishes in huge numbers.

In retrospect, reconstruction might have been better served by smaller, more localized projects. That was essentially the strategy that we would prioritize starting in 2005 and accelerate with the surge of

2007, which focused the U.S. military and civilian reconstruction in the provinces and localities.

Nonetheless, at the macroeconomic level, there were many positive developments. The Treasury Department, led by Secretary John Snow and Under Secretary John Taylor, had pulled off a major miracle in 2003, replacing the existing Iraqi currency with a new dinar. Prewar planning for economic recovery had included consideration of how to prevent monetary and financial collapse and stabilize a currency badly in need of reform. Iraq's economy under Saddam had been plagued by rampant inflation, not to mention problems with counterfeit notes. Largely out of public view, billions of dinars had been printed, shipped into the country, and swapped. Iraq's currency was quickly made stable and largely remains so today.

The Iraqis also needed international help with their debt, which included more than $42 billion that was owed to the Paris Club, a collection of creditor states including the G8 countries, and other industrialized nations. Iraq owed an estimated $45 billion to other Gulf States, principally Saudi Arabia. I thought that important enough to ask former Secretary of State Jim Baker to act as a presidential envoy to the G8 and the Arabs, which he agreed to do. Jim negotiated a reduction of the Iraqi Paris Club debt by 80 percent. The new debt framework helped create a basis for IMF assistance to the Iraqis, capably championed by Anne Krueger.

But the most important task would be to replace the Iraqi Governing Council with an interim government. The Council was by its nature unwieldy, with a change in the presidency every month. The new interim government would have a prime minister and a cabinet to take over as many functions as possible. On January 28, 2004, the NSC met to approve a "transition matrix" that detailed the process for handing over functions to the Iraqis. The new government would also receive sovereignty from the CPA, ending the occupation. And preparation would commence for landmark elections in the Arab world.

The task of forming the interim government to administer the country until the January 2005 elections was entrusted to Lakhdar Brahimi of the United Nations, who worked closely with Jerry Bremer, Bob

Blackwill, and British envoy Jeremy Greenstock. I talked to Blackwill every morning and again before the day ended. I felt that I could do little to help them sort out the complicated process as the fortunes of various candidates for ministerial positions and other posts in the interim government rose and fell.

In time the Iraqi interim government would be formed, with Ayad Allawi serving as prime minister. Allawi is a secular Shia who managed, to some extent, to bridge the sectarian differences that had several times prevented the formation of a more effective opposition in exile, even though many of the personalities were the same. He was not without controversy, sometimes lacking the patience for consultation with his fellow leaders when making decisions. But he would serve well enough to lead the country toward elections.

In the midst of the delicate negotiations to form the government, however, we suffered a major blow militarily when a small SUV convoy in Fallujah was attacked, killing four private security contactors. Images of their charred bodies hanging from a Euphrates River bridge were broadcast worldwide. No doubt the insurgents hoped to attract new recruits and undermine domestic American support for the war effort. Fallujah, in Al Anbar province, had emerged as a stronghold of the Sunni insurgency, a loose confederation of disgruntled Baathists and xenophobic tribesmen. It was also the home of Abu Musab al-Zarqawi, the self-appointed leader of what became known as al Qaeda in Iraq whose suspected WMD laboratories we had discovered before the war. It seemed that the terrorists had decided to fight us on Arab soil, sensing that a defeat of the U.S. military would be an even greater victory than 9/11 had been. And instinctively they knew something that our critics seemed not to understand: that the emergence of a democratic Iraq would be a tremendous blow to extremists' ambitions for a new caliphate that could avenge the loss of the Islamic empire that reigned throughout the Middle East and parts of Europe for centuries. It would also deny the extremists their goal of expelling Western influence from the Middle East.

It's in that context that the deliberations about Fallujah must be understood. Some military commanders and the civilian Pentagon leadership favored an assault on the city, which had become an epicenter of the Sunni insurgency. They reasoned that a large retaliatory offensive could target those who killed the contractors and committed other atrocities and might simultaneously strike a crippling blow to the insurgency.

Although such a campaign would make sense in a traditional battlefield environment, the deliberations over Fallujah quickly revealed how difficult it would be to balance the security and political situation in Iraq. The campaign would occur as government formation was proceeding and just months before the Coalition Provisional Authority was scheduled to transfer sovereignty. Lakhdar Brahimi, the leader of the UN mission in Iraq, said he would withdraw if the United States attacked the city. Even worse, fractures had begun to emerge within the Iraqi Governing Council, with its Sunni members threatening to abandon the effort should the United States assault Fallujah.

I called a Principals meeting to prepare for an NSC meeting with the President on April 5. At that point the marines had just launched Operation Vigilant Resolve, a major offensive to secure Fallujah that constituted the largest mission since the end of major combat operations in May 2003. The forces confronted insurgents whose ruthless tactics were designed not only to murder U.S. troops but also to goad them into attacking civilians inadvertently. They took foreign hostages to undermine the support of our coalition partners. And in a move that was doubtlessly a bid to inflame the Iraqi population against our cause, they took up positions in public buildings such as hospitals and religious sites, forcing our troops to open fire in those heavily civilian environments.

The atmosphere in the Situation Room that day of the NSC Principals meeting was electric, with strong support for the continued assault on Fallujah. Rich Armitage, who represented the State Department, consulted Colin, and the State Department didn't object. As a former chairman of the Joint Chiefs of Staff, Colin always seemed to feel constrained in a situation of this kind—a little like a former CEO wanting to avoid second-guessing his successor. He did intervene on occasion, as he had in the summer before the war, when Don had favored attacking

Zarqawi's laboratories in northern Iraq. But he picked his battles very carefully, and in this one, either he agreed that we should assault Fallujah or chose not to disagree.

The temperature was a bit high for my taste, though, so I introduced a series of what-ifs, especially related to the formation of the government in Iraq. The meeting ended without a conclusion, precisely as I'd hoped. I didn't want the President to be confronted the next day with a unanimous decision of the Principals to continue the assault on Fallujah. After the meeting, Frank Miller caught me in the hallway and said, "There was a lot of testosterone in that room, wasn't there?" I just nodded and went off to see the President, asking him to consider the political context carefully when he made his decision.

Two days later, with the President in the chair, we reviewed the situation. Jerry was on the videoconference at the NSC session and fortunately made the same point I'd made about worrisome political repercussions. Both Brahimi and Sunni members of the Governing Council, he said, were telling him that the assault on Fallujah would scuttle the effort to establish a government. President Bush was receptive to those concerns and indicated that the United States could not risk destabilizing the political situation.

By April 11, U.S. forces and Sunni insurgents had negotiated a cease-fire. Our commanders believed certain tribal leaders seemed willing to back U.S. forces if it would usher in a new era of stability and security, and the expectation was that local security forces would join the fight against the insurgents. So there were now *two* reasons to hold off on an assault on Fallujah. The President concurred, and the Fallujah Brigade was formed. Unfortunately, the next morning's newspapers carried pictures of the commander, General Jassim Mohammed Saleh, who bore an uncanny resemblance to Saddam Hussein. Every step forward in Iraq seemed to come with a step back.

The Sunni insurgent violence in Fallujah coincided with an uprising of Shia militias in the holy city of Najaf and Sadr City, a Shia neighborhood in Baghdad. The militants killed seven U.S. soldiers in April 2004 in response to a call for violence by Muqtada al-Sadr, a radical Shia cleric who emerged as a fiery but influential player in Iraqi politics. Operating from the neighborhood bearing his father's name, Sadr mobilized thousands of Iraqi supporters to take up arms against coalition forces within days of the Sunni uprising in Fallujah. Despite Sadr's wide following, a courageous Iraqi judge had issued an arrest warrant for him in connection with the murder of another cleric at a mosque in 2003. Sadr's militant Mahdi Army was dedicated to destabilizing the burgeoning governance institutions of Iraq and would eventually become a second front of the insurgency against U.S. forces. We discussed many times the wisdom of having the U.S. military act on the warrant and arrest Sadr. (He would take up residence in Iran.) The political risks of doing so always seemed to outweigh the benefits.

EVEN THE INSURGENCY didn't have the counterproductive effect that the prisoner abuse scandal at Abu Ghraib would. That spring, Don asked to see the President. He explained calmly that some U.S. soldiers had allegedly mistreated prisoners at the Abu Ghraib prison in Iraq. Though Don said that there were apparently "sickening" photos, he didn't show any of them to the President. Shortly thereafter, *60 Minutes II* aired photographs documenting the abuses. The President was blindsided and angry. He'd expected something bad; he'd had no idea just how bad. I didn't know until years later that Don had offered to resign over the scandal. Though Don and I had our differences, I felt that the President was right to refuse to accept Don's resignation. He was wrong to let the President be blindsided by the severity of the problem. But the Pentagon hadn't authorized or condoned that kind of behavior. Don's resignation would have obscured that fact.

I felt especially bad not only for the Iraqis who had been abused but for the hundreds of thousands of honorable men and women in uniform who were volunteering, fighting, and dying in dangerous places around the world. Those heinous acts of abuse were committed by a small number of personnel acting in defiance of their orders. Although the Defense Department had authorized military interrogators to use enhanced techniques in their questioning of enemy combatants, the approved techniques were nothing like the reprehensible abuse that occurred at Abu Ghraib. Later, after a wide-ranging investigation into the allegations at Abu Ghraib and other facilities, Vice Admiral Albert T.

Church III would release a comprehensive report concluding that there had been "no link between approved interrogation techniques and detainee abuse." But the few people responsible for those acts became, for some, the public face of U.S. military forces. It was a stain that should never have touched them but did, and regrettably the image of the U.S. soldier around the world became associated with the depravity of Abu Ghraib.

We never recovered fully from Abu Ghraib, which quickly became muddled in the press—and perhaps in people's minds—with the detention facility in Guantánamo, Cuba, and the administration's broader detention and interrogation policies. These provisions had been put into place in the aftermath of 9/11 to detain enemy combatants captured on the battlefield. We also put a premium on collecting time-sensitive information that might prevent another terrorist attack against the United States.

The early debates focused largely on legality and the President's constitutional authority to detain combatants. But the policy implications of the practices began to emerge more clearly by the fall of 2002.

Many of the detainees at the Guantánamo Bay detention center posed a significant and continuing threat to the United States. They include numerous hardened al Qaeda fighters, militants with links to major attacks such as 9/11 and the USS *Cole* bombing, and experienced bombmakers and terrorist financiers. Many of the most dangerous detainees expressed an enduring desire to kill Americans.

Reports began to surface, however, that several other detainees being held at Guantánamo had only a tangential affiliation with al Qaeda or hadn't engaged in hostile actions against the United States. I personally reviewed the case of an Afghan man in his nineties who'd apparently been captured because of some suspected links to al Qaeda. The man was so old he couldn't even recall his exact age, so his questioners estimated that he was about ninety-three based on his recollection of some distant Afghan monarch. It was clear that the feeble elder posed little threat to the United States and its armed forces, and was subsequently released.

In a theater like Afghanistan, where enemy combatants are nearly indistinguishable from civilians, it is understandable that there would be mistaken captures on the battlefield. As I saw it, the challenge we now faced was how to identify those who had been unnecessarily detained and find a way to release them responsibly.

The problem was compounded by misleading allegations that we intended to hold all detainees indefinitely, without any form of redress. In his November 2001 military order, the President required the establishment of military commissions for the very purpose of adjudicating cases against terrorist suspects. The tribunals would be sensitive to our security needs and our intelligence-gathering methods.

Unfortunately, the Defense Department was painfully slow in setting up these tribunals. An order was issued outlining the procedures for military commission trials in March 2002, but it took a full year for Defense Department lawyers to even decide what crimes could be tried before the commissions. Even some of our closest allies, including the United Kingdom and Australia, grew frustrated with the delays and pressured Colin and even the President for access to their citizens and a mechanism for redress.

With the help of my legal adviser, John Bellinger, and General John Gordon, then the deputy national security advisor for combating terrorism, I convened a series of Principals Committee meetings beginning in October 2002 focused specifically on detainee issues. For reasons that I don't fully understand, Don Rumsfeld did not participate meaningfully in these meetings and eventually refused to attend them at all, sending his deputy, Paul Wolfowitz, instead.

That produced one bizarre incident that remains vivid in my memory. I'd convened back-to-back Principals Committee meetings, one on Iraq and the other on detainee issues. (That wasn't uncommon, given the scheduling challenge of convening all National Security Council Principals at the White House at one time.) When the first meeting concluded and I introduced the subject of detainees, Don got up and walked toward the door. "Don, where are you going?" I asked.

"I don't do detainees," he replied as he walked out.

Nonetheless, we made considerable progress thanks to very hard work by Steve Hadley, Paul Wolfowitz, and John Bellinger. First we sought to ensure that detainees were treated humanely. We worked with the Pentagon to grant access to Guantánamo for the International

Committee of the Red Cross (ICRC). Jakob Kellenberger, a quiet Swiss diplomat who headed the ICRC, was a reliable partner in achieving this. Though he harbored deep reservations about our policies, he was more interested in solving problems than generating headlines. I met with him every few months without fanfare to hear his concerns and take steps to address them. I later arranged for him to meet privately with the President. Moreover, we sought to improve conditions for those held at Guantánamo by providing culturally appropriate meals, medical services, recreational activities, reading materials, and time for religious observances. That led one visiting Belgian official to declare it "a model prison."

And we laid the foundation for an effective review process for those detained at Guantánamo as enemy combatants. In May 2004 the Department of Defense announced the formation of an Administrative Review Board (ARB). The ARB assessed whether detainees posed a threat to the United States or its allies in the war on terror and whether other factors, such as a suspect's intelligence value, required his continued detention. There were three options: release, transfer to a third country, or continued detention. In the Administrative Review Board's first round of assessments, nearly 30 percent of detainees whose cases were reviewed were deemed eligible for release or transfer from Guantánamo.

The process of establishing the ARB assessments coincided with the Supreme Court's ruling in *Hamdi v. Rumsfeld,* which held that U.S. citizens detained as enemy combatants "be given a meaningful opportunity to contest the factual basis for that detention before a neutral decision-maker." The Defense Department responded to the mandate in July 2004 by creating Combatant Status Review Tribunals, which would serve as a forum for detainees to contest their status as enemy combatants. The review tribunals were made up of three military officers who had not been involved in the detainees' apprehension, detention, or interrogation. Both the Administrative Review Boards and the Combatant Status Review Tribunals would ultimately allow for the responsible release of those who posed no threat and provide a process—in keeping with our legal traditions and values—for determining the ongoing detention of those who did pose serious threats to our nation's security.

Those provisions would not resolve all of the lingering concerns about our detention policies. Even when we determined that detainees could be transferred or released, we had to ensure that recipient countries had sufficient rehabilitation programs in place to reintegrate former detainees into their societies. And there were places that were off limits for transfer due to concerns about human rights.

Despite their imperfections, however, those changes in policy produced results. By February 2004 the United States had released more than ninety detainees to other countries, including five of the nine British detainees held at Guantánamo. That outcome was not without a significant downside. Recidivism has been a problem, with as many as one in four of those released from Guantánamo suspected of engaging in terrorist or insurgent activity after their transfer. This underscores the difficulty of fighting the war and simultaneously acting on our international obligations concerning detainee treatment. It was a balancing act, and I believe that we eventually got it about right.

But there would continue to be challenges associated with Guantánamo and the administration's broader detention and interrogation policies, and I would ultimately take them on directly as secretary of state.

DESPITE THE Abu Ghraib scandal and the strengthening insurgency, preparations continued apace to transfer sovereignty to the Iraqis and end the occupation. Clearly, responsibility would also transfer from the Department of Defense to the Department of State, which would establish an embassy in Baghdad to conduct "normal" relations with another sovereign nation. Colin proposed John Negroponte to be the first U.S. ambassador to Iraq. John had had one of those storied careers in the Foreign Service that put him on par with some of the greatest diplomats in U.S. history. Colin believed, rightly, that John's calm demeanor, professionalism, and storied career would help him lead what was bound to be a complicated mission where employees' morale would be a constant source of concern.

The plan to return sovereignty to the Iraqis on June 30 was proceeding too, but we were concerned that the insurgents might disrupt the transfer. They certainly seemed capable of spectacular attacks that could undermine the positive message that Iraqis were governing themselves.

I don't really remember who first had the idea, but a number of us began considering making the transfer scheduled for June 30 early in order to "wrong-foot" the terrorists. Jerry Bremer liked the idea and shared it with only a handful of Iraqis, including, of course, Ayad Allawi, who had been elected by the Iraqi Governing Council to serve as the country's interim prime minister. George Tenet wasn't sure that it would matter but thought it worth a try. The British too believed that it might give the coalition the upper hand.

On June 28, we were at a NATO summit in Istanbul and had been on pins and needles that morning awaiting news from Baghdad. A few minutes after the appointed time, I received a phone call from Jerry. He'd handed the letter to Allawi that formally transferred authority from the CPA to the Iraqi interim government. The occupation was over.

I returned to the chamber, scribbled a note, and asked Don to pass it to the President, who was seated directly in front of him. "Mr. President," the note said, "Iraq is sovereign. Letter was passed from Bremer at 10:26 A.M. Iraq time."

I saw the President turn to the man seated next to him, simply by virtue of alphabetical order. George W. Bush and Tony Blair shook hands and acknowledged one step forward in the historic and controversial course on which they had embarked together. President Bush sent the note back to me with a line written across it: "Let freedom reign!"

When I saw the note in the newspaper the next day, the first thing that came to mind was how terrible my penmanship had become. My mother was an English teacher who had always insisted on writing in, as she called it, "a beautiful hand." That was admittedly an odd thought at such a momentous time.

In any case, there wasn't much celebration. The work ahead was getting harder and more complicated, and everyone knew it. The Iraqis had come a long way from the days of the Iraqi National Congress in exiled opposition to the Governing Council in the aftermath of the invasion and now to a sovereign interim government that would help pave the way to the country's first free elections. But Steve Hadley had it right when, sitting in my office a few days after the return of sovereignty in Iraq, he said, "The Iraqis still have to liberate themselves. We've overthrown Saddam Hussein, but this won't work until the Iraqis own their freedom." That would take some time.

19

ANOTHER STEP TOWARD A PALESTINIAN STATE

A RIEL SHARON HAD TAKEN advantage of the defeat of Saddam Hussein and his trust in George W. Bush to make significant shifts in long-held Likud positions in Israel. In accepting the Road Map for Peace in the Middle East and speaking forcefully about the need to make "painful concessions" in 2003, the Israeli prime minister had put himself firmly on the side of a two-state solution. Still, when Dubi Weisglass, Sharon's closest advisor, came to see me at the White House and said that the prime minister was considering a unilateral withdrawal from Gaza, I was stunned.

What Sharon had in mind showed not only how far he'd come toward peace but also his shrewd political leadership. Weisglass said that the prime minister saw an opportunity to split Israeli public opinion on the contentious issue of settlements, thus isolating the minority opposed to a two-state solution. The centerpiece of Sharon's gambit would be a complete Israeli withdrawal from Gaza, settlers and all. The Palestinians would then have a real chance to govern themselves.

As was the case in any conversation with the Israelis, however, there was a "but." To make this advance toward peace, Dubi said, Sharon needed to assure the public that a few of the most established settlements in the West Bank would remain intact in any future peace agreement. Clearly, to make way for a Palestinian state, settlers would have to be uprooted from the West Bank and Gaza. There was little sympathy for those occupying the scattered encampments deep in the West Bank and even less for those in Gaza. The Israel Defense Forces (IDF) no longer wanted to defend those isolated settlements, and Gaza, with its large, angry, and poor Palestinian population, had no future in a Jewish democratic state. But some West Bank settlements, such as Ariel, Ma'al Adumim, Modi'in Illit, and Beitar Illit, were now established Israeli cities. Weisglass said that the prime minister needed to signal that those big population blocks, about 80,000 settlers in all, would be included in Israel when the Palestinian state was created.

The prime minister had sent Dubi to see if President Bush would affirm this principle, in a word legitimizing certain settlements so that the Israelis could begin their withdrawal. Steve Hadley and I listened intently. There was a breakthrough in there somewhere, but it was fraught with dangers for U.S. policy in the Middle East. First, the President couldn't legitimize specific settlements. Second, a unilateral withdrawal from Gaza without negotiation or at least coordination with the Palestinians might signal that the Israelis were prepared to determine the status quo on their own. In other words, even a good outcome, with Israelis leaving disputed territory, might send the wrong message. Third, we were concerned that a withdrawal from Gaza might be perceived as the end of the process, not the beginning: Gaza *first* was one thing; *only* Gaza was not acceptable. We would insist that the Gaza withdrawal be accompanied by the removal of at least some settlements in the West Bank. Eventually, the four northernmost settlements were evacuated.

Over the next month, we came to terms with the Israelis on how to move forward. Dubi and I led the negotiations. Steve Hadley and Elliott Abrams were dispatched to Israel for long sessions with the prime minister to better understand how the process could limit settlement growth and spur movement toward a Palestinian state. The outcome was a letter from President Bush to Prime Minister Sharon that acknowledged the need to accommodate "new realities on the ground," including "already existing major Israeli population centers" in the West Bank, at the time of a negotiated settlement to the conflict.

The letter also addressed indirectly the "right of return," stating that under any realistic solution to the issue, Palestinian refugees would be expected to live in a new homeland, the State of Palestine. The great majority of them would not "return" to their ancestral lands in Israel. That issue had been included in the letter due, in large part, to my interaction with Tzipi Livni, whom I'd met during my first trip to Israel in 2000. She was minister for immigrant absorption when she came to see me in March 2004. We talked for a long time about her personal story as a child of Israeli freedom fighters. She told me that she'd come to the conclusion that Israelis could no longer govern Palestinians and concessions were required. That would mean that there could be no "greater Israel," she conceded. Then she spoke movingly of how hard it was for her to say it since her father's headstone was engraved with a map of Israel incorporating all of Judea and Samaria. Ending the conflict between Arabs and Israelis was her mission in Israeli politics.

But she was worried that even after the establishment of the Palestinian state, there would be demands that Israel accept a large number of Palestinian refugees to fulfill the Arab insistence on "right of return," as embodied in UN General Assembly Resolution 194. Israel did not accept the legitimacy of the resolution, but the rest of the world did. That could change the nature of the State of Israel, which had been founded as a state for the Jews.

I must admit that though I understood the argument intellectually, it struck me as a harsh defense of the ethnic purity of the Israeli state when Tzipi said it. It was one of those conversations that shocked my sensibilities as an American. After all, the very concept of "American" rejects ethnic or religious definitions of citizenship. Moreover, there were Arab citizens of Israel. Where did they fit in?

I took a deep breath and tried to understand, and slowly I came to see what she meant. Most of us thought of the creation of Israel in the context of the horrors of World War II and the Holocaust. But for most Israelis, their country's birth had instead been the fulfillment of a long historical and religious journey to reestablish "the Jewish state." The right of return for Palestinians was inconsistent with the conclusion of that thousands-year-old process. Despite the dissonance that it stirred in me, I suggested that the President include the line that made clear that Palestinian refugees would be expected to live in Palestine. That would allow the democratic state of Israel to be "Jewish."

On April 14 Ariel Sharon came to the White House and stood with the President on the long red carpet of the Cross Hall, the stately corridor that leads to the East Room. The night before, I met with the prime minister for more than three hours to go over the letter and what it meant. I was especially concerned that the Israelis not say that the United States was legitimizing settlement activity. There had been some indirect references to this already in the press, and we suspected that the Israelis had been busy "backgrounding" the story that way. The prime minister said that he understood and would not betray his friend.

There were audible gasps from the press as the President read from the text, which marked a major departure in U.S. policy toward the Middle East. The line that said that all of the issues had to be "mutually agreed" was drowned out in the press by the focus on how we "legitimized" settlements and "rejected" the right of return.

After the press conference, I got into the car and headed to the U.S. Naval Academy in Annapolis, where I was scheduled to give a speech. I checked in with Bill Burns, the assistant secretary for Near Eastern affairs, at the State Department. In his preternaturally calm way, Bill relayed the turbulence that was breaking out in the Middle East in response to what had been said, just as he'd done two years earlier after the President had given his Rose Garden speech calling for Palestinian democracy and the removal of Arafat. By the time I finished at the Naval Academy and returned to the White House, there were messages from the Jordanians, Saudis, and Egyptians waiting for me. The Jordanians, in particular, argued that the President would need to give assurances to the Arabs just as he had to the Israelis.

We had a way of breaking old taboos in the agreed script concerning the Israeli-Palestinian conflict. But for all the commitment to the "peace process" over the years, it had failed to create a Palestinian state or provide decent leadership for the Palestinian people. There was still a lot to be done, but there was movement forward. The Israelis were getting ready to withdraw from Gaza, and the Palestinians would have their chance to show that they could govern themselves.

The letter to Sharon also launched a process to attack the age-old problem of Israeli settlement expansion. Dubi had suggested that we simply name the settlements that would be grandfathered in a final-status agreement. That would require finally understanding what the Israelis meant by the slippery term "natural growth." It seemed logical that until a peace agreement was signed, there would need to be limits on the expansion of those "cities." Steve and Elliott sought a detailed understanding of the ever-shifting Israeli arguments about building within municipal lines, within built-up areas, building horizontally, vertically, and on and on. We could never get an agreed definition for a settlement freeze based on those parameters.

We did, however, agree informally with the Israelis that they would take certain steps to limit settlement growth. First, they would end all special government subsidies to settlers. Second, there would be no new settlements, although in reality the expansion within settlements was more often the problem. Third, they would expropriate no more land for settlement construction. And fourth, they would pass what I came to call the "Google Earth test": there would be no building outward. Though the growth of existing settlements continued to be a bone of contention between us for the next five years, there were no new settlement blocks built from 2004 to 2009, and the settler population grew at a lower annual rate than at any other time since the 1967 war. There was some confirmation that what we had done mattered when the Sharon government was accused of turning its back on settlers to appease George W. Bush.

20

FOUR MORE YEARS

AS THE SUMMER APPROACHED, the attention of the White House turned to the reelection campaign and I reminded myself to stay focused on the tasks of national security. Steve and I decided that one of us would always travel with the President on the campaign trail; it was the first presidential election since 9/11, and the President needed senior national security support at all times. Once in a while Bob Blackwill, who was experienced and had been a Vulcan in 2000, could spell us. On the trail we could also support the President as he faced a barrage of questions about the war, terrorism, and the other security controversies day after day.

Amid the inevitable distractions of the campaign, I gave a lot of thought to how to keep the President's preferences central to what the agencies were doing operationally. It crossed my mind that there might be more than a few career people in the agencies hoping to see George Bush retire to Texas. Maybe it was an unfair thought, but it was there, and I wanted to be sure that no one gave in to the temptation to treat the President, who was facing a tough campaign, as a lame duck.

Because national security was at the crux of so much of the debate, I decided to make a series of speeches around the country to explain what we were doing. It wasn't lost on me that this might be seen as "campaigning" and in contravention of the long-standing tradition by which the national security team stays out of politics. I did indeed speak in a number of battleground states. But I spoke in Texas and Kentucky too, hardly in play in electoral politics. I was careful to avoid political messages in my speeches, but I did take on the President's critics. Could anyone have been surprised that I wanted George W. Bush reelected? I thought that it would help the cause if I explained the policies outside Washington's echo chamber. Still, there was a good deal of tongue wagging about what I was doing and even an investigation by the Office of Special Counsel. It found nothing to suggest that I'd crossed the line.

How did we bear up amid all the contentiousness? Clearly it is miserable to be the incumbent, constantly defending every aspect of your record and answering charges of incompetence or, worse, venality. When the record included September 11, Afghanistan, and Iraq, the task was obviously formidable. I felt each morning as if we were shackled in medieval stocks in a public square, with people throwing fruit at us. I told my cousin that there were days when I felt like Wile E. Coyote in the *Road Runner* cartoons. The unfortunate coyote would catch on to a branch to keep from falling over the cliff and then hang on, his feet in constant motion above the pit below as the road runner chopped away at the branch.

Each morning seemed to bring some new charge or leaked intelligence. In the last week of the campaign, a story appeared that the insurgency was getting many of its weapons from unguarded depots that the military could not account for. The image of our troops being attacked by weapons stolen from stockpiles that were supposed to be under our control became a cause célèbre.

The story just wouldn't go away, every news cycle bringing fresh reports about the connection between the insurgency and unguarded weapons depots. After many entreaties from the White House, the Pentagon finally decided to call a press conference and refute the stories as best it could, since frankly the evidence was pretty compelling. The apparent thievery that was taking place was another consequence of the manpower shortage we were experiencing.

I was on the road with the President when the press conference took place. Since I never wanted to be seen at a rally, I usually stayed on board Air Force One if the stop was short or perhaps hung back in the staff holding room at the event. An ingenious press person at Defense had found a young army captain who'd led the team that secured many of the weapons depots. He was perfect: clean-cut, earnest, and patriotic. Larry Di Rita, the Pentagon spokesman, introduced him but did so with a long, confused windup that undercut the crisp message of competence that was intended. I sat there with the press people yelling at the TV, "Larry, get off the stage!" Finally he did, but the moment had passed and the captain's message was lost on the press corps.

That story, though, was nothing compared to the bombshell that dropped four days before the election. We were in Ohio when we got word that Osama bin Laden had released a tape threatening the United States. It must have been meant to undermine confidence in George W. Bush and contribute to his defeat. But bin Laden didn't understand American politics. I know that John Kerry's people thought it helped the President by reminding the American people of the man who had stood on the rubble of the World Trade Center and rallied them in defense of the country. Our press people worried, but I think the Kerry camp's assessment was more likely right. In the end, it may never be clear which way the tape moved the needle or if it mattered at all.

THE DAY BEFORE the election, we flew to Dallas for a huge rally and then spent the night at the ranch. Karen and I shared the guesthouse, and I tossed and turned as she spent the bulk of the night on the telephone. Before heading back to Washington the next morning, the President wanted to make one final appearance in Ohio to show his appreciation for all the campaign volunteers there. On Air Force One after the event, I followed the election coverage on television and on my favorite website, Realclearpolitics. Just as we were about to land, Karl received news on his BlackBerry that was clearly unwelcome. His face was ashen as he began to read off the early exit polls: down in Ohio; down in Michigan; up one in Alabama. *Up one in Alabama?* I thought. *This is going to be a landslide defeat!*

The President and Laura came into the staff cabin as Karl continued the devastating readout. The President said very quietly, "Too bad." Overcome with sadness, I rushed out of the cabin and into the nearby restroom. I didn't know what to say to the President. I didn't know what to say to my friend.

Air Force One landed at Andrews Air Force Base, and we then disembarked and climbed aboard Marine One to take us to the White

House. Karl noted that exit polls are sometimes wildly wrong and suggested that everyone just suspend judgment until the information was better. It was hard to do.

As I was sitting in my office, again glued to Realclearpolitics, Sean McCormack poked his head in the door. "You know," he said, "something is wrong with these data. For one thing, the percentage of women in the sample is almost twice what it should be." It was a ray of hope, anyway.

I decided to go home. I tried to sleep, having failed to do so the night before, but couldn't. So I took a shower and returned to the White House, where we would view the election returns. A few minutes after I arrived, President George H. W. Bush stopped by my office. "It's not looking too good," he said.

"I don't know," I replied, "Karl is telling everyone that the composition of the survey sample for the exit polls seems to be skewed against us."

"Let's hope so," he said with a little resignation in his voice.

The plan was to have the senior staff and spouses watch the returns on TV in the Roosevelt Room. After about an hour, I couldn't stand it any longer. *I'm going to find Karl,* I decided.

I found him upstairs in the family dining room, where he'd set up a kind of war room. "Can I make myself useful?" I asked, not wanting to just sit around and do nothing. "Yes. You can follow Ohio," he said, taking the time to show me how the computer program worked. Slowly but surely the electoral votes began to pile up. Indeed, the exit polling *had* been wrong. When Karl's program showed that we'd won Ohio, the room broke into pandemonium. The verdict was confirmed a few minutes later on several television broadcasts. I hugged Karl. "We tried to screw it up for you," I said, referring to the series of mishaps and leaks of the last month of the campaign. "But he pulled it off!"

As the hours passed, though, it became clear John Kerry wasn't ready to concede. *Here we go again,* I thought. *Can the country handle another recount?* With the celebration postponed, I went home at 3:00 A.M., uncertain of the results. But this time there would be no recount. Senator Kerry conceded the next morning. The President had won another term.

I walked into the Oval Office shortly after he'd heard the news. "Congratulations, sir!" He thanked me for all I'd done and then said that we needed to talk about the future. In the weeks prior, he'd said a couple of times that Colin was ready to step down and that he wanted me to be secretary of state, so I knew what was coming. I deflected the conversation for the moment, saying there would be time to talk at Camp David, where we'd go for a long weekend the next day. It was November 3. In eleven days I'd be fifty, and I was about to become the secretary of state. But the President and I needed to talk first, as directly as we ever had. I'd liked being his national security advisor, but a lot would change when I left the White House and crossed into Foggy Bottom, as the State Department was informally known. He and I both needed to understand how we'd handle the new relationship, one that, historically, hadn't always been smooth: the interaction between the President of the United States and the secretary of state.

21

SECRETARY OF STATE

I MUST ADMIT that the prospect of becoming secretary of state stirred mixed emotions in me. Obviously, I was honored that the President wanted me to become his chief diplomat. The historic significance of becoming Thomas Jefferson's sixty-fifth successor wasn't lost on me.

After four years as national security advisor, I was ready to be a line officer with the authority that only Cabinet secretaries have. I was tired of coordinating others and tired of the mismatch between authority and responsibility that is an everyday challenge for the NSA. My good friend and mentor George Shultz had predicted this when I left for Washington. "One day you're going to want to run your own shop," he said. He was absolutely right.

I also thought that I could help the President with the State Department and help the department with the President. The President had been burned by leaks of the kind Dean Acheson had described as "What the President meant to say." That had led to some lingering distrust. And I felt that many people in the Foreign Service didn't really understand or appreciate the strengths of the President. Given my strong ties to him, I felt that I could bridge the distance between Foggy Bottom and the White House.

I knew too that there was a lot of work to do going forward to strengthen diplomacy as a matter of both reality and perception in the Bush administration's policies. We had of necessity taken a lot of difficult and controversial steps after 9/11, and many people, particularly in Europe, had hoped that the tough-talking Texan would be sent home. But he would be President for four more years.

The eminent Yale historian John Lewis Gaddis had come to visit shortly before the election and over lunch said something that resonated with me. "Never forget how really dependent the world is on America. And they know it. After all the upheaval of the last few years, this is a time for reassurance," he counseled. A colleague from France had put it a different way: "After 9/11 we knew that you would do what you needed and wanted to do. We just hoped to know your intentions even if we couldn't always influence them." I thought that an overstatement, but, thinking back on the reaction to the National Security Strategy, it may well have been indicative of how others felt. Then one morning I saw the postelection cover of *The Economist*. "Now, Unite Us," it read. I kept that issue in my upper desk drawer at the State Department for the four years of my term.

As I contemplated the job ahead, I also had to acknowledge that I was tired—bone tired. I knew that the secretary of state would need to travel and travel and travel. In fact, it's much easier as secretary of state to drive the agenda when you're abroad. When you are in Washington, you're competing with the latest headline; when you're overseas, you have a press corps eager to report on your every meeting. Usually you have a time change working in your favor so that you're not making news in the middle of the cycle, and you have compelling visuals that help emphasize policies. Being on the road is a good thing for the secretary of state. But I understood why Colin had been concerned about extensive time abroad: he didn't trust either the White House or the Pentagon and always feared that something was happening behind his back when he was on the road. Frankly, I don't think he needed to worry so much about it, but he did. Yet with all the technological possibilities of phone and video, diplomacy is best practiced in person. I knew that, and it ran counter to my own preference for the normalcy (such as it was) of being at home. I like my own bed and my routine.

But most of all I wondered what moving down to C Street would do to my relationship with the President. As national security advisor I had seen him every day, often five or six times a day. I was well aware of the importance of keeping the connection to the Oval Office and concerned that, despite our best efforts, it would be hard to do. Steve Hadley would become national security advisor, and that was comforting because I trusted him to let me know—bluntly—if any distance was emerging between the President and me. I never wanted to leave the President wondering what I was thinking and doing.

It was in that frame of mind that I walked the short distance from my cabin to the President's office in Laurel Lodge at Camp David on the Friday morning after the election. I entered the room and looked around at the photographs on the wall. There, prominently displayed, was a picture of the two of us in the Oval Office a few days after his inauguration. The President was on the phone, and I was standing at his desk, looking down pensively. Eric Draper, the President's photographer, took the shot in silhouette, with the morning sun shining through the windows behind us. I thought of all we'd been through in the last four years.

The President didn't waste time with chitchat. He simply said, "I want you to be secretary of state." I responded by saying how honored I was but that there were a few things we needed to talk about. I said that I hoped he wouldn't take what I was going to say as criticism of the last four years. After all, I'd been deeply involved in the decisions. But recounting Gaddis's admonition, I noted that we had repair work to do with the allies and that we'd need to reaffirm the primacy of diplomacy in our foreign policy. That would also mean reaffirming the primacy of the secretary of state as the principal agent of the development and execution of that policy. We talked about how to make it work, particularly the need to do what we'd done for more than four years: never let distance develop between us that others, foreign or domestic, could exploit. "How am I going to know what you're thinking if I don't see you every day?" I asked.

He replied that we could talk anytime. "You know how it is in the White House," he said. "I'll get busy and forget to call, so you have to call me."

"Okay," I replied, "you'll hear from me every day," only partially in jest.

I'd later tell my colleague Henry Paulson, when he became treasury secretary, to spend time alone with the President. Cabinet secretaries are busy people with big organizations to run and many, many demands on their time. But you have only one boss: the President. You have to find the time to air your differences privately and early. Then, having established the parameters, the secretary can execute policy freely on behalf of the government. I didn't want to be in the position of having to phone home every time I needed to make a tough call on behalf of the United States. The President had to trust me to know when I needed guidance and when I didn't. Before my confirmation, I gave the President a copy of a biography of Dean Acheson and of Acheson's own memoir, *Present at the Creation*. Acheson had succeeded in staying close to President Truman and thus retaining authority and credibility as the voice of U.S. foreign policy. Together, they had led the United States and the world through turbulent times.

I then turned to one substantive issue that was on my mind. "Mr. President," I said, "we need to get an agreement and establish a Palestinian state." He said that he wanted to do so but asked if I thought it could be done. We were both anxious to take advantage of the impending withdrawal of the Israelis from Gaza and the upcoming election of a new Palestinian president, who was predicted to be Mahmoud Abbas, someone we both liked. "We'll get it done," he said after a little more discussion. "What about my offer?"

I said that I needed a little time to digest our conversation and asked if we could talk the next morning. We didn't wait until the next day. When we talked again after dinner, I said yes, I would be honored to become the sixty-sixth secretary of state.

I TURNED FIFTY on November 14 and had invited a number of family and friends to Washington to celebrate the occasion with me. My cousin Lativia and her husband, Will, my Aunt Gee, Uncle Alto and his wife, Connie, my stepmother, Clara, and my stepbrother, Greg, all made the trip from as far away as California to mark the big "5-0" with me.

We'd gone to a fancy dinner at a downtown restaurant, Galileo, on Friday. So I decided to do something low-key on Saturday night—or at least I thought so. I suggested dinner at a favorite casual restaurant, Café Deluxe, on Wisconsin Avenue. I just wanted downtime with my family—nothing formal.

As the Secret Service SUV barreled down Massachusetts Avenue toward the restaurant, I sat back and closed my eyes, having decided not to think at all for the rest of the night. Only my Aunt Gee knew that the President had asked me to be secretary of state. My family never talked to the press and I trusted them, but it just seemed safer to wait a while before telling too many people.

Suddenly, the car turned in to the British Embassy instead of proceeding up Massachusetts Avenue. *This is strange,* I thought. Then it dawned on me that maybe my friends the Mannings were inviting me for a surprise champagne toast before dinner. When we pulled up to the entry, David came out, and he was wearing a tuxedo. "Oh, Catherine and David must have a dinner afterwards," I thought.

David escorted me from the car into the foyer. There I suddenly saw a hundred of my dearest friends and family dressed in evening gowns and tuxedos. It's funny what your eye catches when you're totally surprised. I focused immediately on the guests who'd come from farthest away: Carmen and Gail Policy, Mariann and Dan Begovich, Susan and Michael Dorsey, Fred Weldy, Randy Bean, and others from California. People from all phases of my life were there, arrayed beautifully along the two spiral staircases of the ambassador's residence.

I was just thrilled, and then I thought, *My God, am I underdressed!*, standing there in my black slacks, turtleneck sweater, and red jacket. Fortunately, the Mannings, with the surreptitious help of a member of my staff, Sarah Lenti, had taken care of that too. I was whisked upstairs, where my hairdresser, Bruce Johnson, was waiting for me, along with a stunning, red satin gown by my friend Oscar de la Renta, who'd designed it just for me. Within about an hour I emerged like Cinderella and celebrated through the night. Van Cliburn played the national anthem and "Happy Birthday," and the President gave the toast. We danced late into the evening. It was another of those fairy-tale-like moments.

At one point, I looked across the room at Colin and wondered what he was thinking. With the exception of the President, the First Lady, Andy Card, and Aunt Gee, he was the only other person who knew that I was going to become secretary of state. We didn't mention it to each other that night. He'd done a remarkable job under the circumstances. None of us could have known in 2001 how much our service would be shaped by war and conflict. The Pentagon commands the spotlight in wartime. I couldn't help but wonder how Colin's tenure might have been different in less tumultuous times.

THREE DAYS LATER, the President and I stood in the Oval for a few minutes alone before heading into the Roosevelt Room for the announcement. What an unlikely pair: a scion of a Republican political dynasty—albeit one with a Texas accent—and a middle-class black daughter of the South. We'd been through a lot since that meeting in Kennebunkport. Cataclysmic events and our response to them had shaped his presidency thus far. Now, with the dust settling, we had a chance to build a firm foundation for U.S. foreign policy in the changed circumstances of the post-9/11 world.

I listened to the President's remarks as he introduced me to the press as his nominee for secretary of state. But frankly, I didn't want to listen too closely and become observably emotional. After he finished, I said a few words—very few—and returned to the Oval with him. "Go get 'em," he said. I laughed and said, "Yes, sir!" and left for Capitol Hill to begin the process known colloquially as confirmation. It's more correctly called "the consent of the Senate to the President's nomination." I liked the sound of that and the knowledge that it had been done only sixty-five times before in our nation's history.

The Transition

WITH THE President's agreement, Steve Hadley and I decided that Steve would, in effect, begin to act as national security advisor as of December 1. That would give me time to prepare for confirmation hearings and plan the transition at State. Because Steve and I had worked so closely together—he'd been far more than a deputy, and the President trusted him completely—the handoff would be seamless.

It would also give me time to deal with a nettlesome and long-standing health problem. I'd been cursed with uterine fibroids for more than twenty years. There was a new, minimally invasive procedure that my physician, Sharon Malone, recommended I have. After meeting with Dr. James Spies at Georgetown University Hospital, I decided that I should have the minor surgery.

The President was traveling to Chile for an Asia-Pacific Economic Cooperation (APEC) meeting, and we'd decided that Steve would accompany him. I could have used the transition as an excuse for skipping the trip, but with all the attention generated by my appointment as secretary of state, it was a certainty that the press would learn of my overnight hospitalization.

I decided to release a statement about my medical condition. As Sean McCormick put it, it was better to make the announcement myself rather than allow speculation that I was dying of something horrible. Nonetheless, I was a bit surprised by the coverage the announcement received, including a long segment by Dr. Sanjay Gupta on CNN about the nature of uterine fibroids, complete with illustrations, and the details of the treatment that I would undergo. Obviously nothing was ever going to be truly "personal" again. I told myself that perhaps I was helping millions of women suffering from the same condition. But to be honest, I really resented the intrusion.

Fortunately, everything went smoothly with the procedure, and I convalesced at home over Thanksgiving weekend. The next week I continued my visits to Capitol Hill with Deb Fiddelke, the White House legislative staffer who was responsible for guiding my confirmation through the Senate. Deb was thorough and insightful and made the process far less stressful than it might otherwise have been. Her only fault was her undying love of the Nebraska Cornhuskers.

The meetings with senators were actually interesting and revealing. Obviously, one is trying not to make a mistake that might sink confirmation, but it was useful to hear what was on their minds. As staff to the President I'd had some contact with Congress, briefing selected senators in the run-up to the Iraq war and forwarding the case for funding Iraqi reconstruction. And I occasionally briefed on other issues of importance to the President, such as the Middle East. But the interaction with Congress is not a formal part of the NSA's job. As a constitutional officer, on the other hand, the secretary of state has obligations to the institution established in Article 1 of the Constitution. Members of Congress will remind you from time to time that the founding fathers established the legislative branch first. In line with that, I resolved to always take my responsibilities to the House and Senate very seriously indeed.

The State Department's portfolio was breathtakingly broad. Individual senators tended to pursue their state's parochial issues, such as this or that water treaty, an environmental problem with our neighbors to the north or south, or agricultural and trade issues with friends and foes alike. But there are also the myriad administrative concerns related to embassy management—everything from a multimillion-dollar construction program to salary competition with the private sector for the best local staff. The Foreign Service is unionized, and the Hill maintains an interest in work rules and benefits for even the most senior officers. There was a lot to learn before taking the reins at State. I felt grateful for having been provost of Stanford University, where I had been, in effect, the chief operating officer and had come to love budgets and day-to-day management. I'm not kidding—I *loved* it.

During my meetings on Capitol Hill, I came to appreciate most those senators who brought thoroughness and expertise to foreign policy issues. I'd expected this of such people as Richard Lugar, John Kerry, Chuck Hagel, and Joe Biden. But I learned quickly that James Webb of Virginia knew Southeast Asia in great depth, and I was impressed with Wisconsin's Russ Feingold, who possessed knowledge of and concern for Africa. George Voinovich of Ohio was deeply involved in Eastern Europe, and Alaska's Lisa Murkowski was the reason that I became conversant on Arctic affairs.

As I approached my hearings, I knew that there were some senators who, given the war in Iraq, would never support my confirmation. The fact that we had acknowledged on January 12, 2005, that we had called off the search for weapons of mass destruction served to heighten criticism of the administration in advance of my hearings. But I was in a good position overall, and there was little doubt that, barring a big mistake on my part, I'd be confirmed.

My hearings were set for January 18. I'd enjoyed the six weeks of the transition. Every day I'd go to the department for briefings that covered practically every office within it. I studied every evening so that I'd know the issues in detail. I'm an academic, and I don't like to "float" at thirty-thousand feet. I'm most comfortable when I can engage an issue in far greater depth than the "talking points" prepared by the staff.

On the day of the hearings, I awoke and went through my usual routine. Running on the elliptical trainer, I didn't review the issues. Few people doubted that I knew the substance of the job, but there was a pervasive concern that I'd just be the White House proconsul at the Department of State. The question on the table was what kind of secretary of state would I be. As the *Christian Science Monitor* put it, "When Condoleezza Rice goes to the Senate next week . . . she will appear before a row of senators as something of an enigma . . . a national security advisor who oversaw a steady shift of authority over foreign policy toward the Pentagon and the vice-president's office, and is now taking over the agency she helped eclipse." The assessment was lacking in nuance, but frankly, it was emblematic of what people were thinking.

I thought the critique unfair. We'd been at war, and the Pentagon carries a disproportionate share of the responsibility in combat. Nonetheless, I had to deal with the perception. There was even a suggestion in the press that I really wanted to be secretary of defense. The President and I had talked about my suitability for the job in passing, sometime around the Abu Ghraib incident, when Don had offered his resignation, and briefly again before the election. The idea of being the first woman to run the Pentagon did appeal to me at some level.

But I'd known for a long time that the President wanted me at State. As the impact of the wars on our alliances and our standing in the world was being felt, State was where I thought I could do the most good. I decided to use a phrase in the hearings that would make clear where I stood and to repeat it as often as possible. "The time for diplomacy is now" was meant to convey that I intended to rebalance U.S. foreign policy toward diplomacy—and its execution toward the Department of State. I also acknowledged the charge of unilateralism. "Our interaction with the rest of the world must be a conversation, not a monologue," I said. "Alliances and multilateral institutions can multiply the strength of freedom-loving nations. If I'm confirmed, that core conviction will guide my actions." The message was meant for our friends in the world and my colleagues in the administration.

The hearings began with Dianne Feinstein, the democratic senator from California, presenting me to the Senate Foreign Relations Committee. This is a nice tradition by which the nominee is introduced by a senator from his or her home state. I'd known Dianne and her husband, Richard Blum, for many years. Her strength was on full display that terrible day when Mayor George Moscone and Supervisor Harvey Milk were murdered in San Francisco. She was then a young, untested local politician who demonstrated remarkable fortitude and pulled the wounded city through its grief. Though she was of the other party, I respected Dianne for her tenacity, knowledge of foreign affairs, and good humor, and I was honored to have her present me to the Senate.

My relationship with the other senator from California, Barbara Boxer, was, to put it mildly, less cordial. That became very clear during the hearings when she suggested that I had been dishonest in presenting the intelligence in advance of the Iraq war. She should have been more careful with her talking points before the hearings, because I'd been tipped off by the press that she was going to accuse me of allowing the Iraq mission to overwhelm my respect for the truth. I fired back that I'd never lost respect for the truth in the service of anything. It wasn't the last time that we'd have angry exchanges when I testified before the committee. Barbara Boxer and I had a history. She knew that I'd worked for every California Republican who'd tried to defeat her. And perhaps she bristled at speculation that I'd one day take her on for that seat. She needn't have worried, but it was never just a policy difference for Senator Boxer; she always managed to descend into a personal assault.

About halfway through the first day, the wiry junior senator from Illinois took the floor. His questions were sharp but not rude, and he actually seemed interested in my answers. We volleyed back and forth a few times, and I was really impressed. That was my first encounter with then Senator Barack Obama. He'd vote for my confirmation despite objections from some in his camp, and we would become friendly. We didn't always agree, but I always knew that our exchanges would be without personal animosity or rancor.

A low point of the hearing came late on the first day. Almost everyone had gone home—the press, the senators, most of the staff. The hearing room was noticeably darker without the klieg lights of the networks that had illuminated it earlier in the day. Only the chair, the obviously tired Senator Lugar, Senator George Voinovich of Ohio, and Senator Kerry remained. When asked whether he had further questions, Voinovich demurred, saying that he was there only to keep the chairman company. He left shortly after yielding his time to Senator Kerry.

Perhaps smarting from his defeat in the election two months before, the senator from Massachusetts launched on a long rhetorical journey through most of the points he'd made in the campaign. After having testified for nearly nine hours, I was exhausted and ready to go home, but I kept telling myself that this was really about him, not about me. It helped that I held then and hold now a great deal of respect for John Kerry's knowledge of the issues. So I tried to answer the questions without exhibiting any annoyance. Finally, well after 7:30 P.M., the hearings adjourned. Senator Lugar said that a few other senators wished to ask questions and asked if I could return the next day. I did, and the hearings wrapped up without incident. The committee went into a "business session" and voted 16 to 2 to recommend my confirmation to the full Senate. I was well on my way to becoming secretary of state.

The White House had hoped to have a vote in the full Senate immediately after the President took the oath of office on January 20. But some legislators, led by Senator Robert Byrd of West Virginia, insisted on a floor debate. I was annoyed because the debate would have no real effect; the whole purpose was to provide time for further indictment of the Bush foreign policy.

Thus I attended the inauguration not as the secretary of state but as the secretary of state–designate. At lunch in the Capitol Rotunda, Majority Leader Senator Bill Frist picked up my name card, scratched out "national security advisor," and wrote in "secretary of state," joking that it was clearly his fault that I wasn't yet confirmed. Colin would continue as secretary for a few more days.

My good friend Gene Washington accompanied me to the inaugural balls that night. The fact is that those events are more like stand-up cocktail parties than dances. The President and First Lady make an appearance at each and then depart for the next.

Back in 2001, I'd been very excited about the inauguration and the evening's festivities. I'd bought a new dress and invited scores of friends and family to attend. This time I wanted to skip the whole evening. I dutifully went to three events (wearing the Oscar de la Renta from my birthday party) where I never got past the crunch of well-wishers at the front door. I asked Gene if he minded skipping the rest of the parties. He and I went back to my apartment and, dressed in our inaugural finery, ate leftover ham sandwiches. I went to bed early and slept like a very tired baby.

Six days later, on January 26, the Senate voted 85 to 13 to confirm me. At about seven o'clock, Andy Card administered the oath of office at the White House, and I became the sixty-sixth secretary of state. A few minutes later, I walked out of the West Wing basement door and into a vehicle protected by Diplomatic Security. My time as national security advisor was over.

Two days later there would be a formal swearing-in ceremony in the Benjamin Franklin room of the Department of State. The elaborate rooms on the eighth floor of the State Department look as if they belong in European palaces, not in the 1950s building at Foggy Bottom. But they are the United States' attempt to capture the seriousness and the grandeur of diplomacy. Those rooms, named for the founding fathers, house remarkable artifacts of our nation's history, including Thomas Jefferson's desk. The Franklin room is my favorite, decorated in warm rose and beige colors and dominated by an enormous portrait of our most beloved founding father hanging above the fireplace. Franklin was the United States' first diplomat, having been dispatched to Paris in December 1776.

With the President and my Aunts Gee and Mattie and Uncle Alto looking on, my friend and Watergate neighbor Supreme Court Justice Ruth Bader Ginsburg read the oath of office. As I repeated it, I took in every word: "I do solemnly swear that I will support and defend the Constitution of the United States against all enemies, foreign and domestic; that I will bear true faith and allegiance to the same; that I take this obligation freely, without any mental reservation or purpose of evasion; and that I will well and faithfully discharge the duties of the office on which I am about to enter. So help me God." Then I thanked all those who'd helped me, especially the generations of Rays and Rices who'd always thought such a day possible. I glanced up at the portrait of Franklin. What would *he* have thought of this great-granddaughter of slaves and child of Jim Crow Birmingham pledging to defend the Constitution of the United States, which had infamously counted her ancestors "three-fifths" of a man? Somehow, I wanted to believe, Franklin would have liked history's turn toward justice and taken my appointment in stride.

That night my closest friends; Chip Blacker, who had come from Stanford; Mary Bush; the Hadleys; my family; and I had dinner at the restaurant in the Watergate Hotel. I didn't want to do anything elaborate because I was ready to stop celebrating my appointment and get on with doing the job. But it was quite a moment to be with this collection of extraordinary ordinary people who had been so important throughout my life. We talked a lot about my parents, John and Angelena, who I was sure were there in spirit, looking over the whole incredible scene and happy about it, if not surprised. Before going to sleep I prayed that I'd never take for granted the charge that I'd been given or the sacrifices of those who'd made it possible.

Assembling the Team

THE NEXT DAY I stood on the steps of the lobby of the State Department, employees surrounding me on all sides. It wasn't the most elegant of settings in which to introduce myself—and, of course, the microphone gave off one of those annoying feedback sounds as it was passed to me—but my purpose in calling everyone together was to let them know that I expected a lot from them and that in return they could expect an energetic voice in foreign affairs.

I deliberately drew an analogy to the period immediately after World War II, when heavyweights in the department from George Marshall to Dean Acheson to Paul Nitze had shaped the future and laid a foundation for victory in the Cold War forty years later. I wanted to evoke a narrative of a revered time in the department's history—a time of great consequence and success in U.S. foreign policy.

My biggest challenge in taking the reins at State was to ensure the active loyalty of the Foreign Service. I use the modifier "active" because

I don't mean to suggest that people were disloyal. But they did sometimes appear less than enthusiastic about the President's policies, and, at worst, some (but not all) kept a kind of psychic distance from the more controversial decisions that had been made. In blunt terms, Iraq had to be the Department of State's war too—not Bush's war, not the Pentagon's, but *America's* war. And the President's vision for a democratic Middle East had to be more than a slogan that diplomats repeated without believing it to be possible.

Shortly after my appointment I had assembled a small team of trusted aides to help plan the transition and accompany me to State. They were, for the most part, people whom I'd come to rely on at the White House. I asked John Bellinger to become my legal advisor. The development of the legal framework in the war on terror—issues such as the role of the Geneva Conventions, interrogations, and Guantánamo—had left a bitter taste with some of our allies and with many in the legal community at home. John would be indefatigable in addressing those concerns in a serious manner. He would be neither a constant skeptic nor an unthinking proponent of the international community's supposed code of conduct. That would be good for us abroad and critical in the domestic debates at home.

Jim Wilkinson would join me as senior advisor. A whirling dervish with an idea a minute, Jim was unlike anyone else I'd ever known. He was a Texan who had come from humble circumstances but was extremely well read and had a wonderful "eye" for public relations and image. Jim would help me send the right messages to the American people and to the world about what we were trying to do and how we would do it. Later, Colby Cooper would also join me from the White House to help Jim in developing and executing the public side of my diplomacy.

Brian Gunderson would become my chief of staff, but ironically, we first met when I interviewed him for the position. I say "ironically" because the chief of staff is usually the closest person to a principal, and Brian would become an extremely close confidant. He'd worked for Bob Zoellick in that position, and it was Bob who had recommended him. Brian was a taciturn Minnesotan who, like Jim, had worked for Congressman Richard Armey and possessed impeccable conservative credentials. He was thorough, calm, and had terrific political instincts.

I wanted a chief of staff who would never think of himself as a "gate-keeper" but rather as facilitating contact to me. That is a hard balance to maintain, because not everyone should be able to get to the secretary. Yet some of my predecessors had become known for their "palace guard." The organization needed to be as flat as possible. Ruth Elliott had worked for me in the Provost's office when she was a freshman at Stanford and had come to the White House with me in 2001. She became Brian's deputy, bringing a touch to the job that only someone who has known you for so long can.

Sean McCormack would join me at State as assistant secretary for public affairs and spokesman, the positions he'd held at the NSC. Sean was a Foreign Service officer whose expertise was in economics, not media relations. He'd served in several complex posts abroad, including Algeria and Turkey. Moreover, he had a strong interest in the emerging phenomenon of social media and wanted to modernize the department's media and public relations operations. But mostly I trusted Sean to be on the front lines with the press every day. He'd been with me through the 9/11 Commission, "the sixteen words," and countless other press crises, and I'd never once seen him with his hair on fire.

I rounded out my inner circle with two appointments meant to ensure that I'd be challenged intellectually—in the academic sense of the word. Phil Zelikow would become my counselor. The role of counselor varies greatly in accordance with the secretary's wishes. Colin didn't even have one. But the role has often been one of in-house critic, a kind of licensed kibitzer to push the thinking of the department beyond established bureaucratic boundaries. My long association with Philip, dating back to the first Bush administration, and our coauthorship of a book on German unification had taught me how to take advantage of Philip's talents. He wouldn't be shy in debating me, and he'd be a provocative and creative colleague. Phil's elbows are a bit sharp and he doesn't lack self-confidence, but he is very smart and he would challenge our assumptions going forward.

Steve Krasner, my longtime colleague and an eminent political scientist from Stanford, would become the director of policy planning. Like counselor, this position had waxed and waned in importance depending on the secretary's vision for it. Paul Nitze had written NSC-68 while holding the position and was generally viewed as its most influential occupant. At its best, the small policy-planning staff would push the envelope and prevent "group think" within the department. Many thought of it as a long-range planning apparatus looking years out into the future. I wanted someone who'd bring rigor and new ideas to the current problems we were facing. In the midst of two wars and the fight against terrorism, I didn't have time for speculation about 2020.

When he came to the State Department, Steve brought together a terrific staff of "young guns" to push new ideas. One of his most inspired appointments came in 2006, when he hired the twenty-something Jared Cohen, who'd been a student at Stanford and had taken a four-month sojourn on his own in Iran. He would use his position at Policy Planning to begin to integrate social media into our diplomatic tool kit. That would pay off handsomely some years later, when Twitter and Facebook became accelerants of democratic change in the Middle East.

When it came to the most senior line positions, I wanted to select people whose appointment would send a message of competence, independence, and bureaucratic weight. In that regard, the deputy secretary of state had to be someone with unquestioned foreign policy credentials and recognized intelligence. At times, the person has also functioned as a kind of chief operating officer for the department, running the day-to-day management of the huge organization. With 57,000 employees worldwide located in some 180 countries over twelve time zones, that is no small task. But beyond that critical function, the department needed someone who could carry weight in the foreign policy debates in Washington and abroad and who could powerfully represent the United States diplomatically. I was more than happy to pick up some of the day-to-day tasks of managing the department since, frankly, I liked "making the trains run on time."

Bob Zoellick, who'd been the U.S. trade representative (USTR), was my first choice for the job. He'd bring not only brilliance and intellect to our work but deep expertise in matters of economics and trade. As USTR Zoellick had held Cabinet rank and had some understandable qualms about becoming a "number two." The President helped me assure Bob that he would be my alter ego and that he could make a unique contribution as the deputy secretary.

The President very much liked the idea of Zoellick, whom he knew and trusted, occupying this position. Some in the administration had raised John Bolton's name, but I did not want to repeat Colin Powell's experience. I wasn't sure that I could fully trust John to follow my lead at State, and I didn't want a clash later on should John be—or appear to be—insubordinate. Nonetheless, it seemed to me that he'd be a fine ambassador to the United Nations, where his skepticism about the organization was an asset with conservatives and, from my point of view, a corrective to the excessive multilateralism of our diplomats in New York.

I asked our ambassador to NATO, Nicholas Burns, to become under secretary of state for political affairs, the third-ranking position in the department and one traditionally held by a senior Foreign Service officer rather than a political appointee. Nick and I had known each other from the administration of George H. W. Bush, when he had served first as special assistant to Zoellick at the State Department and then as my deputy for Soviet affairs at the NSC. He hadn't been an expert on the Soviet Union when I asked him to join me at the White House in 1990, but he was one of the brightest young people in the Foreign Service at the time. His career after that had risen meteorically. He'd served as the spokesman for Clinton-appointee Secretary of State Madeleine Albright, causing raised eyebrows among some of the political folk when he was nominated by President Bush to be NATO ambassador in 2001. But by the time he became "P," as it is called, Nick had more than demonstrated his commitment to the President's agenda. A polished, creative diplomat, Nick would become my "go-to guy" for the most difficult negotiating assignments.

The appointment of the under secretary for public diplomacy was closely watched as well, because there was strong sentiment in the foreign policy community and on the Hill that the United States was terrible at projecting its values and a positive image abroad. That stemmed in part from a somewhat rosy view of U.S. public diplomacy in the past. Radio Free Europe, Radio Liberty, and Voice of America had been unqualified successes during the Cold War. The populations of Eastern Europe and the Soviet Union had relied on them to break through the propaganda and lies of the governments that subjugated them.

The circumstances of the post–Cold War world were fundamentally different, though. Not only had media changed, replacing radio waves with satellite TV and the Internet, but the target of America's outreach, the Muslim world, possessed little of the affection for the United States that was so deeply held by the anti-Communist populations of the Soviet bloc. The question "Why do they hate us?" was a complex one that tended to equate dislike of U.S. policies with hatred of the United States. A degree from an American university or college was the most revered credential in the world. And people lined up for blocks to get an entry visa to the United States. The problem was, our policies had rarely been popular with them, long before George W. Bush came to office. For many in the Arab world, the United States was associated with authoritarian regimes—not freedom, as in Eastern Europe. Their suspicions about the messenger overwhelmed the message.

I therefore had less ambitious goals for public diplomacy than some others in the foreign policy establishment had. It would be a huge task just to counter the propaganda of Arab satellite TV on a twenty-four-hour news cycle, to give more people—particularly young people— access to the United States and Americans, and to empower our diplomats abroad to engage the peoples of the places they served. The State Department's public diplomacy apparatus needed reform to make it more nimble and central to the department's mission abroad; public diplomacy shouldn't be an afterthought.

Reflecting on it, I realized there was only one choice for that job with outsized public expectations: my friend from the White House Karen Hughes. Karen was the best and most creative communicator I'd met; she was close to the President; and, though she wasn't a foreign policy expert, she'd been centrally involved in the execution of our policies from the beginning. After a lot of arm-twisting by everyone I could enlist, including the President, Karen agreed to take the job. In my last year, this critical role would be filled by Jim Glassman, who, after a distinguished career in journalism, editing, and publishing, had most recently served as the chairman of the Broadcasting Board of Governors.

The Bureau of Educational and Cultural Affairs would be the most important group within Karen's organization. ECA, as it was called, oversaw most of the exchanges with foreign students and civil society activists. As a result it would be key in our efforts of outreach to the Muslim world and the Freedom Agenda. The Bureau had carried out its functions expertly but not very creatively. That had been the case since I had been an intern there in 1977. I asked a dynamo, Dina Powell, who had directed the Presidential Personnel Office in the White House, to become the ECA assistant secretary. An Egyptian American, fluent in Arabic and passionate about America's promise, Dina would bring energy and new ideas to the bureau. She would launch several effective initiatives, including public-private partnerships and a program near to my own heart that made sports ambassadors of such athletes as the figure skater Michelle Kwan and baseball greats Cal Ripken Jr. and Ken Griffey Jr. She would become, in the course of my term, one of my closest and most trusted advisors.

The post of under secretary for economic, business, and agricultural affairs was also crucial, and I settled on Josette Sheeran. Josette had been Bob's deputy when he was USTR, and she brought energy and expertise to the position. Her career path had been a bit unusual, including a stint as the managing editor of the conservative *Washington Times*.

Later, when Josette left to become head of the UN World Food Programme, Reuben Jeffery, who had worked with Jerry Bremer in Iraq, took on that crucial role in economic affairs. Reuben was a former Goldman Sachs partner who brought deep expertise in financial markets and the global economy. As national security advisor I had seen the increasing relevance of economic power to our international position. There was no doubt that I would spend a good deal of time as secretary of state on issues of trade and the economy. With both Josette and Reuben, State had a strong voice in matters that were increasingly of equal weight to military and political issues in our policy.

Henrietta Holsman Fore became under secretary for management. The Department of State is a huge operation with all the attendant problems of personnel and facilities. Henrietta had founded her own small business and had most recently overseen a dramatic remaking of the management structures of the U.S. Mint. Henrietta and her strong deputies Pat Kennedy and Rajkumar Chellaraja had the skills and the good common sense to make certain that the department was well run. There were administrative practices that needed attention as well. I was shocked, for example, to learn that the Department had over fifty differenct cell phone contracts as opposed to a consolidated account, which could cut costs significantly. Tim Warner, who had been my closest advisor when I was provost at Stanford, helped lead critical reform efforts that improved the management of the Department.

Finally, I retained Paula Dobriansky as under secretary for global affairs, a relatively new creation of the Clinton years, which oversaw multilateral matters from the environment to women's issues to human trafficking to relations with UN agencies. Paula and I had known each other in the 1980s, when we were young East Europeanists participating in the events that would lead to the end of communism in Europe. Paula had distinguished herself earlier in carrying the thankless brief on climate change at a time when suspicions of the administration were at their height. Eventually we would add the word "democracy" to her title, making her the under secretary for democracy and global affairs, a fitting addition given her long commitment to a U.S. foreign policy based on values. In that work Paula was joined by Barry Lowenkron, with whom I had worked in the George H. W. Bush years. As assistant secretary for democracy, human rights, and labor, Barry oversaw key elements of the Freedom Agenda.

These appointments at the level of under secretary gave me a strong team of people who could lead on issues and make decisions so that not every question floated to the top for resolution. Yet I needed to maintain a direct link to the all-important assistant secretaries for the regions of the world. These were the people to whom I looked to represent us abroad and give coherence to U.S. policy. They helped set the substantive policy course, oversaw the embassies, maintained relations with foreign governments, and negotiated on behalf of the United States. The Pentagon had combatant commanders for each region; similarly, the assistant secretaries were my diplomatic commanders and the vital counterparts of and counterweights to the military commanders around the globe. They had to be fully empowered and respected to be able to access high-level officials in foreign capitals and to be seen as speaking for me and for the President. I insisted that they have strong deputies who could run the bureaus in Washington so that they could stay on the road as much as 50 percent of the time. The assistant secretaries had to be seen as the faces and heard as the voices of U.S. foreign policy in their regions.

At any given time, the mix of political and career appointments to those crucial positions has varied. Under George Shultz, for example, a little more than one-half of the regional assistant secretaries were political appointees, not Foreign Service officers. The figure was two-thirds under Madeleine Albright. But I wanted to make career appointments to those positions wherever possible. It would be a signal to the Foreign Service that I valued them and a message that I expected commitment to the President's agenda in return. In the final analysis, five of the six regional assistant secretaries came from the career ranks.

The one noncareer appointment brought Jendayi Frazer to the department as assistant secretary for African affairs. Jendayi had left the White House to serve as ambassador to South Africa. When deciding who would succeed Connie Newman, the highly effective assistant secretary under Colin Powell who continued serving until August 2005, I never considered anyone else. Jendayi had been an architect of the President's highly acclaimed Africa policies and was trusted and admired throughout the region.

When it came to the other appointments, two Foreign Service officers who'd already demonstrated their competence and dedication while serving on the NSC staff quickly emerged as the lead candidates. As special assistants to the President they'd been an integral part of his inner circle at the White House, and he knew and trusted them. They were equally well respected in the Foreign Service and in the capitals of the regions they would oversee.

I asked Daniel Fried, who'd been ambassador to Poland and then special assistant for European affairs at the NSC, to become assistant secretary for European affairs. Dan and I had a long history, going back to 1989, when he was a young desk officer for Poland in the State Department. We'd conspired to push administration policy faster toward recognition of the events that were leading to the collapse of Soviet power. When Dan couldn't get the ultraconservative State Department to sign off on his position papers, he would "bootleg" them to me and I would use them to shape White House policy.

Dan would be on the front lines in repairing relations with the allies, but he was tough-minded and would do so sympathetically but without apology for all that had transpired. He was well respected as a first-rate diplomat in both the department and the capitals of Europe.

Tom Shannon had also served at the NSC as special assistant for Western Hemisphere affairs. As I've noted, the President and I thought it important to reenergize our policies in the neighborhood. He'd come to office hoping to make Latin America a key priority, but we hadn't yet managed to exhibit the energy and creativity in that region that he wanted. Tom Shannon was a trusted aide and a renowned diplomat and could carry that brief. He'd also managed the Cuba issue very well. The President and I shared a deep disdain for Communist Cuba and had very little tolerance for calls to "reach out" to the bloody dictator, Fidel Castro, whom I remembered mostly for his shortsighted decision to place Soviet missiles aimed at the United States on his territory. But in Europe and in some foreign policy circles this unrelenting attitude toward Cuba was viewed with disapproval. Tom proved to be very capable in managing the issue, largely because he was himself deeply committed to a more democratic Latin America—a vision that wouldn't be fully realized until the Cuban people were free. And he capably handled the thorny domestic politics of the issue as well.

I asked David Welch, then serving as U.S. ambassador to Egypt, to take up the critical post of assistant secretary for Near Eastern affairs, overseeing the Middle East. David is one of the finest diplomats of his generation, a well-respected Arabist, and he had served in some of the toughest places. He'd been in Pakistan when our embassy was burned in 1979 and Syria during the Lebanese civil war. And as was the case with Dan Fried, I'd known David and worked closely with him during the George H. W. Bush administration.

David had been somewhat skeptical of the decision to invade Iraq, and I knew that. But he brought deep expertise to the issue, having negotiated the still-working ceasefire between the two major Iraqi-Kurdish factions in 1998. David was also cautious with regards to the democracy agenda in the Middle East. Our conversations convinced me that the differences were ones of tactics not strategy: a little tension on that score wouldn't be a bad thing. And if we were to make progress on the Palestinian issue, David would have to be at the heart of it. All the major players respected him, and that would be key to success.

Dan, Tom, and David were self-evident picks. That wasn't the case with the assistant secretary for East Asian affairs. The region presented numerous problems, everything from managing the rise of China to strengthening relations with Southeast Asia to dealing with North Korean proliferation. Asia had no mature regional institutions like NATO or the European Union, and relations between the major players were contentious, with many unresolved issues from World War II. How did one deal with a maturing democratic ally in Korea who harbored deep suspicions of our long-standing Japanese ally? What about Russia's unresolved conflicts with Japan and Tokyo's strained relations with China? What of the tensions between Seoul and Beijing? East Asia was a thicket of bad bilateral relations. The United States was struggling to maintain good relations with each of the powers and often found itself caught up in the hostility of a region that had not yet put World War II behind it.

East Asia was also the region with the most assertive Pentagon profile. The combatant commander for the Pacific was always something of a proconsul, a four-star admiral operating from his base in Hawaii and prone to pronouncements on matters that at best blurred the boundaries between diplomacy and military policy and at worst shattered them. And it didn't matter who held the post; it seemed to be a permanent feature of the command. The department needed someone who would develop good relations with Pacific Command but stand toe-to-toe with the admiral when necessary.

Moreover, I needed someone who would think differently about East Asia. In the Foreign Service there were Koreanists and Sinologists and those who knew Japan (often referred to derisively as "agents of the Chrysanthemum throne"), but there were no real regionalists in the way that David knew the whole Middle East or Dan all of Europe. I turned to Christopher Hill, who was as close to a generalist as one will find in the Foreign Service, though most of his work had been in Europe. Returning from a successful posting as ambassador to South Korea, Chris had an understanding of the region yet none of the innate prejudices that so bedeviled long-standing specialists. He was a creative thinker and a tough, persistent diplomat who had helped Richard Holbrooke face down Slobodan Milošević in Serbia.

The remaining bureau was a new and crucial one: South and Central Asia. I've mentioned the reaction that I had on September 15 at Camp David when we rolled out the map of Afghanistan. The immediate concern was to strip al Qaeda of its safe haven, but the strategic value of Afghanistan lay in its geography. There was a reason it had always been an object of the great powers' attention in what had historically been known as the "Great Game." Sitting above Pakistan and India to the South, Central Asian states to the north, and Iran to the west, a stable and democratic Afghanistan had the potential to transform the entire region. It would not happen quickly, but if it were ever to happen, the first step was to redefine the territorial confines of South Asia. That meant that the Central Asian states of Kyrgyzstan, Uzbekistan, Tajikistan, Kazakhstan, and Turkmenistan had to be thought of as relating to South Asia, not Europe. The reason those states had been lodged in European Affairs in the State Department was the legacy of their past incorporation into the Soviet Union. I decided to break them out and combine them with the South Asian countries to create a new bureau that represented the current and future geopolitics of the region. There were some howls from traditionalists, including some in those countries who didn't particularly like being lumped with backward Afghanistan instead of developed Europe. But Afghanistan would never grow economically and politically without a regional home that made sense.

The South and Central Asian Bureau would need a senior person to bring it into being and to fight off the many bureaucratic challenges to this new entity. Christina Rocca, the assistant secretary for South Asian affairs under Colin, worked diligently with me over the next year to facilitate this effort. To lead the reorganized bureau, I chose Richard Boucher, who'd been Colin's spokesman but was also a senior Foreign Service officer with a concentration in economic affairs, reasoning that many of the early efforts at regional integration would be on the trade and economic fronts.

Finally, I was stunned to learn that there was no independent Iran desk in the Department of State. It turned out that the department thought in terms of "relations" with countries. Since we had no "relations" with Iran, it didn't warrant its own desk. Amazing. We created an Iran desk and later an outpost in Dubai to follow Iranian affairs from a place with geographic proximity to Tehran. The idea was borrowed from the 1920s, when the United States had maintained an outpost in Latvia to watch events in the Soviet Union prior to the establishment of diplomatic relations. Because the Dubai station processed visas for Iranians, for instance, we were able to learn about events in Iran from people coming through. The Iran desk reported directly to Nick Burns to give it stature and proximity to the seventh floor—the secretary's floor.

Shortly after 9/11, it had become clear that there were new threats and challenges such as terrorism that were not confined to any one geographic area. Coordinator positions have traditionally been established within the State Department to fill this void. These offices report directly to the secretary and draw on functional, as opposed to regional, expertise to manage the U.S. government's response to a particular issue across agencies. To lead the Office of the Coordinator for Counterterrorism, which directed the development and implementation of U.S. counterterrorism policy, I chose Henry "Hank" Crumpton, a former CIA officer who had led the Agency's Afghanistan campaign in 2001 and 2002. In 2004, Colin Powell had established the Office of the Coordinator for Reconstruction and Stabilization, which led efforts to institutionalize the U.S. government's civilian capacity to rebuild post-conflict societies. Carlos Pascual was the Department's first coordinator and did remarkable work in shaping the position at its inception. I selected former U.S. Ambassador to Ukraine John Herbst to succeed him in 2006. John's leadership would prove instrumental in launching the Civilian Response Corps, a rapidly deployable force of civilian employees trained and equipped to assist in post-conflict reconstruction efforts. The Corps would allow the military to focus on security without the additional strains of fulfilling objectives more suitable for civilian specialists in the field.

But the best personnel decision that I made was to bring the incomparable Liz Lineberry back to the State Department with me. Liz had been an assistant to James Baker, Warren Christopher, and Madeleine Albright. Wanting a change, she'd come to work for me at the NSC and was with me practically every day. Liz just knew how to get things done. And she knew what I needed before I did. When I became secretary, Liz came back to Foggy Bottom. She kept my calendar and helped me keep my sanity, reminding me from time to time to have dinner with friends, call my family, or take a Sunday afternoon off to play golf or music.

Liz and my executive assistant, Steve Beecroft, a wily senior Foreign Service officer with a wicked sense of humor, made sure that the front office had warm and open relations with the staff. That is absolutely critical, as the secretary is busy and operates under a good deal of stress. If the front office exacerbates the constant sense of crisis, everyone will feel it and efficiency will decline. Liz and Steve, and later Joe Macmanus when Steve left to become ambassador to Jordan, did just the opposite: they were calming influences. That was an indispensable contribution to me and to my work.

MY FIRST days in the office were largely devoted to getting to know my "building," as it is called, and getting used to being called "S." It was as if I'd lost my proper name since I heard everyone refer to me that way. "S" says this. "S" needs that. I learned quickly not to think out loud lest I set off an entire bureaucratic process to deliver what "S" wanted.

The organization also needed to be flatter. In both of my stints at the NSC I'd marveled at the bureaucratic hierarchy of the State Department. Everything took a long time because several people and offices had to approve even the simplest policy paper. As national security advisor I was always amused that our morning calls would often expose the fact that I knew what was going on in Don's or Colin's building before they did. My one special assistant for a given region would have given me a heads-up on a department's position while it was still making its way step by step up to the secretary. I asked very simply if we could cut down the number of clearances, passing paper through the hands of only those who really needed to be in on a decision. "Of course," everyone told me. But four years later I was still asking. When something was going to "S," everyone with even a passing interest wanted to have a say in it. Eventually I took the step on certain occasions of asking to be briefed by the desk officer who had actually written the paper.

There were also a number of immediate management problems that had come to my attention during the transition. The Bureau of International Narcotics and Law Enforcement Affairs, for instance, was overseeing huge budget expenditures for the training of police in Afghanistan and Iraq. The recordkeeping, though, and thus the accountability for that work was less than adequate. The serving assistant secretary was resistant to the changes that needed to be made. That would have been fine, and I certainly would have allowed him to make his case. But when Brian, my chief of staff, walked into my office late one evening and told me that the gentleman had gone behind my back to complain to his patrons on the Hill, I decided that the bureau needed new leadership. The message had to be clear that I encouraged open disagreement but that this kind of behavior was unacceptable.

Nancy Powell, a senior Foreign Service officer on leave between assignments, became the bureau's acting head. Then I appointed Anne Patterson, an outstanding officer who would later become ambassador to Pakistan. There was no stronger manager and leader in the Foreign Service than Anne.

She took over the bureau, which had inadequate processes to deal with the crushing workload of two huge simultaneous nation-building projects. Matching resources and responsibilities is critical to the success of any organization, and I paid personal attention to problems like that.

Nothing, though, would take more time than trying to make the department's personnel policies more flexible and responsive to our needs. From my position as national security advisor I'd watched the State Department struggle to deploy senior Foreign Service officers to Afghanistan and Iraq. The service is small, about eleven thousand officers globally. Bob Gates and I would later joke that there were as many people in military bands as in the Foreign Service. The numbers had at least improved, thanks to Colin's initiative to hire more than a thousand new officers over the four years of his term. But we were still woefully short of the people we needed, particularly in hardship posts where families couldn't accompany the officers. Since the State Department uses a system where people bid for posts, the least desirable ones often went unfilled—particularly at the midcareer level, where family considerations were salient.

Moreover, the officers we did have were not properly apportioned to the tasks at hand. We had nearly as many officers in Germany, which had a population of 80 million, as in India, which had a population of 1 billion. That was, in large part, a legacy of the Cold War, when Europe had been at the center of the national security agenda. Bob Zoellick led an effort to look at redeployment of our personnel. I'd talked about transformational diplomacy in my confirmation hearings. By that term, I meant that the work of diplomacy was now active democracy promotion, AIDS relief, rebuilding failed states, and the like. The department's most treasured function, political reporting through long cables, was simply less important in a world of instant communication. The Foreign Service needed to embrace new functions and perform them in more remote and sometimes highly volatile places.

All this demonstrates the breadth of the secretary's portfolio. Policy issues and crises dominate the agenda. But the department has to function properly if policy execution is to succeed. I well understood that I should not micromanage. Yet there is a level of knowledge about the details of what is going on in one's building that is absolutely necessary. As I would experience several times, bureaucratic screw-ups usually reached my desk when it was already too late to do much about them. Playing catch-up with the press and Congress agitated and looking for answers is hard. At my first staff meeting I sent a message that I didn't like mistakes but could understand them and that I'd work with people to find a solution. But I hated surprises. "Never fail to tell me something that I should know before people outside this building know," I pleaded. Early warning is the key to good management, but it's very hard to achieve.

MY PREOCCUPATION with the daily work of the department occasionally gave way to the remarkable moments that reminded me of the incredible honor of being secretary of state. Attending the President's State of the Union address in 2005 was one of those times.

I stood just outside the chamber of the House of Representatives, peering in through the door at the assembled members of Congress. I'd always loved the State of the Union, rarely missing the televised annual spectacle that affirms the institutional legitimacy and stability of American democracy. "Mr. Speaker, the President's Cabinet."

The doors flung open, and the bright lights of the press were suddenly and blindingly apparent. I started down toward the front, reaching out to shake the hands of members on both sides of the aisle. At the time of the establishment of the country only four Cabinet positions were created: secretary of state, secretary of the treasury, secretary of war, and attorney general. That order is used in all formal protocol settings. And the secretary of state is fourth in the line of presidential succession after the Vice President, speaker of the House, and president pro tempore of the Senate. As the senior member of the Cabinet, the secretary is always seated first and thus leads the processional of cabinet members just before the arrival of the President.

When I reached the front row, I realized that I'd walked a bit quickly, not wanting to hold up the line. My colleague Treasury Secretary John Snow was well behind me, shaking hands and enjoying the moment. I made a mental note to walk more slowly the next year. After a few minutes the applause stopped, and there was a moment of silence and anticipation. "Mr. Speaker, the President of the United States." As he passed, the President and I exchanged glances. Then he ascended the podium to wild applause. "Members of Congress, I have the high privilege and the distinct honor of presenting to you the President of the United States," said Speaker Dennis Hastert. And so it went: my first State of the Union as secretary of state and a moment when I felt intensely the tradition and the history that attended my role.

I came to relish every historical tidbit about the position, learning, for instance, that the secretary of state is the keeper of the Great Seal of the United States of America. One day I found myself signing hundreds of documents, including certificates commissioning other Cabinet officers. "Why am I signing these?" I asked.

"You are the keeper of the Great Seal," someone said.

"And when did I become the keeper of the Great Seal?"

"Thomas Jefferson was the keeper of the Great Seal," I was told.

One could imagine the founders deciding that an infant republic separated from great-power politics by vast oceans would have minimal foreign policy concerns. Tom Jefferson needed more to do. Why not give him that administrative function? I'd never understood why Henry Kissinger had been required to sign Richard Nixon's resignation letter in 1974. Now I did. The secretary of state had to affix the Great Seal and sign any official document; I was the nation's notary. I had the Great Seal—a mechanical device that imprints the stamp— prominently displayed in the State Department's Exhibit Hall and created a traveling exhibition to commemorate its 225th anniversary.

22

Promoting America's Interests
and Values Abroad

T HE DAY AFTER the State of the Union, I left on my first trip abroad. I'd been in office just a week, and by going on the road right away, I wanted to send a message of openness and outreach to our friends.

I arrived at Andrews Air Force Base and boarded the plane that said simply, "The United States of America." The "blue and white," as it's called, is a Boeing 757 with dated decor, circa 1980. But as I walked into my cabin at the front of the plane and sat at the desk for the first time, I felt a real sense of wonderment and pride. Before I could sink too far into my thoughts, my spokesman, Sean McCormack, came in and said that after takeoff I'd need to go back and brief the traveling press corps, most of whom were assigned permanently to the Department of State. It was a ritual event just after takeoff to try to set the tone for the trip through the initial press stories that the journalists would file upon landing. I dutifully went to the back of the plane, trying to stand up straight despite the slight turbulence that rocked us back and forth.

The journalists were in a good mood, probably giving the new secretary a bit of a honeymoon. They were senior members of their profession who knew foreign policy issues inside out. Steve Weisman of the *New York Times*, Glenn Kessler of the *Washington Post*, Anne Gearan of the Associated Press, and Andrea Mitchell of NBC News had all been around the block more than a few times. The State Department press corps had a reputation for being "foreign policy nerds," as opposed to the generalists, who loved the spotlight of the White House beat. They were going to be my companions for four years in a quasi-adversarial relationship that I hoped would generate mutual respect. That would be in the best tradition of the "fourth estate." We were going to be together a *lot*, so as a nice gesture I gave each one an atlas with which to track our travels.

Jim Wilkinson, my senior advisor, Sean, and the rest of the team had carefully constructed the trip so that the first stop would be in Great Britain, "our closest friend." I learned, by the way, never to say that because even though everyone understood the "special relationship," it was not good to risk insulting other close friends. Indeed, I'd always use the construction "one of our closest friends." That was safe.

The Brits were anxious to help me get off to a good start. My day began with a solid interview with the venerable journalist Sir David Frost. I then met with Prime Minister Blair at Number 10 Downing Street. Walking into Winston Churchill's former dwelling was pretty special. Yet I was struck once again (it was my third or so time there) by its modesty. It's just a town house—but the pictures on the wall go back to the days of nineteenth-century Prime Minister Benjamin Disraeli. I felt very calm before that first encounter as secretary of state because, as national security advisor, I already knew the leaders of most countries well, and I knew Tony Blair best of all; the press availability with him was a comfortable way to begin my public engagement with the world.

The meeting with Jack Straw, the foreign secretary, was also productive and friendly, followed by a formal, extensive press conference. There are two types of press encounters: the "availability," where the participants will just walk out in front of the press, make a few extemporaneous remarks, and perhaps take one or two questions; and the "press conference," with podiums in gilded halls, prepared remarks, and what can seem like an endless number of questions. As Jack and I walked out into the ornate gold-and-white room and onto the stage, I was somewhat taken aback by the huge number of press. *Steady,* I thought to myself. *Posture. Stand up straight. You've done this a thousand times before. Well, maybe not a thousand but enough.*

Jack made his statement, and I made mine. Then the questions began. Much to my surprise, there was very little about Iraq. On January 30 millions of Iraqis had cast ballots in a powerful demonstration of what the path to democracy could look like in the Middle East. Coupled with the breaking news about the involvement of UN personnel in the Oil for Food scandal, our decision to overthrow Saddam Hussein looked a bit better, even to critics, than it had a few months before. The press has a tendency to change the subject when the sense of crisis abates. The journalists' attention had shifted to Iran and the perceived chasm between the United States and its allies on how to approach Tehran's nuclear ambitions.

As I listened to the questions, it dawned on me that the Europeans somehow saw themselves as mediating between the United States and Iran. Washington was viewed as part of the problem, not a partner in finding the solution. *How did we get into this situation?* I wondered. Question after question probed for evidence that the United States was intending to initiate military action against Iran. Though Jack tried to moderate the perception of a split, he too seemed to think that Europe and the United States weren't on the same page. *The Iranians must be loving this*, I thought. I resolved to talk to the President about that very troubling development by phone that night. He needed to know how much distance there was between our friends and us.

That afternoon we were "wheels up" for Berlin. The German capital is one of my two favorite cities in Europe (the other is Rome) and one that provokes historical memories both good and bad. I'd been deeply involved in the unification of Germany and remembered long conversations in Bonn cafés about whether Berlin should again become the capital of Germany. Some thought the great city too irrevocably associated with militarism and two world wars. Fortunately, the Germans decided in favor of Berlin, a capital that is appropriate for a great power.

But in truth, the unified Germany was still coming to terms with its role as the most populous and economically prosperous country in Europe. When one would say something about German "power," an interlocutor would delicately remind you that "power" was not a word with which Germans were comfortable. The definition of Germany's role was complicated, wedded to the European unification project meant to subsume Berlin's "power" by integrating it into a larger, peaceful framework. The country's relationship with the United States had sustained the divided Germany throughout the Cold War and helped to successfully overcome that division near the end of the century. Still, the new Germany was still defining its foreign policy identity. Gerhard Schroeder's decision to link arms with Vladimir Putin in opposing intervention in Iraq was an echo of Germany's historical tendency to sometimes swing eastward. I didn't want to make too much of it, but I thought that our relationship with Germany, more than any other ally, had been seriously damaged by the split over Iraq. The unified Germany was still in the process of defining its policy orientation, and I didn't like the early returns.

We walked into the new building housing the offices of the chancellor. It's been called the "washing machine" for its cylindrical central tower that mimics a perpetual swirl of motion. I love traditional German architecture but find German modernism unsettling and thought to myself that this building was an uneasy companion to the nineteenth-century Bundestag across the square, even though the stone dome of the Reichstag had been replaced with glass to emphasize the transparency of the Bundesrepublik. That I was so focused on the buildings is perhaps a bit strange, given the importance of the meetings I was about to have, but for whatever reason, the architecture was what caught my attention.

We took the elevator to Chancellor Schroeder's office, where he greeted me warmly. Then, after a cordial meeting, the two of us walked down a narrow pathway toward the press availability. As we entered the room, I was literally blinded by the camera flashes. There were hundreds of journalists crowded into a lobby intended for far fewer people. They were pushing and shoving one another to get a picture of the two of us. "Condi, over here!" "Look, Secretary Rice!" "Condi, look at me!" Cameras were flashing in every direction. I kept walking alongside Schroeder, but I was absolutely stunned by the commotion around us.

When we reached the podium, the chancellor made warm remarks about the importance of U.S.-German relations and our shared values. He underscored the contribution that Germany was making to rebuilding Iraq, concentrating on the effort to train security forces. I then delivered remarks that also focused on the future, not the past. The question-and-answer period was much like that in London, probing on Iran, not Iraq, and edgy though not hostile.

At one point I called on a German journalist when it was actually Schroeder's turn to recognize a member of the press. "Woman power!" he yelled awkwardly in his thick German accent. Oh, well, it was meant to be funny—I think. At the end of the press conference, Schroeder leaned over and kissed me on the cheek. The next morning's coverage of my trip to Berlin included a huge picture of the German chancellor and me in a friendly embrace. That photo said more about putting the past behind us than any words could have, and I was grateful for that. Later that afternoon, on the flight from Poland to Turkey, President Bush called and we chuckled about how close the chancellor and I now appeared to be. But on a more serious note the President said that I was setting exactly the tone that he'd hoped; it was time to move on from the wounds of the Iraq split and unite the alliance in the cause of promoting shared values.

No place was more evocative of the potency of those democratic values than Poland, and my stop in Warsaw was intended to remind everyone to think of history's long arc, not the day's headlines. Not only had the Poles participated early and enthusiastically in the liberation of Iraq, they'd done so for the right reasons. They believed in the universality of liberty and were grateful that the free world hadn't forgotten them during the long twilight of the Cold War. That had led the Poles to want to do the same for captive peoples everywhere.

Four years earlier, when visiting Warsaw with the President, I'd become quite emotional at the arrival ceremony. Listening to the two national anthems under not just the U.S. and Polish flags but also the NATO banner, I reflected on how unlikely this scene would have seemed in the dark days of Soviet domination of Eastern Europe. I remembered, too, my trip to Poland in 1989 with George H. W. Bush, who'd helped set off the revolt against the communist regime with his visit to Gdańsk and unequivocal support for the opposition movement Solidarity. Poland was a vivid reminder that U.S. foreign policy, grounded in both power and principle, had helped change what seemed to be immutable circumstances.

If only Europe "old" and "new," together with the United States, could focus energy and attention on troubled regions, particularly the Middle East, we could build a balance of power that favored freedom. It wouldn't be easy, of course. But who would have thought in 1945 that the U.S. President, sixty years later, would review a Polish contingent of NATO troops—still goose-stepping, Central European style—thanks to Poland's recent membership in the Warsaw Pact? Who would have thought it in 1985?

Yet we understood that the challenge was exacerbated by the United States' uneasy relationship with the Muslim world. My next stop in Turkey would underscore that point.

Turkey was a longtime ally and had been a member of NATO since 1952. But until recently it had been only quasi-democratic, with an assertive military and a political elite that enforced secularism—sometimes brutally—on the population. Kemalism, as the doctrine of secularism was called, had allowed Turkey to modernize but not to fully democratize. Religious expression was all but prohibited outside the mosque. Now, with the election of the AKP (Justice and Development Party), avowedly Islamic leaders had taken the reins. They insisted that they had no intention of turning Turkey into a theocracy but merely wanted to rebalance the society and give religious expression and religious people a place in the public square. Tensions were evident as the old elite (wedded to Kemalism) and the new leaders clashed about the future course of the country. Even the fact that the wives of AKP officials often "covered" with head scarves was a source of discomfort for many Turks, who were fearful of the Islamization of their country. I saw Turkey as the frontline state in the historic struggle to reconcile the principles of Islam and the demands of individual liberty.

That struggle is still playing out in the Middle East today. If there is to be democracy in the region, it will likely evolve as it has in Turkey. As in that country, there will have to be a resolution of the tensions between individual rights, including the rights of women, and the tenets of Islam. The place of religion and religious people in politics, resolved in Europe hundreds of years ago, will have to be determined anew in the Muslim world.

Thus the struggle in Istanbul and Ankara and throughout the vast country is of monumental historic significance. I went to Ankara aware of Turkey's centrality to the Bush administration's reorientation of U.S. foreign policy toward the Freedom Agenda.

President Bush's second inaugural address had put the pursuit of human freedom squarely in the middle of U.S. foreign policy. The President had had a direct hand in the address from the beginning of its development, and it had become a deep reflection of his personal convictions regarding human dignity and freedom. The President was following in a long line of American leaders who believed that U.S. interests, in the long run, are best secured by the advance of freedom. "The survival of liberty in our land increasingly depends on the success of liberty in other lands," he said. Still, U.S. policy for sixty years had pursued something very different in the Middle East: stability at the expense of democracy. We had gotten neither. The decision to cast aside the "stability over democracy" mind-set toward the region became the last element of our foreign policy response to 9/11 and the final piece of the Bush Doctrine.

The evolution of our thinking—from the tactical goal of pursuing al Qaeda to creating a strategic agenda for freedom in the Middle East—did not take place overnight. Of course, from the very beginning the President had a deep personal belief in the power of liberty and an instinct toward a U.S. foreign policy based on values; that was evident in the way he viewed the prospective Palestinian state and in his insistence that the United States would help to build a *democratic,* not just a liberated, Iraq.

The second inaugural address made the choice of promoting freedom in the Middle East and elsewhere explicit and set off a debate among policy makers, analysts, and academics about the place of idealism and ideology in U.S. foreign policy. Realists ran to the barricades to sound the alarm that "interests," not "idealism," should guide the United States' interactions with the world. What they failed to see was that the Freedom Agenda was not just a moral or idealistic cause; it was a redefinition of what constituted realism, a change in the way we viewed U.S. interests in the new circumstances forced on us by the attacks of that horrible day. We rather quickly arrived at the conclusion that U.S. interests and values could be linked together in a coherent way, forming what I came to call a distinctly American realism.

Our overall response to 9/11 was in one sense similar to the U.S. response to Pearl Harbor and its experience after World War II. Roosevelt didn't enter the war to democratize Germany and Japan. When the war was over, the Europeans, particularly Great Britain, cared less about the form of the new German government than about containing its power.

Churchill is reported to have said that he liked Germany so much that he wanted there to be as many Germanys as possible. In other words, he wanted to dismember it and return it to its pre-1871 state; safety lay in getting the balance of power right, and that meant a weak Germany.

The Americans, though, had a different view. There was indeed a moral dimension to their insistence on democratic processes and institutions. But there was a practical reason as well: Truman, Acheson, Marshall, and others began to equate a new and stable order with a permanent change in the nature of the defeated regimes, a change that could be secured only with democracy. They believed that the balance of power could be improved in our favor if democratic states emerged in Europe. This linking of our interests (the balance of power) and our values (democracy) was at the core of our strategic thinking. Later the United States and our allies would embed West Germany in a new kind of security alliance, one based on democratic values. NATO would both prevent the further advance of Josef Stalin's Soviet Union and create a security umbrella under which old adversaries would become democratic partners in peace. In Japan this would take the form of a defense alliance with a new government and a Constitution that looked much like the American one. This was an early practical manifestation of a belief that would later emerge in an academic theory called the "democratic peace." Historically, it can be demonstrated that democracies have not fought one another. Therefore democracy and stability—both within states and between them—can be mutually reinforcing.

The belief in the power of democracy to overcome old rivalries and establish a basis for peace and prosperity did not transfer verbatim to the Middle East. Still, the echoes of it were unmistakable in the way that we came to view that troubled region after the horrors of 9/11. The immediate problem was to hunt down al Qaeda, defend our country, and deal with WMD proliferators who might pass the devastating weapons to terrorists. But surely there was some larger message lying in the ruins of the Twin Towers and the Pentagon. It was, we came to believe, the toxic effect of the "freedom gap" in the Middle East and the unforgivable association of the United States with the defense of the authoritarian status quo.

The intellectual origins of the link between the freedom gap and terrorism are complex. The works of Bernard Lewis and Fouad Ajami were influential with all of us, but the single most impactful document for the President, and certainly for me, was the 2002 Arab Human Development Report, sponsored by the United Nations Development Programme. In the report, Arab intellectuals laid out the costs of authoritarianism in the Middle East over sixty years. "The Arab world is at a crossroads," they said, and it risked being left behind. The authoritarian status quo had led to three deficits that stifled progress: in knowledge and education, women's empowerment, and freedom. By identifying the primary sources of the problem, the report helped clarify the way forward.

The absence of freedom in the Arab world had not meant the absence of politics. The comfort many people had in the essential stability of the region was a false comfort. Authoritarians, many of whom were our friends, had set up a false choice: stability or democracy. "Islamist extremists or me," they would say. They then engaged in self-fulfilling policies that made the dichotomy true. Healthy political forces were repressed, and advocates for reform were jailed, beaten, and prevented from organizing. Meanwhile, the Islamists took refuge in the mosques and madrassas, emerging as political forces and in many places purveyors to the population of social services that the corrupt authoritarians did not provide. Hezbollah in Lebanon, Hamas in the Palestinian territories, and the Muslim Brotherhood in Egypt became associated as much with their good works among the poor as with their radical views.

In the most unvarnished case of a kind of Faustian bargain, the Saudi royal family, frightened by the attack on the Grand Mosque in Mecca after the Iranian Revolution in 1979, made a pact with the radical Wahhabi clerics. The attitude of the monarch could essentially be summed up as "The mosque is yours; the public square is ours." Once on a visit to one of King Abdullah's extraordinary residences, I was flabbergasted to find myself walking through an enormous aquarium—populated by tropical fish and sharks! I asked one of the princes how they kept the sharks from eating the fish. "Oh, if you feed the sharks enough, they have no interest in the fish," he said. Steve Hadley later joked that it was exactly how the House of Saud had treated the extremists: feed them, and they won't eat you. That bargain came crashing down with the attack on the World Trade Center and then, two years later, in the brutal attacks on the Saudi kingdom itself. The new virulent ideology had manifested into al Qaeda, which was determined to expel the United States from the Middle East, destroy the "puppet regimes" that we had supported, and clear the way for an Islamic caliphate. So in essence the absence of decent political forces had left a void, which had been filled by extremists who had become the outlet for "politics" in countries experiencing a "freedom gap."

Only the emergence of democratic institutions and practices could defeat terrorism and radical political Islam. We knew that the path would not be easy and there would undoubtedly be trade-offs in the short term. The United States could not radically reorient its foreign policy, refusing to deal with friendly authoritarian regimes such as Saudi Arabia and Egypt on matters of strategic importance.

The Freedom Agenda was meant to be a long-term strategic shift in the way we defined our interests, not just a genuflection toward our values. We developed new international institutions through a series of programs called the Broader Middle East and North Africa Initiative. The Forum for the Future, created in 2004, brought representatives of civil society and governments from throughout the region together to discuss individual rights, women's empowerment, and economic development. Officials from the United States and Europe joined ministers from monarchies such as Jordan and Saudi Arabia and dictatorships such as Syria in sessions devoted to human rights and democracy. The goal was to push on different dimensions, supporting civil society and pressuring governments. The presentations at those sessions were, not surprisingly, sterile and sometimes even a little hostile toward us. Still the participants—representatives of governments and members of civil society—attended, and political reform was on the agenda at every meeting.

In this we attempted to replicate the Conference on Security and Co-operation in Europe (CSCE), which had been formed in 1975. At the time many American conservatives had worried that the CSCE would confirm the status quo, since the Soviet Union and Eastern

Europe participated as equals with the countries of free Europe. But it did just the opposite. Its charter enshrined human rights as one of three "baskets" (the others were security and economics), and dissidents repeatedly used the language to embarrass their rulers, who had, after all, signed on to the document. And the many exchange programs and conferences of the CSCE provided an opportunity for Soviet and Eastern European citizens to meet one another and to engage activists from the West in a protected environment. When the Cold War ended, many former dissidents credited the work of the CSCE in hastening communism's collapse in Europe.

The Freedom Agenda, we knew, would be the work of generations. Nonetheless, in the short term it was important to have some concrete manifestation of the possibility of its success. Iraq's future was too uncertain to provide that example. Turkey was a stable country that, in its transition, was providing evidence that democracy and Islam could exist side by side.

Turkey was important for another reason: it was by geography and history an uneasy bridge between the Middle East and Europe. The great political scientist Samuel Huntington had written an article in 1993 called "The Clash of Civilizations?" and later a bestselling book. In them he argued that there was no such thing as universal values and that the Muslim world, among others, was an entity unto itself. That fact would eventually produce a clash, most likely violent, in which the Western principles of religious tolerance and secular politics would run headlong into political Islam. After 9/11 Sam Huntington sounded like a prophet.

I'd gotten to know Huntington while I was a visiting fellow at his research center at Harvard, the Center for International Affairs, in 1986. He'd been an important mentor to me, sharing my fascination with theories of civil-military relations. There were few minds as fertile as Sam Huntington's. He thought in grand philosophical and historical terms. His book was like that, sweeping in its analysis and even more so in its implications.

After 9/11 I read Sam's book again, this time with considerable alarm. But it seemed to me to understate the ability of institutions to shape events, not just to be shaped by events. History provided many examples. Under the NATO umbrella, Germany and France had become friends. At the end of the Cold War, many had feared ethnic violence in Eastern Europe, but with the exception of the former Yugoslavia it hadn't materialized. Rather, Hungary, Romania, and Bulgaria had overcome conflicts that, a century earlier, would have exploded onto the battlefield. The East and Central Europeans had made a peaceful transition to democracy. Their two lodestars had been NATO and the European Union; membership in one or the other or both had pointed the way.

Turkey was a member of NATO but wanted desperately to accede to the European Union. The strict requirements for membership, both economic and political, had in part driven Turkey's democratization to that point. But the Europeans were ambivalent in the extreme about integrating more than 70 million Muslims. The Turks felt that Europe was going through the motions of negotiating their entry but unlikely ever to finish the process. Their fears were not unfounded. One didn't have to probe too deeply to discover that many Europeans didn't really see Turkey as belonging to Europe. That attitude, I believed, would make Sam Huntington's prophecy true: a Europe that insisted on a new divide between Muslim Turkey and Christian Europe would make a huge strategic mistake.

So I went to Ankara with a deep desire to understand what was going on there and to strengthen our friendship with the Turks. My encounter with the Turkish leaders reinforced my belief that the country could be at the epicenter of a transformed broader Middle East, one that would embrace democratic values and ultimately defeat terrorism.

Foreign Minister Abdullah Gül, who would later become president, has a wrestler's build and speaks fluent English, though with a heavy accent. Although one should always be on guard against reacting to a foreign colleague based on personality, we're all human. Chemistry matters, and with Gül it was immediately good.

As we talked in the car about the future of Turkey, I was convinced that he was a democrat at heart. He acknowledged the discomfort of some Turks with the fact that the AKP was avowedly Islamic, saying that people would eventually see that it was evolving toward something like the Christian Democratic Union (CDU) of Germany. "They're not very Christian anymore," he quipped. He seemed almost hurt that people criticized his wife for wearing a head scarf, saying that it should be a matter of choice. "I have female relatives who cover and some who don't," he said. He then turned to the issue of the Kurdish minority in Turkey, expressing a desire to treat them better than previous governments had and thus awaken their Turkish identity. All in all, I saw nothing to dislike about my colleague—and that holds to this day.

Prime Minister Recep Tayyip Erdoğan was somewhat harder to read. Sitting in his rather dark office with heavy red curtains and surrounded by photographs of Mustafa Kemal Atatürk, the father of modern Turkey, I had a momentary sense that Turkey is indeed not quite European. Though the prime minister said all the right things about democracy and Islam, his defense of the AKP felt more political than had Gül's.

The conversation turned to Iraq and the tensions surrounding Turkey's refusal to allow U.S. troops to transit its territory in 2003. I assured Erdoğan that the President had put the refusal behind him and was now focused on the extremely important relationship between Turkey and Iraq. Erdoğan expressed anger at the continuing attacks by Kurdish rebels using bases in northern Iraq. I promised to take the problem back to Washington, and, indeed, it would become one of the critical issues of the relationship. Erdoğan promised that Turkey was committed to rebuilding Iraq as a stable, unified, and democratic neighbor.

Finally, we established common ground very quickly on the desirability of Turkey's joining the European Union, and I made assurances to intensify the United States' already considerable efforts to make the case to our allies. "We're not members of the EU," I said, stating the obvious reason that our urgings could accomplish only so much. "When we get in, we will propose you for membership," he said. At least he had a sense of humor.

While boarding the plane that was headed for Jerusalem, I felt very good about my visit to Turkey. I liked the Turks as people—tough, exotic, and engaging. They reminded me a bit of the Russians, struggling to fit between Europe and Asia. And I knew that I'd spend a lot of time with them, trying to avert a "clash of civilizations."

The Holy City

THERE'S SOMETHING otherworldly about the light in Jerusalem, especially with sunrise or sunset as a backdrop to the "old city." Whenever I arrived there, I found myself involuntarily praying "for the peace of Jerusalem," a line that has been put to music in one of my favorite religious songs by the English composer Sir Hubert Parry. I'd last been in Jerusalem in 2003 while trying to breathe life into the Aqaba accords. Now, as secretary of state, I felt personal responsibility for the thicket of issues preventing Middle East peace. It's been said that U.S. secretaries of state are drawn to the Israeli-Palestinian conflict like moths to a flame. The implication is that flying too close to this combustible problem is likely to result in being burned. But on that February trip there seemed to be as good a chance as there ever would be to midwife the birth of a Palestinian state.

Mahmoud Abbas had been elected president of the Palestinian Authority on January 9 and had immediately made clear that he believed only in a negotiated solution to the conflict. In his remarks, not just to outsiders but to his own people, the vocabulary of resistance and the intifada was nowhere in evidence. We welcomed Abbas's election by offering to donate $200 million annually to the Palestinians. The President also encouraged the wealthy Persian Gulf states to dramatically increase their aid. That the appeal would fall largely on deaf ears was my first lesson in how stingy the Arabs could be toward the Palestinian cause that they so zealously championed.

Major changes were under way in Israel, too. Ariel Sharon was preparing to take the plan for withdrawal from Gaza to the Knesset in a few weeks. After all the failed negotiations, Israel was about to voluntarily and unilaterally remove settlements and settlers from Gaza and the West Bank. We'd helped Sharon immensely with President Bush's letter of April 2004 in which he acknowledged the need to accommodate major Israeli population centers in the West Bank. Now the world would be able to see the benefits of the significant changes that we'd made to the old script for the peace process. There was a new, internationally respected leader in Palestine and a conservative Israeli prime minister who was ready to divide the land. The U.S. President now had the conditions that he'd insisted on in June 2002 despite the howls of traditionalists at the time.

THE APPROACH to the prime minister's office reminds one that Israel still considers itself to be in a state of war. Every leader in the world lives and works in a protected compound. But the level of security at the Israeli complex is obviously higher than most. Once inside the building, you're struck by its ramshackle appearance: it looks a little like a run-down high school building with bare tile floors and walls that could use a coat of paint. Inside the prime minister's tiny office, half the size of mine at the State Department, Sharon and I reviewed his thinking on withdrawal from Gaza. I reiterated the importance of coordinating with the Palestinians and asked that he meet with Abbas to do so soon. The prime minister assured me that he would but reminded me that he had a lot of work to do in Israel first. "Have you seen those blue flags on the cars?" he asked.

"Yes." I replied. "I thought they were for some kind of holiday."

"No," Sharon said, "they're meant to be a sign of support for the settlers." After my staff and I left the compound and turned back out onto the road, we noticed many blue flags.

That afternoon I was driven to the headquarters of the Palestinian Authority, the Muqata. The long, straight highway through the barren desert always made me wonder why anyone wanted this land. Because of my religious beliefs, I always took a moment to imagine Jesus walking the dusty, and at some points quite steep, pathways of the Holy Land. Then I would return to my discussions with our consul general for Jerusalem, who was seated with me in the back of the armored SUV. We couldn't have an ambassador because Palestine was not a state. Hopefully that was about to change.

The approach to the Muqata runs through Ramallah, a rather

prosperous-looking town with shops, government buildings, and nice apartments. Ramallah, Jericho, and a few other towns were the exceptions for the Palestinian people; most lived in squalid conditions.

When we reached the Muqata, the SUV was turned sharply to avoid the gravesite of Yasir Arafat. It was a delicate moment. I didn't want to seem disrespectful, but I felt it was important to be far enough away that I wouldn't have to get out and acknowledge his grave. My security detail had obviously practiced the maneuver, and we drove just the right route, ending up in front of the assembled Palestinian delegation. Again the shock for me involved the press coverage. Palestinian journalists were roped off to the side, but they were yelling and I could still see the camera flashes. As I got out of the car and was greeted by Abbas's trusted aid Saeb Erekat, they were screaming, "Secretary Rice!" "Over here!" "Please, just one shot!" I thought to myself that I'd have to get used to it.

My meeting with Abbas covered much of the ground I'd traversed with Sharon. Abbas doesn't speak English well, but he understands it and can sometimes respond to questions. An elegant man with a shock of white hair, he seems confident and anxious all at once. He did seem genuinely glad to see me and expressed his hope that I would "stay really involved. We need you," he said. At the conclusion of the meeting we held a press conference in a dingy room with a portrait of Arafat behind us. Well, I hadn't avoided the "leader" after all. As I had in Israel, I declared that this was a period of "great optimism." The news on the way to Paris that Abbas and Sharon had agreed to a summit in Sharm el-Sheikh in Egypt seemed to vindicate that judgment. The two would pledge to cease acts of violence against their counterparts in a mutual ceasefire. We'd come a long way since the darkest days of the intifada in the spring of 2002.

My initial voyage as secretary of state was going better than I could have dreamed. I felt energetic, and people reacted well to my message of vigorous U.S. diplomacy.

It was in that mood that I headed for Paris, knowing that the French love to chatter and gossip about U.S. diplomats. The morning began with a visit to the Hector Berlioz Conservatory, where the students performed Berlioz and Beethoven. Listening to the music was a nice way to connect with the French people and to soften the edges of America's image, which most Europeans at that time associated with terrorism and war.

But the centerpiece of the visit was to be my speech at the Sciences Po, a leading French university. My words would be closely watched for their content, signals, and messages. And also, I had to concede, my suit would be closely watched for its style. I know it's terrible to think that the U.S. secretary of state has to worry about such things. But that's a fact of life if you're female. So I chose carefully: a navy blue Valentino suit with pleats and a bow at the bottom of the skirt, pearls, and navy pumps. The French loved it.

With that hurdle out of the way, my message was well received. The speech called upon the Alliance to stop squabbling about today's headlines and join together in the great work of helping to free people from tyranny. Some journalists reacted to the message about the Freedom Agenda with characteristic comments about American naiveté. There was a deep cynicism among the Europeans about the universality of freedom. It was as if they'd forgotten their own history and the lengths to which others (especially the United States) had gone to defend their liberty. Occasionally I'd remind them that Germany had come recently to democracy. "Oh, but we had a tradition of it," a German would say. "What tradition would that be?" I would counter. "Bismarck, the Kaiser, or maybe the brief interlude that brought Adolf Hitler to power?" It was a rhetorical punch, but it backed our friends away from their patronizing view of the "readiness" of others to govern themselves.

When I met with President Chirac, I realized that I still harbored considerable animosity about Iraq. I told myself that I wouldn't be baited into an argument with the prickly and proud French president. I needn't have worried. When, to break the ice, I asked Chirac about his views on the Middle East, he surprised me with his cogent analysis, even if his dismissal of democracy in the Middle East was disquieting. Nonetheless, we engaged in a true back-and-forth at the strategic level, focusing particularly on what we could do to help Lebanon.

At the press conference with the foreign minister, Michel Barnier gently referred to me as "my dear Condi," signaling his obvious desire to publicly put difficulties behind us. The same was true in Brussels at NATO headquarters and the European Commission, and later in Luxembourg, which was holding the six-month presidency of the European Union. It was crystal clear that the Europeans were desperate to repair the relationship with us. I felt that it was time to reciprocate fully.

Our allies can be frustrating and patronizing, treating the United States as a bigger and stronger but less refined and less cultured younger brother, who needs to be reined in from time to time. I found the European Union to be a strange institution, perhaps best summed up by Henry Kissinger's question "If I want to call Europe, whom do I call?" The truth is, you had to call both Brussels *and* the European capitals.

But with all the challenges, we need Europe, with its considerable wealth and values, to achieve a freer, more prosperous world. The close ties of kinship have been diluted somewhat by the United States' multiethnic character, but the great ideals of the Enlightenment and the principles on which we were founded remain and tie us to Europe as to no other place. And the alliance of Europe and the United States has been the most stable and successful free association of states in international history. Together we stood fast until the Soviet behemoth collapsed, and Europe is now whole, free, and at peace. That bodes well for what a united alliance can do in the future.

ONLY TWO WEEKS after my trip, the President was scheduled to go to Europe for a NATO summit. Sitting in the Oval the day after I returned, we talked at length about what I'd found: an alliance hungry to heal its fissures but deeply split with us about Iran. "They're just sure that we want to take on Tehran next," I told the President.

The President asked how dramatic a shift in policy we needed to reassure the Europeans, clearly indicating that he wasn't ready for anything dramatic. There were two small decisions pending: whether to remove our objection to the Iranians' beginning the process of negotiating membership in the World Trade Organization; and whether to agree to allow them to buy some spare parts for aging American-built civilian aircraft, conceding that the latter could even be considered humanitarian since we didn't want Iranian passenger jets dropping out of the sky due to maintenance problems. By showing flexibility on those issues, we could possibly leverage agreement with our allies to unify our policies and toughen their stance toward Tehran. The timing was propitious because the Europeans had become frustrated with Iran's intransigence in the negotiations that had been going on and off since 2003. The President could use his trip to Europe to confirm my view of the situation for himself and feel out the allies on a new direction.

In fact, that plan bore fruit. When, during his trip, the President signaled this potential change, the allies jumped at the possibility of aligning themselves with us. Two months later we would announce our decision to take modest measures to support the European diplomacy. They, in turn, would agree to refer Iran's case to the UN Security Council if no progress was made. That was the first step in building an international coalition to deal with the Iranian problem.

Freedom's Forward March

EARLY IN 2005 it looked as if the forces of freedom would triumph in a matter of months, not years. Late in February, President Mubarak asked Egypt's Parliament to allow for direct, multi-candidate presidential elections for the first time in the nation's history. And even though women were excluded from the vote, Saudi Arabia conducted its first nationwide election to select half of the members of municipal councils. Taken together, those breakthroughs, combined with the parliamentary elections in Iraq, suggested that the Middle East was moving—or, perhaps more correctly, lurching—toward its first steps of political reform.

But nowhere were developments more stunning than in Lebanon. I've been asked many times through the years, about any number of events, "Were you surprised?" The truth is that you can often see the kindling collecting underneath a structure. The surprise comes from never knowing when a spark might ignite and engulf the structure in flames.

The spark in Lebanon was a car bomb that killed Rafik Hariri, the former prime minister, and twenty-two others. I was standing at my desk at State when images of the carnage started to play across the television screen. My mind flashed back to the only time that I'd met Hariri. He'd come to the White House to ask President Bush to back a donor conference to retire Lebanon's debt. We liked the affable billionaire but joked that he could have simply paid off the debt personally. Indeed, he'd used a good deal of his personal wealth to improve the infrastructure of his country. The sudden and violent death of someone I'd met always shook me for a moment. This time was no different, and it crossed my mind that Hariri was more than a former prime minister; he was about to become a martyr for a cause.

Later that afternoon, I received a recommendation that we recall our ambassador to Syria. Syria's military forces occupied Lebanon, supported Hezbollah, and had long intervened in Lebanese politics. Syria's leaders hated Hariri, who had deep ties to the West, especially to the French. Everyone believed that Syria's fingerprints were all over the assassination, so I talked with the President and we decided to withdraw our ambassador from Damascus to underscore Syria's suspected complicity and put them on the defensive.

At the time the decision seemed wise, but once she was pulled, it was hard to send her back. On several occasions over the next three years it would have been helpful to have had a senior diplomatic presence in Damascus. I never asked the President to recall another ambassador, despite provocations in Venezuela and Belarus.

Events moved quickly in Lebanon. On February 28 the pro-Syrian Prime Minister Omar Karami resigned, ensuring a struggle over the future direction of the country. Remarkably, the pieces were falling into place to begin unwinding Syrian power and influence in Lebanon. The foundation of that outcome had already been laid in 2004 by a coalition led by the unlikely partners George W. Bush and Jacques Chirac.

During a visit to France in 2003, Chirac had challenged President Bush, saying that he was always speaking of democracy in the Middle East. Why couldn't something be done about democracy in Lebanon, which had once had relatively free political institutions? "We should save them from Syria," Chirac said. President Bush was intrigued, and Chirac's advisor Maurice Gourdault-Montagne and I were told to develop a strategy. We settled on a UN Security Council Resolution demanding the withdrawal of Syrian forces and warning Damascus not to interfere in Lebanese affairs. The resolution passed the night that President Bush was nominated at the Republican National Convention in New York City. There were nine positive votes and six abstentions; no one voted against the resolution. In fact, I personally called the foreign minister of the Philippines at three in the morning to secure the final "yea."

At the time, the resolution didn't seem to mean very much. In fact, Damascus scoffed at it and basically told the United Nations to mind its own business. But now, less than a year later, in the aftermath of the Hariri assassination, international opinion shifted hard against the Syrians. Crown Prince Abdullah of Saudi Arabia, who hated Syrian President Bashar al-Assad the younger (he had hated his father too but respected him for his toughness), publicly warned Damascus to get its forces out of Lebanon.

The British had decided to hold a meeting in support of the Palestinian Authority in London on March 1 and 2. Though I'd been to Europe twice since becoming secretary, Tony Blair asked the President to send me to the meeting. The Europeans were always looking for leadership roles in expressing solidarity with the Palestinians. This was one such effort, and the President wanted to oblige his good friend.

That morning I was due to meet with French Foreign Minister Michel Barnier, and with the gathering storm in Beirut we decided to call jointly for Syria to remove its forces. The press took note of the new era of cooperation between France and the United States. It didn't take long to establish a "new era" in the age of instant communication.

Before dinner that night I returned to my suite in the Churchill Hotel and flipped on the television. Tens of thousands of Lebanese were in the streets, carrying posters bearing the likeness of the martyred Hariri. Car horns were honking as people yelled epithets at the Syrians, telling them to get out. For one moment I worried that Tony Blair's Palestinian conference was being overshadowed; then I reminded myself that no one was more devoted to freedom's forward march than the British prime minister. What a good way for his Middle East conference to end.

On March 5 Syria announced its intention to withdraw its military forces from Lebanon. Damascus would still have significant influence and covert intelligence personnel deployed in Lebanon through which to exercise it, and it would have its association with Hezbollah. But the balance of power in the Middle East was shifting: on March 14 hundreds of thousands of Lebanese rallied against the presence of Syrian forces in Beirut. A new, pro-Western movement, bearing the name of that historic date—March 14—was born under the leadership of Saad Hariri, the slain prime minister's son.

23

HIGH MOUNTAINS AND DIRT

I RETURNED TO WASHINGTON from London for only ten days before setting out for South and East Asia. Since becoming secretary I had been in Washington a total of seventeen days, long enough to testify on behalf of the State Department budget before Congress but with time to do little else. The proposed budget requested a 13 percent increase in funding for diplomatic activities. But my preparations to defend it convinced me that the department's budget process was deeply flawed. "How much do we spend on democracy promotion?" I asked. No one could answer since the line items were arrayed by accounts that related to the offices they supported, not to policy priorities. "How much do we spend on foreign assistance for Nigeria?" Well, they would have to get back to me, because the budgets of USAID and the State Department for foreign assistance were not unified. When one of the very able briefers answered one of my questions about a $1 million item by saying (gently) that I didn't need to know the details, I resolved to institute budget reform within the department. "I'm not satisfied turning to the staff for an answer if a member of Congress asks about this," I replied. "One million dollars here, one million dollars there, pretty soon it's serious money." I had been a budget officer as provost of Stanford. The budget is the statement of priorities, not just a collection of numbers. Steve Krasner, the director of policy planning, led an effort to reform the process for allocating foreign assistance, and the staff prepared for far more detailed briefings the next time around.

Then, boarding my plane for the fifth time in two months, I had to remind myself that I'd signed up for "personal diplomacy" and couldn't complain. Jim Wilkinson, my senior advisor, started tracking my miles, hoping that I'd become the most traveled secretary of state in U.S. history. It was a fun parlor game but a title I wasn't sure I wanted to have.

My visit to India and Pakistan was principally to establish personal contact with the key players there: Pervez Musharraf and his generals, the Indian leadership and its opposition. But I also met Sonia Gandhi, the leader of the Indian National Congress Party, for the second time. The Italian-born widow of the slain son of Indira Gandhi had come to the White House when I was national security advisor. At the time, the Indian National Congress Party was not in office and there was some question from regional experts about the appropriateness of meeting with her. We did meet, and she returned the favor on this trip. People remember whether you're willing to see them when they're out of power.

Now the challenge would be to push forward on the agenda for expanded U.S.-Indian relations that President Bush had begun despite the ascendance of the left-leaning coalition in New Delhi. Sonia Gandhi was a real political power in the country as the leader of Prime Minister Manmohan Singh's party. Her opinion mattered, and it was unlikely that the prime minister would take controversial steps without her approval. Our cordial conversation in the sunlit living room of her modest home convinced me that she would be willing to provide the space that Prime Minister Singh and his government needed to stay the course with us.

After an abbreviated tour of Mughal emperor Humayun's tomb outside New Delhi, I met with Singh and the opposition leader, L. K. Advani, then held a brief press conference with my counterpart and headed to Islamabad. That was the nature of those whirlwind trips. I wanted to pay appropriate respect to the culture of the countries I visited, maybe even take in historical sites that I'd always wanted to see, but there was so much to do that any attempt to enjoy the flavor of a place felt very rushed. Over my years as secretary the cultural events got shorter and shorter, until we eventually abandoned them altogether. I've seen a lot of the world from the vantage point of government buildings and meeting rooms, yet missed much of the color and wonder of the ancient lands I've visited. That was my loss, but there was little that I could do about it.

The whole picture of the post-9/11 world came into sharp relief as I looked out of the window of the C-17 military transport descending into Kabul. Flying over the Hindu Kush and then the border between

Pakistan and Afghanistan, it was easy to see why the territory had become the epicenter of Islamic terrorism and extremism: tall mountains with narrow passages and caves were everywhere. No wonder terrorists chose to hide there.

I landed in Kabul and met with our troops and diplomats, something I always loved to do. The secretary of state always addresses the embassy personnel in what is called a "meet and greet." It's a chance to thank the men and women of the Foreign Service for the hard work that they do abroad. The practice of expressing appreciation is particularly important with respect to the locally engaged staff, the citizens of countries around the world who do the bulk of the work in the embassies. In fact, of the 57,000 embassy personnel worldwide, more than 35,000 are foreigners, many of whom have worked a lifetime for the State Department. Kabul had one particularly extraordinary employee, a man who'd personally kept the key to the U.S. Embassy during the long civil war and reign of the Taliban. When Kabul was liberated, he proudly handed it to U.S. forces so that they could reopen the dilapidated building. I was delighted to thank him personally for his service.

In war zones such as Kabul and Baghdad, I started the practice of greeting both the civilians and our military personnel. Places such as Afghanistan and Iraq were truly a combined effort; there was no tidy division between the tasks of the warriors and those of the diplomats.

After the meet and greet we drove into downtown Kabul. I don't know what I expected. I did know that Afghanistan was the fifth poorest country in the world and that it had been wracked by decades of civil war. As we drove along the one existing main street, I could see Afghan merchants sitting in the mud behind little stands selling food or clothes or occasionally homemade tchotchkes. They were clearly industrious and determined but desperately poor. I turned to Phil Zelikow. "The Afghan people have been given nothing but high mountains and dirt," I said. That map on the table at Camp David after September 11 hadn't done justice to the difficulty of our task.

And if our job was hard, Hamid Karzai's was herculean. I'd met the Afghan leader several times in Washington, but seeing him in his own environment was instructive. This man, who'd put his life on the line at the time of Operation Enduring Freedom, was struggling to govern

a country that had throughout its history largely lacked central authority. Karzai appeared genuinely proud of his achievements to that point.
The first freely elected president in Afghanistan's history, he talked of
his people's bravery and determination as we walked through the recently restored gardens of the Presidential Palace. "You should see them
building little mud houses out of bricks that they find along the road,"
he said. Yet the whole scene had an air of unreality about it. Karzai
couldn't go far from Kabul because so much of the country was still
controlled by warlords, who'd been in loose alliance with him during
the war but were now reasserting their authority. The Afghan national
army barely existed, and the police were even more a force in name
only. Prolific poppy production significantly hurt the Afghan economy
by fostering corruption. I was incredulous as Karzai talked glowingly
about Afghanistan's excellent dates and pomegranates, as if a limited
agricultural sector might form the basis of growth going forward. He
noted too that his experts had found old maps that showed oil and gas
deposits in the north. Now, with the liberation from the Taliban, they
were free to explore them. I'd never been to a place where there was a
greater distance between the aspirations of a leader and his people and
the reality of their circumstances.

Yet the Afghans *had* made progress. I visited a women's democracy
center and thought how impossible that would have seemed a few short
years before. There I met a woman police recruit, dressed proudly in a
new uniform and wearing no head cover at all—this in a country that
under the Taliban had punished women for showing even a little bit of
ankle. I left Kabul feeling that the Afghans could succeed, but it was
going to be a long struggle.

Landing in Islamabad again, I was reminded that Afghanistan's fate
was not its own to determine. Pakistan held more than a few keys to its
neighbor's stability. That was not a good thing.

My stop in Islamabad lasted about twenty-four hours. My security
detail was always concerned about Pakistan and never wanted to chance
more than one night there. The agenda with the Pakistanis was familiar
to me from my time at the White House: fight terrorism and extremism; reform the army and the security services; turn your attention
from India to al Qaeda, the Taliban, and Afghanistan. The interaction

was familiar, too, with Musharraf, sitting in his living room at Army House in Rawalpindi, emphasizing all that he was doing to modernize his country and fight extremism. I found myself sympathetic to him, although I didn't care much for people who lead military coups. But Pakistan was such a mess, and I couldn't escape the fact that the United States was partially responsible for its radicalization. The point was underscored at the dinner given that night by my counterpart, Foreign Minister Khurshid Kasuri, who could appear somewhat puffed up. But as the evening went on, a different side of him started to emerge. The "off-script" conversation that night was among the Pakistanis, who talked about what their country had been like in the decades before the war in Afghanistan. They admitted that General Zia ul-Haq had sought legitimacy by supporting Muslim extremists in the early 1980s. That had been a consequential policy choice.

Nonetheless, they rightly pointed to the United States' support for the mujahideen's struggle against the Soviet Union as playing a large role in Pakistan becoming a transit point for jihadists. After the war, some had stayed in Afghanistan, forming the core of the ethnically Pashtun Taliban. Others, including a fair number of Saudis and Egyptians, had returned to Pakistan and now gathered in urban mosques and madrassas and in the tribal areas bordering Afghanistan, recruiting and training a new generation of radicals. Pakistanis knew that they were responsible for the deeply rooted extremism in their country, but the United States had contributed to it. And then, with the defeat of the Soviet Union, we'd lost interest in—and ultimately contact with—Islamabad, until al Qaeda's rise had shoved us back together.

With all that would occur later, it's hard to remember that in 2005 we thought that the Afghan project was in relatively good shape. We did not yet know that Musharraf was contemplating a new peace accord with tribal leaders in North Waziristan, cutting a deal to live and let live in exchange for stopping the passage of militants across the Afghan border. That policy would ultimately lead to a new safe haven for the Taliban and a downward spiral in Afghanistan, one that we were unable to halt before the end of our term.

Indeed, the news of the trip related instead to an easing of the tensions that had plagued South Asia. Pakistan and India informed us that they'd begun a quiet back-channel dialogue on the most vexing issue: Kashmir. My long conversation with both leaders convinced me that they were serious and that they might succeed. But the next day, as I began my visit to East Asia with a stop in Tokyo, we got a reminder of Pakistan's troubles. Twenty-five people were killed when a bomb ripped through a crowd gathered at a shrine in Baluchistan. The glow from positive developments in Pakistan was always short-lived.

A New Direction in Asia

IN THE SAME WAY that I'd begun my trip to Europe with a visit to "one of our closest friends," I landed first in Japan to underscore the centrality of our longest-standing alliance in Northeast Asia. Usually, the arrival ceremony for the secretary of state was a boring affair. The secretary descended the stairs to the waiting handshake of the chief of protocol, who looked the same in every country, no matter how exotic. Then there were a few photographs with the assembled government officials before boarding the motorcade.

My senior staff suggested that we make my arrivals different by establishing the practice of "greeters," who would represent the culture of the country. Sometimes the participants were predictable, such as the little girls with bread and salt in Ukraine or the local pop stars who showed up from time to time.

But once in a while they were unique. That was certainly the case in Japan. I once mentioned that I liked sumo wrestling, an interest I'd developed while teaching at the National Defense Academy of Japan when I was a professor at Stanford. So, Jim reasoned, it made sense for me to be greeted by one of these revered athletes. At the bottom of the stairs of the plane, I found myself suddenly swept up in the embrace of Konishiki Yasokichi—professionally known as "the Dump Truck"— who lifted me off my feet and into his gigantic arms. I was startled but managed to keep my composure and laughed at the front-page newspaper coverage the next day. In any case, it was a far better greeting than one a few months later in Kyrgyzstan, where the local hero was a falconer. There I looked at the bird of prey, which was eyeing me suspiciously from his master's shoulder, and decided that there would be no more greetings involving animals. I made quick work of the ceremony and fled into the safety of my car.

The goal of the trip to Japan was to affirm our relationship with Japan but also to put it in the context of a regional strategy for Asia. In my speech at Sophia University, I intended to make the case for a safer Asia built around the efforts of three great democracies: the United States, Japan, and South Korea. The difficulty of doing so had been underscored a week before, when South Korea had scrambled military jets in response to a Japanese plane that had flown over the disputed Liancourt Rocks (called Dokdo by the South Koreans and Takeshima by the Japanese). Yet over the years we'd make progress toward improved bilateral relations between our two allies—albeit in fits and starts.

Ironically, one source of conflict between them had the potential to induce cooperation—with China included in the equation. The North Korean nuclear program had engendered tension among the regional states, each of which, of course, was looking toward its own interests.

Japan was concerned principally about resolving the abduction cases from the 1970s and 1980s. For Tokyo, positive movement toward Pyongyang was sometimes seen as evidence of insufficient concern about that humanitarian tragedy. Seoul wanted North Korea's nuclear program halted but feared that any confrontational step might worsen tensions on the peninsula. Beijing worried that a nuclear North Korea would encourage Japan—or possibly South Korea—to go nuclear but worried more about the stability of the North Korean regime, fearing a crack-up that could produce floods of refugees into China. In other words, everyone wanted a denuclearized North Korea, but other priorities prevented concerted action to attain the goal.

The Six-Party Talks, which also included Russia, had thus made almost no progress since their establishment in 2003. I believed that there was promise in them, particularly if we could develop a longer-term framework that pointed the way toward denuclearization *and* a resolution of the underlying tensions in the region. We started at State to develop an approach that would do precisely that. It would be hard to get agreement among the six parties. But the first task was to get agreement in Washington, where the divided opinion on North Korea had been pronounced from the very beginning of the administration.

Before departing for Asia, I'd engaged the President and Steve Hadley in a "heart-to-heart" about the North Korean problem. The President needed to be comfortable with the idea that we might have to talk to the North Koreans to achieve what we wanted. It was surely a long shot, but maybe Kim Jong-il could be induced, step by step, to give up his nuclear ambitions in exchange for benefits, which would also be doled out step by step. For instance, Kim's agreeing to let inspectors return might bring renewed fuel deliveries. If that succeeded, we might start down a political track: action for action. We wouldn't give up very much until the North Koreans acted. My diplomats would need room to maneuver in negotiations, and Washington's micromanagement, so evident in the first term, needed to end. The President could trust me to keep my own negotiators in line.

To make the strategy work, we'd have to do three things. First, we'd have to unite the other five powers so that the North couldn't get benefits from any if it didn't live up to its obligations. North Korea was one of the most sanctioned countries in the world, but we needed help enforcing the constraints. We couldn't have China, South Korea, Japan, and Russia each going its own way. That was an easy sell with the President.

The second precondition for a workable strategy, it seemed to me, was making it clear to all the players that a change in regime policy, rather than the regime itself, would be sufficient to begin negotiations—for the time being. The North Korean leader was loathsome; could the President stomach an approach that might leave Kim in power if only the dictator changed direction?

And third, we needed to pursue the development of defensive measures, specifically: blocking the sale of North Korean nuclear material, denying overflight rights for suspicious cargo, and bolstering the missile defense systems of our allies in East Asia. The diplomatic and defensive tracks worked together, as we reinvigorated the Six-Party Talks.

The President thought long and hard about it, and then he delivered one of his strategic insights that always surprised me—even after years of experiencing it. "Well, maybe we'd have to put up with him for a while," he said. "But that place can't stand true sunshine." He was referencing the discredited policy of cordial relations that South Korean President Kim Dae-jung had adopted toward the North. The President suggested that Kim Jong-il might try to reform, but he would do the same thing that most dictators do in such circumstances—bring about his own demise. Then he said something quite startling: "Maybe we could call his bluff and offer him a peace treaty if he gives up his weapons and opens up to the world."

That was a little further than I was willing to go, but I asked my counselor, Philip Zelikow, and Bob Zoellick to start thinking about the idea. Was the answer to the North Korean nuclear program a diplomatic big bang to end the conflict? It was a question worth asking. We saw too that if progress were to occur, the Six-Party Talks might evolve into something even more significant: the basis of a security mechanism for Northeast Asia.

I called Henry Kissinger and asked to have dinner with him. We shared a background as academics, and he'd also been national security advisor and secretary of state. He'd opened China and was one of the greatest strategic thinkers ever to occupy the office. Like my friend George Shultz, Henry was always there to help me rise above the day's preoccupations and explore the strategic changes that were unfolding. He immediately saw the big picture and the possibility for a grand design in Northeast Asia that might ultimately end the conflict and lead to the unification of the Koreas. All that, of course, was far into the future.

In the meantime, I'd go to Seoul and Beijing armed with the knowledge that the President was willing to think big. That allowed me room to suggest a restart to the Six-Party Talks in which the United States would be prepared to be flexible.

The South Koreans were, of course, thrilled to hear that we wanted to restart the talks. But our condition was absolute unity in our approach to Pyongyang. When the North got nasty (which it would undoubtedly do), or if it failed to live up to its obligations, Seoul would have to take a tough line. My interlocutors nodded agreement, but it wouldn't be that easy.

My meetings in Beijing were more difficult. Earlier in March, the

Chinese had publicly questioned the reliability of our intelligence on the North Korean program and suggested that the United States take up the problem bilaterally with Pyongyang. My goal was to let the Chinese know that such an approach was a nonstarter; our participation in solving the problem required theirs too.

As my motorcade sped down the wide boulevard toward the Great Hall of the People, I thought about how much the country had changed since my first visit there in 1988. At that time, on any given day one might have seen on the streets of Beijing a few horse carts, a few cars, and a lot of bicycles. Now cars were everywhere, and my agenda with the Chinese leadership would focus as much on issues associated with Beijing's economic rise as the security problems before us.

We arrived at the front door of the massive Stalinist structure. Ascending the steps, I was startled by the customary salute in which the Chinese guards yell and snap to attention. Even though I visited the Great Hall several times after that, I never quite got used to the guards' bloodcurdling yell, which always made me jump involuntarily.

I was then ushered into an enormous room where at least twenty members of the Chinese delegation stood in front of their seats, awaiting Hu Jintao's arrival. Finally the Chinese president appeared, and we posed for photographs. In China the press people didn't yell out questions; they do that only in democracies. President Hu and I sat down and literally had to use microphones to carry on our stilted dialogue across the cavernous hall.

Hu delivered his welcoming remarks and then launched, as the Chinese always did, into a monologue about Taiwan. I'd already heard the script from the foreign minister, Premier Wen Jiabao, and State Councilor Tang Jiaxuan, who'd talked for forty-five minutes of our one-hour meeting.

More than twenty years after Mao Zedong's Communist regime consolidated its power, Washington finally recognized the People's Republic of China and established diplomatic relations with it. But the "one-China policy" carried a contradiction within it since the United States continued to arm and support Taiwan, which by 2005 was a vibrant democracy. That was a source of constant tension with Beijing, which saw the United States' position as interference in China's domestic affairs. Therefore every meeting with the Chinese started with a lecture about the "one-China policy"; the "three joint communiqués" (signed individually in the 1970s and 1980s); and the evils of arms sales to Taiwan. At that particular time, the harangue also included attacks on the hated president of Taiwan, Chen Shui-bian, who was seen as a particularly aggressive secessionist.

I listened patiently and then returned the favor with my own ritualistic statement of U.S. policy. Yes, we had a one-China policy based on the three communiqués. But we also had the Taiwan Relations Act, which required the United States to help Taiwan defend itself, and we would tolerate no unilateral changes to the status quo. The Chinese had just passed an "anti-secessionist" law, and we were worried that it would bait Chen into his own provocation. (The Taiwanese president didn't act up immediately, but in time he would take dangerous steps that challenged Beijing, causing us to break with him—a step that greatly pleased China.)

After the "exchange of views" on Taiwan, I turned to the problem of intellectual property and China's miserable record of protection. Hu answered woodenly, explaining all that Beijing was doing to stop piracy. We then turned to a cursory review of the situation in North Korea. I couldn't say anything remotely consequential in that setting, and neither could he.

My mind wandered as Hu delivered his talking points. These set-piece "discussions" with the Chinese leadership in a space that felt the length of a football field wouldn't work. I asked our ambassador, Sandy Randt, to see if he could condition the Chinese to smaller meetings with more give-and-take. On average, 70 percent of U.S. ambassadors are career diplomats, but the President reserves the right to appoint certain ambassadors from outside the ranks of the Foreign Service. Sandy, who'd been the President's fraternity brother in college, was one of those noncareer political ambassadors who defied the stereotype: he spoke fluent Mandarin, having lived eighteen years in Hong Kong, and, according to none other than Hu Jintao, knew "more Chinese people than he did." The estimable Ambassador Randt undertook to talk to the

Chinese, and fortunately, on my next visit, Hu's staff suggested a small meeting after the formal one. Well, small by Chinese standards: there were six on each side.

I finished my trip in Beijing thinking that I'd failed to deliver the message that I'd intended. But the Chinese, it turned out, had heard me loud and clear. They let Sandy know that they were anxious to resume the Six-Party Talks and would "explore" the North's willingness to do so as well.

TWENTY-FOUR HOURS later, I headed for the President's ranch and a meeting of the grandly titled but modestly ambitious Security and Prosperity Partnership of North America. The Mexicans and Canadians dutifully showed up with huge delegations, including commerce and homeland security ministers. Don't get me wrong: an effort to "implement improvements in aviation and maritime security" and "improve productivity through regulatory cooperation . . . while maintaining high standards for health and safety" was certainly worthwhile. It just seemed as if there wasn't really an agenda for the secretary of state to pursue. It was another one of those "home owner's meetings."

Yet the trip to Crawford was an opportunity to spend time with the President in a relaxed setting and to catch my breath. I'd been on the road six of the eight weeks that I'd been secretary of state. When we returned to Washington, I intended to stay home for a while to complete congressional hearings on the budget; work on plans to coordinate the Israeli withdrawal from Gaza; and spend some time helping the Iraqis form a government. But then the news came that Pope John Paul II had died. I'd be back on a plane the next week, accompanying President and Mrs. Bush, President Clinton, and President George H. W. Bush to the Vatican for the funeral.

We arrived in Rome two nights before the funeral and were immediately escorted to St. Peter's Basilica to view the late Holy Father in repose. The car ride was a bit uncomfortable because, for security reasons, all five of us had to ride in the presidential limousine, which comfortably seats four. On long rides I was wedged for the entire trip between President Clinton, who talks a lot, and President George H. W. Bush, who talks very little.

In the darkened space of the basilica, I tried to concentrate on my prayers rather than the eeriness of the scene as we knelt a few yards from where the Holy Father lay. Frankly, it was spooky, and I didn't sleep very well that night with the images of the funeral bier fresh in my mind.

The events on the morning of the funeral were, however, glorious. I was seated five rows from the front with the former presidents and several foreign ministers. The President and First Lady were in the second row, the first having been reserved for royalty, including the king of Lesotho in a huge leopard hat.

As the three-hour High Mass drew to a close, I got up to move toward the front. The Vatican had told us to leave first, given the length of our motorcade. I was assigned the difficult task of getting the two ex-presidents out of the crowd and staged for departure. Just as I reached Laura and the President, the pallbearers came down to carry the pope's coffin back into the basilica. The bells of St. Peter's began to peal, the choir blending with them in an ethereal and mournful anthem, and in the square were hundreds of thousands of people, many of them waving the flags of Poland and Solidarity. It was quite a send-off for this man, who had symbolized the moral force that had brought communism to its knees.

Then the pallbearers lifted the coffin and turned it toward the crowd. The day had been cold and windy and gray. At that very moment, the sun burst through the clouds as if to acknowledge John Paul's ascendance to his father's throne. "Did you see that?" Laura Bush asked me. I nodded but I was struck dumb and couldn't speak. As we reentered the basilica and passed the *Pietà,* I thanked God for the gift of eternal life.

Flying back on Air Force One, we talked about that moment and what it had meant. I asked people who'd watched on television if the press had mentioned it and learned that no one had. Months later in Argentina, the foreign minister would recall the same sequence of events. Perhaps only believers saw this powerful affirmation of the truth of the resurrection. I was grateful to have been there.

A week later the College of Cardinals would select Joseph Cardinal Ratzinger as Pope Benedict XVI. In 2004 I'd accompanied President Bush to the sixtieth-anniversary commemoration of the Normandy landing in France, and my luncheon partner had been none other than Cardinal Ratzinger. The conversation had been mostly about our shared love of Mozart. He, too, played the piano. We exchanged a few words about the future of religion but nothing profound enough to recall. Oh, how I wished I'd listened more closely.

24

THE COLOR REVOLUTIONS MULTIPLY

THE EVENTS THAT had been unfolding in the Middle East, most dramatically in Lebanon, mirrored the revolutionary events that had already occurred on Russia's periphery. Eduard Shevardnadze, the Georgian president, was revered in the West for his seminal role in the peaceful collapse of the Soviet Union. I'd gotten to know him during my many trips to Moscow accompanying Jim Baker at the end of the Cold War, the return trips to Washington, and in the relaxed environment of the secretary's mountain home in Jackson Hole, Wyoming.

A dignified man with a shock of white hair, Shevardnadze had a delightful sense of humor and was always kind to me, expressing some wonderment at my fascination with Russia. As foreign minister, he'd helped Mikhail Gorbachev reorient Soviet foreign policy toward cooperation with the West. And in the Soviet Union's last days, when it appeared that hard-liners were trying to turn the clock back, Shevardnadze had resigned while warning ominously of growing reactionary resistance to Gorbachev and his reforms. When Gorbachev fell from power and the Soviet Union collapsed, Shevardnadze returned to his home in the now-independent Georgia and became its first president.

But more than a decade later, Shevardnadze was an aging and somewhat pathetic figure surrounded by corrupt family members and associates who were dragging Georgia into a downward spiral of stagnation and decline. The situation had gotten so dire that President George W. Bush asked Jim Baker to visit his old friend and suggest that it was time to go. Shevardnadze didn't heed that advice and was unceremoniously removed from power when hundreds of thousands of frustrated Georgians took to the streets to demand an end to authoritarianism and corruption. This so-called Rose Revolution in 2003 was the first in a series of revolts to sweep through former Soviet states that came to be known as the color revolutions.

At first the Rose Revolution didn't particularly trouble the Russians, who harbored resentment toward Shevardnadze for his role in the collapse of the Soviet Union. But when the Georgians elected as their president Mikheil Saakashvili, an American-educated firebrand who could not hide his disdain for Moscow, the relationship between Russia and Georgia moved from latent tension to open hostility.

Territorial issues had long been a problem between the two countries. Saakashvili made it clear that he would defend the integrity of Georgia against the Moscow-supported secessionists in the breakaway regions of South Ossetia and Abkhazia. The Russians, on the other hand, believed the Georgians were tolerating—if not facilitating—Chechen terrorism in the Pankisi Gorge, high in the mountains between the two countries.

The latter claim led us to undertake a major effort in the first term to train some of the Georgian military forces in counterterrorism, thereby reassuring the Russians that their neighbors were an asset, not a liability, in the war on terrorism. Chechen terrorism was a constant source of conflict with Sergei Ivanov, Russia's defense minister and my principal interlocutor when I was national security advisor. He would call frequently to denigrate the Georgian effort. In one conversation, he screamed, "If the Georgians don't clean this up, the Russian army will!" I sometimes found it useful to bluntly rebuff these bluffs. "Sergei, no Russian general is leading his troops into the Pankisi Gorge," I said. "And both you and I know it, so stop threatening to do what you aren't going to do." The Russians wanted no part in the rats' nest of Chechen and al Qaeda fighters in that godforsaken place. Eventually Ivanov and even Putin had to admit that the Georgians were having some success against the terrorists.

But Moscow's animosity toward Saakashvili was about something more deeply rooted than mere security or political concerns. Many Russians have an irrational hatred for the Georgians as a people. The average man on the street will tell you without too much prompting that the dark-skinned inhabitants of the Caucasus are thieves and thugs. Once when staying in a somewhat seedy Moscow hotel, the Ukraina,

I returned from dinner to be told by an agitated "hall lady" (in the old Soviet Union these senior citizens stayed up all night to "watch" the comings and goings of hotel guests) that some Georgian men had been asking after me. Her unvarnished anti-Georgian screed was delivered without her apparently noticing that I, too, was dark-skinned.

Moreover, at a political level, the Georgians were remembered as the rough and dangerous "muscle" of the Bolshevik Revolution. Josef Stalin was, of course, Georgian. So too was Lavrenti Beria, the hated chief of the intelligence services, who was executed in 1953 for trying to overthrow fellow members of the Politburo after Stalin's death. And then there was Sergo Ordzhonikidze, a man so vile that a purge was named for him.

Notwithstanding all this, a Western-oriented revolution in Georgia in the short term was tolerable, if troubling. Upheaval in Ukraine was quite another matter.

The shock waves that Ukraine's Orange Revolution produced in Moscow can be understood only in the context of how disoriented most Russians felt after Ukraine declared its independence from the Soviet Union in August 1991. It has been said that, for Russia, losing Ukraine was like the United States losing Texas or California. But that doesn't begin to capture it; it would be like losing the original thirteen colonies. Slavdom, including the Cyrillic alphabet, had roots in Kiev and had spread to Russia. Ukraine had belonged to Poland during the near collapse of the Russian Empire in the seventeenth century and Germany had recognized Ukraine's short-lived independence at the end of World War I. Some Nazi leaders had also dangled independence in exchange for collaboration in World War II. For the Russians, that proved simply that only in weakness had Moscow been unable to defend the unity of the Slavic people—Ukrainians and Russians.

In 1954 Nikita Khrushchev gave the Crimea, along the Black Sea, to the Ukrainian people to celebrate hundreds of years of Russian-Ukrainian friendship. It didn't matter at the time. The collapse of the Soviet Union, however, revealed that move to be a strategic error; Russia suddenly found itself with important assets and a large part of its population trapped in the newly independent Ukraine. The Russian navy's most important base, at Sevastopol, now resided in a different country, along with almost 700,000 ethnic Russians, roughly 70 percent of the city's population. Both from the perspective of Russia's strategic interests and its national identity, the Orange Revolution was a tremendous blow to Moscow.

During the Soviet period and after it, I'd visited Russia and Ukraine several times. It was quite apparent that the Ukrainians—particularly in the western part of the country—did not feel warm fraternal ties with Russia. It was also apparent that the Russians underestimated how much antipathy the Ukrainians held for them. The Ukrainians were still ethnically and linguistically distinctive people despite generations of intermarriage. With their misplaced expressions of the unbreakable bonds of brotherhood between the two peoples, Russians only further alienated Ukrainians. So although it was no surprise to me that the leaders of the Orange Revolution could barely disguise their anti-Russian sentiments, Moscow seemed to have been caught off guard.

It didn't take long for Putin to recover his footing after the shock of the events in Kiev. I came face-to-face with that reality when I visited the Russian president at his dacha outside Moscow in May 2004. It was several months before the presidential elections in Ukraine. Putin took me on a tour of his newly refurbished office. Within a few minutes Viktor Yanukovych emerged from a side room. "Oh, please meet Viktor," Putin said. "He is a candidate for president of Ukraine." I greeted the pro-Russian politician and took the message that Putin had intended: the United States should know that Moscow had a horse in the race to defend its interests.

But the election produced a result that the Kremlin didn't welcome. Viktor Yushchenko and Yulia Tymoshenko's blocs won the election, and the two pro-Western politicians formed the government as their orange-clad supporters cheered in the streets. For the next five years they would struggle to define a path and identity for Ukraine.

As in any country emerging from tyranny, elections were but a first step toward democracy. Institutions were weak, corruption was rampant, and there was thus a tendency for personalities—and personal animosities—to overwhelm politics. Unfortunately, as time passed, the Ukrainian leaders would increasingly turn on each other and the struggle would become more about them than about the future of their country.

It was against that backdrop that I took my first trip to Russia as secretary of state. A month before, Kyrgyzstan had joined the growing list of color revolutions, prompting President Askar Akayev to flee his people's wrath for the safety of Moscow. Needless to say, upon my arrival I found a Russian president who appeared outwardly cool but quite bothered by the direction of events on his country's periphery.

I established a pattern that I would follow in my visits to Moscow. My counterpart, Sergei Lavrov, was, of course, my host. Lavrov had been the Russian ambassador to the United Nations for almost ten years. He spoke nuanced English and was widely regarded as a tough-minded but capable diplomat. He loved fine wine, good food, and hunting in the wilds of Siberia. Well, he was Russian, after all.

We developed a good relationship, slightly formal and sometimes contentious. He was, like me, a natural debater who didn't mind verbal combat. That sometimes unnerved our European friends, but we were usually able to work our way through and make progress on an issue—at least until the Georgian war, when our relationship broke almost irreparably.

Early on, though, I liked working with Lavrov, principally because he was respected enough in Moscow to get things done. Over the years, the colleagues I valued most were those who could move the policies of their governments. It was fine to have perfectly nice and friendly relations, but too often I was forced to work alongside a number of counterparts who were good dinner companions yet feckless politicians.

Before that April 2005 visit to Moscow, Lavrov and I had already met in Turkey shortly after I became secretary of state. There, for almost an hour, he delivered a list of Russian complaints about U.S. policy. I listened patiently but told Bill Burns, then our ambassador to Russia, to get the message to him that our interactions would have to improve or our meetings wouldn't be worth my time. I expected to engage in an exchange of ideas, not listen to a monologue. Moreover, foreign ministers should concentrate on big issues, not every niggling problem between us. When Lavrov and I met in Moscow, the conversation was somewhat better, and over time we got to a place where we could really engage each other rather than just go through our respective lists.

After seeing Lavrov, I would usually meet with President Putin, sometimes in his ornate Kremlin office and sometimes at his government dacha. Russians love their dachas, or summer houses, which can range from small, unheated shacks to grand mansions. Needless to say, Putin's was in the latter category, located about fifteen miles outside Moscow. Along the road leading out of the city's center, one could view the ostentatious character of the new Russia: the route was a kind of Russian Rodeo Drive, occupied by the likes of Dolce & Gabbana and Rolls-Royce. Clearly the days of Soviet autarky were over.

Putin and I rarely met more than two-on-two, and increasingly over the years we would meet one-on-one. We covered a few issues, but as time went on, he'd use the conversation to expound not just on his many "disappointments" with U.S. policy but on his own notion of democracy. *"Tui znaesh nac"* (you know us), he would say, referencing my academic background. The phrase usually introduced a long disquisition on how Russia would come to democracy: through a strong hand (his) and the gradual development of "factions" within his party, which could then represent varying points of view. He thought of it like the factionalized Liberal Democratic Party in Japan, which had been, aside for a brief period in the early 1990s, the ruling party in Japan since 1955 and had varying voices within it. The Russians were a fractious bunch whose many revolutions always turned out badly, he would note. They had to be led.

Though this was radical for a former Marxist, it was quite distant from our modern notions of democratic development. At our meeting that April, Putin did not yet say explicitly that the color revolutions were a U.S. tool to throw Russia off this planned course, but the implication lurked just beneath the surface. Putin told me that he opposed any "revolution from the streets." Saying that it was silly to talk about re-creating the USSR, he nonetheless reminded me that the newly independent states had taken their institutions and wealth from the Soviet Union. It was therefore not surprising that Moscow would have a "continuing interest" in them.

On this particular occasion, the upcoming sixtieth anniversary of the end of the Great Patriotic War, as the Russians called World War II, gave Putin significant cause for concern about our approach to the neighboring states. President Bush had agreed to come to the commemoration of this seminal event in Russian history, but he would visit the Baltic states first. The President had asked me to tell Putin that he would do nothing to embarrass Russia but that the new members of NATO would expect him to address their long, troubled history with Moscow. Putin used the meeting with me to excoriate the Balts for trying to relitigate the past. "They want me to apologize for the Molotov-Ribbentrop Pact," he said. "Maybe they can't read because we already did that in 1989." In fact, there had been a halfhearted acknowledgment by Mikhail Gorbachev of the sinister deal between Adolf Hitler and Josef Stalin. It could hardly have been called an apology.

I decided to let the point go, recognizing how bitter the wounds of World War II remained in Russia; the Soviet Union had lost an estimated 26 million people to German aggression. The history was too complicated to debate at that moment. One year before, at the French observance of the D-Day Normandy landing, we'd all witnessed how sensitive such historical narratives can be. I was seated behind German Chancellor Gerhard Schroeder—who'd been invited, ostensibly, to underscore the reconciliation of France and Germany—as he glared, stone-faced, at a scathing (but accurate) video portrayal of his country's past crimes against humanity. I felt very bad for him, remembering our first encounter, when he had told a touching story of finding a photograph of his father, who had been killed on the eastern front when Schroeder was a baby. "It was my face," he had said in broken English. It was a good reminder that the lives of many ordinary citizens on both sides of the conflict had been changed by that war. It was a good reminder that that was true in any war.

I returned to my message to Putin that the President would make a statement that tried to heal old wounds, not reopen them. Seemingly satisfied, Putin went on to say that he was delighted that the secretary of state was a Russia specialist. "That will mean that the relationship will be central to you," he said. I don't know if he really thought that or if it was meant to be flattery. I made a mental note not to underestimate the Russians—both the help they could provide and the damage they could do.

Putin went on to other issues on the agenda, including a plea to be included in the G7 finance ministers group. Moscow cared about status and bristled at having been excluded from the economic group while being allowed to participate in the political discussions of the G8. "I know our economy is ranked sixteenth," he acknowledged, but he maintained that it was still an important economy. The statement was on the face of it contradictory, and I moved on to Russian membership in the WTO.

That night, I had dinner with Sergei Ivanov, who at the time of this first visit was the minister of defense. I have earlier described my relationship with Ivanov. Owing to our long association, I was able to talk with him candidly. He was no Jeffersonian democrat, but he was—and still is—a modernizer. That was always the true divide in Russia: Slavophiles versus modernizers, not democrats versus authoritarians. He talked about reforming the backward Russian armed forces from a brutal conscript military to a modern one, and he wanted Russia to become technologically more sophisticated and make a contribution to the global economy. Ivanov, it turned out, was one of the two men whom Vladmir Putin pitted against each other two years later to decide who would succeed him as president. Ivanov would lose.

Though that election was in the future, its outcome was clear to me when I returned to Moscow with President Bush the next month for the Great Patriotic War celebration. The streets were decked out with banners commemorating the victory of Soviet forces in World War II. There on light posts in front of stylish European stores were signs saying *"Dyen pobedi"* (day of victory) and *"Slava narodoo"* (glory to the people). I flashed back to my days as a graduate student in the Soviet Union; the slogans were eerily familiar. Then I looked closely at one of the banners. "Brought to you by Nokia," it said. Things had indeed changed.

But it was at the parade on Red Square that I made my very early prediction about Ivanov's future. As minister of defense, Sergei stood in the back of a black ZiL limousine and reviewed the thousands of Russian military personnel arrayed along the cobblestones in front of

Lenin's tomb. Saluting the assembled armies of the Russian Federation, he yelled congratulations to each contingent. He looked, well, presidential. *Putin will never let him become president of Russia,* I thought. *He will not want a strong successor and rival in the Kremlin when he finally moves on.*

Thanks to President Bush's having kept his promise in the Baltics, the atmosphere of the Moscow visit was good. I hadn't been so sure that the Russians would react well to the President's speech in Latvia just prior to our arrival in Moscow. Baltic leaders, including Latvian Prime Minister Aigars Kalvītis, Estonian President Arnold Rüütel, and Lithuanian President Valdas Adamkus, had gathered to hear the U.S. President tell them that their accession to NATO in 2004 meant that they could never be threatened with impunity again. Old men and women cried at the thought of never again having to fear Russian occupation.

But the President also reminded the Balts that they would have to live with their neighbor and that the many ethnic Russians among them should find a place in their new multiethnic democracies. The message struck just the right balance. Clearly the Russians got that point and appreciated it.

In that regard, I was glad that our trip to Tbilisi, Georgia, would come after—not before—the visit to Moscow. Among Georgia's citizenry, anti-Russian sentiments were more pronounced. The overflowing crowd that had gathered in Tbilisi's Freedom Square sang a stirring rendition of the national anthem a cappella after the recorded music tract had failed. We didn't know at the time that a man carrying a live grenade had been caught not far from President Bush.

DRIVING BACK to the hotel from Red Square after the Great Patriotic War celebration, I had been struck by the sight of young Russian families strolling along, eating *morozhenoe,* tasty Russian ice cream. It felt like just another holiday in any country—a time for kids to be out of school and for families to enjoy a warm spring day. The image was in stark contrast to the occasional glimpses of old veterans who'd been honored on Red Square and were hobbling along in the streets. Russia was finally pushing from its national memory the psychic weight of the Great Patriotic War, which Stalin had used to justify repression and the people's meager lives. Their "greatest generation," the peasant boys who'd been recruited from the villages to repel the German armies, were quickly dying off. I wondered if the commemoration of the war's end would have any resonance at all for the country when the seventieth anniversary rolled around.

This was indeed a new Russia. Despite the approaching authoritarian backslide, Russians enjoyed more personal freedom than at any time in their history. I'd first been in Moscow in 1979, when people never looked you in the eye; they just trudged along and looked down at their feet. These days, things were much different. Now, although mortality and morbidity rates rivaled those in the developing world, the population was so much better off. Ordinary Russians traveled and talked to foreigners in a confident, engaging manner. They lived in private apartments decorated with items from the huge IKEA furniture store just outside the city. There was plenty to eat, and stores had great variety. That had been Vladimir Putin's bargain with the Russian people: "I will give you order and prosperity and dignity; you will leave politics to me."

The hardening of Putin's resolve to enforce the second part of that bargain would test our relationship increasingly over the next years. A few months before I became secretary, Putin proposed radical new legislation that went a long way to centralize political power in the Kremlin. In the name of strengthening unity after the terror attack in Beslan, Putin proposed doing away with the election of the country's 89 regional governors. He wanted the Kremlin to appoint them instead. As with a number of other proposed reforms during his tenure, Putin succeeded in pushing his plan through parliament (which his party controlled) and strengthening his grip on Russian politics.

The independent media also became a target. In 2006 the campaign against the press turned violent with the murder of the journalist Anna Politkovskaya, an unrelenting critic of the regime. I met with some of her associates in Moscow shortly after her death and could see the pain and fear in their eyes. Though Putin promised to investigate the crime, it wasn't too hard to imagine that she'd been killed by allies of the Kremlin, with or without its knowledge. Independent television and radio stations were disappearing at an alarming rate, replaced by state-run channels that were increasingly indistinguishable from one another in their full-throated defense of the regime. Then, when ABC News conducted an interview with the Chechen rebel leader Shamil Basayev, Moscow expelled the American network and its correspondents. The message was clear to journalists, both foreign and Russian: don't criticize the Russian state.

The campaign against the media was well under way, but it was only an early phase of the Kremlin's crackdown. An assault on the independent judiciary was also launched as politically motivated corruption and "tax evasion" cases were brought against Russian oligarchs. When Mikhail Khodorkovsky, the best known of those men, came to see me at the White House when I was national security advisor, he talked boldly of using his fortune to change the nature of Russian politics. But he made the mistake of trusting the legal system and decided to stand and fight the charges against him in court. He is still in jail today. Others simply fled, including Boris Berezovsky, whom the Russians pursued all the way to London. Those men hadn't just made the mistake of getting rich; they had tried to use their money to support political causes. That was unacceptable to Vladimir Putin.

The oligarchs were easy targets because in the chaotic days after the breakup of the Soviet Union many had exploited the absence of enforceable regulations to acquire their wealth. It wasn't hard for the Kremlin to make a populist case that the men had pilfered the riches of the country, privatizing oil, gas, and minerals for their personal gain at the country's expense. In the Russian psyche, those arguments resonated.

In fact, Gorbachev had once shared with President George H. W. Bush a little parable about the "egalitarian" tendencies of Russians long before the Soviet period. A peasant finds Aladdin's lamp, the story goes. "What would you like me to do for you?" the genie asks. "Look at my neighbor. He has a good family, good crops, and the latest means of conveyance," the peasant says. "Look at me," he continues. "My wife is awful, I have no harvest, and I don't even have a means of conveyance." "So do you want me to make your life like his?" the genie asks. "No," the peasant responds. "I want you to make his life like mine."

Those were the realities of Putin's Russia: increasing consolidation of power in the Kremlin, an all-out assault on the independent media, and the vindictive use of the judiciary.

In time, the list of hard-line policies would include a campaign against foreign NGOs, which would be forced to register with the Russian government to prevent "subversive activities and corruption." Perhaps we should have seen it coming, but this Putin was different from the man whom we had first met in Slovenia. The Russian leader we thought we knew—who'd helped so much in Afghanistan after 9/11 and talked of strategic cooperation—seemed to be disappearing. Whether the catalyst was the accretion of power in one man, increasing unease as the color revolutions spread, or both, authoritarianism was rising in Russia. And as authoritarianism rose within Russia, it would be matched by harsher policies toward Russia's neighbors, particularly those that had the nerve to act on their independence from the former imperial power. The trend would only be exacerbated by the rising price of oil. Those developments, not the great global issues of the time, would become the core of the conflict between Moscow and Washington.

The exploratory committee in March 1999 dedicated to electing Texas Governor George W. Bush President of the United States. *AP Photo/Donna McWilliam*

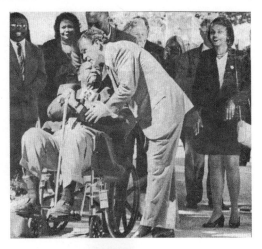

Governor Bush and my dad at a campaign stop in Palo Alto, July 1999. John Wesley Rice Jr. was a lifelong Republican. *Palo Alto Daily News*

Paul Wolfowitz and I cochaired a group of foreign policy specialists (nicknamed the Vulcans after my home city of Birmingham, Alabama) to advise the governor during the campaign. *AFP/Getty Images/ Paul Buck*

One of the most distinguished men in Washington, General Colin Powell was a natural choice as the President's secretary of state. He remains a close friend. *George W. Bush Presidential Library/Tina Hager*

Speaking in the Oval Office with Steve Hadley, my closest confidante and associate in government. He would later become the national security advisor. *George W. Bush Presidential Library/Eric Draper*

Conferring with Vice President Cheney in the White House bunker on September 11, 2001. *Presidential Materials Staff, National Archives*

Outside the Pentagon on September 12. When I returned to the White House, my clothes were covered in soot. *Courtesy of Donald Rumsfeld*

At Camp David, CIA Director George Tenet briefing the President, White House Chief of Staff Andy Card, and me on CIA operations in Afghanistan. *George W. Bush Presidential Library/Eric Draper*

Greeting one of my personal heroes, Nelson Mandela, in the Oval Office. The South African ambassador to the U.S., Sheila Sisulu, looks on. *George W. Bush Presidential Library/Eric Draper*

I had the great honor of playing Brahms with Yo-Yo Ma in April 2002. *George W. Bush Presidential Library/ Paul Morse*

In the White House Situation Room, Don Rumsfeld and I discuss plans for military operations in Iraq. Seated at the table are senior military commanders, Generals Richard Myers and Tommy Franks. *George W. Bush Presidential Library/Eric Draper*

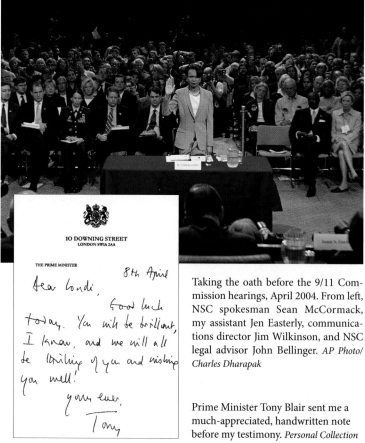

Taking the oath before the 9/11 Commission hearings, April 2004. From left, NSC spokesman Sean McCormack, my assistant Jen Easterly, communications director Jim Wilkinson, and NSC legal advisor John Bellinger. *AP Photo/ Charles Dharapak*

10 DOWNING STREET
LONDON SW1A 2AA

THE PRIME MINISTER

8th April

Dear Condi,

Good luck today. You will be brilliant, I know, and we will all be thinking of you and wishing you well!

Yours ever,

Tony

Prime Minister Tony Blair sent me a much-appreciated, handwritten note before my testimony. *Personal Collection*

Sharing a light moment with Laura Bush at the ranch in Crawford, Texas. *George W. Bush Presidential Library*

My family and closest friends gathered for my surprise fiftieth birthday party at the British Embassy. *MAI/Greg Mathieson Sr.*

Dancing that night with my mentor and friend former Secretary of State George P. Shultz. *MAI/Greg Mathieson Sr.*

Senator Dianne Feinstein of California introduced me to the Senate for my confirmation as secretary of state. *Jay Clendenin/LA Times*

I signed the oath of office with my closest family members looking on. Justice Ruth Bader Ginsburg swore me in. *State Department Photo*

During a 2005 visit to a German military base in Wiesbaden, a photograph of me in a stylish long coat and knee-high boots caused quite a stir when it appeared on the *Washington Post*'s front page. I just wore them because it was snowing. *Reuters/Kevin Lamarque*

In 2005 I welcomed the election of Chancellor Angela Merkel, who embodied Germany's transformation as a former East German politician elected to the country's highest office. *Getty Images/Sean Gallup*

Greeting Her Majesty Queen Elizabeth II of the United Kingdom before performing a piano recital at Buckingham Palace. *State Department Photo*

British Foreign Secretary Jack Straw and I attended a ceremony in my native Birmingham to honor the young victims of the 1963 Sixteenth Street Baptist Church bombing. *AP Photo/The Birmingham News/ Bernard Troncale*

Sitting across the table from Russian President Vladimir Putin. *AFP/Getty Images/Alexander Zemlianichenko*

Greeting children at the Abu Shouk refugee camp in Darfur, where I also met with women who had been victims of rape. Never had I felt raw emotion and pain like that. *AFP/Getty Images*

At the American University in Cairo, I said that for sixty years my country had pursued stability in the Middle East at the expense of democracy. Now we were taking a different course. *Getty Images/Cris Bouroncle*

During my meetings with Egyptian President Hosni Mubarak, I told the aging leader that he needed to provide his people with a voice in their democracy. He refused. *AP Photo*

Observing sheep with Israeli Prime Minister Ariel Sharon at his farm in southern Israel. The strong Israeli leader would eventually demonstrate his commitment to pursuing the establishment of a Palestinian state. *U.S. Embassy Photo Tel Aviv/Matty Stern*

Walking with Afghan President Hamid Karzai along the West Wing colonnade at the White House. *Presidential Materials Staff, National Archives*

Karzai and Pakistani President Pervez Musharraf traded barbs as we sat with nervous smiles on our faces during a 2006 dinner in the White House family dining room. *Getty Images/Eric Draper*

Standing next to Lebanese Prime Minister Fouad Siniora at a press conference in Rome during the 2006 war between Israel and Lebanon. *WPN/Andreas Solaro*

Although we disagreed on Iraq, UN Secretary-General Kofi Annan became an important partner in the aftermath of the immediate invasion and in the Middle East more broadly. *AP Photo/Plinio Lepri*

At an August 2006 meeting of the United Nations Security Council, I cast the United States' vote in favor of a resolution that would finally put an end to the month-long war in Lebanon. *AP Photo/Frank Franklin*

Meeting with King Abdullah of Saudi Arabia in Riyadh. The Saudi king and many other Arab leaders privately expressed relief when we decided to double-down in Iraq amid the deteriorating security situation. *AP Photo/Saudi Press Agency*

An NSC meeting at Camp David in June 2006, five days after a U.S. air strike killed Abu Musab al-Zarqawi, the leader of al Qaeda in Iraq. *Contact Press Images/ Charles Ommanney*

With Canadian Foreign Minister Peter MacKay in Halifax, Nova Scotia, to mark the fifth anniversary of the 9/11 attacks. Canada had welcomed displaced passengers following a grounding order for all aircraft in U.S. airspace. *CP Photo/ Andrew Vaughn*

With Defense Secretary Robert Gates, Treasury Secretary Hank Paulson, and Labor Secretary Elaine Chao during the President's 2007 State of the Union address at the Capitol. *AP Photo/ Lawrence Jackson*

Meeting with our top military and civilian officials in Iraq, General David Petraeus and Ambassador Zalmay Khalilzad, at the beginning of the surge in February 2007. *Agentur FOCUS/ Tina Hager*

With General Ray Odierno, who had been my Pentagon liaison, and Marty Kraus, the head of my security detail, after arriving at the Baghdad airport in late 2007. *State Department Photo*

Greeting Iraqi President Jalal Talabani, a Kurd who would emerge as a unifying leader in the free Iraq. *State Department Photo*

Addressing the press at the U.S. Embassy in Baghdad during a visit to Iraq with Defense Secretary Don Rumsfeld, Army General George Casey, and Ambassador Zalmay Khalilzad. *AP Photo/Jim Watson/Pool*

Meeting with Iraqi Prime Minister Nouri al-Maliki in 2007. Maliki, whom I came to like and respect, was the first democratically elected prime minister under Iraq's new constitution. *AP Photo/Wathiq Khuzaei/Pool*

Conferring with Saudi Foreign Minister Saud al-Faisal at a joint press conference in Jeddah. *AFP/ Getty Images/ Hassan Ammar*

Meeting with King Abdullah II of Jordan, one of America's best allies in the Middle East. *AP Photo/Nader Daoud/Pool*

Being served a strawberry drink in Dubai during a visit with Sheikh Abdullah bin Zayed al-Nahyan, foreign minister of the United Arab Emirates and a member of the ruling family. *AFP/Getty Images/Mandel Ngan*

In 2007 Australian Foreign Minister Alexander Downer traveled with me to California, where we met with former First Lady Nancy Reagan in her private office at the Ronald Reagan Presidential Foundation and Library. *Cliff David/Ronald Reagan Presidential Foundation*

Convening a trilateral summit in February 2007 with Palestinian President Mahmoud Abbas and Israeli Prime Minister Ehud Olmert at the David Citadel Hotel in Jerusalem. *U.S. Embassy Photo Tel Aviv/ Matty Stern*

Greeting Russian President Vladimir Putin in July 2007 at the Bush family home in Kennebunkport, Maine. *AFP/Getty Images*

In November 2007, after months of preparation, we held the Annapolis Conference on Middle East peace, where the Israelis and Palestinians agreed to launch formal bilateral negotiations. *Colby Cooper*

Meeting with UN Secretary-General Ban Ki-moon and former UK Prime Minister Tony Blair, who became the official representative of the Middle East Quartet. *Getty Images/Rick Gershon*

With Salam Fayyad and Israeli Defense Minister Ehud Barak in March 2008 at the King David Hotel in Jerusalem. Fayyad would prove to be a welcome partner in building reliable governing institutions in the development of the Palestinian state. *U.S. Embassy Photo Tel Aviv/Matty Stern*

President Bush and I during a break at an April 2008 NATO summit in Bucharest, Romania. *George W. Bush Presidential Library/Eric Draper*

Meeting with President Hu Jintao at the Great Hall of the People in Beijing after speaking with victims of the May 2008 earthquake in Sichuan province. *AP Photo/Oded Balilty*

With my counterparts from the P5+1 countries (the five permanent members of the UN Security Council plus Germany): Chinese Assistant Minister of Foreign Affairs He Yafei, French Foreign Minister Bernard Kouchner, British Foreign Secretary David Miliband, German Foreign Minister Frank-Walter Steinmeier, Russian Foreign Minister Sergei Lavrov, and EU Foreign Policy Chief Javier Solana in May 2008. The P5+1 would become the principal international body dealing with the Iranian nuclear problem. *AP Photo/Sang Tan/ WPA Pool*

I frequently sought the wise counsel of former Secretary of State Henry Kissinger to get his perspective on key issues in foreign affairs. *AP Photo/ Keystone/Laurent Gillieron*

I visited the Pakistani Embassy in Washington, D.C., to sign a condolence book following the death of former Pakistani Prime Minister Benazir Bhutto. *Getty Images/Brendan Smialowski*

Libyan leader Muammar Qaddafi struck me as unstable during my September 2008 meeting in Tripoli, the first such visit by a U.S. secretary of state since 1953. *AP Photo/ Nasser Nasser*

With Indian Foreign Minister Pranab Mukherjee on October 10, 2008, signing the historic U.S.-India civil nuclear agreement. *State Department Photo*

French President Nicolas Sarkozy and I discuss the ceasefire he negotiated to end the 2008 Russia-Georgia conflict at his estate in the south of France. *AFP/Getty Images*

The best personnel decision that I made when I became secretary of state was to bring with me my executive assistant, the incomparable Liz Lineberry. *Agentur FOCUS/Contact Press Images/Tina Hager*

Reviewing a document with my chief of staff Brian Gunderson in my inner office on the seventh floor of the State Department. *Agentur FOCUS/Contact Press Images/Tina Hager*

One hour before I left the State Department on my last day as secretary, Israeli Foreign Minister Tzipi Livni and I signed a memorandum of understanding on terms for an end to the latest conflict in Gaza. Tzipi is a strong leader and a good friend. *AP Photo/Luis M. Alvarez*

Bidding farewell to the State Department staff on my last scheduled workday as secretary of state. Lining the stairway are some of my senior staff, including (from left to right) Assistant Secretaries Dan Fried and Jendayi Frazer and the Deputy Secretary of State John Negroponte, one of our nation's most distinguished diplomats. *Reuters/Jonathan Ernst*

25

BAGHDAD AND CAIRO

EVENING TRIPS OUT TO Andrews Air Force Base always made me feel a little melancholy. I'd already worked an entire day, sprinted home to pick up my luggage, and jumped into the limousine headed to whatever country was next on my relentless travel log. "Otis, what are you going to do this weekend?" I'd ask my driver as we headed out along Suitland Parkway.

"My daughter's got a basketball game, and I have to get out for a long run," he would answer.

I would ask because it is important for the folks who help you to know that you care about their families and their lives. But the answer always made me sad. I'd lost all conception of weekends.

Otis had been a noncommissioned officer in the army from 1975 until 1995, when he'd become a civilian driver for the government. He'd been the personal driver of two former secretaries of defense and a former CIA director when he joined the State Department's Diplomatic Security Bureau to serve as Colin Powell's driver. Like Steve Estelle, my Secret Service driver at the White House, he was one of those dedicated African American government servants who just did their jobs without any fanfare despite long, crazy hours. Otis and Steve knew every route in Washington, D.C., and could magically turn a twenty-minute trip into a ten-minute one if need be, just by finding a shortcut. I gave Hillary Clinton only a few tidbits of advice about personnel; "Keep Otis" was at the top of the list.

On the morning of May 14, though, the journey out to Andrews was different. I was on my way to Qatar to board a military plane that would fly me to Erbil in Iraqi Kurdistan and then on to Baghdad for the first time as secretary of state. I was so excited that I could barely contain myself. For security reasons, only a handful of staff knew where I was going, and I'd made the decision never to tell my family when I was traveling to Iraq or Afghanistan. They would just have worried.

After the brief stop in the northern Kurdish region, we took off in the military's human transport plane, the C-17. The flight's commander asked if I'd like to sit in the cockpit, which I readily agreed to do. With about thirty minutes left until landing, the flight crew brought me my armored vest and seat—yes, an armored plate that you sit on just in case a missile comes from below. On that occasion we landed without incident, though that was not always the case. Once, flying into Baghdad, we suddenly diverted upon approach. "What was that?" I asked the pilot.

"The airport is being mortared," he said. "We don't know if it's random or if it's meant for you."

"I guess it doesn't really matter," I joked. We eventually landed about forty minutes later.

On another trip, I was to fly from Baghdad to Israel, which required us to fly over Jordanian territory. I spotted a plane off our right side and asked the pilot what it was.

"Oh, ma'am, that's just a Syrian fighter making sure we don't cross into his airspace," he said calmly.

"Well, I hope we have good navigational gear," I quipped.

"Ma'am, don't worry about ours," he replied. "Worry about his."

Iraq was very much a war zone, but I loved going there despite the secrecy and extraordinary security. And I always felt preternaturally safe. On my first trip I wore the helmet that I was given, making me look like a re-creation of the much-maligned photograph of Michael Dukakis riding in a tank during the 1988 presidential campaign. After that I decided to forgo some of the armor, particularly the headwear, when getting off the plane.

The final step in the trip was boarding a Black Hawk helicopter with young gunners protecting its flanks. Swooping down into the fortified International Zone, more commonly known as the Green Zone, I felt tremendous anticipation and excitement. I was finally in Baghdad and ready to carry the message that the United States maintained its confidence in the ability of Iraqis to secure a democratic future. Arriving at the beautiful Presidential Palace, I was reminded that Baghdad had indeed been a cradle of civilization—the source of ancient wonders and antiquities of Mesopotamia and Babylon, including the Code of Hammurabi. This was not Afghanistan; Iraq's cultural and political weight really could reshape the Middle East.

My certainty was shaken somewhat once I entered a room with Iraqi Prime Minister Ibrahim al-Jaafari. He enjoyed a reputation for honesty but had hardly been chosen to lead the transitional government because of his widespread popularity; the Sunnis had by and large not participated in the January legislative elections, and he had run unchallenged for the office largely because no other consensus candidate had emerged. Jaafari was an odd man with the bearing of a humanities professor. He spent the first thirty minutes of our meeting waxing lyrical about U.S. history, various founding fathers (usually confusing them somewhat), and the inspiration that he had drawn from my personal story about having grown up in the segregated South.

I thanked him but turned quickly to my agenda. The great challenge in the spring of 2005 was to include the Sunnis in the county's political institutions and especially to gain their support for a new Iraqi constitution. There would be a referendum on a draft charter in October, and though the Shia and Kurds might be able to bring the constitution into force without the support of the Sunnis, it would be disastrous if a sizable minority did not endorse the new Iraq's founding document. Under Saddam the Sunnis had represented roughly 30 percent of the population but nearly 100 percent of the political power. Now they were 30 percent of the population and terrified of being marginalized by a Shia-led government. It was that fear that had helped fuel the Sunni insurgency.

If a democratic state is to be stable, "one man, one vote" cannot mean the disenfranchisement of minorities. Respecting that reality is one of the hardest problems of democratic governance anywhere. But getting this right in Iraq would mean a new start for marginalized groups across the Middle East. Today in Bahrain and Saudi Arabia (where Sunnis rule over largely disenfranchised Shia populations), we can see the urgency of finding a political formula that works.

It was unsettling that Jaafari seemed to have only a marginal interest in that fundamental problem. He said the right things about wanting to reach out to the Sunnis but gave no indication that he knew how to do it. Perhaps, I told myself, he was just unfocused in our conversation. One thing was clear, though: he was not the man to lead Iraq.

IRONICALLY, MY CONVERSATIONS with the Iraqis were better than my interactions with General George Casey, the U.S. commander of coalition forces on the ground in Baghdad. I liked George. We'd both studied at the University of Denver's Graduate School of International Studies, and he was a decent, honest four-star officer. But I was becoming increasingly frustrated with the Pentagon's attitude toward Iraq, and the tensions between us were growing.

Toward the end of 2004, the briefings for the President had devolved from incomprehensible to inexplicable. The reports about the security situation usually focused on "metrics": How many weapons caches had we destroyed? How many Iraqi security forces had been trained? How many incidents of live fire had there been? Few of those metrics bore much relationship to the deteriorating security situation and the strengthening insurgency. Attacks on reconstruction projects, particularly on the pipelines and electrical grid, were rising. Suicide bombings seemed to occur almost daily. And the highway between the airport and Baghdad had become virtually impassable because the bad guys owned the road.

When pressed on those facts, the Defense Department's answer was largely the same as before: the security situation would improve when the political situation improved. That, of course, begged the question of how Iraqis could run for office while running for their lives.

Shortly after arriving at State, I asked my counselor, Phil Zelikow, to take a quiet fact-finding trip to Iraq. He was accompanied by then Lieutenant General Raymond Odierno, my liaison from the Joint Chiefs of Staff who had led the 4th Infantry Division during the initial invasion. The Pentagon assigns a senior officer to advise the secretary of state on the military aspects of her job and provide connectivity to the Defense Department. I had the remarkable good fortune to inherit Ray from Colin. He is a giant of a man—an imposing six feet, five inches but soft-spoken, decent, good-humored, and generous in spirit. Dealing with him every day, it would have been easy to overlook his toughness until one remembered that it was he who had commanded the unit that captured Saddam Hussein. We immediately hit it off, drawing on our common love of football to break the ice; he loves the New York Giants and was always too kind to ridicule my Cleveland Browns.

Ray was a "thinker" too. Military officers who had led the early campaigns in Operation Iraqi Freedom—David Petraeus, James Mattis, Peter Chiarelli, H. R. McMaster, Ray, and others—had returned from the battlefield between 2004 and 2006 determined to understand why we were not succeeding. The initial effort to remove Saddam Hussein from power had largely been accomplished, but stability had not been restored, and relations with the Iraqi population lay somewhere between indifference and outright hostility toward our presence. In part because we could not protect them from the growing insurgency, people were hedging their bets. In warfare of this kind, a population that is passive toward or intimidated by the terrorists enables their success. When you cannot separate friend from foe, it is hard to win, and increasingly the insurgency and the population were blending into one.

Moreover, in this dense, urban, complex fighting environment, our heavy military firepower in pursuit of insurgents and terrorists often ended up inadvertently alienating the population even further. U.S. soldiers raided towns and villages in search of enemies and often returned to the safety of their bases. The average Iraqi was left to deal with the consequences of those actions. The population had to believe that our forces had the capability and the will to protect them.

A new Army/Marine Corps Counterinsurgency Field Manual was emerging out of those concerns. Either militaries adapt on the battlefield, or they die. It was impressive to watch men like then-Colonel McMaster, an officer who had written a highly influential history of the Vietnam War for his PhD dissertation, and other young officers under the protection of the senior generals look for answers. Their thinking was not immediately welcome in the highest reaches of the Pentagon, but it would eventually lay the groundwork for the successful military surge of 2007.

I understood that it was not my role to change the military's doctrinal approach to the Iraq war. But I, too, had studied counterinsurgencies in history, and I knew that they require civilian support to succeed. David Kilcullen, a retired Australian army officer who served as my special advisor on counterinsurgency, gave the State Department deep expertise in these issues. Winning the support of the local population required economic assistance, reconstruction, and good governance. Tensions were growing between the Foreign Service and a military whose most common assessment was "State is not in the fight." It was true that too few diplomats, especially experienced ones, were deploying to Iraq. There were huge gaps in civilian expertise, often filled by military reservists or National Guardsmen. And there was a perception in the military, on Capitol Hill, and in the White House that the situation reflected the State Department's ambivalence at best and resentment at worst toward the Iraq war.

My charge to Ray and Phil was to look over the situation in Iraq and come back to me with recommendations about how we could improve State's support of the military effort and be responsive to the growing clamor for a change in the United States' approach to the war. Their findings would lead to the deployment of Provincial Reconstruction Teams (PRTs) in Iraq, a kind of hybrid force first established in Afghanistan that included military officers, diplomats, and reconstruction workers from various civilian agencies, including the Departments of Agriculture and Justice and the U.S. Agency for International Development (USAID). The struggle to improve State's contribution was just beginning at the time of that first trip; it was one that would take enormous effort and a redefinition of what diplomats are expected to do in war.

The most immediate conclusion of Phil and Ray's trip was the need to clarify what we were trying to do in Iraq. During my October 2005 testimony before the Senate Foreign Relations Committee, I used a phrase that seemed to capture the essence of the effort. "In short, with the Iraqi government, our political-military strategy has to be to clear, hold, and build," I said in my opening remarks. "To clear areas from insurgent control, to hold them securely, and to build durable national . . . Iraqi institutions." It was a rather catchy phrase but very descriptive of the tenets of counterinsurgency doctrine. In fact, it was an articulation of the strategy that Colonel McMaster had successfully used to retake the northern Iraqi city of Tal Afar. Because it was one of the few statements of our objectives that was easy to understand, it captured enormous press attention. I heard through the grapevine that Don was annoyed and told some that I was out of my lane. I really didn't care. *Somebody has to be able to explain what we're doing,* I thought.

I had not intended, however, to blindside anyone, most especially George Casey. I had thought that Ray had briefed him on my testimony. So when I returned to Iraq in November to inaugurate the first Provincial Reconstruction Team in the country, I was surprised when George asked to see me alone. "Clear and hold" are military functions, he fumed. "I don't like the State Department talking about military doctrine."

I tried to stay calm, reminding myself that he was under enormous pressure. "George, I'm sorry that you were blindsided," I said. "That's wrong. But let's get one thing straight. I'm the secretary of state, not the State Department. That means I am one of the President's chief advisors on this war, and I will say what I please." I then repeated that I thought he had been briefed and would make sure that we had better coordination.

This wouldn't be the last time we would clash. More disagreements over the direction of the war effort would come later. But when I took off from Iraq after my first visit as secretary, I looked down on the terrain—two glorious rivers, fertile agricultural land to the north, oil to the north and south, and the majestic buildings of the nation's beautiful capital. I called the President from the plane. "Baghdad will be a great city," I told him as Iraq faded into the distance. "This will truly be a great country." And I sat back thinking of all that had to be done before that prediction could come true.

IRAQ WAS ONLY one of the pieces of the puzzle in transforming the Middle East. The region seems always to mix hope and despair, and that was certainly the case in the spring and summer of 2005. On the one hand, Lebanon was free of Syrian forces; the Iraqis were debating a new constitution with the participation of Sunni Arabs; Egyptians were moving rapidly toward the most open presidential elections in their history; and the Kuwaiti Parliament had passed a law that gave women the right to vote and run for office. In Kuwait, I was presented with a T-shirt that I still wear—"Half a democracy is no democracy at all," it said. On the other hand, Mahmoud Ahmadinejad, the lightly regarded but undeniably hard-line mayor of Tehran, had been elected in Iran to succeed the more moderate Mohammad Khatami.

Yet the outlines of a different Middle East—one that was more modern and democratic—were emerging and might, if given time, provide less fertile ground in which al Qaeda and Islamic extremists could spread their hatred. It was critical that the United States continue encouraging, cajoling, and persuading our friends to reform. We knew that each nation would move at a different speed. Iraq would need to stabilize its new democracy and reintegrate itself into an Arab world that had essentially expelled it at the time of Saddam's invasion of Kuwait. Lebanon was an unusual state, with its confessional groups locked into a formulaic sharing of power. Still, in the elections just three months after the withdrawal of Syrian troops during the Cedar Revolution (named for the cedar tree on the Lebanese flag), the moderate March 14 political alliance had won a major victory. With our help the Lebanese stood a chance of diminishing not just the role of Damascus but also the destructive influence of Hezbollah. Anti-U.S. forces seemed to be falling back across the region. We believed that we could use the momentum to unite our Arab friends to resist and counter Iranian aggression and penetration into the Middle East.

The role of Egypt in the overall equation was crucial. Iraq, bordered by six neighbors, including Iran, was one of the most important countries geographically. But Egypt was the cultural and political heart of the Middle East. A democratic Egypt would change the region like nothing else.

It was in that spirit that I went to the American University in Cairo in June 2005 to deliver a speech on democracy in the Middle East.

Before leaving Washington, I sat with my speechwriter, Chris Brose, Assistant Secretary for Near Eastern Affairs David Welch, and other key advisors. I told them that I needed to be bold. In his second inaugural address, the President had challenged the world to end tyranny by supporting democratic movements in every nation and culture. I saw the upcoming speech in Cairo as an opportunity to expand on that theme and lay out its implications for U.S. policy in the Middle East. I asked Mike Gerson, who had drafted the President's address, if he wanted to join me on the trip. He did, and there in my cabin as we flew toward Egypt, Mike, Chris, David, Phil Zelikow, Sean McCormack, Brian Gunderson, and I went over every word, saying each one aloud, teasing out its meaning. I wanted to make clear that the United States meant it: the time had come for change—democratic change.

Before arriving in Cairo, I met with Egyptian President Hosni Mubarak in Sharm el-Sheikh, as I would many times over the next years. The aging president increasingly preferred to work at the seaside resort city. We reviewed a number of issues, including the upcoming Israeli withdrawal from Gaza. Then I asked him if we could speak alone. I wanted to talk about democracy and reform, but I didn't want to embarrass the president in front of others. After he shooed everyone from the room, I moved closer to him. Mubarak was very hard of hearing and too proud to wear a hearing aid. So I talked loudly and looked directly at him, hoping that the elderly leader could hear me or, if necessary, read my lips. "Mr. President," I said, "you have a chance to do something great for your country. It's time to give your people a voice. You don't have forever to do it because soon they will demand it. Do it now."

Mubarak sat up straight, leaned forward, and looked directly at me. With his broad nose and hooded eyes, he looked like a pharaoh. "I know my people," he began. "The Egyptians need a strong hand, and they don't like foreign interference. We are proud people."

After listening to him for several minutes, I tried to appeal to that pride and his vanity. "You saved your country from ruin after Sadat's assassination," I told him, referring to his predecessor, who had been gunned down in 1981. "Now take your people forward." I ended our encounter by telling him what I would say in Cairo. "I don't want you to be surprised," I said. He nodded and reminded me that Egyptians don't like to be told what to do.

I felt immediately at home in the academic setting of the American University in Cairo's auditorium. About six hundred students, faculty, and members of civil society were crowded into the relatively small room, made very warm by the glaring television lights. Mubarak's warning was in my head, and I knew that there was great skepticism about the United States in this audience. Yet, as I made my way through the speech to the lines about our mistake in supporting authoritarian regimes, the mood in the room shifted. "For sixty years, my country, the United States, pursued stability at the expense of democracy in this region here in the Middle East—and we achieved neither," I said. "Now we are taking a different course. We are supporting the democratic aspirations of all people." At that moment and later with a group of democracy activists, I felt elated by the connection I'd made with Egypt's impatient patriots. Only later would I wonder if I'd unintentionally promised more rapid change than anyone could deliver, most especially the United States.

As I watched the increasingly isolated Hosni Mubarak struggling to hang on to power in February 2011 while his people ridiculed him from the streets, I thought back on my conversation with him and my speech at the American University in Cairo. He would allow relatively free and very noisy presidential elections that fall of 2005. Steve Hadley and I had invited Mubarak's confidant Omar Suleiman, the head of Egypt's intelligence service, to dinner at the Watergate restaurant prior to the elections. There, in a dark corner of the room, we talked about how the United States could support a democratizing Egypt and what would be required if Egypt's upcoming elections were to be truly democratic. I talked to Mubarak twice in August, urging him to keep the electoral environment free and fair. Then we watched as he campaigned from city to city for the first time in his life, seemingly rejuvenated by the democratic process. Egyptian coffeehouses were alive with political debate, and the Egyptian press commentary exulted that Egypt's politics would never be the same.

But soon thereafter Mubarak reversed course. During the subsequent parliamentary elections in November and December, the regime was accused of deploying attackers wielding machetes and other weapons to intimidate voters. The next year Mubarak refused to carry through on his promise to repeal the hated "emergency law," which limited free speech and assembly. In 2007 he held a public referendum on constitutional amendments that would, among other things, give him authority to dissolve the Egyptian Parliament without the public's consent. The government announced that nearly 76 percent of voters approved the amendments, leading to allegations of election fraud. When we criticized his handling of the elections, Mubarak fumed that U.S. foreign assistance didn't give Washington the right to interfere in Egypt's internal affairs.

His problem, though, was not with us; it was with his people. I thought at the time that they'd never accept going back to the old ways where they were denied a voice in their political future. It was that frustration and anger that spilled out into the streets six years later and swept the confused and isolated Mubarak from power in 2011.

AFTER MY TRIP to Egypt I went on to meet with Crown Prince Abdullah of Saudi Arabia, the first time I'd meet him as secretary. Abdullah, then in his early eighties, would soon ascend to the throne with the death of King Fahd and, like his predecessor, become the Custodian of the Two Holy Mosques in recognition of the Saudi monarch's role in overseeing the two holy sites in Mecca and Medina.

I had met the crown prince during my time as national security advisor. He had initially been suspicious of me at the time, given the rumors that I'd told other Arabs that the Muslim Brotherhood wasn't a threat to the region. I never knew where that misquote had come from but chalked it up to the kind of gossip that ricochets around the Middle East regularly. I had a theory that the Egyptians might have started it. Fortunately, I'd had the opportunity to clear up the misconception when Abdullah visited Crawford in April 2002. I'd received him at the airport and escorted him back to the President's ranch by bus. The Saudi leader had refused to ride in a helicopter.

During that roughly hourlong trip, the crown prince and I had talked about religion and values. I wasn't sure how he'd react to the news that my father had been a Presbyterian minister and that I was unmarried. The latter he thought sad, but he reassured me that I'd probably still find a mate. The former, though, he found reassuring. It was good that I was a believer—even if in Jesus Christ, not Mohammed. By the time we arrived in Crawford, Abdullah had decided that I was a good person and conveyed those kind words to the President himself.

Arriving in Riyadh as secretary years later, I experienced that night what every former secretary of state had described to me. I went to the hotel about nine and waited. And waited. And waited. Finally at about eleven o'clock the crown prince was ready to see me. It seems that the Saudis prefer late-night meetings, having gotten out of bed in the afternoon, dined after nine, and then and only then readied themselves to receive guests.

The crown prince welcomed me warmly at his palace and then said that he wanted me to meet several other Saudi ministers. The princes were lined up in order of seniority, and each came forward, nodded, took my hand, and greeted me. The princes near my age all said hello with an accompanying "I'm a Trojan" (for USC) or "I'm an Aggie" (for Texas A&M). There was even one "I'm a Pioneer" (after my own alma mater, the University of Denver). Some of the most senior princes, such as my counterpart Saud al-Faisal, had attended elite American schools. Saud was a graduate of Princeton.

I'd read that the kingdom had educated the young royals in the United States until the 1980s, when there had been a turn toward conservatism in response to the Iranian Revolution. The younger princes had thus been sent to King Fahd University, where they had studied mostly religion at the expense of gaining technical and linguistic skills. This encounter vivified for me Abdullah's preoccupation with sending more students to the United States, something that had become harder in the post-9/11 environment. By the end of the administration, thanks largely to a push by the President and our ambassadors to the kingdom, James C. Oberwetter and Ford M. Fraker, the number of Saudis studying in the United States exceeded pre-9/11 levels. Education in the West was not a guarantee of liberal thinking; three of the 9/11 suicide hijackers had studied in Germany. But going to school in the United States created more familiarity with—and hopefully more respect for—our system than if Saudis remained isolated from the West.

After the introductions were made, the crown prince and I went into his sitting room with only my trusted interpreter Gamal Helal joining us. The crown prince pulled out a gift-wrapped package. "I have a gift for you," he said. I had become accustomed to Abdullah's gifts, usually jewels that I couldn't afford to keep, given federal ethics rules requiring me to purchase any offering over a certain minimal value. This time, though, I opened the package and realized that it was a full-length, beautifully embroidered abaya, the black robe and veil Saudi women traditionally wear. "I had it made especially for you," he said tenderly. "Our women wear them."

Yes, as a sign of oppression, I thought. But it was so dear, and he meant well. "Thank you, Your Majesty," I said. "It's so beautiful."

We then sat together for two hours, reviewing the landscape of the Middle East, talking about Saudi Arabia and the "modernization" of the country and, of course, Iran. The crown prince exhorted me to deal with Tehran and to resolve the Palestinian conflict by pressuring Israel. Those were views with which I was familiar. But his discussion of his own country was more surprising. I'd come to know Abdullah as something of a reformer in this most conservative of countries. He spoke of the need to hear his people to know what they were thinking and stressed the importance of getting out of the palace and visiting remote parts of the country. He'd authorized the practice of elections for half of the seats of the country's municipal councils, prompting lawyers, businessmen, professors, and tribal leaders to stand for election. Women weren't permitted to vote or run for office, but Abdullah thought that might come in time. He did receive groups of women from time to time to hear their concerns.

The crown prince talked of his plans to change his country's higher education system by building a technical university to give Saudi men—and women—the skills needed for the twenty-first century. One shouldn't overstate the case, but Abdullah was different from his half brothers, who were known for their wealth, even corruption, and their death grip on power. He was a pious man who wanted to change his country—albeit slowly and within very conservative parameters. Later President Bush and I would talk about how we could help Abdullah guide Saudi Arabia toward reform. We felt that we would be pushing on an open door; we might not be able to expect national elections anytime soon, but we could encourage the kingdom to continue redefining the relationship between rulers and ruled. In Saudi Arabia that would be revolutionary in its own right. I could not help but wonder, though, *At eighty-one years old, does he have enough time?*

The Arab world had been isolated from the worldwide movement toward democracy during the second half of the twentieth century, but change was coming, even if it was frustratingly slow. Another key part of the equation would be to find an answer to the decades-old Israeli-Palestinian question. It was not that reform in the Arab world was dependent on resolution of the conflict, though our friends often made that claim. In fact, it was a kind of talisman of legitimacy for otherwise illegitimate governments. When the authoritarian rulers needed to appease "the street," as they referred to their people, the plight of the Palestinians was a convenient rallying cry.

That led me to challenge a group of Arabs on this point early in my tenure as national security advisor. "If you care so much about the Palestinians," I asked, "why have each and every one of you expelled them from your country at some point in time?" It was a slightly exaggerated rhetorical point, but indeed there sometimes seemed to be more concern for trumpeting their cause rather than actually helping the Palestinians. I can't count the number of phone calls I made to the rich Arabs, begging them to give just a little bit of their excess oil revenue to Mahmoud Abbas and the Palestinian Authority. It was sad to watch the dignified Palestinian leader visit his Arab brethren, begging for money, and then have to call me, the U.S. secretary of state, and ask me to press his case with them.

Yes, reform in the Middle East needed to take place whether or not a Palestinian state came into being. That did not, however, diminish the urgency of finding a solution for those beleaguered people. The Palestinians and their leaders were admirable for their perseverance, their relative tolerance of religious difference (some Palestinians are Christian, others Muslim), and their industriousness. They needed their own state, and a democratic Middle East would be incomplete without a democratic Palestine.

In the spring and summer of 2005, the pending Israeli withdrawal from Gaza offered the potential to jump-start movement toward a two-state solution. President Bush had insisted that the Israelis cooperate and coordinate with the Palestinians so the withdrawal wouldn't leave chaos in its wake. James Wolfensohn, who had recently retired as president of the World Bank, agreed to be an envoy on behalf of the Middle East Quartet (an association of the United States, the European Union, the United Nations, and Russia) to facilitate that coordination.

Jim was indefatigable in pushing the process forward, though he was outwardly suspicious of the Israelis, causing some heartburn in Tel Aviv. But through his efforts funding was put into place for the Palestinians to take advantage of the Israeli withdrawal as a step toward statehood. There were, for example, massive greenhouses in Gaza growing world-class vegetables. Private sources, including the Bill & Melinda Gates Foundation and Jewish Americans such as Mort Zuckerman and Leonard Stern, put up the money to buy them from the Israeli settlers. Also, USAID prepared several social projects, including much-needed water purification efforts, that could immediately be started in the newly Palestinian-controlled territory.

We all worried about settler violence, so I went to Israel in July, the third time since becoming secretary, to check in with the prime minister. This time Sharon asked if we could meet at his farm in the Negev in southern Israel to speak in a more relaxed atmosphere. I was somewhat surprised at the invitation; I guess I had never thought of Sharon relaxing. But he was different in that environment, calmer and more reflective. He'd lost his beloved wife several years before, and her photos were everywhere. He talked about how in the years after being viewed as responsible for the tragedies in the Palestinian refugee camps at Sabra and Shatila, he'd effectively retired to the farm. The Sharons would get up in the morning and have breakfast, and he'd go out to work the fields. "Sometimes I got so carried away out on the land that I forgot to come home for lunch," he said. Referring to his wife, he added, "She hated that." It was such a tender moment with this very tough man.

Then he asked if I wanted to see his sheep. I told him that I was a city girl and hadn't ever seen sheep up close and personal. He delighted in giving me my first experience, explaining that he knew them individually, not just as a flock. Walking among the smelly creatures, Sharon suddenly turned serious. "I want you to come back in the fall," he said. "Come back here to the farm. We need to talk about the future." I nodded in agreement.

As I was getting ready to leave, I asked a second time how he felt about the prospects for a peaceful withdrawal from Gaza. My first inquiry had elicited a perfunctory though reassuring answer. The IDF was disciplined and would succeed, he said. This time, though, he took another tack. He told me a story of going to visit settlers to explain why they had to withdraw from Gaza. "One man asked me to get up and come with him," Sharon said. "He took me to the door, and above it was a mezuzah," a Jewish symbol containing portions of the Torah that deal with keeping God in one's everyday life. " 'You nailed it up there yourself,' the man said to me," Sharon continued. " 'You told me that it was good for the Israeli state that my family moved here to Gaza to claim Jewish lands. Now you tell me to leave.' " Sharon was suddenly very emotional. Now I understood that his speech a few years before about "painful sacrifices" had not been meant just in the political sense. Those sacrifices were deeply personal for him.

The Israelis would complete their withdrawal on September 12. As it turned out, it took only four weeks, and settler violence was minimal.

The Palestinians' behavior in response did not, however, inspire confidence that they were ready for statehood. Hamas took to the streets to celebrate the "expulsion" of the Israelis from Gaza, inflaming opinion in Tel Aviv and Jerusalem. Palestinian thugs trashed the greenhouses that could have produced food for them. I called Bill Gates and Jim Wolfensohn to apologize for what had happened to their private investments. "I would do it again in the cause of peace," Gates answered graciously.

Despite those small setbacks, the Israelis were out of Gaza and four small settlements in the West Bank. Soon after, Ehud Olmert, Sharon's deputy, came to Washington with a message from his boss. The Israelis had further plans for disengagement from the West Bank, and Sharon would leave Likud and charter a new political party, Kadima, to support the establishment of two states, Israel and Palestine, living side by side in peace and security.

26

A Heartbreaking Place Called Darfur

D EVELOPMENTS IN THE MIDDLE EAST seemed to warrant my full attention; so much was changing, and so much was at stake. Nonetheless, there were other pressing matters that couldn't be put on the back burner. The President was heading to the G8 at the Gleneagles Hotel in Scotland, and though foreign ministers didn't generally travel with their heads of government, we talked about whether I should go. This was a kind of test of our new relationship; I wasn't his national security advisor anymore, but surely I would continue to travel with him.

I recommended that I go instead to Asia. The North Koreans were acting up, and the members of the Six-Party Talks needed to be corralled into a unified response. China thought the North was ready to return to the table, and South Korea was providing fuel oil again. I thought my time could better be used there. The President agreed.

Further into my tenure as secretary, I traveled less with him and more on my own. As we moved toward the end of the administration, he'd call and ask jokingly, "Is this trip important enough for you to go on?" Maybe we both missed the good old days a bit, but the truth is that when traveling with him I felt a bit like a fifth wheel. As national security advisor you staff the President on the road, deal with the press on his behalf, and manage the other agencies during the visit. Now Steve had those responsibilities. The secretary of state sits there like a potted plant. The President would turn to me fairly frequently, particularly when some leader was complaining about what hadn't gotten done. But ambassadors were quite capable of handling such situations.

I could hear the echo of Jim Baker telling me that the time would come when I wouldn't want to travel with the President. *He's got to be kidding*, I'd thought then. But he was right; we rarely needed to be in the same place. It made sense, to be sure, for state visits and summits, but for most international meetings it was unnecessary. And frankly, it was better to travel on my own plane with my own schedule. Air Force One isn't that comfortable when you don't have a bed.

I did go back to Asia, starting this time in Southeast Asia, specifically Thailand, and then moving on to meetings in China, South Korea, and Japan. While I was on the road, the North Koreans agreed to return to the negotiating table on July 25, so there was a lot of work to do to get ready. For that reason I decided to skip the ASEAN summit scheduled for late July and send the deputy, Bob Zoellick, instead. I was surprised by the reaction overseas. You would have thought that the U.S. had broken diplomatic relations with all of Southeast Asia. My absence was taken as a sign of disinterest in the region. It didn't matter that Bob was being sent as a direct representative of the President. No matter how much I affirmed the importance of the region to the United States, the charge stuck throughout the Bush administration. That was the problem for the secretary of state. It wasn't acceptable to insist that there were priorities; everyone needed your time. Having learned that lesson, the next year, when the ASEAN summit happened to be scheduled in the middle of the Lebanon war, I flew all the way to Malaysia from the Middle East and back.

I ended the summer in Sudan, where events had taken a turn for the worse since the conclusion of the Comprehensive Peace Agreement (CPA) at the beginning of 2005. Sudan had been on the President's radar screen since we first arrived in Washington. He wanted to end the decades-long civil war between the South and the North that had resulted in the deaths of millions of people. Evangelical Christians in the United States had long championed the cause of Christians in the African South of Sudan, who had been oppressed by Arab Muslims in the North. In 2001 the President and Colin decided to appoint former senator John Danforth as special envoy for peace to Sudan. He could overcome congressional constraints on policy choices, they reasoned, and as an Episcopalian priest, he could mobilize the religious constituency.

Danforth proved to be an inspired choice, obtaining a provisional ceasefire in January 2002. His work, along with that of Jendayi Frazer, the African affairs specialist at the White House, and Walter Kansteiner, the assistant secretary of state for African affairs, would eventually lead to the aforementioned Comprehensive Peace Agreement, a set of agreements and protocols that finalized power sharing and territorial arrangements and set into motion a referendum process that would ultimately lead to the South's secession in July 2011.

With assistance from the international community the agreement was signed on January 9, 2005. Colin had directed the U.S. effort, intervening personally in the end to get the deal done. Several times the negotiations had almost broken down, but he and Danforth had persevered. We could always tell when the parties were getting close to success. The celebration was apparently to include sacrificing a white cow, so when Colin called to say that the participants had ordered the animal I was excited by the sign of progress but also sorry for the animal that had been selected. The preparations were a bit premature that day, but the negotiations succeeded soon after. Twenty-two years of civil war—one of the longest conflicts in Africa—had ended. It happened, as it should have, on Colin's watch.

Unfortunately, the end of the civil war in the South came as another crisis in Sudan further deteriorated. In 2003, in a northwestern region of the country called Darfur, two loosely affiliated rebel groups, the Sudan Liberation Movement/Army (SLM/A) and the Justice and Equality Movement (JEM), had launched a series of attacks on government military posts. The rebels' chief complaint was that the Muslim-dominated central government had neglected and marginalized the region's black African ethnic groups. The Sudanese government responded by mobilizing proxy militias called the Janjaweed, which carried out widespread and savage killing of civilians and wholesale destruction of villages. Those atrocities, which to date have displaced an estimated 1.9 million people and killed an estimated 450,000, threatened to undo the CPA. In March 2005 the UN Security Council voted unanimously to deploy 10,000 troops and more than 700 civilian police for an initial six-month period to help enforce the CPA in Sudan. The Council's resolution also signaled that the United Nations Mission in Sudan (UNMIS) would also reinforce efforts to foster peace in Darfur, though it notably eschewed language that would declare the atrocities there to be genocide.

The term "genocide" is often used rather loosely and synonymously with mass violence against a people. In international law, though, it has a precise definition, which comprises two components codified in the 1948 Convention on the Prevention and Punishment of the Crime of Genocide. One is the mental element, the *intent* to "destroy, in whole or in part, a national, ethnical, racial or religious group." The second is the physical element, which includes five specific acts outlined in the convention. To call atrocities genocide, both legal elements must be fulfilled.

American slavery, as awful as it was, would not, for instance, qualify as genocide, though hundreds of thousands of Africans died as a result of the American slave trade as well as at the hands of white American slave owners. The Holocaust, on the other hand, was clearly genocide, because at a certain point Nazi Germany's extermination policy became intentional.

Because genocide is a powerful term, Colin appointed a group of specialists to assess the case in Darfur. When they returned with a finding of genocide, the situation in Darfur took on new urgency. U.S. policy shifted from implementation of the CPA to include trying to save the people of Darfur.

It was for that reason that I traveled to Sudan and Darfur. The beauty of Sudan is striking. Khartoum sits at the intersection of the two tributaries that compose the Nile River and is thus lush despite being largely desert. My visit began with a meeting with John Garang de Mabior, the man who had led the southern Sudan People's Liberation Army long enough and well enough to achieve an end to the violence against his people in 2005. Garang was a huge man, well over six feet tall, with skin color so black that it appeared almost blue. He looked a bit out of place in the palace in Khartoum, where he now sat as vice president in accordance with the CPA, which appointed a southerner to the second-ranking post. He was a man of the bush and of armed struggle, yet he was prepared to try to lead his people as a politician. He was warm and charismatic and deeply grateful for what the United States had done for the people of Sudan. His death in a helicopter crash in late July, only six months after the signing of the CPA, left the South without one of its seminal leaders and made the process of ending the Darfur tragedy and finding justice for the Sudanese people a much harder task.

After meeting Garang we entered the Presidential Palace to meet with the president of Sudan, Omar al-Bashir. In March the UN Security Council had referred the situation in Darfur to the prosecutor of the International Criminal Court. U.S. support for the action had been a source of intense debate within the administration since the United States is not a state party to the treaty. Though his administration had signed it, President Clinton did not recommend the treaty to the Senate and advised his successor to do the same until the United States' concerns were fully addressed. President Bush strongly opposed the ICC on the grounds, among others, that its prosecutor is not accountable to any government. For us this was an issue of sovereignty and a step that looked a bit too much like "world government."

Yet when the genocide issue of Darfur reached the Security Council, I did not want the United States to let the perpetrators off the hook just to make an ideological point about the construction of the court or the Rome statute. After much back-and-forth and strong dissent from John Bolton, I talked to the President and we agreed that the United States would abstain from voting on, not veto, the resolution. Darfur was referred to the ICC on March 31, 2005.

So I was about to meet the man who had overseen the genocide in Darfur and who would later be indicted by the International Criminal Court for three counts of genocide, five crimes against humanity, and two counts of murder. Jendayi Frazer, our assistant secretary of state for African affairs, had warned me that Bashir spoke English but retreated into Arabic when he wanted to be difficult. As I shook his hand, reminding myself not to smile, I looked behind me and noticed that with the exception of my personal assistant, Liz Lineberry, and my personal security detail, I was alone in the room. Bashir's security thugs had held up my delegation, including the ambassador. I was furious and refused to talk to Bashir until my delegation assembled. So we just sat there staring at each other. I loathed him, and I'm sure he felt the same about me.

Finally Sudanese security men dressed in dark suits and wearing sunglasses burst through the doors, shoving my aides along in front of them. I took a deep breath and delivered the message that we expected the Sudanese government to stop the violence against civilians and cooperate with the United Nations, but I could barely concentrate on what I was saying. Bashir spoke slowly, moving his head back and forth, from side to side. He looked as though he was on drugs. It was a truly weird scene.

A few minutes later the American press was shoved through the door, where a scuffle ensued but outside of my line of vision. When I got onto the plane, I learned that my press corps had been roughed up. Andrea Mitchell had been manhandled and pulled out of the room when she asked Bashir a question. I got the U.S. ambassador on the phone and told him to go back to Bashir and tell him to apologize or he'd never see me again nor any other U.S. diplomat. He'd just made the U.S. secretary of state his enemy, and that couldn't be good for him. By the time we landed, the Sudanese foreign minister had apologized.

But that was only one strange experience. As I left Darfur, I was expected to see the wali, or governor, of the province of Darfur. My visit to a refugee camp wouldn't leave time for a meeting, though. And frankly, this wali was such a bad guy that we didn't want to legitimize him. Anyway, as I headed toward the plane I encountered commotion and confusion. Mike Evanoff, the head of my security detail, came over and said that the wali was insisting that we meet in a reception room inside the airport.

"Okay," I said, "it will only take a minute."

"But we haven't swept that room," Mike pleaded.

"Well, I'll have to take my chances," I said.

We walked into the room and confronted a bizarre gathering of at least fifty men in white robes yelling "Allahu akbar!" at the top of their lungs and banging long walking sticks on the floor. The noise was deafening, and Mike was tightening up beside me. "Just keep walking," I said. He drew closer to me, so close that I was finding it hard to move. The wali came over, and we sat down side by side. "I have gifts for you," he said through a translator. There on the floor were boxes too numerous to count. Mike must have been thinking that one of them had to be a bomb. I finished the encounter as quickly as I could and headed for my motorcade. We'd avoided a diplomatic incident, but not without some risk.

Nothing had prepared me, though, for the most disturbing scenes of my trip to Sudan. After I arrived in Darfur, we boarded the motorcade and started out into the dusty desert of Darfur to the location of the Abu Shouk refugee camp. As we approached, there were children lining the road holding huge homemade signs that said "Welcome, Secretary Rice." "Hello Miss Condi." "Thank you America." Soon we were at the camp, and as I got out of the car, kids came from all directions trying to touch me and hug me. There were so many of them. I reached out to a few and then walked toward a makeshift meeting tent. On one side was a "kindergarten" with three- and four-year-olds happily playing in the dirt as relief workers acting as teachers led the older kids through their lessons. All I could think was, *My God, I pray that these kids won't grow up here.*

We walked past a group of women learning to make pasta noodles in the hope that they could export them. But the flies that covered the food suggested that it would fail to pass even minimal food safety inspection. I didn't say anything; I just joined everyone else in marveling at the workers' industriousness.

Then at last I was led into a tent with a few women relief workers and about ten female victims of rape. Each woman tried to tell her story, slowly, deliberately, stopping to gather her thoughts and then plunging ahead. A few finished, but most did not. "I went to get some water one morning, and some soldiers came up to me on the road," one victim began. "They pulled me by my hair for a long time. I kept begging them to stop. They threw me into a tent." She stopped. She didn't have to say more about what had happened. The relief worker got up and put her arm around the woman, who started to sob.

I have never, ever felt raw emotion and pain like that, and I didn't know what to say to them. Everything that might come out of my mouth seemed either irrelevant or unresponsive to their grief. Finally, I just said, "I'm sorry. I am so sorry."

I left Darfur so incredibly sad, full of regret, and deeply offended by what I had seen. How could the so-called international community tolerate that kind of misery and barbarity? I reminded myself of the United States' long heritage of compassion, of providing AIDS relief and food assistance and caring for refugees. As I got into the car, I turned to the USAID administrator, Andrew Natsios, and asked what we could do to help the women. A religious man, Andrew has served the world's dispossessed for most of his professional life. In 2006, he served as U.S. special envoy for Sudan and was later succeeded by Richard Williamson. Andrew quickly put into place a unique multi-pronged program to address sexual violence in Darfur. One of its most important contributions was that it overturned the notion that adjudication of such cases could happen only after a conflict ended. With a few convictions (including a police officer and a military officer) the program was able to help survivors combat impunity at the community level. After experiencing the tragedy and circumstances of Darfur, my respect for those angels of mercy—relief workers in the hardest of circumstances—grew. It was important to honor their sacrifices and to do my best to help them in their work.

Those efforts included combating sexual violence on a global scale. As I left Darfur I reflected on whether we could do more to punish those who violated people in this way since, at the time, the international community had not criminalized rape as a weapon of warfare. My initial efforts included developing the Women Leaders' Working Group. On September 23, 2006, I invited some nineteen women leaders (including the president of Liberia) for the group's inaugural breakfast meeting. I created the group to promote women's empowerment and to address issues of great importance to women: education, political and economic development, and access to justice. By the time of the last meeting in September 2008, the group had grown to nearly sixty.

Ambassador Shirin Tahir-Kheli spearheaded the effort to highlight issues of justice and the empowerment of women. Shirin had been with me at the National Security Council, where she had worked with the First Lady's staff to commission a state-of-the-art children's hospital in Basra. Childhood mortality rates in southern Iraq had been persistently higher than in other countries, with cancer rates among children estimated to be eight to ten times higher in Iraq than those in the West. The planned facility in Basra, which would provide much-needed oncology, medical, and surgical care to thousands of children, would become the first new hospital to be constructed in Iraq since the 1980s. Laura Bush and I became the hospital's sponsors, drawing support from numerous nongovernmental organizations such as Project HOPE and individual and corporate donors organized by the Kuwaiti

Embassy in Washington. With the support of the State Department and the U.S. Army Corps of Engineers, the Basra Children's Hospital opened its doors in 2010, reflecting not only the successful leadership of the burgeoning Iraqi Ministry of Health but also the commitment of Iraqi nurses, doctors, and medical professionals who fill its halls.

Shirin and I shared a view that efforts of this kind were the best form of diplomatic outreach, reflecting the compassion of the United States. And in championing the empowerment of women we were also building a powerful tool against poverty and injustice. If you want to do something about overpopulation, educate women and they will be less likely to have their first child at twelve or give birth to ten offspring. If you want to do something about human trafficking, educate women and they will be less likely to end up in brothels in Southeast Asia, Eastern Europe, and—yes—even the United States. If you want to do something about poverty, give women a microloan and they can build small enterprises in their villages that will employ people and spread prosperity. Societies that treat women badly are dangerous societies. The empowerment of women is not only morally right, it is also practical in the positive impact it has on so many social ills.

The most dramatic cases of injustice toward women related, as in Darfur, to those caught up in conflict and war. In time, the women foreign ministers confronted the United Nations and the world with the view that rape was being used as a weapon of war; it was not just a consequence of it. It is a deliberate strategy to humiliate adversaries who cannot protect their women from degradation. Alarmingly, it isn't always rebels or soldiers who commit rape; many UN peacekeepers had been accused of the same thing. Before our efforts the United Nations had been slow to shine a light on its own transgressions.

The work culminated on June 19, 2008, when I chaired a Security Council thematic discussion on sexual violence during armed conflicts, and I used the U.S. presidency of the Security Council to pass Resolution 1820. The resolution declared rape a weapon of war, criminalizing sexual violence in warfare and making the acts punishable under war crimes statutes.

Finally, my experience in Darfur gave me a renewed appreciation of the role the United States has played in advocating on behalf of and resettling refugees caught in the horrors of war and conflict. George Washington promised that "the bosom of America is open to receive . . . the oppressed and persecuted of all nations and religions." And it has, assisting in the resettlement of tens of thousands of refugees each year.

For instance, after the President determines how many thousands of refugees the United States will admit the following year, the secretary of state personally takes the President's directive to Congress and reports on the number of refugees the administration expects to admit. When I first learned of the obligation, I couldn't understand why, unlike many other tasks, this one could not also be delegated. But after my experience in Darfur I gladly and humbly went to work with longtime refugee proponents such as the late Senator Edward Kennedy, who advocated on behalf of displaced people for more than thirty years. I also came to appreciate the efforts of others in Congress such as Representatives Zoe Lofgren of California and Christopher Smith of New Jersey and of celebrities such as Angelina Jolie, who during my term served as the UN ambassador for refugee affairs. Like Bono on matters of Africa, Angelina brought not just celebrity to the cause but real knowledge and passion.

Like almost everything else, September 11 had a significant impact on this issue. In order to more comprehensively pursue terrorists, the REAL ID Act of 2005 expanded the legal definition of terrorist organizations and barred admission to the United States to anyone who was found to have given material support to terrorist groups. Fortunately, the act permitted the secretary of state, in consultation with the Department of Homeland Security and the attorney general, to conclude that the material-support criterion does not apply to a certain person or group and to issue a waiver. I issued the first waver in May 2006 in order to admit Burmese Karen refugees living in the Tham Hin camp on the border of Thailand. The Karen are a religious and largely peaceful ethnic minority in Burma who have fought for independence from the country's illegitimate government. They have been persecuted, slaughtered, and driven out of their homeland and into refugee camps on the border of Thailand. Given their past support for efforts against the oppressive military junta, many of the Karen had been denied U.S. immigration visas. Eventually the Karen people found their voice through various representatives in Congress. A few months after I issued the Karen waiver, I would announce that we planned to issue waivers to several other groups of refugees. I later heard the life stories of those who had been released from the squalid, miserable camps near Burma in order to start a new life in the United States, and I was proud of what we had done. It has left me to wonder, though, about the countless refugees around the world who are not as fortunate as to have powerful advocates within our system.

The refugee issue was also significantly complicated by the growing number of displaced people from Iraq—an initial trickle that would become a flood as the security situation deteriorated in 2006. Though I knew that opponents of the war were using the issue to embarrass us, they had a point. The United States had a special obligation to the displaced, particularly to those who had worked for us and were being pursued by insurgents.

I had many unhappy conversations with the Iraqi leadership about economic support for displaced people who wanted to leave the country. The proud Iraqis couldn't bring themselves to sympathize with those who wanted to emigrate when they were needed at home. During one encounter with Prime Minister Nouri al-Maliki, he asked in a voice tinged with emotion how he could help some people leave while encouraging others to stay and fight for their country. It was indeed a balancing act, one of those issues of principle that defied simple and consistent application.

In 2007 I appointed James B. Foley to a new position as senior coordinator for Iraqi refugees. The new senior coordinator would manage assistance, guide decisions about particular cases, and work with Iraq's neighbors to help our efforts.

The challenge was particularly evident in Syria, where the majority of the Iraqis had been absorbed. I had to appeal personally to the President to permit James Foley to visit and work with Syria. No one was keen on working with Bashar al-Assad and giving the Syrian dictator a chance to crow about the stream of Iraqis leaving their country in the wake of our overthrow of Saddam Hussein. But even despite our efforts, as in so many cases, the Syrian regime was not cooperative.

27

KATRINA

I'D BEEN TO FORTY-SIX COUNTRIES and traveled 171,628 miles in nine months. I just wanted a vacation and took my annual trip to the Greenbrier, but it wasn't much of a vacation, given the Israeli withdrawal from Gaza, which kept me on the phone day and night. I did, though, pick up a golf club seriously for the first time that summer when my cousin's husband, a very good golfer, insisted that Lativia and I learn to play. I loved it, especially just being outside, and vowed to keep the ball moving forward while I was in Washington. *Really* learning to play would have to await my return to California. Fortunately, I would find Alan Burton, the pro at Andrews Air Force Base, who'd help me learn the game far faster than I ever thought possible. I'll always remember that August for discovering a new passion, not for the vacation, which signaled how hard it would be to get away as secretary of state.

Since any opportunity to break away from the daily grind was appealing, when friends asked if I'd like to join them in New York for the US Open tennis championships the last few days in August, I readily agreed. As I'd done a couple of years before, I planned to spend a few days in New York City, take in a show, shop, and then go out to Arthur Ashe Stadium for the championships. Mariann Byerwalter and Randy Bean, two of my closest friends from California, were coming out to join me.

I didn't think much about the dire warnings of an approaching hurricane called Katrina. My under secretary for management, Henrietta Fore, was on top of the State Department issues. The State Department had a passport office in New Orleans, and we made backup arrangements for our people in Houston. I attended a Homeland Security principals meeting on Thursday, August 30, and returned to the State Department to check once more on plans for securing our offices in the Gulf of Mexico. Then I flew to New York.

That evening, upon arriving at the Palace Hotel, I flipped on the television. Indeed, the hurricane had hit New Orleans. I called Henrietta, who said that the main issue was making sure our people were safe. She'd also convened a departmental task force because offers of foreign assistance were pouring in. I called Secretary of Homeland Security Mike Chertoff, inquiring if there was anything I could do. "It's pretty bad," he said. We discussed the question of foreign help briefly, but Mike was clearly in a hurry. He said he'd call if he needed me. I hung up, got dressed, and went to see *Spamalot*.

The next morning, I went shopping at the Ferragamo shoe store down the block from my hotel, returned to the Palace to await Randy and Mariann's arrival, and again turned on the television. The airwaves were filled with devastating pictures from New Orleans. And the faces of most of the people in distress were black. I knew right away that I should never have left Washington. I called my chief of staff, Brian Gunderson. "I'm coming home," I said.

"Yeah. You'd better do that," he answered.

Then I called the President. "Mr. President, I'm coming back. I don't know how much I can do, but we clearly have a race problem," I said.

"Yeah. Why don't you come on back?" he answered.

I actually hadn't expected that from the President. *That's odd,* I thought. *He'd been so insistent that I go and get some rest. He's really worried.* "Maybe I can go to Houston to represent you," I said.

"Well, just come on back, and we can talk about it then," he replied.

A few minutes later, my senior advisor, Jim Wilkinson, walked into my suite. "Boss, I should have seen this coming," he said. He showed me the day's *Drudge Report* headline on the Web: "Eyewitness: Sec of State Condi Rice laughs it up at 'Spamalot' while Gulf Coast lays in tatter." "Get a plane up here to take me home," I said. I called Mariann and Randy and apologized and then sat there kicking myself for having been so tone-deaf. I wasn't just the secretary of state with responsibility for foreign affairs; I was the highest-ranking black in the administration and a key advisor to the President. What had I been thinking?

When we landed in Washington, I went directly to the State Department, where Henrietta had convened the members of the task force. We needed to be gracious in accepting the many offers that were coming in from around the world, touching expressions of concern such as the $100,000 donation from Afghanistan. Self-sufficiency was one thing; haughtiness was quite another.

When we were asked by the press about aid from foreign countries, Sean McCormack, the State Department spokesman, responded, "Secretary Rice, after consulting with the White House, has made it clear that we will accept all offers of foreign assistance. Anything that can be of help to alleviate the difficult situation, the tragic situation of the people of the area affected by Hurricane Katrina will be accepted." Forty-four countries would eventually send aid, some of it useful and some of it not. But the principle was the important thing; the United States of America would not close its doors to the generosity and good wishes gushing forth from around the world.

On the Friday morning after my return to Washington, the President convened the National Security Council. It reminded me just a little of the days in the aftermath of 9/11. The President was clearly distressed by the inability of the federal government to deal with the unfolding chaos. We focused on the horrible scene at the Superdome, where order had completely broken down. The Defense Department seemed uncertain of the laws concerning the Posse Comitatus Act of 1878, which did not allow active-duty military to carry out law enforcement within the United States.

Don opined that the American people would be shocked to see the military in the street and might react badly. I'd been silent in the meeting but now decided to speak up. "Mr. President, the American people want to see something different in the streets. They need to believe that their government is on top of this. They'll welcome the sight of the military." Josh Bolten, now chief of staff, supported the point. Indeed, the face of the reestablishment of order would become Lieutenant General Russel Honoré, a native of Louisiana, who took command of military relief efforts under Joint Task Force Katrina. It was a godsend that he was also black.

The President still had a serious race issue, however. Many self-described black leaders were accusing him of all manner of venality and prejudice because of the impact the hurricane had on the African American population. People who had means, including several of my friends and relatives of friends, had evacuated as the hurricane approached. Those left behind were the least capable of helping themselves. It was a sad picture with an overwhelmingly black face.

I asked the President if we could speak alone after the meeting, and I proposed two things. I would go see the displaced in Houston (the travel of a high-ranking official to New Orleans might disrupt the relief efforts) to show the flag for the administration as well as to express my personal concern for the people affected. I would also reach out to the new president of the NAACP, Bruce Gordon, and suggest a meeting between the President and him. Bruce could not have been more gracious and, despite some criticism, made the trip to the White House to sit down with the President. Later, the administration would also reach out to Donna Brazile, an influential Democratic activist, who was a native of New Orleans and who to this day acknowledges the President's generosity toward her hometown.

We ultimately decided that I'd go to Mobile in my home state of Alabama instead of Houston. It was a Sunday, so I'd have to go to church before visiting the victims of the hurricane. I attended the 10:30 A.M. service at the Pilgrim Rest AME Zion Church, a black Methodist church where the preacher had to cut his sermon short due to my presence. I wanted to sink underneath the pew as he repeatedly informed the congregation that he had to move things along because "the secretary has to get out of here in two hours." I wasn't sure how I'd be received, but the parishioners were wonderful, responding with an enthusiastic amen to my entreaty that "The Lord is going to come on time—if we just wait." A minister's daughter has a genetic disposition to know what to say in church.

My visit concluded in Mobile, consoling Southeast Asian shrimpers who'd lost everything. The cases of these immigrants were particularly sad. They had left in the aftermath of the Vietnam War and started new lives, only to see their small businesses wiped out by Katrina.

There's never much opportunity at the time to reflect on a crisis like Katrina. In retrospect, the hurricane's aftermath was the first in a spiral of negative events that would almost engulf the Bush presidency. Clearly the response of the federal government was slower than the President himself wanted it to be, and there were many missteps, both in perception and in reality. I'm still mad at myself for only belatedly understanding my own role and responsibilities in the crisis.

Yet for me the lingering wound of Katrina is that some used the explosive "race card" to paint the President as a prejudiced, uncaring man. It was so unfair, cynical, and irresponsible. At the end of my visit to Mobile, I told the press, "Nobody, especially the President, would have left people unattended on the basis of race." I am to this day appalled that it was necessary to say it.

KATRINA RECEDED into the background as my attention turned to the upcoming UN General Assembly (UNGA) in New York. Every year the world quite literally comes to Manhattan. Heads of government and foreign ministers from almost every country attend at least some part of the two-week event. Though I grumbled each year about having to move into the stately Waldorf-Astoria for fourteen days, there was also considerable benefit in taking up residence there since the crazy schedule began with early breakfasts and ended with very late dinners. The point was to cram as many meetings into the allotted time as possible. At least it saved me some travel. Meetings with heads of state and ministers of small states paid dividends. They left satisfied that they'd seen the U.S. secretary of state, and there was no need for me to visit yet another country. It was a fair trade.

The annual gathering afforded an opportunity for nongovernmental organizations to command the world's attention too. President Bill Clinton launched the Clinton Global Initiative in New York at the same time. The forty-second President called and asked if I would join Prime Minister Blair and King Abdullah II of Jordan in a panel discussion on global issues and poverty. It was a chance to showcase the administration's considerable commitment to development assistance in general and Africa in particular. And I wanted to be responsive to President Clinton. In my years as secretary he was unfailingly supportive of me, calling to offer thoughts on some of our challenges and always checking in before and after foreign travel. He did so without fanfare; I never saw a reference to those calls in the media unless the two of us agreed that it would be useful to publicize our contact.

The UN General Assembly also allowed me to gather foreign ministers together in regional or functional groupings. Over the years I would meet the P5+1, which had responsibility for Iran; the ASEAN foreign ministers; the Haiti contact group—well, you get the picture. At this first UNGA, I met the members of the Gulf Cooperation Council (GCC). Everyone read talking points, and despite the unfolding events in the Middle East, absolutely nothing interesting was said. I resolved at that moment to change the dynamics of the group, suggesting that the next time we should invite Jordan, Egypt, and Iraq. They weren't quite ready for the Iraqis, but our meetings would evolve significantly and the GCC would become critical to coordination with our allies in the Middle East.

That September, the other major breaking news was the resumption of the Six-Party Talks on September 13. Surprisingly, by the time we arrived in New York the Six-Party delegates in Beijing were making real progress. Chris Hill, our assistant secretary of state for East Asian and Pacific affairs, called late on the evening of the eighteenth to say that he was close to getting agreement on the Joint Statement that would set a framework for the denuclearization of the Korean peninsula. When the talks stalled, I took advantage of the presence of the foreign ministers in New York to call together the other four participants in the talks, Russia, China, South Korea, and Japan. The Chinese liked to say that they were just convening the talks, meaning that they had no responsibility for making them succeed.

Then, in the presence of his counterparts, Li Zhaoxing was considerably more accepting of China's responsibilities. He sent a message back to Beijing and apparently to the North Koreans. The delegates made further progress. But at midnight Chris called to say that the North Koreans were demanding the construction of a new light-water reactor before abandoning its nuclear weapons program. I called Minister Li, waking the poor jet-lagged man out of a deep sleep, and negotiated new language sitting on my bed in the Waldorf. It was one time I was very glad to have the President's confidence (and the flexibility that

that afforded me). We decided that the Chinese would offer a compromise proposal allowing the North Koreans to keep the nonthreatening elements of their current infrastructure that were clearly related to peaceful nuclear energy purposes. The statement would mention—only mention—the possibility of the North receiving a light-water reactor at some point, but only after it satisfactorily (meaning satisfying the United States) abandoned its nuclear weapons efforts.

I called Steve Hadley and told him about the compromise, which represented a significant shift in U.S. policy. We had always refused to discuss, even mention, a light-water reactor. Though it cannot theoretically be used to build nuclear weapons, there was concern that the North might be able to adapt it to that use.

"I'll tell the President about the proposal in the morning and call you if there's a problem," he said.

"Steve, there can't be a problem," I said. "I've committed us to the language."

I could hear Steve swallow hard. "Okay," he said. Steve had my back on that one.

The next morning the headlines stated, "North Korea Says It Will Abandon Nuclear Efforts" and "North Korea Vows to Quit Arms Program; Nuclear Agreement Set at 6-Nation Talks." Unfortunately, the North Korean issue would soon settle into a kind of predictable pattern: cooperation from Pyongyang and progress in negotiations followed by misdeeds and stalemate. In November, the talks stalled once again, and they would lie fallow for more than a year as North Korea probed for division among the parties and an opportunity to walk back past agreements. Still, the Joint Statement from September was a breakthrough document that would govern the Six-Party Talks for the next three years. And within a couple of days the Iranians signaled to the Europeans that they wanted to restart talks. Good things on the proliferation front often seemed to come in pairs.

AFTER TWO WEEKS at the UNGA, I returned to the road with a trip to troubled Haiti. Colin's visit ten months before had been accompanied by violence and gunfights, and my own visit could be equally risky. But

I knew that it was important for the administration to show its support for the struggling political process of the Western Hemisphere's poorest country. Haiti's elections were scheduled for November (they would be delayed until February of the next year), and I went to the country to encourage the National Election Commission to finalize its work on the rules to ensure fairness.

Driving into Port-au-Prince, I was struck by the extreme poverty—and I'd been in some pretty terrible places. The nature of poverty in the developing world is different than it is in pockets of the developed world; I always noticed in particular that the children weren't playing. In Haiti, as in other impoverished, underdeveloped countries I'd visited, the children were just standing around. It was as if the seriousness of their surroundings—the poverty and violence—had robbed them of their youth.

The commission members sitting in the dilapidated Presidential Palace said all the right things about elections and governance, but there was a surreal character to the whole encounter. Despite all of Haiti's best efforts, the country has been locked in a cycle of intractable poverty, conflict, and natural disasters. No matter how hard they, and the international community, try to transform the country, instability plagues the people of Haiti. I went back to Washington determined to focus my personal attention on the country and began holding periodic teleconferences with the members of the contact group for Haiti.

A contact group is a diplomatic device to unite key countries to handle a crisis or to support a nation in crisis such as Haiti. The group comprised Brazil, which was commanding the UN peacekeeping force; Canada, which was responsible for training the police; the United States; France; the UN Special Representative for Haiti; and the Organization of American States (OAS). We worked together seamlessly, and Haiti was finally able to hold its first presidential elections since Jean-Bertrand Aristide was ousted from office two years before. While there was some balloting contestation and a few protests, the elections were marked by high turnout and much lower violence than had been expected. Three months later René Préval was sworn into office. It was one of those small diplomatic successes that rarely grabs headlines but would have garnered much attention had it failed.

Unfortunately, the country was unable to capitalize on that rare moment of success. Haiti remains unstable and poor, having experienced repeated setbacks, most recently in the devastating earthquake of 2010.

But as troubled as Haiti was (and is), working in the rest of the Americas, through the OAS, was both challenging and rewarding. In June, the OAS met for the first time in the United States in thirty-one years, and I noted that of the twenty-three member states in 1974, ten had been military dictatorships. By contrast, the majority of the Latin American countries in the OAS now firmly believe that political and economic liberty is the only road to success. Furthermore, the central divide in the region was not between "Left" and "Right" but between freedom and tyranny.

Early on, I'd backed the election of José Miguel Insulza, a Chilean diplomat, to the post of secretary-general of the OAS. The United States had earlier refused to support Insulza because he was thought to be a bit too leftist. Instead, Washington had encouraged a Mexican, Luis Ernesto Derbez, to challenge Insulza. But the Chilean had the backing of most of the region, and our continuing to oppose him would have been an embarrassment for our friends in Santiago, particularly President Ricardo Lagos, who'd championed his candidacy.

At the April meeting of the Community of Democracies in Santiago, Chile, I changed our position and negotiated a solution, with the unhappy Derbez withdrawing and Insulza being elected by acclamation. I asked my good friend the capable and strong foreign minister of Colombia, Carolina Barco, to make the announcement.

I tell this story because it illustrates several perennials of diplomacy relating to events offstage that take enormous effort and are rarely reported. First, the lobbying for international diplomatic positions is intense, with countries putting forth candidates who then organize sophisticated campaigns. The United States has to be careful to throw its weight at the right time: too soon, and the person is branded as "Washington's guy"; too late, and the logrolling might bring someone to office that is unacceptable. Second, other countries appreciate a U.S. approach to those elections that isn't heavy-handed: the decision to switch to Insulza would buy goodwill for me as the incoming secretary. Third, the gratitude doesn't last very long. Though I liked José

Miguel personally and we maintained good relations, he was extremely cautious about his left flank. That made it difficult to mobilize the OAS on troublesome places such as Venezuela and Cuba. The principles of the OAS Democratic Charter were too often forgotten amid a mushy consensus and reflexive silence about dictators in the region. But the organization was at least neutral rather than supportive of the region's bad boys, and on issues such as Haiti it played a very useful role.

By the way, the OAS General Assembly in Fort Lauderdale also led to an embarrassing moment as secretary. As the U.S. secretary of state, I was the chair of the event, but due to multiple crises in Washington I had to leave the meeting early. At lunch I thanked the delegates for their attendance and said that I was sorry to leave but I had to "return to the United States." The laughter in the room confused me until Carolina told me what I'd said. When you travel as much as I did, sometimes you forget where you are.

28

Bringing Back the All-Nighter

A SHORT TIME LATER I traveled to Central Asia, where I secured long-term rights to an air base in Kyrgyzstan. The negotiations were tense, with Kyrgyz President Kurmanbek Bakiyev trying to put off the decision yet again. I sat in his office while he negotiated with his team. When he returned to me, he said he needed more time on the details. Since we had a big foreign assistance package—dressed up as more money for basing rights—on the table, I told him there was no more time. It was now or not at all. It was a bit of brinksmanship because we needed the base. But it worked, and we announced the agreement before I left.

Unfortunately, my visits to Central Asia were always briefer than warranted by the importance of the region. I had recognized the geographic significance of these countries at the time of the invasion of Afghanistan. They were key, too, because of their strategic location in terms of energy resources and their vast transportation networks for oil and natural gas. Kazakhstan, in particular, was an energy-producing giant—a place that I had first visited as a Chevron director in the early 1990s. Its president, Nursultan Nazarbayev, was one of the region's strongmen but a modernizer who we hoped might take an interest in regional economic development. Leading a state that bordered Russia and China, Nazarbayev was cautious but desired a relationship with us to help him maintain "balanced independence," as he once told me. The region deserved more attention than I could give it but we enjoyed relatively good relations with its leaders, with the exception of Uzbekistan's Islam Karimov.

AFTER THAT BRIEF TRIP to Central Asia, I stopped in Paris and Moscow before heading to London. When I landed in the British capital, I called home to get a briefing on the polling concerning the October 15 ballot measure on the Constitution of Iraq. Sunni Arab opponents had been working to rally enough voters to defeat the referendum, knowing that the passage of the document in majority Shia and Kurdish territories and its failure in predominantly Sunni areas would have been disastrous. Fortunately, as I went out to Chequers to meet Tony Blair the next day, word came that the Constitution had been adopted. More than 78 percent of Iraqi voters had approved the referendum, sending a firm signal about those citizens' yearning for democratic governance as enshrined in their newly adopted charter. Of the more than 21 percent that opposed the referendum, however, most were Sunni Arabs; in the predominantly Sunni Al Anbar province, for example, about 96 percent of voters rejected it. Though we were both relieved, the British prime minister and I sat over lunch on a peaceful and lovely fall day and reflected on what the vote meant for the work ahead: the Sunnis weren't yet fully on board, and that portended trouble.

In fact, although the Freedom Agenda had progressed significantly, the end of the year brought several reminders of the treacherous road ahead. The first UN report on the assassination of former Lebanese Prime Minister Rafik Hariri pointed to the involvement of high-ranking Syrian and Lebanese security officials. Though the current Lebanese government of Fouad Siniora had responded bravely, promising to cooperate with the investigation and punish the perpetrators, the screams of indignation and veiled threats by Hezbollah reminded us all that the moderate March 14 political alliance was not fully in control of the country.

Then an awful event in Jordan reminded us that the war on terror was still very much with us. On November 9, 2005, suicide bombers struck three hotels in Amman in what appeared to be coordinated attacks, hitting the Grand Hyatt, the Radisson SAS Hotel, and the Days Inn. While targeting American hotel franchises might have been intended as a message to us, the victims, as they often are, were Muslims. In fact, according to a report from the Combating Terrorism Center at West Point, the vast majority of al Qaeda's victims are Muslims: from 2006 to 2008, a striking 98 percent of them were inhabitants of countries with Muslim majorities.

A wedding reception with several hundred guests had just begun at the Radisson when two suicide bombers entered the building and one detonated his vest in the ballroom. His wife's vest failed to explode, and she was later detained by the Jordanian police forces. Another blast had hit the lobby of the Grand Hyatt, and a third hit the Days Inn. The attacks, which were suspected of being coordinated by Abu Musab al-Zarqawi in Iraq (given his resentment of the Jordanian monarchy), killed more than fifty-seven people and left more than a hundred wounded.

I'D ALREADY PLANNED to return to the Middle East one more time before the end of the year. The withdrawal from Gaza was complete, but another major issue had arisen between the Israelis and Palestinians. Since the President's 2002 Rose Garden speech, we'd argued that the composition of the Palestinian state would be as important as its borders. It needed to be democratic, decent, and capable of delivering for its people. In Salam Fayyad, now the prime minister of the Palestinian Authority, we'd found a leader who believed the same. Salam would often say that he intended to build the state even under occupation. Helping him do so, we believed, would accelerate progress toward an end to the conflict. The Israelis would finally have to admit that they had a partner for peace.

To support this goal, the President exercised a congressionally authorized waiver to channel $50 million in direct assistance to the Palestinian Authority. Though the United States has offered assistance to the PA since the Oslo Accords were signed in 1993, in 2005 we significantly increased economic aid through supplemental appropriations and reprogramming. Convincing congressional appropriators and Israel's friends on the Hill that it was safe to do so took some effort. Our support extended to building security forces appropriate for a democratic state—in other words, unraveling the gangs that had served Arafat in the name of security and professionalizing the forces. Within two years we would offer assistance in the form of direct budgetary support to the Palestinian Authority. This would be a breakthrough and a signal of trust since it allowed the Palestinians to spend the money as they saw fit rather than tying it to specific programs.

With the Israeli withdrawal having set a tone of conciliation, it seemed time to press for a breakthrough. The opportunity came in the form of an agreement between the parties to reopen the border crossing at Rafah between Egypt and Gaza. With no Israeli presence, there was justifiable concern about terrorism in what was already proving to be ungovernable territory in Gaza. Yet the crossing was critical for the Palestinians to be able to move their goods.

I was not going to leave Jerusalem without an agreement on movement and access for Palestinians and their goods. In 1979 Israel and Egypt had signed a peace treaty that included the establishment of a buffer zone between Egypt and Gaza, a strip of land known as the Philadelphi Corridor. Rafah, the only checkpoint not located on the Israeli border, was a high-traffic smuggling route for illicit goods and weapons. Security at the Rafah crossing was handled jointly by Israel and Egypt, though the Israelis worried that the Egyptians could not or would not confront the smuggling. It was a difficult dilemma: the crossings had to be effective enough for people to be able to get perishable goods across the border before they spoiled, for instance, but thorough enough to keep weapons out. After Israel's withdrawal from Gaza, new rules were needed to govern the crossing, which had been closed for two months. We had to get a movement and access deal accomplished so that the Rafah crossing could be securely opened.

David Welch went ahead of me to begin the negotiations, but when I arrived at the airport, little progress had been made. On the way to Ramallah I called Defense Minister Shaul Mofaz and Dubi Weisglass. "We're going to get this done," I said. "Send somebody to meet with David who can speak for the prime minister." I then visited President Abbas and asked who would represent him. He said that Mohammed Dahlan, the chief of security, was already in Jerusalem.

After my meeting with Abbas, I called David from the car to see how it was going. "Not well," he said. When I got to the David Citadel Hotel, I went immediately to the room where the negotiations were being held. The participants were clearly stuck on a number of points. I'd promised to go to Jordan to lay a wreath at the Radisson and pay respects to the king after the bombing. "When I get back, I want this solved," I told David.

In Amman I found it hard to keep my mind on my ceremonial duties. Indeed, the scene at the hotel was horrific, with bits of glass and spots of blood still on the banquet room floor. I went before the cameras to offer condolences to the Jordanian people and signal defiance in the face of continued terrorism. Afterward, I visited briefly with King Abdullah, who was more than happy to cut our meeting short so that I could return to the negotiations.

It was after one in the morning when I arrived back at the David Citadel. The rest of the night I shuttled from room to room; the Palestinians and Israelis were now negotiating in separate sessions with David and Elliott Abrams, the NSC's Middle East expert. The talks almost broke down several times, with Mohammed Dahlan yelling at me, "If I sign this, I'll be a dead man!" when I suggested that the PA would have to hand over the names of suspected terrorists for a watch list to facilitate screening at the crossings. At about four, I decided that everyone was tired. "Go to bed," I told the negotiators, "and we'll start again at seven." David came over and whispered that if the Palestinians went home they'd never get back through the Israeli checkpoints so the meeting could resume in three hours. "Then get rooms for them here," I said. Then I went to bed.

The next morning we started again. We almost had agreement, but some issues had not been resolved. I called Defense Minister Mofaz and asked him to come over. The Israelis, like most people in the Middle East, don't relish doing business in the morning. But he did come, and the agreement was settled.

Javier Solana, the European Union's high representative for foreign affairs (essentially its foreign minister), and Jim Wolfensohn were in Jerusalem, and I asked them to come over and join me for the press conference. Making the agreement stick would require a lot of international support. They needed to share in this rare moment of achievement.

At about ten I went downstairs to face the press. "After difficult negotiations I'm happy to report that we have an agreement on movement and access." There was an audible gasp of approval in the room. Somehow my eye caught that of Robin Wright, a veteran Middle East reporter who'd been a critic of the administration on just about everything. *She knows this is an important moment*, I thought. Then I went on to describe the agreement.

There wasn't much time. I called Dubi and President Abbas to thank them and congratulate them, as well as Ahmed Aboul Gheit, the Egyptian foreign minister. Then I boarded the plane to meet President Bush at the APEC summit in South Korea. Deputy Executive Secretary Carol Perez had worked her travel magic again. Somehow I'd managed to get from Israel to Jordan back to Israel and then on to South Korea in about thirty-six hours. I was a day late, but it had been worth the time. In all the excitement I'd completely forgotten that it was my fifty-first birthday. When I boarded the plane, I received a cake and a card from the press. "Thanks for bringing back the all-nighter," one comment said. The press loved the high drama and pure adrenaline of the eleventh-hour agreement. So did I.

By the time my flight touched down in South Korea, word of the agreement had spread. I didn't have time to brief the President, who was walking into his meetings with the Malaysian and then Indonesian presidents, both from countries with large Muslim populations. "Thank you so much for what you've achieved for Palestine," they said to the President. Teasing me a little after the meeting, the President asked, "What did I do for Palestine, and what did you agree to?" Steve Hadley had, of course, briefed him, but he wanted to know the full story. He laughed as I related the details of the all-night session. "They're going to expect this all the time," he said, referring to the raised hopes in the Middle East. "Then we'll just have to get it done," I said.

It was a good end to an incredible first year as secretary of state. I felt exhilarated as I headed for Christmas break. The team at State was functioning well, and in both perception and reality, we were emphasizing the primacy of diplomacy in U.S. foreign policy. I loved the freedom to speak authoritatively for the United States of America. My relationship with the President was different from before but very good indeed. And the Freedom Agenda seemed to be taking hold across the Middle East. I couldn't wait for 2006 to begin.

29

CAN ANYTHING ELSE GO WRONG?

T HE NEXT YEAR, though, would turn out to be miserable—an almost 180-degree turn from the positive direction of the year before. After those many months of setbacks, the President called on me at the first Cabinet meeting of 2007 to give a brief report on the foreign affairs situation. "Well, Mr. President," I said, "the forces of repression struck back last year. It was a bad year for the forward march of freedom. But we'll bend history's arc back toward justice." It may have been too poetic a response, but it seemed as though we all needed a little bucking up. There were so many nights in 2006 when I remember arriving home at the Watergate after a long, long day and wondering, *Can anything else go wrong?* After a while I stopped asking because the answer seemed always to be, *Yes, it can and it has.*

The year began with a crisis in Europe, underscoring the geopolitics of oil and gas. I realized early in my time in Washington that any New Year's celebration would be brief and involve no travel. Usually I went with my cousin and her husband and a few friends to the "pops" concert at the Kennedy Center, followed by dinner and dancing back at my apartment until very late—say, 1:00 A.M.

As I prepared to leave for the concert, I got word that Vladimir Putin was planning to announce that Russia would cut off the flow of natural gas to Ukraine the next morning. That would not just harm Ukraine but disrupt the supply of gas to Europe. I recalled a conversation between President Bush and German Chancellor Schroeder a few years earlier. Told that the German government was dismantling its remaining nuclear capability, the President had been incredulous, noting that Germany would be even more dependent on Russian gas. Schroeder had not been concerned, calling Russia a "reliable partner." We were all stunned when just a few days after leaving office he became board chairman of a pipeline project connecting Russia to Germany across the Baltic Sea. Now the implications of Germany's dependence on Moscow were clear.

The next day Putin made his announcement, claiming that there were no politics involved, only economics that required Ukraine to finally pay the market price for gas. When I said publicly that Russia was using oil and gas as a weapon, reminding vulnerable states that they shouldn't challenge Moscow, the Kremlin fumed. That led to an angry retort from Russian foreign minister Sergei Lavrov, who accused me of hypocrisy. "You're always talking about the free market," he said, "but when we apply those principles to *your* friends [meaning democratic Ukraine], you aren't so principled." I answered that I had no problem with the free market but that Ukraine needed time to adjust. "And Sergei," I countered, "the next time you want to make an economic argument, don't send your President out on New Year's morning to announce the cutoff."

One would have thought this episode to be enough to spur the Europeans to develop a common energy policy to lessen their dependence on Moscow. But there were simply too many conflicting interests. France was already largely shielded, as it derived 80 percent of its generating power from nuclear energy. The northern-Scandinavian tier was self-sufficient, as was Great Britain. But the East Europeans, who were completely hostage, dependent on Russian pipelines for their supplies, didn't carry a loud enough voice within the European Union. And there were jurisdictional issues between the European Commission, which handled trade policy, and the individual states, which held the reins on economic and energy issues. Trying to seal all those fissures in the cause of making Europe less dependent on Russian energy transportation networks was almost impossible.

Later, I would appoint a senior official, Boyden Gray, who had previously been our ambassador to the EU, to promote a common strategic energy policy with our allies. It was fiendishly difficult but needed: the geopolitics of oil and gas would increasingly warp diplomacy, revealing the timidity of the Europeans—particularly the Germans—toward Moscow. The Kremlin had fired a warning shot that the color revolutions were vulnerable to pressure by playing the "energy card." And we didn't really have a good response.

LATE IN THE DAY on January 4, I was sitting at my desk in the inner office, reviewing some of the cables concerning Moscow's gas cut-off. My dark-paneled office was undeniably gloomy in the winter, with little light penetrating the "security" windows meant to protect me. There had been a flurry of phone calls that day from panicked European foreign ministers, particularly in the Baltics and Hungary, who feared escalating pressure from the Kremlin. I was tired and thought I might just go home early and finish my reading in the comfort of my den.

Suddenly my eye caught a cable news bulletin saying something about Ariel Sharon. Before I could sort it out, Brian Gunderson came in, saying that Dubi Weisglass needed to speak with me urgently. "The prime minister has had a devastating stroke," Dubi started before pausing to gather himself. "I'm on the way to the hospital, but I don't think it looks very good." Sharon had experienced a neurological episode about a month before but had made a considerable recovery. I was about to ask if the two health crises were related but realized that Dubi was just trying to get through the call. He was deeply emotional. Sharon was not just the prime minister but Dubi's closest friend.

I simply said, "I'll pray for him."

"Thanks," he answered. I heard the phone click. Sharon had given me an antique Torah for my birthday the year before. I walked over and picked it up. I said a brief prayer for Sharon and for Israel. Then I called the President. "My God, I hope he survives," I said.

"I know," he answered. "I guess all we can do is pray."

Somehow I felt that only the President and probably Steve felt as I did at that moment. We'd come to see Sharon as crucial to peace, a view that would have been unthinkable in the dark days of 2001, when he had ordered Israeli forces to crush the second Palestinian intifada. He was a member of Israel's warrior generation that had secured the state against Arab armies. As such, he had the credibility to make peace with the Palestinians by dividing the land. After all, who could question Ariel Sharon's commitment to Israel's security?

A few months before, I'd come to understand the importance of the generational divide in Israel. Attending the commemoration of the tenth anniversary of Yitzhak Rabin's assassination, I'd been surprised by Sharon's remarks. Rabin and Sharon were hardly cut from the same political cloth; one was associated with peace, the other with war. So when Sharon called him a "brother whom I loved," it was stunning. In fact, they were "brothers" who had in their own way helped to secure the Jewish democratic state of Israel. Their generation was disappearing and with it the moral authority to make hard decisions about Israel's future.

Only months before his stroke, Sharon had decided to split the Likud party and form Kadima, a party that came to be identified with finalizing Israel's borders. There would be many disagreements within Israel about what those contours would be, but Sharon had shifted the political ground so that most Israelis accepted the "two-state solution." The withdrawal from Gaza had been only the first step. I was confident and so was the President that Sharon was willing to take the remaining ones toward the establishment of Palestine.

The next day Dubi called to say that the prime minister would probably not recover. I closed my eyes for a moment. My mind flashed back to standing with the rotund Sharon, tending his sheep. I recalled his words to me. He'd called a few days before the end of the year to discuss the aftermath of the Gaza withdrawal. "How are your sheep?" I'd asked.

"Missing you," he'd answered. Then he had repeated his earlier invitation, "Come back in the fall—here to the farm. We need to talk about the future." When I opened my eyes, I was surprised that they were filled with tears.

The Israeli Knesset met in emergency session the next day and named Ehud Olmert the acting prime minister. I called Olmert to offer condolences and a promise to stand by Israel as it made the difficult choices that lay ahead. It wasn't the time to talk about what those choices might be, but Olmert immediately reminded me that Sharon had sent him to the United States the year before to outline plans for further "separation" from the Palestinians. I didn't like the sound of that term but thought that it could be shaped to mean a negotiated solution—not a unilateral one—to the Palestinian question. We agreed to talk about it all another day.

In fact, our next conversation would be just four days later to discuss the upcoming Palestinian legislative elections. The Israelis were nervous and so were we about Fatah's ability to carry them out. Olmert expressed concern that the Palestinians might "again" delay the timetable.

A few weeks before the end of the prior year, NSC and State Department officials, including Elliott Abrams from the NSC and David Welch, the assistant secretary for Near Eastern affairs, had gathered in my conference room, along with John Hannah from the vice president's office. Steve Hadley and I had begun organizing Middle East strategy sessions that brought the relevant folks together, the goal being to bridge any divide between the White House and Foggy Bottom on the fast-moving events in the Middle East.

On this day, the subject was the upcoming elections. Should we encourage Abbas to postpone the vote? Would Fatah win? There was some concern that the Palestinian people might punish Fatah for the deep and unaddressed corruption of the party—though Abbas himself was not implicated. After open debate back and forth, Elliott said what we were all thinking. "Fatah isn't going to be in better shape six months from now." We agreed that we should encourage Abbas to keep to the timetable. There was no indication that he wanted to delay the vote in any case. And the Israelis were on board to help with movement and access issues—even in troublesome Gaza—so that the poll would be free and fair as possible.

I relate this story in some detail because a myth has survived that Abbas and the Israelis resisted U.S. pressure to go through with the elections. That simply isn't true. Everyone—Olmert, Abbas, and the U.S. government—was in agreement that the elections should proceed. In retrospect, we should have insisted that every party disarm as a condition for participating in the vote. Arms needed to be held only by the security institutions of the governing body—in this case the Palestinian Authority. We'd proposed this idea to the Quartet at a meeting in November, and all had agreed, even the Russians. I'd asked David and Elliott to call Abbas just to let him know what we were about to say. He demurred, saying that such a statement would be seen as an effort to exclude Hamas. Only the participation of all Palestinians would make the election legitimate, he argued. So everyone was on the

same page: the elections should proceed, and Hamas should participate. But failure is an orphan, and when the results were announced,
the finger-pointing began.

The morning of the January 25 legislative elections, I attended the
President's Daily Briefing at the White House. The intelligence that
morning concerning the polling was unremarkable. Fatah would win
a narrow victory, though the decision to split tickets in some localities made several candidates vulnerable. I checked in periodically with
our diplomats in Jerusalem and Ramallah throughout the day. As I was
preparing to go home, Liz Cheney, the deputy assistant secretary, came
into my office. Liz, the Vice President's daughter, was a fierce proponent
of the Freedom Agenda and sometimes disruptive (helpfully, from my
point of view) to the status quo preferences of the department.

"Some of our people on the ground think Hamas is doing better
than expected," she said.

"Well, that isn't good," I answered and returned to tidying up the
day's chores before heading home. The Operations Center gave me a
final report just before I went to bed. All was as we expected; Fatah was
going to squeak by.

The next morning, I put on my gym clothes and went to exercise,
flipping on the local news as I always did. As WRC-TV News 4's Barbara
Harrison reported on the latest murder in the District the night before, I caught sight of the runner on the screen. "Fatah officials resign
from Palestinian Authority in wake of Hamas victory," it said. *That isn't
right,* I thought, pumping a little faster on the elliptical. My heart was
suddenly beating harder—but not from exercise. Again the runner—
"Fatah officials resign in wake of Hamas victory." I decided I'd better
call the department. "Who won the Palestinian election last night?" I
asked the operations officer.

"Hamas," he answered.

"What?" My mind started racing. *It would have been good if someone
had called to let me know that,* I thought. I was a bit disoriented and
asked, inexplicably, to speak to our ambassador in Lebanon, confusing him momentarily with our consul general in Jerusalem. The ambassador was a little taken aback at my question about the Palestinian
elections but reported that Lebanese officials were in shock. Eventually

reaching both the U.S. ambassador to Israel, Dick Jones, and our consul general, Jake Walles (the senior official who dealt with Palestinian affairs), I got confirmation that, not surprisingly, there was confusion and chaos in the region too. I asked the operations center to set up a phone call with Israeli foreign minister Tzipi Livni, who was in an emergency Cabinet meeting. She would be available in about two hours. It was going to be a long day. There were twenty minutes left in my exercise routine. I decided to finish and take a moment to clear my mind.

When I arrived at the office, I immediately called President Bush. He was calm, having always thought Fatah vulnerable due to its corruption. "What do you think we should do now?" he asked.

"The elections were free and fair," I said.

"So we'll have to accept the result," he responded.

I told him that I'd be in touch with the Israelis, our Arab allies, and the Europeans. There was a little time before we'd have to say something. In fact, I was scheduled to deliver a message by videoconference to the World Economic Forum gathering in Davos very shortly. We agreed that I should restate the U.S. principles, including our refusal to deal with Hamas until it renounced terrorism. A few minutes later I agreed to some language with Steve Hadley and ran it by David Welch and Sean McCormack.

I reached Tzipi Livni. She was worried and sounded a little shell-shocked. "This is a disaster. The world can't recognize Hamas as legitimate." The good thing about Tzipi is that she is a problem solver and we'd developed a relationship of trust. I read the statement to her that we'd prepared and said that it would hold things in place until we could confer with our allies. She hung up to return to the emergency Cabinet session. Israel seemed suddenly isolated and vulnerable, even to me. How could the Palestinian people have elected a group of terrorists devoted to the destruction of the state of Israel?

In fact, the Palestinian people had elected politicians whom they thought less corrupt and more capable than those of Fatah. Hamas had said little about "resistance" in the campaign, focusing instead on its good social works and piety. Indeed, the group maintained a network of orphanages, clinics, and schools, particularly in Gaza. Poor Palestinians welcomed those services, and many identified Hamas with alms.

Still, by all accounts, the Hamas leadership had expected to do well but hadn't expected to win; it was an outcome engendered by Fatah's ineptitude, especially the mistaken electoral strategy of allowing multiple candidates for seats they contested. The Palestinian Authority had also failed to campaign effectively. Jim Wilkinson had gone to Ramallah to advise Abbas on how to mount a vigorous defense of his leadership—even helping the PA to construct a proper press facility so that the still-popular Abbas could communicate with his people. But Abbas refused to campaign, wanting to stay above the fray. Fatah's mistakes handed the election to Hamas. The Middle East had just sustained a significant shock. It was now my job to find a new equilibrium for our policy so that we could push ahead toward Middle East peace.

First we had to accept the outcome of the election: it had been free and fair, even if we didn't like the victor. But it was one thing to acknowledge that Hamas had won and quite another to accept its program. We had a choice: as long as the terrorist organization refused to renounce violence and accept the agreements that the PLO under Arafat had made with Israel, we did not have to give it international legitimacy or foreign assistance. Yet we wanted to continue to assist the Palestinian Authority. Since Hamas had won legislative elections, Abbas, who'd been elected president in his own right the year before, was in fact the executive authority in Palestine and the address for foreign aid. A few days after the elections, he formed a caretaker government under Prime Minister Ahmed Qurei, also known as Abu Alaa, who was well known to us since he was a veteran negotiator in the peace process. As President, Abbas would be responsible for the overall direction of the Palestinian Authority and had the mandate to negotiate on his people's behalf. Qurei would oversee the daily functions of governing. Hamas controlled the legislature but would, for the time being, have no responsibility for either negotiations or the government.

The United States could thereby continue to support the Palestinian Authority, which had renounced violence, pledged adherence to existing agreements with Israel, and affirmed the right of Israel to exist. At our urging, Abbas made a statement reaffirming those pledges to that effect. Now we could make a distinction between Hamas and the Palestinian Authority.

I called a few key legislators and promised that no money would ever go to the terrorist organization. Representatives Eric Cantor of Virginia, Ileana Ros-Lehtinen of Florida, Gary Ackerman of New York, and my venerable friend Tom Lantos of California were always helpful touchstones in making sure we could sustain congressional support. As a safety valve, the President withheld aid for a time until we were certain that we had a secure conduit to the PA that Hamas couldn't access.

It was critical, though, to make the policy multilateral, since European aid to the Palestinians was significantly greater than that of the United States. I asked my colleagues in the Middle East Quartet—the UN, the European Union (represented at the time by Austria), and Russia—to meet on the margins of a scheduled meeting on Afghanistan in London, three days after the elections. The Europeans also classified Hamas as a terrorist organization, and thus the argument to them was simple: you can't fund terrorists.

But Russia had a different policy, recognizing Hamas as a legitimate actor in Palestinian politics and maintaining contact with its leadership in Damascus. Sergei Lavrov and I argued vociferously that night about what the election meant. But he understood that the Israelis would sit on the sidelines and refuse to negotiate if they were forced to accept Hamas as a part of the Palestinian political landscape. The isolation of Hamas was a bitter pill for Moscow but a sacrifice worth making to keep the peace process alive. In general, the Russians were helpful partners concerning the Palestinian-Israeli issue. The end of the Cold War had led to thawed relations—even good relations—between Moscow and Tel Aviv, sustained by the one million Russian Jews who also held Israeli citizenship. Russia agreed to a unified position, and the Quartet stated that future aid to the Palestinian Authority would be weighed against its commitment to nonviolence, recognition of Israel's right to exist, and acceptance of previous agreements and obligations. That was a direct shot at Hamas.

At the end of the evening, Lavrov told me that he would deliver to Hamas our message: "Find a way to accept the Quartet's conditions." In an afterthought he asked, "What will you do if they comply?"

I thought about it for a second. "If they do," I answered, "the United States will have to reconsider its position too." Only the President and

Steve ever knew that the message had been passed. We would have had a difficult decision to make had Hamas accepted the conditions. But it didn't. Several months later I received a rambling letter from Ismail Haniyeh, the putative leader of Hamas. Perhaps it was supposed to be a response to Lavrov's entreaty. But it said nothing about the Quartet's conditions. I let the matter drop and didn't answer. We never heard any reply at all from Khaled Meshal, the real power within Hamas, who was in exile in Syria.

Though the Arabs refused to acknowledge their support for the Quartet's conditions publicly, the Egyptians and Saudis made clear privately that they would tailor their aid so that it could not reach Hamas. We'd achieved the isolation of Hamas. But with that came new problems. Gaza, Hamas's stronghold, would become economically paralyzed, a growing humanitarian concern, and a place of escalating militancy. And the cutoff of aid to Hamas created an opening for Iranian assistance. Though the Palestinians, like all good Arabs, were deeply suspicious of the Persians, a more radical element of Hamas grew closer to Tehran, accepting arms and alms from it and turning Gaza into a terrorist wasteland that would explode repeatedly over the next three years.

A Strategy for the Iranian Problem

THE QUARTET'S CONSENSUS on Hamas was not the only good news of the London trip. The effort to harmonize our policies toward Tehran with those of the Europeans was succeeding. The Europeans (in particular France, Germany, and the United Kingdom) had agreed with us that any further refusal by Iran to negotiate should lead to referral of the case to the UN Security Council (UNSC), requiring the cooperation of the Russians and the Chinese. I was in London for a conference on Afghanistan. The Europeans and I decided to invite Sergei Lavrov and the Chinese foreign minister, Li Zhaoxing, to join us at U.K. foreign secretary Jack Straw's official residence, Carlton Gardens, on the evening of January 30. This group became known as the P5+1—the five permanent members of the UN Security Council plus Germany.

Germany, France, and Great Britain had been negotiating on behalf of the European Union since 2005. Britain and France, along with the United States, Russia, and China were on the Security Council. Germany was, thus, the "plus one," though German foreign minister Frank-Walter Steinmeier preferred the term EU3+3 to camouflage the fact that Germany was not a member of the Security Council. The P5+1 would become the principal international body dealing with the Iranian nuclear problem.

The meeting began with dinner—just the ministers plus one aide each, the restricted participation intended to allow candor and real negotiation. I was accompanied by Nick Burns, the State Department's under secretary for political affairs, who'd earlier met with his counterparts and reported to me that the Russians weren't keen to even mention any kind of enforcement in conjunction with the Iranian case.

Jack, French foreign minister Michel Barnier, Frank-Walter, and I had met for a few minutes before the Russians and Chinese arrived. We wanted the outcome to include a promise to refer the case to the UNSC if Iran balked at negotiations. We all agreed that the Russians were unlikely to accept everything we wanted. But if the meeting broke up in failure, we would embolden Iran. At this early stage, the immediate goal was to unite the international community. We were prepared to take less than a full loaf, if we had to, in order to make the first step toward unity and avoid a break in the ranks.

In fact, the Iranians had gotten wind of the gathering and were "working the phones" around the globe to find out what was going on. That would become a familiar pattern. Before every meeting of the P5+1, Tehran would launch a major diplomatic offensive, holding out a carrot of cooperation with one hand and threatening retaliation with the other. It wasn't very effective. Rather, it usually reminded people, especially the Russians, why Tehran was not to be trusted.

The negotiations didn't get off to a good start. Before the salad course could even be served, Sergei Lavrov stated the unequivocal Russian position that threatening the Iranians wasn't an option. The Iranians, he said, had a right to civil nuclear energy under the Nuclear Non-Proliferation Treaty (NPT), and even though they'd been caught cheating (failing to report enrichment and reprocessing activities to the

International Atomic Energy Agency [IAEA] for *eighteen years*), negotiation, not confrontation, was the way out.

I spoke next, Sergei having talked through most of the main course.
"You of all people should consider an Iranian nuclear weapon unac-
ceptable," I said. "You live in the neighborhood. They can reach the
Caucuses with their medium-range missile force. Do you trust them?"
Lavrov retorted that no one trusted the Iranians, but Russian policy was
to provide civil nuclear power for them by building a plant at Bushehr.
Moscow would run the plant, collect the spent fuel, and return it to
Russia. The Iranians didn't need to enrich and reprocess—he under-
stood that—but we had to give them an alternative for civil nuclear
power and a face-saving way out.

The two of us argued back and forth through dessert, coffee, and
cordials—which everyone refused. At one point, Lavrov accused me of
hypocrisy when I said that the United States wasn't trying to deny Iran
civil nuclear power. Rightly, he noted that the United States had never
accepted the Russian effort at Bushehr. "Would that make a difference
to you?" I asked. He seemed caught off guard by the question and didn't
answer. I let the point go, knowing that the United States was prepared
to drop its objection to the Russian-built plant. We just hadn't said so
forcefully, though we'd publicly softened our opposition. In fact, we
would come to embrace Moscow's approach as an answer to Iran's demands for civilian nuclear energy. That shift in policy would strengthen
our hand with the Russians and make it harder for the Iranians to claim
that we were blocking their pathway to a legitimate program that would
have no military use.

Lavrov and I returned to the main point. "Okay," I said. "You don't
like my idea of referral to the UNSC. What's yours?" This was a reprise
of a conversation that Steve and I had had over dinner with Lavrov late
in 2005. He had told us that he worried that pressure on the Iranians
might drive them out of the NPT altogether. "Then they will expel the
inspectors and we will have no way to monitor the program," he had
said. But when we pressed for an alternative, Lavrov admitted that he
really didn't have one. That had not changed by the time of Jack's dinner in London several months later.

The atmosphere was getting pretty tense, which always made the

Europeans nervous—particularly the Germans. "Now, Sergei and Condi—" Frank-Walter began.

Lavrov cut him off. "Well, your idea in Iraq didn't work out so well," he said.

I felt my blood pressure rising. "This isn't about Iraq, and you know it," I replied.

Jack tried to calm things down. "Let's get back to the statement," he said.

Then there was a breakthrough. "Suppose we adopt two parallel tracks," I offered.

"What do you mean?" Lavrov asked, and then answered his own question. "Do you mean we offer to negotiate and then plan to take action if they don't come clean?"

"Yes," I said.

This back-and-forth between the two of us wasn't unusual in those meetings, particularly when the setting was informal. It was not that the others had no views, or failed to express them. But Lavrov and I were the outliers. The allies—and, early in the process, China—could accept the terms that Russia and the United States could agree to.

The Russian then changed tack, saying that the International Atomic Energy Agency, not the UNSC, was the proper forum to force compliance. That was enough of an opening, and we agreed that the first step would be a referral to the IAEA, but I laid down a marker that a judgment of noncompliance should lead to referral to the UNSC. In an example of how diplomacy works when foreign ministers are empowered, no one had to "phone home" for approval to the language.

The weary Jack Straw faced the press gathered at the entrance of his house and read a brief statement of agreement. The five of us stood stoically behind him. The scene was a bit surreal, with only the camera lights illuminating the very dark doorway. It was 1:30 in the morning, but the P5+1 had reached an agreement on how to proceed.

The President called as I was packing up to leave London. "You're on a roll," he said. "Thanks, Mr. President," I said. I was really tired and looking forward to that nap on the plane. I thought, *It isn't even February.*

We now had a new strategy for the Iran problem. The P5+1 would negotiate to come to a unified position that would be taken to the IAEA. The IAEA Board of Governors would then refer the matter to the Security Council.

The idea of two parallel tracks was also established. This meant that Iran was presented with an offer to talk but a threat of sanctions if they refused negotiations. The United States had levied unilateral sanctions on Iran for many years dating back to the takeover of our embassy in Tehran in 1979. And though we would continue to use the power of our own unilateral penalties, multilateral sanctions—even weaker ones—added to the pressure on Tehran. Once we had a Security Council resolution we also anticipated a "halo effect." Other like-minded countries could use the fact of a UN resolution as cover to gain the support needed to impose their own national penalties. Security Council resolutions also had a way of unsettling international corporations and financial institutions doing business in Iran and slowing investment (even if it did not end). Future investment decisions would have to take into account the fact that no one knew if there was another shoe to drop. The goal was to increase international isolation of Iran and engender change in its behavior. This strategy would persist beyond our time in office.

The outcome of that first P5+1 meeting was only the first step. Shortly after the meeting in London the IAEA Board of Governors referred Iran's case to the UN Security Council. Several weeks later, as the diplomacy continued, a headline saying "World's Top Powers to Display United Front on Iran" seemed to sum up the strategy. Keeping everyone united would be no easy task, and getting the Iranians to respond would be even harder.

30

TRANSFORMATIONAL DIPLOMACY

NOT EVERY ISSUE in the first month of the year related to the Middle East, though it seemed that way. I needed to keep advancing the agenda for transformation of the department, where management challenges were stacking up. In particular, I was determined not to produce a budget through the bottom-up logrolling process that was in place. I decided to give a speech at Georgetown University that laid out the reform agenda for State. The speech was a bit wonkish, but the foreign policy community took note, and that was the point.

Referring to the phrase I'd used at confirmation, I talked about transformational diplomacy, focusing on the need to foster the growth of well-governed democratic states. The point was that the work of diplomats should focus less on political reporting—we really didn't need long cables about British politics since I talked to the Brits every day—and more on deeds. What we needed was an expeditionary foreign service that would work on AIDS relief in Botswana; democracy promotion in Egypt; and women's education in Afghanistan.

We established a number of American presence posts, which would allow us to place a single Foreign Service officer in a foreign city where we did not have (and couldn't afford financially) to establish a consulate. This was in recognition of the increasing importance of regions and cities outside the capital, such as the industrial hub of Pusan in South Korea.

I also made a major push to encourage the study of critical languages. Don Rumsfeld, George Tenet, Margaret Spellings, and I launched a "Critical Languages Initiative" to support the study of Farsi, Chinese, Arabic, and other "hard" languages. I reminded everyone that the National Defense Languages Act had done the same during the Cold War to increase the number of speakers of Russian and

East European languages. The U.S. government needed to do the same for the post-9/11 world.

In my Georgetown speech, I said hundreds of Foreign Service officers would be shifted from Europe to Asia and the Middle East. Anyone seeking promotion to senior rank would need to gain expertise in at least two regions. I acknowledged the growth in hardship posts around the world and gently suggested that working in Vienna and Paris was not the future of the Foreign Service. That would soon lead to a *Time* magazine article highlighting State's new breed of officers, who were dubbed, aptly and affectionately, "the Hellhole Gang." Among those featured were Anne Patterson, our ambassador to Colombia and later Pakistan; David Satterfield, an Iraq advisor who'd also served in Lebanon; David Welch; and others. Ryan Crocker, who'd been serving in Pakistan and would soon head to Iraq, belonged on the list too. The message was clear: the future was in hard places doing hard things.

To help ensure the State Department was thinking innovatively about these initiatives, I appointed an outside advisor committee on transformational diplomacy cochaired by Barry Blechman and former U.S. Ambassador to the United Nations Thomas R. Pickering. To assess the Department's democracy promotion efforts, I convened a similar panel of outside experts led by Anne-Marie Slaughter, then the dean of Princeton's Woodrow Wilson School of International Affairs and later director of policy planning under my successor.

The most controversial aspect of the Georgetown speech, though, was the creation of a new office of director of foreign assistance to unify the budgets and development policies of the U.S. Agency for International Development (USAID) and the State Department. USAID had always considered its mission to be separate from and yet equal to that of State. Development was thought to be a long-term process and—theoretically—free of political and strategic motivations: a kind of U.S. largesse at the taxpayers' expense.

In many countries, Britain for example, the two agencies were completely separate. This led to bizarre circumstances in places such as Afghanistan, where the British foreign secretary could not direct foreign assistance to support the war effort. Thankfully, in the United

States, USAID was not a stand-alone agency, its budget being determined by and defended before Congress by the secretary of state. But there was still a kind of uneasy tension in which the USAID administrator reported through the secretary of state, though precisely what that meant was left a bit fuzzy. I made clear that USAID needed to keep its institutional integrity but had to be subject to the secretary's direction.

The problem was that the cultures of State and USAID were very different, the latter eschewing the idea that it was involved in "U.S. foreign policy." That attitude, I was sure, would have come as a shock to taxpayers, and I referenced that disconnect in defending my proposed changes to Congress. While I was a proponent of compassion (as in the President's AIDS relief effort), I needed to make the point that the United States is not a nongovernmental organization. We can't simply focus on a single issue at the expense of others. I saw—and still see—nothing wrong with the proposition that development assistance ought to support broader U.S. foreign policy objectives.

The Bush administration was in a strong position to make this case since we had dramatically increased foreign assistance worldwide. In our view, U.S. interests were tied to democracy and good governance, and development assistance was critical in achieving those goals. What good was it to elect a new democratic government if it couldn't provide for its people? Sometimes the United States needed to give foreign assistance for purely strategic purposes—even if the recipient wasn't a poster child for democracy. But we wanted those cases to be the exception and not the rule.

I ASKED Randall Tobias, who'd launched PEPFAR, the President's AIDS relief program, to take the job as director of foreign assistance and, concurrently, administrator of USAID. His tenure was pretty rocky—Randy could be heavy-handed—but he achieved a lot. Most important, when I conducted budget reviews, the regional administrator for USAID and the regional assistant secretary presented a unified budget. I could finally answer questions such as "How much money do we spend on Nigeria?" without referencing twenty different accounts.

And I could make a reasonable argument that our money was going to encourage democratization and development as well as fight corruption—if not always successfully.

A visit to a small credit union in Mexico, where I spoke with a tiny woman receiving a microfinance loan to expand her ceramics and crafts store, or to the highlands of Guatemala, where farmers once living at subsistence levels were now shipping produce to Walmart, made our efforts come to life. The farmers even took the opportunity of our visit to chastise the Guatemalan president for failure to deliver a promised road. Democracy was alive and well in that remote place. The experience fitted my conception of the changed nature of diplomacy. We needed to be involved in transforming people's lives, not just reporting on the activities of their governments.

I felt even better about those countries that were granted aid through the Millennium Challenge Corporation. The secretary of state chaired the board of the institution that I'd helped the President design in 2003. So much foreign assistance had been wasted over the years, pocketed by corrupt leaders whose wives wore expensive jewels while their people suffered in poverty, ignorance, and disease. The MCC used strict criteria and a process of negotiation to create compacts between aid recipients and the United States. The countries that were selected were certified using quantitative indicators such as governing wisely, fighting corruption, and investing in their people. For countries that did those things well and earned an MCC contract, the sums of money were large: $698 million to Tanzania, $547 million to Ghana, $697 million to Morocco, and $461 million to El Salvador, to name a few. But we set the bar high, and not every country scored well enough to be certified, at least at first. Countries that weren't quite ready were given threshold awards that targeted specific areas of reform. If threshold countries implemented the reforms and took the program seriously, they could become eligible for a full MCC contract and potentially hundreds of millions of dollars in assistance.

The incentives started to change behavior, and we saw leaders from practically every poor country show up with a paper demonstrating why they would be good MCC candidates. Since a compact had to have the support of civil society (farmers' cooperatives, labor unions, environmentalists, businesspeople), the process also brought governments closer to their people. The successful recipients formed "MCC University," where they shared their experiences with prospective candidates.

The work was slow, and sometimes the Congress—and eventually the President—complained that the appropriations weren't being spent expeditiously. And sometimes countries fell back—including when the newly elected Sandinistas in Nicaragua began to unravel democratic and market-oriented economic reforms in 2008. Eventually John Danilovich, who'd been our ambassador in Brazil, took over as chief executive officer of the MCC, replacing Paul Applegarth, who'd successfully launched the program. John brought new energy and focus, and the money started to flow. Yet with all the ups and downs, the MCC garnered bipartisan support and remains to this day a successful innovation in the delivery of foreign assistance.

I was especially proud when, toward the end of our term, we were able to certify Liberia's eligibility for an MCC threshold program. Liberia stood for all that we'd tried to do in Africa: ending civil wars, promoting democracy, and providing hope and a chance at prosperity. Two years after we helped to liberate that country from Charles Taylor's brutality, the Liberian people elected as president a Harvard-trained World Bank economist, Ellen Johnson Sirleaf. She liked to be called "Mother" or "Ma Ellen" by her people, and she fit the part. A heavyset, bespectacled woman who favored brilliantly colored traditional African dress, she looked as though she was *determined* to pull her people out of poverty and despair—by the ear if necessary.

First Lady Laura Bush and I attended her inauguration in Monrovia on January 16. We arrived that morning because there was no place to stay. Even the ambassador's residence was basic, with intermittent electricity and water. In the hot midday sun, we listened to Johnson Sirleaf's optimistic charge to her people to claim their future. I was reminded of the close connections between African Americans and Liberians when the choir sung "The Heavens Are Telling" from Haydn's *Creation*, a song that was a favorite of the choirs of historically black colleges.

The assembled African leaders, gathered to welcome the first woman into their ranks, applauded heartily as she spoke—at least until she said members of her administration would be required to publish their personal finances. "In this respect I will lead by example," she said. "I will be the first to comply by declaring my assets." That drew silence. No other leader really wanted to follow her lead in that regard.

After the ceremony, Laura and I walked down the street to our car. We had to avoid potholes and cracks in the sidewalks that might catch our high heels and send us tumbling. The Liberians had done their best, but the infrastructure was the worst I'd seen anywhere in the world. When the Pentagon decided to establish a separate command for Africa, called AFRICOM, Johnson Sirleaf lobbied to place its headquarters in Monrovia. A U.S. military presence would bring infrastructure improvements, she reasoned. It was a good idea, but the Pentagon demurred, citing the monumental investment that it would require.

I would return to Monrovia with President Bush in 2008. The Liberian people were so grateful for what we'd done. We were met at the airport and driven to the President's office, where the elevator malfunctioned. The President and Johnson Sirleaf climbed the five flights of stairs—the fit George Bush stopping on each landing to "rest," so that his friend could rest too.

Shortly after that, we were led to a creaky stadium to watch President Bush review the newly minted security forces while a band played John Philip Sousa. Apparently, a retired U.S. colonel had decided to devote a couple of years to giving the Liberians a proper military band. And then the Liberians put on the best lunch they could—delicious despite the insistent flies—and invited the President to dance with their leader, an invitation he took up, much to the delight of his hosts and a bit to the dismay of his staff.

That scene would be repeated whenever we visited the African continent: women in Tanzania, wearing skirts with the likeness of the American President emblazoned on them; the President dancing with the Ghanaian first lady and "raising the roof," blending in so effortlessly, in fact, that Assistant Secretary Jendayi Frazer questioned his bloodlines. There were numerous other examples. Responding to a question in 2008 about African pride in candidate Obama and whether they looked forward to his election, the Tanzanian president said that it was, of course, for Americans to decide. Then he added,

"For us, the most important thing is, let him be as good a friend of Africa as President Bush has been." I loved it. Africa was emotionally satisfying for me—not surprisingly, since I was the descendant of slaves. Curiously, it felt like George Bush's home turf too, and that made me very proud.

I RETURNED to the Middle East in February to continue to lay the groundwork for a resumption of negotiations between the Palestinians and the Israelis. The Quartet's position on Hamas had allowed the Israelis to follow suit and distinguish between Abbas and the PA and the Hamas legislature. The Arabs were upbeat, believing both in the President's commitment to Middle East peace and in their capacity to keep Hamas at bay. I always found the press conferences a bit distressing since the Arabs would never admit what they had told me: that they wanted to see Hamas out of business. But it was good enough to have them quietly engage in policies to isolate the terrorists who they feared almost as much as the Israelis did.

I'd just boarded the plane in Egypt heading to Riyadh. David Welch followed me into my cabin. All the blood had drained from his face. A powerful bomb had exploded at the Askariya Shrine in Iraq. Called the "Golden Mosque" because of its gilded dome, the shrine is one of the most revered religious sites in Shia Islam. I got hold of Zal Khalilzad, our ambassador in Baghdad, who said that he'd been making the rounds of Iraqi leaders. We'd quickly learn that the attack had been the work of Abu Musab al-Zarqawi, whom Osama bin Laden had hailed as the "prince of al Qaeda in Iraq." Zarqawi was a fanatic who hated Shia. He was also diabolically brilliant and had decided to set Shia against Sunnis in a bid to spark an Iraqi civil war.

The attack had come in the aftermath of national elections, as the Iraqis were trying to form the first government under their new constitution. Yet, for the moment, they seemed to be responding to the tragedy with maturity. Iraqi leaders from across the religious and political spectrum boldly condemned the attack using similar terms. Zal said that the leaders wanted to visit the shrine together to show interfaith solidarity. I thus landed in Lebanon focused not on Iraq but on the work ahead to support March 14, the political alliance dedicated to Lebanon's independence, in escalating pressure on Syria.

Lebanon is a beautiful country with an alpine climate to the north and Mediterranean vistas along the coast. On this particular February day—perhaps it was the sense of possibility—Beirut seemed to be sparkling. The forces that had come together after Hariri's assassination just one year before were clearly in control. Syria, Hezbollah, and their Iranian patrons were off balance and seemingly in retreat.

We made the turns through the streets of Beirut toward the Grand Serail, a distinctly Ottoman-themed sandstone building with beautiful multicolored tiled floors and walls. Fouad Siniora, the prime minister, came forward to meet me as I rushed past the crush of press. We paused briefly and posed for a picture and then moved into Siniora's cavernous conference room. Fouad was almost an accidental prime minister. He was known as an honest but somewhat uninspiring economist who'd taken the job largely because Rafik Hariri's son Saad was not seasoned enough just yet. Fouad spoke very quickly, sometimes making it hard to understand him, and he was not an imposing presence. But as time passed, we'd come to marvel at Siniora's toughness and competence and long for similar leadership in Afghanistan and Iraq.

Fouad was circumspect in what he said as we sat sipping Middle Eastern coffee. His government, balanced between Lebanon's political and religious groups, included more than a few Syrian sympathizers, such as the foreign minister, a Shia, who was at the table. I told myself to be careful to say nothing that would force Fouad into an uncomfortable dialogue about Syria or Hezbollah. There was no doubt in my mind that the foreign minister would be on the phone to Damascus moments after I left the building. I even managed to invite the gentleman to Washington, though I sincerely hoped he wouldn't come.

After almost an hour, Fouad asked to see me in his private office. There he gave full voice to his hopes and his fears—reminding me that he was walking a tightrope, trying to lead Lebanon toward greater sovereignty and democracy with Syria and Hezbollah ready and able to pounce at any time. He asked for economic assistance, help in building the army, and one other favor: Could I talk to the Israelis about returning Shebaa Farms? The roughly ten square miles that constituted

Shebaa Farms weren't objectively worth very much. The land had been occupied in 1967 and was tied up in the dispute between Syria and Israel over the Golan Heights. The Israelis now maintained an important surveillance post there.

The United Nations had determined that Shebaa Farms was a part of Syria, so when Israel pulled out of Lebanon in 2000, the United Nations had certified the Israeli withdrawal and declared the matter closed, as all Lebanese land had been vacated. But some Lebanese didn't accept that view and dredged up old maps to "prove" their case that it was Lebanese land. Hezbollah seized on Shebaa as a convenient rationale for their militancy. I promised to talk to the Israelis about it and thought that I had a fair chance of convincing Olmert of the wisdom of evacuating Shebaa Farms.

At the time of my February 2006 visit, there was a dispute about Émile Lahoud's presidency because his term had been extended at Syria's behest in contravention of the Lebanese constitution. Lahoud was not, to put it mildly, a friend of democracy or the United States, and our allies wanted him out. Publicly, I stayed out of the controversy, saying only that the Lebanese needed a president in whom they had confidence and who would defend their sovereignty. But I pointedly decided not to meet with him. As his Syrian connections were well known, the message was clear enough.

When I had met him in 2005 on my first trip to the country, he had been dressed in a mustard-colored suit that only highlighted his almost cartoonish artificial tan. After I shook his hand, I felt like I needed a shower. I didn't mince words with him, saying that he needed to press his "sponsors" to fully comply with UN Security Council resolutions that called on Damascus to respect Lebanese sovereignty. Lahoud made his case that he was a Lebanese patriot first and, of course, wanted his country to control its own affairs. *Right,* I thought and ended the session as quickly as I gracefully could. This time I hoped that the decision not to meet with him would fully underscore our disdain for him and what he was doing to his country.

After an audience with the Maronite Catholic patriarch of Lebanon at a monastery high in the mountains, and a meeting at the equally cloistered residence of Walid Jumblatt, the former Communist who now led the Druze community (one of Lebanon's politically important religious minorities), I felt I'd touched all the necessary bases. Lebanon was a very complicated place and every trip there required the utmost in tact and discretion. I loved Beirut but was always relieved when it was time to leave.

THIS WASN'T the case in the United Arab Emirates, where the ruling family was disciplined, organized, young, and direct. I always felt relaxed and at ease in the UAE, the only federal state in the Arabian peninsula. True, there was the complication of having to meet two separate royal families: the ruler of Dubai and the bin Zayeds in Abu Dhabi. There is a big difference between the two most powerful emirates. Abu Dhabi is conservative and controls most of the oil and power in the confederation. That oil wealth is being used to fund an Arab renaissance with great museums and concert halls and cutting-edge international business investments.

Dubai, on the other hand, is known for its man-made island in the shape of a palm tree, its claim to have the tallest building in the world, and its indoor ski slope—yes, an indoor ski slope—right in the middle of the desert. It would soon become known too for profligate spending and near bankruptcy. But in 2006 it was the banking center of the Middle East and a growing international business hub.

So I headed toward the UAE focused on the upcoming conversation about the war on terrorism, Afghanistan, Iraq, Iran, and the Israeli-Palestinian issue. I looked forward to my meeting with the mother of the bin Zayeds, Sheikha Fatima. A power in her own right, she was a fierce defender of her family and a real patron of women's education and empowerment. She wore an abaya (the black robe) and a traditional silk mask that covered all but her eyes. Yet it wasn't hard to see that Sheikha Fatima had a major voice with her sons and thus in the direction of her country. The sheikha didn't meet men outside her family, but she could meet with me. There were some real advantages to being a female secretary of state in the culture of the Middle East.

I landed in Abu Dhabi, the capital, feeling more relaxed and glad that I had only one more relatively easy stop before returning home from a grueling trip. When I got in the car, however, the ambassador asked what I would say about the Dubai Ports World controversy. I knew that there was a simmering problem because the huge conglomerate had purchased a company that operated terminals in six U.S. ports, including New York. For more than a week, there had been angry congressional reaction to the proposed deal, but I assumed it would pass. I called the President just to make sure. "Tell them we believe in the deal, free markets, and our friends," he said.

I visited first with the ruler of Dubai, who was visiting the capital, and delivered that message, moving quickly to talk about the other issues on my agenda. Over dinner with Mohammed bin Zayed al Nahyan, the crown prince, and his brother Abdullah, the foreign minister, I repeated what the President had told me. When I left the UAE, I assumed that all was well.

I flew home to Washington. A few days later the President called. "We aren't going to be able to fade the heat on Dubai Ports World," he said. "You need to call the Emirates and tell them." That afternoon I called Abdullah bin Zayed al Nahyan to deliver the bad news. I invited him to Washington so that we could show that our relationship hadn't been affected by the collapse of the commercial deal. Perhaps we could sign the civil nuclear deal that had been pending for a while. Abdullah accepted my invitation but said that it might be better to wait. (We eventually signed the agreement for Congress's consideration in January 2009.)

Dubai Ports World pulled the offer to manage the ports on March 9. To this day I don't know why we didn't see it coming. Arabs, ports, New York—that should have been a red flag. When I teach this case to my business school students at Stanford, they're unfailingly critical of our being blindsided. I try to explain the factors that led to the deal's demise—among them the fact that the clearance of the acquisition never got beyond the deputy secretaries because there was no national security issue; overconfidence that others saw our relationship with the UAE the benign way that we did; and a deep belief in the importance of low barriers to foreign investment. There were many reasons. But we should have seen the uproar coming, and we didn't.

31

Building a New Relationship with India

THOUGH IT CONTINUED to make headlines, the Dubai Ports World debacle didn't occupy our attention very much longer. On February 28, the President left for India, Pakistan, and Afghanistan. The trip required the most delicate balancing act to get the messaging right in each of the places. Our delinking of relations with Islamabad and New Delhi was working—there was no more talk of U.S. policy toward India-Pakistan, or Indo-Pak, as it was sometimes called. We now had distinct approaches to both important countries. And we were doing really well with India: while there the President would sign the landmark civil nuclear deal.

The nuclear deal was the centerpiece of our effort to build a fundamentally different relationship with India. From the earliest stages of the 2000 campaign, it had been our intention to change the terms of U.S.-Indian engagement. As I noted earlier, the crucial nuclear agreement required breaking many taboos. India had refused to sign the NPT in 1968 and had then conducted a nuclear test in 1974. Only five countries had been "grandfathered" as nuclear powers in 1968—the United States, the Soviet Union, Great Britain, France, and China. Any country that subsequently acquired a nuclear capability was deemed to be in violation of this important set of prohibitions. In 1978 President Jimmy Carter signed a bill that cut off all nuclear trade with India.

The United States thus maintained a web of restrictions on technology transfer and cooperation with India. The list of prohibitions grew over the years, with the condemnation reaching its height in 1998. That year, in response to a long-range missile test by Pakistan, Prime Minister Atal Vajpayee authorized the Indian military to conduct a series of underground nuclear tests, including India's first test of a thermonuclear weapon. When Pakistan followed up with its own nuclear test, the two countries became linked as the poster children for crimes against the non-proliferation regime. Their behavior was different, however. India had developed an excellent record of respecting proliferation safeguards in terms of not transferring technology to other countries. Pakistan—well, it was the home of the nuclear proliferation entrepreneur A. Q. Khan, who had spread nuclear enrichment technology to North Korea and Iran, among other places.

India needed civil nuclear power and wanted to break out of the constraints on high-technology cooperation that were stunting its growth. The proposed civil nuclear deal would make it possible for the United States—and American companies—to help India develop its potentially rich market for this environmentally friendly energy source. But the breakthrough was not just about nuclear power—it would unlock a wide range of possible areas of cooperation with a country that was an emerging power in the knowledge-based revolution in economic affairs. The Indians made clear, too, that they hoped to become a customer for U.S. military hardware. That was an exciting prospect for the defense industry. And for us, even though we were not seeking to "balance" China, cooperation with another emerging power in Asia, especially a democratic one, was a welcome development.

The interests of the United States and India were in substantial alignment. But any change of this magnitude brings resistance. In Washington, the high priests of non-proliferation accused us of gutting the NPT, a treaty that had significantly limited the emergence of nuclear weapons states.

Our problems were considerable in 2006 but Indian Prime Minister Manmohan Singh's were far more complicated, stemming from the Indian national security elite's almost existential attachment to the "independence" of its nuclear program. For some officials, the requirement to place India's nuclear reactors (only the existing civilian ones and any new ones) under IAEA supervision amounted to nothing less than an attack on India's sovereignty. Many of those Indian bureaucrats and pundits also valued their country's "non-aligned status," a relic of the Cold War, when India had declared itself as belonging to neither the Soviet nor the American "bloc." When confronted with that argument, my Indian counterpart, K. Natwar Singh, said, "The Cold War is over. Exactly against whom are we non-aligned?" Good point. But for many in New Delhi the idea of close technological cooperation with the United States was just too much to swallow.

As a result of these tensions, the deal suffered several near-death experiences before and after Singh and Bush signed it in New Delhi. The first had come a year before in Washington, when Prime Minister Manmohan Singh visited the United States in July 2005.

The two leaders were expected to sign a framework document to end the moratorium on nuclear trade and pave the way for a full agreement on civil-nuclear cooperation. I met the day before with my Indian counterpart Natwar Singh in his suite at the Willard Hotel. Frankly, there was so much buzz around the State Department that we wanted to work in a location away from the press and where the atmosphere was more informal. I also thought it a sign of respect to go to him, even though we were in Washington. Natwar was adamant. He wanted the deal, but the prime minister wasn't sure he could sell it in New Delhi. We pushed as far as we could toward agreement. Finally, Natwar said that he would take the document to the prime minister and let me know.

That evening, Nick Burns asked to see me. With Bob Zoellick, the deputy secretary, and several members of the senior staff, Phil Zelikow, Brian Gunderson, and Sean McCormack, in tow, he came down the hall from his office and entered mine. "It isn't going to work," Nick said. "The foreign minister tried, but the prime minister just can't sign on to the agreement."

I was a bit surprised, perhaps having misread Natwar's determination as an indicator that he had the authority to speak for his government. It was late, and I was tired. "Well, if they don't want to get out of the nuclear ghetto, I can't do anything about it," I said. "Why don't you go and meet with the Indians and try one more time." I called the President. "It isn't going to work. Singh just can't make it happen," I said.

"Too bad," he answered and didn't press further. Later that night Nick called to tell me what I already knew—there wouldn't be a deal. I went to bed, constructing a script in my head for the press the next day about needing more time for the negotiations. *That sounds lame*, I thought as I drifted into a fitful sleep.

I woke up at 4:30 A.M. and sat straight up in bed. *I am not letting this go down,* I thought. I called Nick at 5:00 A.M. "I am not prepared to let this fail. Arrange for me to see the prime minister," I said. The meeting with the President was set for ten. "How about breakfast at eight?" Nick called while I was exercising to say that the prime minister didn't want to meet. "Get the foreign minister," I answered. Natwar picked up the phone. My heart was beating pretty fast—maybe from the exercise, maybe from the sense of an important initiative slipping through my fingers. "Natwar, why won't the PM see me?"

"He doesn't want to tell you no," he said. "I've done my best. I told him that the United States wants to take this thirty-year millstone from around your neck. You should do it. But he can't sell it in New Delhi."

I wasn't ready to surrender. "Ask him again," I pleaded. A few minutes later, Natwar called to say that the prime minister would receive me at his hotel at 8 A.M.

I went to the office for a few minutes and then to the Willard, having called the President to tell him I would try personally one more time. Steve asked if I wanted him to go with me. "No, I think I need to do this alone," I said. I entered the prime minister's suite and sat there with Natwar and his boss—all three of us not bothering to touch the pastries and coffee that had been served.

"Mr. Prime Minister, this is the deal of a lifetime. You and President Bush are about to put U.S.-Indian relations on a fundamentally new footing. I know it's hard for you, but it's hard for the President too. I didn't come here to negotiate language—only to ask you to tell your officials to get this done. And let's get it done before you see the President." Prime Minister Singh, a mild-mannered man who speaks slowly and softly, pushed back but eventually gave the nod to his people to try again.

I went directly to the White House and told the President what I'd done. When the Indians arrived, our negotiators and theirs sat in the Roosevelt Room, trying to find agreement, while the President, Prime Minister Singh, Natwar, and I sat nervously in the Oval pretending to focus on other matters. Finally, I got a note to join the negotiators. Natwar and I entered the room to the smiling Nick Burns and his counterpart. "We've got it," Nick said.

The two leaders released the framework agreement to the press, most of whom were already writing stories of failure. Bob Zoellick came into my office. "Sometimes the secretary of state gets tested. You wouldn't take no for an answer," he said. I felt very good, but the *New York Times*'s editorial board soon reminded me that there would be a push back. The U.S.-India deal, it opined, would cause responsible NPT signatories to "be more inclined to regard the non-proliferation treaty as an anachronism, reconsider their self-restraint, and be tempted by the precedent that India has successfully established and that now, in effect, has an American blessing."

The arguments from the non-proliferation community were not without merit. The whole premise of the regime was that countries who pursued civilian nuclear power under safeguards—inspections, reporting, and so on—would *not* pursue military weapons programs. It was too easy, it was thought, to divert technology from one to the other. That, some said, had been the argument vis-à-vis Iran. How could we argue that India was different?

It was a good question, but, unlike Iran, India was not lying to the IAEA about its enrichment activities and the fact of the existence of a military program was well known. Though ideally India—or Pakistan, for that matter—would not have built a nuclear weapons program, this was now a fact of life. The key from our point of view was to get India within the IAEA regime, even if they could not and would not be party to the NPT. Our thinking tracked closely with that of Mohamed ElBaradei, the head of the IAEA and thus the guardian of the NPT. Better to have India in the tent in some fashion, even if New Delhi could not formally join the NPT. ElBaradei understood this point.

At least new construction of reactors would be under safeguard. India already had more than enough nuclear material for its military program. It needed help on the civilian side and we needed the strategic breakthrough with this emerging, democratic power.

The work to move from that initial announcement of a civil-nuclear deal in 2005 to a more detailed framework agreement by March 2006, when the President would visit New Delhi, was extremely difficult and the effort almost failed several times. The prime minister had indeed encountered difficulty when he returned home from Washington in the summer of 2005. By the time of the trip, the Indian delegation was trying to walk back some of the language on IAEA safeguards. Steve and Nick went to the Foreign Ministry to try to hammer out a solution. I thought that I would stay away this time, giving us another bite at the apple should they fail. After several ups and downs and near misses over a period of eight hours, they succeeded. The United States and India had a civil-nuclear deal. Now the really hard work would begin. The reality was that the deal could not go into force until we met a number of criteria stipulated by U.S. law. But we'd lived to fight another day—and that was good enough for the time being.

The nuclear deal was the news of the President's visit to India. Yet other elements of the trip demonstrated why it was time to change the relationship with this emerging global power. I remember well the President's meeting with students at the business school in Hyderabad, a center of technological sophistication that personified India's potential as a high-tech leader and economic dynamo. *This could be Stanford,* I thought.

There was a lot of discussion—but no commitment—regarding India's pursuit of a permanent seat on the UN Security Council. The Indians had a good argument and one for which I had some sympathy. The UN Security Council did not reflect the changes in the balance of power that had taken place with World War II. International institutions are like the rings of a tree—you can date their birth by looking at their membership. The original permanent five members of the Security Council (those with veto authority) were the Soviet Union (Russia became the successor state in 1991), China (with the PRC replacing Chang Kai Shek's ROC in Taiwan in 1971), France, the UK, and the United States. But now there were other important powers and whole continents that were not represented. What about Japan, the world's third largest economy? What about the Middle East? And of course the emerging market powers of Brazil and India did not hold permanent membership either.

The United States had long championed Japan's case but frankly the politics of UNSC reform were just too complicated to take on. The incorporation of India was opposed by China. Brazil's candidacy raised the question of Mexico's exclusion. The Africans could never settle on a candidate to represent a continent split between the Arab north and the

Sub-Saharan black south. And reform would have raised a sticky question for our closest allies. Germany wanted membership, too. Did it make sense to have three European representatives—particularly when the European Union was supposed to have a common foreign policy?

We adopted a strategy of acknowledging the importance of reform and welcoming reasonable proposals, but we never acted on any of them. That said, the continued focus on the issue by emerging powers such as India underscored their growing insistence on a voice in international affairs.

BY WAY of contrast to our time in New Delhi, the trip to Pakistan began with the news upon arrival that there had been an attack on the U.S. consulate in Karachi. A U.S. consular officer had been killed. The President, always gracious to his hosts, endeavored to convince the Pakistanis that this in no way cast a shadow on the visit. But of course it did. There was an air of unreality as we fought to make the visit appear normal. The Pakistanis had been insistent that the President sleep just one night in Islamabad to show that it was safe. After a lot of debate, he decided to push the Secret Service beyond its comfort zone and grant the Pakistanis' request: we'd stay at our ambassador's fortresslike home.

The contrasts continued. The meetings with Prime Minister Singh had been focused on technological cooperation and removing bureaucratic barriers to foreign investment. The President met for lunch with the members of a joint U.S.-Indian CEO council. But the meeting with Pakistan's President Musharraf was dominated by talk of terrorism and our response.

And it wasn't just the conversation that was different. In India, we were treated to a beautiful dinner outdoors on the veranda of the Presidential Palace, a fresh breeze blowing through as we looked out across the beautifully manicured grounds. In Pakistan, aware that we needed to be wheels up for Washington that evening, we sat in the Palace for a hurried two-hour dinner and a "cultural performance" that oddly featured a Western-style fashion show.

Still, the visit to Islamabad allowed us to see a glimpse of a different Pakistan. Musharraf, a classic "man on horseback" who came to power in a military coup, was making important changes in his country. I was struck by the presence of strong women ministers representing the Pakistani government in our meetings. It was also encouraging to see a vibrant press corps peppering both presidents with questions about everything from the possibility of a civil-nuclear deal with Pakistan—not possible from our point of view—to expectations about coming elections in the country. For all his limitations, with the freeing of the press and of the judiciary, Musharraf had laid the groundwork for a civilian government to return. Ironically, those changes would soon turn out to be his undoing.

India and Pakistan were successfully delinked. Unfortunately, the stop in Kabul underscored a link of another kind—Pakistan and Afghanistan were tied together more than ever as the problem of cross-border terrorism deepened. And a proposed policy change in Pakistan would only exacerbate the problem.

In September 2006 we had first gotten wind of a possible deal between the Pakistani military and the tribal leaders in North Waziristan, the territory deep in the mountainous region between Pakistan and Afghanistan. Negotiating with the Pakistani Taliban, Musharraf agreed to withdraw troops from their territory in exchange for assurances that the tribal leaders would cease attacks on the military and stop the infiltration of militants across the Afghan border. The territory has been ungoverned throughout its history. The British had tried and failed, and the Soviet Union had simply left the suspicious, pious, and xenophobic tribes to their own devices. Pakistan had rarely interfered in the area either, but the war on terror required military engagement in the region, as al Qaeda and the Taliban had fled there after our invasion of Afghanistan.

The Pakistani military proved unequipped and poorly trained for the mission and reluctant to transform its capabilities to do a better job. Still focused on India, the Pakistani army was ready for an engagement in Kashmir but not in the Federally Administered Tribal Areas (FATA) and the North-West Frontier province. Though we had already given Pakistan more than $4.5 billion in security-related assistance by October 2005, Pakistan had accomplished very little in restructuring its armed forces. In fact, Islamabad's primary concern was the release of the F-16s that had been purchased and then withheld in 1990 when Pakistan was suspected of secretly producing nuclear weapons. The President had acceded to Musharraf's plea to deliver the airplanes. "This will make it easier to work with my military and build a spirit of partnership," Musharraf told me on one occasion. But it said something about the mind-set of the Pakistanis that high-performance aircraft, rather than the nuts-and-bolts of equipment and training for counter-terrorism, dominated our conversations.

The truth is that the Pakistanis had no stomach for fighting in the rugged border region between Pakistan and Afghanistan. Musharraf decided to cut a deal with the tribal leaders—a kind of live and let live. In exchange for a stand-down of the Pakistani military, the tribes agreed to control their "guests," the terrorists. Only the first half of that deal was realized and the region became a safe haven for several terrorist groups: fighters commanded by Baitullah Mehsud; the Haqqani network, still active after we left office; and remnants of al Qaeda.

In late September 2006, Musharraf would come to Washington to present this deal to the President. We told Musharraf that the United States wouldn't criticize him publicly and that we'd give the deal a chance to work. But the President made clear to him in the Oval Office meeting that the United States would take action itself if we learned of an imminent threat to our territory or if we learned that key al Qaeda figures were being harbored there. Musharraf was told point blank that we considered it our prerogative to act without permission or—possibly—Islamabad's knowledge.

That night, the President invited Musharraf, Afghan President Karzai, and their respective ambassadors to a small dinner in the family dining room at the White House. The Vice President, Steve Hadley, and I joined President Bush at what turned out to be a contentious affair.

The dinner started routinely enough, with Karzai and Musharraf sharing their thoughts about how things were going against the Taliban and al Qaeda. But after about an hour, Musharraf started to explain the agreement that he'd made with the tribes. Sugarcoating the facts and overselling the potential benefits, he talked for more than thirty minutes. Karzai suddenly interrupted, saying that Musharraf had made a deal not with the tribal leaders but with the terrorists. When Musharraf protested, Karzai dramatically pulled out a piece of paper from his long flowing cape. "See, it says right here that the Taliban will not be disturbed," he said. Musharraf tried to answer, but Karzai was on a roll, stopping just short of accusing the Pakistani of complicity in the cross-border raids into his country.

Things were getting pretty hot. The ambassadors were shifting in their seats, and, frankly, so were we. It was as if we were watching a heavyweight bout where one overmatched fighter had somehow gotten into the ring by mistake. Karzai was proving to be a brilliant prosecutor, and Musharraf had few answers; he seemed suddenly not to know what he'd signed.

President Bush interjected the thought that perhaps they could monitor the progress on the deal together. It was a bit lame but about all anyone could think of at the moment to separate the verbal combatants. It didn't work, and the two were getting hotter under the collar by the moment. A photograph from that dinner says it all: Karzai and Musharraf glaring at each other while we, the ever-sunny Americans, sit with nervous—almost silly—grins on our faces.

Finally Karzai mentioned something about a joint *loya jirga* (tribal council) that he'd proposed. He'd never received an answer. We jumped on the opening, turning the conversation to getting such a council established. I said that I'd call Ryan Crocker and Ronald Neumann, our ambassadors in Islamabad and Kabul, to help coordinate the establishment of the *jirga*. When the two men left, the Vice President, Steve, the President, and I looked at one another in amazement. "They almost came to blows," the President said. Everyone nodded in agreement.

The management of the relationship between our allies in the war on terror suddenly seemed daunting in the extreme. However, the relationship between the two men had soured well before that dinner, and the strains were very much on display as we visited Afghanistan during the President's trip on March 1, 2006, months before their Washington encounter. When we arrived in Kabul, Karzai vented about Musharraf, whom he accused of wanting to annex Afghan Pashtuns into Pakistan. Musharraf had made a similar claim about Karzai's desire for a greater Pashtunistan during our time in Islamabad.

The President turned the conversation with President Karzai to the training of the Afghan security forces, fighting corruption, and—most troubling—the failing effort to rid Afghanistan of poppy. The President gently suggested that we might have to use some of the methods that had succeeded in Colombia, including aerial spraying.

Hamid Karzai is a proud man, and, as had been the case in my encounter with him the year before, he tended to emphasize the positive. But it was frustrating as he declared problem after problem to be under control. "We're making real progress with the governors on poppy eradication," he said, a statement belied by the estimates of numerous monitoring organizations. "All we need are some alternative crops—maybe pomegranates—for them to grow," he continued, only to note that the road network didn't allow for the transport of perishable fruits and vegetables to market. "So we need roads, roads, roads—as quickly as possible," he added. There was always a story of villagers who'd come to him promising to plant good crops, not bad ones.

In fact, it was good that Karzai was an optimist—maybe that was what got him up in the morning to do one of the hardest jobs on Earth. But sometimes I couldn't tell if Karzai believed what he was saying or just thought that we might. He did not want to even acknowledge the possibility of dramatic measures such as crop destruction through aerial spraying. The issue would be a source of tension between our two countries for the remainder of the President's term. But as frustrating as the relationship with Karzai sometimes was, he was the elected president of Afghanistan. Though in time we would come to see the importance of the governors of the provinces in addressing the country's challenges, there was no alternative to Karzai, who stepped up to be the first freely elected president of his country.

That afternoon, the President and Laura, Karzai, our ambassador Ron Neumann, and I cut the ribbon dedicating the gigantic but not particularly attractive new U.S. Embassy in Kabul. The President asked if I'd had anything to do with the architectural design. I made clear that I hadn't. But the big, ugly building would serve its purpose and it sent the message that, for better or worse, we were in Afghanistan for the long run.

32

Democracy in Latin America and Beyond

O NLY FOUR DAYS AFTER arriving home from South Asia, I was scheduled to travel to Indonesia and Australia. But that March itinerary would be a clear demonstration of why the secretary of state has a dedicated plane. It turned out that Chile had elected its first woman president, Michelle Bachelet—exciting both because of her gender and because Chileans were managing to orchestrate the transfer of power peacefully. Our ambassador had sent a message that the President-elect very much wanted me to go to Santiago for the inauguration. She would consider it a personal honor if I did. I wanted to protest that Chile was somewhat out of the way in getting to Southeast Asia and Australia. I didn't. I just got on the plane on March 10 and headed for the momentous event. I'm glad I did.

That morning I met with Bachelet, discussing with her briefly the challenges in the region. I noted our concerns about Hugo Chávez and accepted her promise to defend democracy in Latin America. I knew, though, that Chile would keep its head down and never confront Chávez. Bachelet had to watch her left flank, and there were many in the country who sympathized with Chávez's radical views. My purpose there was to acknowledge Chile's long and difficult path to democracy. Seeing little girls all dressed in white who'd come to see history made was inspiring. And watching Ricardo Lagos, Bachelet's predecessor, escort her to the podium before leaving the stage—an act that underscored the peaceful transfer—was remarkable too. Chile had endured so much trouble with military coups and socialist revolutions. The show of democratic stability was worth the trip. And I was really glad that the United States of America had shown up when I spotted Hugo Chávez there to mark the moment. He saw me too—but from across the room. Our paths didn't cross.

Earlier in the day, however, I'd met two of Latin America's new leftist presidents, both expected to be allies of Chávez. (We were observing a worrying trend toward radical populism in the hemisphere's elections.) Evo Morales in Bolivia and Tabaré Vázquez in Uruguay could not have been more different, though. Vázquez, an oncologist by trade, was thoroughly professional. I liked him immediately, especially his emphasis on trying to improve the lot of his people—and his invitation to have the United States join him in doing so.

Morales, on the other hand, seemed completely out of his depth. He had no ideas—only slogans. When he handed me a ukulele, saying that he knew I was a musician, I didn't think much of it. At the press availability shortly after, the two of us walked out and held the "gift" up for the cameras to see. Later, members of the press told me that it was decorated with coca leaf, a banned substance that Morales had threatened to legalize in his country. I was appalled, and it spoke volumes about his immaturity. I told the President that he would like Vázquez and that we could work with the Uruguayan. Not so with Morales, who was a clone of Chávez, only lacking his master's cunning.

Nonetheless, as I boarded the plane for Jakarta, I felt good about what I'd seen in Latin America. It was easy to focus on Chávez and Morales, but for a region that had until recently been known largely for military dictators, our neighbors had come a long way.

And the countries of Latin America were not the only places that were moving forward. When President Bush came to office, Indonesia was a troubled place. The longtime dictator Suharto had been overthrown. Elections had produced two weak governments, including one headed by Megawati Sukarnoputri, the daughter of Indonesia's first authoritarian president, Sukarno, and a well-meaning but ineffective leader with an allegedly crooked husband. The terrorist challenge from the al Qaeda affiliate Jemaah Islamiyah was threatening to make the Indonesian archipelago a safe haven and hub of operations across Southeast Asia.

But with the election of Susilo Bambang Yudhoyono, known as SBY, in September 2004, Indonesia had come back from the brink. SBY was a military officer who'd been trained in the United States. He was the personification of the success of our International Military Education and Training program. One of the first decisions I made as secretary was to reinstate the program with Indonesia, which had been suspended in light of Jakarta's crackdown on the breakaway (and soon to be independent) region of East Timor.

Paul Wolfowitz, who'd been ambassador to Indonesia, had for years been advocating that the United States restart the exchanges. He was right. Often the United States severs ties with militaries in protest of human rights violations. Though such action is an important signal and sometimes has an effect on the policies of governments, it does have a downside, as the United States loses contact and influence with those institutions. The impetus for this severing often comes from the Congress, where a few senators use the power of the purse to force changes in the policies of the executive branch. In this case, Patrick Leahy of Vermont had been the loudest proponent of the suspension. Fortunately, when I called him and told him that I was going to recertify the program he surprisingly didn't fight back.

SBY is a thick-framed man of few words who brought stability and competence to the presidency. And he was tough—tough on terrorists despite Indonesians' well-deserved reputation for preferring conciliation to conflict. SBY turned out to be a great counterterrorism partner, and after the bombing in Bali that killed 202 people in October 2002, he was able to mobilize his security forces and his population to support him.

Moreover, the world needed examples of the peaceful coexistence of Islam and other religions. Indonesia was turning out to be a wonderful case. When I visited a local madrassa, I didn't know what to expect. But there I found boys and girls studying together, and I had fun joining forces with someone dressed as Elmo to launch an Indonesian version of *Sesame Street*. I will long hold in my mind's eye a picture of little girls frantically waving their hands to answer my questions while the little boys seemed quite shy. *If only this same scene plays out in the Middle East someday,* I thought as I left the elementary school classroom.

My geographically challenging journey ended in Australia, where at least I was in the same country for several days. The United States' relationship with the Aussies was so smooth that there seemed to be little real work to do. The two countries were so bonded that, in fact, the government of John Howard was doing a lot of heavy lifting in Iraq and Afghanistan. President Bush and Prime Minister Howard were much alike: tough, resolute, and not at all afraid of controversy. Australia was taking on and solving conflicts in the South Pacific. Because the U.S. secretary of state is the address for almost every issue, it was a relief to have an ally like Australia that was willing to fix problems, not just talk about them. It was a joy to get a call from Alexander Downer, the foreign minister, simply saying, "We're handling that issue in the Solomon Islands," or "We're working on East Timor." "Is there anything I can do to help?" I'd ask. "No. I'll let you know if I need anything," he'd answer. It was great to hear.

On that particular trip, Alexander had arranged several relaxing activities to complement our long strategic discussions. Oh yes, I spoke at the university and faced, as I often did, several noisy protesters. I always found that simply letting them shout their slogans and then reminding people of the blessings of democracy and free speech usually brought the crowd—even an unsympathetic one—to my side. "People are now able to speak out in Kabul and Baghdad too," I'd say. Some of the press there remarked that I'd taken questions that I hadn't seen in advance. Apparently that was a bit risky or unusual. *Why would anyone expect to see the questions in advance?* I thought. There were some advantages to having been a university professor for many years, where one could always rely on having to face a nineteen-year-old who wanted to play "gotcha" with the professor. I was used to it.

And I got to attend the swimming competition at the Commonwealth Games. I found that my love of sports, like my love of music, often gave me an easy bridge to the population. Sitting with the great swimmer Ian Thorpe, or "the Thorpedo," as he was called, was a real thrill, as was the chance to present the medals to the winners. There were some really fun perks that went along with my job.

The truth is, though, there was little time to take advantage of opportunities in the beautiful places that I visited. Not too long after my trip to Australia, I was in Nassau for a meeting of the Caribbean Community (CARICOM), chaired by the Harvard-trained Bahamian Foreign Minister Fred Mitchell. The organization unites all of the small countries of the Caribbean. I'd built good relations with the foreign leaders of the island states, more than anything by showing up personally and engaging them on their problems of tourism, disaster relief, and security for the world cricket championships. They were fun people and always asked if I wanted to stay for a few days to enjoy the superb weather, beaches, and golf. I could never do it. Usually I stayed for less than twenty-four hours and headed home—to repack and hit the road again.

In fact, I didn't mind the travel so much—my staff and plane made it fairly easy. I tried to keep a regular routine, even on the road. In Washington, I got up every morning at 4:30 A.M. and trudged upstairs to work out so that I could be at my desk by 6:30 A.M. I tried to go to bed no later than 10:00 P.M. On the road, few foreigners wanted to meet at 6:30 A.M., so I got to sleep in until 5:30 A.M. I usually flew overnight, sleeping on the plane and working out immediately upon arrival. By the end of the day I was tired and able to sleep despite the time change. I will admit that I sometimes slept for a few moments in the car while moving from place to place. This meant that the U.S. ambassador in the country had to shorten his or her briefing so that I could take advantage of my uncanny ability to fall into a deep sleep for ten minutes and awake refreshed and ready to go.

Unless negotiations demanded it, I rarely attended meetings late into the night, telling my counterparts that dinners needed to end no later than 9:30 P.M. "You don't want me making decisions on behalf of the United States on four hours' sleep," I told my staff early on. And I tried to stay away from local "delicacies." That was easier than one might have thought. Food is largely homogenized around the world these days. It isn't hard to get grilled fish or meat and cooked (always cooked) vegetables. I made an exception in the Middle East because I love meze (hors d'oeuvres) and the tasty rice and meat dishes. The discipline of exercise, diet, and enough sleep kept me healthy throughout my tenure and the crazy travel schedule that I endured.

But I loved nothing more than a few days in Washington when I could enjoy a sense of normalcy. My exceptional house manager, Amy Gilbert, took care of me, and it wasn't really necessary for me to grocery shop or run errands. Yet I liked to show up at the Watergate Safeway once in a while, my security detail trying not to intrude as I walked along the rows of foodstuffs. Heads would turn a bit, but people usually left me alone to fend for myself in the vegetable aisle.

In addition to my own workouts, I trained twice a week—or whenever possible—with Tommy Tomlo, a former marine who had no mercy on his fifty-plus-year-old subject. Tommy, who is also from Alabama, is an Auburn and Redskins fan, but we somehow got along anyway. I enlisted him to participate with me in the Susan G. Komen walks/runs for breast cancer awareness—something that he still does to this day.* Tommy made it hard—but fun—to stay in shape.

And I tried also to set aside time each week for activities that I enjoyed. I'd learned a hard lesson after 9/11, when I became tired and rattled after working thirty-nine days in a row. Sunday afternoons became my refuge. I'd get up and make phone calls around the world, including a standing call with the British foreign secretary. Then I'd attend church at National Presbyterian at 11:00 A.M., listening to the inspiring sermons and sometimes calling on the pastoral care of my friend Reverend Eunice McGarrahan.

When I came home, I tried not to work, often playing golf at Andrews Air Force Base with my friends Sandy Langdon, Anne Johnson, and Mary Bush, or my great friend and golf pro Alan Burton would meet me and walk the course—even in 37-degree weather, my lower limit for an outing. On one occasion, the ground was so frozen that Alan had to hammer the tee into the ground with a club. Well—I didn't have much time to play, so a little cold weather couldn't be a deterrent.

At other times I'd watch the NFL or play music with my quintet. I just cherished those five or six hours when it was possible—sometimes—not to think about all that was swirling around me. But at 7:00 P.M. or so I'd check in with the Operations Center and get my head back into the game for the upcoming week. I actually experienced what I came to call "sundowning," a little sense of dread that Monday morning was nigh.

---

*The Susan G. Komen for the Cure was founded by my friend Nancy Brinker, our energetic former ambassador to Hungary and chief of protocol.

33

A Change of Leadership in Iraq

T HAT APPREHENSION was warranted as events turned increasingly sour, particularly in Iraq. The relative calm that had characterized the Iraqi reaction in the immediate aftermath of the Golden Mosque bombing in February didn't last. Insurgent attacks were escalating, and in Al Anbar province there was open warfare. Al Qaeda in Iraq, under the leadership of Abu Musab al-Zarqawi, had established a foothold in the province. We were losing more U.S. soldiers too, not just in Al Anbar province but in Baghdad and in the South, where the Iranians had stepped up support for the radical Shia militias. The Iraqis were descending into a sectarian conflict that stood at the precipice of all-out civil war.

And the country was staggering forward in a leadership vacuum as attempts to form a government stalled. After the elections, Ibrahim al-Jaafari had been nominated to be prime minister by his party as a kind of compromise candidate. But no one really wanted him to *be* prime minister, and he couldn't garner enough votes. A stalemate ensued and lasted for four months. Every day the Iraqis made clear that Jaafari would never receive enough votes in Parliament to become the country's leader. Yet he was stubborn and defiant, saying that he couldn't disappoint his people by withdrawing.

Prime Minister Blair and President Bush conferred and decided that it would be a good idea if Jack Straw and I visited Baghdad together. That would show the solidarity of Britain and the United States and our resolve to get a handle on the worsening security situation. We knew, though, that we had really only one mission: to get Jaafari out!

I picked Jack up in London for the trip to Baghdad. We'd become close friends as well as close colleagues. In the fall of 2005 I'd taken Jack to my hometown of Birmingham, Alabama, having vowed to take foreign ministers outside Washington so that they could get a feel for the country. The deeply personal journey to the place of my birth had done more than that—it had given Jack a feel for how far the United States had come. We visited my father's church and my childhood home. Jack and his wife, Alice, didn't say it, but I know they were stunned at how modest my beginnings had been.

Birmingham had rolled out the red carpet and our visit coincided with the dedication of a memorial to the four little girls killed at Sixteenth Street Baptist Church in 1963. I participated in the dedication, a very personal event for me since my kindergarten classmate Denise McNair had been one of those killed. Jack and I walked the short distance from the church to Kelly Ingram Park, holding the hands of four little girls all dressed in pink and white for the occasion. The experience was powerful, particularly when we were told of how the bomb had blown out almost all of the windows—except one. That window, showing a likeness of Jesus Christ, had withstood the blast, but there was a hole—the face of our Lord was gone.

Still, I wanted the Brits to see the new Birmingham too, so we visited the University of Alabama at Birmingham's first-class medical center. I explained how this steel town had become a technological powerhouse thanks to Governor George Wallace's successful plan to turn the one-time commuter school into a first-class university.

Then there was one more thing to do. On Saturday we went to Tuscaloosa. Jack and I walked through the tunnel with more than eighty thousand Crimson Tide fans cheering wildly in anticipation of the big matchup with Tennessee. Jack is a politician and he glowed, basking in the adoration of the crowd. I wanted to tell him that the Alabama faithful would have cheered a squirrel coming out of the tunnel at that moment. This was the big leagues—SEC football! I flipped the coin, and Alabama won. "Nice flip," drawled Brodie Croyle, the Alabama quarterback. I'm sure my British friends didn't understand much about the game, but they were excited anyway. Alabama won, and all was well. We ended the evening with a messy deep-fried meal at Jim 'N Nick's Bar-B-Q. My friends loved the South.

Jack returned the favor at the beginning of 2006, inviting me to his electoral district in Lancashire. There were the predictable protests, which every host always apologizes for unnecessarily. At the concert that night, one of the performers sang the Beatles' "Hey Jude," substituting anti-war lyrics for a good portion of the song. She tried gamely to get the crowd to join in but it was the wrong crowd and most of the audience sat in stoic silence, giving the whole thing a comedic twist.

The next day we went to Jack's neighborhood outside the city, a district with a large Muslim population, mostly from Pakistan. It was easy to see why the Europeans have had so much trouble integrating a disaffected minority population. Many of the people there clearly didn't really see themselves as British, and it seemed as if the feeling was mutual.

Jack had arranged a one-hour discussion with Muslim leaders, all of whom viewed me skeptically, since I was the face of the Bush administration abroad. But the session couldn't have gone better. I was honest with them about what we were trying to do and about the United States' own troubled history with minorities. The ice broke when I said, "When America's founding fathers said 'We the People,' they didn't mean me." After that the questions turned to how a black woman from Alabama had come to be secretary of state. Had I ever encountered prejudice? One woman asked how she could have her say when men wouldn't stop talking. In my tenure this scene would be repeated many times—among Afro-Brazilians in Bahia, Chinese students at Tsinghua University, and journalists in Turkey. A black female secretary of state simply didn't fit with the stereotypes that most people held about the United States. Tony Blair may have summed it up best when he said that he'd been struck by the sight at the first Camp David meeting of the President flanked by Colin Powell on one side and me on the other. *Could this happen in Britain?* he asked himself. *Not yet,* he said he answered silently. *Not yet.*

The trip was eye-opening for me and, despite the press focus on the protests, largely successful. But during a question and answer session after my remarks at the BBC–Chatham House Lectures in Blackburn, I said something that was interpreted in a way I did not intend. I was asked to give examples of lessons learned from some of the mistakes that had been made over the prior three years. After giving a lengthy discussion about how difficult it is to determine in the midst of an historical event whether a decision, tactical or otherwise, is ultimately good or bad, I concluded by quipping, "I know we've made tactical errors—thousands of them, I'm sure. But when you look back in history, what will be judged is, did you make the right strategic decisions? And if you spend all of your time trying to judge this tactical issue or that tactical issue, I think you miss the larger sweep."

Because I thought my point—of missing the larger sweep—clarified my previous remarks, I didn't think much of what I had said until I saw the news clips that evening. "Rice Admits to Thousands of Mistakes in Iraq," they read. I'd used the word "tactical," so the military assumed I was shifting blame to them. I tried to clean up the mess, telling journalists that I hadn't been literal. "I say I've done that a thousand times. I don't mean I've *literally* done it a thousand times," I protested. But it didn't help. The story lived on for days. I just didn't anticipate how my words would be heard. It wouldn't be the last time.

So, by the time Jack and I were sent off to Baghdad together on April 2, 2006, we were good friends indeed. When Jack got onto the plane, he was really sick with the flu. I watched him preparing to sleep on the floor for the overnight flight. "Jack, you take the bed in my cabin," I said. "I'll sleep on the floor." He was grateful and felt better the next morning. I didn't think anything of it, but it was a story the next day. "Is it true that you took Secretary Rice's bed and she slept on the floor?" Jack was asked by the members of the press. I still can't figure out why it seemed so odd that I'd make the offer or that Jack would accept. The press could make a story of just about anything.

Flying into Baghdad that morning we encountered very bad weather. It wouldn't keep us from landing, but we were told that helicopters were grounded. Both Jack's and my security details were adamant. We'd either wait until the weather cleared or go to another part of Iraq—perhaps up to Kurdistan. The issue was that the Baghdad Airport Road, or "Death Street," as the Iraqis called it, known for lethal insurgent attacks, was the only road from the airport to the international zone. Deaths from roadside bombs were common, and there had been no time to even attempt to secure the highway.

Jack and I conferred and agreed that as the Iraqi leadership was waiting for us in Baghdad, we would take our chances. When we landed, we piled into a black suburban with our ambassadors and started the precarious, six-mile trip to the center of the city. Suddenly the motorcade screeched to a halt. The Iraqis had set up a roadblock, and traffic had slowed to a crawl. On both sides of the SUV there were buses and trucks, any one of which was a potential bomb carrier. There was nothing to do but wait. I wasn't particularly frightened, though I was vaguely aware of the danger. But I was relieved when we finally broke through and passed the security guards standing watch at the gates of the protected Green Zone.

As it turned out, the trip in wasn't half as bizarre as our meeting with Jaafari, which can only be described as surreal. Striking me—as he had before—as more suited to a professorship than political leadership, Jaafari welcomed us and described in detail his plans once he became prime minister. *Is he living in some other world?* I wondered.

Jack and I had agreed that we'd take turns making the argument that he had to end his pursuit of the prime minister position: I would go through the basic facts of the situation, and Jack would appeal to him politician to politician. Everything we tried met with stubbornness and obtuseness. "I can't disappoint the people who nominated me," he said. I was tempted to say, "*No one* wants you to be prime minister— even the people who nominated you." I held my tongue and let Jack try again. After a while, though, I just said to Jaafari, "You aren't going to be prime minister. You have to step down. This isn't because the United States wants it this way. The Iraqis don't want you, and that's what matters." Jack appeared a little taken aback, but I'd learned to be direct with Jaafari, who now looked hurt as the translation rolled forward. But he held his ground.

We went to see other Iraqi leaders who asked us point-blank if we'd convinced Jaafari to step down. *Why are you depending on us to do your dirty work?* I wondered. Not convinced that we'd gotten through, we went back to Jaafari, and this time, with only our interpreter in the room, delivered the message again. Even though he resisted, we knew we'd gotten through this time. He began publicly to suggest that he might have to withdraw and did so about three weeks later, on April 20.

On the twenty-first, Nouri al-Maliki was nominated by the Shia coalition and elected by Parliament. Iraq had its democratically elected leader. A new era had begun.

Less than a month after my visit with Jack Straw to show British-American unity, President Bush decided that I should travel to Baghdad again—this time with Don Rumsfeld to show Pentagon-State unity. I was okay with the idea, though I doubted it would stem the tide of "Don hates Condi" and "Condi hates Don" stories that had become standard fare in Washington. Admittedly, my relationship with Don was testy. He'd resented my role as national security advisor because he didn't like "White House" interference in his affairs. Now, as secretary of state, I think I seemed, to him, to be too indiscriminately flexing my figurative muscles, pushing into the Pentagon's lane.

We'd crossed swords, for instance, on Uzbekistan where, after bloody riots in May 2005, State had issued a tough human rights report against the regime. The Uzbek president, Islam Karimov, had responded by threatening to expel us from the military base that he'd allowed us into at the time of the invasion of Afghanistan. Let us recall that we'd paid a small fortune for the privilege, but the dictator felt no obligation to honor that deal and said so.

Don called me to say that we needed to back off. "The military needs that base," he said. "Our security is at stake." I told him that I was sympathetic to the Pentagon's plight but that, in my view, the United States could not soften its position on human rights as a quid pro quo for the military presence in Uzbekistan. "What's more, now that he's threatened us, we can't afford to cave," I told him. Don somehow heard this as "human rights trumps security" and told Steve Hadley to take the issue to the President. The President obviously wanted to keep the military base, but he didn't tell me to tone it down, so I didn't. Eventually Karimov would carry through on his threat, but I would negotiate basing rights in Kyrgyzstan and the Tajiks would make it clear that we could use their territory "as needed" too.

This was just one of my dustups with Don. The truth is, we'd never quite repaired our relationship after the Iraq Stabilization Group incident in the fall of 2003. And the gulf between us had widened after the President had endorsed "clear, hold, and build," which, as previously mentioned, I'd introduced in October 2005 to explain publicly what we were trying to achieve in Iraq.

For all that, the tensions between Don and me weren't personal; we still had a civil—even social—relationship. But on policy matters, we often clashed. I was skeptical of a joint trip to Baghdad. Don was downright hostile to the idea. Preparations for the trip were extremely difficult for my staff because every decision on the Pentagon's side, no matter how small, seemed to need Don's okay. Finally we were ready to go. We flew into Baghdad separately: I came in from a NATO foreign ministers meeting by way of Greece and Turkey, Don from Kuwait.

The meetings with Iraq's leaders went well but were marked by tragedy. The sister of Tariq al-Hashimi, a Sunni Arab leader who served as one of Iraq's two vice presidents, had been shot and killed by insurgents the day we arrived. Hashimi had already lost one brother just two weeks prior in a separate shooting, and his sister had been gunned down a day after Hashimi stood with his Shia and Kurdish counterparts to issue a unified call to crush the insurgency. It was increasingly clear that the terrorists would spare no effort in seeking to intimidate, threaten, and prevent Iraq's leaders from forming a unified, stable democracy.

Don and I both found Nouri al-Maliki, the incoming prime minister, a reassuring figure, largely because he seemed to know what he wanted to do. He hadn't yet been installed, so most of his ideas were conceptual, but at least he had ideas. That was a stunning contrast to Jaafari.

Every public appearance with Don was a disaster, though. It started when we held our first press availability. During a roundtable with members of both the Pentagon and State Department press corps, Janine Zacharia of Bloomberg asked whether our "secret" arrival said anything about the security situation. Well, of course it did, and what it said was not good about conditions on the ground. But one learns to just answer and not cause a scene. Don shot back, "I guess I don't think it says anything about it. . . . I just don't see anything to your question." I tried to smooth things over by saying something about the improvements in Iraqi security forces and then took the next question. In fact, I took several of the next questions while Don doodled conspicuously on a piece of paper. I was mortified and signaled Sean to end it. He did.

Don left. I would spend the night in Iraq for the first time. Our performance had just solidified the narrative of discord between us, and there wasn't much to do about it.

Frankly, that was the least of our problems. Iraq was descending into chaos, and a lot was riding on the success of its new prime minister. That night I asked to see Maliki alone at Zal's residence.

The soon-to-be prime minister was wearing a brown suit and sporting what looked to me like a five o'clock shadow. We sat together in Zal's living room with just the translator, getting to know each other and talking about the future of his country. He told me that he understood the need to improve security but that it would take a long time. If he could deliver electricity quickly, people would feel an immediate improvement. Could I help him do that? I said that we'd do what we could, but I knew in my heart that the two were inextricably related, and in that moment I reflected on all the failed efforts to deliver power thus far.

My overwhelming impression was favorable, though. Maliki was down to earth and spoke very little English. He'd spent his exile in Syria, not Tehran, because he couldn't stand the Iranians. He had a blunt, direct character that I really liked. "The Iraqi people have had enough," he said. "And if we don't demonstrate that we can govern, then we're not going to be able to do this. All will be lost if we can't demonstrate we can govern." I was surprised. It was the first time an Iraqi leader had taken things upon himself rather than simply asking what we, the United States, could do. And when I said that most Sunnis didn't feel safe when they saw the Shia-dominated Iraqi security forces, Maliki showed a sense of black humor. "I don't feel safe when I see them either," he said. I really felt good about Nouri al-Maliki. When I was wheels-up from Baghdad the next day, I was more hopeful than I'd been since the bombing of the Golden Mosque four months before.

34

SHIFTING COURSE ON IRAN

THE TEMPORARY SENSE of ease about Iraq allowed me to focus my attention again on the continuing problem of Iran. By the spring of 2006 we'd taken a number of small steps to unify the international community on the Iranian issue. I met with my P5+1 counterparts in New York on the margins of several meetings at the United Nations to try to move the process forward, but there seemed to be little motivation to levy Security Council sanctions against Tehran. In fact, the uneasy consensus that we'd developed in London was already showing signs of strain, with the Russians signaling publicly that they didn't favor punitive actions. We needed to make another move.

The big carrot for the Iranians was U.S. participation in the negotiations. As Javier Solana, the EU foreign policy chief, put it, "They want America. That's all they want—America." We were not prepared to enter the negotiations unconditionally, but might it be time to call the Iranians' bluff? What if we offered to join the talks in exchange for a suspension of Iranian enrichment and reprocessing activities?

Getting consensus around a U.S. policy shift of this magnitude would not be easy. I wasn't even sure that I could get the President to that point. Over the Easter break I did what I often found helpful: I wrote a paper outlining a possible policy shift. Sometimes with the daily crush of events, it is hard to step back and think. I found it useful to take time out, usually on a weekend or a holiday, to write a paper to clarify my own thinking. This time I wanted to be sure I had my arguments in order before approaching the President.

I first discussed these ideas with the President shortly after Easter. The President was not immediately convinced that we ought to offer to join the negotiations. We kept going back and forth in each of at least six separate encounters. He was still not ready to make a decision by the middle of May, and his NSC Principals were hardly of one mind on the subject. As the President processed the pros and cons of the proposal, he'd call with a question or a thought. "The President is on the phone," Liz would say.

"Yes, sir?"

"I was just thinking, suppose we play this card and the Iranians just drag out the negotiations?" he asked on one occasion.

"We can always walk out after a prescribed period of time—maybe six months," I offered.

"No," the President disagreed, "you know we'll never be able to do it. I can hear our friends now begging to have the negotiations continue just a little bit longer. We'll be trapped."

During one of our Sunday-morning phone calls, the President raised another concern: "Suppose we do this and the Europeans or the Russians just give lip service but don't carry through with sanctions?"

"That's a risk, sir," I replied. "But right now we're dead in the water. We need to take a risk."

Finally I asked if we could have dinner with Steve Hadley and figure out a way forward. I needed to make this move in advance of a scheduled trip to Europe at the beginning of June. I hoped to get the P5+1 together at that time. "Come on over tomorrow night," he said.

The next night, I joined the President, the First Lady, and Steve for dinner in the dining room where the first couple ate their daily meals. On several occasions when I joined them, we engaged in friendly conversation over several courses—the President mostly interested in dessert. But on that particular evening, we ate quickly, and then the President, Steve, and I retired to the office upstairs in the residence. As I described earlier, it is the room in which he made the critical decisions on September 16, 2001, that led to the war in Afghanistan. The room was always cold and bleak, not sunny and inviting like the Oval Office. That night it felt particularly chilly—or maybe it was just the fact that I didn't seem to be getting anywhere. We reviewed all the relevant factors: the stalemate that the Iranians were exploiting while they continued to improve their capabilities; the slippage in the international coalition; and the stepped-up aggression against our forces led by Iranian allies in Iraq. The last made the President and other members of the NSC wonder whether "rewarding" the Iranians with an offer to talk made any sense while they were killing our soldiers.

At a later NSC meeting on the subject, though, there was less resistance than I expected from the other principals. The Vice President said little except to underscore the point the President had made before: we had to make sure the Iranians didn't read the offer as an expression of weakness. Don said nothing. Quite unexpectedly, the President asked whether we should make the offer to enter the negotiations unconditional. That idea quickly faded as we focused on how critical it was that we verify suspension of the program. The worst possible outcome would be negotiating while the Iranians continued to improve their capabilities.

At the end of the meeting the President again demurred, saying that he needed to think about it. I cornered Steve outside the Situation Room. "What is he still thinking about?" I asked.

"He just considers it a big deal," Steve replied. "I think he'll get there."

When I got back to the department, I called the President. "Why don't you call Blair, Chirac, Merkel, and Putin?" I suggested, hoping that those conversations would move things along. "Put the proposition to them and see what they think." He noted that Blair was coming to the White House; he'd speak to him then. And he'd ask Blair to feel out the others too. "I'll call Putin," he said.

The conversation with Blair was, as usual, wide-ranging. But when the prime minister turned to Iran, the President deferred, saying he wanted to talk about it at lunch. After some small talk around the rectangular table in the family dining room, the President suddenly said, "Tony, Condi has this idea, and I want to know what you think." I almost swallowed my scallop whole. Blair smiled. Leaders who knew us well had gotten accustomed to the somewhat unusual and sometimes informal interaction between the President and me.

"Well, what does she have up her sleeve?" Blair asked.

The President then described the idea and asked whether the Europeans were ready to levy tough sanctions on Iran if Tehran failed to negotiate in good faith. Blair said that he favored the change in strategy and would of course be willing to take tough steps if Iran balked.

He didn't want to speak for others but would see Chirac and Merkel at the upcoming European Council meeting and put it to them directly. Within a few days the two leaders called the President with the message he needed: they would not "go soft" on Iran if we made the shift. Putin was equally categorical and delighted that we were finally "taking Russia's advice."

"You don't need a secretary of state," I joked. "You can do this diplomacy stuff yourself." We laughed, but I had what I needed. I'd given the job of drafting a statement on the matter to Bob Joseph, who had headed proliferation policy for me both at the NSC and now at State. Bob was a hard-liner but also a clear and broad thinker. In fact, I often asked Bob to come in and debate issues with me to force me to confront hawkish objections to my diplomatic efforts. The final statement on Iran bore his imprint. When I sent it to Steve for interagency coordination, he said, "This is pretty tough," obviously pleased by its tone.

"It has to be," I said. I wasn't just protecting our right flank at home. I wanted to be sure that the Iranians didn't misread the approach. Things were not going well in Iraq. I didn't want Tehran to think that it had gained the upper hand.

On May 31, I faced the press to announce the shift in U.S. policy. In exchange for Iran's verifiable suspension of its enrichment and reprocessing activities, the United States would join its EU-3 partners (the United Kingdom, France, and Germany) and sit face-to-face with Tehran's representatives in negotiations. I also made clear that all issues—not just nuclear—would be on the table.

The latter offer was key. We were signaling to Tehran that there might be a political thaw in the bargain too—we could talk about regional issues, such as Afghanistan, Iraq, economics, and trade. Our European allies, the Russians, and many other countries believed that the big prize for Iran was an improved relationship with the United States and recognition of its role in international politics. We were testing that proposition. If Iran were looking for a path toward normalizing relations with the United States, nuclear negotiations could be the starting point. But there would have to be a change in the regime's behavior. Left unsaid was the central point: we were not, in the short run, seeking regime change. Frankly, from our point of view, if Iran took the carrot and carried through on the obligations to verifiably suspend its nuclear activities, it would be a very different regime in any case.

"President Bush wants a positive relationship between the American people and the people of Iran," I stated, "a beneficial relationship of increased contacts in education and cultural exchange, in sports, in travel, in trade, and in investment." But the nuclear issue was not the only obstacle standing in the way of improved relations. "The Iranian government supports terror," I reminded the international community. "It is involved in violence in Iraq, and it is undercutting the restoration of full sovereignty in Lebanon under UN Security Council Resolution 1559."

So Iran was far from being a responsible state, but, together with the Europeans, we were willing to offer a path toward its reconciliation with the international community. That was the carrot. The stick would be tougher sanctions and further isolation.

Several hours later I got on the plane for Vienna, Austria, and a meeting of the P5+1. I felt a great sense of relief at being able to engage my colleagues on firmer ground. The Iranians predictably reacted to the "disrespectful tone" of the statement, and Sergei Lavrov said that the approach could have been more "diplomatic." The Russians weren't as cooperative as I'd hoped, given the big step we'd made; they again repeated their arguments about not backing Iran into a corner. But they and all the others knew that the shift in U.S. policy had put Tehran back on the defense. The P5+1 was united, and we now had a really firm basis from which to move toward UN Security Council sanctions.

MY RESERVATIONS about extending an olive branch to Tehran were compounded by my growing sense of our vulnerability in Iraq. It was becoming painfully obvious that we had neither the right military strategy in Iraq nor enough forces to carry out the flawed one that we were pursuing. NSC meetings were becoming increasingly frustrating with shifting metrics and claims about the number of Iraqi security forces being trained. After one such briefing I told my chief of staff, Brian Gunderson, that I would never again use the Pentagon's train-and-equip numbers when briefing the Congress. "I don't believe them myself," I told him.

When it came to financial accountability for the war effort, I relied on the meticulous work of Stuart Bowen, who, as the special inspector general for Iraq reconstruction (SIGIR), oversaw the expenditure of funds for Iraq relief and reconstruction activities. Though Stuart performed a tremendous public service, I dreaded our meetings, as they were a reminder of the high costs of reconstruction efforts in highly insecure environments. Whenever the Iraq Stabilization Group had tried to focus the Pentagon on protection of critical infrastructure—pipelines or the electrical grid, for instance—the Defense Department would repeatedly say, "We don't have enough civilians in the fight."

I accepted the criticism that State needed more people in Iraq, and we were making personnel changes to make that possible, including finding a way to send qualified Arabists from posts such as Cairo while allowing their families to stay in the region. Before that change, a family would have to pick up roots, sometimes in the middle of the school year, and return to Washington while the officer was deployed to the war zone. I even threatened to require Foreign Service officers to serve in Iraq. This was a radical break with the practice of voluntary bidding on posts. It hadn't been done since Vietnam. Ultimately I didn't have to because enough people of all ranks volunteered. But I was prepared to do so and to face down the American Foreign Service Association—a kind of union for U.S. diplomats—before Congress and the American people if necessary. I really resented the implication by the Pentagon and in some corners of Congress that State was to blame for the mounting failures in Iraq.

The issue came to a head in an NSC meeting in May. When I presented an update on the number of civilian personnel willing to deploy to Iraq, George Casey, the commanding general in Iraq, blurted out, "Ma'am, that's a paltry number." And he had done it in front of the President.

At that time I had defended my agency, signaling that the Pentagon wasn't exactly covering itself in glory. "General, when you can protect forty times the civilians we have on the ground now, I promise to send more," I said.

"Okay, on that happy note we will adjourn," the President interjected, abruptly concluding the meeting.

I left for Camp David that afternoon and upon arrival called George to apologize for embarrassing him in front of the President. But when Steve mentioned before dinner that everyone, including the President, had been uncomfortable with the confrontation, I simply told him that it had to be said. I wouldn't allow the Pentagon to get away with that nonsense. "You and George okay?" the President asked at dinner.

"Yes," I answered. I didn't elaborate, and the President didn't ask for further details.

In the summer of 2006 I would answer questions about Iraq by stating bluntly the challenges we were facing and then describing what we were trying to do. But in truth, I worried that we were in danger of losing. Newspapers worldwide were filled with dire stories of suicide bombings, roadside attacks on coalition forces, and—most poignantly—U.S. troop casualties in the *Washington Post*'s "Faces of the Fallen." I made myself look at every photograph of each soldier so that I wouldn't become inured to the war's human cost.

I'd begun to visit Walter Reed Army Medical Center and the National Naval Medical Center every few months. New Year's Day and Good Friday were particularly good days to go because there were fewer visitors than on Christmas or Easter. I never took the press or told them; I'd just arrange to go spend time with the patients, their families, and the dedicated medical staff; listen to their stories; and talk about the challenges of recovery. When I thanked the injured service members for their sacrifice and received their thanks for what I was doing for the country, the reciprocal gesture never felt quite right. *I don't deserve that,* I remember thinking. Often a soldier would say that he just wanted to get back into the fight. The courage of J. R. Salzman was particularly inspiring. As he led a fuel convoy near Baghdad, a roadside bomb exploded by J.R.'s Humvee. He lost his left hand and his right arm below the elbow. Before joining the 34th Infantry Division, J.R. was a serious athlete, and he was determined to compete once again, grateful he still had his legs. Upon his discharge from Walter Reed, J.R. went on to win two world titles in logrolling. I never scheduled events directly after these visits because it was so emotional to see what those patriotic young men and women were enduring and trying to overcome.

One young man will always stay in my mind's eye. The doctor at

Bethesda had warned me that his particular case of traumatic brain injury was worse than most. The soldier's unit had been hit head-on by several improvised explosive devices (IEDs), but he had miraculously survived. "I wouldn't take you in there," the doctor said, "but his mom wants to meet you." I steeled myself and went into a darkened room where a young black man was crying out and screaming uncontrollably. I flashed back to my father's own anoxic brain injury when he had done the same thing. At the time, the doctor had said that it was the brain repairing itself. It sounded as though Daddy had been flung into the depths of Hell. It was the same with this young man.

His mother walked away from the bed and greeted me. "I'm so sorry for what's happened to your son," I said hesitantly.

"He's a little better sometimes," she answered. We had a picture taken together, and I promised to pray for them. I asked from time to time about the young man. I eventually learned that he hadn't made it.

Though the human toll was difficult to witness, I deeply believe that the sacrifice was not in vain. The new Iraq could be the foundation of a more peaceful and prosperous Middle East. Yet in the summer of 2006 that goal seemed far away indeed.

The deteriorating situation on the ground was eroding support at home with a rapidity that was terrifying. All kinds of radical ideas were being proposed. Senator Joseph Biden and Leslie Gelb, the former president of the Council on Foreign Relations, coauthored an article in which they suggested that Iraq be partitioned into three autonomous zones along sectarian and ethnic lines—a spectacularly bad idea that gained credence only because nothing seemed worse than the current circumstances. NBC News declared Iraq to be in a civil war, a term that we assiduously rejected. I made a visit to Capitol Hill to check in with the leadership on both sides of the aisle. I expected the Democrats to be in full revolt, but I found bipartisan despair. The Republicans didn't relish going home that summer with the Iraqi millstone around their necks. "Something has to change before the fall," Senator Mitch McConnell told me. "I can't hold the caucus too much longer." I respected Mitch as one of the best legislators I knew. His warning couldn't be ignored.

And we were getting nowhere inside the administration. The more pressure we put on the Pentagon, the less flexible it became. Every NSC and Principals meeting ended with Don clinging to the notion that only an improvement in the political landscape would solve the security situation.

In the midst of those horrors, we finally received good news. The chaos in Iraq had, in part, been the handiwork of Abu Musab al-Zarqawi, who was suspected of orchestrating the February bombing of the Golden Mosque. Though Ayman al-Zawahiri, bin Laden's second in command, had criticized the so-called emir of al Qaeda in Iraq for perpetrating violence against other Muslims, Zarqawi's plan to destabilize Iraq had worked, plunging the Iraqis into civil conflict—if not outright war—between Sunnis and Shia. On June 7 I was at my desk when I got the news: Zarqawi had been killed in a strike by U.S. warplanes. A few months later, the unit that killed him gave me a stone with the initials AMZ and the date 6–7-2006. The gruesome souvenir occupied a treasured spot on my bookcase at the State Department. Today it sits on a shelf in my office at Stanford. I have recently reflected on how I became hardened enough emotionally back then to celebrate a human being's death without the slightest feeling of remorse. But in truth, I was almost giddy when I heard the news. Maybe Zarqawi's demise would deflate the Sunni insurgency and give us a chance to fight on one front—not two—as we dealt with the threat of Muqtada al-Sadr's Mahdi Army in the south.

What we didn't immediately see were the changes in the Sunni heartland that were beginning to shift on the ground in our favor. My first hint had come not from the intelligence agencies but from an e-mail that a friend passed on to me. It had come from his son, a young officer serving in Anbar who talked about the improving environment and cooperation with the locals. Apparently, al Qaeda and the insurgent fighters were turning out to be very bad guests among the tribal communities in Al Anbar province. The sheikhs were tiring of the intimidation by these foreigners, who compelled cooperation through the most brutal of tactics—delivering the severed heads of children to their parents, for instance, to ensure loyalty to the terrorist cause. Reportedly, quite a few daughters of the tribes had been forcibly married off to the insurgents too. Zarqawi's successor, Abu Ayyub al-Masri, apparently escalated those practices, and in time the tribal leaders had enough. The seeds of the Anbar "awakening" had been sown, and we'd soon have new allies in the rough-and-tumble Sunni heartland.

The summer marked a kind of awakening in Washington too. Individually and together, several of us began looking for new approaches to Iraq. On June 6 Philip Zelikow, the department's counselor, and James Jeffrey, a senior Middle East hand who'd served in Iraq, sent me an eleven-page memo called "Possible Political-Military Strategy for the Summer of 2006." Reflecting the view that we couldn't sustain our troop presence for much longer, they recommended a "selective counterinsurgency" strategy. The United States wouldn't try to be everywhere in the country, but we *would* add troops temporarily to contest for major strongholds, create a better atmosphere for the newly trained Iraqi forces, and then withdraw. I found the memo thought-provoking and sent it on to Steve Hadley. We agreed to start an informal process between our staffs to discuss options. Not surprisingly, Steve had the President's authority to look for a different path in Iraq.

35

THE MIDDLE EAST PLUNGES INTO WAR

WITHIN A COUPLE of weeks, though, events in the Middle East and Asia exploded, diverting my attention from Iraq for the better part of two months. I'd just returned from a trip to Vienna for a U.S.-EU summit and to Budapest for the fiftieth anniversary of the Hungarian Revolution. The latter event was emotional for me as a student of communism in Eastern Europe—especially so when the Hungarians unearthed my long-forgotten academic article called "The Soviet Decision to Invade Hungary." The trip ended on the twenty-fourth, and I was to leave again for Pakistan and Afghanistan.

On June 25, a calm Sunday morning, I sat sipping coffee in my Watergate kitchen, hoping to have a few hours to myself and perhaps play golf before departing the next day. The phone rang. It was Tzipi Livni, the Israeli foreign minister. Eight Palestinian militants in Gaza, including members of Hamas, had entered Israel through a secret tunnel and killed two Israeli soldiers, wounded three others, and kidnapped a nineteen-year-old corporal named Gilad Shalit. I could hear the rage in Tzipi's voice. "The Israeli people will demand that we do something," she cried out.

"Tzipi, stay calm and don't just react," I said. "Hamas will pay a price internationally for what they've done." But I knew that it wouldn't be long before Israel avenged the attack and we'd again be deep into a crisis in Gaza.

After hanging up, I called the President. "They [the Israelis] are loaded for bear," I said. "Do you want to call Olmert?"

"No, what is he going to tell me except what you've already heard?" he asked quite reasonably.

"Do you want *me* to call him?" I asked.

"Yes," said the President, "and give him my condolences."

Sometimes it was better for me to make the first call, allowing the President a "second bite at the apple," if we needed one—and when the situation on the ground was clearer.

The conversation with the Israeli prime minister was much like the one with Tzipi. I made some points about the need to be cognizant of the vulnerability of civilians in Gaza. Olmert acknowledged that responsibility but said that the attack would not go unanswered. It was better that he had the conversation with me. You don't want to put the President of the United States in the position of asking for restraint when you know the request will fall on deaf ears.

I left the next morning for Pakistan and Afghanistan, trying to concentrate on the problems there while awaiting the news—certain to come—of an Israeli attack in Gaza. My agenda in South Asia was a familiar one: to continue to push for cooperation between these unlikely and prickly partners in the war on terror. But in Pakistan the news took a different and consequential turn. My dinner with the foreign minister had gone later than expected, and it was already midnight when we met the press. I expected to take a few questions critical of India and of Karzai, call for cooperation, and end the encounter.

The last question was from a journalist who noted that the United States had not called for "free and fair elections." Frankly, I wasn't sure if he was right, and I didn't want to blindside my host. But what else could I say? "The United States stands for free and fair elections and will help the Pakistani government to achieve them." At that moment I had no idea how elaborate my involvement would become. Within a year I would arrange a deal between Benazir Bhutto and Pervez Musharraf, insisting that the general take off his uniform to facilitate a return to civilian rule. And I would help clear the way for Bhutto's tragic reentry into Pakistan.

My attention to matters in South Asia didn't last, however, because the Middle East was erupting. By the time I arrived in Moscow to meet with my G8 counterparts and lay the groundwork for the upcoming summit, the expected Israeli response was unfolding in Gaza. The Israel Defense Forces (IDF) were sent into southern Gaza, where they conducted air strikes against bridges and energy infrastructure. Israeli forces also seized members of Hamas in the West Bank. The clashes in

Gaza had a predictable rhythm. Hamas would provoke, Israel would respond militarily, and the international community would wring its hands. This time was no different. With the help of Peter MacKay, the Canadian foreign minister, I fought back the idea of a G8 statement urging the Israelis to cease their military action. "Who are we kidding?" I said to my colleagues. "We can call for a ceasefire until we're blue in the face. It isn't going to happen until Israel has completed its operation."

The problem was that the Israelis always seemed to overreach. Initially, there was some sympathy for a response but sooner or later the inevitable Al Jazeera pictures of civilian misery would turn the tide of public opinion. Israel, determined to damage Hamas and to send a message of deterrence, was never sufficiently aware of when it was running out of time before it, and not the terrorists, was considered the aggressor. It was the job of the United States—and the secretary of state in particular—to walk the fine line that affirmed Israel's right to self-defense and protected U.S. interests with a broad set of allies and friends. Every secretary of state since 1948 has had to do that. I sometimes wonder how many more of us will come and go before that challenge goes away.

THE FIGURATIVE EXPLOSION in the Middle East would soon give way to headlines about a literal one in Asia. On the Fourth of July, North Korea test-fired seven missiles, including a Taepodong-2 ICBM. The North Korean issue had festered since the breakdown of talks almost a year before. Seeking to blame the United States, the North had offered to return to the Six-Party Talks on condition that the U.S. unfreeze Pyongyang's assets in a Chinese-owned bank in Macau. The money in Banco Delta Asia totaled only $25 million, but it was symbolically important to Kim Jong-il. When the President met with Chinese President Hu Jintao at the White House in April, Hu asked him directly to unfreeze the assets so that the talks could resume. At the time, the President reminded Hu that the problem was not one of sanctions but of North Korea's threats and bad behavior. The missile test put the Chinese in a corner.

I called my Chinese counterpart, Li Zhaoxing, and told him that the time had come for Beijing to step forward. North Korea had had plenty of warning not to conduct the test but had gone ahead anyway. In fact, the prospect of the test had led us to mobilize for the first time our nascent missile defense system. Using components in Alaska and at sea, the Pentagon had cobbled together the ability to shoot down a North Korean missile should it threaten the United States or U.S. assets. I'd favored the idea but told the President that it might cost us internationally or even on Capitol Hill. (The issue of missile defenses was still sensitive, and seeing interceptors put into position might trigger a negative response.) It did neither. Our allies, Congress, and even the Russians seemed to see the wisdom of a "defensive" challenge to North Korea's aggression.

Li and the Chinese were isolated internationally and they knew it. In Paris at a previously called meeting of the P5+1 to discuss Iran's nuclear activities, the Chinese had first refused to send a representative, claiming scheduling conflicts, but had ultimately dispatched Li's third in command. I am convinced that it had little to do with Iran. Li didn't want to talk about North Korea, so he avoided the meeting. Sitting in the French Ministry of Foreign Affairs on an unbearably hot day with no air-conditioning, I found myself angry at Beijing for this policy of avoidance. I made a mental note to tell Li that China was a great power but never acted like one. Then a little voice inside my head whispered, *Maybe that's for the best.*

Despite China's reticence the Japanese and United States sponsored a Chapter VII UN resolution imposing strong sanctions on the North. On this issue the Chinese had never voted for Chapter VII, which called for all necessary means to protect against a "threat to peace and security." In the end, they weren't ready to do so on this occasion either. But when John Bolton, the U.S. ambassador to the UN, called me only one week after the missile test to say that he had UNSC agreement on imposing sanctions if we would delete the reference to Chapter VII, I readily agreed. John had cleverly used much of the language of the more consequential resolution in this new draft. Now China was on record agreeing to sanction its client. Pyongyang's missile test had been too much for even Beijing. More importantly, these steps laid the foundation for much tougher action against Pyongyang when in a few months

Kim Jong-il again, to quote President Bush, "threw his food on the floor in a very noisy way" by exploding a nuclear device.

AS THE NEGOTIATIONS on North Korea were unfolding, I was on my way to meet the President for his bilateral sessions with his European counterparts. On the heels of the trouble in Gaza, more consequential and dangerous events were taking place in the Middle East. Hezbollah had launched an attack across the Blue Line (the internationally recognized border between Israel and Lebanon), killing Israeli soldiers and kidnapping others. After conversations with Tzipi Livni and Lebanese Prime Minister Fouad Siniora, I issued a statement condemning the attack. The region was exploding again.

I caught up with President Bush in Germany, trying to keep tabs on what was transpiring in the Middle East without detracting from the visit meant to showcase our friendship with Berlin. Chancellor Angela Merkel decided to stage a German barbecue dinner for the President, complete with a whole roasted pig. The scene was a little odd, as if the cultural event had been flipped on its head—the Texans sitting there in their cowboy boots with Chancellor Merkel similarly attired. But it was a very nice outing, and I spent a good deal of time with Merkel's husband, a professor with whom I shared stories about the crazy goings-on in universities.

But by the time we reached the Konstantinovsky Palace just outside St. Petersburg, the situation in Lebanon was deteriorating quickly. I had been looking forward to a brief, somewhat routine stop there to attend a bilateral between the President and President Putin before the G8 summit of heads of state. Foreign ministers didn't usually attend the meeting with their bosses, and I was glad to head for Washington for an extended home stay—two whole weeks before heading to Southeast Asia.

My room was in a separate building on the palace grounds from where the President was staying. After several calls with the Israelis, I called Steve Hadley to see if the President was available. "He says you should come on over," Steve said. I dressed hurriedly while my security detail figured out how to get the car to me quickly. The Russians had decided that there would be no cars on the premises, so my agents were also without transportation. A nearby golf cart seemed the quickest way to get to the President.

Having so recently been angered by the Gaza provocation, Israel was in no mood to be counseled to exercise restraint. There was little doubt that Olmert—needing to show that he was as strong as his predecessor, Sharon—would come down hard on Hezbollah. Within a day, Hezbollah compounded the problem by launching a near-continuous assault of rockets into northern Israel. The pictures across Israeli television of citizens scrambling into bomb shelters further enraged public opinion.

In response to the Hezbollah infiltration, Israel blockaded the Lebanese coast and began a bombing campaign against Lebanon's main airport, hitting fuel tanks that caused dramatic and fiery explosions. When I later asked Olmert's aides why they'd gone after fuel tanks, he was honest. "Because we needed the Israeli people to see that we were doing something spectacular," he said.

The G8 always seemed to be dominated by an unforeseen crisis. The year before, it had been the attack on the London public transit system that had killed fifty-two people. A tragedy of that kind at least permitted the G8 to be immediately united in its response—no one favored terrorist attacks. But reacting to the outbreak of hostilities in the Middle East is a much more complicated matter. And the response would follow the familiar pattern seen a month before in Gaza: sympathy for Israel; alarm at the civilian toll resulting from the response; and a turn against the Jewish state, which would within a matter of weeks be seen as the aggressor. The difference this time was the magnitude of the confrontation. This wasn't a raid into the Gaza Strip and a nasty skirmish with Hamas; it risked an all-out war between Israel and the state of Lebanon, which was held captive by Hezbollah.

The President, Steve, and I talked about taking advantage of the G8 to craft a joint statement from the summit participants that would set the terms for the coming international debate about Lebanon. It helped that the French had no sympathy for Hezbollah and Jacques Chirac was a fierce defender of Lebanese sovereignty; it had been the United States and France that had spearheaded the effort to get Syrian troops out of the country. Even the Russians were furious at Hezbollah's leader, Hassan Nasrallah, and were prepared to back strong language. They largely supported the view that a ceasefire had to ensure that Hezbollah could never again cross the Blue Line and attack Israel.

Knowing their sentiments, Steve and I drafted a statement for the leaders of the G8. "Where are we going to get somebody to type it?" he asked.

"I type eighty words a minute," I replied, explaining that my mother had insisted on typing lessons "just in case" I needed secretarial skills. What irony! I certainly needed secretarial skills in this case—of both the clerical and diplomatic variety.

We composed a statement that had several elements. First, the statement firmly laid the blame for the violence at the feet of the extremists who were responsible: Hamas in Gaza and Hezbollah in Lebanon. The Israeli operations were in direct response to brazen cross-border raids by the Iranian-sponsored groups. Hamas and Hezbollah had picked the fight, and it was important for the international community to affirm that.

Second, it expressed our deep and growing concern about the human toll of the violence. The conflict was killing civilians, damaging infrastructure, and disrupting thousands of lives and livelihoods. We were sure Israel would get most of the blame for the perilous humanitarian situation; often overlooked, however, was how Hamas and Hezbollah worsened the crisis by deliberately enmeshing themselves among civilians.

Third, the statement urged Israel to operate with utmost restraint, while reaffirming its right to defend itself. We couldn't blame the Israelis for wanting to respond to the attacks on their territory, but how they responded mattered. The Israeli operations had strategic and humanitarian consequences, and we urged the Israelis to take the greatest care to avoid killing or injuring innocent civilians, as well as to avoid undermining the democratically elected government of Lebanon.

Finally, it called for the cessation of violence by all sides—but, importantly, not on any terms. The fighting needed to end on terms that were positive and sustainable, and the framework for achieving this outcome had been outlined by previous Security Council resolutions. In Lebanon, this meant the disarmament of Hezbollah and the redeployment of the Lebanese Armed Forces to the south of the country, where they had been prevented from operating for decades. Only by reasserting its writ across its territory could the Lebanese government credibly enter dialogue with Israel and resolve the long-running—but not insurmountable—obstacles to lasting peace.

That evening we met with the French and British national security advisors over dinner to agree to a text that we'd jointly present to the Russians the following day. There was back-and-forth about some of the exact terms, particularly concerning arms embargoes that clearly targeted Syria. The Russians were always careful to say nothing that might constrain their lucrative arms trade with Damascus.

By lunch the next day, the statement was ready to be presented at the leaders-only meeting that afternoon. I told Steve that I'd likely go ahead and leave. He suggested that I stay. Referencing the President, he said, "He'll want you around for this." I returned to my room to make calls to European allies and check in with the Israelis.

After about an hour, I received a call on the secure phone (though the Russians could undoubtedly "hear" us talking) from Jared Weinstein, the President's personal aide. "The boss wants you to come over," he said. The President had called Steve as well, and the two of us jumped in another golf cart and went to the building where the leaders were meeting.

When we arrived, the President, apparently having forgotten that he had summoned Steve, called me to the table with the other leaders and said, "Condi is going to work out the rest of this language." I looked around and noticed that Blair and Putin were not at the table. They'd gone into a small room to discuss the terms. I joined them, motioning for Steve to come with me.

When we walked into the room, Blair said, "Come on in, Condi." In a relatively short time we had an agreement on precisely what the United Nations would be asked to do; that had been the sticking point, with the Russians wanting a larger UN role in "investigating" the circumstances of the attack and the Brits knowing that it would be unacceptable to Israel. The work finished, we went back into the other room and adopted the statement.

I looked over at Steve. "What's wrong?" I asked.

"I can't be his national security advisor if he doesn't trust me to do these things for him," he said. "I have to resign."

It hadn't occurred to me that the President's decision to call me in had put Steve in an embarrassing position. He was right about the implications for how he would be viewed. I'd been in his place, knowing what it was like to occasionally have the President take me for granted in front of his peers. "I'll talk to him," I said.

"No, don't do that," he insisted. "I have to handle this myself."

We went back to where the President was staying, and I asked to see him. "Mr. President," I said, "you just cut the legs out from under Hadley. He doesn't think you trust or value him."

The President looked surprised. "I just needed you to negotiate that language—I didn't want to do it," he said.

"I know," I said, "but that's not how Steve took it. And it might not be how others took it either." I left. The President called Steve over and apologized. It was a bad moment with a very good ending. The two men would become incredibly close after that—it was different from the relationship the President and I had but equally close. And it would matter a lot when Steve took up the cause of redirecting our faltering effort in Iraq.

The G8 statement was a good start but it was not a substitute for active diplomacy. Whenever there's a conflagration, particularly in the Middle East, people expect the U.S. secretary of state to go and try to resolve it. The President, Steve, and I talked about whether I should go and when. Blair had said it best when he told the President, "Condi will have to go but she can't go too soon. When the American secretary of state goes, something has to happen." We all knew that nothing was going to happen for a while, so I returned to the United States to monitor events from Washington.

I've been asked many times to describe my hardest challenges while in government service. There were many, but a disproportionate number seemed to cluster in 2006: Iraq in flames, Hamas in the Palestinian government, North Korea flexing its muscles in Asia, Iran marching toward a nuclear weapon, Afghanistan deteriorating. Some days it was hard to see a way out. I would read the biographies of the founding fathers, and it reminded me that impossible things had been achieved before. *The United States of America should never have come into being,* I thought, *after a war against the greatest military power of the time and with Hamilton and Jefferson at each other's throats.* But it did. *And who would have believed that the Soviet Union could collapse peacefully? You can do this!*

But even in a terrible year there is always something that stands out. And in 2006 it was the war in Lebanon, which was truly debilitating. As the conflict dragged on, I felt personally responsible for trying to stop it—and very much on the spot. Yet I knew that we had to have the right ceasefire terms so that Hezbollah was not handed a victory for its aggression.

Each day brought new horrors as Hezbollah fired rockets at the Israeli population, and in response the IDF laid waste to Lebanon's infrastructure. The government of Fouad Siniora was caught in the middle. His government was in no way responsible for Hezbollah's raid. It had known nothing about it in advance. But it was paying the price. Never had a government looked so helpless—unable to stop either the splinter terrorists, who were theoretically a part of the government, or the IDF, which in retaliation was destroying the country.

My efforts in the early stages were reduced to practically begging the Israelis to back off—just a little, at least, in recognition of the precarious position of the Siniora government. I gained the Israelis' agreement to spare the power grid, thereby avoiding misery for the Lebanese who lived beyond the Hezbollah-controlled South. For the time being, Israel also did not use its ground forces to a significant extent. Meanwhile, the international community was moving from despair at the humanitarian toll to the predictable stage of blaming Israel. Pressure for a ceasefire was growing.

The President called the National Security Council together on July 19. There was broad agreement that the Israeli offensive would continue no matter what we said. Furthermore, it was probably a good thing that Hezbollah sustain more damage to its infrastructure and forces so that the terrorist group wouldn't be tempted to launch attacks again in the near future.

But there was also a great deal of sympathy for Siniora and the Lebanese people. We agreed to press the Israelis on all fronts to refrain from attacks that punished our allies in Beirut. It was admittedly a fine line but one that we had to walk for a while.

After the meeting, the President and I walked back to the Oval. "Are you ready to go?" he asked.

"I think so," I said. The night before, I'd seen a CNN report—one of many in the news—asking precisely when the U.S. secretary of state was going to show up. There had even been one of those snap polls asking people if I could bring peace. I don't remember the numbers, but most people thought I could. *This is getting pretty personal,* I thought.

"What will you do there?" the President asked as we continued down the hall.

"Well, I don't know just yet," I said. "David Welch has been working on terms for a ceasefire, and I'll try to get both sides on board." I would go first to the United Nations, where I'd called for consultations. My colleagues from around the world had readily agreed. Ministers didn't like sitting on their hands, and at least we could *look* as though we were doing something in New York.

Two days later I left for Lebanon and Israel to cobble together the terms of a durable, sustainable ceasefire. By that time, the international community was overwhelmingly in favor of an immediate ceasefire. I kept asking my colleagues to focus not on the timing but on the terms—our strategy had to be to try to lay a more secure foundation for Israeli and Lebanese security to avoid a Hamas-like repetition of the conflict. It was frustrating trying to get people to do the right thing. It was hard to negotiate an agreement that would actually matter—and very easy to call for an end to the war.

I landed first in Lebanon to try and move the various factions toward agreement on terms for a ceasefire. Fouad just wanted to end the war as quickly as possible, but he said he couldn't do it alone. Could I talk to Nabih Berri, the speaker of Parliament and leader of the Shia political party, Amal?

No friend of the United States, Berri was nonetheless key to an agreement that would send the Lebanese army into the South and prevent

Hezbollah from reestablishing its presence there. The meeting was un-
pleasant and tense. "Do you expect me to make a deal with the Israelis,
who are killing my people?" he started out.

"I'm very sorry for the losses of life," I said, trying to keep my cool.
At one moment he had me believing that he actually cared about his
people, but the next I suspected that he was just playing the political
advantage that he clearly had over me. I got nowhere with Berri, but at
least he wasn't inclined to oppose the movement of the Lebanese army
into the south of the country. I realized at that moment this was the
most important step we could take: reestablishing the national army
throughout the country would be a victory for Lebanese sovereignty as
it took up positions that Hezbollah and Syrian forces had once held. It
wouldn't change the political balance immediately, but it was one step
toward strengthening the power of our allies in Beirut. Couple that
with a more capable and empowered multinational force and it would
be possible to conceive of a more sustainable security environment after
a ceasefire.

When I returned to meet with Siniora, he again raised the unresolved
issue of the Shebaa Farms, a region disputed between Israel, Lebanon,
and Syria. He quickly agreed to some other elements of the ceasefire, including the army redeployment and the need for a peacekeeping force.
But he wanted it to be the United Nations Interim Force in Lebanon
(UNIFIL) with a new mandate. That was, I knew, a nonstarter for the
Israelis, who rightly had no confidence in UNIFIL's ability to keep the
peace in the South when the Israel Defense Forces withdrew.

I then went on to Jerusalem, meeting with Olmert, Livni, Barak, and
others. It was clear that the Israelis were just beginning their operation.
The end of the conflict was nowhere in sight. I finished my discussions
in Jerusalem and Beirut having made little progress, particularly on the
central element of an international peacekeeping force to replace the
Israeli army once it withdrew. I told the parties that I would return after
the international conference to be held in Rome. I had agreed to go to
show support for the Lebanese and because I'd need Italian and French
assistance on any new force presence.

In fact, it had been a colossal mistake to attend. The Europeans
wanted to show activity—a bit like the meeting in New York—and that

was the real purpose of the gathering. But knowing as I did that the United States might be isolated in refusing to call for an immediate ceasefire, I went anyway, trusting my skills and my colleagues' assurances that we'd reach unanimity in what we said.

I arrived in Rome intending to meet with Javier Solana and UN Secretary-General Kofi Annan. Javier was quickly becoming one of my most valued colleagues. A former NATO secretary-general, the Spaniard was a strong supporter of ties with the United States and keenly aware of how much the European Union needed to work with us to succeed diplomatically. His position as the European Union's high commissioner for foreign affairs was structurally weak—he could do little without agreement from the EU member states. Still, he was an exceptionally good and capable diplomat. One of Javier's strengths was his calm demeanor; he was not given to wild swings of emotion, whether in the face of crisis or in everyday work.

Just before he arrived, I got word that the IDF had mistakenly attacked a UN bunker, killing several personnel. Javier warned me that he'd spoken with Kofi, who was very upset and couldn't see how the Israelis had made such a mistake. The contradictory stories coming out of Tel Aviv didn't help. The Israelis said that the bunker was a Hezbollah command post. Unfortunately, it was filled with UN personnel. Furthermore, the IDF had just hours later suffered tough losses in a fight for a key town—they were in a foul mood and the fog of war made it hard to get the facts right. Had Hezbollah used the UN workers as human shields? Had the Israelis been careless in their targeting?

I asked Kofi to join us. He'd already made a statement that came close to accusing the Israelis of an intentional attack on UN personnel. I promised to call Olmert immediately and get the Israelis to order an investigation of what had happened. The Israelis apologized but the atmosphere was souring quickly against our friends, even as the calls for an immediate ceasefire were getting louder. That night I called Steve and told him, "Tomorrow will be rough, but I think I can keep the temperature down."

The next morning I met with the Italian foreign minister Massimo D'Alema. Massimo, a former Communist, was nonetheless someone with whom I worked well. He made it clear at the breakfast meeting that he had no intention of isolating the United States. We agreed that the conference statement would reference the need for a ceasefire and the terms but with no reference to the timing. The word "immediate" was to be avoided at all costs.

The session proceeded as expected with each participant expressing solidarity with the Lebanese people and—depending on the speaker—some combination of anger at Hezbollah and anguish about Israel's response. I delivered a U.S. position that focused on what we needed to achieve to prevent Hezbollah from profiting from its aggression and a strong push to strengthen Lebanon's sovereignty over its own territory by deploying the national army in the South for the first time in thirty years. There would need to be a more capable international peacekeeping force than the hapless UNIFIL, which had been in the country for decades but, alas, with a mandate so weak that it had been a spectator whenever trouble arose.

Fouad Siniora took the opportunity of the conference, not surprisingly, to excoriate Israel and push for an immediate ceasefire. But he cleverly presented a seven-point program that dovetailed nicely with what we wanted to do. The centerpiece was strengthening the Lebanese national army and making it—not militias (read: Hezbollah)—the protector of the state. The plan, which also called for international aid to rebuild the shattered country, struck exactly the right balance between blaming Israel and weakening Hezbollah. It was a very impressive outing.

The meeting was about to close with unanimous support for the Italian-drafted statement when all of a sudden the French foreign minister, Philippe Douste-Blazy, raised his hand. "The statement has to say immediate ceasefire," he blurted out. "That is what the Lebanese people expect." I was furious. The Russians, the Arabs, even the Lebanese had raised no objection to the statement, knowing that ultimately I was the one who was going to have to deliver the Israelis. Now Douste-Blazy, a medical doctor whom Chirac had appointed not for his expertise but for the management of his internal coalition, had thrown this stink bomb into the room. *Does he know what he's doing, or is he just clueless?* I wondered.

Whatever his intentions, Douste-Blazy managed to blow up the conference. After several attempts to find common language—most notably by the Brits—I called a halt to the proceedings and said that I couldn't accept the word "immediate." The statement was passed without the time constraint. But it took about five seconds for word to leak out of the room that the United States had been isolated in support of Israel. I caught up with Karen Hughes on my way to the press conference. "Well," she said, "it seems we're the only ones who want the war to continue."

Several hundred journalists were crowded into a room intended for, at most, one hundred people. As I stepped on stage with Kofi Annan, Massimo, and Fouad, I took a moment to wipe my forehead. It was unbearably hot and I didn't want to be seen sweating through the press conference. *I wish I had worn a lighter-weight suit,* I thought. I then proceeded to explain that the United States would work as quickly as possible for a ceasefire, but the key was to get terms that would prevent a return to the previous status quo. I looked at Fouad, whom I admired so much. This dignified man was in so much pain and begging the world to stop the war. I had to stand next to him and say that the time had not yet come to do so. The next morning, the *New York Times* carried a front-page picture of the press conference. I was wiping my forehead, but it looked as though I was experiencing a case of the vapors. There was nothing to be done about the image; sometimes a picture *isn't* worth a thousand words, I told the press on my plane as I headed off to Kuala Lumpur, Malaysia.

I'd missed the ASEAN Regional Forum (ARF) meeting the year before and didn't have an option to skip it again. I felt ridiculous heading to Southeast Asia while trying to negotiate an end to war in the Middle East. But I decided to just accept the contradiction and make quick work of the stop nearly five thousand miles from where I should have been.

But the ARF presented me with another problem. A silly tradition had grown up whereby the foreign ministers from the non-ASEAN countries performed musical skits. Colin had done a version of the Village People's "YMCA." Madeleine and the Japanese foreign minister had performed a song from *Evita*. You get the picture.

I wanted no part of it, finding the whole thing undignified and not very funny—particularly in the age of YouTube. That was even more the case in the midst of a devastating war in the Middle East. But I couldn't refuse to perform and decided to do something serious instead. "I can actually play the piano," I told my chief of staff, Brian Gunderson, "so tell them I'll play Brahms." I thought it would be nice to play a piece with a well-known Malaysian musician, and so, in addition to soloing the Brahms "Intermezzo," I teamed with the first violinist for the Malaysian National Symphony Orchestra and performed a movement of the Brahms *Violin Sonata No. 3 in D Minor*. I knew the pieces well and had run through them upon arrival. There was one awful moment when the violinist got lost about halfway through the piece, but we managed to end together. Both offerings were well received. "I didn't know you could play like that," Sergei Lavrov said. "It was really beautiful. You're really good."

Did you think I was lying about being able to play? I thought. *Stop being uncharitable and just say thank you.* "Thanks, Sergei. I'm glad you enjoyed it," I said. By the way, the Russian skit was hilarious, something about ASEAN taking over the world and peppered with references to the "rice" harvest from the United States. A couple of years later, the ARF ministers decided to kill the idea. Hence Hillary Clinton has been spared that particular frivolity.

WHEN I RETURNED to the Middle East, I landed in Jerusalem, where we had made little progress on terms for deployment of an international peacekeeping force. We were running out of time because the Israelis were nearing a decision on whether to widen the war with a major ground offensive deeper into Lebanon.

I went immediately to dinner at Prime Minister Olmert's house and reviewed the state of the negotiations. My major concern was to prevent a widening of the war while we tried to achieve terms for a ceasefire. Additionally, I wanted to impress upon the Israelis the need to relieve the escalating humanitarian crisis by allowing relief workers time to work without fear of IDF air strikes. Olmert promised to talk to his defense minister, Amir Peretz, and get back to me.

I went to the hotel to try to get some rest before the next morning, when I was to meet with the chief of staff of the IDF and Defense Minister Peretz. After a brief meeting with our delegations in which I focused on the humanitarian issue, Peretz and I met one-on-one. I told him that time was running out and I couldn't hold the ground against an immediate ceasefire for much longer. As I was warning against any escalation of the war, his BlackBerry went off. He took a look at it and then returned to the conversation. As we wrapped up, I told him that I was leaving immediately for Lebanon and would return to Jerusalem within a day or so. I'd decided that personally shuttling back and forth was necessary to find a resolution of the war.

Then, suddenly, David Welch interrupted the meeting and showed me his BlackBerry. He had received an e-mail from our ambassador in Lebanon informing us that an Israeli air strike had caused major civilian casualties. An apartment building in Qana had collapsed in the strike, killing more than twenty Lebanese civilians. I immediately realized that Peretz had known about the incident but hadn't told me. I confronted him and he finally admitted that, yes, something had gone awry. He said they were investigating but were not yet sure of the details.

David, Sean, Brian, and Karen were waiting for me when I came out of the meeting. We rushed up to my suite and flipped on the television. The pictures were awful as bloodied bodies were pulled from the wreckage. The Arab world was now inflamed, with denunciations of Israel coming in from across the region.

I called Siniora. "I assume I shouldn't come," I said to him.

"It's best if you don't," he answered. "This has got to stop. It has got to *stop!*" he shouted into the phone.

"Fouad, I'm so sorry," I began. But he was just silent. I hung up and asked to see Olmert, who agreed to meet me within an hour. I was furious at Peretz. Now I would have to tell the press that I had sat through a meeting with the Israeli defense minister not knowing that the IDF had killed numerous Lebanese civilians in an attack. The press was more interested, though, in the fact that I'd canceled my return trip to Lebanon: "Does this mean that the United States has lost its ability to broker a deal?" I kept my comments short—words of condolence to the Lebanese and a promise to find an end to the war. I didn't address the implication in the question that I'd lost the moral high ground by supporting the Israelis too long. But when I saw Olmert, I was more direct. "Get it over with," I said. "After today, you have no ground to stand on. And I'm not going to let the United States go down with you." We quickly negotiated a forty-eight-hour halt on air strikes for humanitarian purposes. As I was taking off for the United States, the fragility of the brief cessation was clear; the IDF had reduced its air activity, but fighting continued. Nonetheless, the half measure gave a little breathing space to relief workers to replenish the dwindling supplies of food and medicine.

Upon my return I went immediately to the White House to meet with the President. We reviewed the situation and the diminishing international support for our position. He too was very worried that the Siniora government might be in real danger of collapsing. "They're caught between a rock and a hard place. People are questioning whether America can be counted on to help its Lebanese friends," I said. The President agreed to call Olmert and impress upon the Israelis the urgency of finishing the operation quickly.

The problem was that the Israelis didn't really have a firm grasp on their strategic objectives. They kept saying that they wanted to damage Hezbollah, but they understood that they wouldn't succeed in destroying the terrorist organization. They wanted to punish Hezbollah, but they admitted that they were now doing more damage to Lebanon—and potential friends—than to the terrorists. They kept threatening to launch a major ground offensive, but they didn't want to reoccupy Lebanese territory from which they'd withdrawn in 2000. Since they didn't know what they were trying to achieve, they didn't know when they'd achieve it. A full independent review of Israeli decision making (the Winograd Commission Report) would later conclude that the war had been badly managed from a political-military point of view. Israel had gone to war with uncertain objectives. And we were paying the price.

We decided to work with France and the United Nations Security Council to draft a resolution that would end the war. I couldn't wait any longer for the Israelis to determine what they were trying to do. Steve would work directly with the Élysée Palace through the foreign policy advisor to President Chirac. I would work with the Lebanese, the Israelis, and the United Nations.

The elements of the agreement would be the following: the entry of the Lebanese army into the South so that it controlled the entire country; a beefed-up UN peacekeeping force under Chapter VII with real teeth to replace UNIFIL so that the IDF could withdraw; a border-monitoring system to close off the arms flow across the Syrian land border and at sea so that the Israeli blockade could be lifted; and some wording that promised to revisit the Shebaa Farms question. A cease-fire would come into effect upon deployment of the security forces.

For the next week, we attempted to get agreement on these basic points. Not surprisingly, Siniora was simultaneously negotiating with me and with the various factions in his government. Olmert had splits in his coalition too. Hawkish elements in Jerusalem, particularly in the military, wanted to keep the war going. Some in the IDF were push-ing to expand operations, despite the uneven success thus far. I knew, though, that Tzipi Livni and Olmert were looking for a way out of the predicament. I just needed to help them find it.

The biggest challenge was to find a formula that both Siniora and Olmert could accept on the peacekeeping force. With our concur-rence, Olmert wanted a force with a robust mandate under Chapter VII of the UN Charter, which would authorize it to take military action. The Israelis felt it important that their withdrawal not be followed by Hezbollah's swift rearmament, and authorizing the peacekeeping force under Chapter VII would have enabled it to prevent that and better assist the Lebanese army to reassert its authority. Chapter VII was a nonstarter for Siniora and the other Lebanese parties, who felt that a force with such a mandate would spark fighting and ultimately threaten civil war. The Lebanese demanded a Chapter VI mandate, which, un-like a Chapter VII resolution, would limit the force to using peaceful means. Ultimately we achieved a compromise that both parties could accept—an expanded UNIFIL force, operating under Chapter VI but with a mandate to "take all necessary action" to ensure southern Lebanon would not be used for hostile purposes.

During negotiations with the parties, our friends in Paris suddenly dropped from sight. I cannot to this day explain what happened, but their active efforts to find a solution just ceased. We suspected that Chirac's civilian advisors were telling him Hezbollah would attack any French peacekeepers in Lebanon. Therefore France had wanted a cease-fire and a peacekeeping force only after all of the political issues were settled—including a mechanism to deal with Shebaa Farms. Not even Siniora was suggesting that there had to be a political agreement before a ceasefire—that wasn't going to happen. We toyed with the idea of two resolutions, one to end the war and then one to deal with the politics. The French tried to reverse the order. After several days they just stopped working toward a deal. Kofi Annan took up the slack, becoming my negotiating partner in a way that I could never have imagined given his anger at the Israelis that day in Rome. Because he could also talk to the Syrians—warning Damascus not to stand in the way of an agreement—his work was essential.

The focus of the negotiations was now the UN with John Bolton working toward a resolution. Each night I would talk with John as his day ended in New York, and I'd go home to a flurry of phone calls with the parties in the region to move the ball forward. The next morning we'd start again, but, as Nick Burns said, it felt like *Groundhog Day.* I'd go to bed thinking we had an agreement only to wake up to find that something had unraveled overnight. David Welch kept helicoptering back and forth between Israel and Lebanon.

The President was in Crawford, and he asked me to join him there so that we could work together on Lebanon. I arrived on August 5 and briefed him on where things stood. The next morning, we had a regularly scheduled NSC meeting by videoconference. The President asked me to bring everyone up to date, which I did. I was stunned when the Vice President said in reply that we shouldn't be seeking a resolution. "We need to let the Israelis finish the job," he said. I scribbled a note to the President. "Where has he been for the last two weeks?" The President didn't respond. The Vice President continued with a soliloquy that revealed his *ex parte* (from my point of view) conversations with the Israelis. I was furious. Had he been negotiating with some people within the Israeli government behind my back and suggesting that the United States might support an extension of the war? It was quite unlike the Vice President, whom I'd come to know as straightforward even when we didn't agree. It occurred to me that this might have been another "staff-driven" view, but it was unacceptable.

When he finished, I explained patiently that I had—along with Steve Hadley—been working with the Israelis and the Lebanese on terms for a ceasefire. We were getting close and would likely go to the United Nations to vote on a resolution in a few days. There could be no turning back now. And our allies in Lebanon were in danger of collapse. If the NSC principals felt differently, I had to know.

The Vice President repeated his view that the war should continue. "Do that, and you are dead in the Middle East," I said to the President— loud enough for others to hear. The President called a halt to the meeting and said he would get back to everyone. I followed him out of the videoconference room. "I've been out there negotiating a resolution, and now we don't want one?"

By the next morning the President had produced—in his own hand—a document about the Middle East. The essence of the argument was that too much was at stake to allow the war to continue—including our posture in Iraq and his desire for a push toward Palestinian statehood. He noted insightfully that we couldn't abandon the democratic forces and their foothold in Lebanon and sustain the Freedom Agenda. With that bit of internal discord resolved, I returned to Washington to push for a ceasefire.

The ups and downs continued, but by Wednesday evening, John Bolton thought he had an agreement on the language. Then there was another disruption: the Arab League decided to send its foreign ministers to Washington to demand a ceasefire. "It's gone pretty sour here all of a sudden," John reported from New York. "They want to wait for the Arabs to get here." I needed that like a hole in the head because it would mean days of grandstanding while those who wanted to expand the operation gained ground in Tel Aviv.

After a long day on the phone with Kofi trying to nail down support of the parties for the resolution, Margaret Beckett, the British foreign minister, called. "I'm coming to New York," she said. "Tony has decided that it's time to go to the UN, particularly since the Arabs are going."

"Margaret, I'm worried that we'll just sit there and look stupid if the resolution isn't ready," I said.

"I can look stupid in London, or I can look stupid in New York," she replied. "I guess I'd just as soon look stupid at the UN." I agreed to meet her in New York on Friday to make a last push.

By the time I arrived in New York, we'd nailed down almost all elements of the resolution. David Welch was in Lebanon sitting with Siniora when I arrived in my suite at the Waldorf. Steve was working furiously with the Israelis, solving yet another overnight problem. An earlier version of a resolution draft that didn't reflect Tel Aviv's changes had somehow ended up on Olmert's desk. Shalom Turgeman, Olmert's diplomatic advisor, had called Steve, furious that the United States was putting on the table a solution that Israel couldn't support. Steve made certain that they had the right version of the resolution. Only several years later did I learn that John Bolton had been sharing information with the Israelis through their UN ambassador without permission to do so. That practice had backfired, as the Israeli ambassador was one step behind the discussions between the White House and the prime minister's office.

As John was in the Security Council chamber preparing to present the resolution at three o'clock, I suddenly saw a television report that threw everything into a tailspin. Israeli tanks were crossing deeper into Lebanon; the IDF had begun a ground invasion moments before the UN vote.

I'd been on the phone with David Welch and Siniora, finishing last-minute details, when the news report caught my attention. "Get Tzipi on the phone!" I yelled to Liz Lineberry, who was standing nearby. When I heard Tzipi's voice, I just couldn't contain my anger. "What are you doing?" I demanded. I could immediately tell that she really wasn't sure of the answer to that question. It occurred to me that the IDF might have jumped the gun, launching the escalation of the war that some in the defense establishment had favored. Maybe the Israelis were trying to send a message that time for diplomacy was running out. It was a pretty dramatic way to get our attention.

I called Steve and asked him to get hold of Olmert's office, and then I phoned Olmert himself. He said something about having a stronger position from which to begin the ceasefire. It didn't really make sense.

I decided on the spot to keep pushing through to the resolution. "Tell John to tap-dance for a few minutes," I said to Brian, who immediately told Bolton to stall in the chamber. Then, with the prime minister of Lebanon on one phone and the prime minister of Israel on the other, I nailed down the final wording. Just before entering the room, Kofi called me into his office. "How much time will the Israelis need before they begin to withdraw?" I called Olmert again, and we settled on the ceasefire taking effect within forty-eight hours.

After John presented the ceasefire resolution that we'd negotiated, I entered the chamber and cast the U.S. vote in favor of it. UN Security Council Resolution 1701 passed unanimously on August 11. Siniora had angry words for Israel, but the most recent Lebanese war was about to end—just about a month to the day after it had begun.

That night on the plane I allowed myself to sip a glass of white wine, something I hadn't done in weeks due to the round-the-clock negotiations. I didn't really feel a sense of satisfaction, but I did feel relief. The Israelis would withdraw, capable security forces would come in, and Fouad Siniora's government had survived. Somehow we'd threaded the needle and protected the interests of both our friends. On Sunday morning I awoke to a *Washington Post* opinion piece. "The Middle East Is Condi's Now," it was titled. "In the wake of the devastating war in Lebanon, the secretary of state will have to make sense of the crumbling order in the Middle East." *That's absolutely right,* I thought. *I have to, and somehow I will.*

Several days later, I left for the Greenbrier, where I spent most of the day on the telephone, working to raise troop contributions for the new peacekeeping forces. It's always hard to assemble those forces, particularly since the United States has long been reluctant to put substantial forces into a UN operation that it does not dominate. And in the case of Lebanon, the U.S. military would have been an inviting target, as it was when the marine barracks there were bombed in 1983. But thanks largely to the Italians, the "new" UNIFIL came into being. The French, still sulking, had refused to lead the mission until the Italians (led by, once again, my friend D'Alema) said that they would. Then Paris relented and agreed to command, with Italy, Spain, and Turkey providing the bulk of the forces.

Resolution 1701 was then and still remains controversial, particularly among conservative commentators and certain "friends" of Israel. Indeed, though it ended the war, it didn't solve all of the security problems in Lebanon. We were never able to get a practical solution to the Syrian land-border issue. Siniora was simply afraid to put international forces on the border and directly challenge Syria. Until the day I left office, I continued to look for a solution, including deploying technical personnel from Germany who could quietly monitor the border. Nothing really worked. As a result, Hezbollah continued to receive arms—albeit at a reduced rate—in direct contravention of Resolution 1701.

The Winograd Commission said, however, that the resolution was an "achievement" for Israel. The Lebanese army did deploy to the South, and Hezbollah was weakened by the reality and perception of displacement from its area of influence by the national forces. The Lebanese people cheered when, for the first time in thirty years, the national army entered the South. And UNIFIL has been a capable force in keeping the peace.

So, though it wasn't a perfect solution, UNSCR 1701 was an important victory for Siniora, who delivered his people from the horrors of a war that he didn't start. Hassan Nasrallah, Hezbollah's leader, tried to claim victory. But the terrorist organization had achieved nothing but displaced people, a weakening of its own infrastructure, and the entry of the Lebanese army and an international force where its fighters had once roamed. Later Nasrallah would admit that he wouldn't have started the war had he been able to predict the Israeli reaction and the conflict's aftermath.

The Israelis would complain bitterly about the failure to secure the land border with Syria, and some hawkish elements would suggest that they should have continued the war. But we bailed Tel Aviv out of a poorly executed response to an admittedly unprovoked attack. Olmert and Livni have at least had the decency to acknowledge that the diplomatic solution was delivered just in time.

And unlike in the ceasefire of 1996, Damascus was a bystander, surprisingly kept in check by Kofi Annan's warnings to stay out of the way and its weakened position given its troop withdrawal in 2005. When Secretary of State Warren Christopher had negotiated the resolution to the previous outbreak of hostilities in 1996, he'd been "protected" by Syrian forces that lined the streets of Beirut—their dominance on full display. Chris, as he was known, had made more trips to Damascus than he had to Beirut, and the final agreement had been between Syria and Israel. Now, in 2006, one would have been naive to assume that Syria had no influence. Yet, having the Lebanese negotiate on their own behalf was a big step forward in the long saga toward the reestablishment of Lebanese sovereignty. The United States of America had salvaged a lot from the flames of Israel's war with Hezbollah.

36

REVISING THE FRAMEWORK FOR
THE WAR ON TERROR

T HE MONTH-LONG WAR in Lebanon had demanded my undivided attention. But problems were piling up elsewhere: there were the deteriorating situation in Iraq; North Korea's continuing intransigence, which was now taking the form of a possible nuclear test; and the need to advance the Palestinian-Israeli negotiations. Most immediately pressing, however, was the need to respond to those who were challenging our policies concerning detainees and to make the legal framework for the war on terror as sturdy as possible.

In late June of 2006 the Supreme Court ruled in *Hamdan v. Rumsfeld* that the military commissions system to try detainees was inadequate for failing to guarantee certain judicial protections that the Court argued were afforded to detainees by domestic and international law, such as the right to appear at trial and the admissibility of certain kinds of evidence. The Court had also concluded, contrary to the legal opinions of Justice Department lawyers, that the provision known as Common Article 3 of the Geneva Conventions applied to our conflict with al Qaeda and that al Qaeda members were entitled to certain minimal guarantees contained in that provision.

In policy terms, the Court's conclusions regarding Common Article 3 actually had little effect on how detainees in U.S. military custody were treated. President Bush had determined early on that, as a matter of policy, all such detainees would be treated humanely and, where appropriate, in a manner consistent with the principles of Geneva. There was never any question on this issue. Furthermore, the ruling did not repudiate the use of military commissions outright—it rather struck down the tribunals in their current form and pointed toward congressional authorization as the key to establishing their legitimacy. In the immediate aftermath of 9/11, I supported the President's decision to take every action that was deemed necessary and legal to prevent another attack. I believed then, as I believe now, that those actions saved American lives, both by removing enemies on the battlefield who were targeting U.S. troops and by generating intelligence that helped us identify and prevent potential terrorist attacks.

Yet early in my tenure as secretary of state it became increasingly clear that those policies were creating their own security challenges. Diplomatic relations with our allies, particularly the Europeans, were increasingly strained by the mistaken perception that the United States' detention and interrogation policies operated outside the bounds of international law. Given the transnational nature of the threats, we depended heavily on our allies' cooperation in intelligence gathering and battlefield operations. Even our closest ally, the United Kingdom, had expressed deep misgivings over the continued detention without trial of four British nationals in Guantánamo.

From my first days at the State Department, I was determined to act on the President's desire to bring our policies into the light, frame them for the public, and gain legislative authorization for them. He had expressed a desire to do so when I was national security advisor, and now, as secretary of state, I could pursue them from the strength of my Cabinet position.

My legal advisor, John Bellinger, and counselor, Philip Zelikow, worked tirelessly through the interagency process to develop options for overhauling the administration's detention policies. In consultation with Bellinger and Matthew Waxman, my former executive assistant at the National Security Council who was now serving as one of the Pentagon's primary officials on detainee affairs, Zelikow and then-acting Deputy Secretary of Defense Gordon England authored a nine-page memorandum in June 2005 recommending that the administration seek congressional approval for its policies and formally accept as a matter of policy the minimum standards for detainee treatment articulated in Common Article 3 of the Geneva Conventions—two of the very reforms that the Supreme Court would ultimately require us to make a year later.

Additionally, the memorandum recommended that the Central Intelligence Agency transfer a small number of high-value detainees out of secret detention facilities that it operated overseas. Those so-called black sites had been established in the chaotic aftermath of 9/11 and had held terrorist suspects such as Khalid Sheikh Mohammed, the mastermind behind the 9/11 attacks, and Abu Zubaydah, who had provided information that helped lead to KSM's capture. There had been precedent for the CIA's overseas detention program: for decades the United States and other countries had used renditions to transport terrorist suspects from the country in which they were captured to other countries in which they could be held or questioned. By 2005, though, it appeared that detainees with little or no additional intelligence value could be transferred out of the CIA detention facilities to their home countries or to Guantánamo to await trial.

Gordon and Zelikow's recommendations ran into stiff resistance from the Defense Department and the Vice President's office. The memo apparently angered Don, particularly because his acting deputy had worked on it without his direct authorization. He also objected to taking over responsibility for the CIA detainees should they be transferred to Guantánamo. The Vice President's staff opposed the formal adoption of Common Article 3 standards. Although the President had publicly committed to closing Guantánamo earlier that year, we couldn't find a way to do so safely.

Ironically, one of the most debilitating aspects of those programs was the secrecy surrounding them. It was difficult to explain what we were doing and the protections that were in place if we couldn't even acknowledge the basic facts of the situation. This contributed to misinformation and allegations that were not only untrue but had deadly consequences. In May 2005 *Newsweek* had published an article accusing U.S. soldiers at Guantánamo of desecrating a copy of the Koran by flushing it down a toilet. The story had turned out to be false, and *Newsweek* had subsequently retracted it—but not before it sparked violent protests against the United States in Afghanistan, Pakistan, and across the Muslim world. The riots left at least fifteen people dead.

In November 2005 the *Washington Post* ran a front-page story revealing the existence of the CIA's secret overseas detention facilities, prompting a firestorm of criticism. The story appeared just a month before I was scheduled to fly to Berlin for a NATO meeting. I received panicked phone calls from my counterparts across Europe who had been summoned by their parliaments to answer allegations of complicity with the CIA. That led to a flurry of formal inquiries directed at me as secretary of state. "I hate to send this to you," Margaret Beckett, the British foreign secretary, had said, "but I have no choice." I reassured her and everyone else that I understood their predicament. But I also knew that it would be the only issue on the table when I landed in Europe. I had to address it head-on.

I called CIA Director Mike Hayden and told him I needed to say something substantive before leaving for Europe. The first draft that the Agency sent was far too coy, and I called Mike again. He promised to do what he could to be helpful. After we painstakingly negotiated the text, Sean McCormack called the press together at Andrews Air Force Base before my flight. That was highly unusual—I normally briefed the press on the plane—but we wanted the stories to circulate in Europe before I arrived.

Standing at the hastily arranged press conference, I delivered a statement to the press: "For decades, the United States and other countries have used 'renditions' to transport terrorist suspects from the country where they are captured to their home country or to other countries where they can be questioned, held or brought to justice." I made clear that, "In conducting such renditions, it is the policy of the United States, and I presume of any other democracies who use this procedure, to comply with its laws and comply with its treaty obligations."

I had hoped that my statement would be enough to satisfy the press's inquiries. On the plane, however, reporters continued to question me about the CIA's secret sites and tried to get me to confirm whether they existed. I found myself in a bind: I wanted to discuss the administration's policies, but any answer would ultimately force me to reveal classified information that had not been authorized for release.

"I can't continue to stonewall on this," I said to my staff. "I have to be able to acknowledge the CIA's practices so I can explain them." I called Steve Hadley in Washington, and he got the President and the NSC Principals to agree on an approach that would allow me to say that as a matter of U.S. policy our international obligations "extend to U.S. personnel wherever they are, whether they are in the United States or outside of the United States." The statement hinted that the CIA was indeed operating facilities overseas.

In Europe the statement was big news. I defended our practices vigorously because I believed in them. And I made headway because I reminded everyone that such intelligence operations were not unique to the United States—and that the information gathered was used to defend them, not just us. "If you don't learn what terrorists are planning, thousands of innocent people die," I said. "This isn't like law enforcement, where you punish the crime after the fact."

The Belgian foreign minister Karel De Gucht held a dinner that night before a NATO ministerial meeting. "Don't worry," he said, "I will make sure this issue doesn't dominate by telling people that we will address it at the end."

"No," I said, "we'll address it at the beginning." When Karel gave me the floor, I said, "An eight-hundred-pound gorilla is sitting in the middle of Karel's lovely table. Let's talk about the detainee issues. I'm prepared to stay here until everyone has had his say." It was cathartic and open. After the session, we were on better footing with our allies. They might not have agreed with everything that we were doing, but they no longer felt that it was out of arrogance or disregard for international norms. The next day several media outlets noted that I had made some progress on the issue. And when I returned to Washington, a well-known left-leaning journalist said to me, "You play two deuces better than anyone I know."

The *Hamdan* ruling six months later allowed us to go even further in pursuing the goal of establishing an improved legal framework for the war on terror. A principal problem with the military commissions, the Supreme Court argued, was that Congress had not authorized their establishment. Although I was disappointed that the Supreme Court had struck down the military commissions in their current form, I was confident that by securing Congress's authorization we could create an even more robust tribunal system that would both protect our intelligence operations and guarantee detainees certain due process rights. Steve Hadley was working on behalf of the President to get suitable legislation. I also felt that the Court's ruling regarding the application of Common Article 3 to our detainees would at least reassure our European allies that we were indeed operating in ways that were consistent with international law.

So I was taken aback when, soon after the ruling, some members of the administration argued the President should support legislation that would essentially overrule the Court's decision. Rather than seek Congress's authorization to establish a military commission system, the President, they argued, should simply demand that Congress recognize his authority to do so on his own. That approach would effectively signal to the world that the administration did not even respect the opinions of its own Supreme Court on these matters, let alone those of its allies. "Mr. President, you cannot reverse the Supreme Court," I pleaded at an Oval Office meeting to review the *Hamdan* decision. Ultimately, the administration worked with Congress to secure passage of the 2006 Military Commissions Act, which legislatively authorized the tribunals.

No one was trying to walk away from our decisions in the chaotic aftermath of September 11, most especially me. They had been made at a time when we had an opaque understanding of al Qaeda's operations and its internal structure. Less than a month after 9/11 we were confronting anthrax attacks and later a smallpox scare, and many worried we were facing the first in a wave of threats against the American people.

By 2006 many of these facts had changed. We had gained a much better grasp of al Qaeda's structure and future plots, in no small part because of the mechanisms we had put in place in the early days after 9/11. We had taken the fight to the enemy overseas, disrupting al Qaeda's capacity to carry out attacks by denying its safe haven in Afghanistan.

Early in his second term the President decided that the time was right to revisit these decisions in light of the progress we had made in the war on terrorism. He and his top advisors well understood that national security decision-making inevitably requires doing what is legal and necessary to protect the country while remaining true to the values at the core of our nation. The President was determined to strike that balance without compromising the effectiveness of the program and what the American people would deem acceptable for ensuring their security.

In that regard, I felt strongly that the time had come to acknowledge that we were holding Khalid Sheik Mohammed and other notorious terrorists. We couldn't allow them to remain "disappeared" and outside the reach of any justice system. I reminded the President of his guidance that we had to lift the veil on our operations and engage the people's representatives in Congress in the formulation of a legal framework for the war on terror. That is what democracies do.

Not everyone agreed, however, and this issue would turn out to be one of the most contentious between the Vice President and me. Our differences came to a head during a National Security Council meeting in August 2006 held in the Roosevelt Room. (The Situation Room was being renovated.) I argued, as did others, that the President should publicly acknowledge the CIA's detention and interrogation programs and transfer all remaining detainees in the CIA's overseas facilities to Guantánamo Bay, where they could face trial. The Vice President objected, arguing that the detainees should remain in CIA custody given that they might have continued intelligence value. He worried that revealing the existence of the prisons would betray the trust of countries that had agreed to host them within their borders. I told the President that the secret sites were having a corrosive effect on the nation's ability to secure intelligence cooperation and that he should resolve the issue rather than leaving it for his successor. "Mr. President," I said, "don't let this be your legacy."

For several minutes the Vice President and I went back and forth; no one else spoke. It was the most intense confrontation of my time in Washington, but it was civil—not personal. I knew that Steve Hadley and Josh Bolten, then White House chief of staff, shared my views. I didn't know what the President was hearing from the attorney general. For once I couldn't read the President, and when he said he needed to think about it, I prayed that he understood the consequences fully.

He did. At his direction, a speech was prepared that he delivered in the East Room of the White House on September 6, 2006. President Bush announced that fourteen high-profile terrorists, including 9/11 mastermind Khalid Sheikh Mohammed, would be transferred to the detention facility at Guantánamo Bay, where they could be tried by military commissions authorized by Congress. The President told the American people that a small number of suspected terrorists had been held and questioned outside the United States in a program operated by the Central Intelligence Agency. He also acknowledged that in a limited number of circumstances the CIA had used alternative interrogation procedures to question terrorist suspects and that such procedures had been reviewed extensively by the Justice Department to ensure that they complied with our laws, our Constitution, and our treaty obligations.

These issues would arise again the next year when the CIA sought the President's policy approval to renew its interrogation program, which had been suspended following the passage of the 2005 Detainee Treatment Act (DTA) and the Supreme Court's *Hamdan* ruling. These events had raised some uncertainty about what was permissible under these legal standards, so the CIA requested that the Justice Department conduct a new legal review of its program to ensure it was consistent with the DTA and Common Article 3 of the Geneva Conventions. It also sought an executive order from the President that would interpret the Justice Department's findings and in effect give the CIA policy authorization to restart the program.

When the draft of this executive order was circulated for my approval, I concluded that I could not endorse its findings. My legal advisor John Bellinger had determined that the CIA's proposed program as currently constructed was inconsistent with the Supreme Court's application of Common Article 3. I agreed with his judgment and refused to concur with the order. As a result, the program remained suspended until the CIA determined it could eliminate some of the more aggressive techniques without sacrificing the effectiveness of the program.

We would continue to revisit these issues throughout the rest of our time in office. Some of our goals remained unfulfilled: the President had been unable to close Guantánamo on his watch, a task that has proven equally difficult for his successor. But the modifications President Bush put into place has allowed the Obama administration to employ—and in some cases accelerate the use of—national security programs that had their foundations in the immediate aftermath of 9/11.

I was pleased that the administration was able to place our detention policies and other counterterrorism tools on a more sustainable footing. As I stood in the East Room in September 2006 listening as the

President lifted the veil on these programs, I gazed at the families of 9/11 victims who'd assembled to hear the address. Some applauded; some cried; some looked skyward as if to pray. I had a feeling then that we'd turned a corner as a nation; 9/11 would be avenged, and its suspected planners would face justice.

GEORGE W. BUSH had been transformed on that September day in 2001 into a wartime president and all of us into members of a war council. As secretary of state, I was now the chief diplomat and engaged in so many issues and activities that seemed quite distant from that September 11. But I too had been marked by the attacks on the World Trade Center and the Pentagon in ways that wouldn't easily be erased. I realized that yet again when, on the fifth anniversary, I had a sudden and unexpected reaction that almost caused me to call it quits.

The President had gone to New York to observe the passing of five years since the attacks. The Cabinet, led by the Vice President, attended a church service at St. John's Episcopal Church as had been done each year since 2001. Afterward, we gathered on the White House lawn for a moment of silence. As we were standing there, I looked up as a plane made an approach to Reagan National Airport along the Potomac. For a moment it seemed to be headed straight for us. I was terrified but after what seemed like several minutes (but was only a moment), I realized that it was on a normal flight path. *I have been doing this too long,* I thought. *Tomorrow I am going to tell the President that I want to leave at the end of the year. I can't do this anymore.*

Since the President would lead the commemoration in New York and the Vice President the one in Washington, I'd decided to do something with an international flavor. Canada, particularly its eastern coast, had responded to 9/11 in the most remarkable way, taking the aircraft that had to be grounded immediately and harboring the suddenly displaced passengers. Nova Scotians had taken hundreds of Americans into their homes; the hosts were total strangers who were just lending a helping hand when needed. My friend and colleague, Foreign Minister Peter MacKay, was from Nova Scotia. I decided to go to his home province to thank Canada for what it had done.

After a nice ceremony at which several pairs—passengers and their hosts—spoke movingly about that day, Peter, who is single, hosted me for a "family" dinner at a lodge on the Atlantic coast. It was just what I needed—relaxed and low key. That night I slept very well with the cool ocean breeze coming through my open window.

The next morning, Peter and I walked to a local coffee shop for breakfast. During his introductory remarks before a speech I was to deliver that day, Peter began by saying that I had slept well. "And she left the window open last night," he added, repeating what I'd told him. I immediately heard a soft snicker among the crowd, and I tried to laugh his comment off at the beginning of my speech. But the scene had been set: The next day, Helene Cooper, the *New York Times*'s diplomatic correspondent, wrote about our supposed flirtation. Noting the foreign minister's good looks and my black pencil skirt, Helene made a mountain out of a molehill. I have to admit it was kind of funny, if misdirected. When I got home, I called Peter. "A girl can't be seen with you without some scandal," I joked. Peter was kind of embarrassed. He is a good friend. And I've never told him that without the levity and refreshment of that visit, I might not have regrouped and returned to Washington to fight another day.

37

Iraq Spirals Downward

A ND WHAT A FIGHT it would be. The summer had been a time of reckoning for all of us involved in the President's decision to invade Iraq. I knew that we couldn't afford to lose; U.S. credibility and power would have been diminished more severely than at any time since the Vietnam War. Arguably, given the relative importance of the Middle East, the damage would have been deeper and more lasting. When President Bush was asked about those who criticized the war effort, he often said, "Count me among them." I felt the same way and struggled to find my own center—a compass to guide me forward. Withdrawal was not an option. Maintaining the status quo was not an option. The current circumstances were unacceptable, but a new path was difficult to imagine. What in the world were we going to do?

Steve was asking the same questions and had quietly begun an informal review process within the NSC to look anew at our options. General Peter Pace, the chairman of the Joint Chiefs of Staff, had tasked a group of colonels to do the same. I asked Phil Zelikow, along with my senior Iraq advisor, Jim Jeffrey (and later his successor, David Satterfield), to "think outside the box" and find a way out of the abyss into which we had sunk. In searching for alternative strategies, I told them to conduct a no-holds-barred assessment, to question our assumptions and develop options that would address both the political challenges and the sectarian violence that threatened to tear the country apart. I did so for three reasons. First, I was haunted by the lead-up to the war. We had planned and planned and even tested our plans in war games. But we had not—I had not—done a good enough job of thinking the unthinkable.

Second, I wasn't certain that the military was prepared to develop and execute a new strategy. Over the next several months of assessing new options, I was initially skeptical about whether a "troop surge" would work. It was not that I didn't want more troops deployed; I had come to favor a larger presence when it became clear that our forces could not secure the areas they had cleared of insurgents. But more U.S. troops doing the same thing—pursuing the same flawed strategy—would only result in more casualties. I hadn't been insistent enough as national security advisor when the President had accepted the Pentagon's assumptions about what it could achieve in Iraq. As secretary of state, I didn't want to make that mistake again.

Finally, I did not trust the Iraqis to do what had to be done to stop the violence against one another. It was unclear to me whether they lacked the will or the capability—or perhaps both—to bring an end to their sectarian bloodletting. Frankly, I was beginning to wonder if Iraq's leaders were determined to commit suicide and drag their newly liberated country along with them. If they were, I saw no reason for U.S. forces to die trying to prevent them from doing so.

The debates within and among the State Department, Pentagon, and the National Security Council would continue throughout the summer and into the fall. Despite all of the uncertainty that would color our deliberations, one thing was clear: Iraq stood on the precipice of disaster. It was in that frame of mind that I left for yet another visit to the Middle East.

After a short stop in Saudi Arabia, I arrived in Cairo to meet with the Gulf Cooperation Council (GCC) "plus two," the two being Egypt and Jordan. We met over an Iftar dinner, the traditional meal that Muslims enjoy after a long day of fasting during Ramadan. I knew it would be an important session because the GCC+2 represented the more moderate, anti-Iranian coalition within the Middle East. I'd developed a relationship of trust with them, and our meetings were frank and often contentious. They would push for a more active role in the Israeli-Palestinian peace talks. I would counter that I had been to Israel more than any other country in the world, secured direct U.S. budget support for the Palestinians, and criticized Israeli settlement policy publicly. I would then remind them that their budgetary support for the Palestinians did not match their rhetoric. And we would move on.

They would then press me to "do something about the Persians." I had the feeling that they would happily hold our coats in a confrontation with Tehran. But with the exception of the Bahraini foreign minister, Sheikh Khalid bin Ahmed al Khalifa, no one wanted to say anything publicly. So I would try to allay their fears and explain that the United States had no intention of permitting Iran to become a nuclear power.

Then I would exhort them to support the young Iraqi democracy. They would express the view that Nouri al-Maliki was a Shia and therefore pro-Iranian. I would counter that he was an Arab first and had spent most of his exile in Syria because he detested the Iranians. I argued that if the Shia Arabs are isolated and oppressed by their Sunni Arab brethren and have nowhere else to turn, they're likely to find Tehran's pull irresistible. "Unless you acknowledge Iraq's Arab identity, you will force them into the arms of the Iranians," I would say. We would then go round and round about the need for the Arab states to send credentialed ambassadors to Iraq as a sign of support. Eventually, a year and a half later, the GCC+2 would become the GCC+3 when Iraq was invited to join the group. We needed to institutionalize the Arab world's relationship with Iraq and believed that the GCC+3 could help bridge differences. It was a major step forward, but the GCC was a conservative group of Sunni authoritarians. Perhaps Hoshyar Zebari, the Iraqi foreign minister and a Sunni Kurd, had it right when he once told them, "You treat us like a virus. I don't know what makes you more nervous, the Shia part or the democracy part." Now, in the fall of 2006, I desperately needed the Arabs to rally around the Iraqis.

Arriving at the Egyptian Foreign Ministry just before sundown, I was greeted by Foreign Minister Ahmed Aboul Gheit. Ahmed favored fine suits and nice wines. He was the quintessential "secular" Egyptian, distrustful of the Islamists and proud of the fact that a significant number of women in his ministry did not wear the veil. He could be a bit patronizing. "The president thinks of you like a daughter," he would say, referring to the aging Hosni Mubarak. *Sure,* I thought. *He probably hates my guts because of what I've said about democracy in Egypt.* But Ahmed was a good diplomat, and we forged a productive working relationship on everything from the peace process to Iraq. Egypt had even been the first Arab state to send a diplomat to be ambassador in Baghdad. Unfortunately, the envoy had been kidnapped and killed in

July 2005, and Cairo had been understandably cautious about sending another representative to replace him.

Ahmed took me downstairs, where the ministers were beginning to assemble for the ceremonial breaking of the fast by eating dates. After joining them—and enjoying the tasty, sugary bites—the more conservative Gulf Arabs left to engage in prayers. "We'll be right back in about fifteen minutes," one of them said. "But if *your* Shia were here, it would take an hour," he continued, drawing out the *your* to make it clear that he meant the U.S.-backed Iraqi government.

I stood there with the Egyptian and the Jordanian waiting for the others to finish praying. *What a weird place the Middle East is—full of contradictions and chasms,* I thought. Before I could reflect too much more, prayers were over. They had taken less than fifteen minutes.

We entered the banquet hall. I was, of course, the only woman among them. I've been asked whether it felt strange to be a female secretary of state in a part of the world where women are clearly second-class citizens—if one can even use the term "citizens." The fact is, when you're the U.S. secretary of state, no one wants to offend you; you're just the secretary of state. Occasionally my gender was an advantage—for instance, in meeting and getting to know the matriarch of the UAE. And once in a while there was a moment when I was so glad that I was a woman secretary of state. One such moment came in a meeting with the late Abdul Aziz al-Hakim, the leader of the Supreme Council for the Islamic Revolution in Iraq (SCIRI). SCIRI had close ties to Iran, and Hakim, a conservative Shia cleric, couldn't even shake my hand because I'm a woman. But after our breakfast at the U.S. ambassador's house in Iraq, Hakim said that he wanted to ask a favor. *What is this about?* I thought.

"My thirteen-year-old granddaughter loves you," he said. "Would you send her a note and then see her when she and her mother are in the United States?" He was beaming as only a grandfather can. I was stunned but readily agreed to do so.

The Hakim women arrived at the State Department a few months later. In bounded a cute girl wrapped in a scarf but also wearing a pink T-shirt. "I have seen you on TV," she said in perfect English. "I want to be foreign minister too." Hakim clearly had great hopes for his granddaughter. Maybe that was evidence of a small crack in the wall of resistance to progress for women in the region. It was good to be a woman—and the United States' chief diplomat, particularly in the Middle East.

The Iftar that night in Egypt had focused more than usual on the Israeli-Palestinian question. My colleagues encouraged me to push for direct negotiations between the parties, particularly in light of the Lebanon war. I couldn't have agreed more and had written a memo to President Bush suggesting the same. We could use the end of the Lebanon war to reinforce a strategic framework for the Middle East. We could rally the anti-Iranian coalition to support democratic governments in Lebanon and Iraq. Yes, it was a little strange to rally the authoritarians to the cause of freedom—I was nevertheless counting on Tehran's divisive reputation and behavior to unite us through our common interests, if not our values.

But though the road to the Freedom Agenda went through Baghdad and Beirut, the road to common purpose with the Arabs went through Jerusalem. I wanted to square the circle—that is, push for a Palestinian state to end the conflict but insist on a democratic Palestine to help lay the foundation for a "new Middle East." I'd used that phrase in the context of Lebanon, referring to the war as the "birth pangs of a new Middle East." The comment had drawn a rebuke from across the region, including a political cartoon showing me pregnant with the new Middle East, blood dripping from my teeth. Point taken. So I dropped the reference and started to talk about a "different Middle East." Words mattered a lot in a region that loved to say one thing and do another.

My trip to Jerusalem and Ramallah convinced me that we had a chance to make progress on that vision. The Palestinians had helped their cause with the Israelis and with us by keeping the condemnatory rhetoric about the war in Lebanon to a minimum. Mahmoud Abbas and the Palestinians hated Hezbollah and harbored no sympathy for them whatsoever. But no Arab could speak openly about his disdain for the terrorist organization; to do so would invite retribution for appearing to side with Israel in a time of war. Yet, with the war over, they were ready to resume negotiations toward statehood as soon as possible.

Moreover, fighting had erupted in previous weeks between Hamas and Fatah in Gaza—reminding everyone, including the Israelis, that there were two very distinct Palestinian factions, one devoted to peace and the other to conflict. Abbas was fuming at Hamas when I arrived to see him, and though there would be a tentative "ceasefire" a few weeks later, the dustup with the rival faction reminded him that his best card was to deliver a Palestinian state—something that Hamas could not do. In the Middle East peace process it was a thin reed of cooperation—but it was enough. The Israelis and Palestinians, for different reasons, were ready to negotiate.

YOU KNOW that times are rough when the Palestinian-Israeli issue is the bright spot in a trip to the Middle East. I left Jerusalem for Baghdad. There the gloom that I'd felt in Washington deepened. It would—without a doubt—be the worst trip of my entire time as secretary of state.

The politics in Iraq were in an absolutely poisonous state in all directions as sectarian violence raged between the Sunnis and Shia. Before arriving in Baghdad, I told the press that it was not up to the United States to heal the divisions. "They are going to have to resolve these issues among themselves," I said.

When I shuttled over to the Presidential Palace for a meeting with Prime Minister Nouri al-Maliki, though, it became clear that the Iraqis had a long way to go. Reading off a list of accusations against the Sunnis, the Shia leader seemed to have lost all concept of his own responsibility to bring his people together. I'd expected better from him, particularly after the promises he made to the President in June during a surprise trip to Baghdad. At a joint meeting of the two leaders and their respective Cabinet officials—the President sitting with the Iraqis and the U.S. Cabinet participating by videoconference from Camp David—Maliki had impressed all of us by presenting his own strategy for securing the country and rebuilding the Iraqi economy. Shortly thereafter he had even delivered an address to the Iraqi parliament, laying out his proposal for national reconciliation and healing sectarian divisions.

But as the summer dragged on, the Shia prime minister seemed to cloak himself in sectarian garb. Maliki's government dragged its feet in cracking down on Muqtada al-Sadr's Mahdi Army, no doubt because of the repercussions—political and otherwise—he would suffer if he went after the forces of one of Iraq's most powerful Shia leaders. Instead, it was easier to blame the violence on somebody else. Some of his advisors even intimated that the Shia death squads that his government had failed to eradicate might well have been a figment of the Sunnis' imagination.

My dinner with Jalal Talabani did not go much better. The rotund Kurd who was Iraq's president confirmed that everyone felt shut out of important decisions. Dining with Jalal was always an unnerving experience. He ate with both hands, literally shoveling massive amounts of food into his mouth while simultaneously plopping huge portions of chicken, lamb, and rice onto my plate. Yet he was emerging as a statesman and a force for good. *We're in deep trouble, though, when the Kurds are the best hope for Iraqi unity,* I thought. I promised to impress upon Maliki the need to be more inclusive.

By the time I reached the residence of Zal Khalilzad, our ambassador to Iraq, I was really tired and annoyed with the Iraqis. Zal had arranged for me to meet with a number of Sunni political leaders, including the leader of the parliament's Sunni bloc, Adnan al-Dulaimi. I would then see a group of Shia officials to get their perspective on the violence.

The meeting with the Sunnis started on a bizarre note. The speaker of Iraq's parliament, Mahmoud al-Mashhadani, related a story that was meant to be a compliment but made my skin crawl. He told me that he had been in prison at the time of the 2003 invasion. Apparently, the inmates followed the news of the U.S. buildup, including my aggressive language against Saddam. "We put your picture up on the wall," he said. "We loved you." I'm not sure if it was true, but it was a novel way for the speaker to introduce himself.

The Sunnis then pulled out unbelievably graphic pictures of what the Shia death squads had done to their people. The images displayed severed heads and limbs and bloodied bodies mutilated beyond recognition of human form. I looked at them—I'd become inured to gore—and expressed some sympathy. I took their point that they were taking considerable risk upon themselves by taking part in Maliki's government, finding their families the targets of death threats and assassination attempts for what the extremists felt was a betrayal of their cause.

But as I listened to the Sunnis, they seemed to place the blame squarely on the Shia without recognition of their own responsibility to press their Sunni compatriots to lay down their arms. In fact, they were seemingly oblivious to the havoc that Sunni insurgents were causing. After nearly an hour of hearing more complaints about the Shia, I finally snapped. "Let me tell you something," I said. "We have a saying in America: you can hang together, or you can hang separately. If this situation doesn't improve, when I come back here in six months you will all be swinging from lampposts. It is time to make your peace with each other."

I would convey the same message to the Shia parliament leaders who visited me as well. Their complaints and accusations sounded almost identical. "Americans understand fighting al Qaeda," I told them. "We even understand that some Iraqis think we are occupying your country and that you don't like it. But Iraqis killing Iraqis—Americans don't get that, and we're not going to put our bodies in the middle of your blood feud."

Later, well after 10:00 P.M. and totally exhausted, I met with Maliki again. I challenged him, saying that we couldn't solve the Iraqis' civil conflict for them. "By reconciliation, I don't mean that you have to love each other," I said. "But you have got to get a hold of the army and the police. I hear that people are punished for killing Shia, but you are not going after Shia who kill Sunnis. This can't last. Your words don't match your actions, and the United States will not stay here if you don't fix this." Then I repeated the warning I had delivered earlier: "If this situation doesn't improve, in six months you'll all be swinging from lampposts."

It was quite difficult to sleep that night at Zal's residence. All night long helicopters skirted back and forth, patrolling the imperiled Green Zone. Earlier in the evening there had been mortar fire aimed at the house. Perhaps the rounds had been meant for me, or perhaps they were just random; haphazard gunshots had become common fare in Baghdad.

The next morning I flew to northern Iraq to meet with Massoud

Barzani, the president of the Iraqi Kurdistan region, and urged him to spend more time in Baghdad. He and President Talabani had an uneasy relationship; the two Kurdish leaders had once led rival factions, but, after signing a ceasefire agreement negotiated by David Welch in 1998, they had put aside their differences to confront Saddam Hussein. We needed both of those leaders to invest in a unified Iraq, and we particularly needed Barzani to crack down on the Kurdistan Workers' Party (PKK), a Kurdish militant group that launched cross-border attacks against Turkey.

I tried to appeal to Barzani's sense of pride in overthrowing Saddam and—frankly—to his vanity by saying that he was a founding father of the democratic Iraq. He always listened and always promised to cooperate with the leaders in Baghdad. He would even offer to come down from the mountains of Erbil to help govern. He rarely followed through, but he needed to feel respected lest he distance himself too far from Iraq's central government. My time with him was necessary, if not wholly effective.

After the meeting with Barzani, I went to the airport but was told that I shouldn't board the plane. I worried that there might be some unfolding incident, but in a short while I learned that the problem was a mechanical one. Some debris on the runway had apparently been sucked up into the engine of the C-17 and rendered it inoperable. I was due to meet my colleagues in London for an important meeting of the P5+1 and European Union foreign policy chief Javier Solana. I watched the frantic scene as my staff, including Air Force General Will Fraser, my Joint Staff liaison, worked the phones to find another plane. It was always good to have a senior military officer around to get the Pentagon's attention in circumstances like this.

Two hours later, a backup military plane took me from Turkey to the United Kingdom. So that I'd make it on time, a London police helicopter met me at Heathrow and lifted me to the downtown meeting. The sights of the grand British capital at dusk were stunning—and soothing. For the first time since I'd gone to Iraq in 2005, I was grateful to be out of the country.

. . .

WHEN I ARRIVED in Washington, I went to see the President and told him what I'd encountered in Baghdad. He was troubled because, despite all of the difficulties we faced in Iraq, I'd always been able to step back, keep perspective, and maintain a modicum of optimism. The President, the Vice President, Steve, and I were alone—and I was as unvarnished in my assessment as I could possibly be.

"They have a Bull Connor problem," I said, referring to the segregationist that patrolled my native Birmingham. "In my neighborhood, when the police showed up, it wasn't good news. That's how it is for the Sunnis, and I'm not sure Maliki cares. But this isn't just about him. It's all of them: Hashimi, Mashhadani, Dulaimi, Barzani, Talabani. No one wants to act on behalf of Iraq—it's all about each of them and their sectarian and personal agendas."

"How do you know that?" the President asked with a little anxiety in his voice.

"They don't even acknowledge the problem anymore," I said. "The average Iraqi has no one to trust—not the government, not us. Life in Iraq isn't even approaching normal, and it isn't going to until the security situation improves."

Steve and the Vice President said nothing. The President and I were locked in a pretty intense exchange. He was so frustrated with the situation and with the Iraqis. I knew that he was seriously considering a surge of U.S. forces, and he would later tell Maliki that he was prepared to add troops if the Iraqis stepped up. I was tired, emotional, and on edge. I looked straight at him. "Mr. President, what we are doing is not working—really not working," I said. "It's failing."

"What would you do?" he asked. "How can we make this work?"

I had launched an effort at State to look for answers. I thought about the situation in Iraq constantly. Still, I didn't want to engage on "solutions" at this moment. "I don't know," I replied. "Let me go and think." That was my moment of deepest despair about Iraq. I wasn't sure that there was an answer to the President's question. But that wasn't an acceptable response. I was secretary of state and one of his closest advisors—and I was as responsible as anyone for the course we were on and the dilemma we faced.

38

An Explosion in Asia and a Challenge for U.S.-China Relations

THE LIFE-AND-DEATH DECISIONS concerning Iraq were building to a fever pitch. Yet the rest of the world didn't stop so that we could deal exclusively with that overwhelming challenge. North Korea had continued its insolent behavior, and it now appeared ready to raise the stakes with its nuclear program. In early October we were receiving reports that Pyongyang might be planning an underground nuclear test. The July missile incident had been bad enough, but exploding a nuclear device would be of another order of magnitude.

On the morning of October 9 the North Koreans made good on their threat. The event had been preceded by a frantic phone call to President Bush from Hu Jintao. The Chinese had been given only a one-hour notice by Pyongyang. The President reminded Hu that North Korea's action was a slap first and foremost at Beijing and asked what China was prepared to do given the embarrassment that the North Koreans had caused. Hu didn't answer directly, but there was little doubt that, this time, Kim Jong-il had gone too far.

Mike Hayden, the CIA director, called me at about ten o'clock on the night of October 8—already the ninth on the Korean peninsula—to say that the expected test had taken place. I immediately arranged a conference call of the other five ministers in the Six-Party Talks, reaching them in the wee hours of the morning. The Chinese foreign minister, Li Zhaoxing, said very little, but it was clear that we were united in the need to go to the United Nations. Within six days, reflecting the international community's outrage over the incident, the UN Security Council unanimously passed Resolution 1718, with Beijing casting a "yes" vote in a direct strike at its client in Pyongyang. Sanctions targeting military equipment and luxury goods (which the regime fancied) bolstered the resolution, this time under Chapter VII authority.

Given the anger at Kim Jong-il, the resolution was not unexpected. But the real tests of our relationship with China were still to come: How far would Beijing go in pressuring the North? Could we count on the Chinese to do the right thing? Beijing understood the dangers of a nuclear North Korea but feared an unstable one even more. That trade-off limited China's willingness to pressure Pyongyang to the point that might bring the regime down. And the Chinese were aware too that Kim Jong-il's collapse might hasten unification on the peninsula—totally on South Korea's terms.

The Bush administration's relationship with China had begun in an inauspicious manner with the downing of the U.S. reconnaissance plane in April 2001. But over the next few years, the interaction had become more stable and productive. The task of managing China's rise as an economic and political power was critical to the future of the international system. Shortly after arriving at State, I asked Bob Zoellick to take special responsibility for nurturing the U.S.-China interaction. On his first trip to Beijing, Bob gave an important speech, encouraging China to become a "responsible stakeholder" in international affairs. It took some time for the Chinese to find a translation for the phrase, but they liked what it meant when they finally figured it out: the United States would welcome, not fear, China's rise and wanted Beijing to be an active partner, commensurate with its growing influence.

That was easier said than done. The problem wasn't that Beijing was too active. Rather, the Chinese exhibited a studied passivity that was detached in an almost Socratic way: they commented on issues but rarely worked to resolve them. I got so tired of hearing their standard refrain—"China will always act in the interest of peace and prosperity"—that one day I finally stopped Li in mid-sentence. "No, you won't," I said. "You'll act in your own interest." He was a bit startled, but I felt better having said it even though the next time he returned to the same empty language. I once asked a Mandarin-speaking colleague if there was something about the language that made the Chinese always seem to be speaking in slogans. He assured me that there was not.

Slowly but surely, though, we made progress in getting the Chinese actually to act in a useful manner. China reacted quickly after September 11, 2001, sharing information more fully than we'd expected about terrorists' activities in Central Asia and in the ethnically troubled regions abutting their territory. Cooperation was delicate because, as with Chechnya in Russia, the terrorism issue was tangled up in an ethnic conflict—in this case with the Uighurs. Though some Uighurs were indeed extremists—we found a number of them fighting in Afghanistan—they were largely acting in opposition to Beijing's heavy-handed repression of minorities.

The Chinese also came to appreciate the President's patient and even-handed treatment of issues concerning China's economic growth and the escalating demands in Washington to "punish the Chinese" for trade protectionism and currency manipulation. The huge trade imbalances were always a source of significant tension with the Congress. Only months before the 2004 election, the President refused to accept a "dumping" petition (a claim that a foreign country is "dumping" goods into another country's economy at a lower price than that charged at home to gain market share) for sanctions against Beijing. The Chinese could see that George Bush had gone the extra mile to protect the relationship and would not succumb to easy opportunities to blame China for the United States' economic difficulties. Unfortunately, Beijing rarely reciprocated.

The management of the economic relationship benefited from the arrival of Hank Paulson as secretary of the Treasury. At Goldman Sachs, Hank had been deeply involved in myriad matters concerning the Chinese economy and U.S.-China relations. He had excellent contacts across the Chinese government and was well regarded.

Hank came to see me shortly after his appointment. As we lunched on the eighth floor of the State Department, he somewhat hesitantly floated an idea. He wanted to establish a U.S.-China Economic Dialogue that he would cochair with the Chinese vice premier. The dialogue would address issues of the environment and trade as well as general economic issues. I learned later that he'd proposed the notion to the President. "I'm not sure how Condi will react," the President had told Hank. "She might think that you're trying to be secretary of state for economics." He shouldn't have worried. I was confident that State would retain influence over any key decision, and I would ask the deputy secretary to accompany Hank whenever the Dialogue met. Anyway, it seemed to me that a separate channel for the thicket of economic issues was a good idea. I was never a fan of linkage politics and didn't really believe that threatening the U.S-China economic relationship in retaliation for differences in the security field or on human rights would work. We needed to solve economic issues with China because of their centrality to the health of our own and the global economy. Still, when necessary I could reinforce Hank's message, and he could reinforce mine that the totality of the relationship mattered even if there were no actual quid pro quos. That said, I was by no means off the hook for purely economic issues.

So prevalent were these problems in my meetings in Beijing that, after yet another desultory conversation about China's horrendous record on intellectual property rights (IPR), Hu had a surprise for me one day. "You're always talking about IPR," he said. "Let me introduce you to the woman who is in charge of making sure that piracy is prosecuted." In walked Madame Wu Yi, a stoutly built woman standing no more than five feet tall. I had, in fact, met her before in my office as national security advisor. Back then we had laughed at both of us being included in *Forbes*'s "Most Powerful Women in the World" list. She was indeed formidable, a former petrochemical plant manager who had become the government's dependable troubleshooter. Wu had, for instance, overseen the successful effort to contain the SARS pandemic in 2003. But the challenge she faced this time was on full display when on my way back to the hotel—no more than two miles from the Great Hall of the People—I saw many a street vendor selling pirated goods.

My portfolio intersected a great deal, therefore, with the economic team. In addition to a seamless relationship with Hank, I enjoyed a close and easy interaction with the trade representatives, Robert Portman and later Susan Schwab, with Commerce Secretary Carlos Gutierrez, and with Sam Bodman at the Energy Department. As national security advisor, I had worked on economic issues, mostly concerning Russia, with Commerce Secretary Don Evans and Energy Secretary Spence Abraham. But as secretary, economic issues were a more regular part of my day, particularly trade problems.

In this work, Susan and I became and remain great personal friends, sharing a love of shopping and performances at the Kennedy Center. We also enjoyed a laugh once in a while at how much we stood out in the red suits that we wore among the dark-suited men in the room. Susan had a tough job because trade policy is always as much about domestic politics as it is international relations. I tried to help as much as possible, carrying many a message about opening the beef market in Korea, the pork market in Russia, and the financial services sector in China. "What do you want me to say?" I'd ask her in a customary phone call or meeting before I traveled.

"You know the script," she'd answer. "There is nothing wrong with our—fill in the blank. Open your market!" She would then send me backup materials that made me more conversant about Russian claims of trichinosis in American pork or Korean concerns about mad cow disease in beef. I became more knowledgeable about such issues than I had ever expected—or wanted—to be.

The truth is, I never felt any of the tension that is often reported between State's "strategic" view of China and that of the President's economic advisors. Perhaps there were strains at lower levels, but at the Cabinet level I don't remember a single conflict concerning economic policy toward China—or, for that matter, Russia or Europe—that required the intervention of the President. My colleagues respected my overall leadership of key relationships, and I understood their special task in managing the challenges of an integrated global economy.

The ease in our relationships was especially important given the increasing overlap of security and economic matters. As national security advisor, I'd added the treasury secretary to the regularly attending members of the National Security Council. We became very dependent on the Treasury to help pressure bad actors—utilizing the power of executive orders, Section 311 of the USA PATRIOT Act, and other measures to blacklist individuals and financial institutions for supporting WMD proliferation, money laundering, and terrorism.

Sitting in my cabin on a return trip from the Middle East, Stuart Levey, under secretary of the treasury for terrorism and financial intelligence, spoke with my counselor, Phil Zelikow, and me about what more we could do with regard to Iran. He indicated we could take the use of these tools to a new level by pressing international financial institutions and corporations—even in the absence of formal sanctions—to limit their investments in and dealings with Iran.

I'd been impressed with our ability to mobilize international financial action against North Korea without having to go to the United Nations. A briefing early in my tenure as secretary of state by David Asher, a senior advisor on East Asian affairs and the coordinator of our North Korea policy, had outlined, persuasively, the strengths of this approach. The process worked liked this: The Treasury would designate entities—front companies, for instance—that it identified as supporting terrorism or weapons proliferation or, in the case of Section 311 sanctions, as being "of primary money laundering concern." Once "listed" by the Treasury, an entity would often be denied access to the U.S. financial system, and any other institution—say a German bank—that conducted business with it would risk being similarly restricted from the U.S. market.

The early results of such efforts had been dramatic. After the United States had designated the Macau-based Banco Delta Asia as an entity "of primary money laundering concern" for facilitating suspicious transactions on behalf of the North Korean regime, many financial institutions had reportedly severed their ties with Pyongyang. Few foreign banks were willing to risk losing access to the U.S. financial system simply to do business with the "Hermit Kingdom."

Iran had much deeper ties to foreign countries and companies and was better integrated into the international system. If we could keep international banks and corporations from doing business with Iranian entities, it would help shut them out of the international financial market. And since the euro, dollar, and yen were the currencies that mattered in the global economy, we could avoid having to get the Russians and Chinese on board.

Although these measures were on occasion better in theory than in practice, they would nevertheless become one of our most important levers. We had to be careful not to use this economic tool for blatantly political purposes. Treasury was a vigilant guardian, making certain that the evidence gathered supported the contention that a suspicious entity was indeed supporting proliferation or terrorism.

The sanctions and other financial measures codified in Treasury rules and executive orders didn't immediately cripple the Iranians, but they made their financial transactions more expensive and far more difficult. We eventually succeeded in blacklisting some of Iran's biggest banks, including Bank Saderat Iran and Bank Sepah, as well as companies and individuals affiliated with Iran's Islamic Revolutionary Guards Corps (IRGC), which supervises the regime's unconventional weapons program and is suspected of maintaining extensive ties to terrorist organizations throughout the Middle East. Given how deeply entrenched this military apparatus had become in economic affairs of the state, our thinking was that legitimate entities would want to limit their interactions with Iranian businesses—even those that had not been specifically blacklisted—to avoid running afoul of the U.S. financial system.

The process of getting other countries to join us in this effort was slower than we expected. But forced to choose between their activities in Iran or access to the United States financial system, many Western institutions opted to scale back their operations in Tehran. Hank Paulson and Stuart Levey's leadership was crucial in achieving that result, and I understood why it worked. I'd been a corporate director for two financial institutions. Reputation was their most important asset, and no CEO wanted to face the board of directors and say that a banking partner had been found to be supporting the Islamic Revolutionary Guards Corps.

IRONICALLY, THE COOPERATION with Treasury on sanctions that began with North Korea would come full circle as we tried to find a way back to the Six-Party Talks. The North Korean issue was both a blessing and a curse in our relationship with China. I was reminded of the Chinese characters *wei ji*, which seemed to capture the situation. *Wei* means "danger" and *ji*, "opportunity." Together they form the Chinese word for "crisis." The challenge with the North Korean nuclear problem was to turn the crisis into an opportunity rather than a danger to the larger relationship with Beijing and the region more broadly.

Although it faced a number of regional security challenges, Asia lacked robust institutions to deal with them. Unlike in Europe, where

NATO provided a multilateral alliance for the democracies on the continent and across the Atlantic, the United States maintained separate bilateral defense arrangements with South Korea, Japan, Australia, New Zealand, Thailand, and the Philippines. The Organization for Security and Co-operation in Europe (OSCE) gave multilateral cover to efforts to defuse so-called frozen conflicts from the Cold War era in the Caucasus and Eastern Europe. Though the organization was not always successful in its pursuits, in large part due to Russian intransigence, the OSCE could be helpful in lending legitimacy and focusing the diplomacy of multiple parties. There was no such thing in Asia. Rather, the Pacific Rim was a web of bilateral—and mostly bad—relationships: Japan with South Korea; South Korea with China; Japan with Russia; Japan with China. All bore the unhealed wounds of World War II. The United States thus became the hub of a wheel with spokes radiating in several directions. We succeeded over the course of the administration to cultivate better relations with each of the parties than they had with each other. But the challenge posed by North Korea, given the many competing interests and priorities among the key regional players regarding the fate of Pyongyang, pushed the bilateral approach to its limits.

The original rationale for the Six-Party Talks had been to prevent North Korea from playing the parties off one another. But it occurred to us that it could do more: it could become a security forum where the parties of Northeast Asia dealt with nuclear proliferation, terrorism, and ultimately even security disputes among themselves. There was no intention to replace the strong bilateral ties that we enjoyed, only to augment them. In fact, we had significantly modernized our defense alliances with South Korea and Japan. The implementation of the Defense Policy Review Initiative, for example, was an ambitious effort aimed to adapt the Japan-U.S. alliance to twenty-first-century security threats. There were also the regular meetings of the 2+2, a joint summit between the U.S. secretaries of state and defense and their Japanese counterparts. I held trilateral meetings with Japan and South Korea, as well as with Australia and Japan. We engaged our allies in numerous fora. Nevertheless, the President had immediately seen the potential of a multilateral forum through the Six-Party Talks that would include China.

This led to language in the Joint Statement of September 2005 that anticipated the establishment of a "peace and security mechanism" once the nuclear issue was resolved satisfactorily. We deliberately left open the timing and definition of what would constitute "satisfactorily" so that we could preserve flexibility in discussing broader issues beyond North Korea's nuclear program when we deemed it appropriate.

In our most ambitious designs for the forum, we thought that the Six-Party Talks might ultimately lead to a final resolution of the Korean War, even a peace treaty. This would have been a big leap from where we were presently, but it was worth contemplating. What if the North could be persuaded to give up its nuclear weapons—really give them up verifiably—in exchange for the recognition that would come from actually ending the Korean War legally? Would the tyrannical regime of Kim Jong-il be strengthened by such a step, or would the end of the conflict deprive the dictator of a raison d'être in the way that the end of the Cold War destroyed East Germany? Would Kim be willing to open North Korea to international institutions such as the World Bank in a bid to improve the lives of his people, only to find that his vampire-like regime couldn't live in the bright sunlight? It was a bold idea and one that I wasn't sure would sit well with the President, who'd let it be known that he loathed Kim Jong-il.

We first discussed the new approach in an NSC meeting in early 2005. I laid out the case, careful to say that the North would not receive any concessions without serious movement toward disarmament. Not surprisingly, the Vice President was not persuaded, but he didn't dismiss the notion out of hand. Don, on the other hand, was remarkably supportive. "Sometimes when you've got an insoluble problem [North Korean nukes], it is best to enlarge it—make it bigger," he said helpfully. He promised to have the Pentagon look into what post–Korean War security arrangements might look like, both bilaterally and multilaterally. Don's interest was sparked too by his view that the South Koreans needed to take more responsibility for their own defense and free up our forces. That was certainly one way to bring about that redistribution of obligations.

The President didn't say much at the first session; he simply took in the arguments. But one evening at dinner at the White House, he turned to the issue again. "Do you think Kim will give up his weapons if he thinks we'll let him survive?" he asked. I replied honestly that there was no way to know the answer to that question without testing the authoritarian leader. "Let's test him, then," the President said.

"Are you going to be comfortable with what we'll have to do?" Steve asked, suggesting that such overtures would mean that "regime change" was off the table.

"No," the President said. "It's just regime change by other means. He'll never survive if that place is opened up."

In April 2006 Hu Jintao came to Washington for an official visit—with nearly all the trappings of a state visit. The distinction is lost on most people who are not steeped in the finer points of diplomatic protocol. But I can assure you it was of great importance to our guests, who knew precisely what activities were included in each level of recognition. A *state* visit entailed a South Lawn welcoming ceremony, complete with the Colonial Fife and Drum Corps, which was led by a drum major in a large hat made of bear fur. Those visits culminated with an elaborate state dinner in the State Dining Room. An *official* visit, on the other hand, might simply be an Oval Office meeting with the President, followed by a working lunch with members of the Cabinet. It was possible to mix and match a little, but state visits were rare; there were only eight in the Bush years, and they were reserved for leaders with whom we wanted to highlight our extraordinarily close relationship.

The Chinese presented a problem in this regard. They wanted all the trappings, but in a Washington environment where Chinese currency issues and trade surpluses made management of the relationship hard enough, it was better not to appear too close. That was true too from the point of view of our significant differences on human rights and religious freedom.

We decided on a South Lawn ceremony but a fancy lunch instead of a dinner. The Chinese were satisfied—or at least they were until a Falun Gong protester shouted out from the press riser as Hu was delivering his remarks. It was a moment of deep embarrassment both for us and for them—but Hu soldiered on and managed to appear unfazed by the outburst. Hopefully, he didn't notice that the White House announcer had introduced him as the president of the Republic of China. That, of course, would be Taiwan.

Despite those hiccups, the visit proceeded smoothly, but the President encountered the problem that I had had in Beijing during my earlier visit. Every meeting with Hu was too large to discuss really sensitive matters, and the President had a particularly sensitive one in mind. He wanted to tell Hu to communicate the grand bargain to Kim Jong-il: give up your nuclear weapons, and we'll give you a peace treaty that ends the Korean War and recognizes your regime. That message couldn't be delivered with too many people around.

By the time we reached lunch, there had still been no opportunity to raise the issue. So the President became his own social secretary, rearranging the seating so that I sat on one side of Hu and he on the other. Then he politely turned to the others at the table: William Daley, the former commerce secretary; Michelle Kwan, the Olympic figure skater; and Richard Levin, the president of Yale. "Condi and I have something to talk to President Hu about," the President said. "Excuse us for a moment." The translator, Hu, the President, and I then conducted our conversation. Hu nodded his understanding and said that he would deliver the message. We reinforced the message through Henry Kissinger, who used his long and deep contacts with the Chinese to add his own assessment that the President was serious. It was a real turning point in how we approached the North Korean issue and in our interaction with Beijing.

From that moment on we pursued the denuclearization of North Korea with three goals in mind: increasing the transparency of Kim Jong-il's nuclear program by "getting our people on the ground"; reducing the ability of the North to make, sell, or use nuclear weapons by retarding Kim's capacity to produce plutonium; and, if Kim was willing to give up his weapons, ending the Korean conflict. And perhaps through diplomacy—not just confrontation—we could end the loathsome regime itself.

The President had made a strategic leap in his thinking. That was what permitted us—through Chris Hill, the assistant secretary for East Asian and Pacific affairs—to pursue active negotiations with the North that we'd eschewed in the first term. It was *not* a softening of policy toward the North; the President was not abandoning regime change in favor of the State Department's well-known desire to negotiate with rogue regimes. Rather, it was a kind of strategic gamble—a safe one from the United States' perspective because the North would get no real benefit until it demonstrated its willingness to give up its nuclear arsenal. North Korea was one of the world's most sanctioned regimes, and those instruments would be the stick in our hands. We would remove constraints selectively if we made progress. And we were confident that with this bold approach we could keep the five parties of the six united in pressuring Pyongyang.

Ironically, the nuclear test gave us an opening to launch this strategy. I set out for Northeast Asia with three goals: to reassure our allies; to get support for full implementation of UN Security Council Resolution 1718, which had imposed stiff sanctions on the transfer of large-scale weapons, nuclear technology, and luxury goods into the North Korean state; and to deescalate the crisis expeditiously and move back to the Six-Party Talks. I've always thought that the argument about whether to "talk" to bad guys was misleading. Sometimes in diplomacy you have to negotiate with rogue regimes. You can't overthrow every one of them by force, and diplomatic isolation, though perhaps psychologically satisfying, is not always effective. But if I have to negotiate with an adversary, I want to do it from a position of strength. Suddenly, because of the North's aggression, we had the upper hand. What better time to engage Pyongyang than when it had lost all international support, including that of Beijing?

After an NSC meeting at which we established the policy framework for dealing with the crisis, I headed to Northeast Asia on October 17 and began my trip in Japan. The Japanese were relatively calm, reassured by the strong statements that the President had already made reaffirming the United States' security commitments to them. My meeting with Prime Minister Shinzo Abe was productive but rather typical of my usual engagements with the Japanese. It was quite unlike meetings with Prime Minister Koizumi, who had always been an animated personality. When engaging foreigners, the Japanese are known for their reserve—hiding their emotions and obscuring messages in impenetrable formality. That was never the case when we dealt with Koizumi, who was as ebullient, open, and candid an interlocutor as any of the leaders with whom we dealt. I'd first met him when he visited

Camp David early in the President's first term. There he talked openly about Japan's stagnation and what he wanted to do to reform the economy and society—and he largely delivered. He also sang Elvis Presley songs; quoted lines from his favorite movie, *High Noon;* and tossed around a baseball with the President in full view of the press. He was a fierce defender of the U.S.-Japan alliance and of the Freedom Agenda, committing Japanese forces to support missions in both Afghanistan and Iraq.

By contrast, Prime Minister Abe was a more traditional and reserved leader, but I found him quite forceful on that particular day. When we talked about what North Korea had done, he was very clear that he had no intention of raising the prospect of a Japanese nuclear option should the North go further. "But," he cautioned, "there are many who want to do exactly that, and their voices are getting louder." It was useful to have those noises from Japan, so that Beijing could see that an unchecked North Korean nuclear program had real consequences. Still, Japan was deeply distrusted in the region, not just by China but by our South Korean friends as well. A little bit of posturing about what Japan might do was helpful—but not *too* much.

Tokyo wanted North Korea's program stopped but feared that we might make a deal with Pyongyang before the tragic Japanese abduction cases could be resolved. While Foreign Minister Taro Aso mentioned the issue of the abductions at our joint press conference, I focused on the nuclear issue at hand and the Security Council resolution. I didn't want to get a deal to halt North Korea's nuclear program only to have to resolve the abduction issue fully before it could go into effect. It would be a constant balancing act throughout the next two years.

I left Japan having affirmed, as expected, the government's willingness to carry out the comprehensive sanctions of UNSCR 1718 faithfully and to take the toughest possible stance against North Korea. What, though, of Seoul? The South Korean president, Roh Moo-hyun, was hard to read. He would sometimes say things that suggested an anti-American streak, such as his lecture to me on an earlier visit suggesting that South Korea needed to act as a balancer between China and the United States.

Then there was the incident the following year that summed up his erratic nature. As their meeting was coming to a close, Roh asked the President to state his willingness before the press to move toward normal relations with the North if it gave up its nuclear weapons. There was nothing new in that; it had been a part of the September 19 framework agreement of 2005. The President dutifully restated the promise when the press entered the room. Suddenly Roh turned to the President and said, "I think I might be wrong—I think I did not hear President Bush mention the—a declaration to end the Korean War just now. Did you say so, President Bush?" The President, somewhat surprised by this intervention, repeated his statement. "If you could be a little bit clearer in your message, I think—" Roh insisted. Now everyone was embarrassed. The shocked interpreter stopped translating, but Roh looked at her and insisted that she continue. After that drill the President called a halt to the press availability. The two leaders shook hands, and Roh smiled and thanked the President—seemingly unaware of how bizarre the moment had been.

Aware of his unpredictable behavior, I frankly did not know what to expect in South Korea. Through my first couple of years as secretary, I'd relied on my foreign minister colleague, Ban Ki-moon, to "interpret" his president. But Ban had left the ministry to become secretary-general of the United Nations. His replacement, Song Min-soon, was also very capable and broad in his thinking. Yet I had the sense that he was more reluctant to challenge his president's unorthodox thinking.

I needn't have worried. The North Koreans had succeeded in toughening Seoul's stance considerably. There was not an inch of daylight between the United States and South Korea on the sanctions or their implementation. Even the usual pro-North protesters had disappeared from the streets this time.

In Beijing, I found a Chinese leadership that was tougher in private on North Korea than I'd ever seen them, if still engaged in sloganeering in public. Hu had sent the third-ranking Chinese official, State Councillor Tang Jiaxuan, to North Korea after the nuclear test. Tang's visit "had not been in vain," I was told, but I was not given further details at the time. I learned through other channels that the Chinese had quietly cut off the supply of spare military parts to Pyongyang. That news made me take more seriously my Chinese interlocutors' insistence that they'd not let Kim Jong-il off the hook for his ill-advised nuclear gambit. The Chinese appeared willing to discuss the future of the North.

Tang had another message, though. Pyongyang knew that it had made a mistake—despite the public blustering about sanctions being an act of war. Would the United States consider a resumption of the Six-Party Talks? I'd agreed to allow Hill to attend a quiet trilateral meeting in Beijing with the Chinese and the North Koreans. I was furious when I learned that the Chinese had showed up only long enough to get the meeting started and then departed, leaving Chris in a bilateral with his North Korean counterpart. That night at my hotel, Chris had called from the putative trilateral to explain what was happening. "End it as soon as possible," I said. "I'll raise it with the Chinese tomorrow."

I asked to see Hu with only a couple of advisors present. This time, the Chinese acceded to my request. He made very short work of the formal session, ended it, and we went into a back room, three on three. Sandy Randt, our ambassador, and Chris Hill accompanied me. I told Hu and Tang that China had to stop acting like the meeting planner and take real responsibility for making the Six-Party Talks work. The North's aggressive act in testing a nuclear device had changed the circumstances. I couldn't hold President Bush behind the current strategy if Beijing didn't play its role more actively. But I said I thought the President might be willing to restart the talks based on a clear understanding with China of how we would proceed. This tactic of holding the President's agreement in reserve was very important in getting things done. The President and I would often choreograph moments like this. "You deliver the message of what we want. But tell them you'll have to convince me," he would say. It was always good for the secretary of state to be the negotiator but to make clear that there was a hard-to-convince President who would ultimately make the decision. Hu asked if Chris could stay a day longer: China would work with us to develop a proposal to move the process forward.

MY FINAL STOP in Northeast Asia was Russia. The Kremlin had been generally cooperative in the Six-Party Talks and particularly interested in the peace-and-security mechanism, which, I suspected, it saw as a way to bolster Moscow's relatively weak influence in the region.

I didn't expect any difficulty concerning what to do about North Korea and I found none. There were, however, many other sticky issues to address, including a number of economic problems that were holding up negotiations on Russia's accession to the World Trade Organization (WTO). And there were real storm clouds concerning Georgia, where the tensions were increasing between Putin and Saakashvili.

I arrived in Moscow and went to my hotel to await the phone call that Putin was ready to see me. Usually the call came within a matter of minutes—sometimes I just went ahead to the Kremlin knowing that any delay would be a short one. This time, though, we were told that the President wanted me to meet him at Meiendorf Castle, a presidential retreat just outside Moscow in Barvikha. Fine, I thought, patiently watching tennis on a Russian sports channel and working a little bit on my language "ear." After waiting around for two hours after the scheduled appointment, I was told that we should leave for the meeting.

"What is this about?" I asked Bill Burns, our ambassador in Moscow. He surmised that Putin was testy and trying to send a message that he was not to be taken for granted. *And I am to be taken for granted?* I put my ego aside and my smile on.

When we walked in the front door of the estate, I was stunned. There, around a huge rectangular table, sat the entire Russian National Security Council. I'd experienced this once before as national security advisor, when Putin had gleefully invited me to meet them at his dacha. "I'll bet you've always wanted to see what this was like," he said, vaguely referencing my academic background as a specialist on Russian security affairs. I didn't know then whether it was meant to be a kind gesture or a manipulative one.

This time I had no doubt. "We're having a birthday party for Dmitri and Igor," he said, referring to the future Russian president and national security advisor. "We thought you might like to join us." Bill and I then sat through a bizarre encounter with the Russians, drinking special reserve Georgian wine—the likes of which they'd just embargoed in an effort to cripple the Georgian economy—and listening to their crude jokes about the "Gruzini," a Russian term for Georgians.

At one point the discussion turned to terrorism, Putin feigning concern for the inmates at Guantánamo. "You have to treat them humanely," he said. I could barely keep down my dinner, thinking of what the KGB officer had undoubtedly done to people vastly more innocent than the residents of Guantánamo.

Finally, I said, "Mr. President, this has been fun but we have a number of things to talk about. Could I talk to you alone?" In this more private discussion, he wanted to include Lavrov, which was fine, and I brought along Bill Burns. We repaired to a room adjacent to the increasingly raucous party.

THE DISCUSSION STARTED OFF cordially enough. We quickly went through a list of Russian legislation on intellectual property and market access that needed to change, Putin explaining that it would be easier to change after the United States had signed the accession agreement admitting Russia into the WTO. "It will give us an argument with the Duma," he said, empowering the puppet legislature with more authority than it had. Nonetheless, it did make sense that there were interest groups that needed to be appeased. I promised to take the idea back to the President and see if we could go ahead with the agreement before the Russian legislation to conform their laws to WTO standards passed.

I then changed the topic to Georgia and simply said that I had a message from the President. "We are concerned about the rhetoric toward Tbilisi and the embargo," I said calmly. "Any move against Georgia will deeply affect U.S.-Russian relations." In an instant Putin stood up, peering over me. "If Saakashvili wants war, he'll get it," he said. "And any support for him will destroy our relationship too." It was a physical posture clearly meant to intimidate. So I stood up too and, in my heels, rose to five feet eleven over the five-foot-eight or so Putin. I repeated the President's message. For a distended moment we stood there face to face—well, almost.

Lavrov decided to defuse the situation, and we soon returned to the agenda. I softened my posture and voice too, saying that we just didn't want any misunderstandings between us about the importance of Georgia to the United States. I said that I would talk with Sergei about reenergizing the "friends of Georgia" to look for a solution. There the confrontation ended, and Bill and I left. "He can be scary," I said to Bill, who kept his own counsel.

Successes on the Proliferation Front

WITHIN TWO WEEKS North Korea had agreed to resume the Six-Party Talks, but we did not rush to arrange a first session. I needed time to strengthen the resolve of the other parties and test Beijing's commitment.

That chance came in Hanoi three weeks later, on November 18. The Asia-Pacific Economic Cooperation (APEC) summit was my favorite multilateral event. The organization united the vibrant economies of the Pacific Rim, starting in Chile at South America's tip and circling up, around, and all the way back down to New Zealand. It was always reassuring that the global economy could depend on these engines of growth and that the United States stood as the glue between the two continents. The talk of growth, trade, and private enterprise stood in stark contrast, for instance, to the Summit of the Americas, where the likes of Hugo Chávez and Néstor Kirchner spewed anti-capitalist, anti-American venom.

This particular summit carried even deeper messages about the power of markets given its location in Vietnam. I remember my first encounter with the Vietnamese, a meeting of the Southeast Asian states on the margins of our first UN General Assembly in 2001. "The most important thing for Vietnam is to join the World Trade Organization," the prime minister had said. *Ho Chi Minh must be spinning in his grave*, I thought. Then, seeing Vietnam for the first time during the APEC meeting, I was sure that the immediate victor in the long and painful war that I knew as a child was indeed turning in his still carefully preserved mausoleum.

I don't know what I expected but Vietnam was the greatest surprise of my entire time in government. The incredibly young population—there seemed to be no older people—was ambitious, entrepreneurial, and very pro-American. President Bush couldn't go anywhere without a gaggle of young women defying the Secret Service and getting close enough to take a picture with their high-tech cameras. One of the best meals that we had anywhere in the world was in Ho Chi Minh City, where a young restaurateur had taken over a deep bunker, made it into a wine cellar, and brought in a great chef from Italy. The stock exchange that we visited was still small but thriving, with serious-looking traders fresh from business school. Only the names—Hue, Haiphong Harbor—reminded me of what had transpired there. Hearing them stirred unexpected emotions in me. Colin Powell once said that the United States needed to see Vietnam as a country, not a war. It wasn't hard to make that transformation when standing on the streets of the vibrant young nation.

The political situation had not kept pace with the economic boom, however. Vietnam's Communist Party, the VCP, was hanging on through the usual means: repression of opposition and punishment of those who crossed the line into political dissent. There had been a little—very little—progress on religious freedom, even for nonregistered churches. But there was a lot of work to do to push the VCP toward political change. Still, the Vietnamese version of repression was less visible than that of many other authoritarian states, and the people did seem to enjoy a modicum of personal freedom.

Even the leaders of Vietnam seemed to sense the irony of the Communist Party's devotion to free markets. The foreign minister called me aside after the meeting with the prime minister. He had a favor to ask: "Would the President just go over and meet with the general secretary of the Communist Party? He can make a lot of trouble if he feels ignored." I wondered why the request hadn't been made earlier but raised it with the President and Steve. We decided there wasn't much downside, forgetting about the "setting" for the meeting. I would shortly see why advance people are so important. We walked into the room where President Bush and the Vietnamese president were seated under a giant statue of Ho Chi Minh and the general secretary seated to their side. "The great leader foresaw the cooperation between the United States and Vietnam," intoned the general secretary. *When exactly did he foresee that?* I wondered. The meeting was mercifully short. There were still some "contradictions," as Karl Marx would have put it, to be sorted out in Vietnam.

The morning of the APEC summit two days later gave me the chance to lay the groundwork for the resumption of the Six-Party Talks on our terms. I asked the Vietnamese to host a breakfast for the Chinese, Russians, South Koreans, Japanese, and me. I asked that Australia, Indonesia, and the Philippines (as the head of ASEAN) be included. The idea was to talk about security in the region. Everyone showed up, and it couldn't have gone better. The Chinese heard every foreign minister, including Russia's, deliver a strong message in support of the Six-Party Talks but with the proviso that it had to achieve something. "North Korea has endangered the whole international system," minister after minister said. The Chinese were stunned at the ferocity of the condemnation of Pyongyang. They had received the message, and as we ended the year I was confident that we would find a way back to the talks—and a chance to do something about one of the two big proliferators.

I felt good too about our prospects concerning the other one. On the heels of the change in U.S. policy in May, we'd finally united the P5+1 to seek and pass a resolution in the UN Security Council in July. The Chapter VII resolution for the first time demanded that Iran suspend all enrichment-related and reprocessing activities, and it gave Iran by the end of August to comply or face possible economic and diplomatic sanctions.

As is almost always the case in international politics, however, the deadline came and went. Still, we were making progress in pushing toward another resolution. In fact, in the fall we'd make yet another push to get the Iranians to the negotiating table—and we almost succeeded.

In advance of the UN General Assembly that September, and after talking to the NSC Principals, I went to the President with a plan to take another step with our allies in the P5+1. I wanted to use the meetings in September either to get the Iranians to the table or, failing that, to get a tougher resolution. I personally developed a calendar of events and moves that we would make from the summer until the meetings in New York: steps we took unilaterally were in one color; actions by our allies in another; UN Security Council moves in a third. I took the proposed schedule to a breakfast meeting with the President and Steve. It was so complicated and had so many colors and lines that Steve said what the President was thinking: "I can't make heads or tails of this." Okay, so maybe I'd gotten a little elaborate with my calendar.

The point was actually pretty simple. We'd turn up the heat on the Iranians by placing financial restrictions on a few more entities, hopefully in concert with the Europeans, then give them a face-saving way to change course. It would require a little Kabuki theater, though.

Tehran contended that it could not suspend without "negotiations" first. That was obviously unacceptable to us, since suspension was a precondition for our involvement in the talks. We decided to have Javier Solana, the EU foreign policy chief, negotiate a suspension with the Iranians, Europeans, Russians, and Chinese at the table. I would then join the talks immediately after the suspension was agreed. All this was to happen within a matter of a day or so at the UNGA in New York. Javier communicated the idea to his Iranian counterpart, Ali Larijani. Everything was set.

Two days before I left for New York, my consular affairs officer came in to say that the Iranians had suddenly requested extra visas and there wasn't time to process them. *This is a ruse,* I thought. I told her to keep our consulate in Bern open throughout the night and get it done. When the Iranians were presented with all the visas they'd requested, Larijani suddenly needed another one for a second translator. "Get it done," I told Consular Affairs.

Now out of excuses about visas, Larijani refused to come to New York anyway. We still don't know what happened. Some reporting suggested that he didn't want to negotiate while his radical new president, Mahmoud Ahmadinejad, was in New York for the first time. The Russians said that there had been a last-minute refusal by Ayatollah Khamenei to go along with the gambit. Whatever the case, the Iranians managed to unite the P5+1 even further. It took several months of haggling, but the UN Security Council adopted Resolution 1737 two days before Christmas. It was the toughest yet.

Resolution 1737 condemned Iran for failing to stop its enrichment activities and imposed sanctions that would remain in effect until the regime fully complied. The resolution targeted Iran's ability to import the materials it needed to advance its nuclear and ballistic missile programs, and it froze the assets of individuals and companies with ties to the programs. Importantly, it created a Security Council committee to manage the list of entities subject to financial restrictions, and it granted the committee flexibility to add to the list over time, thus enabling the sanctions to become progressively tougher without additional resolutions. It also laid down another deadline, sixty days this time, by which Iran would have to verifiably halt its nuclear program or be subject to "further appropriate measures" by the Security Council.

Both proliferators were under pressure by the end of 2006. I felt that our willingness to energize the diplomatic track and show flexibility was paying off. I was under no illusion that the unity of the international community would last indefinitely or that the Iranians and North Koreans were ready to make a deal. But we were in much better shape than we'd been in January. Even conservative lawmakers and commentators were prepared to give us a little space to make the new approaches work.

Shortly after my announcement that the United States would join the negotiations with Iran if it verifiably halted its nuclear activities, I held one of my periodic off-the-record sessions with the "Fox Tong," a group of Fox News personalities. I often asked journalists to come for a session of this kind so that I could explain what we were doing without creating untimely news stories. David Ignatius, Tom Friedman, David Brooks, and others would join in from time to time because it also gave them a context for the policies that were emerging. The Fox group usually included William Kristol, Charles Krauthammer, Jim Angle, Mort Kondracke, Brit Hume, Fred Barnes, and Juan Williams. To my surprise there wasn't much criticism of the shift—skepticism, certainly, but no accusations of having gone soft. The sessions allowed me to gauge the politics surrounding our decisions—but these were also quality thinkers who made me sharper in assessing and defending the policy. This was particularly true of my interactions with Krauthammer, who is simply one of the best minds in D.C. At the session concerning Iran the consensus view could be summed up as "Hope it works." It was well understood that we didn't have the bandwidth for unilateral confrontation with Iran and North Korea, given the situation in Iraq. The strategy had, at the very least, provided multilateral management tools to address the proliferation threat. In a year that was memorable for its troubles, that was a welcome achievement.

39

PLAYING THE LAST CARD

I T WAS ALMOST UNBEARABLE to watch the pressures on the President to change course in Iraq in the fall of 2006. One morning I stopped by the Oval on the way to a National Security Council meeting just to talk. I related my conversations on Capitol Hill and noted the growing hostility even from Republicans about our effort. We discussed the impending release of the Iraq Study Group report. The bipartisan study group, cochaired by former Secretary of State Jim Baker and former Democratic Congressman Lee Hamilton, had been the brainchild of Representative Frank Wolf of Virginia, who sought to find "common ground" concerning the Iraq war. When Frank came to see me about the proposal in early 2006, I thought that it was a good idea and told him that I would speak with the President. Though concerned that he might be perceived as outsourcing foreign policy, the President clearly understood that he needed the help of the august group of commissioners to stabilize support for continuing the war in Iraq—and to give us a bipartisan "landing zone" for a new policy. It was a bitter pill to swallow that many commentators subsequently depicted the commission as a gathering of wise men from the administration of George H. W. Bush, who would teach his prodigal son a thing or two about realism and competence in foreign policy.

Now, as I sat in the Oval with the President, I suggested that the report might give us a chance for a "reset" in Iraq. I knew Steve agreed. But the President wasn't going to give anyone a blank check on Iraq policy. He wouldn't reject the findings—many of which would turn out to be in line with his own thinking—but he made clear that he would find his own way to move forward. "I am *still* the commander in chief," he asserted. The phrase hung in the air.

As we left the Oval, I asked Steve if he thought the President was capable of acknowledging how deep a hole we were in. We agreed that he did—but he is "one tough hombre," Steve said. "That he is," I agreed.

Throughout the summer, the President's top security advisors and their agencies had continued their reviews of the situation in Iraq. Steve and I called our teams together in mid-October for a no-holds-barred debate of our options. The NSC staff—guided ably by J. D. Crouch, Meghan O'Sullivan, William Luti, Peter Feaver, and Brett McGurk— had coalesced around an option to "surge" U.S. forces and reorient the military toward a "counterinsurgency" posture. In a densely urban environment such as Baghdad, where plainclothed insurgents appeared virtually indistinguishable from innocent civilians, the military's use of heavy firepower to eliminate enemies risked civilian casualties. Such collateral damage had in the past inflamed local citizens and undermined their support for our forces. By contrast, counterinsurgency would emphasize securing the Iraqi population, not just gunning down insurgents, as the military's strategy for defeating the enemy. By patrolling the streets of major cities and remote provinces and securing reconstruction projects, U.S. forces would be able to demonstrate their commitment to Iraq and hopefully convince the Iraqis to invest in their own future as well by laying down their arms.

Such an approach would force our troops to make tough choices and take on greater risk to themselves by venturing out of secure areas. The doctrine would expect them to restrain their fire at times, even if under attack, to avoid shooting into crowded marketplaces, for instance.

I had come to believe that counterinsurgency was the right approach for the complex battlefield in Iraq. In June I had passed along a memo to Steve that recommended a "selective counterinsurgency" option that would essentially implement this doctrine in key regions of the country. Developed by Phil Zelikow and Iraq coordinator Jim Jeffrey, the proposal had called for a temporary infusion of U.S. forces to execute such a strategy. But after the dreadful summer of unrelenting sectarian violence, I was no longer convinced that conditions were ripe—either in the Pentagon or in Baghdad—for this new strategy to succeed.

The successful implementation of this counterinsurgency doctrine depended heavily on the military's ability to adapt to its tenets. Change within such a massive organization is difficult to accomplish even in times of peace, let alone in the middle of a conflict. I worried that the Pentagon leadership was not prepared to implement this new strategy.

More importantly, as I've previously noted, I wasn't sure of the commitment of the Iraqis themselves. Because they lacked either the capacity or the will, the Iraqis were not doing their part in quelling sectarian violence. If it was a lack of capacity on the part of their security forces, maybe an infusion of troops would help in the short term. But if it was a lack of will on the part of the Shia-led government to crack down on the violence—a suspicion I worried might be true—it seemed ill advised to put more U.S. forces in the middle of the slaughter.

It was obvious that Steve favored a "surge" of U.S. forces to stem the violence and give the Iraqis a chance to practice politics. I continued to be skeptical. Our staffs went back and forth, with Phil Zelikow developing a different plan to scale back U.S. involvement. In its baldest incarnation, the emerging proposal from the State Department would seek to reinforce the current balance of power among the Iraqis to stabilize the country and condition our continued engagement on the government's ability to rein in sectarian feuds. According to this proposal, if the government continued to support sectarian killings or even organized its own program of ethnic cleansing, the United States would announce and execute a pullback of its forces out of the cities. The hope was that the credibility of this threat would give us leverage and put the onus squarely on the Iraqis themselves to stop killing one another. I was not convinced that this would work—but I wasn't sure that surging more U.S. forces would work either. At least this way, fewer Americans would die.

Then, a few days before the midterm elections, the President called to ask me a question that began to reset my own thinking. "What do you think about Bob Gates as secretary of defense?"

I could barely contain my joy. "That would be great," I replied. "Why didn't we think of it before?" Gates and I had a long-standing friendship going back to the heady days of the end of the Cold War in the George H. W. Bush administration. We'd remained friends as he took on academic roles at the George Bush School of Government and Public Service at Texas A&M. He ultimately became the university's president.

I'd been careful not to involve myself in the decision about Don Rumsfeld's fate. There was something unseemly about one secretary, no matter how close to the President, appearing in any way to be trying to vanquish another. The President knew how I felt. The closest I'd come to an opinion about Don had been in our initial conversation at Camp David when the President had asked me to be secretary of state. "I don't intend to spend my energy sparring with Don," I'd said. "I'm going to lead U.S. foreign policy, and I don't need his input." The President had simply acknowledged the statement, a little taken aback, I think, by the sharpness of the comment. Again, it was nothing personal with Don. I just wanted him out of the diplomatic lane.

I promised to call Bob and tell him how much I would welcome his appointment at Defense. Bob had kindly told the President that working with me would be easy and productive. More important, I was confident that the Pentagon might now face the challenge in Iraq head-on and creatively. In November 2006, the day after the midterm elections, President Bush announced that he would nominate Bob to serve as the next secretary of defense. My faith in a new start was reinforced when I later learned that Bob intended to appoint David Petraeus to succeed George Casey.

Still, I had reservations about the surge option and continued to press the President to consider alternatives. Steve thought that we might involve Hank Paulson in the discussion—not to draw on his expertise as treasury secretary but to get "fresh eyes" on the problem. It was a great idea. On the Sunday after Thanksgiving, the national security team gathered in the White House solarium with the President. Don was there—continuing to act as secretary of defense until Gates could be confirmed—along with the Vice President, Joint Chiefs of Staff Chairman Peter Pace, Paulson, Hadley, and his deputy, J. D. Crouch. I was struck by the fact that in six years I'd never been in that particular room.

Surrounded by windows that bathed the room in sunlight during the day, the solarium had been host to a meeting where President Dwight Eisenhower had launched a strategic review of Cold War policy in the light of the early gains by the Soviet Union. I don't know whether the room had been selected for our Iraq review with that historical precedent in mind or if the President was just looking for a change of venue. Either way, I hoped that we might channel the thinking of our predecessors more than fifty years later. We would need all the help we could get.

At one point, J.D. suggested what we all knew: the NSC staff favored a troop surge. I questioned again what the troops would do. "Improve population security," he said. I challenged, "So are we now responsible for the security of the Iraqi population or is that the job of their government?" I probed the issue of Maliki's commitment to his own people. I argued that we could not allow the Iraqi leader to take the presence of U.S. troops for granted. The discussion was raucous and intense but led to no final resolution.

The next day, I departed with the President for the Baltics and a NATO Summit in Latvia. *Who would have dreamed that a U.S. President would one day attend a NATO summit in Riga?* I wondered. It was another chance to reflect on history's long arc—and offered reassurance that tough decisions can ultimately change that arc's direction.

The chance to test that proposition came into full relief two days later when we met with Maliki in Amman, Jordan. The President spent more than an hour with the Iraqi one-on-one. While the two men were meeting, Steve, Zal Khalilzad, and I talked with the prime minister's advisors, including his national security advisor, Mowaffaq al-Rubaie. I was stunned when Rubaie suggested that government-sanctioned Shia violence against the Sunnis simply didn't exist. I exploded at him: "Either you're lying to us, or someone is lying to you." Steve and Zal intervened with supporting but less direct comments. I'm glad they did, because even though I really liked and respected Mowaffaq, I wanted to punch him at that moment. *When are these people going to get a grip on the problem?* I asked myself. Right about then we were called back into the room.

Maliki had given the President his own plan for stemming the violence in Baghdad. The President told him that if he was ready to step up, the United States was prepared to put in more forces. "I'll put in tens of thousands if that's what's needed. But you have to be ready to do difficult things." The President gave him a long list—related mostly to even-handedness in regard to sectarian violence. *He's going to surge our forces,* I thought. *But before he does, the military had better know they*

*have to change course on the ground. Bob Gates will figure this out. We'll
be okay. God willing.*

I separated from the President and went on to Jericho and Jerusalem
to give another push to the Palestinian-Israeli peace talks. But my mind
was not on that conflict—we were going to stand or fall on what happened in Iraq.

That became even clearer when I met with the foreign ministers of
the Gulf Cooperation Council plus Egypt and Jordan (GCC+2). The
findings of the Iraq Study Group report had begun to leak out, and
it looked to all the world as though the recommendation would support withdrawal—not a precipitous one but withdrawal nonetheless.
The best that could be said was that there was some room for one more
push before the United States left—but the goal was clearly to get out,
one way or another. The GCC+2 foreign ministers were terrified that
we were about to leave Iraq and abandon the Sunnis. "It hurts me as
an Arab to say this," the Egyptian said, "but you need to increase your
presence and finish the job. We will all be done if you don't."

The foreign ministers were unsettled too by the buzz around the report's insistence on a new diplomatic push that would involve talking to
Iran—a kind of regional solution to the Iraq problem. They were rightly
suspicious that the Iranians would use their enhanced diplomatic perch
that would come with U.S. consultations to further their influence in
the region, and the ministers wanted a promise that the United States
was not about to sell out to Tehran to end the war in Iraq. "We're not in
a position of strength right now," I acknowledged. "But we're not that
weak either. We have no intention of inviting Iran into the Middle East."

Several of my GCC colleagues countered, "They [the Iranians] are
fishing in troubled Arab waters. They smell blood. You have got to be
stronger in confronting them."

We then issued a public statement that said nothing about Iran. The
Middle East was a place of contradictions and fictions. Yet my fellow
ministers were right; it was no time to let Tehran sense wavering on
the part of the United States. That was the lesson that I took from those
conversations, and it started to change my view of the surge.

. . .

I RETURNED to Washington in time for the release of the Iraq Study Group report, confining my own reaction to the suggestion in the report of a "diplomatic offensive" toward the Israeli-Palestine negotiations and high-level talks with Iran and Syria. We were deeply engaged in the first, so I eagerly embraced that idea. But as to Tehran and Damascus, I made it clear that it was a nonstarter. "If they have an interest in a stable Iraq, they will do it anyway." My own view was that it was worth probing them—particularly Syria—but I was not going to petition these hostile regimes on bended knee to help us in Iraq.

Two days after the Iraq Study Group report was released, we met with the President for yet another NSC strategy session on Iraq. I pushed again on the question of Maliki's commitment but as before didn't single out the prime minister. "They're all at fault," I said. "This isn't just about Maliki. It is about Talabani and Hashimi and Hakim—all of them." I said bluntly that they might have to kill one another for a while before they got the point. If they didn't want to secure their own populations, why would the United States be able to do it for them? Without their commitment the surge wouldn't work.

"So what's your plan, Condi?" The President was suddenly edgy and annoyed. "We'll just let them kill each other, and we'll stand by and try to pick up the pieces?"

I was furious at the implication that I cared less about winning in Iraq than those supporting the surge. "No, Mr. President," I said, trying to stay calm. "We just can't win by putting our forces in the middle of their blood feud. If they want to have a civil war we're going to have to let them." There was a lot of shifting of feet around the table. The President and I were on the edge of a confrontation right then and there—something we'd never had in the company of others.

Thankfully the meeting ended shortly after that. I followed the President into the Oval. "You know that's not what I mean," I said. "No one has been more committed to winning in Iraq than I have."

"I know," he said softly. "I know." I felt terrible. His pain was so visible, but he was determined to find a way out and prepared to put everything on the line.

I called Bob Gates and asked when we could spend some time together. We met for dinner on December 12 and talked about the options before us. He clearly favored a surge but shared a lot of my concerns. He told me at that time that he wanted Dave Petraeus to assume the command of the coalition forces in Iraq, replacing George Casey whom he would promote to be army chief of staff. I'd known Petraeus from the earliest days of the war and respected him enormously for his intelligence and his strategic sense. He'd participated in the drafting of the Army and Marine Corps's new counterinsurgency field manual, so I was confident that he would be able to carry out exactly the kind of change in strategy that needed to accompany an influx of troops. I was feeling a lot better about the prospects for the surge, but I had to make one last call. Ray Odierno had been my Joint Staff liaison and was now a lead commander in Iraq. I always tried to respect the chain of command, but this decision was too important to stand on ceremony. "Ray," I said after apologizing for calling him directly, "do you favor more troops? Can you use them to reinforce the Anbar Awakening?" He told me that he did and that he could. That sealed it for me.

AFTER CHRISTMAS, the NSC team gathered at the ranch to review the Iraq strategy one last time. I drove up to the President's house and found him on the back porch, looking out over the lake and the great expanse of the ranch. "You're going to do it, and it's the right thing to do," I said, not even having to say the word "surge." "I'm there, and I'll do everything I can to support it. But, Mr. President, this is your last card. It had better work," I concluded and walked away.

The United States was about to take a monumental gamble and double down in Iraq. We had a fighting chance; there was new leadership in the Pentagon; there would be additional manpower and a new strategy. And we would signal to both the region and the world our commitment to finish the job in Iraq. Still, the surge was a risky strategy because it depended on the Iraqis to deliver their end of the bargain. But it was our best option—and probably our last one.

Thus we could leave no stone unturned to make it work, and as secretary of state that meant bringing civilian support to the military effort. Every obstacle had to be removed; business as usual and State

Department processes had to get out of the way. I called my closest staff together and told them that I was pretty sure the President had decided in favor of a surge—leaving just a little ambiguity so as not to preempt the announcement. "I want the best team in Iraq and Provincial Reconstruction Teams that are fully staffed with experienced people. I will direct people to serve if they don't volunteer," I said. "I want Ryan Crocker to be the ambassador. He knows how to work with the military," I continued, alluding to his effective service in Pakistan. "Tell the D Committee to give me the recommendation," referencing the process that the department's deputy led to generate a recommendation for the ambassador. "And I want to see Ryan myself to convince him to do it. He's going to get everything he asks for—directly from me."

On December 30 Saddam Hussein was executed. The political slate had been wiped clean, and the monster of Baghdad had been brought to justice. But the demons beneath his horrific regime hadn't been vanquished—sectarian violence and terrorism were threatening to control Iraq's destiny. The President of the United States was determined to fight them and chart a different path. *I hope to God the Iraqis are ready to lay claim to a democratic future,* I thought. *One way or another, the die is cast.*

40

A Diplomatic Surge

S O HOW DID IT GO?" the President asked. It was the day after his January 10, 2007, announcement of the "surge" of more than 20,000 additional U.S. troops to Iraq, and I'd come directly to the White House from my testimony before the Senate Foreign Relations Committee.

"Not very well," I said, taking the seat next to him in front of the roaring fire. "We have a tough sell."

"Tough sell" doesn't even scratch the surface, I thought. I'd certainly expected considerable skepticism from the senators; Iraq wasn't going well, and no one wanted to be in support of our effort. The day before, Senator John McCain had called to warn me. "Don't take any guff from any of them," he said. "You're in a position to stand your ground." It was a kind of pep talk, and frankly, I appreciated it.

But the questioning was more brutal than I had expected, with senators essentially implying that the administration could no longer be trusted. In fact, those were precisely the words that Senator Bill Nelson of Florida used. "I have not been told the truth," the Democratic senator said. "I have not been told the truth over and over again by administration witnesses, and the American people have not been told the truth." What could I say to that? I tried to stay calm and responded that I'd always told the truth as I knew it—sometimes we'd been wrong, but we'd never intended to mislead. The exchange was one of the lowest moments of my entire career in government.

Listening to those legislators working to outdo one another in criticizing the President was painful. I kept trying to focus on what the surge would do: integrate military and civilian counterinsurgency efforts and deploy U.S. personnel among the people to deliver population security, reconstruction, and governance. I also emphasized that the new way forward in Iraq would take place against a broader regional diplomatic strategy in the Middle East, pitting moderate reformers against militant regimes in Iran and Syria. *Stay focused,* I told myself. *Keep delivering the message.*

Nebraska Senator Chuck Hagel called the President's decision "the most dangerous foreign policy blunder in this country since Vietnam." And he was a *Republican.* Many senators excoriated Iraqi Prime Minister Nouri al-Maliki, with most suggesting that we'd reached the point of no return: the war could not be won.

After a near-relentless barrage of criticism, California Senator Barbara Boxer provided one of the few openings during which I could take the offensive. She inexplicably suggested that I could not understand the sacrifices of those lost in conflict because I had no children. Not only was it a dumb thing to say, it was deeply offensive. *Would anyone have said that to a male secretary of state?* I wondered. *I didn't realize that having children had anything to do with one's fitness to lead.* I decided not to engage her on that point and instead responded that I fully understood the sacrifices that our men and women in uniform were making. "I visit them," I stated. "I know what they're going through. I talk to their families. I see it." She backed off but was broadly criticized for the bizarre comment.

I made it to the end of the hearings without losing my cool and having defended as best I could the strategy about which I'd been an early skeptic. "That was pretty rough," my chief of staff, Brian Gunderson, said as we drove away from Capitol Hill.

"Could have been worse," I replied.

In fact, I was feeling somewhat better about the prospects for a successful surge. Bob Gates was now at the Pentagon, and we could work together to unify our civilian and military efforts. Later in the year, Lieutenant General Doug Lute would join the NSC staff as the President's principal advisor on Iraq and Afghanistan, building on the extraordinary work of Meghan O'Sullivan in coordinating these two engagements. Steve Hadley and I had also had dinner with then Lieutenant General David Petraeus just before Christmas, and I had great confidence in him. "This is the second time we were supposed to get together," Dave said when we arrived at the Watergate restaurant. I didn't understand what he meant. "I had made an appointment to come and see you at the National Security Council before leaving for Iraq in 2003," he recalled. "Secretary Rumsfeld found out about it and insisted that I cancel." Thank goodness those struggles of distrust and secrecy with the Pentagon were over.

THE DAY after my testimony I headed to the Middle East. I was focused on the upcoming meeting with the GCC that would take place toward the end of my trip, where I was sure I could secure support for the surge. But during my first stops in Ramallah and Jerusalem, I made unexpectedly good progress on the Palestinian-Israeli conflict, securing an agreement with Olmert and Abbas to conduct a three-way dialogue, with the United States as an active participant. It was a breakthrough that signaled that the President and I had gained the trust of both sides. The Israelis typically preferred bilateral talks with the Palestinians and separate bilateral talks with us, worried that they'd be forced into a corner in a tripartite framework. They preferred to "agree to a position with the United States" and then talk to the Palestinians. "That won't work," I had explained, making clear that I needed to be an honest broker. I announced the deal in Egypt, trying to show respect for Cairo's special role in the peace process. If we were going to get a deal, we needed the Arabs.

As I'd expected, Mubarak was focused more on Iraq and Iran than on the Palestinians. He, like King Abdullah of Saudi Arabia, was thrilled that the President had doubled down on Iraq. Those leaders had worried that the United States would cut and run, leaving them to face chaos in Iraq and enhanced Iranian influence in the region. *They don't know George W. Bush very well,* I thought.

At the GCC meeting the next day, the surge proved wildly popular. My Persian Gulf counterparts were as supportive as Congress had been dismissive. The ministers of the Gulf states, Egypt, and Jordan tried to outdo one another in thanking the President for his decision, and this time they issued a public statement of support. When facing skeptical questions about Baghdad's inability to govern earlier that day, I had been delighted to hear Saudi Foreign Minister Saud al-Faisal come to the Iraqis' defense. "Why speculate on such dire consequences?" he asked. Invoking Iraq's historic legacy as part of the cradle of civilization, Saud continued, "I cannot for the life of me conceive that a country like that would commit suicide given the goodwill and the desire of all to help in this." Standing next to him during the press conference, I was so grateful to him for his comments. I then had a passing thought: *I hope to God he's right.*

One of our biggest concerns during the closed meeting was our decision to engage Baghdad's neighbors, including Iran, in a conference about Iraq's future. "Why do you want the Iranians there?" I was asked. I explained that the Iraqis wanted to include all neighbors and the United States wouldn't object. "Just don't let them gain a foothold in Iraq that way," the ministers warned. My announcement a few days earlier that we had arrested Iranian operatives in Iraq helped tamp down their anxiety. President Bush had authorized a series of raids against Iranian agents who were providing sophisticated explosive devices and other weapons and training to the Shia militias. The action had sent shock waves across the region. "Tehran needs to know that its militants will not be permitted to operate with impunity in Iraq," I'd told the ministers. Since one of those captured was a high-ranking Quds Force officer, Tehran had to worry about the exposure of its clandestine activities inside Iraq. There's no doubt that for a while the Iranian regime pulled in its horns after his arrest.

I moved on to discuss the progress in the Israeli-Palestinian conflict. The GCC ministers were pleased, but there wasn't a lot of discussion. *This is pretty interesting,* I thought. *The Israeli-Palestinian issue has fallen down the list of priorities. Iran is number one, two, three, and four.*

I returned to Washington fully prepared to exploit this new reality. I arranged to return to the region a month later, in February, for the first trilateral talks with Israel and the Palestinian Authority. My Middle East Quartet colleagues from the United Nations, the European Union, and Russia joined me at the State Department on February 2 to give a push to the upcoming negotiations. There was considerable optimism about the peace process, now that the United States had taken the lead.

My goal was to get agreement to accelerate progress on the Road Map—the document developed in 2003 that outlines the parties' step-by-step obligations toward the creation of a Palestinian state. But I hoped, too, that we could agree to begin a dialogue on the final status issues: borders, security, refugees, and Jerusalem. I knew that Israeli Prime Minister Ehud Olmert was reluctant to engage on these "core" points of contention. He argued, as had his predecessor, Ariel Sharon, that the Palestinians needed to show a stronger commitment to fighting terrorism before these issues could be discussed, in effect halting progress on the Road Map at its first stage.

The argument had become stale, though, and I believed that the Israelis would—in the context of trilateral discussions with me—begin to negotiate these issues seriously. President Mahmoud Abbas and his Palestinian Authority were locked in a low-level war with their extremist Hamas rivals in Gaza, with near-daily fatal clashes between their respective security forces. It would be hard for the Israelis to claim that they didn't have a partner against terrorism with the bloody conflict between the Palestinian factions playing out every day.

Little did I know that King Abdullah of Saudi Arabia was reading the Palestinian landscape too—but with increasing alarm. He was no friend of Hamas, given its connection to the Muslim Brotherhood, which often challenged the legitimacy of the region's authoritarian regimes. Yet the sight of Palestinians killing one another was more than he could bear. According to his advisors, the king had been watching a wall full of televisions that he keeps playing at all times in the palace. On every screen, the bloodshed in Gaza was visible. "The Israelis have got to be stopped," he'd said. When told that it wasn't Israelis but Palestinians who were firing on one another, he decided to "do something." The king got on the telephone, called Mahmoud Abbas and Khaled Meshal, the leader of Hamas, and summoned them to Mecca. When a call comes from the Custodian of the Two Holy Mosques, no leader in the Arab world can refuse to answer.

I held my breath as we waited for news of what the agreement would say. There was little doubt that there would be a pact, because the Palestinians weren't foolish enough to embarrass the Saudi king. When word came that there was a deal, it was a devastating blow. My trusted interpreter Gamal Helal rushed down to my office. He'd been on the phone with Abbas's people and had been following the Al Jazeera coverage as well. "How bad is it?" I asked. "It's a piece of sh—t!" he exclaimed, quickly apologizing for his language. Hamas would enter into a unity government with the Palestinian Authority, and the party's putative leader in Gaza, Ismail Haniyeh, would become prime minister. With that agreement, the distinction between the moderate Fatah and extremist Hamas factions was immediately blurred since the Palestinian Authority would now allow officials from a group that we, the Europeans, and the Israelis listed as a terrorist organization into the Palestinian government. Any prospects for Israeli-Palestinian negotiations were now dead on arrival.

Olmert was on the phone in what seemed like a matter of minutes. "I won't negotiate with terrorists," he yelled. I didn't challenge him, knowing that no Israeli prime minister would talk to a Palestinian government that counted Hamas among its members. I said I'd get back to him and tried to phone Abbas, who was, to be frank, ducking my call. The next day I finally reached the Palestinian Authority president, telling him bluntly that any chance for negotiations had been destroyed by the "unity pact." He begged me to understand that, sitting in Mecca with the king of Saudi Arabia, he had had no choice but to sign it. Our other Arab allies were equally contrite but unwilling to do anything to repair the damage.

My trip to Jerusalem for the trilateral meeting with Olmert and Abbas was to take place a week later. "I'm going ahead with it," I told Steve and the President the next morning in the Oval. "Maybe I can keep the whole thing on life support if I can get the two of them in the same room." After all, if Abbas could not negotiate, by default Hamas' agenda, "no negotiations," would win outright. The President agreed, and when Olmert called him to protest, he asked the prime minister to go through with the meeting. After much back-and-forth, the Israeli agreed, making sure we knew that he'd have no discussion of "anything substantive."

It wasn't the best start to a diplomatic initiative, but at least the two had agreed to talk. I had very low expectations for the meeting; I was just hoping to keep the encounter from blowing up. I told the press that we'd discuss how to map out a "political horizon" for the establishment of a Palestinian state. The two parties needed to be convinced that there could be an end in sight to the conflict. The term was deliberately vague and could mean anything from broad philosophical ruminations about the future to the minute details of final-status negotiations. Olmert said he would confine their discussions to the former, Abbas the latter. Throughout the trip journalists would ask if the situation was too complicated for a meeting. "If one waited for the perfect time to come to the Middle East," I replied, "perhaps you wouldn't get on an airplane." But some times were better than others. This one wasn't very good.

The David Citadel Hotel was always enormously helpful and accommodating during my numerous trips to Jerusalem. This time, though, we quickly realized that there wasn't a proper room for a tripartite meeting. Karen Hughes and my advisor Colby Cooper, who had been with me since the White House days, went to look at the one option, a voluminous ballroom that swallowed a little table where the three of us were supposed to sit. They did their best, bringing in potted palms and Israeli, Palestinian, and American flags to make the setting slightly more intimate. And I learned later that there had been a last-minute swap of the table for one that was fair to all parties—the original had a Star of David emblazoned on it.

After the obligatory camera spray with the three of us smiling stiffly and awkwardly shaking hands—it's rather difficult to shake the hands of two leaders at once—the press left and we sat down, just the three of us. The table was tiny and the room enormous. "I feel like I'm in a train station," Abbas said. Olmert took up the hostility in the room. "How could you hug Khaled Meshal?" he asked Abbas. The Palestinian kept trying to explain that he had no choice when the Saudis pushed for an agreement, but Olmert clearly had the upper hand. Soon the two were exchanging a steady volley of insults as I sat silently in the middle. "Well, you should never have had the elections," Olmert said, referring to the 2006 vote that had brought Hamas to power in Gaza.

"We didn't *want* to have elections," Abbas shot back.

I furrowed my brow at that one. *What are they talking about?* I asked myself. *They both wanted elections.* But I decided that I had an opening to put them on the same page. "Okay," I said, "*we* wanted the elections. The United States wanted the elections. All right?" They sat back in their chairs, satisfied to let the American take the blame. "Now can we go upstairs to my suite and talk about the future?" I pleaded. They agreed, and, much to the surprise of our aides and the hotel staff, we trundled onto the elevator and headed for the ninth floor.

Once we were upstairs, the mood lightened considerably. We walked out onto the balcony overlooking the Holy City. Olmert pointed out all of the construction he'd overseen when he was mayor—not really a helpful line of discussion. Abbas half-jokingly said, "Yes, and you built those ugly apartments in front of the Damascus Gate."

"I built them for the French and the Americans," Olmert countered. Everyone laughed.

I then added that I had my own "final-status issue." "Do you know that the Protestants don't have a place in the Church of the Holy Sepulcher?" I asked. "I want them to when you finally settle Jerusalem." That lightened the mood even more, and we went inside where the two talked about their desire to settle the conflict. There were no negotiations and no breakthroughs, but under the circumstances it was a diplomatic victory. At least they were talking.

I decided to make a press statement on my own—without the two of them—not wanting to risk unraveling the fragile comity we'd achieved. "Can I say that you'll meet again?" I asked gingerly. They nodded in agreement. "I'll be back next month," I said, and went out to face the press.

"They only agreed to meet again?" someone asked.

"Yes," I responded. "They will meet again." *You have no idea how relieved I am to be able to say that,* I thought. I packed up and headed home.

THE DEPARTMENT was finally taking the charge seriously to fully mobilize for duty in Iraq. Bob Zoellick had decided to step down as deputy, a step I regretted. We'd worked well together, but Bob acknowledged that he'd never quite accustomed himself to being number two. He remained a good and valued colleague and a sounding board for the various issues I would continue to confront during my tenure.

His departure came at a bad time, though, with all the trouble swirling around in the Middle East. I knew I wanted John Negroponte to be my deputy, but he was then serving as the nation's first director of national intelligence (DNI). He wanted to come to State but didn't want to send the message that the DNI was a job so fraught with bureaucratic infighting that he couldn't last even a year. The President insisted on finding another candidate for the DNI before he would release John to take the job at State. I understood all of those concerns, but it made the management of the department even more difficult. Though Nick Burns served capably as acting deputy, it looked to the outside world as if the team was falling apart—especially when my counselor, Phil Zelikow, decided to leave too. Since no one knew that Negroponte would become the deputy, there was a good deal of scuttlebutt that I'd run into management trouble at Foggy Bottom. I was relieved when John finally joined me; he was the perfect choice. One of the most revered Foreign Service officers of his generation, he'd been on Henry Kissinger's delegation during the 1972 opening to China, worked in Vietnam, and served as ambassador five times, including a tour in Iraq. His authority and popularity in the Foreign Service were enormously helpful in supporting some of the tough calls that I had to make regarding personnel assignments to difficult places.

Another factor that helped bring the department on board was the President's request for a huge increase in the State Department's budget to support the needs of transformational diplomacy as well as the surge. The increase would fund 254 new positions for critical countries such as India, China, Indonesia, and Lebanon, as well as 57 new positions in the Office of the Coordinator for Reconstruction and Stabilization so that we could rapidly deploy our civilian capacity to respond to crises and stabilize missions overseas. Additionally, the request provided for $6 billion in supplemental funding for Afghanistan, Iraq, and Lebanon.

The initial discussions with the Office of Management and Budget hadn't been very promising; it is the OMB director's job to "green-eyeshade" government spending. But we were at war, and though everyone talked about the importance of civilians in the fight, no one wanted to fund them. I was tired of hearing from the Pentagon that State wasn't doing its job, and I was grateful to Bob Gates when he called for greater foreign affairs funding in a much-admired speech around that time.

The department was seriously stretched—in terms of both operations and foreign-assistance funding—to help the multiplying newly democratic states dependent on America. I'd pledged $770 million at a Paris Donors' Conference for Lebanon. It was imperative that we support Prime Minister Fouad Siniora's government, which was still trying to rebuild from the war and hold militant forces at bay. A similar pledge of $10.6 billion to Afghanistan at a NATO ministerial meeting was necessitated by growing evidence of the Taliban's resurgence. When I started adding those commitments to what we were already dedicating to Iraq, I realized how stretched we were.

I never believed, though, that the entire bill should fall on the U.S. government. Thanks to the innovative work of Dina Powell, the Egyptian American assistant secretary for educational and cultural affairs, who was working under Karen Hughes, we pioneered public-private partnerships in both Lebanon and later in the Palestinian territories. The former brought together such high-level executives as Craig Barrett from Intel, John Chambers from Cisco Systems, Jay Collins from Citigroup, and the Lebanese businessman Yousif Ghafari to fund reconstruction and community service projects throughout the country. Siniora needed an answer, particularly in the Shia South, to the largesse Hezbollah bestowed on the population. The business community was often quicker and more efficient at providing help than our government could ever be.

We launched a similar effort with the Palestinians later that year. I called Walter Isaacson of the Aspen Institute and invited him to come over. "Walter, how would you like to do something for peace?" I asked. He readily agreed and organized the U.S.-Palestinian Partnership, an association of private business and foundation leaders such as Ziad Asali and Jean Case. Their early efforts helped raise more than $1.4 billion in investment commitments to help Salam Fayyad make the West Bank economically prosperous and secure.

Such efforts, however, could only augment, not supplant, U.S. government assistance. When I got the OMB's calculation of how much funding the State Department merited, I called my friend Rob Portman, the OMB director, and said that I would appeal. He understood fully; it was nothing personal between us. The Vice President, who oversaw the appellate process on behalf of the President, was very sympathetic and assured me that he would help make the case for adequate funding.

We also changed the designation of the State Department to a "national security agency," placing it in the same category as the Departments of Defense and Homeland Security. As it concerned the budget, the distinction meant little, but it sent a signal that diplomacy was an equal partner in the conduct of the wars in Afghanistan and Iraq and essential to the success of the Freedom Agenda.

The additional funding and the emphasis on the need for a civilian surge caused me to strengthen even further the Provincial Reconstruction Teams, doubling the number of PRTs in Iraq and hiring about three hundred civilians to carry out reconstruction tasks. The PRTs operated far from the fortified Green Zone in Baghdad. They merged diplomats, aid workers, and military personnel in units that could carry out counterinsurgency doctrine as it was intended. There was little distinction between war and peace. Rather, the teams were responsible for governance and reconstruction in areas that were far from peaceful and where security was always in question. Obviously, it was dangerous work.

The civilians in the PRTs, however, needed to have their protection seamlessly integrated into the functioning of the combined civilian and military unit. I learned that this had caused a big turf war between State and the Pentagon about who would be in command of PRT personnel. "Well, of course it will be the brigade commander," I told my chief of staff, Brian Gunderson, when he said that our folks were looking for guidance.

"The embassy objects," he said, noting that the ambassador didn't want "his people" reporting to someone else.

"Well, they're *my* people," I told Brian, "and they'll report to the brigade commander. Ask them if they have any other ideas about how to stay safe since none of them carry guns." That ended the controversy, and the integrated teams of diplomats, aid workers, and military personnel became one of the really successful experiments of the Iraq war.

Very often, particularly in wartime, necessity *is* the mother of invention. Most people who served in PRTs found them rewarding and effective. And the President, who had enormous respect for what the military was doing in Iraq and Afghanistan, gained a new appreciation for what diplomats could do, too. Sometimes in person but often by video, he encountered stories of these civilian PRT "veterans," people in their fifties and sixties who were risking life and limb far from the comforts of embassies and capitals.

As an influx of civilians began deploying to Iraq, we became increasingly reliant on contracted security forces to guard and transport diplomats and aid workers around the country safely. There simply weren't enough soldiers to carry out those tasks, and frankly, the military's job was really to fight insurgents, not protect American civilians. The State Department's Diplomatic Security bureau is in charge of protecting the secretary of state and is also dedicated to the protection of the embassy. "DS," as it is known in the department, is enormously capable but small. Though I increased the number of DS special agents by more than two hundred, there was simply no way that the security arm of the Foreign Service could protect the large contingent of civilians in the war zones of Iraq and Afghanistan. When officers could be spared, they were largely engaged in protecting high-ranking officials and foreign dignitaries. Our only choice was to contract security out.

For the most part the arrangement worked well. But we learned the hard way that there were real liabilities to the system. One morning in September I woke up to reports that personnel working for Blackwater USA—at that time our largest source of private security contractors in Iraq—had opened fire in a Baghdad square. Although it was unclear how the shooting had started, seventeen civilians had been killed in the incident. Shortly after I heard the news, I walked into the Oval Office for a scheduled meeting with the President. "You look like you've lost your last friend," he said. I told him about the Blackwater incident and said it was big trouble. It was. The Iraqis began demanding that Blackwater leave the country, and there were hearings and numerous investigations into the shooting. I tried to stem the crisis by testifying on the subject before Congress, conducting internal reviews of how we manage our contractors and making major adjustments to the way they were overseen. I ordered DS to deploy dozens of additional agents to accompany Blackwater security details moving through Iraq. Defense Secretary Bob Gates and I even agreed to place armed contractors that operated in the battlefield under the supervision of the Pentagon. And I asked the fine officer who headed the department's Diplomatic Security bureau to resign.

As our forces begin withdrawing from Iraq and Afghanistan, the United States will likely grow even more dependent on those forces. In June 2011 the State Department signaled that it would spend close to $3 billion on private security contractors to protect its diplomats in Iraq after the U.S. military completed its drawdown in the country at the end of the year. Many experts question whether we should be relying on these contractors, particularly as they undertake missions that have been traditionally reserved for our military or other governmental entities. These are valid concerns, many of which I share. But unless we increase the number of personnel within the government to provide this capacity in-house, we will have to rely on these forces, at least in the short term. In a tough budgetary environment that isn't a realistic option. This does not negate the need for enhanced oversight of and accountability for these contractors. Both State and Defense will need to ensure that the rules under which they operate, particularly those pertaining to how they use force, are more closely aligned with those of our military, without compromising the quality of security they provide for our diplomats.

I BEGAN TO SENSE that in the corridors of the Pentagon and among congressional hawks, complaints about how State was not pulling its weight in the fight were dissipating. Since becoming secretary, I'd fiercely defended the Foreign Service against the Pentagon and Congress, and, thankfully, our efforts seemed to be paying off.

There were always exceptions, though. I'll never forget the day John McCain came to see me to complain about the Department's role in Iraq. John and I are old friends, and it started off with civility. But all of a sudden he was yelling and red in the face. "We're about to lose the second war in my lifetime, and State isn't in the fight!"

I let him finish his tirade because I knew that he could be emotional. And then I led him through the changes we'd made and encouraged him to meet Ryan Crocker, who'd just become the U.S. ambassador in Iraq. Ryan would have everything he needed, I told John, including a team of people with ambassador-level experience working for him. "John, you know that no one is more dedicated to winning in Iraq than I am," I said.

"I know," he replied quietly.

He's just a patriot who has given a lot and demands the same, I thought. *It's okay. Don't return fire with fire.* Our meeting ended amicably.

THE ROLE of diplomacy in support of the Iraq effort continued to grow, demanding more and more time. The remaining tensions with friends and allies who had opposed the war initially had been largely overcome, replaced by a general sense of alarm at the war's disastrous course. Some of our original partners had already left—Spain due to the election of the leftist government of Prime Minister José Luis Zapatero, Italy because it simply couldn't maintain domestic support for the war any longer. In February 2007 Great Britain announced a drawdown of about 1,600 of its 7,100 troops. But while domestic pressures on our co-alition partners to get out were growing, recriminations about how we had gotten into Iraq were rarely heard. Now we were all united in trying to find a way to leave a stable country behind.

In that regard, there was a collective sigh of relief when I announced U.S. support for an Iraqi-led conference that would solicit input from its neighbors about how to stabilize the country. Frankly, I didn't expect much of Syria, and I was sure that Iran had no intention of helping, but at least a gathering would put some international pressure on them to stop making trouble. We were taking a tougher line toward Tehran with the arrests of their personnel in Iraq and the passage of a second round of sanctions in the United Nations concerning Iran's nuclear program.

Thus in March, David Satterfield, my able coordinator for Iraq, and Zal Khalilzad, our outgoing ambassador to Iraq who would be assuming our top diplomatic post at the United Nations, joined Iraq's neighbors, including Iran and Syria, at a conference in Baghdad. There was a brief "pull-aside" between our folks and the Iranian representatives. It was the first face-to-face meeting in three years. "Just don't give them anything to crow about, Zal," I'd told the ambassador. I needn't have worried. The Iranians were so nervous to be in the presence of Americans that they read their talking points verbatim, barely made eye contact, and made quick work of the whole thing. Ryan Crocker would meet in Baghdad with his counterpart. The meeting was equally unproductive.

The scene wasn't terribly different when I attended the minister-level meeting for Iraq's neighbors, the Iraq Compact Conference, held in Sharm el-Sheikh, Egypt. Most of the news coverage from the event focused on my discussions with the Syrian foreign minister. Our encounter would be the highest-level contact Washington had had with Damascus since we had recalled our ambassador in 2005. I was late for the prearranged meeting, having been delayed by another meeting. When I got there, the rotund Walid Muallem, who looked a little like an Arab version of Ariel Sharon, was relieved that I'd come. "I thought you might not show up," he said.

"Why would I do that?" I answered. That was perhaps the most momentous part of our discussion. I delivered my points about Syria's interference in Lebanon and its failure to stop terrorists in their country from crossing their border into Iraq.

"It's hard to stop them," he said, but I was having none of it.

"They're coming through Damascus airport," I countered. The whole exchange reminded me of something an Arab minister had said when I asked about the prospects for cooperation with Syria: "You can't buy the Syrians. You might be able to rent them, though. The only problem is, you never know how long they'll stay rented." I decided then and there that cooperation with Damascus was a one-way street. The siren song of engagement with the Syrians has attracted many U.S. diplomats. I lost my appetite for any such effort that day in Sharm after talking to Muallem.

There were no preset plans for me to meet my Iranian counterpart, Manouchehr Mottaki, who was something of a cipher in any case with no real authority to do anything. But when I arrived at lunch, I noticed that the Egyptian foreign minister—my buddy Ahmed Aboul Gheit—had placed the Iranian in my direct line of sight. Only the Saudi foreign minister sat between us. "Did you say hello to Condi?" Ahmed asked with a twinkle in his eye. "Or did you mean her too, when you said,

'Peace be upon you'?" The Iraqi, the Saudi, and others in earshot were chuckling, but Mottaki looked stricken. "Hello," I said to get the poor guy off the hook. He nodded and went back to his lunch.

That evening Ahmed tried again. The Egyptians had planned an elaborate dinner by the sea. I arrived a little late because I had a number of press interviews that ran long. When I got to the table, there was an empty chair next to me, which Ahmed had reserved for the Iranian. Mottaki left before I got to the dinner, however, complaining that he was offended by the entertainment, a Ukrainian violinist wearing a rather revealing red dress. Sean McCormack quipped to the press that it was unclear whether Mottaki had been fearful of the woman in the red dress or the woman in the black pantsuit, my chosen apparel for the evening.

So I never had a real conversation with my Iranian counterpart. After a while I found it useful to tweak him in my press conferences, offering to meet him anywhere, anytime, to talk about anything—if Iran would just suspend its nuclear program. That never happened, but the offer helped me keep the P5+1 united and the Iranians isolated.

It was unfortunate that the nature of the regime made it impossible to pursue rapprochement with Iran. The Iranian people are among the most pro-American in the region—and, ironically, the most supportive of the Freedom Agenda. Anecdote after anecdote from those who visited Iran made this point. Australian Foreign Minister Alexander Downer related how he attended a meeting at the University of Tehran, only to be confronted by the students for not speaking clearly about democracy "like George W. Bush." My advisor at State Jared Cohen found that when people in Iran learned he was American, he rarely had to pay for anything. And my Stanford colleague William Perry, a former secretary of defense, was once asked during a visit there if he personally knew me. "Yes, I do," he said, to which the individual explained how much he admired me. It turned out that the U.S. secretary of state was popular for confronting the regime.

We thus tried to reach out to the Iranian people. In 2006 I requested $75 million in supplemental funding to support our democracy and cultural diplomacy programs in Iran. I told the Senate Foreign Relations Committee that during the 1970s about 200,000 Iranians had studied in the United States; by 2006 that figure had fallen to 2,000. The requested funding would be used to increase our "exchanges" with Iranian professionals and students as well as improve our radio broadcasting service to enhance the prospects for true democracy in the country. "I've read that it is forbidden in some quarters to play Beethoven and Mozart in Tehran," I told the senators. "We hope that Iranians can play it in New York or in Los Angeles." I even supported a U.S. wrestling team traveling to compete in a tournament in Tehran. But there were U.S. flags in the stadium, and the regime eventually clamped down on "sports diplomacy."

In May 2007 a group of young Iranian artists came to the United States to display their work at the Meridian International Center in Washington, D.C. I addressed the group and made some remarks to the press, avoiding any political messages that might make it difficult for our guests. When we suggested a reciprocal visit for American artists, though, the regime refused. The mullahs no doubt understood how popular the United States and Americans were—and it terrified them.

41

A New Approach to Latin America

I N FACT, WE HAD many major foreign policy initiatives under way, but in the atmosphere created by Iraq, it was difficult to get attention for them. By the beginning of 2007, we'd begun to significantly restructure our approach to Latin America. While reactionary leaders such as Hugo Chávez in Venezuela, Daniel Ortega in Nicaragua, and the ever-difficult Kirchners in Argentina were grabbing headlines, the region was making considerable progress toward democratic consolidation and free-market reforms.

U.S. foreign assistance to Latin America and the Caribbean had doubled from $860 million a year to $1.6 billion, and the United States had invested nearly $900 million through Millennium Challenge compacts with El Salvador, Honduras, and Nicaragua and a threshold agreement with Paraguay. We enjoyed excellent relations with Colombia, Chile, Peru, Brazil, and most of Central America. But were we still undervaluing our friends through too much attention to our adversaries?

We decided that we were and that, more troubling, we were allowing the "bad boys" of the region to set the terms of the debate. While we talked about trade and foreign investment, they spoke of social justice. While we talked about economic growth, they spoke of health, welfare, and jobs. Why should we allow Chávez to appropriate the language of the people's well-being when those words rang hollow?

The President set off for a six-day tour of Latin America to deliver this new message. It was a message that our friends had longed to hear from the United States. Hank Paulson developed an initiative to deliver loans to small businesses; the Overseas Private Investment Corporation provided additional funding to underwrite mortgages for working families in Mexico, Brazil, Chile, and Central America (an effort that had obviously started before the housing crisis in the United States); and we announced a $75 million partnership for English-language training for Latin American students. The trip was the culmination of a long interagency effort led by Dan Fisk of the NSC and Assistant Secretary Tom Shannon who was held in the highest regard in the region. We also enlisted the president of the Inter-American Development Bank, Luis Moreno, who had served as the Colombian ambassador to the United States, to support programs to strengthen some of the poorest countries in the region.

We did one other thing too. The President and I stopped talking about Hugo Chávez, who'd actually gone to Argentina to hold an anti-Bush rally during the trip. By the time we arrived in Uruguay after a stop in Brazil, Chávez began conjuring up theories about why the President wouldn't mention him and protested publicly. Our tactic was working. He loved it when we would criticize him because he could then stand as the defender of the poor against the "gringo" to the north. Ignoring his provocations worked better.

The same held true the next year with the Russians. In "retaliation" for our response to the war in Georgia, Moscow flew Soviet-era "Blackjack" bombers along the coast of Venezuela. Bob Gates later joked that the United States would have been happy to carry out search-and-rescue missions if one of the old planes crashed. I simply pointed out to the press that unarmed Soviet-era bombers didn't change the balance of power in the Western Hemisphere. We made light of those ridiculous actions.

But Chávez was dangerous nonetheless, accused of rigging elections in the region and even funding and arming FARC narco-terrorists against the Colombian government. We found it more effective to counter him quietly rather than with great fanfare. And building up your friends with aid and assistance is one way to diminish your enemies. That was the new course we set in Latin America.

We tried again to strengthen our relationship with Mexico, too. When I visited my counterpart, Patricia Espinosa, toward the end of my term, I was struck by questions in our press conference about the violence perpetrated by the drug cartels that roamed the U.S.-Mexican border region. When the newly inaugurated president of Mexico, Felipe Calderón, met with President Bush for the first time in March 2007, he was very blunt about what he faced. "We need your help in training the army to do the work that the police can't," he said. It was shocking to hear the Mexican president ask for the help of the Americans in a matter of internal security, since Mexico's stance for years had been to defend proudly its "sovereignty" from the "gringos" to the north. The Mérida Initiative, a $1.4 billion joint partnership to train and equip our Mexican and Central American neighbors' militaries and law enforcement officers, was put into place, but not without congressional turbulence. It seems that Senator Patrick Leahy was concerned that the funding would fall into the hands of Mexican army officials guilty of past human rights abuses. When I couldn't convince Pat to release the funding bill from committee for a vote, I called the senators of California, New Mexico, Arizona, and Texas (states that bordered Mexico and suffered from spillover violence) and told them the problem. They had no trouble convincing their fellow legislator from Vermont that the Mérida Initiative was a national security priority.

I wish that we could have done more. There are parts of Mexico that are beginning to resemble a failed state. My counterpart Patricia had chosen for our meeting the relaxed setting of Puerto Vallarta. Sitting there by the beach, she related statistics to me that were shocking at the time: I was told that five thousand officials had been killed or kidnapped, and many thousands of civilians had been caught up in drug-related violence as well. Killings by drug cartels had spread beyond border cities such as Ciudad Juárez to the major economic centers such as Monterrey.

Sometimes an event is a powerful metaphor for a situation. In 1996, as Stanford's provost, I'd accompanied the football team to the Sun Bowl in El Paso. It was a wonderful time with a grand gala dinner across the border in Ciudad Juárez, complete with a "bloodless" bullfight. When I returned to Stanford in 2009, the Cardinal won its way to the Sun Bowl again. This time our trip materials carried a warning that essentially told us, "Don't cross the border into Ciudad Juárez. Your life is in danger there."

I could never shake the feeling, born that day many years before at President Vicente Fox's ranch, that we never reached our full potential with Mexico. But at least the relationship between the two democracies, which had faced so many challenges in the past, was clearly one of friendship.

THE MOST DEVASTATING FAILURE in our dealings with Mexico had less to do with foreign policy than with domestic affairs. The President had come to office wanting to push forward comprehensive immigration reform in the United States. He'd discussed it with Fox and then Calderón, and it would have been a wonderful achievement in the United States' relationship with its southern neighbor. But that wasn't the principal reason why George W. Bush wanted to fix immigration. As Texas governor he'd been a proponent of dealing with the deepening wound of undocumented immigrants living in the shadows—hardworking people without whom California grapes wouldn't be picked and Texas roofing would come to a standstill. No fan of "amnesty," he envisioned a "guest worker program" to allow people to stay in the country legally as long as they had a job. There would be a penalty for breaking the law, but eventually people might even achieve citizenship by paying a fine and learning English. In the Senate the bill had the notable support of Republicans John McCain and Jon Kyl and Democrat Ted Kennedy.

I had rarely seen the President more disappointed than he was the day the bill failed. He was sitting slightly slumped in his chair in the Oval. "I'm so sorry," I said.

"Yeah, me too," he said. Publicly, he would say, "The American people understand the status quo is unacceptable when it comes to our immigration laws. A lot of us worked hard to see if we could find a common ground. It didn't work."

It didn't work, and it still hasn't. I'm convinced that fixing immigration is one of the critical tasks facing the United States today. I believe in upholding our laws, and I'm certainly one who believes in the "melting pot" and the need for everyone to learn English (though it wouldn't be bad to learn Spanish too). But the grainy video on cable news of Mexicans crawling across the border does not enrich the dialogue about this hard problem. I don't recognize my country when people talk of denying citizenship to the children born here of illegal-immigrant parents. I don't see why we should continue to educate engineers and scientists and scholars from around the world—and then send them home.

The United States is a country of immigrants. For generations, the most ambitious people have come here from across the world to be a part of this great experiment. Immigrants keep us refreshed and immune from the sclerotic demographics of Europe, Japan, and Russia. Singapore's founding father, Lee Kuan Yew, once asked me if I knew why America would always be great.

"Why?" I asked.

"Because you can tolerate difference," he said. "And that makes every smart young person want to go there. An immigrant can never be German or Chinese or Japanese—but they can be American." He was absolutely right.

I've been asked many times what I regret about my time in Washington. There were many disappointments but maybe none greater than the failure to get immigration reform when we had a chance. The United States has prospered by drawing on talented people from around the world to enrich us. My parents and grandparents believed in the transforming power of education to lift lives and break through racial and class barriers. Immigrants often hold those views, too, and the determination to act on them. I have always felt a deep kinship with them.

Unfortunately, by 2007 we were out of steam and out of ammunition—sapped by 9/11, Afghanistan, and Iraq. After the attack on the Twin Towers and the Pentagon we had to make trade-offs and pick our battles. Maybe the battle for immigration reform came too late.

Yet, despite some disappointment that we didn't achieve more in the region, the real story in Latin America was the progress of democratic forces—not perfect and certainly fragile, but well under way. In Washington, I addressed a conference sponsored by the OAS and the African Union to draw lessons from one another on democratic transitions. It was a big step for the nations of the Western Hemisphere, which still talked in terms of "noninterference" in one another's affairs.

And nowhere was the language of noninterference heard more often than in the case of Cuba. It wasn't a secret that Fidel Castro was going to die—one day. But our Latin American friends did not want to advocate for democracy for the Cuban people even as they increasingly enjoyed it themselves. Only little Costa Rica and its Nobel Laureate president, Óscar Arias, dared to challenge the orthodoxy about Cuba.

Yet, when word came that Castro had fallen ill, we thought there might be an opening to engage the Latin Americans and the Europeans about Cuba's future. The President had appointed a Commission for Assistance to a Free Cuba to mobilize the U.S. government in building a foundation for the democratic transition when the time came. The commission undertook the most extensive U.S. government assessment of Cuba's development needs and identified how we could help meet them. Commerce Secretary Carlos Gutierrez and I cochaired the effort. Carlos was a Cuban American who had fled the island with his parents and brother a year after the 1959 revolution. Carlos was lucky to leave with his parents. Thousands of young refugees, known as the "Peter Pan" children, fled without their parents to avoid conscription and many never saw their families again. Not surprisingly, Carlos had a deep attachment to Cuba and to the desire of its people for freedom. Yet he was not an ideologue; he genuinely wanted to promote change and was prepared to support creative ideas. There was some jealousy at the State Department that the commerce secretary was clearly taking the lead in this diplomatic endeavor. I felt none of that, preferring to be Carlos's "wingman" as we tried to push against the seemingly immovable force of the Castro brothers. That they remain in place is a tragedy for the Cuban people.

Despite our efforts, Cuba remains a lone outpost of oppression in our hemisphere. In 2002 President Bush said he would engage Congress to ease the embargo and begin to normalize our diplomatic relations if Cuba were to undertake a democratic political opening, commit to elections, and respect human rights and fundamental freedoms. The Cuban response was the Black Spring of 2003, when Cuban authorities arrested and imprisoned seventy-five democratic activists.

The Bush administration took a number of other steps to reach out to the Cuban people. We used technology to overcome Castro's efforts to block the free flow of information. For instance, we broadcasted TV and Radio Marti from aircraft to avoid Cuban signal-jamming efforts, and we authorized the shipment of cell phones, direct TV decoders, and computer equipment to help Cubans connect with the outside world. In an effort to promote safe migration, we increased the number of refugees we would take each year. And in response to the devastating hurricanes and tropical storms in 2008, we offered significant humanitarian and reconstruction assistance to Cuba, even indicating a willingness to work through the regime to ensure the Cuban people received what they needed to survive and rebuild their communities. Regrettably, the regime turned down several offers of such assistance.

Though there was a growing chorus of politicians calling for us to accommodate the Castro regime, we never wavered in our support for political freedom in Cuba and for a peaceful transition to democratic rule. Someday Cubans will have the same basic rights as the other peoples of the Americas. And when that day comes, after the Castro era, we will have left the Cuban people with no doubt that we were on their side.

Progress in the Six-Party Talks

NORTHEAST ASIA WAS again an active front in the early months of 2007. I was returning from a trip to the Middle East and stopped in Berlin to meet with Chancellor Angela Merkel and my German counterpart, Frank-Walter Steinmeier. Shortly after landing, my chief of staff, Brian Gunderson, said that Chris Hill, the assistant secretary for East Asia, wanted to see me for a few minutes at the hotel. Chris had just concluded a secret meeting with the North Koreans. (Berlin was chosen for the meeting because North Korea, one of the most isolated countries in the world, had diplomatic representation there dating back to its Soviet-era relations with East Germany.)

I arrived at the Adlon, a spectacularly beautiful prewar hotel across from the Brandenburg Gate, where the Wall once divided East from West. Overlooking the Bundestag, my suite was comfortable, with a grand piano in it that I often played to release the tensions of the day. The wonderful staff of the hotel made it easy, having acquired scores of some of my favorite Brahms pieces. The only discordant element was a frightening portrait of Kaiser Frederick the Great in the dining room.

His piercing glare seemed directed at me, and I reflexively diverted my eyes when in his presence.

That night I arrived around six, and Chris was waiting for me. He was clearly excited about his encounter with Kim Kye Gwan, the North Korean negotiator for the Six-Party Talks. The North Koreans were prepared to shut down their reactor at Yongbyong and readmit IAEA inspectors. "What do they want? A light-water reactor?" I asked skeptically, referring to the type used theoretically for civilian energy purposes.

"No," he replied. "They want their money back."

Chris was referring to the $25 million in frozen North Korean assets that we were holding. The money had been frozen under the executive order that sanctioned North Korea for illicit activities, including counterfeiting our currency. "That's going to be a tough sell with the President," I said. Chris handed me a piece of paper that he'd drawn up with Kim. It was a step-by-step plan to move the Six-Party Talks forward, and it included unfreezing the assets. The North Koreans would be in town for one more day. Chris was guessing that Kim had acted somewhat beyond his instructions from Pyongyang. If he went back without our agreement, we might be back to square one. It looked like a reasonable approach, but I knew it would be a tough sell in the interagency process.

I decided to go directly to the President. I called Steve on the phone and told him what had happened. "I need you to take this to the President directly," I said. As any good national security advisor will do, Steve protested that he needed to convene the Principals. "I don't have time for that, Steve. I'd like to talk to the President." Steve got the President on the phone. "Sir, we have a chance to get this thing off the ground but it won't be there tomorrow," I said.

"Send me the paper," he answered.

I did and then waited until about 1:00 A.M. Berlin time (7:00 P.M. in Washington) before calling again. The President had approved the paper. He had, of course, consulted the Vice President, and Steve had talked to Bob Gates, who had no problem with the approach. Within a month the Six-Party Talks generated an agreement based on the outline that Chris and Kim had prepared. Pyongyang would receive $400 million in aid and fuel oil in return for disabling the nuclear facilities in Yongbyong and allowing the return of nuclear inspectors. And the North Koreans would eventually get their $25 million.

It turned out that it was really hard to get around a Treasury 311 sanction once it had been levied. No financial institution wanted to touch the money, lest it be accused of money laundering. Hank Paulson called every finance minister who might be able to help. No one would. The most remarkable reaction came from the Bank of China. "We have an international board," Hank was told. "They don't want us dealing with frozen North Korean assets." Hank tried to convince responsible officials that the United States *wanted* this transfer, so there would, of course, be no action against them. Still, no one wanted to be involved. Even the President intervened, calling me in Berlin while a gathering of people, including former chancellor Helmut Kohl, waited to give me an award for my role in German unification. "Is there something else that will satisfy the North Koreans?" he asked.

"No, sir, there isn't," I said.

"Are you tired?" he asked, perhaps hearing the strain in my voice

"No, just frustrated," I said.

Finally Hank came up with an idea: he arranged for the New York Federal Reserve, working with a private bank in Russia, to accept the money from Banco Delta Asia, the bank that held the funds. That didn't end the drama, though. It would take several more months before finally, in June, the money could actually be transferred to the North. Nothing was simple in dealing with the "Hermit Kingdom."

The resolution of the problem allowed Chris Hill to make a trip to North Korea, the first by an official in the Bush administration since Jim Kelly's star-crossed visit in 2002. And it allowed me to meet my North Korean counterpart on the margins of an ASEAN forum in July 2008, along with the other foreign ministers of the Six-Party Talks. In the brief encounter, the hapless and nervous official said virtually nothing. But it was a photo-op that moved the process forward—slightly.

42

IMPROVING THE DAILY LIVES OF PALESTINIANS

I RETURNED TO THE Middle East as promised in late March for talks with Abbas and Olmert. The atmosphere was tense, particularly since the Palestinians had acted on the basis of the Mecca agreement and actually established their "unity government." Since the Israelis weren't prepared to sit down with Abbas, I engaged the two sides in "parallel talks," shuttling between them.

The time wasn't right to make progress on the core issues, but I did think that there was a lot of low-hanging fruit in the everyday interaction between the parties. When the press talks about "the peace process," it focuses on borders, security, Jerusalem, refugees, water rights—matters that must be resolved to end the conflict. But there are other complex problems concerning the daily lives of the Palestinians and security for the Israeli people.

The goal of the first phase of the Road Map is to give the Palestinian people as normal a life as possible while respecting Israeli security concerns. Anyone who'd traveled in the Occupied Territories saw long lines of Palestinians at roadblocks set up by the Israel Defense Forces. Sometimes it could take as much as six hours for a Palestinian family to travel a few miles, since individual family members are regularly searched and questioned in an effort to prevent terrorists from moving freely. There had been terrible stories of women in labor who had lost their newborns while waiting for the ambulance to be searched. The movement of goods—agricultural products, for instance—was difficult too, sometimes taking so long that the produce spoiled along the side of the road. And there were a few direct routes that Palestinians simply were not permitted to take, which sometimes turned short trips into daylong slogs.

I spent endless hours working with the Israelis to remove as many of these roadblocks as possible. I became used to negotiating the lifting of important obstacles one by one. Since no Israeli defense minister wanted to wake up one day to find that a terrorist had crossed through a recently lifted border check, the process was arduous and frustrating.

The other major on-the-ground issue was facilitating the training of Palestinian security forces so that they could take responsibility for more of the territory where their people lived. When Palestinians were able to provide security, the population didn't have to live in the shadow of the IDF—and there was thus far less friction between the two peoples. But the Israelis weren't going to turn over territory to security forces that might ignore or, worse, facilitate terrorism, and I knew it would be a nonstarter to ask Congress to fund these forces under the unity government. The key was to train Palestinians who were competent and trusted to do the job (so that Israelis didn't have to), but to show that Hamas had no role.

Fortunately, both the Israelis and the Palestinians trusted the Americans to help them achieve these goals. And the IDF trusted the U.S. military in particular. So after becoming secretary I asked Don to assign a three-star general to work on the problems of security, movement, and access. The first general chosen was William "Kip" Ward, an outstanding army officer who laid the foundation for the training of the Palestinians. Lieutenant General Keith Dayton succeeded Ward and labored at these tasks for five years. He masterfully built trust between the rapidly improving Palestinian security forces and the Israelis. He banged heads with the Israeli Defense Ministry practically every day to get roadblocks removed and towns turned over to the Palestinians. And he hammered on Abbas and his people to root out corruption and incompetence in their police forces.

When Keith could go no further, he called me. I would then call Israeli Defense Minister Ehud Barak, Salam Fayyad, or Mahmoud Abbas and fuss about the lack of progress. On some trips to the Middle East I would insist on seeing Barak and Fayyad together so that, with me present, they could accuse each other face to face of failure to carry out obligations. "Get this solved before I come back," I'd say, feeling a little bit like a parent.

The painstaking work rarely made headlines, but it made a difference.

One of Barak's key aides paid me a great compliment when he said, after we left office, that he missed Sergeant Dayton and Corporal Rice. That was indeed the level of our work. But it would pay off as we looked to foster negotiations on the final-status issues. It was getting harder for the Israelis to claim that the Palestinians weren't fighting terror—and harder for them to claim that they had no partner for peace.

Despite the tensions concerning the unity government, the March trip did result in an agreement that Olmert and Abbas would meet weekly. The next day on March 28, after four busy days in the region, the Arab League reaffirmed the Arab Peace Initiative of 2002, which was welcome news. Unfortunately, the good words were undone by the Saudi king's sudden rant at the same Arab League meeting in which he called the U.S. presence in Iraq illegal, stating that in Iraq "the bloodshed is continuing under an illegal foreign occupation and detestable sectarianism." The outburst left the Saudis scrambling to reassure us that the king's frustration did not mean that he wanted us out of Iraq. "Really?" I said to the Saudi ambassador. "You could have fooled me." Sometimes the hypocrisy of the Arabs was more than I could take.

We didn't comment publicly, but it was one of the many examples of Arab leaders saying one thing in private and the near-opposite in public. I believed that on some level their hypocrisy grew from an absence of accountability. It was not a product of being Arab, of course, but rather of being autocrats. Lacking in popular legitimacy, many of the Arabs felt the need to grandstand and play off populist passions. That they often had to throw the United States under the bus to do so rarely stopped them.

In this case King Abdullah's comments could not have been more ill timed. Domestic pressures were rising with both houses of Congress expressing discontent with the Iraq mission. Back in February, the House of Representatives had passed a resolution repudiating the surge—seventeen Republicans breaking ranks and joining the 246–182 majority. On March 23 the House adopted a spending bill with a timetable for withdrawal, and four days later the Senate put forward a bill with a nonbinding withdrawal timetable, setting a goal of withdrawing all U.S. troops from Iraq by March 31, 2008.

We desperately needed something to go right, but things just got worse. On April 12 a suicide bomber killed eight in an attack on the Iraqi Parliament, which was located in the supposedly safe Green Zone. Four days later, six members of the Iraqi Cabinet resigned on Muqtada al-Sadr's orders. I had the sickening feeling that the surge had come too late.

In the middle of these difficult days, George Tenet, who'd headed the CIA during the World Trade Center and Pentagon attacks and during the subsequent invasion of Afghanistan, released his memoirs. Suddenly George, who'd told the 9/11 Commission that I'd "gotten it" when he had "warned" of an impending attack, was saying that I'd ignored his clear signals. *What clear signals?* I thought. *Back when CBS discovered the August 6 memo that supposedly warned of an attack, you didn't even remember it. You'd told me you'd been somewhere on a beach in New Jersey that day.* To counter George's revisionist narrative, I went on the Sunday-morning shows and dutifully recounted what we'd done in the run-up to 9/11, reminding people of what George had said at the time. It was hard to get very worked up about it, though. I was confronting too many real problems around the world to worry about a retrospective blame game. Iraq would have been enough. But there was also the task of rescuing the Middle East peace process; we needed an answer to a growing humanitarian crisis in Sudan; and out of the blue we were in a war of words with Moscow about missile defense and conventional forces limitations in Europe. Was the Kremlin trying to resurrect the Cold War?

Relations with Moscow Sour

OUR RELATIONS with Moscow had been somewhat testy for a number of months. The Kremlin had complained about our decision to place missile defense components in Poland and the Czech Republic, making clear that the offense was linked to the status of the two as former members of the Soviet bloc. "Put your interceptors in Turkey," Sergei Lavrov had said at the time.

Now we were moving toward implementing agreements with our

allies. The Czech and Polish foreign ministers came to Washington, and it was no secret that we were moving ahead.

We tried not to make it a zero-sum game, continually insisting that the systems that we were contemplating were no threat to Moscow's deterrent and reiterating an offer to Moscow for partnership in the area of missile defense. Bob Gates and I made the case in an op-ed in the *Daily Telegraph*, suggesting that the NATO-Russia Council would be an excellent forum for cooperation in this area.

Still, the Russians bristled, and I was prepared for fireworks when Sergei Lavrov paid a visit to NATO headquarters. I had no idea, however, just how incredible the encounter would be.

It was always satisfying to see the Russians come to NATO and sit there among members that included a unified Germany, the three Baltic states, and seven former members of the Warsaw Pact. We'd advocated strongly for the incorporation of the East Europeans into the Alliance, and they'd been the staunchest defenders of the Freedom Agenda throughout the world, including in the Middle East. But the East Europeans never let the Russians forget that they'd lost the Cold War, and they sometimes treated the Russians in a manner that bordered on ridicule, which made me uncomfortable.

At that particular session, however, the Russians deserved what they got. Just before the NATO ministerial meeting, I learned that Putin had declared a suspension of the Conventional Forces in Europe (CFE) Treaty. In a speech to the Russian Parliament, he derided what he perceived to be an unequal treaty that disadvantaged the Russian Federation. Indeed, the Russians hated the agreement, which called for limiting the number and location of troops in Europe. It had been negotiated at the end of the Cold War, at a moment of supreme weakness for the dying Soviet Union. They had a good point about the need to further revise a treaty that, despite having undergone some changes in the 1990s, was originally written to balance the forces of NATO and the Warsaw Pact. The latter had, of course, ceased to exist, and some of its members had been incorporated into the former.

Sergei Lavrov had come to Oslo, Norway, to rally support against our plans for missile defense. It was an old game that the Russians were playing, splitting the allies from the United States by playing on the fears of the Europeans, particularly the Germans, of conflict with the Kremlin. But Putin's announcement had soured sentiment toward Russia. When Lavrov launched into his remarks—which were vaguely threatening about missile defense and dismissive of Russian obligations under CFE—he lost any hope of winning support. Minister after minister excoriated Russia for Putin's announcement and supported the idea of missile defense. Those who had reservations about our plans to put components in Eastern Europe kept their opinions to themselves. The Czech minister of foreign affairs, Karel Schwarzenberg, said only one thing: "Pshaw—fine thing to come here *after* threatening to abrogate a treaty commitment." It was a wonderful moment of confrontation between a Czech who was plenty old enough to remember 1968 and a Russian who did too.

Lavrov had also come to lobby for cooperation between NATO and something called the Collective Security Treaty Organization. He brought slides explaining the CSTO—a pitiful attempt to re-create a Warsaw Pact–like structure. Its members were Russia, Kazakhstan, Belarus, Armenia, Kyrgyzstan, Tajikistan, and later Uzbekistan—all states comprising the stub of the old Soviet Union. I felt bad for him at that moment.

Finally, Sergei (who just wanted to get out of the room) concluded his comments. He couldn't resist one final shot: "I've heard the arguments about missile defense—the same argument, just in different languages." He promised to seek areas of cooperation, but it was pretty clear that he didn't really mean it.

It would have been totally satisfying were it not for the fact that we really did need to work with Moscow on a problem of growing urgency. The violent breakup of Yugoslavia had resulted in the establishment of six independent countries: Serbia, Croatia, Slovenia, Montenegro, Bosnia and Herzegovina, and Macedonia (or the Former Yugoslav Republic of Macedonia—more about that later). But there was one piece that remained unresolved: Kosovo. Kosovo was an impoverished and ethnically charged enclave of Serbia that had been brutally cleansed by Slobodan Milošević's armies. Kosovar Albanians, who make up more than 90 percent of the population, clamored to secede from Serbia, but

Serbia would not countenance independence. Indeed, one of the most famous and most remembered battles in Serbia's history was the loss of Kosovo to the Ottoman Turks in 1389.

Much of the world had accepted that Kosovo would secede and become independent. But Russia, long an ally of Serbia, was not prepared to do so. The Kosovars wanted their independence and were ready to take it by force if it was not granted to them. We had to find a diplomatic solution and Moscow stood in the way. The charged atmosphere of the Oslo ministerial meeting did nothing to improve the chances for cooperation on this dangerous problem. In May I went to Moscow on a mission to improve at least the tone of the relationship. Putin and I had a direct conversation in which we both acknowledged responsibility for the pall over U.S.-Russian relations.

A couple of weeks after that I met Sergei Lavrov at the G8 ministerial in Potsdam, Germany. Frank-Walter Steinmeier was so proud of the beautiful restoration of Cecilienhof Palace, where the Potsdam Conference had been held in 1945 as World War II was drawing to a close. The flags of the victors were displayed in the corners of the conference room—the Stars and Stripes of the United States; the Union Jack of Great Britain; and the hammer and sickle of the Soviet Union— here in the unified Germany. *Amazing,* I thought. *What would Truman think? What would Stalin think?* The sentiment of the moment was suddenly disrupted by the comment of my unpredictable friend, the Japanese foreign minister, Taro Aso. "But for a few turns in the war, it could have been the flags of Germany, Italy, and Japan," he blurted out. *Okay,* I thought. *Time to move on.*

Sergei and I used the occasion to spar over Kosovo and missile defense despite the promises of Moscow weeks before to find areas of agreement even when our policies did not coincide. The Europeans tried as usual to mediate—unsuccessfully. The scene that day was a harbinger of what was to come: an increasingly difficult relationship with the Kremlin for the next eighteen months, until the end of the Bush years.

Relations thawed briefly when the President invited Putin to the Bush family home at Walker's Point in early July, hoping to appropriate some of the warmth that the Russians felt for George H. W. Bush, whose respectful diplomacy at the end of the Cold War was greatly appreciated in Moscow.

After the Presidents Bush took Putin fishing—Putin caught the only fish—President George W. Bush and Putin settled back at the house for the meeting, and President George H. W. Bush went off to prepare dinner. Sitting in the same pastel chintz living room where I'd first talked with the then governor about foreign policy, the Russian and U.S. presidents relaxed and talked openly and candidly about the problems in the U.S.-Russia relationship. Looking past them, one could see through the window an extraordinary view of the Atlantic Ocean.

Putin was as tough on Iran as I'd ever heard him, making very clear that he had no love for Ayatollah Khamenei or Mahmoud Ahmadinejad. But he said that Russia had to deliver on the fuel shipments to the Bushehr reactor that had been held up for months. "Our companies will start to lose money because of the contract," he explained calmly. The President asked only that the Russians make no announcement without full coordination with us. Putin agreed and kept his word. It was one incident but emblematic of the relatively good cooperation on Iran—far better than the public perception.

The two men then turned to missile defense, agreeing to find a way to cooperate. I believe now that there was some miscommunication between them but I didn't catch it at the time. The President was trying to make clear that he wouldn't reverse the decision to place sites in Poland and the Czech Republic. Putin was offering alternate sites. Yet we were encouraged by Putin's reference during the press conference that afternoon to missile defense as an area of "strategic partnership" and his proposal that we continue the conversation in the forum of the NATO-Russia Council. The President and Putin agreed to have Bob Gates and me follow up with a visit to Moscow. The next day, Lavrov and I issued a joint statement reaffirming our desire for a post-START treaty. George W. Bush and Vladimir Putin did have good chemistry, and on this occasion it helped to calm the waters—temporarily—of our increasingly choppy relationship. After a dinner of lobster and swordfish (not the fish that Putin had caught) the Russians left and everyone felt better.

. . .

IN SOME MATTERS we worked very effectively with Moscow. This was certainly the case in the Middle East, where Sergei's support in the Quartet of our approach to the Israeli-Palestinian issue was unwavering. In fact, the Middle East Quartet was a very effective mechanism for coordinating policy toward all aspects of the peace process.

The prospects for forward movement were once again on the rise. Predictably, Hamas and Fatah were not able to live in harmony under the Mecca agreement. The isolation of Gaza had exposed the weakness of the Hamas-led government. As a Palestinian friend told me, "It just showed that they aren't the great resistance movement—they're just a bunch of politicians who can't make the sewer system work either."

Indeed, the "unmasking" of Hamas was one of the unexpected but welcome benefits of their victory in the elections. I'd often argued that it was preferable to force extremists to prove that they could govern, not just blow up innocent people. Hamas couldn't do the former, so it decided to launch a preemptive strike against the rapidly improving security forces of Mahmoud Abbas. Everyone knew that Hamas had the upper hand in Gaza but believed that the Fatah forces were at least capable of putting up a fight. They weren't. While Fatah's national security advisor (and one of the former security chiefs), Mohammed Dahlan, was in Egypt for surgery on his knee, Fatah forces were routed, the final indignity being Hamas's takeover of Abu Mazen's Gaza compound.

The Palestinian Authority had been pushed back into the West Bank. But there was both good news and bad news in that. Obviously Gaza would be an even bigger terrorist safe haven than before. Yet the PA could now concentrate on building reasonable institutions and economic growth in the West Bank. It would have the support of the international community in doing so—including the Israelis, who would restart the flow of tax revenue to the government of Salam Fayyad. It would also allow Olmert to begin, in earnest, to pursue political talks with Abbas, who'd rid himself of the albatross of Hamas.

The timing coincided with Tony Blair's decision to step down as prime minister and cede the office to his intra-party rival Gordon Brown, the chancellor of the Exchequer. Blair sent a private note to the President and asked him to share it with me. It asked whether the

United States would support the creation of a position for him as the Quartet's special representative for Middle East affairs.

"Tony wants to do this, but he doesn't want to step on your toes," the President told me, standing at his desk in the Oval. I read Blair's letter, which laid out an agenda of strengthening Palestinian institutions. He explained to the President that the United States would have to deliver the negotiated solution.

"It's fine," I told the President. "I think we can work together and he can go places and do things that I can't."

"Like what?" the President asked.

"Go to Gaza," I answered. The other Quartet members quickly came on board with the idea, and Blair was named to the post.

Tony Blair would bring new energy to the effort to build the Palestinian institutions and foster economic development in the West Bank. Olmert and Abbas were finally ready to negotiate seriously toward a final-status agreement, meeting at Sharm el-Sheik on June 25 and announcing their intention to do so. If they succeeded, Hamas would have to make a choice. If Hamas opted for continued resistance, it would lose the Palestinian people, who wanted decent lives. And if it accepted the agreement, it was finished as a terrorist organization. The pieces were falling into place for a big push toward a resolution of the Israeli-Palestinian conflict. It was during those summer weeks that I began, very discreetly, to lay the ground for what would be the historic Annapolis Conference. There could be no better accelerant for the Freedom Agenda in the Middle East than, at long last, the establishment of a democratic Palestine.

I FELT VERY GOOD about the cooperation that we were achieving in the Middle East. But there were some issues that made me want to pull my hair out in pursuing common ground with the "international community." Sudan was exhibit one.

The Comprehensive Peace Agreement, so painstakingly brokered by Bob Zoellick in 2005, was in serious danger of unraveling under the worsening circumstances in Darfur, and the May 2006 Darfur Peace Agreement was failing for a variety of reasons including a lack of signatures and limited scope. I'd seen firsthand the suffering in the refugee camps, and the continued reports of violence against civilians were fueling—properly—cries of outrage from human rights groups and NGOs. The crisis was one of those front-page stories with enormous celebrity attention and daily calls for the administration to do more.

In fact, no one wanted to do more than the President. He was fed up with the fecklessness of the United Nations and the international community—and sometimes, I thought, fed up with my explanations for why nothing was moving forward. Why couldn't the world do a simple thing such as mobilize peacekeeping forces to protect innocent people and deploy them to Darfur, even if it meant ramming them down the throats of the war criminals in Khartoum?

The answer was simple. There was little will or stomach for a confrontation with the Sudanese government, particularly since the Security Council was stalemated due to China's reluctance to impose penalties on the oil-rich regime. Sudan's president, Omar al-Bashir, did just enough to keep pressures from mounting to the point of action, usually by feigning agreement with entreaties to admit UN forces only to find numerous excuses to keep them from deploying.

He could count on the inefficiency of the United Nations as well. It was like pulling teeth to get the peacekeeping bureaucracy to recruit forces and pay them. When I learned from the Ethiopian prime minister, Meles Zenawi, that he was ready to send forces—capable troops—to Darfur, I was delighted. He called later to say that it would take six months—not because his military was slow but because the United Nations insisted on building barracks for them and that would take time. "I told them the army can travel on its stomachs," he said, referring to their ability to build their own encampments along the way. I called UN Secretary-General Ban Ki-moon and lost my temper when he defended the peacekeeping office. "This is why people hate the U.N.," I said, feeling an immediate sense of regret for my rudeness. Ban Ki-moon was not the problem. He was a good man with the right values, but he headed the worst bureaucracy in the world. The secretary-general couldn't even fire people without a vote of a committee of the General Assembly. "I'll try again," he said meekly. "I know, I know," I answered.

My most uncomfortable meetings with the President were always about Sudan—because I couldn't give him good options. The Principals Committee meetings that we held in advance of the NSC sessions rarely achieved much as attendees reviewed over and over again the impediments to international action. The President's frustration finally boiled over, and he told his assembled War Cabinet that he was considering unilateral military action and wanted options. Jendayi Frazer, the assistant secretary of state for African affairs, who'd advocated for a tougher response, was very excited but soon reported that the working-level sessions had become bogged down. Not surprisingly, the Pentagon had made it clear that it opposed any military involvement in Sudan. Its argument was compelling: we can't take military action in another Muslim country, especially one in which a vital national interest isn't at stake. As frustrated as he was, the President acceded to the reality of that circumstance.

That left us with no course but to return to the slog of international cooperation. The President did levy new U.S. sanctions in May, and I was directed to consult with the United Kingdom and other allies on multilateral sanctions and an expanded embargo on arms sales to Sudan.

The problem, of course, wasn't the United Kingdom or any of the Europeans. In fact, the May election of Nicolas Sarkozy in France strengthened the coalition against Sudan. The French president called seventeen countries, including China and Russia, as well as diplomats from regional and international organizations, to Paris for an international meeting on Darfur. He was wonderfully blunt, saying that the international community was not meeting its responsibilities.

That June I went to visit Sarkozy in Paris. The energetic president of France and his foreign minister, Bernard Kouchner, made quite a pair. Sarkozy had cleverly reached across the political aisle to select Kouchner from the opposition Socialist Party. Kouchner is a Nobel Prize winner for his extraordinary work in founding Médecins Sans Frontières/Doctors Without Borders, which delivers medical assistance around the globe. Sarkozy is a pro-American son of a Hungarian immigrant who values freedom and human rights. The two of them were quite a contrast to the cynical Chirac, who thought in terms of French grandeur and great-power politics and had a colonialist disdain for the democratic aspirations of people in the Middle East and Africa.

Whenever I met Sarkozy, he greeted me by saying, "I love this woman." He didn't mean it literally, of course. But we saw eye to eye on almost everything. I couldn't help but think how different it might have been to confront the problem of Saddam Hussein with Sarkozy instead of Chirac in the Élysée Palace and Angela Merkel instead of Gerhard Schroeder in Berlin. France could do little, though, to move the needle on Darfur. Beijing was the obstacle. Sudan was perhaps the best example of China's mercantilist-style foreign policy—concerned first and foremost with its economic interests. Sudan was a major supplier of oil to China, and Hu Jintao, who was chasing an average 10 percent growth at home, was in no mood to challenge Bashir over the cost of human lives in Darfur.

In July we would succeed in securing a UN Security Council resolution, 1769, calling for a joint peacekeeping operation with the African Union. That year, the African Union/United Nations Hybrid Operation in Darfur (UNAMID) deployed 26,000 troops to allay the violence. There was never a doubt that violence against civilians ebbed wherever the international peacekeepers deployed. But until the day that I left the State Department there was no greater source of frustration than Sudan. Sudan represented the international community at its worst—smug and self-righteous about its principles, including the "responsibility to protect," and almost completely ineffective in actually acting on them in hard cases.

The horrific situation in Burma was another egregious example of the international system's inability to act. The Burmese junta was so repressive and isolated that it had actually refused international help for its people after a monstrous cyclone devastated the country in 2008. Thousands of people died needlessly while the generals deliberated and stalled. We finally managed to get some assistance through, using the good offices of Admiral Timothy Keating, the commander of U.S. Pacific Command, who was able to appeal to his counterparts in the Burmese leadership. Nearly ten days passed before the Burmese military junta permitted the first U.S. aid shipment into the country, and by that time the cyclone had killed up to 32,000 people and impacted millions of others. Even after those initial deliveries, Admiral Keating was forced to withdraw four U.S. Navy ships from the region after fifteen failed attempts to convince the government to allow them to deliver more aid.

This behavior was not surprising given the nature of the regime. Aung San Suu Kyi, the leader of the opposition, had long been under house arrest and had become a symbol of the junta's repressions. Laura Bush had taken up her plight as a personal cause, giving voice to the United States' support for the Burmese people. But India and China always blocked real action in the Security Council, citing their long borders with Burma and fears of instability.

Then, on the second day of the UN General Assembly in 2007, the sheer brutality of the regime burst onto television screens. The activist religious community in Burma, monks who engaged in peaceful resistance, had always been a center of opposition. But on September 26 they took their protest into the streets for the ninth straight day, chanting the name of Aung San Suu Kyi. The junta cracked down hard, and violence soared.

Coming as it did during the UNGA, the events were deeply embarrassing for Burma's supporters, especially the Southeast Asian states that had maintained a posture of noninterference in their neighbor's affairs. I happened to have a meeting with the ASEAN leaders the next afternoon. When the press entered the room, I delivered a strong condemnation of the events, turning to face the Burmese foreign minister. I knew that it would make my Southeast Asian colleagues uncomfortable, since they tended to avoid conflict—a cultural trait, I was always told. I continued to attack the Burmese minister when the cameras left. He tried to talk about trade. "You can't ignore what your government is doing in the streets. You and your leaders are despicable," I said. Finally, a few ministers spoke up, particularly my friend Alberto Romulo, the foreign secretary of the Philippines, who was more direct than others at the table. But still no UN action followed. There was just a weak UN Security Council Presidential Statement (the mildest form of condemnation). Within a few weeks, we imposed tougher unilateral sanctions on Burma. Multilateral penalties would have been more effective, but we didn't have that option.

There would be one other example of the international community's inability to act. The plight of the people of Zimbabwe under the aging dictator Robert Mugabe would capture headlines worldwide, particularly when a cholera outbreak underscored the consequences of his authoritarian rule: a contaminated water supply with no purification chemicals and a collapsed health-care system. Zimbabwe had once been the breadbasket of southern Africa, but it was now experiencing widespread famine. Mugabe's failure to address these crises was just one example of his callous neglect for his own people. Yet some African leaders, particularly those in South Africa, were reluctant to break publicly with Mugabe because of his fervent opposition to apartheid decades ago. The Russians and the Chinese, too, were reluctant to interfere in Zimbabwe's internal affairs. This left those who wished to do something about the regime—the United States, Europe, and a few African countries—without the Security Council's backing for multilateral sanctions.

The United Nations had much to commend, particularly some well-run agencies such as the World Food Programme and UNICEF, ably led by Josette Sheeran and Ann Veneman respectively. It also conducted some very successful peacekeeping missions overseen by talented public servants such as American Jane Hall Lute. In addition, the UN was a place to convene the world to discuss important problems, and the Security Council was a way to express the collective will of the international community on matters of peace and security. But the UN is in the final analysis a collection of independent states. The diplomacy was hard, and I had great help in dealing with the organization. Kristen Silverberg, my assistant secretary for international organizations, was tenacious and fortunately more patient than I. When the time came to do hard things, it was exceedingly difficult to align the interests of its members. I therefore came to value more the ad hoc arrangements, sometimes called "coalitions of the willing," that could actually get things done.

Thus, I always bristled when the press or experts accused us of unilateralism. Yes, sometimes it would have been better to bring the international community along. But experiences such as Burma and Zimbabwe exposed just how hard it was to get others to do difficult things. The United States was sometimes accused of "moralism," but at least there was real concern for the plight of those living under tyranny, a quality that seemed in short supply among the broader community of states.

While unilateral sanctions were not always effective, "name-and-shame" efforts were surprisingly powerful. The State Department issued several reports each year that assessed various countries' progress on human rights and religious freedom. Two of the most watched were the annual human rights report—which was sure to draw a rebuke from countries that were cited for abuses—and the human-trafficking report. President Bush put modern-day slavery on the international agenda with a speech to the UNGA in 2003, followed by the issuing of a National Security Presidential Directive aimed at eradicating human trafficking.

Some of the saddest stories in the world emerged as people began to pay closer attention to the tragedy of human trafficking and slavery: young children sold as sex slaves globally—particularly in Southeast Asia and Eastern Europe; children forced into slave labor making cigarettes, bricks, and other items or brutalized and enslaved as household servants, porters, or camel jockeys; children smuggled across borders and sold into "adoptions." These crimes had been perpetrated for years, but our efforts helped bring them into the light. Each year we ranked countries on their commitment to fighting these awful practices. The ambassador at large for combating and monitoring human trafficking, a position held first by former congressman John Miller and then by Mark Lagon, gave visibility to the cause. And countries hated to be listed in Tier III, the worst offenders. Because virtually no government wanted to be associated with modern slavery, we were able to make real progress in getting countries to change laws and prosecute offenders. Our efforts were also greatly enhanced by the work of Assistant Secretaries of State for the Bureau of Democracy, Human Rights and Labor, Barry Lowenkron and David J. Kramer. Still, as I write this, the State Department's Office to Monitor and Combat Trafficking in Persons estimates that 12.3 million adults and children are trafficked for forced labor, bonded labor, and forced prostitution around the world. The struggle against these crimes continues.

43

IRAQ AND THE HOME FRONT

I'D PLANNED TO GO back to Africa during the summer. There was a lot of work to do, including continuing the work of mobilizing the African Union to deal with the mess in Darfur. We had appointed Cindy Courville as ambassador to the African Union, making us the first country to accredit diplomatic representation to the organization. The step was widely welcomed as a sign of our respect for the continent's efforts to manage its own affairs. Moreover, a number of African leaders wanted me to visit to affirm the popular programs of the Bush administration and give a little domestic push to their initiatives. This was particularly true in Ghana, a Millennium Challenge compact recipient, a partner in disposing of Charles Taylor in Liberia, and a great example of outstanding leaders, John Kufuor.

It seemed as if since 2005 the trip to Ghana never materialized. I'd been on the road one out of every three weeks and sometimes two out of every three weeks, negotiating and trying to advance Middle East Peace, tending to our relations with allies on several continents, and urging Iraqi and Afghan leaders to remain focused on the tasks at hand. My job was to be on the road—because diplomacy didn't work remotely.

That changed in the summer of 2007. The President and I had one of our periodic dinners late in June. He talked at great length about the situation in Iraq, noting that there were some hopeful signs on the ground. Conditions in Al Anbar province had improved significantly, even before the surge was fully implemented. Like many of our battles in Iraq, success was facilitated by the cooperation of local provincial governors and tribal leaders. In Al Anbar, tribal sheikhs collectively decided to resist al Qaeda and directed their local security forces against the Sunni insurgents. The Anbar Awakening, as it was called, was very much a story of local initiative by the Iraqis and their U.S. military partners, whose innovative application of counterinsurgency principles would become the foundation of the 2007 surge strategy. But the home front was darkening, and the President worried aloud that we might not be able to hold a domestic consensus long enough for the surge to work.

One month before, the President had vetoed an Iraq supplemental funding bill because the $124 billion had come with strings attached. Included in those strings was an arbitrary deadline for withdrawal of U.S. forces. A revised bill removed the timetable but laid out a series of difficult-to-meet "benchmarks" for progress by the Iraqi government. David Petraeus and Ryan Crocker would be summoned back to Washington in September to report on the state of the war. The President and I had met with the Republican leadership, which had told the President that the situation in Iraq was "endangering the future of the Republican Party." Despite the President's cool, I could see how much that comment hurt. *The Republican Party?* I'd thought at the time. *What about the future of the country and America's credibility?* But it was crystal clear that the domestic dénouement was fast approaching.

"I want everyone to stay home and fight the fight here," he said. "I need you and Bob Gates meeting with Congress, meeting with the press—I need you out there defending the policy and buying time." At first I didn't quite get it. Did he mean I needed to stay home too? He did. The next morning, I canceled all but essential travel for July and turned my attention to the war at home.

More than ever, I needed the State Department fully mobilized and fully behind me. Ryan Crocker had sent a memo saying that he wasn't getting the personnel that he needed in Iraq. It leaked to the press, and I used the moment to make a more draconian change in our personnel policies. I called the director general, a high-ranking Foreign Service officer with responsibility for all career-related decisions and management of the corps, to come in for an extended session on our challenges in Iraq as well as Afghanistan. Harry K. Thomas had been a good choice for the job. Much like his excellent predecessor, George Staples, Thomas was creative and unafraid of controversy, though his deft touch kept the latter to a minimum. "What more can I do?" I asked. "Do I have to direct people to go?" Coincidentally, both Harry and George were black officers in this position, one of the highest ranking jobs in the foreign service.

Thomas asked for a few days to think about it, and when he returned he suggested that I declare that no bids would be accepted on posts *until* the Iraq and Afghanistan jobs were filled. I accepted his recommendation and made a statement to that effect. It was a heavy-handed policy, and I knew that it would be unpopular as officers around the world waited to learn what their next assignment would be. But it worked, and Ryan got the people that he needed. Eventually, four former ambassadors—Charlie Ries, Marcie Ries, Adam Ereli, and Margaret Scobey—would join him, making the Iraq embassy team the most experienced in the world.

Another crucial step was getting my entire team behind me—not just the political folks such as Brian Gunderson and Brian Besanceney, who'd replaced Jim Wilkinson. I knew where they stood on the war. Eliot Cohen, an extraordinary scholar from the Johns Hopkins School of Advanced International Studies, had replaced Phil Zelikow, and he too was a proponent of the war, though somewhat critical of how we'd conducted it. No, I needed the senior management of the department, particularly the career officers, to be with us.

The opportunity to discuss with them the challenge of Iraq came at the end of June. I'd begun scheduling annual two-day retreats outside of Washington for the senior staff to review priorities and set direction for the next year. This year, we met at the Airlie Center in Virginia late on the afternoon of the twenty-eighth. The group consisted of just the key regional assistant secretaries, the under secretaries, and my front office.

Sitting down in an overstuffed chair in front of them, I asked what they wanted to talk about. A few people spoke up about various problems around the world. After a few minutes, I stopped the discussion. "Doesn't anyone want to talk about Iraq?" Someone later told a journalist that it was like a weight had been lifted from the room. Each assistant secretary related his or her fears that we were losing in Iraq. "We can't afford to lose—America *can't* lose, and the whole world thinks we *are* losing," one person said. I let people vent for a long time, and then I talked about what we were trying to do. Everyone, to a person, said that Iraq would become a greater personal priority as they thought about their work. We *had* to win.

. . .

THE DAYS were long and stressful in the summer of 2007, and I tried once in a while to get away from the pressures by playing the piano or visiting friends. Dog-tired, I decided to take a real holiday for the Fourth of July weekend, inviting my cousin and her husband to Washington. The President's birthday is July 6, but Laura always threw a party at the White House for him on Independence Day. After launching my own diplomatic reception for foreign dignitaries at the State Department, I would join the White House festivities and watch the fireworks from the Truman Balcony.

In 2007 Tiger Woods started holding a tournament at the Congressional Country Club over the holiday weekend. The President invited the professional golfers to his birthday celebration. It was great fun to sit with Fred Couples and Phil Mickelson and talk about my newly discovered love of golf.

Since the tournament honored veterans, I decided to go the next day to support that cause and to enjoy a day outside the office. I sat with wounded warriors, watching those amazing golfers. Suddenly, my security detail tried to dive in front of me as I watched Phil's duck-hooked two-iron whiz by me. It didn't come as close as it looked—I'm sure. *Boy, he must have really caught that way early,* I thought. A week later, the *Washington Post* published a snippy little piece suggesting that I seemed to have too much time on my hands. *I can hardly wait to get out of this town,* I thought.

THINGS WERE STARTING to improve in Iraq, and for the first time in almost two years I felt that we'd turned a corner. The surge was beginning to have an effect on population security, both in perception and reality. Sectarian violence was down due to gains in Al Anbar province, where the military had secured the cooperation of the tribes. My meeting with the sheikhs of the Anbar Awakening on November 1 was encouraging—if a bit odd. Our allies were tough and rough-hewn, and one wondered about their long-term commitment to pluralistic politics. Nonetheless, they were patriots who were determined to take their territory back from al Qaeda, and they represented our best chance for stability in Iraq. More than anything, these men represented what Steve Hadley had talked about the day the statue of Saddam fell in Baghdad. Finally, the Iraqis were determined to liberate themselves—it was *their* fight now, not just ours.

Along the way I had seen glimpses of the political evolution in Iraq, too, when I had visited the city of Mosul in 2005 and met with the town council there. Mosul promised to be one of the most difficult places in the country in which to establish political institutions. It was an ethnically mixed city, challenged by Kurdish-Sunni rivalries that had often been violent. The Provincial Reconstruction Team working there was among the most experienced in Iraq—with a seasoned diplomat, Jason P. Hyland, leading the political effort. I walked into the conference room—which was badly in need of a coat of paint—and listened to the briefing by the team. After a few minutes, the Kurdish head of the council was asked to make remarks. He was one of the toughest-looking characters I'd ever seen; "five o'clock shadow" didn't do justice to the mask covering his lower face.

The discussion started off pretty well, with the council chief talking about the need for everyone to work together and his commitment to democracy and tolerance. Then he turned to his deputy, a Sunni, who began to talk about the rights of his people and expressing views about elections in the region that were clearly *not* consistent with those of the wider council. All of the members were now shifting uncomfortably in their seats. I could see that tensions were rising, and my first impulse was to say something to calm the situation. Then something inside of me said, *Keep quiet—see how they handle this.* I'm glad that I didn't intervene. The Sunni finished his remarks, and the council chief simply said, "Thank you for your views." It was killing him, but somehow he knew that in the "new Iraq," he had to let people have their say. *Maybe,* I thought, *they have a chance at decent politics after all.*

Those moments had been all too rare early on but the Iraqis were slowly maturing politically as the surge took hold. Indeed, I found myself defending the Iraqis more vigorously than I would have thought possible after my difficult encounter with them in October of the year before. Suddenly, it seemed churlish and self-righteous when members of Congress chastised the Iraqis for failure to pass a budget. *How long has it been since the United States passed a budget on time?* I wondered. I started to draw more and more on the United States' own experience. How long had it taken for even our mature democracy to deal with minority rights? It was only in my lifetime that black people finally achieved a guarantee of their right to vote. The United States, more than any other country in the world, should be patient.

Fortunately, the Iraqis were starting to show that they could take advantage of the moment and that they had one great asset that most new democracies don't have: wealth. They announced that they'd spend $7.3 billion of their own money to train, equip, and modernize their forces. That was relatively easy to achieve. But we had to pressure Maliki to also use the country's resources for reconstruction in the provinces and to target a substantial portion of it for the Awakening.

Not surprisingly, the Shia prime minister was suspicious of the loyalties of the sheikhs. We'd go back and forth with the Iraqis about getting support to their new allies in Al Anbar province. Finally, the President's frustration relative to this led him to convene a meeting in Al Anbar province late in 2007 with Maliki, Talabani, Second Vice President Tariq al-Hashimi, and the sheikhs. Maliki looked as if he were being dragged to a hanging. He sat in an almost fetal position as the Sunnis demanded project after project for reconstruction as recognition of their role in securing the heartland. But Jalal Talabani was all over it. "You, the great sons of Al Anbar, will get what you want. Yes, you should have a military academy! We have heard you." What a politician. It was suddenly clear why this Kurd was the most unifying figure in the country: he knew how to play the game like the best Chicago ward boss.

But the clock in Iraq and the one in Washington weren't in sync. The President had been right to focus our attention on the home front, where in September there would be a formal review of progress. We needed to hold the line until then and hope that there would be enough positive news to sustain the effort. Bob Gates and I held briefings for Congress on each aspect of the effort in Iraq, with Bob bringing new credibility to the assessments that we were presenting. In addition to the large briefings in both houses, Bob, Steve, and I met individually with influential legislators and as many members of the press as possible. We were just trying to hold ground in the face of the harsh head winds blowing against the war. When the President released an interim report in July on the congressional benchmarks, Senators John Warner and Richard Lugar responded with a call to begin drawing up plans to redeploy U.S. forces from the front line to border security and counterterrorism. There was no one on the Hill more respected than those two Republicans. They were known for their national security knowledge and steadfastness. Hence their call for troop redeployment was a shot across our bow that time was running out—indeed, it had already run out with the American people.

Then there was a breakthrough—not in Iraq but in the pages of the *New York Times*. Michael O'Hanlon and Kenneth Pollack of the Brookings Institution published an opinion piece in that paper in late July arguing that the Iraq war strategy was accomplishing its objectives and the military should be given more time to play it out. Both men were highly regarded and had been critical of the war effort. And since Brookings was hardly a hotbed of Republicanism, the article sent shock waves through Washington. Maybe the terms of the debate were changing—or at least some of the policy elites were starting to take a fresh look.

We'd been in discussions about how to respond to the September review—for example, should the President hint at a coming drawdown? I believed that the American people needed reassurance that our combat presence would indeed come to an end someday. Bob Gates and Steve agreed, thinking that it was better for us to control the conversation about withdrawals than to leave it to others. In retrospect, there was less friction inside the administration on that point than one might have thought. Now that things were going better in Iraq, we could talk about the "end in sight" without the implication that we were cutting and running. It was in that vein that we began to consider how a framework arrangement with the Iraqis—both a status-of-forces agreement and a political document to govern the relationship—might bring an end to the war. The President had only eighteen months left; Iraq needed to be on a sustainable footing when our transfer of power occurred.

When David Petraeus and Ryan Crocker came back in September to testify on progress in Iraq, the mood in Washington had shifted. There were still those who argued for withdrawal on a timetable, but the sense that the war was irretrievably lost had disappeared. The President had courageously played his last card in authorizing the surge. It had turned out to be a winner.

The progress in Iraq was starting to reverberate in the region as well. Finally beginning to see a pathway to a stable Iraq, the GCC countries agreed to invite Iraq's foreign minister to join them in a meeting with me. And the Arabs began to make plans to reenter Iraq diplomatically, with Saudi Arabia announcing its intention to send an ambassador to Baghdad. The hard work wasn't finished, and the Arabs still viewed the Shia-led government with suspicion. But the situation was a far cry from the darkest days of 2006.

EVEN AS conditions improved in Iraq, a new storm was brewing in the region, this one between the Kurds and the Turks. On October 21, the Kurdish terrorist group PKK launched an attack across the Turkish border from northern Iraq, killing seventeen Turkish soldiers. Instability on the border had already prompted the Turkish Parliament, a few days earlier, to authorize the deployment of forces into Iraq to crack down on the militants. Obviously, this was a provocative and dangerous move, putting the young Iraqi government on the spot in the face of a clear violation of its sovereignty. There was a good chance that it could even ignite a small-scale war, because Massoud Barzani's militia—the armed wing of the Kurdistan Democratic Party—would likely resist a Turkish incursion. Now, with this latest provocation by the PKK, it wasn't clear that Turkey could be restrained.

I called Turkey's prime minister, Recep Erdoğan, asking him to delay his decision and promising that the United States would put pressure on our Kurdish allies to take action against the militants. I called Barzani and told him that time was running out. Either he would deal with the militants or the Turks would. And I believed the Turks were in the right. Then I told the press about the conversation, leaving out the point about the Turks being in the right. I wanted to calm public opinion in Ankara, but I didn't want to hand Erdoğan a pretext for invading northern Iraq. I said simply, "I made the very clear point [to Barzani] that the KRG [Kurdish Regional Government] needs to separate itself from the PKK in a very, very clear and rhetorical way. . . . The [KRG] is not going to prosper in conditions in which there is instability in northern Iraq, and the PKK is a serious source of instability in northern Iraq."

I was scheduled to go to the second Iraq neighbors conference in Istanbul at the beginning of November. To buy some time, the President decided that I'd go to Ankara first. We asked the Turks not to do anything until my trip. On October 26 Erdoğan signaled publicly that he would delay his decision to deploy forces until he could meet with President Bush.

Still, landing in Ankara, the extent of the public's anger was clear; it was hard to escape patriotic banners and signs denouncing the Kurds. I held a press conference with my colleague, the young foreign minister Ali Babacan, promising to put the full weight of the United States behind an Iraqi crackdown on the PKK. I reminded the press that the United States didn't discriminate among terrorists, and explained that I had confirmed with the prime minister that we considered the issue "a common threat—not just a threat to Turkey but a threat to the interest of the United States as well." I said that the President would meet with Prime Minister Erdoğan on November 5 to further the discussions. Taken aback when Ali seemed to suggest that the PKK's resurgence was a result of our invasion of Iraq, I gently reminded him that Turkey had had problems with the PKK well before 2003.

In my meetings with Erdoğan and President Abdullah Gül, it was easy to see that the Turks really didn't want conflict. But they were being pushed to the limit by public anger and—it seemed, though they didn't say it—a military that was spoiling for a fight. When the President and Erdoğan met, they set into motion planning for the United States, Iraq, and Turkey to deal with the PKK. A year before, I had asked retired Air Force General Joseph Ralston to act as a special envoy on the issue. It was tedious work, and he met with considerable bureaucratic resistance inside the U.S. government and in Turkey. He had returned to private life before this crisis unfolded, but he laid significant ground-work toward a solution.

Over the next year, crucial elements of military and intelligence cooperation were put in place. Barzani and the Kurdistan Regional Government became more helpful, pulling away from the PKK and its violent methods. Relations with Turkey improved as the seriousness of the U.S. effort became clearer. Most important, Turkey didn't carry through with the threat to deal unilaterally with the PKK—at least for the moment.

The delicate diplomacy was almost derailed, though, by the U.S. Congress. The powerful Armenian American lobby has for years pres-sured Congress to pass a resolution branding the Ottoman Empire's mass killings of Armenians starting in 1915 as genocide. There are many historical interpretations of what happened but it was clearly a brutal, ethnically motivated massacre. Still, the killings did occur in 1915.

My first experience with this problem had come in 1991, when I was working in the White House under George H. W. Bush. It had fallen to me, as acting special assistant for European affairs, to mobilize an ef-fort to defeat the resolution in the House of Representatives. The Turks, who had been essential in the first Gulf War effort, were outraged at the prospect of being branded for an event that had taken place almost a century before—under the Ottomans!

Back then I had succeeded in my assigned task, and in the years that followed every U.S. president and secretary of state had tried to fight off the dreaded Armenian genocide resolution. It was not that anyone denied the awful events or the tragic deaths of hundreds of thousands of innocent Armenians. But it was a matter for historians—not politi-cians—to decide how best to label what had occurred.

Now, in 2007, in the midst of tensions on the Turkish-Iraqi bor-der and with Ankara's forces on high alert, the House Foreign Affairs Committee voted in favor of the resolution. I'd begged House Speaker Nancy Pelosi to do something to prevent a vote, but she said there was little she could do. Defense Secretary Bob Gates and I delivered a press statement outside the White House, reiterating our opposition and say-ing that our own commanders in Iraq had raised the prospect of losing critical bases in Turkey. Eight former secretaries of state signed a letter opposing congressional action on the issue. All this occurred over a resolution condemning something that had happened almost a hundred years before.

We managed to convince the Turks that we would do everything possible to prevent a vote in the full House, which we eventually did. But that was just one example of how the tendency of the Congress to grandstand on hot-button issues can severely interfere with the conduct of foreign policy. This case was all the more galling because the democratically elected Armenian government had little interest in the resolution. In fact, it was engaged in an effort to improve relations with Turkey, and it didn't need it either. The separation of powers didn't always work to the advantage of U.S. interests. Few countries were willing to believe that the President of the United States couldn't prevent a vote of that kind if he really wanted to.

44

THE ROAD TO ANNAPOLIS

IN GENERAL, THOUGH, the situation in the Middle East was improving. The atmosphere was particularly propitious concerning the Israeli-Palestinian conflict, where we were seeking to launch bilateral political negotiations on all the big issues. In the early years of the Bush administration, the time had never seemed right for an international conference—certainly not at the time of the intifada, nor in the middle of the Israeli withdrawal from Gaza, nor when Hamas had won legislative elections, and certainly not when the Palestinians had formed their unity government. But in the wake of Hamas's stunning and violent takeover of Gaza and its expulsion of Fatah officials from the area, the situation was different. Abbas needed an agreement with Israel, and Olmert seemed ready to give him one. Olmert and Abbas both told me in June that they were ready to talk about "core issues." It was time to give the two-state solution a real push. An international conference could achieve that.

I'd raised the idea of a conference in my weekly meeting with the President in early June. He was immediately skeptical but not hostile to the idea. He rightly pointed out that an international conference could be hard to manage. Delegates might think it their responsibility to begin to negotiate rather than simply support the bilateral negotiations between the two sides. And then there was the matter of expectations: if we called the world together to discuss Middle East peace, people would expect something momentous to happen.

"How do we keep expectations from getting out of control?" he asked. "What if we can't get an agreement?" I said I thought we had to take the risk. The key would be to promote the conference as simply a forum for endorsing the work that the parties were already doing, though it might actually launch formal negotiations too. It could also be a forum for the Arab states to demonstrate their own commitment to the peace process. The Palestinians in particular would find an international send-off helpful. Reviewing all the progress that Palestinian Authority Prime Minister Salam Fayyad was making in the West Bank, I said that a conference would help sustain the good guys by giving international momentum to the process. We'd always argued that the Palestinians needed new leadership before they could have a state. Now they'd fulfilled their part of the bargain; we needed to fulfill ours. It would also discipline the Europeans and Arabs by highlighting *bilateral* negotiations, but giving these other players some pride of ownership and some responsibility. We could pursue increased support for building the institutions of a Palestinian state, particularly from the Arabs.

The President wanted to restrain expectations and be sure that the Israelis were on board. "I'll call Olmert, but I need to know that you want to do this," I said. "The Israelis are going to hate the idea because they don't like international 'interference' in the peace process. So when I call Olmert, I have to know that when he calls you, you're ready to say that you support the idea."

The President asked that I get together with Steve and sketch out how an international gathering might work. "And can we call it a meeting?" he asked. Somehow that sounded less grandiose.

"Fine with me," I said. "It's a meeting."

We structured the meeting around three elements, or "tracks," for progress toward Palestinian statehood. First, we'd accelerate progress on the first phase of the Road Map—matters such as removing checkpoints and improving security cooperation to show the Palestinians that the occupation was receding. Second, we'd launch bilateral negotiations on the "core issues" that were key to ending the conflict. And third, we'd make implementation of the political agreement subject to the completion of Road Map obligations.

The last point helped to resolve a sticky "sequencing problem." The original Road Map had a strict three-phase structure. Political negotiations were not to begin until the third phase, when the Palestinians would, in effect, have created all their institutions and defeated the terrorists. That had been a key element in Sharon's acceptance of the document. Yet to assure further progress on the first phase, the building of institutions, we needed a political track. So we rearranged the sequence but agreed that implementation of a peace treaty and the creation of the Palestinian state would be subject to completion of the Road Map obligations, particularly concerning the restructuring of Palestinian security forces. That was acceptable to both the Palestinians and the Israelis.

Still, the Israelis were uncomfortable with the idea of an international gathering (conference, meeting, whatever). Olmert had a long-scheduled meeting in Washington on June 19. Fortuitously, the Palestinian unity government, which had brought together Fatah and Hamas, collapsed less than a week earlier. With Fatah's temporary partnership with Hamas over, Olmert had fewer reasons to object to an international meeting, as long as it wasn't expected to accomplish much. "I'm ready to negotiate," he said. "But I don't need the Europeans and others in the middle of it." The point of the meeting then would be to launch bilateral negotiations between the parties, not to substitute for them. The President announced four weeks later that he'd hold an international meeting on Israeli-Palestinian issues before the end of the year. He didn't give a date or a place. There was still too much work to do in preparing the meeting. We'd invite participants only when that work was done.

The prospect of an international meeting on Middle East peace was wildly popular with my colleagues in the Middle East Quartet—both the Russians and the Europeans. My biggest problem was to prevent them from running to the microphones before the President could announce his own meeting. I knew that in preparing the meeting I'd have little trouble with those colleagues. The Arabs would be somewhat harder.

After years of begging for a peace conference, the Arabs suddenly had all kinds of reservations, worries, and demands. David Welch, the assistant secretary of state for Near Eastern affairs, was spending hours on the road and on the phone with them. During my trip two weeks after the announcement, I met with the Egyptians and the Saudis. They refused to sign on to the idea, leaving me to explain to the press that I didn't expect anyone to accept an invitation that hadn't yet been issued. Well, it was a good talking point anyway.

I would return to the Middle East four more times before the meeting—the last trip being my twentieth to the region since becoming secretary. We'd committed to holding an international meeting in Annapolis at the end of November. Unfortunately, there was little agreement about what it would do, and we were determined not to send out any invitations until everyone had privately agreed to come. Several times the whole thing seemed in danger of coming apart.

But by early November the pieces had started falling into place. We had announced that the international meeting would be held at the U.S. Naval Academy in Annapolis, a city that had been the host to a past peace process of historic significance. It was in the Maryland capital that Congress had ratified the 1783 Treaty of Paris, which had formally ended the American Revolution and brought our country into being. The venue would provide a secure location outside Washington for the various ministers and heads of state to launch a peace process of a different kind at the historic site.

At the beginning of the month I attended the Saban Forum in Jerusalem and delivered a well-received speech that strongly and emotionally affirmed our friendship with Israel. My first visit to Israel had been "like coming home to a place I'd never been," I said. At Olmert's request, I didn't say much about the international meeting. "I need to do this in my own way," he'd told me in a phone conversation the week before. Speaking after me, he proceeded to deliver a truly pathbreaking speech in which he made it quite clear that he was ready for negotiations, strongly endorsing the meeting in Annapolis. And he did it in Hebrew, making sure that it was broadcast live to the country.

It was somewhat more difficult to secure Arab cooperation. During my trip the month before, the Egyptian foreign minister had actually suggested postponing the meeting. It wasn't clear what we were supposed to achieve as a result of the delay. So I knew that I had my work cut out for me at a dinner of the Arab League and the Middle East Quartet in Cairo. I found myself defending the decision to even hold a meeting, flabbergasted at the seeming lack of enthusiasm. Finally

Saudi Prince Saud al-Faisal revealed the code, saying that they all badly wanted a meeting but feared failure. He cited yet again the violence that had broken out after Camp David. *You've wanted a meeting for four years to show that the Bush administration is involved in the peace process*, I thought. *Now you're afraid of failure?*

I answered by saying that my favorite movie line was from *Apollo 13*: "Failure is not an option." Everyone smiled, and Saud publicly said for the first time that Saudi Arabia believed some good could come of an international meeting.

Now with support for the idea of a meeting, I undertook the task of drafting the invitation, which would reveal what the meeting was intended to do and which both the Arabs and Israelis presumed they could word. The Arabs wanted the invitation to set the terms for a peace agreement. The Israelis wanted little more than the time and place. The Arabs wanted a reference to the 2002 Saudi peace initiative as a basis for negotiation. That was unacceptable to the Israelis, who didn't see it as a basis for anything. We agreed on mentioning it without characterizing its role. The Palestinians wanted the core issues—borders, security, refugees, and Jerusalem—spelled out. "That will bring down my government," Olmert said. The Arabs wanted a deadline for the conclusion of an agreement. "In the invitation?" I asked. They dropped the idea.

Then there was the matter of who should be invited. No one suggested Iran, but Syria was a more difficult matter. Bashar al-Assad was hated by most of his colleagues, but no one was willing to leave the Syrians out. The Egyptians had assured us before the President announced the conference that they didn't care if Syria was invited; now they insisted that the Syrians participate. I talked to the President and to Olmert, who finally agreed that we could extend an invitation to Damascus. But before accepting, the Syrians said they would come only if there was a reference to a track to negotiate the return of the Golan Heights, disputed territory on the Israeli-Syrian border. Lebanon wanted a mention of Shebaa Farms. We decided to say that the meeting was about the Israeli-Palestinian track but to mention the other outstanding issues as key to a comprehensive peace.

The final issues came to a head in a weekend meeting of the Arab League a week before we were to convene in Annapolis. The Arabs made clear that they would vote as a bloc on whether to attend the meeting. Here we were, ten days before the intended date, and we didn't have agreement on who would come or what the invitation would say. I made more than twenty phone calls that weekend, mostly through the Egyptians, the Jordanians, and Abdullah bin Zayed al Nahyan of the United Arab Emirates. At one point I had even gotten the Arabs to agree, only to have the Israelis dig in their heels. A week earlier I'd gone to Crawford with the President, and at each meal that weekend he'd ask me, "Is it done yet?"

"No, sir, but it will be," I'd answer. At least, I hoped so.

Finally, on Sunday night, I got the pieces into place, and on Monday the President sent the invitation. Olmert hit the roof when he saw it, saying that there were references to the Saudi peace initiative that he hadn't approved. He called the President, who didn't want to undermine me. "Talk to Condi," the President told him. Finally, I just said that the offending references had been the result of last-minute negotiations but that they weren't going to change the nature of the meeting. I'd take the blame if anything went off track in Annapolis. That seemed to calm him down. We were ready for the international meeting, which, by the way, had come to be called a conference after all.

45

EMERGENCY RULE

P REPARING FOR AN international meeting on the Israeli-Palestinian conflict could have been a full-time job. But, of course, it was one of many urgent priorities. No problem was becoming more pronounced in the spring and summer of 2007 than the crumbling political situation in Pakistan.

Opposition to Pervez Musharraf was rising from several quarters as presidential elections approached. The Pakistani president was locked in a controversy with the country's Supreme Court over the constitutionality of his decision to run for reelection while still in uniform: could the president of Pakistan serve simultaneously as its army chief of staff? In March 2007, before the court could weigh in on that question, Musharraf suspended the chief justice from office. That prompted months of protests from lawyers and other parts of civil society. The Pakistani press was also increasingly critical of Musharraf's rule.

At the same time, a confrontation between the Pakistani government and Islamic militants, who had occupied Islamabad's Red Mosque since 2006, came to a head. The Pakistani military stormed the site on July 10 and, much to the relief of the population, ended the siege. Still, some saw the action by the military as part of a larger campaign that blurred the lines between militants and Musharraf's political opponents.

I'd been keeping a wary eye on unfolding events in Islamabad, staying in close contact with Anne Patterson, our ambassador. Anne was rightly considered one of our strongest ambassadors in the entire world. She was well connected in Pakistan, with close ties across the political spectrum.

Anne was always cool as a cucumber, but I could hear the concern in her voice when she called urgently to speak with me on August 8. The cables from the embassy had been tracking reports that Musharraf might declare emergency rule. Now, Anne said, he was about to do it. She would meet with him the next morning. Later in the day I had a previously scheduled meeting with President Bush, and we talked about the need to keep Musharraf from "doing something stupid." I went home that night deeply unsettled by all that I'd heard.

There was an eight-hour time difference between Islamabad and Washington. My phone rang, jerking me out of a deep sleep at about 1:00 A.M. Anne was going in to see Musharraf, but she was even more concerned that he was on the verge of imposing martial law than she'd been the night before. I told her to call when she finished her meeting, and I tried to go back to sleep. Thirty minutes later the phone rang again. I'm unsure if I'd fallen asleep or not, but I was startled.

"Ma'am, Ambassador Patterson needs to speak to you urgently," said the young officer on watch in the State Department operations center.

"I think you'd better call him," Anne said without much of a windup.

"Now?" I asked.

"Yes, Madame Secretary," Anne replied. "I think he's going to make an announcement before the day is over."

"Make the arrangements," I said, and got up to wash my face and gather my thoughts.

At two o'clock, I got Musharraf on the phone. "Mr. President," I said, "I've heard that you have a difficult decision before you." I was trying to be respectful but firm. He explained that a national state of emergency was necessary because of the violence in Pakistan. He would still hold elections in the fall, but he had to, as he put it, save his country.

I implored him not to do it. Pakistan had been taking tentative steps toward democracy, with elections scheduled in a few months. Suspending the constitution by declaring a state of emergency would be a huge step back, and it was hardly clear that it would quell the violence; in fact, it might exacerbate it. Musharraf would also, we believed, damage his presidency irrevocably. "You will have no credibility, and I don't see how you can run for president after you've imposed a state of emergency," I said, hoping that the argument would register. We talked back and forth for fifteen minutes or so. I pleaded with him one more time not to do what I feared had become inevitable. There wasn't much more that I could do. Several hours later, though, Musharraf publicly reaffirmed his commitment to the upcoming presidential and parliamentary elections; he said nothing about a state of emergency.

"You pulled it off," the President said when I spoke with him the next day.

"For the time being," I responded.

"Do you think you gave him the right advice?" the President asked. "Suppose his enemies come after him now? He'll blame us."

"Maybe he'll just blame me," I answered. "Your relationship with him hasn't been implicated."

It was clear, though, that Musharraf was on borrowed time in Pakistan. I thought he'd run out his string of luck, a view not widely shared within the administration. The question was how to use the time we'd bought to create better conditions for the upcoming elections. The answer, we believed, lay in forging an alliance between the two strongest political forces in the country: Musharraf and former Prime Minister Benazir Bhutto.

At the beginning of 2007, Musharraf had asked for help in bridging his differences with Bhutto, the powerful opposition leader who'd lived in self-imposed exile throughout his rule. It seemed a long shot, but if the two rivals could come to a power-sharing arrangement, it would shift the weight of politics toward the moderates and undermine the Islamists, as well as Nawaz Sharif, a former prime minister who, more so than other prominent figures in Pakistani politics, was suspected of maintaining close ties to the militants.

Richard Boucher, the assistant secretary for South and Central Asian affairs, became the point man for the United States in exploring a deal. Shuttling back and forth between the parties—usually meeting Bhutto in London—Richard got them close enough to make a face-to-face meeting possible. That encounter took place in the United Arab Emirates in late July, but their discussion was inconclusive. When I talked Musharraf out of declaring a state of emergency, I promised to redouble our efforts to bring the two of them together.

Boucher shuttled back and forth several times in the fall. By early October, there were four outstanding issues: when would Musharraf shed his military uniform (before or after the elections); would Bhutto and her party colleagues be immunized in the multiple corruption cases against them (including the one against her husband); could she become prime minister despite a constitutional prohibition against a third term (she'd already had two terms); and finally, would Musharraf support her return to Pakistan before the elections?

I put those questions to Musharraf in a phone call on October 3 at 4:47 P.M. At 5:47 P.M. I got back to Bhutto with his response. At 6:18 P.M. I talked to Musharraf again. At 6:53 P.M. I called Bhutto. That continued every half hour until 11:28 P.M., with nine more calls back and forth.

Bhutto was suspicious of Musharraf's motives and he of hers. A phone call would bring us one step closer to a deal, only to have the next call unravel what had been accomplished. Benazir kept saying that she had to bring her party conference along because they didn't want a deal with Musharraf. I argued that she had to do it for the good of the country—only an alliance between the two of them would allow elections to take place in a stable environment.

As I shuttled from phone call to phone call, I asked myself again and again if I was doing the right thing. Power-sharing arrangements are fraught with difficulty because, in general, the parties don't really *want* to share power. I was also concerned that we might be accused of interfering in the democratic process. Why not just let elections happen and the chips fall where they may? And frankly, both of them had major liabilities and assets: Musharraf had come to power in a coup, but he controlled and was admired by the all-powerful military; Bhutto and her family had severe corruption problems, but she had emerged as a symbol of reform in Pakistan and had generally liberal political impulses. Both rivals were moderates who were willing to fight extremism—at least as much as any Pakistani politician could. A power-sharing arrangement between them would be only one step toward democracy in Pakistan, but I thought it an absolutely essential one before the country could move ahead.

I went to bed at about midnight, only to be awakened at 12:41 A.M. by Musharraf. Well, I had said he could call anytime. I called Bhutto at 4:58 A.M. and relayed the latest offer. The next morning, I talked to each of them one more time. They had a tentative deal—not firm but detailed enough that Bhutto would be permitted to return to Pakistan to stand in the parliamentary elections that would be held by mid-January.

The deal had been complicated by rumors that Musharraf planned to take off his uniform only after the presidential elections had taken place; he would stand for president as Pakistan's army chief of staff. Bhutto had told me that she didn't trust him to follow through with his pledge. "I'm taking this as a U.S. guarantee that he will," she'd said.

The deal was announced on October 4. When Bhutto returned to Pakistan on October 18, her homecoming was met with an assassination attempt as two bombs exploded at the festive rally celebrating her return. She was spared, but nearly 140 people died in the attack.

Musharraf's "victory" in the presidential elections on October 6 only served to inflame the situation. Throughout that month, the Supreme Court considered a petition that would invalidate the results on the grounds that Musharraf had violated the Constitution by standing for election while serving in a military post. As the decision neared, Musharraf became more agitated—apparently worrying that he might face treason charges if the court acted. This time no amount of intervention on my part—or on the part of the President, who warned him against doing so—could stop him from declaring the state of emergency. On November 3 Musharraf suspended the Constitution and fired several top judges, including the country's chief justice.

"HE'S DONE," I told the President that morning in the Oval Office. "I don't think so," he responded. "He's got the army with him."

The President then became emphatic. "I don't want anyone pulling the rug out from under him. The United States isn't going to be in a position of trying to bring him down." I didn't disagree, but we were on record as favoring Pakistani democracy, and Musharraf had just blown up any chance for a peaceful transfer of power.

"Mr. President," I said. "I'm on the hook for him to take off his uniform and allow Bhutto to run for prime minister. He made a direct promise to the secretary of state of the United States. If he backs off that now, we'll have no relationship at all in Pakistan—even if we have one with Musharraf."

The only other people in the Oval were the Vice President, Steve, and Josh Bolten, so we could be very direct with one another. "I don't want people trashing him," the President said. The Vice President added that Musharraf was essential to the war on terror.

"But he's got no credibility left with the Pakistani people," I said. "It's only a matter of time until he's done." I reassured the President that I'd say nothing publicly to undermine Musharraf but insisted that we'd have to criticize the imposition of martial law. We ultimately did, prompting Musharraf to excoriate Anne Patterson for our "abandonment" of him. The President said that he would personally use the time until the upcoming parliamentary elections to counsel with Musharraf and get him to do the right thing: keep his promise to make the contests free and fair. It was a difficult task, but the President pursued it tirelessly.

The situation in the country continued to deteriorate. We were urging Musharraf almost daily to commit to lifting the state of emergency and holding elections. Finally, on November 11, he promised to hold the parliamentary elections in January but defended his decision to impose martial law. President Bush was asked about the situation, and, as we had agreed, he called on Musharraf to hold elections and restore the Pakistani constitution. But trying to balance our interests, the President defended the Pakistani's role in cracking down on extremists and made clear that he was still our ally. Some thought this position came a little too close to absolving Musharraf for what he'd done. The President and I talked about it. We were in an untenable position. Musharraf needed to lift the state of emergency.

Bhutto went before the television cameras at her compound in Lahore, where she had been put under house arrest. She told the world that she'd no longer deal with Musharraf, dashing any remaining hope for a power-sharing agreement and setting up a confrontation in the January elections. The plan had been to have Bhutto become prime minister should her party win the largest share of seats in Parliament, with Musharraf remaining president. That way moderate forces would be united.

Now the state of emergency allowed Bhutto to back away from the deal. "My dialogue with him is over," she said. I called and asked her to reconsider, but she was firm. Several days later Nawaz Sharif returned to Pakistan from exile. Musharraf's house of cards was crumbling.

The final act for the beleaguered Pakistani president came as it grew increasingly clear that he was losing support among the army, the institution on which he counted to support his continued rule. After painstaking negotiations, he resigned his military post as he'd promised, handing over command to General Ashfaq Parvez Kayani, the day before he was sworn in as president. He finally lifted emergency rule on December 15. He would remain president for eight months. But the political reign of Pervez Musharraf was essentially over. Pakistan would have free and fair parliamentary elections, and when Musharraf eventually stepped down, he would do so peacefully. Given the circumstances, that was a significant achievement, and it was in no small part due to the President's persistent work with him.

46

Final-Status Talks Begin

MUSHARRAF TOOK OFF his uniform on November 27, the day of the Annapolis Conference for Middle East peace. The days in the run-up to the meeting were dominated by haggling among the parties about whether there would be a joint statement and what it would say. Again the Palestinians looked for as complete a recitation of the terms of an agreement as possible. The Israelis wanted the document to say very little.

Our preference was to have a framework that enshrined the three elements of a deal: performance on the Road Map; support for direct bilateral negotiations between the parties on the core issues; and a provision that would make implementation of an agreement subject to completion of the Road Map obligations. We were also prepared to establish a timeline for completion: one year. The last provision was controversial and risky. If the parties didn't conclude an agreement, everyone would talk about failure. But as I told anyone who asked, the Bush administration had a deadline anyway. Within a year there would be a new President of the United States, whether an Israeli-Palestinian peace had been brokered or not.

Two days before the conference, there was still no agreement on a joint statement. The Israelis and Palestinians had been negotiating on their own with the help of David Welch. I met separately and then together with them throughout the afternoon, but we couldn't agree on language.

That night I took Tzipi Livni and the Palestinian negotiator, Ahmed Qurei (also called Abu Alaa), to dinner at the 600 Restaurant at the Watergate. The management was always helpful and gave us a private room for the dinner and discussion. "I'm not going to negotiate language tonight," I told them. "But you have got to find common ground.

We can't start the conference with disagreement." The evening was pleasant, but perhaps the fact that the waiter mixed up the orders—serving the kosher meal to the Palestinian and the beef to the vegetarian Livni—was a metaphor for the confusion of the moment.

The night before the conference there was a kickoff dinner in the Ben Franklin Room at the State Department. The delicacy of Middle East diplomacy was very much on display, as we had to work hard to make sure that the paths of the Israelis and the Saudis didn't cross. I'd promised Saud that he wouldn't be forced into an awkward handshake with the foreign minister of the Jewish state of Israel. It would have been a nice breakthrough but not worth the trouble: We would need Saudi Arabia to make far more important decisions if we could get close to an agreement. After the dinner, I met again with the negotiators, and we made a little more progress. But by the morning of the conference, David, who had been at it all night, told me we still didn't have a document.

I arrived at the White House for the helicopter ride to Annapolis with the President. "Do you have an agreement?" he asked hopefully.

"No, sir," I replied. "You're going to have to do it yourself. I've got them within striking distance. Now you'll have to deliver the deal." The President smiled broadly. I could tell that he was relishing this moment to try his hand at Middle East peace. We agreed that he'd have a private meeting with Olmert and Abbas when they arrived at the Naval Academy. I would continue to work on the negotiators.

After a few minutes alone with the two leaders, the President called the rest of us into the room. "Okay, we want a deal," he said. "That's what my friends and I have agreed. Now, Tzipi, Abu Alaa, and Condi, go get one." That was really all we needed because the clock was ticking. Olmert spent a few minutes with Livni, and the Palestinians caucused. We finished the statement about ten minutes before the conference was to start.

Steve Hadley took the document and began to search for a staff aide who could put it into a form that the President could read, meaning in big type. "Give it to me," the President said. "I'll just read it as is."

The three men proceeded together toward the conference hall—a cordon of midshipmen lining the way. Displayed on the Naval Academy campus were U.S., Israeli, *and* Palestinian flags. It was not universally noticed, but that was the first time the Palestinians had come to an international peace conference under their own banner. Abbas was very proud.

When they entered the crowded room, there was great anticipation of what they would say. The betting money was that there would be no joint statement. So when the President, using his reading glasses, which added drama to the already electric moment, read out the agreement, there was an audible sigh of relief. The conference already had a successful outcome: formal bilateral negotiations to end the conflict between Israelis and Palestinians had been launched.

The two leaders then delivered remarks, Olmert's frankly a little more conciliatory than Abbas's. But there sitting at the table was Saud al-Faisal, the foreign minister of Saudi Arabia. Saud had made a special effort to be there, despite his poor health that day. He was wearing his robes, though the Princeton-educated man often wore Western dress when in the United States. I knew that Saud would leave after he spoke, but his presence meant everything. It was also the first time the Saudis had come under their flag to publicly sit across the table from the Israelis. It was a great moment as the representative of the Custodian of the Two Holy Mosques applauded the speech of the Israeli prime minister.

After the President, Olmert, and Abbas departed, I took over the chair of the meeting. I welcomed the ministers and made a few remarks about the task at hand, emphasizing that we were present to support the parties, not negotiate for them. I called on Saud early in the queue so that he could leave. The speeches were overwhelmingly positive. Even the Syrian was conciliatory, and I made sure to treat him with respect. Of course Damascus had sent its *deputy* foreign minister. *That's fitting*, I thought. *One foot in the international community and one foot in terrorism.*

Everybody who wanted to be seen as a "player" had lobbied to be at Annapolis, the first Middle East peace conference in almost twenty years. It was quite a gathering, including some ministers whose country's interest in the Middle East would have seemed remote, to say the least. Brazil laid claim to a spot ostensibly because of its large Palestinian population. The Vatican asked for a representative. Who could say no to the Holy Father? Several small European states just traded on their good relations with the United States to get an invitation. It was quite a scene, with more than fifty delegations in attendance.

I found it challenging to sit and seem interested in every speech, no matter how irrelevant to the chances for a successful negotiation. I even suggested that not everyone had to speak. Fat chance of that—every minister did.

Finally, at the end of a long day, I began my comments to wrap up the conference. I'd prepared some fairly innocuous remarks restating U.S. support for the negotiations and employing standard language to reiterate our core positions. But I looked out at the gathering and decided to put my prepared speech to the side.

"We have said the words 'two-state solution' so often that it now sounds rather bland and meaningless," I began extemporaneously. "But we're talking about people's lives that could be changed forever. You see, I know something of what the Palestinians and Israelis feel. I grew up in Birmingham, Alabama, at a terrible time for black people. I think I know what it's like for a Palestinian mother to tell her child that she can't travel on that highway—because she is Palestinian. And the anger and humiliation that comes with that. My mother had to do that—because I was black and there were places that I couldn't go just because of the color of my skin. But I know too what it's like for an Israeli mother to put her child to bed and not know if a bomb will kill him in the night. My parents had to comfort me when my little friend was killed in that church in Birmingham in 1963. They must have wondered if I was ever truly safe. People shouldn't have to live that way. So we need to create a Palestinian state to live in peace and security with the Jewish State of Israel not because of politics. We need to do it for the changed lives— Palestinian and Israeli—that it will bring."

When I finished, the place exploded in applause. I closed the meeting, and minister after minister came up to me to thank me for the commitment I'd shown. Tzipi Livni and Abu Alaa said almost the same thing: "You really do understand." As secretary, I rarely let my emotions show. My style was to be coolly analytical and, if necessary, unfailingly tough. I hadn't planned this more emotional appeal; it had just felt right, and I followed my instincts. I was glad I did.

ANNAPOLIS WAS EMBLEMATIC of more than forward movement in the Palestinian-Israeli conflict. The countries represented there—with the exception of Syria—were also the bulwark of resistance to Iran. We'd hoped to get one further UN Security Council resolution before the end of the year. Hank Paulson and I had unilaterally designated Iran's Islamic Revolutionary Guards Corps (IRGC) as a proliferator of weapons of mass destruction and its elite and brutal Quds Force as a supporter of terrorism, the first time that we'd blacklisted entire government institutions in Iran. We also designated three Iranian state-owned banks: Bank Melli and Bank Mellat for their involvement in proliferation activities and Bank Saderat as a terrorist financier. No U.S. citizen or private organization would be permitted to engage in financial transactions with these entities or their members, and foreign businesses would likely be deterred from doing so as well, given how pervasively entangled the IRGC had become in the Iranian economy.

Hank had also launched his "road show," as the former investment banker called it, warning European financial and corporate executives of the dangers of doing business in Iran. It was his own terrific idea—a kind of whisper campaign in which the secretary of the treasury would remind those global economic and financial giants that Iran was a complex place where enterprises' associations with terrorism and weapons of mass destruction weren't always apparent. He pointedly asked, do you want to wake up one day to find that the Iranian bank or company that you've been dealing with is actually an IRGC front? Do you want to risk your reputation? It was very effective. German Chancellor Angela Merkel was so impressed that she planned a meeting with her country's business community to urge them to cut back on financial ties with Iran.

Then, in November 2007, we received a National Intelligence Estimate that judged with "high confidence" that Iran had halted its suspected nuclear weapons program in the fall of 2003. Anyone who read that assessment would be shocked, since the implications of this finding were very different from those of the estimate presented two years prior. More worrisome to us, though, was the manner in which the phrasing of the 2007 NIE seemed to downplay the equally significant judgments contained within it. The mere fact that a nuclear weapons program had even *existed* in Iran, regardless of when—or indeed whether—it was halted, suggested to us that the country's supreme leader had intended to pursue nuclear weapons at some point in time. Furthermore, if the assessment was accurate, it had developed this program in defiance of its obligations under the Nuclear Non-Proliferation Treaty.

The key statement was buried in the middle of the declassified version of the estimate: "Iran's civilian uranium enrichment program is continuing." This finding struck at the heart of the argument: the technical capabilities that Iran was actively pursuing through a civilian program could be converted clandestinely to produce nuclear weapons. Given its past pursuit of a secret nuclear weapons program, it would not be unreasonable to assume that Tehran might intend to pursue one again. But we knew that in the public sphere this conclusion would be overshadowed by the NIE's more prominently featured assessments.

In the NSC, we debated for several weeks precisely what to do about the estimate. Given the failed intelligence of the Iraq war, we were suspicious of its assessments. The Vice President argued briefly that we should simply reject the NIE. But that didn't seem feasible, given the failure to find WMD in Iraq and what that had done to our credibility regarding intelligence. So the President decided to declassify the estimate's main findings and release them before they leaked. At least that way we could provide context for the information.

When we released the declassified version of the NIE in December, few of our closest allies accepted its central findings—not the British, not the French, and most especially not the Israelis. All told us that they believed the estimate to be wrong. The Russians crowed that they'd always said there was no military element to the Iranian program. We were trapped. And the poorly constructed NIE, today universally recognized as flawed, did damage to our diplomatic efforts.

I felt especially bad for Nick Burns, who was trying to negotiate sanctions with his counterparts when the NIE became public. He hadn't been able to tell the other negotiators what was coming. Needless to say, the momentum toward a resolution stalled. And Chancellor Merkel canceled her meeting with the German business community.

A Day of Great Tragedy and Mourning

AS THE END of the year approached, the world was serving up new problems, but I was by now accustomed to the fact that my inbox never got smaller. With the Middle East a little better, I took a trip to Ethiopia, calling together the African Union to address the deteriorating situation in the Democratic Republic of the Congo, Darfur, the implementation of the peace agreement in Sudan, and the instability in Somalia.

Shortly after Christmas 2006, the Islamic Courts, a group of fundamentalist militias, had overrun the minimal resistance of Somalia's security forces and started to take over strategic parts of the country. Meles Zenawi, the prime minister of neighboring Ethiopia, had warned that the situation in Somalia was becoming intolerable for his country. He was worried about the possible spillover effects of having a violent extremist group gain a foothold in territory adjacent to his country.

On December 29 Meles called me. At the time I was with my cousin at her house in Atlanta for a few days of vacation before returning to Washington. "I will make this quick, and I want to be out as soon as possible," he said. I knew exactly what he meant—he planned to deploy Ethiopian forces across the border into Somalia to rout out the militants. Frankly, I didn't try to dissuade him. The disciplined Ethiopian troops expelled the Islamists and occupied the upper third of the country. I was relieved that the al Qaeda–associated groups had been denied a safe haven.

But now almost a year later, Ethiopian troops were still in the country. The longer they stayed, the greater the instability seemed to grow as they became a target for terrorism and tribal opponents.

The meetings in Africa at the end of 2007 were in part intended to push the African Union and the United Nations to take on greater responsibility in stabilizing Somalia. Every effort in the last several decades to govern the country had failed, and the territory had consequently emerged as a safe haven for terrorism. The latest transitional government was a pathetic collection of decent people who hadn't even been able to reside in the country before the Ethiopian invasion.

I met the putative Somali president in Addis Ababa, Ethiopia, and knew right away that he had no chance of stabilizing his country. He and his colleagues were a government in name only. The meeting ended as so many did—with a call to find an answer through the international community and an increased deployment of African Union (and perhaps UN) peacekeepers. I was getting tired of this.

The chaos in Somalia had brought the world face-to-face with an age-old problem: pirates. These armed raiders had become a scourge in the Gulf of Aden, attacking cargo ships off the horn of Africa and taking refuge in Somalia's weakly governed territory. After several high-profile incidents of armed robbery by these pirates, the United Nations Security Council unanimously adopted a Chapter VII resolution in December 2008 authorizing states to conduct land-based operations into Somali territory to pursue the perpetrators. As I worked on this problem, I could not help but reflect on the fact that Thomas Jefferson had confronted the Barbary pirates at the dawn of the Republic. Some things, I guess, never change.

WHEN I HELD an end-of-the-year press conference to review all that we'd done in every region of the world, I felt good about 2007. We'd recovered a lot of lost ground from the year before. In our last meeting before Christmas, I told the President that I was looking forward to one last year in which we could tie up a lot of loose ends and maybe— just maybe—declare the creation of a Palestinian state. *Don't tempt fate,* something inside me whispered.

Two days after Christmas, that little voice turned out to be prophetic. I was sitting in my den—having decided to work at home in advance of my trip to Atlanta the next day—when CNN flashed a news bulletin. Benazir Bhutto had come under attack as she was campaigning in Rawalpindi; there had been gunfire and an explosion, but the extent of her injuries was not known. I called Anne Patterson, who was hearing from Bhutto's people that their leader had been mortally wounded. Within a few minutes that news was confirmed. Benazir Bhutto was dead. Images of mourning and chaos rushed across the screen. Pakistan was again in a deep, deep crisis.

The following day we held an NSC meeting on the situation in Pakistan. There was little to do except assess the situation and wait for the chaos to begin. I visited the Pakistani Embassy and signed a condolence book. "This is a day of great tragedy and great mourning," I said at the embassy. "She was a courageous woman . . . the way to honor her memory is to continue the democratic process in Pakistan so that the democracy she so hoped for can emerge."

I got into my waiting car and experienced a feeling of deep sadness and emptiness. Benazir Bhutto's death was very bad news for Pakistan—and for the United States. And for me it was a personal blow. I'd helped Bhutto return to Pakistan in the hope that she could lead her country out of crisis. Now she was dead. It felt as if yet another chance for a democratic and stable Pakistan had died with her.

47

A FINAL YEAR

THE PRESIDENT BEGAN his last year in office with a trip to the Middle East—one of two that he would make in a matter of six months. There was an air of anticipation, even optimism, as we departed for Jerusalem. September 11, 2001, had highlighted the malignancy of the region, particularly the freedom gap and the virulent ideologies that filled the vacuum. We had been drawn deeper in, trying to address the void with support for democracy—sometimes from afar and sometimes, as in Iraq, on the ground through the sacrifice of American lives and treasure. A new historical epoch had begun, and like all transformative change it was a rocky road. Yet, with one year left, the outlines of a different Middle East were discernible: a fragile democratic pathway for Iraq; Lebanon enjoying greater sovereignty and freedom; and, for Palestine and Israel, negotiations toward a two-state solution, living together in democracy and peace.

I knew how much the President had looked forward to his trip to Israel and to seeing its people. Walking together in Capernaum, where Jesus had lived, we shared the religious power of the moment. And at Yad Vashem the President closed a historical chapter by admitting that the United States should have bombed the railways in Europe leading to the death camps. Holocaust scholars and survivors had been waiting to hear that for more than fifty years. The President had been beloved in Israel since the early days of the administration, when he had steadfastly supported the right of Israel to defend itself and challenged the Palestinians to find new leadership untainted by terrorism.

No trip to the Middle East ever unfolded without controversy, however. The President decided, against the wishes of the Israelis, to travel *by car* to Bethlehem in the West Bank. When one goes by helicopter, it is easy to miss the ugliness of the occupation, including the checkpoints and the security wall. I insisted that the President needed to see it for himself and it would have been an insult to the Palestinians if he didn't. Riding in the car with him, I could see the look on his face. We sped through wide-open barriers, but the graffiti-laden wall couldn't be ignored, even at high speed. "This is awful," he said quietly.

"Yes, it is. That's why there has to be a Palestinian state," I said. He nodded sympathetically.

Once in Bethlehem, we were able to see what the Palestinians had achieved under new leadership—though the trash along the streets seemed to suggest that the Palestinian Authority hadn't completely mastered the task of governing. The city center, however, looked beautiful, still sparkling from the successful open-air investment conference in Nativity Square for one thousand investors the previous spring. It was a far cry from the days when Israeli gunfire had damaged the Church of the Nativity. The luxury hotel had guests this time, a change from my trip to the city a year before. The situation in the West Bank was improving.

I'd warned the President that the Church of the Nativity was a tad overwhelming for low-church Protestants like the two of us. When I'd visited, I had been put off by some of the icons, including the cherublike, porcelain Christ doll lying in the manger. The President missed the display, because apparently the little icon is taken upstairs to lie on the altar during the Christmas season—and was still there when we visited in January.

But the most troubling aspect of my visit had been a near confrontation between a Franciscan priest and a Greek Orthodox bishop. The Church of the Nativity is divided into three sections, each controlled by a different Christian sect. The elderly Greek, excited by my visit, had unfortunately crossed into the Franciscan sector. "You don't belong here! This isn't your place!" the protective friar had barked. I was startled and appalled. *Lord Jesus,* I thought, *look at what your people have done to your memory.* Fortunately, during the President's visit the warring factions kept to their own pews and everything went smoothly.

Earlier in the day, the President traveled to Ramallah to be received by President Abbas and his government. Abbas had called me to say that he didn't think they had a proper place for a meal with the President.

"You've been to the Muqata [the headquarters of the Palestinian Authority]. It isn't very nice," he said. I'd assured him that the President would be just fine with the accommodations—and that the food was, in any case, very good.

We drove through the gate and up to a red carpet, where the proud Abbas stood flanked by his newly minted U.S.-trained security forces. The Palestinians played our national anthem and the song that they would use when they had a state. It was a nice moment, as the President acted as if they already had one. As we went to lunch, we passed through hallways that wore a coat of paint so fresh that you could still smell it.

I then accompanied the President to Kuwait and the UAE and broke off to visit Iraq to acknowledge the progress there. Arriving in Saudi Arabia in time for dinner with the king, I walked into the palace and saw the President sitting there in a light blue ski sweater. "It's a gift from His Majesty," he blurted out as if to keep me from saying something about it that I might regret. I was grateful that he had given me a heads-up.

We had a big agenda with the Saudis that included Iraq, Israeli-Palestinian peace, and Afghanistan, but the king mostly wanted to talk about Iran. He didn't leave much doubt about what he thought. He wanted the United States to take decisive action against the Iranian regime.

These conversations were always uncomfortable because the President, though keeping his options open, had no intention of going to war against Iran. There was no easy path ahead. One could not destroy the nuclear program by just attacking a few targets. And the mullahs had made certain that any strike on those facilities would have to take place near major population centers, exposing civilians to danger. Most experts believed that limited military action might actually strengthen the regime—provoking a unifying nationalist response and undermining the reformers. This was a point that we also made repeatedly to the Israelis, who faced an existential threat from the Iranian nuclear program.

The unintended consequences of war with Iran, particularly given the still fragile situation in Iraq, were just too great. In a later meeting with the king, Bob Gates would be considerably blunter about the prospects of a U.S. attack on Iran, saying that the President of the United States would face the wrath of the American people over such a decision. That angered Abdullah, who somehow held out the hope that George W. Bush might be willing to "take care of Iran" before leaving office, this despite the fact that the king would periodically meet with the Iranians and even, on one occasion, actually hold hands with Ahmadinejad. Given that fraternization, the Saudis' advocacy for tougher action was a little hard to take.

And while the diplomatic track was slow, we were making progress despite the unfortunate framing of the conclusions from the Iran NIE. Shortly after returning from the Middle East, I attended a P5+1 meeting in Berlin and tried to resurrect the Security Council resolution that had been shelved at the end of the year. Most of our meetings had been held in intimate settings such as the British prime minister's residence or the small room in the French Foreign Ministry. The surroundings helped make the discussions conversational and informal.

The minute we walked into the room in the German Foreign Ministry, though, I knew we had a problem. The room was huge, with a big round conference table and booths for simultaneous translation. The coldness of the room synced perfectly with the chilliness of the interaction. Sergei Lavrov and I sparred as we always did, and when we were still on item number one (of four), after an hour, I asked for a break. Nick Burns and I called Lavrov and Deputy Foreign Minister Sergei Kislyak aside. "Let's find something we can both live with and then have Nick and Kislyak negotiate the terms of the resolution," I said. "Then we'll take it to the others." I didn't want to offend our hosts or the other Europeans, but getting Russia and the United States on the same side would save time and frustration. Surprisingly, we came to agreement on a draft text for a UN Security Council resolution against Iran. It would take almost two months to pass the third resolution, but the very fact of the agreement that day in Berlin had stunned the world—especially the Iranians. Coming only a month after the release of the NIE, it was critical in getting us back on track.

In fact the foundation for agreement with the Russians had been laid in the last months of 2007. At the UN General Assembly in September, I'd asked to see Lavrov alone. I told him that we needed to see if we could crack the Iranian problem before the Bush administration left office. Taking him into my confidence, I told him about an idea that I'd discussed only with the President and Steve Hadley, though Nick Burns and a few others at the department were aware of it. I wanted to put a U.S. interest section in Tehran. An interest section handles routine matters within a foreign country, such as advocating for U.S. citizens who are in trouble and issuing visas to foreign citizens who want to travel to the United States. The Foreign Service officers who staff them are not engaged in high-level diplomacy, and having one does not mean that relations are on a normal course. We have long maintained such a presence in Havana, for instance.

When a country does not have an interest section, it is represented in such matters by a "protecting power," in our case Switzerland. If we could take on these tasks for ourselves we would gain one key advantage: firsthand knowledge of the terrain. U.S. diplomats had been out of Iran for almost thirty years. The last Americans to serve in Iran were nearing retirement or had already left the Foreign Service. We had few Farsi-speaking officers in the diplomatic ranks or in the intelligence services. More important, we had no eyes and ears on the ground. Rather, we were forced to rely on our friends in Australia or the United Kingdom to give us diplomatic reporting on the place, which was so crucial to our interests.

One day while sitting with the able Australian ambassador as he relayed his impressions of the unfolding events in Iran, I was reminded that we were making policy toward Iran with one hand tied behind our back. By establishing the Dubai station in the UAE, which could make visas available to Iranian citizens, we'd tried to give ourselves better access to the people of Iran and a window on what was going on there. But there's no substitute for the on-the-ground presence of experienced diplomats, who, even just through osmosis, can pick up key signals and important trends. It might even give us a platform from which to get to know and engage dissidents in the country. The interest section in Cuba had done so for years. Iran maintained an interest section in the United States. Why shouldn't we do the same?

When I told Lavrov, he was very excited and wanted to discuss it with the Iranians right away. I explained that I had a lot of work to do at home if we were going to move in that direction. "Sergei, this can't be seen as a favor to the Iranians," I said. "This is a hardheaded calculation of what is in *our* interest, but I wanted you to know what I'm thinking."

I then asked him whether President Putin could get in direct contact with Ayatollah Khamenei in order to gauge whether there was really a possibility of resolving the nuclear issue. President Bush had often remarked that dealing with the Iranians put us into a position where we could never negotiate directly with the decision maker. Ali Larijani, their negotiator on nuclear issues, Foreign Minister Mottaki, and even President Ahmadinejad didn't have the authority; that rested with Khamenei, whose thinking no one seemed to know. The President wanted a way to know directly what Khamenei was thinking. He had made the point to Putin at Kennebunkport, drawing interest from the Russian in what he might personally be able to do.

Lavrov said that he'd go back to Moscow and talk to Putin. "This can't leak," I said. He agreed, and it didn't.

Putin, he said, could easily get a message to Khamenei and see what it would take. "Can he mention the interest section?" he asked.

"No," I answered, "I don't think so—at least not yet." Two weeks later I was in Moscow with Bob Gates to talk about missile defense cooperation. Putin pulled me aside and said that he'd gotten Lavrov's message. He said I should tell the President that he'd see Khamenei at a summit of the five Caspian nations the following week.

When he returned from the summit on October 16, Putin called to tell the President that he'd delivered a message to Khamenei that the Americans wanted to solve the problem. But the Iranians did not take up our diplomatic outreach, as Larijani unexpectedly resigned several days after Putin's conversation with the Supreme Leader. Most people saw this as a signal that the more radical elements of the Iranian regime had further consolidated control of the nuclear program. Though the Russians complained about the U.S. announcement, five days later, of sanctions against the IRGC, they were more upset with Iran's decision to reject yet another opportunity to resolve the nuclear stalemate. By the end of October 2007, the Russians' attitude toward the Iranians had soured significantly. From that time forward, it would be more difficult to get Beijing's agreement to penalties against Iran than Moscow's.

China was becoming more insistent on defending its own growing economic interests in Iran, particularly as a source of oil and gas. That was a shift from the more passive Chinese posture of the years before.

The release of the NIE in December would temporarily cause the Russians to back off their support for new sanctions. But they hadn't forgotten that Putin had gone to Tehran and gotten nothing in return from Khamenei. The Islamic Revolutionary Guards had further poisoned the atmosphere by harassing and provoking three U.S. Navy ships on January 6, 2008. The U.S. commander had demonstrated admirable restraint, but the Pentagon warned the Iranians that they were playing with fire. Moscow—along with everyone else—was relieved that the incident hadn't flared into open confrontation. Tehran was once again digging itself into a diplomatic hole. And as a result, the moment to establish an interest section never came.

Yet, by the time of the Berlin meetings in January we were back on track for sanctions. The third resolution, negotiated in Germany, was passed in March in New York. Collectively, the three rounds of UN Security Council sanctions against Iran had blacklisted dozens of Iranian individuals and entities for their suspected ties to Iran's nuclear program. The sanctions prohibited arms exports from Iran as well as the sale of certain equipment or technology that could contribute to the development of a nuclear capability. And alongside measures the United States had taken through Treasury rules and executive orders, we had increased pressure on the Iranians who were beginning to feel the squeeze of the sanctions on their economy. Iran might not have verifiably disarmed by the time we left office, but it would be forced to make a choice: suspend its nuclear program or risk further isolation for its intransigence. That strategy is still in place today.

THE BERLIN meeting was the last for Nick Burns, who'd done a superb job as my point man on Iran for three years. At the end of 2007 he'd come to me and said that he needed to leave; it was time for him to retire from the Foreign Service after twenty-seven years. Nick said he needed to go into the private sector to sustain three daughters in expensive educational institutions—a dilemma I fully understood. It was what it was.

That said, I was so sad to see him go. He'd been my wingman on this tough issue and many others, and he had my trust. Nick had taken no small amount of abuse, particularly from the Russians. In fact, at a dinner in 2006 Lavrov had taken the unusual step of chastising Nick, leading British Foreign Secretary Margaret Beckett to defend him. "I don't take kindly to ministers assaulting other people's [lower-ranking] officials at my dinner table," she'd said. Nick was tough enough to get the Russian's attention and grudging respect. Replacing him wouldn't be easy.

I turned to the one person whom I thought capable of a last push on a number of issues, especially the Iranian challenge: our ambassador to Russia, Bill Burns. He had the advantage of also being an expert on the Middle East. Bill didn't want to leave Moscow, a city that his wife and daughter loved and where he was indeed doing a fine job. But he agreed to return to Washington as "P," or under secretary for political affairs and the third-ranking officer in the department. He'd carry forward our efforts to crack the Iranian problem before our time ran out.

I left Berlin and headed to the World Economic Forum at Davos, the gathering of the globe's economic and political elites high in the Swiss Alps. It was my last year as secretary, and I'd promised the forum's founder, Klaus Schwab, that I would appear during my term. The trip over the Alps to the conference was worth the effort. The sight from the window of the Swiss army helicopter was easily the most breathtaking I've ever experienced. I've always been most at peace in the high mountains, such as the Colorado Rockies of my teenage years in Denver. But I'd never seen anything like this, and on my return that night it was even more extraordinary—timeless and spiritual.

I decided to use the occasion of my speech at the conference on January 23 to take on some of the shibboleths about the Bush administration and to send one last message to our friends and foes alike. "Well, I can assure you that America has no permanent enemies," I said, "because we harbor no permanent hatreds." It was not meant as an unconditional outreach to Tehran or Pyongyang; rather, it was intended as a conditional invitation to jointly find an end to the nuclear crises through diplomacy rather than confrontation. Neither regime would last; of that I was sure. The question was whether they'd collapse before becoming full-blown nuclear threats. That seemed less likely. Iran was starting to produce small amounts of enriched uranium. The North Koreans were considered a threat because of their ability to process plutonium and enrich uranium—and then sell the product and their knowledge to the highest bidder. Iran and North Korea were already heavily sanctioned, but what was the time frame in which penalties might work? We might not have time to bring about regime change absent wars that we couldn't afford to launch. Could we change the policy of the regimes instead? I was determined to ask that question as creatively and aggressively as possible in the time left to us. At least the world and the next U.S. President would know that we'd tried to give our enemies a chance to change course.

Free Trade in the Americas

I WAS HOME from Switzerland exactly twenty-four hours before boarding a plane for Medellín, Colombia, with nine members of Congress in tow. The trip was intended to rally support for passage of the United States–Colombia Free Trade Agreement (CFTA). Together with planned free trade agreements (FTAs) for Panama and South Korea, the CFTA would complete the Bush administration's bilateral trade agenda and perhaps give a spur to the flagging prospects for a successful end to the Doha Round of the World Trade Organization.

The President was an enthusiastic free trader, believing in the power of open markets to spur economic growth. The economic arguments were powerful, as was the political rationale globally. The United States was the strongest proponent of free trade because it helped spur economic growth at home and abroad and created a basis for a more stable and peaceful international order. That had been the reasoning behind the establishment of such free-trade institutions as the General Agreement on Tariffs and Trade (GATT) at the end of World War II. In 1945 the United States accounted for an enormous share of the world's GDP. At the time it might have seemed logical to protect that share. But the United States took a different course, believing in free trade as a way to expand the global economic pie. In succeeding years it eschewed the "beggar thy neighbor" protectionism that had helped spur conflict and war.

Yet though there were large numbers of winners, undeniably there were losers too—industries and workers displaced by cheaper labor and lower expenses abroad. This circumstance led to powerful veto groups, particularly organized labor and, increasingly, environmental interests, that wanted to impose U.S. standards on developing countries. In response, our trade representatives negotiated agreements with very tough labor and environmental requirements. The proposed FTAs with Colombia and Panama reflected the trend.

So it was something of a shock when opposition arose in Congress over labor protections and human rights, particularly concerning the deal with Colombia. The claim was that the Colombian government had to be held accountable for the deaths of labor organizers at the hands of the paramilitaries, some of whom had been associated with President Álvaro Uribe's party during the near–civil war with the FARC. The Colombian government was actively prosecuting those responsible, even if they were members of the party, the government, or in some cases close relatives of the leadership. Yes, Colombia had a history of violence toward labor, but the level of violence faced by union members was now less than that faced by the general population, in part because of special protections for labor leaders. The fact is that opposition to the United States–Colombia Free Trade Agreement was thinly disguised protectionism.

I joined Sue Schwab, Hank Paulson, and Carlos Gutierrez in an all-out effort to get the agreements passed. Speaker of the House Nancy Pelosi said she was not opposed to the agreements. I'd known Nancy for several years, since we are both from the Bay Area, and I took her at her word. In numerous private sessions she claimed to be hamstrung by the Democratic Caucus. The idea of traveling to Colombia with a congressional delegation had come out of one of these meetings.

Medellín was the perfect place to send the message of Colombia's resurrection from a failed state to a democratic ally of the United States. The city had once been synonymous with Pablo Escobar, the notorious drug kingpin, and trouble. Now it was an up-and-coming urban success story with kids playing peacefully in its parks. We were taken to reeducation centers where former paramilitary members—men and women—received employment training. We also visited a nursery where women were now picking flowers to export to the Netherlands—women who, a year before, had been armed combatants. The message was clear. Colombia's stability depended on jobs, and the FTA was key to economic development and job creation.

The members of Congress who accompanied me were clearly impressed by what they'd seen. We ended the day meeting with Uribe, who can be impressive in his defense of his country's course. At this particular session, though, he was a bit loquacious with his guests, who still faced a five-hour plane ride home. But he was well meaning, and I left Colombia feeling that we'd won over more supporters.

Still, despite many more meetings, briefings, and sessions with Nancy and Senate Majority Leader Harry Reid, who also professed his support for the agreement, we couldn't get it done. Two years after the Bush administration left office, it *still* hadn't been completed.

The inability to pass the Colombia and Panama FTAs and KORUS (the South Korean agreement) made the collapse of the Doha Round of international trade negotiations on our watch even more painful. The round had begun in November 2001. In the last six months of his time in office, President Bush made concluding the round successfully a personal goal, holding numerous meetings in the Oval Office with Sue Schwab, the economic team, and me. He raised the issue with Manmohan Singh of India, Luiz Inácio Lula da Silva of Brazil, and Hu Jintao of China, trying to get the "emerging-market countries" to grant better access to their markets for services and manufactured goods. He worked directly with the Europeans to find a "package deal" that the developed countries could propose to the developing world.

Agriculture was always the killer, however. It's remarkable how much farm policy—subsidies in particular—can hinder the free-trade agenda. Even though the President offered to get rid of all U.S. farm subsidies in exchange for expanded access to agricultural markets around the world, we could never get a deal. His veto of the subsidy-laden farm bill in May 2008 was overridden by the Congress.

Unable to make progress on these bigger trade agreements, we tried one last time, launching an effort to join the Trans-Pacific Partnership, whose original members were Singapore, Brunei, Chile, and New Zealand. I worked hard to get people to sign on but couldn't help feeling that free trade was dead on our watch—and probably for sometime to come. The United States has led the world toward a free-trading global system and in doing so has helped lift millions of people out of poverty. But it has not shown the same degree of leadership on this issue in recent years. For the sake of the economy, this hiatus should be short-lived.

48

It Seems Like Yesterday—
It Seems Like Forever

I WAS VERY AWARE in 2008 of doing things for the last time. That was true for just about everything, including social events such as the perennial Washington dinners: those of the White House Correspondents' Association, the Gridiron, and the Alfalfa Club. The last is a membership organization that I'd been tapped to join as a "sprout" in 2002, along with, among others, the President's brother Marvin Bush and my childhood heroine, the Olympic figure-skating champion Tenley Albright. The Alfalfa dinner is one of those gatherings at which official Washington gets together to roast the President and other luminaries in a sometimes slightly forced show of bipartisanship.

I didn't mind the dinners, though they tended to go on well past my bedtime. In the tough years, the jokes had an anti-Bush edge that was a bit uncomfortable. The President always managed to disarm the audience, though, with self-deprecating humor. And the appearance of the marine band at the evening's beginning was always the event's highlight. I never liked John Philip Sousa until I heard it played by "The President's Own," as the band is called. It was nice too that at the Alfalfa dinner there was only one toast—that being simply, "To the President."

I invited my friends Freeman and Jackie Hrabowski to my last Alfalfa dinner, not thinking much about the significance of asking a man who had grown up down the street from me in segregated Birmingham and had gone on to become president of the University of Maryland, Baltimore County. That night as I looked out from the dais—the secretary of state sits at the head table—I thought about our parents and our past: *only in America.*

Two nights later, I looked around as my car headed up Pennsylvania Avenue past the brilliantly lit white government buildings and toward the Capitol for the President's final State of the Union address. I'd made this ceremonial trip several times before, attending six State of the Union speeches, two inaugural addresses, and a joint session of Congress on September 20, 2001, when the President had comforted and rallied a stricken and terrified nation. *It seems like yesterday that I came to Washington,* I thought. *No, it seems like forever.*

Inside the Capitol that night, I lined up in the anteroom with my Cabinet colleagues. "Ladies and gentlemen, the President's Cabinet," the cloakroom manager announced. And as the door flung open, I could see the blinding camera lights and the outstretched hands of legislators lining my path. I stepped forward to lead the Cabinet as secretary of state one last time.

THE MOMENTS of reflection were always fleeting though as the next crisis emerged. Iraq was continuing to improve, but not without violence and occasionally a mystifying and deeply regrettable mishap such as a mistaken strike on Iraqi civilians instead of the intended al Qaeda target. The Iraqis were taking more and more control of their own affairs—not always a good thing. In February they passed a law that threatened yet again to enrage the Sunnis, pushing the limits of de-Baathification to the point that the jobs of many ordinary people were imperiled. It was a sign of the hatreds simmering just beneath the surface of the new inclusive democratic institutions.

But it was Afghanistan that now seemed most at risk. After Musharraf's deals with the tribal leaders, the region in Pakistan near the Afghan border became a more secure safe haven for Taliban fighters. Consequently, the Pashto heartland of Kandahar and Helmand provinces in southern Afghanistan were increasingly violent and difficult to govern. NATO, which had enthusiastically taken on the military mission to defeat the Taliban, was experiencing enormous strain as unequal distribution of responsibilities—and casualties—became a source of conflict among members of the coalition. The governments of Canada, the Netherlands, Denmark, and Great Britain, in particular, bristled as they watched other countries restrict their military presence so their soldiers would be exposed to minimal conflict. For their allies it meant facing even greater risks. And the Karzai government, which was somewhat incompetent, was showing signs of venality—even deep-seated corruption.

Eliot Cohen, who'd succeeded Phil Zelikow as counselor in the department, took responsibility for digging into the Afghan issue. The counselor has no defined portfolio and can take on directed assignments of that kind. What he found was disturbing. We all knew that the effort in Afghanistan was floundering, but Eliot thought it was nearing catastrophic failure. Steve Hadley had begun a thorough review with an eye to a revised strategy. The NSC would develop two different types of policies, ones that we could implement before leaving and others that we could at least start, leaving the next administration with a better platform from which to improve the situation.

Coordination with the allies was one of the problems that needed immediate attention. Therefore, David Miliband, the British foreign secretary, and I set off together for Afghanistan to demonstrate unity of purpose. I also wanted to see firsthand what was happening *outside* of Kabul, so we decided to go to Kandahar. Our meetings with the joint military task forces—Canadian, British, U.S., and others, known as RC-South—were unsettling. I was accustomed to the tight integration of American civilians and military in Iraq through the Provincial Reconstruction Teams. We certainly had our problems, but here in Kandahar it looked as if the civilians and military had no idea what each other was doing. I kept getting less-than-satisfactory answers to my questions, and when one general said, "Well, that's not possible," in response to a question about better governance in one area, I became furious. "I'm an American," I said. "Nothing is impossible." There was silence for a moment or two, and pretty soon the meeting dissolved. I made a mental note to talk to the President and Bob Gates about what I'd experienced. It was imperative that we get a handle on the effort in Kandahar in particular, as it was the Taliban's home and its stronghold.

Later in the day Karzai met with David and me. I'd been vaguely aware of the Afghan president's claim that the British were scheming against him. The charge rested on his knowledge of the activities of two diplomats who were holding discussions with former government officials who were, according to Karzai, out to overthrow him.

Much to my astonishment, he took the opportunity of our meeting to accuse David and the United Kingdom of trying to oust him. "Either you know what's going on, or your people aren't telling you what they're doing," he said, leaving little room for an acceptable response. David tried to reason with him that Britain was doing no such thing. Karzai would not be mollified. Finally, I spoke up for the Brits, but he just shut me down. "America doesn't have anything to do with this treachery," he said.

David and I had the same thought: *Better to end this meeting now.* It was a very troubling moment but not the last time that Karzai's conspiracy gene would get the best of him. Then, at lunch, he was like a different person—all smiles and happy host. "Try this wonderful pudding, it's an Afghan delicacy." *Wow! What's going on here?* I wondered.

When I got home, I told the President that we needed to stay *really* close to Karzai. He agreed and intensified his personal contacts with the Afghan. Perhaps it was just the stress of governing the ungovernable, but Karzai sometimes seemed to believe the worst about the foreigners trying to help him. That day it was the Brits. It was only a matter of time until those feelings would apply to *us* as well.

NOT LONG after returning from Afghanistan, I joined the President for his final trip to Africa and an opportunity to celebrate all that he'd done for the continent. But, as the President made his way across the region, the biggest stories were about the unfolding violence in Kenya and the threat of civil war.

Africa was clearly making progress toward democratic governance, with peaceful transfers of power in countries like Benin, Mali, Sierra Leone, and Liberia. In several places, though, elderly strongmen had signaled their desire to hold on to power. Because the President of the United States was well respected in Africa, having launched AIDS and malaria programs and large increases in foreign assistance, it fell to him to gently encourage—even cajole—those leaders to move on. Nelson Mandela had once told the President that his people had begged him to run for a third term. "I told them that I want African leaders to see that it's okay to retire," the jovial Mandela had said. The President compared him to George Washington, who'd refused to become king. "Your country is lucky that he was that kind of man," Mandela said. "Africa doesn't have enough of them."

The President recalled that discussion with Mandela many times. In 2006, when President Olusegun Obasanjo of Nigeria sidled up to the President and suggested that he might change the Constitution so that he could serve a third term, the President told him not to do it. "You've served your country well. Now turn over power and become a statesman," he'd said.

After a strong public rebuke from the United States and condemnation of his efforts by the international community, the Nigerian Senate rejected the constitutional amendment proposal that would have allowed Obasanjo to serve a third term. The crestfallen Obasanjo was initially angry, accusing Jendayi Frazer of undermining him in the press and with his own people. "I'll never deal with her again," he told the President.

The President responded, "Well, she's a good person. But the main thing is that your country needs you to do the right thing." Obasanjo did cede power—to a handpicked successor—but at least he was unsuccessful in changing the Constitution.

Before Obasanjo, the President had had the same "fireside chat" with longtime Kenyan President Daniel arap Moi, who'd come to the Oval Office in 2002, hoping to convince the United States that his country needed him for stability. The President delivered the tough message: when the Constitution says it's time for elections, you need to step down. Moi, also under pressure from African leaders, relented, and elections for his successor were held in December 2002.

Fortunately, the elections in Kenya went smoothly. Mwai Kibaki defeated Moi's handpicked candidate by a large margin. When the aging Kibaki was elected, there was great hope that Kenya had turned the corner toward a stable democracy. We even invited Kibaki to the White House for a rare state visit, made somewhat difficult by his fragile physical condition as the result of a near-fatal accident during his campaign. Nonetheless, he had seemed to be an honest, if hardly inspiring, choice for the post-Moi era.

But he, and particularly the people around him, had turned out to be intolerant of opposition and determined to stay in power. When Kibaki's run for reelection in December 2007 proved inconclusive and allegations of fraud began to spread, conflict erupted in Kenya that would last well into the first few months of 2008.

The election was so poorly run that it isn't clear to this day who really won. As December turned into January, both sides continued to claim victory. A key problem was that Raila Odinga, the challenger, who had many of the characteristics that Kibaki did not (youth, charisma, and energy) was from the marginalized Luo ethnic group, and Kibaki is from the traditionally more powerful Kikuyu. Both groups claimed their candidate as the winner, and the post-election confusion threatened to plunge the country into civil war.

Former UN secretary-general Kofi Annan was asked to mediate the conflict. I tried to help from a distance, phoning Odinga, then Kibaki, then Odinga again to encourage a power-sharing arrangement. By the time the President and I landed in Benin, a republic on Nigeria's western border, the situation in Kenya had worsened. Armed gangs "representing" each of the contenders were engaged in open warfare that began in the western town of Kisumu and spread to the slums of Nairobi and beyond.

The press hounded the President at every stop: "What is the United States doing to stop the violence in Kenya?" "Are you afraid of civil war?" It was one of those times when I wanted to cry out, "Does every problem in the world belong to the United States?" But of course I didn't. The President and I decided that I should break off from his trip and go to Kenya. I called Kofi and asked, "Can you use my help?" He was grateful for my offer and we agreed that I'd come the next day.

I decided to leave after the Tanzania portion of the trip. It was an important stop from a policy perspective. Tanzania had received an MCC grant and was a model AIDS relief recipient, and its president, Jakaya Kikwete, was one of the bright, young democratic leaders of Africa. I also wanted to be present when the President greeted the families of the victims of the 1998 U.S. Embassy bombings. So I attended the events in Dar es Salaam, including a dinner that I'll never forget. Often the social dinners are routine and blur one into another. But that night I sat with the foreign minister and several others who'd been on the border at the time of the Rwandan genocide. "At first we didn't believe the stories we were hearing," one official said. "And then people started to stumble into refugee camps—missing limbs, hacked off hands and feet."

"We should have done something," another said.

Suddenly no one had much of an appetite. My mind wandered back to our visit to Rwanda—sitting with President Kagame and listening to his recounting of his own participation in the military confrontation with the genocidaires. And then there was the genocide museum in Kigali. One exhibit was a letter from a young boy who had expressed faith that the UN troops would come in time to save his family. They didn't, of course. *I'd better get on that plane tomorrow and make something happen in Kenya,* I thought. *Once ethnic violence begins, you never know where it's going.*

The next morning I got on the plane for Kenya. The route we traveled filled me with awe, as our plane flew right over Mount Kilimanjaro. I made a mental note to return when I could enjoy the view. There wasn't time right then, but one day there would be a chance to witness this natural wonder without the pressures of my current job.

I arrived in Kenya and headed for the Nairobi Serena Hotel, where Kofi had taken up residence. In the car, our ambassador Michael Ranneberger handed me a newspaper. The headline was an appeal to both Kibaki and Odinga. "Don't Kill Our Kenyan Democracy," it said. "This is the headline in every newspaper and on every television station," he said. "It's a coordinated effort by civil society and the press to push the leaders toward agreement. The Kenyan people don't want a civil war."

"Then there's something to work with?" I asked.

"Yes," he replied, "it's just you've got two bullheaded politicians who can't see past their own interests."

When we reached the hotel, Kofi greeted me at the door. He'd already been in the country for a month and looked a bit tired. I'd worried that I might be "bigfooting" him by swooping down as the U.S. secretary of state. That wasn't how he saw it, however. He needed help, and it wouldn't be the first time we'd worked as a team. But I promised him that I would make clear that my efforts were in support of his. After all, I'd soon be back on a plane and he'd have to carry the negotiations forward to conclusion. We held a short press availability so that the point could be made at the start of my visit.

Then I went to see the parties—first Kibaki and then Odinga. The president and his aides were gathered in his very hot second-floor offices. *I guess the air conditioning isn't working today,* I thought. *Or maybe the Africans just like it hot. Or maybe they're trying to make me uncomfortable.* Whatever the explanation, we sat there in the stultifying heat discussing the future of Kenya. Kofi had gotten the two men to agree to share power, but the devil was in the details. Odinga wanted to be a prime minister with real powers; Kibaki was determined to thwart him. The challenger wanted the Finance Ministry and Defense. The president wanted to give him no powerful posts at all.

I started by reminding Kibaki of the great promise that everyone had seen in him when he had first been elected. He'd told the President at the time that he'd institutionalize democracy in his country. Now he had a chance to deliver on that promise. The stubborn old man just kept repeating that he'd won the election, but he seemed to go into and out of focus, suddenly losing his train of thought several times. It was then that I realized that his "people" might be more the problem than he. It's often the case that advisors have as much to lose as the principal, particularly in Kenya, where political power is often accompanied by considerable wealth.

In a stroke of good luck, one of the individuals in the room was Kibaki's coalition partner Uhuru Kenyatta, whose sister had gone to Stanford with Jendayi, the assistant secretary for Africa. I asked Jendayi to call Kenyatta aside and see if he could establish a real bottom line. They agreed to continue their talks after the formal meeting broke up.

I then went to see Raila Odinga and his advisors at their party headquarters. He was very focused and clear, making the negotiations easier. He wanted enough power as prime minister to govern the country. He also wanted two or more important ministries. He didn't want to be a figurehead. Then I looked across the table at one of my own former Stanford students, Sally Kosgei. Ironically, here in the middle of this conflict, were two individuals with Stanford ties, each on a different side. But they knew each other, and they knew Jendayi. "They are all children of Kenya's elites and have known each other since grammar school," Jendayi explained. These contacts proved to be useful back channels.

Finally, I met with the business community and civil society and confirmed what the ambassador had said. The dispute was not one that the Kenyan people wanted or supported; no one wanted civil war.

In the end we were able to help Kofi bring about a power-sharing arrangement, with Odinga in the newly created—and somewhat vaguely defined—position of prime minister, responsible for coordinating government business, and Kibaki as chief of state and head of the armed forces in the role of president. A few months before we left office, Odinga came to see me at the department. He was on a mission to recruit foreign investment to Kenya in his role as head of government. "How are you and the president getting along?" I asked.

"Not bad," he answered. "I try to respect him for his age. It works okay."

I felt very good about the work I'd done in Kenya, most of it without much fanfare. When I returned to Stanford, Diane Comstock, a friend whose church works in Kenya, sent me a note. It was the story of a woman who'd been so moved by what I'd done to "save Kenya" that she had named her daughter Condoleezza. *Wow!* I thought. *That's unbelievable!* Then I had to laugh as I imagined the little African girl learning to spell "Condoleezza." "She'll have a head start on the alphabet," I told my friend. Being secretary of state had its moments. This was one of them.

49

WHITHER CHINA?

J OSH BOLTEN, the White House chief of staff, had given all of us a little "countdown" clock, ticking away the remaining days of the Bush administration. I put it on the corner of my desk. There was still a lot to do, and I was very aware that we'd soon come to a "crossover point," when other governments would start to look past us to the next administration. The flip side was that several leaders wanted to "finish" important business, since they believed that "the devil you know is better than the devil you don't."

I wondered which camp Kim Jong-il would fall into. In the first quarter of 2008, it seemed that he wanted to "finish" the business with the Bush administration. There had been a thaw in 2007 during which the North Koreans carried out their obligations, allowing IAEA and U.S. inspectors on the ground where, as one press member put it, they "crawl[ed] all over the place," even destroying equipment related to the nuclear program. The improvement in Pyongyang's compliance coincided with the election of a new, tough-minded president in South Korea. It helped too that U.S.-China relations were on a solid footing. For a moment in the winter of 2008, it looked as though we might just get the North Koreans to make better choices. The North desperately wanted to be removed from the terrorist list, which identified countries engaged in and supporting terrorism. Somehow the North Koreans seemed to believe it signaled acceptance internationally, though they remained heavily sanctioned. But we were holding out until we could get a look at the declaration of their nuclear facilities, sites, and activities promised in the step-by-step plan that Chris Hill and Kim Kye Gwan had worked out the year before. Still, we were making progress and it was nice that the inauguration of South Korea's new president could take place without a crisis on the Korean peninsula as the backdrop.

I headed the U.S. delegation to the event, enjoying my chance to get to know a distinguished guest accompanying the group, Hines Ward, the Pittsburgh Steelers' receiver. Hines is half Korean and wore traditional garb, a gesture that was greatly appreciated by our hosts. Sitting on the dais and looking out over the huge crowd, it was easy to forget that South Korea had come to democracy just two decades earlier having been ruled by autocratic leaders such as the staunchly anti-Communist Syngman Rhee since before the Korean War. The conservative businessman turned politician Lee Myung-bak addressed the crowd and then reviewed the troops of the Republic of Korea. It was an incredible sight in a country that had once been a military dictatorship. Then the Seoul Philharmonic Orchestra played Beethoven's "Ode to Joy," a fitting end to a remarkable celebration of freedom.

I met with the new president later that day. We talked only briefly about North Korea since he was short on time and—not surprisingly—attention on his inaugural day. Yet I was really moved as I listened to his impassioned concern for the people of North Korea. "They are our brothers and sisters," he said, showing an empathy that was a far cry from the Korean official a few years before who'd despaired at integrating "brain-damaged midgets" should reunification occur. The administration had appointed a special envoy for human rights in North Korea. Jay Lefkowitz, a Washington lawyer with whom I had worked at the White House, had tried to find an entry point with our allies in the region to tackle this difficult problem. Many commentators and some in Congress criticized the State Department as insufficiently active in pursuing the cause of human rights in North Korea. But without a strong partner in the South there was little that we could do. For instance, Seoul under Roh had refused to enhance their abilities to broadcast into North Korea. Now, with a South Korean president with greater interest in the human rights issue across the thirty-eighth parallel, I thought that we might make a new start—even in the waning days of the administration. That night I called the President to talk about my visit to China the next day. "Lee is going to be a great partner for you in the Freedom Agenda in Asia," I told him. I was just sorry that the two of them wouldn't have longer to work together.

It was very clear that the Chinese were sorry they wouldn't have longer to work with George W. Bush too. Our relationship had come a very long way from the downing of our aircraft on Hainan Island in 2001 and tensions over Taiwan arms sales. We'd navigated a lot of turbulence with Beijing over the eight years. The Chinese didn't appreciate our consistently raising human rights cases and the Tibetan issue, but they tolerated it. Even when the President met repeatedly with the Dalai Lama in the residence of the White House, the howls from Beijing were somewhat muted. The protests increased when the President participated in the presentation of a Congressional Gold Medal to the Dalai Lama in 2007. But in relatively short order, the fit of pique subsided. In fact, we set the terms of engagement on these difficult issues early: we vowed to be respectful but determined in challenging China on human rights. And we held fast to the belief that time was not on the side of authoritarianism in a country that was rapidly growing more prosperous.

We repeatedly told the Chinese that we believed that their economic growth was good for the international economy. They listened but probably ignored us when we said that it would be good for there to be a liberalization of Chinese politics too.

Yet I firmly believe that political change will come to China. Labor unrest, ethnic riots, product safety negligence, censorship on the Internet, and disasters that have repeatedly caused massive loss of life due to shoddy construction pose a serious challenge to China's development. One has to wonder how China's hierarchal and rigid political system can effectively respond. The country's internal dynamism is boiling under Beijing's tight lid, and I hope, in the coming years, the party leadership will let off some steam. Perhaps this is why Premier Wen has now several times raised—albeit cautiously—the need for political reform. I can't help but think that some of those Communist officials who are planning the 2012 Party Congress recognize the strain prompted by the most rapid social and economic transformation in human history. Some of them must be asking, "How can we liberalize *without* becoming Gorbachev?"

The U.S. can and must continue to advocate for a democratic China. With a country of China's size and complexity, the U.S. government's direct tools for influencing internal development are few. They're essentially limited to leveraging the power of open markets and helping make sure that the Chinese people are exposed to the world through universities and companies. Other more frontal approaches are likely to be resisted and can even backfire.

THUS, THERE WAS never much of a question as to whether the President would attend the Olympics in Beijing. We all understood that it was China's coming-out party; any attempt to get something in return would most certainly have been resented and resisted. The President announced early and often that he'd attend the Olympics as a sporting event, taking the issue of quid pro quo off the table. The Chinese came to appreciate the administration's nuanced policy, knowing that we'd take a stand when we had to—for instance, on the Dalai Lama—but that we'd show respect when we could, as with the Olympics.

And sometimes our interests came together in unexpected ways. Such was the case with Taiwan. From the time of his election, Taiwan's president, Chen Shui-bian, had been a thorn in our side, not just Beijing's. The Taiwan Strait issue, as the relationship between mainland China and Taiwan has come to be known, is one of those international problems that requires delicate balancing. It's important to prevent open conflict, though the issue defies resolution—at least for the time being. The United States is committed to helping Taiwan defend itself in the event of Chinese provocation or attack. But there is no interest in Washington in helping a Taiwan that provokes China. That was the problem with Chen Shui-bian.

Taiwan was where the Kuomintang had fled after the 1949 revolution. The island grew economically and eventually became democratic. China has always held that Taiwan must be reintegrated into the mainland, whereas the Taiwanese have claimed that the mainland is theirs. But as the PRC has grown more powerful, Taiwan has shifted to a position of trying to maintain its autonomy. The United States has supported that ambition but not a declaration of formal independence. Chen constantly walked toward the precipice of declaring independence, which was a serious violation of the principle that neither side should try to change the status quo.

At the end of 2007, Chen announced that he'd hold a national referendum on joining the United Nations in the name of Taiwan. This thinly disguised ploy to get the people of Taiwan to vote for independence sent Beijing into a tizzy. It threatened all kinds of retaliation. We agreed that the referendum was provocative, and I said so publicly.

The Bush administration had been a good friend to Taiwan, securing Congressional support for an arms-sale package and working tirelessly to convince China to allow Taipei's participation in world bodies such as the World Health Organization. No one was particularly sympathetic, therefore, to Chen's entreaties to his few remaining friends in Washington. There were a few phone calls from members of Congress but no real support for Chen's position.

When I arrived in Beijing the day after the Korean president's inauguration, the foreign minister asked if I'd call the referendum a provocation again, this time in front of the Chinese press. I'd expected this request and had talked it over with the President the night before. The Chinese press was primed to ask the question—and to receive the answer. I avoided using the word "provocation" again, but that night my carefully worded rebuke was played over and over on television. It was played in Taiwan too, where the referendum began to lose support almost immediately. Most people understood that Taipei could not be on the wrong side of the United States.

Thanks to both the Taiwan issue and the President's decision to attend the Olympics, the Chinese were in a very good mood about U.S.-China relations. They believed too that we were doing all we could to resolve the North Korean issue. "I just hope you can pass on the administration's policy to the next President," Foreign Minister Yang Jiechi told me during that visit.

"Jiechi," I said, "you have lived in Washington [as political counselor and ambassador], and you know that's not how it works."

"Well," he said, "we can hope."

A few months later, I visited Chengdu, China, the site of a devastating earthquake that spring that had caused seventy thousand deaths.

The relocation site was very orderly, and the Chinese citizens seemed grateful for their lodgings, which were likely to be their homes, we were told, for up to three years. A twelve-year-old boy walked up to me and said, "You're that lady from America." I answered that I was. He smiled and hugged me. I always loved those moments with kids when you could feel what America means to people of all ages. But I also saw something that made me wonder about China's remarkable development. We had to pass through a village to get to the relocation camp. It was right out of the nineteenth century—just a few miles from the gleaming, modern metropolis of Chengdu. *That's the problem,* I thought. *They've pulled more than 500 million people out of poverty, but they have so many more to go. And inequality is widening. How does a Marxist government handle that?*

From that perspective, the rise of China looked a little different— less certain and potentially more chaotic. We'd come to office knowing that managing the U.S.-China relationship would be one of our most important tasks. The international system has not always been good at accommodating rising powers. One of the reasons that we were confident we could was the strong web of alliances that we enjoyed. The United States was an established Pacific power, both militarily and economically. South Korea, Japan, and Australia were strong democratic friends, more than capable of holding their own in the changing region.

But Japan was emerging as a weakening link in that chain. I've mentioned Prime Minister Koizumi's determination to undertake long-delayed, much-needed bureaucratic and economic reforms. When he left office, Japan fell back into consensus politics again, with essentially interchangeable prime ministers who never seemed to move the country forward. It was increasingly depressing to go to Japan, which seemed not only stagnant and aging but hamstrung by old animosities with its neighbors. And I was concerned too about my personal chemistry with the Japanese, who believed I was too interested in resolving the North Korean nuclear issue and unwilling to hold the line on the abductions. It began to feel as if the Japanese wanted the Six-Party Talks to fail lest they lose their leverage with us to help them with the admittedly tragic abduction issue.

For the remainder of the term, I'd fight to avoid linkage between the two issues. We could only say that we'd press the North Koreans to resolve the questions about the kidnapped Japanese citizens but if we could constrain—even end—Pyongyang's nuclear program, we needed to do that. Maintaining that position was very difficult. Tom Schieffer, the President's good friend and former co-owner of the Texas Rangers, was ambassador to Japan (having already served as ambassador to Australia). Tom was a great guy but sometimes a little too insistent in making Tokyo's case. After one incident in which Tom called the President—not me—about Japan's complaints, we had a discussion about the appropriate chain of command. He hadn't meant to cross the line, and we never had difficulties again. But I know it was hard on Tom because the Japanese were hypersensitive and insecure. Therein lay the problem: we needed a confident Japan as a partner in a changing Asia, and with the end of Junichiro Koizumi's term in office in 2006, those days had seemed to disappear.

50

OLMERT MAKES AN OFFER

I RETURNED FROM ASIA and headed almost immediately to the Middle East. The prospects for a framework agreement between the Palestinians and the Israelis were brightening as the spring approached. During the President's trip in January, we'd both been impressed by Olmert's desire to get a deal. After the Annapolis Conference, he'd placed Tzipi Livni in charge of the Israeli side of the negotiations, and President Abbas had tapped Abu Alaa. There was something of an asymmetry since the Palestinian team was experienced, having negotiated the issues for more than fifteen years. Like the back of their hands, the team members knew the ins and outs of the maps, the nuances of the phrases, and the history of the conflict. Tzipi admitted that she didn't know the issues as well but she came up to speed very quickly. I traveled to the region even more frequently, holding meetings with each side separately and several times jointly. The progress was slow but steady. At one point, to better understand the Palestinian concerns about the Israeli settlement of Ariel, Tzipi even suggested a joint field trip to see it. I was convinced that the parties were trying very hard.

In March I made two trips to the region, and I made another in April. With those trips, I had fallen into a pattern, meeting with the Arabs through the GCC and covering everything from Iraq to Afghanistan to Annapolis. I'd then go on to meet with the Palestinians and the Israelis, starting in Jerusalem with dinner at Olmert's house. At first, I'd take Elliott Abrams, who traveled with me from the White House, David Welch, and the ambassador. Shalom Turgeman and Yoram Turbowitz, Olmert's close advisors, usually accompanied the prime minister. After dinner, Olmert and I would go into his study. He'd smoke a cigar, I'd drink tea, and we would go deeper into the issues that had come up at dinner.

But when I arrived in Jerusalem in May, I got word that Olmert wanted me to come to dinner alone. I was a little surprised, but we'd met one-on-one at least once before. When I got to the residence of the prime minister, he didn't waste much time on pleasantries.

"Tzipi is a hard worker, and she has my complete confidence," he began. *Why is he telling me that?* I wondered. Then he made himself clear. "The problem is that the process with Abu Alaa isn't going to get it done in time. Israel needs to get an agreement with the Palestinians before you leave office," he said. He continued without waiting for me to respond. "I want to do it directly with Abu Mazen," he said, referring to Mahmoud Abbas by his nom de guerre. "You are going to see him tomorrow. Tell him that I want to appoint one person. I have someone in mind. He is a retired judge that I trust. I want Abu Mazen to appoint a trusted agent too. We can write down the agreement in a few pages and then give it to the negotiators to finalize," he said. I started to ask about the relationship between what he was proposing and what Tzipi was doing. I felt kind of awkward because it was pretty clear he hadn't told her what he was telling me. But as I opened my mouth, Olmert started talking again.

"I know what he needs. He needs something on refugees and on Jerusalem. I'll give him enough land, maybe something like 94 percent with swaps. I have an idea about Jerusalem. There will be two capitals, one for us in West Jerusalem and one for the Palestinians in East Jerusalem. The mayor of the joint city council will be selected by population percentage. That means an Israeli mayor, so the deputy should be a Palestinian. We will continue to provide security for the Holy sites because we can assure access to them." *That's probably a nonstarter,* I thought. *But concentrate, concentrate. This is unbelievable.* He continued, "I'll accept some Palestinians into Israel, maybe five thousand. I don't want it to be called family reunification because they have too many cousins; we won't be able to control it. I've been thinking about how to administer the Old City. There should be a committee of people—not officials but wise people—from Jordan, Saudi Arabia, the Palestinians, the United States, and Israel. They will oversee the city but not in a political role." *Am I really hearing this?* I wondered. *Is the Israeli prime minister saying that he'll divide Jerusalem and put an international body in charge of the Holy sites? Concentrate. Write this down. No, don't write it down. What if it leaks? It can't leak; it's just the two of us.*

Olmert was on a roll. "I will need your help on security. The IDF has a list of demands—some of them probably are okay, but the Palestinians won't accept all of them. I need the United States to work this out to the satisfaction of the military. Barak will work with you. I can sell this deal, but not if the IDF says it will undermine Israel's security. That's the one thing no prime minister can survive. And one other thing, I need to know that you won't surprise me by offering other ideas before we've had a chance to talk about them. I'm taking an enormous risk here, and I can't be blindsided by the United States." Olmert had been leaning forward; neither of us had touched our dinner, and when the server had come in, he'd shooed her away. Now he sat back in his chair, exhausted by the recitation of the extraordinary details of the deal as he saw it.

"Prime Minister, this is remarkable, and I will try to help. I will talk to Abu Mazen tomorrow," I promised. "Be careful where you speak to him because people may be listening," he said.

After dinner, I hurried back to the hotel and related the details to David and Elliott only—minus the proposal on an international committee to oversee the Holy sites. I trusted my advisors, but a slip of the tongue on that one would have been devastating to Olmert. "You must not tell anyone," I said sternly, knowing that they wouldn't. Then I called Steve Hadley and told him that I had some extraordinary news but didn't feel comfortable—even on a secure phone—repeating what I'd heard from Olmert. After all, I was in an Israeli hotel; one never knew who might be listening. "Tell the President he was right about Olmert. He wants a deal. And frankly, he might die trying to get one," I said, recalling that Yitzhak Rabin had been killed for offering far less. I hung up the phone and looked out my window at the Holy City. Maybe, just maybe, we could get this done.

The next day I went to see Abbas and asked to see him in the little dining room adjacent to his office. I sketched out the details of Olmert's proposal and told him how the prime minister wanted to proceed. Abbas started negotiating immediately. "I can't tell four million Palestinians that only five thousand of them can go home," he said.

I demurred, saying that he should make his concerns known to the prime minister. "Are you ready to talk with him alone?" I asked. Abbas said that he would but could not appoint a trusted agent—he wanted to do this himself. I sensed that the internal politics of the Fatah party were such that he could not sidestep Abu Alaa, a power in his own right and sometimes a rival within the party. *This is going to be a problem,* I realized. *But just get them together, and see what happens—one step at a time.*

I called the prime minister before I left and said that Abbas was ready to talk but wanted to do it himself. The prime minister said that he'd arrange a meeting. "What language will you use?" I asked.

"English," Olmert replied.

"Remember that you speak it better than he does. He'll be at a disadvantage," I countered.

"It isn't my intention to put him at a disadvantage," he replied. *I think he really means that,* I thought. "I'll be in touch, Prime Minister," I said. "And I'll tell the President about our discussions."

Olmert ended by saying, "Remind him of our first meeting when I said that I wanted a deal."

When I returned to Washington, I had a very good idea of what we, the United States, needed to do. General Will Fraser had taken the task of Roadmap coordination. I would ask him to accelerate his efforts. General Jim Jones had assumed the role of special envoy, and I asked him to think about how to approach the IDF on security arrangements for the new Palestinian state. It occurred to me that some of the Israeli demands—for instance, for a permanent IDF presence inside the new Palestinian state to guard the Jordan Valley—might be accommodated by a "regional solution." In other words, I could possibly try to convince the Jordanian king to place his troops alongside others, even NATO forces, on that border. I raised the idea of a NATO role with the Alliance's Secretary General, Jaap de Hoop Scheffer, saying that he should do nothing and tell no one for the time being. The Israelis might be convinced to accept Jordan's forces because they trusted them, and the Jordanians would certainly accept U.S. help. I was not at all confident that the Pentagon or NATO would want to play such a role, but if we were that close to a deal, it might be possible. Other concerns, such as control of air space or border security, might have technical solutions. Perhaps the United States could accelerate sharing of early-warning radar data with Israel—and help with the Iranian threat at the same time. I talked to Bob Gates and asked if the Joint Staff could help Jim Jones. Gates readily agreed, though there was some resistance in the Joint Staff to becoming deeply involved in what was seen as the "peace process." My view was that without reliable security arrangements for Israel there would be no agreement. The new Palestinian state had to come into being in a way that enhanced rather than detracted from regional—and Israeli—security. The State Department couldn't deliver those conditions, but the Pentagon could.

I wanted to make sure that the key Arabs knew what was going on too, though I was pretty sure Abbas was briefing them. The Saudi ambassador to the United States, Adel al-Jubeir, was the king's most trusted advisor. Adel's grandfather had worked for the king's grandfather; he was as close as possible to being a member of the royal family without actually being in the al-Saud bloodline. I told Adel what I'd heard from Olmert, presenting the ideas about Jerusalem as my own so as to shield the Israeli. He promised to share the information with the king only. I assumed he'd also tell Saud al-Faisal, the foreign minister. That was fine. One good thing about the Saudis was that they didn't leak.

Before leaving the region, I had talked to the king of Jordan. I didn't ask him for any specific commitments, but I knew that he would come along if and when a deal was imminent. In fact, no Arab was going to fully commit until we were on the cusp of an agreement; my job was to get Olmert and Abbas to that place and then ask the Arabs for help.

The Egyptians were somewhat more complicated interlocutors because they *do* leak. Nonetheless, I took the foreign minister into my confidence, as well as Omar Suleiman, the chief of internal security and the closest person to Mubarak. The Egyptian president apparently told his advisors that we'd never succeed and I'd crash down in a heap. But of course he didn't say that to my face. The truth was that Mubarak had never really forgiven me for my Cairo speech of June 2005, in which I'd used unprecedented language to call for political reform in Egypt and the region. I understood that, but I needed Egypt in order to conclude a deal.

The President, Steve, and I sat in the Oval and reviewed the bidding. "It sounds like he's serious—really serious," the President said.

"Yes, he is," I replied, "and he knows he's running out of time." The rumor mill was churning away about Olmert. An investigation was under way into a variety of corruption allegations, including charges that he had diverted political contributions for personal use. The word "indictment" was being thrown around with some regularity. We agreed that we'd ignore the storm clouds and work with the prime minister until it was no longer possible to do so. And I would intensify my work with Abu Alaa and Tzipi to see if we could sync the two negotiating tracks—or at least get them closer. It was not the process that we'd envisioned at Annapolis, but it was the one we had—and it had a chance of succeeding.

When we returned to Israel later in May for the sixtieth anniversary of its founding, the President addressed the Knesset. It was clear that Israelis believed they had no better friend than George W. Bush. His speech was emotional and showed great empathy for Israel's continued sense of vulnerability.

I had reviewed and approved the speech. Now, listening to it, I thought it should have done more. Somehow the President should have used the moment to challenge the Israelis to make tough decisions—the peace process wasn't even mentioned. *How did I let that happen?* I wondered. I'm certain that there would have been no objection to language about Annapolis—but somehow it didn't get done. It was a missed opportunity for diplomacy but a triumph for U.S.-Israeli friendship.

Publicly challenging the Israelis to make a bold move might not have been the right call, though, given the need to bolster Olmert against the growing storm clouds of legal and political trouble. The President said later that watching the members of the Knesset sitting next to the prime minister reminded him of sharks circling their prey as they suspiciously eyed both him and one another. That was precisely the state of affairs. The prime minister's days were numbered.

. . .

THE ISRAELI-PALESTINIAN issue was starting to take a lot of time. After years of criticism that we hadn't been active enough, there were suddenly those—both in the press and in the expert community—who implied that we were wasting our time. My trips to the region were increasingly mocked as useless talking sessions with no discernible progress. Arshad Mohammed of Reuters and others pressed me endlessly on what we were trying to achieve. After meeting with Abu Alaa and Tzipi, I could only point obliquely to the "seriousness" of the parties. Indeed they were methodically going through the issues and coming to agreement on a few—some of consequence, including the need to negotiate on the basis of the 1967 line with agreed swaps (and, as Tzipi always added, taking into account the population realities on the ground, meaning the settlements). I could, of course, say even less about what Olmert and Abbas were doing. I swallowed my pride as pundits held forth about the empty Annapolis process. *Keep your head in the game and your ego in check,* I told myself. *They don't know what they are talking about.*

So Much Left to Do

IN MY LAST YEAR, I was finding it hard to deliver on all of the promises that I'd made to make "one last visit" to other parts of the world. In all honesty, my focus was on the Middle East peace process where I thought we might get a breakthrough; solidification of the progress in Iraq; and finding ways to reverse the growing negative trends in Afghanistan. I felt too that we had to make one last push in the Six-Party Talks and the P5+1 to stop the forward progress of the North Korean and Iranian nuclear programs. I managed a quick stop in Iceland on May 30, a visit that I promised in exchange for the leadership's agreement to our redeployment of four F-15 fighters and 1,200 servicemen and -women from the base at Keflavík to areas around the world where they were needed more. Don Rumsfeld had first raised the issue in 2001, noting correctly that there was no Soviet threat to confront in Icelandic airspace. The Icelanders had gone crazy, claiming that we were reneging on the 1951 U.S.–Republic of Iceland bilateral defense agreement. It took five years, but we finally worked out a deal that signaled our continuing commitment to our ally *and* permitted the sensible redeployment. My brief visit to the country, which is built on volcanic rock, was short but not without controversy. As I arrived, I learned that the Icelandic Parliament had passed a resolution condemning Guantánamo. At the press conference, I simply suggested that the Parliament do its homework and referred it to the assessment by the Belgian official who had called it a "model prison." I was tired of nonsense like this and was perhaps less diplomatic as my time wound down.

On the other hand, Latin America was not just a stop to fulfill a promise. I had really wanted to go back to the region and found the time in March for a two-day trip. My brief stop in Chile felt rushed, and I was sorry for that. The foreign minister, Alejandro Foxley, had been a terrific colleague, and I was glad that we found time to launch a program of educational exchanges between our countries in 2007, as well as a Chile-California partnership during my 2008 trip. Not long after becoming foreign minister, Alejandro had mentioned the desire to improve the English-language skills of Chileans so that they could pursue graduate education in the United States. We showed that bureaucracies could get things done rather quickly.

I'm a firm believer in the importance of educational exchanges. That comes in part from my own experience at Stanford with foreign students who are exposed to the United States and our values. In fact, when I was provost at Stanford, we started a program called the New Democracy Fellows for students from Eastern Europe and the Soviet Union. I have encountered some of them now working at high levels of government and business, including Alexei Sitnikov, my PhD student, who regularly advises the Russian presidency. Clearly, not all experiences are positive. But overwhelmingly, foreign students come to appreciate Americans as people even if they don't like our policies. And many of those young people go on to become leaders in their countries.

Unfortunately, after September 11, 2001, we experienced a precipitous decline in the number of foreigners studying in the United States. The necessary tightening of our visa programs produced unintended consequences. Often the visa application process was so lengthy that a student missed the start of the school year. It became difficult for students to take up their studies, go home for vacation, and return in time for the new semester due to the need to apply for a visa each time. Those were real constraints. But there were problems of perception too, a feeling that the United States did not want foreign students and indeed feared them.

The issue would come up in almost every conversation between the President and foreign leaders—and not just in the Middle East. I remember sitting with the prime minister of Singapore, who introduced his Cabinet members, each of whom had studied in the United States. "You are jeopardizing one of your greatest strengths," he had said. "Our young people think you don't want them in the United States, and they're going to other places like England now." The President was appalled to learn how dramatically student exchanges had been curtailed, and when I became secretary it was one of the issues he asked about most frequently: "How are we doing at getting students into the United States?" By 2007 I was able to tell him that we'd recovered from the post-9/11 slump and students again were studying in the United States in increasing numbers.

Still, I felt that exchanges shouldn't be a one-way street. Americans are notoriously monolingual and, frankly, a bit provincial. I've long been an advocate of study-abroad programs. Education Secretary Margaret Spellings and I teamed up to spotlight the importance of student exchanges, holding the U.S. University Presidents Summit on International Education in 2006. One great strength of the American higher education system is its diversity, so we invited leaders from community colleges, liberal arts schools, and private and public research universities. Margaret would visit countries in South America, the Middle East, Africa, Europe, and Asia with several university presidents to further emphasize the importance of the issue.

If the stop in Chile underscored our commitment to educational exchange, my trip to Brazil was a chance to showcase the administration's— and particularly *my*—advocacy of minority rights in Latin America. It was very difficult to get the press to pay attention to issues beyond the Middle East, Europe, and Asia. I was determined to structure my trip to Brazil in a way that brought focus to the breadth of our efforts in Latin

America. Our ambassador, Cliff Sobel, had the perfect idea: why not go to Salvador da Bahia, the cultural home of Afro-Brazilians?

I'd visited Brazil for the first time in 1993 as a Chevron director. The company named oil tankers after members of the board of directors, and when my turn came, the christening ceremony was in Rio. In a grand ceremony, accompanied by five days of parties, I launched the *Condoleezza Rice,* a 136,000-ton supertanker. Anna Perez, who worked for Chevron (and would later work for me at the White House), had thoughtfully suggested renaming the ship when I became national security advisor, rightfully fearing that it might draw the attention of an enterprising terrorist. So the *Condoleezza Rice* is no more, but it was fun to have a supertanker bear my name for a while.

During the trip, I was somewhat taken aback by the racial divide in Brazil. Brazilians had always protested that they had no race problem. Yet it seemed to me that the field hands were Africans (dark-skinned), the service personnel were mulatto (biracial), and the government officials were European/Portuguese. Brazil was the country most similar to the United States in its ethnic makeup, but it seemed to have experienced little of the civil rights revolution that had changed the face of American politics and society.

Latin American leaders were comfortable talking to me about their struggles with racial equality and efforts at affirmative action. Indeed President Uribe of Colombia had called me the day that he announced the appointment of his first Afro-Colombian to a cabinet post. Perhaps leaders such as Uribe were comfortable because I was honest with them about America's own struggles. In fact, as I often said, the U.S. State Department was no model of racial diversity. "I can go all day and not see another person who looks like me," I told the director general in advocating for more aggressive minority hiring. There were of course legendary black Foreign Service officers—among them Ambassadors Ruth Davis, Edward Perkins, and Horace Dawson—but they were few and far between. I appointed the department's first chief diversity officer, Barry L. Wells, and championed programs like the Pickering Fellows and the Rangel Fellows to interest minorities in Foreign Service careers. Still, even after the terms of consecutive black secretaries of state, the racial makeup of the diplomatic corps hardly "looks like America." This is a tragedy for a country that is the model of multiethnic democracy. I know that Colin felt the same way.

But as disappointing as the U.S. record is on this score, the rest of the world is still light-years behind. Thus, I took note when President Lula criticized his own country's record on race relations, condemning discrimination in unambiguous terms in a November 2007 statement. Before departing Brasilia, I signed the U.S.-Brazil Joint Action Plan to Eliminate Racial Discrimination with the Afro-Brazilian minister Édson Santos and my counterpart, foreign minister Celso Amorim.

Then I headed for Bahia, the heart of Afro-Brazilian culture and life. I loved it. We went to a church that had been built by African slaves. It had taken one hundred years because the men had constructed it on their one day off, Sunday. Simple yet elegant, the small sanctuary was as spiritual as any I had ever seen. Then we emerged into the square, lined by the citizens of Bahia. Yes, there were a few protesters who made the evening news. But my memories will always be of the black faces and outstretched hands—citizens happy to see a fellow daughter of the African diaspora.

The night before, the governor had thrown a dinner for me quite unlike the stuffy, formal affairs to which I was accustomed. The food was great—a bit like my Louisiana grandmother's Creole cooking—and the dancing, even better. Gilberto Gil, the best-known Afro-Brazilian jazz musician, entertained and then we all got up and danced, first in the room and then on the patio in the warm Brazilian night. I love Brazil and the Brazilians. I told myself, *You'll come back here when you can really have fun!*

Maliki the Leader

TO BE HONEST, there just wasn't much time for experiences like Bahia, even though I thought them important to my work as secretary. The core tasks of the administration's last year were pretty clear and most involved the Middle East. Nothing, of course, was more critical than to stabilize Iraq before the end of the President's tenure. And fortunately, there was finally something to work with. There was almost universal acknowledgment that we'd turned a corner, and the chorus of voices decrying our involvement in a "civil war" had largely fallen silent.

The security situation in Iraq had definitely improved, but it was more than that. The government was beginning to function, unevenly but more effectively, and Prime Minister Maliki and the other leaders were showing maturity in their leadership of the country. As we approached the third neighbor's meeting, scheduled for April 22, the Iraqis, as David Welch put it, were back. When we convened in Kuwait that morning, the atmosphere couldn't have been more different than in Sharm el-Sheik about a year before. Then there had been a mournful recounting of the troubles of Iraq.

Now country after country stood to congratulate the Iraqis on their progress and pledge cooperation with them. "This is so different," I said to David and Ryan Crocker. "They almost seem deferential."

"Oh, they are," my expert Arabists said. "The Arabs don't like the Iraqis, but they do respect them. They're hoping not to have to fear them again." I suddenly got it. But the Iranian representative seemed to have pulled the wrong script from his briefcase. He was still talking about the collapse of Iraq and blaming the chaos on the United States. Most of the delegates just rolled their eyes.

The night before the conference when I arrived in Kuwait City, Ryan Crocker rode with me to see Maliki. "You need to get him to be a little more gracious in his comments tomorrow," Ryan told me.

"Okay, but what is he planning to say?"

"He'll tell you," the ambassador said, chuckling.

Maliki and I talked about the upcoming meeting and what we wanted to achieve. He said he didn't want much from the other countries and would simply report on Iraq's progress. Then he told me how he'd open his remarks, and I understood Ryan's concern. "I'm going to say thank you to all of you who stayed with us through tough times— especially those who helped us early. That will mean the United States and some of the Europeans," he said. "Then I'm going to turn to my 'brothers' [meaning the Arabs] and say, 'And to the rest of you, the hell with you,' " he declared with a twinkle in his eye.

I laughed with him and replied, "Prime Minister, let's work on that a little bit." His speech was, of course, fine—but it did have a little edge, reminding the gathering that some had doubted the Iraqi people. It was a very good moment for him. I had come to like and respect Nouri al-Maliki.

I wouldn't have expected that scene several months before. In late 2007 Maliki had experienced a near revolt in the leadership circle. The prime minister was making no friends with his high-handed leadership style and inability to get anything done. He apparently held secret meetings to which he didn't invite other stakeholders and sometimes called meetings of the leadership and then refused to show up. The Iraqis were making minimal progress on the checklist the U.S. Congress had demanded on everything from passing budgets to transferring funds to the provinces to passing an oil law and new de-Baathification standards.

Bob Gates had taken a trip to Baghdad and returned to tell the President that Talabani, Hashimi, and First Vice President Adel Abdul-Mahdi were plotting to overthrow the prime minister—constitutionally, of course. Their idea was to force a vote of confidence in the Parliament, which they were sure Maliki would lose if the United States made clear that it had lost faith in the prime minister. Or, even better from their point of view, maybe we could just get Maliki to resign. Bob told the President that he was worried; perhaps he hadn't shot the idea down as forcefully as he should have. "They might think this is what we want," he said. "They know we're not happy with him either."

I'd scheduled a trip to Baghdad the following week, on the heels of a trip to the Middle East to talk about the Annapolis Conference. "You need to make sure they understand we're not for overthrowing Maliki," the President told me. I said I would deliver the message.

Arriving in Baghdad, I went first to see the prime minister. We met alone (along with my trusted interpreter Mustafa Sayid). I didn't wait long to broach the subject. "Mr. Prime Minister, you have real trouble with the other leaders. But I am here to tell you that the United States does not want to see your government dismissed. We are not in favor of a change of prime minister," I said. Maliki was visibly relieved. Then I continued a little beyond my guidance from Washington. "But you're doing a terrible job. You're failing. And we aren't for that either," I said sternly.

I don't know what I expected, but certainly not what he said. "I've been waiting to have this talk for weeks. I'm so happy you came. Thank you." As Sayid translated, I couldn't believe my ears. *Did he hear me tell him that he's doing a terrible job?* I wondered. I asked Sayid to repeat what I'd said. "Yes, yes. I am so glad to talk about this," he repeated, smiling broadly. I was floored but decided to go with it.

"Let's work on a program to get you out of this mess." I then suggested a series of steps including regular meetings with the other leaders.

"Okay, that's a good idea," he replied. I asked him to repeat the steps three times. He dutifully did.

"Now, Prime Minister, I have one more request," I said, pushing my luck a bit. "I have a meeting with President Talabani and the others; come and go with me."

That was a bridge too far. "No, I'll meet with them later," he countered.

"No, we have to go now," I said. So we did. I got into my car, and he followed me to Talabani's house, where the surprised president of Iraq welcomed his "brother" the prime minister with a big bear hug. I went through the details of what we'd agreed to do, and Maliki left. Talabani could tell right away that there would be no U.S.-sanctioned constitutional coup. Over lunch the others complained about Maliki, but the plotting was over.

The choice to back Maliki had been a wise one, a fact that became clear in March 2008 when the prime minister took a chance to demonstrate his leadership. Iraqi security forces had finally begun to take on the Shia extremists beholden to Muqtada al-Sadr in the south of the country, particularly in Basra, Iraq's third-largest city. Dave Petraeus had worked out a careful plan with the Defense Ministry, one that put the Iraqis in the lead but relied on significant U.S. support. Everything was going well and proceeding deliberately.

Then the Iraqis suddenly accelerated the timetable without Dave's knowledge. Providing just a few days' notice, the Iraqi army rushed south on March 24, accompanied by Maliki himself, who personally oversaw the operation from the field.

There was a National Security Council meeting that day with, as usual, Dave Petraeus and Ryan Crocker attending by videoconference. The two of them were ashen. "He's gone and done it now. This could fail. Then what will we do?" The general and the ambassador took turns excoriating Maliki for his incompetence and recklessness. Then each of us took turns doing the same. No one had anything good to say about him. We were all trying to figure out how to stop him.

The President hadn't said anything. Then he did. "I think he's showing leadership," he said. "Maybe it's not the way I would have done it. But he's the prime minister of his country. Maybe he knows what he's doing." George W. Bush was right. His politician's instinct told him that Maliki needed to demonstrate courage and control and that he was doing precisely that.

The Basra adventure was a resounding success. The Iraqi army rode triumphantly into the city, taking back the key port of Umm Qasr as the Iranian-backed Mahdi Army abandoned its posts. For better or worse, Iraqis were going to do things their way—not ours.

UNFORTUNATELY, EVEN as Iraq and the Palestinian situation were improving, Lebanon was worsening. The pro-Western March 14 government of Fouad Siniora had survived crisis after crisis. In the early part of the year, the March 14 ministers had actually slept in their offices, refusing to bend to the Hezbollah-inspired mobs in the streets or the assassins who were trying to systematically eliminate their majority in the Parliament by quite literally eliminating (killing, in other words) the parliamentarians. It was a crazy place.

Tensions had been high since Siniora's government had made clear that it would support the UN commission of inquiry into the assassination of former Prime Minister Rafik Hariri. Though the investigation's preliminary findings pointed to the involvement of Syrian and Lebanese intelligence, by late 2007 the inquiry had a new lead. A break in the case involving the alleged hit team's cell phone records would lead to a new and even more controversial conclusion: it would directly implicate Hezbollah. And it would raise already simmering sectarian tensions to a boil, leading to skirmishes between extremist and democratic forces, with neither side able to gain the upper hand.

In May the usually careful Siniora made a mistake. He fired a security official with ties to Hezbollah and tried to assert state control over the group's telecommunications network. Hezbollah reacted in rage, sending its militia out into the streets and pursuing government supporters. The group's gunmen took over parts of Beirut and some surrounding towns and villages, including Druze enclaves under the protection of March 14 supporter Walid Jumblatt.

Hezbollah had demonstrated what it could do by force. Meanwhile, the Lebanese army stood by, fearful that its entry could spark a civil war. The Qatari ruler eventually worked out a power-sharing arrangement that ended the eighteen-month stalemate over who would become the country's next president. The head of the national army, Michel Suleiman, was elected as a compromise candidate, and the Parliament finally reconvened. There was no doubt that Hezbollah and its allies, whose walkout had started the standoff, had won something of a victory. The March 14 forces felt despondent and defeated.

The government had clearly sustained a blow, but Hezbollah had paid a price too. In cafés and on street corners throughout Beirut there was dismay at Hezbollah's turning its arms on Lebanese. Hezbollah was supposed to be a resistance army against Israel, but it had showed itself to be just another violent faction, willing to kill Lebanese and throw the country into turmoil. For the time being, though, the extremists had regained their footing, exerting a power that was based on fear.

I decided to go to Lebanon in June after the Qatari deal to show support for the March 14 politicians. It was the least I could do. I told Steve Hadley that I felt we'd been unable to do enough to help our friends in Lebanon—or to punish our enemies. But that was Lebanon: a country in a perpetual state of instability and deadlock.

I had a trip planned to Jerusalem and decided to stop in Beirut on the way home. We didn't announce the visit but almost everyone assumed I'd go to Lebanon while in the region. My security detail didn't want me to fly the "blue and white" into the airport, which was known to be "owned" by Hezbollah, particularly since there had been some threats on extremist websites. "We can fly to Cyprus and chopper onto the embassy grounds and then drive to the meetings," Marty Kraus, the head of my security detail, said. But I had a different vision. "No. We're landing the blue and white at the airport. I am going to get off the plane and be received by the foreign minister in front of the cameras and then we'll drive to the meetings. The secretary of state isn't going into Lebanon under cover as if we think it's a war zone." It was the only time I overruled Marty. It was so crucial in this circumstance that the United States be seen as having a presence. Everything we'd achieved since Syrian forces left was on the line. We were going to signal support for the sovereign government—and show no fear. And, as I told Marty, Hezbollah wasn't suicidal. Did it really want to kill the U.S. secretary of state and bring the force of the United States down on itself?

It was my last trip to Lebanon. There had been so many ups and downs. But at least there was a legitimate democratic government—even if the extremists had to be tolerated within it. And though it would take a year to do so, the Lebanese people would punish Hezbollah for the use of the militia against their countrymen. In the 2009 elections, the "Party of God" lost badly. Hassan Nasrallah was reduced to complaining that the electoral districts had been poorly drawn. That was at least a step forward, even if one could be sure that there would be steps backward as well. A completely free and democratic Lebanon was still a long way off. But thanks to the withdrawal of Syrian troops and the deployment of the Lebanese army to the southern border, it was closer than when we began.

51

Completing the Task of Building a Europe Whole, Free, and at Peace

THE FOUNDATIONS OF THE old Middle East were beginning to crumble. I felt every day the urgency of securing a new democratic basis in the region for the post-9/11 era. But the job of building on our gains in post–Cold War Europe proved equally demanding. The spring of 2008 would present several crucial challenges: the situation in Kosovo; the future of Georgia and Ukraine in NATO; and, perhaps most delicate of all, the relationship of Russia to the new Europe. This final challenge would become increasingly difficult as we moved toward the last six months of the administration.

President Bush was a fierce believer in NATO and had, from the beginning of his administration, worked to strengthen and expand the Alliance. We'd expended enormous energy on modernizing NATO'S capabilities, bringing them more into line with the needs of the post–Cold War era. Initially there had been some resistance to the idea that missile defense was an important part of that new concept. At the first summit in 2001, only the Czech leader of the revolution that had brought communism down in 1989, President Václav Havel, had unreservedly backed the President's call for an all-out push in that area. The President never forgot Havel's support, which he took, rightly, to be an example of the differing sensibilities of the newer members of NATO from Central and Eastern Europe. By the time of the Bucharest summit in April 2008, though, missile defense was hardly controversial any longer and the Alliance had agreed to pursue joint efforts to defend its territory—all the while hoping that cooperative arrangements could be worked out with the resistant Russia.

NATO's writ had expanded dramatically too, with the Alliance having taken on major training activities with the Iraqi security forces and, more consequentially, a central role in the battle for Afghanistan. The latter mission was both a blessing and a curse. For someone like me, who as a young scholar had debated the appropriateness of "out-of-area" (meaning out-of-Europe) engagement for NATO, its involvement in Afghanistan was a stunning development. Still, the war exposed both the disparate capabilities of the members and radically different views of the use of military power. The discussions at every meeting walked a fine line between grateful acceptance of contributions and frustration at the number of caveats that some members placed on their forces. The divide between "fighters" and "peacekeepers" grew every day, until some armies were seemingly relegated to never leaving their barracks.

Not surprisingly, countries whose soldiers were doing the heavy lifting and exposed to grave danger resented the constraints on other militaries, particularly the Germans. I took a somewhat more charitable view. How could we expect Berlin to suddenly embrace a war mission? We'd been working for sixty years for a German army that wouldn't fight in foreign wars. I was personally grateful for whatever the allies could do, though I knew that the disparity in contributions would remain a source of tension.

Another innovation within the Alliance was the decision to open our meetings and consultations to non-European democratic allies, specifically Japan, Australia, South Korea, and New Zealand. Though some of our friends thought this might dilute NATO, making it a "global policeman," I thought the development welcome, since those countries' forces were also deployed in Afghanistan. And though we couldn't announce it during the President's term, we knew that President Nicolas Sarkozy had made the decision to reintegrate France into the NATO military command structure that it had left in 1966. All of this activity made it hard to recall the early post–Cold War days, when there were some who had pronounced the Alliance dead.

In fact, NATO had become a vital instrument in the stabilization of post-Communist Europe. Together with the European Union, it gave aspirant states from the former Eastern Bloc a lodestar as they sought to reform and to end old rivalries between them. This was a replay of NATO's original mission at the end of World War II. Though many remembered the Alliance principally as a barrier to Russian expansion, there had been a second purpose: NATO's founders saw it as a democratic umbrella under which old rivals could resolve their differences. Thus the early hope had been that Germany could be rebuilt and rearmed within an alliance with France, its bitter enemy. War between the two great European rivals would then become unthinkable. At the time it was a bold and risky notion—but it worked. Now, in the twenty-first century, the Central and East Europeans and eventually the states of the Balkans would follow the same course.

The fulfillment of this vision required the continuous expansion of the Alliance, however. President Clinton had begun that process, adding the Czech Republic, Poland, and Hungary in 1999. President Bush continued it, adding in 2004 Romania, Bulgaria, Slovenia, Slovakia, and, most consequentially, the Baltic states that had been forcibly incorporated into the Soviet Union. Moscow had swallowed hard and accepted the accession of Latvia, Lithuania, and Estonia. The next tranche would clearly be countries recovering from the Balkan wars: Albania, Croatia, and Macedonia.

The last would be delayed due to a somewhat bizarre dispute with Greece over the name of the country. After the breakup of Yugoslavia, Athens had lodged its objection to the use of "Macedonia" as the official name of the newly independent republic. For reasons I still do not fully understand, the Greeks claimed that its modern-day usage for a former state of Yugoslavia would somehow diminish the cultural heritage that Greeks ascribe to an empire that existed more than two millennia ago. Perhaps they felt that the population in its modern-day incarnation would somehow not live up to the legacy of the ancient homeland of Alexander the Great. As a result, the new country was called the Former Yugoslav Republic of Macedonia. But the leaders of the country wanted to enter NATO under their preferred name—who wants to be called the "former republic" of something? The Greeks objected. Tireless efforts, including through Matthew Nimetz, a special envoy for the issue, could not resolve the dispute.

I would get frustrated with the Greeks over the issue, I admit. In one meeting with my counterpart, Dora Bakoyannis, with whom I had otherwise very good relations, I lost my cool. "It was two thousand years ago!" I said with exasperation. "Who cares?"

"I have a feeling you Americans just don't understand," she countered.

"Yes, you're right," I answered, "I don't understand." But she wouldn't budge, saying that a change in policy would bring down the Greek government.

On the other hand, I couldn't understand the rigidity of the Macedonians either. I guess I felt like the Georgian who told his Macedonian counterpart, "You can call us the 'Stupid Little Republic of Georgia' if we can get into NATO." But the Macedonians persisted too. Thus, when Albania and Croatia were admitted, Macedonia was not and is still awaiting a resolution of the "name" debate before its membership in Europe's greatest military alliance can be consummated.

Despite setbacks of that kind, however, I firmly believed that the Alliance was in better shape than we'd found it as we headed toward the President's final summit in Bucharest, Romania.

But there was one issue that threatened to overshadow NATO's progress. As the Alliance moved steadily east, Moscow's tolerance was being tested. Through the establishment of the NATO-Russia Council in 2002, we'd tried to demonstrate the point that the expansion of the Alliance was meant not to antagonize Russia but to enhance stability and military cooperation in Europe. The council had made little progress largely because the Kremlin never fully embraced it. Russia's alienation from NATO was growing under the pressure of rising authoritarianism at home and irredentist policies toward the former Soviet bloc. Georgia and Ukraine were next in the queue to be considered for the Membership Action Plan (MAP). The MAP does not confer membership, but it is the process through which countries prepare for membership, undertaking necessary political and military reforms. When the question of deepening the relationship of NATO to Ukraine and Georgia by giving them a Membership Action Plan arose, Moscow's strained tolerance broke.

I'd assumed that we would not push this step within the Alliance before the President left office. When I'd met with Ukrainian President Viktor Yushchenko on the margins of Davos earlier in the year, I had told him that there was very little chance that Ukraine would be granted MAP. Sitting in a tiny chalet and noting that the very tall Yushchenko's legs were cramped practically to his chin, I realized right away that we had a problem. The Ukrainian president almost cried. "It will be a disaster, a tragedy, if we don't get the MAP," he pleaded.

Yushchenko had been elected president after the Orange Revolution and was in a testy coalition with Yulia Tymoshenko, a blonde bombshell who was a very popular political figure. Yushchenko still bore the scars of a strange incident of poisoning that had left his face distorted and his skin color an eerie purple. Though it couldn't be proven, Yushchenko and many others believed that the Russians had been responsible and that they had intended to kill him. The Ukrainian president was thus a sympathetic character, if a somewhat mercurial politician. The tensions among the "Orange forces" were exceedingly high. Tymoshenko had been coy about her support for MAP but Yushchenko had managed to make MAP a litmus test of his ability to deliver his Western friends.

We'd heard similar views from the Georgians, and, given the pressures that Moscow had been placing on Georgia, Mikheil Saakashvili's government had a good claim for the MAP as a counterweight to Russia as well. Ukraine and Georgia considered it an essential affirmation of their pro-Western orientation and—though unsaid—a shield from Moscow's pressure.

The question of what to do about granting the MAP related not only to the Kremlin's reaction but also to the reticence of some Alliance members, particularly Germany, to admit Ukraine and Georgia. Chancellor Merkel didn't trust the Georgians, whom she saw as still corrupt, and she made the point, correctly, that the Ukrainian governing coalition was a mess. France was undecided but leaned toward supporting Berlin. On the other hand, the Central and East European states saw the MAP as a test of NATO's fealty to the defense of the former Soviet territories.

So we faced a dilemma. At the NSC meeting held to consider our position, I presented the pros and cons with no recommendation. Frankly, I didn't know what to do. Though the status was not the same as membership in NATO, everyone knew that no MAP country had ever failed to gain membership, though it had taken Albania nine years. This was a big step, and the opponents would not be assuaged by the de jure differences between MAP status and actual membership: both were objectionable.

The President listened to the arguments and then came down on the side of Ukraine and Georgia. "If these two democratic states want MAP, I can't say no," he said toward the end of the meeting. I admired his principled stand. It was what I loved about George W. Bush as President—what was right mattered. *But I have to deliver this,* I thought. *This is going to be really hard.*

The President then reminded us that the stakes were high for another reason. He'd accepted an invitation from Vladimir Putin to visit Sochi, Russia, immediately after the Bucharest summit. How could the U.S. President sit down with the Russian if he failed to deliver MAP for Ukraine and Georgia? He couldn't. *But Putin is going to be in a really foul mood if the Alliance does vote for granting the MAP.* There didn't seem to be a good way out.

AS THE BUCHAREST SUMMIT approached, we intensified consultations with the Germans, trying to find a solution, Steve Hadley working closely with his German counterpart. At one point we thought we had an answer—a kind of enhanced cooperation that looked like the MAP, smelled like the MAP, but wasn't called the MAP. Unfortunately, it satisfied no one, since the Germans weren't anxious to push the relationship with the aspirants too far beyond where it currently stood. Then we tried a tactic of fixing the end of the year as a deadline for making a final decision on MAP. That didn't satisfy anyone either. We left for Bucharest with no agreement in hand.

I hated showing up for an important meeting with the crucial issue unresolved. The press is always full of predictions of failure, and in this case I had a sinking feeling that they might be right. When I arrived at the airport, I was greeted by Victoria Nuland, our ambassador to NATO. Toria, a career Foreign Service officer, had worked for the Vice President before being appointed our representative to the Alliance in 2005. She was the first woman to hold the job and she was extremely capable and well regarded among her diplomatic peers. Thus, when Toria told me that we had big trouble with the Germans, my heart sank. At the hotel, I met up with Dan Fried, the assistant secretary of state for European and Eurasian affairs, who'd been trying to find a face-saving solution that would be acceptable to both the Germans and us. None was in sight.

The President, Steve Hadley, and I conferred briefly before the evening dinners were to begin. The President would join the heads of state and government, and I would dine separately with the foreign ministers. As it turned out, the leaders spent little time on the issue, hoping that the ministers would resolve it. As a result, the issue dominated our dinner and produced one of the most pointed and contentious debates with our allies that I'd ever experienced. In fact, it was the most heated that I saw in my entire time as secretary.

The Romanian foreign minister asked me to speak first, but I demurred, allowing Frank-Walter Steinmeier of Germany to take the floor. I didn't want to put him on the spot, but I'd decided that it was better to have him make Berlin's arguments, then have the East Europeans speak. That way I would have the last word.

Steinmeier made the German arguments, concentrating on the weakness of the Ukrainian coalition, a point everyone understood. But then he strayed into territory that he shouldn't have. He said that the "frozen conflicts" in Georgia made it impossible to grant MAP. After the breakup of the Soviet Union, Abkhazia and South Ossetia, territories that were ethnically distinct from Georgia and with a heavy Russian population, had tried to secede from Georgia. Moscow had taken their side in the ensuing conflict. The regions were balanced on a knife's edge, with sporadic fighting and increasing encroachment of Russian military forces (sent there in the early 1990s as international peacekeepers) into the disputed areas. Diplomatic efforts had failed to resolve the problem, hence the term "frozen conflict."

"If NATO had taken that view, West Germany wouldn't have been admitted in 1949," one of the Central European ministers countered. "You were one big frozen conflict until 1990," another offered. *Uh-oh*, I thought, *this is getting ugly*. The Polish foreign minister, Radosław "Radek" Sikorski, took the floor. Radek, a U.S. educated politician who is married to an American journalist, was a fierce defender of the prerogatives of Central Europe and a great orator. I sat back in my chair. "We've tried to be sensitive to German concerns in the EU," Radek said. "You're always saying, 'Germany needs this and Germany needs that.'

Well, this is a matter of national security for us. And now you come and tell us you are more worried for Moscow than for your allies." *That's not really what Frank-Walter said,* I thought. Then, referencing the Munich appeasement of 1938 without saying the words, Radek reminded the German that Eastern Europe's forty-year captivity under Soviet rule had been thanks to Berlin.

Frank-Walter was devastated. He would later say it was the most brutal experience of his time as foreign minister. But I couldn't intervene on his behalf; in fact, I needed to press the advantage. "There are times when allies have to stand together," I said. "MAP does not confer immediate membership, but it is of great value to Ukraine and Georgia—and it is deeply desired by our new members. Moscow needs to know that the Cold War is over and Russia lost. We can't let it split the Alliance."

Nobody came to Frank-Walter's defense, and the meeting ended. The next day, Chancellor Merkel told the President that she was never again leaving me alone in a room with her foreign minister. But I wasn't the one who'd done the damage. It was the East Europeans, recalling the inglorious German past, who'd set the tone. I didn't think we'd get MAP, but I did believe the Germans might be ready for a deal. Christoph Heusgen, the chancellor's foreign policy advisor, asked to see Steve the next morning along with the French and the British. There would be "plus ones," people to take notes. Steve and I decided I would be the "plus one." We invited the Poles and the Romanians too. There wouldn't be any more backroom deals between the old members of the Alliance at the expense of the new ones.

The meeting was inconclusive, but it was clear that Germany wanted to avoid a confrontation, as did we. The language that was worked out was acceptable, including a promise to have the foreign ministers review Ukraine and Georgia's progress toward MAP at the next meeting in December. There was a lot of forward-leaning language about the two country's prospects for MAP in the future.

When we arrived in the meeting room, the President asked me to go over the statement with the chancellor. She agreed, and behind a curtain adjacent to the hall, Heusgen, Hadley, Sikorski, and I finished the work. Radek had been certain that Poland would concur and that would bring along the other East Europeans. But when the general session started, the Polish president objected, saying simply, "We want MAP now!" *What happened?* I wondered.

The chancellor and I huddled again and then called the East and Central European leaders over to a corner of the room. Then she did something quite remarkable and very savvy: she sat down in the middle of the group of her peers—she, after all, had been raised in East Germany. Patiently, we went over the language in the only common language we had: Russian. After a little while, I walked away and went back to talk to the President. Jonas Gahr Støre, the Norwegian foreign minister, came over. "You'd better go back over there," he said. "I'm not sure this is coming out right in English." I hastened over to the group. The language now read, "Ukraine and Georgia *will* become members of NATO."

The Alliance had failed to grant immediate MAP status but was bestowing the now-certain prospect of future membership onto those countries, a point I made to the somewhat skeptical press. Before our agreement, I told reporters, it had not been clear whether NATO would even consider Ukrainian membership, and many had suggested that its expansion into the Caucasus was off-limits. "That question has been answered with language that NATO welcomes Ukraine's and Georgia's Euro-Atlantic aspirations for membership," I said. "We agreed today that these countries will become members of NATO. And so those questions are now off the table, and it is a matter of when, not whether." I was happy with the outcome. We could work with the agreed formulation. The document passed by acclamation.

LATER IN THE DAY, Vladimir Putin arrived at the NATO summit for the last time as Russia's president. In a few months, he would step down to become prime minister, leaving the presidency to his handpicked successor, Dmitri Medvedev. No one expected a diminution of his power, but it was a change of leadership of sorts.

Putin's valedictory was for the most part unremarkable—a string of complaints about how Russia had been treated despite its outstretched hand of friendship. Toward the end he seemed to make a threat against Ukraine, reminding the assembled that the now-independent state's eastern part was Russian, both ethnically and historically. Nonetheless, one couldn't help but feel that Putin's appearance only underscored the defeat of the Soviet Union at the end of the Cold War. After all, George W. Bush, Angela Merkel, and Nicolas Sarkozy were not speaking before the Warsaw Pact. Moscow's European military alliance had long since ceased to exist.

We headed for the car and encountered Putin on the steps of the palace. "I'll see you in Sochi," Putin said, with more than a hint of uncertainty in his voice.

"Yes," the President confirmed. "I'll see you in Sochi." Somehow we'd split the difference enough to make the last major meeting of the U.S. and Russian presidents possible.

THE SOCHI VISIT in April was a bit anticlimactic. Putin proudly took us on a tour of the facilities for the 2014 Olympics. I remember being struck by the ramshackle appearance of the city and the proposed sites for athletic events. *They have a lot of work to do,* I thought.

We did manage to issue a declaration on U.S.-Russian relations that demonstrated that—despite the problems—our cooperation had been productive. In reading through it, I was reminded how much the two countries had done in the areas of counterterrorism and counterproliferation. Our joint achievements included proposals for an international fuel bank to prevent countries from independently enriching uranium; a nuclear terrorism initiative; cooperation in the Proliferation Security Initiative; and work on future generations of proliferation-resistant nuclear reactors. On Iran and North Korea, we didn't always see eye to eye on tactics, but we had managed successive rounds of sanctions. And on counterterrorism the two cooperated through joint actions in law enforcement, intelligence sharing, terrorism finance, and technology and transportation security.

The paper affirmed our desire to keep working toward a missile defense solution, building upon our agreement in principle at Kennebunkport the year before. But despite the fact that Bob Gates and I made two trips to Russia, we were unable to move the ball very far on that issue. Kennebunkport had given both sides hope that we might find a solution. The Russians still didn't like the idea of missile defense components in Poland and the Czech Republic, but Putin had demonstrated a willingness to at least listen to our proposals. He had told us that the ideas seemed creative and promising, and he had gone out of his way to emphasize before the press the goodwill between us. In advance of a follow-up meeting in Moscow, Steve, Bob Gates, and I had browbeaten the bureaucracy into a far-reaching set of ideas—including the stationing of Russian military personnel at the missile defense bases. Bob had even offered to leave the missile launcher silos empty until the United States and Russia had a common understanding of the long-range ballistic missile threat from countries like Iran.

Then we met with Lavrov and the military, and the "experts" devoured the proposals, inserting their standard refrains and qualifiers that had bogged down previous agreements. That pushed us further away from resolution. To be fair, our own draft of the proposal, which the Pentagon and the State Department had sent to the Russians to follow up on our visit, had been long on bureaucratic conservatism and short on innovation. The Czechs and the Poles themselves were none too happy with the idea of Russian soldiers on their territory, noting that the term "presence" had been used as a euphemism for "occupation" during the Cold War.

In fact, I saw this sentiment firsthand. In the Czech Republic, there was some resistance to the deployment in Parliament, but many Czechs, mostly young people, had organized themselves to rally votes in favor of missile defense. During one visit to Prague I met with Czech Foreign Minister Karel Schwarzenberg, who looks like he could have been a Hapsburg aristocrat, to reaffirm our missile defense intentions. After a black-tie dinner, Karel asked if I would accompany him to his favorite pub. Overruling my security detail on this one, I decided to go along. My savvy and good-humored assistant Anne Lyons, who later came to California to lead my staff, was caught off-guard. There, in a dark basement bar, we met with the organizers of the campaign for missile defense while Anne and my detail frantically tried to cover up raunchy posters on the walls. It was quite a scene. The organizers looked as though they should be protesting a war, and we were still in our formal wear; but I was delighted to meet them, take pictures, and down a very good Czech pilsner. I was sure the Czechs would be solid against Russian pressure, but we would still have work to do.

Bob and I kept pushing our own bureaucracies and had traveled to Moscow in October 2007. This time the atmosphere was somewhat chillier. Putin kept us waiting in the anteroom for more than thirty minutes after we had been announced and followed to his office by the press. In the meeting, he complained that the negotiations weren't moving and that the papers that we kept sending showed none of the creativity that Bob and I had expressed orally. Despite a more cordial discussion at a second meeting in March 2008 where we negotiated language in the Sochi declaration, we still could not make substantial progress on the issue. Success in getting a detailed plan that was acceptable to both sides eluded us. My own surmise is that the general staff didn't really want a deal. It hated the idea of missile defense, despite all of our efforts to remove any elements that could have been thought to be remotely threatening. I also suspect that the geographic location of the sites was more important than anything else; Poland and the Czech Republic had been members of the Warsaw Pact. The Russians couldn't swallow the "encroachment" eastward. By the time of Sochi in April our efforts had run out of steam.

The Sochi declaration wasn't exactly the landmark Basic Principles of U.S.-Soviet Relations that Henry Kissinger and his Soviet counterpart, Andrei Gromyko, had signed at the height of the Cold War. That document had had the feel of two superpowers dividing up the responsibility for running the world. But at least there was a framework document that defied the conventional wisdom that our relationship had been all about conflict. Kissinger himself later remarked that he would have "loved to have had a document of that kind."

Sochi also gave President Bush a chance to spend a little time with Dmitri Medvedev. I'd met him several times, and though I doubted he'd be powerful enough to challenge his political sponsor, he was interesting in his own right. Medvedev came from a different generation: he was a university student when the Soviet Union collapsed, and, unlike the former KGB official whom he would soon replace, Medvedev had never actually been a member of the Communist Party. I remembered one particularly enlightening encounter with him, a meeting that revealed the generational shift that was taking place.

I had met earlier in the day at the U.S. ambassador's residence with a group of young Russian entrepreneurs—bankers, lawyers, and businesspeople. When I launched into my points about the absence of independent television stations in Russia, I expected a sympathetic response. "Your television looks like it did when I was a graduate student here in 1979," I said, suddenly realizing that that must have seemed like ancient history to them.

"Yes, I know," one of the young men responded. "Here is what our news looks like: The first story is about the great man [Putin]. The second is about agricultural production being up. The third is about whatever innocent people the United States killed today. The fourth is about the chosen successor to the great man." *That about sums it up*, I thought. But then he asked, "But who watches television? We're all on the Internet."

Shortly thereafter, I went to see Medvedev and delivered the same points about the media. "I know," he said, taking little time to defend the system. "But who watches television? We're all on the Internet." I was struck by the fact that he'd used the same argument that the young entrepreneurs had made, an almost identical dismissal of the importance of television. Maybe things were changing in Russia.

We sat with Medvedev at the small, festive dinner that Putin had arranged at the official presidential residence in Sochi. The president-in-waiting didn't seem particularly confident, and he was determined to avoid substantive issues. So the evening turned out to be mostly a social occasion with traditional Russian dancing, which the President unwisely tried to join. I couldn't believe my eyes when George W. Bush attempted to do one of those Cossack splits, almost failing to get up despite his legendary fitness. Well, the Russians appreciated the effort. And the evening seemed a bit like a last lap for U.S.-Russian relations in our term.

In engaging Medvedev, I did have a sense that we were encountering not just a leader from a different generation, but one who, left to his own devices, might alter Russia's path. Since becoming president, Medvedev has championed Russia as a leader in the knowledge-based economy. He has argued that his country should not be content to be principally an exporter of oil, natural gas, coal, and metals—a profile more befitting a developing country. (Approximately 80 percent of Russia's export revenues come from these natural resources.) The Russian president rightly makes the point that his country has brilliant mathematicians and software engineers. But this obscures the fact that many of Russia's most talented entrepreneurs have chosen to emigrate or at least to work as green-card holders in Palo Alto and Tel Aviv. The unreliability of contracts, insufficient intellectual property protections, and the inconsistent application of the rule of law all hinder the emergence of a knowledge-based economy.

Medvedev's vision for Russia clashes not only with its current economic profile but also the power structure that supports it. Vladimir Putin is a defender of a statist economy. Personal fortunes and a fair amount of political violence have been characteristic of that course— one that has been fueled by high oil prices and sustained by Putin's authoritarian grip.

Russia will always be a major exporter of oil and natural gas. But will it be more able to capitalize on the industriousness and innovation of its people to ascend to higher levels of the global economy? It is a question that has implications not just for the country's domestic development but for its interaction with the world as well.

52

WAR BREAKS OUT IN GEORGIA

SOCHI WAS THE high point of our last year with Putin's Russia. By the summer of 2008 tensions were growing over Kosovo, and the ever-simmering Russian hatred of Georgia was reaching a boiling point.

The denouement on Kosovo had been approaching since our discussions with Russia and NATO regarding the Conventional Forces Treaty the year before. The Balkans, which had been dubbed the "powder keg of Europe" for the early twentieth-century wars that had begun there, was relatively quiet for the bulk of our term. Some countries—Albania, Croatia, Macedonia, and Slovenia—were doing rather well, economically and politically. Bosnia and Herzegovina was and still is a mess, with three presidents and three separate security forces. The Dayton Accords had signified the end of the tragic Bosnian war, but they had also established two governments and one autonomous district: the Federation of Bosnia and Herzegovina, which is populated mostly by Bosniaks and Croats, and Republika Srpska, populated by Serbs. A third self-governing district belonging to both the Federation and Srpska, the Brčko Municipality, is mostly Muslim. I tried, in 2005–2006, to coax those substates toward constitutional reform to strengthen the integration of the state. By constitutional requirement the presidency of Bosnia and Herzegovina must be occupied by three individuals: one rotating chair of the presidency and two other members. The head of state must consist of one Croat, one Serb, and one Bosniak. When, in 2005, the three presidents showed up at the State Department, I knew that it was a fool's errand to try for greater integration. I had to make sure that each one spoke in turn, and I needed to address all three, by name, every time I spoke. *This is going nowhere,* I thought. And it didn't. The constitutional referendum to consolidate the government failed in 2006, but Bosnia and Herzegovina was no worse off than it had been before we tried.

Conversely, the problem of Kosovo threatened to break into another open conflict. During the 1990s NATO air campaign to remove the murderous Slobodan Milošević from power, the Albanian Kosovars, who constituted more than 90 percent of the population of the region, were subjected to ethnic cleansing. Milošević's Serbian troops evacuated entire towns—forcing the women and children to march to Kosovo's borders while slaughtering the men and dumping their bodies in mass graves. In total, Milošević's troops forced 1.3 million Albanian Kosovars from their homes. When he was finally stopped by NATO and deposed, the United Nations established the Interim Administration Mission in Kosovo (UNMIK) to control the region and manage conflicts. Several diplomatic efforts failed to adequately resolve Kosovo's status situation. So in 2007 the highly respected Finnish former president Martti Ahtisaari, acting on behalf of the United Nations, tried once again to find a solution to the problem. When he could not, he presented the Comprehensive Proposal for the Kosovo Status Settlement (also known as the Ahtisaari Plan), a report that effectively recommended eventual independence for the Kosovars.

We were firmly in support of the Ahtisaari proposal, and I asked Ambassador Frank Wisner, a seasoned retired diplomat, to act as special envoy to help us implement the plan. The French, British, Germans, and most of the other Europeans were united behind the effort. The Russians, though, were adamantly opposed, taking the side of their allies the Serbs. The Europeans and we were unable to come to agreement with Russia and decided that we had no choice but to back independence for Kosovo. That resulted in a messy process. It wasn't possible to go to the Security Council for a vote establishing an independent Kosovo; the Russians would surely be joined by the Chinese in a veto, since Beijing was worried about the secessionist precedent for Taiwan and Tibet.

The only choice was to manage the problem in a way that prevented violence, convincing as many countries as possible to recognize Kosovo. Our task was to hold the allies together in the face of Moscow's resistance and to deliver a decision before the Kosovars became impatient and took to the streets. And I felt strongly that we needed to find a way to placate the Serbs, for whom I had some sympathy. The Serbians had elected a Western-oriented president, Boris Tadić, who wanted badly to integrate into Europe and NATO.

Dan Fried was the point person for the diplomacy, working closely with Wisner, Judy Ansley on Steve's staff, and with the Pentagon. The United States had troops in the region, and there was great concern that any violence might embroil them—and the much more substantial European contingents—in a civil war. The other major concern was that Belgrade might try, little by little, to annex the upper third of Kosovo, where the radical Serbs lived. I was pretty sure that Moscow didn't want that, but the Russians weren't very helpful in restraining their ally's incendiary talk.

As the summer of 2007 wore on and the Kosovars became more agitated, I pressed the Europeans to act. Our idea was that we would recognize the new state in concert and bring as many others along as possible. The NATO allies, particularly the French and the Germans, kept stalling, hoping for a miraculous change of heart in Moscow. Every meeting ended with a promise to get on with it but more and more time passed. When, in mid-June, the French insisted on another month's delay, the President was furious. At an NSC meeting the next week, I found myself defending the allies' desire for more time, despite my own reservations. The President called Putin, who told him what Lavrov had told me: "We can accept anything that the Serbs accept."

That, of course, wasn't helpful. At the G8 summit in Heiligendamm, Germany, Nicolas Sarkozy proposed another 120 days of negotiations at the conclusion of which, if an agreement had not been reached, the Security Council would endorse the Ahtisaari Plan. After the Heiligendamm Summit, on June 9, the President called for Kosovo's independence at a press conference in Rome. He repeated his support for independence and the Ahtisaari Plan in Albania the following day. "One more month," the President told me. "And then we recognize them if we have to do it alone. I've promised them, and we have to carry through." The President would eventually agree, however, to the Sarkozy proposal extending negotiations another 120 days only with the understanding that it would be the final delay.

On February 18, 2008, we officially recognized Kosovo, as did many other European states. By the end of the year, fifty-three states would recognize Kosovo: most of the European countries, the United States, Canada, Australia, and several countries in Africa, Latin America, and the Middle East. Tadić survived, helped by a decision that the United States made to secure a place for Belgrade within NATO's Partnership for Peace. The Serbs had been blocked from joining because they hadn't yet hunted down and handed over the Balkan war criminals Ratko Mladić and Radovan Karadžić. I felt strongly that we couldn't wait for that to happen. Serbia needed some evidence that there would be a place for it in Europe and NATO if the wound of Kosovo were ever to heal.

Today Kosovo is independent (though Moscow does not recognize it) and Serbia is moving closer to Europe, despite continued bitterness. On the day we recognized Kosovo, Brian Gunderson asked if I felt comfortable creating yet another weak state that might be unsustainable. "What choice did we have?" I asked. And added, "But in time Kosovo will be alright. It was the right thing to do."

THE KOSOVO PROBLEM paled in comparison to the brush fires igniting in Georgia. Over the previous year tensions had been growing in the already unstable regions of Abkhazia and South Ossetia, much of it fueled by Moscow. In the spring of 2008, every week seemed to bring some new provocation to South Ossetia, from increases in the number of Russian troops (ostensibly to engage in railroad construction) to plans to issue Russian passports to the citizens living in what was Georgian territory. Lavrov had sent me a long memo detailing Russia's grievances with Saakashvili and the Georgians—some of it legitimate, some of it concocted. It was, nonetheless, a warning sign. It was only a matter of time until a spark ignited open conflict in the area.

During a visit to Germany on June 23 for a conference on Palestinian state building, Frank-Walter Steinmeier and I developed a diplomatic plan to respond to the deteriorating situation in three phases: the first phase would include assurances that force would not be used by any party (one of Moscow's demands of the Georgians); the second phase would involve the return of refugees and practical cooperation on the development of institutions; the third phase would be the final settlement of Abkhazia's political status. Frank left for Tbilisi, Abkhazia, and Moscow shortly after. He told our diplomats a few days later to say that he was making progress.

I went to Tbilisi a few weeks later, on July 10, on the heels of a trip to the Czech Republic to sign the missile defense agreement that the Russians had tried to prevent. The press tried to link the two: was this a trip intended to poke a stick in Moscow's eye? It was not, though I am sure the Kremlin read it that way.

Saakashvili met me on the terrace of Kopala Restaurant, which featured breathtaking views of the city. The Georgian president, who is big and demonstrative, pointed out the beautiful restoration work that was under way on monasteries, churches, and other historic buildings. He was very proud of his leadership of the country and rightly so: Georgia's corruption levels (according to the Corruption Perception Index) had declined dramatically beginning with Saakashvili's police reform initiatives in which thousands of corrupt officers had been fired and the department completely rebranded. The country was also trying to shield itself from Russia's pressure, by attempting to use gas from Azerbaijan instead of Russia. And despite Moscow's embargo of Georgian goods, the economy continued to grow even though large segments of the population still lived in dire poverty.

It was, nonetheless, hard to get Saakashvili to see that all of his gains were at risk because of the worsening situation in Abkhazia and South Ossetia. He's proud and can be impulsive, and we all worried that he might allow Moscow to provoke him to use force. In fact, he himself successfully provoked conflict in another breakaway part of the country, Adjara, and benefited when it had been reintegrated into Georgia through domestic and international pressure. The precedent, we feared, might make him think that he could get away with a repeat performance in the territories located closer to Putin's beloved Sochi.

"Mr. President," I said, trying to shift his attention away from the rooftop tour of the city, "you need to sign a no-use-of-force pledge."

"How can I do that when Putin is doing the things he's doing?" he answered, suggesting that he'd sign only if the Russian gave him something in return.

"I'll talk to the Russians, but you don't have a choice," I told him.

"You can't use force, and so the threat to do so doesn't do you any good. Sign the pledge now while you have international support."

We went back and forth for more than an hour, Saakashvili stubbornly refusing to yield. Finally, I thought I'd better get tougher. "Mr. President, whatever you do, don't let the Russians provoke you. You remember when President Bush said that Moscow would try to get you to do something stupid. And don't engage Russian military forces. No one will come to your aid, and you will lose," I said sternly.

He got the point, looking as if he'd just lost his last friend. I tried to soften what I'd said by repeating our pledge to defend Georgia's territorial integrity—with words. He asked if I'd say so publicly. I did, avoiding any language that might be misinterpreted as committing us to Georgia's defense with arms.

THE END OF JULY had been brutal with travel to Europe, the Middle East, Singapore, Australia, New Zealand, and Samoa—all in the space of two weeks. *If I can just get to August 8! I'll play golf and visit with friends at the Greenbrier,* I promised myself. *And then in two weeks, I'll be off to Beijing for the close of the Olympics. Just get to August 8!*

There had been some violence in and around South Ossetia during the first days of August. Yet diplomatic activities were continuing, and there had been a relatively good report from a meeting between the European envoy and his Russian counterpart. I was a little unnerved when Dan Fried and Kurt Volker, his principle deputy, dropped by on the evening of the sixth to say that Matthew Bryza, a deputy assistant secretary for the region, was on the ground in Georgia and reported that the fighting was increasing. I was quite alarmed when I learned that Russia had evacuated more than eight hundred people from the area.

On the night of August 7, the dam broke. Despite Georgia's unilateral ceasefire earlier in the day, South Ossetian rebel forces continued shelling ethnic Georgian villages in and around the capital, Tskhinvali. In response, the Georgian military commenced a heavy military offensive against the rebels after a senior Georgian military official declared that Tbilisi had decided to restore "constitutional order" in South

Ossetia. Only thirty minutes after Georgia began its offensive, Russia came to the aid of the South Ossetian rebels, moving its 58th Army tanks through the Roki Tunnel into Georgian territory.

Dan Fried updated me throughout the night. I waited anxiously at my apartment on the morning of the eighth, trying to decide whether to go ahead to the Greenbrier. My family and friends had gathered for the trip by car to West Virginia and I was their ride, since my security detail could go only if they were taking me. The stranded vacationers sat in my living room eating turkey sandwiches while I tried to sort out the problem. After a little while, I decided to set out for the Greenbrier. I could always come back if I needed to.

Or . . . I could just stay on the telephone in my cabin. It was August, and, as Steve Hadley often put it, we were maldeployed. The President was attending the Olympic Games in Beijing, and Bob Gates was in Munich. The time difference with China made it difficult to conduct conference calls, but at least twice a day I talked with the President. He had found himself sitting next to Putin at the Olympic opening ceremonies, engaging in awkward conversations in which the Russian alternately accused the Georgians of genocide and feigned ignorance of what Russia's troops were doing.

We decided that we didn't want the conflict to become a U.S.-Russia row and that the European Union and the Organization for Security and Co-operation in Europe (OSCE) should be actively involved in the diplomacy. I talked repeatedly to Bernard Kouchner, the French foreign minister, and Alexander Stubb, the Finnish foreign minister and head of the OSCE, trying to guide the two of them toward a common message. I issued a statement calling on Russia to "cease attacks on Georgia by aircraft and missiles, respect Georgia's territorial integrity and withdraw its ground combat forces from Georgian soil."

By August 11 the Georgians claimed that they'd withdrawn their forces from South Ossetia. Frankly, the remoteness of the area made it hard to tell, and the information that we were receiving was mixed. We continued to pressure the Georgians to stop any military activities, hoping to remove any pretext for Moscow's continued assault.

Then, that afternoon, Sergei Lavrov called me for the second time during the crisis. The first call had been largely a stream of invectives against the leadership in Tbilisi. But this time he was very calm. "We have three demands," he said.

"What are they?" I asked.

"The first two are that the Georgians sign the no-use-of-force pledge and that their troops return to barracks," he told me.

"Done," I answered.

Saakashvili would have to swallow hard, but I was sure we could insist that he accept the Russian terms. But then Sergei said, "The other demand is just between us. Misha Saakashvili has to go." I couldn't believe my ears and I reacted out of instinct, not analysis.

"Sergei, the secretary of state of the United States does not have a conversation with the Russian foreign minister about overthrowing a democratically elected president," I said. "The third condition has just become public because I'm going to call everyone I can and tell them that Russia is demanding the overthrow of the Georgian president."

"I said it was between us," he repeated.

"No, it's not between us. Everyone is going to know." The conversation ended. I called Steve Hadley to tell him about the Russian demand. Then I called the British, the French, and several others. That afternoon the UN Security Council was meeting. I asked our representative to inform the Council as well. Lavrov was furious, saying that he'd never had a colleague divulge the contents of a diplomatic conversation. I felt I had no choice. If the Georgians wanted to punish Saakashvili for the war, they would have a chance to do it through their own constitutional processes. But the Russians had no right to insist on his removal. The whole thing had an air of the Soviet period, when Moscow had controlled the fate of leaders throughout Eastern Europe. I was certainly not going to be party to a return to those days.

The next morning I gave up on any notion of a vacation and returned to Washington. The President was back from Beijing, and Steve was able to gather the NSC for a meeting. The session was a bit unruly, with a fair amount of chest beating about the Russians. At one point Steve Hadley intervened, something he rarely did. There was all kind of loose talk about what threats the United States might make. "I want to ask a question," he said in his low-key way. "Are we prepared to go to war with Russia over Georgia?" That quieted the room, and we settled into a more productive conversation of what we could do.

Our sources of information were not very good, often filtered through the panicked Georgian political and military officials. Admiral Mike Mullen, the chairman of the Joint Chiefs of Staff, had established a link with the Russian chief of staff, largely to prevent any miscalculation between our forces. It was also a very useful channel to take the pulse of the Russians. French President Sarkozy had succeeded in negotiating a ceasefire, but the Russian forces seemed to be ignoring it. The confusion was exacerbated by the fact that Medvedev kept insisting that his forces had withdrawn when they hadn't. The new Russian president didn't seem to be on top of the situation. That was a problem too.

As we sat in the Situation Room, dark reports were coming from the Georgians that the Russian army was headed for Tbilisi, having forced the Georgian army out of Gori, a small town only forty miles west of the capital. Saakashvili kept calling the White House to say that his government was about to be overthrown. After the second desperate call, we decided that our friends needed visible help. We sent humanitarian supplies by military transport—a visible statement of support that might at least back Moscow off. And we decided that I'd go to Georgia.

Since the French were now leading the diplomacy, the President called Sarkozy and offered to send me to Paris too. The French president was in the south of the country and did not want to go back to the capital. So, on August 14, we met on the veranda of the magnificent presidential vacation home, Le Fort de Brégançon, in Bormes-les-Mimosas on the Mediterranean.

I asked Sarkozy how I could help. He explained that he needed the Georgians to sign the document that he'd negotiated, but that Saakashvili was hesitant. That was surprising since the Georgian had told President Bush that he just wanted the war stopped. Then I looked at the document and immediately saw the problem. The French had negotiated a "15 km security exclusion zone," in which Russian troops would be permitted to stay for an unspecified period of time. Georgia isn't very big, and the zone seemed to permit the invaders to occupy key roads in the country as well as the town of Gori, located only about sixty-four kilometers from Tbilisi.

I asked whether anyone had looked at a map to see what the zone covered. Much to the astonishment of our delegation, they hadn't. Jean-David Levitte, who was Sarkozy's advisor on foreign policy and a terrific diplomat, protested that the agreement could not possibly have that effect. "I will call our ambassador in Tbilisi and ask him about the geographic limitations," he said. The chagrined Levitte came back to say that the consequences of the exclusion zone were exactly as we'd feared.

Now the question was how to save French diplomacy from its own mistake and end the war. We agreed that Sarkozy would write a letter to both Saakashvili and Medvedev that was specific this time about what the exclusion zone meant and how long the Russian forces could stay. I'd take that letter to the Georgians and get their agreement. We took advantage of Chancellor Merkel's meeting in Sochi with the Russian president to secure Moscow's final consent.

When I arrived in Tbilisi, it was easy to see the stress on the faces of the Georgian leaders. They looked so young—indeed, the oldest was about forty—and they were really tired, having failed to sleep for several days. We met in Saakashvili's office, the television blaring in the background. When I handed him the letter, he asked if they could have a moment to look it over. "Take as much time as you want," I said. There was an audible sigh of relief.

"The French just gave us the paper and said sign it," Eka Tkeshelashvili, the foreign minister, said. Though I doubted that it had been exactly like that, I was determined to take some of the pressure off of them.

"We'll work through it together, but get your lawyers to look it over carefully," I said.

Finally we had an agreement. I asked Dan Fried to call Jean-David Levitte to see how it was going in Moscow. The two went back and forth on the phone as I was talking with Saakashvili and his senior advisors. After intense work on both sides, the agreement was signed, though it would be several more days before their forces complied with the terms and Russian forces never completely withdrew to their pre-conflict positions. And even then, two weeks after we announced the agreement, Moscow would declare Abkhazia and South Ossetia independent, further exacerbating the hostility between Georgia and Russia.

Saakashvili and I walked outside to meet the press. It was unbearably hot in Tbilisi, and I was anticipating a short encounter. I was also worried about the capricious, emotional, and exhausted Georgian president and what he might say. "Mr. President, just thank the Europeans and the Americans for standing with you. Say something encouraging to your people about ending the war. Leave any comment about the Russians to me," I said.

The press conference began smoothly, but as he kept speaking, I could see that the Georgian's blood pressure was starting to rise. With halting speech he continued, as if trying to decide what to say next. Saakashvili speaks wonderful English, so I knew that wasn't the problem. All of a sudden his language became aggressive. He started calling the Russians barbarians and claimed their tanks were "on a roll" and would not stop. *Okay,* I thought, *I expected some tough words to the Russians. We're still all right.* Then he started in on the Europeans, referencing Munich and appeasement. *Oh no! What is he doing?*

After he finished his twenty-minute tirade I tried to repair the damage by explaining the French participation in the ceasefire and exhorting the Russians to end the conflict. *Time to get out of here,* I decided. The press conference ended. I was so mad at Saakashvili that I couldn't even speak. I shook his hand and got into the car with Eka, the foreign minister, for the short ride to a hospital to visit victims of the war. "He's blown it," I told her. Eka arranged for us to give a last-minute press statement at the airport, where we both thanked the Europeans before I left.

We held a NATO foreign ministers meeting in Brussels a few days after the agreement was signed. I found the allies surprisingly charitable toward Saakashvili, but a few did say that he had demonstrated why MAP for Georgia was not a good idea. I tried to keep the focus on the Russian transgressions, and indeed the NATO-Russia Council was suspended indefinitely for their incursion into Georgia. The Alliance issued a declaration of its support for Georgia and called on Russia to remove its troops from the area. Most important, NATO reiterated its intention to "support the territorial integrity, independence and sovereignty of Georgia and to support its democratically elected government and to deny Russia the strategic objective of undermining that democracy." The next day, I went to Poland to sign a missile defense agreement. I didn't intend to send a message to Russia; the time had simply come. But it was, of course, taken that way. Partially that was due to the Poles' perception of the situation, not ours. The Russo-Georgian conflict had a huge effect on Poland—the Polish public was alarmed and worried about Russian aggression as a result of what had happened to Georgia. So while we went to Poland to sign the missile defense agreement regardless of the conflict, the Polish public shifted public perception of the intention of the agreement to defense against Russian aggression.

Moscow paid a price for its invasion of Georgia, largely because the Kremlin overreached. There was a lot of anger at Saakashvili, whom many Europeans accused of provoking the crisis. But Lavrov's insistence that the Georgian president must be removed was a bridge too far. Moscow could still invade a small neighbor and defeat its army as in the old days. But it could no longer march to the capital and overthrow the government. And the integration of Russia's economy into the international system turned out to be a constraint as well. The Russian stock market appeared to have been punished viciously for the instability the Kremlin had caused, necessitating the suspension of trading on the exchange for two days.

At the UNGA a month later, Sergei Lavrov and I met for the first time since the war. "Sergei," I told him in private, "you did what I could never have done. You made Misha Saakashvili the darling of the international community. Now the Georgians have more reconstruction money than they can spend [$1 billion], and your troops are stuck in South Ossetia with the resounding diplomatic support of Hamas and Nicaragua." The press was all over us, wondering if our relationship had survived the events in Georgia. At our meeting we agreed to pass a Security Council resolution on Iran simply reaffirming past resolutions. The reason was to send a signal to Iran that the Georgian war had not caused us to abandon our joint efforts toward Tehran. It was never quite the same, but we managed to work together for the rest of our term. Nonetheless, I'm sure Lavrov looked forward to the arrival of another team in Washington.

It was a rather bitter end to what had been a hopeful start for U.S.-Russia relations at that first meeting in Slovenia. I gave a speech at the German Marshall Fund in Washington that September to put it all in perspective. Essentially I reminded the world of all we'd done to reach out to Moscow and some of our cooperative efforts. But the problem, I told my audience, lay in Russia's inability to come to terms with the post–Cold War order. The relationship hadn't fallen apart around Iran, North Korea, or arms control. We had achieved good cooperation in the Middle East and excellent collaboration in the fight against terrorism and nuclear proliferation. The problem had to do with the Russian periphery and former sphere of influence. Moscow believed that it still had special privileges on the territory of the former Soviet Union and the Warsaw Pact. We believed that the newly independent states had the right to choose their friends and their alliances. That had turned out to be an irreconcilable difference.

53

CEMENTING KEY RELATIONSHIPS
WITH IRAQ AND INDIA

I RETURNED TO BAGHDAD on August 21 to try to solidify the terms of a status of forces agreement, as well as an accompanying strategic framework agreement, which would set the foundation for our long-term bilateral relationship with a fully sovereign Iraq. The United States signs status of forces agreements, or SOFAs, with foreign countries to define the parameters under which our military is able to maintain a presence within their jurisdictions. The President wanted to regularize our presence in Iraq in anticipation of major U.S. troop withdrawals, first from the cities and towns and then from the rest of the country. The draft agreement with Iraq was almost done when I arrived, but Prime Minister Nouri al-Maliki had balked at some of the language that granted immunity to U.S. troops from Iraqi law. Given that our forces were already subject to strict codes of conduct and a system of military justice, we believed adamantly that no U.S. soldier should be subject to Iraq's nascent judicial system, even when off duty or outside U.S. military bases. Our SOFAs with other countries differed somewhat on that point, but there was simply no other way to protect our forces from misplaced reprisals in Iraq's underdeveloped legal structures.

The other major issue was what we'd say about timetables for eventual withdrawal. Maliki was facing nationalist pressures and needed, for political reasons, to be able to say that all U.S. forces would be gone by a specific deadline: the end of 2011. The Iraqis had already been taking on more responsibility for security and would assume full control over Al Anbar province on September 1. But we'd hoped to avoid setting a firm date for departure in order to allow conditions on the ground to dictate our decisions. Some also expressed concern that a firm date might give an impression of being driven out of the country. There were many arduous negotiating sessions between their team and ours, which was led by Brett McGurk, the senior director for Iraq and Afghanistan at the National Security Council. But we couldn't come to an agreement.

When I went to see Maliki in August, I left thinking our team had nailed down the final details of the language. If the security situation remained stable, the United States was prepared to remove all U.S. combat troops by the end of 2011 but leave a contingent force of as many as 40,000 soldiers to assist the Iraqis with training and logistics. However, when I got back to Washington, he reneged, calling for the withdrawal of *all* U.S. forces by the end of 2011.

The process of negotiating the agreement was arduous. Every time the consensus failed inside the Iraqi political system, Maliki asked for more concessions. The President swallowed hard but pushed forward; he, more than anyone else, saw the strategic significance of the agreement.

Eventually we found suitable language, and Maliki, against pretty tough odds, was able to pass both the SOFA and the strategic framework agreement through his parliament. We'd given quite a lot of ground on issues such as a withdrawal timetable, consenting to the removal of all U.S. forces by the end of 2011, and we even conceded a limited level of Iraqi legal jurisdiction over our troops in cases of certain "grave premeditated felonies" when such crimes occurred off-duty and off-base. Ultimately, the compromises we made proved beneficial because the resulting SOFA put the end of the war in sight and left the new U.S. President a firm foundation for a successful conclusion of our presence there.

That late-summer trip was my last to Iraq, and it was very emotional. For the first time, the security situation permitted me to travel into the Red Zone, the region outside the fortified Green Zone, to visit some of the Iraqi leaders who lived there. A year before, that would have been impossible; we'd only been able to get to this point because of the extraordinary efforts of General David Petraeus, then commander of Multi-National Forces-Iraq, and Ambassador Ryan Crocker, one of our nation's finest Foreign Service officers. I would later bestow the Secretary's Distinguished Service Award, the highest honor I could give, on both members of this highly effective civil-military team.

As we turned the corner onto the main street in Baghdad's Red Zone, I spotted a little boy standing in a field where kids were playing soccer. That would have been impossible a year before as well. The child, maybe eight years old, put his hand to his head in a salute. He'd apparently gotten used to seeing U.S. military convoys and thought we were one of them. He seemed quite unafraid of his surroundings or us. I raised my hand and returned his salute—even though by then we'd already passed him.

BEFORE THE Russian invasion of Georgia, I'd given serious consideration to resigning my post in September. I would lead the official U.S. delegation at the closing ceremonies of the Beijing Olympics, and that would be it. What a way to go out! I was really tired, and I also thought that it would be perfect to have my deputy, John Negroponte, become secretary of state for the remainder of the term. There had been few Foreign Service careers as distinguished as John's; it would have been a fitting coda to his service. When I told Steve of the idea, he laughed. "The President will never go for it," he said.

"Well, I'm going to try," I said. But there never seemed to be a good time to bring up the idea, and once the Georgian war began, I knew I couldn't leave.

Moreover, there were still a few loose ends, to put it mildly. I was especially concerned about completing the international components of the civil-nuclear deal with India. The historic accord announced by President Bush and Prime Minister Singh in July 2005 had actually been only the beginning. The U.S.-India deal took more than three years to finalize and demonstrates perfectly how difficult it can be to achieve a major foreign policy shift even if the heads of state of both countries are fully supportive and engaged. After the deal was announced in the summer of 2005, it had to go through several complex stages, including amendment of U.S. domestic law (the Atomic Energy Act of 1954) to permit civilian nuclear trade with India; negotiation of a bilateral "Section 123 Agreement" between the United States and India, which detailed India's obligations and rights under the deal; an India-IAEA safeguards (or inspections) agreement; and the grant of an exemption for India by the Nuclear Suppliers Group, an export-control group of then forty-five countries. Finally, the U.S. Congress had to vote again to approve the "Section 123 Agreement."

Each step was fraught with difficulty. Under secretary for political affairs Nick Burns served as my chief negotiator for the deal along with India expert Ashley Tellis. The pair moved mountains to negotiate the first detailed outline of the deal in early 2006. I personally testified before both houses of Congress in April of that year, and Nick, with his aide Anja Manuel, spent many hours explaining to skeptical senators and representatives why amending U.S. law to permit civilian nuclear trade with India made sense. The deal's environmental friendliness was an advantage. One of the arguments that ended up having traction with Democrats in particular was that the deal would enable the United States—and American companies—to help India develop an emissions-free energy source, and thus to rely less on its highly polluting domestic coal to generate electricity. In July and November of 2006 the House and then the Senate voted overwhelmingly, in bipartisan fashion, to amend U.S. law. Meanwhile, Anja and other State Department officials traveled to India a half-dozen times to hammer out the details of the "123 Agreement," the implementing document, which was finally concluded on August 3, 2007.

But the marathon continued. Prime Minister Singh had to face down critics of the deal within India and would barely survive a no-confidence vote that almost brought down his unruly coalition government. After India finalized its own agreement with the IAEA, we needed the endorsement of the IAEA's board of governors, a step that was achieved relatively easily in August 2008 after India agreed to give IAEA inspectors wider access to its civil nuclear facilities. Securing the consent of the Nuclear Suppliers Group was much harder.

The major nuclear technology suppliers—Russia, China, France, the United Kingdom, and, of course, the United States—all backed the deal. But there was significant resistance from the Austrians, the Irish, and the Nordic countries, all of which considered themselves guardians of the non-proliferation regime. John Rood, one of our primary negotiators and the acting under secretary for arms control and international security, was having little success in bringing these countries on board.

Jonas Gahr Støre, the Norwegian foreign minister, tried to help, writing language that I approved to bring the recalcitrant states along. I was in Algiers during the negotiations and stayed up all night making phone calls. (They were in addition to the more than twenty that I'd made before leaving Washington.) Finally it came down to the Austrian foreign minister, Ursula Plassnik, who was at a European Council meeting in Brussels. I asked German Foreign Minister Frank-Walter Steinmeier to track her down and get her agreement. She apparently didn't want to be found. But Frank-Walter persisted, and she instructed her negotiator to agree. John called the next morning to say that he had secured international consent from the Nuclear Suppliers Group to move ahead with the deal.

The next step was to get congressional approval before the end of the legislative session, and time was running out. Jeff Bergner, the assistant secretary for legislative affairs, told me we were short on votes. But a last-minute deal satisfied New York Congressman Gary Ackerman, and with him came the requisite Democratic votes. The House passed the legislation 298 to 117.

Congress's arcane rules made it much easier to get a vote in the House than in the Senate. Unfortunately, the Senate was out of time, and it had apparently been the administration's fault. When the White House had communicated to the Senate leadership the administration's priorities, the civil-nuclear deal was somehow not on the list. That had begun a comedy of errors that almost cost the President one of his signature foreign policy achievements. When my legislative people at State told me what had happened, I called Steve and then Josh Bolten. The chagrined Josh admitted the mistake and said he'd do what he could. I talked to Senate Majority Leader Harry Reid. He indicated that he could now only bring the bill to the Senate floor through a unanimous-consent agreement, but he couldn't get that done because an anonymous hold had been placed on the bill. Unanimous consent could be achieved only once the hold was lifted, and that seemed a far way off.

I called the President. "Hi," he said. "What's wrong?"

I don't know if he heard the irritation in my voice that quickly or if Steve had told him. "Mr. President," I said, "thanks to a White House screw-up, Barack Obama or John McCain is going to be signing your treaty with India." I then explained what had happened.

The President hung up, and a few minutes later Josh called back. "We'll get it done," he said. I still don't know to this day what Josh did, but we got the vote.

The historic agreement passed the Senate 86 to 13, and the President signed the United States–India Nuclear Cooperation Approval and Nonproliferation Enhancement Act into law on October 8 in an East Room ceremony. With domestic approval from Congress in hand, I joined my Indian counterpart, Pranab Mukherjee, in formally signing the agreement at the State Department two days later. The accord would now permit the United States to exchange peaceful nuclear technology with India and, perhaps more important, establish a foundation for a new strategic partnership with New Delhi. I was proud of what we had achieved, especially of the core team that had gotten it done.

But it was also a moment when cooperation between the executive branch and Congress had overcome strong resistance to change. I looked around at the legislators gathered in the East Room at the President's signing ceremony. Two of the House members who'd been most helpful in getting the legislation started—as in so many other matters—weren't there. Henry Hyde, a former Republican congressman from Illinois, and my great friend Tom Lantos, the former chairman of the House Foreign Affairs Committee, had both died within the last year. I especially felt the loss of Tom. The northern California congressman was a Hungarian refugee from the Nazi terror and Communist repression and the House's only Holocaust survivor. Tom was a fierce fighter for human rights and freedom; he had even been arrested about two years before his death while protesting outside Sudan's embassy against the government's mass slaughter of civilians in Darfur.

Tom and I would get together from time to time, and he was always there for me, even when we didn't agree. I'd become close to his family. One day during one of our meetings, Tom was almost in tears. His beautiful granddaughter, Charity Sunshine, then twenty years old, had been diagnosed with a very rare and almost always fatal disease, idiopathic pulmonary hypertension. She was an operatic soprano who possessed, as he put it, "the voice of an angel." Right then and there we came up with an idea: I'd accompany Charity in a performance at the Kennedy Center to raise awareness of the disease. The night of the performance was very special indeed. Doctors, researchers, and patients for whom the disease had become a way of life all turned out. So too did many diplomatic personnel and members of Congress. Tom and his wife, Annette, beamed as Charity sang some of their favorite show tunes. Remarkably and thankfully, even after a double lung transplant, she's still singing today. And we did raise the awareness of those who hadn't known about this near-orphan disease—including me.

When Tom died, I really missed him—his wisdom and warmth. At his memorial service I spoke about him as a conscience of the Congress on matters of human freedom. From time to time he would visit, and he would always bring me a plant or a flower. The last time he came he brought an orchid, but it didn't bloom. On the morning of his memorial service, I woke up to see a white flower on the previously dormant plant. It was just like Tom to send a gentle reminder that he was still there.

54

HE LIVES IN HIS OWN HEAD

THE LAST FEW MONTHS did not go quietly or without consequence. They even brought historic moments—none more so than
my much anticipated visit to Libya to meet with Colonel Muammar
Qaddafi. When the Libyans gave up their weapons of mass destruction
in 2003, there was a clear diplomatic quid pro quo: in exchange, we'd
help them to return to good standing in the international community.
But it would not be easy and not only because of Qaddafi's long record
of brutality.

Libya had arrested five Bulgarian nurses and a Palestinian doctor
several years before on trumped-up charges that they had deliberately
infected more than four hundred Libyan children with HIV. The medics insisted that they were innocent, but the Libyan courts had sentenced the group to death. The United States repeatedly urged Libya
to find a way to release them, and I was grateful for the dedication and
leadership of European Commissioner for External Relations Benita
Ferrero-Waldner on the issue. Libya's decision in 2007 to commute the
sentences and allow the medics to return home was due in large part to
Benita's resolve.

We had to make sure, too, that we were sufficiently attentive to the
sensitivities and needs of the families of the victims of the colonel's
decades-long reign of terror. I withheld my visit until we could secure
a Libyan claims settlement for families whose relatives had been killed
in attacks such as the bombing by Libyan agents of Pan Am Flight 103
over Lockerbie, Scotland, in 1988. My upcoming trip gave me powerful
leverage in these negotiations because Qaddafi desperately wanted me
to visit Tripoli.

There were two reasons for this: one traditional and the other, well, a
little disconcerting. Obviously, the first visit by a U.S. secretary of state

since 1953 would be a major milestone on the country's path to international acceptability. But Qaddafi also had a slightly eerie fascination with me personally, asking visitors why his "African princess" wouldn't visit him.

I decided to ignore the latter and dwell on the former to prepare for the trip. The arrangements were not easy, with all manner of Libyan demands, including that I meet the leader in his tent. Needless to say, I declined the invitation and met him in his formal residence.

Stopping first in Portugal and staying with my friends Ambassador Thomas Stephenson and his wife, Barbara, I took advantage of Foreign Minister Luis Amado's knowledge of Libya and Qaddafi. He suggested that I open the conversation with a discussion of Africa. "And don't be surprised when he says something crazy," he cautioned. "He'll get back on track."

When I arrived in Tripoli, I was asked to wait at one of the only Western-style hotels in the city. There was no doubt that the capital had once been a beautiful place, but it appeared run-down and tired. The only bright lights seemed to be those illuminating the many, many billboards of Qaddafi and his "inspirational" sayings. In speaking with Libyans, a distinct generational divide manifested itself. While the senior staff spoke English fluently and reminded me of my European colleagues, younger officials appeared to have had fewer educational opportunities and little contact with the West. It was another reminder of the sad consequences of Qaddafi's monstrous rule.

After several hours, we were summoned to the residence, where I greeted the Libyan leader and sat down to hundreds of camera flashes. Qaddafi said a few completely appropriate words, as did I, and the press left. We began the conversation as Amado had suggested, talking about Africa in general and Sudan in particular. Libya, he promised, would help with alternative routes for humanitarian supplies to the refugees. *This is going pretty well,* I thought. *He doesn't seem crazy.* Then, as Amado had predicted, he suddenly stopped speaking and began rolling his head back and forth. "Tell President Bush to stop talking about a two-state solution for Israel and Palestine!" he barked. "It should be one state! Israeltine!" Perhaps he didn't like what I said next. In a sudden fit, he fired two translators in the room. *Okay,* I thought, *this is Qaddafi.*

It was Ramadan at the time of my visit, and after sundown the "Brother Leader" insisted that I join him for dinner in his private kitchen. Colby Cooper, who had overseen the arrangements for the trip, protested that this hadn't been the plan. My security detail did as well, especially when they were told to stay outside. I thought I could take care of myself and went in. At the end of dinner, Qaddafi told me that he'd made a videotape for me. *Uh oh,* I thought, *what is this going to be?* It was a quite innocent collection of photos of me with world leaders—President Bush, Vladimir Putin, Hu Jintao, and so on—set to the music of a song called "Black Flower in the White House," written for me by a Libyan composer. It was weird, but at least it wasn't raunchy.

The press was fascinated with my trip, and I sat down for an interview with CNN's Zain Verjee (who often worked with producer Elise Labott on State Department coverage). Zain asked me about my personal impressions of Qaddafi. I remember that I came away from the visit realizing how much Qaddafi lives inside his own head, in a kind of alternate reality. As I watched events unfold in the spring and summer of 2011, I wondered if he even understood fully what was going on around him. And I was very, very glad that we had disarmed him of his most dangerous weapons of mass destruction. There in his bunker, making his last stand, I have no doubt he would have used them.

55

One Last Chance for North Korea

THE NEGOTIATED END to Libya's weapons of mass destruction program was evidence that rogue states could be convinced—with the right incentives—to give them up. Occasionally, President Bush would say, "Dictators don't give up their weapons," and then he'd immediately correct himself. "But Libya did," he'd add in amazement. The prospect of a tyrant facing his last days with the ultimate weapon to protect himself is reason enough to seek an end to such programs. So too is the possibility of a dictator who, playing out an endgame scenario or perhaps in need of funds, detonates a nuclear bomb or sells the world's most dangerous weapons to the highest bidder.

It was concerns such as those that made us accelerate efforts to end the North Korean nuclear program. Our negotiations with the North Koreans had been guided by three breakthrough documents. The first, the Joint Statement signed by the six parties in September 2005, had established the basic framework for an agreement on nuclear disarmament of the Korean peninsula. In it, the North had committed to abandoning its nuclear programs in exchange for the gradual granting of benefits (such as heavy fuel oil deliveries) and the eventual normalization of relations with the United States, Japan, and South Korea. As I have discussed previously, these benefits would be delivered only after verifiable progress had been made by the North toward declaring, disabling, and eventually dismantling its nuclear program.

In February 2007 and again in October 2007 the six parties signed two detailed implementation plans that laid out specific steps to meet the terms of the 2005 Joint Statement, including the shutdown of the nuclear reactor at Yongbyon, the resumption of inspections, and "a complete declaration of all nuclear programs" in North Korea. These were agreements Chris Hill, the assistant secretary for East Asian and

Pacific affairs, had worked out with Kim Kye Gwan and then his Six-Party counterparts, and they required the United States to take a series of steps, including the return of the $25 million in frozen assets and the removal of North Korea from the U.S. list of state sponsors of terrorism, once the North Koreans had met their side of the bargain. The Chinese had played a major role in drafting the document.

The whole process had encountered a number of ups and downs, with diplomatic breakthroughs in 2005 followed by North Korean missile and nuclear tests in 2006. There was a surge of progress throughout much of 2007, followed by Pyongyang's backsliding toward the end of the year, when the North failed to meet a year-end deadline for providing its nuclear declaration and disabling fully three of its Yongbyon nuclear facilities.

By 2008, though, the diplomacy had also produced some results. Even though Pyongyang had not completely disabled its known capability, the North had taken significant initial steps toward this goal, sealing and breaking down much of the infrastructure associated with Yongbyon. It had also readmitted weapons inspectors, including experts from the United States, who'd begun to "crawl all over" the nuclear site and verify its disablement. Rendering inoperable the North Koreans' plutonium production capacity was a significant achievement, as we were worried that they might transfer the material to others.

We were focused at the beginning of the year on getting the North to submit its declaration. We expected Pyongyang to provide a full disclosure of all of its plutonium-related activities. Since the program's existence was well known, the North Koreans seemed prepared to do this to a fairly acceptable level; we also had other sources of information in any case that could fill in any gaps.

But despite our successes on the plutonium side, serious concerns remained regarding our suspicions that the North Koreans had developed a second route to a nuclear weapon through uranium enrichment. It had been a problem since the earliest days of the administration, when we had received intelligence that the North had been pursuing a highly enriched uranium capability. The discovery had caused the postponement of Assistant Secretary Jim Kelly's visit to Pyongyang in 2002. When the visit took place, the North Koreans seemed to admit that they had a program and then denied its existence. Confronted with the accusations, they responded by expelling weapons inspectors from the country in 2002 and withdrawing from the Nuclear Non-Proliferation Treaty the following year. We now needed the North Koreans to acknowledge their uranium enrichment capability in their declaration so that facilities and research associated with it would be covered by the inspection regime that we'd employ as a part of the agreement. This was no small matter; it was, in fact, the crux of the issue.

Chris Hill and his North Korean counterpart, Kim Kye Gwan, worked on the declaration for months. I knew that everyone in the government was nervous about what was transpiring. Steve Hadley scheduled interagency meetings for Chris to apprise his colleagues about the course of diplomacy. Unfortunately, Chris often acted as if they were an intrusion into the considerable flexibility that I'd won for him with the President. By all accounts, he answered questions somewhat petulantly, only reinforcing concerns in the Pentagon, the Vice President's office, and even the National Security Council staff.

There was a tendency, too, in the Washington press corps to attribute every breakthrough exclusively to Chris's negotiating skill, which would only reinforce the misguided notion that State was somehow winning a bureaucratic battle against other agencies that opposed the course we were on. A few too many such stories appeared throughout the spring, and it was a problem for me and for Chris. We agreed after a while that he wouldn't talk to the press about the negotiations. I'd take any questions so that I could deflect criticism of him from the right, on Capitol Hill, and within the administration. Chris also stepped back from the day-to-day negotiations with the North, handing that responsibility to an excellent Korean-speaking Foreign Service officer, Sung Kim, with Paul Haenle representing the NSC. This created something of a firewall since Paul could represent Steve and the White House directly and help keep the interagency process better informed. I can honestly say that Chris never operated outside his guidance, but the overhyping press coverage made it seem as if he was freelancing—*successfully* freelancing was the impression, but that didn't earn him any slack. In any case, the personality dynamics made the already difficult issue even harder to manage.

THE NORTH KOREANS finally presented their formal declaration of their nuclear program on June 24, 2008. A few days later, they blew up a water-cooling tower at the nuclear facility in Yongbyon. Although the demolition was covered on CNN with great fanfare, this spectacle could not make up for serious deficiencies in North Korea's declaration report. There was a fairly comprehensive accounting of their plutonium program, but the report revealed nothing about North Korea's suspected uranium capability. And there was an accounting of the amount of plutonium the North had produced, but the declaration did not cover the issue of how many "devices" the North might have made with the plutonium it had harvested. Nonetheless, knowing how much material they had made allowed us to estimate how many devices there might be.

By prior arrangement, the delivery of the declaration was meant to trigger the removal of restrictions on North Korea from the Trading with the Enemy Act and also the lifting of the country's designation as a state sponsor of terrorism. The latter was subject to a forty-five-day waiting period once the President notified Congress of his intention to do so.

The inadequacy of the North Korean declaration had been evident for some time, prompting a debate within the administration about whether to go ahead and remove the North from the United States' state sponsor of terrorism list, which singled out countries that supply a terrorist organization with training, logistics, or material or financial support. Technically, the North Koreans should have already been removed from this list much earlier; there had not been, at the time, any known terrorist incident involving Pyongyang for two decades. But the signal that removing them from the list would send was important, all the more so since North Korea valued the step as legitimating its regime in the eyes of the international community.

The Japanese were lobbying hard against lifting the designation, though. They worried, as before, that there would not be enough pressure on the North to resolve the abduction issue. We'd tried to help, and indeed, Pyongyang had agreed to some small steps, including a plan to reopen investigations into the abductions issue and answer questions about the fate of the victims.

The Vice President was dead set against removing the North Koreans from the terrorism list, saying that it would reward bad behavior since the North hadn't lived up to its obligations in filing the declaration. At one of the several NSC meetings held on the subject, one participant said, "We have to get the North Koreans to tell the truth." I sometimes wondered if that was a quixotic fantasy. *The North Koreans say that their country is paradise and South Korea is a prison camp,* I thought to myself. *They aren't acquainted with the truth.* But the point was well taken; we had to find some way to get a handle on the uranium enrichment issue.

We decided to go at the problem from another angle. The North Koreans would also have to agree to a verification protocol to govern the on-site inspection of all aspects of their nuclear program. That protocol, if properly structured, would give us access to sites both declared and undeclared, meaning that we'd have the right to inspect a building or facility even if the North hadn't put it on the declaration. We could then trigger inspections of sites that were suspected of being associated with uranium enrichment.

We were also seeking an acknowledgment of North Korea's alleged proliferation of nuclear technology and know-how to other entities. This issue was meant to deal with a very troubling problem: strong suspicions and evidence of North Korean assistance to Syria in the building of an undeclared nuclear reactor that had been discovered the year before.

The covert facility had been destroyed in an Israeli air strike, after President Bush had refused an Israeli request that we carry out the operation ourselves. We met as a national security team on this issue for the better part of two months. The Vice President favored U.S. action, while Bob Gates and I stood against it. When Mike Hayden, the CIA director, told us that he couldn't certify with anything other than low confidence that the reactor was part of a nuclear weapons program, the President decided against a strike and suggested a diplomatic course to the Israeli prime minister. Ehud Olmert thanked us for our input but rejected our advice, and the Israelis then expertly did the job themselves.

As can be imagined, though, this complicated even more the question of what to do about North Korea. In April 2008 the Central Intelligence Agency released images of the Syrian reactor, elements of which were strikingly similar to some of the construction and engineering components at North Korea's Yongbyon nuclear facilities. "How can we deal with a country that lies on its declaration, is still pursuing nuclear weapons and is suspected of helping Syria build a reactor for its own program?" That was a very good and penetrating question asked by the opponents of continued diplomacy with the North. But I felt strongly that we had to go the last mile to see if we could stop Pyongyang's further development of nuclear weapons. And I thought that if we could just get people on the ground—good, well-trained U.S. inspectors—we might really learn what was going on inside this isolated, dangerous country.

The forty-five-day waiting period on the "state sponsor of terrorism" designation came and went as we worked feverishly to get the North to improve the tenets of a proposed verification protocol before we would consider removing Pyongyang from the list. There is little doubt in my mind that the Chinese were helping put pressure on the regime this time. Of all nations, China has the most influence on North Korea. But the Chinese cannot dictate to the North, and sometimes it was wearisome to watch Beijing's own frustration with Kim Jong-il.

I'll never forget one such incident. At a meeting of ASEAN in Malaysia, I asked our hosts to convene a meeting of interested foreign ministers to talk about nuclear proliferation. The Six-Party Talks had stalled again, and I thought we might bring some international pressure on the Chinese and the North to move forward. My counterpart, Li Zhaoxing, had agreed to attend, but when the meeting started he was not present. We forged ahead, but there was a lot of mumbling that he'd stiffed the other participants—most especially me. About halfway through the meeting, Li appeared, visibly shaken. He said nothing. But when the session ended, he came up to me and apologized. "I've never been talked to that way!" he said, referring to his discussions with the North Koreans. He was quite furious and physically agitated. I later learned that he'd tried to bring the North Koreans to the meeting, only to be chewed out by the political commissar who was accompanying the hapless North Korean foreign minister. Sometimes even China couldn't make Pyongyang budge.

Finally, in late August, the North Koreans began to push hard for a resolution to the terrorism list issue. They could count, and they knew we were several days past the forty-five days that had followed our notice to Congress. North Korea announced that it would be suspending its disablement of its nuclear facility in Yongbyon because the United States had not kept its end of the bargain. We decided that Chris should go to Pyongyang in search of a breakthrough, and he seemed to get one in early October. The parties agreed to verification measures that would give inspectors access to all declared sites related to the plutonium production program and, based on "mutual consent," access to undeclared sites as well. As Chris noted at the time, we'd have to have consent anyway since we weren't going to shoot our way into the facilities. The inspectors would also be able to carry out "scientific procedures" such as sampling and forensic activities—which were key to understanding what materials and chemicals were being used and thus the nature of the activities at any given site. Perhaps more important, the North Korean negotiator, Kim Kye Gwan, committed verbally to creating a separate document that would address outstanding issues—namely, North Korea's suspected uranium enrichment program and allegations of proliferation.

The verification measures were far from perfect, and for eight days we debated whether to complete the process and remove the North from the state sponsors of terrorism list. Again the President faced contradictory advice, with the Vice President saying no and me arguing that we needed to take this one last step. The six parties would now work to put in writing what the North had committed to Chris verbally. The resulting verification protocol would have to be clear about what we were allowed to do because I wasn't asking anyone to trust Pyongyang. But, I argued, we had no other way to get on the ground where we knew troubling activities were taking place. We'd obtained information about North Korea's nuclear activities that had come from the approximately eighteen thousand pages of documentation that the North had handed over earlier that spring. These papers included operating records that dated back to 1986. The quid pro quo was worth a try, and anyway, removing the North from the terrorism list would have little if any effect on the sanctions we imposed on the regime. These measures had been codified in acts of Congress, executive orders, and UN Security Council resolutions that would remain intact. The United States wouldn't make any additional concessions to the North without a satisfactory verification protocol. And if the North didn't give us one, we would suspend the energy assistance that each of the six parties was scheduled to deliver as part of our previous agreements.

I thought I'd made a compelling argument. On the evening of

October 9, I was at a State Department retreat just outside Washington, D.C. The President and I had talked numerous times about the decision he faced. At one point, he asked whether there was something else the North might accept. I asked Chris Hill the question. "They would accept a visit by you," he answered.

I relayed the option to the President. "No! That would really legitimize him," he responded, recalling the star-crossed trip to Pyongyang of Madeleine Albright, who had been made to endure a cultural event in which the citizens of North Korea carried out elaborate card displays.

That night, he called me several times, clearly struggling with the decision. I talked to Steve Hadley, who was also struggling, but he had decided he agreed with me on the decision. The President did too. I asked if the President wanted me to come back to Washington immediately. He did. I made my apologies to the State Department management and leadership and returned home. Knowing that the President had made the decision, I called several members of Congress. Most were fine, but some, such as Senators Jon Kyl and John Ensign as well as Congresswoman Ileana Ros-Lehtinen of Florida, were deeply troubled. Those were people whom I'd come to trust and respect, and it bothered me that they were so concerned.

I thought that the argument was solid for trying—one last time—to get the North Koreans to deal. That's the way diplomacy works. But I knew that I'd asked the President to walk out on a limb and that if the North Koreans didn't deliver he'd be subject to fierce criticism. That is, unfortunately, precisely what has come to pass.

Despite our best efforts, the North balked and would not write down the understandings we had agreed to orally. The final Six-Party Talks broke down on our watch on December 11. On December 12 we announced that we wouldn't go forward on energy assistance absent progress on verification. We thought the Chinese and Russians had agreed, but they indicated that they would complete their share of energy assistance. South Korea, on the other hand, would not.

A month later, the North Koreans made a statement saying they wouldn't allow nuclear inspections unless the United States' "hostile policy and nuclear threat to the North are fundamentally terminated." That was an old canard that Pyongyang employed when it didn't intend to cooperate. The Six-Party Talks had come to an end.

Much later, in 2010, nuclear physicist Siegfried Hecker, a former director of Los Alamos National Laboratory, would be invited to North Korea and shown an industrial-scale facility capable of producing enriched uranium. According to Hecker, the state of the facility demonstrated "without a doubt" that Pyongyang had pursued uranium enrichment for many years. We'd been right about uranium enrichment but unable to use diplomacy to confirm our suspicions or do anything about it.

The fact is there are constraints in dealing with North Korea that limit the options available. In debates with the Vice President, I would often make that point and ask what option he was proposing. He could never come up with one that was actually feasible. Those discussions always demonstrated that there was no perfect solution to the problem.

The military option against Pyongyang was not a good one; it was fraught with unintended consequences and the near-certainty of significant damage to Seoul. Kim Jong-il maintains missile batteries whose projectiles can reach South Korea's capital city in a very short period of time. Though august figures such as former Defense Secretary William Perry suggested we threaten to launch air strikes against the North's ballistic missile site before their July 2006 test, President Bush and his advisors did not seriously consider military action. The Pentagon maintains military plans for war against North Korea. The day may come when a President has to use them, but everyone wants to avoid that outcome if at all possible.

A second option would have been to adopt a sanctions-only approach, trying to squeeze the regime until it either collapsed or changed its policy. The first outcome seemed unlikely. The Kim dynasty had survived for more than half a century despite isolation from the United States and the international community.

The possibility of simply squeezing the regime into submission was tempting but likely to fail. The North Koreans were already heavily sanctioned and still they had detonated a nuclear device and proliferated nuclear knowledge to Syria. There was no evidence that sanctions alone were changing their behavior or slowing their path to even more sophisticated nuclear technology.

The punitive measures that were put in place undoubtedly helped spur the North toward sporadic cooperation. Still, the imposition of sanctions in the absence of a willingness to negotiate seriously serves only to isolate the United States from its allies. Maintaining a coalition against Kim Jong-il required us to keep the onus for recalcitrance on the North. And in truth, without concerted actions from others, American unilateral penalties were unlikely to bring an end to North Korea's ambitions. In the final analysis, Beijing was willing to go only so far in pressuring the North. While a nuclear North Korea was unwelcome, the collapse of Kim's regime was thought to be worse given that the resulting instability could spill over into bordering Chinese territories. That concern, which heightened after Kim's stroke in 2008, was a serious constraint.

Confronted with these options, we chose to give multilateral diplomacy—backed by the punitive measures already in place—a chance. This produced a careful set of requirements that China, Russia, Japan, South Korea, and the United States placed upon the North. The diplomacy had produced results. When Pyongyang complied with its obligations—producing information that we otherwise would not have had, disabling significant parts of their nuclear infrastructure, and permitting American inspectors on the ground—we took reciprocal steps of our own. When Pyongyang refused to meet its obligations, we, in response, refused to move forward.

We had to make a choice: allow the North Koreans' expanding nuclear capability (which included processed nuclear material that could be sold or transferred) to continue unchecked and unmonitored, or try to enlist the Chinese to stop them. The idea that we could bomb the Syrian reactor to make a point about proliferation in the face of uncertain intelligence was, to put it mildly, reckless. I told the Chinese that the North Koreans had done something stupid and venal in assisting Damascus and that it was time for Beijing to step up. But they (and the rest of the region) would have never tolerated the military strike that the Vice President recommended. In the eleventh hour of the administration, we decided to make one more diplomatic push. As a result, the North Koreans remained isolated in the region and the incoming President was not confronted with a crisis on the peninsula on day one of his term.

At least in giving the diplomatic track its best shot, the United States can't be blamed for what North Korea has done. But the truth is that until the tyrannical regime is gone, no one can rest easily, given its dangerous possession of a nuclear capability.

56

THE FINANCIAL CRISIS OF 2008

WHEN THE PRESIDENT asked me to come back to Washington, we didn't want to tip the press that an announcement about North Korea was coming. There were scores of State Department officials with me, and my sudden return to the capital was bound to be noticed. "Tell them you have to come back and help on some matters related to the financial crisis," the President said.

"Well, I do," I said. It wasn't just a ruse.

In the summer of 2008, we were experiencing a number of problems in the global economy. Oil prices spiked to nearly $140 a barrel, causing problems for growth as well as driving food prices skyward and sparking riots around the world. The sudden surge enhanced the diplomatic leverage of such U.S. adversaries as Hugo Chávez and the Iranians. When I was a Chevron director, I had often commented that the politics of oil was geopolitics with a capital "G," and now we were experiencing that firsthand. Chávez, for instance, was using his excess profits to influence elections across Latin America.

It was very difficult to address the energy problem coherently within the international system, but we did manage to put together a number of energy partnerships, largely through the good work of Gregory Manuel, whom I had brought to the State Department. Greg had been my student at Stanford and had worked for me at the NSC in the economics directorate. I needed someone who would be indefatigable and dogged in bringing the various interested parts of the State Department together to pursue energy initiatives. He worked with Reuben Jeffery to push work in the area forward and to maintain at least a dialogue with other countries.

That work paid off, yielding—as just one example—a comprehensive partnership with Brazil in the area of biofuels as an alternative energy source. Given the obvious benefits of energy policies that could reduce individual nations' dependence on oil, it should have been easier to bring the countries of the world together. I had, for instance, hoped to draw the Central Asians—particularly Kazakhstan—into greater dialogue about energy security in South-Central Asia and beyond. But it was hard, and I never really had the time to devote to that important portfolio. It was an area that cried out for international leadership.

We were under such pressure on so many other issues that, too often, longer term economic issues of that kind did not receive the consistent effort they deserved. But in the fall of 2008, despite North Korea, Iran, Middle East peace, Iraq, and a host of other issues, the financial crisis was suddenly front and center and demanded attention.

My most important role in that regard was to support Hank Paulson in a period of extraordinary crisis that reminded me of the early days after 9/11. Each development brought new uncertainties, which demanded a mobilization of financial and economic resources on a scale not seen since the Great Depression. At Hank's request, I sent Reuben Jeffery from State to work alongside David McCormick, the under secretary of the treasury for international affairs. Reuben would stop in to brief me on the latest news at the beginning and end of each day. As the crisis unfolded and then accelerated, Hank and I met with the President most mornings during the time usually reserved for the intelligence briefing. Hank would enter with yet another horror story of a bank failure and news that lending had ground to a halt. The economy was in grave trouble. One night at a reception in the East Room, Josh Bolten called me aside. "You probably ought to know that Goldman and Morgan Stanley could fail tomorrow," he whispered.

"What?" I said. That's the way it was—every day brought very bad news.

I didn't have anything to offer in terms of economic advice, but it wasn't hard to see the effect on leaders and diplomacy. Hank would handle relations with the first-order countries, but I promised to help with those that he didn't have time to reach. I just wanted to show the world that we were on top of it, so every morning I'd call Hank's chief of staff, Jim Wilkinson, who'd previously worked for me as a senior aide. "What are we saying today?" I would ask. It was dizzying and disconcerting.

In the depths of the crisis, the President held a meeting at Camp David with French President Nicolas Sarkozy and José Barroso, the president of the European Commission. Sitting at the same table where we'd responded to 9/11 and planned two wars, I listened to the leaders' dismay at their inability to stem the tide of the crisis. Economic policy had so many more moving parts than even the complicated issues I was used to managing. The President and Sarkozy agreed to hold a meeting of the G20 leaders, just to reassure them and show confidence. Right before our eyes, a new international balance was unfolding. No one spoke of convening the G7 or G8. China, Brazil, India, and others had to be at the table. All of a sudden, Sarkozy said, "It has to be in New York! The crisis started in New York, so it has to be there!"

I was shifting in my seat. "You got something to say, Condi?" the President asked.

I was a little startled but plowed ahead. "New York isn't the entire U.S. economy," I said. "Maybe you should hold the meeting somewhere that doesn't feel like a crisis." Then I whispered to the President, "If you do it in New York, every out-of-work trader will be interviewed by the networks worldwide."

"No kidding!" the President replied. He suggested that I mention the point to the French leader before dinner. When we broke for cocktails, I talked to him, making the point about the potential news coverage. The President was able to convince Sarkozy and in the end the meeting was held in Washington, D.C.

The crisis was evolving in the context of the coming election too. The President was careful to brief both John McCain and Barack Obama. The problem was obviously going to outlast our time in office. The fact of the impending change of power gave every decision a slightly surreal feel. I was increasingly aware that I was making choices that would condition the environment for whoever came after me. That was really the context of the election for me. Certainly, as a citizen—and political junkie—I watched the contest with interest. But I was secretary of state, and I didn't want to become too emotionally involved in what was going on. And I'd been there at the beginning with George W. Bush. I had little energy left for politics.

The day after the election, I was sitting in my usual morning staff meeting. "Are you going to say anything about the election?" Sean asked.

"What do you mean?" I asked. "To whom?"

"To the press," he said. "They will want to know how you feel about the election of the first black President."

"Proud," I replied. And so I hijacked the first minutes of Sean's morning briefing and told the press what I was feeling. I explained that as an American, and as an African American in particular, I was especially proud because of the long journey our country had traveled in overcoming wounds regarding race. "One of the great things about representing this country is it continues to surprise; it continues to renew itself; it continues to beat all odds and expectations," I said extemporaneously. "You just know that Americans are not going to be satisfied until they really do form that perfect union."

Preparing the Handover

THE DAYS WERE growing short for our administration as a new team prepared to take the reins. I wanted to ensure as orderly a transition as possible, something that is easier to do in the State Department than in the White House. When the presidency changes, even if there's no change of party, the White House staff leaves en masse. But in the agencies, the career service carries on. This is tremendously beneficial to the country. For instance, Bill Burns continued as Secretary Clinton's number three, able to bridge the two administrations.

I also wanted to make sure that my successor, Hillary Clinton, had all that she needed to get off to a good start as quickly as possible. We met several times, including at my apartment for dinner. Our relationship was—and is—an easy one, going back to the day she brought her prospective freshman daughter, Chelsea, to Stanford when I was provost. It helps too that there really is, even in difficult times, a kind of "fraternity" of secretaries of state. We all know what the job is like, its stresses and strains, and therefore there is great empathy among us. Perhaps now it would be better to call it a "sorority" since three of the four most recent secretaries—Madeleine Albright, me, and Hillary Clinton—have been women. Indeed, when Secretary Clinton finishes her term it will have been at least sixteen years since a white male held the office of secretary of state.

The transition was very smooth. But there is one source of awkwardness in the interim ten weeks between the election and the inauguration. Though there's only one president at a time, it's important to make certain that the incoming commander in chief is kept up to date on critical matters as they unfold.

There were a number of "hot" diplomatic issues, and the President and I decided that I would communicate with President-elect Obama directly. It wouldn't have been appropriate to do so with Hillary because until a Cabinet officer is confirmed, the Senate frowns upon that person "acting in the role." And so the President-elect and I spoke several times about the negotiations with North Korea, the Gaza problem, and—most urgently—the events that unfolded in South Asia in late November. We talked for the last time a few days before the inauguration. "Mr. President-elect," I said, "this is probably our last conversation before you enter the Oval Office. I am proud of your election. Good luck and Godspeed."

57

MUMBAI

O N NOVEMBER 26, I was preparing for the arrival of my family for the Thanksgiving holiday. I'd taken off a little early, but the phone was ringing as I arrived home. The operations center was on the telephone. David Mulford, our ambassador in India, and Anne Patterson in Pakistan were both calling. I flipped on the television as the watch officer described what had happened. There was carnage everywhere from ten coordinated attacks by Islamic terrorists across Mumbai, India's most vibrant commercial city. Over the next three days, more than 150 people would be killed and almost twice as many wounded.

The President and Laura Bush had kindly invited my family and friends to Camp David for one last Thanksgiving dinner. Mariann and Dan Begovich, Gene Washington, and my Aunt Gee were all excited to attend. I didn't want to disappoint them, and in any case it would be helpful to be with the President as we tried to manage the crisis.

Ambassador Mulford's message was stark. "There is war fever here," he said. "I don't know if the prime minister can hold out. Everyone knows that the terrorists came from Pakistan." I then talked to Anne. Her message was just as clear. "They have their heads in the sand," she said.

Needless to say, I didn't do much celebrating, showing up for meals and nothing else. We were issuing statements of support for India and trying, through Anne, to get the Pakistanis to say something useful. Then, on Saturday, I realized just how bad the communication between the parties really was.

I was leaving my cabin to join others for "chip-and-putt" golf on the lawn behind the President's residence when the Camp David operator called and said that Judy Ansley at the NSC was on the phone. Judy was one of Steve's deputies. "The Pakistanis say the Indians have warned them that they've decided to go to war," she said anxiously.

"What?" I said. "That isn't what they're telling me." In my many conversations with the Indians over the two days, they'd emphasized their desire to defuse the situation and their need for the Pakistanis to do something to show that they accepted responsibility for tracking down the terrorists.

I asked the operations center to get the Indian foreign minister on the phone, but they couldn't reach him. Now I was starting to get nervous. *Is he avoiding my call because they* are *preparing for war?* I wondered. It still didn't make sense, but it was India and Pakistan, and anything could happen.

I called back again. No response. By now the international phone lines were buzzing with the news. The Pakistanis were calling everyone—the Saudis, the Emiratis, the Chinese. Finally Mukherjee called back. I told him what I'd heard.

"What?" he said. "I'm in my constituency." (The Indians were preparing for elections, and Mukherjee, who was a member of Parliament, was at home campaigning.) "Would I be outside New Delhi if we were about to launch a war?" he said. Apparently, he explained, the Pakistani foreign minister had taken his stern words in their recent phone call the wrong way. "I said they were leaving us no choice but to go to war," he said. *This is getting dangerous,* I thought.

I was scheduled to go to Europe in a few days for my last NATO summit. The President asked if I could go to India and Pakistan first. I agreed but thought it wise to stop in London on the way. Sitting in London, I had a strong sense of déjà vu. Hadn't we been here before with the Brits, trying to head off a war in South Asia in 2001? I'd once said that I knew it was time to step down as provost when issues that I thought I'd resolved in year one came back around in year six. *South Asia,* I thought. *Here we go again.*

But when I arrived in India, I could see and feel the difference. A lot had changed since 2001; most important, the Indians trusted us. They didn't want war, though they were being pushed hard by the press and public opinion to avenge the attacks. When I arrived at Prime Minister Singh's home that night, it was easy to see how much pressure he was under. But he was determined to avoid war. The foreign minister felt the same. "But you have to get Pakistan to do something." Clearly the impending elections made the situation even more difficult.

When I arrived in Islamabad, it was obvious that a lot had changed there too. Musharraf hadn't always been effective, but he had exuded confidence, in part due to the loyalty of the army to him personally. Now I was face to face with a new, weak civilian government headed by Benazir Bhutto's widower, Asif Ali Zardari. The Pakistanis were at once terrified and in the same breath dismissive of the Indian claims. President Zardari emphasized his desire to avoid war but couldn't bring himself to acknowledge Pakistan's likely role in the attacks. Pakistani Prime Minister Yousaf Raza Gillani, who I also met, launched into a long speech about how Pakistan fought extremists too. They had been told that the terrorists who had launched the attack had nothing to do with Pakistan.

"Mr. Prime Minister," I said, "either you're lying to me or your people are lying to you." I then went on to tell him what we—the United States—knew about the origins of the attack. I didn't accuse Pakistan's government of involvement; that wasn't the point. But rogues within the security services might have aided the terrorists. It was time to admit that and to investigate more seriously. Finally, I went to meet the chief of staff, General Ashfaq Pervez Kayani. Our military liked him and considered him honest and effective. He was the one person who, even if he couldn't admit responsibility, understood that Pakistan would have to give an accounting of what had happened. That was a start.

When I left South Asia, I wasn't certain that I'd achieved what I intended. But as the days went on, the crisis eased. Almost a month later, on December 27, Zardari admitted that "nonstate actors" existed in Pakistan and had to be rooted out. It wasn't a great statement, but, taken together with earlier promises to investigate the Mumbai attacks, it was enough. Singh's party had won overwhelmingly a few weeks before in the provincial elections, and the prime minister no longer had to placate the war caucus.

Several days after returning from South Asia and Europe, I attended the Kennedy Center Honors for the last time as secretary of state. I always loved the event, which honors our finest artists. On Saturday night, the secretary hosts a gala dinner in the Ben Franklin room at the State Department at which the recipients receive their honors. It was one of my favorite nights of the year, a chance to sit with Itzhak Perlman, Joshua Bell, Robert Redford, Elton John, Diana Ross, and Aretha Franklin, among others.

Then, on Sunday night, the President hosts a reception for the honorees before the performances at the Kennedy Center. There is a nice ceremony at which the achievements of the recipients are recalled. That year, the last award was dedicated to the wonderful actor Morgan Freeman. The President introduced him by recalling his role in the movie *Deep Impact,* which is about a black man who is President of the United States when a meteor hits the earth. "That's about the only thing that hasn't happened in the last eight years," the President quipped.

When he returned to his seat, I leaned over and said, "Don't tempt fate. We've still got a few weeks left."

58

ONE LAST CHANCE FOR A PALESTINIAN STATE

IN THE WANING MONTHS of our time in Washington, we tried one last time to secure a two-state solution. The Olmert proposal haunted the President and me. In September the prime minister had given Abbas a map outlining the territory of a Palestinian state. Israel would annex 6.3 percent of the West Bank. (Olmert gave Abbas cause to believe that he was willing to reduce that number to 5.8 percent.) All of the other elements were still on the table, including the division of Jerusalem. Olmert had insisted that Abbas sign then and there. When the Palestinian had demurred, wanting to consult his experts before signing, Olmert refused to give him the map. The Israeli leader told me that he and Abbas had agreed to convene their experts the next day. Apparently that meeting never took place. But I knew what had been proposed, and I asked Jonathan Schwartz, a State Department lawyer with many years of experience in the issue, to construct an approximation of the territorial compromise. I wanted to preserve the Olmert offer.

I talked to the President and asked whether he would be willing to receive Olmert and Abbas one last time. What if I could get the two of them to come and accept the parameters of the proposal? We knew it was a long shot. Olmert had announced in the summer that he would step down as prime minister. Israel would hold elections in the first part of the next year. He was a lame duck, and so was the President.

Still, I worried that there might never be another chance like this one. Tzipi Livni urged me (and, I believe, Abbas) not to enshrine the Olmert proposal. "He has no standing in Israel," she said. That was probably true, but to have an Israeli prime minister on record offering those remarkable elements and a Palestinian president accepting them would have pushed the peace process to a new level. Abbas refused.

We had one last chance. The two leaders came separately in November and December to say good-bye. The President took Abbas into the Oval Office alone and appealed to him to reconsider. The Palestinian stood firm, and the idea died.

Now, as I write in 2011, the process seems to have gone backward. The Palestinians are speaking in the UN General Assembly of unilaterally declaring statehood. There are familiar squabbles about Israeli settlement activity. I certainly know the frustration of Israeli announcements of building new housing on disputed land; it often felt as though those bulletins were issued just after the secretary of state had traveled there. It happened to me several times. Not only would I call Olmert and Livni to complain, but I would also publicly denounce what Israel had done, reminding everyone that the United States would not recognize unilateral alterations of the status quo at the time of negotiation. But I never let progress on the settlement issue become a U.S. precondition for negotiations. I believed that once there was an agreement, the question of settlements would be moot.

In the end, the Palestinians walked away from the negotiations— and soon a new Israeli prime minister would walk away too. Abbas was told by numerous Israelis, including some of Olmert's closest advisors, that the lame-duck prime minister did not have the legitimacy to deliver the deal. But had he expressed a willingness to accept the extraordinary terms he'd been offered, it might have been a turning point in the long history of the intractable conflict. It might be a long time before another Israeli prime minister offered anything as dramatic again. I turned over the negotiating file to my successor. The conditions were almost ripe for a deal on our watch, but not quite. Still, I have to believe that sooner or later, there will be a two-state solution. There is no peaceful alternative.

Gaza Again

INDEED, THE CONFLICT exploded one last time as 2008 came to a close. Tensions had been rising in Gaza throughout November and into December as Hamas fired rockets into southern Israeli population centers in violation of a fragile summer ceasefire. During his last visit to

Washington, Olmert made clear that the situation was becoming intolerable. He told the President that he could not let Israel's enemies take advantage of what they might read as a political vacuum, pending elections.

On Christmas Day, Tzipi Livni called to say the Israelis would have to act. The Israelis never asked for permission, and we never gave it. Thanks to the warning, though, I wasn't surprised when, on December 27, Israel launched a massive attack into Gaza, hitting a hundred preplanned targets within a span of 220 seconds. The bombardment continued, leading ultimately to a ground invasion on January 3. Needless to say, my last holiday week was not as I'd imagined. I sat in my cousin's home, on the phone trying to get the Israelis, the Egyptians, and the Arabs to establish terms for a ceasefire.

When it came to Israel's responses to provocations, I'd become accustomed to the diplomatic pattern of initial outrage at the terrorists, followed by human suffering, culminating in a condemnation of Israel. Under pressure from the Arabs, the UN Security Council called a meeting on the situation in Gaza. I left for New York, hoping to avoid a formal resolution because I didn't want the United States to veto an end to the war.

I called Olmert and tried to get a sense of when he could end the operation. He was noncommittal, saying that he had to wipe out the threat to the civilian populations. I told him I'd try to hold off a resolution. Olmert said that Sarkozy was in the same frame of mind. *Good,* I thought. *With the support of the French* and *the British we ought to be able to avoid a resolution.* I went to bed assuming that we'd prevented a diplomatic crisis, and, with that in mind, I planned to go home the next day, after the Security Council meeting in New York.

What happened next was bizarre. The Arabs had gathered and asked to see the members of the P5. Lavrov had not attended the meeting, and neither had Chinese Foreign Minister Yang Jiechi. Bernard Kouchner and David Miliband, my French and British counterparts, and I went to meet with the Arabs. I fully expected unity, but after hearing their hostile and emotional presentation, Kouchner suddenly said, "You're right. There should be a resolution to stop the fighting." I looked at David, who just shrugged. We left the meeting.

"What are you doing?" I asked Bernard. "Your President told Olmert there should be no resolution."

Bernard was a bit defensive but retorted, "The Arabs won't accept no resolution. I have to go with them." *Now what?* I thought.

I rushed back to the holding room and called Steve Hadley, describing what had happened. He reached his French counterpart, but there was clearly a split between the Élysée Palace (the presidency) and the Quai d'Orsay (the Foreign Ministry). I returned to the room with the Arabs and said that we'd work with them on a resolution. "I will stay here tonight to see if we can find a solution," I said. My own view had been colored by a call from Abbas, who had begged me for a resolution. "There will be a 'day of rage' tomorrow, and I'm not sure we can keep the West Bank quiet. Salam [Fayyad] is very worried."

After many hours—we worked until about nine at night—we negotiated a resolution. It was far from perfect. I would have preferred a stronger condemnation of Hamas, but it did not condemn Israel and at least mentioned the need to stop terrorism.

Olmert, when he called me in New York, was enraged. He thought I'd double-crossed him by agreeing to a resolution. "Your problem, Prime Minister," I told him, "was with the French. I thought you said Sarkozy was with you."

Tzipi Livni, who would stand for election as prime minister in a few weeks, called too. "This is a disaster," she said.

"You haven't even read it," I countered. "Would it help if the U.S. abstains?"

"Yes, it would," she answered.

I dialed the President and caught up with him in the White House residence. He'd just heard from the angry Olmert.

All of my colleagues were gathered in the Security Council chamber. I knew that everyone would vote yes, and I had, after all, negotiated the resolution. "How do you want me to vote?" I asked the President.

"How do *you* want to vote?" he responded.

"On balance I would vote yes, but I'll certainly understand if you want me to abstain."

"We need to abstain," he said.

And so I did, casting the only vote that wasn't in the affirmative. As I was leaving, the Saudi and UAE foreign ministers came over to the car. "You are a good friend," they said, thanking me for letting the resolution go forward. "This helps us immensely."

I felt bad that my last vote in the United Nations was, in a sense, against the Israelis. In reality, it was worse than that: it wasn't for anyone, and it wasn't against anyone. Sometimes that's the best you can do, but it felt empty. The next day Olmert told the press that the President had overruled me. *You snake!* I fumed. I called him and yelled at him about it and I told the President I would never trust Olmert again. *It doesn't matter,* I told myself. *We're done.*

But we weren't quite done. The Israelis didn't stop their offensive right away, and Tzipi and Olmert needed our help in getting a basis on which to do so. As I'd done so many times, I shuttled by phone among the Egyptians, the Israelis, and the Palestinians to find a solution. The question was whether we could find a reliable way to close the tunnels Hamas was using to smuggle weapons into Gaza. If the Israeli government could tell its people that that had been achieved, it could end the military operation.

After several days, we were pretty close to an agreed-upon set of arrangements, with the Egyptians playing a major role—supported by our training and technical assistance—in shutting off the arms supply.

It was Thursday, January 15, a day before I would leave the State Department for good. Tzipi Livni was on the phone. "I need to come there and sign the document. We need a visible demonstration that the U.S. will guarantee these arrangements," she said.

"Tzipi, there isn't time. I'm leaving office tomorrow. Why don't we just make an announcement in our respective capitals?"

But she persisted. "I'm leaving tonight, and I'll be there tomorrow morning." I realized that the Israelis needed this one last show of support and that Tzipi, because of her bid to become prime minister, needed it most of all. *I guess I can do this one more time,* I decided.

And so, one hour before I said good-bye to the State Department, I sat in the Treaty Room and signed a memorandum of understanding on terms for an end to the latest conflict in Gaza.

I said good-bye to Tzipi at the seventh-floor elevator. "Thank you," she said, "for your friendship and your support of Israel. Come to visit.

You'll always be welcome." I hugged her, thanked her for all we'd done together, and wished her good luck in the elections.

Then I walked back to my office and wrote a little note to Hillary Clinton. It's customary for the outgoing secretary to leave last thoughts. I didn't say anything elaborate, and what I did say will remain between the two of us. I was very, very glad to be done.

"Time to go," I said to Brian as we headed down the elevator and into the lobby where the State Department's employees were gathered. I looked out at the faces, some of which I knew well and some I didn't really know at all. I thanked them all just the same and walked out of the front door for the last time as "S." My car was waiting to take me to Camp David, where I'd meet up with the President and some of his closest senior staff. The weekend was busy because there were myriad details that had to be tied down in association with the Gaza agreement. But I tried to enjoy it and take in the atmosphere one final time.

I remembered my first time at Camp David. The President and I had decided to go to the gym to work out. We had gotten horribly lost, disoriented by the blinding snowstorm all around us. "They may never find us," I said.

The President laughed. "Great first headline—the President and the national security advisor lost in the snow," he joked.

On Sunday morning the presidential party attended church, as we'd done so many times before, in good times and bad. The Camp David staff gathered in the hanger to say good-bye, and then we flew off in Marine One. There is a nice tradition at Camp David: each time the President arrives, the flag of the commander in chief is raised just as he lands. It is lowered the minute he leaves, only to be raised again upon his return. This time when the marines lowered the flag, it was for the last time. I looked over at the forty-third President, who was quietly gazing out of the window. I wanted to say something, but it was better not to. I closed my eyes and let scenes from the last eight years flash in front of me. And then I thanked God for the improbable events that had brought me to this place. There had been no higher honor.

EPILOGUE

AS THE WHITE HOUSE Soviet specialist at the end of the Cold War, I witnessed the liberation of Eastern Europe, the unification of Germany on Western terms, and the beginning of the peaceful collapse of the Soviet Union. It is difficult in retrospect to remember just how unlikely those events once seemed as the Soviet Union cast its shadow across Eastern Europe. Few people personally remember the Hungarian Revolution of 1956 and fewer still the Berlin crisis of 1948. When I returned to Stanford in 2009, I was startled when I realized that some of my students had not even been born when the Berlin Wall fell, and many had never seen the hammer and sickle fly above the Kremlin.

As the Cold War's darkest days fade from memory, what once seemed impossible now seems to have been inevitable. In reality, the peaceful resolution of the Cold War was the product of farsighted decisions made at a time of great uncertainty. After World War II, the United States and its allies set out a vision and built institutions to guide us through the "long-twilight struggle" to victory. The foundation of that strategy was an unyielding trust in the ability of free nations to outperform and then to outlast those that denied their people freedom.

In my last major television interview on *Meet the Press*, David Gregory thanked me for all the time I'd given to the program. He told me that it was my twentieth appearance on the show. *Twenty times. My God, that's a lot of Sunday mornings.* David asked a version of a question that I've been asked repeatedly since: What will be the legacy of the Bush administration? Often accompanying such queries is the implication—well, more than an implication—that the turmoil of 9/11, Afghanistan, Iraq, and the Middle East would forever scar the eight years that we served. I've answered honestly that my own experiences affirm that "history has a long arc," and I do believe that "it bends toward justice."

The past decade has tested that proposition and those who have been responsible for leadership of the country through these turbulent times. There have been three great shocks to the international system since 2001. The first two, 9/11 and the global financial crisis, bookend the presidency of George W. Bush and strike at the heart of our nation's most vital interests—our security and our prosperity. The third is the Arab Spring.

Since the beginning of this historic year, the people of the Arab world have challenged the autocratic order in at least a half dozen states. Some governments have fallen; others teeter; a few have regained their balance. Still others have not yet faced the unrest but brace for the day that will undoubtedly come. The desire for freedom will persist until it is secured.

As Americans, this should not surprise us. The United States has a view of how human history ought to unfold. In 1776 we claimed our inalienable rights and insisted on their universality. As the United States grew into a great power and then a superpower, it has not been neutral in the struggle between freedom and tyranny.

The events of the Arab Spring have vindicated the belief in the universality of our values. Those commentators who today reduce the demands of the people in the streets of Tunis and Cairo to only economic grievances do them a disservice. Certainly people want a better life, but they can only demand it and hold their government accountable if they have a right to change their leaders. If they can't do that peacefully, they will turn to violence to achieve their goals.

The events of September 11 brought the practical implications of that dynamic into sharper focus. The terrorists responsible for those devastating attacks hailed from countries where oppressive governments had closed peaceful outlets for political reform, creating conditions ripe for violent extremism. These terrorists were able to operate in weak or failing states that allowed them to recruit, train, and plan their attacks with relative impunity. President Bush and his foreign policy team understood those implications and adjusted course after 9/11. We pursued the Freedom Agenda not only because it was right but also because it was necessary. There is both a moral case and a practical one for the proposition that no man, woman, or child should live in tyranny. Those who excoriated the approach as idealistic or unrealistic missed the point. In the long run, it is authoritarianism that is unstable and unrealistic. This is because every dictator fears the "Ceausescu moment," described to us by the Romanians when President Bush visited Bucharest in 2002.

In 1989 Nicolae Ceausescu, then secretary general of the Romanian Communist Party and overseer of a repressive regime, went into a square in Bucharest thinking he had sufficiently quelled the growing discontent in his country. His speech began with a recitation of all he'd done for the Romanian people. At the time revolutions were spreading throughout Eastern Europe—in Poland, Czechoslovakia, Hungary, East Germany, and beyond.

As he was speaking, an old lady suddenly yelled, "Liar!" Then ten people joined her, then one hundred, then one thousand, and soon one hundred thousand. An unnerved Ceausescu turned to run but the military delivered him to the revolutionaries instead. The hated Romanian leader and his wife, Elena, were executed.

That is the Ceausescu moment, when the only thing standing between the dictator and his people—fear—breaks down, and there is nothing left but anger. An old lady yells "liar," a policeman refuses to fire at the Berlin Wall, a soldier turns his tank turret away from the crowd in the square, and suddenly the tides have turned in favor of the oppressed. We had hoped that the authoritarians of the Middle East, particularly our friends, would change the basis of their relationship to their people before the Ceausescu moment came to them. But some of them did not. As I write, people across the region are clamoring for their liberty and demanding a voice in how they will be governed.

While freedom and democracy sustain each other, they are not the same thing. Democracy is both a process and a system of governance that protects freedom. The process is begun with elections—a first step toward stable democracy. The harder task is to construct institutional arrangements that define the relationship of the individual's rights to the state's authority and sustain that contract over time.

The United States, more than any other country, should understand that the journey from freedom to stable democracy is a long one and that its work is never done. After all, when the Founding Fathers said, "We the people," they didn't mean me. My ancestors were counted as three-fifths of a man in the deal that permitted the founding of this country. My father had trouble registering to vote in Alabama in 1952 due to poll tests and harassment of black voters. And I didn't have a white classmate until I moved from Birmingham to Denver at age twelve.

Still, we are also an example of why institutions matter in moving toward justice. When Martin Luther King or Rosa Parks—one a recognized national leader, the other an ordinary citizen—wanted to challenge the status quo, they could appeal directly to America's own principles. They didn't have to ask the United States to be something else, only to be what it professed to be. That's the value of democratic institutions, even if their promise is not completely fulfilled immediately. At first, constitutions or bills of rights may exist only on paper. But they exist. And as people begin to appeal to them, to use them, to insist on respect for them by those in positions of authority, these institutions gain legitimacy and power.

Yet political change is necessary but not sufficient in itself for the success of democracy. When people choose their leaders they tend to expect more of them in terms of economic prosperity and social justice. That is why support for democracy must be accompanied by support for development. The Millennium Challenge Corporation was created with this in mind. Those who are governing wisely and democratically can use foreign assistance to deliver for their people—better health care, education, and prospects for employment. Ultimately, good leaders will free their economies and their markets and attract private investment. But they need help at the start, and our investment in them will pay off many times over as the number of stable, responsible democracies grows.

It is why, having helped Afghans and Iraqis win their freedom, we have an ongoing stake in the maturation of their nascent institutions. If the governments are called to fulfill the contract their people have with them, the democracies will over time stabilize and mature. Citizens will use those institutions to address their grievances and to pursue remedies. Most important, they will know that the ultimate weapon is in their hands: they can change their leaders peacefully. And in time, terrorists and hostile neighbors will find it more difficult to shake the foundations of these governments.

Nowhere is this truer than in the Middle East where the Arab Spring has freed millions. Americans can help to channel the developments there in a positive direction. We have influence with the militaries in Egypt and Tunisia; with civil society and political activists, many of whom we've helped to train through America's nongovernmental institutions; and with entrepreneurs and businesspeople who need a way to access the power of international markets to deliver jobs and prosperity.

In other places, our friends—particularly the monarchs of the region—still have a chance to reform now before it's too late. The United States can coax these monarchies to adopt constitutions and reforms that give greater voice to their people. The changes will strengthen moderate voices across the region, including in the Palestinian territories. The Palestinians have made great strides toward building democratic and accountable governing structures—even in the absence of statehood. The United States and the international community—but most especially, Israelis and Arabs—have an interest in providing a framework toward peace in which those hard-won reforms can be sustained.

And to our enemies, the Syrian and Iranian regimes, we should say, "Your time has come. Whatever follows you is unlikely to be worse, for your people and for the world, than who you have been."

To say that democracy is ultimately stabilizing is not to say that the pathway will be smooth and without setbacks, even violence. Because reform has come late in the Middle East, the most organized forces are the extremists who gathered in radical mosques and madrassas while authoritarians pushed decent political forces out of the public square. The radical Islamists will likely contest in elections. But perhaps it's better that way. In the light of day, they will have to answer questions about individual rights and religious freedom and about the role of women. They will have to explain too how they intend to improve people's lives. When the only vision they have to offer is one of oppression and destruction, they will surely fail, removing not only the threat they pose to the region but also across the globe.

It all sounds like very heavy lifting, and as I've traveled abroad since leaving office, people ask me if the United States is still prepared to be a catalyst for democratic change and a partner for those who seek it. The question is often sparked by the second of those great international shocks: the financial crisis and its aftermath. Is America out of steam, confidence, and optimism? I don't believe that we are—and I don't believe we have a choice to retire to the sidelines.

I told President Bush a few months before leaving office that people were tired of us. After 9/11 we dared to think in broad historical strokes, believing that many of the old assumptions about stability and security no longer held. I realize now that it may have seemed unsettling—and exhausting—at home and abroad. But the legacy of 9/11 is a reminder that indeed our interests and our values are linked. That lesson was never more evident than when the consequences of the freedom gap in the Middle East exploded here at home.

As secretary of state I was always aware of the constraints of the world as it *is* and resolved to practice the art of the possible. But I also tried not to lose sight of the world as it could be, and insisted on a path toward that end. This is the long-term work of diplomacy. History will judge how well we did. I can live with that, and I am grateful for the chance to have tried.

NOTE ON SOURCES

In composing this memoir, I drew upon a variety of materials to supplement my own recollections of the consequential events that shaped my time at the White House and State Department. I relied on my daily calendars and official trip logs to recall various meetings and travel over the course of my eight years in government. I am enormously grateful to Liz Lineberry for keeping such meticulous records.

I also drew heavily on the public papers of the George W. Bush presidency as well as those released by the State Department from 2005 to 2009, including speeches, public statements, reports, publications, and transcripts of briefings, congressional testimony, interviews, and press conferences. These materials are publicly available on the archived websites for the George W. Bush White House (http://georgewbush-whitehouse.archives.gov/) and the State Department (http://2001–2009.state.gov).

In addition, I consulted documents housed at the George W. Bush Presidential Library and my papers at the State Department. On several occasions, Peter Haligas made it possible for me to review my NSC papers at the library's temporary facility in Louisville, Texas, and he, Shannon Jarrett, and David Sabo assisted in processing declassification requests. Clarence Finney, director of the office of correspondence and records at the State Department, made it possible for me to review my papers in California. I am indebted to the dedicated employees of the National Archives and Records Administration who are preserving these documents from this consequential period of American history not only for me but also for future generations of scholars.

A number of my colleagues and former associates in government generously participated in interviews for this book and helped sharpen my memory of key events. The Presidential Oral History Program at the University of Virginia's Miller Center of Public Affairs hosted roundtable discussions with some of my senior staff members at the State Department. I am grateful to Russell Riley, the chair of the program, Bryan Craig, Katrina Kuhn, Barbara Perry, Marc Selverstone, and Seyom Brown for organizing these. Many other colleagues provided helpful answers to my various inquiries throughout this process.

I reviewed secondary sources as well, including news reports in print and broadcast media, to supplement my own recollections. I consulted articles in the *New York Times*, the *Washington Post*, the *Wall Street Journal*, and other publications in conjunction with broadcast transcripts from programs produced by CNN, Fox News, ABC News, CBS News, NBC News, and other networks. Archived news coverage was accessed through online subscription databases made available by the Stanford University Libraries & Academic Information Resources.

A partial list of sources appears below.

Bush, George W. 2001. "Statement by the President in His Address to the Nation." Oval Office, White House, Washington, D.C., September 11.

———. 2001. "Address to a Joint Session of Congress and the American People." United States Capitol, Washington, D.C., September 20.

———. 2001. "Remarks by the President to the United Nations General Assembly." United Nations Headquarters, New York, N.Y., November 10.

———. 2002. "State of the Union Address." United States Capitol, Washington, D.C., January 29.

———. 2002. "President Bush Delivers Graduation Speech at West Point." United States Military Academy, West Point, N.Y., June 1.

———. 2002. "President Bush Calls for New Palestinian Leadership." Rose Garden, White House, Washington, D.C., June 24.

———. 2002. "Remarks by the President to the United Nations General Assembly." United Nations Headquarters, New York, N.Y., September 12.

———. 2003. "Address to the Nation." Cross Hall, White House, March 17.

———. 2003. "Address to the Nation." Oval Office, White House, March 19.

———. 2004. "Letter from President Bush to Prime Minister Sharon," April 14.

———. 2005. "Second Inaugural Address." United States Capitol, Washington, D.C., January 20.

———. 2007. "Address to the Nation." Library, White House, January 10.

Commission on Intelligence Capabilities of the United States Regarding Weapons of Mass Destruction. "Report to the President of the United States." March 31, 2005.

Director of Central Intelligence. "Iraq's Weapons of Mass Destruction Programs." October 2002.

Iraq Study Group. *The Iraq Study Group Report: The Way Forward—A New Approach.* New York: Vintage Books, 2006.

Joseph, Robert G. *Countering WMD: The Libyan Experience.* Fairfax, Va.: National Institute Press, 2009.

National Commission on Terrorist Attacks Upon the United States. *The 9/11 Commission Report.* 2004.

National Security Strategy of the United States of America. September 2002.

Office of the Director of National Intelligence. "Iran: Nuclear Intentions and Capabilities." National Intelligence Estimate. November 2007.

Performance-Based Road Map to a Permanent Two-State Solution to the Israeli-Palestinian Conflict. United Nations Security Council Document S/2003/529.

Rice, Condoleezza. "Promoting the National Interest." *Foreign Affairs.* January/February 2000.

———. 2004. Testimony at the Ninth Public Hearing of the National Commission on Terrorist Attacks Upon the United States. Hart Senate Office Building, Washington, D.C., April 8.

———. 2005. "Remarks at the American University in Cairo." Cairo, Egypt, June 20.

———. 2005. Testimony before the Senate Foreign Relations Committee. "Iraq in United States Foreign Policy." 109th Cong., 2nd sess., October 19.

———. 2006. "Transformational Diplomacy." Georgetown University, Washington, D.C., January 18.

———. 2007. "Remarks at the Centennial Dinner for the Economic Club of New York." New York, N.Y., June 7.

———. "Rethinking the National Interest." *Foreign Affairs.* March/April 2008.

United Nations Development Programme, Regional Bureau for Arab States/Arab Fund for Economic and Social Development. *Arab Human Development Report 2002: Creating Opportunities for Future Generations.* New York: United Nations Publications, 2002.

U.S. Army/Marine Corps Counterinsurgency Field Manual. U.S. Army Field Manual No. 3–24/Marine Corps Warfighting Publication No. 3–33.5. Chicago: University of Chicago Press, 2007.

U.S. Senate Select Committee on Intelligence and U.S. House Permanent Select Committee on Intelligence. "Joint Inquiry into Intelligence Community Activities Before and After the Terrorist Attacks of September 11, 2001." 107th Cong., 2nd sess., S. Report No. 107–351, H. Report No. 107–792, December 2002.

Acknowledgments

Writing this book has afforded me the opportunity to revisit the historic and challenging events of my eight years of government service. In doing so, I have felt enormously grateful for the chance to work with such wonderful people, many of whom became and remain dear friends.

During those years in Washington the pressure was often high, and I was sustained by the love of my family and their unwavering support. The extraordinary, ordinary Rays and Rices were always there—just a phone call away.

This book simply would not have been possible without the dedication of Cameron Bell and Theo Milonopoulos. Cam and Theo led the project from its inception to its final stages, providing exemplary leadership and research, keen insights, and scrupulous attention to detail. Their drive for excellence greatly enhanced the manuscript.

I want to thank my senior research associate, Leisel Bogan, who contributed to story lines, offered helpful feedback, and supplied background information, as well as my invaluable research team: Kia Ghorashi, Justine Isola, Charles Nicas, and early on, Daniel Slate. Their precision in fact-checking and copyediting was both humbling and essential. The book also received important contributions from Mohammad Ali, Jenny Arriola, Amir Badat, Dianna Bai, Carolyn Forstein, Avery Halfon, and Philippe de Koning.

My team in California has been a blessing to me as they balance and support my many commitments. My new, indefatigable chief of staff, Georgia Godfrey, along with her excellent predecessors, Anne Lyons and Colby Cooper, have provided leadership and wise counsel over the years. Caroline Beswick and Julianne Jochmann kept me on schedule and organized, and my longtime assistant Marilyn Stanley remained indispensible throughout the production process. Others in my office—Natalie Davies, Blair Dawkins, Taylor Jackson, Emma Welch, Molly Welch—offered cheerful assistance.

The continued support of the Hoover Institution and Stanford University allowed me to complete this project. John Hennessy, John Etchemendy, John Raisian, Garth Saloner, Steven Denning and Roberta Bowman Denning, George and Charlotte Shultz, and Thomas and Barbara Stephenson have continuously welcomed me back home to Stanford with open arms.

I'd like to thank the team at Crown Publishing—specifically Tina Constable, David Drake, Laura Duffy, Linnea Knollmueller, Elizabeth Rendfleisch, Nathan Roberson, Robert Siek, and Penny Simon for their efforts on behalf of this book. And thank you to my talented editor, Rick Horgan, who challenged me to reflect and then gave me the space to write my story.

I am grateful for the trusted friends and colleagues who helped make the experience of government service a meaningful one. Many shared their thoughts, memories, and anecdotes for this book. President Bush and First Lady Laura Bush were gracious in doing so. Steve Hadley, Steve Krasner, and Anja Manuel reviewed the manuscript, as did my Stanford colleagues David Kennedy and Amy Zegart. Thanks also to John Bellinger, Dan Fried, Jendayi Frazer, and David Welch, who read and commented on matters related to their expertise.

Many former colleagues also answered research inquiries as they arose. To Bill Burns, Nick Burns, Victor Cha, Eliot Cohen, Bob Conquest, Alexander Downer, Brian Gunderson, Carlos Gutierrez, Albert Hawkins, Michael Hayden, Chris Hill, Reuben Jeffrey, Anne Krueger, Jay Lefkowitz, Greg Manuel, Cindy Marble, Sean McCormack, Frank Miller, Kori Schake, Tom Shannon, James Sheehan, Shirin Tahir-Kheli, Fran Townsend, Matt Waxman, and Phil Zelikow, thank you for your kind and generous help.

During my research, the Miller Center of Public Affairs at the University of Virginia invited me to participate in their Presidential Oral History Program. Russell Riley, the program chair, and Katrina Kuhn, the program administrator, conducted useful group interviews with my former State and White House team. I am grateful to them for this terrific forum.

The professionals at the National Archives and Records Administration at the George W. Bush Presidential Library were relentless in their search for records and documents. Shannon Jarrett, the supervisory archivist, and archivists Peter Haligas and David Sabo guided me through the archives, and Jodie Steck willingly tracked down photos from my days at the White House.

I also appreciate the people in Washington who helped me access key records and documents. Those who facilitated the declassification review process deserve my particular thanks for their patience and efficiency. It was a pleasure working with Peggy Grafeld, Mark Ramee, and Clarence Finney at the State Department, and Bill Leary at the NSC.

Finally, I wish to thank Harry Rhoads and Liz Morrison at Washington Speakers Bureau as well as Suzanne Gluck, Wayne Kabak, Teri Tobias, and Steve Neal for their continuing support and advice.

INDEX

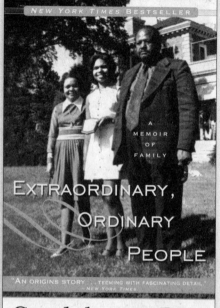

Books of Merit

The Fire Thief

the
fire
thief

STEPHEN

GUPPY

Thomas Allen Publishers
Toronto

National Library of Canada Cataloguing in Publication

Guppy, Stephen, 1951–
    The fire thief / Stephen Guppy.

ISBN 0-88762-142-2

I. Title.

PS8563.U577F57   2004   C811'.54   C2003-906705-X

Editor: Patrick Crean/Sarah Williams
Cover and text design: Gordon Robertson
Cover image: Kristin Sjaarda

Published by Thomas Allen Publishers,
a division of Thomas Allen & Son Limited,
145 Front Street East, Suite 209,
Toronto, Ontario M5A 1E3 Canada

www.thomas-allen.com

**Canada Council
for the Arts**

ONTARIO ARTS COUNCIL
CONSEIL DES ARTS DE L'ONTARIO

The publisher gratefully acknowledges the support of
the Ontario Arts Council for its publishing program.

We acknowledge the support of the Canada Council for the Arts, which
last year invested $20.3 million in writing and publishing throughout Canada.

We acknowledge the Government of Ontario through the
Ontario Media Development Corporation's Ontario Book Initiative.

We acknowledge the financial support of the Government of Canada
through the Book Publishing Industry Development Program (BPIDP)
for our publishing activities.

08 07 06 05 04   1 2 3 4 5

Printed and bound in Canada

For Nelly, Sebastian, Izabel

Nür die Fülle führt zur Klarheit.

—— NIELS BOHR, 1927

Part One

1

Boomtown

Buried deep beneath the porous ground of the Danforth Nuclear Reservation, there are 828 radioactive beagles. The dogs are encased within the six-inch-thick stainless-steel walls of a cylindrical vault sunk forty-seven feet beneath the surface. Nearby, in an identical storage tank, one of several others in that particular tank farm, is every single drop of every piss and crap those beagles ever took. There are just over sixteen tonnes of radioactive beagle waste in total. The dogs were used in an experiment to test the effects of radioactivity on animals. They were exposed to radiation in carefully measured doses, and the effects of the exposure were observed and recorded. Then the dogs were bred and the incidence of birth defects noted. When the experiment was deemed complete, the beagles were destroyed.

There are also entire freight trains buried out at Danforth, as well as cores from the reactors of nuclear submarines, and bulldozers that were contaminated when they were used to move radioactive waste. In the opinion of some physicists, the tank farms at Danforth may be the last artifacts of mankind to survive on this planet, as by the time the plutonium and other radioactive matter in those subterranean tanks becomes inert, the human race will almost certainly be extinct.

This is where I grew up: Atomic City, USA. The drive-in where I hung out with my friends was called Nukie's. The mascot of the high school football team—the Bombers—was a freshman dressed up as a mushroom cloud. There was a street called Plutonium Crescent. You get the idea.

My stepfather rarely spoke about his job at "the Area" when I was growing up. Neither did the fathers of the kids I went to school with. If Clyde discussed the details of his work with my mother, Betty, she never passed any of it along to me. I understood that he had a responsible position at the nuclear plant, that the function of the plant had something to do with nuclear energy and the defence of the country in the event of a war, and none of us questioned the morality of what he and his employers did. In the late fifties and early sixties, there was nothing particularly remarkable about working in a nuclear plant or a disposal site for radioactive materials. We rarely mentioned or thought of the risk; we were marching straight into the future, and the rest of the world seemed obsolete.

2

The Madhouse Choir

My biological father, Alfred Wheeler, was one of the last Canadian soldiers to be killed in the Second World War. He died in the town of Nijmegen, not far from the Dutch-German border. It was six weeks past VE day, long after he should have been safely on his way back home to his pregnant wife and family. According to family legend, at the very moment that my father's heart stopped beating, Aunt Alice—my father's twin sister—woke up in bed beside her fiancé and screamed, *Suffering Jesus! Alfie's dead!* This happened in a cheap motel in Greeley, Colorado. My aunt and the boyfriend, Joel Kaiser, were on their way to Los Angeles to audition for a radio show. They were going to make it big in country music. After Aunt Alice had her flash of intuition, they turned around and headed north.

Everyone in my father's family played an instrument of some sort. Years ago, before I was born, they had toured the Prairies as a family act, Daddy Bill and His Nine Spinning Wheelers. My grandfather, Daddy Bill, was a fiddler and my grandmother, Kitty, played guitar and did much of the singing. My uncles played upright bass, dobro and drums. Alfred and Alice, the twins, sang duets. In the photos I have of them, taken back in the middle thirties, they're two bright-eyed farm kids with snow-white hair, both of them smiling artlessly toward the photographer's lens. My father's wearing a cowboy shirt and jeans with the cuffs rolled up, and Auntie Alice has so many crinolines on that her guitar seems to rest on her skirt. The camera loves them. They're so perky it gets on your nerves.

My mother became a registered nurse the year after my father died—1947. She had started her training during the time of her husband's absence, taking six months off to look after her new baby. When she heard about a job in a psychiatric clinic on the coast she accepted it without hesitation. We moved to New Westminster, on the north side of the Fraser River, half an hour's drive from Vancouver, and Betty settled in to raise her child alone. A couple of years of weekly letters and anxious phone calls later, my grandparents, Floyd and Billie Arnott, sold up their pharmacy in Mainprize, Saskatchewan, and moved out to join us on the coast. This was the family I knew as a child.

Betty's job was at Riverdale, which was just a few miles up the Fraser River from our house. Riverdale was (and is, although the name has been changed) a hospital for the mentally ill—the *insane*, they probably would have said in those days. Betty worked as a psychiatric nurse. She had to commute to work from our bungalow in New Westminster; usually, she left me with a neighbour or hired a girl to babysit me while she was away. Most of the time, this arrangement seemed to work okay—I got to know several of the families in the neighbourhood quite well, and I also became acquainted with a succession of sullen, bored-to-tears-by-children teenage girls. The summer I was six, however, Betty's system broke down: the neighbours all went on vacation at once, and the girls got better-paying jobs or simply grew up and moved on.

"You'll have to come along to work," my mother announced one morning. "You can see what I do for a living up close, and we'll save a few bucks in the process."

I'd been out to Riverdale once or twice before when Betty had to drop by on one of her days off to pick up a paycheque or meet with a doctor, but I'd never made it past the reception area. It was raining when we pulled up outside the clinic, and as a consequence none of the patients or staff was outside on the grounds. The building was an unadorned, forbidding-looking rectangle faced with beige sandstone, four storeys high with a flat roof and rows of puny windows. Brutally drab, rather than sinister—but to me it might as well have been Dracula's castle. Insane people, after all, lived there. People too crazy to have their own houses. Only the reassuring presence of my mother made me willing to go inside.

Betty got me set up in a little nurses' lounge on the third floor, which was where she was working. She'd brought along a colouring book and a couple of my favourite toys, as well as some apple juice in a plastic bottle and cookies for my snack. She'd drop in as often as she could manage, she told me. Meanwhile, I was to stay in the lounge, talk to no one who wasn't dressed exactly like her, and play with my trucks and my crayons. The ward clerk at the nurses' station just outside would let her know if I had any problems. Then she kissed me and disappeared down the hall.

It was warm in the lounge, I can remember that quite clearly. The building, I guess, had hot-water heat, and the cranky old cast-iron radiators moaned and clanked incessantly as they filled the room with warmth. The lounge smelled of antiseptic and cigarette smoke, so that the air, stained yellow by the roll-down blinds on the narrow windows, seemed alternately caustic and stale. I coloured Mickey Mouse royal purple on a field of lurid yellow, drew polka-dots on Goofy's nose and gave Daisy Duck a brilliant grass-green halo. Footsteps came and went in the hall outside the open door, and each time I heard someone passing I looked up in expectation, hoping it was my mother coming back. Finally, a couple of nurses came in on their coffee break and sat on the leatherette sofa while they smoked their cigarettes. One of them was blond and young and the other was grey-haired and heavy-set and acted like she had kids or even grandkids of her own. She asked me sensible questions about the pictures I was colouring and wanted to know if I'd had cookies or something to drink. The younger woman also tried to take an interest in what I was doing, telling me what a lovely dump truck I had and so forth, but she was clearly anxious to get the other nurse's attention so that she could tell her about how her boyfriend had taken her skiing. When they'd finished their coffee and cigarettes they stood up and straightened their uniforms; then they went back to their jobs, the older one ruffling my hair as she passed.

After what seemed like a very long time, I began to get lonely for my mother. Remembering what she'd said about the ward clerk, I wandered out the door of the lounge and started down the hall. The nurses' station, when I found it, was unattended: the ward clerk, whoever that might have been, had obviously taken a powder. Perhaps, I thought, he or she was through the doors I could see at the opposite end of the hallway. Or maybe Betty was through those doors. Either way, it was worth a look.

I pushed the heavy metal-clad door open with some difficulty, and found myself in another corridor. I was greeted by the muffled sound of voices. Most of the doorways, on both sides of the hall, stood open. I peered cautiously into a few of these rooms, noting the beds with their drawn white curtains and again the clinical smell of antiseptic, then made my way down to the end of the hall. The room there was filled with sunlight—it was, I would find out later, called the "sunroom"—and it was occupied by six men in bathrobes, five of whom were playing cards. The card-players were sitting on folding chairs, hunched over a bockety card table, squinting pensively at the cards in their hands. The sixth man sat bolt upright on an old sway-backed couch, pawing at a magazine as if he'd left something important wedged between its pages and was frantically trying to find it. The light was both exhilarating and blinding. The room had a very high ceiling, and the windows seemed to reach beyond my sight.

"Who dealt this garbage?" the tallest man at the table said. He was a barrel-chested, rumbling-voiced giant, but I couldn't see his features, as he was back-lit against the glare ice of the windows.

"The Holy Ghost," another man answered. This voice was trembly and almost feminine in its sweetness. "It was his deal. Almost always is, isn't it?" The owner of the tremulous voice, a hunched shape whose slippers kept making sliding sounds on the lino, followed up his brief speech with a slippery glissando of a giggle.

"No wonder I'm holding this bunch of bananas, then," the giant said. "I think ol' HG likes to watch me lose. Einstein couldn't win diddly-squat with a handful of rat-shit like this."

"Just listen to him, will you, bluffing his butt off! Expects us to swallow a story like that, the old reprobate." The new voice was assertive and had a trace of some hard-edged foreign accent. "You think he used that poker face on quarterbacks when he was playing? Lulled them into a stupor before he snapped their stupid heads off their necks?" By the time he'd finished talking, my vision had cleared sufficiently that I could see his face as he glowered at his companions over a fan of cards. He was sallow, squat and heavy-browed, and his eyes were dark and filled with bitter fire. I must have taken a step toward this compelling figure, as he'd hardly stopped talking before the group at the card table finally noticed my presence.

"Oh, look, O'Malley, a leprechaun. Conjured up in your honour, I have no doubt. Perhaps this means your luck is going to change!" said the man with the quivering voice. The ascending arpeggio of his giggle again filled the air.

"A what?" asked the giant, not yet deigning to look up from his cards.

"A kid in the ward, for Chrissakes," said the squat man. "Where the Sam Hell'd he spring from? One of them scrawny hens on Level 3 go and hatch herself an egg?"

"Mind your French, Szokey," Trembling Voice whispered.

The giant finally dropped his cards and regarded me with dark blue, apparently myopic eyes that hung beneath the cantilevered eaves of lush grey eyebrows.

"A kid," he breathed. "A real one."

The incandescent room was still and silent. All five of the card-players stared at me in silence—Trembling Voice, Fire Eyes, the Giant, a spindly man with a mist of white fuzz on his mottled eggshell scalp, and another man—the Holy Ghost?—whose hair was long and scarecrow blond and whose eyes seemed blank as marbles.

I could feel myself starting to pout and then sob, my lower lip jutting involuntarily out and my eyes misting over with confusion and fear under the gaze of these huge silent strangers. I was just beginning to bawl in earnest when the Giant got down on one knee and put his hand—large and loose as a turkey wing—on one of my shoulders.

"Hey, kid," he said, "you want to play rummy?"

By the time Betty found me, I had beaten Fire Eyes twice at snap, and Trembling Voice, who by then had been introduced to me as Arthur, was helping the Giant to teach me the basics of rummy. Betty had apparently been standing in the doorway of the sunroom watching us play for quite some time before she cleared her throat and interrupted the game. She was so relieved at finding me safe, she told me later, that she completely forgot to chew me out for disobeying her and wandering away from the lounge. The fact that she'd found me with a half-dozen certified loonies didn't bother her at all.

"He could do worse," she told my grandparents over the phone that evening. "If being cracked is your only failing, you're more reliable than most folks I know."

For the next few days I spent my time playing hand after hand of cards with the men of Level 5. Betty'd drop me off at the sunroom every morning, check on me at coffee breaks and take me to the lounge for lunch at noon. We'd eat our sandwiches and drink our weak tea and I'd tell her about all the interesting things I'd been learning. Mostly, I was becoming increasingly expert at various card games. The Level 5 boys stuck pretty much to rummy, but the presence of a child in their midst seemed to bring out the latent teacher— or some long-buried paternal instinct—in several of them. The Giant was particularly good at showing me how to shuffle and deal the cards; he was patient and reassuring, and his massive frame and deep, gentle voice made me feel secure and confident as I fumbled around with the deck.

Level 5 was the chronic ward—the long-term clientele, as Betty called them. The Giant, O'Malley, had been a professional wrestler, and before that he'd played for Green Bay and three different teams in the Canadian Football League. He'd played DE, and been noted for pulverizing quarterbacks. He'd had a half-dozen major nervous breakdowns, starting in his college days at UCSB, when he ran a fumbled ball he'd recovered all the way up the stairs into the cheap seats and refused to come back down. The game had been decided years ago, he shrieked at the coaches and paramedics as they tried to reassure and calm him; he and his teammates were shadows of the real, long-vanished players. They were dim, incomplete projections of a lost archetypal world.

Trembling Voice, Arthur Jameson, had been an accountant for a shady firm of wholesale clothiers with a sideline as racing touts and loan sharks. Sent to jail when the government audited his bosses' accounts, he had developed a case of agoraphobia so acute that even the limited vertical space of the sunroom made his naturally feminine voice trill and quaver and his delicate fingers shake. Walter Szoke—Fire Eyes—had tried to kill his girlfriend, then in a fit of repentance poisoned himself by drinking homemade beer laced with caustic cleanser. No one seemed to know who the Holy Ghost had been in whatever life he had before he landed up in the asylum. Perhaps he really was an angel, a wandering exile from some more lucid and tranquil dimension—the Mormon Angel Moroni, who lived in the American West before the coming of the Europeans, and who walked with the New World Jesus in the dry lakes of western Nevada.

There were two other sunroom regulars. Carapaldi was a gaunt-faced Italian who never actually joined in the daily rummy game, but always seemed to be hanging around, leafing frantically through dog-eared back issues of *Maclean's* and *Reader's Digest* or minutely examining the carpet and drapes for stains. And Hotchkiss was thin and looked like

Einstein. Neither of these fellows said a word that I can remember, and they remain in my mind as a silent Greek chorus, an audience for their more loquacious fellow inmates.

At the end of my second week of rummy games with the Giant and his friends, my grandparents arrived in New Westminster. Betty took the afternoon off to pick them up from the CNR station, and before we left she took me on a quick tour of the floor to say goodbye to the various new friends I'd made among the nurses and ward clerks who worked on Level 5. The women made a fuss over me, which embarrassed and delighted me and made my mother beam and flush with pride. When the last of the "gals from the ward," as Betty called them, had finally finished tousling my hair and telling me what a brave little soldier I was for waiting with the "boys" while Mama worked, Betty took my hand and led me down the hall towards the sunroom.

"I expect you'll want to say thanks to Mr. O'Malley and the other fellows for putting up with you these past two weeks," she said.

"Aren't we going to play cards any more today?" I asked, having momentarily forgotten all about picking up Floyd and Billie. "Szokey said it was dealer-calls poker after lunch, and he's going to show me how to cheat. He's really good at dealing from the bottom."

"I'm sure Mr. Szoke was only joking, Sonny. Anyways, the patients are having a singalong this afternoon. Mr. Riordan from the Baptist Church in Haney is going to bring his accordion and lead them in some songs."

It would have been just after noon when we got to the end of that hallway, and the sunroom, which had been practically incandescent with angling light all morning, had mellowed into golden shafts and shadows. Though the doors were closed, we could hear the humming, nasal sound of the accordion quite clearly as we approached.

"Be quiet, now. They're listening to Mr. Riordan," Betty cautioned, raising one finger with its red, tapered nail to her lips. She pulled back the door a few inches and peered through the narrow opening, then smiled as if someone inside had greeted her. Assured of our welcome, she pushed me gently into the room. I stood there feeling stunned, my senses fogged with umber light and mellow, buzzing music. Then, as if on cue, the music stopped and everyone applauded.

"That was lovely, Mr. Riordan," one of the nurses said— there were two or three in the room with the inmates. The accordionist, an elderly, glum-looking fellow with streaks of pure white in his sandy-blond hair, nodded shyly at the compliment, then went immediately back to playing. I smiled up at the men who had been my friends and playmates for the past two weeks, searching each of their faces for a hint of recognition, but they were all too intent on reading the words of the song from the mimeographed sheets that each of them held (some in hands that visibly shook with the tension of reading and following the song); no one paid any attention to me. I was about to say something, music or no music, shout out a greeting of some sort to the Giant or Walter Szoke or Arthur, when the tallest of the nurses in the room raised her hand as if she were an orchestra conductor, and everyone stumbled together into song. The voices of the women, strong and surprisingly musical, rose clearly out of the general hum. I could hear O'Malley's deep-bass drone and the guttural, half-shouted words of Fire Eyes. Carapaldi and Hotchkiss didn't try to join in with the others, though the Italian's mouth was working as if he had swallowed a thorn. It took me a moment—almost until the end of the song, in fact—to locate the owner of the lovely, leaping tenor that soared up over the voices of the nurses. The Holy Ghost was singing, his blue, blank eyes uplifted toward the distant plaster ceiling with its bare nests of electrical conduits and its gaping, cobwebby ducts.

Amazing grace, how sweet the sound
That saved a wretch like me
Oh, I was lost, but now am found
Was blind, but now I see . . .

3

A Wedding in the Family

The Wheelers, my father's people, were mythical figures to me. My cowboy-singer father and his talented twin were two distant angels beaming from an album crammed with snapshots, their haloes of platinum hair vivid as coronas ringed around a double star. Then, in the summer of 1954, when I was eight years old, my father's twin sister arrived at our front door. It was Saturday, so Betty was home, and Floyd and Billie had dropped over to help her with some chores around the house. Billie and my mother were out on the little back porch that had been built onto the kitchen, feeding laundry through the wringer of the washer and then pinning up the clothes on the line that stretched out to a post on the far side of the yard. Floyd had rigged up the clothesline for them and now he was in the bathroom, installing a medicine chest that he'd built us, and I was sitting on the toilet seat, watching him measure things (*Measure twice! Cut once!*). When the doorbell rang, Floyd went on waving the measuring tape around and humming through the half-dozen nails he invariably kept between his lips when he was working on the house. I just sat there until I heard Betty hollering, "One of you boys'll have to get that; we're up to our elbows in bluing back here!" I ran to the front door and opened it, expecting to find Johnny Wilkerson from next door. Before I got to the door, I was already composing my excuse for not coming out to play with Johnny; I was having a good time just hanging out with my grandfather and didn't want to do anything else. When I swung the front door open, my eyes were looking straight ahead, where I expected Johnny Wilkerson's face to be. I found myself looking at a wide red patent-leather belt, which was wrapped around Aunt Alice's midriff. The belt went with her striped white suit, her pumps, her wide summer hat. She was wearing bright red lipstick and pinky-red eyeshadow. Even her handbag was shiny and red. I thought she looked just like a film star.

"Good Lord!" she shrieked. "You look exactly like your momma!" I heard someone drop something out on the porch, and then Betty came running, a wad of wet dishtowels still in one hand.

"Oh God! It's Alfie's Alice!" she said. She deposited the towels on the arm of a chair, looked Auntie Alice up and down, and then started tugging frantically at the rag she'd used to tie up her hair.

"Jesus Christ! I look a terrible fright! Excuse me for a minute!"

She turned and ran off towards the bathroom, where she collided with her father, who was just coming out the door.

Auntie Alice winked at me and took a cigarette out of her handbag. We waited in silence while Betty and Floyd disentangled themselves and Billie came in from the porch. Alice was the first Wheeler I'd ever met; or at least the first member of my father's family I was old enough to remember meeting. Grandpa Bill and Kitty were still in Mainprize, two of the boys had died in the war, and my other aunts and uncles had settled down back east. But I'd seen enough snapshots of my father; it was easy to see that he and Alice were twins.

She stayed an hour, then asked us to call her a taxi. She was catching a boat that evening, she said, to Victoria, over on Vancouver Island. Joel Kaiser was waiting there to show her the house he'd just rented; they had decided to give up performing and were finally going to marry and settle down. After she left, my mother and grandparents sat around drinking coffee until late in the afternoon, rehashing everything Alice had said and ignoring all the chores they'd left unfinished. *Didn't she look marvellous? Wasn't that some outfit! With the matching bag and shoes! Do you really think, my grandmother asked, that her and that Joel will settle down? Alice Wheeler has ants in her pants!*

My mother met the man who would become her second husband, Clyde Alonzo Cateret, in the summer of 1959, when I was thirteen years old. My stepfather was an electrical engineer, a "double-E" from Michigan State: the classic Illinois prairie boy with a talent for wiring up gizmos. Years after he died, I found out that he'd worked on the experiments that led to the discovery of the transistor, and that he'd been recruited by one or two of the earliest of the semiconductor firms that were starting up in the Santa Clara Valley. Plenty of engineers of his generation had gone on to ride the big waves of microwave technology and consumer electronics, but Clyde had chosen, for whatever reasons, to stay in the calm, placid waters. He'd spent his working life at the Nuclear Reservation in Danforth, Washington, devising monitoring systems for the canisters of nuclear waste.

Clyde had a cousin who lived in Surrey, across the Fraser River from New Westminster. Zinnia worked with Betty at Riverdale, as a typist in medical records. Like Betty, she was a widow, her husband having been killed in a logging accident, and like Betty, she was the mother of a budding adolescent. Her daughter was a bucktoothed girl named Shirley who lived for horses and modern dance. Betty and Zinnia got together for coffee or lunch in the nurses' lounge on Level 3 once or twice a week to discuss their parallel lives. Every month or two Zinnia would drive up to our place in New West on a Saturday afternoon to do some shopping at the Woodward's store with my mother, and less frequently Betty and I would drive to her place and spend the day with them on their acreage. It was there that Betty ran into Clyde.

It was one of those heavy summer afternoons when even the insects thrumming through the hayfields seemed lethargic. What wind there was brought nothing but humidity off the river. Betty and Zinnia had been talking endlessly about movie stars over tea at the kitchen table ever since we'd arrived, while I tagged along after Shirley as she went about her chores. Shirley was sociable, you had to give her that much, but nothing she wanted to talk about held a great deal

of interest for me. We walked to the barn, which was a minia-
ture version of the sort of thing you'd find on a real working
farm, and she fussed over her horse for a while, then we fed
the few chickens while she talked about dance lessons and
the horse shows she was going to compete in that coming
summer. When we made our way back to the kitchen, Zinnia
and Betty were sitting at the Arborite table smoking cigarettes and chatting with a man I'd never seen before. He was
so tall that he had to sit sideways at the table with his legs jutting out into the room. His arms were thin and red from the
sun, and there was a day's growth of sandy stubble on his
long, sunburned face.

"Sonny, come on in here and meet Clyde," Betty told me.

"Clyde Cateret, this is Sonny Wheeler," Zinnia said. She
was smiling, enjoying the idea of formally introducing a
thirteen-year-old kid to an engineer in his mid-forties. Clyde
got laboriously out of his chair, unwinding those basketball
player's legs of his and stretching out an arm the length of a
construction crane to shake me by the hand.

"Pleasure to make your acquaintance, young man," he
told me. The voice was deep but gentle, and he spoke with a
sort of drawl that sounded vaguely American to me; I eventually learned it was a Midwestern accent. He reminded me
of some film star, Henry Fonda or maybe Jimmy Stewart—
someone calm and strong in a way that didn't hint at a potential for violence.

Clyde and the two women talked right through lunch.
He was, I guess, an easy man to talk to—gentle, direct, with
a soft, teasing humour that Zinnia and Betty seemed to like.

The conversation was of trivial matters, mostly, and I can't imagine, looking back on that afternoon, what subliminal signals were passing between Clyde Cateret and my mother. He reappeared a few weeks later, apparently seized with an uncontrollable desire to visit his cousin. Over the next year or so, he was a frequent guest at Zinnia's and an equally frequent visitor to our house.

Not long before Christmas, Betty came into my room before I went to sleep one evening and announced that she and Clyde were getting married. I nodded and managed a tentative smile, unsure of my own emotions. She stroked my hair the way she had when I was four or five years younger, then reached into the pool of yellow light from the lamp on my bedside table and gently clicked the bedroom into night.

For me, my mother's wedding was a Cook's tour of unfamiliar emotions. The day had been filled with the bustle of adults running about, hastily preparing for the wedding. Betty was in a state from the moment she got up that morning. She couldn't find nylons that didn't have runs, and where the heck had she put the marriage licence, and were you supposed to invite the JP to the reception or not, and would her supervisor out at Riverdale be offended at not being invited, and so on and so on and so on. Billie oscillated between trailing around after her distraught daughter and sneaking into the dining room to fortify herself with tiny nips of almond cream sherry. Floyd wandered around with his thumbs tucked in his braces, reminiscing to no one in particular about weddings he'd attended in the past. Dizzy with anticipation, I hid behind an old *Sports Illustrated* and tried to stay out of the way.

Before lunch, Floyd took me with him to the dry cleaner's to pick up Betty's wedding outfit and the suit that he'd be wearing; then we stopped at the florist's for boutonnieres and corsages. My grandfather used the trip as an opportunity to lecture me on the necessity of adapting to changes. I'd have a father now, he said, for the first time, and that was something I should value: make it easy for your new dad, and he'll reward you with the leadership and security that fathers provide for their children. Think of your mother, too: she'll have a couple of men to look after now, not just you. You'll have to adjust to sharing her attention. Floyd meant well, I'm sure, and he said what he did out of genuine concern for the difficulties he foresaw for me in my life with a stepfather, but his words hit my heart like the strokes of a hammer. I didn't say a word for the rest of the drive.

Betty and Clyde were married in the registry office in New Westminster, British Columbia, in July of 1960. Floyd and Billie were there, as were Zinnia and Shirley and a couple of Betty's nurse friends from work. Clyde arrived half an hour before his wedding, having been held up by heavy traffic at the border. Joel Kaiser, Alice's perpetual fiancé, who had been drafted to stand in as best man, was even later than the groom. Auntie Alice finally turned up at the reception, which was held at a Chinese restaurant down on Pender Street in Vancouver. She had a steady gig performing on a cruise ship that ran up and down the coast to Alaska, and she was wearing the huge fur coat she'd bought to keep herself warm in the frozen north, which made her look like a bear with incredible legs. Already plastered from the end-of-the-cruise party on the cruise ship, she burst into the restaurant shrieking, "Oh shit, I'm so goddamn sorry, Bette! I missed the fucking wedding! I'm such a hopeless idiot! I missed the fucking wedding!" and had to be calmed down by three Chinese waiters and coaxed into her seat.

Joel, I remember, had been greatly moved by the spectacle of someone getting married, even in a registry office, and removed his glasses at intervals to blink at us over his Number Five Combination Plate through moony, tear-filled eyes. Auntie Alice, having exhausted her supply of apologies, took her pumps off and put them on the table beside her rice-wine glass.

"These doggies of mine are killing me!" she exclaimed. "I ran all the damn way from the dock to the foot of Burrard Street. You'd think you could find a taxi in a city the size of this one, eh? Listen, I practically had to take my panties off before I could persuade one to stop!" After dinner, we all piled into Clyde's Studebaker, the adults flushed with rice wine and excessive amounts of almond chop suey and moo goo gai pan and me so full of boneless sweet-and-sour pork that I settled into the plush seat and immediately fell asleep. We drove out on Kingsway to Floyd and Billie's place, where I would be bunking down for the duration of my mother's honeymoon, and where Joel and Alice were staying the night. After tearful goodbyes in the doorway, Clyde and Betty headed south.

When the happy couple had departed, my grandparents, Auntie Alice and her husband all settled down for a cup of coffee. I collapsed into an armchair, quite prepared to keep up my end of the conversation, whatever it might be about. Billie, however, had other ideas. I'd no sooner sat down than she ordered me upstairs to wash up and get my teeth brushed. Fifteen minutes later, I was fast asleep again, this time in bed.

I woke up to the sound of people shouting. It was still night, and at first I thought it was a TV show, Desi giving Lucy hell about forgetting to polish his conga drum or something, but gradually I recognized the voices. It was Joel and Auntie Alice, and she was mad as a wet hen. She was doing far and away the greater part of the yelling and carrying on, and Joel's end of the conversation was pretty much confined to saying, "Lord, Alice!" and "Calm down a little, Ally, you're deafening!"

"Well, I don't want to work in some damn store, on my feet all day getting varicose veins and kissing people's asses so's they'll buy a ukulele for their grandson!" I heard Alice roar. "And I sure as hell don't intend to play housewife!"

"Lord, Alice! Try and keep your voice down. There's people a couple of provinces away who're trying to get some sleep!"

"That's all you ever want from me, Joel Kaiser. Sit down and shut up and act like a wife! Well, I ain't your wife nor no one's! I won't never be a shopgirl nor some mealy-mouthed coffee-klatch cunt!"

"But Alice, if we bought a store we could live like normal people! I've had it with all this traipsing around, eating hot-plate food and waiting for buses. I'd just like to stay in one spot for a while, have a place I could call my own."

The argument died down eventually, and I could hear Floyd and Billie going downstairs and a lot of muted talking, punctuated by someone sobbing as if her heart were about to break. After that, I must have gone to sleep. When I woke up next morning, sun was shining in through the upstairs window and my room was bright and warm. I made my way downstairs in my pyjamas and located my grandmother, who was already hard at work at the kitchen sink, peeling apples for apple-fritters.

"Is Auntie Alice still asleep?" I asked.

"Alice has gone," Billie told me. "She had to get back to her cruise ship. They're sailing for Alaska or the Yukon or someplace today."

"But Auntie Alice said the cruise ship job ended yesterday!" I protested.

Billie gave me a tight-lipped look. "Maybe it did and maybe it didn't, young Mister Know-It-All. Now get yourself out in the yard and help your grandfather. You know how difficult he finds it to waste time without your capable assistance. If you don't get out there right away, he's liable to do something useful, and then both of us will die of surprise!"

Three weeks later, my mother and her new husband came back from Las Vegas. They had brought me some poker chips with "Caesar's" embossed on the backs and a "Big Daddy Roth Weird-O" T-shirt they'd picked up on a side trip to L.A.

"Put these somewhere safe, Sonny," Clyde said as he reached into the pocket of his slacks and pulled out a handful of bright new silver dollars. "They're not exactly worthless, but they look too darned pretty to spend."

I thanked them for the gifts and went to find a place in my suitcase for the money. Everything that Betty and I owned had already been packed up and taken away by the men from Western Line moving: our little house in New Westminster was empty and up for sale. First thing next morning, we loaded my cardboard suitcase into the trunk of Clyde's Studebaker and said our goodbyes to Floyd and Billie. As I waved to them through the back window of the car, I felt like a boy on a raft that was being carried out from shore by the current: everything I knew was receding, I was drifting away from my life.

4

Satori in Smallville

The first few days in Danforth, I hardly went outside the house. I felt like a cat that's been shut inside a cardboard box and then released in an unfamiliar location: all I wanted to do was cower under a bed or a sofa until my internal alarm-bells stopped ringing and I felt that it was safe to show my face. In the meantime, I moped around peering at the neighbour-hood through the gaps in the curtains and gradually exploring the house.

My room was upstairs, on a corner of the house that faced northwest, away from the river. From the window in the gable-end, I could see Saddle Mountain, which Clyde had told me had once been a Wanapum vision quest site, and from the dormer I had a view of some bare desert hills. When I got up first thing in the morning, the mountain was brilliant with sunlight, and towards evening I could watch the shadows creeping up its flanks as the day grew dark. In my first weeks in Danforth, I did that quite a bit. Those weeks were sheer misery for me. I missed my grandparents, the kids from our old neighbourhood and the familiar sights and smells of our little house. Most of all I missed my mother: even though Betty was now home all the time, I felt as if everything between us had changed. Betty was completely preoccupied; she had thrown herself into her new role with surprising ferocity. I guess this was really the first chance she'd had to sample married life, my father having disappeared so soon after they were married, and she immersed herself in what she apparently imagined to be her wifely duties from the moment she got up in the morning until last thing in the evening, when *Gunsmoke* or *The Ed Sullivan Show* had ended and we all went off to bed.

Clyde had moved into a "Q" house—most of the houses in Danforth were built to one of a limited number of plans— to accommodate his new family, and Betty's first project in her incarnation as the Model of Suburban Womanhood was to decorate our new home. We soon acquired a washing machine and automatic dryer, an RCA television with a rabbit-ears antenna, a hi-fi in a blond-wood cabinet, pole lamps with plastic seashell fixtures, a dinette set in fiesta-patterned Arborite, and a Danish-modern living-room suite with a boomerang-shaped table. I tagged along listlessly in Betty's wake as she bustled around the furniture stores and Bapco paint franchises, then stood wordless as a sentinel while delivery trucks and painters arrived and our rooms began to fill and change colour. My mother metamorphosed to blend in with her new environment. The nurse's shoes, cardigans and men's slacks quickly vanished, replaced by the vivid plumage of a Danforth engineer's wife. She strode through the house in crisp pastel dresses, mouth slicked with lip gloss, hair as puffed and flipped as Jackie Kennedy's, high heels tapping efficiently on the lino-tile floors. Once in a while, my glum looks and pointed silences would penetrate her aura of self-absorbed contentment, and she'd purse her frost-pink lips and treat me to one of her omniscient stares.

"Don't waste your time throwing sulks, Sonny. I know you miss the way things were, but life isn't about standing still."

"Nobody asked me if I wanted to come here," I'd mutter—my new Danforth mantra, repeated as required.

That would get me a dismissive shrug, then the clicking of her heels down the hallway. "We're here, and here we're staying. You'll just have to make some new friends."

In the absence of old friends or new ones, I passed the last weeks of summer reading comic books or watching the TV. My taste in comics was narrow: all I read was DC Superman stuff, in its various permutations—*Superman, Superboy, Justice League of America*, and so on. Flipping meditatively through the pulpy, luridly coloured pages as I sprawled out on the sofa in the family room, I gradually conceived the notion that the Man of Steel and I were alike. We were both aliens, in one sense or another, though Krypton may not have been completely identical to New Westminster. We both lived in small towns located in the nebulous American heartland, towns whose defining characteristic was their banality. Neither town seemed plausible even to the most uncritical observer; they were stage sets that belonged on a Hollywood backlot. (Someday, I thought, a high wind would come up and blow down all the houses in Danforth, send their cardboard false fronts whirling through the windbreaks and over the river into the scablands far beyond.) Danforth, like

Smallville, was an impossibly flawless embodiment of the mythical American community, yet both towns had been the site of cosmic conflagrations, the crucible in which ordinary men and supermen engaged in battles of apocalyptic magnitude with weapons of unimaginable power. Superman's adoptive parents, the Kents, were Mr. and Mrs. Average American, as were Clyde and the newly transformed Betty, at least to my adolescent eyes. Both Superman and I were orphans, and he communed with the spectre of Jor-El just as I did with the vagrant shade of my real father, Alfred.

The Man of Steel's life and mine differed in some fairly dramatic ways, of course. For one thing, I didn't have a lot of trouble with the machinations of fiendish arch-villains. Superman had to contend with the devious Lex Luthor. Then there was Brainiac, the Bizarro Superman, and Mr. Mxyzptlk, the gnome from the Fifth Dimension, whose powers were equal to Superman's and who could only be subdued by being tricked into saying his name in reverse.

Kltpzyxm!

In September of 1960 I started at Danforth High. My first day in my new school began with General Science. The teacher was a frail-looking man with a rooster comb of snow-white hair and a fine-boned face that seemed to chip at the air like a woodpecker's beak as he fielded questions from his students, turning from one to another with twitchy, nervous movements. The eyes were grey and gave off light; the voice was soft but urgent. I must have been staring at him more openly than I realized: he looked up from between a couple of girls whose fluting, adenoidal voices had been fluttering around him like chicks demanding food from their mother, and those cool grey eyes zeroed in on me for an instant, two noncommittal lasers probing quickly across the room. I lowered my eyes and started to leaf through *Adventures in Physics*.

After the bell rang, Crashaw waited until the buzz of voices had died down and quietly said, "Good morning." When he was sure that he had our attention, he jerked his head toward the portrait above his desk. "Manya Sklodowska," he said. "Better known as Madame Curie."

I looked up at the photograph, as did very nearly everyone else in the classroom. It was large, about fourteen by eleven inches, and framed in heavy wood. I was surprised I hadn't noticed it earlier. Perhaps my time in Canadian schools had made me used to seeing a picture of a woman at the front of each classroom—for years I had looked up at the Queen every morning and paid no attention whatsoever to her presence. While the portraits of the Queen in my old schools had been hand-tinted in powdery pinks and delicate gilt, Manya Sklodowska's face in the photograph was a smudge of oily shadow. She was dark and had deep-set, intense-looking eyes, you could see that much clearly enough, but apart from that it was difficult to distinguish her from anyone else you might see in a badly lit, grainy old photo.

"The history of science is the history of inspiration," Crashaw announced. "The man, or possibly woman, who first noticed that round things could be moved more easily than square ones and then applied that observation to the fashioning of a wheel was inspired, and his or her inspiration gave a gift beyond any price to mankind. That inventor's society was probably a group of primitive nomads or cave-dwellers, but suddenly they were more advanced, capable of doing more complex and difficult tasks more competently and quickly than any other group of people on the planet. Generations later, their chariots rolled across the Middle East and they conquered everything in their path. Knowledge is power, young ladies and gentlemen. Knowledge is power!"

Crashaw went on for most of the period, talking about the role of scientists in advancing the fate of nations. What he said was interesting enough, I'm sure, but no lecture could have held my attention. I was far too absorbed in the vastly more important task of scoping out my fellow adolescents to listen to some old guy jawing about science.

The other students treated each other with an easy famil-iarity that seemed to exclude me absolutely. They leaned across the aisle or turned around in their desks when they thought the teacher wasn't watching and conversed in brief bursts of whispers and giggles. Notes were passed from hand to hand, and glances flashed across the stuffy, neon-lit space above the tops of hardwood desks. Once in a while, one of the kids would turn in his or her desk and look me over with a quick and apparently uninterested stare. At the same time, I began to pick out the more interesting faces from the two dozen or so other students in the room. Every face in the room was white, of course: I'd caught sight of two or three Negro boys in the halls—which was more black kids than I'd have seen in a year in New Westminster—but none of them seemed to be in my class.

I already knew a couple of the boys, Gregory Durst and Richie Deacon. Richie was a popular boy, brash in the polished way of a professional salesman. He kept his black hair neatly combed and greased into place with Brylcreem, and his snap-tab shirts were crisply ironed and buttoned at the wrist. Gregory Durst was never called "Greg": his nickname was "Professor." He and his dad had their hair cut side by side in Joe Cliff's barber shop on Ruthium Crescent every Friday afternoon at exactly five o'clock—short back and sides, grease on the cowlick. No one was ever less cool. Deacon and Durst and I had one thing in common: our fathers—stepfather in my case—were Danforth engineers. We'd been thrown together at barbecues and patio parties a few times over the summer, and out of that unasked-for proximity a tentative sort of friendship was beginning to evolve.

Durst sat front row centre, the traditional suckhole's position, but he paradoxically seemed utterly bored by what Crashaw had to say. While the teacher spoke, he amused himself by taking apart a couple of Paper-Mates from the half-dozen or so in his breast pocket. Deacon was joking with a short red-haired girl who sat behind him, jostling the books on her desk with his elbow and whispering things that made her feign anger and shock.

There were a few quite presentable girls the class, I noticed. A tallish young woman who sat in the front corner near the window particularly caught my eye; she was long-limbed and looked as if she might be athletic; what interested me most about her was the way she allowed her hair, which was soft and honey-blond, to fall in haphazard strands around her shoulders, rather than teasing it up into a bouffant frosted with hairspray like most of the other girls. Perhaps she felt my eyes on her, or perhaps she was simply curious enough to want to sneak a glance at the new boy in class. In any case, she turned around and gave me a look that was cool but somehow open, like the gaze of a thoughtful child. Her eyes were the blue of cornflowers and remarkably calm and serene. She looked at me until I flinched and looked down at my notebook. When I raised my eyes again, those eyes were fixed intently on the blackboard.

This, of course, was Karen Sullivan, appearing for the first time in the story of my life. That she was the daughter of a longhair, and thus a member of Danforth's ruling class, a fairy-tale princess of the new atomic kingdom, was something I'd find out soon enough. That I'd love her and mourn her for most of my life was a thing I could never have dreamed.

When the period was almost over and his diatribe on the wonders of science was finally wheezing to a close, Mr. Crashaw put down his chalk and elaborately brushed the white dust off his hands.

"Say goodbye for now to our friend Madame Manya," he said. "You'll be seeing a lot of her over the next ten months."

Some of the students waved at Madame Curie's portrait and yelled "Bye-bye, Manya!" A boy in the back of the room wolf-whistled, and somebody moaned, "What a pooch!" Then the bell rang, and General Science was over.

Leaving the science lab, I found myself walking through

the halls toward my next class in the company of Gregory Durst.

"Enlightened?" he asked me. "Filled with inspiration? Old Man Crashaw's lectures are supposed to have that effect on the uninitiated, you know."

"Not particularly."

"Well, he's a pompous old fart, I grant you that much, but he does have a point."

"Does he?"

Gregory gave me a quizzical look.

"Of course he does, Wheeler. Didn't you catch any of that sermon of his?"

"Not a lot."

"Jesus, Wheeler. You're on your way to the beatnik life already, I can see that. You'll be beachcombing down in California, eating seaweed and sleeping under a pile of old driftwood, while the rest of us are driving jet-powered Cadillacs and taking holidays on the moon."

"All right, all right. What did Old Man Crashaw say that was so important?"

"He talked about scientists, Wheeler. Longhairs like Fermi and Teller. The men who made the A-bomb. And this city, for that matter. Scientists are going to be the ones who rule the world."

"Could be, I guess. But you didn't seem any more interested in what Crashaw was saying than I was."

"Heard it all before. He talks about the atomic scientists all the time in science club. I've been going to the meetings for a couple of years."

Durst followed me into the boys' room, holding forth about how he was going to get an A in General Science, take physics at Stanford, do research, etc., etc. I relieved myself, then took out my plastic pocket comb and ran it quickly through my hair while he stooped to retie the laces on his Hush Puppies.

A couple of tough-looking boys in leather jackets strode into the washroom, the steel taps on their pointed shoes rapping fiercely on the ceramic-tile floor. Durst looked up from his labours and nodded toward them.

"Hoods," he said, with the demeanour of an expert woodsman identifying the spoor of some predator that was killing off all the game.

The two hoods whipped out rat-tail combs and began to preen their ducktails in the mirror above the sinks.

"Hey, Professor Durst," the taller of them said, his eyes still locked on his own image in the mirror. He was thin and blond, with a long perfect nose and full lips that made him look petulant and childish. "What're you hanging around in here for? You conducting an experiment or something?"

"Sometimes it floats and sometimes it doesn't, Prof," the other hood contributed, raking his comb through black hair that glistened with hair oil. "Everybody knows that. You're wasting your time."

The hoods had a good laugh about that one; then the blond boy said, "I saw you and your old lady hanging around with Old Man Sullivan outside the clubhouse last weekend, Durst. Her and Lionel Sullivan got a thing on the side, or have you been porking Lionel's sexy little daughter?"

"Ignore them," Durst told me. He straightened up and headed for the door.

"Hey, I wouldn't mind doing a little lab research on Queen Karrie Sullivan myself," the dark-haired boy said. "The angle of the dangle equals the mass of the ass, you know, all kinds of good shit like that." He glanced over at Gregory and me, his hazel eyes meeting mine briefly. He seemed, on first impression, an archetypal figure of the fifties. Sal Mineo without the effeminate pout. High, almost Indian cheekbones.

The hoods' names were Jarvis and Deerborne, Gregory informed me as soon as we'd left the washroom. Alan Jarvis, the thin blond boy, was the son of a judge, and in the light of that embarrassing fact, his status as a teenage rebel was understandable. Even the teachers treated him with sympathetic condescension. His dark-haired friend had no such excuse: Deerborne's dad was a mechanic. The son was a gearhead, like his father. They belonged to that shadowy class of Danforth residents who didn't make their living at the Area. Deerborne, Sr. ran the Esso garage on Lincoln Boulevard, which was more or less the main street of Danforth, and Bobby spent his weekends pumping gas.

"You have to join the science club," Durst said as we walked to our next class. "Every year we do a project. All the brainier kids are in it, everyone who wants to be an engineer or a longhair."

"All right," I said. "Maybe I will."

5

Whiz Kids

The Danforth High School Science Club met every Wednesday after school at Mr. Crashaw's house. Crashaw and his wife had married late and had their first and only child when he was already in his middle forties. His wife died in childbirth, and the care of their daughter was left to a woman who lived across the river in Pasco and who had to be home to her husband by five. There was an understanding among the teachers and administrators at the high school that Mr. Crashaw could not be expected to remain at the school after the end of classes, and he had been excused from participating in extracurricular activities—except for the science club, which he had apparently found himself unable to give up.

Meeting at the teacher's house was the best thing about being a member of the club. Mr. Crashaw lived in a two-storey saltbox that was out of step with the new-as-tomorrow look of everything else in Danforth. I suppose it had been a farmhouse in the days before the Company had evicted all the farmers. We gathered in the kitchen, having been ushered in by the great man himself, who was still in the tweed coat and baggy dress flannels he wore in all weathers to the school. There were six members of the science club apart from me—Gregory Durst; a plain girl with braces and the unlikely name of Chenille; a tiny, rodent-toothed blond girl who never seemed to have any interest in anything we said; two guys named Ralph—one blond, pink-cheeked and chubby, and the other short and dapper-looking, with glistening mouse-brown eyes; and Karen Sullivan. Gregory, as usual, made himself at home, lounging in a spindle-backed chair and absent-mindedly fingering the knick-knacks on the maple colonial hutch. The rest of us sat around the table as stiffly as toy dolls propped up in front of a tea set by some imaginative child.

"Rockets, that's what I want to build this year," Gregory announced. "Solid-fuel, two- or three-stage jobs with nose-cone chutes and mercury switches between stages. Crashaw can show us how to build them."

The two Ralphs giggled in unison, and the little blonde with the rat teeth rolled her eyes in disgust. I looked involuntarily toward the open doorway, expecting Mr. Crashaw to march in and disembowel Durst with a kitchen knife for having neglected to refer to him as "Mister." When the teacher returned a few minutes later, however, he looked so distracted that I doubt he would have noticed if Gregory had accused him of being Leon Trotsky's brother-in-law and offered to burn down his house.

"My apologies, young ladies and gentlemen, for keeping you waiting," he said. "My daughter required my attention. She has a dance recital Sunday, you see, and she needs me to look in at intervals while she rehearses. Now, I suggest we all introduce ourselves, and then we'll move along to setting our agenda."

With Mr. Crashaw's arrival, the meeting settled into the pattern it would maintain every week for the next several months. Durst quizzed the teacher about the rockets he wanted us to build for our project, and then Mr. Crashaw talked at length about some episode from the history of nuclear physics. The rest of us said practically nothing, though every once in a while the tiny girl with the rodent teeth would lean against Chenille and whisper something rapidly into her ear, after which Chenille would blush and both girls would cover their mouths and giggle.

Crashaw had just begun to tell us about Lord Rutherford's discovery of the atomic nucleus when the front doorbell rang.

"Excuse me," Crashaw muttered distractedly. He got out of his chair and darted toward the foyer, with that nervous, coiled-spring energy that he seemed to be unable to tone down, even in his own house. We all sat in silence as he unlatched and opened the front door to see who had arrived.

It was Deerborne, the hood I'd seen at school. I wondered what he wanted from Mr. Crashaw. Maybe he'd come to cut the lawn or something. I almost felt sorry for him as he stood there in Crashaw's doorway, shifting awkwardly from one foot to the other in his needle-point shoes, white socks and black denim skinnies.

"Mr. Deerborne," Crashaw said, in that half-courtly, half-sarcastic way of his. "I see you decided to join us after all.

Did the book on rocket propulsion interest you at all?"

Deerborne looked embarrassed, but muttered that yes, he guessed he had enjoyed the book all right. He unzipped his windbreaker and pulled out a large-format book, which he handed over to the teacher.

"Come in, come in, Mr. Deerborne," Crashaw said. "We're just getting organized, as it happens. Mr. Durst has been lobbying for rocketry as this year's project. The two of you seem to be following the same trajectory."

Deerborne slipped his shoes off and followed Mr. Crashaw into the kitchen. The teacher offered to get Bobby a chair from the dining room, but Deerborne said he'd just as soon stand. He took up a position across the room from the rest of us, leaning against the range.

Crashaw introduced Bobby Deerborne to all of us except Durst and Karen Sullivan, whom Deerborne already knew. He introduced me as a "new addition from north of the border," and Bobby took a step away from the counter and I got up from my chair so that we could shake hands, which was something I hadn't expected. Where I came from, the tough boys might nod or sneer, but they would never allow themselves to do something as normal as shake someone's hand. Either all Yanks did these things differently, I noted, or Deerborne was an odd sort of hood.

"Well then," Crashaw said. "That's everyone?"

We exchanged the shy, confused looks of teenagers who are never sure when an adult is asking a rhetorical question. Chenille shrugged and showed off her braces. The rat girl huddled into her bony shoulders as if to appear as inconspicuous as possible. The two Ralphs sniffed and giggled. The Professor went on fiddling with a horse brass. Bobby Deerborne stared morosely at the fridge.

"That's everyone," Karen Sullivan said.

"All right, let's talk about rockets."

For the next half-hour, we discussed the possibility of building a model solid-fuel rocket. Model rocketry was a popular enough pastime in those days; the glamour of the space program had affected most adolescents and kids to one degree or another, and most of us blithely assumed that travelling through space in rocket-ships would be a part of our common future. We were all potential Jetsons; we saw ourselves soaring effortlessly up from the translucent dome of Atomic City, USA, to visit Mars and Venus and spend our weekends on the moon. The Professor roused himself from his apparent lethargy long enough to make a strong case for rocketry as our project for the year, and Deerborne, curiously, backed him up with the occasional "Yeah" and "That's right." We voted, little democrats every one of us, and passed the Professor's motion, with only the rat girl—who had a passion for crystal radios—opposing. Even Chenille caught the space-travel virus and neglected to vote with her friend.

We were deep into a discussion of the more pragmatic aspects of our project—how we would purchase materials, whether we'd need some kind of licence, where the launches could take place—when Crashaw's daughter, Curie, came into the room. Ignoring the fact that her father had guests, she marched up to the teacher, who was speaking to Gregory about some fine point of telemetry that I couldn't understand, and tugged at the sleeve of his blazer. This was typical of Curie Crashaw, as I was to discover. In all the years I knew her, I rarely saw her looking absent-minded or distracted. She moved through the moments of her life with a sense of urgent purpose, and she would invariably focus her attention on one particular person, transfixing him or her completely with the spotlight of her need. Usually it was Crashaw, of course, who was the object of his daughter's fierce attention.

"Daddy, I need you to help me. I can't get this right."

"Curie," the teacher said. "Are you finished with your new routines already?"

"Didn't you hear me? I can't even start. Mrs. Turnbull scratched the record on the hi-fi."

"How dreadful!" Crashaw answered, his voice dropping to a whisper. "Shall we have her shot? Putting scratches on the *Sacre de Printemps!*"

"Daddy! I'm serious! Help me!"

Curie turned in the doorway, a furious elf in a midnight-blue leotard, her feet in their ribboned pink slippers stomping out of the room and up the stairs.

"Ladies and gentlemen, you must excuse me," the teacher told us. "The world, it seems, is ending. I must go and rescue Igor Stravinsky." He stood up and dashed from the room.

Our meeting survived two more of Curie's interruptions before Mr. Crashaw finally announced that it was getting close to dinnertime and that our families would doubtless be expecting us to come home.

The Professor and the two Ralphs piled into a Nash American driven by Gregory's mother, and Chenille and her friend walked off in the direction of the high school. Unable to think of any plausible reason for hanging around, I left Karen Sullivan standing on the Crashaws' porch, waiting for her ride, and set off on foot toward home. Bobby Deerborne had stayed in the living room talking to the housekeeper, Mrs. Turnbull, whom he apparently knew, and I heard his metal taps clattering on the stone walk as he left.

"Hey, Wheeler, wait up," Deerborne shouted.

I paused while he jogged up to meet me.

We trudged on for a couple of blocks in relative silence, each of us trying to spark up a conversation. Bobby asked me a couple of questions about Canada—Did they drive a lot of small English cars there? Had I played much lacrosse and hockey?—and mentioned that he'd seen the minor-pro hockey team up in Seattle. I told him that I guessed a few of our neighbours drove English Fords or Austins and that, no, I hadn't played a lot of hockey.

We walked another block without speaking.

"So, you been interested in rockets long?" I asked, not knowing what else I could say.

He shook his head.

"No, I don't have much interest in rockets. Rocket-powered dragsters, now, that could be a whole other thing."

"Rocket-powered cars?"

"Yeah," he said. "They're building some already, right? Walt and Art Arfons. They run them at the Bonneville Salt Flats."

I didn't want to say anything that might reveal my total ignorance of the subject. "Sounds cool," I said. "I bet they really travel."

"Fuckin' A," he said.

The wind had begun to get up as the sky above the river grew darker. The trees along the boulevard were bending a little in the gusts. There was wind-blown dust in the air, tiny, invisible atoms of grit. There were dust storms fairly often that fall, and I already regarded them as a regular part of life in the Washington desert.

"Termination winds," Deerborne said.

I must have looked puzzled.

"Termination winds," he repeated. "That's what the old-timers called them, the boys who came to build the plant, you know, back when the war was still on. They'd be living out here in bunkhouses, crammed in nose-to-asshole, Negroes in one camp and white guys in another, right? The wind would get up and blow for days, and those sorry sons-of-bitches would be out there working steel and pouring concrete in the middle of the desert, the wind blowing grit in their eyes and up their noses. Every time it started to blow, damn near half of them would pack up and quit."

"I bet they did," I said. "That dust is pretty hard to get used to."

We walked along in silence until we came to the next cross street.

"I go south here," I said.

Deerborne had already turned the corner. He raised one hand in a lethargic wave but didn't look back. I watched him walking inland, his head slouched down as if he were watching the pavement, the collar of his windbreaker turned up against the wind.

The science club became one of the focal points of my adolescent life. I didn't know it at the time, of course, but that high-school club included all the bright stars of my private constellation. Karen. Bobby. Curie. Old Man Crashaw himself, I suppose. Even the Professor, though he'd drift out of my life forever after high school.

Our meetings were spent listening to Crashaw. Every week he would recount for us another chapter in the history of the development of the A-bomb. He began with Madame Curie. Manya Sklodowska as a schoolgirl in Poland. Manya suffering through years as a governess in an obscure town in rural Poland. Manya, a small figure in shabby black shawls, moving purposefully across a frozen white background. Manya in Paris, piling overcoats, scarves, framed paintings, even chairs on top of her bed to keep warm in her unheated apartment. The years with her husband, shovelling through great heaps of pitchblende in search of infinitesimal traces of radioactive elements, their laboratory a shed with no heat and a broken roof. Marie and Pierre working tirelessly night after night with their sore, swollen hands, unaware that their experiments were giving them radiation burns. Rain and snow falling on the indefatigable Sklodowska.

"After Roentgen's discovery of radiation," he told us, "scientists all over Europe were struggling to find the cause of these emanations that could pass through solid metal, that could allow you to see the bones beneath your skin. That search led to the discovery of the structure of the atom, and it led Madame Curie to discover two new elements, polonium and radium. Two additions to the list of the essential things that make up the universe. Can you imagine how important that is?"

Madame Curie was Crashaw's private Muse, but the story of her life was only the beginning of his epic: its true and central subject was the invention of the Bomb, and every major physicist of the century had a part to play in one or more of its elaborate cantos.

"In Berlin, in the 1920s," he told us, "there was a man named Leo Szilard. He was a physicist; he worked with Lise Meitner." We'd all heard about this Meitner in earlier discussions, of course. She was almost as familiar a figure to us as Einstein or the eternal Sklodowska.

"Wasn't Szilard at Los Alamos?" Gregory asked.

"He *caused* Los Alamos," Crashaw said. He went on to tell us about how Szilard had gone to see Einstein about the threat of a Nazi A-bomb, a visit which had convinced Einstein to contact President Roosevelt about the necessity for an American bomb.

"Szilard wasn't just a scientist. He was a man who had a vision of a better, more humane and efficient world. He wanted to set up a council of enlightened scientists who would guide the progress of mankind into the technological age. He called them the *Bund*—the Brotherhood, I suppose you could say."

"So what happened to this Brotherhood?" I blurted. It

took Crashaw a moment to focus his attention on me—hardly surprising, considering the fact that I generally sat through our meetings in silence.

"*This* happened," he said, smiling incredulously. "This city we live in. The power that can change the world. The end of war. The Bomb."

I was used to Crashaw's rhapsodies about the glorious nuclear future, but it was simple history I wanted, not a vision.

"But what about the Brotherhood itself—those people? I mean, it's not like there's a gang of scientists telling everyone what to do."

My ignorance was too much for Gregory.

"Come on, Wheeler!" he blustered. "This whole country's built on technology! Without scientists, we'd be nothing but hunters and farmers!"

"No, Wheeler's right, Durst. Szilard's vision never really came to fruition, though I think you'd all agree that scientists, chemists and nuclear physicists, in particular, exert tremendous influence over public policy all over the civilized world these days. Behind the Iron Curtain, as well as here in the USA."

"My father says that physicists are remaking the world," Karen said. "That the power of the atom will change our lives completely. Like we won't even recognize the world in fifty years."

"It's scary, kind of, isn't it?" I asked. "Releasing all that energy without really understanding what might happen? Couldn't it start a chain reaction or something?"

Crashaw gave me a condescending smile. Durst looked away in embarrassment. Chenille and the two Ralphs giggled. Bobby Deerborne examined his nails.

"The universe is made of energy," Crashaw began. "Planets and stars. Animals, including ourselves. The seven seas. The air. You and I—our very bodies. Why, the sun itself is a nuclear reactor! Without nuclear fusion, there would be no life on Earth. The idea that a nuclear event—even the detonation of a hydrogen bomb—could cause some kind of massive chain reaction is pure science fiction, I'm afraid. You've been watching too many movies, Mr. Wheeler."

After almost every science club meeting, I would hang around the Crashaws' place as long as I could, hoping to catch Karen Sullivan alone. Too often, Karen's mother would already be waiting in front of the house: she'd beep the horn impatiently the minute we came outside, and Karen would jog toward their Plymouth Fury, school books huddled to her chest and her hair bobbing up and down and falling into her eyes. Once in a while, Mrs. Sullivan would be late, and her daughter would have to wait on the Crashaws' porch for five or ten minutes until her mother's blue Fury pulled into the street. The first time this happened, I told Bobby Deerborne I had to talk to Mr. Crashaw about my science homework and then hovered in the living room, sneaking covert glances through the window at Karen while the two Ralphs and the other girls got into their winter coats and headed off down the street. Finally, after what seemed like an hour of goodbyes between various members of the club, there was no one on the porch but Karen Sullivan. I grabbed my coat from the rack and dashed outside.

"Hi," I said. Karen was sitting slightly forward on the porch swing, her toggle-coat open and her books clutched to her pink sweater. She smiled but said nothing.

"Great swing," I said. "Can I try it?"

Karen slid herself over to the far side of the swing, and I sat down gingerly and settled back on the cold wood-slat seat of the trembling contraption.

"Feels a bit rickety, doesn't it?"

This got me a perfunctory smile. There didn't seem to be anything to say.

"So, what do you like about the club?" I finally asked. "Are you interested in building rockets?"

She stared across the street again, her blue eyes focused as they often seemed to be on some object in the infinite distance, as if she were looking *through* the scene instead of *at* it.

"Nothing really," she said. "I don't really care about science."

"But you're so good at it! You're always getting A's on Crashaw's quizzes!"

"It's mostly pretty easy. You don't have to study or anything."

"Maybe *you* don't," I told her. "Keeps me pretty busy sometimes. Clyde—that's my stepfather—helps me out quite a bit if he's home. Otherwise, I'd probably be failing. Or getting C-pluses or something, which is just as bad as far as Clyde's concerned."

"Science is just numbers and tables. There's nothing *real* about it. They make it sound so incredibly important, but it's really just a game."

"I guess that's true," I told her, although I wasn't at all sure it was. "I just wish it was a game I could play a little better, that's all."

Karen smiled and leaned forward on the swing seat, hands thrust deep into the pockets of her toggle-coat, and turned her face toward me. I found myself staring into the absolute cerulean blue of her calm, noncommittal gaze. I returned her smile, feeling speechless and stupid and hating myself, then she turned away and looked out at the Crashaws' lawn, the branches of the ornamental tree in the centre of the little front lawn. I gave up and joined her in staring across the street at the neat row of Company houses, the white picket fences, the blank desert sky. A couple of minutes later, Karen's mother's car pulled up in front of the house. Karen gathered her books and brushed past me, filling my senses with the smell of her shampoo, the textures of her scarf and coat, the tawny blond light of her dishevelled hair as it fell around her shoulders.

"See you in school, I guess," I told her.

She paused and turned toward me. "We could study together some time, if you want. I go down to the library after classes. You could meet me if you wanted to, Sonny."

I smiled, feeling suddenly, unexpectedly blessed. "Sure, I'd like that," I said. Karen gathered her books to her chest and strode away. I waved to Mrs. Sullivan, who chose not to see me, and watched her daughter bound down the Crashaws' front steps and hurry through the gate. In a moment, the Fury was gone.

6

Day's Pay

The morning of August 9, 1945. There was an air raid alarm earlier, but nothing has come of it, and some of the people of Nagasaki have started to emerge from the underground shelters. It is a day of moderate heat in the Urakami Valley. The dome of the heavens is cloudless and blue. A woman is hurrying home through narrow, empty streets. She is young, perhaps twenty. She hears the drone of engines, and looks up for an instant before turning to run back to the shelter. She sees the sun glint off the silver bell of the Urakami Catholic Church. There is an explosion of intense white light, light coming from everywhere and nowhere, light filling the bowl of the valley, instantly illuminating every detail on the ridge of hills that separates the Urakami Valley from the neighbouring regions. Then the woman is gone, the cells of her body vaporized as rays of 3,000-degrees-centigrade heat flash outward from the epicentre of the explosion. Her atoms disperse as the nuclear wind blasts out of the bowl of the valley at 300 metres per second.

On the far side of the mountain ridge, in the Nishiyama Valley, an old man is sitting at a green metal desk in the Katsuyama Primary School. He sees the flash of solar fire reflected in the smooth, abstract lake of the desk. He sees the bones of his arthritic hands, the bones of his legs beneath the desk, the iron beams that hold up the flooring. As he raises his head and shifts his glance toward the window, the absolute light is almost instantly replaced by an equally absolute darkness. The atomic cloud has eclipsed the sun. Seventy thousand people are dead. Three hours from now, as the old man climbs as hurriedly as he can from floor to floor, directing the teachers and neighbours, ushering children into already crowded classrooms where they will not encounter the wounded, the primary school begins to fill with refugees, people bleeding from every orifice, people draped in blood as if in the ceremonial robes of some apocalyptic religion, people blinded by light or by fear of light, people struck blind by infinite darkness.

Towards nightfall—the true night of the turning world, which follows in due course the false night of airborne debris and fallout—the old man discovers himself sitting slumped against a concrete wall in the building's basement. The wounded, the terrified, continue to stream past him. Others now direct them to the crowded, fetid upstairs rooms or, if it is obvious that they will die very soon, simply allow them to stagger or be dragged into a corner, where they lie down on the cold, bare floor. There is nothing left of the old man's world—even his memories seem to be shredded, torn into delicate, colourless scraps that flutter on the hollow, booming flute notes of his heartbeat. When he raises his eyes, he sees a woman walking slowly, painfully toward him. Her entire face is missing. In its place is a charred black wound. As she approaches, the man discerns that the woman's features have been burned from the bone completely, cartilage, muscle and skin incinerated, and the massive wound, the net of wounds, so perfectly cauterized by the heat of the explosion that there is very little visible blood.

The bomb that destroyed Nagasaki was made with plutonium 239 generated in a breeder reactor in Danforth. My stepfather helped to design and build that reactor. A lanky young man in spectacles, benign as Gyro Gearloose, he sat in a dingy office in a makeshift hut while dust storms whipped the windows and termination winds howled across the desert; he doodled rectangles, jagged lines, intricate loops and circles—wiring diagrams—on a yellow Big Chief writing pad. His doodles were refined into blueprints, the blueprints became roadmaps of circuits, dimensionless Mondrian landscapes through which particles thrummed from minus to plus, flowing through gates or frustrated by switches. The road map intersected with other such maps: cooling pipes, hydraulic lines, railway tracks ferrying uranium ore from the mines of Nevada and Utah, the emerging grid of interstates over which heavy trucks conveyed plutonium buttons to a base in the Arizona desert, flight patterns of B-52s moving east and across the Pacific, the trajectory of *Day's Pay*, the aircraft that carried the warhead.

The house in which we live was built for the purpose of making the atomic bomb that exploded over the Urakami Valley. So was the street outside, the town, the Danforth Inn, the Tri-Cities Public Library, the town clock, the streetlights, the ditches. Clyde and most of my friends' fathers,

Crashaw and the rest of my teachers, the majority of my neighbours live in Danforth for no other reason than to make atomic bombs. Even Betty, my mother, has joined them. I alone am different. I am exiled from another world—an alien, a spy.

My stepfather tied his own flies on his workbench in the basement. He'd busy himself for hours down there, working with scissors, hackle pliers, and a little Thompson model-A vise. He'd built himself a cabinet full of tiny drawers for storing the various improbable materials—antelope hair, porcupine quills, muskrat fur, and white-tipped turkey tail feathers, for example—that he used to fashion his delicate flies, and on the bench itself were bobbins holding several types of thread.

The fly-tying bench was separate from and vastly neater than the bench on which he assembled his electronic gizmos. These were strewn across the second bench and much of the floor beneath it; they weighed down shelves and burst out of cupboards: fuses, transistors, vacuum tubes, resistors, capacitors, chassis assemblies, plastic knobs and oscilloscopes, God alone knows what else.

During my first months in Danforth, I tried to avoid being alone with Clyde. However unjustly, I blamed my new dad for the loss of my mother. His physical presence—the sandy hair on his long-boned arms, the scurf of his whiskers, the smell of his tobacco and wintergreen Speed Shave— seemed alien and vaguely repellent. Betty didn't help matters much. Instead of giving me time to get used to my new situation, she'd push me into spending time with Clyde. Eventually, however, Betty's urgings—and sometimes sheer boredom—would get the better of me, and I'd go down to the basement in the evenings and watch as my stepfather worked.

Clyde Cateret was a quiet, private man who didn't generally talk a lot when he was working, and his shop became a place of calm and contemplation for me, as I suppose it had always been for him. I can remember it clearly—the chalky, slightly damp smell of the exposed concrete walls, the ribbed rubber treads on the staircase, the little pool of light from the gooseneck lamp above Clyde's bench that was the only source of illumination in the basement, the shelving stacked with apple crates and jars full of resistors, screws of all conceivable shapes and sizes, gauges with dusty glass faces, and spools of electrical wire.

"How's that club of yours going?" he asked me one evening after I'd returned from Mr. Crashaw's.

"All right," I said. "We were talking about Oppenheimer and Teller and all those guys today. Oppenheimer seemed kind of interesting."

"I met him once, did I tell you?"

"You met Robert Oppenheimer?"

Clyde smiled. "That's right. Back in '45, right before the end of the war."

"When you started at the Area?"

"Before I started, actually. I was out here on contract, working for Dupont. They built the reactors here; that was back before GE came along."

Clyde fished around in his pocket and produced his pipe and pouch.

"Open the hatch for me, will you, Sonny?"

The hatch was what Clyde called the one small window in that end of the basement, a single wood-framed pane that covered a foot-high horizontal slot above the concrete of the wall. I got down from my perch and pried the recalcitrant window open, then fastened its little eyebolt to the brass hook that hung from one of the joists.

"Thanks," Clyde said. He struck a wooden match and held it to the bowl of his pipe.

"A few of us were working on the water-cooling system. Heat diffusion pipes, a pumping system, filters. Fairly straightforward stuff, from a purely mechanical point of view, but in those days we had no clear idea about acceptable levels of contamination, the diffusion of radioactive isotopes in water, the effect of turning loose a whole bunch of thermal energy into a river system used for breeding salmon, irrigating farms, and so on. In a perfect world, there would have been time to look into all these nuances more exhaustively, but there was a shooting war on in the Pacific and we had to move things along. We cut as few corners as we possibly could, scratched our heads with considerable vigour, and tried not to make costly mistakes. It was a cowboy show, though, no matter how you looked at it. We were flying by the seat of our pants."

Clyde leaned back in his chair and directed a stream of pipe smoke toward the open window.

"One morning, we were hanging around in my office, working over some preliminary sketches of the system, just kicking a few ideas around, trying to anticipate possible glitches. 'Getting the drop on the gremlins' was what we called it. Brainstorming, I guess you could say. Anyway, in walks Bill Wilton, who was a management type from Dupont. 'Gentlemen,' he says, 'There's a couple of longhairs from Los Alamos coming up here in a half an hour.'"

"Gregory talks about longhairs," I said. "Physicists, chemists. I think he wants to be one after college."

"That sounds about right," Clyde said. "I think Gunther and Elsie Durst fed that boy equations with his Pablum. They're determined he's going to be the next Einstein. Or better yet, a bigwig at GE."

"Did you know who the longhairs were?"

"No. Fermi had been around, and so had Szilard, Edward Teller, people like that. They used assumed names, of course, to throw off Axis spies, but everybody seemed to know they were there. I hadn't run into any of them, though. Too busy with my own job to worry a lot about longhairs or anyone else just passing through. Tourists, as far as I was concerned."

Clyde took off his glasses and laid them carefully on the bench.

"We didn't have a lot of use for pure science. We were engineers, you understand, and we liked to think of ourselves as problem-solvers, practical people. Fermi and those guys were experimentalists at best, and at worst they were wild-eyed dreamers, spinning theories. They'd figured out atomic fission, sure, but they could no more make a reactor work than fly."

"So what was he like?"

"Thin," Clyde said. "Tall enough, about your height, I guess, but so skinny you could have used him for a shoelace. Looked almost like a woman, in a way—very fine, very delicate features."

"What did you talk about?"

"Nothing much. Wilton gave him some crap about how well things were going, we all grinned a little, a couple of the guys made jokes. The usual empty talk you make when someone's passing through. Then the management fellows ushered him out. That was the one and only time I ever saw him."

"Did you know who he was, Dad? I mean, the father of the A-bomb and all that?"

"Oh, I suppose so, he kept a pretty high profile even in those days, and the world of atomic research was still very small. Not that his reputation would have made a lot of difference to me and the fellows I worked with. He was just some prissy-looking longhair, as far as I could see. Surprised me, though. I heard a long time later that he was quite a serious outdoorsman. Spent a lot of time up in the Sangre de Cristos. Went there every summer, right up until the war."

I didn't have a lot to say to Clyde about his story, but I remember I felt a certain degree of pride in the fact that he had once met a famous man of science—the father of the A-bomb himself. It made me feel connected, in some tenuous way, to the mythology of the atom, the stories Old Man Crashaw had drummed into us all at the science club and in his class. A few nights later, though, I woke up in a caul of sweat, mummified in bedsheets. The moon was full and the streetlights on Argon angled in through my window—my bedroom seemed as light as early morning, though it was only 1 a.m. by the phosphorescent travel clock—a gift from Aunt Alice—that squatted underneath my bedside lamp. I'd been dreaming, and tatters of my sleeping mind still fluttered in my head. In the dream, I'd been sitting at the table with my parents. They were gaunt and pale, eyes heavy with sleep, cheeks hollowed as if from starvation. We were eating birds, the three of us, bloody gouts of meat and feathers. A narrow man, so thin he seemed to disappear when he reached for the salt cellar, then shimmer back into being as he settled in his chair, sat directly across from me, between Clyde and Betty. His eyes were as blue and as filled with incalculable distance as Karen's, but his hair was lush and shadow-black, curled in tendrils around his ears. The thin man was the father of the A-bomb. He too seemed drugged or half-asleep. He ate nothing of our terrible meal; his passion was for grains of salt. He shook them on his empty plate, stirred them with spidery fingers. His mouth worked as if his mind were rehearsing some vital and difficult utterance, but if he spoke I wasn't able to hear him.

Awake, I peeled the blankets and sheets from my body, got out of bed and went to the window. Outside, the sky was indigo, electric with glacial moonlight. I could see the hump of Saddle Mountain arched against the sky. I imagined that the A-bombs had dropped on our city, though nothing was damaged or out of place. I stood there a long time, just watching. The whine of a motorbike knifed through the night.

We never did finish those rockets. Gregory Durst's parents eventually bought him a rocket that came in a kit, and he and his father launched it in the park beside the river one windless Sunday morning in late April. Clyde drove me down to the park to watch, and the two of us leaned against the side of his Studebaker and craned our necks backwards as the suddenly minuscule needle of the Professor's toy spacecraft etched a faint line of hydrogen mist against the uniform blue of the sky.

"Goes reasonably well, doesn't it?" Clyde said.

"Yeah," I said. "Not bad."

"Someone waiting for you over there," Clyde continued. "Isn't that Lionel Sullivan's girl?" He nodded toward a park bench across the boulevard, where Karen and Bobby were sitting with little Curie Crashaw. Curie's father and one of the Ralphs were over in the centre of the playing field, talking to Gregory and his dad.

"See you in a minute."

"Take your time." Clyde pulled out his tobacco pouch and started pinching threads of Virginia Plain into his meerschaum.

Bobby turned his head and nodded to me as I jogged up to him and Curie.

"We have liftoff!" I said.

He nodded. "Damn straight." Then, "Sorry," he added, glancing at Curie.

"Oh God!" Curie said, not looking at Bobby or me. "I'm not a baby!"

She stood up and ran toward her father. Karen called to her a couple of times and then gave up. We all watched Curie running across the empty baseball diamond until she reached the distant figures of Mr. Crashaw and the others. Crashaw was pointing up toward the apex of the sky, where the vapour trail from Gregory's rocket had zigzagged into a jagged thread as fine as a crack in the air.

"Pretty cool, eh?" I said.

"Yeah," Bobby admitted. We talked about the launch for a while—I knew enough about the basics of rocket propulsion by this time to carry on a reasonably intelligent conversation.

"I got to split," Bobby finally said. "Larry needs me to crew for him. Alex is sick. My old lady's looking after the Esso tonight, if you can imagine Lida working a gas pump."

Bobby's father, Larry, drove a sprint car at the oval track across the Columbia River on most summer weekends. Bobby's mother did the books for the family business, but rarely showed her face in the garage. That was men's work and they were welcome to it, as far as she was concerned.

"See you in school," I said.

"Whatever," Bobby told me. He turned and started to walk back toward the downtown strip, shoulders hunched in his leather jacket, needle-points scuffing the sidewalk.

"He's nice, really, isn't he?" Karen asked. "I mean, he seemed like such a hood." She'd been watching Bobby walk away, or watching me watching him, one or the other.

"Yeah," I said. "Bobby's okay."

"You kids want a lift?" I heard my stepfather call from across the street. He was leaning against the side of his car, squinting into the sunlight, looking loose-limbed and skinny as a boy.

"I think I'll walk back home, Dad."

"Good choice," he said, getting back in the Studie. "Nice to see you, Karen," he added. He rolled up the window and pulled slowly away.

"That was great," Karen said. "I never thought poor Gregory would actually get that rocket launched. It was getting so every time he brought it up, Mr. Crashaw changed the subject!"

"Now, if he had made it a nuclear-powered rocket . . ."

Karen laughed. "Old Man Crashaw would have built the thing himself!"

We stood and watched the small, gesticulating figures on the playing field. Crashaw, the Professor and his dad examining Gregory's toy spaceship. Curie an agitated spark a few feet distant from the others, her stance a ballet of impatience.

"Want to go over and talk?"

"I'd better be getting home for dinner."

"Me too. Come on, let's cut through the park."

I offered her my arm. She slipped her hand in the crook of my arm and we wandered along enjoying the cool air that rose off the river.

"Are you really interested in science, Sonny?" Karen asked me. "I mean, you don't say very much at the meetings."

"I'm not really crazy about model rockets. I'm going to take physics, though, in college."

"Is that your best subject?"

"English lit's my best subject. That's just because it's easy, though. Physics is tougher for me. All that math."

"My father says only physicists really understand anything. Everyone else is just buying and selling. Watching TV and football and waiting to die."

"Maybe he's right."

We were climbing a hillock where the bedrock broke the surface of the lawn. Karen stumbled or slipped on the smooth, mossy granite, and I wrapped my arm around her narrow waist reflexively to keep her from falling. Then we were body to body; I could feel her warmth, her breath on my face, the solidity of her slim, athletic frame. We laughed, or at least I giggled nervously while she gasped and then gave a little shriek. Then, of course, it happens. We're looking at each other's eyes—so close she's out of focus. Her lips begin to part—hesitantly, perhaps, but avidly enough to reveal her excitement and hunger—and her eyelids drift down as our mouths come together and touch.

When we turned the corner into Uranium Crescent, Karen's parents were just getting home. Her mother was in tennis whites, but her dad was wearing a shirt and tie, though he'd taken off his jacket in deference to the warmth. I guessed that Karen's mom had picked up her father from the plant and driven him home, as she was driving and the car—the powder-blue Fury—seemed more suited to her than to him.

"I thought you were coming to the club," Karen's mother said. She looked right past—or through—me. Her husband walked into the house without stopping to say hello. I caught a glimpse of him, though, and the impression stayed with me. Tall, very thin, full of taut nervous energy, his hair lank and thinning, but worn long enough at the front that he had to brush it out of his face as he walked. He looked, I thought, European somehow, or like an English country doctor who had somehow wound up in the northwestern states. It was, of course, the look and style of a career academic of exactly that time and place, a man of science, but I was ignorant of such niceties in those days. Karen's mother was also thin, though with generous enough hips and breasts to look feminine in a refined, Grace Kelly sort of way. Her legs looked athletic under her brief tennis dress, and she walked on the balls of her feet.

"I went to the park," Karen said to her mother.

"They were launching a solid-fuel rocket," I chipped in.

Karen's mother completely ignored me.

"Dana and Iris expected you, you know. Laura Lees said Dana had been hanging around since lunchtime, hoping you'd show up. Laura'd booked you girls a court for one-thirty."

She opened the trunk and picked up a small bag of groceries, which she handed to her daughter, then she walked around the car and up the steps.

"I need you to help with dinner," she said over her shoulder. She opened the door and went into the hall, leaving the door standing open.

"Your mom looks so young," I said, thinking I guess of Betty.

"Yeah," Karen said. "I better go and help her."

She turned away and started to walk slowly up the wide, semicircular steps to the front door. From inside the house came the sound of her mother talking and the faint strains of music—Mantovani, I think, or something equally vague and benign.

The afternoon was turning cool. There was wind getting up in the branches of the lindens that lined the Sullivans' street. I turned and headed back across the park.

7

Century 21

The crowd is moving slowly through the glass doors of the United States Science Pavilion. I hang around just inside the entrance, listening to the taped voice of the commentator endlessly repeating information. *Science is essentially an artistic or philosophical enterprise, carried on for its own sake. In this it is more akin to play than to work. But it is a quite sophisticated play in which the scientist views nature as a system of interlocking puzzles. He assumes that the puzzles have a solution, that they will be fair...*

My entire grade at Danforth High School has been bussed up to Seattle to see the Century Twenty-One Exhibition. We've spent the morning exploring the pavilions. I've been through the International exhibits, John Glenn's space capsule and the rest of the NASA displays; then I wandered through the Hall of Industry gazing at the Johnson's Wax display and H. J. Heinz exhibit, took in the Simulated Space Journey, the Bubbleator and the Seattleite car-of-the-future. It's past noon now, and all I can think about is how hungry I am. My friends, though, are intent on seeing everything before we have to leave.

"Let's head for the Gayway," Richie yells. The presence of three of the more interesting girls in our grade is making it difficult for him to speak at a normal volume. He is practically bellowing over the buzz of the crowd.

The girls are Karen Sullivan, Lana Crosson and someone named Linda, whose last name I don't know. Lana, Karen's best friend, is dark and has a downturned mouth she emphasizes with frost-pink lipstick. She's flirting with Richie—a preliminary skirmish before the serious warfare of going steady—which I assume is why the girls are putting up with us at the moment. Linda's shorter than her friends and not as slim. All three are dressed for the occasion—white gloves, sleeveless pastel dresses, summer heels. Lana and Linda have backcombed and teased their hair into luminous, satiny bubbles. They emanate the heady scent of Revlon hairspray and Evening in Paris perfume.

"I'm going to hang around here," Durst says. "I'll see you guys later."

He heads off toward the exhibits.

"We'll meet you here in a couple of hours!" I call after him. "If you miss us, just go to the bus!"

I think I see Durst nod, but he doesn't turn around. That's Gregory, totally unconcerned about getting lost in the crowds or losing track of his friends.

We start to follow Richie Deacon along the East Boulevard toward the stadium.

"Have you been to Show Street yet?" Lana asks.

"Not yet," I say. "What's it like?"

"We haven't been there yet either. My brother says they have stripteasers there. Burlesque queens, he called them. He's such an absolute sex fiend, I'm sure he spent the whole day there, just drooling all over the ground."

"Lana!" Linda says. "Do you have to be so disgusting! Knock it off!"

"What's disgusting about that?" Karen says. "Nudity's perfectly natural. Everyone has a body, after all."

"Yeah, but some of us have more interesting bodies than others!" Richie says. He turns around and leers at Lana, who slaps him on the shoulder.

We walk across the Friendship Mall, past the Standard Oil and Bell Telephone exhibits.

"We have to turn here," Richie says. He is consulting his program and guidebook at every second step. "The Gayway's right next to the place where the Monorail stops."

"I want to try that Monorail!" I say.

"We had a ride already," Karen says.

"Yeah?" I ask. "What's it like?"

"It's boring," Linda says. "You only go about half a block, then the stupid thing just ends. It's like riding the bus, only you're stuck there with your wheels off the ground."

"I thought it was terrific," Karen says.

"That figures, Karen," Lana says. "You always did have a one-track mind!"

Richie laughs at about ninety decibels.

The Gayway seems familiar somehow after the resolutely futuristic look of the other exhibits. It's a carnival, a county fair, with rides and cotton-candy booths. There's a great deal of neon light flashing from the rides and exhibits. The whole scene reminds me of Playland at the Pacific National Exhibition, which Floyd and Billie took me to every summer when I was living up north.

"Let's find the Wild Mouse," Richie says. "That's supposed to be the best."

Richie takes Lana's hand, a move that surprises everyone except Lana, who clicks along happily after him on her white summer heels.

"You guys go on if you want to," I say. "I think I'm going to head for the Food Circus."

"I'm hungry too," Karen says. "I slept in too long to have breakfast and still get to school before the bus left."

"You two go on, then," Lana says. She gives her friend Karen just the shadow of a conspiratorial look. "Come on, Linny. Let's go."

"I don't know," Linda says. "I'm kind of hungry too. I could maybe use a hot dog or something."

"For the love of Mike, Linda," Lana hisses. "Quit thinking about your stomach. We'll find you a candy bar or some popcorn."

"Popcorn? Who wants popcorn? I was talking about *food* . . ."

"Come on, for Pete's sake. You're going to make us miss the burlesque show."

Lana and Richie walk off toward the stadium, dragging the reluctant Linda in their wake. I can hardly believe I'm all alone with Karen.

"Which way is the Food Circus?" Karen asks. The bars of

variegated light swarm down her face and body. She looks like a space girl from a movie, her flowing hair frosted with light from the throbbing bars of neon and her ice-blue eyeshadow and pale lipstick coloured bronze, magenta, orange as the Ferris wheel whirls.

"It's over there, just past the Monorail Terminal."

"I hope they have good burgers. I'm so hungry."

"I bet they have better stuff up in the Needle," I say. "You want to go up and have a look?"

Karen looks surprised. "Sure. All right. Let's try that."

We stand there for a minute smiling at each other, the neon from the Gayway rides swirling over us in multicoloured patterns.

"Let's go," I say. "This whole place is making me dizzy."

She laughs and slips her arm under mine. We walk toward the Space Needle. It is getting late, and the air has cooled off from the heat of the early summer afternoon.

Twenty minutes of standing in a lineup later, we're sitting at our table in the restaurant. I'm feeling exhilarated, almost light-headed. The ride up the elevator to the disc of the Needle is at least partially responsible for this euphoria—Karen gave a little shriek as the car started upwards, like a kid on a roller coaster, then grasped my hand and held it as we soared up from the earth. I'm feeling the wonderful sense of power that comes to you at certain moments of that terrifyingly beautiful time between adolescence and adulthood, thinking, I'm doing something adult now, sitting in a fancy restaurant with a beautiful, intelligent young woman. The restaurant's futuristic theme places it in an era that doesn't quite exist yet—not just the future but *our* future, our own time, mine and Karen's—and that makes the sense of having escaped the mundanity and frustration of childhood even more acute. I look out the window at the radiant triangle of Mount Rainier and the stratum of misty cloud along its base, wishing I could live forever in the manufactured future of the fair.

"I'm absolutely famished," Karen says. "I hope they don't take long." She folds her hands on the varnished tabletop and smiles across at me.

"This is great, eh?" I say, meaning the World's Fair, the day.

"Yeah," Karen says. Those luminous blue eyes gaze frankly at my face, a look that seems merely trusting and open, as if no one and nothing in the world could mean her harm.

"Pretty crowded, though," I go on. "All those lineups and people."

"You should see Disneyland. We went there a couple of years ago. This is just about as bad."

"I guess you've heard that joke about the Seattle World's Fair doll? You wind it up and it waits in line?"

"No," Karen says without laughing. "Where did you hear that? Was it a comedian on TV or something?"

"Maybe it was. I don't remember."

The conversation falters, caught up in some entropy that neither of us seems to be able to overcome. We smile across the blond-wood table for a while, the horizon sliding past outside the windows, and then, in desperation, I ask her which of the exhibits she liked best.

Karen seems to have to think about that for a minute.

"The International pavilions, I suppose."

"You'd like to travel, right? See the world?"

"I'm thinking about the Peace Corps. After college, I mean. Lana's older brother, Geoffrey, he's a Peace Corps volunteer. He's been to Malaysia and someplace in Africa. Rhodesia? The Congo? Somewhere like that."

I don't know much about the Peace Corps. If I think about the future at all, I imagine a job, marriage, children. I'm not sure I want any of these things, but I can't visualize any other way of living. Betty and Clyde expect me to go to university, and I'm willing enough to go along with their plans, but apart from that I have no very compelling dreams—no realistic ones, anyway. I want a Corvette, a boat I can run on the river, most of the girls who follow Elvis around in *GI Blues* and *Blue Hawaii*, maybe a drum set or a Fender guitar. I suppose I lack the American sense of destiny. After three years south of the border, I'm still Canadian at heart. Our foreign wars have already been fought, by my father and his generation. Neither the Peace Corps nor the Army has any relevance for me.

"Yeah," I lie. "I've thought about the Peace Corps too. Be cool to go to Africa or Malaysia. See the world."

"It's helping people that interests me," Karen says. "Did you know they have no flush toilets in Malaysia?"

I almost laugh, God help me. The vision of all those Malaysians looking frantically for a toilet, hopping through the paddies with their legs crossed, is very nearly more than I can bear.

"No, I hadn't heard that."

We sit there and work on our burgers for a while. When I happen to glance up and catch Karen's eye, she doesn't give me one of those automatic smiles, just chews her food and looks at me calmly. I like that: it makes me feel like she's really content to be sitting there across from me, living this particular moment, not just behaving the way she thinks people are supposed to, not just acting out a role.

After we've finished the burgers, we pick at our fries and compare notes about the exhibits.

"Did you see the Bayanihan Rice Dance?" Karen says. "It was so beautiful. I love the primitive dancers. They all seem so natural, so untouched by anything commercial or chintzy."

"Maybe you'll go there sometime," I say. I have no idea who these Bayanihan people are or where it is they come from, but I'm not about to ask.

"I wonder how Linda and Lana and your friend are doing."

"Having a ball, I bet. Richie will be, anyway. Wandering around on Show Street with two girls. I hope he doesn't drive them both crazy."

"Oh, I don't think they'll mind too much. Not Lana, anyway."

We both laugh kind of nervously, embarrassed at the thought of Richie and Lana's mutual attraction, then she turns away and looks out the windows.

"Want to see the view a little better?" I ask her.

"Okay. Sure."

We split the tab and follow the crowds of tourists to the observation room. There are telescopes you can look through, but each of them has a long lineup, so Karen and I content ourselves with staring through the vast panes of glass at the city and the waters of the sound. After we've taken in the sights for a few minutes, I swallow hard and reach to take her hand. As soon as our fingers touch, she looks away over the fairgrounds again, but she lets her hand rest in mine without complaint.

"I wish it was dark," I say. "Being up here would be like being on a spaceship. We could imagine we were flying to the stars."

Karen smiles and says, "I like this all right. There's nothing I really want to see on Venus."

"It's probably just like here anyway," I tell her. "Just some houses and white picket fences. High schools and field trips and Pioneer Day parades."

"I don't think so somehow," Karen says. "I think that there'd be nothing there. Just ice and rocks and dust storms. Like the world will be after the Bomb." She takes her hand away and carefully pulls on her gloves.

We take the elevator back to earth and make our way across the fairgrounds towards the pavilion. In the Plaza of the States, the evening wind is whipping the dozens of national flags around. The crowds seem to be thinning, as if some people have gone home for dinner.

"We'd better get moving. Bernard and Old Man Crashaw will be waiting."

Karen giggles. "Poor Bernard. He looked so worried when we got off the buses. I'm sure he thinks we'll blow up the fairgrounds or something!"

Bernard is Bernie Jenkins, our principal. He and Mr. Crashaw are our chaperones on this field trip. They've given us strict instructions to meet back at the Friendship Mall in front of the IBM pavilion at six o'clock—the principal, who was once in the Marines, insisting on referring to this location as the "mustering point."

We run up the steps of the Science Pavilion, past the endless, oracular voice of the taped presentation on the loudspeaker system, and join yet another lineup. We don't have to stay there long, though. The line hasn't moved more than five or six feet forward before Mr. Crashaw and his daughter come out from the exhibit with the Professor loping distractedly along in their wake. Among the floral pastels of the rest of the girls and young women in the crowd around the doors to the pavilion, little Curie is a study in monochrome. She's wearing white tennis shoes, black pedal-pushers that seem incongruously baggy on her skinny legs, a black T-shirt with a small white bow at the throat, and of all things a flat black beret. She is also wearing sunglasses, black ones with harlequin frames and lenses that seem completely opaque; they make her face look elfin and tiny.

"Wheeler. Karen. I hope you've had a chance to see the pavilion," Mr. Crashaw says.

"Sure. It was cool," I tell him. Karen nods in agreement, though I can tell from her look that the science stuff inside didn't interest her much.

"I suppose your father has already described the pavilion to you in detail, Karen," the teacher adds. "I'm told Lionel had a role in the selection of the exhibits." He pronounces Karen's father's name with a certain plummy richness, as if the word were a sweet piece of fruit.

"Let's go home now, Daddy," Curie pouts. She tosses her head and glares up at her father.

"Of course we're going home," her father tells her. "I don't believe we have any choice. Mr. Jenkins will be waiting at the buses."

"If they haven't all turned into pumpkins!" Karen says, and suddenly starts to laugh. The Professor strides past us and heads across the courtyard alone, the shadows of the international flags whipping under his feet like flames. We all turn away from the lineup and start walking.

8

Satellite

In the summer of 1965, my wandering Aunt Alice re-entered my life. The phone rang while we were in the middle of dinner. It was late June and school had just about finished. Clyde and I were talking about my chances of getting accepted at CalTech when Betty picked up the phone.

"Don't eat all of that potato salad," Betty said when she'd finished talking to my aunt. "Alice is bound to be hungry. Sonny, go and get some clean sheets from the laundry cupboard; we'll have to put Alice in your bed. Clyde, do you mind running down to the station?"

I wondered where my mother thought I was going to sleep, but I figured she must have something in mind. I went upstairs and stripped the sheets off my bed, then I did what I could to make the room presentable. When I'd finished stacking up comics and car magazines and checking under the bed for dirty socks and discarded jockey shorts, I took the sheets down to the laundry and then ran back upstairs to get some fresh ones. I finished remaking my bed, then I went back down and gave Betty a hand straightening up the living room. By the time we'd arranged the throw cushions and fanned the last half-dozen issues of *Look* on the boomerang-shaped coffee table, Clyde's car was pulling into the driveway.

"She's only staying for a week or so," Betty said. "She's landed a job in Vancouver. Good money, too, for singing in some nightclub. Since she split up with Joel, the jobs have been harder to land."

Seeing us at the window, Alice waved as she got out of the car. Betty and I waved back and then went to the front door to greet her. My stepfather was taking suitcases, three or four of them, all different sizes, out of the trunk.

"Jesus, Bette," Alice said when we opened the door. "This looks like the place where the Cleavers live. Whole town does, come to that. All manicured and washed-behind-the-ears. It's a long way from Mainprize, though, ain't it?"

"Fifteen years and three thousand miles, more or less," Betty said. "But it's good to see that some folks don't change. Alice, I swear you don't look any older than you did the day Clyde and I got married."

"A whole bunch less pie-eyed, though, I hope," Alice said. "Lord, Bette, don't bring up your wedding. I'm still so damned embarrassed I could practically pee down my leg!"

Betty was right. Auntie Alice hadn't changed much. She was getting a little bit thicker in the hips, but there was still that crown of platinum hair and those red lips and nails that made her seem so bright and vivid. She smelled of cigarettes and violets, and her red pumps clattered emphatically as she strode up the stairs behind Betty—to fix her hair, which already seemed pretty much perfect, and "freshen up." Clyde wandered in after her, lugging her bags.

"Still the same Alice," he muttered.

"You bet," I said. "Here, let me take those." I grabbed my aunt's cases and bounded upstairs.

The job, if it ever existed, fell through, and Alice settled in for the summer. I moved to a storage room in the basement, right next to Clyde's workshop, and slept on a rollaway cot. It was cooler there than it was upstairs, anyway, though the racket of the oil-fired furnace made it hard to sleep on chilly nights.

Years of playing gigs at night had made my aunt nocturnal; she couldn't get to sleep before 1 or 2 a.m. at the earliest, and it was often near dawn before she finally went to bed. You'd hear her opening drawers and the doors of cupboards, navigating the complexities of our unfamiliar kitchen. The hi-fi would come on suddenly in the small hours some nights, as if it had been turned on by a poltergeist. I'd wake up to Percy Faith and Rosemary Clooney, Dean Martin, Van Cliburn, whatever Alice could unearth amongst my parents' records, and then lie there and listen to Alice padding restlessly back and forth in the living room until I drifted back to sleep.

That summer, I was starting to keep pretty late hours myself. I was eighteen and working part time at the Esso, pumping gas and fixing flats and washing windshields. I was going out with Karen too, although our relationship hadn't really progressed very much since that first kiss at the rocket launch. We "went out" every week or two, at least when

Karen wasn't out of town or dragged along to some country club do with her parents. For our dates I'd borrow the Studie from Clyde, and we'd drive along Plutonium next to the river. Karen was passionate about a lot of things in those days: the pettiness of her girlfriends—many of whom were country club types I hardly knew—the tedium of high school and the insularity and unreality of the town we had both grown up in; but every subject that concerned her, however harmless on the surface, inevitably brought her circling back to the one thing she seemed to care about. Her father.

Whatever ambiguity and guilt I felt then—and perhaps still feel now—about my own father or fathers was a smouldering match beside the terrible fire of Karen's feelings about Lionel Sullivan. She loved him the way a lapsed Catholic must love God, needing desperately to believe in his omnipotence and wisdom and just as desperately to convince herself that he was an empty straw statue, a fraud.

"Lionel talks, but I think he hardly sees me," she said. "It's as if he's a writer—you know, a novelist or something—and he's already written the story of my life. He wrote it a very long time ago, actually, when I was just a little girl. My life is finished, over. He can't understand why I'm still around the house."

"What happens to you in his story?"

"Well, first I grow up and go to university, where I meet some nice young man and get married. The young man worships my father, of course, and of course he's a professional of some sort. Not a scientist, you understand—the world

only needs a few good scientists, and after Einstein, Oppenheimer and Lionel Sullivan, the angels broke the mould.
Maybe he's a doctor or a lawyer. He sails, he golfs, he drinks
single malt and water, and if he plays around he's sure to
keep it quiet. He knocks me up with two-point-five children. We live on Flawless Street in Perfect City, where no
one's sick or black or poor. We've been buried for a decade
before we realize we're dead."

"Oh yeah?" I asked her. "What finally wakes you up?"

"The sound of our children pissing on our graves."

I glanced across at Karen. I was looking at an optical illusion. There she was looking just as she always did, hands
folded in the lap of her pristine white Levi's, unruly hair
feathering over the shoulders of the fitted French-blue
T-shirt she favoured that summer—the archetypal American
princess—but her heart, at times like this, seemed as volatile
and corrosive as anything the longhairs could have conjured.

"Soon," I said, wanting to lighten the tone of the conversation, "*real* soon, right after graduation, we should get the
hell away from here. The Area, the longhairs, this whole
phoney town. Go and live somewhere *normal* for a change."

"We could drive to California." She turned and ignited a
diamond-white smile, hair sweeping over her cheekbone.
The changeling, the dark twin, had vanished. "Wouldn't that
be incredibly fabulous?"

We made it as far as the River, then I pulled the Studie
over by the side of the road and the two of us ran down the
steep, grassy bank. The Columbia was smooth as polished

marble. We could hear a party somewhere, voices distant in the stillness, and the thrumming of an outboard far down-river, but there was no one on that stretch of shore but us.

"I love that smell," Karen said. "Water. Just the way the river smells this time of year." She sat down and tugged at a few blades of couch grass. "You can smell the winter runoff. All the snow in the Sierras. All the minerals in the rock."

I sprawled out beside her, ran the flat of my palm up her long, narrow back.

"Sonny," she said, as if she'd just recognized me, picked the one familiar face out of a crowd. She turned to me and lay back, brushed her lips across my cheek. We kissed, our tongues probing, my hands on her hips, then her breasts, which seemed impossibly soft and lush beneath her T-shirt. She swung her leg over me, mounted my hips and ground herself into me, her breath in my ear.

"It's all right," she whispered. "My mom made me go to her doctor." She pulled herself up, kneeling above me, hips grinding slowly back and forth. "Couldn't risk me getting knocked up by just *anyone,* you know."

She leaned forward onto me, blood-warm and nuzzling, and I watched the river shimmer through the curtain of her hair.

One night, a week or so after Alice arrived, I came home from working late at the garage to find her in the living room, just sitting there alone on the dark. It was almost one, and Clyde and Betty had probably been asleep for a couple of hours.

"Don't mind me," Alice said.

"Sorry," I whispered. "Didn't see you."

"Think nothing of it, Sunshine. Us ghosts get used to people looking right through us. Comes with the territory. Once in a while we'll rattle our chains a bit or throw something out of a cupboard, just to see if it makes anyone jump."

I laughed, then remembered that Betty and Clyde were asleep up in their bedroom and put my hand over my mouth. The next thing I knew, I was stifling a series of yawns.

"Long day, eh?" Alice asked me. "You must be feeling ready for some shut-eye."

"Not really," I whispered. I was tired all right, my arms ached from wrestling with tire irons and stacking cans of Penzoil on the racks in the garage, but I didn't feel ready for bed. I sat down on the opposite end of the couch from Aunt Alice and reached for the switch on the pole lamp.

"You mind?"

Alice shrugged. "At your own risk, kiddo. I took off my makeup an hour back."

I turned on the table lamp, leaving the tri-light at its lowest setting.

"Everything okay?" I asked. Aunt Alice was looking at me intently, as if she saw something unusual in my appearance.

"You remind me of your dad sometimes."

"Mom says I look like him."

"More like her, by and large, but your eyes and mouth are certainly like Alfie's. And mine, come to that. Which is good news for you, buddy-boy. All us Wheelers are good-looking."

"What was it like, when he died?" I asked. "I mean, you being his twin and all that?"

I realized I'd probably made one of those unforgivable blunders that only adults were aware of, but once I'd opened my mouth I couldn't stop myself.

Alice looked up at the ceiling for a moment, then lowered her eyes and picked at the fabric of her housecoat.

"We were out on the road, me and Joel. Someplace way up in Rockies. Colorado, I guess it was. We had this audition in Los Angeles all set up. This fellow who'd worked at the radio station in Winnipeg had heard us, and Joel had got to know him. He promoted things, concerts and dances and so forth. Anyways, this Winnipeg guy knew some other guy who was an announcer on WZEK, Los Angeles. *The Hayride.* Boy, that was really something in those days. Our big chance, like getting in the movies. All the hotshots sang on *The Hayride.* Rose Maddox and her brothers. Patsy Montana.

"So anyways, we stopped at this auto court someplace up north of Denver. You wouldn't believe the air up in those mountains. You could have reached right up and tickled God's ass, if you'd wanted. The moon and stars looked close enough to touch. We were there when I heard about Alfie."

She sucked on her lip for a minute, staring at the dead green eye of the console TV as if she expected it to light up with scenes from her earlier life.

"Mom said you didn't hear. She said you just knew."

Alice smiled, however sadly. "Sounds crazy, doesn't it? Stuff like that happens with twins."

"What about the audition, Aunt Alice? Did you ever get down to L.A.?"

"Nope," Alice said. "And I always regretted it. God, but I

wanted to sing on that station! I told myself it wouldn't have meant much, you sing a few numbers and bugger off home none the wiser. But you never know, do you? Me and Joel, we might have got a chance to make a record, sing some more on other stations, who knows?"

"That would have been great."

"What about you, Sonny? You ever get the urge to sing? Pick up a guitar or toot a trumpet or something?"

I shook my head, embarrassed for no good reason by her question. Like every kid who grew up in the fifties and sixties, I'd entertained a few wild dreams of living like a rock star. The closet in my bedroom contained a Silvertone guitar from Sears Roebuck, but I hadn't used it for much except for posing in front of the mirror above my dresser while I threw myself around and mimed the words to "You Really Got Me." My rare attempts at singing had convinced me that I took after my mom's side of the family in more than just looks. The Wheeler gift for music had entirely passed me by.

Alice gave me an appraising look, as if she were looking through the person I seemed to be and into my real self, my future.

"Just as well, I guess," she told me. "Singing never did much for the rest of us. Certainly not me, at any rate."

"Hey, at least you can do something special."

Alice smiled. "I bet you can do something special too, Sonny."

"Change tires, you mean? Wash windshields and check people's oil?"

"Takes a lot of skill to fiddle that dipstick, Sonny boy. Not many guys can do it right. Just ask your old Aunt Alice— I know."

I must have been blushing. Alice fished another Pall Mall out of the crush-pack on the end table and lit it with Clyde's marble table-lighter.

"You'll do okay in life, Sonny, I'll bet you." She leaned back and blew a stream of smoke into the shadows. "You've got a good heart, like your mama, and you're sharp at school like she was as well. Pretty soon you'll be an engineer, like Clyde."

"That's what Mom would like, all right. Turn me into Clyde, Junior. Get me up there at the Area, splitting atoms."

"Well, if that don't work out you can always come see your Aunt Alice. Where I come from, most people don't even split hairs."

Alice replaced the heavy lighter on the table. She brushed at some imaginary lint on her housecoat, her platinum hair, which she'd caught up in a filmy scarf to keep it off her face, burnished gold as pirate's treasure in the lamplight.

"You better turn in pretty quick if you're planning on getting up before dinner," she finally said.

I stood up and ran my hand over my brush cut, feeling suddenly washed out with fatigue. "See you in the morning."

"Not unless there's a three-alarm fire. I'll be sawing logs till lunchtime, if not later."

I washed up in the main-floor bathroom and then headed downstairs to my bed. Half an hour later, as I drifted off to sleep, I could hear Aunt Alice pacing across on the ceiling.

9

The Cosmic Dwarf

In the fifties and sixties, every household in Danforth was visited once a month by the FBI. A pair of agents would arrive together, athletic-looking men in charcoal suits getting out of a nondescript Ford Fairlane. These interviews were low-key, just a couple of representatives of the government touching base with the families of some of Uncle Sam's most valued employees, but the object of the exercise was difficult to miss.

"Great neighbourhood you have here," one of the G-men would comment. "Nice view of the river and all. Must be pleasant with the park so close by."

"That's a well-kept house next door," the other Fed would add. "Really caught my eye as we were parking. Roland, I said to my partner here, that's as fine a suburban house as you'd wish to see."

Mrs. Typical-Danforth-Housewife would nod cautiously as she poured them their coffees and offered the pound cake around. Her husband, who inevitably worked at the nuclear plant, would be even more reserved.

"Bet they're not the sort of folks to have loud parties," Agent 1 would continue, keeping the conversational ball rolling. "I wouldn't imagine they'd be unusually heavy drinkers or anything like that."

"I often say to my wife that you can tell a heavy drinker's house just by driving past it in your car," Agent 2 would add.

Finally the penny would drop, and someone in the family would assure the FBI men that, no, as far as she knew the MacNeils weren't particularly fond of drinking. And no, they'd never heard them having parties.

We had a visitation from the G-men a couple of weeks after Alice moved in. I'd been mowing lawns all morning and had sprawled out in my usual position on the sofa, avoiding the heat outside. On my stomach was a slim stack of *Superman* comics, which I was studying with the rapt attention of a rabbinical student poring over the Talmud. When the FBI agents arrived, I gathered up my comic books and headed for the kitchen, intending to escape through the sliding doors and find a chaise lounge to lie down in on the deck. Betty waved me back into my seat, however, as she bustled to the door to greet the agents.

One of the Feds was our regular, a big man in his twenties, six-four or -five with a boyish blond brush cut and the shoulders of a born defensive lineman. His name, I remember, was Ford. The other guy I didn't know; he was older, maybe forty, and his cropped hair was greying and thin on the crown. He was as unusually short as his partner was remarkably tall, a fact which gave the pair of them a comical, Mutt-and-Jeff air. The short guy, for all his lack of stature, looked threatening in a way that Ford didn't; his eyes were grey and hooded, and his wide face seemed as hardened as a boxer's.

"Hey, Sonny!" Agent Ford called after Betty had shown him and his partner into the living room. "How's football?"

Football was all right, I told him. We chatted about the Bombers' chances in the coming season while Betty took the agents' hats and put them up on the shelf in the entrance, and then Ford and his partner took a seat on the sofa, both of them hitching their polyester slacks up carefully and thanking my mother for offering them a seat.

The Feds fitted neatly into my comic-book fantasies. They were extraterrestrials, intergalactic villains sent to kill the Man of Steel. The tall guy was an android, that much was obvious, and his partner was the Cosmic Dwarf, Mr. Mxyzptlk. In one of the Superman shorts I'd watched at the movie theatre back in New West, Lex Luthor tricked Superman into using his X-ray vision to transmute base metals into plutonium. Then Lex faked his death and came back to life as Atom Man, with superhuman abilities that matched his archrival's. These cops were quite obviously Lex Luthor's confederates. They had come to Atomic City to defeat the Man of Steel.

Aunt Alice came wandering down the stairs from her room just as Betty was serving Mxyzptlk and his buddy a cup of tea. My aunt was wearing pale-blue cotton shorts with a polka-dot pattern and had a pink shirt tied in a calypso knot underneath her breasts. There was an unlit Pall Mall hanging from her lips, and she had the preoccupied expression of someone who is looking for something and can't think where it might be. I was sitting on the couch beside the younger of the G-men, breathing in his smell of aftershave and sweat and squirming with embarrassment and impatience, and I could see Aunt Alice poking around among the pencils and string in the junk drawer under the kitchen counter.

"Gentlemen, I don't think you've met my sister-in-law, Miss Wheeler. Alice, this is Agent Ford," Betty said. "Alice is staying with us for a couple of weeks."

"Roland," the tall cop said, standing and shaking my aunt by the hand. "My partner, Agent Blankenship," he added.

Mxyzptlk looked Alice over from beneath his hooded eyes, then stood up and smiled as he offered his hand.

"My pleasure, Miss Wheeler. I trust you're enjoying your visit?"

"You bet," Alice said. She sashayed around to the couch and sat down beside Agent Ford, who moved over to give her some room.

"Mrs. Cateret been showing you the local attractions?" Blankenship said.

"We've been down the hardware place a couple of times, if that's what you mean by 'attractions,'" Alice said. "And Betty here's been threatening to take me out bowling."

Mxyzptlk smiled. "Fine sport, bowling. Very enjoyable way to relax."

"Oh, yeah," Alice continued, "and Sonny and his girlfriend took me swimming. That's a serious river you've got here."

"Certainly is," Mxyzptlk said. He sat back and cradled his teacup in his hands. We all sat there in silence for a moment while the adults sipped their tea. There was something absurd about the two men, the hulking Agent Ford and his hard-eyed, burly partner, sitting there in stiff suits balancing Betty's delicate heirloom china in their huge, blunt-fingered hands. I noted, possibly for the first time, the value tough men place on maintaining an air of courtesy and gentleness, particularly in the presence of women. I was seeing their Clark Kent personae, I decided: their secret identities would be something else entirely—hard words and .38s and toecaps in your balls.

"Had a chance to see the Area, Miss Wheeler?" Ford finally said. "I'm sure Mr. Cateret would show you around. I expect you've heard a lot about what they do there?"

Mxyzptlk tightened his lips.

"I'm sure Miss Wheeler wouldn't find much of interest in an industrial facility, Roland," he said softly.

"No, I guess not," Ford echoed, straightening up.

My stepfather chose that moment to emerge from his workshop. We heard him close the basement door and the swishing of his slippers on the runner in the hall. By the time he got to the living room, the Feds had placed their teacups on the coffee table and stood up to shake hands. From that moment on, the talk was primarily of fishing. When they'd finished their tea and shaken hands all round, the agents took their leave.

"Nice boys," Alice commented after the FBI men had driven away. "Real spiffy dressers, too. Reminds me of a morticians' convention me and Joel played in Weyburn. A clothes-moth would have ruptured itself trying to munch its way through one of those suits."

Betty laughed and started picking up the teacups. Clyde wandered into the dining room and came back with a *Popular Science*.

"What are those guys, anyways? Insurance peddlers or something?" Alice asked.

"They're FBI agents," Betty explained. "They think Clyde's John Dillinger and Sonny here's Pretty Boy Floyd. Me, I guess, they mistake for Ma Barker. We generally hide the machine guns until they leave."

Clyde shot her a peeved look. "They're just checking for security risks," he said. "It's their job. This is, after all, a dual-use facility. A lot of the stuff we do is still for the army."

"FBI, eh?" Alice said. She swirled the last finger of her tea around in the bottom of the cup. "What's that stand for? Fucking Big Idiots?"

Everything seemed to stand still for a minute while Alice's remark sank in. I buried my nose in my *Justice League of America* comic. Clyde sniffed, wiped at his nose with the back of his hand, then stood up and walked out of the room. Betty bit her lip until her husband was safely out of earshot, then started to make barely-audible whimpering noises, like a cat that's chasing mice in its sleep.

"A visit from the Fucking Big Idiots," Alice drawled. "Now that's something to write home about, ain't it?"

My mother managed to restrain herself for a couple of seconds longer, but then the dam finally burst. Soon she was hooting with laughter, and then Alice let loose with a rebel whoop and the two of them collapsed on the couch.

"Oh Jesus Christ, Alice!" I heard Betty giggle. "You're a wicked, wicked woman. I haven't laughed like that in eighteen years!"

"Been a while for me too, Bette. I guess I ought to come down here more often. These Yanks seem to tickle my funnybone."

The weekend before Aunt Alice left, my parents threw a party. They invited their friends from the Area, the engineers Clyde worked with and their wives. Durst and Deacon always tagged along with their parents, and I invited Karen. I also mentioned the party to Bobby when we were working together at the Esso.

"Sounds pretty weird, Wheeler," Bobby said. "All those brass-ass types from the Area standing around grilling meat. Is that a nuclear-powered job, your barbecue? Clyde using briquettes or plutonium rods?"

"Factory stock," I told him. "Mom won't let Clyde soup it up. She doesn't like T-bones that glow in the dark."

"You sure you want me to come? I mean, some of those country club broads might have a hard time staying faithful with me hanging around."

"We'll just have to take that chance, I guess. Come early, Clyde never buys as much Rainier as he should."

Our guests started to arrive about six o'clock that Saturday evening. It was August and the weather was still reasonably warm, but you could feel a kind of softness in the air. The men were wearing short-sleeved shirts and a few wore

Dacron Bermuda shorts, the kind with pleats and belt loops and a razor-edged crease, just as if they'd taken the pants from their leisure suits and hemmed them at the knees. Most of their wives wore light summer dresses, though a few had dressed more formally. Richie Deacon's mother, who was small and elfin, with brilliant dark eyes and a wide, sensual mouth, had just had her hair cut fashionably short. She did a slow pirouette in the entrance so that Betty could admire her new style.

"Fabulous!" Betty said. "You look like Leslie Caron. What's the word they use, 'gamin'?"

"Gam-*een*," Mrs. Deacon corrected. She smoothed her cap of glistening black petals and floated past my mother into the dining room, where Clyde was arranging chip dip and pretzels on the table.

Richie's dad was as thin as his son, but three or four inches taller. He wore his thinning hair in a brush cut, which was probably supposed to make him look boyish. He was no sooner in the door than he went into a boxer's crouch and faked a couple of punches at my stomach. "Hey up, Sonny boy!" he bellowed. He did that every time I saw him.

My aunt, who'd been hiding out upstairs in what had once been my bedroom, didn't put in an appearance until most of the guests had arrived. By the time she came downstairs to join the party, the living room was almost full, and there was a whole flock of women in the dining room and kitchen, putting out the hors d'oeuvres and dips they'd brought and talking about their kids. Alice was wearing a halter top and pedal-pushers, strappy white sandals with extravagant heels. She'd combed her platinum hair away from her face *à la* Marilyn Monroe, stroked blue and red eyeshadow over each eye, and painted her mouth with shockingly bright red lipstick.

"Lord!" I heard one of Clyde's engineer friends sigh. "Va-va-*voom!*" Richie Deacon's dad muttered.

"Seen Bette?" Alice asked. She was teetering a little on her heels, as if she'd just bought her first pair.

A couple of the men pointed dumbly toward the kitchen.

"Right this way," Mr. Deacon said. "I'll bet you're Alice Wheeler, right? Sonny's aunt from way up north?"

Alice allowed herself to be steered through the wide double doorway to the dining room. A minute or two later, I heard her jangling laugh ring out above the hum of conversation, and then my mother saying something I couldn't quite hear. Clyde drifted out of the kitchen a few minutes later, smiling vaguely and toting what appeared to be a Scotch-and-water. If I knew my stepfather, he'd be nursing that same drink all evening—an alcoholic drink was a prop to Clyde, something you posed with at parties. It would never have occurred to him to put away enough booze to get drunk.

"Keep an eye on your aunt, Son," he whispered as he passed me. "I think she primed the pump with a few rye-and-sevens while she was fixing her hairdo upstairs. Seems to be a habit with the Wheelers."

"Right," I said, wondering what my stepfather meant. Clyde winked and drifted away through the throng in the living room.

"Not really the party kind, is he?" Karen asked me.

"I imagine he'd rather be fishing," I said. Alice's unmistakable laughter pealed through the smoky air once again. Someone turned up the hi-fi, and the soothing voice of some crooner my parents liked—Jack Jones or Perry Como, probably, someone like that—drowned out the drone of voices in the room. "Come on," I said. "Let's go somewhere quiet."

Karen held my hand, stepping tentatively on the basement stairs, which were narrow and steep. The gooseneck lamp above Clyde's workbench cast just enough light for us to see where we were going. The "hatch," as Clyde called it, was open, and I could feel a draft across the musty space.

"Is this your room?" Karen asked.

I laughed. "Over there," I said, pointing towards the door to the basement bedroom. "That's where I'm camping out, anyway. Just until Aunt Alice goes home."

I pulled out my stepfather's swivel chair and offered it to Karen, who perched on the edge of the leatherette seat as if she were afraid it might swallow her whole.

"Your dad's workbench, right?"

"Yeah. This is Clyde's inner sanctum. Where he tinkers with his electronic stuff. A little different from Lionel's study, I bet."

Karen smiled. "I think I like this better. Daddy's den always reminded me of those cabinets magicians use. You know—to make things disappear? He'd step inside it right after dinner, and immediately he'd vanish for the evening. We couldn't find a trace of him, no matter how hard we looked."

Karen stretched out her long legs and rested her feet on my knee. She leaned back, stretched, and lifted her hair as if to feel to cool of the cellar on her nape. I slouched in the arm-chair—a legacy of our New Westminster place—and watched her eyes grow thoughtful. We were far enough along in our friendship by then ("affair" doesn't seem the right word for people of our generation, and in those days a "relationship" was something that happened between nations or compan-ies) that I could stare at her without either of us feeling self-conscious. I cupped my hand over her ankle, felt her warmth and the prickle of tawny stubble on her skin. She closed her eyes and did a neck-roll. The amber light from the goose-neck lamp made her tan seem even darker, lent a sheen to her long, downy legs. She looked so American, somehow. The perfect California surfer girl, careless of her own youth and beauty.

Karen was idly shuffling through the papers on Clyde's workbench. She fished out a single sheet of plain white paper with a diagram on one side.

"That's weird," she said. She handed me the paper.

It looked like a tuning fork or a narrow, square arch. The two sides of the diagram were pillars, and there was—or seemed to be—a third pillar, about the same size as the others, right between them. As my eyes followed the middle pillar up towards the horizontal line of the lintel, it vanished into the sides of the two bounding pillars. The archway had two supporting pillars or three—it was impossible to say which. I blinked as the illusion strained my eyes.

"It's a blivet. An optical illusion. Some engineer some-where came up with it, and Clyde and his cronies at the Area have been passing this one around."

"Kind of hurts your eyes, though, doesn't it?"

"I bet I can cure that," I said. I flipped the blivet back onto the workbench, then leaned forward, my hand on Karen's knee. "Come here."

"You come here!" Karen protested.

"Meet you halfway. Don't keep me waiting."

She leaned forward and we kissed, tentatively at first, then hungrily, our tongues exploring each other's mouths. I slid my hand along her thigh and under the hem of her shorts.

"Sonny, your parents are right upstairs!"

"They're busy. Clyde's cooking burgers and Mom will be mingling or something."

"What about your aunt Alice?" Karen giggled. "If she comes downstairs every man at the party will follow. Not that she'd make it in those heels."

Our laughter was interrupted by the sound of the door swinging open.

"Sonny? You down there?" my stepfather said.

I leaned back from Karen's arms, squinted up at the shaft of yellow light in the stairwell. "Yeah? What's up?"

"Soup's on. Come up and get a burger when you want."

"All right. We'll be up in a few minutes."

The door closed. I lifted Karen's hair from her face, let it ribbon through my fingers. She was smiling, and her eyes seemed unfocused, her thousand-mile gaze turned inward.

"I guess we've been discovered."

"Caught in the act."

She arched her back lazily, buttery light pooling in the smooth sides of her throat.

"Christ," I said. "Don't you ever wish we were grown up and married? So we could just do whatever we want?"

"Yeah, I bet you'd like that!" Karen said. The cobalt eyes met mine, her gaze as open as a toddler's yet somehow frustratingly opaque. "Maybe that's what I'd like too." I reached to take her hand, but she stood up and started to straighten her clothes. "I think we'd better go now. They're waiting."

Karen and I made our way upstairs. The party had crystallized into four or five small groups, each in a separate room. We drifted into the family room, where some of the men were in a huddle in front of the TV. At first I thought they were watching football. Then Mr. Deacon straightened up and said, "He's rolling. He's rolling that thing around like a pinball! What a kick that must be, eh? Doing barrel rolls in space!"

"Where is he?" someone said.

"Right here, I think."

"Approximately, anyways," someone else added.

"He's orbiting over America. Right at this minute. Right now."

"Hope he's looking the other way," another voice said. "Didn't get around to mowing the lawn like I'd meant to today."

Karen stood watching the group of older men around the television, as if she were interested in the space flight, and I busied myself pouring a fresh glass of Coke from one of the bottles on the coffee table. It was an ordinary moment, I suppose, nothing special—the glory days of the space program were still far ahead, with the space walk and moon landing.

We were already accustomed to the idea of someone being blasted out of the Earth's fragile envelope and transformed into a temporary moon. Still, the picture remains in my mind with perfect clarity: a period piece, like a Norman Rockwell illustration of hicks around a big RCA wireless with expressions of incredulity on their ruddy, child-like faces.

This was the latest of the Gemini flights. John Glenn had gone up in '62, and my friends and I had seen the actual Friendship 7 capsule in Seattle. Now Gordon Cooper was orbiting the Earth. From a hundred miles up, he could still see the rivers, roads, even smoke pouring out of the chimneys of houses. He could see the Great Wall of China, the terraced hillsides of Ceylon, the long scar of the Trans-Siberia Railway etched faintly on the barrens of Urkutsk. When he looked down on America, he could see the lines of interstates, densely interwoven in the north and east, loose and random in the prairies and the deserts of the west. He must have felt like he was looking at a Rand McNally map.

"Let's go outside," somebody shouted. "I want a look at this little old hot-damn of a capsule!"

Mr. Deacon and a couple of the other men laughed, and someone quietly pointed out that there wasn't much chance of seeing anything, given the relatively tiny size of the capsule. No one paid any attention to his observation; we all began to wander out the doorway and into the yard. Soon a couple of dozen people were spread out in groups across the level green of the front lawn; half a dozen more were standing on the porch and front stairs, leaning on the wrought-iron railings and staring up into the clear starry sky.

"There it is!" someone yelled, and instantly two or three people were pointing up towards the apex, where the Big Dipper was drifting at a glacial pace toward the western horizon, which still glowed faintly red from the sunset.

"That's an airplane!" Mr. Deacon said.

"Sure it is. Deek's right," another fellow said.

We watched the red blip anyway, tracing its arc across the Little Dipper and away toward the dark edge of the world.

Just then, I heard the ominous *thump* of a souped-up V8 contrasting weirdly with the smooth, crooning voice of some saccharine pop star on a car radio as a '57 Chevy tooled slowly down the block.

"That's Bobby!" I said. "He turned up after all!"

Karen turned to watch as Bobby's Chev made a preliminary pass in front of our house and then turned around and came thumping back down the street. I could see Sherri leaning out of the passenger-side window and waving at no one in particular as they passed the row of parked cars in front of our lot. When they finally found a place to park, Bobby gunned the Chev a couple of times before shutting off the ignition, and by the time he and Sherri came strolling down the driveway, the whole crowd of adults on the lawn was watching the two of them instead of the stars.

"This some kind of traditional Canadian rain dance, Wheeler?" Bobby asked. "You Eskimos enjoy this kind of stuff?"

"That's right," I said. "We're trying to speed up summer. We do this every year up north, just before the big breakup begins."

Bobby laughed and flicked his cigarette butt high into the air. It flared and trailed a shower of sparks as it arced above our heads.

"Look," he said. "A sputnik! Those fucking Russians aced us again!"

Sherri, Bobby's girlfriend, had made her way over to where my mother and Aunt Alice were standing. She and Betty were both looking up at the sky, and Sherri was saying something to my mother. Alice, who was clearly drunk, was leaning on my mother for support. Every time she looked up, she apparently made herself dizzy, which in turn made her whoop with crazy laughter.

"Your aunt's really having a ball," Karen told me. The vigil on the lawn had made her thoughtful, and she was staring at the houses up and down the block with a look of detachment and wonder, as if it were she who was orbiting far above the planet, gazing down on our paltry suburb with the eyes of some alien god.

We stood on the lawn for a long time. Aunt Alice held on to my mother, and we all stared up into the sky, which was so full of stars it seemed exaggerated and unrealistic, like the night sky in a Technicolor movie. After a while, some people began to wander back into the house, and soon only Bobby and I and Karen and Sherri, along with my mother and Alice and two or three others, were still standing pointlessly out there. Far above us, hundreds of miles away, a man was spinning slowly in a cone of polished metal, blazing with reflected light, a forlorn and tiny planet. Farther still, the constellations wheeled, their light already ancient. Someday, hundreds of thousands of years away, those same stars would shine on this bare North American desert, through the soil of which a fan of radioactive isotopes bled west to the Pacific, the last remaining evidence of human life on earth.

Part Two

10

Revolutions

In the middle sixties, Danforth High had one of the highest rates of college entry among its graduates of any secondary institution in the country. Most of the kids from my graduating class went on to university or college. Karen enrolled at the University of Washington, in Seattle. She was going to study education. Richie Deacon was headed for Oregon, and Gregory Durst had been accepted at Caltech. I went back to Canada, the country of my birth, to study physics at the University of British Columbia; it was my way, I guess, of paying a debt to both my fathers and betraying or abandoning neither.

I passed the first few months of my career as a student in that fog of lost connections in which so many newcomers to large universities find themselves engulfed. By Thanksgiving I was down to three courses (a fact I hadn't bothered to tell my parents or even Floyd and Billie, in whose house I was living), and any dreams I might have had of becoming an engineer or a physicist were memories.

Floyd and Billie had moved to a bungalow in Port Moody, near the south bank of Burrard Inlet; from their living-room window they could have seen across the water to Pleasantside and Sunnyside, if they ever set foot in the living room or opened the curtains more than a quarter of an inch. They had entered, during the six years that Betty and I had been living down in Washington State, the twilight world of the very old. They lived in the dark, day and night, seemingly oblivious to the fact that their curtains were closed on the brightest of days and that there was only the light in the hood above the electric range to see by.

My room was in the basement, next to a workshop which was cluttered with empty paint tins and jam cans filled with nails. There was a narrow bed and a straight-backed chair that I used to hang my clothes on while I slept. Billie's ancient foldaway Singer sewing machine, which like my grandfather's tools had fallen into disuse, served as a desk, and the sill of the little window became a bookcase. At night, I'd lie there in the dark and listen to my grandparents shuffling through the lightless rooms above me. Neither of them slept much any more; they'd watch their eternal TV shows until it was almost midnight and then fuss around for an hour or more getting ready for bed. By one-thirty they'd be sleeping, and by three they'd both be up. Floyd would sit in the kitchen reading a Zane Grey Western and smoking, while Billie reminisced in a hectoring voice and made cup after cup of weak tea. They'd head back to bed around dawn.

Every couple of days, I tried to get a phone call through to Karen. She was sharing a townhouse with the daughter of a friend of her family; the girl, whose name was Ariel, would invariably let the phone ring eight or nine times before answering, and when she finally picked up the receiver she would breathe "Hello" with such exaggerated lassitude that you felt she might expire at any moment. "Karen's out," she would tell me, and only reveal where her roommate had gone if you wheedled and begged her. One call in five, I got Karen.

"Sonny," she would say, as if reassuring herself that such a person existed. She too invariably seemed lethargic or exhausted. She was studying hard, she told me. She was also reading widely, she said, though when I tried to talk books with her, she would only say that she was working her way through some "philosophical stuff" and let the conversation falter and die. She was equally uninterested in gossiping about old friends. Lana, she said, was "marrying some dentist or doctor," and her other good friend, Linda Miller, was "wasting her time in some office." She rarely mentioned Danforth, and when she did she made it sound like a place we'd visited briefly years ago, on a rainy and tedious vacation.

Early in December, I called her to talk about Christmas. The phone rang the requisite half a dozen times, then Ariel's breathy voice said, "Karen? Yeah, she's here." There was a lengthy pause and the sound of a guitar being strummed, tentative arpeggios that clattered to a halt on the same discordant phrase every time. Finally, Karen picked up the phone.

"Sonny." Her voice seemed thin, attenuated.

"You sound tired."

"Exams," she said. "Studying."

I told her about my plans for the holiday, taking the Greyhound down to Danforth a week before Christmas and staying with Clyde and Betty until a few days after New Year's, when the spring semester began.

"We could meet in Seattle and bus down together. I'm getting out of here on the twentieth. I think the bus leaves around nine or nine-thirty."

"I can't, Sonny," Karen said. There was a minute or two of dead air after she said this. I expected her to explain, but she didn't seem inclined to.

"What's the problem?" I finally said.

"There's this girl I know, Jody Lister?" She said this as if it were a question. "Her father went to Princeton with my dad?"

"Yeah, all right," I said. I'd heard of the Listers plenty of times already. They were the family Karen and her parents went to stay with in Seattle once or twice a year. Other times, they'd gone off on vacations together—skiing trips, Hawaii, stuff like that.

"She's going to school in Pennsylvania. Bryn Mawr. Well, anyway, she's coming home to be with her family over Christmas. She's asked me to stay with them for two or three nights before I go home."

"I guess I could wait a couple of days," I said, though the thought of remaining in Floyd and Billie's basement any longer than I absolutely had to made me feel physically ill.

There was another pause, then she cleared her throat.

"Jody's dad's going to drop me off," she said. "Their whole family's spending Christmas in Squaw Valley. Mom and Dad and the boys and I might join them there for New Year's, I'm not sure."

We talked for a few minutes longer, then I told her I'd see her in Danforth and we both said goodbye. I hung up the phone and headed for my room in the basement.

"You going to watch *Bonanza,* Sonny?" Billie called to me from the living room. We'd eaten our dinner in there—Swanson's Swiss Steak Dinners, with green beans and a little daub of caramel pudding—and Billie and Floyd were sitting in their armchairs with their tin TV tables still in front of them.

"No thanks," I said.

"Homework?" Billie asked.

"Yeah," I said. "That's it, homework."

"Busy, busy, busy," my grandfather muttered. He was reading a Western, peering down at the book through his half-moon reading glasses. "You want to pay some attention to your social life, you know. Boy your age ought to have a girl-friend."

When the term ended, I took the bus south to Danforth alone. Most of my high school friends who'd gone away to college had made it back home for the holidays. We got together at parties and tried out our new personae. We were college men with tentative beards and turtlenecks, coeds in wool skirts and loafers. Bobby had landed a job up at the Area, working construction on the new dual-use reactor. Of all my old friends from Danforth, he had probably changed the least. He was still living with Larry and Lida and helping his dad at the Esso whenever he had a few days off. He was making plans, though, like the rest of us. When I drove down to the garage the morning after my arrival in town, the first thing he told me was that Sherri and he were engaged.

"No shit?" I said. "Christ, that's terrific."

Bobby grinned and shook his head.

"She's fabulous," I added.

He wiped his hands on a grease rag and smiled some more, bouncing a little on the balls of his feet.

Alex, the other mechanic, came in from gassing up somebody's Corvair and shot me a wink as he passed.

"So you heard, eh?"

"He just told me this minute. I don't even know when the wedding is yet."

"We're waiting a while," Bobby said.

"He's going to take some lessons first," Alex chimed in. He rang up the sale and made change. "'Your Wang and What to Do with It.' They have them Wednesday nights down at the Y."

"Yeah, yeah," Bobby said. "Come back here and eat my shorts!" he added as Alex hustled out the door, laughing and jangling a fistful of coins.

"So why the long engagement?" I asked. "Saving up for your own place or something?"

Bobby nodded. "Sherri's got her eye on this rancher. There's another reason we're taking our time, though. I've been offered a full-time gig with Digger Johnson."

"He's the sprint car guy, right?"

"Was at one time. He's into the straight-line stuff these days. Runs a fueller on the NHRA West circuit. Does pretty good too. Thing is, though, he's building a car for the salt flats. Got an Allison V-12 aircraft engine about the size of a fucking house. He wants me to come out to Bonneville, be the gofer on his team."

"Sherri okay with that idea?"

"Long as she gets to come along."

Bobby tucked the grease rag into the pocket of his coveralls and we headed back into the shop. The smell of oil and lanolin cleanser hit me right away, bringing back the feel of working there that summer. There were half a dozen truck tires stacked against the wall, waiting for repairs, and somebody's Olds 88 was up on the hoist, minus its tailpipe and muffler. Larry's sprint car was in the other bay, its engine torn down to the block, and Miss October was still holding court on the wall, though she'd acquired a red-ink goatee since I'd last seen her. The chalk-scrawled *Where's Von Dutch?* on the wall beside the crapper still greeted visitors enigmatically. You wouldn't think an old garage with a greasy concrete floor and pin-ups on the walls could seem homey, but it was.

"So how's things with you?" Bobby asked. "School okay? You getting any smarter?"

"Not a lot. Fact is, I'm thinking of quitting."

"Oh yeah?"

"Yeah. That is, if I pass enough courses to quit. Could be they'll throw me out first."

"You talked to your mom and Clyde yet?"

I shook my head.

"Don't blame you. I gather Clyde kind of figured you for a scientist or something. Local boy makes bombs and all that shit."

"I don't think I'm cut out to be a longhair, somehow. I mean, look at those clowns out at the Area. All that education, just to make a pile of poison that they hope they'll never use. And the way they live is just so fucking boring. Man, they ought to blow up Danforth. Leave the communists alone."

Bobby grinned. "Can't argue with you there, Professor Wheeler. So fill me in about the campus pussy. You finally lose your cherry or what?"

I managed to control my curiosity about Karen's whereabouts until a couple of days before Christmas. Calling her place on the telephone proved useless, however; I got either the cleaning woman or one of Karen's brothers, none of whom seemed to have any interest in his older sister's current location or plans for the future. Finally, I gave up and got Clyde to drop me at the Sullivans' house on his way to a Kiwanis Club meeting.

Karen's younger brother opened the door.

"Hi, Anthony," I said.

He gave me a sullen look, skinny little twelve-year-old in shorts and a Squaw Valley T-shirt, his brush cut on a level with my shoulders.

"Mom!" he yelled. He turned and disappeared inside.

Mrs. Sullivan appeared at the far end of the hallway.

"Come on in the kitchen, Sonny. Have a Pepsi or something. I just got in from the club, as you can see."

I took off my shoes and padded down the hall toward the dining room, slipping along in my stocking feet on the polished oak flooring. Mrs. Sullivan was in the kitchen, which was on the other side of the dining room. Both rooms were done in Danish modern, smoothly finished teak tables and functional, unadorned chairs. A light with several fixtures, each enclosed with a disc of copper-coloured metal like the rings of Saturn, hung above the table.

"Come on in," Mrs. Sullivan repeated. She was standing at the counter with a bottle of Gilby's gin and a bottle of tonic water. She picked up the tonic as she spoke and added a dash to her glass.

"I suppose I should be offering you a proper drink, shouldn't I? Now that you're a college man and all. What would you like? A glass of wine? Beer?"

"Pepsi would be great."

"You sure you wouldn't like one of these?" She nodded towards the bottles on the counter.

"No thanks. Really."

"To each his own," she said brightly. She opened a can of Pepsi and sloshed some into a highball glass. Then she handed it to me and lifted her own glass in a toast.

"Skol!"

"Right, *skol,*" I said, and took a swig of pop.

She asked me a few questions about what I'd been doing— how big was the university, how did I like Vancouver, was I enjoying my studies, all the usual sort of stuff. I told her things were pretty much okay.

"You must miss seeing your friends."

I nodded.

"Karen especially, I expect?"

"Yeah."

She took a sip of gin and gave me a cool, appraising look over the rim of her glass.

"Have you heard from her much lately?"

"Ariel said she's been pretty busy. Exams, I guess, and all that."

"Ariel! My God, what a singular creature that one is! Ralph and Edna Bormann have been concerned about young Ariel, you know."

No, I hadn't known that, I told her.

"Oh Lord, yes! She was debarred from taking two exams this semester. Chemistry and American lit, I think it was. And history too. English history, European history, something like that. Two exams at least."

"That's too bad."

"Well, Ariel has a history, you know. 'Nerves,' is that what they call it?"

I didn't know what she was talking about. I smiled, then I took another sip of my Pepsi so that I wouldn't have to say anything.

"We consented to Karen sharing with Ariel because Ralph and Edna thought she might give Ariel a push in the right direction, be a positive influence, that kind of thing."

She sat down next to me and crossed her legs.

"Lionel and I had some concerns, I can tell you, but we thought, well, Ariel's from a good family. And the offer of the townhouse was difficult to resist. Only now . . ."

The phone rang and Mrs. Sullivan got up and picked up the receiver from the counter beside the fridge.

"Oh, hello, Iris," I heard her say. "How've you been?"

Iris was one of Karen's tennis friends. There were four or five girls she saw at the club, the daughters of Danforth managers and longhairs. I'd run across a few of them with Karen, but most of them I didn't really know.

"Looking for Karen?" Mrs. Sullivan said. She gestured toward the table and I handed her her drink. "She's staying with a friend of hers up in Highlands," Mrs. Sullivan continued. She took a quick sip of her gin-and-tonic. "Jody Lister? She's been seeing quite a bit of Jody's older brother, Jarrold. He's at Yale, I believe, or one of those other schools back east. I expect he'll be home, though, for Christmas."

I drew in my breath and bit my lip. Mrs. Sullivan smiled radiantly at me over her gin glass.

"Happy Christmas, Iris," she said. "I'll tell her you called."

When I got back home, Betty was up and dressed and making dinner.

"Sorry it's a little late, Sonny," she said. "I was on the phone for ages with Alice. She called from Las Vegas."

"I'm not very hungry anyway," I told her. I went into the living room and picked up a copy of *Life* from the array of magazines on the coffee table.

"She's married!" my mother yelled from the kitchen. She was stirring a pot very briskly, making a racket as she whipped up mushroom gravy. The homey smell of the cooking roast drifted in through the doorway along with her voice, though neither of them could penetrate my mood.

"Her husband's a guy called Fangis. Funny name, isn't it? He sounds very nice, though. Has a proper job too. He works at the Nuclear Test Site."

Great, I thought. Married people with proper jobs. Even Alice was Donna Reed these days. I flipped the page in *Life* and gazed absently at a display ad. A family in front of their white picket fence. The mother, who looked a lot like Debbie Reynolds. The dad, who was tall and suavely greying, his smile clenched on the fine stem of his meerschaum. And capering around with the camping equipment behind the three-quarter-view drawing of next year's Rambler wagon, the kids: the boy with his T-shirt and wide, gap-toothed grin, his sister with her pedal-pushers and pigtails, and a toddler of indeterminate gender, chubby hand poised on a tire. Behind them was a white frame house, leaf-green gables and shutters on the four bedroom windows upstairs, a swing on the porch beside the entrance. Beyond it, a skyline of picturesque elms. And beyond that, I decided, an atomic bomb plant. The scablands that lay beyond the stage set.

"I'll grab something later," I called to my mother. I tossed the magazine onto the table and headed upstairs to my room.

The day before I was due to go back to Vancouver, I finally ran into Karen. I'd been getting restive sitting around the house, and when my mother went grocery shopping I'd asked her to drop me in town. I'd wandered down Lincoln as far as the Esso and shot the breeze with Alex; then I'd stopped in a pharmacy and browsed through the magazines, just killing time, until I glanced out the plate-glass window and saw Karen on the sidewalk on the opposite side of the street. She was just saying goodbye to someone—a girl, I thought it was Lana Crosson but I couldn't be sure—and her face changed from smiling sociability to a closed look of inward concentration as she turned from watching her friend's car pull away down the street, bowed her head and gathered her white leather bag to her chest, and started walking east, toward Danforth Hardware and the Western Reserve Bank. I put the *Esquire* I'd been leafing through back on the rack and was out the door before she had gone half a block.

"Oh, Sonny, it's you," she said, turning toward the sound of my voice. Her eyes seemed vague and weary, and she was clutching her cloth winter coat to her throat against the steady wind that had been blowing off the Columbia all morning.

"I was beginning to wonder if I'd see you."

"Oh yeah, I've been up in Seattle."

"I know. I talked to your mom a couple of weeks ago. She said you were staying with the Listers. You have an okay time up there? Do any skiing?"

She shook her head. "We decided not to ski this year. I'm really sick of hanging around Squaw Valley every Christmas holiday, making stupid conversation and pretending it's all such fun. You can't be a kid forever, right? There's more important things in life."

We wandered down to Riverside Park and sat on a park bench, our winter coats tucked carefully under our bottoms to protect us from the cold. Karen stared straight ahead at the slow-moving waters of the river. I looked up into the bare, jagged branches of the elms, remembering the day we'd watched the Professor launch his rocket, our first kiss on the trail beneath the overarching trees.

"How's school? You make out all right on your finals?"

She shook her head. "I passed, I suppose. It doesn't matter. That whole scene's just stupid and boring. It's like being force-fed. Some paid-off establishment lackey pouring saccharine down your throat."

"I'm thinking of dropping out too," I said, making it sound like I had a choice.

Karen gave me a quick, startled glance, those brilliant sapphire eyes of her registering, inexplicably, panic.

"You? I thought you were going to be an engineer or something." She seemed to gather herself together. The blue eyes returned to the river. "It's none of my business. You know what you need."

No, I don't know, I wanted to tell her. *I wanted you with me, to know you, that was all.*

"What about the Peace Corps?" I asked her. She'd mentioned the idea of joining a couple of times over the phone, but that was back at the beginning of the semester.

She kept her gaze focused on the distance, watching the river, the swirl of cold lights.

"That's a front, you know."

"A front?"

"Yeah, that's right. They send these idealistic kids overseas, to places in Africa and South America. They're supposed to be helping the people, and what they really are is salesmen, selling them America the Bountiful, just like you'd sell a Pontiac or some perfume or a bottle of Coke. It's such a lie— If it weren't for us, they wouldn't be starving. If it weren't for America, they'd have their own land and the freedom to do what they wanted. We starve them, we kill them, then we send a bunch of college kids over there to plant seeds and dig irrigation ditches and show them what swell folks we are!"

I looked down and started to tug at the grass between my knees. I was embarrassed, though whether for Karen or myself I wasn't sure.

"Where'd you get all this stuff?" I finally asked her.

She glanced at me quickly and then looked away. "Nowhere," she said. "It's obvious. Look around you. Read the news." She was holding her chin high and her mouth was pursed in a look of what could have been defiance. She reminded me, oddly, of her father. That same expression of certainty, of having access to absolute truth.

"Vietnam, Cuba, Korea. That's the real face of America. Just look at what happens in this country. Segregation. Discrimination. Poverty. The war. I certainly don't need anyone to tell me how things are."

"That guy in Seattle, right? Jarrold Lister?"

Karen turned away, obscuring the curve of her cheek in her hair.

"It's not about some romance, Sonny," she said. "It's not about boys and girls and going on dates and getting married. How can you think about any of that when people are being starved and killed and put in prison? Negro people. Asian people. In Vietnam. In Africa. In the ghettos. In the south."

"And Lister, he's involved in this?"

"He's involved in the Movement. He has been forever. It's his life, you know, politics. He lives what he believes."

"And that's what interests you, politics?"

"Everything is politics, Sonny. People who have power and people who are victimized and exploited. That's the kind of world we live in now. That's America. That's us. I want to help to change all that. Don't you?"

"Yeah, I guess I do," I said. I reached down and picked at some stiff blades of yellow winter grass between my feet. "I mean, you know I've been against this Vietnam thing, just like you have, from the beginning. I wonder sometimes, though, whether human beings can really change. Whether it's just our nature to want to have power over others, if only so they can't have power over us. I mean, that's what the A-bomb's all about, isn't it? A bunch of cavemen gathering sticks and huddling in their burrows. Killing blindly, out of terror. Isn't that who we really are?"

Karen shook her head. "That's bullshit. We're *trained* to believe that anyone who's different from us is our enemy. We're *trained* to believe that white men have the God-given right to rule the world. That's what people like Jarrold and me have rejected. The belief that white Americans are God's chosen master race."

I shredded a blade of grass between my fingers. Wind was ruffling the trees, and the surface of the river winked and sparkled. Karen sniffed, as if she were getting a cold, and began to root around in the pockets of her coat. When she'd found herself a Kleenex, she wiped her nose and sat there staring blindly at the semaphore of meaningless lights on the river, air and water dancing for no reason and to no end.

"I have to go," Karen finally said. "Lionel's driving me

back to Seattle. If I keep the old bastard waiting, he'll expect me to take the bus."

I almost, instinctively, offered to borrow my stepfather's Studie and drive her up myself, but I managed to keep my mouth shut for a change. I stood up, brushing grass off my pants. "Yeah," I said. "Guess I better be getting along as well. Betty needs a hand with the dinners lately. She hasn't been feeling too hot."

We parted and started to make our way out of the park, Karen angling north along the pathway through the gaps beneath the dolmen trunks of giant elms, and I heading south and west toward the playing fields and home.

By the time the end of the term arrived, I was spending more time cruising jazz clubs and drinking beer than I was showing up for my classes. I went out to the university maybe once or twice a week. I was debarred from writing two exams and managed to pass one course. My grandparents took me out for dinner to celebrate the end of my first year. We sat in an almost-empty Mr. Beef's steakhouse just off the Barnett Highway, chewing our baked potatoes and watching headlights slip past in the rain.

"Well, here's to our college man!" Floyd said when we'd finished eating. He lifted his glass and saluted me across the table. He'd sprung for a carafe of the house red, which if nothing else was patriotically domestic.

When summer came, I found myself a job and moved out.

11

Shatter

I went back to Danforth for a couple of weeks in early September of 1967. I'd been living on my own up in Vancouver for more than two years, but Betty and Clyde still kept my bedroom just the way it had been when I left. It was a typical teenage boy's bedroom from the early nineteen-sixties, an exhibit from the Age of JFK: Superman posters, Johnny Unitas and Wilt the Stilt, the Beach Boys and Nancy Sinatra. Some plastic model hot rods on the shelves above the bed. The only thing incongruous was me.

In Vancouver, I'd been stocking shelves at a Wong Lee's Superior Foodstuffs for over a year—the latest in a succession of dead-end jobs. The work was hard and mindless, which was exactly what I wanted. I humped heavy boxes of produce off trucks and lifted flats of cans onto rickety shelves from midnight until seven in the morning, then took the bus home through the empty, rain-swept streets to the studio apartment I'd rented. Once home, I'd spend the morning reading—Kerouac and Burroughs, James Baldwin, Marx and Marcuse, books and articles about the invention of the A-bomb and its use in Hiroshima and Nagasaki, and stacks of dog-eared Superman comics. My apartment was as barren as a monk's cell. I had no TV, and I only used the radio late on weekend nights, when I listened to jazz from Seattle. I was drifting, going nowhere fast, an outsider with few friends and no future. My failure was my greatest accomplishment, of course—I'd shattered the claustrophobic dream world that Betty and Clyde and America in general had envisioned for me. I'd escaped from Atomic City. I was the Bizarro Sonny Wheeler, the evil twin who lives in the basement, Lex Luthor in his cave beneath the world.

I was lying on my bed staring up at the Revell model of the X-15 rocket plane that was hanging from my bedroom ceiling when I heard my mother's quiet knock at the door.

"Come on in, Mom. I'm not busy."

Betty appeared in the doorway. "Bobby's here," she told me. I thought I could sense a note of disapproval in her voice, but I was paranoid enough about my parents' opinion of me and my friends that I might have imagined it. I got up and headed downstairs. Bobby was standing in the foyer, shifting from one boot to the other on the welcome mat and making conversation with Clyde.

I nodded to Bobby and we went out to his car without talking. He put the Chevy into gear and motored down Argon Crescent and onto Lincoln Boulevard, driving like the road was made of eggshells.

"Where we headed?"

"Pasco," he said. He punched the cigarette lighter and fished a crush-pack of Camels out of the pocket of his shirt.

I sat back and watched the storefronts of Danforth slide past as we made our way south along Lincoln. In a few minutes we were cruising across the marshlands, over the bridge and out of town. Bobby pulled into the parking lot behind a beer-and-a-shot joint between a muffler shop and a Dixie Chicken franchise. I could hear the canned music before I'd got out of the car.

The bar was as murky as the inside of a fish tank. What light there was came from the jukebox and the orange neon Coors sign on the wall behind the bar. "Light My Fire" was blasting from the box, bass notes bubbling up beneath the singer's crooning voice.

Bobby lit another Camel, his third since we'd left my house. I signalled the waiter for a couple of beer. He wandered over with his serving tray under one arm and looked us over before he spoke.

"You boys got any ID?"

Bobby screwed up the corner of his mouth, as if he'd eaten something bitter.

"Get fucking serious, pal."

The waiter stared at Bobby for a moment, his fleshy lips working as he sucked at his teeth. "Just trying to do my job," he said. "We could lose our licence."

"Two Buds, in the can," Bobby told him.

When the beers arrived, Bobby sipped his beer in silence.

"Something on your mind?" I asked.

"My number's up, all right? The notice came a couple of days back."

I thought about this for a minute. "You've been drafted?" I finally said.

"Bingo. That's it. I been drafted. They have called up my patriotic ass."

He took a long pull on his Camel and then leaned back in the bar chair and blew a thin, hard stream of smoke toward the fluorescent orange neon of the beer sign.

"What about Sherri? And the job with Digger Johnson?"

"Jesus fucking Christ, Wheeler. You really don't get it, do you? I mean shit, man, you sit up there in Van-fucking-couver on that pacifist Canadian butt of yours and nothing that happens in the rest of the world means dick to you, right?" He scrubbed out the butt of his smoke in the ashtray. "Sherri and me are shit, right?" he said quietly. "The job with Digger, that's also shit. My life from next fucking week to infinity is officially shit. I got the fucking papers to prove it."

"You going to report?"

Bobby put down his beer can and looked at me as if he didn't comprehend what I was saying.

"My dad was a Marine sergeant, Wheeler. So was Uncle Archie from Fresno. One of Lida's brothers served on a cruiser. You giving odds I'll burn my fucking draft card?"

"People do refuse the draft," I said. "A couple of guys burned their draft cards at that Husky Stadium protest. Others have chosen to go to jail. It happens."

"Jail, man? You kidding?"

"It's better than killing people, isn't it? I mean, shit, Bobby, someone has to say no to killing. We can't all just march off like a bunch of fucking robots and blow up anyone inconsiderate enough not to have been born white and wealthy."

"I look rich to you, Wheeler? If I had been born into money, I'd be diddling around at some college someplace on an automatic fucking deferment. Rich dicks like you and Jarvis don't fight wars."

I helped myself to one of Bobby's smokes from the crushpack on the table. He was too deeply into his worries to notice that I'd started to smoke, let alone that I was bumming his Camels.

"So what are you going to do? Pack up and hop the bus for boot camp? Do your two years and hope you survive?"

"And risk your life in a pointless war? Defending what? Coca-Cola? Frigidaires? The Mouseketeers and Ann-Margret movies? The inalienable right of exploited people everywhere to make American businessmen rich?"

"It's all a fucking joke to you, isn't it, Wheeler," Bobby said. "Nobody's ever going to ask you to fight for your freedom. When the Soviets invade Vancouver, you'll just raise the price of vodka in your Communist government stores."

On his two brief visits to my apartment in Vancouver, nothing had troubled my friend more than the fact that you had to line up in a publicly owned store to buy alcohol. *You got to see a bureaucrat to get a fucking beer?* he'd whine. *You cheeseheads need a fucking revolution!*

"Hey, look. I'm sorry I'm a Canadian, okay?"

He took a long, slow drag on his Camel and blew smoke at the neon sign.

"All right," he said. "I suppose I forgive you for being a cheesehead, but there's really no fucking excuse."

"Hey," I said. "Maybe you ought to convert. Take a cruise on up to Van sometime and forget to come back across the border."

"What would I do? Hunt moose? Build fucking igloos?"

"They have the odd industrial plant up there too, you know. Even a car or two. It isn't all snowbanks and Mounties."

"Don't bullshit me, Wheeler. I've been there. Anyways, I don't speak the language."

"You don't know any Canadian?"

"God's truth. Not a fucking word."

Our joking mood lasted about halfway to a party at Bobby's friends' place in Pasco, then Bobby and I both ran out of patter and we drove through the dark streets in silence, the radio in Bobby's Chev turned down to a murmur, a whisper of hillbilly keenings and mournfully twanging guitars.

The next weekend's party was at Alan Jarvis's parents' house, a pillared neo-classical block with Scarlet O'Hara pretensions that stood on an acre or so of trees and lawn overlooking the river. Jarvis's father, the lawyer, was out of town on business. Jarvis himself was home from Brown, in which his parents had enrolled him despite his having barely scraped through high school. He'd been wasting his time—and his old man's money—there for the past couple of years, but he still came home often enough to keep in touch with the social whirl of Danforth.

I'd made the rounds of the party, moving from one group of my old high-school friends to another, feeling vaguely alien and nostalgic at the same time. I felt I had little in common with my old teenage gang, most of whom were on their way to marriage and careers, but I also felt a sense of comfort at settling back into the safe little world of Danforth. Richie Deacon was holding court in the Jarvises' Danish-modern dining room, sprawled in a teak occasional chair nursing a Rainier, and he bellowed a greeting as I wandered through the door from the kitchen.

Not wanting to get caught up in the crowd around the Deeker, I winked at him and wandered through the French doors to the patio. More partiers were draped over the lawn furniture, one or two couples, a drunk kid sitting on a terra-cotta planter with his head between his knees, a couple of girls in pink pantsuits staring at a circular fish pond. The lawn was dry and freshly mown, and it extended in soft, inviting undulations from the edge of the flagstone patio down a gentle slope to the river. I left the vague bubble of light from the windows and strolled into velvety darkness. When I came to the crest of the slope, just before it angled fairly steeply down toward the little wooden slip and the boathouse, I noticed someone walking up towards me. She—even in the dark I could see her slightness and feminine figure—was taking her time ascending the gentle arc of railway ties that had been used to make a long set of giant-sized stairs. I leaned against the smooth trunk of a white birch and watched her, and as I stood there, she lifted her face to the moonlight, and

I realized why her stance and her movements had seemed so familiar.

"Curie?"

She laughed, a little descending arpeggio. "You didn't recognize me," she said. It wasn't a question.

"I do now," I said. "You've grown up a lot."

That, at least, got me a wry sort of smile. She was wearing a skin-tight mini-dress, midnight blue and shiny, and black vinyl boots that came halfway up her thighs. Her hair was elaborately backcombed. She climbed the last few railway ties, taking long giant steps that made her boots flash with light and swinging her matching black purse as she walked, like a little girl carrying a basket.

"Been out for a boat ride?" I asked her.

She shook her head. "Nothing like that. I came down here to look at the river."

"And to get away from that party, I bet."

"Yeah. They do get a little oppressive. Is that why you're out here as well?"

"Yeah. It's all kind of foreign. Sometimes high school seems a long ways in the past."

Curie came to the top of the stairs and positioned herself in front of a large elm as if she were posing for a picture. Everything about her, the shiny dress, her bag and boots, even her fairy-pale skin, seemed to shimmer like the water of the river.

"So how's school?"

"I don't know," she said. "I don't really go there. My father thinks I go there, but I don't." She spun the bag on its narrow strap and watched it flash and twirl. "Not that he cares what I do with my time. I'm an experiment to him, not a person. Radiation Girl, Mr. Science's extraordinary child."

"Yeah, well, I can relate to that."

"You're still in college, aren't you?"

"Not really. I drop by there once in a while. Use the library. Have a beer at the student pub. Place kind of gives me the creeps."

"I know exactly what you mean. People locked up in stuffy rooms, scratching at papers and worrying. I like it here in the woods at night, when there's no one and everything's quiet."

I'd wandered over to the tree where Curie was standing and leaned against its smooth, striated bark. From that angle, I could see the yellow lights of the house, hear scraps of conversation, muffled bass from the stereo set, a joyous drunken shout. Curie looked up at me without expression. She was still the skinny pixie with the knowing, defiant eyes she had been back in the days of Crashaw's science club, though with her backcombed hair and extravagant outfit she looked like a spy from a James Bond flick or the Moon Maid in the *Li'l Abner* comics.

"I never thought you were one of them," she told me.

"Oh yeah?" I said. "One of what?"

"Daddy's little whiz kids. The science club crowd. You just didn't have the look of a true believer. I guess that's why he never really liked you."

It was news to me that Crashaw had disliked me, and it bothered me a little to find out. "What about you?" I asked. "Didn't you like me either?"

She stepped closer and turned her pale moon-maid face upward, her eyes searching mine. "What do you think?"

I touched her cheek, ran the back of my cupped fingers along the arc of her cheekbone. She closed her eyes and opened her lips and I kissed her. I had expected her to feel light and fragile in my arms, a handful of brittle bones under the slick synthetic skin of her dress, but in fact she seemed solid and strong. She pressed her hot, fervid little body against me, grinding her lips against mine. I felt myself getting hard, solar heat climbing me flash after flash.

"Hold on for a second," she whispered.

She sat down on the tender grass and tugged off her boots. Then she stood up and turned around.

"Unzip me," she said. I pulled down her zipper and parted the glistening material, baring her shoulder blades, the delicate arc of her spine. She let her shoulders go limp and shrugged the dress off as I peeled it down her body. As she stepped out of the fallen dress, I ran my hands up her belly, cupped her breasts, and stroked both her firm little nipples.

She bent to roll her panties down her legs. Then I was lying above her, elbows and knees on the cold, giving earth. I touched her little breasts, the nipples hard as candle wax, then kissed them each and licked around the aureoles. Curie arched her back, shuddered, pushed her hips against mine. I stroked her thighs and reached to touch her pussy.

"Don't. Not yet," she told me. We exchanged a long, searching kiss.

"You okay?" I asked her.

She nodded, eyes closed, a twinge of displeasure at the corners of her mouth. "It's all right. Go slowly."

I held her, touching her, taking my time. The grass was soft and cool, and motes of light shimmered and danced through the dark leaves of the overarching trees. Then Curie's breathing quickened, and I felt as much as heard her breath at my ear moaning, *Now you can, now*. And in a moment I was in her, thrusting hard against her squirming hips, her astonished little yips.

"Oh Jesus, I can't hold it!" I muttered.

She shrieked as I pulled out of her, then rolled onto her side and pulled her dress against her breasts.

"Shit, I'm sorry. Happens sometimes, you know. Not much you can do."

She blinked incomprehension.

"It's all right. I'm fine now. Don't worry."

We stood up, got our things back on, and headed for the house. I put my arm around her waist, but she seemed inexplicably shy of my touch. As soon as we reached the Jarvises' patio, she told me she had to get home and slipped off through the shadows towards the driveway. I wandered past the necking couples lounging on the lawn chairs and picked my way through the family room, intending to find a washroom and straighten myself up. I was halfway down the second-floor hallway when someone started shouting my name.

"All right, where have you been, you horny bastard?"

Allan Jarvis was draped against the door frame of his parents' study. The blond quiff had been transformed into a razor-cut shag, and the leathers he'd favoured in high school had given way to a crushed-velvet Nehru, high-collared white shirt, candy-striped bell-bottoms and a pendant.

"Get in here and explain yourself, Wheeler! There's a Scotch with your name on it ready for immediate consumption. Whole fucking bottle of the stuff, if you like. That ought to loosen your tongue!"

He reeled back into the study, still babbling imprecations to himself. I followed apprehensively and was greeted with a wad of wet paper towel, thrown by my old friend the Deeker, who was at ease in a leather recliner with his Beatle boots up on a gorgeous rosewood desk. Bobby Deerborne was sitting beside him, hunched forward with a cigarette dangling from his lips and a cut-crystal whisky tumbler balanced on one knee.

"Here's the culprit, duly apprehended and processed!" Jarvis roared. He fell towards a wingback chair, which toppled against the wall with the impact. Jarvis fell over whooping and giggling.

"So, Sonny my lad," Richie Deacon said. "Rumour has it you've been sighted skulking homeward from parts unknown in the company of a certain science teacher's innocent young daughter. 'They're old enough to bleed, they're old enough to slaughter'—that your hypothesis, Wheeler? Have you anything to say in your defence?"

"Off with his pecker!" Jarvis bellowed. He rolled off the upended chair and lay prone on the carpet, still chortling.

"Mind your own business," I said. "Where's this famous glass of peat moss I was offered?"

Bobby pushed the Glenlivet bottle—liberated from Jarvis, Sr.'s liquor cabinet, no doubt—across the desk toward me.

"Fill your boots, Wheels. You've earned it," Richie said. He leaned back in the recliner and took a pull on his cigar.

The long picture window behind him afforded a panoramic view of the moonlit lawn and trees behind the house. I poured myself a finger of the whisky, sat down, and took a tentative sip.

"Hope you assholes have been enjoying yourselves," I said.

12

The Red Telephone

I was dreaming of Betty when the phone started ringing. She was holding my hand and striding through the halls of the Riverdale Clinic. She was apparently in a terrible hurry, which wasn't unusual for Betty. I was five again, and my head felt unnaturally heavy. I was tired out and needed my nap. Betty kept dragging me down the long hallways. *Slow down, Mom*, I whined, but she just ignored me. There was no sound in the building but the clatter of her heels. And then I heard the telephone ringing.

"That's Alfred," Betty sang out. Her voice sounded cross. "He told me he'd call, but he hasn't. Can't you hurry up, Sonny? Can't you hear the damn phone?"

We raced to the end of the hall and turned left. The ringing of the phone became louder. We were racing toward a sunroom at the far end of a wide yellow hall. I could see the windows blazing with daylight. *Slow down, Mom!* I blubbered. Betty yanked my arm and pulled me along in her wake, my nostrils filled with Evening in Paris.

The sunroom, when we got there, was empty. On the circular table was a telephone, as well as some magazines, *Time* and *Look* and *Life*. On the cover of one of them was a picture of John F. Kennedy. On another was a picture of my father. The telephone rang louder and louder. I sat up in bed and cried out.

It was almost noon on a sunny late-February morning. I'd been asleep since eight-thirty, when I'd come home from the night shift stocking shelves at Wong Lee's. I was staring at a black-and-white picture of Pharaoh Sanders, which I'd cut out of *Downbeat* and framed. I reached for the telephone on the apple crate beside my bed and mumbled a sleep-slurred hello.

"Sonny," a woman's voice said in my ear.

I sat up and automatically tried to flatten my flyaway hair. "Karen?"

"Hey, you recognized my voice. That's great."

"Sure. Of course. Where are you?"

"Seattle, for the moment. I'm coming up tomorrow. Can you meet me?"

"Yeah, sure. I guess. After eight, though. I work until seven in the morning."

"You work until 7 a.m.? What are you, a vampire or something?"

"Pretty close. I'm on graveyard. At a grocery place."

"That's ridiculous, but pick me up anyway. I'll be getting off the bus around ten."

"All right," I told her, "I'll be there."

I spent that afternoon and evening cleaning up my little apartment—an activity as unfamiliar to me as cooking pork chops to a Muslim—and then hurried off to catch my bus to work. Next morning, I walked the seven blocks to the Coach Lines station and guzzled a few cups of high-test java in the coffee bar to keep myself awake until the bus from Seattle pulled in.

When the bus arrived, I wandered out into the staging area and watched the passengers clamber off the bus. Fifteen or twenty people disembarked, and I was beginning to feel a little anxious. But then, finally, there she was, stepping carefully down the metal steps, fleece-lined jacket done up to her neck. She was wearing brown, from her tam down to her rust suede boots. She looked around kind of hesitantly, the way people do when they've just got off a bus and are hoping that someone's there to meet them. I waved and she caught sight of me, hurrying over with the *Georgia Straight* in one hand and an umbrella that had once belonged to my grandfather in the other.

"Sonny, Jesus. What's all this noise?"

She tugged at my new beard, finally full and bushy after a summer of patchy inadequacy.

"Didn't know if you'd recognize me."

She gave me a peck on the cheek and then stood back and looked me up and down.

"Sure," she said. "Same old Sonny. Take more than a few whiskers on the chin to change you!"

The rain held off until we'd arrived at my apartment, so we didn't need Floyd's old umbrella. "Not quite the same as Ariel's place," I said as we climbed the steep flight of stairs to the second floor, our boots thumping bass notes out of the hollow-sounding staircase, Karen shielding her eyes from the bare hundred-watt bulb that cast jagged Fritz Lang shadows on the walls.

"That's cool with me," she said. "That townhouse seems so plastic. I only leave my stuff there in case my mother drops in."

"See a lot of your parents?"

"Not much," Karen said. "They know they don't like where I am in my life, but they can't decide if they want me closer to them or farther away. First they send me to Europe like some black sheep who has to be hidden from the neighbours, then they bitch at me for working in Michigan."

"Certainly sounds like parents, all right," I laughed. "Though Clyde and Mom have pretty much surrendered themselves to having a disaster in the family. I think they put it down to genetics. You remember my aunt Alice, of course."

"Oh yes, I remember your aunt Alice!"

I rummaged around in my pocket for my key. There was no bulb at all in the short upstairs hall, and after the blitzkrieg of light in the stairwell, I was having trouble finding the lock.

"Let me do that," Karen whispered. She took the key and deftly flicked the deadbolt back.

"Pretty cute," I said. "For someone who doesn't live here, you know your way around."

"Good night vision," she told me. "That's what you get from hanging out with panthers."

"Oh yeah?" I said. I flicked on the light on the range hood in the little kitchenette. "You living with the jungle cats these days?"

She smiled enigmatically, then slipped off her suede coat and sat down on one of the kitschy chrome-and-leatherette chairs at my chrome-bound Arborite table—the table from Betty's little house in New Westminster, resurrected from my grandparents' basement after a decade of gathering dust.

"God, Sonny, there's so much to tell you. The whole scene's been getting so heavy. I've learned so much since the last time I saw you. This war has changed everything, really shown us the way the world works."

"Yeah, you feel it here too," I said. "The war's dragging everything down."

I put the kettle on for tea and got a couple of cups from the cupboard.

"You heard any news about Bobby?"

Karen seemed confused for a moment. She rummaged in her purse until she found a pack of menthols and a lighter.

"Bobby from Danforth? The greaser?"

I nodded. "That's right, you remember him. Bobby from old Crashaw's science club."

"Didn't he get his ass drafted?"

"That's right. Last I heard, he was back east in boot camp. I guess he's hip-deep in jungle now, poor bugger. Every time I see a casualty on the news I get worried. I figure it's going to be him."

"I guess I didn't know him all that well." Karen took a drag on her Kool and then exhaled the smoke slowly, the ash-white plume curdling gradually into the rhombus of light from the range hood. "He should have resisted, man. No soldiers, no wars."

"That's about what I told him. We didn't quite see eye to eye."

I opened the cupboard directly above the range hood and pulled out the Colman's powdered mustard tin I used to stash my dope. Then I licked the gummed edge of a Zig-Zag Blue paper and carefully siamesed it to another of the same. That done, I shook some Acapulco Gold I'd scored outside the Phase Four on Fourth a couple of days before onto the papers and proceeded to roll a corpulent joint.

"Now that's abusing the drug!" Karen laughed. She handed me her lighter—a Zippo with a flint-wheel and a shiny chrome case—and watched while I fired up the number.

When we'd done the joint and gulped a hit of jasmine tea to wash away the smoke-taste, both Karen and I decided we were hungry.

"Come on," I said. "Let's go for a walk. There's a couple of hidden benefits to living in the slums. Interesting restaurants, for a start."

We ate at a Chinese place on Pender. Both the service and the decor seemed to have been borrowed from a Jimmy Cagney prison movie, but the food was spicy, aromatic and subtle. We shared a seafood hot-pot, taking turns to delve with chopsticks into the steaming, fragrant cauldron, laughing as we pulled out butterfly prawns, tentacles from translucent celapods, crenellated oyster mushrooms spongy and slick as brains. The conversation was pretty much a monologue; Karen talked about her travels and her work out in the east.

"London, what a waste of time. I was so confused about everything, like university didn't take me where I needed to go, and neither did marching for peace and all that do-gooder humanist claptrap. It's all such bullshit, really. In London, I kind of just let myself go, started tripping on Sandoz and Lebanese hash, hanging out with pilgrims and hippies. I almost went to Kathmandu. This guy I got to know was going out there. We were going to live in an ashram way up on the top of some mountain. Chant and do Zen stuff, stay off of the drugs."

"That sounds all right. I mean, as long as they had TV and all. I wouldn't want to miss a week of *Laugh-In*."

Karen ignored my attempt at humour and went on with her rap. "I backed out, though. I let him go without me. That Buddhist trip is nowhere, really. Pretending that the real world doesn't matter. The world is full of suffering, man, and no amount of prayer and Zen is going to change it. So I flew back to Seattle and called Jarrold."

"Jarrold?"

"Yeah, Jarrold from Seattle, Jody's brother. We were really tight for quite a while, then he went east to get involved with ERAP."

"With how much?"

She smiled. "The Education Research Action Project. It's working with urban kids, families. Trying to educate, help the people in poor communities understand what brought them there and recognize the cause of their oppression."

"That's what you've been doing in Michigan?"

"Yeah, sort of. Political stuff that grew out of it."

Karen went on to describe some of the things she'd seen when she was working in the industrial towns of Illinois and Michigan. It was interesting stuff, or should have been, but my mind was grinding over and over her mention of Jarrold Lister.

"Where you crashing?" I finally asked. When we talked on the telephone she had vaguely mentioned visiting a girl-friend in Vancouver, someone she knew from Michigan, a student at UBC.

"Wherever, man," Karen answered. She looked directly into my eyes. "I thought you might have some suggestions."

"All right," I said. I signalled the waiter, who'd been ignoring us for half an hour. "We can catch a cab back to my place. I guess you're pretty tired from the trip."

Karen smiled. "I'm cool with walking. You can show me the sights."

Vancouver was shining with that vague opalescence that is neither the presence of rain nor its absence. We wandered west on Pender Street toward the shopping district, our arms linked, Karen leaning towards me, her shoulder almost level with mine. I was feeling as if time itself had been folded double, so that the past shone through the blank sheet of the future. Everything familiar about being with Karen—the sweep of her honey-coloured hair as she walked with that long stride she'd inherited from her father, her way of looking straight ahead at some invisible vanishing point beyond the far horizon, her nervous fingers working at my coat sleeve as we walked—was made to seem distanced and foreign by the fact that she was someone from another phase of life.

Back at my place, I opened a bottle of wine—Bulgarian red, the starving student's friend—while Karen went into the bathroom. I had, of course, every young man's idiot vision of his date slinking out of the bathroom naked except for fresh lipstick, but when Karen emerged she was absent-mindedly tucking her T-shirt back into her jeans. I handed her a juice glass half-filled with lethal Iron Curtain plonk, then slipped my hands up the T-shirt and cupped both her breasts in my hands.

"Mind if I have a drink?" she said.

"Good luck," I said, "it's East European."

She took a sip and put the glass on the table. We kissed, once quickly, a tentative, exploratory stab at reconciliation, then pressed our bodies tight and crushed our mouths together in a lush, gasping, open-mouthed kiss.

"Sonny, I'm so sorry," Karen whispered.

I started to say something, to tell her that whatever had happened between us was past and forgotten, but she shook her head, took my hand in hers shyly, and led me to the bedroom, where we stood side by side on my old Persian rug and let our clothes drop on its threadbare mandala. I kissed her throat and nipples, licked the salty, freckled skin between her breasts, then let myself gradually sink to my knees, my tongue licking over her curved, hairless belly, the musk of her cunt in my nostrils.

Karen stayed the rest of the week. I took her around to some of my haunts—the university, the local pub, a couple more restaurants and jazz joints. I'd faked sick and booked off my job for a couple of shifts, but I couldn't afford to be on holiday for long. Thursday night, I was back at Wong Lee's, humping crates. I woke her up coming in, and we made love to the background music of buses grinding their gears along Commercial and garbagemen clanking and banging in the alley behind my apartment. Then I got out of bed and made us some jasmine tea and cornflakes for breakfast. Half an hour later, I was sleeping.

When I got up, Karen wasn't around. I went out to score a paper and some smokes. By the time I got back, she'd returned. She'd started packing things into her suitcase, which was yawning open on the unmade bed, her suede boots and peasant shirt beside it.

"I talked to Ariel while you were out," she told me. "Jarrold's been calling her, dropping around. Things are heating up, this being an election year and all." She reached up and touched my hair gently, the way a sympathetic mother might try to console a disappointed child. "It's time I got back to Seattle."

"Jarrold Lister? That frat boy from Harvard?"

"Princeton. He went to Princeton."

"Harvard, Princeton, wherever."

I waited for her to say something, but instead she started gathering up her things from the floor and the chairs.

"Jesus, Karen, do you really think some pampered Yankee prep-school kid—"

"I'm a Yankee, too, remember? You used to live there yourself."

"All right, I'm sorry. It's not that he's American. But, Christ, he's just such a walking cliché . . . I mean, after everything you've said about Lionel, here you are tagging along after some middle-class phoney who could probably pass as his twin."

Karen's face flashed white, and she flinched as if I'd physically hurt her.

"He's nothing like my father!" she shrieked.

"Not like your father? He *is* your father, for shit's sake. Can't you see that? Thirty years from now he'll be exactly like Lionel. And you'll become your mother, with the two-point-five children and the tennis and the gin."

"You don't understand. Not politics. Not Jarrold. And sure as hell not me."

She threw her makeup case and shirt into the suitcase and closed it, then sat down on the bed and slipped her boots on under her bell-bottoms.

"It's not about Jarrold, Sonny. I've told you that before. It's about the real work, the struggle." She paused and bit her lip, her face looking suddenly drained and tired. "Anyway, Jarrold's just a friend of mine. Someone who's important to the Movement. I hadn't even heard from him in . . . I don't know, weeks and weeks. Ever since we split up in Chicago. He told me that he'd call me, but he must have gotten busy or something."

She stood up and went into the kitchenette. "Look, I'm sorry I have to run off like this. There's this thing I have to get to, this meeting . . ." She gathered up her suede coat and handbag. "Can you tell me which bus I need to catch? I have to get to the Greyhound place by four-thirty. It's the only bus south until tomorrow."

"Stay here," I told her. I was pleading, being pathetic, and I knew that every word I said dug me deeper into a hole. "We can move to the islands, get away from all this shit that's going down. There's lots of people getting out, heads and artists and all that; you can homestead in the Kootenays or on one of the islands. Squat on government land for nothing. Raise your kids the way you want to. Forget the fucking war."

"I don't want to forget anything, Sonny. I want it all to change. I want to change it."

I walked to the bus stop beside her, insisted on lugging her suitcase, wound up sitting silent beside her all the way to the Coach Lines station, trying desperately to think of an argument that would change her mind and make her stay. Why are we so ready to believe that someone's failure to love us is the result of a flaw in their logic, an error that can be argued out of existence? *If only you'd see things clearly, you'd realize it's me that you love!*

Perhaps mercifully, her bus was already boarding when we got to the station.

"I have to go, Sonny," Karen repeated. She leaned forward to kiss me, and I turned away.

"I thought you'd be happy," she said. "This is real, you know. It matters. It changes things, right?"

"Yeah, sure," I said. "Of course I am. Happy, I mean. I'm happy."

There was silence for a moment.

"I really have to go. They've already called for the bus." She picked up her suitcase and started to walk toward the Coach Lines bus. "I'll see you, Sonny. Maybe in Seattle." Then she turned away and ran toward the door of the bus, her suitcase swaying against her leg, her honey hair swirling at her shoulders.

I'm standing in the kitchenette, drinking Tang from the pitcher. The radio's honking out bubble-gum shit, but I don't have the energy to change it. These night shifts are killing me slowly: some days it's too noisy to sleep much past ten or eleven o'clock. The phone rings, once, twice, three times. The damn thing keeps ringing. On the ninth or tenth ring, I pick it up.

"It's Curie. Curie Crashaw? From Danforth?"

"I'm kind of tied up now. Getting ready for work and all that. My shift starts early tonight."

Dead air.

A frisson travels up my spine, a little intimation of danger. I'd seen Curie five or six times since the party at the Jarvis place: the very next day, in fact, she'd turned up without a word of warning at Clyde and Betty's place. Clyde had yelled up the stairs that I had a visitor, and I wobbled down a few minutes later, my brain a throbbing ruin from the demolition-work of the previous night's drinking, and discovered Curie standing in the driveway beside her bike. My shock at running into her in broad daylight wasn't helped by the fact that she'd metamorphosed overnight from Interstellar Moon

Maid Spy Chick into an ordinary small-town adolescent. She looked distressingly like a stalwart of the science club, which by this time she must have been, in her sweatshirt and pedal-pushers, smiling tentatively at me, eyes dangerously luminous behind her cat's-eye glasses. I'd told her I wasn't feeling well—a scientifically verifiable fact at that moment—and asked her to come back in a day or two, which to my growing alarm, she did. Clyde was up at the Area, Betty shopping in town, and we'd wound up on the couch and then up in my bedroom, making love beneath the beneficent gaze of my household gods, Wilt Chamberlain and Nancy Sinatra. This scene had repeated itself a couple of times, then I'd headed north to Vancouver again and put the whole business out of my mind.

"Can't you talk?" she says now. "Just for a minute? I really have to talk to you." Then her voice changed, mutating from pleading to pompous. "There are things we really have to discuss."

"Well, sure, that's cool, Curie. Maybe I could call you back? Or drop around next time I'm down?"

Dead air, then a rapidly indrawn breath.

"I really have to see you. I'm late."

What's she late for? I find myself wondering. An image of little Curie, ten years old and pestering her father about the music for her modern dance rehearsal, swims absurdly to the surface of my mind.

"You're *late?* What are you talking about?"

"I'm *pregnant,* right? I'm going to have a baby."

"Hold on a second," I say. I turn down the radio, put the phone down and take a deep breath. There's another radio on in someone else's apartment, coincidentally tuned to the same channel mine was. The pop song continues, though faint and indistinct. Someone's banging trash cans in the alley.

"You're sure about this?"

Silence.

"I mean, have you been to a doctor and found out for sure? It's not like you're just late or something?"

Silence.

"All right, you're pregnant. And you figure it's mine? Are you *sure?*"

Silence, then the sound of her sobbing.

"What are you planning on doing?"

A couple of minutes' more silence, then Curie seems to collect herself. "I really have to see you," she repeats, her voice calm and businesslike. "Come down here this weekend. I really need to talk to you. Now."

I cover the mouthpiece with my hand and take two more deep breaths.

"I can't do that, Curie. I'm working."

"It's your baby too," she says. "I *really* need to see you."

"I'll call you when I'm down there. As soon as I get a few days off. Maybe Easter or whenever. It won't be very long."

I hear her hang up the phone, but gently. I can imagine her placing one finger on the chrome stud and pressing it down carefully. Then silence. The stellar hum. The music of the void.

13

In the Garden of Eden

My only child, Eden Richard Crashaw, was born July 16, 1968. I didn't hear about his arrival until a few days later, when I was down in Danforth visiting my parents. I celebrated by getting thrown out of the cocktail lounge in the Danforth Hotel and taking a taxi to the hospital, where I slipped on the grass beside the parking lot and tore a piece out of my jeans. The desk clerk at Admissions informed me that Mrs. Crashaw and her father had already left with the baby the day before, and then a nervous-looking kid from Security made small talk about baseball while he walked me to the door. I found my way to the Crashaws' saltbox an hour or so before dawn that morning and woke up Mrs. Turnbull, the housekeeper.

"There's no one home. Go away," she stage-whispered out the window.

I leaned against the wide trunk of a chestnut and peered up at the second-storey window. "Where the hell'd they go?"

"Far away from you, I'd imagine," the old woman said. She closed the window and drew the curtains.

I staggered up the walkway and onto the front porch, intending, I guess, to pound on the door until Old Man Crashaw decided to show himself or Mrs. Turnbull called the cops, but whatever force had driven me this far—anger, fear, belated pride or just plain pissed-drunk self-importance—seemed to drain from my body as soon as I climbed to the porch. Instead, I sat down on the porch swing and stared at the first blush of dawn. The swing seat was wet with dew, I could feel it through my jeans the moment I sat down, but I ignored it and let myself relax. My body felt like bags of sand, heavy, inert and shapeless. I looked through the boughs of the chestnut at the clear summer sky with its aura of pale violet sunrise. The planet Venus, a misty cyclopean eye, hung above the delicate stratum of newborn day. The darkness above the horizontal landscape seemed unusually three-dimensional: all the pale suns of the galaxy flamed at unimaginable distances both from me and from each other. If this were a Disney movie, I decided, one of those little fusion reactors would flare up into a four-pointed star, bright and cheery as a tinfoil Christmas angel, and wink at me reassuringly from heaven.

I tried to visualize my son, but the best I could come up with was a vague, generic baby; I imagined him lying awake in a crib, looking up at a window that framed a smiling moon and Peter Pan stars and planets. When I was nine or ten and living in Vancouver, my mother and Billie had dragged me along to see a musical, *Carousel*. In the film, a man who had died and gone to heaven was gazing down at his sleeping children. Every night he would hang the constellations in the sky, cardboard stars covered in Reynolds Wrap, and his kids would see them shining in the dark. I was maudlin enough to convince myself that my new child would be better off without me: I would die and be a loving ghost—an absent, mythological father.

Filled with grief at my posthumous condition, I finally staggered down the steps and made my way along the street, ignoring the early risers who stared at me apprehensively as they pulled out of their carports and zoomed away to work.

A week or so later, Betty mentioned that Mr. Crashaw had taken Curie to a private institution in Oregon; Curie was recovering from some sort of breakdown, and her father had taken compassionate leave from his teaching position to help her look after the baby. I did my best to keep my expression neutral while she was talking, though I suspected I was incapable of keeping anything from Betty.

"Postpartum depression," Betty pronounced. "Commonest thing in the world. God sakes, after you were born I felt like one of those stupid fish that's climbed up a river and dumped all its eggs in the gravel. I wanted to give up and float back to the ocean. Lasted for a couple of weeks."

I was helping her shell garden peas in the kitchen.

"I know how it feels to have a kid when you're alone, as well. It's not a pleasant prospect, I can tell you. I went through that when Alfie was in Europe, and I went through it all over again when I found out he wasn't coming home. And at least I'd *wanted* to have a kid. Don't expect poor little Curie could say the same."

She ran her thumbnail along the spine of a pod and deftly split the skin. The peas rolled out, plump and fleshy, and went *plock, plock, plock* into the bowl.

"And living in a town like Danforth wouldn't help. People here think any girl who can't keep her knees together deserves to suffer. I'm surprised your old teacher didn't pack her off to an unwed mothers' home as soon as she started showing. Too attached to his little princess, I guess."

"How's the baby?" I ventured. "You heard anything?"

"Surprised you're interested. Didn't think you had much use for babies." She looked me straight in the eyes, her glittery retinas scanning me coldly.

"Just curious, I guess." I stood up and went to the fridge.

"Ironic, isn't it? Your father wanted kids so bad. A son! Well, poor Alfie would have swum across the Atlantic when you were born if the Army wouldn't have shot him for desertion! And he never got the chance to see you once in his whole life, goddamn it. Not once did he see your face."

I pulled out a carton of apple juice, got a glass from the cupboard and poured myself a half-glass of juice.

"It's not my kid, Betty. I don't know whose kid it is. Ask Curie. Ask her damned old man. Could be his, for all I know."

Betty stood up and looked down at me, her hands on the back of the chair.

"You look at him and tell him that. Tell that girl, if you haven't already."

She headed out of the kitchen, slippers shuffling quietly down the hall.

I spent Christmas Eve of 1968 stoned on shitty mescaline, stumbling from one party to another in the East Vancouver rooming house where I'd been living for a couple of months.

The girl I'd been living with, a religious studies student whose father was an ophthalmologist, had tired of my dark moods and unfashionable boozing and moved back into her parents' house on Spanish Banks. Other girls had come and gone.

I'd long since given up my job at Wong Lee's Superior Foodstuffs, and I was supporting myself by dealing mescaline—which seemed to be the college kids' psychedelic of choice—and selling the *Georgia Straight* on street corners downtown. Two days a week, I'd take the number 10 bus out to the UBC campus and set up shop in the student lounge. The mesc went for eight bucks a cap: the mentally deficient biker who fronted it to me got five and half, and the other two-fifty was profit.

The house was full of flotsam that winter. The bikers had parked their Harleys in the front yard, wheels mired to the axles in the crabgrass, and there was a primer-coloured school bus with a homemade glass observation dome taking up most of the sidewalk and effectively blocking the front gate. I could hear the stereo from the front main-floor apartment booming the brainless drum solo from "In-A-Gadda-Da-Vida," a song the cokeheads and meth freaks couldn't get enough of that winter. Voices bubbled up the stairwell, transmuted into pan flutes that warbled unsteadily over the *whump-thump* of Iron Butterfly's bass and drums. The streetlights bled an iridescent oil slick on the threadbare sheet that covered my window.

Around midnight, I got off my mattress and headed outside for some air. The narrow stairs resembled a refugee camp. There was somebody sitting on every second step, little scarecrow hippie girls who looked barely old enough for high school, a couple of smackers with Keith Richard cheekbones and formaldehyde complexions, everything tinted undersea green by the bare painted light bulb above us. The reek of hash and patchouli oil competed with the mildew from the carpets. I had almost succeeded in picking my way to the landing when I heard someone calling *Wheeler, hey, Wheeler* over the din of Iron Butterfly and the shrieking of the runaways as they passed around a bong of hash.

"Hey, Reb, how you been?" I said. The biker who'd been fronting me mescaline, a bearded, greying, snaggle-toothed Albertan with a Molson muscle hanging over his buckle, was leaning out of a first-floor doorway, squinting up at me through the strata of hash smoke.

"Better than you, fuck-ass. Where's the fifty you owe me? Pony up."

"Stuff's moving slow this week, Reb. What's the rush, for Christ's sake? You know you'll get your end."

Reb scowled at me suspiciously. "I better, man. You try rip me off, I might just have to smarten you up."

"Nobody's ripping you off, man. Take it easy. The rest of that mesc'll move in the next few days."

"Whatever you say, man." Reb smirked. "Hey, come on down here, dude. I don't like trying to jabber up a motherfucking hole."

I picked my way through the mob on the stairs and followed Reb into the bikers' apartment. There seemed to be some sort of disorganized party in progress, which was pretty much the usual situation. The living room contained a wooden kitchen table that was completely covered in empties and overflowing mounds of cigarette ash. Bikers sat around in grimy armchairs, their chicks perched on their knees or curled at their feet on the lino. There were two stereos on, both playing the same Iron Butterfly song out of phase with each other, so that the air was filled with dissonant thunderings and the small rooms seemed to echo like a canyon. Most of the bikers seemed oblivious to my arrival—people wandered in and out of the apartment all the time—but one or two scowled and gave me hard looks, as if they were offended by the idea of someone dropping in unannounced.

"That fucking little twat upstairs, Janey or whatever her name is," Reb shouted, his voice barely audible above the music, "she says you laid a cap on her for nothing."

"That's right," I said. "I gave her a hit. She's good for the eight bucks, isn't she? Her old man's some kind of doctor on the Island." The girl, Janice, was a runaway from Nanaimo who'd been crashing with the heads across the hall from my room. She was one of those innocents adrift in the later sixties, too charmed by the mythology of peace and communal living to notice that the hippies she was hanging with carried hunting knives and handguns and had no interest in anyone except as a source of drugs. I had fallen into conversation with her one night on the porch steps outside, and I eventually invited her upstairs for a drink of wine. The next time I saw her, she asked me to front her a cap of my mescaline so that she could get loaded for some concert in town, and I felt guilty enough about preying on a confused little sixteen-year-old to give her what she wanted on credit.

"You take my fucking shit and lay it on runaway bitches, man? You figure I'm ignorant or what?"

"She'll pay, man. Don't worry."

"It ain't the bitch I'm worried about, asshole. I don't let people fuck with me, that's all."

"Be cool, man. It's all taken care of," I said. "Listen, I've got some serious smoke upstairs. I'll go get it. We can do a few bongs and kick back."

Rebel nodded, still looking suspicious. I loped up the stairs, dodging bodies, and was back down to the bikers' apartment in a couple of minutes, a dime bag of dust in one hand and a glass-tube bong in the other.

We'd done a few rounds of the bong when Rebel stood up and headed for the door. "Come on, dude. We got business." He nodded to another biker, a rangy, long-faced man I knew as Blondie, who promptly shrugged off the languid girl who'd been nuzzling his shoulder and followed us into the hallway. A crowd of kids had just blown in the front door, little weekend hippies from the suburbs, most of them more drunk than stoned. They eyed the bikers nervously over their Roger McGuinn granny glasses, doing their best to look cool.

"Got some new shit I want you to move for me, man," Reb said.

"Mesc?" I asked. I was starting to get antsy. Blondie was standing too close, leering down at me from his height, and the kids were jostling past toward an open doorway down the hall.

"Better, man. STP. It's like a super acid. Keep you ripped to the tits for a week."

I had heard about STP, but I wasn't all that anxious to try it. The shit could leave you perma-stoned, turn you into one of those shell-shocked husks with the vacant eyes wandering around in Stanley Park, sleeping under the ornamental shrubs and talking to the angels. Acid got you loaded enough.

"I don't know, man. That shit's a little heavy for the college frat-boy crowd."

"It's stashed in the basement. Let's go," Rebel said. He stumped toward the doorway to the cellar—a plank hatch in the wall below the stairs. The tall guy, Blondie, shoved me from behind and I stumbled after Rebel.

"Take it easy, man. What's the hurry? We'll get there *mañana,* all right?"

The three of us clumped down the narrow flight of stairs to the cellar. Apart from the rusty boiler and its Medusa's-head of ducting, there wasn't a lot to see—one long rectangular room with a couple of lightless antechambers jutting off to one side. The frame of someone's ten-speed. A couple of truck tires. A galvanized metal tub. At one end of the room was a wooden door exactly like the hatch at the top of the stairs. Reb opened it and reached inside, fishing around for something in the joists above the door. When he'd found what he was looking for, he held it up into the lamplight for Blondie and me to inspect.

"Orange barrels," he said. He opened the top of a baggy filled with twenty or thirty squat orange pills and offered it to me. "Better just cop the one, man. That's plenty."

"Later, man," I told him. "I'm kind of whacked out just at the moment." I couldn't very well tell Rebel I'd been sampling his mesc, not when I already owed him.

"Do it, man. Just do it. It'll really set you up." This was Blondie, bending down from his six-foot-five to whisper encouragement in my ear.

"Cop it and we're square, man," Rebel told me. "I'm going to front you some to deal, right? So you'd better know what's what with this shit."

I reached into the transparent bag and pick out a barrel.

"Come on, dude," Reb prompted me. I placed it on my tongue.

"That's cool," Reb said. Blondie laughed, then grabbed me from behind and shoved me hard enough to make me fall. Then both of the bikers were over me, kicking and whacking away with their fists. I turtled and tried to struggle back to my feet, but the two of them shoved me through the doorway of the storage room. The door slammed and everything was suddenly dark. By the time I got up and tried the door, it had been locked from the outside.

There I am, sealed into the null space of darkness: the inside of the door is solid enough to take my blows with nothing more than a dull, muted thumping that barely seems to carry even within the claustrophobic space of the closet. No one can possibly hear me—not, at least, unless he or she is stand-

ing on the other side of the door. Certainly no one will hear
me from upstairs. And there is no one in the basement but
Rebel and Blondie. My only hope is that they'll have a change
of heart, come back and let me out again—which is, of
course, no hope at all. Bikers genuinely *like* to fuck people
up; mercy simply isn't in their repertoire. It isn't long before
I hear the *thump* of heavy footsteps ascending the stairs.

I pound a while longer, hear myself whining *Reb, for fuck's
sake let me out*, half my brain disgusted at my grovelling voice
while the other half childishly clings to the hope that the
morons will tire of their game. Eventually, I let myself slide to
the floor, curl up on the cold, greasy concrete. The space in
which I'm caged is soft, an amorphous black-fleshed lozenge
bleeding off into indeterminacy on every side of my body
except the cold fact of the floor. Which is not cement, I realize, but the backs of hard-shelled beetles. There are hundreds
of them, thousands now, replicating themselves so rapidly
that they cover and obscure each other, layers of them swarming on each other's backs, the whole swarm a throbbing mandala. I jump to my feet and cower against the rough wood of
the door.

Then everything, darkness, enclosure, begins to transform. I am holding the edge of a simple piece of shelving,
one of three or four rows of shelves that line the walls of the
storage room—the room must have been a root cellar back
when this building was the home of a family who canned their
own vegetables and fruit, long before it was chopped up for
apartments. I know this, can feel the grain of the rough-cut
planks against my fingers, but I also know that I am holding

my burned body upright against the side of a tier of bunks on which other victims of the Holocaust are lying. This is the basement of Katsuyama Primary School, in the Nishiyama Valley, concavity of annihilation and nuclear fire. The dead are shadows, shapes of dust, but they moan with all the voices of the elements, wood and stone, dry joists and old foundations creaking. I can see right through the rough wood shelves, through the bunks on which the wounded lie. I can see through my own hand when I hold it up before my eyes, see the frail bones of fingers and forearm and wrist, see the red tree of nerves and veins branching inside me. I am Superman, exile from Krypton, gazing with my X-ray eyes through the flimsy skin of matter. I raise my transparent hand, watch fascinated as the muscles and sinews, streaks of fiery red within the gelatinous cylinder of my forearm, tense and twitch and palpitate. As I watch, my hand blooms into flame, ignited by the thermal pulse of the atomic blast. And then I am music, pure process. I am Kali, god of fire.

For hours, for the rest of that night, I am burning. I flicker between two equivocal dimensions, world of shimmering Kali fire and world of cold planks and concrete floors, echoing wind of my terrified sobbing. At times the insects climb my legs, become my legs, my armoured skin. At times I am insect mandala. At last, as the first rush burns off and I begin to spiral downward, I drift into a fitful doze, waking into neon pulsing darkness, careening down the insect pit, then sleeping, waking, sleeping . . .

And then, I am jolted terrified awake by a vast geological scraping, tectonic plates abrading stone on stone, the belly-scales of submarine dragons. And I turn and find the door is open. I stand up, lever myself painfully to my feet and turn, blinking sparks of diamond light, to face the humming flatland of the cellar. And there, standing in diagonal morning sun from the narrow horizontal pane above the concrete foundation, is a woman with a raw, bleeding wound for a face. She is peeling a red mask of flesh from her cheekbones, hollow sockets of her melted eyes, mandible jutting her charred black dentalia. She stands before me waving in one blackened monkey marionette hand that desiccated mask. . . .

And I see, in a flash of weird clarity, Janice from across the hall, smiling blond innocence, blue eyes looking inward and shifted slightly out of focus with whatever high she's been riding all night, a veil of red lace fluttering from her fingers.

Part Three

14

Termination Winds

I started work at the Danforth Nuclear Reservation in the spring of 1969. My job was at the Zee Plant, a plutonium processing facility. What I did there was simple. I would ride to the gates of the Area every morning at seven in the Studie Hawk with Clyde, or (if I was on one of the later shifts) get on one of the Company's blue buses and stare out the window at the moonscape of Washington desert until I arrived at my place of work. I was doing work that could easily have been handled by a robot, and that probably should have been performed by something other than a sentient being. I would suit up in my overalls, put on my breather mask, stick my hands into the rubber-lined holes of a glove box and watch through a safety-glass window as my disembodied fingers struggled through the heavy rubber protective gloves to remove the slugs of plutonium or U-235 from the triple-wrapped, brass-bound cans in which they arrived from the special nuclear materials vault and place them in transparent plastic bags. When I'd inspected, sealed and labelled each can, I'd take it out of the glove box and place it on a separation rack for shipment to Los Alamos and from there to the Test Site in Nevada.

I'd bought myself a three-dollar haircut in Seattle, but some unacknowledged vanity or terror of being spontaneously transformed back into a clueless teenager convinced me to leave the moustache and most of the sideburns. I told myself I looked exactly like John Lennon on the *Sgt. Pepper* album cover, though I secretly suspected that I really looked more like an accounting clerk who smoked dried banana peels on weekends, took frug lessons at the YMCA, and drove a GTO. In fact, I probably looked like exactly what I was—a stone freak who needed a paycheque.

My stepfather got me the job, of course. I applied on a Wednesday and was at work the next week. My first morning at my new job, I sat down to breakfast with Betty and Clyde at seven-thirty, feeling seriously out of sync with reality. I was a savage who'd been dragged in out of the bush, dressed up in workman's clothes, and painstakingly trained to perform simple, repetitive tasks in order to demonstrate some noble, dreary hypothesis—the brotherhood of God's creatures, perhaps, or the dignity of labour. A wild child, suckled by timber wolves or Washington desert coyotes. Or an alien who'd landed on Earth and survived by taking on the physical form and activities of the Earthlings: Jerry Lewis in *Visit to a Small Planet*, mugging as he climbed out of his spacecraft and confronted the pastel landscape of Kodachrome, USA. What I was experiencing was common enough among the young men and women of my generation; we were changelings, every one of us, stolen from our beds and transformed irreversibly by the genie LSD.

My parents, like parents everywhere, had invented a convenient fiction to explain their wayward son's reappearance, years after high school graduation: I was saving up money before going back to school to complete my degree. The Area paid its workers well, and living with the folks would allow me to build up enough cash for a few years' tuition. Before long, I'd sign up at UW and get my life back on the rails. They couldn't possibly have believed this little exercise in suburban PR, but I suppose it gave them something to say to the neighbours when they were asked why the prodigal son had come home.

For myself, going back to Danforth was a painful last resort. I had run out of options in Vancouver, and the night I'd spent locked in the basement had apparently bent some sprockets in my head. It was a subtle thing, I guess you'd say—I wasn't *quite* one of that legion of befuddled ghosts created by the wonders of love, peace and psychedelia, but I wasn't fully functional either. Mainly, I just felt tired. I knew the grey exhaustion of the ill and the very old, although at twenty-three I was hardly ready for the rest home. Also, there was something slightly haywire in my perceptions— I'd be looking at someone, just conversing, and his face would seem to shift, the shadows would rearrange themselves and I'd feel as if I were seeing him from a totally different angle than I had a moment before. Objects would do this dance as well; I soon learned to restrain myself from getting up and adjusting paintings or ornaments around Clyde and Betty's living room, even when they seemed to be shimmering, caught in an invisible gust of wind that was jostling their molecules around. Instinctively, perhaps, I had crawled back to the safest place I knew to nurse my fucked-up senses, like a wounded animal returning to its lair. The job was just part of the package.

The day of my interview, my stepfather drove me home; we both knew I'd scored a job, but neither of us could admit it yet. Personnel would call in a couple of days, telling me to drop in and fill out my withholding-tax forms and so forth, but for now we chatted about the Danforth High football team, which seemed to be struggling along reasonably well without me, Clyde's plans for the vegetable garden, the new hotel that was being built out toward the Pasco bridge.

"We'll stop by that café on Lincoln," Clyde finally said. "They do a reasonable fish-and-chips there. Not too greasy. Your mother's not feeling too hot this past couple of days. I expect she could use a night off cooking dinner."

"Mom's been under the weather a lot lately, hasn't she? You should talk to her, Dad, make her go see the quacks."

Clyde nodded, but didn't say anything. We drove up the main street in silence until Clyde had located the fish-and-chips joint. When we'd pulled into the lot behind the restaurant, I opened my door and started to get out.

Clyde put his hand on my arm. "Stay here for a minute, Sonny. There's something we need to talk about. Your mom."

I closed the car door and settled back. Something in my stepfather's voice made me want to avoid his eyes. I stared out the window at the blue-metal Dumpster and the grimy stucco rear wall of the restaurant.

"Your mother has lymphoma," Clyde started. "There's no easy way to tell you this, but she's been seriously ill for quite a while."

"How serious do you mean?"

"The cancer's been in remission for a couple of years now. We were hopeful—the oncologist in Seattle seemed quite optimistic—that the remission might last for a very long time. This kind of lymphoma is technically incurable, you understand, but lengthy remissions aren't uncommon. After ten years, after twenty, you can think of the remission as the next thing to a cure."

"Yeah? So what do you mean? Is she still in remission or what?" I felt, inexplicably, anger more than terror or grief. "Why didn't you tell me, Clyde? Jesus. I don't understand you. She's my mother, right? I should have been told."

Clyde sighed. I glanced to my left and saw him slumped in the driver's seat, his hands cupped on the spokes of the steering wheel. He looked, for the first time since I had known him, like an old man, drained of vitality; the backs of his hands were mottled with liver spots, and his wrists seemed too thin for his cuffs.

"What are we going to do, Dad?"

He sighed again. "I don't know, Son," he said. "I really can't imagine. I try to think of something, but I can't."

An elderly couple came out of the restaurant, the old man adjusting the bill of his hunting cap, his wife clutching a brown paper bag that was already spotted with grease stains.

"It's the plant, you know," I finally said. "It's Danforth. It's poisoned the river. It's leaking radiation." The old folks scuttled off toward their pickup. I turned to Clyde and slammed the palms of my hands against the dashboard. "Why the hell did you have to bring her to this goddamn cancer sink?"

Clyde shook his head in denial, but his whole frame seemed to crumple with the impact of my words. He hunched above the dashboard, gripping the steering wheel as if he were clutching the hull of an overturned boat.

We sat there for several minutes in silence. More people came out of the fish-and-chips place, got into their cars and drove away. I saw a young woman glance nervously at us, two men in a car going nowhere, then she gathered her fawn lambskin coat to her body and hustled in the back door of the restaurant. Everything about her—her fur-trimmed coat, fashionable boots, little bright-coloured miniskirt twitching as she hurried up the steps, the swept-back hairdo, seemed absurd to me, almost offensive. The moment that had held us both had already flashed and vanished; now the planet was revolving into night.

After the first round of chemo, my mother began to lose her hair. She put on some weight, or retained too much water, and her face took on a bloated look, slack and pouchy along the jaw. When she was feeling well enough to get up and potter around the house, she rummaged through her dresser drawers for silk scarves that could be converted into makeshift turbans. She'd soon unearthed a sizable collection of them in a wide range of bird-of-paradise colours.

"Presents from your Auntie Alice, mostly," she told me. "The gift shops on cruise ships must sell them."

"Maybe the croupiers in Vegas have been passing them out with the chips."

Betty laughed. "That's certainly a possibility. At least the more recent ones don't have polar bears and gold pans for a pattern. The roulette wheels and dice are more attractive."

Betty was in touch with Alice every couple of weeks. Alice's husband, Eugene Fangis, had died of cancer only the previous winter, so Alice was one of the few people Betty could speak to frankly about the disease—most folks, myself included, were too overwhelmed with sorrow and confusion to offer much beyond inarticulate expressions of sympathy.

Betty and Clyde had aged a lot in the years I'd spent up in Vancouver. The compass of their lives had narrowed. Every second week, they drove up to Seattle so that Betty could have her treatments and consult with her oncologist. Sometimes they'd be away a couple of nights, and other times they'd drive home that same evening. Clyde seemed to have distanced himself from his job at the Area. He still went to work every weekday morning, but seldom stayed late at his office and never went in on the weekends. He had also apparently lost interest in fishing; he'd banter about the trout lakes with old friends he ran into in Danforth, but he didn't accept any of their invitations for fishing trips and he never drove up to the lakes himself. Instead, he'd sit and watch TV or wander around in the garden. Betty slept a lot, especially in the afternoons, and spent a lot of time on the phone.

Superficially at least, my life wasn't all that different from my parents'. Nights, I sat on the couch beside Betty and stared without interest at *The Glen Campbell Goodtime Hour* or *Here's Lucy* or *Green Acres*. Days, I trooped around after my supervisors, and stared—again, without interest—at glove boxes, CAM alarms, walls of dials and switches. I sat through orientation and safety committee sessions, the archetypal unmotivated, clock-watching industrial worker. In spite of myself, I gradually began to pick up the argot of the natives. Canary suits and mine-safety appliance masks when working in hot zones. Inactive hoods containing greater than 100 grams fissile material require a 91-centimetre minimum spacing between the hoods and any fissile material near them. CAM stands for constant air monitoring system; too many rems and the buzzer goes off. Triple-wrapped brass containers from the special nuclear materials vault are transported on a little red wagon with separators to keep the materials from going critical. Blow up your gloves before putting them on to make sure there aren't any pinhole leaks. Get yourself crapped up, the radiation monitors make you strip and take a shower; then they give you a contact slip, send you home for a couple of days without pay.

Like a lot of people with tedious and potentially dangerous jobs, I came to rely on the company of my workmates to get me through each shift. Their antidote to the fear of radiation poisoning was irony—they were maestros of the apocalyptic witticism, the glow-in-the-dark innuendo.

"Hey, Sonny," Rena Walters called out one lunch break as I was pouring myself a second cup of gritty instant in the lunchroom. "You heard there's an opening in the Hot Zone? Perfect fit for an ambitious young stud like yourself. You could be the new Atomic Man. A genuine working-class hero." Rena was a couple of years older than I, already divorced, and addicted to Anne McCaffrey novels, which she read on almost every break and (reputedly) in the women's john during her shift.

"Atomic Man?" I asked. "Who's that, the local superhero? How come I've never heard of him? Am I one of the bad guys or something?" I pulled up at chair at the Formica table where Rena and another of the younger workers on my shift, Ron Belten, were finishing off their sandwiches and coffees.

"Probably, Wheeler," Belten told me. Belten was a working-class kid from Aberdeen; he and I had quickly developed a hippie-and-greaser comedy routine consisting of mutual needling. He was one of the two Area workers I felt close to; the other was a tall, heavy-set guy in his early thirties who went by the nickname of "Warthog." "But what kind of dip-shit superhero would waste his time on you? You stoners tend to atomize yourselves."

"Fuck off, Ron," Rena said. She fished a pack of menthol Kools out of her handbag and reached for Belten's lighter.

When she'd fired up the smoke, she continued. "Atomic Man's going back a ways. You were probably still out in the real world back then."

"Probably. The only Atomic Man I know about is the one from the old Superman shorts they used to play in the movie theatres when I was eight or nine years old."

"There was this old guy who worked here up until a few years ago," Rena told me. "Guy in his sixties, maybe six months from retirement."

She picked up her smoke from the black plastic ashtray, took a quick, nervous drag, and deposited it in the ashtray again.

"Anyway," she continued, "this old fucker'd been working here a dog's age, they probably built Zee Plant around him. One of those 'slow and steady does it' types, watches the clock and stays out of trouble. One night he's up here in 242Z on nuclear-process work, keeping an eye on the columns."

"What the old guy doesn't know," Belten interjected, "is that some lawn dwarf had left some radioactive shit . . ."

"Americium and processing resin in solution," Rena said. "You have to work your way around Professor Belten's technical jargon. These intellectuals are always hard to follow."

"Yeah, radioactive shit, just like I said. There'd been a shutdown for four or five months in that part of the show— operators went out on strike."

"That's right. And the stupid buggers left this americium solution in a separation column. Regs say pretty clearly that you can't leave americium in solution for more than ninety days, otherwise it starts to react with the nitric acid in the solution and all holy hell can break loose."

"Which is exactly what happened to Atomic Man. This americium shit in the column started smoking, great fucking big clouds of red smoke came farting out and covered the whole goddamn room. Then of course the whole shebang blew up. Covered the poor fucker with glass fragments and nice buzzy, glow-in-the-dark diarrhea. He only got out by crawling on his knees."

"Must have been a riot, eh? Monitors howling, alarms going off. Happens a lot in my nightmares."

"What happened to Atomic Man?" I asked. "Did he croak?"

"Should have, in theory," Rena said. "He'd ingested more radioactive material than anyone else has—ever. They flushed him out in hospital, got the americium out of his system. It was a couple of months before anyone could touch him. His family couldn't stand in the same room with the guy without putting on lead-shielded aprons, like they were working in an X-ray lab or something. But the stubborn old fucker survived."

"And because he was already getting on in years, the down-the-road cancer risk didn't much matter, right?"

"Company was lucky on that one, all right. Anyways, he got to be known as Atomic Man. Hell of a way to find fame."

"No shit," I said. I scrunched my candy-bar wrapper into a ball and tried a hook shot. It missed the trash can by two or three feet.

"Whiff!" Rena said. "Good eye there, Kareem. You're a pistol."

In early July, my fifth month back in Danforth, I ran into Karen's friend Linda. She was getting out of a Pontiac in front of the bank. I watched as she said something to the straight-looking dude who was driving, then called her name as she hurried to the crosswalk on the corner.

"Oh, Sonny!" she cried. "Didn't recognize you for a minute there! Must be that cookie duster! It makes you look so *serious*, a professor or something like that!"

We filled each other in on our current events—she was married to the Pontiac guy, who sold real estate up in Olympia, and had just come down to Danforth for the weekend to see her folks.

"Do you hear anything from Karen?" she asked me.

"Not for quite a while," I said. "I think she's out east someplace. Ann Arbor or somewhere like that."

"No, no, she's back in Seattle. Lana Crosson—remember her?—told me Karen's living in some communal house with a bunch of student-radical types. I guess her folks could give you the address."

I had told myself I wasn't going to ask about Karen. I was suffering through withdrawal, but determined to break my addiction. *That* addiction, anyway. The rest I intended to cultivate—I was working on the assumption that they cancelled each other out.

"You see her much, Linda?"

"Never. We kind of don't see eye to eye any more. I guess we sort of went our separate ways."

I looked at Linda's polyester office-girl outfit, her back-combed bouffant, the figure that was already expanding into complacent middle age: it wasn't hard to imagine her and Karen losing touch.

Linda rattled on about her husband and their honeymoon and the rancher they'd just purchased, but my mind was full of images of Karen. The next day, I phoned her parents' home and asked Anthony for his sister's address. He said he had absolutely no idea where she was living, his bored voice implying that he didn't much care. I tried Ariel's borrowed townhouse next, though I thought she'd most likely have moved on or married or finally freaked out and starved herself to death. The phone rang six or seven times, then Ariel picked up.

"What?" she said. "Who is this?"

"Sonny Wheeler. You might remember me. I'm a friend of Karen Sullivan's. She came up to see me in Vancouver a year or two ago." I explained that I was looking for Karen.

"Just wait," she said. "I have to look."

I held for several minutes, the whistle of dead air punctuated by the sound of someone dropping solid objects. I wondered if Ariel was dismantling a bookcase or looking under furniture for something she had misplaced.

"Four-oh-two-seven Winterhaven Street, don't ask me where that is. Someplace near the Ave., I suppose. That's where all the hippie imbeciles live."

"Is there a phone number, Ariel?"

"Of course not. Everyone who wants her calls me."

I wasn't sure if she was pissed off or proud about being Karen's receptionist. She hung up without saying goodbye.

15

The Transmutation
of Elements

The Winterhaven house was a two-storey box on a shady street. There was a conspicuous head house a half-block away, the gables painted purple and the trim a lurid orange, but Karen's place just looked rundown. The only clue that the inhabitants weren't just ordinary Northwest working folks was the Volkswagen van with American flag curtains and an "I FLASH DAILY" bumper sticker that was parked outside. That, and the faint strains of "Pleasures of the Harbor" wafting through the half-open windows. I made my way up the rickety stairs and across the sagging porch.

After I'd knocked a couple of times, I noticed someone watching me from the window. The sheet that served as a curtain was pulled back a couple of inches and I could see someone's fingers and the vague shape of a body in the room at the front of the house. Whoever was sizing me up couldn't have found it easy going, as the window faced the same way as the door. I stepped back to show myself and waved at the shadowy figure, who promptly let go of the sheet and disappeared. A couple of minutes later, the door creaked open an inch or two, and a woman's voice said, "What do you want?"

"I'm looking for Karen," I said. "She around?"

There was a pause, the sound of shuffling feet, a staccato burst of coughing, then the woman's voice returned.

"She isn't around. You can't come here."

The door closed, so I knocked again. Eventually, whoever was jerking me around condescended to open the door a crack and tell me to go away.

"Where's Karen?" I said. "You'd better tell me. I'll stand here and shout my fucking head off. You really sure you want that kind of static? Just tell her who it is and then I'll go."

More shuffling. More coughing. A conference of whispers from somewhere inside.

"All right. What's your name?"

I told her who I was. "I'm going down to Southern Star Chili. She can join me if she wants to," I said. I made my way back down to Clyde's Studie, which I'd borrowed for the day, and headed out into the Ave. I was into my second bowl of Texas chili when Karen came in the door.

"Sonny," she said. She was wearing an army-surplus jacket, despite the fact that it was 75 degrees outside and reasonably sunny, a tank-top, paint-splattered jeans, and sneakers. Her voice sounded tired and resigned, as if seeing me were an obligation, like being forced to watch some sitcom she had liked once and no longer cared for.

"I heard you were back," I told her. "Thought I'd drop in and see how you were."

She poured herself a coffee from the carafe on the counter and sat down across the table from me. "I've been really busy, working. Getting ready for Chicago. There's a fuck of a lot to do."

"Too much to come to the door, eh?"

Karen's face seemed to stiffen. "We have to maintain security. Winterhaven's a safe house. Who gave you the address? Ariel, right?"

I nodded.

"That's so like her. She loves to cause trouble. I've told her no one's allowed in the house except leadership and cadre. She'd probably give my address to the pigs, the stupid bitch."

"I thought you were back in Chicago." I told her about running into Linda.

"Yeah, right. Last month. I went out for the SDS convention. I was only back in Illinois for a couple of weeks, then we drove back in a Volkswagen bus, took our time and made some contacts. We had to get the word out to the people."

"Sounds like a trip," I said.

Those blue eyes, wearier now but still as clear as heaven, lit up at the memory of where she'd been.

"Man, you should have been there! Magic Annie and Gloria Lee were up on their folding chairs, screaming like the fucking Eumenides. *Ho, Ho, Ho Chi Minh! Vietnam is gonna win! Ho, Ho, Ho Chi Minh! Vietnam is gonna win!* Those Progressive Labour pigs had their backs to the fucking wall!"

"I have to be honest, these protests don't seem to be cutting much ice. People get their heads busted open, and the next day not a whole lot has changed."

"Everything's changed, man. The whole fucking axis has shifted. It's not about protesting the war any more, don't you see that? We're *all* in the war now. We're bringing it home."

"That's easy to say, Karen. But the only way this war gets back to America is in a pine box with the body of some kid. That and the *ABC News at Eleven,* which is pretty bloody easy to turn off."

"That's what's different about Chicago. We're not going there to protest, man. We're going there to fight."

"You figure you can fight the American government? That's a pretty tall order. Takes a lot of rocks and Molotovs to make a serious dent in a tank."

"That's our strength. No one believes us. Like no one believed that the Viet Minh could chase the French out of Southeast Asia. We're not about fighting tanks and bombs, anyway. What we're fighting is people's ideas. If we change enough minds, all the brain-fucked five-star piggies in the Pentagon won't beat us. We'll be the People's Army. Many raindrops wear through stone."

As if she wished to end the discussion on that epigrammatic note, Karen stood up and swilled down the dregs of her coffee. I polished off the last of my chili, picked up the tab for both of us, and followed her out onto the street.

"Come on," she said. "Walk with me. Let's check out the Ave. for a while." Her voice had softened, her eyes sought my face. Some internal wind had changed direction, and she was once again the girl I'd known in Danforth.

A couple of blocks along the Ave., Karen stopped for a minute to rap with a lanky kid in ripped jeans and an army surplus jacket that was the twin of her own. He looked rest-

less as a meth freak, scuffling unlaced workboots on the concrete and bobbing his head arrhythmically as we approached.
Karen and he did the usual "Hey, man, what's happening?"
shit for a few minutes, both of them scanning the street with
sidelong glances as they talked, as if they expected a SWAT
team of armour-clad science-fiction brain police to materialize like ectoplasm out of someone's laurel hedge.

"Later," Karen said finally, dismissing the boy with a word,
and we went on our way along the Ave.

"That's Buster," she told me. "He hangs around the house.
He's not really cadre, but he's useful at times."

"I thought you said only cadre and leadership . . ."

"He's working toward a genuine revolutionary consciousness." She rolled her neck, honey hair swinging, and canted
her face upwards, enjoying the sunlight. "Jarrold says he's all
right," she added, as if that settled the issue.

The sidewalks were quiet enough for a Saturday afternoon—a few freaks and student types trolling the shops,
some square johns, mostly old guys who looked like retired
insurance salesmen and their Donna Reed old ladies, taking
care of the weekend shopping or just wandering around in
the sun. Half an hour later, we were walking up Winterhaven
toward Karen's house. The necessity of maintaining security
apparently forgotten, Karen took my hand and led me up
the rickety stairs to the porch. I followed her into the living
room, which was dark except for the lozenge of sunlight that
sprawled through the doorway. The room contained a sagging
sofa which, from its worn burgundy brocade and the ornately
carved mahogany facing on the arms, probably dated from

the forties, and a huge wicker peacock chair with a fraying full-moon back. A bare mattress lay in one corner, someone's sleeping bag crumpled half-open on the striped, sweat-stained ticking. The windows were closed despite the heat—sealed shut with decades of paint, I found out later—and the air was barely breathable, rank with rotting compost smells and the musty reek of mildew.

There were six or seven people hanging out at the Winterhaven House that afternoon, but I only remember the few who would become a part of my life over the next several months. The woman who'd answered the door when I first came looking for Karen was called Gloria Lee. She was maybe five-one or five-two, certainly no taller, and had heavy hair in a nondescript brown that she parted in the middle and allowed to hang in her eyes. Between the hair and her glasses, which were round and tinted khaki green, you could hardly see her face. Magic Annie looked more hippie than radical, a waifish blonde in tattered bell-bottoms and a wispy cotton peasant blouse with puffed sleeves. The only one I recognized was Tom Brownschidle—tall and lanky with dark hair that was already thinning, Tom had organized a free lunch program for itinerants and occasionally did some writing for the *Helix*. He was a well-known figure among the local hippies and even showed up on KING TV at times, as an unofficial spokesman for the street kids. He was slumped on the burgundy couch under the Viet Cong flag that was the only attempt at decoration, French-inhaling a roll-your-own. He lifted one long-fingered hand lethargically when Karen introduced me.

I took out a baggie of smoking dope and some Zig-Zags and rolled a spliff to pass around. The blond chick, Annie, brought a half-finished gallon of a murky homemade bingo from the kitchen. The afternoon drifted past in slow motion, people leaving and arriving, Karen dozing on the couch. I laid off the vino after sundown and by eight or nine considered myself straight enough to drive home.

"I better split," I told Karen.

She looked at me with sleepy eyes. "Stay, man. Hang out. You can crash here tonight."

"I've got to split," I protested, but an hour or so later she and I were in the kitchen, leaning against the gurgling old Frigidaire and exchanging long, wine-musty kisses, and my hands were up her shirt. Eventually, Tom Brownschidle came in and stood there watching us disentangle ourselves, taking nervous little hits on his roll-your-own and scowling.

"Let's get to work," he finally said.

Karen laid her palms against my chest.

"Can you make yourself scarce for a while, Sonny? We're working out some problems. Some shit left over from the high school recruitment thing. You can hang out upstairs if you want."

I found my way upstairs, lay down on a mattress, stoked up a joint, and thumbed through a copy of *Ramparts* that was lying on the floor beside the bed. I couldn't get into the magazine, however. I'd had enough of the weed that little shifts of perspective were beginning to haunt my vision. The bedroom I'd chosen to hang out in, smallest of the three but paradoxically the least cluttered, seemed at one moment vast and unstable, a barn loft fraught with shifting winds, and at the next moment suffocating and claustrophobic. I glanced up from an article on Ken Kesey, startled by the sob of a high-pitched, indrawn scream from the floor below, to catch the unreliable angles of the mottled plaster walls around me turning themselves subtly but unmistakably inside out, as if the whole room were an M.C. Escher etching. When I quickly lowered my eyes to the page again, the print seemed illegible hieroglyphics, an insect swarm of cuneiform scratches, and I could only read one large boldface subhead: *The Chili's Getting Hot: The Merry Pranksters Are Having Pot.* The headline, innocent as it was, seemed suffused with secret meanings. *I had been eating chili when Karen arrived. Things were heating up politically—or was Karen's political rap just an excuse to appear and disappear in my life? Did the heat mean the heat of her body? Was it nuclear fire in the reactor? Who were the Merry Pranksters? Karen's radical friends? What prank were they planning to play?*

I got up and made my way to the top of the staircase, walking silently on tiptoe. I would spy on the pranksters and catch them. I hovered in the dark of the unlit upper hallway and copped a quick glance around the corner.

Buster, the tall kid we'd run into on the Ave. that afternoon, had turned up and ensconced himself in the corner at the foot of the stairs. He puffed at a smoke and looked sullen, bopping his shoulders around at unpredictable intervals as if he'd heard a few bars of music in his head. A couple of others were sitting on the bottom stair with their backs to me, a woman with dark gypsy tresses flowing over a long patchwork poncho and a boy who by his scrawny neck and slender frame must have been another high school recruit.

Karen's voice rose above the ebb and flow of someone sobbing or gasping for air.

"The rest of us were passing out leaflets, rapping to the ones who showed some interest. Talking up the Chicago action. Gloria wasn't into it. She wouldn't approach the kids near the school doors or do anything but stand there and look like she'd rather be somewhere else. Home with a good book or watching TV. Watering the motherfucking lawn."

The pranksters' voices rumbled. *Right on, man! She let down her comrades!* Headlights, shining in obliquely from the street, raked over the wall above the stairs and disappeared.

I edged down the stairs, which lurched in perspective, Buster and the other kids an enormous distance below me and then suddenly very close. To my left I could see the Winterhaven cadre on the couch, the floor, and a couple of chrome-and-vinyl kitchen chairs, in a ring around Gloria Lee. Karen leaned forward in the wicker peacock chair, only her hand and one leg visible behind its convex eclipse.

"I can't. I can't just talk to people," the woman sobbed. "I can't do that."

"Why?" Karen shrieked at her. "Because you're too *clean*? Too white bread? Too *precious*?"

Gloria Lee took off her glasses, wiped at her eyes with the sleeve of her army shirt, then started to examine the frame of the glasses, turning them over and over in her hands as if she suspected they might be broken.

"She doesn't want people to think she's a Communist," Tom said. "She doesn't want people to see her as a nigger, as trash. To give up her white-skin privilege. She has no pride in being one of us. In fighting the people's fight."

The girl started to whine *I do, I do* but her words drowned in asthmatic wheezing. As she sobbed and coughed, glasses off, face slick with snot and tears, Karen and the others continued to rant at her, a circle of gaunt faces bronzed into demonic masks by the glow of a single candle dripping viscous rivulets down the sides of a Thunderbird bottle.

Spineless selfish honky bitch!

Spoiled creep! Bourgeois princess! You'll never be a revolutionary soldier!

"I'll work hard to improve myself . . ." Gloria Lee blurted. Then her breathless gasps overwhelmed her again.

The circle broke and a few of the cadre got up and went into the kitchen. Tom, who was still holding court in the middle of the sofa, began to lecture Gloria Lee in a soft, confiding voice. *Always look to your comrades for guidance. Do what they do. Say what they say. Think of Comrade Che and Comrade Fidel in the mountains. Remember our Viet Cong comrades. Try to feel their isolation and the pain of their oppression. Try to grasp their nobility, try to make it your own. . . .*

The evening uncoiled into spiralling arcs, each a flickering underground movie. My poltergeist perception shifts continued to dog me, people's faces phasing from highlight to shadow, doorways morphing unexpectedly into three-pillared tuning-forks. I coped the way I usually did, by bumping up the wine-to-weed ratio until my whole warped sensorium softened and blurred. Somewhere before dawn I woke next to Karen on a lumpy mattress sprawled on the fir floor in one of the upstairs rooms. We'd been dozing for a couple of hours; now Karen had stoked up the joint we'd been working on earlier and was lying on her side facing the window, through which the street lamp cast vertical slashes of halogen yellow on the stained plaster wall.

"You want a hit?" she asked. She waved the doobie vaguely above her shoulder.

I took the proffered number and managed to pinch it long enough to draw a lungful of smoke before it burned me.

"We did some good work tonight, Sonny. You must have felt the vibe, right? We were cutting through the bullshit, making progress."

I exhaled and reached for the wineglass on the floor beside the bed.

"That was pretty rough, eh? You always that tough on Gloria?"

"She let down her comrades."

Karen lay back and took a leisurely hit on the J. She passed it back to me, held her breath for a minute, then directed a column of smoke at the wall.

"Criticism, self-criticism, is an essential tool of cadre transformation. It's painful to hear your comrades when they analyze your weaknesses and point out your indulgences and moments of self-delusion; it's like your best friends have turned into predators, like they're wounding you, tearing your flesh. But it's energizing also; it cleans you, burns away the shit we've been consuming ever since we were deluded little kids. All that crap that we were fed in school, the glorious march of science. White bread and Betty Crocker. *Father Knows Best.*"

"Your friend downstairs—what's her name? She doesn't look too energized. Wiped out is more like it. You people really kicked her around."

"We, all of us, everyone who lives here, we're all in pain, suffering. Cadre transformation is like that. We have to be stripped to the bone, to burn away all the illusions, so that one day new men and women, revolutionary fighters, can rise from our dust and be born."

I took a hit, snuffed the roach between my thumb and forefinger, popped it into my mouth, and chased it with a mouthful of Ripple.

"What about Jarrold?" I said. "Are you and he . . . ?"

She sat up on the mattress, rumpled blankets whirlpooling around her, raked her fingers through her hair to sweep the long strands from her face.

"There's no more monogamy here, like I told you. No more torture-chamber families like the ones we grew up in. Families are a microcosm of oppressive white society— have you read R. D. Laing? That's the *first* thing we have to destroy, the fucking American family."

She stood up, slipping out of the bedclothes, and started to walk naked toward the door.

"Where you going?"

She waved without turning around, and I assumed she'd gone off to use the john. When she hadn't returned ten or fifteen minutes later, I sat up on the mattress and softly called her name into the darkness of the hall.

"All right, don't come back," I finally said. I giggled, flopped over and buried my head in the pillow. When I heard her footsteps returning, I reached out and grabbed at her ankles.

"It's cold in this room," an unfamiliar voice said calmly. Someone's foot kicked playfully at my arm. I turned on my side and looked up at Magic Annie.

"'Scuse over, I'm freezing."

She kicked the blanket off the side of the mattress and snuggled in beside me just as if we'd been sleeping together for years. I inhaled a hit of patchouli, a sharp note that might have been hashish, the moist, loamy musk of her hippie-chick sweat.

"Where's Karen?" I whispered.

I felt her shrug under the blanket.

"She just took off a minute ago." I sat up and peered around for my Levi's.

"Hey, don't get distracted," Annie whispered. She reached up, put her hand on my shoulder, pulled herself up into a sitting position and slid her palms over my chest, fingers caressing my nipples, tickling and teasing my skin. I turned and pushed her back down on the mattress.

"Slow down," I said. "Karen's in the john, right? She'll be back in a couple of minutes."

Annie smiled and shook her head. "Why don't you just pretend I'm Karen? It's not like it makes any difference. Everyone is everyone. We're all the same—right?"

She cuddled up and nuzzled my throat, the tip of her tongue darting little teasing flicks across my ticklish skin.

Then her hand skated over my belly. "See?" she said. "I get the same reaction as Karen, right? There's really no difference at all."

I woke up sprawled half on the mattress and half on the dusty fir floor of the bedroom. Annie was curled up beside me, blond hair a river eddying over the pillow-slip, face calm and childlike in sleep.

The john at the end of the hall was in use, so I stumbled downstairs, bladder bursting, with the intention of taking a leak in the backyard if I had to. My hair was the dishevelled mess it always was when I first got out of bed, my beard itched, and my face and hands felt greasy with sweat. The house below was quiet, and I thought for a moment that the living room was unoccupied. Then, just as I came to the foot of the stairs, I saw Karen lying on the mattress. She was still asleep, sleeping bag bunched around her hips like the robe of a bathing woman in a Renaissance fresco, hair obscuring her face. Beside her, lying on his back, bare-chested, was a dark-haired man who looked a few years older than Karen or me. His face was thin but strong-boned, his cheeks dark with stubble. He too had pushed the sleeping bag down to his waist, and he lay with his arms extended, palms open as if in supplication.

The next step I took made the rickety stair moan like a nail being pulled out of heartwood. Karen didn't wake, but the dark man's eyes opened. He sat up and scratched absentmindedly at the hair on his chest. His eyes were as cool blue as Karen's.

"So who the fuck are you?" he said softly.

"Sonny Wheeler, man," I told him. "I'm a friend of Karen's, you know . . ."

He smiled. "Ah, the high school sweetheart! Well, don't just stand there looking stupid, dude. Find a doorway and put yourself through it."

"I'll talk to you later," I said. I was suddenly weak-kneed and covered in sweat. I sat down on the stairs and put my head between my knees. When I raised my eyes again, the man had flopped over and was apparently dozing.

Karen lifted herself on her elbows. "You okay, Sonny?" she asked me. She sat up and gave me a radiant smile. "Where's Annie? Still asleep?"

16

Alchemical Wedding

My child's head turns slowly toward me. The blue eyes, transparent near the pupil though rimmed with simple midnight, open sleepily. My father's eyes. Alfred's.

Eden—the name Curie chose for her son—is thirteen months old. He can walk, though unsteadily, exploring his terrain like an astronaut setting foot on an unfamiliar planet. He coos monosyllables, feeling his way into the shaped sonorities of language. The last time I saw him, he repeated "Hi!" several dozen times, to me, to my mother, to Curie, to the stuffed bear he carries everywhere and periodically cuddles and chews on. He regards me noncommittally, as if I were a feature of the landscape, then closes his eyes, snuffles and, shuddering faintly, drifts back off to sleep.

The visits are Betty's idea. Curie called her from the hospital in Oregon; I can only imagine the conversation, as my mother won't tell me anything about it except to say that Curie "wasn't feeling too hot these days," and Curie stopped calling me soon after Eden's birth. The Crashaws, so Betty said, had decided that it would be best for Eden if I were to have some part in his upbringing. Curie might be ill for some time, who could tell, and the old man and his housekeeper could hardly be expected to run and play with a growing child. They needed help, and I would be the one to provide it. Betty'd laid all this out for me one evening at home. She'd come into my bedroom and sat down on the foot of bed. "We're meeting with Richard Crashaw and Eden next weekend," she'd said. "You're going to be spending some time with your boy."

Before I could speak, she added, "I know he's yours, Sonny. Curie told me, and if that wasn't enough I've seen him myself. Blond hair, white and fine as cornsilk. The spit of your father. Those eyes."

She crossed her legs under the bright, flowing muumuu with its pattern of tropical flowers. She was wearing pink lipstick that went with her dress and a silk scarf she'd wound around her head.

"When you're young, when you're your age, you make the mistake of thinking that you're someone. When you're older, when you've had your kids and seen the world pass by you, you begin to understand it isn't true. What you are is a place something's passing through. Like wind in a wheat field. Water in a stream. Everything you and I are, all we know, just comes to nothing. But the movement flows through us, becomes someone else. It's time for you to recognize your place."

The first of the visits was painful for everyone—except perhaps Betty, who cooed over Eden and insisted on picking him up when he stumbled on his pile of wooden building blocks and bumped his shoulder on the cherry-wood table in the Crashaws' front room. Crashaw, to his credit, had the courtesy to leave us—Betty, Mrs. Turnbull, and me—alone with the little boy and repair to his study, which was some-where upstairs.

"Well, go on, Sonny," Betty said. "You can talk to kids too, you know. They're a whole lot like adults that way."

"What you building, Eden? That a train?" I asked. I realized how stiff and tentative I must have sounded, how obvious it must have been that I was totally inexperienced at dealing with children.

Eden stared at me, expressionless, wobbling slightly as he struggled with the unfamiliar business of standing erect, his eyes filled with wintry Saskatchewan sky. He wasn't, of course, aware that I was his father: that revelation we'd agreed to save for later, when Curie came back from the hospital, when he'd learned that I was someone to trust.

I held out one finger, and was momentarily thrilled to see the little boy stagger unassisted toward me. He stumbled, of course, before reaching my extended hand, pitched forward and belly-flopped onto the carpet, lay howling for a second while I sat there befuddled and helpless, was finally scooped up and cuddled into whimpers by Mrs. Turnbull, who was now his nurse as she had long ago been Curie's.

"You have to move faster than *that,*" Betty said.

"They take a lot of watching," Mrs. Turnbull contributed.

Eden snuffled as Betty handed him across to the old woman. Shot me a glance full of fear and alarm. After that, he clung to Mrs. Turnbull until my mother and I left.

This time, Eden looks genuinely pooped out. He's been drifting between sleep and waking ever since my mother and I arrived.

"How's Curie?" I ask Mrs. Turnbull.

That gets me a sniff of disapproval. "You'd have to ask Mr. Crashaw. She's doing as well as can be expected, I suppose."

We sit there a while, at a loss for conversation. Betty, who's having one of her off days, her times when the chemo and the disease itself seem to have worn her threadbare, sits at Eden's feet on the long, fussy-looking French provincial sofa, his bare foot cradled in one of her hands like a sleeping mouse curled in the straw. Mrs. Turnbull sits totemic in an armchair, antsy from lack of cigarettes, which she normally chain-smokes. When the little boy moves or twitches, I notice, her hand twitches with him, as if the urge to straighten and fuss with his blanket and clothes is very nearly too strong to resist. Crashaw is out somewhere. He's retiring from his teaching job, but still goes to the high school every once in a while, ostensibly to wrap up his duties but actually—according to Betty, at least—to take his mind off the worry of his family.

"We might as well go," Betty finally says. "This kid is enjoying his *siesta* way too much to pay any attention to anyone else. He'll be conked out till dinnertime now."

"I'll put him to bed for a proper nap," Mrs. Turnbull says. "He'll roll off and hurt himself here." She stands up and begins to lift Eden.

"Let me take him," I find myself saying. I've never actually held Eden. He's past the age when they have to be carried everywhere, and I've been too afraid of freaking him out and sending him off into a fit of terrified shrieking to just lift him up spontaneously or give him a friendly hug.

Mrs. Turnbull looks questioningly at Betty.

"He used to play receiver in high school," she says. "Good hands."

The old woman passes the sleeping child into my arms.

"It's his brain that doesn't function," Betty adds.

Betty shows me how to cup the boy's thigh in one hand, index finger forming a secure ring with the thumb, how to cradle his head on my arm. I take the stairs slowly, one cautious step after another. Eden's eyelids flutter, cornflower irises rolled up in sleep, and he fidgets at the unfamiliar feeling of motion, but he doesn't wake up, not even when I lower him gently into the crib in Curie's bedroom. I stand there for a few minutes, just taking him in. His face is soft with baby fat, but the features are delicate, the skin beneath the rosy glow of sleep as startlingly pale as Aunt Alice's. Betty's right: he has the Wheeler genes for sure. I touch the little straw-white curls, damp from the heat of his body, feel the softness of his baby skin, then turn away and leave him to get on with his nap. I don't go back downstairs to Betty and Mrs. Turnbull right away, though. This is the first time I've ever been in Curie Crashaw's bedroom, and I take the opportunity to have a look around. The decor is probably typical enough of a middle-class girl's room at the dark end of the sixties. Some records—Janis Ian, Leonard Cohen, that sort of thing—are stacked neatly beside a monaural record player; there's a stiff bouquet of joss sticks poking out of a crystal bottle; a poster from the Judy Collins concert at the Arena. On the vanity, unframed and propped against a couple of perfume bottles, is a five-by-seven snapshot of a group of teenagers standing on a playing field with Curie's father. It is, I suspect, the science club, though a later edition than the one that Karen and Bobby and the Professor and I were in. There's seven kids with Crashaw; Curie is the only one I know. It's a bright day in late spring or summer. The photographer must have his or her back to the sun, as everyone in the photo is squinting. Crashaw, his hair a white acetylene flame against the uniform blue background, peers straight into the eye of the camera, as do most of the kids. Only Curie has looked away at the moment that the camera's shutter spasmed. Her face is turned sideways, so that the photographer must have seen her in profile, though from the blurring between her bloodless face and the cap of Leslie Caron hair, she obviously turned too quickly for him or her to abort the shot.

Before I leave the bedroom, I open the top drawer of Curie's white-enamelled writing-desk and leaf through the papers inside. I don't know what I'm looking for—some doorway into Curie's world, a place which has always seemed opaque to me. There are, of course, no letters. Curie has few friends in Danforth, none at all I've heard her mention in the larger world beyond. In a plain manila envelope, however, I find a sheet of official-looking heavy stock, a treasure worth exploring for a moment. I draw it out and balance it on my fingertips, taking care not to soil its whiteness. Eden's birth certificate, on which are inscribed his full name and date of birth and the name of his mother as well as the signatures of some strangers whom I take to be functionaries in the local registry of births and deaths. I slip the card back in the envelope and carefully replace it in the desk.

"The Crashaws don't want money," Betty tells me later. We're driving back across town in her new Chevelle.

"You *asked* Old Man Crashaw?"

"I asked."

I say nothing, concentrate on driving. *Keep your eye on the road at all times!* I remember Clyde telling me, years ago when he was teaching me to drive. Right at this moment, it seems like excellent advice.

"I figured maybe fifty a month would be all right," Betty tells me. She too is staring straight ahead.

"But I thought you said . . ."

"No, I told you what *he* said. Richard Crashaw. What *I* said was fifty a month. You can put it in a bank account for Eden if his granddaddy's too damn stiff-necked."

I was lying on my bed, half-heartedly paging my way through the latest *Cheetah*, which I'd picked up the previous weekend in Seattle, when Betty rapped at my door and came in. She and Clyde had been shopping, making the rounds of the supermarket and the hardware place where Clyde liked to look at garden tools and check out the latest trends in bug sprays.

"Bobby's home," Betty said.

"Yeah? Really?"

She nodded, strain coming into her face, as if even nodding her head required effort and resistance to pain.

"His mother called. Lida. She said he'd caught the bus from San Diego."

"That's wonderful. I mean, Jesus, he did it, eh? He went to Nam and survived."

"I think he's still on active service, Sonny. He doesn't get his discharge for a couple of months yet, from what Lida said. I guess he's on leave for a while."

After Clyde and I had eaten the dinner I'd warmed for us—some leftover burgers from the weekend with Uncle Ben's Converted Rice and frozen Birds Eye Vegetable Medley—I borrowed Clyde's Studie and drove across town.

The Deerbornes' house looked small and rundown, somehow, as if not just Bobby but the whole Deerborne family had been away for a couple of years. I parked behind Larry's pickup and headed up the red concrete walk. The front lawn needed cutting, hawkweed sparking up out of the bluegrass, and the flower beds looked sparse and unkempt. I noticed Bobby's 'Cuda in the carport, up on blocks with its mag wheels missing.

Lida answered the door in her housecoat.

"He's in the kitchen," she said. "Tell him to eat something, will you? Beer on an empty stomach, he'll wind up with gastritis like his dad."

I followed her into the kitchen. Bobby was sitting at the colonial table, a can of Rainier in one hand. He was wearing a T-shirt that looked freshly laundered, over Red Tabs, and his hair had been buzzed down to a flat-top.

"The military look," I said. "It suits you."

Bobby stood up and offered his hand. I felt strange about shaking hands with an old friend—this was probably the first time we'd greeted each other so formally since that meeting in Mr. Crashaw's kitchen.

"Good to see you, Sonny. I been meaning to give you a ring. Listen, where's my manners, sit down. You want a Rainier?" He waved the can absent-mindedly.

"Maybe later," I said. I sat down at the table. Bobby lowered himself into his chair again, angling his body cautiously, as if he were having trouble with his back.

"I'll leave you boys to catch up," Lida said. She wandered off through the living room, her slippers hissing softly on the hardwood.

Bobby smiled, then looked down at the polished yellow maple of the tabletop.

"So how'd it go, man?" I asked him. "You made it okay?"

He shrugged and took a hit on his Rainier. His eyes slid away toward the window.

"Oh, you know, just regular army shit. Ugly food. Plenty of walking."

"You didn't get wounded or anything? You're okay?"

He shook his head. "No, shit, I'm all right. You sure I can't get you a brewski? They're Larry's, but he doesn't care. Buys a case every week out of habit. Hardly drinks at all these days. Digestion, you know. Getting old."

"All right, you twisted my arm, but let me get it." I got up and helped myself to a can of cold Rainier from the fridge. The beer summoned up a little wave of nausea, reminder of an evening at the Fission Hole, but I chugged on it anyway and waited for the icy glow to overwhelm the sickness. Like they told us in high school, perseverance pays off.

"I hear you're free in a month or so. You planning on moving back home?"

Bobby shook his head, looking down at the table. "No idea, man."

"Take it easy for a while, eh? Thought about travelling or anything like that?"

"I been travelling. Join the Army, see the world."

"Right. I guess you have."

We sat there in silence for a few minutes, both of us admiring the view of the back garden—a rotary clothes-hanger, metal garden shed, two rows of bedraggled tomatoes.

"Seen Sherri at all? She in town?" I asked him.

I knew perfectly well that Bobby's old girlfriend was living outside Pasco, sharing a trailer with a guy who worked construction at the Area. She'd got herself an office job, receptionist or whatever, and changed her hair from red and long to short and kind of sandy.

"Don't know, man. That's over. I'm starting again, I guess. Clean slate."

"I can relate to that, all right."

More silence. More looking out the window.

"How about you? Surprised me to hear you were back here. Get tired of Vancouver or what?"

"Not really. Betty's been pretty sick. Cancer. Figured I'd be better off home."

"Lida told me. I'm sorry. The medicals been any help?"

"Not a lot in the long run. Costing Clyde a bit to keep up the chemo, but I'm not sure it does any good."

Bobby nodded. "How's Clyde holding up?"

"He's a rationalist, basically. Used to solving problems, finding ways to get things done. This thing Mom has, this cancer, he sees it like a glitch in the cosmos, a walking refutation of the logic of the world."

"My first few months out, I worked with the medics. Can you believe it? Doctor Deerborne is in, man. What a motherfucking farce. You'd get these guys with sucking wounds, their whole chest full of shrapnel. Give them morphine, plasma, pack the wound. Might as well have bought them a soda."

He picked up his beer to take another hit, and I noticed that his hand was trembling slightly.

"Clyde figures he's to blame, I think. He brought her here to Danforth, exposed her to radioactive waste, that iodine that fucks up your lymph glands."

"Yeah? What do you think?"

"Could easily be, I suppose. I mean, they've had eight reactors strung along the goddamn river since the middle of the fifties, mostly cranking out plutonium for bombs. The Public Health over in Oregon said that the Columbia's the most radioactive river in the world. Doesn't exactly make you want to swim there."

Bobby smiled, a tight-lipped grimace, his narrow face reflected in the murky auburn waters of the table. "You been studying up on this stuff, Sonny?"

"Yeah," I said. "Up in Vancouver. A lot of the information's classified and socked away in some lead-lined vault in the

Pentagon with a couple of three-star generals jerking off outside the door. There's still enough on Danforth to make you pray it had never existed. This place will still be buzzing when the stars have all burnt out."

"Sounds like the Nam, man. We've dropped so much shit on that poor fucking country—not to mention the claymores and the Bongs' fucking tripwires—one fart could send the whole place to Neptune."

"Fucking amazing what we do with the world, eh?" I laughed, but Bobby shook his head sadly.

"So how do you square that with working up at Zee Plant?"

"I don't know, Bob. I wish I could tell you. I need to get inside the thing, to know what it is the evil shits are building." I was conscious as I spoke that I was lying to myself—I wanted to curl up small and die, and Danforth was my spawning stream, my nest.

"Then what? You figure you can change it?"

"I doubt it, man. Whoever builds things like Danforth, they don't give a shit what we think. Not to mention the fact that you can't just wave a magic wand and make several hundred ares of reactors and nuclear waste turn into fairy dust or something. It's a question that doesn't really have an answer."

Bobby shook his head, still staring at his own reflection. Then he looked up and grinned at me, the first real smile I'd seen on his face since I arrived.

"Blow the fucker up, man," he said. "That's the answer to anything. Just go and blow the stupid fucker up."

We finished our beers and wandered outside. I'd intended to say goodbye at the front door and be on my way, but Bobby followed me out into the driveway.

"'Cuda's looking good," I said. "Seems to have survived okay without you."

He rested one foot on the nose of the Barracuda, smoothed his pant leg and stared at the windshield, on which our reflected faces shone like white stones in a pond.

"Machines, man. What's the point of the fucking things? Shit-heaps of metal and plastic, that's all, but you can feel more about a bucket of bolts than you can for some people you run into. A lot of guys are totally obsessed."

"You'd see that in the military, I guess. They love their technology, don't they?"

"Shit, there's all kinds of outrageous mechanical junk in the Army. You name it, they got a few thousand. Most of it's decent stuff, too. Quality engineering and reasonably well maintained. Nothing haywire, you know what I mean?"

"This country's full of Clydes, man. Why not?"

"I can relate to old Clyde, man, let me tell you. The time I've spent on this damn thing, you absolutely would not believe. Pile of scrap, that's all it is. Good for fuck all but melting down for beer cans. But light it up, man, and you're riding a hurricane. Like a wild horse in a thunderstorm. Damn straight."

"You getting it back on the road?"

"Yeah, in time for my discharge, anyway. Needs some work, you know. Things I didn't get around to before I shipped out."

He ran his hand over the smooth metal hood, came away with his palm grey with dust.

"Might even give it a wash." He batted the dust from his hand on his jeans, grinning like the kid I'd known in high school.

17

Jet City Breakdown

"She's probably gone down the Ave., man," Gloria Lee told me. "We were all down there this afternoon, and it looks like there might be some action tonight. The Alki beach thing really pissed the people off."

"All right, maybe we'll check it out."

"Who's that dude you're with?" she added, then put her fist in front of her mouth and started coughing.

"Don't worry about him. He's cool." Bobby, with his regular army buzz-cut and that tight T-shirt over his muscles, was so blatantly *un*cool that he couldn't possibly be an FBI plant or a narc. Normally, I wouldn't have brought him anywhere near Karen's radical friends, but that particular evening I was feeling up and ready to raise hell with anyone, the Weather gang included. It was one of those wonderful late summer evenings; there was a glow suffusing everything, golden light washing over the peeling green paint of the Winterhaven house's front porch, and it had washed away, for a few hours at least, the shadows that had filled my mind ever since I'd left Vancouver. August sunset in the Pacific Northwest—you could bottle it and sell it to the tourists.

"Later," I added, and Gloria Lee nodded and started to head back inside the house. I bounded down the rickety steps to Bobby's Barracuda, which was making *basso profundo* thumping noises as it idled at the curb.

"No Karen?" Bobby asked.

"They figure she's down the Ave."

"Whatever."

We pulled away from the curb with a roar and a chirp of the Goodyears and tooled through the streets toward the Avenue. Bobby had been working on the 'Cuda for most of his leave, and this was the first time he'd driven it any distance. He'd picked me up just after lunch, and we'd blasted up the I-5 with the tape player pounding out *The Doors* and *Wheels of Fire*, a six-pack of ice-cold Rainiers on the console and Bobby periodically leaning his crew-cut head out the window.

"You trying to find out how aerodynamic your head is, Deerborne?" I'd asked him.

"Air, man. I need fresh air."

"Some people wouldn't call the atmosphere over the I-5 'fresh.'"

"It ain't jungle sweat either, man. The air's so thick in the Mekong, man, you have to chop it up with machetes to breathe it. I hate that fucking jungle more than anything on earth. There's a million species of ugly bug and mud like diarrhea, and the air's so goddamn humid it's like you're sweating inside your lungs."

"Getting to be a jungle right here in Jet City, man. All kinds of crazy shit going down now."

There'd been riots and near-riots all week in town—
I knew that from the TV news, if not from any first-hand
information. The craziness had started the previous week,
across the inlet from the Ave. on Alki beach. There'd been an
open-air concert there with some of the local bands, just an
organized party really. The cops had showed up, as they normally would, but they'd kept their distance and let the kids
enjoy the music and the sunshine. Then some genius had
decided to liven things up by dropping a paper cup filled
with gasoline into one of the police cruisers and chasing
it with a lighted match. After that, the cops had charged
the crowd, who'd responded by pelting them with whatever
came to hand. The night after the Alki riot, the action shifted
to the Ave. The usual street crowd was hanging around, and
kids came in from the suburbs all fired up for an entertaining evening of civil disobedience, as if it were a fashionable
new dance craze. The results were fairly obvious: a few of
the storefronts we passed were boarded up, the glass having
been shattered by the rioters, and there were cop cars parked
conspicuously at intervals on either side of the street.

We cruised the Ave. for several blocks before I caught
sight of Karen.

"Over there, man, by the Korean place."

Bobby angled the Barracuda over to the curb. We were
thirty or forty feet past Karen, who was huddled with Nina,
Tom Brownschidle's girlfriend, and a gangly kid in Davey
Crockett fringes who was probably one of her high school
recruits. Bobby fed the parking meter while I rapped with
Karen. Her friend, the young guy, mumbled "later" and loped

off down the sidewalk with Nina. Bobby and Karen and I went into the Korean takeout place, located a table and ordered a round of coffees.

"Jesus, man, what happened to you?" Karen said. She was looking with obvious amusement at Bobby's army crewcut. "Been walking around under a helicopter?"

Bobby shook his head, his eyes on the Formica tabletop on which his elbows rested.

"Bobby was in the Nam, Karen. I told you in Vancouver."

"You were in Vietnam? In the Army, man? Fighting?"

Bobby lowered his head.

"Bobby did his hitch. He's out now." I took a sip of my java, which tasted as if it had been hanging around in the pot for a while. "What's all this shit about street-fighting? Radio's full of it. What the fuck's been going down?"

Karen paid no attention to me. She was staring straight at Bobby. "You look like a fucking Nazi, man," she said.

Bobby ran a hand over his cropped hair and smiled at his reflection in the Formica.

"You kill a lot of peasants, man? Gut them with your bay-onet? Machine-gun some innocent children?"

Bobby finally lifted his head and met Karen's eyes. "So I guess you're the princess of peace now, that right?" he said softly. "Marching with the placards. Shaking your fist. Burn-ing the fucking flag. Good shit like that?"

"Karen's been working with the peace movement for years, Bob. Ever since the demonstrations started."

Karen kept her eyes on Bobby.

"We don't want peace with fascist America, man. We want war."

"You don't have to *want* war, Queen Karrie. It's like Uncle Fucking Sam. It wants you."

"Must have wanted *you* pretty bad, Deerborne. Patriots like you are hard to come by."

"I did what I had to, that's all."

"Hey, I *bet* you did, hotshot. I bet it really gave you a hard-on, too. Big John Wayne stud from white-bread America running the whole fucking world. Put those little yellow bastards in their place."

"Yeah, I guess that was it all right," Bobby told her. He fingered a Camel from the pack on the table and helped himself to my chrome Zippo lighter. "Whatever you say."

Silence. The Korean man and woman behind the counter eyed us with obvious concern.

"All right," I said. "Let's just chill out and take things easy. We're all getting way too worked up."

"Sure, Sonny. What's a few hundred thousand dead peasants? Nothing to get worked up about, right?"

Bobby ran his hands through his cropped hair as if something were irritating his scalp.

"I guess you know a lot about all that shit, Karrie? All those poor Asian peasants and so forth?"

"I understand politics, Deerborne. That's more than some dumb honky greaser like you can figure out."

"You don't know dick, girl. I was shit-scared from the minute I got there till the minute they shipped my ass out.

There I am marching around the fucking paddies, belt full of hand grenades and mortar on my shoulder, GI fucking Joe from one end all the way to the other, and all I wanted was to fly back home to Danforth and curl up underneath my bed. Get me home to Lida and Larry, man, and let the Bongs have the rest of the world."

"We never should have been there, man," I said. "We never should have been there."

Bobby laughed that wild-ass, maniacal laugh of his.

"What we should have done, man, was nuke Charlie's ass. Somebody should have seen that from the get-go. You dick around, you perish. That's the way it always has been in a motherfucking war."

"Somebody ought to nuke your fascist ass, greaseball!" Karen stood up, her chair scraping backwards with a shriek and our cups slopping coffee onto the table.

"Hold on, man," I muttered. "I'll be back in a minute."

"Whatever," I heard Bobby whisper as I opened the glass door and followed Karen out into the street. The long-legged stride of hers had already taken her halfway down the block, and I had to do a quick jog to catch her.

"What was that supposed to accomplish?" I asked.

Karen hunched her shoulders and strode along, her profile obscured by the collar of her army coat and the swirls of her dirty-blond hair. I grabbed at her arm to make her stop, and, while she shrugged off my hand, she slowed down a few steps later and finally turned to confront me.

"What the fuck are you doing with a greaseball like that? I told you—"

"He's an old friend. I thought he was a friend of yours too, you know. The science club, all that good shit. High school."

"High school was a prison, Sonny. A training camp for fascists. We talked about it often enough. Assholes like Deerborne, they were convicts like the rest of us, they were just too dumb to know it."

"Bobby's all right. He's been through the Nam thing and all that. It's changed him, made him see how things work."

Karen shook her head. "Greasers, man. You're wasting your time." She turned and started walking, hands buried in the pockets of her coat, towards the corner of Forty-second, where a crowd of kids was spilling off the sidewalk.

"Give me a minute," I told her. "I'll just get my lighter and shit."

I went back to the Korean joint and caught Bobby coming out of the doorway. We'd planned to hit a couple of bars and then head out to see some Army friend of his who was renting a house up in Ballard. I told him I'd decided to stay with Karen. *She's wired up on politics. She's always felt things strongly. It's really nothing personal, right?* That got me another "Whatever."

"You need a ride home tonight, man?" Bobby finally asked.

"I'm all right. I'll hop a bus tomorrow or something."

He nodded and headed for his car. I had just caught up with Karen, who was wandering along the sidewalk looking into the windows of the little boutiques on that part of the Avenue, when the 'Cuda rumbled past us, Bobby punching one brief bleep of sound from the horn. For the next few hours, we strolled up and down the Ave., rapping with people Karen knew, some of them familiar to me from the Winter-haven house, others just local street hippies. The August sun-set was slowly replaced by the chemical sheen of streetlights and storefronts. Everyone was talking about the riots.

"There's Tom and Nina," I told Karen. Tom Brownschidle, unmistakable with his stoop and rangy stride, crossed the Avenue through traffic and loped toward us. Nina's black hair and poncho swung rhythmically as she hurried to keep up. Now that it was getting dark, the Ave. and the surround-ing streets were rapidly filling with shifting, apparently aimless crowds. Most of the faces on the street were strangers—kids hitching in from the suburbs, street people drifting into the District from downtown. Everything was quiet, though; an evening stroll through a busy tourist district would have seemed about the same. Then, an hour or two before mid-night, a police siren blipped and howled a block away, and a ripple of latent energy drew the crowds off the sidewalk and into the traffic lane to see what had happened.

"Somebody's trashed a storefront. Looks like Queens-bury's." Queensbury's was a men's shop, a relic of the pseudo-British boutique craze from a couple of years before.

"What the fuck for? Queensbury's ain't exactly a CIA front."

"Property is theft, man," Nina chirped. "The street should belong to the people."

She had to raise her voice to a scream for us to hear the end of the sentence—a police car equipped with a howler had angled into a side street, and its oscillating avian screech seemed to instantly overwhelm and distort our perceptions. We clamped hands to ears and ran, hunched over as if from the hurricane force of the sound waves, down the sidewalk and into the relative quiet of doorways and the narrow mouths of alleys. Karen, Nina, Tom and I wound up huddled in the entrance of a bookshop. Tom nudged me in the ribs and said, "Here, stash this." He passed me a two-foot length of pipe, lead, about an inch and a half in diameter, concealing it under his arm as he slid it inside my jacket. "Just whip it through the glass as you run, man," he shouted into my ear.

"Fuck, man, you trying to get us busted?" I tried to hand the pipe back, and, when he raised his hands, palms out, in a gesture of refusal, let it drop.

Tom's face flashed through panic to anger. The howler cruised closer. Nina was shouting and pointing at a tableau of agitated figures on the opposite side of the street, where someone had lit a trash fire in one of the city's garbage containers and rolled it into traffic, tonguing gasps of pinwheel fire. Karen dropped to one knee between us, scooped the length of pipe off the concrete, and deposited it casually into her shoulder bag, as if it were a hairbrush or a fresh-baked baguette.

Across the street, some kids had started chucking rocks in the direction of the cop car. From somewhere out of my range of vision, police were bellowing warnings through a bullhorn. *You are ordered to disperse! You will be removed by force! You are ordered to disperse!* On the next block, blue-grey smoke drifted up above the crowds and cars. The mass of people on the sidewalks seemed to twitch and spasm away from the cloud, a complex and vulnerable organism recoiling from some predator's claws.

"Tear gas!" someone shouted. The shattering oscillations of the howler died down for a moment, then resumed at an even more sickening volume, though apparently from another location.

"Let's move!" Tom bellowed, and the four of us began to jog, deking and swerving through the loiterers on the sidewalk. Soon everyone seemed to be running, some jogging a few steps then pausing to crane around and check out the action, others pelting down the sidewalks as if the concrete were collapsing behind them, some darting into traffic and across the clotted Ave. At some point, I lost touch with Nina, Tom and Karen, and found myself running beside two or three young dudes I'd never seen before. We jogged in a pack for a half-block, shoulder to shoulder, then the others sheared away to the left and went hurtling into a cross street. A few moments later, I caught up with Karen, who was crouching in front of the display window of a clothing store, rummaging in her cloth bag for the pipe. I jogged up to her, panting and gasping, unable to speak, and stood staring at the mannequins in the window. The window dresser had apparently booked off in the middle of changing the display. A little group of mannequins, naked and sexless, gazed blankly at some vanishing point within or beyond the storefronts across the way. Mommy and Daddy and Buddy and Sis. Serene in their nakedness as Adam and Eve.

The night was stretched taut as a drum skin. I could feel a pressure building, someone's thumbs on the backs of my eyes. *Why did nothing ever happen? Why was time so thick and slow?*

"Give me that, for fuck's sake!" I screamed at Karen. She looked at me quizzically, then handed me the length of lead pipe. I stepped toward the plate glass, squinted up at the mannequins, then turned and bolted back the way I'd come, raking the pipe laterally across the glass as I ran down the length of the window. The effect was spectacular. Glass shattered back onto the floor of the display space, a shower of shards and splinters glinting horizontally away from the end of the pipe; then, a heartbeat before I completed the sweeping motion and arrived at the end of the window, the whole pane collapsed and crashed down onto its frame, spilling forward to explode against the concrete. The mannequins remained impassive, apparently unimpressed.

18

Tranquility Base

"He burned her face!" Curie sobs. "He burned her with acid! She doesn't have a face!"

I'm sitting in the Crashaws' living room. Curie's perched on the edge of the colonial sofa, huddled around a frilled gingham sofa cushion. Her face is streaked with tears. "He burned her face!" she keeps sobbing. "He burned all her skin off. She doesn't have a face!"

The talking head on the network news is rattling off the details of the story. The victim was a secretary, he tells us: she worked in a finance company in downtown Seattle. Three days ago, she went out for a drink after work with her friends from the office. She was, or so the story goes, a shy and well-mannered young woman, engaged to a man she had been going with since high school. She rarely accepted her colleagues' invitations to come along with them to a tavern, but this time she had agreed.

Behind the talking head, taped footage of an ambulance, a stretcher with a human body covered in a brilliant red blanket being unloaded from the back doors of the vehicle in a huddle of paramedics. An IV on a metal stand. A crowd of people screaming and jostling. The stretcher being set to earth. Its legs and wheels descending. Network cameras. Flashbulb fire. A man in a grey suit, arms spread like a basketball guard, trying futilely to herd back the crowd. Then paramedics pushing the stretcher. The footage expands to eclipse the network talking head; now it fills the entire screen of the Crashaws' twenty-one-inch mahogany-veneer RCA console. Everyone, everything, surging left toward the doors of a building. The doors are blue metal, dented and studded with rivets. The camera bumps our heads against the metal. We see the stretcher sucked inside. The doors close. The crowd is swarming over them. Then everything is swallowed up. The talking head appears.

Curie has been home a few weeks. Childbirth and depression have changed her; the wire-thin spark of incandescent energy who had marched in and out of our science club meetings is gone, replaced by a limp, skeletal, largely silent young woman with streaked hair, ash-blond over auburn, and a sun-deprived complexion she accentuates with kohl-black Max Factor smeared in rings around her eyes. Exhausted, stunned with Librium, she sleeps most mornings, spends the afternoons curled up in an armchair, legs tucked under her fleshless body, one arm draped over her tummy as if she were still pregnant, staring at her father's new colour TV. She speaks to me seldom, seems to blame me for the breakdown that followed Eden's birth. On the few occasions I've tried to touch her—gently, the tips of my fingers on her wrist or her shoulder—she recoils as if burned. On my visits, she tolerates my presence but rarely meets my eyes. I bring Eden down from his bedroom—his grandfather has paid a couple of recent dropouts from the high school to remodel the upstairs guest room—and watch him play with his blocks and trains on the living-room carpet while his mother gazes blankly at soaps and ancient reruns, placidly ignoring us both.

The victim's name is Liesl Potter. She was born in Eugene, Oregon, and moved to Seattle after high school. She is single and enjoys jogging and playing the piano. She is twenty-eight years old. The man who raped her and burned her face with acid is forty-two, an unmarried sales clerk. His name—if in fact the police disclosed it—slips through my memory without leaving any permanent trace. He was arrested within hours of the incident, which occurred on a strip of waste land not far from Tacoma, a place to which Liesl Potter's abductor apparently drove her in a rented panel van. The fact that the vehicle was rented, the distance from the place where Liesl left her friends to the place where she was abandoned, blind and mad with agony, implies that the abduction and assault had been planned. The man is in custody, no one says where. The talking head pronounces a few words regarding the unavailability of further information, then the newscast shifts to other, unrelated matters. A plane is lifting off from an anonymous airport runway. Then the VP, Spiro Agnew, enters a building in a crowd of other men. He's the only one I recognize. That balding head and Uncle Tonoose nose.

Curie heaves and gasps for breath as if the air in her house is no longer her natural element. Her reaction to the news report is the first real emotion I've seen from her in the days since she's been home. She is drowning in history, in the terror that underlies and illuminates in lurid, shifting colours every instant of our lives. I gather Eden into my arms and start to carry him up the stairs, his little blond head lolling in the crook of my arm. Before I can reach the second floor, however, Curie's retches turn into razor shrieks, and Eden, startled, jolts awake and begins to whine in sympathy. Luckily, the racket brings Mrs. Turnbull running from her cleaning chores upstairs. She halts at the top of the staircase to appraise the situation, and I dash up and thrust the squalling child into her arms.

"Get him settled down, *please!*" I tell her. I race back down the staircase and throw myself onto the couch beside Curie.

"Her pills are in the bathroom!" the old woman yells as she disappears down the upstairs hallway toward little Eden's room.

"I'll get your medication," I whisper to Curie, who has run out of screams and subsided back to soundless, wrenching dry heaves. Then I comically launch myself back up the stairs and run into the upstairs bathroom, where I pull a dozen or so bottles off the glass shelves of the mirrored cabinet above the sink in search of Curie's downers. Librium in hand, I careen back to the living room and carefully dole out two, then, what the hell, three, of the spansules. Then I'm into the kitchen to pour her some water and back to the couch just in time to hand her the glass before she chokes trying to swallow her pills between her uncontrollable whimpers.

"Take it easy," I say stupidly, as if I'm talking to a spooked horse or a dog that's caught a whiff of the neighbour's cat.

"He burned her face," she moans again, quietly this time, and sadly. Her makeup has pooled in the hollows underneath her eyes and streaked her face in rivulets, blue, black, pink, purple. She lifts her striated, crumpled face toward the ceiling, the rack of her anorexic chest sobbing pitifully against me as I hold her, mumbling platitudes and wishing I was anywhere but where I am.

After half an hour, Mrs. Turnbull appears. She asks if I've given Curie her medication, then nods and goes into the downstairs bathroom, from which she emerges with a facecloth with which she dabs at Curie's face. Minutes later, Richard Crashaw arrives. He throws his coat on an armchair and hurries across the carpet to his daughter. Curie is now semi-conscious. Her eyes flicker open, she mumbles something inaudible.

"What did you say to her, Wheeler?" Crashaw says. "What did you do to upset her?"

I shake my head and walk past him, gather my jacket from the coat stand and head for the door. "Ask her," I say over my shoulder. Then I'm outside, in a cool wind that ruffles the leaves of the chestnut, walking east toward my parents' place, alone.

A couple of weekends later, I got up while Clyde and Betty were still asleep and headed out into the yard. Clyde had left the car keys in the ashtray as always: I started up the engine, gunning it a couple of times to get it running smoothly, and pulled out of the driveway, kicking up a little spray of gravel as I let out the clutch. As I drove away, I could see the woman in the house across the road part her bedroom curtains and sneak a look at me. I smiled through the car window and gave her the finger. Tell that to the Fucking Big Idiots.

I motored across town to the Crashaws'. It was still pretty early on a Saturday morning, and the oak-lined street was empty except for a couple of plush-looking ginger cats who were sunning themselves in mottled light on the sidewalk a couple of doors down from the Crashaws' whitewashed box. I hadn't been by to see Eden in weeks.

I prodded the doorbell a half-dozen times, cursing under my breath with impatience, then finally Mrs. Turnbull opened the door and asked me what I wanted.

"My kid," I said. "I'm here to see Eden."

"Is it your day to see Eden?"

"Sure it is, Tuesday, Wednesday, whatever. Where is he? Upstairs in the playroom?" Crashaw had converted one of the upstairs bedrooms into a playroom for Eden; it was at the rear of the house, on a hallway that joined the master bedroom to Curie's old room.

Mrs. Turnbull looked around nervously. "Mr. Crashaw isn't feeling well. I think you'd better come back tomorrow."

"I'm not here to see Crashaw," I told her as I shouldered past.

"Mr. Crashaw is sick!" the old woman protested.

"This whole fucking country's sick," I said. I looked around the foyer, and then headed for the stairs. The woman followed me, clucking about her boss being sick and her not having the authority to let me into the house and so forth. "Where's Curie?" I asked her.

"I don't know. You'd have to ask her father."

My boy was in the playroom, right where he usually was before breakfast, sitting on the carpet watching cartoons on the colour TV.

"Where's Grandpa?" he asked me. He sounded apprehensive, as if he wanted his grandfather there to protect him, and that faint tinge of fear in his delicate little-boy's voice took all the anger out of me, made me feel as if I'd been walking into wind for miles and it had suddenly died down.

"What's Uncle Scrooge doing?" I asked him. He turned his head and went back to looking blankly at the animated images on the TV screen.

"It's not Uncle Scrooge," he said, matter-of-factly.

He was right. It was Ludwig von Drake, the professor duck who was often in the more educational Disney cartoons. Ludwig was explaining something to the three little Disney-ducklings, Huey, Dewey and Louie. He swept his pointer across the surface of a blackboard, and it was instantly covered in a forest of mathematical equations. The duck-kids looked suitably impressed.

"That Ludwig, you know, he's one of those longhairs," I said. I pulled at my own recently cut hair and Eden looked away from his cartoon long enough to treat me to a tentative smile.

The door of the family room opened and Mr. Crashaw looked in. He was wearing a tartan dressing gown over his pyjamas, but his hair was neatly brushed and he'd shaved.

"Eden? Are you all right?" he asked.

"He's fine," I said. "Absolutely ducky."

The old man ignored me. "Mrs. Turnbull, will you come here for a moment, please?" he shouted as loudly as his asthmatic-sounding lungs would allow him.

The old woman appeared in the doorway behind Crashaw, peering nervously over his shoulder and plucking at the collar of her apron.

"Keep an eye on the child," Crashaw said. "Sonny and I have things to discuss."

"Come along, Eden," the woman said.

"You don't have to do what they say," I told Eden, but he got up off the floor and, giving me a fragment of a smile as he walked past, docilely followed the housekeeper down the hall.

Crashaw shut the playroom door.

"What the hell do you think you're doing?" He lifted his little banty-rooster head, the muscles in his scrawny, old man's neck clenching, and glared at me out of those arctic-blue eyes. I had the urge to smash him against the wall, grasp his skinny little chicken neck and shake him until he dropped.

"Eden's my son," I said.

"He carries your genes," Crashaw said, his voice quivering. "Apart from that, I'm not sure I know what you mean."

I stepped back, hands on my hips, shaking my head with frustration. Clenched and opened my fists.

"You know I have rights, Richard. You and Curie wanted it, it wasn't just my idea."

"It wasn't your idea at all," Crashaw said. He was keeping his voice down to a whisper so the housekeeper couldn't hear.

"Well, it was Curie's. She wants me with Eden, no matter what you may think."

The lined face jerked upward, and he sniffed, mouth pursed into a net of wrinkles, glacial eyes flashing. "This has been a dreadful time for my daughter, Wheeler. Dreadful." He paused and sniffed again, as if he were having trouble drawing breath. "She was too young for this, much too young to have children. She was always a fragile girl. High-strung, too much like her mother."

Crashaw fingered the frogged lapel of his dressing gown. His hand was blue-veined, pale as wax.

"Giving birth was the death of Curie's mother, and Curie's always blamed me for that, I suspect. Not consciously, but deep in her feelings. This Potter woman she goes on about is part of a pattern. Men make women pregnant, they seduce or they rape them, women die."

He stepped away from the door to the playroom and lowered his voice.

"I'm an old man, Wheeler. I've already raised a child alone. I've my own life to think of. My health. It's time for you to face up to your responsibilities. To be a proper father. You have a job, Wheeler, even if it's only as a labourer. Your parents have some money. It's you who should be responsible for Eden. When Curie's feeling herself again, when she's older and more able to cope with this business . . ."

"I can't marry Curie, if that's what you mean."

A flicker of anger came back into the old man's eyes. He raised his jaw combatively, though his lower lip was trembling.

"That didn't stop you from getting what you wanted, though, did it?"

"That's not the way it is any more, man. I'm free, so's Curie. We did what we wanted, that's all."

"You and your free love! Generation of traitors and cowards, the whole bloody lot of you! I pity poor Eden and the rest of his kind—brought up by people who are babies themselves! They're the ones who'll have to live with your betrayals."

Crashaw's face crumpled and he covered his eyes with his sleeve and retreated toward the doorway to his bedroom.

"Just go now," he muttered. "Just go."

Back in the car I popped the clutch and peeled away from the curb and down the block, where I let the Studie get away from me long enough to make it fishtail and screech its tires before I headed for the highway.

Three hours later, pretty good time even by my stepfather's standards, I was parking in front of the Winterhaven Street house. As I ran up the front steps, I noticed that an ancient couch from the upstairs had been dragged outside and left to rot in the damp of the narrow veranda. A bottle-green blanket, thick with dog hair, was balled up in the doorway, as if someone had been using it for a doorstop. The living room was pretty much empty, and there were two good-sized holes in the back wall about a foot above the baseboard. I heard the sound of someone hammering or pounding away at something in the back of the house, and for a moment the logical if unlikely possibility that someone was trying to renovate the place crossed my mind. When I got to the kitchen, I could see what was making the noise. Buster was kicking a hole in the wall. He'd already knocked out a sizable cavity beside the kitchen table, and now he was working on a strip beneath the window. His workboot was white with Sheetrock dust and he was red-faced and sweating from the effort.

"What's happened to Karen?" I asked.

Buster just glared at me and went right on kicking holes in the plaster. Gloria Lee kept her head down, but at the sound of my voice she started rocking, knees up to her chin, face buried in a nest of tangled brown hair, rocking herself into fetal security like some hopelessly autistic child.

Magic Annie wandered in from the backyard. She seemed distracted, hardly paying any attention to my arrival—or to the fact that one of her roommates was systematically destroying the house. She was holding a four-inch paintbrush that was clotted with dried purple paint, and she seemed to be having trouble finding somewhere to put it down.

"Karen's been busted," she said. "The pigs picked her up on the Ave. after midnight. Her and a couple of dudes from the Wesley Street house have all been indicted. Conspiracy to incite or some such bullshit. Jarrold got his old man's lawyer down there first thing this morning. He figures they might kick her on bail."

"Shit," I said. "Where the fuck is she?"

"I don't know," Annie said. She gave me a wistful smile and lifted the paintbrush. "Maybe the courthouse?"

"So where the hell is Jarrold?"

"Vanishing," Magic Annie said. She looked at her clotted paintbrush as if she were noticing it for the first time and then turned and went back out the door into the yard.

"Vanishing? What the fuck does she mean?"

Buster stopped kicking the Sheetrock and glared at me.

"The tunnels, pig," he said. "Everybody's living in tunnels. We're digging in, burrowing, chopping out dirt. Pretty soon, there won't be nobody left above ground but you pigs."

I turned away and walked through the rubble in the living room, leaving Buster kicking in the wallboard and Gloria Lee whimpering into her nest of hair.

Downtown, there were five or six hippies hanging around outside the courthouse. A couple of them were trying to hassle the clerks who came and went, but it was nothing you could call a demonstration. I recognized a dumpy blond girl from the meetings around the ROTC demonstration and asked her what was happening.

"I don't know, man. Karen and Diana Jameson and Clint and some other dude from Wesley Street got made for incitement. The bail hearing's set for this afternoon, I hear. Word is the pigs are going to keep the people locked up until the trial date."

I bounded up the steps and made my way through the crowd in the entrance. I was looking for someone to ask directions when I saw Tom Brownschidle picking his way through the throng.

"What's happening?" I asked him. "Where's Karen?"

"It's cool, man," he told me. He brushed past, headed for the front doors in a hurry, hands thrust into the pockets of his pea jacket and his shoulders hunched as if he were striding into a heavy wind. "Jarrold's lawyer got her kicked. She's up at his parents' place in Highlands. Him and his old man made bail."

I followed him out onto the front steps of the courthouse.

"What happens now?"

He stopped and turned to look at me. "Nothing. There'll probably be a hearing. Then they have to set a trial date. Could take weeks or even months."

"So what are we supposed to do?"

"Nothing, man. Just try to keep your mouth shut and stay cool." He shouldered his rucksack and trudged off down the stone stairs to the street.

I got home just after sunset. I parked the car in the driveway—Betty's car was in the carport—and put Clyde's keys back in the ashtray. The house was dark when I went inside, and I thought for a minute that Clyde had gone out. I wandered into the kitchen and helped myself to a couple of Dad's chocolate chip cookies from the jar beneath the window. It was pretty much dark outside by this time, and all I could see of the backyard was the line of the fence, pure black against relative darkness, and the silver glints of the tinfoil Clyde had put up around the vegetable patch to discourage hungry birds. The sun was down, but there was still a dusty crimson stain like a vein of ore running horizontally across the western sky. I stood there for a minute and stared at it, and that was when I heard my stepfather coming in through the double glass doors from the deck.

"Going to be cool tonight," he said. "Wish I'd thought to put those cloches on the peppers and tomatoes."

"Yeah," I said. I opened the fridge door and took out a carton of milk.

"Your mother's asleep," Clyde said.

I nodded.

"She'd been sleeping since just after noon," he continued. "I suppose that it's good for her to sleep as much as she can. Might give her a chance to build up her strength." He turned the light over the range on and surveyed the room, as if he were surprised at what it looked like in the light.

"When's the next operation?" I asked, though I already had a pretty good idea when it was.

"A week from tomorrow," Clyde said. "I'm driving her up to Seattle the night before. We'll get a hotel room."

I took a long swig from the carton of milk and then finished the rest of the cookie. Clyde took his penknife out of the pocket of his polyester slacks and started scraping out the bowl of his pipe. I waited for him to mention the fact that I'd taken off with his car for two days, but he didn't seem inclined to broach the subject.

"You know, when I started here in '46, you never heard much talk of cancer. Now they talk about it all the time. Eating meat, they say, causes it. Other foods, some of them pretty darned innocuous. You've heard this stuff about strontium 90?"

"In milk?" I asked. I drained the last of the milk from the carton and held it up to show him.

"I remember ten or twelve years ago, we'd sometimes take a Geiger counter and drive up across the bridge to where the old village of Danforth used to be, before the military expropriated everything and started constructing the nuclear reserve. We'd drive up every second or third dirt road we came to and wander around on the farms. You know that country, Sonny?"

"You drove me up there once, with Mom. She wanted to see some farms, I think."

"Yes," Clyde said, "I guess we did. That would have been when your mother was thinking a lot about where she grew up. Saskatchewan. The little town she and your grandparents lived in."

"Mainprize," I said.

"That was it," he said. "Mainprize, Saskatchewan. Wheat country, I believe she said. Hundreds of acres of barley and wheat."

He shook out the bowl of the pipe above the sink and ran some water.

"When we came across sheep or cattle on the farms," he continued, pushing his glasses up against the bridge of his nose and looking towards the window, which was now so black he couldn't have seen much of anything except his own reflected face, "we'd check them out for radioactivity. Put the counter right up against the animal's neck, to check for radioactive isotopes of iodine in the thyroid. Some of them were all right, you know, within acceptable limits in any case, not much hotter than you and I might get working in restricted zones up at the Area. Others, quite a few, were pretty bad. Once in while, fairly often, we'd put the machine against the neck of a cow or a sheep and the needles would go right off both scales. Those animals were hotter than pistols."

"They were downwind from the Area?"

Clyde nodded. "That's right," he said. "You could draw a straight line from the Area halfway to Spokane, and count on finding cattle that had got themselves a dose of radiation. There was plenty of other ways of telling, of course. Cows were throwing deformed calves, some of them black and twisted, like nothing you could ever imagine. Others would throw calves early; there were a lot that just aborted. Others would die, just lie down in the fields like they'd worn themselves out, and the vets couldn't find any plausible reason. They didn't have any known diseases, they hadn't been injured, they just damn well decided to lie down and die."

His mouth knotted up as he spoke, as if he were trying not to let himself seem angry.

"You've known about this since then?" I asked. "Before Betty and I even came here?"

"I knew," Clyde repeated, looking down at his pipe, which he was packing with a wad of fresh tobacco, even though he had just cleaned it out.

"And Betty, had you told her?"

Clyde shook his head.

"Security, right?"

Clyde nodded. He fished a match out of the pocket of his short-sleeved shirt and snapped it alight with his thumbnail. "People know," he added. "Did anyone ever tell *you?*" He puffed at his pipe to get it going, and then we both stood there in the kitchen in silence for a while, neither of us in any hurry to end the day and get to bed. I looked at his hands as he cradled his meerschaum. They were highlighted by the warmth of the small incandescent bulb in the range hood, and Clyde seemed to me a figure in a painting, someone half obscured by shadows at the border of a group scene, only his wrist bones and fingers visible in a fragile sphere of light. I looked at him and thought of my father. Had either of them chosen his war?

"Mom will be seriously pissed if her prize tomatoes get hit with the frost," I said. "Let's go put out those cloches of yours. We can turn on the lights on the deck."

"Good idea," my stepfather said. "You go and switch the lights on. I'll start bringing the cloches out from under the porch."

We were out there for close to an hour, working quietly and slowly in the dim yellow light from the deck. Neither of us said anything; possibly Clyde was worried about waking up the neighbours. The work was finicky anyway; you had to position each of the cloches carefully over the tomato or pepper plant, making sure not to knock the green fruit off the branches or damage the tender spreading plants. We finished the job at five to twelve, then we stood there with our hands on our hips looking around at Betty's garden.

"Only Betty would put a garden in the middle of the desert," Clyde said. I was surprised to hear him call my mother "Betty"; he usually referred to her as "your mother" or "Mom," and to strangers he called her "my wife." We stayed there a few minutes longer, two men with nothing much to say in a suburban yard near midnight. Then Clyde knocked out his pipe against the heel of his deck shoe, and both of us went back inside the house to get some sleep.

19

Return to Bizarro Planet

Late February. A Saturday blank as onyx. We were sitting in Ariel's townhouse. Karen phoned me at Clyde and Betty's place and asked me to drive up to Seattle and give her a hand to move some stuff. When I arrived, I found Karen packing. She was balling up her clothes and stuffing them into a garbage bag, one of those big green vinyl trash-catcher jobs. Ariel had shut herself in the larger bedroom before I arrived, but after I'd watched Karen sort and pack for five or ten minutes, she burst out of the bedroom and dashed into the john. Minutes later, I heard coughing and retching.

"She all right? What's going on?"

"She's puking, for Christ's sake. Can't you hear?"

"Sounds pretty bad. She seen the doc?"

"She doesn't need a doctor. She's not really sick."

"She sounds pretty sick to me."

Karen stopped packing long enough to stare at the bathroom door.

"Women learn to do that."

"To throw up?"

That got me a scornful look. She strode into the bedroom and came back with an armload of tie-dyed shirts and blue jeans. "Women internalize their oppression." She stopped and pushed the bathroom door open. Ariel was slumped beside the bathtub in a tight fetal curl. "Her body is America. It's full of fat and peasants' blood. She's vomiting to purge herself. To puke up her father and mother. It's the only thing left that'll make her feel clean."

"You sound like Curie Crashaw."

"Yeah? Little Curie's developing a revolutionary consciousness despite herself, is she? I wonder who's responsible for that."

I fished a cigarette out of my shirt pocket and snapped it alight with my Zippo.

"Fucked if I know."

"Oh yeah? That's your story and you're sticking to it, right?"

I exhaled a plume of smoke between my knees and deposited the cigarette in an ashtray. "Things happen, Karen. It doesn't mean there's anything between us."

"Hey, none of my business, right? You don't think I have problems of my own?"

Since the last time I'd seen her, Karen had been out to Chicago, where she'd managed to get herself busted again. Thousands had been expected to converge on the city to bring the war home to the streets of America; a few hundred showed up. They ran through the streets trashing storefronts, smashing windows, lighting fires. Quite a few of them wound up getting clubbed by cops and hustled into holding cells to wait for their parents to come up with bail. Karen's trial date was next spring; the Seattle trial was apparently going to happen around the same time. She'd chopped her hair into spiky tufts since I'd seen her last and dyed it a chemical blond. Her voice and gestures had taken on a frantic edge: she spoke and moved like a figure in an out-of-sync home movie, a few revolutions too fast for real life.

"What's this shit about going underground? That just Buster making noises?" I picked up a copy of *T. V. Picture Life* from the end table. *Jackie Gleason & His Sweetheart Split After 15 Years! This is the Baby Liz Montgomery Thought She Could Never Love!*

Karen stared at me, cobalt eyes registering suspicion. "Buster? What did he tell you?"

"That everyone's vanishing, was pretty much what he said. Disappearing so the federal pigs can't find them."

"Fuck," Karen hissed. She dropped the Glad bag into which she'd been shoving clothing, paced to the window, then came back and pulled my Camels out of the pocket of my shirt.

"You're welcome," I said. I fished around in my jeans and found my lighter.

She held her hair away from her face and leaned towards the flame.

"Classified information, right?"

She took a long, luxurious drag and French-inhaled the smoke, then blew it in a stream toward the ceiling.

"That stupid son of a bitch had no goddamned business telling anyone anything. That's only been discussed in the collective. Fuck, he shouldn't even *know* about shit like that. Some idiot's been mouthing off too much."

"So it's true?"

Karen sat down, took another drag, and levelled her entomologist's gaze on me. *This creature exhibits slight signs of intelligence.*

"We're purging anyone who isn't ready for direct action, Sonny. All the contacts will be cut off, including you and Buster and some of the others. The rest will work in focals— independent cells, maybe three or four people, that's all. They'll execute their own local actions. Identify targets and strike them. That way, the FBI pigs can't root out the whole organization. No one but the Weather Bureau will really know what's going on."

"And you're cutting me off? What's that about, Karen? Some head game of Jarrold's, I bet."

"Jarrold thinks you're a plant, man. You know that?"

"A *plant?* What d'you mean? Like an FBI snitch? Did you tell that cunt I've known you since, what was it, sophomore year? Did you tell him what went down at the demo?"

Three strides took her back to the window. She inhaled, funnelled smoke against the wet Seattle landscape, paced back to square one and stuffed a few more wrinkled skirts into the Glad bag.

"You need to prove him wrong, man. Get involved in some more actions. Demonstrate a genuine commitment." She lifted her head as if listening carefully, analytically, to Ariel's constricted inhalations. "Otherwise"—the blue eyes sliced sideways—"why wouldn't he think you're a pig?"

By nightfall we washed up across town at Winterhaven Street. It was nine or nine-thirty. Ultimate Spinach had spun itself into silence, and I lifted the tone arm, removed the record and slipped it back into its sleeve. Rain and wind made soft sounds in the trees along the street. Jarrold had settled himself into the peacock chair and Karen was on the carpet at his feet. I was conscious of both of them watching me as I crossed the room and sat down on the couch. When I looked up, they were staring at me intently, as if they expected me to make some sort of announcement or spontaneously combust. The room was quiet except for the sound of Gloria Lee's asthmatic wheezing, which she was doing her best to muffle behind her hand. Everyone seemed to be waiting for something to happen.

It was Tom Brownschidle who finally spoke.

"Criticism self-criticism," he said simply. "Sonny, you can stay this time. The collective has decided to include you in the work today, since you carried out your organizational duties around the ROTC demo all right."

The demonstration at the UW Air Force ROTC building had been strictly a women's action, but I'd helped out painting signs and finding spray-bombs for the women who were going to do the scene. I'd used Clyde's car to ferry the half-dozen women to the campus, and then I'd followed them as far as the doors of the building to make sure they didn't get hassled by campus cops or ROTC creeps. I watched as Karen, who was wearing my old Danforth High football helmet, spray-painted black for the occasion, disappeared into the building with her comrades. Since the night we'd smashed the window on the Ave., she'd been treating me more as an equal, more like someone involved in the larger struggle, and less like a tedious, occasionally welcome old boyfriend who couldn't stop hanging around.

"Things are heating up all over the city," Tom continued. "Our collective needs to make plans for a decisive action. Something that will galvanize the people's frustration. Make them want to kick the pigs until they drop."

Tom pushed his glasses back onto the bridge of his nose and swiped his lank brown hair off his forehead. As he spoke, some of the others muttered "Right on!" and held up three fingers in a stiff-armed salute. Jarrold, arrayed in the peacock chair with the light from the antique standing lamp burnishing his unshaven cheeks and highlighting his cheekbones, nodded pensively in agreement.

"What's this thing with the fingers?" I whispered to Magic Annie, who was sitting beside me on the couch, bare feet tucked under her bottom. "A peace sign with a penis?"

Annie giggled. "That's the fork, man."

I must have shrugged or registered incomprehension. Karen, who'd apparently been watching us, spoke up from across the room.

"When the Manson people offed that bourgeois Hollywood bitch and her friends, man, they stuck a fork in her pregnant belly. 'When they'd killed the pig, they stuck a fork in her,' that's what Bernadine said at the Flint thing, man. So now that's our sign, right? The fork."

"Are you a pig, man?" Magic Annie said. She grinned wolfishly and jabbed at my ribs with her fingers. "Stick a fork in him, see if he's done!"

"You look about ready to eat, yourself." I skimmed a finger along the top of her peasant blouse and tugged gently at the elastic. I shot a glance sideways, but Karen was already deep in conversation with Nina and didn't meet my eyes. Gloria Lee's asthma got the better of her for a moment, and she started into a fit of shallow, gasping coughs. Though she seemed to be in some distress, none of us did anything to help her. When the noise of her attack had died down, Tom continued with his rap.

"The Bureau's been concerned about monogamous things happening between people here. The word from the Bureau is smash them. Smash monogamy, man."

"Right on," Nina said. "Who needs that bourgeois shit?"

The elimination of monogamy was one of Weatherman's more recent objectives. No families. No parents. No husbands and wives. Sex should be communal, like everything else. I'd heard talk of orgies at Weatherman houses, the famous Weatherman Wargasm, but what I'd seen at Winterhaven was pretty much what you'd expect at any local head house—some one-night stands, some couples whose relationships were as stodgy and predictable as any suburban marriage, some people who didn't seem to be in on the action at all.

"Tom," Gloria Lee said, "what about you and Nina?"

The question hung in the air with the shoals of cigarette smoke.

"We're comrades," Tom said decisively. "The work comes first for both of us. Anything else is just a side trip."

"That's such a copout," Gloria Lee said. Tom began to argue in a reasoned, unhurried manner, explaining the distinction between bourgeois monogamy and a sexual relationship between two dedicated revolutionaries. I found myself losing track of the conversation, partially because I'd heard Tom's bullshit several times before, from him and from Karen and from others, and partially because Magic Annie kept coming on to me, stroking my leg with her bare foot and tugging playfully at my hair.

"Open wide," she finally said. "It's time for your medicine." She showed me a square of blue blotter paper that was balanced on the tip of her finger. "Windowpane. It's really, really mellow. You'll love it. I just copped a couple myself."

"I'm not into chemicals these days."

She giggled. "This is more like a hash high. Just try it."

I opened my mouth, and she delicately dropped the paper on my tongue.

The criticism of Nina and Tom went on for what seemed like an hour or more, with Gloria Lee attacking and Tom and Nina defending themselves adroitly, Tom arguing his case in professorial tones that suggested a knowledge of critical theory far beyond anyone else's, throwing in quotes from Debray and Marcuse, and Nina angrily accusing her accusers, regardless of gender, of being closet male chauvinists who merely wanted women as playthings—both of them, in other words, relying on their trump cards to get them through what seemed to me a stylized and pointless discussion. Neither Jarrold nor Karen said anything.

Tom shifted in his armchair to confront me.

"Sonny, there's still the question of where you fit in."

Magic Annie prodded me and giggled. Everyone else stared expectantly, as if I were an amateur magician who was about to pull a rabbit from his hat. The silence stretched out like Silly Putty.

"He fits in everywhere, right?" Jarrold finally said. "He's young Mister Manythings, our Sonny. The original all-purpose solvent. One minute he's protesting nuclear arms, the next he goes home and makes A-bombs. He's Uncle Ho and McNamara in one convenient tinfoil package, and he's probably an archbishop on Sundays. He's the pigs and the revolution and Sergeant Joe Honky Nigger-Killing Greaser, and you get them all bundled up in one. Is that an irresistible bargain or what?"

Karen leaned forward and took a hit of Ripple from the twenty-sixer on the table. "Jarrold's right on, Sonny. You work at a death plant. You manufacture death."

"It's important to me, working at the Area," I said. My throat felt dry and tasted of metal, as if the blotter were cut with meth. "It's one thing to talk about the evil of America, it's another to observe it up close."

Jarrold huffed in exasperation. He turned himself sideways on the peacock chair and draped one leg over the arm.

"That's absolute criminal shit, man," Karen said. "You work at the bomb plant because that's what your mom and Clyde programmed you to do. You can't let go of Danforth. You're a little kid who can't leave his mommy."

I laughed, my voice seeming distant and tinny. "Hey, it's a living."

"You're not Bobby Deerborne. You don't have to think like a greaser."

I blinked at her, trying to clear my vision. The acid had started to kick in, and I could feel myself ascending the first coil of the spiral. I felt both very far from myself and very deep within my body. The effort of trying to speak seemed enormous: words were bubbles of thick, viscous liquid—slippery, unstructured, and heavier than air.

"You're a pig, man," Jarrold said. He spun back in the peacock chair to face me. "You cling to your white-skin priv-ilege. You're a lying bourgeois pig!"

"Fucking pig," Buster echoed. Gloria Lee's shrill, birdy voice took up the chant, "Pig! Pig! Pig! You're just a lying fucking pig, man, a lying fucking arrogant honky pig!" Then all of them were standing up, chanting: "PIG PIG PIG PIG MOTHERFUCKING PIG!"

Backlit figures circling a fire in the wastes of a vitrified desert. I lurched up and staggered to the doorway, which instantly veered away from me, elusive as a surface in a mirror. The door was a pillar and the pillars of the door frame were doorways. I stumbled out onto the porch, down the stairs. I could hear Buster screaming from the doorway, "RUN, PIG, RUN!" Then jagged arpeggios of laughter.

Hours later, I was sitting on a rain-wet bench on the boulevard beside a children's playground, shivering like a dog left out all winter. I'd come down enough to understand where I must be. The topography of the skyline, distant tow-ers against a hemisphere of clouds bathed in light from the city, seemed familiar. I also recognized Tom Brownschidle's

Volkswagen bus. I watched it without interest as it hissed to a stop, blunt nose angled up against the sidewalk. There were three or four people inside, I could tell. The passenger door opened and Karen stepped out.

"Jesus, man. You're hard to find."

I stared at her, my oldest friend. Rain slithered from my waterlogged hair.

"Come back now and be one of us. We're your family now, your brothers and sisters. There's no one else on Earth but us. Come back and be one of the tribe."

I stood up, the whole landscape lurching, and wandered slowly back to the bus.

The purest light flows from the window. Curie has her back to the window wall, and the shaft of morning brightness angles diagonally from the sky across the avenue to her feet on the red oak flooring, so that she is standing at the base of a slanted prism. In the past few months, Curie has transformed herself. Her body, blurred and vague since childbirth, has sharpened into focus. In her diaphanous empire-waisted dress and bone court heels, she is all geometry, verticals, angles—the cosine of bell sleeve, planes within the narrow back, triangle from clavicle to rib cage. She has starved herself to a filament, and the process has rendered her gestures and glances incandescent. Her eyes, rimmed in mascara, crimson eye shadow, brittle streaks of liner—the full Max Factor arsenal—regard the space above my head as if some purer, more rational, form of my spirit were hovering a foot or two above me.

I am kneeling on the carpet, watching Eden.

"I've spoken to her. Liesl. She's in hospital down in Los Angeles. I can't tell you where exactly. They're trying to kept her whereabouts secret."

"You talked to her? On the phone, you mean?"

"That's right. On the telephone."

Eden turns. He too is made of light, though in the shadow of the colonial sofa, his usual luminescence has been dimmed to gold and amber. He reaches toward me, his gaze on the tips of his fingers, as if the gesture were a simple act of nature like the opening of petals or the flicker of a bird's wing— something he has witnessed but not willed. I also reach, hold up one finger. He clasps it in his chubby fist, shakes it as if to test my strength and durability, then releases it and toddles in the direction of his mother.

"Is there anything they can do for her? Plastic surgery, I mean."

"Perhaps. Maybe someday. I mean, you couldn't ask her, could you?"

Curie turns to the window. She looks up into the canopy of the chestnut outside.

"She's been given some land, near Sacramento."

This comment strikes me as bizarre. It makes me think of what has happened to Liesl Potter as a part of some terrible primitive ritual for the selection and deification of a goddess. She is mutilated and given some land.

"Some women will take care of her. Only women."

As if to emphasize her point, to symbolize the theme of separation, Curie steps out of the shaft of light and crosses to the end of the sofa, the sound of her heels bright and metallic on the hardwood, then muffled by the thickly woven rug. She places her hand on the curved maple arm of the sofa, strokes it as if feeling its smoothness.

"I think I'm going to live there too. With Liesl, on the commune, if they'll let me."

Eden watches Curie solemnly. I wonder what he hears and sees. Adult words, their music of relentless hooves, their quick dance of pause and inflection. Adults facing each other, frozen in poses, oblivious to the possibilities of dust motes and sunlight and space.

"You think you'd be happy with that? A bunch of women living on a commune?"

"What have men brought into the world? Rape. War. The A-bomb. All those wonderful people that Dad used to talk about. Oppenheimer, Szilard, Fermi. Look what they brought into being. The bomb is so typical, just another natural product of that male need to hunt down everything untamed and inexplicable. The deer in the forest. The unpeopled islands. The dancing at the centre of an atom. To smash it and kill it and make it their own."

Eden has discovered the sunbeam. He reaches from relative darkness, rotates his chubby hand in its radiance. Then, emboldened, he steps into the luminous rhombus and is suddenly haloed with light.

"What about your namesake, Curie? Don't forget your old man's muse."

"She was trying to be something she wasn't. A man in a man's world. That's often an intelligent woman's mistake."

"That's such crap. She was a scientist, just like Einstein and the others. She started the process that led to the bomb."

"She believed in the purity of science. A male myth. She was wrong."

The issue, I understand, is settled. Curie sits on the couch almost sideways, knees together. She gasps, then exhales a racking sob, hand open over her face. Eden mewls like a distressed kitten, stumbles over to her, eyes moist and expectant. She cups her free hand on the top of his head as if to convey a blessing. "Go to Sonny," she whispers, her voice trembling slightly but otherwise under control.

"You take things too seriously, Curie," I tell her. She straightens, drops her hand from her face, which is wet with tears and already streaked with rivulets of liquefied makeup.

"And you don't? The wrong things . . ." She sobs again. I get up and pass her some Kleenex. We remain in that pose for several minutes, a tableau, Curie alternately sniffling and dabbing her face, me kneeling a foot from her bare knees on the floor, as if this were a freeze dance in high school.

"So what about Eden?" I finally ask. "You're a mother now. You have a kid. It's not like you can just take off and leave him."

"I'm not a mother."

"You're Eden's mother. Eden's your child."

Curie glances around the room as if she's looking for something she's misplaced. "I never *had* a mother. How can I be one myself?"

"I don't think you have a choice, Curie. Someone has to look after Eden."

"Mrs. Turnbull can look after Eden. She was my nanny, wasn't she? What's the matter with her?"

"Nothing, I guess."

I get up from my knees and offer my hand to my son, who clasps it reflexively and follows me out of the room. Mrs. Turnbull's in the kitchen, wiping counters with unnecessary vigour. I wonder how much she's been able to hear. She gathers the boy to her wide, solid body and packs him outside into the glassy greens and blues of afternoon. When I get back in the living room, Curie hasn't moved. She's crumpled, though, curled into herself so that her forehead almost touches her knees. She's still sobbing, quietly, and the Kleenex I gave her is balled in her fist. I walk to the front door and let myself out.

20

Precognition

In the first week of March, a bomb went off in a townhouse in New York City. Three people were killed, all of them members of a Weatherman cell. Two women escaped, one having to pick her way over the rubble of the building's collapsed upper floor and walk naked out into the street. One of the dead was identified by a single fingerprint: all that was ever found of her was one finger. One of the others was never found at all; he had been making an anti-personnel bomb, taping roofing nails to bundles of dynamite; his body was disintegrated by the violence of the blast. The Winterhaven cadre watched the televised reports of the explosion on the colour set at Ariel's townhouse. Ariel, who had been hospitalized twice for anorexia in the past year, sat on a stool at the bar in the kitchen and prodded a plate of carrot sticks like a lethargic cat teasing a mouse. Her cheeks were concave and heavily rouged, and she had cut her hair short and dyed it blond in obvious imitation of Karen's new ragamuffin look.

"Why do you care if they're dead?" she kept saying. "They're idiots. Boring people. Morons."

Jarrold, who claimed to know one of the survivors, slouched in Ariel's La-Z-Boy and glared at her every time she spoke. Karen sat on the floor with her head in her hands, feathers of platinum hair jetting up between her fingers, not even watching the TV. Tom Brownschidle, Nina and Magic Annie had taken the only couch. I sat on the floor in the opposite corner of the small room from Karen and wondered what I was doing in Seattle. It was Sunday night. I had to be at work back at Zee Plant in less than twelve hours. The drive alone would take close to four, if I wanted to get home without getting a ticket. I was bone tired from sleeping on floors for two nights and working the previous five. I would have to pop uppers to make it.

"Ted Gold was in that apartment," Karen said. "I saw him at Flint, in the General Ballroom. He did this incredible rap . . ."

Karen's idea tailed off into silence. Nina leaned back on Tom's lap and blew cigarette smoke at the ceiling. We stayed like that, frozen, even Ariel keeping her mouth shut, until finally Lister lifted his head from his hands and spoke.

"We need to do something serious, for fuck's sake. Hit the pigs in their fat, slimy bellies."

He leaned forward and put his hands together, palms open and fingertips touching, as if in meditation or prayer.

"We need to plan an action. A gesture that will embody our rage and disgust for all time. Something Mr. and Mrs. White-Bread America won't easily forget."

"A monument to the Freedom Fighters, man," Tom Brownschidle whispered.

Nothing much had changed since the winter. Karen and a few others were still out on bail, awaiting trail on the incitement charge from the previous summer. Karen also faced charges in Chicago. She was waiting for something to happen, it seemed, and so were the rest of the cadre.

"Let's rip off the Area," I said.

There was silence for a moment.

"The *what?*" Jarrold finally said.

"The Area. Danforth. The bomb plant."

There was a moment of silence, as if everyone were thinking my suggestion over.

"Shit, man," Jarrold said finally. "That's dumb. I mean, where the fuck is Danforth? Who knows about that? Who cares?"

"Jarrold's right, man," Tom added.

"Fuck, no!" Karen said. "You ought to fucking listen to Sonny. He's right-on about this. What do the pigs fear most? A-bombs, right? A gang of righteous revolutionaries with a nuke at their disposal would really make them shit their britches, wouldn't it? Talk about bringing the war home! What a trip!"

She looked around the room at each of us, her mouth hanging open and her ice-blue eyes alight.

"What about it, Wheeler?" Jarrold said.

I hesitated for a moment. I'd thought about this quite a bit—all those nights in my time-capsule teenager's bedroom on Argon Crescent feeling disgusted with myself for working at the Area, imagining ways to cripple the reactors, kill the monster that was slowly killing Betty, shut down the death plant forever.

"Well?" Karen asked. Her eyes locked in on mine. She was sparkling, bright with life and energy in a way I hadn't seen since we were kids in Danforth.

"It's doable," I said. "The AEC and the contractors who run the Area are more concerned with espionage than they are with people breaking in and fucking up equipment. Security isn't as tight as you might think."

"What's doable?" Brownschidle said. "Sabotage? Demonstrations? Building a bomb?"

"Stealing a plutonium button."

"Right on!" Karen whispered.

"What's the point, Wheeler? Where does it get us?" This was Jarrold. He sat back in the armchair and stroked his two-day stubble.

"Jarrold's right," Brownschidle said. "What use is this plutonium if you don't have expertise? You need someone to tell you how to use it. There can't be many people around, even physicists, who could really make an A-bomb."

"That's not the point," I said. "You just get the button out, that's all. Then you start to make demands."

"It's theatre, man," Karen interposed.

"That's right," I said.

Karen stood up. "Dig it," she said. Her razored hair tufted around her head like a burning corona. "The Weather Theatre presents the Apocalypse. One performance only. A holocaust right in your own fucking home!"

"Right on," Nina said, and a couple of the others also muttered their approval. Karen flashed me a mad grin. Ten minutes later, she had followed Jarrold out to his Alfa for the drive into the city. It was the last time I'd see her alive.

Mr. Crashaw was in the living room, a space that was in theory used for entertaining guests but which under normal circumstances seemed purely ornamental—this was the first time I'd seen anyone actually sitting on the *faux*–Louis Quatorze brocade. I hovered in the doorway for a few moments while Crashaw completely ignored me. He was gazing into the fireplace, which contained nothing but a set of handsome brass fire dogs that had clearly never been exposed to a flame.

"Where's Curie?" I finally asked.

"Gone," the old man told me.

While I waited for him to elaborate, I wandered into the room and took a seat on a small brocade hassock. Crashaw registered my presence with a flick of his eyes, but he didn't—as I'd half expected him to—try to order me off his furniture and out of the room.

"She's gone off to a farm in California. A *commune.*" He pronounced the word with a terrible bitterness and finality.

"The Liesl Potter thing, right?"

He pursed his lips and stared at the vacant fireplace. "Apparently someone has donated the land and some money: it's a considerable amount of money, as it happens—ten or twelve million dollars, I believe. The land is in California, the northern part of the state, near Ukiah or Sacramento. The Potter girl will live there, and the intention is for several other women to live there with her, presumably to look after her needs."

I guess I must have nodded.

"Doesn't interest you, I take it? The mother of your child runs off to a commune and leaves you—or me, I suppose—with the infant, and all you can do is sit there and nod like an owl?"

"Yeah. That's about it, I guess." I stood up and headed for the door. If Curie's departure didn't interest me, it was probably because she'd barely acknowledged my existence, or anyone's, in the months since she'd come back from the clinic. And I certainly hadn't busted my ass to acknowledge hers. Her presence in my life was both a reprimand and a threat—I was sick with guilt at the way I'd treated her and scared shitless that I'd be tied to her and Eden and my job at the Area forever, one more drone with a loveless marriage, a kid to support, and a dead-end job. "I'm going to take Eden down to the playground," I said as I retrieved my jacket from the coat rack in the foyer. "That all right with you?"

Crashaw continued to stare at the fireplace. He opened his mouth as if to speak, then sighed and began to rub his forehead with the tips of his fingers. "He's your son, Wheeler. Just let Mrs. Turnbull know. She worries."

A few weeks later, a single sheet of plain white bond in a business-sized envelope arrived, addressed to me, care of Clyde and Betty Cateret, 3542 Argon Crescent, Danforth, Washington.

Sonny,

Take care of Eden. He belongs, of course, to neither of us, but we created him, however blindly. However poorly qualified you may be to do so, try to save him from himself. Father's old and I am leaving now, forever. You must try to find the father in your heart.

Curie

I was fixing myself a sandwich when the phone rang.

"Yeah?" I said into the receiver.

"She's dead," a voice said. It was a woman's voice, distant and muffled. Gloria Lee? Curie? Magic Annie?

"What? I can't hear you."

"She's dead. Your little friend Karen. The house blew up. She's dead."

Curie. It had to be Curie. But where could she be calling from? Potter's commune in the mountains?

"I can't hear you," I said. "Speak up."

"She's dead. Karen Sullivan. She blew herself to smithereens. They're all dead now, all of them, Mommy and Daddy and Buddy and Sis. Their creepy old house just went *poof!*"

No, I decided, that wasn't Curie Crashaw's voice. I felt a chill snake up my spine.

"I can't hear you," I said. "This is a bad connection. I can't hear you."

There was a *click,* and the line went dead. I stood there and listened to the dial tone. This is the sound of nothing, I thought. What was it before there were telephones? Wind?

The absence of wind, the hole in the air when the wind stops? The ozone air after a cloudburst?

The dial tone. That's the sound of the world without God, or at least it is for someone who came into this world when I did. Dead air. The blank rush of mortality. A connection you just couldn't make.

I put down the phone, then picked it up again and dialled Karen's parents' home number. I got her brother Anthony, who didn't seem any more morose and uncommunicative than usual.

"She's living in Seattle now," he said, giving an exasperated thrust of emphasis to the name of the city. What was I, completely retarded? Didn't I even know that Karen hadn't lived at home for years?

I had just hung up, convinced that the call I'd received had been an ugly practical joke, the local narcs or the Fucking Big Idiots playing head games or some freak from the Winterhaven house making trouble, when the telephone rang again. This time I knew the voice.

"Sonny, it's Tom. Karen and Gloria and Annie, they're dead. And Indian Jimmy from Frisco. They were making a pipe bomb. The fucking thing blew up. Nina got out okay, but nobody else. You'd better keep your head down for a while."

There is no public funeral. Karen's parents shut themselves inside their house, her brothers disappear from school, Lionel takes a leave of absence. They have gone out of the country, moved to Seattle, been transformed into sparks of moonlight like children in a myth. The local rumours add up to nothing. Not that any of it matters. Karen's death is an aura that radiates from my body. I feel her as an absence, the shadow of a running woman burned into a wall.

Three weeks after the bomb blast, I am sitting in a co-op house a few blocks from the Ave. The remnants of Seattle Weatherman are draped on the usual thrift-shop furniture—Tom Brownschidle sits on a swaybacked couch, Nina with her bare feet tucked under her thighs, head lolling on Brownschidle's shoulder, Buster with his head between his knees on the rug in front of them, Jarrold Lister in Peter Fonda aviator shades and the scurf of a burgeoning Che Guevara beard in a chair beside the stereo. I've drifted here from the Ave. with Nina and Tom, whom I ran into while trying to score some MDA from a kid outside the Korean restaurant. I don't know what I'm doing back in Seattle—I've been daring myself to go and see what's left of the Winterhaven house, but I can't seem to get any closer than my old haunts on the Ave. Some part of me is still denying that the accident ever occurred; Karen has been somewhere, just hiding, and soon I'll wander into a coffeehouse or deli and see her sitting at a table in the corner, scanning the latest *Helix* while she sips her espresso black.

"This changes nothing," Tom Brownschidle says.

"What the fuck do you mean, man? Karen's dead. Gloria Lee and the others. They're dead." There's a genuine anger in my voice as I say this, but I'm hoping that he'll vehemently deny it. How well the creeps in the White House and the Pentagon understand us: we crave deniability, long to be told that their obvious venality and viciousness—and ours—is an optical illusion, that the acts of treachery and murder we observe and commit are mere shadows in a meaningless dream.

"How many Vietnamese people die every day?" Tom said. He stopped pacing and turned on me with a look of righteous anger. "Karen was a soldier, man. An anti-imperialist freedom fighter. How the fuck can you grieve for her death and not grieve for the thousands of Vietnamese peasants who are burned and bombed and bayonetted every year? How can you be so fucking arrogant? Jarrold's right, man. You're a motherfucking pig."

"What good did that bomb do the peasants?"

Tom shakes his head and leans back on the couch. Nina, who seems to be nodding off, nuzzles her face into the shoulder of his blue-flannel shirt.

"It tells the pigs that the war isn't something you see on Walter Cronkite. That you can't change the channels and make it all vanish," Jarrold said. His voice was calm and gentle, hardly louder than a whisper. "It tells them that the next bomb might go off in one of Boeing's death factories or in some pig recruiter's office or in Betty Crocker's fucking kitchen for that matter. It tells them that their sons and daughters hate what America's become, hate it so completely that they're willing to die to bring change. It tells them that the Vietcong are *here*."

Tom glances at Jarrold, who meets his eyes and then stands up and walks to the door. "You need to *commit*, Wheeler. There's no room in a revolutionary army for irony or selfishness or doubt. You have to commit yourself completely. Until you can do that, you're no fucking use."

Jarrold stands framed by the doorway, lush hair swooping over his forehead, his stubbled tan glowing with sweat.

"That's the difference between Karen and you, Wheeler," he whispers. "She danced to the end of the music. A jerk-off like you, man, all *you* do is talk. Is it really any wonder she dumped your sad ass?"

I'm on my feet and across the room before Lister's finished talking. Buster tackles me before I can do much more than shove Jarrold back against the door frame and land a clumsy kick on his upper thigh. Brownschidle grabs my arm, and he and Buster and I dance awkwardly sideways, kicking and flailing ineffectually at each other, like a trio of slightly spastic male Rockettes. Jarrold laughs but not before I see a genuine twinge of fear in his eyes. Then he turns and limps out of the room.

"All right, back off," I tell the other men.

Brownschidle steps back and nods across to Buster, who's panting with the effort of trying to wrench my left arm behind my back.

"Let him go, man. It's over. Jarrold was completely out of line."

I give the boy a push at the moment he lets go of my arm, and he falls back and stumbles into a bookcase. A heavy glass ashtray explodes on the hardwood floor.

"Time to step off the precipice, Wheeler," Brownschidle says as I turn to leave. "Are you one of us, or are you a pig?"

Outside, I find Lister waiting at the foot of the stairs. I shrug off my army-surplus fatigue jacket and get my guard up in preparation for round two, but he crouches over, rubbing his thigh with one hand and waving me off with the other.

"My fault, man. I fucking deserved it. It's the Winterhaven thing, right? I've been out of my head ever since."

I sit down on the bottom step and nod agreement. Both of us just hang there for a minute, chests heaving with the aftershock of violence—two fierce revolutionary soldiers, trembling from the trauma of an awkward schoolyard brawl.

21

Contamination

The day began with a mystery and ended in the scream of alarms. I had gone through my usual beginning-of-shift routine, changing into my canary suit, adjusting the breather mask, and then heading on down to Special Nuclear Materials to check out my quota of triple-wrapped brass cans. I'd removed the first few cans from the fifty-five-gallon storage drum, placed them a reasonable distance apart on my little red wagon, and moved along to my glove box to start checking the U-235 and plutonium buttons and packing them in tuna cans. Belten and Warthog were ahead of me, the Wart working at a glove box and Ronnie-boy staring at the sign-out sheet.

"Good reading?" I asked him.

"Fascinating," he said in his best Mr. Spock voice. I laughed, but he just continued staring at the sheet.

"Come on, man, let's get shaking. I want to make my numbers without putting these hockey pucks too close together. I hate it when they start to chain react."

"Yeah, whatever." He scanned the list once again and then shook his head. "There's something fucking screwball here.

I've got one too many tuna cans or one too few motherfucking buttons. How do you figure that?"

"I don't, man. I tote that barge and lift that bale and keep my fucking mouth shut. Most of all, I make my quota. Toss the can back into storage and forget it."

"Good advice, Dudley Do-Right. And when the control folks check the numbers, they'll dis-employ my ass."

"So hide the stupid fucker. Take it home and make yourself an ashtray."

"Yeah, right. And what'll I tell Security when they find it in my lunchbox?"

"Tell them you really like tuna. Now get out of my fucking way."

Belten grumbled a little, but he finally took the hint and wandered off. I checked out my quota and got down to work. If I considered the matter at all after that, it was only to reflect on my co-worker's stupidity in worrying about a simple metal can. If a button had really gone missing, every alpha-particle detector in Zee Plant would be screaming like Tippi Hedren and the Mod Squad folks would kick the door off its hinges and stick machine guns down our throats.

Half an hour before quitting time, the CAM alarms went crazy. I was coming in the door from the john when it happened. Rena had packaged up a button in her glove box, wrapped the tuna can in double plastic outer bags, and taken it out of the glove box for shipping. At that point, inexplicably, the package had burst into flame. Belten grabbed a fire extinguisher and blasted the problem with chemical foam, which put out the fire in a hurry, all right. It also sprayed carcinogenic dust around the room.

"Get the fucking shit off me!" Rena was screeching. "Get it off! It's on my clothes!"

"Rena's crapped up, man," I heard someone shout. Then a couple of radiation monitors ran into the room, breather masks over their faces. One of them started trying to wrestle the extinguisher away from Ron Belten while the other one got down on one knee a few feet from Rena and waved a dosimeter in front of her feet and legs. Belten apparently realized that the extinguisher had caused the problem and let the monitor take it from his arms. The alarm was screaming, screaming in the neon-white light of the room.

I found myself backing slowly away from the crowd, staring at the knot of white-suited radiation monitors, Warthog and Belten, the terrified Rena still sobbing and staring at her feet as if she expected them to mutate into tentacles. As I stumbled backward, my foot hit something solid, there was a dull metallic ring, and I glanced sideways in time to see Belten's extra tuna can go slithering across the floor towards the doorway. The scene seemed to freeze and clarify, and I felt as if I were somewhere high above the momentary fury of the accident. I had a look around and ascertained that no one was paying any attention to me; everyone in the room was too busy fumbling around with extinguishers or just standing there yelling at each other to notice me at all. Then I carefully kicked the tuna can through the doorway and across the hall, where it came to rest beside the row of lockers.

"You're *all* crapped up," I heard one of the monitors yelling. "Get out of your canaries and head for the showers."

"Does this mean we get fucking contacted?" Belten said.

"You'll all be getting contact slips, fucking rights," the monitor told him.

"Like I can afford a fucking holiday. This sucks, it really sucks."

We showered, changed our clothes and reported to our supervisor. Rena, Belten and the Hog were given contact slips and told to report back to work in five days. The boss man treated me to fifteen minutes of supreme shit for entering a contaminated area after an alarm had sounded, though I kept repeating that the CAM hadn't actually gone off until I was halfway through the door.

"They contact you, man?" Belten asked me. We were sitting in the changing room after quitting time, our bodies limp with the bone-deep fatigue that invariably seems to follow a crisis.

"Not this time. How long you off for?"

"Five." He offered me a stick of Wrigley's Spearmint.

"We're going to be cleaning up this situation for a month," I said, leaning forward in my chair to take the gum. "Mops and pails and Mary Mild. What a pain in the fucking ass."

"You might be, *hombre*," Belten said. "Me, I'm fucking off-ski. I've had a gutful of worrying about getting fucking irradiated, sterilized and barbecued in plutonium sauce every time I come to work. Life's entirely too short for that crap."

"What about the bread?"

"There's other jobs. My brother-in-law does concrete work in Arizona. Be a relief to work in fresh air for a change."

We shot the shit for a few more minutes while the last of the incoming shift got suited up and went off to their posts, then Belten said goodbye and left the building. When he'd gone, there was no one in the changing room but me. I unzipped my fresh canary suit and pulled out the mystery tuna can. I'd scooped it up from its hiding place next to the lockers on my way back from the supervisor's office. I turned it over in my hands, trying to focus clearly on the chain of events that I was contemplating putting into play. There were cracks in the world you could pass through, I thought. Crevasses you could leap across, if only you had the jam. Karen had already made that leap, made it long before the accident that destroyed her. Her luminous trace was a pathway I could follow. It was my turn to pass through the void.

I put the can in my lunchbox and wandered out of the building, taking my time and chatting to a couple of guys I barely knew who were arriving with the afternoon crew. It was day shift, so I knew I could probably catch a lift home with Clyde. I hung around outside the plant, smoked a couple of cigarettes and waited. Finally, at quarter past six, I saw my stepfather's Studebaker turn into the lane. I waved, and he pulled over.

"How's it going, Dad?"

"Business as usual," Clyde told me. He looked wrung out, as if he hadn't been eating or sleeping, which was pretty much the way he'd looked for months. We drove to the main gates in silence, the Studie's V8 thrumming in our ears.

"Afternoon, Mr. Cateret," the security guy said. "Going up to the lakes this weekend?"

Clyde shook his head. "I doubt it, Will. Those trout'll have to get along without me."

The guard smiled and waved us through.

Two days later, I was sitting in the Weatherman house just off the Ave., watching Jarrold Lister turn the tuna can over in his hands.

"We could take a bunch of photos," I told him.

"Photos of what? A tin can?" He drops the tuna can on the coffee table. "What exactly is that supposed to prove? There must be some jobber who makes these cans, right? We could have boosted one from his factory, or built one in a shop. Why would anyone believe we stole it from Danforth?"

Tom reached across the table and picked up the can, then rotated it in his hands as if seeing it from just the right angle were the key to understanding its use.

"People are sick of demonstrations and protests. They don't react to anything. They've seen it all before. You have to hit them in their gut, do something that affects them in a physical, visceral way."

"White Americans have been so safe and pampered, they don't understand what it means to be hunted and hungry and afraid for your life," Jarrold said. He jumped up from the couch and paced nervously to the window. "You have to hurt the fuckers. Let them feel a little fear."

"What if we start a scram?"

Jarrold and Tom exchanged glances. "A scram? What the fuck is that?"

I explained about the emergency shut-down procedures at Zee Plant.

"Still not good enough," Jarrold insisted. "It's too easy for the pigs to dismiss it. An accident, a glitch in the system. They have to *see* the liberating forces. To know that the Americong can reach into their death machine and tear out its motherfucking heart."

"Like we're going to charge into a nuclear plant—is that what you're saying? Rip off plutonium right under their noses? That's suicide. We might get into the Area, but there's no way we'd get back out."

"What about you, man? You're already in. Your old man's a boss in the plant, right? You're one of the nuclear family. You lead the action from inside the facility, the rest of us work from the outside."

I tried to explain the sheer size and complexity of the Area, how difficult it would be for intruders to get from the fence to the plutonium processing facilities without being seen. Jarrold and Tom kept repeating their mantra: *We have to make a show of force.* I kept chanting back at them: *With luck, we can create an illusion.* Nina and Buster, the only other remaining cadre (or the only ones I was trusted to see, at any rate) wandered in and out, supplying inspiration in the form of a glass bong or new bottle of Thunderbird. Somewhere past midnight, we agreed on our plan.

When I woke on the sofa next morning after a night of blissful unconsciousness, my first since the Winterhaven explosion, Tom and Jarrold were ready to get down to details. After the action, we agreed, it would be necessary for all of us to vanish, ideally in different directions. Weatherman cells across the country had been dropping out of sight for the past several months, assuming new identities and continuing the struggle as individuals or in small cells of two or three people, cutting off any connecting threads along which the pigs could navigate. We would dissolve into the underground, a web of ghosts connected by a vision, and wait until the time was right to rise and strike again.

"There's a couple of scams you can use, man. Both of them stick pretty good."

Tom pushed his glasses back onto the bridge of his nose. He peered at me intently through the little oval lenses. You could go through microfilm newspapers in the university library, he went on, until you found the obituary of someone who'd been born around the same time as you had and died at an early age. The birth would be on record, and you could apply for a new birth certificate claiming that the death date was a mistake. The other routine was to go to a supply store and buy yourself a baptismal certificate, then fill that out yourself and use it to apply for an official birth certificate from the government.

"For an action as risky as this one, we'll fix you up with two sets of papers, each in a different name. That's in case you get blown and have to re-establish cover. Nina will do the thing with the government; we don't want the pigs being able to trace anybody from the commando by checking with the census bureau clerks."

"So I'll be using the name of some kid who died back in the forties?"

"Right. One of your IDs will be in that name. The other name you can make up yourself."

I took a sip of jasmine tea.

"Clark Kent," I said. "Anybody else using that one?"

"Yeah, no one would ever cop to that being an alias. Sounds as natural as plastic dog shit. Great idea."

"Clark Kent Mainprize, then. How's that sound? His parents liked Superman comics."

"Whatever, man. You're the one who's betting his life on it, not me."

Between coffee and lunch, I wander into the changing room to cop a few minutes' downtime. The scent of pot smoke greets me as soon as I open the door. My initial reaction is to wonder if I'm experiencing some weird olfactory flashback—then I glance to my right and see Ron Belten sprawled out in one of the vinyl-covered chairs in the lounge, his sneakered feet perched happily on the butt of an overturned trash can. He gives me the Groucho Marx eyebrows in greeting and goes back to what he was doing, pinching a roach to his lips and inhaling. I wander to the urinals, peel my canaries down to my knees, unzip my jeans and start to take a leak.

"Toke?" Belten asks me.

"Think I'll pass, thanks. This place is psychedelic enough." I give the works a parting shake and do up my zipper, then park my butt in the chair next to Belten's and put my feet up beside his on the can.

"Your loss. It's sensimilla. A buddy of mine grows it in his hothouse. Veddy, veddy mellow, my man. Veddy *subtle*. Caresses the brain cells as if they were nipples."

I glance towards the doorway.

"And you're not concerned, I take it, about the Mod Squad dropping by?"

"The Keystone Kops?" Ron shifts to an unctuous Asian accent. "I welcome them with open arms. I take them to my breast and embrace them." He waves his arms expansively. "I love them as I love all God's creatures, no matter how repugnant and slimy. We are all brothers under the scales."

"Still planning on packing it in, I take it?"

He drops the Reverend Moon routine and goes back to being Belten. "Three or four days, man. Just waiting for my ride down to Scottsdale. Middle of next week and I'm gone."

Ron scrunches the roach into a ball between his fingers and flicks it towards a urinal. "In the interim," he continues, his voice now plummy English, "as no doubt you've gathered, old thing, one does one's best to stay amused."

A couple of weekends later, I took a bus up to Tacoma and checked in at a motel. After watching TV for an hour or so, I got off the bed and answered the door. Tom Brownschidle came in out of the drizzle, his fuzzy freak hair tucked up under an Australian bush hat, the brim of which partially obscured his face. He glanced at the television and said, "Leave it on. Fucks up the shotgun mikes the pigs are into using."

He sat down on the bed, slipped a small leather satchel

from his shoulder, and pulled a manila envelope from the inside pocket of his heavy winter coat.

"Looks kosher, right?"

We spread out the two birth certificates on the polyester bedspread. Charles William Watson. Clark Kent Mainprize. Two people who didn't exist.

"Yeah," I said. "Pretty convincing. To me, anyway. Let's hope they fool the border dicks and cops."

"Border, man? You planning on travelling?"

"Could be."

"Canada's cooler than here, right?"

"Long as you can negotiate the border. I'm not sure where I'm headed yet. Maybe Canada, maybe not."

"That's up to you, man." Tom flashed a friendly smile, though his eyes seemed to be sizing me up, examining my demeanour for fault lines and flaws. "You get backed into a corner, there's a number you can call." He rattled off a ten-digit phone number. I didn't recognize the area code. "If you use it, your name is 'Delgado.'"

"Delgado," I repeated. I was apprehensive about the whole operation, but I had to fight the urge to crack a smile. Phoney passports. Getaway plans. Now even secret code names. I felt like I was talking to Q.

I went into the kitchenette and fished out a couple of cans from the six-pack of Rainier I'd scored on my way from the bus station to the motel.

Then I carefully unfolded a ragged chamber-of-commerce promotional map that I'd lifted from the glove box of Betty's Chevelle. "Here's a map of Danforth. I've marked the garage and the road out to the Area. Is everybody clear about the time?"

Brownschidle looked slightly offended. "They're cool," he said. "We've been doing manoeuvres every night. Calisthenics and cross-country training. We're ready, man. We'll be there on time."

"Who's driving?"

That got me a suspicious look.

"What do you care who's driving, man? You look after your end, we'll take care of ours."

Tom stood up and headed for the door, buttoning his coat as he went. "Later, man." He turned and looked me in the eye. "Look me up when we're running the government." The smile again, and he was out the door. I noticed the satchel as soon as I turned around, but Tom was already halfway across the parking lot before I could call him back.

"That's yours, man. May it serve you well." He flashed me a three-fingered peace sign. Loped off past the concrete block buildings, the muffler shops, the Dixie Chicken franchise.

I dumped the bag on the kitchenette counter and rummaged inside until I found the Walther. I hefted it in my palm. Ran the tip of my finger over the slick, matte-black metal. Touched the jaunty Walther banner, incongruously festive on such a pug-nosed, aggressive machine. It was, I reminded myself, a theatrical prop, nothing more. Dropped it into Tom's satchel. Grabbed the room keys, and went to check out. I never even knew if it was loaded.

As if to reflect my state of mind, my supervisors at the Area transferred me from glove box duty to the transport of materials from the special nuclear materials vault to the Hot Zone. The move delayed our evolving plans—a welcome delay, though it freeze-framed me into a purgatory state between the will to act and the act itself, like a parachutist dangling from the plane. More importantly, as far as my own shit-scared sensorium was concerned, it spiked me that much deeper into marrow: I clumped in my canary suit through the hollow, irradiated rib-cage of Zee Plant, the clinical geometry of hallways and jack-ladders fish-eyed into wobbly, unstable tunnels by the cyclopean visor of my breather mask and hood. Paralyzed with anticipation, I borrowed Clyde's Studie most evenings and drove around town looking at the mundane blocks of houses—most of them prefab and built to predictable plans. I bounced from the Fission Hole to the bar in the Danforth Hotel, methodically immersing my cortex in alcohol without ever really succeeding in getting drunk. I seemed to be losing the ability to break free of my psyche. Not even the Fission Hole's famous submarines could help me escape. One evening, I stood for almost half an hour on the field of my old high school, doing nothing more than watching the shadows of goalposts and bleachers elongate and finally dissolve into blue desert night. The next evening, zero hour minus a couple of days, I drove around to Bobby's place and parked next to his Barracuda in front of the little square lawn.

"He's in his room. Just go on in," Lida told me.

I waited until she had disappeared and then padded down the carpeted hall to Bobby's room and rapped softly on the door.

"Sonny," Bobby said when he opened the door. "Come on in."

The walls of Bobby's bedroom were bare. A ziggurat of hardbound books—automotive manuals or something equally utilitarian, by the look of them—garnished with a couple of *Hot Rod* magazines, squatted on one edge of his desk, the rest of which was naked as moonlight. He had systematically defoliated the walls of their posters, garbaged the girlie mags, sold his LPs and the wire rack of singles, even removed the mirror in which he used to preen his duck's-ass and practise that hard-eyed stare. There wasn't even a radio or a clock beside the bed. I had assumed that he'd moved out of this room when he was drafted, possibly in expectation of moving into his own house with Sherri if and when he made it home. It occurred to me that there might have been another explanation for the orderly, monastic sparseness of his surroundings: like Curie, like Ariel, like me for that matter, he had been starving himself in some symbolic and intensely personal way. He had stripped his life of everything that held him to the earth.

"I'm bugging out," Bobby told me. "Going out to the salt flats. See if I can still catch on with Digger."

"You figure the job is still open?"

"Not really—but what the fuck. There's nothing I need to do here, that's for damn sure." Bobby dragged on his cigarette. Rubbed hard at the arcs of his eyebrows, as if there were something irritating just beneath his skin. "You go over the Sierras, man, that's a *genuine* desert. Salt flats and baldies, riverbeds that dried up a century ago. It's the opposite place from a jungle. I think I can breathe there. Get some wind in my lungs."

I could have said that Danforth was a desert. I could, at least, have listened. I was trembling with energy, fire in my bones.

"When you leaving?" was all that I asked him.

"Couple of days, I guess. Whenever."

"I'm gonna need a ride, man. Take me with you."

Bobby put his smoke to his lips as if to take another drag and then seemed to change his mind. He held the cigarette, glowing end up, and examined its corona of ash. "You want to go to Utah?" he asked me. "What the fuck for?"

I drew in a slow, anxious breath. This was Bobby, I told myself. My best friend since junior high. Bobby who gave not one shit about authority, propriety, whatever. If I couldn't trust him, what was the use?

"We're going to do an action," I told him. "Me and some of Karen's people. I'll have to disappear for a while."

"'Karen's people'? Those Jerry Rubin dickheads? You serious, man?"

I glanced around at his sterile monk's cell.

"Think where they brought us up, Bobby." I was whispering, placing my words as carefully as I would have placed my steps if I were walking a tightrope. "In a little slice of Disneyland on a radioactive river. My dad, Clyde, is a nice man who makes fucking A-bombs. My mother, she's dying of cancer. Everyone's dying of cancer. We're all radioactive, man, we just don't fucking know it. Yeah, I'm serious. Why wouldn't I be?"

Bobby swept his hair off his forehead. He'd let it grow out since he'd come home, and the lank black strands curtained his eyes.

"What you ought to do, Sonny, is get fucking lost. Just lose yourself, walk up a mountain. There's canyons and valleys a goat couldn't find. Get a gun and go bush, man, walk into the hills. Shoot the first cunt that walks up the trail."

He rubbed his eyes with the ball of his thumb. "I used to think about that over in Nam, quite a bit. You'd see all these hills under haze, far away. You'd be slogging along through the bugs and the sweat, and you'd catch a quick glimpse of these mountains. I used to think about taking a wrong turn someday. Just strip off my dog tags, let them drop in the muck. Go live in the clouds like a Buddhist."

"I can't just walk away now," I told him. "Karen's dead, man. The rest of us have to shoulder her load . . ."

Bobby exhaled a grunt of soundless laughter. Took a drag on his Camel. Exhaled again, taking his time.

"Get serious, Sonny. Those cunts are just rich brats trying to piss off their folks. Twenty years from now, this revolution bullshit will all be forgotten. They'll be living up in Highlands with three Caddies and a pool."

"They will if nothing changes, man. If no one tries to change it. You have to do what Karen did, Bobby. You have to stop talking and act."

Bobby huddled on the bed, head down, hair shadowing his features. He took another drag on his cigarette and exhaled again, funnelling smoke at his feet.

"All right, man, whatever. Your funeral. You tell me where to meet you. I'll be there."

22

Scram

Minus twelve hours and ticking: after dinner, I pleaded a headache and went straight to my room. I had entered the universe of last things. The last time I'd eat dinner with Betty and Clyde. The last time I'd hear the comforting drone of the TV from downstairs. The last time I'd look out my window at the hump of Saddle Mountain obscuring its crescent of dark starless sky. The last time I'd lie on my narrow single bed with the posters of pro athletes and Hollywood babes gazing down at me, as if they were holy icons and pop culture were some idiot religion. The last night I'd sleep in my home.

When I'd closed myself into my bedroom, the only light a circle of buttery yellow from the table lamp next to the bed, I opened the drawer of my bedside table and took out Tom Brownschidle's Walther, unwound the multicoloured petals, Betty's old dust rags, that I'd wrapped around it, and balanced it, muzzle toward me, on the palm of my outstretched hand. It was compact and surprisingly heavy. I could feel its reptilian coldness. The proximity of death occurred to me then, as suddenly and unexpectedly as a blow from a falling object. It was easy to die. I could vanish. I could snap the clip into the handle, remove the safety catch, insert the barrel of the gun in my mouth, and in an instant the pain would be gone.

I heard my mother's step—unmistakable, painfully tentative—on the staircase outside my room. She ascended the last few stairs cautiously, but I resisted the impulse to rush out and help her. I swaddled the weapon in its nest of bright remnants and nestled it into the drawer beside a stamp album, some baseball cards, a pair of dysfunctional flashlights, and a Honeytone 12 Transistor with a snazzy chrome-mesh grille. Then I got up and opened the door.

"I had a call from Richard Crashaw," Betty said.

"He heard from Curie lately?" I couldn't work up much interest in Curie and her father at that moment; she was gone to wherever to lead some kind of life I couldn't imagine, and Eden was with his grandfather. That was that. I focused, instead, on the pattern of tiny rosebuds on the wallpaper in the landing. The flowers seemed repellent and cloying, little wheels of ersatz petals in a cloud of curdled pink.

"He's getting old, and he worries about what's going to happen to Eden. Who's going to look after him when Richard's finally gone? God knows it won't be Curie. That girl's no use at all."

"Things'll work out," I said. I glanced around the landing, which suddenly seemed small and confining.

"You should ask him for custody. You're the only real choice."

Betty's eyes searched my face, then she turned and propelled herself slowly toward the rail around the head of the staircase, reaching out into the space above the landing as if she were walking in darkness. When she'd traversed the distance to the railing, she used it to support herself and started down the stairs.

"Good night," I said, and closed the door. She may, I suppose, have answered, but I didn't hear her voice. I sat on the bed for a long time, just listening to myself breathing. The idea that I would never speak to my mother again revolved in my chest like an icy planet. No matter what occurred in life or in whatever infinities lay beyond it, I would never again be able to call for my mother, to recite for her the inventory of my unimportant days as I always had, forever and forever. I had spoken the last heart-breakingly trivial syllables of our lifelong blood relationship, words which contained neither magic nor wisdom but only the meaningless echo of the void beyond my voice.

I reminded myself that what I was about to do I had envisioned and planned for Betty. I drew a line as bright and sharp as a laser-light from the seething alchemical cauldron of Zee Plant to the cancer that was eating through her body. I woke up a couple of times in the night, feeling nauseated. When the alarm went off, I was sweating and curled into a tight fetal ball on the edge of the mattress, but the sickness in my belly had dissolved. I got out of bed and headed for the bathroom off the landing. I locked the bathroom door, checked it a couple of times to be sure, and then took my time getting ready for work, going carefully and methodically over the plan for the action as I peed and brushed my teeth.

I would dress in my usual T-shirt and jeans, but under them I'd wear a thin black turtleneck and lightweight black cotton pants that wouldn't bunch up too much under my Levi's. I'd carry a ski mask in one of my pockets, and the Walther would be tucked into the other. I'd hit the control wall and set off the scram, then I'd duck into a janitor's closet or one of the cans, strip off my canary suit and stash it, along with my regular clothes, and make a quick cameo appearance on the catwalk to the west of the control room, just to make sure that someone got a look at the disguise—a genuine terrorist, larger than life. After that, I'd lose the pistol and clamber back into my canaries. I could stash the commando gear later, in a wastebasket perhaps.

While I was inside Zee Plant, Jarrold and Buster would get on with their own part of the action, which was simply to cut through the heavy wire security fence a mile or so from the entrance gates to make it look as if someone had broken in. Their driver, who'd have cruised past the gates and killed some time exploring side roads, would turn around and scoop them up. By early the next morning, Tom and Nina would be dropping off copies of a communiqué describing the incursion into Zee Plant and the theft of a plutonium button and demanding that the American government acknowledge its guilt in the ongoing racist murder of Asian civilians. The copies would be accompanied by prints of the tuna can in the hands of a terrorist in a black shirt and ski mask.

The action would be attributed to the Karen Sullivan Brigade of the Students' International Committee for an

End to Imperialist Violence. In reality there was, of course, no brigade, no committee, no action. The terrorists who had escaped from the Area had never broken in. The masked infiltrator was a labourer playing dress-up. The stolen plutonium button wasn't stolen. The whole gig was an optical illusion. A *blivet*, as Clyde would have said.

Betty was still asleep when I went downstairs to fix myself breakfast. This wasn't unusual. She often didn't feel up to getting out of bed until long after Clyde and I had left for work. A district nurse came by every day around lunchtime to make sure she had everything she needed. By the time we got home from the Area, she'd be out of bed and pottering around. Clyde had already finished his breakfast and put his dishes into the dishwasher—a recent purchase, the first on our block—and he was standing at the kitchen counter putting together some sandwiches for lunch. I helped myself to Frosted Flakes and slopped a little milk into my bowl, pausing to take a sip of Maxwell House before beginning to spoon up the flakes.

"Macaroni loaf okay?" Clyde asked. He held up a plastic-wrapped package of lunch meat.

"Whatever. Sure."

"Mustard?"

I nodded and went back to shovelling cereal into my mouth. By the time I'd had all I could stomach, Clyde had packed both our lunches and headed for the car. I sat staring out the window at the familiar scenes as we left town and headed towards the Area. The nausea of the previous night had returned, and I was afraid my voice would tremble if I tried to make conversation. Fortunately, Clyde was doing enough talking for both of us. For the entire time it took us to drive to the Area, he went on about the recent demise of the Seattle baseball team. The American League had approved the sale of the Pilots to Milwaukee interests in April. They would be moved and renamed the "Brewers." Seattle would never, in Clyde's opinion, have the opportunity to host another major league baseball franchise. Jet City, and all of Washington State, would languish in bush league oblivion forever.

We turned at the gates and headed along the river toward the 100 Area. Clyde pulled up as near as he could to 105 Building and let me out. "Pick you up later?"

"It's okay, Dad. I'll hitch a ride with Rena or whoever."

Clyde smiled. The Hawk pulled away, its aging exhaust rattling noisily.

A few minutes later, I was inside the changing room, pulling on my canaries and listening to Belten and Warthog and the others shoot the shit. So far, so good: the security guard at the gate had no interest in me, and there was no one guarding the entrance to the building—no one would bother to check the son of a long-time employee for weapons, at least. The Danforth bosses were still living in the fifties: nuclear spies concerned them; the possibility of nuclear terrorism hadn't occurred to them just yet.

As I picked my way through the scrum in the doorway a few minutes later, canaries on and breather mask securely in one hand, Warthog grabbed my arm and steered me a few steps away from the others.

"Keep an eye on Ronnie, eh? He's been juiced or ripped most of the week."

"I'd noticed. What the fuck though, eh? You can't fire someone who's quit."

"Getting canned is the least of his worries. The Hot Zone is no place for pissing around half-crocked."

I shot Wart a thumbs-up and headed for the special nuclear materials vault. My job was transporting plutonium slugs through the Hot Zone to the workers—Rena, Warthog and, for the moment, Belten among them—on glove-box detail. At the vault, I signed in, and I was given my payload of tuna cans under the gaze of two security people, one from Nuclear Material Control and one from Operations. I was too tense for small talk—not that I knew these dudes any-way—so I stood around looking surly while they went through their little routine. I knew there would be TIDs, "tamper-indicating devices," on the tuna cans, and I also knew that the load would be inventoried at both ends of my route. I didn't intend to follow the flight plan, however. They could keep their green kryptonite forever for all I cared; I just wanted to lay a false trail. I did a couple of dummy runs, forcing myself to pretend it was business as usual so that I could make sure nothing had been changed in the operation of the plant that would affect what I had planned.

By the third run, the vault boys were getting bored; they hardly spared me a glance as I signed in and trundled my cart towards the freight elevator. Once I'd hit B deck, I ripped up the log sheets, ditched the cart in the first cleaning room I came to, and headed for Mission Control. This involved ascending a level on one of the numerous exposed metal stairways that formed the bone structure of Zee Plant, then traversing a catwalk, ascending another flight of stairs, and finally hooking a left through a heavy swinging door. The room itself seemed cavernous and cramped at once: there was plenty of vertical space, but the walls hemmed you in from all directions, metal cliffs inclined at minus-ten degrees reaching up toward a heaven of ventilation ducts and conduits and heavy steel beams. On the control room wall there were rows of switches, twenty-three to a row. The wall was metal, painted the same nondescript industrial grey as the stairs, the beams, the ducting. The rows were numbered in large white digits. At the top of the wall, just above row 30, there was a sign that read "Caution: Bumping Panel May Cause Scram."

The word "scram"—Clyde explained all this to me when I first started work at the Area—comes from the term "safety control rod axe man." When Enrico Fermi designed the first nuclear reactor, there was an extra safety rod suspended from a pulley. In the event of a problem, a man with an axe would cut the rope. According to legend, a logger from the north woods of Michigan was rounded up and hired for the job. He stood with a red, single-bitted axe on his shoulder and waited. If Fermi had given the signal—a chopping motion—he would have swung his axe. The same principle applied in a modern scram, although the mechanism was a little more sophisticated; control rods were inserted into the reactor core to absorb neutrons and shut the reactor down. When Clyde started at the Area, though, things were still pretty haywire. If the engineers wanted to shut down the reactor, he told me, they'd bang on the control room panel hard enough to cause the thing to scram. I was hoping that technique would still work.

Part of the shift engineer's daily routine was checking the external monitors every couple of hours. The control room was empty. Captain Kirk had left the bridge. I stumped across to the panel, sloping walls teetering precariously in my distorted fish-eye vision, and banged the metal panel with my fist. I waited for the shriek of the scram alarms. Apart from a jolt of pain in my hand and a dull wobble-board thump, nothing happened. I belted the switchboard again. Again, nothing happened. I took a few steps backward, angled my shoulder toward the wall, and charged like a television narc trying to break down the door of a coke house. The canary suit padded my shoulder and arm against the impact of the protruding switches, but the shock of hitting solid, unforgiving metal still rattled me down to my bones. Silence. I turned and found Belten behind me. In our visors and canary suits, we were astronauts, aliens, invaders from Mars. He grinned behind his shiny plastic visor, rotated one finger around his temple as if to tell me I was crazy, then sashayed over to the end of the control wall, shuffling like Charlie Chaplin, and calmly pressed a circular red button. This done, he executed an awkward pirouette in his cumbersome canary suit and dithered off toward the exit door. I turned and bolted up the metal stairs to the catwalk, the hairs on the back of my neck standing up. Alarms screamed so loudly they seemed like jolts of agony wired directed into the nerves in my spinal cortex. In the humming heart of Zee Plant, the cylindrical void bound with walls of intractable metal, the nuclear reactor began to shut down.

Bobby picked me up beside the park at quarter to three. My rucksack was stashed in the trunk of the 'Cuda, along with Bobby's suitcase and a couple of cases of beer.

"Well, you do it?" Bobby asked me.

"Yeah, it's done."

Blurred internal Kodachrome of Rena in her canary suit, staring up as I run on a catwalk. My open mouth, devoid of sound. Her visor flashing glare ice. Her quick-shuffle steps out of sight. My helter-skelter flight around corners, shot of pain banging my shoulder on vertical steel rib telltale clang clang clang clang of my feet on the wafer of expanded steel mesh.

"Whatever, dude. Let's get fucking with it."

We tooled through town as if cruising for chicks or heading for a beer over in Pasco. I kept my head down crossing Lincoln, and even Bobby looked furtive and nervous. I was shocked, in some utterly illogical way, that the houses and streets of Danforth still existed. I had wiped the board clean just an hour ago, hadn't I? Passed my hand across the bright screen of memory and obliterated everything I knew. The world of my adolescence, my past and family had been annihilated in the demon scream of howlers as the Zee reactor scrammed. I had finally succeeded in becoming Bizarro Superman, my own distorted image, the negation of myself. Yet here, in this world, there were people calmly walking with their children in the sun. The ordinary houses, some with galvanized metal trash cans waiting on neatly clipped boulevards for the garbage truck's arrival. The fleshy, lichened trunks of the catalpas beside the street. The way light reinvents itself when it shines through leafy canopies. I had lost all this, betrayed it, and I felt a growing panic at the finality of what I'd ridiculously, thoughtlessly, talked myself into. The universe still existed; it was I who was destroyed. I had vanished like my father. I had left behind my son.

"Let me out, man. I have to get out." We were nearing the perimeter of the city; the access road to the highway was just up ahead.

Struggling numb-fingered into canary suit. Faster! Move! Fumbling. Hawk-shriek of scram alarms. Hard footsteps outside the john doorway must be the Mod Squad freaks. Coming to slice me to shit with their guns. Can't get my footing here. Slither on toilet tiles. For Jesus' sake get moving! Keep moving!

"Why? What's the hassle?"

"Eden, man. I have to take Eden."

Bobby looked at me but didn't stop driving.

"Let me out, man," I repeated. "I have to take my son."

Bobby flicked his cigarette butt out the window.

"Whatever," he said. He whipped the 'Cuda onto the gravel shoulder, hauled the wheel to the left and gunned it, kicking up a rooster-tail of gravel and dust as we made a tight U-turn. Five minutes later, we were parked a block from Mr. Crashaw's saltbox.

"Shit," I said as I got out of the car. "I should have brought something to put Eden's stuff in. A suitcase or a garbage bag or something."

Bobby leaned around the headrest and grabbed an empty duffle bag, service-khaki, stained on one end with a blotch of something mottled and dark. "Use this, man."

Unseen through a stretch of hall turning shouldering painfully open the door cowering across the room and bursting (saved and trapped) into the cubicle just in time spewing coffee breakfast flakes bile into the waiting white porcelain mouth of the shitter American Standard O Lord yes I burn I am burning.

I took the duffle, glancing at the red stain as I bundled it up and stuffed it in my shirt.

"That happened when I was doing my Medevac gig. An Air Cav gunner bled to death. That bother you?" He shot me a grin, the hint of a challenge in his eyes. "I consider it a kind of souvenir."

"This won't take long," I said. "I'll tell them I'm taking the kid for a walk. Going down to the playground or something."

I folded up the duffle bag and stuffed it under my jacket; then I jogged down the sidewalk and hopped the Crashaws' fence. Mrs. Turnbull answered the door, as I'd expected. Old Man Crashaw would still be hanging around at the school.

"Eden ready?" I asked. "Got his coat on?"

The old woman seemed flustered, as if she thought I suspected her of negligence for not having Eden all tricked out and ready to roll. "I wasn't sure when you'd be coming," she said.

"I'm going to take him some spare jeans. Where's his backpack?"

"The usual place. Hanging on the door of his closet."

"All right, I'll get it. Could you give him a hand with his shoes?"

I bounded up the staircase and into Eden's bedroom. Ducks and bears watched me noncommittally as I ransacked his closet and dresser, stuffing shirts, pants, socks and underwear into Bobby's duffle. He'd need his friend Tuffy, I decided. The raggedy old teddy bear went into the sack with the clothes. A couple of Dr. Seuss books, a favourite multicoloured ball and a plastic truck with goggly eyes instead of headlights, and the duffle bag was pretty much full. I pulled up the window and let the bag roll onto the soft grass, behind the cover of some roses and a trellis. When I'd done that, I padded as softly as I could down the hall, Mrs. Turnbull's voice drifting up the vault towards me as I hurried by the head of the stairs.

"You must try and keep your feet dry. There's puddles near the swings this time of year."

Nothing had changed in Curie's room. In some compartment of his mind, Crashaw was still waiting for his daughter to come home. I crossed to the writing desk and fumbled around in the drawer until I came up with Eden's birth certificate. I folded it once and stuck it inside my faded denim shirt.

A retroactive vision: I had caught a ride from the Area with a couple of guys who were working construction on a new disposal site. My clothes were a collage of conflicting intentions. My canary suit was on the floor of a john stall, shucked off like the skin of some reptile. My work clothes I'd discarded in a janitor's closet, all except a cotton shirt, which

I'd retrieved to slip over my black commando gear. The ski mask had been in my pocket, but I'd apparently lost it in my hopeless headlong flight out of Zee Plant. I had been swimming upstream, against the tide, as engineers in lab coats and Hot Zone workers in full protective canary gear swarmed across the catwalks in the panic of the scram.

The getaway car was luck, pure luck: I'd waved it down and hopped in, and no one at the gates had blinked an eye. I had ridden into Danforth in paralytic silence. And it is, I suppose, an indication of my blurred and cocooned state of being that I could watch stupefied as the long fence that separates the Area from the scablands, miles of implacable geometry, rows of diamonds streaming to infinity, flashed past without my seeing—not, at least, until months later— the lack of a hole in the wire. That elusive perception leapt belatedly into my conscious mind, a rainbow trout breaching the surface, one ordinary sun-washed morning as I walked from my Floral Fantasies delivery truck to a coffee shop in a North Las Vegas strip mall: *What had happened to Jarrold and Buster? They hadn't cut a hole in the fence.*

Part Four

23

The Loneliest Highway
in America

We headed south through Portland, then zigzagged east and south again through Klamath Falls, Weed and Red Bluff before veering toward the Sierras. Bobby did most of the driving; he was wired on pills and soaring, and the rhythm of the road seemed to chill him out, give his energy a channel to flow through. We travelled nights and holed up in the daytime, spending my pay from the Area on burgers and roadside motels.

There is no way of describing how it feels to be on the run. If I had imagined where my actions at Zee Plant might lead me, it was only in terms of fantasies—the romantic rebel gunned down by the forces of oppression, the freedom fighter holed up like a prophet in the mountains, waiting for the grinding-wheel of history to revolve. I had not imagined waking up at noon in an airless motel room, a little boy sobbing for his Grandpa in the Hide-A-Bed beside me, every muscle in my body knotted tight as wire with fear. Or finally drifting back to sleep, down a well of sheer exhaustion, only to dream the thunder of the cheap plywood door splitting open, the boots of federal agents crashing whip-cracks on the lino, the bullets ripping fissures in my flesh and smashing bone.

It was only in the lost hours of the night, when we were driving, that I felt a delusive sense of calm, as if the 'Cuda were a bubble on some swiftly flowing stream. Bobby, who clearly didn't care about the danger I'd placed him in, drove as if the car and he were being sucked into a vacuum, half-hunched above the steering wheel, his shoulders bopping absently in sync with the eight-track as Hendrix and the Zeppelin marched us east into the dawn. Eden slept or watched the night flow past, spent hours talking nonsense into the raggedy ear of his one stuffed bear. Daylight was torture, though; the coming of day reduced me to an insect on a table. I scrabbled from doorway to doorway, pulling poor Eden along in my wake, a centipede flushed unhappily out of its nest of forest shade.

Past Ely on Route 50, the "Loneliest Highway in America," Bobby dropped us off on the side of the road. He was headed into Utah, to the Bonneville Salt Flats, trying to dredge up old connections, find a doorway back into his life.

"You going to be all right?" he asked. "I can run you down to Vegas, no problem."

I shook my head. "It's better you don't, Bob." He must have known what I was thinking—that the cops might be looking for his car by now—but all he did was grin and rev the engine.

"Hang on," I said. "I'll get Eden's stuff out of your duffle."

"Take it, man. Maybe it'll bring you luck. Got me through some pretty tight stuff back in Bongville."

I nodded thanks and busied myself shepherding Eden off to the shoulder of the road. Bobby leaned across the seat and flashed us a thumbs-up. Then he gunned the Barracuda and popped the clutch. There was a moment of unholy smoke and noise, and then he was gone, fishtailing off into Utah. We stood there with the acrid smell of burned rubber in our nostrils, both of us looking down the empty stretch of road toward the east.

"Is Bobby coming back?" my little boy asked me.

I shook my head. "Not for a while," I told him. "He has some things to do now. So do we."

To my surprise, he accepted this without complaining. If I could be his daddy, then Bobby could drive away into the heat haze on the Nevada-Utah border and find us again at some point in the future, just as if we were all in different rooms of one house. Children trust us because they don't understand how dangerous the world is and how helpless we really are. I suppose we trust each other—and ourselves— for pretty much the same reason.

I took my son by the hand and we started to walk south along the side of the road. It was late in the morning already, and I had no clear idea of where we were going to eat or sleep or where we should expect to be by nightfall. I've never felt so lonesome in my life.

Three hours and two rides later, we were sitting in a booth in the Premier Cafe in Humboldt, Nevada. Eden was mixing the dregs of his milk into my Orange Crush, then stirring the concoction frantically and sticking his nose into the mouth of the glass to inspect the results. I was finding out a lot of things about my son, one of which was that he liked to mix things up and stir them. Maybe he was going to be a scientist someday, just like his grandfather's idol, Madame Curie. My hamburger sat on the chipped plate in front of me, a forlorn piece of pop Americana. I should have been hungry enough to gobble five or six greasy burgers and a mountain of fries, but in fact I didn't feel much like eating. Eden had poked a few fries into the puddle of ketchup on the plate and devoured them, then he too had lost interest in anything but pouring and stirring. I wondered how on earth I was going to keep him healthy when I didn't know what or how much he needed to eat, or anything else about being a father. I needed my mother, and Eden needed his—the mother he might have had if she weren't Curie Crashaw. But Curie had no interest in Eden, and Betty was back home in Danforth. Aunt Alice would have to do.

I had pretty much decided not to spend the night in Humboldt. We'd rest a little longer, then try our luck on the highway, head further south. Eden must have been exhausted, though you certainly wouldn't have known it to watch him enjoying himself with the Orange Crush and milk. I was about to ask the waitress if there were any decent motels that wouldn't cost us too much on the road down to Vegas, when I heard the door of the café swing violently open and a woman started yelling with a voice like a three-alarm fire.

"Pour me a fucking coffee, Jacquie," she shouted at the waitress. "If it don't taste like petrified rat piss. The last cup I had here made diarrhea strained through an old sock look good."

The waitress smiled. "That must have been the gourmet stuff," she said. "You look like you could use a cup of something, though, that's for sure."

"What I could use is a fucking machine gun. I'd blast the balls off every single son of a slut in Nevada. Cowboys first, the other bastards later."

"Man trouble, Lois?"

"You just said the same thing twice, honey. That some kind of fucking speech impediment or something?"

I did my best to ignore the conversation, but Eden was sufficiently interested to take a break from his mad scientist routine and stare with rapt attention at the woman.

"Hey, lady," I finally said. "You want to keep the language down a little?"

The woman swivelled around on her heels for a while, squinting as if the light were bad and trying to get a bead on whoever had spoken. Miraculously, given her condition, she finally settled on me.

"Who the sanctified blazes are you?"

"Clark Kent," I told her.

"Damn, I been waiting a long time to run into you, pal. Hey, Jacquie, this peckerhead here thinks he's the Man of Steel."

"Don't they all?" the waitress asked.

"Tell him my name," the woman said. She stood there wobbling on her pointy heels and grinning.

"Her name's Lois Lane," the waitress informed me.

"Lois Lane of the *Daily Planet?*" I asked.

"Nope," she said. "Lois Lane of Joe Carigoli's All-Star Rest 'n' Relaxation Ranch. Hookers and whores for hire, best rates in Nevada. At least I was till this morning, when I told that cheap guinea son of a bitch to go suck his own dick for a change."

"This is my son," I said. "He's three. Luckily, he doesn't always understand what adults are saying."

I was wasting my breath. The woman, Lois Lane, had lost interest. She was telling the waitress how much she hated the State of Nevada.

"I'm getting straight into that car of mine right this minute," she said, "and I'll be goddamned if I won't just drive all night and day until I'm someplace else entirely. Argentina, maybe. Or Denver. My ex-husband used to live around there, till his girlfriend kicked him out."

The waitress, Jacquie, leaned her chin into her elbow on the counter. She waited until her friend had run out of rocket fuel, then she watched the woman stagger out the door and went right back to wiping the counter.

Eden lost interest in his chemistry experiment about the same time I gave up on my burger. I paid the bill and we headed outside. The woman who had called herself "Lois Lane" was standing on the sidewalk beside a dusty late-fifties T-Bird with Colorado plates. She had taken her car keys out of her handbag and was trying unsuccessfully to open the car door. A thin, dark man with a greased-back quiff was standing beside her on the sidewalk, his hands in the pockets of his powder-blue leisure suit. Something about the way they were standing there, Lois Lane and the stranger, made me curious enough to walk towards them until I could hear the dark man's voice.

"You fucking owe Joe fucking money, you cunt," the man said. He was glancing both ways as he spoke, as if afraid of causing too much of a scene, and he kept his voice down to a threatening whisper.

I picked up Eden, who was sleepy enough to welcome a chance to get off his feet, and walked over to the girl.

"You ready to go home now, honey?" I said. "I think our little boy here needs his nap."

The greaseball stopped talking long enough to look me up and down.

"Who in fuck is this?" he whispered to Lois.

I handed Eden to Lois, who had the wit to take him in her arms and give him a cuddle. I was expecting him to burst out crying or at least to make some sort of objection to being dumped into the arms of some woman he didn't know, but he calmly let his head rest on her shoulder so that they looked for all the world like mom and child.

"I'm Lois's husband," I said. "You mind watching your language around the kid?"

The greaseball kind of grimaced, like there was something in his mouth he didn't much like the taste of. He stood there running his thumb and forefinger up and down the skinny lapel of his suit. Then he straightened the knot on his electric-blue silk tie, shot me one of those heavy-lidded, next-time-is-payback-time looks, turned on his heel and walked off in no particular hurry.

"Give us a ride," I told Lois Lane. "Even if it's just out of town. We need to get south, down to Vegas."

"Yeah, yeah, whatever," Lois said. Her attention wasn't on Eden and me, however; she was watching the retreating figure of the greaseball. "Clark's a state trooper," she yelled after him as he crossed the street. "So fuck off before he puts your stupid homo ass in the slammer, you ugly fucking guinea asshole creep! And watch your fucking mouth around my kid!"

When the hard case was out of sight, I took Eden from Lois and helped him into the back seat of the T-Bird. Then I grabbed the keys that were dangling from the woman's hand, walked around the car and settled into the driver's seat, leaving her standing on the sidewalk.

Lois knocked on the passenger-side window, and I punched the power window switch and eased down the glass.

"What the fuck you think you're doing?" she asked me. "This is my car, in case you hadn't noticed. That means I'm the driver. So get the fuck out of my seat."

"When you sober up," I told her. "Right now I think it might be better if I drive."

She looked a little put out, but she climbed into the passenger seat anyway. Fifteen minutes out of Humboldt, both she and Eden were fast asleep. I drove for somewhere over a hundred miles, as far as a place called Caliente, then pulled up in front of a roadside motel. I left Lois and Eden sleeping in the T-Bird and went in and booked us a room. By the time I came out of the office with the key to our unit, Lois Lane had woken up.

"I'm getting too beat to drive," I said. "Can't keep my eyes open much longer. This is just north of Vegas, some little hick place."

"I know where it is." She lifted her shades and scanned the dust of the parking lot as if it were the surface of the moon. "Caliente."

She climbed out of the car and I got Eden.

"You book us a unit?" she asked, nodding at the room key on its scuffed wooden paddle.

"Yeah," I said. "Just one, though."

"What am I supposed to do? Sleep in the fucking Bird?"

"You can stay with us if you want to."

"Yeah, right. You got a two-bedroom?"

"It's a one with a foldaway. You mind?"

She didn't have anything to say to that, but she pursed her lips a little bit and looked at the ground as she followed me over to the door of 17.

"Look, you're welcome to stay if you want to," I said. "I'll sleep on the floor or whatever. The boy here can sleep on the sofa. The bed and the bedroom's all yours."

The unit was poky and dark, but at least it was cooler than outside. I laid Eden down on the double bed and surrounded him with pillows so he wouldn't roll onto the floor in his sleep, then I walked down the highway to a store that sold groceries and bought us some canned soup, milk and bread. When I got back, Lois was dozing on the sofa and Eden was making that whimpering, unhappy sound he generally seemed to make waking up.

"You mind if I turn on the TV?" I asked.

"You go ahead, partner. I'm going to see about freshening up." She picked up her handbag and headed through the single bedroom to the washroom.

I flicked the channel selector around until I found a *Tom and Jerry* cartoon and then settled in on the lumpy sofa next to Eden. My son watched the show with meticulous attention, mouth slightly open, little forehead creased with concentration. I cupped my hand against the back of his head, brushed at his uncombed tufts of straw-white hair with the tips of my fingers. He flinched and glanced at me, then angled his body slightly forward on the sofa and went back to staring mesmerized at the antics of the cartoon cat and mouse.

When Lois came back from the washroom, she seemed sleepy but reasonably sober. She had washed her face and swept her brassy hair back from her cheekbones. She wasn't, I decided, a bad-looking woman.

"What's your name, sweetie?" she asked Eden. He looked up at her boldly enough from the shelter of his blond bangs, but he wasn't about to answer her question.

"Eden," I said. "His first name is Eden."

"Eden?" she said. "Christ, what kind of name is that to give a kid? Whose idea was it, his old lady's or yours?"

"Hers, originally, but it was pretty much the only thing we ever agreed on," I said. "That and wishing we were anyplace but Danforth."

"Danforth? Where's that?"

"On the coast," I said vaguely. I reminded myself that I needed to forget that I had ever been to a place called Danforth, that I had ever been inside a nuclear plant, that I had ever known anyone who worked there or lived there. I had to reinvent myself, make the fictional Clark Kent Mainprize a whole bunch more real than Sonny Wheeler. It was going to be a harder thing to do than I'd imagined, that was obvious: I apparently couldn't say three words to anyone without feeling the need to bring up my hometown.

Lois didn't seem particularly interested in my revelations; geography obviously wasn't her subject. She wandered into the kitchenette and started poking through the grocery bags.

"That all you got?" she asked. "Canned soup?"

"That's right," I said. "It's not a proper supermarket or anything, you know. They only had a few shelves of canned stuff."

"Couldn't you have picked up some ripple chips and dip or whatever? Just soup?"

"Just soup," I said. The cartoon ended, and I flicked around the channels until I found the TV news.

"It's not even Campbell's," Lois said.

Lois Lane and I got it on in the lumpy bed while Eden slept soundlessly, his small body curled up on the couch under one of my flannel winter shirts. I had, I confess, uncharitable thoughts about the possibility of contracting what's politely known as a social disease, though why Lois's past should have concerned me more than that of any of the hippie girls and runaways who'd found their way into my bed would have been a difficult question to answer. Free love and Weatherman Wargasms notwithstanding, I was a child of the tight-assed fifties at heart, and the idea of having sex with a prostitute, even a retired one, still brought with it an aura of danger and dirt.

When I'd shot my wad, I rolled off Lois's hips and lay there and stared at the water-marked ceiling. Lois was lying on her back with the covers pulled down to her waist to cool off. She had her eyes closed and was breathing very slowly. I ran the palm of my hand along the curve of her side in what was intended to be a gesture of affection.

"Shit," she said, knitting her brow as if in pain.

"Little late for a headache," I said.

"Tell that to Jack Daniel's." She sat up and grimaced, licking her teeth and scrunching up her eyes. "I need a little Jimmy, that's what."

She got out of bed, picked up her purse from the Naugahyde armchair, and headed for the bathroom. When she got back, she was sniffing and rubbing her nose. She got into bed and pulled the sheet up to her chin.

"Your name really Lois Lane?" I asked.

"Almost," she said. "It's really Lois Lansky. Got tired of saying 'no relation' when I was talking to folks from Las Vegas."

"You not from Nevada, then?"

She rolled over onto her back and reached for her pack of cigarettes and the Bic. "Not from anywheres, really," she said. "My first dad was LDS, Mormon. We farmed outside

St. George, Utah. He threw my mom out the year I was five, and I guess I just naturally tagged along with her." She lit up and slowly blew a column of smoke toward the water-marked ceiling. "My next two dads worked construction mostly, when they could be bothered to hold on to a job. We lived in Alberta, Montana, Idaho, Oregon, and for a while in San Diego, which at least had a good place to swim. Just bounced around from here to there, Mom and me living in trailer camps, moving on when the booms died or the men up and quit."

"So how'd you wind up turning tricks?" I said.

She sat up and examined the glowing end of her Kool menthol.

"Shit happens," she whispered, her voice going distant and cold.

"You got that right," I said. "Even Superman has serious problems these days."

I turned away and rested my head on the pillow, my whole body aching with fatigue. I dimly heard what may have been Lois Lane sobbing quietly to herself, but the next thing I knew it was morning, and Eden was cooing to his ragged old bear.

24

Phantom Zone

We were in Las Vegas by ten that morning. I stopped in front of the Westward Ho on the Strip and used a pay phone to call Alice. It rang about eight times before anyone answered, but she finally picked up the phone. I told her I was travelling with my son and my girlfriend, though I wasn't particularly confident that either of my companions had any interest in filling those roles. We would get ourselves set up with a hotel room, I said, and drive around to see her in the evening.

"Forget the hotel," Alice said. "They're tourist traps anyways. You can all come stay with me. Since Eugene died this place damn near echoes."

"You sure you have room?"

"Come on over and look for yourself. I'll mix us some drinks while I'm waiting."

"Eden takes his apple juice straight, just for the record," I said.

I hung up the phone and got back in the car, feeling as if there might be some hope for me and my son after all.

Alice's place was in North Las Vegas. We drove up Las Vegas Boulevard and made a left onto Sahara, then swung over to

Decatur and headed north. I'd envisioned a townhouse or condo, but 2351 Bella Vista was a stucco bungalow with a vaguely art deco look. It was L-shaped, with the two wings of the L elided by a quarter-circle entranceway with glass block sidelights flanking the bright red front door. The steps leading up to the door were red concrete arcs that echoed the shape of the entrance, and the sidewalk to the street was also red. A small tribe of lawn dwarves, some shouldering picks or shovels, smiled up from the edge of the flower beds beneath the front windows. Everything seemed reasonably neat and clean, at least.

"Weird," Lois said as she helped Eden out of the back seat of the Bird.

"Yeah," I said. "You could say that." I touched her arm. "Hang fire a minute. There's some stuff you need to know."

Lois shook her head, smiling to herself. "You know, I bet I've heard this song before."

I took off my sunglasses, wiped sweat from my eyes with the back of my wrist.

"My name isn't Clark. It's Sonny Wheeler."

"Big piss in the wind, sport. Half the people I run with don't use their own names."

"My aunt here, Aunt Alice, I haven't seen her for a while." I replaced the shades, rolled my neck to work out the stress of the drive. "There's things she doesn't need to know about. Political problems. Trouble."

She turned away and watched as Eden ran back and forth kicking at the pebbles on the sidewalk, his bright new runners flashing in the oppressive midday glare.

"'Political problems'? Jesus, that's a new way of putting it. You mean the folks you ripped off didn't vote the same way as you?"

"It's complicated," I told her.

"Whatever you say, sport." Lois shouldered her handbag and followed the child toward the house. When she'd reached the gate in the ranch-style fencing, she turned and looked at me for a minute through her round blind-man's shades. "How about I start calling you 'Sonny' and let you worry about the rest?"

I fetched my duffle and Lois's suitcase from the trunk of the car and headed for the door. I stood there for a minute. Did I really think my family could shelter me now?

"Jesus, what are you, shy?" Lois said. She reached around me and pressed the doorbell. I heard the chimes inside the entranceway play the first six notes of "Keep on the Sunny Side."

"This is definitely the place," I said.

"Cute, real cute." Lois rolled her eyes.

Eden giggled and started stretching frantically for the doorbell, which was too high for him to reach.

The front door swung open and Aunt Alice stepped outside.

"You want to ring it again?" she asked Eden. "Lift him up, Sonny. Poor little guy's gonna bust a gut."

I hefted my son reluctantly, my back still giving me grief from spending the night on a swaybacked motel bed. He pounded the button a few times, chortling at the happy song that issued from the doorbell.

"Gosh, he's cuter than a bug's ear, isn't he? Hair just like his grandpa's, too. Like me, I guess, at one time. Lucky little bugger's got that genuine Wheeler hair."

Alice's own hair was chrome silver. It was teased and backcombed up into a hard silver bubble that surrounded her emaciated and heavily made-up face.

"My Nancy Sinatra look," she said, patting the wig and smiling.

"Sorry," I muttered. "Didn't mean to stare."

"Help yourself," she said. "I can't say I'm looking forward to the day I don't get stares." She batted her eyelashes coquettishly and did an exaggerated Jayne Mansfield pout. "Anyways, let's all go in and get off this porch. I opened a can of apple juice, just like you said, and there's a fresh jug of mai-tais for us grown-ups. Come on through to the patio; it's cooler out in back."

She took Eden's hand and led him into the dark interior of her house, the two of them chattering away at each other about doorbells and apple juice and so forth. Eden had obviously found a friend.

Lois shot me a quizzical look. I shrugged as I picked up our luggage: Bobby Deerborne's well-travelled duffle bag and Lois's Samsonite briefcase.

"Cancer?" I whispered.

It was Lois's turn to shrug.

The house was small and crowded with furniture, much of it upholstered in pastel velour; we made our way through the living room and dinette, Lois practically turning her ankles as she plowed through the shag in her heels.

The patio wasn't noticeably cooler than the inside of the house, although the cinder-block fence cast a certain amount of shade across the patio stones at that time of the day. The yard was small, the sort of thing you'd expect to see behind a townhouse rather than a separate residence. There was a white plastic patio set just outside the doors, four chairs and chaise lounge, a little round table with an umbrella poking through a hole in its centre. Alice, or someone, had planted some bougainvillea along one of the fences, and there was another troop of Disney dwarves hanging around at the foot of the back fence, squatting pensively on red concrete mushrooms or leaning on their picks.

Alice told us to sit down and pulled out a chair for Eden; then she went back inside the house to get our drinks. In a couple of minutes she was back, balancing a tray with obvious difficulty. I started to get up to help, but she waved me back into my seat. She put the tray of drinks on the plastic lawn table and sat down next to Eden. "Here's the drink you ordered, sir. One apple juice straight from the tree, stirred not shaken!"

Eden giggled and looked up at her with obvious interest.

"How have you been?" I asked. "Mom told me about your husband. I'm sorry."

Alice brushed past my poor attempt at sympathy and asked me about Betty and Clyde. "You poor kid," she finally said, reaching out to touch Lois's arm. "You must be bored half to death by all this family talk. Sonny, let's change the subject."

"Don't change nothing on my account," Lois said. "I'm used to hearing stuff about people's lives. You could say

I'm a real good listener. Had plenty of occasion to practise."

She grinned up at Alice from the edge of the low chaise lounge.

"Well, anyways, this little man of yours is ready for beddy-byes, isn't he?"

We'd all been ignoring Eden, who had slouched in his chair with his head against Lois's arm. He was drowsy with the heat and the boredom of listening to adults, and was accustomed to taking an afternoon nap.

"Yeah," I said. "Is it okay if I put him down on the sofa?"

"Well, of course it is. We'll set him up properly in the sewing room later on. I want you all to treat this place as home." Alice started to pull herself out of her chair. "I'll give you a hand to get him settled."

"Sit down, for God's sake, finish your drinks," Lois said. "I'll take care of Eddie." She scooped the somnolent Eden into her arms. "You come along with me now," she whispered.

Aunt Alice and I watched Lois carry Eden through the open sliding doors into the house. Then my aunt's face grew serious. She cleared her throat and looked me in the eyes.

"Didn't anybody tell you I was dying?"

I shook my head, unable to think of anything sensible to say.

"Well, I'll be damned. I kind of thought your mother would have told you. Me and her had a couple of heart-to-hearts a month or so ago. She mentioned you were back with her and Clyde and working at that idiotic bomb plant. She holding up all right, is she? Through the treatments and all that, I mean?"

I nodded, feeling baffled. The air was too hot and the surroundings too unusual for me to think about anything very clearly. Ever since I'd crossed into Nevada, I'd been feeling out of step with the rest of the world. Probably I was in shock at the enormity of what I'd done back at Zee Plant. The desert air didn't help much, though. The sky looked strangely false to me, as if it were a backdrop from a movie, some cheesy science-fiction thing you'd see in a Saturday matinee. I expected alien spaceships to zip past at the periphery of my vision or robots to crash through the fence from the neighbours' yard and zap us with their sterilizing rays.

"She's doing about as well as you'd expect," I finally said. "The cancer's spread to her hip joints, but the doctors seem to figure they might have caught it. Betty thinks they're full of shit."

Alice laughed. "I bet they won their medical tickets in the same poker game that mine did. Mine were always going on about how they'd stopped this damn cancer, right up until they told me I was finished."

"Betty never mentioned you'd called."

She looked off into the impossibly blue Nevada sky.

"People like us get secretive. You figure there's no one else on earth who knows about what you feel. Only dead folks, who aren't real talkative, and those of us who are in the same boat. Betty feels a little lonely sometimes, I would imagine. She hasn't seen any of this bullshit before, not like I have. I'm practically a world-class freakin' expert."

"Jesus, I'm sorry."

"Nothing you can do about it."

Alice stared into the ozone-clear sky above the back fence for a minute, her eyes focused on infinity, or on something in the past. Then she brightened and gave me her liveliest, career-entertainer smile. "It's a heck of an excuse to wear wigs, though. I always did like wigs. Right after the first time on chemo, I went out and bought myself close to a dozen. One for each of my favourite film stars. I don't wear this silver one much, though. Makes me look like a '56 Buick. My Ann-Margret hair's my favourite; it's orange as a safety cone and goes halfways down my back."

"We won't stick around long, me and Eden," I told her.

"You move in for as long as you want. I'd be glad to have some company for a change. This damn town's an anthill full of strangers. You could live here for a hundred years and never meet a soul."

Lois and I took the spare bedroom, and I made up a bed for Eden in a room hardly bigger than a closet that Alice referred to as her "sewing room," though it appeared to contain nothing but cardboard file boxes; the only Singer in sight was her. I had nothing to read Eden for a bedtime story, so I told him about the times I'd gone fishing with Clyde, which seemed to hold his attention well enough. Before I'd come to the part about catching my first cutthroat, his eyes had closed and his breathing slowed down. I kissed him and turned out the lamp.

Coming out of the bathroom, I paused outside my aunt's room, which was pink and full of lace and frills, from the skirt around the double bed to the valance above the curtains. Her dresser, which was white and curvy, held a couple of hand mirrors, some bottles of cream, a carnival-glass ash-tray overflowing with strands of coloured pearls, and eleven disembodied plaster heads, ten of which were covered with wigs.

"I'll start looking for someplace to stay tomorrow," Lois said when we were lying together in bed. "There's a girl-friend of mine lives down in Henderson. I can look her up tomorrow. You'll have to think of something to tell this aunt of yours, though, I guess. Maybe we could fake a fight or something." She had scrubbed off her makeup for the first time since I'd seen her, and her face seemed young and pale beneath the feathers of frosted blond hair.

"Stick around if you want. Eden and I will have to make a move before long anyway. Kick back for a few days and go with the flow. I don't think Aunt Alice gives a shit." The minute I'd said this, I felt like a fool. What did I know about this woman, after all? A crazy drunk, a sometime hooker. Worst of all a smacker, if the night before was any indication. After the road I'd been down since high school, I wasn't in any position to be critical of anyone, I knew that, but my life on the low side had taught me what kind of people I ought to avoid. Hookers and junkies were high on the list. Still, there were advantages to travelling with a woman—a man with a small child was more likely to be noticed than an ordinary family of three. And Vegas was always full of newcomers, people trying to catch on at some job or other and make themselves a better life. If I could bring myself to play house with Lois, I could fade into the woodwork for a while.

25

The Wall of the
Cold War Martyrs

We spent the next day at Alice's place, relaxing and taking life easy. I'd expected Lois Lane to be worse than useless around the house, but she shook off her hangover quickly enough to find Eden a cartoon show on television and help my aunt get out the Wheat Chex and orange juice for breakfast. After we'd eaten, Lois drove Aunt Alice into town. There were, she'd said, a few things she wanted to pick up. She'd dug out some tennis balls and a souvenir teddy bear she'd won at a fair up in Reno—Luna the Moon Bear, a friend for Eden's own shopworn favourite, Tuffy. That was all there was in the way of kids' toys, but Eden and I made the best of it. We went out in the little backyard and played catch beside the patio. When Eden had had enough of the tennis ball stuff and started to get fussy, I rustled us up some sandwiches and put him down for a nap on the couch. I was nodding off in a chaise lounge outside when the women got home. Alice dumped a bag on the counter beside the fridge and wandered out to see what I was up to.

"Eden's having a little snooze," I told her. "Let me give you a hand with that stuff."

"Relax. I'm managing fine." She made her way back inside just as Lois emerged from the bedroom. I noticed them talking, then pulled my ball cap back down over my eyes and returned to the serious work of soaking up sunlight. Lois, who must have been chased outside and told to relax almost as quickly as I was, sprawled out in the other lounge.

"Your aunt's fixing mai-tais," she said.

"Mai-tais?" I whispered, craning my neck around to sneak a look through the patio doors. Alice was busy at the wet bar, all right. I could see her lifting bottles and doling out shots of this and that with her mottled scarecrow arms. "What is this, *Hawaii Five-O?*"

"Hey, I really like that show!" Lois protested. She lay back and put on her Ray-Bans.

My son had also surfaced. I could hear him babbling happily to his great-aunt, then he came careening through the patio doors, sporting some new Mickey Mouse ears that Alice had bought him and brandishing a Buck Rogers raygun. I scooped him up as he darted between Lois and me and gathered him onto my lap. He sat there squirming and giggling, all scraped knees and tanned, panting rib cage, his hair white as straw beneath the ludicrous plastic ears.

"You dead!" he informed me. He pointed the gun at my face and pulled the trigger.

I lolled my head as if I'd been levelled by a blast of killer protons. "Book 'em, Danno," I said.

Alice appeared with her tray of drinks, and Lois got up and helped her to a chair.

"You should have been here back in the fifties," Alice said, "everything atomic was all the rage. Bartenders were mixing up 'Atomic' cocktails—vodka, brandy and champagne, if you can imagine that—there were 'Atomic' hairdos, people dancing the 'Atomic-bomb bounce.' You could look up the street and see mushroom clouds rising in the early morning sky, right there at the end of the Strip. Then the earth would be trembling, the buildings start to shake. There's a rumour Howard Hughes had a pendulum installed in his suite up at the Desert Inn, so's he could tell how much the ground had moved every time there was a test shot."

She laughed and glanced sideways. Eden was sitting on the little patch of lawn, prodding with a swizzle stick at a hole in the level grass.

"You come down here much in those days?"

"Sure, every couple of years back in the fifties. I worked a few small clubs down Henderson way, dreamed big dreams of playing the Sahara while I ate beans and slept in some fleabag motel. That was me and Joel Kaiser. You remember old Joel, don't you, Sonny?"

"Yeah, sure I remember. I liked him. He was quiet, but always real friendly and nice."

"He was nice, all right. Too damn nice. I wanted to walk on the wild side in those days. Poor old Joel, I think he just wanted a wife."

She swished a plastic swizzle stick around in her drink.

"It's a funny thing, how life turns out. I ran off from Joel and married a guy who wasn't appreciably different. Eugene was just an ordinary, stay-at-home sort. Sometimes what you really need is right in front of your nose. You only have to take the time to see it."

She turned and smiled at Eden, who was poking at the sandy soil, an archaeologist uncovering relics.

"I remember the first time Joel and me came down here," Alice continued. "We drove west through all those hick states and mountains, then we crossed into Nevada pretty late on a Wednesday night. We'd been keeping musicians' hours for years by that time, getting up in the afternoon and going to bed at sunrise, so I guess it seemed natural to travel in the dark. We'd come as far south as a place called Pioche, up on 93, when I decided I was starving and we better pull over and eat. It ain't exactly God's country up there, as I guess you most probably noticed. Dead sheep and sagebrush and that's about it."

She stopped her soliloquy long enough to stare off at the bougainvillea that snaked along the top of the patio wall.

"Joel parked the car up a lonesome little side road. Then we got out and laid our picnic stuff on this blanket and sat down to eat our food."

There must have been something in her voice that foreshadowed what was coming. I could feel a cold tremor writhing up my spinal cord in spite of the afternoon heat.

"We'd hardly started eating when we saw this flash of light. It was unearthly, like nothing I'd seen before. A light so clear that every little rock and twig of sagebrush seemed to leap into your vision. You could see every fold in the mountains, the grainy, glassy texture of the black valley sand on the slopes. I swear I had the feeling that I could see each of the colours of the rainbow separately within that white light. The sky was blue and grey and red and white, all at the very same time. Then there was silence, just absolute silence. We looked at each other, kind of holding our breath. Then the cloud came up over the mountain, like a bruise or a house on fire. Oh Christ, it was so damned enormous. And then there came a rumbling noise and the roar of this ungodly wind."

She paused and drew a long, slow breath. I heard some sort of animal scratching around on the opposite side of the patio wall, a neighbour's chihuahua or whatever.

"The bomb tests?" I asked her, not that what she'd described could have been anything else.

"Shot Smoky," Alice said. "August 15, 1957. Of course I didn't find that out until bloody near fifteen years later. Friends of mine at the downwinders group have the name and date of every damned above-ground shot and underground event those bastards at the Test Site ever made."

"You think that was what made you sick?" I asked. "Exposure to radiation from the bomb test?"

She shrugged. "Could be, I guess. None of the Wheelers had cancer." She took a long sip from her mai-tai. "We didn't have a whole lot else, come to that."

That evening, after I'd tucked Eden into bed, Alice and Lois and I sat in the living room, the TV flickering aimlessly with the volume turned down to a whisper. I asked Alice, innocently enough, how she was managing since her husband died.

"I get by okay, no thanks to Uncle. You know, I haven't seen a cent of Eugene's pension. Let alone any compensation for what those sons of you-know-what's did to Eugene and me. I wrote the AEC over thirty times in the past ten years, and what do you think it got me?"

She pulled herself to her feet and wandered into the hallway to rummage in the drawer of the telephone table. When she came back, she was holding a wad of letters, some still stuffed into envelopes and others bound in packets with variously coloured rubber bands.

"Thirty-six times I wrote to the government," she said. "The director of the AEC. Army lawyers. The Governor His Lordly Self. Three whole sets of useless assholes representing the Silver State of Nevada. Doctors out at Nellis Air Force Base. Others at the hospital here where they operated on Eugene. Not a speckled-arsed one of them did nothing."

She fanned the letters and envelopes out on the coffee table and sat there, her wasted face sculpted in lamplight and shadows, picking at the papers as if they were the shedding hair of some familiar but faintly repugnant animal.

"I don't understand those people at the Site," she continued. "They've got to know what the radiation does, but they carry on pretending it's pretty much harmless, the Lord alone knows why. Eugene, by the time he left that place, he was so damned tired all the time he could hardly put his clothes on in the morning. He looked like an old man, worn out and good for nothing, though he was only fifty-eight when he retired. They'd send him down into the hot holes on recovery work, over and over. It was because he'd been raised to believe that you did your job, no matter how shitty it was, without complaining. Those bastards knew they could send Eugene just about anyplace and make him do about anything they wanted. There was other guys who bitched if they thought the work was getting the least bit dangerous, but my Eugene just went and did his job, no matter what it cost."

"Didn't you know he was in danger, working out at the Test Site and all that?" Lois asked.

"He mostly didn't talk about his work there at all, let alone about the danger. Nobody who worked at the Site did. A little radiation, what was that? The longhairs from Los Alamos and the AEC guys were always going on about how the fallout from a nuclear test let off less radiation than the dial of a Timex wristwatch or some such ridiculous bullcrap. And people like us believed them, which seems incredible to me now. Once in a great while, mostly when Eugene and me had gone down to Charmaine's or Scotty's Texas Barbecue and had a few drinks, he'd mention how he'd got a dose at work that day, how they'd sent him down in the hot holes and his dosimeter was way the hell and gone up past the limit. He'd mention it, most often, in kind of a joking way, but in the last few years he spent there, I could tell he was getting worried. Towards the end he never mentioned it at all."

Alice paused to cough and then glanced at the desert outside.

"Before he died," she said, "his tongue had swollen up so big it filled his whole mouth. His throat was like a bag of bloody tumours. At the end, Lord forgive me, I just wanted him to die."

Alice got up and went into the kitchen. The electric blender whirred, and I heard her clinking glasses around.

"No more for me, thanks," Lois said. "I'll be dreaming about palm trees as it is." She yawned and pulled herself off the couch, then padded barefoot down the hallway to our room.

"You get around to calling your mom?" Alice asked. She handed me my mai-tai. "She's not the worrying type or anything, Betty, but she'll be pleased to know you've turned up all right."

Alice had garnished my drink with a plastic swizzle stick poked through a wedge of canned pineapple. I fiddled with it, wondering how much I could say. Alice waited, motionless and watching, her haggard face a dolmen in the lamplight.

"Betty doesn't know I'm here," I finally said.

"I figured that somehow. Does she know you're with Eden?"

I shrugged. "Yeah, I imagine she does by now." I dropped the plastic stick into my glass and placed the glass carefully onto a coaster. "I had to get out in a hurry. I ran into problems, some trouble. I couldn't tell Betty and Clyde." I raised my eyes and faced her, reminded of the time we'd sat up and talked in Clyde's living room after my shift at the garage.

"None of my business," Alice said. She stood up and gathered our glasses. "I won't lie to Betty, you know that. But I'm not going to snitch on my family. Your old man was no kind of saint, let me tell you. Come to think of it, neither was I."

"I stole a can from Zee Plant."

She paused, the tumbler in her long-fingered hand glowing faceted gold in the lamplight.

"A can of what, tuna? Heinz beans in tomato sauce, maybe? And for that you had to run off to Nevada? Shit, those judges up in Washington must be tough!"

"The can for a plutonium button. It was empty at the time, as it happens. I expect they didn't know that, though. Not that it matters. They'll be looking for me, either way."

Alice lowered herself to the arm of a chair. I told her as briefly as I could what had happened.

"Come here," she said finally. "There's something I've been meaning to show you." She stood up and headed down the hallway, the highball glass in both hands like a chalice. I slumped along after her, all the fatigue from days of driving south pressing on my body like the weight of a tidal wave. The hall seemed claustrophobic, the spackled ceiling gloomy and low.

"This was Eugene's room," she said. "His study. Not that he ever studied anything, you understand, but he needed a place for his keepsakes and stuff. He collected things, just junk, I guess you'd call it." She opened the door, and I followed her into the study, which looked about nine or ten feet square, a dim cube of knotty-pine panelling with a student's desk and plenty of shelving. The air was stale and perfumed with an artificial pine scent, something manly and outdoorsy that you could purchase in a can. A couple of shelves held a collection of beer cans, all different brands. Baseball caps hung from a pegboard. There were neat piles of matchbooks on one corner of the desk.

The back wall, the one that ran across the gable end, was nine or ten feet high, rising to a vaulted ceiling, and very nearly covered in photographs. The images were of various sizes, though most were simple snapshots, the kind you'd take with an Instamatic and a flashbulb. Some were colour, but most black-and-white. There were animals in some of the pictures. A sheep with two extra legs draped across its woolly flank, hooves hanging uselessly almost to the earth. A two-headed cow or bull, Janus-faced and mythic. Then a row of six mongoloid children, moon-faced and jovial, grinning for the camera in front of what looked like a rural school. A gaunt, balding woman, her age impossible to estimate, displaying the scar where her breast had been removed. Close-ups of hands with blackened, twisting nails. Asymmetrical faces, bulbous with swelling or sunken as sump-holes beneath the ordinary orbits of terrified eyes. I passed along the wall slowly, touching some snapshots with the tips of my fingers.

"Who are they?" I asked.

"Downwinders. Farmers from east of the Test Site. NTS workers like my poor Eugene. Cowboys and men from uranium mines. Vets who did manoeuvres under fallout. Their kids who were born wrong—retarded, deformed. Baby animals from up around Tonopah."

"You collected these?" I asked her.

"People gave them to us, mostly. We've been trying to work up a class-action suit. Make the government pay for the damage they've done. Not that anything could pay for what happened."

I should have been shocked at the images, I suppose. Instead, they seemed familiar. These were the shapes that shimmered at the edge of my adolescent nightmares. Desert ghosts barely visible through the bland façade of Danforth. I squatted on my haunches and ran my fingers down the brittle, curling edges of the overlapping snapshots. They felt like the coarse, peeling bark of some oak. The dark, inverted shadow of the World Tree.

26

The Return of the
Cosmic Dwarf

Lois found a job slinging drinks in a nightclub, and Alice convinced a friend of hers who owned a florist's shop to give me some part-time work making deliveries. The job was okay, as far as it went. They need a lot of flowers in Vegas, home of the push-button wedding and the drive-through divorce. We were living rent free at Aunt Alice's place, and the fifty a week or so I made with the florist bought enough booze and groceries to make me feel I was earning my keep. A certain amount of what Lois earned went up her nostrils, but I had the impression that she was trying to keep her scag problem under control. On top of that, she was always bringing chocolate bars and Cheezies home for Eden, and she took us all out for dinner at a surf-and-turf joint once a week.

Alice's days were measured out in phone calls and naps: she spoke to other downwinders and their relatives almost daily, though she rarely felt strong enough to go to their meetings or to involve herself in the ongoing frustration of their lawsuit. Her close friends were few, and most of those she didn't see. Between age and illness, the compass of her life had narrowed. She sat beneath the gaudy umbrella on her patio and sipped her beloved mai-tais, reminders of a time of Tiki lounges and cars with fins and chrome.

Lois and Alice and I were keeping late hours. We'd got into the habit of having a tequila or two before turning in at night; we'd sit outside and watch the few visible heavenly bodies in the neon-tinted atmosphere wheel gradually toward the horizon. Alice was mostly awake at these times as well; she didn't seem to need a whole lot of rest any more, and when she did sleep it was more often in the daytime than at night. Nights when Lois was working, we could find ourselves up pretty late: cocktail waitresses don't work bankers' hours, and it was generally 2 or 3 a.m. anyway before she got home from the club. She'd be tired as hell but wound up from weaving through a crowd of sweaty Shriners with Nelson Riddle tunes rattling her brains. She needed a margarita before she could sleep.

I'd settled into my pretend life with Lois and Eden and Aunt Alice, and on a good day I could almost forget who I really was and what I'd done. I'd go along perfectly well for a while, hours at a time if I was lucky, just shooting the bullshit with Alice and Lois and helping to keep Eden entertained. Then I'd be doing something innocent, taking a leak in the john, watching TV, whatever, and the weight of my situation would crush me. My lungs would clamp down so I couldn't draw breath, and the muscles in my arms and legs would tense up so tight I felt as if my tendons would snap. I knew absolutely, at those moments, that the FBI would find me;

a lifetime of *Dragnet* and *Highway Patrol* had taught me that cops were invincible, that the good guys would always win out in the end. I'd even taken to sitting in the bedroom that Lois and I were using, perching on the edge of the bed and peering through a crack between the fussy lace curtains, scoping out every car that passed, every heat-stroked jogger or doddering old lady on the street. In the night, I'd hear noises and sit up in bed, my whole body drenched in sweat despite the portable air conditioner in the window.

One hungover morning, I sprawled in the fussy fuchsia armchair in the bedroom as Lois stirred and began to surface from her sleep. I'd been up all night, my mind full of trap doors and narrowing hallways. I was locked into the Phantom Zone like some comic-book criminal from Krypton. I had sentenced myself to existence in the void.

"Jesus Christ, Sonny," Lois said. She sat up and raked her fingers through her frosted hair. "You look like you just chased a fart through a barrel of nails. You come to bed at all last night? You sure as hell don't look it."

I stood up and pitched myself onto the bed. "I been thinking," I told her.

"You think a whole lot, partner," she said. "What you need is a dose of stupid. This sleepless brooding vampire shit'll kill you."

She went out into the hallway and came back with the little chrome-legged stool that Alice used to get into her higher kitchen cupboards. She carried it to the closet across from the bed and stood on it, bare feet arched like a ballerina's, while she fumbled around with the ceiling tile above the shelf. When she stepped down, she was examining a heavy plastic freezer bag.

"I been trying to stay off this garbage," she muttered. "Couldn't bring myself to flush it, though. Like throwing silver dollars down the toilet."

I rolled on my side on the bed, and Lois lay down beside me. She spread the plastic bag on the coverlet between us and peeled the Zip-loc mouth apart. Then she licked the tip of her index finger and inserted it into the bag. Her finger emerged coated in heroin, the chipped crimson fingernail frosted white as if with ice.

"You crank this stuff?" I asked her.

She shook her head. "Nope. You get to like the needle rush. That's what really gets you wired. You're better off to horn it. Keeps life simple."

"What's the matter? You afraid of commitment?"

She winked. "Always have been. Footloose and fancy-free." She sniffed powder from her fingertip, pinched her nostrils closed and then inhaled hungrily.

"Your turn." She proffered the bag.

"You're a fine moral influence, Lois," I said. I slipped a finger into the bag and took a hit. The smack felt cool and dusty on the membranes in my nose. "I'd like to introduce you to my family someday. You're just the type of girl they had in mind."

"You can kiss my ass, cowboy." She frosted her fingertip again and huffed the power up her nose. "I've already met your family, as it happens."

"Yeah, I guess you have." I rolled on my back, a ripple of nausea quivering through my stomach.

Two more snorts and I could close my eyes and see the fields of ice expanding. Mandalas of lucent dawnlight etched on darkness. I was breathing Annapurna winds, the frigid night blossoming, enfolding. I turned and smiled at Lois. We were Superman and Lois Lane, alone in the Fortress of Solitude, a million miles north of everything, on the crystalline roof of the world.

Another Nevada morning. Another run for the roses in the Golden Moments van. I was supremely hungover after a night of margaritas, but I had to get to work. I bolted a Maxwell House instant and said goodbye to Eden and Alice, who were watching *Crusader Rabbit* over Wheat Chex.

The alcohol had upset my digestion, and by ten or so I'd already had to make a couple of pit stops to deal with a case of the runs. I was getting behind with my list. Bruno and Edna, the husband-and-wife proprietors of Golden Moments Floral Fantasy, had already given me grief a couple of times about not keeping up with the schedule, and I wasn't anxious to tangle with either of them again. Around ten after ten, I hustled through the lobby of the Lancer, a downmarket hotel-slash-casino that catered to vacationing Kmart clerks and other high-rollers. Most of the tonier places ran to their own florist, but the Lancer's brochures had to brag about the convenient ice machines and the Gambler's Special, steak and eggs for $1.95 a plate. I noticed, out of the corner of my eye, a couple of dudes about my age who seemed to be observing my progress as I headed for the elevator; I barely registered their presence at the periphery of my vision, and if their drab suits hadn't looked so out of place among the lurid Hawaiian prints and souvenir T-shirts on most of the other lurkers in the lobby, I'd probably never have noticed them at all.

Upstairs, I wandered around the halls until I tracked down the suite I was looking for. I knocked, hung around getting antsy for a minute, then knocked again and took a step backward as a guy about six-five and two hundred pounds opened the door. I tried to look past him, expecting a woman; the arrangement was one of those I-really-fucked-up-honey-please-forgive-me specials, with a few dozen longstems in passionate orange, baby's breath, lots of glossy leaves, what have you. Right out of *The Guy's Guide to Giving Flowers*. Instead of a chick, there was another guy much like the first. He was sitting on the couch, suit jacket folded on the arm right beside him, tie loose and the first few buttons of his Arrow shirt open, drinking Coke and watching televised golf. Okay, I thought, whatever moves you. I handed the first guy the foliage and waited for my tip.

"What's your name, pal?" the guy said. He turned and dropped the flowers on an armchair.

"Clark," I said.

"Clark," he repeated. He dug out his billfold and peeled off a single. The flowers were already paid for.

"There you go, Clark. Have a happy day, all right?" He smiled at me, his expression bland as a Ken doll's, his bulky shape filling the doorway.

I thanked him and pocketed the two-dollar bill, then I headed down the hall toward the elevator. When I glanced back, the door of the suite was still open, but I couldn't see if anyone was watching.

Things in the lobby had livened up considerably. A busload of junketeers, Chinese or Japanese folks who must have been from San Francisco or someplace like that, judging by their fluent American-accented English, had flooded the space between the desk and the elevators like the chorus in a musical rushing out onto the stage. Flashbulbs were going off like Roman candles on Independence Day; little knots of middle-aged Asians were gathering here and there to grin their way into a quick Kodak memory. As I passed through the mob and made for the doors, I noticed the two guys who'd watched my arrival. They were slumped in a pair of armchairs at the perimeter of the tourist invasion, but one of them jumped to his feet and snapped a picture, flashbulb glaring, at exactly the moment I passed. I turned, startled, mouth no doubt gaping, and the fellow who was standing fired off another flash. Half blinded, I bulled through the entrance and hurried down the street toward the van. As I pulled out of the roundabout, I checked all the mirrors carefully to see if anyone had followed me outside. My scalp was cold and tingling.

The mirrors stayed clear all the way to Flamingo. I turned north and headed for my employer's place, taking deep breaths to calm myself down.

The rest of the day passed uneventfully. A couple of mai-tais, heavy on the Bacardi, smoothed the wrinkles from my cerebellum and stopped my inner smoke alarm from scream-ing. In a couple of days, I'd let the whole business slip quietly from my mind. Then, that weekend, while Lois and Eden played catch in the backyard, Aunt Alice called me back into the kitchen.

"I've been having a talk with your mom."

"How is she?" I asked hesitantly. Of my many betrayals, leaving Betty seemed the worst, and I'd had to try hard to push the thought of her illness from my consciousness ever since I'd left Danforth. Like the body in the lake in a mystery story, however, it kept bobbing to the surface of my mind.

"Pretty worried, what with her health and Clyde having problems at work."

"Clyde's having trouble at Zee Plant?"

She shook her head. "You left some dirty laundry behind you."

I turned away so that Alice couldn't see my face. A cold fan of nausea was flooding through my torso, and my skin felt like it was flashing back and forth from ice to flame to ice. I fiddled with the junk on the mantel, pictures of Eugene in little brass frames, a lump of quartz crystals the size of a fist, a couple of Grand Canyon sno-globes.

"You told them I was staying here?"

"I should have told Betty ages ago. She's your mom. She has a right."

I sat down on the armchair next to Alice and tried to think things through. "They'll know," I said. "Betty'll tell Clyde, that's certain. Old Man Crashaw too. She'll figure he might be worried about Eden."

"Why wouldn't he be? Why wouldn't Betty be too, for that matter?" Alice shook her head, not a hair of the Fonda shag moving.

I slumped beneath the weight of her disapproval, head in hands, the jazzy paisley carpet curdling between my feet.

"Did she ask if I was coming back?"

"No, she didn't say a lot. She's got worries of her own, you know." Alice stood up, wincing as she always did at the pain in her side. I'd learned not to offer to help her, so I had to just sit there and wait until she'd worked her way up to her feet.

"There's something else," she added. "I'd like you to take my picture."

"For the wall?"

She nodded. She was looking, though, not at the walls but out through the patio doors to the yard where my son was running in and out of the lawn sprinkler's spray to keep cool. "Not today, though," she added. "I'll say when it's time."

27

Life During Wartime

The phone rang. I scanned the street through the smudged glass panes of the telephone booth. It rang again and a third time. I told myself to stay cool and took a couple of long slow breaths while I listened to the stupid goddamn ringing.

"Yes?"

I gulped a breath, unprepared to say anything.

"Yes?" the voice repeated. "Who is this?"

"Delgado. I think I've been made."

There was a moment of dead air, then I could hear the voice, muffled and distant, yelling, "Some Italian guy, Delgracci or whatever." Then someone else answered, but I couldn't make out the words. Then silence, as if someone had placed his hand over the phone.

I shifted my weight back and forth as I waited. Left foot. Right foot. Listening to nothingness. Then another voice, also male, sharper and deeper than the first: "There's nobody here by that name, pal. I'm sorry. You got the wrong number."

The man on the other end hung up before I did. I stood there for a while not knowing what to do, the receiver slick with sweat in my hand.

Lois was in our bedroom dressing Eden when I got home.

"Eddie's been down to the playground. His pants got a little bit dusty, so I thought I'd stick these clean ones on him so's he won't look too messy when Alice gets home. Had fun though, didn't you, babe?"

Eden was grinning up at me, and I tried to look reasonably cheerful for him, though all I felt was fear. "Where's Alice gone?"

"You know. She told us about it yesterday. Remember?"

Alice saw her oncologist every couple of weeks. A friend of hers had picked her up and would be bringing her back after lunch.

I told Lois what had happened at the Lancer. I started off well enough, stating the facts as I remembered them without getting flustered or embroidering the truth. Then the vision of Ford and Blankenship—or their spiritual descendants— in the lobby of the Lancer rose up in my mind, and I found myself babbling about the Cosmic Dwarf Mxyzptlk and joggers cruising past the house and so on.

"This is like, what, ten or twelve years ago you last saw these guys?"

"Yeah. Eight years, maybe ten."

"And you're sure they're the same dudes? I mean, a lot of guys look pretty much alike, right? Cops look like other cops, for instance."

"Help me pack," I said. "I'll have to borrow Alice's car and hope it get us to the coast."

Lois finished pulling Eden's T-shirt over his head and then straightened his clothes and brushed his unruly hair off his forehead with her fingers. I stood there shifting my weight from one foot to the other, electric with impatience and fear. Every cell in my central nervous system was zinging with the primitive need to cut and run, and I couldn't understand why Lois wasn't hustling to run for it with me.

"Did Auntie Alice brush your teeth? Go on in the bathroom, sweetie."

"Jesus! Don't worry about that. Just start packing everything you need. Where the fuck is Alice anyway? I thought she was supposed to be home right after lunch."

Lois piloted Eden through the doorway, her hands on his shoulders, and got him started in the direction of the bathroom. Then she turned and came back into the bedroom.

"I'm not going with you, Sonny. I'm staying here with Alice and Eden."

I stopped talking and considered what she'd said. I'd visualized, for some reason, the three of us taking off and heading for the border. I hadn't decided which border just yet, though Canada seemed dauntingly far from where we were.

"Eden's coming with me. You can stay here if it's okay with Alice, I suppose. You can sort things out with her after we're gone."

"That's it? After a year? 'Just sort things out yourself'?"

"It's not like I have a lot of choices here, Lois."

"You go if you have to. Just leave Eden."

"He's my kid. He has to go where I go."

"Even if where you're going is straight to the joint?" She turned and walked into the kitchen. "What if you get your ass wasted?" she whispered. "Do you really think those FBI shits wouldn't shoot you?"

"How can I leave him here? How could my aunt look after anyone? She's dying, for Christ's sake. She's on her way out."

"Try to keep your voice down. Think of Eden."

She opened the fridge and started taking things out— peanut butter, Velveeta cheese, margarine, two kinds of jam. I thought she was going to let the conversation die, but as I turned to leave the kitchen, she dropped a heavy jar, a peanut-butter jar, on the Arborite and yelled, "What about me, you stupid bastard?"

I turned around expecting her to haul off and hit me, but she was crying instead of fighting for a change.

"He could stay with me. I'm here too, not just Alice."

"What makes you think you could look after him?" Even in my agitated state of mind, I realized the cruelty of what I'd just said the moment I said it. "I mean, Jesus, what if something should happen to you?"

She gave me a wounded look, a flash of bitter wisdom in her normally guarded eyes.

"Like an OD, you mean? Like me going back to my old kind of work?"

"Jesus, Lois, I mean . . ."

"I know what you mean, Sonny. A druggie and a washed-up fucking hooker. The original unfit mother, isn't that right?"

She was holding herself away from me, cringing against the counter, like a kid who's grown accustomed to being hit.

"That's not what I meant, for Christ's sake," I said. "It's just that we only met a while back, and you and me aren't anything legal. Alice at least is a relative of his."

"Thirteen months. That was over a year ago, up in Humboldt."

I reached to touch her bare arm, but she flinched.

"I never promised you anything, or lied about who I was. You knew what was what when you came here."

"Yeah, sure. I knew from experience exactly who you were. I sure as hell should have, at least."

"Just help me get Eden's stuff together," I said. "I'm going first thing in the morning."

She turned and walked out of the room.

When I'd packed my things and Eden's into the trunk of Aunt Alice's Montego and made sure I had enough apple juice and cookies to get us through at least the first day of our journey, I lifted Aunt Alice's camera box down from the shelf of the closet in the hall. I had cleaned Eugene's Leica and loaded it with film a few days earlier, in case I needed it in a hurry. I assumed it was in good working order, although I really had no way of knowing if any photos I tried to take with it would turn out. It was a beautiful instrument, Eugene's old camera, and I spent some time fiddling with the turned metal knobs and peering at the little Zeiss lens in its bright metal bezel while I waited for my aunt to get ready. By the time Lois came out of the bedroom and told me that Alice was waiting, I had almost succeeded in convincing myself that I was capable of doing what needed to be done.

Alice had turned out the light in the bedroom, and all I could see as I entered was her narrow shape standing beside the carefully made twin bed. She was wearing her flowered housecoat and pink rubber thongs, and I clearly remember thinking that she looked like she was heading for Hawaii. She'd taken off her hair and wrapped her head in a fuzzy pink bath towel, and her face was slick and shiny, as if she'd washed it with some sort of moisturizing gel.

I set up the tripod as quickly as I could and tested the flash a couple of times, just to be sure it was working, filling the bedroom with unearthly blue-white light each time. My aunt watched me work without speaking, her emaciated features leaping out of the relative darkness each time I tried the flash. I pictured her standing in the barren field behind her parents' house in Mainprize, a woman lit by lightning in the cool of a mid-summer storm.

"You ready?"

She nodded. I'd been surprised by her reaction when I told her I was leaving, though I shouldn't have been, I suppose. She came from a world where you lived with your choices. She would let me make my choice, whatever she thought of it.

I bent to the eyepiece and fooled with the focus ring until every line on the skin of her face was as sharp and distinct as a crack in a worn piece of slate. Alice shrugged her flowered housecoat off her shoulders and let it fall to the carpet, then she stepped out of her rubber thongs and kicked them aside. Naked, she was so frail I wondered how she could keep herself standing. Her arms and legs were mottled with lesions. A semicircular bruise that looked like curdles of sour black milk had spread from her crotch to her navel. There were surgical scars on her throat and her stomach. One breast had been removed, leaving a patch of burned red flesh, its edge a puckered seam.

Inevitably, I thought of all the pictures I'd seen of Holocaust survivors and Africans caught in a famine, their arms mere sticks of fleshless bone: every age must have its icons of human suffering, I suppose, and those were the ones I'd grown up with. I couldn't fit my aunt into history, however; nothing as real as the sight of her dying body could be theorized or expressed as an abstraction. The aunt I loved was standing in a white, consuming fire; I could see her, hear her rasping breath, but there was nothing I could do to save her. I carefully set the shutter speed and twisted the aperture ring around until I was reasonably sure of getting a decent picture. Then I put my eye to the eyepiece, cutting Alice's dying body free of the living world around it and enclosing her in a frame of light, transforming her into physics, the mute, indifferent interplay of photographic emulsion and light.

I took her picture smiling, then again with her face at rest.

"We're done now," Alice said. "Just take out the film before you go. I never was a lot of use with cameras."

28

Amargosa

Aunt Alice's Montego died in Amargosa Valley. The temp gauge hit the red-line and the radiator gave up the ghost. I got out, squinting into harsh midday sunlight, and popped the hood to have a look. Eden was curled up on the back seat asleep. To the west were the Amargosa dunes and beyond that the Funeral Mountains, which lie roughly north-to-south along the California-Nevada state line.

I opened the back door of the car and stood there, helpless as a kid myself, looking down at the sleeping Eden. His white mop was hanging in his eyes as he slept, and I brushed it as gently as I could from his forehead. I put my hand on his arm to wake him, but he was too far gone to pay me much attention. With the unquestioning faith that children have in their parents, he let me lift him out of the car without waking. I hefted him up to my chest and started walking up the side of the highway. It was dusty and hotter than I was used to, even after months in Vegas, but it didn't seem to matter to Eden: the poor little guy was so exhausted he'd have slept on the top of a stove.

Half a mile up the road we came to a country store. It was one of those jack-of-all-trades places you run into in the boonies, half groceries-cum-hardware and the other half hamburger joint. I settled Eden into a leatherette booth and asked the waitress for a sandwich and milk.

"There a pay phone?"

The waitress waved me toward the back of the room, where a heavy black telephone clung to the faded floral wallpaper like a beetle on a leaf. It took six rings for Alice to answer.

"The car's had the biscuit," I told her. "I'm leaving it here. I'm sorry, I never seem to bring you much but trouble." I gave her directions and the number of the store.

"How's Eden? Is he managing all right in the heat?"

"Pretty tired. We had to walk a ways."

"You sure he's going to be all right?"

"Don't worry. I'll look after him."

"You going to take the bus?"

"Maybe. Hang on for a minute, Alice."

I covered the Bakelite mouthpiece. "The Trailways stop here?"

She paused in her work, a yellow plastic mustard bottle in one hand. "Sure does. Should be one along any minute."

"Which direction?"

"Vegas. The Reno bus already went."

I nodded and uncovered the phone. The woman went right on with what she was doing, herding the sugar dispensers together at one end of the counter and then unscrewing the chrome tops.

"There's a Trailways up to Reno later on," I lied. "We'll catch it if we can't hitch a ride. Or I might rent a car up in Beatty."

Dead air. Silence. I could hear Aunt Alice breathing. "Catch the Vegas bus, Sonny. There's one comes past Mercury every afternoon. Eugene used to ride it home once in a while."

"I don't think I can do that," I told her.

Another few heartbeats of silence. "That desert ain't a playground. You have to bring Eden back here."

I turned around and leaned against the wall. The waitress was checking the plastic squeeze-bottles of mustard and ketchup. She hardly glanced up when I spoke, but I could tell she was listening to my conversation from the look of concentration in her eyes.

"Where's Lois?" I finally said.

She hesitated before she answered. "Out. She went out before lunch." Her voice was thin and burdened with fatigue, as if the effort of speaking were too difficult to maintain.

"You're alone there?" The sun was still high enough that the interior of the restaurant was shady, but the dry heat pervaded the air. If I leaned toward the door to the kitchen, I could just catch a breath from the rotary fan. "You going to be okay there, Aunt Alice?"

"I'll manage," she said. She was wind in an empty culvert. "It's not like I'm betting scared money. Every new day's a jackpot, far as I'm concerned."

I drew a breath and leaned against the wall again. There was a transparent plastic pastry case behind the counter in front of me, and I found myself staring at the meagre display of pastries, a couple of slices of pecan pie, some butter tarts, about a third of a lemon meringue. Next to that was the window to the kitchen, through which I could see the fat, balding chef going stoically about his business, his roll-your-own dripping cigarette ash as he waddled back and forth.

"All right, I was wrong. I can't take Eden. I'll put him on the quarter-of-three Trailways. Can you get him at the station, for sure?"

"I'll call right now and book a cab."

When I got back to the booth, our sandwich was ready. Eden looked up at me through sleep-reddened eyes, then nuzzled against my side like a bear cub. His eyelashes flickered and he drifted into sleep. I gradually eased him down to the seat. Then I got up and found myself a stool at the counter.

"I have to put my boy on the Vegas bus," I told the waitress. "I got this new job up in Beatty. I have to be there for the night shift. Can you sell me the tickets, or does the driver look after all that?"

"You can get them from the driver," she told me.

There was something like hate or contempt in her eyes, but I was in no mood to consider her feelings. It occurred to me later, though, that she may have been where Eden was at one time, back when she was a kid. Left behind by rootless parents, put on buses, passed along.

"Where's his mama?" she asked. "She waiting for him back in Vegas? I mean, he's only a little guy, ain't he? He shouldn't be alone on that bus."

"He'll be okay once he's on the bus. His mother will be there to meet him."

When the bus arrived, I carried Eden up the stairs and found him a seat near the front. His eyes fluttered open. I explained that I had to go away for a while, that the bus would take him home to Lois and Aunt Alice.

"Where you going, Daddy?"

"Daddy has to see some people, Eden."

He looked puzzled for a moment, then his eyes brightened.

"Is it work, Daddy?"

"That's right. I have to go to work."

He smiled at my lie. "You go work now, Daddy," he whispered. He closed his eyes and cuddled against my side. When I was sure he was asleep again, I got up to talk to the driver. He nodded when I asked if he'd keep an eye on Eden, who had drifted back to sleep. The bus driver squinted at me through his blue-tinted glasses, his pouchy features taut with suspicion. I told him that the little boy's mother would meet him in Vegas. I explained that I would call her and make sure she was there on time.

"You sure he's all right?" he said. "You sure this is okay?"

I stumbled my way down the steps again and into the blistering heat. The heavy hydraulic door hissed shut. My head was full of noises, like a radio stuck between channels. I walked west away from the bus stop, my shadow dark as oil against the dusty desert ground.

By nightfall I was passing through Beatty, looking down at the storefronts from the cab of a Kenworth semi. The trucker let me off at the junction of routes 95 and 190, and I walked toward the Funeral Mountains with Bobby's duffle slung over one shoulder. I was headed for Death Valley, which seemed appropriate enough. I thought more than once of heading back, but my feet kept trudging hopelessly in the direction of the mountains, and I stuck out my thumb as if by reflex at every car that came racketing past.

The truck that pulled over had more bare metal than paint. In another life it must have been a pickup, but the bed had been stripped off and replaced by rough planks, on which rested a gas-powered pump or air compressor that looked as sandblasted as the truck.

The guy who was driving gave a sort of grunt of recognition as I clambered up into the cab. He was old, one of those sun-reddened old codgers you run into all over the southwestern desert, most of them driving hosed-out trucks as beat up as the one this fellow drove.

"Going west?" he asked, rather redundantly. I nodded. He eased down the handbrake and let the pickup roll back onto the highway. Those words were the only conversation we made in more than two hundred miles, and the truck had no radio or tape deck. We listened to the windless air, which seemed to my ears to be ringing.

Someplace beyond the mountains, I woke up from a shallow sleep. I stole a look over at the old man who was driving. He was still in exactly the same position he'd been in when I fell asleep somewhere back on the other side of the mountains. Even the expression on his face was just the same.

I can't remember where he let me off or how many rides it took me to get across Death Valley. The next thing I remember is vivid enough, though: I am waking up in the middle of the night underneath a freeway bridge near Oildale, California. I can hear the cars going over, the *whoosh* of their engines and the rhythmic *thud* of their tires on the metal spacers between the sections of paving. I sit up, one side of my face raw from sleeping on dirt, and squint across the greasy-looking canal at the flares of the refinery smokestacks blazing up into the dark.

From Oildale, I drifted north, traversing California longitudinally through its arid interior regions. Near Fresno I fell in with migrants, fruit pickers working the melon fields and vineyards, some of them likely illegals. Concealed among the shambling men and the Spanish and Asian voices, I slept in the beds of transport trucks and numbed my heart with Thunderbird and whatever pharmaceuticals—meth cut with strychnine and baby powder, angel dust and trash psychedelics—I could score for a few bucks in working-men's bars, or freeload crashing parties. I holed up for three days, pole-axed with red wine and misery, in an abandoned bus at the verge of someone's stump ranch near Crater Lake. Danforth and my parents' house were a few hours straight up the freeway. All other roads were infinite, twisting out toward the vertigo of exile. On the third day, I packed up my sleeping bag and the balance of my worldly possessions and hiked down to the county road, heading for Highway 101 and the circuitous route to Vancouver. The federal police and the duplicitous ghosts of Zee Plant no longer concerned me. What prevented me from going home was shame.

Eight months later, in the fall of 1974, I was sitting in the sunroom at Riverdale, the mental home where my mother had once worked, an hour's drive outside Vancouver, squinting through a haze of medication and trying to decide if the high-pitched roaring I could hear was the sound of some appliance or the insects in my head. By this time I was no longer someone named Wheeler. I was Charles William Watson, born 1942 in Tacoma, Washington, USA. That was the name the Vancouver street worker who'd fished me out of the downtown lockup and had me admitted to Riverdale had found on the ID card in my wallet, and it sounded all right to me, although I couldn't remember anyone named Watson. In my mind, sometimes, I was Gene or Eugene Fangis, who lived inside the tunnelled earth of Frenchman's Lake, Nevada. Other times, I was convinced I was the Atomic Man from Zee Plant, my body a bright nest of swarming electrons. Once in a while I was Superboy, walking home through the sad streets of Smallville. More often, I was light, pure light, streaming in like sorrow through the smeared, reluctant glass.

29

Spinning Wheel

A morning came, sculpted of crystal. The windows of the sunroom glowed. My head flushed with intricate silence. The chittering insects had died in their sleep—or gone deep into burrows to wait out the day, cicadas hived into root-soil. I wandered the hallways in my inmate's green pyjamas and terry-cloth robe. I could see things in proportion, each object in its place. The radiators hissed to themselves as I passed, but their iron coils were no longer breathing. I noted the regular rhomboids of doors. The lino floor shimmering daylight.

A woman with a trolley emerged from a door. She was wearing a yellow cotton dress, which marked her as a passing spirit, one of those who smiled but rarely spoke—a practical nurse or a ward clerk. A memory bubbled up out of the fog, a soft sphere that slowly rotated. Within it, I was walking through fields with a girl. She was skinny, red-haired, and had big rabbit teeth. In the kitchen, her mother was laying out lunch. Betty was there, her hair swept up in a glistening, hairsprayed bouffant. She was smiling and making conversation.

The practical nurse smiled at me too, benign apparition, as she passed.

My mother's old friend Zinnia. Clyde's cousin.

"You're Zinnia," I muttered, surprised at my voice. I wondered if the woman could hear me. She glanced up, the shocked little O of her lips replaced in a heartbeat with a distant, professional smile. Then her trolley clattered past me and away down the hall. Days later, I woke from a nap to find her sitting by my bed. I lay between fear and anticipation, waiting. The red hair, I noticed, was now a henna rinse. The narrow face was slack along the jawline. But the eyes were wide and friendly still, the mouth as buck-toothed as her daughter's.

What I looked like I can only imagine.

"You're Sonny Wheeler, aren't you? I must have seen you here before, but I guess I didn't recognize you. Sorry." She pulled a crumpled Kleenex from the sleeve of her cardigan. "Got a cold." She smiled. "Sorry."

"Zinnia? You're still here?" I managed to ask her, my voice a fractured croak.

"Well, sure I am. Only now I'm a practical. It pays a little more." She dabbed at her nose with the Kleenex, then looked down at her lap. "I was real sad to hear about your mother."

"Is Betty here with you?" I asked.

She looked at her lap.

"You didn't know, Sonny?" She balled up the tissue, fingers working nervously. "Does Clyde know you're here?"

I guess I must have shaken my head.

"He's living in Yakima. That's where he moved after Betty passed on. He came up here fishing last summer."

I considered this idea for what may have been quite a while. My mother reappeared to me as a nest of subtle textures. Her crisp blouse and slick lips. Her powdered cheeks. The Arborite counter in the kitchen of our New Westminster house, also dusted with a skin of soft powder. I felt her absence suddenly, the translucent, impermeable membrane that divided forever our separate worlds.

"My mom died?" I whispered to Zinnia. She reached and touched my arm.

"Do you want me to tell Clyde I saw you? I talk to him on the phone, you know. Not often, just once in a while."

The shock of Clyde's presence—that he could still exist after all that had happened—trembled through me. I had left him when Betty was dying. I had stolen his magical fire.

I shook my head. "He won't want to see me."

"Don't sell Clyde short," she whispered. "He's a pretty smart fellow, my cousin."

I turned and faced the sterile wall. I felt Zinnia's gentle touch on my shoulder. Then her footsteps retreated toward the hallway. Then the door hissed as it closed.

I drifted into a shallow sleep, the voices and sounds from the corridor a garbled fugue that seemed to be percolating out of the past. I was hunched on a park bench back in Danforth in the rain. Karen Sullivan was sitting right beside me. She laughed and said, "Open your mouth when you kiss me." In her hand were swollen berries and a single glossy leaf. I was Alfred, dead in wartime. I was wearing a soldier's uniform, though the sleeves were torn to rags. Karen nuzzled against me, her tawny hair clouding my vision, her breath as warm as blood against my cheek. *"The universe is made of energy,"* she whispered. *"Planets and stars. The animals. The seven seas. The air."* She brandished her poison leaf and placed it on my tongue. It tasted of rock salt and thunder and rain. *"You and I. Our very bodies. We are burning. Deserts. Fire."*

When I woke, the dream was residue, a dull ache in my eyes. I rose from my bed and shuffled in my slippers to the window. Heat from the radiator flushed up my legs as I stared between venetian blinds at the shadows on the hospital lawn. A car with a noisy exhaust traversed the distance, motoring beyond the poplars that protected the grounds from the highway. I thought of Bobby's 'Cuda howling, fish-tailed, into Utah, and the memory seemed to comfort my guttering spirit just as surely as the creaking hot-water pipes beneath the window warmed my skin.

My old friend had gone into the mountains. The distance had drawn him inside it. I imagined him driving faster and faster across a horizontal plane, his car and his body blurring as he was transmuted from mass to light. Karen Sullivan too was among the transformed, and Alice, and Curie and Betty. My life was a blank sheet of paper. They had all turned into light and disappeared. Only Clyde remained to graft me to my memories. And somewhere, somewhere, Eden, the child whom I had sacrificed to fear and chance and fate.

Weeks later, I was lying on my hospital bed, an issue of *Time* magazine splayed open on my lap. I had just that morning acquired a new roommate, an older guy with a baseball cap and a perpetual look of wounded incomprehension. When an intern appeared in the doorway, the middle-aged guy looked up expectantly and began to rise involuntarily from his chair.

"Mr. Watson, you have visitors," the intern said. "Do you want to come down to the sunroom?"

My roommate sat back down and began to examine his fingers as if he suspected his hands might not be clean.

"I never have visitors," I said.

"Well, I guess this must be the exception." The intern smiled. He was a small, fit-looking man in his twenties with strawberry-blond hair that was prematurely receding.

"I don't want to see anyone. Tell Clyde I'm not feeling well. I'm sleeping."

The young man looked puzzled. "I don't think that was the name, actually. Anyway, they're waiting in the sunroom." He turned and walked into the hallway, the soles of his white sneakers chirping.

"Visitors, eh?" my roommate shouted, his voice unnecessarily loud. I glanced across to find him nodding encouragement. "Visitors. That's nice. That's good." His face, still smooth enough for a man his age but fleshy and heavy in the jowls, was bright with perspiration, as if the effort of trying to strike up a conversation had made him break out in a sweat.

"It's a mistake," I said quietly. "It's not for me." I stood up, ignoring his crestfallen expression, and left him to fidget and examine his hands. I walked out into the corridor and stole a glance toward the sunroom, which was down the hall, past fifty feet of laundry carts and open doors and recently waxed linoleum. I could see a woman standing in the distance, her figure starkly outlined against the wall of brilliant glass. Back-lit in that radiance, she was archetype and absence, an angel bodied forth from fire, a shadow etched in stone. I thought, of course, of Betty, her crisp white dress and shining eyes as she sang to a wheezing accordion with the Holy Ghost and Fire Eyes and the Giant. I thought, as well, of Curie, daughter of radium, mother of my moonlight son, and of Karen. She was all of these and no one, a stranger in a waiting room in an antiseptic clinic, and I gasped as she turned to face me, her features resolving as she stepped into the hallway, the fringes on her buckskin jacket swinging. Lois Lane had arrived in Vancouver.

I flinched from her open smile. I could see her right in front of me, in Alice's house in Vegas, picking up the jar she'd dropped, the family-size Kraft peanut butter. She was holding the jar in one hand and rubbing at the tears in her eyes with the other. *He could stay with me, Sonny. I'm here too, not just Alice.* Her mouth turned down like a girl's in her sorrow. And I, in my stubbornness, my need to possess and own my child if I could own nothing else under heaven, reciting for her the litany of her failings and mistakes.

"Hey, Sonny," she said.

There was a tremor of apprehension in her eyes, though it melted into pity when she saw me shuffling awkwardly toward her in my institutional pyjamas and tatty striped robe.

"Where is he?" I managed to ask her.

"Well, he ain't on a bus to Las Vegas," she muttered. She turned towards the doorway to the sunroom just as Zinnia and Eden came out.

My little boy had lengthened and his features seemed more delicate. The eyes were Richard Crashaw's now, grey and curious, probing briefly at my stubbled face and then glancing up once or twice more shyly as he hid behind Zinnia's legs. I smiled down at him, but he clung to Zinnia's hand and wouldn't meet my eyes again.

"I called Clyde," Zinnia said. "I guess it wasn't really my business, but you'll be needing help and family. You're going to have to leave here soon, you know."

"People don't stay in detox forever," Lois chimed in. "Believe me, I've tried it. It starts to get on your nerves."

"Was it Clyde that sent you up here?" I asked her.

"He called, left a message. That was right after Alice died. You know how it goes." She brushed a stray swirl of hair off her face, glitzy rings and silver bangles winking.

"You should go and see Clyde, Sonny," Zinnia said. She sniffed and pulled a Kleenex from her sleeve.

"He knows I can't go back there," I muttered. The proximity of so many familiar people was making me feel jittery and confused. Their obvious concern overwhelmed me. I wanted, however irrationally, to retreat into my impersonal room and curl up in my bed.

"I think you may be wrong about that," Zinnia said. "Clyde told me his bosses had deep-sixed the issue, that whatever you'd done was forgotten. He said they were experts at burying grief." She shook her head sadly, as if the world that her cousin inhabited were incomprehensible to her.

Lois reached out and squeezed my hand. Her palm was cool and supple. "You been running from shadows, my friend."

Ten days later, Lois and Eden drove out from their motel in Vancouver to collect me. I said my goodbyes to Zinnia, signed the forms for my release, and sat down on a banquette near the entrance door with the shopping bag that held my few possessions. A clutch of nurses strode briskly past me, brilliant white uniforms catching the light. I glanced up and ventured a smile as they passed, but they were chatting happily to each other and ignored me. A patient was wheeled in by an ambulance crew, his body a cordillera of bone beneath sheets, one huge hand hanging down from the stretcher. At last I saw Lois's rusty T-Bird pull in. She circled the lot, found a vacant space and parked. I was surprised to see that Eden could open the door and clamber out of the car without help. Lois took his hand and they crossed towards the entrance door together. They swung their arms and began to run, and just as they came to the top of the steps, she lifted him clean off the pavement and whirled him, his sneakered feet and bright checked jacket flying. In a moment they were bursting through the door.

Acknowledgments

My sincere thanks to Patrick Crean for his faith in this project and for helping me to find a path through the forest. Thanks also to Sarah Williams for some useful suggestions, and especially to Nelly Kazenbroot, whose support and insight made this book possible.

My main source for information on the history of Richland, Washington (the basis of the fictional Danforth), and the lives of nuclear workers was Paul Loeb's *Nuclear Culture: Living and Working in the World's Largest Atomic Complex* (Philadelphia: New Society Publishers, 1982). Michael D'Antonio's *Atomic Harvest: Hanford and the Lethal Toll of America's Nuclear Arsenal* (New York: Crown Publishers, 1993) provided additional material about Richland, as did Michele S. Gerber's *On the Home Front: The Cold War Legacy of the Hanford Nuclear Site* (Lincoln, Nebraska: Univ. of Nebraska Press, 1992) and S. L. Sanger's *Hanford and the Bomb: An Oral History of World War II* (Seattle: Living History Press, 1989). Much of the information about the Seattle street riots of the sixties came from Walt Crowley's detailed first-person account *Rites of Passage* (Seattle: University of Washington Press, 1995). His timelines were particularly useful. The background for the depiction of the Seattle

Weatherman cell came largely from *With the Weathermen* by Susan Stern (Garden City, N.J.: Doubleday, 1975), though the characters who make up my fictional Weatherman cell are entirely invented. The following publications provided more general information about the Weatherman era: Ellen Frankford's *Kathy Boudin and the Dance of Death* (N.Y.: Stein and Day, 1983); Larry Grathwohl, *Bringing Down America* (New Rochelle, N.J.: Arlington House, 1976); and Harold Jacobs, *Weatherman* (Berkeley: Ramparts Press, 1970). Some books that helped me envision the impact of the atomic tests on the population of the American southwest include *American Ground Zero* by Carole Gallagher and Keith Schneider (MIT Press, 1993); *Under the Cloud: The Decades of Nuclear Testing* by Richard L. Miller (Two-Sixty Press, 1999); and *Children of the Atomic Bomb: An American Physician's Memoir of Nagasaki, Hiroshima, and the Marshall Islands* by James N. Yamazaki, M.D. and Louis B. Fleming (Duke University Press 1995).